When should I travel to get the best airfare?
Where do I go for answers to my travel questions?
What's the best and easiest way to plan and book my trip?

frommers.travelocity.com

Frommer's, the travel guide leader, has teamed up with **Travelocity.com**, the leader in online travel, to bring you an in-depth, easy-to-use resource designed to help you plan and book your trip online.

At **frommers.travelocity.com**, you'll find free online updates about your destination from the experts at Frommer's plus the outstanding travel planning and purchasing features of Travelocity.com. Travelocity.com provides reservations capabilities for 95 percent of all airline seats sold, more than 47,000 hotels, and over 50 car rental companies. In addition, Travelocity.com offers more than 2,000 exciting vacation and cruise packages. Travelocity.com puts you in complete control of your travel planning with these and other great features:

Expert travel guidance from Frommer's - over 150 writers reporting from around the world!

Best Fare Finder - an interactive calendar tells you when to travel to get the best airfare

Fare Watcher - we'll track airfare changes to your favorite destinations

Dream Maps - a mapping feature that suggests travel opportunities based on your budget

Shop Safe Guarantee - 24 hours a day / 7 days a week live customer service, and more!

Whether traveling on a tight budget, looking for a quick weekend getaway, or planning the trip of a lifetime, Frommer's guides and Travelocity.com will make your travel dreams a reality. You've bought the book, now book the trip!

Other Great Guides for Your Trip:

Frommer's Denmark

Frommer's Sweden

Frommer's Europe

Frommer's Europe from $70 a Day

Here's what the critics say about Frommer's:

"Amazingly easy to use. Very portable, very complete."
—*Booklist*

♦

"The only mainstream guide to list specific prices. The Walter Cronkite of guidebooks—with all that implies."
—*Travel & Leisure*

♦

"Complete, concise, and filled with useful information."
—*New York Daily News*

♦

"Hotel information is close to encyclopedic."
—*Des Moines Sunday Register*

Scandinavia

19th Edition

**by Darwin Porter
and Danforth Prince**

HUNGRY MINDS, INC.
New York, NY • Cleveland, OH • Indianapolis, IN

ABOUT THE AUTHORS

Co-authors **Darwin Porter** and **Danforth Prince** have written numerous best-selling Frommer's guides, notably to England, France, the Caribbean, Italy, and Germany. Porter was a bureau chief for the *Miami Herald* when he was 21, and Prince was formerly with the Paris bureau of *The New York Times*. They are also the authors of two other Scandinavia titles: one devoted to Denmark, another to Sweden.

Published by:

HUNGRY MINDS, INC.

909 Third Ave.
New York, NY 10022
www.frommers.com

ISBN 0-7645-6355-6
ISSN 0278-1069

Editor: Lorraine Festa
Production Editor: Stephanie Lucas
Design by Michele Laseau
Cartographer: Elizabeth Puhl
Photo Editor: Richard Fox
Front cover photo: Vindel River in Lapland, Sweden
Back cover photo: Historic Bryggen in Bergen, Norway

Production by Hungry Minds Indianapolis Production Services

SPECIAL SALES

For general information on Hungry Minds' products and services please contact our Customer Care department; within the U.S. at 800-762-2974, outside the U.S. at 317-572-3993 or fax 317-572-4002. For sales inquiries and reseller information, including discounts, bulk sales, customized editions, and premium sales, please contact our Customer Care department at 800-434-3422.

Manufactured in the United States of America

5   4   3   2   1

Contents

List of Maps xi

1   The Best of Denmark   1

1 The Best Travel Experiences 1

2 The Best Scenic Towns & Villages 2

3 The Best Active Vacations 4

4 The Best Festivals & Special Events 5

5 The Best Castles & Palaces 5

6 The Best Offbeat Experiences 6

7 The Best Buys 7

8 The Best Hotels 7

9 The Best Restaurants 8

2   Planning a Trip to Denmark   9

1 The Regions in Brief 9

2 Visitor Information & Entry Requirements 10

3 Money 10

    The Danish Krone 12

    What Things Cost in Copenhagen 13

4 When to Go 14

    Denmark Calendar of Events 15

5 The Active Vacation Planner 16

6 Adventure & Alternative Travel 17

7 Health & Insurance 18

8 Tips for Travelers with Special Needs 20

9 Getting There 23

10 Getting Around 31

11 Organized Tours 33

    Suggested Itineraries 33

    Fast Facts: Denmark 34

3   Introducing Copenhagen   38

1 Orientation 38

    Neighborhoods in Brief 40

2 Getting Around 42

    Fast Facts: Copenhagen 44

3 Accommodations 46

    Family-Friendly Hotels 52

4 Dining 56

    Family-Friendly Restaurants 65

    Quick Bites 67

4   Exploring Copenhagen   70

    Suggested Itineraries 70

1 In & Around the Tivoli Gardens 71

2 Amalienborg Palace & Environs 73

    Frommer's Favorite Copenhagen Experiences 76

3 Rosenborg Castle, Botanical Gardens & Environs 78

4 Christiansborg Palace & Environs 79

v

5 In the Old Town
(Indre By) 80

6 More Museums 81

7 The Churches of
Copenhagen 82

8 A Glimpse into the Past
Outside Copenhagen 83

9 Literary Landmarks 83

10 Architectural Highlights 84

11 Of Artistic Interest 84

12 Especially for Kids 84

13 Copenhagen on Foot: Walking
Tours 85

Walking Tour 1:
The Old City 85

Walking Tour 2:
Kongens Nytorv to
Langelinie 88

14 Organized Tours 91

15 Active Sports 92

16 The Shopping Scene 93

17 Copenhagen After Dark 97

18 Side Trips from
Copenhagen 102

5   Exploring the Danish Countryside   117

1 Funen 117

2 Bornholm 132

3 Jutland 140

6   The Best of Norway   157

1 The Best Travel Experiences 157

2 The Best Scenic Towns &
Villages 158

3 The Best Active Vacations 159

4 The Best Festivals & Special
Events 159

5 The Best Museums 160

6 The Best Buys 160

7 The Best Hotels 161

8 The Best Restaurants 161

7   Planning a Trip to Norway   163

1 The Regions in Brief 163

2 Visitor Information & Entry
Requirements 164

The Norwegian Krone 166

What Things Cost in Oslo 167

3 Money 167

4 When to Go 167

Norway Calendar of Events 168

5 The Active Vacation Planner 170

Tracing Your Norwegian
Roots 172

6 Health & Insurance 172

7 Tips for Travelers with Special
Needs 172

8 Getting There 173

9 Getting Around 175

10 Organized Tours 178

Suggested Itineraries 179

Fast Facts: Norway 180

8   Oslo   183

1 Orientation 184

Neighborhoods in Brief 185

2 Getting Around 186

Fast Facts: Oslo 188

3 Accommodations 190
  Family-Friendly Hotels 194
4 Dining 198
  Dining Secrets of Oslo 202
  Family-Friendly Restaurants 204
5 Seeing the Sights 208
  Suggested Itineraries 208
  Frommer's Favorite Oslo Experiences 212
  The Man Behind The Scream 217
6 Especially for Kids 219

7 Oslo on Foot: Walking Tours 219
  Walking Tour 1: Historic Oslo 219
  Walking Tour 2: In the Footsteps of Ibsen & Munch 222
8 Organized Tours 226
9 Active Sports 226
10 Shopping 228
11 Oslo After Dark 230
12 Side Trips from Oslo 235

9   Bergen   240

1 Orientation 240
2 Getting Around 241
  Fast Facts: Bergen 243
3 Accommodations 245
4 Dining 249

5 Seeing the Sights 251
6 Outdoor Activities 255
7 Shopping 256
8 Bergen After Dark 257
9 Side Trips from Bergen 259

10   Exploring the Norwegian Coast   261

1 By Coastal Steamer 261
2 The Fjords 265
  Frommer's Favorite Offbeat Adventures 266

3 Trondheim to Narvik 276

11   The Best of Sweden   291

1 The Best Travel Experiences 291
2 The Best Scenic Towns & Villages 291
3 The Best Active Vacations 292
4 The Best Festivals & Special Events 293

5 The Best Museums 293
6 The Best Offbeat Experiences 294
7 The Best Buys 295
8 The Best Hotels 295
9 The Best Restaurants 296

12   Planning a Trip to Sweden   297

1 The Regions in Brief 297
2 Visitor Information & Entry Requirements 297
3 Money 298
4 When to Go 298
  The Swedish Krona 300

  What Things Cost in Stockholm 301
  Sweden Calendar of Events 301
5 The Active Vacation Planner 302
6 Health & Insurance 304
7 Tips for Travelers with Special Needs 304

8 Getting There 305
9 Getting Around 308
10 Organized Tours 310

Suggested Itineraries 311
Fast Facts: Sweden 312

13   Introducing Stockholm   315

1 Orientation 315
   Neighborhoods in Brief 317
2 Getting Around 318
   Subway Art in Stockholm 319
   Fast Facts: Stockholm 320

3 Accommodations 322
   Family-Friendly Hotels 325
4 Dining 332
   Family-Friendly Restaurants 339
   Perfect Picnics 342

14   Exploring Stockholm   345

   Suggested Itineraries 345
1 On Gamla Stan & Neighboring
   Islands 346
   *Frommer's Favorite Stockholm
   Experiences* 347
2 On Norrmalm 348
3 On Djurgården 349
4 On Kungsholmen 353
5 On Södermalm 353
6 Near Stockholm 354
7 A Literary Landmark 354
8 Architectural Highlights 355
9 Especially for Kids 355
10 Stockholm on Foot: Walking
    Tours 355

   *Walking Tour 1: Gamla Stan
   (Old Town)* 355
   *Walking Tour 2: Along the
   Harbor* 359
11 Organized Tours 361
12 Spectator Sports 362
13 Outdoor Activities 362
14 Shopping 362
15 Stockholm After Dark 367
    *The Capital of Gay
    Scandinavia* 370
16 Side Trips from Stockholm 373
    Gamla Uppsala 378

15   Gothenburg   383

1 Orientation 383
2 Getting Around 385
   Fast Facts: Gothenburg 385
3 Accommodations 387
4 Dining 391

   Perfect Picnics 394
5 Seeing the Sights 395
6 Especially for Kids 399
7 Shopping 399
8 Gothenburg After Dark 401

16   Skåne (Including Helsingborg and Malmö)   404

1 Båstad 405
2 Helsingbor 410
3 Malmö 418

4 Lund 428
5 Ystad 433
6 Simrishamn 435

17 Exploring the Swedish Countryside 438

1 The Göta Canal 438

2 Dalarna 440

3 Gotland (Visby) 447

4 Swedish Lapland 453

Holiday on Ice 456

The Lapps (Sami) in Sweden 459

18 The Best of Finland 464

1 The Best Travel Experiences 464

2 The Best Scenic Towns & Villages 465

3 The Best Active Vacations 466

4 The Best Festivals & Special Events 467

5 The Best Museums 467

6 The Best Offbeat Experiences 468

7 The Best Buys 469

8 The Best Hotels 469

9 The Best Restaurants 470

19 Planning a Trip to Finland 472

1 The Regions in Brief 472

2 Visitor Information & Entry Requirements 474

The Finnish Markka 475

3 Money 475

What Things Cost in Helsinki 476

4 When to Go 476

Finland Calendar of Events 477

5 The Active Vacation Planner 478

6 Health & Insurance 479

7 Tips for Travelers with Special Needs 480

8 Getting There 480

9 Getting Around 484

10 Organized Tours 486

Suggested Itineraries 487

Fast Facts: Finland 488

20 Helsinki 492

1 Orientation 492

Neighborhoods in Brief 494

2 Getting Around 495

Fast Facts: Helsinki 496

3 Accommodations 499

4 Dining 508

Perfect Picnics 517

5 Seeing the Sights 518

Suggested Itineraries 518

Frommer's Favorite Helsinki Experiences 524

Did You Know? 525

The Building of Finland 526

Walking Tour: Central Helsinki 531

6 Organized Tours 533

7 Spectator Sports & Outdoor Activities 534

8 Shopping 534

9 Helsinki After Dark 540

10 Side Trips from Helsinki 545

Appendix A: Denmark in Depth 550

1 Denmark Today 550
  Did You Know? 551
2 The Natural Environment 552

3 History 101 552
  Dateline 552
4 Dining with the Danes 557

Appendix B: Norway in Depth 559

1 Norway Today 559
2 The Natural Environment 560
  Did You Know? 561
3 History 101 562

Dateline 562
A Sifter of Viking Secrets 565
4 Dining with the
  Norwegians 566

Appendix C: Sweden in Depth 568

1 Sweden Today 568
  Did You Know? 569
2 The Natural Environment 570
3 History 101 571

Dateline 571
Swedish Yankees 574
4 Dining with the Swedes 577

Appendix D: Finland in Depth 579

1 Finland Today 579
  Those Mysterious Genes 580
2 The Natural Environment 581
  Did You Know? 582

3 History 101 583
  Dateline 583
4 Dining with the Finns 587

Index 589

List of Maps

Scandinavia 3

Denmark 11

Copenhagen Accommodations 48

Copenhagen Dining 58

Copenhagen Attractions 74

Walking Tour: The Old City 87

Walking Tour: Kongens Nytorv
to Langelinie 89

Side Trips from Copenhagen 103

Jutland & Funen Island 119

Bornholm 133

Norway 165

Oslo Accommodations 192

Oslo Dining 200

Oslo Attractions 210

Walking Tour: Historic Oslo 221

Walking Tour: In the Footsteps
of Ibsen & Munch 223

Bergen Attractions 253

Sweden 299

Stockholm Accommodations 326

Stockholm Dining 334

Stockholm Attractions 350

Walking Tour: Gamla Stan
(Old Town) 357

Walking Tour: Along the Harbor 360

Side Trips from Stockholm 375

Gothenburg Attractions 397

Skåne 407

Dalarna 441

Lapland 455

Finland 473

Helsinki Accommodations 502

Helsinki Dining 512

Helsinki Attractions 520

Walking Tour: Central Helsinki 529

AN INVITATION TO THE READER

In researching this book, we discovered many wonderful places—hotels, restaurants, shops, and more. We're sure you'll find others. Please tell us about them, so we can share the information with your fellow travelers in upcoming editions. If you were disappointed with a recommendation, we'd love to know that, too. Please write to:

Frommer's Scandinavia, 19th Edition
Hungry Minds, Inc.
909 Third Avenue
New York, NY 10022

AN ADDITIONAL NOTE

Please be advised that travel information is subject to change at any time—and this is especially true of prices. We therefore suggest that you write or call ahead for confirmation when making your travel plans. The authors, editors, and publisher cannot be held responsible for the experiences of readers while traveling. Your safety is important to us, however, so we encourage you to stay alert and be aware of your surroundings. Keep a close eye on cameras, purses, and wallets, all favorite targets of thieves and pickpockets.

WHAT THE SYMBOLS MEAN

✪ Frommer's Favorites

Our favorite places and experiences—outstanding for quality, value, or both.

The following abbreviations are used for credit cards:

AE	American Express	EC	Eurocard
CB	Carte Blanche	JCB	Japan Credit Bank
DC	Diners Club	MC	MasterCard
DISC	Discover	V	Visa
ER	EnRoute		

FIND FROMMER'S ONLINE

www.frommers.com offers up-to-the-minute listings on almost 200 cities around the globe—including the latest bargains and candid, personal articles updated daily by Arthur Frommer himself. No other Web site offers such comprehensive and timely coverage of the world of travel.

The Best of Denmark

Denmark presents visitors with an embarrassment of riches—everything from exciting Copenhagen to historic castles, unusual offshore islands to quaint villages, and more. To help you decide how best to spend your time, we've compiled a list of our favorite experiences and discoveries. In the following pages, you'll find the kind of candid advice we'd give our close friends.

1 The Best Travel Experiences

- **A Week Down on the Farm:** The best way to see the heart of Denmark and meet the Danes is to spend a week on one of their farms. Nearly 400 farms, all over the country, take in paying guests. Stick a pin anywhere on a map of Denmark away from the cities and seacoast, and you'll find a thatched and timbered farm, or perhaps a more modern homestead. Almost anyplace makes a good base from which to explore the rest of the country on day trips. You join the host family and other guests for meals. You can learn about what's going on at the farm, and pitch in and help with the chores if you like. Activities range from bonfires and folk dancing to riding lessons or even horse-and-buggy rides. Although the official agency that used to arrange such holidays is no longer with us, many visitors seeking this kind of offbeat accommodation often surf the Internet for farms that advertise their willingness to receive guests. Or, decide which part of Denmark you'd like to be located in, then contact the nearest tourist office which keeps a list of farms willing to accept paying guests.

- **On the Road on a Bike:** Denmark is relatively flat, making it one of the best countries in Europe for touring on two wheels. You pass green hills, half-timbered villages, castles, manor houses, beech forests, and lakes as you roll along. Cyclists are given high priority in traffic. You can set out on your own, but a company that's loosely affiliated with the Danish tourist office is **Bike Denmark,** Olaf Poulsens Allé 1A, DK-3480 Fredensborg (☎ 48-48-58-00; www.bikedenmark.com). It offers eight different bike tours of Denmark. Some depart from Copenhagen; others cover parts of Jutland and, in some cases, southern Sweden. Tours last for 5 to 10 days, and cover 12½ to 37 miles per day. Detailed maps and directions are given to each cyclist, who proceeds at his or her own pace along itineraries especially selected for their exposure to areas of historic interest or natural beauty. Luggage is transported ahead of time and awaits participants in their hotel rooms at the end of a long day of cycling.

- **A Day (and Night) at the Tivoli:** These 150-year-old pleasure gardens are worth the airfare to Copenhagen all by themselves. They're a little bit of everything: open-air dancing, restaurants, theaters, concert halls, an amusement park . . . and, oh yes, gardens. From the first bloom of spring until the autumn leaves start to fall, they're devoted to lighthearted fun. The gardens are worth a visit anytime, but are especially nice at twilight, when the lights begin to glint off the trees. See chapter 4.

- **On the Trail of the Vikings:** Renowned for 3 centuries of fantastic exploits, the Vikings explored Greenland, North America, and the Caspian Sea from roughly A.D. 750 to 1050. Their legacy endures in Denmark. Relive the age at the Nationalmuseet in Copenhagen, which displays burial grounds of the Viking period, along with the largest and richest hoards of treasure, including relics from the "Silver Age." Even Viking costumes are on exhibit. At Roskilde, explore the Viking Ship Museum. It contains five vessels found in a fjord nearby, the largest of which was built in Ireland around 1060 and manned by 60 to 100 warriors. At Jelling, see two enormous mounds (the largest in Denmark)—one was originally the burial ground of King Gorm. And if you're in Ribe, check out the Museum of the Viking Age, where a multimedia room, "Odin's Eye," introduces the visitor to the world of the Vikings through an all-around sound and vision experience. See chapters 4 and 5.

- **In the Footsteps of Hans Christian Andersen:** To some visitors, this storyteller is *the* symbol of Denmark. The fairy tale lives on in Odense, on the island of Funen, where the shoemaker's son was born in 1805. His childhood home, a small half-timbered house on Munkemøllestræde where he lived from 1807 to 1817, has been turned into a museum. You can also visit the H. C. Andersens Hus, see the large store of memorabilia (including his walking stick and top hat), and take a few moments to listen to his tales on tape. But mostly you can wander the cobblestoned streets that he knew so well, marveling at his life and works. In the words of his obituary, they struck "chords that reverberated in every human heart," as they still do today. See chapter 5.

2 The Best Scenic Towns & Villages

- **Dragør:** At the doorstep of Copenhagen, this old seafaring town once flourished as a bustling herring-fishing port. Time passed it by, however, and for that we can be grateful. It looks much as it used to, with half-timbered ocher-and-pink 18th-century cottages—all with thatched or red-tiled roofs. The entire village is under the protection of the National Trust. A 35-minute ride from the Danish capital will take you back 2 centuries. See chapter 4.

- **Ærøskøbing:** This is storybook Denmark. The little village on the country's most charming island, Ærø, lies 18 miles across the water south of Svendborg. A 13th-century market town, it is a Lilliputian souvenir of the past, complete with little gingerbread houses. You expect Hansel and Gretel to arrive at any moment. See chapter 5.

- **Ribe:** On the peninsula of Jutland, this is the best-preserved medieval town in Denmark. It's famous for its narrow cobblestoned lanes and crooked, half-timbered houses. An important trading center during the Viking era, it's known today as the town where the endangered stork—often the subject of European

Scandinavia

myth and legend—flies back in April to nest. The medieval center of Ribe is protected by the National Trust. From April until mid-September, a night watchman
circles the town, spinning tales of its legendary days and singing traditional
songs. See chapter 5.

- **Odense:** Thousands of Hans Christian Andersen's fans visit the storyteller's
  birthplace every year. Denmark's third-largest city has a medieval core, and you
  can walk its cobblestoned streets and admire its half-timbered houses, including
  the H. C. Andersens Hus. Odense is also a worthwhile destination in its own

right, with many attractions (including St. Canute's Cathedral) in the city and nearby. On the outskirts you can explore everything from the 1554 Renaissance castle Egeskov to a 72-foot-long 10th-century Viking ship (at Ladby, 12 miles northeast of Odense). See chapter 5.

- **Ebeltoft:** On Jutland, this well-preserved town of half-timbered buildings is the capital of the Mols hill country. It's a town of sloping row houses, crooked streets, and local handcrafts shops. The Town Hall looks as though it were erected for kindergartners to play in. In Ebeltoft you can also visit the 1860 frigate *Jylland,* the oldest man-of-war in Denmark. See chapter 5.

3 The Best Active Vacations

- **Biking:** A nation of bikers, Denmark has organized the roads to suit the national sport. A network of bike routes and paths is protected from heavy traffic, and much of the terrain is flat. Bicycling vacations are available as inclusive tours that cover bike rental, ferry tickets, and accommodations en route. Some deluxe tours transport your luggage from one hotel to the next. For more information, contact the **Danish Cycling Federation,** Rømersgade 7, DK-1362 Copenhagen (☎ **33-32-31-21;** www.dcf.dk).

- **Camping:** There are a number of pleasant, well-equipped campgrounds near Copenhagen and elsewhere, and a total of 528 throughout the country. For information about campsites and facilities, contact the tourist information office in the town or region that appeals to you. Or write to a nationwide organization devoted to marketing Danish campgrounds to the rest of the world, the **Campingraadet,** Hesseløgade 16, DK-2100 Copenhagen (☎ **39-27-88-44**).

- **Fishing:** For centuries, much of Denmark relied for its diet on the sea and whatever the country's fishers could pull out of it. Since then, no smørrebrød buffet has been complete without a selection of shrimp, herring, and salmon. The preparation of plaice, cod, eel, perch, and trout are culinary art forms. The seas off Funen's 680-mile coastline, especially within the Great Belt, have yielded countless tons of seafood, and that tradition has encouraged anglers and sport enthusiasts to test their luck in the rich waters of the Baltic. Many outfitters can introduce you to the mysteries of fresh- and saltwater fishing. One of the most consistently reliable, which maintains a permanent headquarters facing the Great Sound on the island of Funen, is **Ole Dehn,** Søndergard 22, Lohals, DK-5953 Tranekær (☎ **62-55-17-00**). Its most popular offering involves half-day deep-sea fishing tours on the Great Sound, which cost 195 DKK ($24.40) per person. The 6-hour fishing experience, from 8am to 2pm, is conducted whenever business warrants.

- **Golfing:** In recent years, golf has become quite popular in Denmark. There are more than 100 clubs throughout the country, most of which welcome visitors— all you need is a membership card from your club at home. Several clubs have a pro trainer, golf shop, clubroom, and restaurant. Contact local tourist offices for a list of the golf courses in the regions you plan to visit.

- **Horseback Riding:** Riding schools throughout Denmark rent horses; local tourist offices can offer advice. Our favorite place for riding is on the Isle of Læsø (off Jutland), which you can explore on the back of an Icelandic pony. After you gallop past salt marshes and birds, you can stop from time to time to relax on the beach. For more information, contact **Krogbækgaard,** Byrum, DK-9940 Læsø (☎ **98-49-15-05**). Boats sail to Læsø from the port of Frederikshavn in North Jutland.

4 The Best Festivals & Special Events

- **July 4 Festival** (Rebild, near Aalborg): This is one of the few places outside the United States that celebrates U.S. independence. Each year Danes and Danish-Americans gather for picnic lunches, outdoor entertainment, and speeches. See chapter 2.
- **Fire Festival Regatta** (Silkeborg): This is the country's oldest and biggest festival, with nightly cruises on the lakes and illumination provided by thousands of candles on shore. The fireworks display on the final night is without equal in Europe, and Danish artists provide the entertainment at a large fun fair. Usually held the first week in August. See chapter 2.
- **Aalborg Carnival:** Celebrated on May 21, this is one of the country's great spring events. Happy folk in colorful costumes fill the streets. Almost 10,000 people take part in the celebration, honoring the victory of spring over winter. The whole city bursts with joy. See chapter 2.
- **Copenhagen Jazz Festival:** One of the finest jazz festivals in Europe takes place in July. Some of the best musicians in the world show up to jam in the Danish capital. Indoor and outdoor concerts—many of them free—are presented. See chapter 2.
- **Viking Festival** (Frederikssund): During this annual 2-week festival (June 19 to July 15), bearded Vikings revive Nordic sagas in an open-air theater. After each performance, there's a traditional Viking banquet. See chapter 4.

5 The Best Castles & Palaces

- **Kronborg Slot** (Helsingør): Shakespeare never saw this castle, and Hamlet (if he existed) lived centuries before it was built. But Shakespeare set his immortal play here—the Bard has spoken, and that's that. Its cannon-studded bastions are full of intriguing secret passages and openings for guns, and it often serves as the backdrop for modern productions of *Hamlet*. The brooding mythical hero Holger Danske is said to be asleep in the dungeon and according to the legend, the Viking chief will rise again to defend Denmark if it is endangered. See chapter 4.
- **Christiansborg Palace** (Copenhagen): The queen receives official guests in the Royal Reception Chamber, where you must don slippers to protect the floors. The complex also holds the Parliament House and the Supreme Court. From 1441 until the fire of 1795, this was the official residence of Denmark's monarchs. You can tour the richly decorated rooms, including the Throne Room and banquet hall. Below you can see the well-preserved ruins of the 1167 castle of Bishop Absalon, founder of Copenhagen. See chapter 4.
- **Rosenborg Castle** (Copenhagen): Founded by Christian IV in the 17th century, this red-brick Renaissance castle remained a royal residence until the early 19th century, when it was converted into a museum. It still houses the crown jewels, and its collection of costumes and royal memorabilia is unequaled in Denmark. See chapter 4.
- **Frederiksborg Castle** (Hillerød): Known as the Danish Versailles, this moated *slot* (castle) is the most elaborate in Scandinavia. Built in the Dutch Renaissance style of red brick with a copper roof, the castle's oldest parts date from 1560. Much of the castle was constructed under the direction of the "master builder," Christian IV, from 1600 to 1620. Now a major national history museum, the castle was ravaged by fire in 1859 and had to be completely restored. See chapter 4.

- **Egeskov Castle** (Kværndrup): On the island of Funen, this 1554 "water castle" is set amid splendid gardens. It's the most romantic example of Denmark's fortified manors. Built in the middle of a moat, it's surrounded by a 30-acre park. The best-preserved Renaissance castle of its type in Europe, it has many attractions on its grounds, including an airplane museum and a vintage automobile museum. See chapter 5.

6 The Best Offbeat Experiences

- **Calling on Artists and Craftspeople:** West Jutland has many open workshops where you can see craftspeople in action; you can meet the potter, the glassblower, the painter, the textile designer, and even the candlestick maker. Local tourist offices can tell you which studios are open to receive guests in such centers as Tønder, Ribe, Esbjerg, Varde, Billund, Herning, Struer, and Skive. One of our favorite crafts studios lies in Jutland, 16 miles west of Esbjerg, near the town of Blåvand, on a farmstead in the tiny agrarian hamlet of Ho. Here, the husband-and-wife team of Asger Kristensen and Inga Sørensen direct the **Havlit Stentøj studios,** at Vesterballevej 1, Ho, DK 6857 Blåvand (☎ 75-27-95-93). Jointly, the couple produces charming ceramics, including hand-painted replicas of birds, some rustic, some more detailed and refined. The artists take their inspiration from the rugged landscapes of West Jutland in their fabrication of such additional objects as urns, pots, and bas-reliefs.
- **Making People-to-People Contacts:** If you'd like to meet Scandinavians with interests and backgrounds like yours, the best "bridge" is **Friends Overseas,** 68-04 Dartmouth St., Forest Hills, NY 11375 (☎ 718/544-5660). There's a $25 fee for your "hookup" in Scandinavia, but for many it's worth the money to have this close encounter with these bright, articulate people, who are among the most educated in the world. Know in advance that there isn't any background investigation of the people you're going to be matched with, and everything is very casual and free-form—basically the Scandinavians listed in the company's handbook are whomever happens to fill out the proper forms. But based on the instincts of company founder, Larry Eisner, and the natural friendliness of the Scandinavians, social encounters usually work out happily, without unpleasant incidents. Contact information is grouped into subcategories that include families with children, couples, and singles. For more information, see "Adventure & Alternative Travel," in chapter 2.
- **Journeying Back to the 1960s:** If you're nostalgic for the counterculture, it lives on in Christiania, a Copenhagen community at the corner of Prinsessegade and Badsmandsstræde on Christianshavn. Founded in 1972, this is an anarchists' commune that occupies former army barracks; its current residents preach the gospel of drugs and peace. Christiania's residents have even organized their own government and passed laws, for example, to legalize drugs. They're not complete anarchists, however—they do venture into the city at least once a month to pick up their social welfare checks. Today you can wander about the community, which has a theater, cafes, grocery stores, and even a local radio station. See chapter 4.
- **Exploring Erotica:** Denmark was the first country to "liberate" pornography, in 1968, and today there's a museum in Copenhagen devoted to the subject. In the Erotica Museum (at Købmagergade 24), you can learn about the sex lives of such famous figures as Nietzsche, Freud, and Duke Ellington. Founded by a photographer of nudes, the exhibits range from the tame to the tempestuous—

everything from Etruscan drawings to pictures of venereal skin disease and sado-masochism videos. See chapter 4.

7 The Best Buys

- **Danish Design:** The simple but elegant lines that became fashionable in the 1950s have made a comeback. Danish modern chairs, glassware, and even buildings have returned. "Old masters" such as Arne Jacobsen, Hans Wegner, and Poul Kjærhom are celebrated; their designs from the 1940s and 1950s are sold in antiques stores. Wegner, noted for his sculptured teak chairs, is now viewed as the grand old man of Danish design. Younger designers have followed in the footsteps of the "old masters," producing carefully crafted items for the home—everything from chairs, desks, and furnishings to table settings and silverware. For the best display of Danish design today, walk along the pedestrians-only Strøget, Copenhagen's major shopping street. The best single showcase for modern Danish design may be **Illums Bolighus,** Amagertorv 10 (☎ 33-14-19-41).
- **Crystal & Porcelain:** Holmegaard crystal and Royal Copenhagen porcelain are household names, known for their beauty and craftsmanship. The items cost less in Denmark than in the States, although signed art glass is always extremely costly. To cut costs, you can shop for seconds, which are discounted by 20% to 50%—sometimes the imperfection can be detected only by an expert. Copenhagen's best centers for these collectors' items are **Royal Copenhagen** and **Bing & Grøndahl Porcelain,** Amagertorv 6 (☎ 33-13-71-81), and **Holmegaards Glasværker,** Amagertorv 6 (☎ 33-12-44-77).
- **Silver:** Danish designers have made a name for themselves in this field. Even with taxes and shipping charges, buying silver in Denmark is about half as costly as doing so in the States. If you're willing to consider "used" silver, you can get some remarkable discounts. The big name in international silver is **Georg Jensen,** Amagertorv 6, Copenhagen (☎ 33-11-40-80)—and you can buy it at the source.

8 The Best Hotels

- **Phoenix Copenhagen** (Copenhagen; ☎ 33-95-95-00): The Danish Communist Party used to have its headquarters here, but the "Reds" of the Cold War era wouldn't recognize this pocket of posh today. It reeks of capitalistic excess and splendor, from its dazzling public rooms with French antiques to its bedrooms with dainty Louis XVI styling. See chapter 3.
- **Hotel d'Angleterre** (Copenhagen; ☎ 800/44-UTELL in the U.S., or 33-12-00-95): Some critics rate this the finest hotel in Denmark. It drifted toward mediocrity a few years back, before a massive investment saved it. Now the hotel is better than ever, and houses a swimming pool and a nightclub. The service is among the finest in Copenhagen. See chapter 3.
- **Falsled Kro** (Falsled; ☎ 62-68-11-11): Funen Island's finest accommodation is this quintessential Danish inn, with origins going back to the 1400s. A Relais & Châteaux property, it has been elegantly furnished and converted into a stellar inn with a top-quality restaurant that rivals the very best in Copenhagen. See chapter 5.
- **Hotel Dagmar** (Ribe; ☎ 75-42-00-33): Jutland's most glamorous hotel was converted from a private home in 1850, and the building dates to 1581. This

half-timbered hotel encapsulates the charm of the 16th century, with carved chairs, sloping wooden floors, and stained-glass windows. Many of the rooms have antique canopy beds. A fine restaurant that serves Danish and international dishes completes the picture. See chapter 5.

- **Hotel Hesselet** (Nyborg; ☎ 65-31-30-29): This stylish, modern hotel on Funen occupies a woodland setting in a beech forest. The spacious bedrooms are artfully decorated, often with traditional furnishings. A library, Oriental carpets, and an open fireplace add graceful touches to the public areas. Many Copenhagen residents head here for a retreat, patronizing the hotel's gourmet restaurant at night. See chapter 5.

9 The Best Restaurants

- **Skt. Gertruds Kloster** (Copenhagen; ☎ 33-14-66-30): The capital's most romantic restaurant serves the most refined cuisine. In 14th-century underground vaults, you dine by the light of some 1,500 flickering candles. Once a medieval monastery, the restaurant now offers delectable international cuisine, including velvety foie gras with black truffles, and venison with green asparagus. See chapter 3.

- **Kommandanten** (Copenhagen; ☎ 33-12-09-90): A house built by a Danish commander for his family in 1698 accommodates this restaurant. The menu reflects the finest continental and Mediterranean influences in such dishes as foie gras with lobster and truffle sauce, and pigeon sautéed with bacon, cabbage, and cherries. Fresh seafood is served in every conceivable way. The wooden floors and beams date to the 17th century, but the Warhol art makes the restaurant look trendy. See chapter 3.

- **Divan II** (Copenhagen; ☎ 33-12-51-51): This early-19th-century slate house was constructed when the lush Tivoli Garden grounds were being laid out. In this romantic setting, you can enjoy both a meal and a view over the lake across from the fairy-tale Hans Christian Andersen Castle. The chefs prepare the gardens' most refined cuisine, ranging from rack of Danish lamb roasted with garlic and sage to mousseline of lobster baked with turbot and served with asparagus spears. See chapter 3.

- **Marie Louise** (Odense; ☎ 66-17-92-95): Glittering with crystal and silver, this dining room, located on a pedestrian street, is one of the finest on the island of Funen. In an antique house, this Danish-French alliance offers excellent cuisine, preparation, and service. Seafood and fish are the favored dishes. See chapter 5.

- **Falsled Kro** (Falsled; ☎ 62-68-11-11): Even if you don't stay here, consider enjoying a meal. A favorite among well-heeled Europeans, it produces stellar French-inspired cuisine, often using seasonal produce from its own gardens. The succulent salmon is smoked on the premises in one of the outbuildings, and the owners breed quail locally. Such care and attention to detail make this one of Denmark's top restaurants. See chapter 5.

Planning a Trip to Denmark 2

In the following pages we've compiled the practical advice you'll need—airline information, what things cost, a calendar of events—so that you may plan your trip to Denmark with ease.

1 The Regions in Brief

ZEALAND Home to Denmark's capital, **Copenhagen,** Zealand draws more visitors than any other region. It's the largest island, the wealthiest, and the most densely populated. Other cities include **Roskilde,** 20 miles west of Copenhagen, which is home to a landmark cathedral (burial place of many kings) and a collection of Viking vessels discovered in a fjord. In the medieval town of **Køge,** witches were burned in the Middle Ages. One of the most popular attractions on the island is **Helsingør** ("Elsinore," in English), about 25 miles north of Copenhagen, where visitors flock to see "Hamlet's castle." Off the southeast corner of the island lies the island of **Møn,** home to Møns Klint, an expanse of white cliffs that rises sharply out of the Baltic.

JUTLAND The peninsula of Jutland links the island nation of Denmark with Germany. Jutland has miles of coastline, with some of northern Europe's finest sandy beaches. Giant dunes and moors abound on the west coast, whereas the interior has rolling pastures and beech forests. Jutland's more interesting towns and villages include **Jelling,** heralded as the birthplace of Denmark and the ancient seat of the Danish kings; here you can see an extensive collection of Viking artifacts excavated from ancient burial mounds. The Viking port of **Ribe** is the oldest town in Denmark. It's known throughout the world as the preferred nesting ground for numerous endangered storks. The resort of **Fanø,** with its giant dunes, heather-covered moors, and forests, is an excellent place to bird-watch or view Denmark's varied wildlife. The university city of **Århus** is Jutland's capital and second only to Copenhagen in size. **Aalborg,** founded by Vikings more than 1,000 years ago, is a thriving commercial center in northern Jutland. It lies close to Rebild National Park and the Rold Forest.

FUNEN With an area of 1,150 square miles, Funen is Denmark's second-largest island. Called the "garden of Denmark," Funen is known to the world as the birthplace of Hans Christian Andersen. Its rolling countryside is dotted with orchards, stately manors, and castles. **Odense,** Andersen's birthplace, is a mecca for fairy-tale writers and fans from around the world. Nearby stands Egeskov Castle, Europe's best-preserved Renaissance castle, resting on oak columns in the middle of a small lake. Funen has a number of bustling ports, including **Nyborg** in the east and **Svendborg** at the southern end of the island. **Æroskøbing,** nearby on the island of Ærø and accessible by ferry, is a medieval market town that's a showplace of Scandinavian heritage.

BORNHOLM   In the Baltic Sea, southeast of Zealand and close to Sweden, lies the island of Bornholm. The countryside is peppered with prehistoric monuments and runic stones, and numerous fishing villages dot the shoreline. Some of Europe's largest castle ruins dot this region of the island. The town of **Rønne** is the site of Denmark's oldest regional theater; it stages numerous concerts and shows year-round. The island of **Christiansø,** off the coast of Bornholm, was the site of Denmark's penal colony. Criminals sentenced to life imprisonment were deported to the island, where they spent their lives in slavery.

2 Visitor Information & Entry Requirements

VISITOR INFORMATION
In the **United States,** contact the **Scandinavian Tourist Board,** P.O. Box 4649, Grand Central Station, New York, NY 10163 (☎ **212/885-9700;** www.scandinavia. com), at least 3 months in advance for maps, sightseeing information, ferry schedules, and advice. Call or write for information; walk-in clients are no longer accepted.

If you contact a **travel agent,** make sure the agent is a member of the American Society of Travel Agents (ASTA). If a problem arises, you can complain to the society's Consumer Affairs Department, 1101 King St., Alexandria, VA 22314 (☎**703/706-0387**).

In the **United Kingdom,** contact the **Danish Tourist Board,** 55 Sloane St., London SW1X 9SY (☎ **020/7259-5959**).

ENTRY REQUIREMENTS
American, Canadian, Irish, Australian, and New Zealand citizens, and British subjects, need only a passport to enter Denmark. You must apply for a visa only if you want to stay more than 3 months. A British Visitor's Passport is also valid, for holidays and some business trips of less than 3 months. The passport can include your spouse, and it's valid for 1 year. Apply in person at a main post office in the British Isles, and the passport will be issued that day.

Your current domestic **driver's license** is acceptable in Denmark—an international driver's license is not required.

3 Money

CURRENCY   Although a member of the European Union, a majority of Danes rejected the euro as their form of currency in September 2000. They continue to use the **krone** (crown), which breaks down into 100 **øre.** The plural is **kroner.** The international monetary designation for the Danish kroner is "DKK." (The Swedish currency is the kronor, but note the different spelling.) At press time, 1 krone equals about 13¢ U.S., or 8 DKK to the U.S. dollar. One krone equals 9 British pence, or approximately 11 kroner to the British pound. These rates are subject to change, so check the current rates shortly before you go.

Denmark

The Danish Krone

For American Readers: At this writing, $1 = approximately 8 kroner (or 1 krone = 13¢); this was the exchange rate used to calculate the dollar values given in this edition, rounded to the nearest nickel.

For British Readers: At this writing, £1 = approximately 11 kroner (or 1 krone = 9 pence); this was the exchange rate used to calculate the pound values in the chart below.

Note Regarding the Euro: The eventual role of the euro (€) within Denmark is less certain than it is within many other countries of Europe, because, in September 2000, a majority of Danes rejected a proposal to adopt it as the national currency. But despite its uncertainty, you're likely to see it listed as one of several price options on some hotel and restaurant bills. But purely as a point of reference, at press time, 1€ = 6.7 kroner (or 1 krone = .15€).

Note: International exchange rates fluctuate, so the figures in this chart may not be the same by the time of your trip to Denmark. Use this table as a guideline.

DKK	US$	UK£	Euro	DKK	US$	UK£	Euro
1	0.13	0.09	0.15	75	9.38	6.75	11.25
2	0.25	0.18	0.30	100	12.50	9.00	15.00
3	0.38	0.27	0.45	125	15.63	11.25	18.75
4	0.50	0.36	0.60	150	18.75	13.50	22.50
5	0.63	0.45	0.75	175	21.88	15.75	26.25
6	0.75	0.54	0.90	200	25.00	18.00	30.00
7	0.88	0.63	1.05	225	28.13	20.25	33.75
8	1.00	0.72	1.20	250	31.25	22.50	37.50
9	1.13	0.81	1.35	275	34.38	24.75	41.25
10	1.25	0.90	1.50	300	37.50	27.00	45.00
15	1.88	1.35	2.25	350	43.75	31.50	52.50
20	2.50	1.80	3.00	400	50.00	36.00	60.00
25	3.13	2.25	3.75	500	62.50	45.00	75.00
50	6.25	4.50	7.50	1000	125.00	90.00	150.00

Bank notes in circulation include 50, 100, 200, 500, and 1,000 kroner. Coins are in denominations of 25 øre; 50 øre; 1 krone; and 2, 5, 10, and 20 kroner. Still in circulation, but being phased out, are 5- and 10-øre coins.

When converting your currency into Danish kroner, be aware of varying exchange rates. In general, banks offer better rates than currency-exchange bureaus, but they do charge a commission. Hotels generally offer the worst rates. If you are cashing American Express checks, you will get the best rate at American Express.

CURRENCY EXCHANGE   Many hotels in Scandinavia simply do not accept a dollar- or pound-denominated check; those that do will certainly charge for making the conversion. In some cases a hotel may accept countersigned traveler's checks or a credit or charge card.

If you're making a deposit on a hotel reservation, it's cheaper and easier to pay with a check drawn on a Scandinavian bank. This can be arranged by a large commercial

What Things Cost in Copenhagen	U.S. $
Taxi from the airport to the city center	16.25
Subway from Central Station to outlying suburbs	1.40
Local telephone call	.35
Double room at the Hotel d'Angleterre (very expensive)	286.90
Double room, with bathroom, at the Hotel Kong Arthur (moderate)	160.00
Double room, without bathroom, at the Hotel Valberg (inexpensive)	75.00
Lunch for one at Restaurant Els (moderate)	26.00
Lunch for one at Ida Davidsen (inexpensive)	12.00
Dinner for one, without wine, at Kommandanten (very expensive)	78.75
Dinner for one, without wine, at Copenhagen Corner (moderate)	28.00
Dinner for one, without wine, at Nyhavns Færgekro (inexpensive)	19.40
Pint of beer (draft Pilsner)	6.45
Coca-Cola	3.40
Cup of coffee	3.40
Admission to the Tivoli	6.15
Movie ticket	8.50
Roll of ASA 100 color film, 36 exposures	10.50
Ticket to the Royal Theater	7.50–75.00

bank or by a specialist like **Ruesch International,** 700 11th St. NW, 4th floor, Washington, DC 20001 (☎ **800/424-2923** or 202/408-1200; www.ruesch.com). It performs a wide variety of conversion-related tasks, usually for about $15 per transaction.

If you need a check payable in a Scandinavian currency, call Ruesch's toll-free number, describe what you need, and write down the transaction number. Mail your dollar-denominated personal check (payable to Ruesch International) to the Washington, D.C., office. When it's received, the company will mail you a check denominated in the requested currency for the specified amount, minus the $3 charge. The company can also help you with wire transfers, as well as the conversion of VAT (value-added tax) refund checks. Information is mailed upon request.

In England, contact Ruesch International Ltd., 18 Savile Row, London W1X 2AD (☎ **020/7734-2300**).

TRAVELER'S CHECKS Traveler's checks are a bit outdated in the wake of ATMs sprouting up around the world, but some visitors still prefer this old-fashioned means of carrying money. Most banks give you a better exchange rate for traveler's checks than for cash. Checks denominated in U.S. dollars or British pounds are accepted virtually anywhere; sometimes you can also get checks in a local currency.

The agencies listed below will replace checks if they're lost or stolen, provided you produce documentation. When purchasing checks, ask about refund hotlines. American Express has the most offices around the world.

Issuers sometimes have agreements with groups to sell traveler's checks without a commission. For example, American Automobile Association (AAA) clubs sell commission-free American Express checks in several currencies.

American Express (☎ 800/221-7282 in the U.S. and Canada) is one of the largest and most recognizable issuers of traveler's checks. Holders of certain types of American Express cards pay no commission. For questions or problems arising outside the United States or Canada, contact any of the company's many regional representatives. We'll list locations throughout this guide.

Citicorp (☎ 800/645-6556 in the U.S. and Canada or 813/623-7300, collect, from elsewhere) issues checks in several currencies.

Thomas Cook (☎ 800/223-7373 in the U.S. and Canada or 609/987-7300, collect, from elsewhere) issues MasterCard traveler's checks denominated in several currencies; not all currencies are available at every outlet.

Visa Travelers Checks (☎ 800/221-2426 in the U.S. and Canada or 212/858-8500, collect, from most other parts of the world) sells Visa checks denominated in several major currencies.

CREDIT & CHARGE CARDS   These are useful throughout Scandinavia. American Express, Diners Club, and Visa are widely recognized. If you see a Eurocard or Access sign, it means the establishment accepts MasterCard. With an American Express, MasterCard, or Visa card, you can also withdraw currency from cash machines (ATMs). Always check with your credit- or charge-card company about this before leaving home.

ATM NETWORKS   Plus, Cirrus, and other networks connecting automated-teller machines operate throughout Scandinavia. If your credit card has a PIN (Personal Identification Number), you can probably use your card at Scandinavian ATMs to withdraw money as a cash advance on your card. Always determine the frequency limits for withdrawals, and check to see if your PIN code must be reprogrammed for use abroad. Discover cards are accepted in the United States only. For **Cirrus** locations abroad, call ☎ 800/424-7787. For **Plus** usage abroad, check www.visa.com or call ☎ 800/843-7587.

MONEYGRAM   If you find yourself without money, an American Express wire service can help you secure emergency funds from family members or friends. Through **MoneyGram,** 7401 W. Mansfield Ave., Lakewood, CO 80235 (☎ 800/926-9400; www.moneygram.com), money can be sent abroad in less than 10 minutes. Senders should call American Express (☎ 800/221-7282 in the U.S. and Canada) to learn the address of the closest MoneyGram outlet. Cash, credit card, charge card, or sometimes personal checks (with ID) are acceptable forms of payment. The fee is $10 for the first $300, with a sliding scale for larger amounts; the fee enables the sender to include a short telex message and make a 3-minute phone call to the recipient. At the outlet where money is received, the recipient must present a photo ID.

4 When to Go

CLIMATE

Denmark's climate is mild for Scandinavia—New England farmers experience harsher winters. Summer temperatures average 61° to 77°F. Winter temperatures seldom go below 30°F, thanks to the warming waters of the Gulf Stream. From a weather perspective, mid-April to November is a good time to visit.

Denmark's Average Daytime Temperatures °F

Jan	Feb	Mar	Apr	May	June	July	Aug	Sept	Oct	Nov	Dec
32	32	35	44	53	60	64	63	57	49	42	37

HOLIDAYS

Some of these dates may vary slightly, so check with a local tourist office. Danish public holidays (and dates of those that do not vary) are New Year's Day (January 1), Maundy Thursday, Good Friday, Easter Sunday, Easter Monday, Labor Day (May 1), Common Prayers Day (fourth Friday after Easter), Ascension Day (mid-May), Whitsunday (late May), Whitmonday, Constitution Day (June 5), Christmas Day (December 25), and Boxing Day (December 26).

Denmark Calendar of Events

Note: Exact dates below apply for 2001. Should you be using this guide in 2002, check with local tourist boards for exact dates.

May

- **Ballet and Opera Festival** (Copenhagen). Classical and modern dance and two operatic masterpieces are presented at the Old Stage of the Royal Theater in Copenhagen. For tickets, contact the Royal Theater, Box 2185, DK-1017 København (☎ 33-69-69-69). Mid-May to June.
- **Aalborg Carnival.** This is one of the country's great spring events. The streets fill with people in colorful costumes. Thousands take part in the celebration, which honors the victory of spring over winter. For information, call ☎ 98-13-71-11. May 20 to 25.
- **Carnival in Copenhagen.** A great citywide event. There's also a children's carnival. For information, call ☎ 33-25-38-44. May 30 and 31.

June

- **Viking Festival** (Frederikssund, 8 miles southwest of Hillerød). For almost a month every summer, "bearded Vikings" present old Nordic sagas in an open-air setting. After each performance, a traditional Viking meal is held. Call ☎ 47-31-06-85 for more information. Mid-June to July 8.
- **Midsummer's Night** (throughout the country). This age-old event is celebrated throughout Denmark. It is the longest day of the year. Festivities throughout the tiny nation begin at around 10pm with bonfires and celebrations along the myriad coasts. June 21.
- **Roskilde Festival.** Europe's biggest rock festival has been going strong for more than 30 years, now bringing about 90,000 revelers each year to the central Zealand town. Beside major rock concerts, which often draw "big names," scheduled activities include theater and film presentations. For more information, call ☎ 46-36-66-13. June 1 to July 1.

July

- **Funen Festival.** This annual musical extravaganza frequently draws big, international headliners. The festival's music is often hard-core rock, but gentler, classical melodies are presented as well. It takes place in the city of Odense, on the island of Funen. For more information, call the Odense tourist bureau (☎ 66-12-75-20). July 1 to 5.
- **July 4** (Rebild). Rebild, near Aalborg, is one of the few places outside the United States to honor American Independence Day. For more information, contact the Aalborg Tourist Office, Østcrågade 8, DK-9000 Aalborg (☎ 98-12-60-22). July 4.
- **Copenhagen Jazz Festival.** International jazz musicians play in the streets, squares, and theaters. Pick up a copy of *Copenhagen This Week* to find the venues. For information, call ☎ 33-93-20-13. July 6 to 15.

- **Sønderborg Tilting Festival.** Dating to the Middle Ages, the "tilting at the ring" tradition has survived only in the old town of Sønderborg on the island of Als in southern Jutland. While riding at a gallop, the horseman uses his lance to see how many times (in 24 attempts) he can take the ring. Parades, music, and entertainment are included. For more information, contact the Turistbureau, Rådhustorvet 7, DK-6400 Sønderborg (☎ 74-42-35-55). Mid-July.

August

- **Fire Festival Regatta** (Silkeborg). Denmark's oldest and biggest festival features nightly cruises on the lakes, with thousands of candles illuminating the shores. The fireworks display on the last night is the largest and most spectacular in northern Europe. Popular Danish artists provide entertainment at a large fun fair. For more information, contact the Turistbureau, Godthåbsuej 4, DK-8600 Silkeborg (☎ 86-82-19-11). August 2 to 4.
- **Fall Ballet Festival** (København). The internationally acclaimed Royal Danish Ballet returns home to perform at the Old Stage of the Royal Theater just before the tourist season ends. For tickets, contact the Royal Theater, Box 2185, DK-1017 København (☎ 33-69-69-69). Mid-August to September 1.
- **Århus Festival Week.** A wide range of cultural activities—including opera, jazz, classical, and folk music, ballet, and theater—is presented. It's the largest cultural festival in Scandinavia. Sporting activities and street parties abound as well. For more information, contact Århus Tourist Office, Rådhuset, Århus C, DK-8000 Århus (☎ 89-31-82-70). August 31 to September 9.

5 The Active Vacation Planner

BEACHES   With some 5,000 miles of coastline, Denmark has several long strips of sandy beach. In many cases, dunes protect the beaches from sea winds. Most beaches are relatively unspoiled, and the Danes like to keep them that way—any polluted beaches are clearly marked. Many Danes like to go nude at the beach. Nudist beaches aren't clearly identified; often you'll see bathers with and without clothing using the same beach. The best beach resorts are those on the north coast of Zealand and the southern tip of the island of Bornholm. Beaches on the east coast of Jutland are also good, and often attract Germans from the south. Funen has a number of good beaches, too, especially in the south.

BIKING   The Danes have organized their roads to suit their national sport. Bikers can pedal along a network of biking routes and paths protected from heavy traffic. The Danish landscape is made for this type of vacation. Most tourist offices publish biking tour suggestions for their districts, a great way to see the sights and get in shape at the same time. The **Danish Cycling Federation (Dansk Cyklist Forbund),** Rømersgade 7, Copenhagen (☎ 33-32-31-21; www.dcf.dk), publishes excellent tour suggestions covering the whole country. The federation can also provide data about package vacations.

FISHING   No place in Denmark is more than 35 miles from the sea, so fishing is a major pastime. The country also has well-stocked rivers and lakes, including fjord waters around the Limfjord. Anglers between the ages of 18 and 67 must get a Ministry of Fisheries permit for 120 DKK ($15); it's available at any post office. Jutland is known for its good trout fishing (salmon is available, but found more readily in Norway). Anglers who fish from the beach can catch eel, mackerel, turbot, sea trout, plaice, and flounder. For more information, contact **Sportfiskerforbund,** Worsåesgade 1 DK-7100 Vejle (☎ 75-82-06-99).

GOLF   In recent years, golf has become very popular in Denmark. The undulating landscape is ideal for the construction of courses. For the most favorable treatment, prospective golfers should bring a valid golf club membership card from home. For information on the best courses near where you're staying, contact local tourist offices.

SAILING   Denmark has about 600 large and small harbors. Sailing enthusiasts will have many opportunities, especially in the open waters of the Baltic or the more sheltered waters of the South Funen Sea between Lolland and Falster, and Zealand. The Limfjord in North Jutland is also ideal for sailing. Many sailboats are available for rent, as are cruisers. For information, contact local tourist offices.

WALKING   Local tourist offices distribute folders that describe short and long walks in Danish forests. Twenty are printed in English; check at tourist offices.

6 Adventure & Alternative Travel

ADVENTURE TRAVEL OPERATORS

In North America, a few companies offer adventure trips to Scandinavia (see chapters 7, "Planning a Trip to Norway," 12, "Planning a Trip to Sweden," and 19, "Planning a Trip to Finland," for specific country information). **Crossing Latitudes,** 420 W. Koch St., Bozeman, MT 59715 (☎ 800/572-8747 or 406/585-5356), offers sea kayaking and backpacking expeditions throughout the region; and **Blue Marble Travel,** 31 South St., Suite 301, Morristown, NJ (☎ 800/258-8689 or 973/326-9533; www.bluemarble.org), features reasonably priced biking and hiking trips in Denmark and Norway.

IN THE U.K.

The oldest travel agency in Britain, **Cox & Kings,** Gordon House 10, Greencoat Place, London SW1P 1PH (☎ 020/7873-5000; www.coxandkings.co.uk), was established in 1758. Today the company specializes in unusual, if pricey, holidays. Its offerings in Scandinavia include cruises through the spectacular fjords and waterways, bus and rail tours through sites of historic and aesthetic interest, and visits to the region's best-known handcraft centers, Viking burial sites, and historic churches. The company's staff is noted for its focus on tours of ecological and environmental interest.

To cycle through the splendors of Scandinavia, you can join Britain's oldest and largest association of bicycle riders, the **Cyclists' Touring Club,** 69 Meadrow, Godalming, Surrey GU7 3HS (☎ 01483/417-217; www.ctc.org.uk). Founded in 1878, it charges £25 ($40) a year for membership, which includes information, maps, a subscription to a newsletter packed with practical information and morale boosters, plus recommended cycling routes through virtually every country in Europe. The organization's information bank on scenic routes through Scandinavia is especially comprehensive. Membership can be arranged over the phone with a credit card (such as MasterCard, Visa, Access, or Barclaycard).

LEARNING VACATIONS

Danish Cultural Institute (Det Danske Kultur Institutu), Kultorvet 2, DK-1175 København (☎ 33-13-54-48; fax 33-15-10-91), offers summer seminars in English, including a course in Danish culture. Credit programs are available, but many courses are geared toward professional groups from abroad. An especially interesting course for those with some knowledge of Danish is "Danmark, Danskerne, Dansk," which includes language instruction.

An international series of programs for persons over 50 who are interested in combining travel and learning is offered by **Interhostel,** developed by the University of New Hampshire. Each program lasts 2 weeks, is led by a university faculty or staff member, and is arranged in conjunction with a host college, university, or cultural institution. Participants may stay longer if they want. Interhostel offers programs consisting of cultural and intellectual activities, with field trips to museums and other centers of interest. For information, contact the University of New Hampshire, Division of Continuing Education, 6 Garrison Ave., Durham, NH 03824 (☎ **800/ 733-9753** or 603/862-1147; www.learn.unh.edu).

Another good source of information about courses in Denmark is the **American Institute for Foreign Study (AIFS),** River Plaza, 9 West Broad St., Stamford, CT 06902 (☎ **800/727-2437** or 203/399-5000; www.aifs.org). This organization can set up transportation and arrange for summer courses, with bed and board included.

The biggest organization dealing with higher education in Europe is the **Institute of International Education (IIE),** 809 United Nations Plaza, New York, NY 10017 (☎ **800/445-0443** or 212/883-8200; www.iie.org). A few of its booklets are free; for $39.95, plus $6 for postage, you can buy the more definitive *Vacation Study Abroad.* The Information Center in New York is open to the public Tuesday through Thursday from 11am to 4pm. The institute is closed on major holidays.

One well-recommended clearinghouse for academic programs throughout the world is the **National Registration Center for Study Abroad (NRCSA),** 823 N. 2nd St., P.O. Box 1393, Milwaukee, WI 53201 (☎ **414/278-0631;** www.nrcsa.com). The organization maintains language study programs throughout Europe.

PEOPLE TO PEOPLE

Established in 1971, **Friends Overseas** matches American visitors and Scandinavians with similar interests and backgrounds. Names and addresses are given to each applicant, and letters must be written before the visitors depart; Scandinavians may not meet visitors unless they have ample time to plan. For more information, write to Friends Overseas, 68-04 Dartmouth St., Forest Hills, NY 11375 (☎ **718/544-5660** after 5pm; www.nordbalt.com). Send a self-addressed, stamped business-size envelope, and include your age, occupation or occupational goals, approximate dates of your visit, and names of your traveling companions. The fee is $25.

7 Health & Insurance

HEALTH

You will encounter few health problems while traveling in Scandinavia. The water is safe to drink, the milk is pasteurized, and the health services are excellent. Occasionally a change in diet might cause minor diarrhea, so you may want to pack some anti-diarrhea medicine. In the summer, arrive at buffets early so that your smørrebrød (open-faced sandwiches) or salads made with mayonnaise are fresh.

Put all your essential medicines in your carry-on luggage, and bring enough of any prescription medications to last through your stay. Bring along copies of your prescriptions written in the generic form.

If you need a doctor, your hotel can find one. You can also get a list of English-speaking doctors from the **International Association for Medical Assistance to Travelers (IAMAT),** 417 Center St., Lewiston, NY 14092 (☎ **716/754-4883;** www.sentex.net/~iamat), or in Canada, Regal Rd., Guelph, ON N1K 1B5 (☎ **519/ 836-0102**).

If you suffer from a chronic illness, talk to your doctor before traveling. For conditions such as heart trouble, epilepsy, or diabetes, wear a Medic Alert Identification Tag, which immediately alerts any doctor to your condition. The tag also provides Medic Alert's 24-hour hotline number so that a foreign doctor can obtain your medical records. The initial membership costs $35, plus a $15 yearly fee. Contact the **Medic Alert Foundation,** 2323 Colorado Ave., Turlock, CA 95381-1009 (☎ 800/ 825-3785).

In case of a sudden illness or the aggravation of a chronic disease, Denmark provides free treatment to foreign visitors, provided they are not deliberately seeking free treatment and cannot immediately return home. Transportation home is the visitors' responsibility.

INSURANCE

Before buying additional insurance, check your homeowner's, automobile, and medical insurance policies as well as the insurance offered by credit- and charge-card companies and auto and travel clubs.

Remember, Medicare covers U.S. citizens traveling in Mexico and Canada only.

Also note that to submit any claim, you must always have complete documentation, including all receipts, police reports, medical records, and other data.

If you're prepaying for your vacation or are taking a charter or another flight that imposes high cancellation penalties, consider getting cancellation insurance.

One final note: The restrictions tied to most of these policies are sweeping and somewhat unforgiving. Check them carefully. If you consider yourself the least bit active, chances are you won't be covered if you're injured in an activity that could be deemed even remotely "athletic." Also, check with your local insurance agent to see if you already have a policy that covers what these policies would cover.

The following companies can provide information:

- **Travel Guard International,** 1145 Clark St., Stevens Point, WI 54481 (☎ 800/ 826-1300 or 715/345-0505), offers comprehensive insurance programs. Prices start at $44. The program covers basically everything, including emergency assistance, accidental death, trip cancellation and interruption, medical coverage abroad, and lost luggage. There are some restrictions, which you should understand before you purchase the coverage.

- **Travelers Insured International, Inc.,** P.O. Box 280568, Hartford, CT 06128-0568 (☎ 800/243-3174 in the U.S. or 860/528-7663 outside the U.S. between 7:45am and 7pm EST; www.travelinsured.com), provides trip cancellation and emergency evacuation policies that cost $5.50 for each $100 of coverage. Travel accident and illness insurance starts from $10 for 6 to 10 days; $500 worth of coverage for lost, damaged, or delayed baggage costs $20 for 6 to 10 days; and trip cancellation goes for $5.50 per $100 worth of coverage (written approval is necessary for cancellation coverage above $10,000).

- **Travelex,** 11717 Burt St., Suite 202, Omaha, NE 68175 (☎ 800/228-9792 in the U.S.; www.travelex-insurance.com), offers insurance packages based on the age of the traveler as well as the cost of the trip per person. Included in the packages are travel-assistance services and financial protection against trip cancellation, trip interruption, flight and baggage delays, accident-related medical costs, accidental death and dismemberment, and medical evacuation.

- **Healthcare Abroad,** c/o Wallach & Co., 107 W. Federal St., Middleburg, VA 20118 (☎ 800/237-6615; www.wallach.com), offers $250,000 of comprehensive medical expense protection, plus the multilingual services of a worldwide travelers' assistance network. Any U.S. resident under the age of 85 traveling outside the country is eligible to participate. Provisions for trip cancellation can also be written into the policy for a nominal cost.

- **Access America,** 6600 W. Broad St., Richmond, VA 23230 (☎ **800/284-8300** in the U.S.; www.accessamerica.com), offers comprehensive travel insurance and assistance packages, including medical expenses, on-the-spot hospital payments, medical transportation, baggage insurance, trip-cancellation and interruption insurance, and rental-car collision-damage insurance. Its 24-hour hotline connects you to multilingual coordinators who can offer advice and help on medical, legal, and travel problems. Varying coverage levels are available.
- **Travel Assistance International** by Worldwide Assistance Services, Inc., 9200 Keystone Crossing, Suite 300, Indianapolis, IN 46240 (☎ **800/821-2828** in the U.S., or 202/331-1596; www.specialtyrisk.com), is another option. It offers on-the-spot medical-payment coverage up to $15,000, or $60,000 for emergency care, practically anywhere in the world, as well as unlimited medical evacuation/repatriation coverage back to the United States if necessary. For an additional fee, you can be covered for trip cancellation/disruption, lost/delayed luggage, and accidental death and dismemberment. Fees are based on the length of your trip and the coverage you select. Prices begin at $65 per person ($95 per family) for a 1- to 8-day trip.

INSURANCE FOR BRITISH TRAVELERS   Most big travel agencies offer their own insurance and will probably try to sell you a package when you book a trip. Think before you sign up. Britain's Consumers Association recommends that you insist on seeing the policy and reading the fine print before you buy travel insurance.

You should also shop around for better deals. You might contact **Columbus Travel Insurance Ltd.** (☎ 020/7375-0011 in London), or, for students, **USIT Campus** (☎ 0870/240-1010 in London; www.usitcampus.co.uk).

8 Tips for Travelers with Special Needs

FOR TRAVELERS WITH DISABILITIES

If you're flying around Europe, the airline and ground staff can help you on and off planes and reserve seats with enough leg room, but you must arrange for this assistance *in advance* through the airline.

IN THE UNITED STATES   Before you go, you might want to contact an agency that can provide planning information. One is the **Travel Information Service** at the MossRehab Hospital in Philadelphia (☎ 215/456-9603, or 215/456-9602 TTY; www.mossresourcenet.org), which provides information to telephone callers only.

For a $35 annual fee, you can join **Mobility International USA,** P.O. Box 10767, Eugene, OR 97440 (☎ 541/343-1284; www.miusa.org). Besides answering questions on various destinations, it offers discounts on videos, publications, and programs it sponsors. One of the best organizations serving the needs of people with disabilities is **Flying Wheels Travel,** 143 W. Bridge St. (P.O. Box 382), Owatonna, MN 55060 (☎ 800/535-6790 or 507/451-5005; www.flyingwheelstravel.com); it offers international escorted tours and cruises.

You can also get the names and addresses of tour operators and miscellaneous travel information from the **Society for the Advancement of Travel for the Handicapped,** 347 Fifth Ave., New York, NY 10016 (☎ 212/447-7248). Annual membership dues are $45, or $30 for senior citizens and students. Send a stamped, self-addressed envelope.

For blind or visually impaired individuals, the best source of information is the **American Foundation for the Blind,** 11 Penn Plaza, Suite 300, New York, NY

10001 (☎ **800/232-5463** or 212/502-7600; www.afb.org). It offers information on travel and requirements for the transport of seeing-eye dogs.

IN BRITAIN   Travelers with disabilities can contact **RADAR (Royal Association for Disability and Rehabilitation)**, Unit 12, City Forum, 250 City Rd., London EC1V 8AF (☎ **020/7250-3222;** www.radar.org.uk), for useful annual holiday guides. *Holidays and Travel Abroad* costs £5; *Holidays in the British Isles* goes for £7; and *Long Haul Holidays and Travel* is £5. RADAR also provides holiday information packets on such subjects as sports and outdoor holidays, insurance, and financial arrangements for people with disabilities. Each fact sheet is available for £2. All publications can be mailed outside the United Kingdom for a nominal fee.

Another good British service is the **Holiday Care,** 2nd Floor Imperial Buildings, Victoria Road, Horley, Surrey RH6 7PZ (☎ **01293/774-535;** fax 01293/784-647; www.holidaycare.org.uk), which advises on accessible accommodations. Annual membership costs £15 (U.K. residents) or £30 (nonresidents). It includes a newsletter and access to a free reservations network for hotels throughout Britain and—to a lesser degree—Europe and the rest of the world.

IN DENMARK   In general, trains, airlines, ferries, and department stores and malls are accessible. For information about wheelchair access, ferry and air travel, parking, and other matters, contact the **Danish Tourist Board** (see "Visitor Information & Entry Requirements," above).

In Denmark, useful information for people with disabilities is provided by **Disabled People's User Service** (run by the Danish Council of Organizations of Disabled People), Kloeverprisvej 10B, DK-2650 Hvidovre, København (☎ **36-75-17-93**).

FOR GAY & LESBIAN TRAVELERS

In general, Denmark is one of the most gay-friendly countries in Europe, and was one of the first to embrace same-sex marriages. Anti-discrimination laws have been in effect since 1987. Most Danes are exceptionally friendly and tolerant of lifestyles of either sexual preference. Obviously, an urban center such as Copenhagen will have a more openly gay life than rural areas. In many ways, the Erotic Museum in Copenhagen illustrates the city's attitudes toward sex—both heterosexual and homosexual. The history of both forms of sexual pleasure is presented in an unprejudiced manner.

IN THE UNITED STATES   To learn about gay and lesbian travel throughout Scandinavia in advance, you can obtain publications or join data-dispensing organizations. Men can order *Spartacus,* the international gay guide ($32.95), or *Odysseus 2001, The International Gay Travel Planner,* a guide to accommodations ($27). Lesbians and gay men might want to pick up a copy of *Gay Travel A to Z* ($16), which focuses on general information and lists bars, hotels, restaurants, and places of interest for gay travelers throughout the world. These and other books are available from **Giovanni's Room,** 345 S. 12th St., Philadelphia, PA 19107 (☎ **215/923-2960;** fax 215/023-0813; www.giovannisroom.com).

The magazine *Our World,* 1104 North Nova Rd., Suite 251, Daytona Beach, FL 32117 (☎ **904/441-5367;** www.ourworldmag.com), covers options and bargains for gay and lesbian travel worldwide. It costs $35 for 10 issues. *Out and About,* 657 Harrison St., San Francisco, CA 94107 (☎ **800/929-2268** or 415/229-1793; www.outandabout.com), has been hailed for its "straight" reporting about gay travel. It profiles the best gay or gay-friendly hotels, gyms, clubs, and other places at destinations throughout the world. It costs $49 for 10 information-packed issues.

International Gay & Lesbian Travel Association (IGLTA), 4331 N. Federal, Suite 304, Fort Lauderdale, FL 33308 (☎ **800/448-8550** for voice mail, or

954/776-2626; www.iglta.com), encourages gay and lesbian travel worldwide. With around 1,200 member agencies, it specializes in putting travelers in touch with appropriate gay-friendly service organizations or tour specialists. It offers a quarterly newsletter, marketing mailings, and a membership directory (updated four times a year). Travel agents who are IGTA members are included in this organization's vast information resources.

IN DENMARK   The Danish organization for gay men and lesbians is **Landsforeningen for Bøsser og Lesbiske,** Teglgaardstræde 13, 1007 København (☎ **33-13-19-48**); there are branches in Århus, Aalborg, and other cities.

FOR SENIORS

IN THE UNITED STATES   Many senior discounts are available, but some may require you to be a member of an association. The **American Association of Retired Persons (AARP),** 601 E St. NW, Washington, DC 20049 (☎ **800/424-3410** or 202/434-AARP; www.aarp.org), is the best U.S. organization for seniors. It offers discounts on car rentals and hotels.

For information before you go, get a copy of the free booklet *101 Tips for the Mature Traveler,* available from **Grand Circle Travel,** 347 Congress St., Suite 3A, Boston, MA 02210 (☎ **800/221-2610** or 617/350-7500; www.gct.com).

SAGA International Holidays, 222 Berkeley St., Boston, MA 02116 (☎ **800/ 343-0273;** www.sagaholidays.com), organizes all-inclusive tours for seniors, preferably 50 years of age or older. Insurance is included in the net price of the tours.

Information is also available from the **National Council of Senior Citizens,** 8403 Colesville Rd., Suite 1200, Silver Spring, MD 20910 (☎ **301/578-8800;** www.ncscinc.org). For $13 per person or per couple, you receive a bimonthly magazine, part of which is devoted to travel tips. Discounts on hotel and auto rentals are available.

Sears Mature Outlook, P.O. Box 9390, Des Moines, IA 50306 (☎ **800/ 336-6330;** fax 847/286-5024), is a travel organization for people over 50. Members are offered discounts at ITC-member hotels and a bimonthly magazine. The annual membership fee ($39.95) entitles members to coupons for discounts at Sears.

Elderhostel, 75 Federal St., Boston, MA 02110-1941 (☎ **877/426-8056** or 617/426-8056; www.elderhostel.org), offers an array of university-based educational programs for senior citizens throughout the world, including Scandinavia. Most courses abroad last about 3 weeks and offer remarkable value—the reasonable cost includes airfare, accommodations in student dormitories or modest inns, all meals, and tuition. The courses, which require no homework, tend to be in the liberal arts. Participants must be at least 55 years old; spouses of any age may attend, but companions must be at least 50. Meals consist of the basic fare found in educational institutions worldwide. Elderhostel programs offer a safe, congenial environment for older single women, who make up about two thirds of the enrollment.

For information on the University of New Hampshire's **Interhostel** program, see "Learning Vacations," above.

Uniworld, 16000 Ventura Blvd., Encino, CA 91436 (☎ **800/733-7820** or 818/382-7820; www.uniworldcruises.com), specializes in single tours for the mature person. It arranges for you to share accommodations with another single person or gets you a low-priced single supplement. Uniworld specializes in travel to certain districts of England, France, Spain, Italy, and Scandinavia, including Denmark.

IN DENMARK   Seniors with valid age identification (such as a passport) are entitled to discounts on rail travel and the ferries to Sweden, plus certain attractions and performances, including those at the Royal Theater. However, you may have to belong to a senior's organization to qualify (an AARP card will suffice) for certain discounts.

FOR FAMILIES

Family Travel Times newsletter costs $40 (online only—www.familytraveltimes. com), and it's updated every 2 weeks. Subscribers also can call in with travel questions but only on Wednesday from 10am to 1pm Eastern Standard Time. Contact Family Travel Times, 40 5th Ave., New York, NY 10011 (☎ **888/822-4322** or 212/477-5524).

The best deals for British families are often package tours put together by some of the giants of the travel industry. Foremost among them is **Thomsons Tour Operators.** Through its subsidiary, **Skytours** (☎ **020/7387-9321**), it offers dozens of air-land packages that have a designated number of airline seats reserved for free use by children under 18 who accompany their parents. To qualify, parents must book airfare and hotel accommodations lasting 2 weeks or more and book as far in advance as possible. Savings for families with children can be substantial.

FOR STUDENTS

IN THE UNITED STATES   A subsidiary of the Council on International Educational Exchange, **Council Travel** is America's largest student, youth, and budget travel group, with more than 60 offices worldwide. The main office is at 205 E. 42nd St., New York, NY 10017 (☎ **212/822-2600;** fax 212/822-2699; www.ciee.com). International Student Identity Cards, issued to students for $19, entitle the holders to receive generous travel and other discounts. Discounted international and domestic air tickets are available. Other offices of Council Travel are at 844 E. Lancaster Ave., Bryn Mawr, PA 19010 (☎ **610/527-6272**); 565 Melville, University City, MO 63130 (☎ **314/721-7779**), and Franklin House Suite 102, 480 E. Broad St., Athens, GA (☎ **706/543-9600**).

Eurotrain rail passes, YHA passes, weekend packages, overland safaris, and hostel and hotel accommodations can also be booked. Council Travel sells a number of publications for young people, including *Work, Study, Travel Abroad: The Whole World Handbook; Volunteer: The Comprehensive Guide to Voluntary Service in the U.S. and Abroad;* and *Going Places: The High School Student's Guide to Study, Travel, and Adventure Abroad.*

For real budget travelers, it's worth joining **Hostelling International/IYHF** (International Youth Hostel Federation). For information, contact Hostelling International/American Youth Hostels (HI-AYH), 733 15th St. NW, Suite 840, Washington, DC 20005 (☎ **202/783-6161;** www.hiayah.org). Membership costs $25 annually; those under age 18 join for free, and those over 54 pay $15.

IN BRITAIN   Campus Travel, 52 Grosvenor Gardens, London SW1W 0AG (☎ **0870/240-1010;** www.usitcampus.co.uk), is Britain's leading specialist in student and youth travel worldwide. Founded to meet the needs of students and young people, it provides a comprehensive travel service specializing in low-cost rail, sea, and air transportation, holiday breaks, travel insurance, and student discount cards.

9 Getting There

BY PLANE

Summer (generally June through September) is the peak season and the most expensive. Scandinavia's off-season is winter (from about November 1 to March 21). Shoulder season (spring and fall) is in between. In any season, midweek fares (Monday to Thursday) are lowest.

REGULAR AIRFARES & APEX FARES

Regular airfares include, in order of increasing price, economy, business class, and first class. These tickets carry no restrictions. In economy you pay for drinks, and the seats are not spacious; in business, the drinks are free, and the seats are wider; in first class, amenities and services are the best.

Currently the most popular discount fare is the **APEX** (advance-purchase excursion), which usually carries restrictions—advance-purchase requirements, minimum or maximum stays—and cancellation or change-of-date penalties.

In addition, airlines often offer **promotional discount fares.** Always check the travel sections of your local newspapers for such advertisements.

THE MAJOR AIRLINES

FROM NORTH AMERICA   Only three airlines offer nonstop flights from the United States to Copenhagen. **SAS** (Scandinavian Airlines Systems; ☎ **800/ 221-2350** in the U.S. or 0171/734-6777 in the U.K.; www.flysas.com) has more nonstop flights to Scandinavia from more North American cities than any other airline, and more flights to and from Denmark and within Scandinavia than any other airline in the world. From Seattle and Chicago, SAS offers nonstop flights to Copenhagen daily in midsummer and almost every day in winter; from Newark, New Jersey, there are daily flights year-round to Copenhagen. SAS's recent agreement with United Airlines, the "Star Alliance," connects other U.S. cities (such as Boston, Dallas/Fort Worth, Denver, Houston, Los Angeles, Minneapolis/St. Paul, New York, San Francisco, and Washington, D.C.) to the three U.S. gateway cities.

SAS offers one of the lowest fares to Copenhagen from New York. With restrictions, and flying during specific off-peak seasons, round-trip tickets can cost as little as $425 for those who pay for their tickets within 2 days after booking and stay abroad between 7 and 30 days. No refunds or changes in flight dates are permitted. A similar round-trip ticket from Chicago to Copenhagen costs $565. Both tickets cost $60 more for travel on Friday, Saturday, or Sunday. These prices can—and almost certainly will—change during the lifetime of this edition. Always confirm prices before booking your ticket.

Delta (☎ 800/241-4141 in the U.S.; www.delta.com) features daily nonstop flights to Copenhagen from JFK, usually at prices comparable to those offered by SAS and TWA.

Nonstop flights to Copenhagen from the greater New York area take about 7½ hours; from Chicago, around 8½ hours; from Seattle, 9½ hours.

FROM THE U.K.   British Airways (☎ 800/AIRWAYS, or 0845/773-3377 in the U.K.; www.britishairways.com) offers convenient connections through Heathrow and Gatwick to Copenhagen. The price structure (and discounted prices on hotel packages) sometimes makes a stopover in Britain less expensive than you might have thought. **SAS** offers five daily nonstop flights to Copenhagen from Heathrow (1¾ hours), two daily nonstops from Glasgow (2 hours), and three daily nonstops from Manchester (2 hours, 20 minutes). Other European airlines with connections through their home countries to Copenhagen include **Icelandair** (☎ 800/223-5500 in the U.S. or 020/7874-1000 in the U.K.; www.icelandair.com), **KLM** (☎ 800/374-7747 in the U.S. or 0870/507-4074 in the U.K.; www.nwa.com), and **Lufthansa** (☎ 800/ 645-3880 in the U.S. or 0845/773-7747 in the U.K.; www.lufthansa-usa.com). Be aware, however, that unless you make all your flight arrangements in North America before you go, you might find some of these flights prohibitively expensive.

BUCKET SHOPS, CHARTERS & OTHER OPTIONS

BUCKET SHOPS   More politely referred to as "consolidators," these agencies buy large blocks of unsold seats from the airlines and sell them to the public, often at dramatic discounts (from 20% to 35% off regular fares). The terms of payment may vary from the last minute to 45 days in advance. Here are some recommendations to get you started.

TFI Tours International, 34 W. 32nd St., 12th floor, New York, NY 10001 (☎ **212/736-1140** in New York State or 800/745-8000 elsewhere in the U.S.) offers service to 177 cities worldwide.

Travel Avenue, 10 S. Riverside Plaza, Suite 1404, Chicago, IL 60606 (☎ **800/ 333-3335;** www.travelavenue.com), is a national agency. Its tickets are often cheaper than those sold by other shops.

All Travel (☎ **800/300-4567** or 310/312-3368) recognizes that its clients collect information on the web, but offers a person to talk to about personal vacation plans, and also assists you with options for making the right decision. It usually features at least 14 "hot deals" of the week, including some off-the-beaten-path treks as well as eco-adventures.

One of the biggest U.S. consolidators is **Travac,** 989 Sixth Ave., New York, NY 10018 (☎ **800/TRAV-800** or 212/563-3303). It offers discounted seats from points throughout the United States to most cities in Europe on TWA, United, Delta, and other major airlines.

UniTravel, 1177 N. Warson Rd., St. Louis, MO 63132 (☎ **800/325-2222**), offers tickets to Europe at prices that may be lower than the airlines charge if you order tickets directly. UniTravel is best suited for passengers who want or need to get to Europe on short notice.

Another option for people with flexible travel plans is available through **Airhitch,** 2641 Broadway, 3rd floor, Suite 100, New York, NY 10025 (☎ **800/326-2009** or 212/864-2000; www.airhitch.org). You tell Airhitch which 5 consecutive days you're available to fly to Europe, and Airhitch agrees to fly you there within those 5 days. It arranges for departures from the East or West Coast, the Midwest, and the Southeast. It tries, but cannot guarantee, to fly you from and to the cities of your choice.

You can also try **800-FLY-4-LESS,** a discount domestic and international airline ticketing service. Travelers unable to buy their tickets 3 weeks in advance can get discounted fares with no advance purchase requirements. 800-FLY-4-LESS (the name is also the phone number) is a nationwide airline reservation and ticketing service that specializes in finding the lowest rates.

CHARTER FLIGHTS   Strictly speaking, a charter is a one-time-only flight between two predetermined points, for which the aircraft is reserved months in advance. Before you pay for a charter, check the restrictions on your ticket or contract. You may be asked to purchase a tour package and pay for it far in advance, and there will be a stiff penalty (or ticket forfeit) if you cancel. Some charter-ticket sellers offer an insurance policy for a legitimate cancellation, such as hospitalization or a death in the family. Be aware that a charter might be canceled if the plane cannot be filled.

Some charter companies have proved to be unreliable in the past. One recommended operator is **Council Charter,** a subsidiary of the Council on International Educational Exchange, 205 E. 42nd St., New York, NY 10017 (☎ **888/COUNCIL**). It can arrange charter seats to most major European cities on regularly scheduled aircraft.

REBATERS   Rebaters are firms that pass along to a passenger part of their commission, although many assess a fee for the service. They are not the same as travel agents, but can sometimes offer similar services. Most rebaters offer discounts averaging from

10% to 25%, plus a $25 handling charge. **Travel Avenue,** 10 S. Riverside Plaza, Suite 1404, Chicago, IL 60606 (☎ 800/333-3335; www.travelavenue.com), is one of the oldest agencies of its kind. It offers upfront cash rebates on every airfare over $300 it sells. In a style similar to that of a discount brokerage firm, the agency prides itself on not offering travel counseling. Instead, it sells airline tickets to independent travelers who have already worked out their travel plans. Also available are tour and cruise fares, plus hotel reservations, usually at lower prices than if you reserve them on your own.

TRAVEL CLUBS   Travel clubs are another possibility for low-cost air travel, offering discounts usually in the range of 20% to 60%. After you pay an annual fee, you're given a hotline number to call to find out what discounts are available. Of course, you're limited to what's available, so you have to be fairly flexible. **Moment's Notice,** 7301 New Utrecht Ave., Brooklyn NY 11204 (☎ 718/234-6295; www.momentsnotice.com), charges $25 per year for membership and is geared for impulse purchases and last-minute getaways. **Sears Mature Outlook,** 3033 S. Parker Rd., Suite 1000, Aurora, CO 80014 (☎ 800/336-6330 in the U.S.), charges a $39.95 annual membership fee and offers members a quarterly catalog, maps, discounts at select hotels, and a limited guarantee that equivalent packages will not be undersold by any other travel organization.

   Encore Travel Club, 4501 Forbes Blvd., Lanham, MD 20706 (☎ 800/638-8976), charges $59.95 a year for membership and offers up to a 50% discount at more than 4,000 hotels, sometimes during off-peak periods. It also offers substantial discounts on airfare, cruises, and car rentals through its volume-purchase plans. Membership includes a travel package outlining the company's services and use of a toll-free telephone number for advice and information.

GOING AS A COURIER   Couriers are hired by overnight air-freight firms hoping to skirt the often-tedious Customs delays that regular cargo faces at the other end. For the service, the courier pays the firm a fee much lower than the cost of the ticket, and sometimes can fly free. Don't worry—the service is legal. You won't be asked to handle any contraband. Also, you don't actually carry the merchandise you're "transporting"; you just carry a shipping invoice to present at Customs when you arrive.

   This cost-saving approach is not for everyone—there are lots of restrictions, and courier opportunities are hard to come by. You're allowed only one piece of carry-on luggage; your checked-baggage allowance is used by the courier firm to transport its cargo. Also, you must fly alone.

   For more information, try **Now Voyager,** 74 Varick St., Suite 307, New York, NY 10013 (☎ 212/431-1616; www.nowvoyager.com), Monday to Friday from 10am to 5:30pm, Saturday from noon to 4:30pm. An automatic telephone-answering system announces last-minute specials and the firm's fees for the round-trip. Courier services are also listed in the yellow pages or in advertisements in newspaper travel sections.

   For a $45 annual membership fee, the **International Association of Air Travel Couriers,** P.O. Box 1349, Lake Worth, FL 33460 (☎ 516/582-8320), will send you six issues of its newsletter, *Shoestring Traveler,* and about a half dozen issues of *Air Courier Bulletin,* a directory of air-courier bargains around the world. The fee also includes access to their 24-hour "Fax-on-Demand" update of last-minute courier flights available for those who can travel on short notice.

A NOTE FOR BRITISH TRAVELERS

Because regular airfares from the U.K. to Scandinavia tend to be high, savvy Brits usually call a travel agent for a "deal"—a charter flight or special promotion. These so-called deals are often available because of Scandinavia's popularity as a tourist destination. If you can't get a deal, the next-best choice is an APEX ticket. Although these tickets must be reserved in advance, they offer a discount without the usual booking restrictions. You could also inquire about a "Eurobudget ticket," which carries restrictions or length-of-stay requirements.

British newspapers typically carry lots of classified advertisements touting "slashed" fares from London to other parts of the world. One good source is *Time Out,* a magazine published in London. London's *Evening Standard* has a daily travel section, and the Sunday editions of almost all British newspapers run ads. Although competition is fierce, one well-recommended company that consolidates bulk ticket purchases and passes the savings on to its customers is **Trailfinders** (☎ **020/7937-5400** in London; www.trailfinder.com). It offers tickets on such carriers as SAS, British Airways, and KLM. You can fly from London's Heathrow or Gatwick airport to Copenhagen, Oslo, Stockholm, and Helsinki.

In London, many bucket shops around Victoria Station and Earl's Court offer low fares. Make sure the company you deal with is a member of the IATA, ABTA, or ATOL. These umbrella organizations will help you if anything goes wrong.

CEEFAX, a television information service carried on many home and hotel TVs, runs details of package holidays and flights to Europe and beyond. On your CEEFAX channel, you'll find a menu of listings that includes travel information.

Make sure you understand the bottom line on any special deal you purchase—ask if all surcharges, including airport taxes and other hidden costs, are indicated before you commit. Upon investigation, people often find that some of these "deals" are not as attractive as advertised. Also, make sure you understand what the penalties are if you're forced to cancel at the last minute.

TRAVELER BARGAINS & WEB ADDRESSES   Savvy travelers can find excellent deals on vacation packages by searching the Internet. Increasingly, travel agencies and companies use the Web to offer everything from vacations to plane reservations to budget airline tickets on major carriers. Although their exact configuration (and their specific offerings) changes as fast as the Internet itself, a good beginning involves engaging your favorite Web search engine and searching on the keyword "travel." Check for tips offered by your search engine on narrowing your search because a simple scan of "travel" could yield 10 million matches. To save you time and effort, we have found some sites that may be useful.

Many travel sites maintained by services and agencies offer basically the same service as the airlines (see Web sites above), but on a much wider and larger scale.

- **www.yahoo.com** is a no-nonsense site that gets the job done efficiently and quickly, offering links to Web sites and search engines all over the globe.
- **www.travelcom.es** allows you to search travel destinations and offers links to travel agencies all over the world and in all 50 states.
- **www.previewtravel.com** is the foremost of these sites. Featured prominently on America Online, it offers vacation, airline, and hotel deals, and updates its offerings daily. The most user-friendly of the travel sites, Preview Travel even lets you book your vacation on its site.
- **www.moments-notice.com** promotes itself as a travel service, not an agency, providing a vacation bargain hunter's dream. Deals are updated daily, and many are snapped up by the end of the day. A drawback is that many of these vacations require you to drop everything and go almost immediately.
- **www.1800hotel.com** offers budget reservations at prestigious hotels all over the world. Prices for many accommodations are up to 65% off, and you can book online instead of through a travel agent.

- **America Online** (www.aol.com) has areas devoted to many of these businesses and can be customized to investigate a particular region of the world you may have trouble finding.

BY CAR

You can easily drive to Denmark from Germany. Many people drive to Jutland from Hamburg, Bremerhaven, and Lübeck. A bridge links Jutland and the central island of Funen. In 1998 a bridge opened that goes across the Great Belt from Funen to the island of Zealand, site of the city of Copenhagen. The bridge lies near Nyborg, Denmark. Once in West Zealand, you'll still have to drive east across the island to Copenhagen.

Car-ferry service to Denmark from the United Kingdom generally leaves passengers at Esbjerg, where they must cross from Jutland to Copenhagen. From Germany, it's possible to take a car ferry from Travemünde, northeast of Lübeck, which will deposit you at Gedser, Denmark. From here, connect with E55, an express highway north to Copenhagen.

BY TRAIN

If you're in Europe, it's easy to get to Denmark by train. Copenhagen is the main rail hub between Scandinavia and the rest of Europe. For example, the London–Copenhagen train—through Ostende, Belgium, or Hook, Holland—leaves four times daily and takes 22 hours. About 10 daily express trains run from Hamburg to Copenhagen (5½ hours). There are also intercity trains on the Merkur route from Karlsruhe, Germany, to Cologne to Hamburg to Copenhagen. The Berlin–Ostbahnhof–Copenhagen train (8½ hours) connects with Eastern European trains. Two daily express trains make this run.

If you plan to travel a great deal on German railroads, it's worth securing a copy of the *Thomas Cook European Timetable of European Passenger Railroads.* It's available exclusively in North America from **Forsyth Travel Library,** 226 Westchester Ave., White Plains, NY 10604 (☎ **800/FORSYTH**). It costs $27.95, plus $4.95 postage (priority airmail) to the United States or $2 additional to Canada.

Thousands of trains run from Britain to the Continent, and at least some of them go directly across or under the Channel, through France or Belgium and Germany into Denmark. For example, a train leaves London's Victoria Station daily at 9am and arrives in Copenhagen the next day at 8:25am. Another train leaves London's Victoria Station at 8:45pm and arrives in Copenhagen the next day at 8:20pm. Both go through Dover–Ostende, or with a connection at Brussels. Once you're in Copenhagen, you can make rail connections to Norway, Finland, and Sweden. Because of the time and distances involved, many passengers rent a couchette (sleeping berth), which costs around £18 per person. Designed like padded benches stacked bunk-style, they're usually clustered six to a compartment.

RAIL PASSES FOR NORTH AMERICAN TRAVELERS

SCANRAIL PASS   If your visit to Europe will be primarily in Scandinavia, the Scanrail pass may be better and cheaper than the Eurailpass. This pass allows its owner a designated number of days of free rail travel within a larger time block. (Presumably, this allows for days devoted to sightseeing scattered among days of rail transfers between cities or sites of interest.) You can choose a total of any 5 days of unlimited rail travel during a 15-day period, 10 days of rail travel within a 1-month period, or 1 month of unlimited rail travel. The pass, which is valid on all lines of the state railways of Denmark, Finland, Norway, and Sweden, offers discounts or free travel on some (but not all) of the region's ferry lines as well. The pass can be purchased only in North America. It's available from any office of **RailEurope** (☎ **800/361-RAIL**) or **Scanam World Tours,** 933 Highway 23, Pompton Plains, NJ 07444 (☎ **800/545-2204**).

Depending on whether you choose first- or second-class rail transport, 5 days out of 2 months ranges from $200 to $270, 10 days out of 2 months ranges from $310 to $420, and 21 consecutive days of unlimited travel ranges from $360 to $486. Seniors get an 11% discount; students a 25% discount.

EURAILPASS If you plan to travel extensively in Europe, the **Eurailpass** might be a good bet. It's valid for first-class rail travel in 17 European countries. With one ticket, you travel whenever and wherever you please; more than 100,000 rail miles are at your disposal. Here's how it works: The pass is sold only in North America. A Eurailpass good for 15 days costs $554, a pass for 21 days is $718, a 1-month pass costs $890, a 2-month pass is $1,260, and a 3-month pass goes for $1,558. Children under 4 travel free if they don't occupy a seat; all children under 12 who take up a seat are charged half-price. If you're under 26, you can buy a **Eurail Youthpass,** which entitles you to unlimited second-class travel for 15 days ($388), for 21 days ($499), 1 month ($623), 2 months ($882), or 3 months ($1,089). Travelers considering buying a 15-day or 1-month pass should estimate rail distance before deciding if a pass is worthwhile. To take full advantage of the tickets for 15 days or a month, you'd have to spend a great deal of time on the train. Eurailpass holders are entitled to substantial discounts on certain buses and ferries as well. Travel agents in all towns, and railway agents in such major cities as New York, Montréal, and Los Angeles, sell all these tickets. For information on Eurailpasses, and other European train data, call RailEurope at ☎ **800/438-7245**, or visit them on the Web at **www.raileurope.com**.

Eurail Saverpass offers 15% discounts to groups of three or more people traveling together between April and September, or two people traveling together between October and March. The price of a Saverpass, valid all over Europe for first class only, is $715 for 15 days, $928 for 21 days, $1,150 for 1 month, $1,630 for 2 months, and $2,013 for 3 months. Even more freedom is offered by the **Saver Flexipass,** which is similar to the Eurail Saverpass, except that you are not confined to consecutive-day travel. For travel over any 10 days in 2 months, the fare is $556; any 15 days over 2 months, the fare is $732.

Eurail Flexipass allows even greater flexibility. It's valid in first class and offers the same privileges as the Eurailpass. However, it provides a number of individual travel days over a longer period of consecutive days. Using this pass makes it possible to stay longer in one city and not lose a single day of travel. There are two Flexipasses: 10 days of travel within 2 months for $654, and 15 days of travel within 2 months for $862.

With many of the same qualifications and restrictions as the Eurail Flexipass, the **Eurail Youth Flexipass** is sold only to travelers under age 26. It allows 10 days of travel within 2 months for $458 and 15 days of travel within 2 months for $599.

Contact Eurail to see which option might be best for your travel needs.

RAIL PASSES FOR BRITISH TRAVELERS

If you plan to do a lot of exploring, you might prefer one of the three rail passes designed for unlimited train travel within a designated region during a predetermined number of days. These passes are sold in Britain and several other European countries.

An **InterRail Pass** is available to passengers of any nationality, with some restrictions—they must be under age 26 and able to prove residency in a European or North

African country (Morocco, Algeria, and Tunisia) for at least 6 months before buying the pass. It allows unlimited travel through Europe, except Albania and the republics of the former Soviet Union. Prices are complicated and vary depending on the countries you want to include. For pricing purposes, Europe is divided into eight zones; the cost depends on the number of zones you include. The most expensive option (£219) allows 1 month of unlimited travel in all eight zones and is known to BritRail staff as a "global." The least expensive option (£129) allows 22 days of travel within only one zone.

Passengers over 25 can buy an **InterRail 26-Plus Pass,** which, unfortunately, is severely limited geographically. Many countries—including France, Belgium, Switzerland, Spain, Portugal, and Italy—do not honor this pass. It is, however, accepted for travel through Denmark, Finland, Norway, and Sweden. Second-class travel with the pass costs £179 for 22 days or £235 for 1 month. Passengers must meet the same residency requirements that apply to the InterRail Pass (see above).

For information on buying individual rail tickets or any of the above-mentioned passes, contact **British Rail International,** Victoria Station, London (☎ **0990/ 848-848** or 0845/748-4950). Tickets and passes are also available at larger railway stations as well as selected travel agencies throughout Britain and the rest of Europe.

BY SHIP & FERRY

It's easy to travel by water from several ports to Denmark. Liners carrying cars and passengers operate from England, Germany, Poland, Norway, and Sweden. Check with your travel agent about these cruises.

FROM BRITAIN DFDS Seaways (☎ **800/533-3755** in the U.S. or 020/7616-1400 in London) runs vessels year-round between Harwich, England, and Esbjerg in West Jutland. The crossing takes 16 to 20 hours. The same line also sails from Newcastle upon Tyne to Esbjerg, but only in the summer, as part of a 22-hour passage. Overnight cabins and space for cars are available on both routes.

FROM NORWAY & SWEDEN   The **Bergen Line** (☎ **800/323-7436** in the U.S., or 212/319-1300) operates vessels from Oslo to Hirtshals in North Jutland.

Stena Line runs popular sea links from Oslo to Frederikshavn, North Jutland (11½ hours), and from Gothenburg, Sweden, to Frederikshavn (3 hours). For information, schedules, and fares, contact EuroCruises, 33 W. 12th St., New York, NY 10014 (☎ **800/688-3876** in the U.S., or 212/691-2099).

FROM GERMANY   From the Baltic coast, ferries operate between Kiel and Bagenkop on the Danish island of Langeland. Reserve tickets at **Langeland–Kiel Touristik,** Oslokai 3, Kiel (☎ **431/97415-0**).

PACKAGE TOURS

For travelers who feel more comfortable if everything is prearranged—hotels, transportation, sightseeing excursions, luggage handling, tips, taxes, and even meals—a package tour is the obvious choice, and it may even help save money.

One of the best tour operators to Denmark, Sweden, and Norway is **Bennett Tours,** 342 Madison Ave., New York, NY 10073 (☎ **800/221-2420** in the U.S., or 212/697-1092). It offers land packages with experienced guides and a wide range of prices.

Other reliable tour operators include **Olson Travelworld,** 1145 Clark St., Stevens Point, WI 54481 (☎ **800/826-4026**), and **Scantours, Inc.,** 3439 Wade St., Los Angeles, CA 90006 (☎ **800/223-7226** or 310/636-4656).

10 Getting Around

BY PLANE

The best way to get around Scandinavia is to take advantage of air passes that apply to the whole region. If you're traveling extensively in Europe, special European passes are available.

SAS'S VISIT SCANDINAVIA FARE   The vast distances encourage air travel between Scandinavia's far-flung points. One of the most worthwhile promotions is SAS's **Visit Scandinavia Pass.** Available only to travelers who fly SAS across the Atlantic, it includes up to six coupons, each of which is valid for any SAS flight within or between Denmark, Norway, and Sweden. Each coupon costs $75, a price that's especially appealing when you consider that an economy-class ticket between Stockholm and Copenhagen can cost as much as $250 each way. The pass is especially valuable if you plan to travel to the far northern frontiers of Sweden or Norway; in that case, the savings over the price of a regular economy-class ticket can be substantial. For information on buying the pass, call **SAS** (☎ **800/221-2350**).

WITHIN DENMARK   For those in a hurry, **SAS** (☎ **70-10-20-00** in Copenhagen) operates daily service between Copenhagen and points on Jutland's mainland. From Copenhagen it takes about 40 minutes to fly to Aalborg, 35 minutes to Århus, and 30 minutes to Odense's Beldringe Airport.

Fares to other Danish cities are sometimes included in a transatlantic ticket at no extra charge, as long as the additional cities are specified when the ticket is written.

BY TRAIN

Flat, low-lying Denmark, with its hundreds of bridges and absence of mountains, has a large network of railway lines that connect virtually every hamlet with the largest city, Copenhagen. For **information, schedules, and fares** anywhere in Denmark, call ☎ **70-13-14-15.** A word you're likely to see a lot is *Lyntog* ("express trains").

On any train within Denmark, children between 4 and 11 are charged half price; they must be accompanied by an adult. Seniors (age 65 and older) receive a 20% to 33% discount on one-way or round-trip tickets at any time of the day or year. No identification is needed when you buy your ticket, but the conductor who checks your ticket might ask for proof of age.

The Danish government offers dozens of discounts on the country's rail networks—depending on the type of traveler, days or hours traveled, and destination. Because discounts change often, it's always best to ask for a discount based on your age and the number of days (or hours) you intend to travel.

BY BUS

By far the best way to visit rural Denmark is by car, but if you want or need to travel by bus, be aware that you'll probably get your bus at the railway station. (In much of Scandinavia, buses take passengers to destinations not served by the train; therefore, the bus route often originates at the railway station.) The arrival of trains and departure of buses are usually closely timed.

For seniors (age 65 and over), round-trip bus tickets are sometimes offered at one-way prices (excluding Saturday, Sunday, and peak travel periods around Christmas and Easter). Most discounts are granted only to seniors who are traveling beyond the city limits of their point of origin.

BY CAR

RENTALS   Avis, Budget, and Hertz offer well-serviced, well-maintained fleets of cars. You may have to reserve and pay for your rental car in advance (usually 2 weeks, but occasionally as little as 48 hours) to get the lowest rates. Unfortunately, if your trip is canceled or your arrival date changes, you might have to fill out a lot of forms to arrange a refund. All three companies may charge slightly higher rates to clients who reserve less than 48 hours in advance and pay at pickup. The highest rates are charged to walk-in customers who arrange their rentals after they arrive in Denmark.

Before you rent, you should know that the Danish government imposes a whopping 25% tax on all car rentals. Agencies that encourage prepaid rates almost never collect this tax in advance—instead, it's imposed as part of a separate transaction when you pick up the car. Furthermore, any car retrieved at a Danish airport is subject to a one-time supplemental tax of 190 DKK ($23.75); you might prefer to pick up your car at a downtown location. Membership in certain travel clubs or organizations (such as AAA or AARP) might qualify you for a modest discount.

Note: The following rates are for 1 week's rental of a Volkswagen Polo (the smallest car available). They include unlimited mileage and are subject to change.

Avis (☎ **800/331-1212** in the U.S.; www.avis.com) maintains two offices in Copenhagen, one at the arrivals hall of the airport and another at Kampmannsgade 1 (☎ **33-15-22-99**). The rate is $339—if you pay 2 weeks before your departure. "Walk-in" customers who don't reserve from North America pay double that rate.

Budget (☎ **800/527-0700** in the U.S.; www.budget.com) has about 14 rental locations in Denmark. That's fewer than Avis or Hertz, but they tend to be in cities and regions most frequented by foreign visitors. Budget's rate is $240 if you pay in North America. The price is considerably higher for walk-in customers. Budget has a large branch at the Copenhagen airport (☎ **32-52-39-00**).

Hertz (☎ **800/654-3001** in the U.S.; www.hertz.com) charges a prepaid rate of $297 and about $346 for those who have not prepaid. Hertz's office in central Copenhagen is at Ved Vesterport 3 (☎ **33-17-90-20**); another office is at the airport (☎ **32-50-93-00**).

Also consider using a small company based in Harrison, N.Y. **Kemwel** (☎ **800/ 678-0678** in the U.S.; www.kemwel.com) is the North American representative for two Denmark-based car companies, Van Wijk and Hertz. It may be able to offer attractive rental prices to North Americans who pay in full at least 10 days before their departure. Seniors and members of AAA get a 5% discount.

INSURANCE   Each rental company builds a certain amount of insurance into its rates, which is adequate for most drivers and most accidents. If you have a mishap and don't have additional insurance to cover the cost of repairs, you'll be responsible for an amount that varies from 15,000 DKK ($1,875)—the amount Budget feels is appropriate for its least valuable car—to the full value of the car (the amount proposed by most of Budget's competitors). Of the big three, Budget usually offers the most favorable insurance arrangements and rates that are competitive.

Additional insurance for the least expensive car is about 100 DKK ($12.50) per day at Budget, and a bit more for equivalent vehicles at the other three companies. Advance payment with certain types of credit or charge cards may eliminate (or at least reduce) the need for additional insurance, depending on the card issuer. Some people use this technique to avoid buying extra insurance, but always verify the fine-print legalities of the individual card issuer. (Be aware that if you choose this method to insure your rental car, your private automobile insurance may be activated to pay for repairs to your rental car, perhaps eventually leading to higher premiums.)

11 Organized Tours

If you'd rather leave the driving and the details to someone else, lots of package tours are available to show you the highlights of Denmark. *Note:* The prices below are per person, double occupancy. Single-occupancy rates tend to be quite a bit higher.

BUS TOURS   Scanam World Tours (☎ 800/545-2204; www.scanamtours.com) offers a tour through the "Heart of Fairy Tale Denmark." You can choose a 3- or 6-day trip through Hans Christian Andersen country, including a visit to Odense (his birthplace) and an excursion to Legoland. Tours begin at $420.

SELF-DRIVE TOURS   Several companies offer self-drive tours, which usually include accommodations, rental cars, and customized itineraries. **Scantours, Inc.** (☎ 800/223-7226) features the 5-day "A Taste of Danish Castles," which is available year-round. Prices begin at $875. The company also sponsors a tour of Danish inns. The 4-day self-drive tour includes accommodations, breakfast, car rental, and an itinerary. Prices start at $325.

BICYCLE TOURS   An excellent way to explore the flat, rolling Danish countryside is on a bicycle. Numerous organizations (including Scantours, Inc. and Scanam Tours) sponsor bike tours through various regions of the country. You can choose one that covers the castles, beaches, and fjords of northern Denmark; the southern Funen islands; the beaches and marshland of western Jutland; or the lake country in eastern Jutland. **Blue Marble Travel** (☎ 973/326-9533) offers 7-day excursions to Hans Christian Andersen country and several small islands in the Baltic for $1,495. **Dansk Cyklist Forbund,** Rømersgade 7, DK-1362 København K (☎ 33-32-31-21), can provide the latest information on cycling tours in Denmark.

Suggested Itineraries

If You Have 1 Week

Days 1–3   Spend your first 3 days in Copenhagen. After a day recovering from the flight, have dinner at the Tivoli Gardens (in the summer) or Nyhavn (in the winter). If you're arriving from nearby and will not have jet-lag on your first day, explore Copenhagen walking along Strøget—the world's largest pedestrian street—then visiting Kongens Nytorv (King's New Square). Spend the morning of the second day taking one of our walking tours (see Chapter 4, "Exploring Copenhagen"); then (in the summer) spend the afternoon wandering through the Tivoli and listening to the free music. Devote Day 3 to more serious sightseeing, including visits to Christiansborg Palace and the Ny Carlsberg Glyptotek.

Day 4   Leave Copenhagen and head north, stopping over at the modern art museum, Louisiana, before heading to Helsingør, site of Kronborg Castle of *Hamlet* fame. Spend the night in Helsingør, or return to Copenhagen.

Day 5   Journey to Odense on the island of Funen, birthplace of Hans Christian Andersen. Spend the rest of the day and evening exploring its many attractions.

Day 6   Stop in Roskilde to see its cathedral and the Viking Ship Museum. Return to Copenhagen and spend the night.

Day 7   Try another walking tour, and schedule interior visits to Rosenborg Castle and, if you have time, the National Museum. Return to the Tivoli for a farewell drink.

If You Have 2 Weeks

Day 1   Recover from jet lag and have dinner at the Tivoli (in the summer) or at Scala, a restaurant complex across from the Tivoli (in the off-season).

Day 2   In the morning, take our first walking tour (see chapter 4). Spend the afternoon wandering around the Tivoli Gardens (in the summer).

Day 3   Take another walking tour and visit Christiansborg Palace and the Ny Carlsberg Glyptotek.

Day 4   Head north from Copenhagen. Visit the modern art museum, Louisiana, and have lunch at Helsingør, site of Kronborg Castle of *Hamlet* fame. Spend the night in Helsingør.

Day 5   Explore North Zealand, with visits to the royal palace at Fredensborg and the 17th-century Frederiksborg Castle at Hillerød. Spend the night in Helsingør.

Day 6   Return to Copenhagen and visit Rosenborg Castle and the National Museum.

Day 7   In Copenhagen, explore the other attractions of Zealand, journeying outside the capital to the open-air museum, Frilandsmuseet. Head to Roskilde for lunch, and visit the cathedral, the Viking Ship Museum, and the Iron Age Village at Lejre.

Day 8   Head south from Copenhagen to explore South Zealand. Visit the old market town of Køge, Vallø Castle, and Selso Slot. Spend the night in a typical inn on Zealand.

Day 9   Go west, crossing mid-Zealand. At Korsør, cross the bridge to Nyborg. Visit Nyborg Castle before driving to Odense to explore the city of Hans Christian Andersen. Stop overnight in Odense.

Day 10   Spend time exploring more of Odense, and then visit the Viking ship at Ladby and Egeskov Castle, outside Odense.

Day 11   Drive south from Odense to Svendborg. Explore the nearby islands of Thurø and Tåsinge.

Day 12   From Svendborg, board a ferry (make a reservation) and head for the island of Ærø. Spend the night in the capital, Ærøskøbing, or at an island inn.

Day 13   Leave Ærø and return to Svendborg by ferry. Drive north toward Odense along Route 9 until you connect with E20 west, the highway into Jutland. In Jutland, take Route 32 at the junction with E20 to Ribe. Spend the night in Ribe.

Day 14   Leave Ribe in the morning and drive to Silkeborg to view Sky Mountain. Ride on a paddle-wheel steamer on the Silkeborg Lakes. Visit the Silkeborg Museum. From Silkeborg, drive to Århus, where you can explore the Old Town. Have fun at Århus's Tivoli amusement park. Spend the night.

Fast Facts: Denmark

Area Code   The country code for Denmark is **45.** It precedes any call made to Denmark from another country. There are no city area codes. Every telephone number has eight digits.

Business Hours   Most **banks** are open Monday to Friday from 9:30am to 4pm (Thursday to 6pm), but outside Copenhagen, banking hours vary. **Stores** are generally open Monday to Thursday from 9am to 5:30pm, Friday 9am to 7 or 8pm, and Saturday noon to 2pm; most are closed Sunday.

Cameras & Film   Film is so expensive that we suggest you bring what you'll need. Processing is also expensive, so wait until you're home. There are no special restrictions on taking photographs, except in certain museums (signs are generally posted). When in doubt, and in the Christiania area of Copenhagen, ask first.

Customs   Nearly all items that can safely be viewed as "personal" are allowed in duty free. Tobacco is limited. You can bring in 250 cigarettes or 250 grams of tobacco. You can also bring in 1 liter (a standard bottle) of spirits or 2 liters of strong wine, depending on whether you're coming into Denmark from an EU or non-EU country. There are no restrictions on the importation of currency. However, nonresidents cannot take out more Danish kroner than they brought in, unless they can prove they obtained it by converting foreign currency.

Upon leaving Denmark, U.S. citizens who have been outside their home country for 48 hours or more are allowed to take home $400 worth of merchandise duty free—if they have claimed no similar exemption within the past 30 days. If you make purchases in Denmark, keep your receipts.

Doctors   Most areas have doctors on duty 24 hours a day on Saturdays, Sundays, and holidays; weekday emergency hours are 4pm to 7:30am. Every doctor speaks English.

Drug Laws   Penalties for the possession, use, purchase, sale, or manufacturing of drugs are severe. The quantity of the controlled substance is more important than the type of substance. Danish police are particularly strict with cases involving the sale of drugs to children.

Drugstores   They're known as *apoteker* in Danish and are open Monday to Thursday from 9am to 5:30pm, Friday 9am to 7pm, and Saturday 9am to 1pm.

Electricity   Voltage is generally 220 volts AC, 50 to 60 cycles. In many camping sites, 110-volt power plugs are also available. Adapters and transformers may be purchased in Denmark. It's always best to check at your hotel desk before using an electrical outlet.

Embassies   All embassies are in Copenhagen. The embassy of the **United States** is at Dag Hammärskjölds Allé 24, DK-2100 København (☎ **35-55-31-44**). Other embassies are the **United Kingdom,** Kastelsvej 40, DK-2100 København (☎ 35-44-52-00); **Canada,** Kristen Berniskows Gade 1, DK-1105 København (☎ 33-48-32-00); **Australia,** Strandboulevarden, DK-2100 København (☎ 39-29-20-77); and **Ireland,** Østbanegade 21 (☎ **35-42-32-33**).

Emergencies   Dial ☎ **112** for the fire department, the police, or an ambulance, or to report a sea or an air accident. Emergency calls from public telephone kiosks are free (no coins needed).

Holidays   See "When to Go," earlier in this chapter.

Language   Danish is the national tongue. English is commonly spoken, especially among young people. You should have few, if any, language barriers. The best phrase book is *Danish for Travellers* (Berlitz).

Liquor Laws   To consume alcohol in Danish bars, restaurants, or cafes, customers must be 18 or older. There are no restrictions on children under 18 who drink at home or, for example, from a bottle in a public park. Danish police tend to be lenient unless drinkers become raucous or uncontrollable. There is no leniency, however, in the matter of driving while intoxicated. It's illegal to drive with a blood-alcohol level of 0.8 or more, which could be produced by two drinks. If the level is 1.5, motorists pay a serious fine. If it's more than 1.5, drivers can lose their license. If the level is 2.0 or more (usually produced by six or seven drinks), a prison term of at least 14 days might follow. Package stores in Denmark are closed on Sunday.

Mail　Most post offices are open Monday to Friday from 9 or 10am to 5 or 6pm and Saturday from 9am to noon; they're closed Sunday. All mail to North America is sent airmail without extra charge. The cost for mail weighing 20 grams (.175 ounces) is 5.50 DKK (70¢). Mailboxes are painted red and display the embossed crown and trumpet of the Danish Postal Society.

Maps　The best map for touring Denmark is part of the series published by Hallwag. It's for sale at all major bookstores in Copenhagen, including the most centrally located one, **Boghallen,** Rådhuspladsen 37 (☎ **33-11-85-11**), in the Town Hall Square.

Newspapers & Magazines　English-language newspapers are sold at all major news kiosks in Copenhagen, but are much harder to find in the provinces. London papers are flown in for early-morning delivery, but you may find the *International Herald Tribune* or *USA Today* more interesting. Pick up a copy of *Copenhagen This Week,* printed in English, which contains useful information.

Pharmacies　See "Drugstores," above.

Photographic Needs　See "Cameras & Film," above.

Police　Dial ☎ **112** for police assistance.

Radio & TV　No English-language radio or TV stations broadcast from Denmark. Only radios and TVs with satellite reception can receive signals from countries such as Britain. News programs in English are broadcast Monday to Saturday at 8:30am on Radio Denmark, 93.85 MHz. Radio 1 (90.8 MHz VHF) features news and classical music. Channels 2 and 3 (96.5/93.9 MHz) include some entertainment, broadcast light news items, and offer light music. Most TV stations transmit from 7:30 to 11:30pm. Most films (many of which are American) are shown in their original languages, with Danish subtitles.

Rest Rooms　All big plazas, such as Town Hall Square in Copenhagen, have public lavatories. In small towns and villages, head for the marketplace. Hygienic standards are usually adequate. Sometimes men and women patronize the same toilets (signs read TOILETTER or WC). Otherwise, men's rooms are marked HERRER or H, and women's rooms are marked DAMER or D.

Safety　Denmark is one of the safest European countries for travelers. Copenhagen, the major population center, naturally experiences the most crime. Muggings have been reported in the vicinity of the railway station, especially late at night, but crimes of extreme violence are exceedingly rare. Exercise the usual precautions you would when traveling anywhere.

Taxes　The 25% VAT (value-added tax) on goods and services is known in Denmark as *moms* (pronounced "mumps"). Special tax-free exports are possible, and many stores will mail goods home to you, circumventing moms. If you want to take your purchases with you, look for shops displaying Danish tax-free shopping notices. Such shops offer tourists tax refunds for personal export. This refund applies to purchases of at least 300 DKK ($37.50) for U.S. and Canadian visitors. Your tax-free invoice must be stamped by Danish Customs when you leave the country. You can receive your refund at Copenhagen's Kastrup International Airport when you depart. If you go by land or sea, you can receive your refund by mail. Mail requests for refunds to Danish Tax-Free Shopping A/S, H. J. Holstvej 5A, DK-2605 Brøndby, Denmark. You'll be reimbursed by check, cash, or credit- or charge-card credit in the currency you want.

For the refund to apply, the 300 DKK must be spent in one store, but not necessarily at the same time. Some major department stores allow purchases to be made over several days or even weeks, at the end of which receipts will be tallied. Service and handling fees are deducted from the total, so actual refunds come to about 18%. Information on this program is available from the Danish Tourist Board (see "Visitor Information & Entry Requirements," above).

A 25% moms is included in hotel and restaurant bills, service charges, entrance fees, and repair bills for foreign-registered cars. No refunds are possible on these items.

Telephone   The country code for Denmark is **45**. It should precede any call made to Denmark from another country.

Danish phones are fully automatic. Dial the eight-digit number; there are no city area codes. Don't insert any coins until your party answers. At public telephone booths, use two 50-øre coins or a 1-krone or 5-krone coin only. You can make more than one call on the same payment if your time hasn't run out. Remember that it can be expensive to telephone from your hotel room. Emergency calls are free.

Time   Denmark operates on Central European Time—1 hour ahead of Greenwich Mean Time and 6 hours ahead of Eastern Standard Time. Daylight Saving Time is observed from the end of March to the end of September.

Tipping   Tips are seldom expected, but when they are, you should give only 1 or 2 DKK. Porters charge fixed prices, and tipping is not customary for hairdressers or barbers. Service is built into the system, and hotels, restaurants, and even taxis include a 15% service charge in their rates. Because of the service charge, plus the 25% moms, you'll probably have to pay an additional 40% for some services!

Consider tipping only for special services—some Danes would feel insulted if you offered them a tip.

Water   Tap water is safe to drink throughout Denmark.

3 Introducing Copenhagen

Copenhagen, the capital of Denmark, got its name from the word *køben-havn*, or "merchants' harbor." It grew in size and importance because of its position on the Øresund (the Sound), the body of water between Denmark and Sweden, guarding the entrance to the Baltic.

In the summer of 2000 the Øresund Bridge was officially opened, linking Sweden and Denmark physically for the first time ever. Today there's a 10-mile motor and railway link between Zealand (the eastern part of Denmark) and Skån, the southern part of Sweden. If you'd like to tie in a visit to Copenhagen with the châteaux country of Sweden, it is as easy as driving across the bridge.

From its humble beginnings, Copenhagen has become the largest city in Scandinavia, home to 1.5 million people. It's the seat of the oldest kingdom in the world.

Over the centuries Copenhagen has suffered more than its share of disasters. In the 17th century the Swedes repeatedly besieged it, and in the 18th century it endured the plague and two devastating fires. The British attacked twice during the Napoleonic wars in the early 1800s. The last major disaster occurred in 1940, when the Nazis invaded Denmark. They held it until 1945, when British soldiers moved in again, this time as liberators.

Copenhagen's canals, narrow streets, and old houses reflect its considerable charm. Its most famous resident was Hans Christian Andersen, whose memory lives on. Another world-renowned inhabitant was Søren Kierkegaard, who took long morning strolls in the city, planning his next work; his completed essays eventually earned him the title "the father of existentialism."

Copenhagen retains some of the characteristics of a village. If you forget the suburbs, you can cover most of the central belt on foot, which makes it a great tourist spot. It's almost as though the city were designed for strolling, as reflected by its Strøget, the longest and oldest pedestrians-only street in Europe.

1 Orientation

ARRIVING

BY PLANE You arrive at **Kastrup Airport** (☎ 32-54-17-01), 7¼ miles from the center of Copenhagen. Since 1998, air rail trains have linked the airport with Copenhagen's Central Railway Station, in the center of the hotel zone, and the whole affair now takes a mere 11 minutes and costs 16.50 DKK ($2.05). The Air Rail Terminal is underneath the airport's arrivals and departure halls, just a short escalator ride from the gates. It has more than 30 check-in counters, ticketing offices, information desks, restaurants, and fast-food chains. You can also take an SAS bus to the city terminal; the fare is 35 DKK ($4.40). A taxi to the city center costs around 130 DKK ($16.25). Even cheaper is a local bus, no. 250S, which leaves from the international arrivals terminal every 15 or 20 minutes for Town Hall Square in central Copenhagen and costs 15 DKK ($1.90).

BY TRAIN Trains arrive at the **Hoved Banegård (Central Railway Station),** in the center of Copenhagen, near the Tivoli Gardens and the Rådhuspladsen. Call ☎ 33-14-17-01 for rail information. The station operates a luggage-checking service, but room bookings are available only at the tourist office (see "Visitor Information," below). You can also exchange money at Den Danske Bank (☎ 33-12-04-11), open daily from 7am to 8pm.

From the Central Railroad Station, you can connect with the **S-tog,** the local subway system. Trains depart from platforms in the terminal. Ask the staff at the information desk near Tracks 5 and 6 which train you should board.

BY BUS Buses from Zealand and elsewhere in Denmark also pull into the Central Railroad Station. For bus information call ☎ 36-13-14-15 (daily 7am to 9:30pm).

BY CAR If you're driving from Germany, a car ferry will take you from Travemünde to Gedser in southern Denmark. From Gedser, express highway E55 north runs to the southern outskirts of Copenhagen. If you're coming from Sweden and crossing at Helsingborg, you'll land on the Danish side of Helsingør. Take express highway E55 south to the northern outskirts of Copenhagen.

BY FERRY Most ferries land at Havnegade, at the end of the south side of Nyhavn, a short walk from the center of Copenhagen. Taxis wait here for ferry arrivals. Most come from Malmö, Sweden; ferries from continental Europe usually land in South Zealand.

VISITOR INFORMATION

The **Copenhagen Tourist Information Center,** Bernstorffsgade 1 (☎ 33-25-38-44), is across from the Tivoli's main entrance. In July and August, it's open daily from 8am to 11pm; in May, June, and early September, daily 9am to 9pm; September 16 to April, Monday to Friday 9am to 4:30pm, Saturday 9am to 1:30pm. Pick up a copy of *Copenhagen This Week* at the tourist center; its "Events Calendar" has good listings for entertainment and sightseeing events.

CITY LAYOUT

MAIN ARTERIES & STREETS The heart of Old Copenhagen is a maze of pedestrian streets, formed by Nørreport Station to the north, Rådhuspladsen (Town Hall Square) to the west, and Kongens Nytorv to the east. **Strøget,** the longest pedestrians-only street in Europe at three-quarters of a mile long, goes east from Town Hall Square to Kongens Nytorv, and consists of five streets: Frederiksberggade, Nygade, Vimmelskaftet, Amagertorv, and Østergade. Strøget is lined with shops, bars, restaurants, and in summer, sidewalk cafes. **Pistolstræde** is a maze of galleries, restaurants, and boutiques, all housed in restored 18th-century buildings.

Fiolstræde (Violet Street), a dignified street with antiques shops and bookshops, cuts through the university (in the Latin Quarter). If you turn into Rosengaarden at the top of Fiolstræde, you'll come to **Kultorvet** (Coal Square) just before you reach Nørreport Station. Here you join the third main pedestrian street, **Købmagergade** (Butcher Street), which winds around and finally meets Strøget and Amagertorv.

At the end of Strøget, you approach **Kongens Nytorv** (King's Square), the site of the Royal Theater and of Magasin, the largest department store in Copenhagen. It's the beginning of **Nyhavn,** the former seamen's quarter that has been gentrified into an upmarket area of expensive restaurants, apartments, cafes, and boutiques.

The national government is centered on the small island of **Slotsholmen,** which is connected to the center by eight bridges. Several museums, notably Christiansborg Castle, are here.

The center of Copenhagen is **Rådhuspladsen** (Town Hall Square). From here it's a short walk to Copenhagen's biggest attraction, the Tivoli Gardens, and to the Central Railroad Station, the main railroad, subway, and bus terminus. The wide boulevard, **Vesterbrogade,** passes by the Tivoli until it reaches the Central Railroad Station. Another major boulevard is named after Denmark's most famous writer. **H. C. Andersens Boulevard** runs along Rådhuspladsen and the Tivoli Gardens.

FINDING AN ADDRESS   Even numbers are on one side of the street, odd numbers on the other. Buildings go in numerical order, with A, B, or C often inserted after the street number.

Neighborhoods in Brief

TIVOLI GARDENS   In the heart of Copenhagen, on the south side of Rådhuspladsen (Town Hall), these amusement gardens were built on the site of fortifications. A total of 160,000 flowers and 110,000 electric light bulbs set the scene. Built in 1843, the Tivoli is made up of a collection of restaurants, dance halls, theaters, beer gardens, and lakes. If you're in Copenhagen in summer, there is no more fun place to dine, and restaurants range from the pricey deluxe dining room with formal service to a beer hall with typically Danish food. The downside? Prices at the restaurants in Tivoli are about 30% higher than elsewhere in the city.

NYHAVN & KONGENS NYTORV   This is the harbor area, for years the haunt of sailors looking for tattoos and other diversions. Nowadays, it's one of the most elegant sections of the city, site of the deluxe Hotel d'Angleterre and many other stellar hotels and prestigious restaurants. The central canal, filled with yachts and boats, and the 18th-century facades of the buildings along the water contribute to the area's ambience and elegance. Kongens Nytorv (King's Square) is the entryway to Nyhavn and the home of the Royal Theater. For years, this was the section of Copenhagen where nobility erected their town houses. At the centerpiece of the square is an elaborate equestrian statue of King Christian V, depicting a quad of classical figures seated submissively under His Majesty's horse. In and around the square, and along Nyhavn, you'll find a selection of the grandest and most romantic hotels in Copenhagen.

NEAR RÅDHUSPLADSEN (TOWN HALL)   This is the very core of Copenhagen—nothing could be more central, or more convenient. This location puts you right near Tivoli Gardens, the pedestrians-only shopping street, Strøget, and the Central Railway Station. Hotels east of the station tend to be more upmarket than those west of the station at Vesterbro (see below). Some of the most expensive hotels in Copenhagen, including the Palace and Kong Frederik are here, but you'll find moderate and inexpensive ones as well. The same holds true for restaurants.

STRØGET   This is the longest pedestrians-only street in Europe, beginning at Rådhuspladsen. The most interesting parts are Gammeltorv and Nytorv ("old" and "new" squares), on either side of Strøget. They're the sites of fruit and vegetable markets, as well as stalls selling bric-a-brac and handmade jewelry. The word Strøget doesn't appear on most city maps (though we've marked it on ours). Instead, Strøget encompasses five streets: Frederiksbrerggade, Nygade, Villelskaftet, Amagertorv, and Østergade. In addition to shopping, this area has a lot of cafes, fast-food places, and some minor restaurants. The better restaurants of Copenhagen lie off the Strøget along adjoining streets, and in other parts of the city.

INDRE BY   This is the Old Town, in the heart of Copenhagen. Once filled with monasteries, it's a maze of old streets, alleyways, and squares. If you cross Gammeltorv and Nørregade, you'll be in the university area, nicknamed the Latin Quarter, as in Paris. Although not a district for hotels, this is one of the best places for dining in Copenhagen, especially for those on a budget or traveling moderately. Most of the restaurants are clustered on or near Gråbrødretorv or "Greyfriars Square" in the heart of Copenhagen's medieval core. Today it's a charming and hip area, especially after dark, when the clubs and cafes are buzzing. Don't expect the architectural grandeur of Kongens Nytorv. What you get instead is a setting that is low-key and unpretentious, representative of the brown-brick buildings that fill most of Copenhagen. The Vor Frue Kirke (cathedral of Copenhagen) is here, as is the Rundetårn (Round Tower).

SLOTSHOLMEN   On this island, site of Christiansborg Palace, Bishop Absalon built the first fortress in the city in 1167. Today it's the seat of parliament and the site of Thorvaldsen's Museum, among others. Bridges link Slotsholmen to Indre By. You can also visit the Royal Library, the Theater Museum, and the Royal Stables. The 17th-century Børsen (Stock exchange) is also here. This is an area to visit for sight-seeing attractions, not a hotel and restaurant district.

CHRISTIANSHAVN   This was the "new town" ordered by master builder Christian IV in the early 1500s, originally constructed to house shipbuilding workers. Visitors come here today mainly to see the Danish Film Museum at Gothersgade 55, and Vors Frelsers Kirke, on the corner of Prinsessegade and Skt. Annægade, where sightseers climb the old church's spire for a panoramic view. Again, this is a section to visit for its attractions rather than hotels and restaurants.

CHRISTIANIA   Within walking distance of Vor Frelsers Kirke at Christianshavn is this offbeat district, once a barracks for soldiers. Entrances are on Prinsessegade. In 1971 many young and homeless people moved in without the city's permission, proclaiming that Christiania was a "free city." It has been a controversial place ever since. Regrettably, the area, founded on idealism, also became a shelter for criminals, especially drug pushers. There are craft shops and restaurants here; merchandise and food are fairly cheap because the residents refuse to pay Denmark's crippling 25% tax. Don't photograph anyone without permission. As some out-of-towners say about New York, "It's a great place to visit but I wouldn't want to live there."

VESTERBRO (THE RAIL STATION AREA)   This district lies to the immediate west of the Central Railway Station. Its main street, Istedgade, runs west from the main rail depot. This area is filled with some of the least expensive hotels in Copenhagen. It is seedy in some parts, gentrified in others. In the early 1970s when Denmark legalized pornography, visitors from all over the world flocked here, and the place took on somewhat of a red-light district aura. Although pornography is still hawked here, the district is also the site of respectable budget and moderately priced family hotels, especially along Helgolandsgade and Colbjørnsensgade. Today with many of its original 19th-century facades restored, the district has been considerably cleaned up. Refugees from Turkey and Pakistan, followed by citizens of other countries, have settled heavily in the area, and you'll find many ethnic restaurants and craft shops.

NØRREBRO Even in the middle of the 19th century, this section—adjacent to Vesterbro—was a blue-collar neighborhood. The original Danish settlers departed long ago, and the neighborhood has increasingly filled with immigrants (the overflow from Vesterbro) who don't always get a friendly reception in Copenhagen. The area also abounds with artists, students, and musicians who can't afford the high rents elsewhere. Nørrebro is rich in artisan shops and ethnic (especially Turkish and Pakistani) restaurants. There are so many secondhand clothing stores—especially in the district around Sankt Hans Torv—that Nørrebro is taking on overtones of a Middle Eastern bazaar. Alleged antiques shops also fill the area along Ravnsborgade, but believe us: many of the furnishings and objets d'art aren't authentic. On Saturday morning a flea market is in full swing along the wall of Assistens Kirkegård, to the west of Nørrebrogade. Although not a hotel or restaurant district, Nørrebro attracts those seeking a look at off-the-beaten Copenhagen.

NEAR NØRREPORT STATION This district lies to the north of Vesterbro and though it may seem inconvenient you can arrive at it in just 15 minutes from the central station. Its chief landmark is Assistens Kirkegard, the largest cemetery in Copenhagen—containing the tombs of Hans Christian Andersen and Sören Kierkegaard—which is now a public park. The area is visited chiefly because it's the setting for one of Copenhagen's best-known budget hotels, Ibsens, and a leading gay hotel, Jørgensen.

FREDERIKSBERG Vesterbrogade runs west from the inner city to the residential and business district of Frederiksberg. It grew up around Frederiksberg Palace, constructed in the Italianate style with an ocher facade. A park, Frederiksberg Have, surrounds the palace. To the west of the palace is the Zoologisk Have, one of the largest zoos in Europe.

DRAGØR This seems to be everybody's favorite spot, after the Tivoli. It's especially recommended if you have time to see only the Copenhagen area and not the countryside. Dragør is a fishing village south of Copenhagen that dates from the 16th century. Walk its cobblestoned streets and admire its 65 red-roofed houses, which have been designated national landmarks. Chances are, you'll patronize one of the restaurants here at lunch, returning to a city hotel at night. However, there are hotels and inns here should you decide to stay.

2 Getting Around

Copenhagen is a walker's paradise, neat and compact, with many of its major sightseeing attractions in close proximity to one another.

BY PUBLIC TRANSPORTATION

A joint zone fare system includes Copenhagen Transport buses and State Railway and S-tog trains in Copenhagen and North Zealand, plus some private railway routes within a 25-mile radius of the capital. You can transfer from train to bus and vice versa with the same ticket.

FARES A *grundbillet* (basic ticket) for both buses and trains costs 11 DKK ($1.40). You can buy 10 tickets for 75 DKK ($9.40). Children under 12 pay half price; those under 5 ride free on local trains, and those under 7 go free on buses. For 70 DKK ($8.75), you can purchase a ticket good for 24 hours of bus and train travel through nearly half of Zealand (worth it for a heavy day of sightseeing); it's half price for children 7 to 11, free for children under 7.

Impressions

What strikes me now most as regards Denmark is the charm, beauty, and independence of the women.

—Arnold Bennett, *Journal,* 1913

The Danes that drench their cares in wine.

—Ben Jonson, "Ode Allegorical," 1603

DISCOUNT PASSES   The **Copenhagen Card** entitles you to free and unlimited travel by bus and rail throughout the metropolitan area (including North Zealand), 25% to 50% discounts on crossings to and from Sweden, and free admission to many sights and museums. The card is available for 1, 2, or 3 days and costs 155 DKK ($19.40), 255 DKK ($31.90), or 320 DKK ($40), respectively. Children under 12 pay half price. For more information, contact the Copenhagen Tourist Information Center (see "Orientation," above).

Students who have an **International Student Identity Card (ISIC)** are entitled to discounts. You can buy a card in the United States at any Council Travel office; for the office nearest you, call ☎ **800/GET-AN-ID.**

For information about low-cost train, ferry, and plane trips, go to **Wasteels,** Skoubogade 6 (☎ **33-14-46-33**), in Copenhagen. It's a travel agency specializing in discount train and plane tickets for travelers age 26 and under, and it's open Monday to Friday from 9am to 7pm and Saturday 10am to 3pm.

Eurailpasses can be purchased at any train station in Scandinavia and are good on local trains in Copenhagen.

BY BUS   Copenhagen's well-maintained buses are the least expensive method of getting around. Most buses leave from Rådhuspladsen. Buses run along the major routes every 10 to 15 minutes, and a basic ticket allows 1 hour of travel and unlimited transfers within the zone where you started your trip. For information, call ☎ **36-45-45-45.**

BY S-TOG (SUBWAY)   The S-tog connects central Copenhagen with its suburbs. Use of the tickets is the same as on buses (see above). You can transfer from a bus line to an S-tog train on the same ticket. Eurailpass holders generally ride free. For more information, call ☎ **33-14-17-01** at any time.

BY CAR

Because of the prevalence of traffic-free walkways, and because of its many parks, gardens, and canalside promenades, Copenhagen is well suited to pedestrians. It's best to park your car in any of the dozens of city parking lots, and then retrieve it when you're ready to explore the suburbs. Many parking lots are open 24 hours a day, but a few close between 1 and 7am; some close on Saturday afternoon and on Sunday when traffic is generally lighter. The cost ranges from 15 to 25 DKK ($1.90 to $3.15) per hour or 55 to 75 DKK ($6.90 to $9.40) for 24 hours. Two centrally located parking lots are **Industriens Hus,** H. C. Andersens Blvd. 18 (☎ **33-91-21-75**), open Monday to Friday from 7am to 12:45am, Saturday and Sunday 10am to 12:45am; and **Statoil,** Israels Plads (☎ **33-14-37-76**), open 24 hours.

BY TAXI

Watch for the FRI (free) sign or green light to hail a taxi. Be sure the taxi has a meter. Københavns Taxa (☎ **35-35-35-35**) operates the largest fleet. **Tips are included in**

the meter price: 22 DKK ($2.75) when the flag drops, then 10 DKK ($1.25) per kilometer (.6 mile), Monday to Friday from 6am to 6pm. From 6pm to 6am, and all day on Saturday and Sunday, the cost is 11 DKK ($1.40) per kilometer. Many drivers speak English.

BY BICYCLE

Many Copenhageners ride bicycles. For 50 DKK ($6.25) per day, you can rent a bike at **Københavns Cykler,** Reventlowsgade 11 (☎ 33-33-86-13). Hours are Monday to Friday 8:30am to 5:30pm, Saturday 9am to 1pm, and Sunday 10am to 1pm.

Fast Facts: Copenhagen

American Express is represented throughout Denmark by **Neiman & Schultz,** Nørregade 7A (☎ 33-13-11-81), with a branch in Terminal 3 of the Copenhagen Airport. Fulfilling all the functions of mainstream American Express except for foreign-exchange services, the main office is open Monday to Thursday from 8:30am till 4:30pm, and Friday from 8:30am to 4pm. The airport office remains open till 8:30pm Monday to Friday. On weekends, and overnight on weekdays, a recorded message, in English, will deliver the phone number of a 24-hour AMEX service in Stockholm. This is useful for anyone who has lost a card or some traveler's checks. As for foreign exchange, you'll find Neiman & Schultz offices scattered throughout Copenhagen, including a branch that's open 24 hours a day at the railway station.

Area Code   The country code for Denmark is **45.** There are no city area codes. Every Danish telephone number has eight digits.

Baby-sitters   Try Students Baby-sitting Agency, Lykkesholmes Alle 33C (☎ 70-20-44-16), open Monday to Friday 1 to 4pm in the summer, 10am to 3pm the rest of the year. The cost is 250 DKK ($31.25) for 1 to 5 hours, plus 40 DKK ($5) for each additional hour. Transportation is extra.

Bookstores   One of the best and most centrally located is **Boghallen,** Rådhuspladsen 37 (☎ 33-47-27-60). The shop carries books in Danish and English. Hours are Monday to Saturday 10am to 5pm.

Business Hours   Most **banks** are open Monday to Friday from 10am to 4pm (Thursday to 6pm). **Stores** are generally open Monday to Thursday from 9am to 6pm, Friday 9am to 7 or 8pm, Saturday 9am to 2pm; most are closed Sunday. **Offices** are open Monday to Friday from 9 or 10am to 4 or 5pm.

Camera Repair   The biggest photography shop and camera supply center in Denmark is **Kontant Foto,** Købmagergade 44 (☎ 33-12-00-29). It's open Monday to Thursday from 8:30am to 5:30pm, Friday 9am to 7pm, Saturday 10am to 2pm.

Car Rentals   See "Getting Around" section in Chapter 2, "Planning a Trip to Denmark."

Currency Exchange   Banks are generally your best bet. The main branch of **Den Danske Bank** (The Danish Bank), Amagertorv 2 (☎ 33-44-30-00), is open Monday to Friday from 10am to 4pm (till 6pm on Thursday). When banks are closed, you can exchange money at **Forex** (☎ 33-11-29-05) in the Central Railroad Station, daily from 8am to 9pm, or at the **Change Group,** Østergade 16 (☎ 33-93-04-55), Monday to Saturday from 9am to 10pm, Sunday 9am to 8pm.

Dentists   During regular business hours, ask your hotel to call the nearest English-speaking dentist. For emergency dental treatment, go to **Tandlægevagten,** Oslo Plads 14 (☎ 35-38-02-51), near Østerport Station and the U.S. Embassy. It's open Monday to Friday from 8am to 9:30pm; Saturday, Sunday, and holidays 10am to noon. Be prepared to pay cash.

Doctors   To reach a doctor dial ☎ 33-93-63-00 from 9am to 4pm or ☎ 38-88-60-41 after hours. The doctor's fee is payable in cash, although some have started accepting credit cards. Virtually every doctor speaks English.

Drugstores   See "Pharmacies," below.

Emergencies   Dial ☎ 112 to report a **fire** or to call the **police** or an **ambulance.** State your phone number and address. Emergency calls from public telephones are free (no coins needed).

Eyeglass Repair   The largest and oldest optical chain in Denmark is **Synoptik,** Købmagergade 22 (☎ 33-15-05-38), with branches throughout Denmark. Most glasses can be replaced in 2 or 3 hours. Bifocals can take 10 to 14 days. Synoptik also specializes in contact lenses, with hundreds of types in stock. Hours are Monday to Thursday 9:30am to 6pm, Friday 9:30am to 7pm, Saturday 9:30am to 4pm.

Hairdresser   Luigi Cassino, Store Kongens Gade 46 (☎ 33-13-28-48), offers any and all hair-related services for both men and women. Call for an appointment. Hours are Monday to Wednesday and Friday from 10am to 6pm, Thursday 9:30am to 7:30pm, and Saturday 8:30am to 2pm.

Hospitals   In case of a sudden illness or accident, even foreigners are entitled to free medical treatment in Denmark. One centrally located hospital is **Rigshospitalet,** Blegdamsvej 9 (☎ 35-45-35-45).

Internet Access   To check your e-mail or to send messages, go to **Copenhagen Hovebibliotek,** Krystalgade 15 (☎ 33-73-60-60), open Monday to Friday 10am to 7pm, Saturday 10am to 2pm.

Laundry & Dry Cleaning   There are coin-op laundries in all neighborhoods. Some are independent, others part of the Vascomat and Møntvask chains that seem to dominate the business. Some of the most convenient are at Borgergade 2, Nansensgade 39, and Istedgade 45. They are open daily 8am to 10pm. **Dry Cleaning,** Vester Farimagsgade 3 (☎ 33-12-45-45), is a block from the Central Railroad Station. It's open Monday through Friday from 8am to 6pm, Saturday 9:30am to 3pm.

Libraries   Try the **Københavns Bibliotek** (Copenhagen Library), Krystalgade 15 (☎ 33-73-60-60). Open Monday to Friday from 10am to 7pm, Saturday 10am to 2pm, it has a large collection of English-language publications.

Lost Property   The Lost and Found Property office at Slotsherrensvej 113, 2720 Vanløse (☎ 38-74-88-22), is open Monday to Thursday from 9am to 5:30pm, Friday 9am to 2pm. For property lost on buses, phone ☎ 36-45-45-45; on trains, ☎ 33-16-21-10. These numbers operate only Monday to Friday from 9am to 4pm (to 6pm on Thursday).

Luggage Storage & Lockers   Luggage can be stored in rental lockers at Central Railroad Station. Lockers are available daily from 4:30am to midnight. The cost is 35 DKK ($4.40) for 24 hours. For information, call ☎ 33-14-04-08.

Newspapers   Foreign newspapers, notably the *International Herald Tribune* and *USA Today,* are available at the Central Railroad Station in front of the Palladium movie theater on Vesterbrogade, on Strøget, and at the newsstands of big hotels.

Pharmacies   An *apotek* (pharmacy) open 24 hours a day in central Copenhagen is **Steno Apotek,** Vesterbrogade 6C (☎ **33-14-82-66**).

Photographic Needs   See "Camera Repair," above.

Police   In an emergency, dial ☎ **112.** For other matters, go to the police station at Halmtorvet 20 (☎ **33-25-14-48**).

Post Office   For information about the Copenhagen post office, phone ☎ **33-33-89-00.** The main post office, where your *poste restante* (general delivery) letters can be picked up, is at Tietgensgade 35-39, DK-1704 København (☎ **33-33-89-00**). It's open Monday to Friday from 11am to 6pm, Saturday 10am to 1pm. The post office at the Central Railroad Station is open Monday to Friday from 8am to 10pm, Saturday 9am to 4pm, Sunday 10am to 4pm.

Religious Services   St. Ansgar's Roman Catholic Church is at Bredgade 64 (☎ **33-13-37-62**); the English Church of St. Alban's (Anglo-Episcopalian) on Langelinie (☎ **39-62-77-36**); the American Church (Protestant and interdenominational) at the U.S. Embassy, Dag Hammarskjølds Allé 24 (☎ **35-55-31-44**); and the synagogue at Krystalgade 12 (☎ **33-12-88-68**). The International Church of Copenhagen (affiliated with the American Lutheran church) holds services at the Vartov Church, Farvergade 27 (☎ **39-62-47-85**), across from the Town Hall.

Rest Rooms   Some free public toilets can be found at Rådhuspladsen (Town Hall Square), the Central Railroad Station, and at all terminals. Look for the markings TOILETTER, WC, DAMER or D (women), or HERRER or H (men).

Safety   Compared with other European capital cities, Copenhagen is relatively safe. However, since the early 1990s, with the influx of homeless refugees from around the world—many of whom have become pickpockets—crime has risen. Guard your wallet, purse, and other valuables as you would when traveling in any big city.

Shoe Repair   The department store **Magasin,** Kongens Nytorv 13 (☎ **33-11-44-33**), has a great shoe-repair franchise, **Mister Minit,** in its basement. Service is available Monday to Saturday, 10am to 7pm.

Taxes   Denmark imposes a value-added tax of 25%, known as *moms* (and pronounced "mumps"). It's included in hotel and restaurant bills, service charges, entrance fees, and repair bills for foreign-registered cars. No refunds are given on these items. For more information, see "The Shopping Scene" in Chapter 4, "Exploring Copenhagen."

Transit Information   Phone ☎ **36-45-45-45** for bus information or ☎ **33-14-17-01** for S-tog (subway) information.

3 Accommodations

Peak season in Denmark is summer, from May to September, which pretty much coincides with the schedule at the Tivoli Gardens. Once the Tivoli closes for the winter, lots of rooms become available. Make sure to ask about winter discounts.

Nearly all doubles come with a private bathroom. Find out, though, whether this means a shower or a bathtub. You can undercut these prices by requesting a room without a bathroom at moderate and inexpensive hotels. Ask if breakfast is included (usually it isn't).

A word of warning: In most moderate and nearly all inexpensive hotels in Copenhagen, the bathrooms are cramped, and there's never enough for ll your stuff. Many of the bathrooms were added to older buildings that weren't designed for bathrooms. Also, get used to towels that are much thinner than you might like.

RESERVATIONS SERVICE At Bernstorffsgade 1, across from the Tivoli's main entrance, the Tourist Information Center maintains a useful hotel-booking service, **Værelsænvisningen** (☎ 70-22-24-42). The charge for this service, whether you book a private home, a hostel, or a luxury hotel, is 40 DKK ($5) per person. A deposit, about 8.6% of the room cost, must be paid, but it's deducted from your bill later. You'll also be given a city map and bus directions. This office doesn't accept advance reservations; it can arrange private accommodations if the hotels in your price range are full. The office is open April 19 to September 30, daily from 9am to 9pm; October to April 18, Monday to Friday 9am to 5pm, Saturday 9am to 2pm.

In the same building, the **Hotel Booking Service** (☎ 33-25-38-44) will reserve hotel rooms in advance.

NYHAVN & KONGENS NYTORV
VERY EXPENSIVE

✪ **Hotel d'Angleterre.** Kongens Nytorv 34, DK-1050 København. ☎ **800-44-UTELL** in the U.S., or 33-12-00-95. Fax 33-12-11-18. www.remmen.dk. E-mail: anglehot@remmen.dk. 124 units. A/C MINIBAR TV TEL. 2,565–3,765 DKK ($320.65–$470.65) double; from 4,095 DKK ($511.90) suite. AE, CB, DC, MC, V. Parking 175 DKK ($21.90). Bus: 1, 6, or 9.

At the top of Nyhavn, this is the premier choice in Denmark. Though it's a bit staid and stodgy, it's impeccably bourgeois and correct—there's no better address in Copenhagen. The seven-story hotel, a Leading Hotels of the World member, was built in 1755 and extensively renovated in the 1980s. Guests have included Hans Christian Andersen and almost every celebrity who has ever visited Denmark. It's a medley of styles: Empire, Louis XVI, and modern. The guest rooms are beautifully furnished with art objects and occasional antiques. Room sizes and views vary, but each has a high ceiling and marble bathroom, complete with robes, hair dryer, phone, and scale. The deluxe rooms are in front, but those facing the courtyard are more tranquil and also receive a fair amount of sunlight—when the sun is shining, that is.

Dining/Diversions: The Bar is popular with everyone from rock stars to CEOs. The moderately priced Restaurant Wiinblad caters to the young and beautiful. Restaurant d'Angleterre is acclaimed for its French cuisine and vintage wines. Light lunches and snacks are also available.

Amenities: Room service (24 hours), laundry, valet parking, in-house video, banquet and meeting facilities, health club, swimming pool, sauna, Turkish bath, solarium.

✪ **Phoenix Copenhagen.** Bredgade 37, DK-1260 København. ☎ **33-95-95-00.** Fax 33-33-98-33. E-mail: p.remillard@arp-hansen.dk. 212 units. MINIBAR TV TEL. 1,650–2,495 DKK ($206.25–$311.90) double; 3,000–6,000 DKK ($375–$750) suite. AE, DC, MC, V. Parking 95 DKK ($11.90). Bus: 1, 5, 9, or 10.

More than any other hotel in Copenhagen, this top-of-the-line lodging poses a serious challenge to the discreet grandeur of the nearby Hotel d'Angleterre. Opened in 1991, the Phoenix was a royal guesthouse, originally built in the 1700s to accommodate the aristocratic courtiers of Amalienborg Palace. Beginning in 1988, tons of white and colored marble were imported to create the elegant Louis XVI–style decor that has impressed guests ever since. Beds are large with firm mattresses, and wool carpeting and chandeliers add graceful notes to the guest rooms. The Italian marble bathrooms

Copenhagen Accommodations

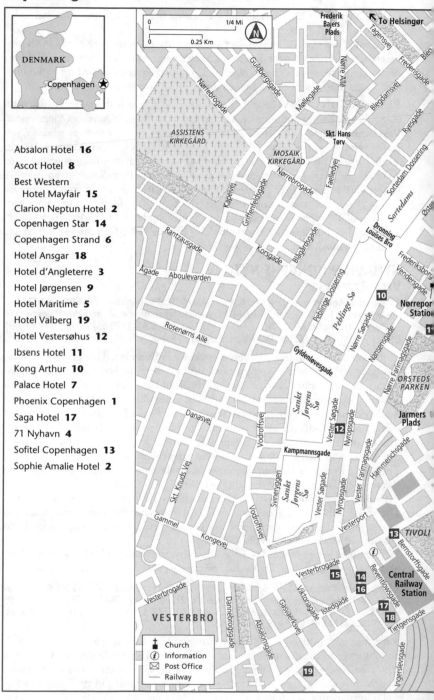

DENMARK

Copenhagen ★

Absalon Hotel **16**

Ascot Hotel **8**

Best Western
  Hotel Mayfair **15**

Clarion Neptun Hotel **2**

Copenhagen Star **14**

Copenhagen Strand **6**

Hotel Ansgar **18**

Hotel d'Angleterre **3**

Hotel Jørgensen **9**

Hotel Maritime **5**

Hotel Valberg **19**

Hotel Vestersøhus **12**

Ibsens Hotel **11**

Kong Arthur **10**

Palace Hotel **7**

Phoenix Copenhagen **1**

Saga Hotel **17**

71 Nyhavn **4**

Sofitel Copenhagen **13**

Sophie Amalie Hotel **2**

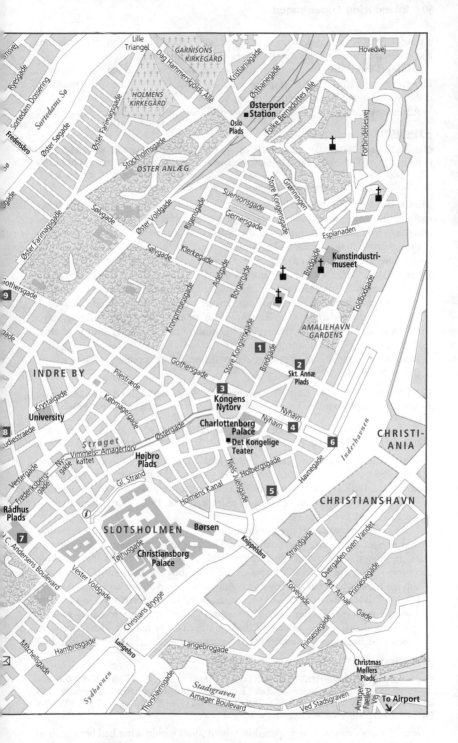

are sufficiently large and contain hair dryers, and robes. The best accommodations also have faxes, trouser presses, and phones in the bathrooms.

Dining/Diversions: On the premises is a Danish-French restaurant, the Von Plessen, as well as an English-inspired pub, Murdoch's. Menus are often based on dishes served in old Danish manor houses.

Amenities: Concierge, 24-hour room service, massage, laundry, nearby salon.

EXPENSIVE

Clarion Neptun Hotel. Skt. Annæ Plads 18–20, DK-1250 København. ☎ **800/654-6200** in the U.S., or 33-96-20-00. Fax 33-96-20-66. www.choicehotels.dk. 133 units. MINIBAR TV TEL. 1,600–1,900 DKK ($200–$237.50) double; 2,200 DKK ($275) suite. Rates include buffet breakfast. AE, DC, MC, V. Free parking. Bus: 1, 6, 9, or 19.

Modernized in 1990, the interior of this 1854 hotel resembles an upper-crust living room, with English-style furniture and even a chess table. Some rooms overlook two quiet, covered interior courtyards. On the hotel's outdoor terrace on the 6th floor, you can order drinks in the summer. The rooms are tastefully furnished in modern style and have trouser presses, hair dryers, and safes. Closets are small, and the tiled bathrooms are only modest in size. Only some units are air-conditioned. Ask for a room that opens onto the courtyard—they are the brightest during the day and the most tranquil in the evening. Suites, most often booked by businesspeople, have dataports and faxes.

Dining: The Gendarmen Café/Restaurant, in an adjoining 1840s building, has a cozy, rustic atmosphere and serves regional Danish fare. A leading Danish food critic recently awarded the restaurant five out of five stars.

Amenities: Room service (24 hours), baby-sitting, business center, access to nearby health club, dry cleaning, and laundry.

✪ **71 Nyhavn.** Nyhavn 71, DK-1051 København. ☎ **33-43-62-00.** Fax 33-43-62-01. www. 71nyhavnhotelcopenhagen.dk. E-mail: 71nyhavnhotel@apr.hansen.dk. 126 units. MINIBAR TV TEL. Mon–Thurs 1,450–1,750 DKK ($181.25–$218.75) double; 2,450–2,900 DKK ($306.25–$362.50) suite. Fri–Sun 1,065–1,525 DKK ($133.15–$190.65) double; 2,125–2,550 DKK ($265.65–$318.75) suite. Rates include breakfast. AE, DC, MC, V. Free parking. Bus: 550-S.

On the corner between Copenhagen harbor and Nyhavn Canal, this red-brick hotel is a restored warehouse that dates from 1804—one of the few buildings in the area spared by an 1807 British bombardment. The warehouse was converted into a hotel in 1971, and thoroughly renovated and redecorated in 1997, but leaving the fine Pomeranian pine beams intact.

Most rooms have a view of the harbor and canal. Nice touches in the rooms include trouser presses and double-glazed windows. The best units also have ironing boards, faxes, and robes, and computer plugs are available at the reception desk. Nonsmoking accommodations are available. Mattresses are firm, but the beds are narrow. Bathrooms are rather small, but are tiled and contain hair dryers; most have a stall shower.

Dining/Diversions: In the cellar, the Restaurant Pakhuskælderen offers rustic charm and good French and Danish food. The menus change constantly to reflect seasonal supplies, and the wine list is among the finest in the city. The hotel also has a small bar.

Amenities: Room service, money exchange, concierge, dry cleaning, and laundry.

MODERATE

Copenhagen Strand. Havnegade 37, DK-1058 København K. ☎ **33-48-99-00.** Fax 33-48-90-91. www.copenhagenstrand.dk. E-mail: copenhagenstrand@arp/hansen.dk. 174 units. MINIBAR TV TEL. 1,195–1,595 DKK ($149.40–$199.40) double; 1,795–2,395 DKK ($224.40–$299.40) suite. AE, DC, MC, V. Tram: 1 or 6.

One of the city's newest hotels opened in July of 2000 within what had been built in the 1800s as a pair of brick-and-timber factories. The savvy architects retained as many of the old-fashioned details as they could, adding a nautical gloss to the lobby—lots of varnished wood, brass hardware, and paintings of sailing ships and the nearby piers that used to service them. There's a bar within the lobby, and a reception staff that works double time mixing drinks and pulling pints. The medium-sized bedrooms are less richly decorated than the lobby, but filled with comfortable, contemporary furnishings. The hotel is rated three stars by the Danish government, but frankly, all that it lacks for elevation into a four-star status is a full-fledged restaurant. In light of the many eateries within the surrounding Nyhavn district, that is hardly a disadvantage. On the premises is a small-scale "business center" where residents can have access to e-mail, a word processor, and a photocopy machine.

Sophie Amalie Hotel. Skt. Annæ Plads 21, DK-1250 København. ☎ **33-13-34-00.** Fax 33-11-77-07. www.remmen.dk. E-mail: anglehot@remmen.dk. 134 units. A/C MINIBAR TV TEL. 1,160–1,230 DKK ($145–$153.75) double; 1,475–2,075 DKK ($184.40–$259.40) suite. Winter discounts available. AE, CB, DC, MC, V. Free parking. Bus: 1, 10, or 28.

The Sophie Amalie is a first-class hotel on the harbor-front, close to Amalienborg Castle. From the rooms facing north, you can see the castle, where Queen Margrethe II lives. Within walking distance of Nyhavn, it's convenient for exploring the business and shopping districts. Dating from 1948, the hotel has been vastly improved and upgraded over the years. Its guest rooms are furnished with the best of Scandinavian modern design. Double-glazing on the windows cuts down on street noise. The beds are rather narrow, but with firm, comfortable mattresses. Closets are large, but bathrooms are small, with mosaic tiles and hair dryers. In the sixth-floor suites, curved staircases connect the two levels. The hotel is named for Sophie Amalie (1628–85), a German duke's daughter who married King Frederik III at the age of 15. The Restaurant Sophie serves Danish cuisine, and the chef is quite good. We've enjoyed the mussels steamed in sorrel and garlic and ravioli stuffed with truffles; the chef also specializes in young rooster with basil and tomato. For dessert, when was the last time you had a rhubarb soup with a parfait of licorice and caramel? Sophie's Bar is a snug little retreat. Amenities include sauna, solarium, laundry service, and baby-sitting.

INEXPENSIVE
Hotel Maritime. Peder Skrams Gade 19, DK-1054 København. ☎ **33-13-48-82.** Fax 33-15-03-45. www.hotel-maritime.dk. E-mail: hotel@maritime.dk. 64 units. TV TEL. 825–1,600 DKK ($103.15–$200) double; 1,600 DKK ($200) triple. AE, CB, DC, DISC, MC, V. Bus: 1, 6, or 9.

Although the guest rooms here are comfortable and tastefully conservative in style, you might be put off by the pretentious and somewhat rigid staff. Ignore them, and relish in your hotel's enviable location near hotels that cost a lot more. The neighborhood lies between high glamour (Kongens Nytorv, site of the Hotel d'Angleterre) and the Nyhavn Canal, a reminder of seafaring Copenhagen. Built more than a century ago, it was converted into a hotel in 1953, and the guest rooms were completely renovated in 1996. The top floor contains a conference center, and the street level has a restaurant.

NEAR RÅDHUSPLADSEN (TOWN HALL)
VERY EXPENSIVE
Palace Hotel. Rådhuspladsen 57, DK-1550 København. ☎ **800/448-8355** or 33-14-40-50. Fax 33-12-75-86. www.palace-hotel.dk. E-mail: reception.palacecopenhagen@principal.co.dk. 162 units, some with shower only. MINIBAR TV TEL. 1,725–2,495 DKK ($215.65–$311.90) double; from 2,500 DKK ($312.50) suite. Rates include buffet breakfast. 25% discount may be available on weekends and in midwinter, depending on occupancy. AE, DC, MC, V. Parking 150 DKK ($18.75). Bus: 2, 30, 32, 33, 34, or 35.

Opened in 1910 and declared a historic landmark in 1985, the Palace Hotel has been a respite for countless camera-shy celebrities. Although the hotel has tried to keep

ⓕ Family-Friendly Hotels

Hotel d'Angleterre *(see p. 47)* This elegant hotel has a swimming pool and in-house video; both help keep children entertained.

Kong Arthur *(see p. 53)* This is a haven near tree-lined Peblinge Lake in a residential section.

abreast of the times, it's no longer the front-runner it once was (that distinction now belongs to some other recommended hotels, including the Kong Frederik). The modern rooms are attractively furnished in an English country style—conservative furniture, floral chintz curtains. Most bathrooms are cramped, but they do have hair dryers. The best rooms are on the top floor, away from street noises. If you're assigned a room on floors 2 and 3, you are still in luck—they have high ceilings and tasteful furnishings and appointments. The reception desk staff is especially helpful in arranging for theater tickets, tours, and transportation. There's also a roof terrace.

Dining/Diversions: Brasserie on the Square, serves Danish and international food. The Palace Bar on the ground floor has a Hollywood atmosphere.

Amenities: Valet; laundry; in-room safe-deposit box; parking garage; executive meeting rooms; health club with sauna, solarium, and massage.

EXPENSIVE

Sofitel Copenhagen. Bernstorffsgade 4, DK-1577 København. ☎ **800/223-5652** or 33-14-92-62. Fax 33-93-93-62. www.accorhotel.dk. E-mail: booking@accorhotel.dk. 93 units. MINIBAR TV TEL. 1,695–2,095 DKK ($211.90–$261.90) double; 3,095–6,495 DKK ($386.90–$811.90) suite. AE, DC, MC, V. Parking 120 DKK ($15). Bus: 1 or 6.

Rich with turn-of-the-century atmosphere, this successful overhaul of an older hotel combines first-class comfort and antique furnishings. Opposite the Tivoli Gardens, the hotel was commissioned by King Frederik VIII in 1913, and has entertained its share of celebrities and royalty. Guest rooms of varying dimension resemble what you might find in an English country house—but with all the modern amenities. Antiques, double-glazed windows, and views from many units make this a good choice; rooms on the top floor have dormered windows. Bathrooms are generous in size, completely tiled, and contain hair dryers and make-up mirrors. There are some smoke-free accommodations.

Dining/Diversions: The Library Bar is one of Copenhagen's most charming oases. Off the lobby, the Flora Danica serves a sumptuous Scandinavian breakfast buffet, and a good lunch that features such dishes as roast beef sandwiches, cognac-flavored blini, and American rib-eye steak with stuffed potato.

Amenities: Room service (7am to 11pm), dry cleaning, laundry, secretarial services, health club nearby.

MODERATE

Ascot Hotel. Studiestræde 61, DK-1554 København. ☎ **33-12-60-00.** Fax 33-14-60-40. www.ascothotel.dk. E-mail: hotel@ascot-hotel.dk. 143 units. TV TEL. 1,190–1,390 DKK ($148.75–$173.75) double; 1,650–2,490 DKK ($206.25–$311.25) suite. Rates include buffet breakfast. Winter discounts available. AE, DC, MC, V. Free parking. Bus: 14 or 16.

This is one of the best small hotels in Copenhagen. On a side street about a 2-minute walk from Town Hall Square, it was built in 1902 (on 492 wooden pilings rescued from a medieval fortification that had previously stood on the site). In 1994 the hotel annexed an adjacent building designed in the 19th century as a boathouse; its black-marble columns and interior bas-reliefs are historically important. The guest rooms have been renovated and modernized, and the atmosphere is inviting. The furniture is rather standard, and the finest units open onto the street. Nevertheless, the rooms in the rear get better air circulation and more light. The tiled bathrooms are generous in size. Same-day laundry and dry cleaning are available. There's also a bar, a fitness center, and a solarium, but no restaurant.

○ **Hotel Kong Arthur.** Nørre Søgade 11, DK-1370 København. ☎ **33-11-12-12.** Fax 33-32-61-30. www.kongarthur.dk. E-mail: hotel@kongarthur.dk. 107 units. MINIBAR TV TEL. 1,280–1,480 DKK ($160–$185) double; from 2,900 DKK ($362.50) suite. Rates include buffet breakfast. AE, DC, MC, V. Free parking. Bus: 5, 7, or 16.

Built as an orphanage in 1882, this hotel sits behind a private courtyard next to tree-lined Peblinge Lake in a residential part of town. It's a terrific value. It has been completely renovated into a contemporary hostelry; a more recent expansion offers more spacious rooms, including 20 nonsmoking units. Each of the comfortably furnished and carpeted guest rooms has in-house video and a safe. The spacious bathrooms are tiled and contain hair dryers. The hotel is equipped with a sauna and provides 24-hour room service and baby-sitting. Breakfast is served in a large greenhouse-like room that's filled with light on sunny days. The hotel's Restaurant Brøchner is recommended for its reasonably priced Danish and French cuisine. A Japanese restaurant, Sticks 'n' Sushi, offers sushi and yakitori. The bar is pleasant, open 24 hours, and contained within a corner of the lobby.

INEXPENSIVE

Hotel Valberg. Sønder Blvd. 53, DK-1720 København. ☎ **33-25-25-19.** Fax 33-25-25-83. www.valberg.dk. E-mail: hotel@valberg.dk. 20 units, none with bathroom. TV TEL. 600 DKK ($75) double. Rates include breakfast. AE, CB, DC, DISC, MC, V. Bus: 10.

Simple but well kept, this five-story hotel, formerly known as the Boulevard Hotel, is about a 10-minute walk from the Central Railroad Station. Renovated in the late 1980s, it's unpretentious and unassuming, with bright, acceptably decorated guest rooms. Each has a sink with hot and cold running water but the toilets and showers are in rooms off the central corridors. Breakfast is the only meal served.

Hotel Vestersøhus. Vester Søgade 59, DK-1601 København. ☎ **33-11-38-70.** Fax 33-11-00-90. www.vestgersoehus.dk. E-mail: hotel@vestersoehus.dk. 44 units, 40 with bathroom. TV TEL. 780 DKK ($97.50) double without bathroom; 1,140–1,240 DKK ($142.50–$155) double with bathroom; 1,460–1,590 DKK ($182.50–$198.75) double with bathroom and kitchenette. AE, DC, MC, V. Bus: 29.

One of the best features of this simple hotel is the view from about half the guest rooms (top two floors). They overlook a canal-shaped body of water, Skt. Jørgens Lake, which the Danes refer to as "the lakes." (The remainder sit above the quiet, more prosaic back yard.) Set in the heart of town, behind a red-brick facade, the Vestersøhus was originally built around 1900 as an apartment house. Its simple rooms are small and furnished in a way that's not particularly imaginative, but is comfortable. If you want to do your own cooking, know in advance that the 12 rooms with kitchenettes are usually booked far in advance with business travelers setting up medium-term lodgings. Only breakfast is served, but it's included in the room price.

INDRE BY

Copenhagen's main hotel drag, Helgolandsgade, is near the Central Railroad Station. The many moderately priced hostelries in this area can be booked through a **central reservations office** at Helgolandsgade 4 (☎ **31-31-43-44**), adjacent to the Triton Hotel. The service is operated by the well-recommended Absalon Hotel, and most people who use the service are referred there. If it's full, lodgings are found at other acceptable hotels in the neighborhood. Colbjørnsensgade, which runs parallel to Helgolandsgade, is the second major accommodations street. From either street, you're within easy walking distance of Rådhuspladsen and the Tivoli Gardens.

In the 1970s this area became one of Europe's major pornography districts, but hotel renovations, much-publicized civic efforts, and the gradual decline of the porno shops led to gentrification, which continues today. With original 19th-century facades generally still intact and often gracefully restored, the district is safer than you might think and offers some of the best hotel values in Copenhagen.

MODERATE

Best Western Hotel Mayfair. Helgolandsgade 3, DK-1653 København V. ☎ **800/ 528-1234** in the U.S., or 33-31-48-01. Fax 33-23-96-86. www.themayfairhotel.dk. E-mail: info@themayfairhotel.dk. 106 units. MINIBAR TV TEL. 1,150–1,195 DKK ($143.75–$149.40) double; 1,800–1,900 DKK ($225–$237.50) suite. Rates include breakfast. AE, DC, MC, V. Bus: 6, 16, 28, 29, or 41.

This older, much-respected hotel retains some of its original architectural detailing after a radical overhaul that brought it up to modern-day standards about a decade ago. Two blocks west of the main railroad station, it boasts conservative decor that might remind you of the furnishings in a well-heeled private home in England. Guest rooms are comfortable, representing better-than-expected value for a hotel that's rated three stars by the Danish government. Guest accommodations have safes, trouser presses, and coffeemakers. The full marble bathrooms are adequate in size, and all contain hair dryers. Some recently upgraded accommodations have sitting areas. The hotel does not have a bar or health club, and serves only breakfast.

Copenhagen Star. Colbjørnsengade 13, DK-1652 København. ☎ **33-22-11-00.** Fax 33-21-21-86. www.accorhotel.dk. E-mail: star@accorhotel.dk. 134 units. MINIBAR TV TEL. 1,190 DKK ($148.75) double; 1,395–1,995 DKK ($174.40–$249.40) suite. Rates include breakfast. AE, DC, MC, V. Bus: 6, 16, 28, 29, or 41.

Located a short walk from the railroad station, this hotel was created in 1990 when a simple older lodging was connected to a neighboring building and upgraded. Its neo-classical facade was originally built around 1880. The outside is lit with neon, and the interior is definitely postmodern, with leather chairs, teakwood tables, and granite columns. Guest rooms are traditionally furnished and well maintained, with such extras as hair dryers and trouser presses. The suites have Jacuzzis. There is a bar on the premises, and only breakfast is served.

INEXPENSIVE

Absalon Hotel. Helgolandsgade 15, DK-1653 København. ☎ **33-24-22-11.** Fax 33-24-34-11. www.absalon-hotel.dk. E-mail: info@absalon-hotel.dk. Summer 830 DKK ($103.75) double; 1,030 DKK ($128.75) triple; 1,300–1,500 DKK ($162.50–$187.50) suite. Winter 1,050–1,300 DKK ($131.25–$162.50) double; 1,250 DKK ($156.25) triple; 1,400–1,600 DKK ($175–$200) suite. Rates include all-you-can-eat buffet breakfast. AE, DC, MC, V. Closed Dec 17–Jan 2. Bus: 6, 10, 16, 27, or 28.

This family-run lodging, one of the best-managed hotels in the neighborhood, consists of four townhouses that were joined into one building and became a hotel in 1938. It has a spacious blue-and-white breakfast room, and an attentive staff directed by Eric and Mogens Nedergaard. The guest rooms are simple and modern, but cramped. Those with private bathrooms also have TVs, trouser presses, and hair dryers. There are laundry facilities.

The Absalon traces its origins to a love story that unfolded at the nearby railroad station. Shortly after the yet-to-be father of the present owners began his first job as a porter at a neighboring hotel, he was asked to go to the station to pick up a new baby-sitter who had just arrived from Jutland. They fell in love, married, and bought the first of the buildings that became the hotel. Two of their children were born in Room 108, including one of the brothers you'll probably meet behind the reception desk.

A short walk from the Absalon, and under the same management, is the roughly equivalent **Selandia Hotel,** Helgolandsgade 12 (☎ 33-31-46-10), where the 80 rooms go for the same prices as in the Absalon. If one of these two hotels is full, management will direct you toward the other.

Hotel Ansgar. Colbjørnsensgade 29, DK-1652 København. ☎ **33-21-21-96.** Fax 33-21-61-91. www.ansgar-hotel.dk. E-mail: ansgar@ansgar-hotel.dk. 81 units. TEL. 1,050 DKK ($131.25) double. Extra bed 200 DKK ($25). Rates include buffet breakfast. AE, DC, MC, V. Bus: 6, 10, 28, or 41.

Although this five-story hotel was built in 1885, its comfortable, cozy rooms have modern Danish furniture. A dozen large rooms that can accommodate up to six are perfect for families, and are available at negotiable rates. There is often free parking outside the hotel after 6pm. Guests arriving at Kastrup Airport can take the SAS bus to the Air Terminal at the Central Railroad Station, walk through the station, and be inside the hotel in less than 4 minutes.

Saga Hotel. Colbjørnsensgade 18–20, DK-1652 København. ☎ **33-24-49-44.** Fax 33-24-60-33. www.sagahotel.dk. E-mail: booking@sagahotel.dk. 79 units, 24 with bathroom. TV TEL. 380–580 DKK ($47.50–$72.50) double without bathroom; 500–870 DKK ($62.50–$108.75) double with bathroom. Extra bed 150–200 DKK ($18.75–$25). Modest winter discounts. Rates include breakfast. AE, CB, DC, MC, V. Bus: 6, 10, 16, 28, or 41.

This is a reasonably priced, acceptable choice on this sometimes-troublesome street. About half of its accommodations tend to be booked by groups of foreign visitors in the summer, and by Danish student and convention groups in the winter. The hotel was created in 1947 from two late 19th-century apartment buildings. The guest rooms, renovated in 1989, are unusual—each has its own layout. The five-story building has no elevator, so hauling luggage upstairs might present a problem. The reception and breakfast areas are one floor above street level. Breakfast is the only meal served.

NEAR NØRREPORT STATION
MODERATE

Ibsens Hotel. Vendersgade 23, DK-1363 København. ☎ **33-13-19-13.** Fax 33-13-19-16. www.ibsenshotel.dk. E-mail: hotel@ibsenshotel.dk. 103 units. TV TEL. 1,050–1,250 DKK ($131.25–$156.25) double. Rates include buffet breakfast. AE, MC, V. Bus: 5, 14, or 16.

A favorite with budget-conscious travelers and families, Ibsens Hotel, built in 1906 and completely renovated in 1998, offers comfortable, well-maintained guest rooms. Most of the traditionally furnished rooms are doubles or triples. They now have private bathrooms, which are cramped. Breakfast is the only meal served, but there are many restaurants and cafes nearby.

INEXPENSIVE

Hotel Jørgensen. Rømersgade 11, DK-1362 København. ☎ **33-13-81-86.** Fax 33-15-51-05. www.hoteljorgensen.dk. E-mail: hotel@post12tele.dk. 24 units; 13 dormitory rms (72 beds). TV TEL. 650 DKK ($81.25) double; 115 DKK ($14.40) per person in dormitory. Rates include breakfast. MC, V. Free parking. Bus: 14 or 16.

This white stucco 1906 building, a former textbook publishing house, became Denmark's first gay hotel in 1984. On a busy boulevard in central Copenhagen, it obviously appeals to gay men and lesbians, but also welcomes straight guests. The staff is most helpful. Prices are reasonable, and the rooms are conventional and well organized. The 13 dormitory rooms, which accommodate 6 to 14 people each, are segregated by gender.

4 Dining

Copenhagen has more than 2,000 cafes, snack bars, and restaurants. Most of the restaurants are in the Tivoli, where you'll pay extra for the privilege of dining there, around Rådhuspladsen (Town Hall Square) or the Central Railroad Station, or in Nyhavn. Others are in the shopping district, on streets that branch off from Strøget.

Reservations are not usually required (except in the most exclusive restaurants), but it's a good bet to phone ahead where reservations are recommended in the following guide. (Nearly everyone who answers the phone at restaurants speaks English.)

TIVOLI GARDENS

Prices at the restaurants in the Tivoli are about 30% higher than elsewhere. To compensate, skip dessert and buy something less expensive (perhaps ice cream or pastry) later at one of the many stands in the park. Take bus no. 1, 6, 8, 16, 29, 30, 32, or 33 to reach the park and any of the following restaurants.

Note: These restaurants are open only from May to mid-September.

VERY EXPENSIVE

✪ **Divan II.** Vesterbrogade 3, Tivoli. ☎ **33-12-51-51.** Reservations recommended. Main courses 290–345 DKK ($36.25–$43.15); fixed-price lunch 345 DKK ($43.15). AE, DC, MC, V. Daily 11am–midnight. DANISH/FRENCH.

In a garden setting, this is the finest restaurant in the Tivoli, and certainly the most expensive. It was established in 1843, the same year as the gardens, and despite its name, it's older than its nearby competitor, the less formal Divan I. The service is impeccable, and the cuisine is among the most sophisticated in Copenhagen. The chefs create excellent meals using the best ingredients, but without audacious inventions. The carpaccio of Norwegian wild salmon marinated with lemongrass and virgin olive oil is a success, as is the terrine of goose foie gras baked with fresh truffles. Everything is elegant and well prepared, whether it be the redfish braised with saffron and garlic (served with sautéed fennel) or médaillons of free-range poultry from Bresse, France, stuffed with squash and served with goose foie gras. Many ingredients are home grown, and those dishes are the most likely to achieve taste perfection—try the rack and leg of Danish spring lamb (in truffle cream sauce) or lightly salted breast of Danish free-range duck with an unusual horseradish beurre blanc sauce. You may think you'll never be hungry again, but then the waiter mentions strawberries Romanoff (marinated in Smirnoff vodka, Grand Marnier, and orange juice), or chocolate mousse, walnut nougat, and a crêpe filled with custard cream and fresh berries—and a spicy cake with raspberry sorbet, all on the same platter. No wonder it's called the chef's "grand dessert."

EXPENSIVE

La Crevette. Vesterbrogade 3, Tivoli. ☎ **33-14-68-47.** Reservations recommended. Main courses 195–298 DKK ($24.40–$37.25); 3-course fixed-price lunch 295 DKK ($36.90); 4-course fixed-price dinner 395 DKK ($49.40). AE, DC, MC, V. Daily noon–11pm. SEAFOOD.

This restaurant offers more varied seafood dishes than any of its Tivoli competitors. Housed in a 1909 pavilion, it has an outdoor terrace, a tastefully modern dining room, and a well-trained staff. The seafood is fresh, flavorful, and prepared in innovative ways—for example, pickled slices of salmon with oyster flan and egg cream with chives, or bisque of turbot with veal bacon and quail's eggs. The imaginative main dishes might include grilled sea bass and scampi on crispy spinach and sautéed eggplant, or fried fillet of red mullet with chive sauce and a delightful "pyramid" of shellfish. Meat and poultry courses are scarce, but you don't come here for that. Finish with a selection of cheeses from France, Denmark, and Italy (served with marinated prunes, a nice touch), or the freshly made pastries of the day. The restaurant has its own confectionery.

Divan I. Vesterbrogade 3, Tivoli. ☎ **33-11-42-42.** Reservations required. Main courses 125–350 DKK ($15.65–$43.75); fixed-price lunch 185 DKK ($23.15); fixed-price dinner 325 DKK ($40.65). AE, DC, MC, V. Mon–Sat noon–11pm, Sun noon–10pm. FRENCH.

Opened the same year as the Tivoli, this popular gardenlike restaurant has been pleasing discriminating diners since 1913. It offers refined French cuisine and service, and a good view of the gardens. The chef prepares one of the largest selections of hot and cold appetizers at the Tivoli. Try freshly shelled fjord shrimp, smoked salmon, or a crêpe stuffed with sweetbreads and sun-dried tomatoes. A symphony of fish is a platter of three fish selections with three sauces. Poultry and meat dishes are likely to include a saddle of Danish lamb with roasted mushrooms and sauce *Périgeux* (Madeira sauce with truffles), or breast of cock from Bornholm roasted with mustard seeds and served with savoy cabbage.

Louise Nimb. Bernstorffsgade 5, Tivoli. ☎ **33-14-60-03.** Reservations required. Main courses 198–295 DKK ($24.75–$36.90); fixed-price lunch 295 DKK ($36.90); fixed-price dinner 335 DKK ($41.90). AE, DC, MC, V. Daily noon–4pm and 5–11pm. DANISH/FRENCH.

Next door to its companion restaurant, La Crevette, this is the most formal restaurant in the Tivoli. It's styled like a Moorish pavilion, decorated with antique accessories. Louise Nimb was a chef who prepared soup in what was then a smaller kitchen. Those modest days are long forgotten, and the present menu is one of the most elaborate in the city; the chef uses only the freshest produce. Your first course might be smoked Baltic salmon, freshly peeled fjord shrimp, or oysters gratinée in lemon sabayon. The chef is rightfully proud of his shellfish medley, which includes Norwegian lobster, mussels, oysters, crab claws, and North Sea shrimp. Other fish choices include grilled red mullet with chive sauce. Meat eaters might prefer tournedos of beef with marrow and red wine sauce. Live piano music is featured at dinner.

Restaurant P.H. Vesterbrogade 3, Tivoli. ☎ **33-75-07-75.** Reservations recommended. Main courses 165–275 DKK ($20.65–$34.40); fixed-price lunch 165 DKK ($20.65); fixed-price dinner 195–425 DKK ($24.40–$53.15). AE, DC, MC, V. Daily noon–10:30pm (last order). DANISH/FRENCH.

One of the most upscale and elegant restaurants in the Tivoli bears the initials of Paul Hemmingsen (1894–1967), an architect, interior designer, and writer whose works are known by virtually every Dane. It's a newcomer to the Tivoli restaurant scene, where owners and venues change very rarely. The restaurant has gained fame since it was established in the late 1990s, thanks to intelligent cuisine and a freshness that older, more jaded restaurants might have lost. The menu draws on French and Danish traditions, with touches of Asian spice to heat things up just a bit, but no traditional Danish heaviness.

For starters, try three varieties of homemade pickled herring with onions and capers, smoked Baltic salmon with asparagus, or even scrambled eggs with Italian summer truffles on the side. North Sea turbot is served with white asparagus, spring cabbage, and tomato fondant. If you want something deeply rooted in the old kitchens of Denmark, try veal cutlet with panade of ham and shallots, served with potato baked in calf's tail confit and creamy morel sauce. The restaurant is in a modern-looking building that Hemmingsen designed, with lamps that a connoisseur might instantly recognize as the designer's.

Copenhagen Dining

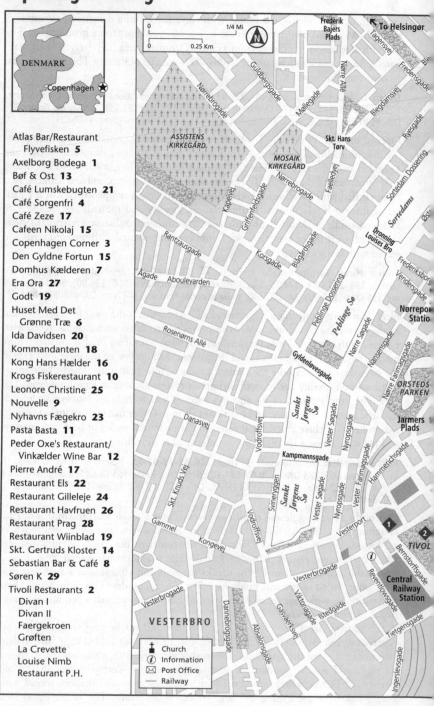

Atlas Bar/Restaurant
Flyvefisken **5**
Axelborg Bodega **1**
Bøf & Ost **13**
Café Lumskebugten **21**
Café Sorgenfri **4**
Café Zeze **17**
Cafeen Nikolaj **15**
Copenhagen Corner **3**
Den Gyldne Fortun **15**
Domhus Kælderen **7**
Era Ora **27**
Godt **19**
Huset Med Det
Grønne Træ **6**
Ida Davidsen **20**
Kommandanten **18**
Kong Hans Hælder **16**
Krogs Fiskerestaurant **10**
Leonore Christine **25**
Nouvelle **9**
Nyhavns Fægekro **23**
Pasta Basta **11**
Peder Oxe's Restaurant/
Vinkælder Wine Bar **12**
Pierre André **17**
Restaurant Els **22**
Restaurant Gilleleje **24**
Restaurant Havfruen **26**
Restaurant Prag **28**
Restaurant Wiinblad **19**
Skt. Gertruds Kloster **14**
Sebastian Bar & Café **8**
Søren K **29**
Tivoli Restaurants **2**
  Divan I
  Divan II
  Faergekroen
  Grøften
  La Crevette
  Louise Nimb
  Restaurant P.H.

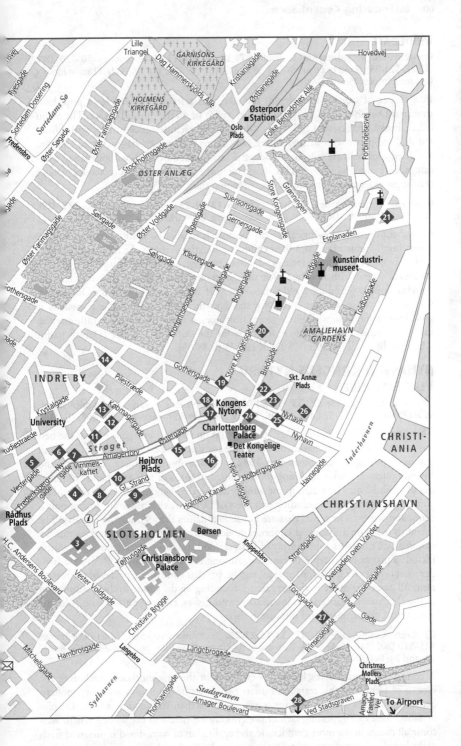

Lille
Triangel

GARNISONS
KIRKEGÅRD

Dag Hammerskjolds Alle

Hovedvej

HOLMENS
KIRKEGÅRD

Kristianiagade

Østbanegade

Østerport
■ Station

Oslo
Plads

Folke Bernadottes Alle

Forbindelsesvej

ØSTER ANLÆG

Stockholmsgade

Øster Farimagsgade

Øster Søgade

Øster Søgade

Sortedam Dossering

Ryesgade

Sortedams Sø

Fredensbro

Grønningen

Store Kongensgade

Suensonsgade

Rigensgade

Gernersgade

Klerkegade

Øster Voldgade

Sølvgade

Sølvgade

Øster Farimagsgade

Gothersgade

Adelgade

Borgergade

Kronprinsessegade

†
■

Esplanaden

21 †

Kunstindustri-
museet

Bredgade

†
■

†
■

20

AMALIEHAVN
GARDENS

Toldbodgade

14

INDRE BY

Pilestræde

Gothersgade

Store Kongensgade

Bredgade

Skt. Annæ
Plads

19

22

23

Krystalgade

Købmagergade

13

University

12

11

Studiestræde

Strøget

Østergade

18 Kongens
17 Nytorv

24

25

26

Nyhavn

Nyhavn

Inderhavnen

CHRISTI-
ANIA

5

6

7

Amagertorv

Nygade Vimmels-
kaftet

15

Charlottenborg
Palace

■ Det Kongelige
Teater

Vestergade

Frederiksberggade

10

Højbro
Plads

16

Niels Juelsgade

Havnegade

CHRISTIANSHAVN

4

8

9

Gl. Strand

Holmens Kanal

Holbergsgade

Strandgade

Rådhus
Plads

ⓘ

SLOTSHOLMEN

Børsen

Knippelsbro

Overgaden oven Vandet

Prinsessegade

3

H.C. Andersens Boulevard

Vester Voldgade

Christiansborg
Palace

Tøjhusgade

Tøjhusgade

Skt. Annæ
Gade

Christians Brygge

27

Mitchellsgade

Hambrosgade

Langebro

Langebrogade

Langebrogade

Prinsessegade

Tovegade

Christmas
Møllers
Plads

✉

Sydhavnen

Thorshavnsgade

Stadsgraven

Amager Boulevard

28

Ved Stadsgraven

Amager
Fælled
Vej

To Airport

MODERATE

Færgekroen. Vesterbrogade 3, Tivoli. ☎ **33-12-94-012.** Main courses 70–170 DKK ($8.75–$21.25); fixed-price lunch 105 DKK ($13.15). AE, DC, MC, V. Daily 11am–midnight (hot food until 9:45pm). DANISH.

In a cluster of trees at the edge of the lake, this restaurant resembles a pink half-timbered Danish cottage. In warm weather, try to sit on the outside terrace. The menu offers drinks, snacks, and full meals. Meals might include omelets, beef with horse-radish, fried plaice with melted butter, pork chops with red cabbage, curried chicken, and fried meatballs. If you like honest and straightforward fare, without fancy trim-mings, and don't like to spend a lot of money, this might be the place for you. A pianist provides sing-along music every evening starting at 8pm.

Groften. Vesterbrogade 3, Tivoli. ☎ **33-12-11-25.** Main courses 85–175 DKK ($10.65–$21.90). AE, DC, MC, V. Daily noon–10pm. DANISH.

Partly because of its low prices, partly because it recalls the rustic restaurants many Danes fondly remember from their childhood vacations, this is the most popular spot in the Tivoli. The outdoor terrace and indoor dining room hold about 750 diners. We always start here with freshly peeled shrimp, though smoked salmon with cream of morels is equally tempting. Cold potato soup with bacon and chives is the Danish ver-sion of vichyssoise. Ask the waiter for the day's fish offering. The chef's specialty is grilled beef tenderloin with bitter greens, tomatoes, olive oil, and black truffle essence. Old-time Danes have come here for years for the skipper's *lobscouse* (Danish hash). Glasses of beer sell for 30 to 45 DKK ($3.75 to $5.65).

NYHAVN & KONGENS NYTORV
VERY EXPENSIVE

✪ **Era Ora.** Torvegade 62. ☎ **32-54-06-93.** Reservations required. Fixed-price menus 495–595 DKK ($61.90–$74.40). AE, DC, MC, V. Mon–Sat 6pm–midnight. Bus 2, 8. ITALIAN.

This reminder of the "Golden Age" (Era Oro) is on virtually everyone's list as the best Italian restaurant in Denmark, and one of the consistently best restaurants of any kind within Copenhagen. Established in 1982 by Tuscan-born partners Alessandro and Elvio, it offers an antiqued dining room painted in tones of soft green and gold; par-ties of up to 12 may be seated in the wine cellar. You're likely to find some remarkably chic people dining here, including members of Denmark's royal family, lots of politi-cians, and writers and artists that are household names throughout the country. The cuisine is based on Tuscan and Umbrian models, with sophisticated variations that are inspired by Denmark's superb array of fresh seafood and produce. Traditional favorites include a platter of 10 types of antipasti. Among them is a variation of Valletta (ten-der roast beef with olive oil, parmesan, and herbs) that's one of the prides of the restau-rant. All pastas are made fresh every day. Depending on the season and the inspiration of the chef, main courses include succulent veal dishes, rack of venison with balsamic vinegar and chanterelles, and ultra-fresh fish.

✪ **Godt.** Gothersgade 38. ☎ **33-15-21-22.** Reservations required. Fixed-price menus 385–510 DKK ($48.15–$63.75). Tues–Sat 5:30–10pm. Closed July and Dec 23–Jan 3. Bus 6, 10, and 14. INTERNATIONAL.

A consistent favorite that's known to everyone in the neighborhood, including the Queen of Denmark, this restaurant offers two floors of minimalist and very modern decor (all in tones of gray) that never exceeds more than 20 diners at a time. Despite its fame, there's an appealing lack of pretentiousness here and the willingness to wel-come all clients in the most democratic and egalitarian of ways. Food is prepared fresh daily, based on ingredients that are the best at the market that day. The repertoire of dishes is splendid, the service is minutely choreographed, and the atmosphere so special it is worth reserving for your final night to kiss Copenhagen good-bye until another time. The chefs have prodigious talent and imagination, and the dishes are constantly changing. The sauces are sublime, as are the herbs and seasonings. Examples might include crab and rascasse soup with leeks; fried Norwegian redfish with a purée of celery and watercress sauce; roasted rack of hare with cranberries and roasted chanterelles; and fresh figs marinated with black currant liqueur, wrapped in phyllo pastry and served with a coulis of pears and chocolate mousse.

✪ **Kommandanten.** Ny Adelgade 7. ☎ **33-12-09-90.** Reservations required. Main courses 250–320 DKK ($31.25–$40); fixed-price menu 630 DKK ($78.75). AE, DC, MC, V. Mon–Fri noon–2pm; Mon–Sat 6–10pm. Bus: 1 or 6. INTERNATIONAL.

Built in 1698 as the residence of the city's military commander, Kommandanten is the epitome of Danish chic and charm. The menu offers a mouth-watering array of classic dishes as well as innovative selections. Each dish of flawless seasonal foods reflects a pleasing personal touch. The finest ingredients are used, and the menu changes every 2 weeks. You might be offered the grilled catch of the day, breast of duck with port-wine sauce, braised turbot with olive sauce, or a gratinée of shellfish. The service is the best in Copenhagen. Make sure you see the three Warhols of Margrethe II in the downstairs dining room.

✪ **Kong Hans Kælder.** Vingårdsstræde 6. ☎ **33-11-68-68.** Reservations required. Main courses 285–410 DKK ($35.65–$51.25); fixed-price menus 595–750 DKK ($74.40–$93.75). AE, CB, DC, DISC, MC, V. Mon–Sat 6pm–midnight. Closed July 15–Aug 15, Dec 24–26. Bus: 1, 6, or 9. INTERNATIONAL.

This vaulted Gothic cellar, once owned by King Hans (1455–1513), may be the best restaurant in Denmark. Its most serious competition is the Kommandanten, which many discriminating critics claim is the best. It's one of the few restaurants in Copenhagen where you're likely to see clients as diverse as Roger Moore, Lars Ulrich (drummer from Metallica), Renée Russo, and various heads of state, all enjoying the candlelit ambience and the medieval setting. The chef creates dishes that one critic credited to "Matisse or Picasso" instead. You may experience the artistry à la carte or by selecting a fixed-price menu (one offered at lunch, five at dinner). A typical three-course dinner would include smoked salmon from the restaurant's smokery, breast of duck with *bigarade* (sour orange) sauce, and plum ice cream with Armagnac. The à la carte menu is divided into "country cooking," including such items as *coq au vin* (chicken with wine) from Alsace and daube of beef; and *les spécialités*, featuring tournedos with foie gras sauce or fresh fish from the daily market, perhaps beginning with an essence and ballotine of quails with truffles. Other stellar examples include cutlets of Danish veal with peanut oil, cèpe mushrooms, and truffle flavored butter; North Sea turbot prepared at table, cooked in a salt crust and served in puff pastry in a mousseline of wasabi mustard; lemon sole wrapped in a crust of seasonal mushrooms and Serrano ham; and fresh Canadian lobster removed from its shell and braised with butter, spices, and herbs. Located on "the oldest corner of Copenhagen," the building has been carefully restored and is now a Relais Gourmands. Hans Christian Andersen once lived upstairs.

✪ **Pierre André.** Ny Østergade 21. ☎ **33-16-17-19.** Reservations required. Main courses 225–355 DKK ($28.15–$44.40); fixed-price menus 395–695 DKK ($49.40–$86.90). AE, DC, MC, V. Mon–Sat noon–2:30pm and 6–10pm. Closed 3 weeks July–Aug. Bus 6, 10, or 14. FRENCH/DANISH.

Everything we've sampled here has been a sheer delight—vivid flavors, masterful technique—ranking with the top restaurants of Paris or London. The chefs have considerable talent and create imaginative, elegant dishes packed with robust flavors, but nothing that's overpowering.

Choosing what to eat at this thriving Nyhavn eatery is a delicious dilemma: You might begin with a house specialty of carpaccio of foie gras "Emilia-Romagna," served with shaved Parmesan and truffles, or a salad of curried lobster with broccoli. Entrees include braised fillet of turbot with mushrooms, leeks, and mango sauce, and wild venison with a bitter chocolate sauce, corn, and cranberries. For a sweet ending, consider the special chocolate cake wherein a partially liquefied filling runs onto your plate in a gooey, glorious mess.

EXPENSIVE

Leonore Christine. Nyhavn 9. ☎ **33-13-50-40.** Reservations required. Main courses 205–255 DKK ($25.65–$31.90); 4-course fixed-price menu 435 DKK ($54.40). AE, DC, MC, V. Mon–Fri noon–3pm, Sat–Sun noon–4pm; daily 6–10pm. Bus: 1, 6, 9, or 650. DANISH.

This restaurant, on the sunny (south) side of the canal, is the best in Nyhavn. It's open year-round, but seems at its best in summer, when the terrace is open and you can dine overlooking the canal and the throngs of passersby. The menu changes weekly, and reflects whatever is seasonal at the time of your arrival. Stellar examples include oven-baked halibut with mussels and saffron; grilled butterfish with squash marmalade and tomatoes; North Sea turbot with fjord shrimp and asparagus; grilled salmon with couscous, fried eggplant, and balsamic vinegar; roasted red snapper with bay leaves, balsamic vinegar, and basil; and sliced breast of wild duck with polenta and wild mushrooms. For dessert, expect dishes such as white chocolate cake with mango sherbet. The restaurant is named for the sister-in-law and bitter enemy of Sophie Amalie, the 17th-century queen of Denmark and wife of Frederik III. As the king's sister, Leonore was "the lady of the land"—until Sophie Amalie arrived.

MODERATE

Café Lumskebugten. Esplanaden 21. ☎ **33-15-60-29.** Reservations recommended. Main courses 168–250 DKK ($21–$31.25); 3-course fixed-price lunch 275 DKK ($34.40); 4-course fixed-price dinner 465 DKK ($58.15). AE, DC, MC, V. Mon–Fri 11am–10:30pm, Sat 5–10:30pm. Bus: 1, 6, or 9. DANISH.

This restaurant is a well-managed bastion of Danish charm, with an unpretentious elegance that's admired throughout the capital. It was established in 1854 as a rowdy tavern for sailors. As the tavern's reputation grew, aristocrats, artists, and members of the Danish royal family came to dine and see what the fun was all about. A gentrified version of the original beef hash is still served.

Two glistening-white dining rooms are decorated with antique model ships. (Two smaller rooms are usually reserved for private functions.) The food and service are excellent. Specialties include tartare of salmon with herbs, Danish fish cakes with mustard sauce and minced beetroot, sugar-marinated salmon with mustard-cream sauce, and a symphony of fish with saffron sauce and new potatoes. A filling lunch platter of assorted house specialties is offered for 185 DKK ($23.15).

Restaurant Els. Store Strandstræde 3 (off Kongens Nytorv). ☎ **33-14-13-41.** Reservations recommended. Sandwiches (lunch only) 42–75 DKK ($5.25–$9.40); main courses 185–238 DKK ($23.15–$29.75). AE, DC, MC, V. Mon–Sat noon–3pm; daily 5:30–10pm. Closed July. Bus: 1, 6, or 10. DANISH/FRENCH.

Restaurant Els preserves its original 1854 decor. Several murals are believed to be the work of Christian Hitsch, the 19th-century muralist who adorned parts of the interior of the Danish Royal Theater. Hans Christian Andersen was a regular here.

Each day there's a different fixed-price menu, and a selection of Danish open-faced sandwiches at lunch for those who want a lighter meal. The cuisine at night is French, accompanied by excellent wines. The menu is based on what's fresh at the market.

Menu items are creative and unusual, and change at least every month. Examples include ragout of whitefish with cabbage and wild rice; breast of wild duck with blackberry sauce; tournedos of beef with beans, shallots, and tomatoes. Starters that are likely to be always on the menu, regardless of the season, include a selection of five "Els" appetizers, or a saffron laced version of mussel soup.

Restaurant Gilleleje. Nyhavn 10. ☎ **33-12-58-58.** Reservations recommended. Main courses 168–218 DKK ($21–$27.25). AE, DC, MC, V. Mon–Sat 11am–3pm and 5–11pm. Bus: 8, 9, or 10. DANISH/INTERNATIONAL.

The nautical decor here is appealing, but diners come mainly for the endless procession of dishes deftly prepared by the skilled kitchen staff. You get tasty fare and plenty of it. You might start with the specialty, a velvety-smooth lobster soup that will make you want to order a second helping (but that would fill you up too quickly). Other special dishes include the Danish herring platter, a popular first course. The fish soup is always savory, as is the whisky steak flambé with grilled tomatoes. For dessert (if you have room), try the Danish crêpes with vanilla ice cream.

Restaurant Havfruen. Nyhavn 39. ☎ **33-11-11-38.** Reservations recommended. Lunch main courses 135–175 DKK ($16.90–$21.90) (until 5pm); dinner main courses 140–240 DKK ($17.50–$30). DC, MC, V. Daily 11:30am–11pm. Bus: 1, 6, or 9. SEAFOOD.

Small and usually full, this restaurant is a cozy, nautically outfitted hideaway with a reputation for serving good fish. A carved wooden mermaid hangs from the heavy ceiling beams. The lunch menu emphasizes salmon, different preparations of herring, and such shellfish as clams and oysters. Dinner is fancier, with platters of whatever was fresh in the fish market. Especially flavorful is Greenland turbot in *beurre blanc* (white butter) sauce, which tastes wonderful when served with a fruity white wine from the Loire valley. The staff can get rather hysterical when the place fills up.

Restaurant Wiinblad. In the Hotel d'Angleterre, Kongens Nytorv 14. ☎ **33-12-00-95.** Reservations recommended. Lunch main courses 60–130 DKK ($7.50–$16.25); dinner main courses 169–238 DKK ($21.15–$29.75); fixed-price menus 295–350 DKK ($36.90–$43.75). AE, DC, MC, V. Daily 11:30am–5pm; Sun–Thurs 5–10pm, Fri–Sat 5–11pm. Bus: 1, 6, or 9. DANISH/INTERNATIONAL.

This is the less formal of the two restaurants in the upscale Hotel d'Angleterre, which is known for selecting some of the city's finest chefs. Many diners prefer Restaurant Wiinblad to its more restrictive and expensive sibling, Restaurant d'Angleterre. Bjørn Wiinblad, a beloved illustrator of children's fables, helped design his namesake's decor. Lunch might consist of *smørrebrød* (open-faced sandwiches), salads, and Danish platters that combine three oft-changing ingredients into a satisfying meal. Dinners are more elaborate, and might include grilled salmon with lobster flavored saffron sauce; shrimp served with Thai-style lemongrass; and tenderloin of Charolais beef with lobster tail and drawn butter.

INEXPENSIVE

Café Zeze. 20 Ny Ostergade 20. ☎ **33-14-23-90.** Reservations recommended. Fixed-price lunch 55 DKK ($6.90); lunch main courses 40–70 DKK ($5–$8.75); fixed-price dinner 89 DKK ($11.15); dinner main courses 90–130 DKK ($11.25–$16.25). AE, DC, MC, V. Mon–Sat 11:30am–4:30pm and 5:30–10pm (last order). Bar and café Mon–Thurs 8am–midnight, Fri 8am–2am, Sat 9am–2am. Bus: 1, 6, 9, or 10. CONTINENTAL.

This is a hip bistro and cafe with a reputation for good food and brisk service. Late night tends to be more about drinking than eating (which accounts for the increased noise level) but overall the place can be a lot of fun. You'll find a cheerful setup with a high ceiling, mirrors, and a sunny yellow interior. Menu items change frequently, but expect a well-prepared medley of dishes that includes sautéed breast of turkey with coconut and chili sauce; roasted guinea fowl with shrimp and braised arugula; and fillets of lamb with shiitake mushrooms.

✪ Ida Davidsen. Store Kongensgade 70. ☎ **33-91-36-55.** Reservations recommended. Sandwiches 35–250 DKK ($4.40–$31.25). DC, MC, V. Mon–Fri 9am–4pm. Bus: 1, 6, or 9. SANDWICHES.

This restaurant has flourished since 1888, when the forebears of its present owner, Ida Davidsen, established a sandwich shop. Today, five generations later, the matriarch and namesake is known as the "smørrebrød queen of Copenhagen." Her restaurant sells a greater variety of open-faced sandwiches (250 kinds) than any other in Denmark. The fare has even been featured at royal buffets at Amalienborg Castle. You select by pointing to your choice in a glass-front display case; a staff member carries it to your table. The vast selection includes salmon, lobster, smoked duck with braised cabbage and horseradish, liver pâté, ham, and boiled egg. Two of them, perhaps with a slice of cheese, make a worthy lunch. If in doubt, a member of the service team, or perhaps Ida's charming husband, Adam Siesbye, will offer suggestions.

✪ Nyhavns Færgekro. Nyhavn 5. ☎ **33-15-15-88.** Reservations required. Fixed-price dinner 155 DKK ($19.40); herring buffet 89 DKK ($11.15); smørrebrød 39–100 DKK ($4.90–$12.50). CB, DC, MC, V. Daily 11:30am–4pm and 5–11pm. Closed Jan 1, Dec 24–25. Bus: 1, 6, or 9. DANISH/FRENCH.

The "Nyhavn Ferry Inn" has a long tradition and many loyal fans. The house is old, dating from the final years of the 18th century. The popular summer terrace offers a view of other 18th-century houses and boats in the canal. Inside, the decor is unusual, with a spiral stairway from an antique tram. Lights serve as call buttons to summon the staff when you want service.

The daily homemade buffet consists of 10 types of herring, including fried fresh herring, rollmops, and smoked herring. Some people make a full meal of it. You can also order smørrebrød—everything from smoked eel with scrambled eggs to chicken salad with bacon. A true Dane orders schnapps or aquavit at lunch. (Denmark has a tradition of making spicy aquavit from herbs and plants.) For dinner you can enjoy one of Copenhagen's most succulent entrecôtes.

NEAR RÅDHUSPLADSEN
MODERATE

Atlas Bar/Restaurant Flyvefisken. Lars Bjørnstræde 18. ☎ **33-14-95-15.** Reservations recommended. Lunch main courses 75–140 DKK ($9.40–$17.50); dinner main courses 105–175 DKK ($13.15–$21.90). DC, MC, V. Atlas Bar, Mon–Sat noon–10pm; Restaurant Flyvefisken, Mon–Sat 5–10pm. Bus 5, 6, or 16. DANISH/THAI/INTERNATIONAL.

The food served at these two restaurants derives from the same kitchen, and adheres to the same culinary philosophy. They include lots of vegetarian food inspired by the cuisines of Thailand, Mexico, and India, always with a Danish overview toward tidiness and coziness. On the street level, the cramped and cozy Atlas Bar, whose walls are painted terra-cotta, serves a busy lunchtime crowd, but slackens off a bit at night, when the wood-sheathed *Flyvefisken* (Flying Fish) opens for dinner. Upstairs, expect a greater emphasis on Thai cuisine and its fiery flavors, including lemongrass, curries, and several of the hot and spicy fish soups native to Bangkok. Although the authenticity of the Thai cuisine has lost just a bit of its zest in the long jump from Thailand, it's still a marvelous change of pace from typical Danish fare. Expect lots of business here, especially at lunchtime, when the place is likely to be fully booked.

ⓕ Family-Friendly Restaurants

Copenhagen Corner *(see p. 65)*   A special children's menu features such dishes as shrimp cocktail and grilled rump steak.

Ida Davidsen *(see p. 64)*   When has your kid ever faced a choice of 250 sandwiches? At the "smørrebrød queen's" cozy eatery, that's what you get. Even the queen of Denmark has praised these sandwiches and ordered them from royal buffets at Amalienborg Castle.

Copenhagen Corner. H. C. Andersens Blvd. 1A. ☎ **33-91-45-45.** Reservations recommended. Main courses 78–250 DKK ($9.75–$31.25); 3-course fixed-price menu 295 DKK ($36.90). AE, DC, MC, V. Daily 11:30am–11pm. Bus: 1, 6, or 8. SCANDINAVIAN.

Surrounded by some of the heaviest pedestrian traffic in Copenhagen, this restaurant opens onto Rådhuspladsen, around the corner from the Tivoli Gardens. It offers well-prepared, unpretentious meals. The menu features the Danes' favorite dishes, beginning with three kinds of herring or freshly peeled shrimp with dill and lemon. There's even carpaccio of fillet of deer for the most adventurous. Soups are excellent—try consommé of white asparagus flavored with chicken and fresh herbs. The fish is fresh and beautifully prepared, especially the steamed Norwegian salmon with a "lasagne" of potatoes, and baked halibut with artichokes. Meat and poultry courses, although not always as inspired as the fish, are tasty and tender, especially the veal liver Provençal.

Restaurant Prag. Amagerbrogade 37. ☎ **32-54-44-44.** Reservations recommended. Lunch main courses 45–85 DKK; fixed-price lunches 198–238 DKK ($24.75–$29.75); dinner main courses 188–265 DKK ($23.50–$33.15); fixed-price dinners 248-358 DKK ($31–$44.75). AE, DC, MC, V. Mon–Fri noon–3pm and 5–10pm, Sat 5–10pm. Closed July. Bus: 2 or 9. DANISH.

Established in 1910 as the Café Sonderberg, and named after Prags (Prague) Boulevard, which runs nearby, this restaurant was revitalized under the direction of the Michelsen family, and today does a thriving business from a position near the SAS Radisson Scandinavia Hotel, east of Tivoli. It resembles a warm Danish *kro* (inn), with dark-wood trim, white stucco walls, and impeccable service. As much attention is paid to the way a dish looks as to the way it tastes. Menu items include lobster bisque with cognac; risotto with shellfish; roasted mackerel with tomatoes and garlic; carpaccio of duck; goose-liver with apples and calvados; and any of several fresh fish of the day, sometimes served with seasonal mushrooms.

Sebastian Bar & Café. Hyskenstræde 10. ☎ **33-32-22-79.** Reservations recommended. Lunch platters 35–70 DKK ($4.40–$8.75); dinner main courses 100–185 DKK ($12.50–$23.15). DC, MC, V. Bar and cafe, daily noon–2am; restaurant, daily 5–11pm. Bus: 6 or 29. INTERNATIONAL.

Long recognized for its role as a gay bar and cafe, this institution opened a restaurant on its premises in 2000. Today, it functions as a catch-all rendezvous for many of the Danish capital's gay men and women to meet, cruise, and kibitz. Expect a cafe ambience at lunch, when sandwiches, salads, and light platters are served in an old-fashioned tavern with yellow walls and lots of wood trim. During the dinner hour, when food service expands onto an upper floor, the venue and menu are both a bit more grand. Thanks to a former chef of Maxim's in Paris, the food here can be more eclectic and urbane than you might have imagined, sometimes with an emphasis on dishes from Mexico, Thailand, India, and France. Still, plenty of people just come for the bar. Expect temporary art exhibitions, often semi-erotic photographs that change frequently. On Friday and Saturday nights the bar is especially busy, a meeting place before a night of clubbing.

✪ **Søren K.** On the ground floor of the Royal Library's Black Diamond Wing, 1 Søren Kierkegaards Plads. ☎ **33-47-49-49.** Reservations recommended. Lunch main courses 65–125 DKK ($8.15–$15.65); dinner main courses 195–225 DKK ($24.40–$28.15); 3-course fixed-price dinner 315 DKK ($39.40). DC, MC, V. Mon–Sat 11am–10:30pm. Bus: 1, 2, 5, 6, 8, or 9. INTERNATIONAL.

Named after Denmark's most celebrated philosopher, this is an artfully minimalist dining room that's on the ground floor of the newest addition to the Royal Library. Opened in 1999, it has the kind of monochromatic gray-and-flesh-toned decor you might have expected in Milan, and big window views that stretch out over the sea. Menu items change frequently, but might include carpaccio of veal, foie gras, oyster soup, and main courses such as veal chops served with lobster sauce and a half-lobster, venison roasted with nuts and seasonal berries and a marinade of green tomatoes. The restaurant virtually never cooks with butter, cream, or high-cholesterol cheeses, making a meal here a health-conscious and savory experience. To reach this place, you'll have to enter the main entrance of the library and pass through its lobby.

INEXPENSIVE

Axelborg Bodega. Axeltorv 1. ☎ **33-11-06-38.** Reservations recommended. Main courses 98–125 DKK ($12.25–$15.65). AE, DC, MC, V. Daily 11:30am–8:45am; bar, daily 10am–2am. Bus: 1 or 6. DANISH.

Across from the Benneweis Circus and near Scala and the Tivoli, this 1912 cafe has outdoor tables where you can enjoy a brisk Scandinavian evening. Order the *dagens ret* (daily special). Typical Danish dishes are featured, including *frikadeller* (meatballs) and pork chops. A wide selection of club sandwiches is also available for 48 to 76 DKK ($6 to $9.50) each. Although the atmosphere is somewhat impersonal, this is a local favorite; diners enjoy the recipes from grandma's attic.

Café Sorgenfri. Brolæggerstræde 8. ☎ **33-11-58-80.** Reservations recommended for groups of 4 or more. Smørrebrød 35–60 DKK ($4.40–$7.50). DC, MC, V. Daily 11am–8pm. Bus: 5 or 6. SANDWICHES.

Don't come here expecting grand cuisine, or even a menu with much variety. Café Sorgenfri, in the pedestrian shopping zone in the commercial heart of town, has thrived for 150 years selling beer, schnapps, and a medley of smørrebrød. Two to four sandwiches might form a reasonable lunch, depending on your appetite. Partly because it holds only about 50 seats, it's likely to be crowded around the lunch hour, with somewhat more space at mid-afternoon. Consider having an early dinner here, if it suits you. Everything reeks of old-time Denmark, from the potted shrubs that adorn the facade to the well-oiled paneling.

Domhus Kælderen. Nytorv 5. ☎ **33-14-84-55.** Reservations recommended. Lunch main courses 38–118 DKK ($4.75–$14.75); dinner main courses 98–168 DKK ($12.25–$21); fixed-price menus 148–225 DKK ($18.50–$28.15). AE, DC, MC, V. Daily 11am–4pm and 5–10pm. Bus: 5. DANISH/INTERNATIONAL.

The good food at this bustling, old-fashioned emporium of Danish cuisine draws a mixed crowd from City Hall's courtrooms across the square to visiting foreigners. The half-cellar room holds memorabilia from 50 years as a restaurant (before that, it was a butcher shop). Lunch tends to be more conservative and more Danish than dinner. It might include *frikadeller* (meatballs) and heaping platters of herring, cheeses, smoked meats and fish, and salads. Dinner could be pickled salmon; prime rib of beef with horseradish; and fine cuts of beef, served with béarnaise or pepper sauce. Also look for the catch of the day, prepared just about any way you like. You get no culinary surprises here, but you are rarely disappointed.

Quick Bites

Copenhagen has many hot dog stands, chicken and fish grills, and smørrebrød counters that serve good, fast, inexpensive meals.

Hot dog stands, especially those around Rådhuspladsen, offer *polser* (steamed or grilled hot dogs) with shredded onions on top and *pommes frites* (French fries) on the side.

The *bageri* or *konditori* (bakery), found on almost every block, sells fresh bread, rolls, and Danish pastries.

Viktualiehandler (small food shops), found throughout the city, are the closest thing to a New York deli. You can buy roast beef with free *log* (fried onions). The best buy is smoked fish. Ask for a Bornholmer, a large, boneless sardine from the Danish island of Bornholm, or for *røgost,* a popular and inexpensive smoked cheese. Yogurt fans will be delighted to know that the Danish variety is cheap and tasty. It's available in small containers—just peel off the cover and drink it right out of the cup as the Danes do. *Hytte ret* (cottage cheese) is also good and cheap.

The favorite lunch of Scandinavians, particularly Danes, is smørrebrød. The purest form is made with dark rye bread, called rugbrød. Most taverns and cafes offer smørrebrød, and many places serve it as take-out food.

You can picnic in any of the city parks in the town center. Try Kongsgarten near Kongens Nytorv, the Kastellet area near *The Little Mermaid* statue, Botanisk Have (site of the Botanical Gardens), the lakeside promenades in southeastern Copenhagen, and the old moat at Christianshavn. Remember not to litter.

Huset Med Det Grønne Træ. Gammel Torv 20. ☎ **33-12-87-86.** Reservations recommended. Sandwiches and platters 35–115 DKK ($4.40–$14.40). MC, V. Mon–Sat noon–2:45pm. Closed Sat May–Aug. Bus: 5. DANISH.

The only drawback here is the hours, which are shorter than those of virtually any other restaurant in the neighborhood. Nevertheless, it quickly fills with shoppers and long-time patrons. Specialties include artfully crafted sandwiches in the open-faced Danish style. Among the least pretentious is herring, sliced and arranged on rough-textured bread with butter. Other versions include hot smørrebrød (more like full-fledged platters, really) garnished with chopped beef, horseradish, chopped onions, and pickles. The *pièce de la résistance* is a "sampler platter" composed of the most-loved culinary specialties of Denmark, including herring, chopped beef, liver pâté, potato salad, horseradish, cheese, and a scattering of radishes, scallions, lettuces, and pickles. Beer tastes wonderful with sandwiches like this, but if you really want to pretend you're Danish, opt for one of 12 kinds of *aquavit* (schnapps). They're 28 DKK ($3.50) a glass. The staff will suggest one that you might find appealing.

INDRE BY
VERY EXPENSIVE

✪ **Skt. Gertruds Kloster.** Hauser Plads 32. ☎ **33-14-66-30.** Reservations required. Main courses 258–310 DKK ($32.25–$38.75); fixed-price menus 415–625 DKK ($51.90–$78.15); children's menu 90 DKK ($11.25). AE, DC, MC, V. Daily 4–11pm. Closed Dec 25–Jan 1. Bus: 4E, 7E, 14, or 16. INTERNATIONAL.

Near Nørreport Station and south of Rosenborg Castle, this is the most romantic restaurant in Copenhagen. There's no electricity in the labyrinth of 14th-century underground vaults, and the 1,500 flickering candles, open grill, iron sconces, and rough-hewn furniture create an elegant medieval ambience. The food is equally impressive, each dish balanced to perfection. Try the fresh homemade foie gras with black truffles, lobster served in turbot bouillon, scallops sautéed with herbs in sauterne, venison with green asparagus and truffle sauce, or fish and shellfish terrine studded with chunks of lobster and salmon.

MODERATE

Bøf & Ost. Gråbrødretorv 13. ☎ **33-11-99-11.** Reservations required. Main courses 125–179 DKK ($15.65–$22.40); fixed-price lunch 95 DKK ($11.90); fixed-price dinner 235 DKK ($29.40). DC, MC, V. Mon–Sat 11:30am–10:30pm. Closed Jan 1, Dec 24–25. Bus: 5. DANISH/FRENCH.

"Beef & Cheese" is in a 1728 building, and its cellars come from a medieval monastery. In the summer there's a pleasant outdoor terrace overlooking Greyfriars Square. Specialties include lobster soup, fresh Danish bay shrimp, a cheese plate with six different selections, and some of the best grilled tenderloin in town. One local diner confided: "The food is not worthy of God's own table, but it's so good for me I come here once a week."

Peder Oxe's Restaurant/Vinkælder Wine Bar. Gråbrødretorv 11. ☎ **33-11-00-77.** Reservations recommended. Main courses 79–189 DKK ($9.90–$23.65); fixed-price lunches 89–108 DKK ($11.15–$13.50). DC, MC, V. Daily 11:30am–midnight. Bus: 5. DANISH.

The building dates from the 1700s, but this restaurant and wine bar attract a young crowd. The salad bar is 20 DKK ($2.50) when accompanied by a main course. It's so tempting that many prefer to enjoy it alone for 56 DKK ($7) per person. Dishes include lobster soup, Danish bay shrimp, fresh asparagus, open-faced sandwiches, hamburgers, and fresh fish. The bill of fare, although standard, is well prepared.

INEXPENSIVE

Pasta Basta. Valkendorfsgade 22. ☎ **33-11-21-31.** Reservations recommended. Main courses 69–150 DKK ($8.65–$18.75). No credit cards. Sun–Wed 11:30am–3am, Thurs–Sat 11:30am–5:30am. Bus: 5. ITALIAN.

This restaurant's main attraction is an enormous buffet (sometimes called the "Pasta Basta Table") loaded with cold antipasti and salads. With more than nine selections, it's one of the best deals in town at 69 DKK ($10). The restaurant is divided into half a dozen cozy dining rooms decorated in the style of ancient Pompeii, with faded frescoes patterned after originals from Italy. It's on a historic cobblestoned street off the main shopping street, Strøget.

Menu choices include at least 15 kinds of pasta (all made fresh on the premises), *carpaccio* (raw marinated fillet of beef) with olive oil and basil, a platter with three kinds of Danish caviar (whitefish, speckled trout, and vendace, served with chopped onions, lemon, toast, and butter), mozzarella with a sauce of pine nuts and fresh basil, fresh mussels cooked in dry white wine with pasta and creamy saffron sauce, thinly sliced salmon with a cream-based sauce of salmon roe, and sliced Danish suckling lamb with fried spring onions and tarragon. Dessert offerings include an assortment of Danish, French, and Italian cheeses, crème brûlée, and tartufo.

SLOTSHOLMEN
EXPENSIVE

Krogs Fiskerestaurant. Gammel Strand 38. ☎ **33-15-89-15.** Reservations required. Main courses 258–445 DKK ($32.25–$55.65); 3-course fixed-price menu 445 DKK ($55.65); 5-course fixed-price menu 565 DKK ($70.65). AE, DC, MC, V. Mon–Sat 11:30am–4pm and 5:30–10:30pm. Bus: 1, 2, 10, 16, or 29. SEAFOOD.

A short walk from Christiansborg Castle, the most famous restaurant in the district was built in 1789 as a fish shop. The canalside plaza where fishers once moored their boats is now the site of the restaurant's outdoor dining terrace. The restaurant serves fresh seafood in a single large room decorated in antique style, with old oil paintings. The well-chosen menu includes lobster soup, bouillabaisse, oysters, mussels steamed in white wine, and poached salmon-trout with saffron sauce. Each dish is impeccably prepared and flavorful. A selection of meat dishes is available, but the fish is better.

Nouvelle. Gammel Strand 34. ☎ **33-13-50-18.** Reservations required. Main courses 265–310 DKK ($33.15–$38.75); 3-course fixed-price lunch 465 DKK ($58.15); 4-course fixed-price dinner 595 DKK ($74.40). AE, DC, MC, V. Mon–Fri 11:30am–3pm and 6–10pm, Sat 7:30–9pm. Closed Dec 22–Jan 6. Bus: 28, 29, or 41. DANISH.

Nouvelle has been one of the capital's special restaurants since 1950. It's on the first floor of an 1870 house beside a canal. If you've won the lottery, the restaurant has a special caviar menu, with Sevruga and Beluga. Otherwise, you can explore the à la carte menu, which changes frequently but is likely to include goose-liver terrine with three kinds of glazed onions, or warm oysters and mussels gratinée. The superb fish dishes include North Sea turbot grilled or poached and served on a tomato, rosemary, and artichoke parfait. Lobster is served as a fricassée with green apples and curry hollandaise. Meat selections are likely to include grilled goose liver with glazed spring cabbage and curry, or lamb medallions with white truffles and new onions.

MODERATE

Den Gyldne Fortun. Ved Stranden 18. ☎ **33-12-20-11.** Reservations recommended. Main courses 178–248 DKK ($22.25–$31); 3-course fixed-price menu 325 DKK ($40.65) Mon–Sat, 295 DKK ($36.90) Sun. AE, CB, DC, MC, V. Mon–Fri noon–3pm; daily 6–10pm. Bus: 1, 6, or 10. DANISH/SEAFOOD.

Popular at lunchtime, this restaurant opposite Christiansborg Castle lives up to its name, "golden fortune." Dating from 1796, it has been visited by Hans Christian Andersen, Jenny Lind, and Henry Wadsworth Longfellow. You climb green marble stairs to enter the formal restaurant, which resembles an English club. Amid crystal chandeliers, modern lithographs, and bubbling aquariums, you can order the kind of dishes that members of Denmark's royal family have requested after shopping expeditions on the nearby Strøget. Choices include a Scandinavian version of bouillabaisse (served only in winter), fried fillet of plaice in butter sauce, fried Danish lamb with red wine and tarragon sauce, oven-baked salmon with Noilly Prat sauce, halibut with red wine sauce and herbs, and fillet of turbot with scallops, fresh tarragon, and *beurre blanc* (white butter) sauce. Dessert offerings include the restaurant's well-known sweet plate, with the day's freshest mousses and pastries, or a range of exotic sherbets that change almost every week.

INEXPENSIVE

Cafeen Nikolaj. Nikolaj Plads 12. ☎ **70-26-64-64.** Main courses 75–155 DKK ($9.40–$19.40). AE, CB, DC, DISC, MC, V. Mon–Sat 11:30am–5pm. Bus: 2, 6, 10, 27, 28, or 29. DANISH.

This cafe, which to some evokes Greenwich Village in the '50s, is on the site where Hans Tausen, a father of the Danish Reformation, delivered thundering sermons in the 16th century. Today no one is thundering—they're ordering an array of typical Danish lunches, including a tasty variety of open-faced sandwiches and homemade soups. You can always count on various types of herring. Danish sliced ham on good homemade bread is a perennial favorite, and there is also a selection of Danish cheeses. The place makes no pretensions of being more than it is: a simple cafe that prepares good-tasting food with fresh ingredients at fair prices.

4

Exploring Copenhagen

In sights and nightlife, perennially youthful Copenhagen offers the charm of the past, the magic of the present, and the promise of the future.

For all the tourist-propaganda emphasis on "life-seeing," amusement parks, shopping expeditions, beer gardens, and bustling nightspots, Copenhagen is also proud of its vast storehouse of antiquities. It holds its own with the other capitals of Europe.

The "fun, fun" slogans and the "wonderful, wonderful" Copenhagen melodies tend to detract from an important fact. The Danish capital is an excellent center not only for pleasure seekers, but also for serious visitors who want to inspect art galleries, museums, and castles.

In the morning, museum-goers can wander back to classical or Renaissance days in such showcases of art as Thorvaldsen's Museum. You can stroll down corridors, inspecting diverse sculptured creatures, such as Cupid driving two wild boars, a she-wolf, even Apollo Belvedere.

In the afternoon, head south to the little town of Dragør on the island of Amager, long connected to the mainland and now almost a suburb of Copenhagen. Here you'll see the legacy of the Dutch inhabitants who lived and farmed on the island for some 300 years, displayed in museums and evident in the architecture.

On a summer evening, visitors can stroll through the Tivoli pleasure gardens, which seem to have emerged intact from the days when the world was young . . . and so were we. The Danes apparently love childhood too much to abandon it forever, no matter how old they get—so the Tivoli keeps alive the magic of fairy lights and the wonder of yesteryear.

Amusement parks, shopping, beer gardens, and bustling nightspots vie with galleries, museums, and castles for your time in Copenhagen. So many hidden nooks wait to be explored that it's hard to decide what to do first. Here are a few ideas.

Suggested Itineraries

If You Have 1 Day

Take our walking tour through the old city (see "Walking Tour 1: The Old City," below), which isn't too taxing if you're still recovering from jet lag. Spend the late afternoon at Christiansborg Palace, on

Slotsholmen, where the queen receives guests. Early in the evening, head to the Tivoli. However, if it's winter, explore Kongens Nytorv (King's New Square) and the now-charming old sailor's quarter called Nyhavn. At some point in the day, climb the Rundetårn (Round Tower) for a glorious panorama of Copenhagen.

If You Have 2 Days

On the first day, follow the suggestions above. On Day 2, visit Amalienborg Palace, the queen's residence. Try to time your visit so that you can see the changing of the guard. It doesn't have the precision or pomp of the changing of the guard at Buckingham Palace, but nonetheless it remains a Kodak Moment. Continue beyond the palace to the city's beloved statue, *The Little Mermaid,* perched upon a rock in the harbor. In the afternoon, see the art treasures of Ny Carlsberg Glyptotek. At night, visit Scala, the restaurant and shopping complex.

If You Have 3 Days

Follow the suggestions above for the first 2 days. On the morning of Day 3, visit 17th-century Rosenborg Castle, summer palace of Christian IV, and wander through its park and gardens. Have lunch at one of the restaurants that line the canal at Nyhavn, the old seamen's quarter. Visit the National Museum in the afternoon.

If You Have 4 or 5 Days

For the first 3 days, see the suggestions above. On Day 4, head north from Copenhagen to Louisiana, the modern-art museum located in a 19th-century mansion on the Danish Riviera. Continue to Helsingør to visit Kronborg Castle, made famous by Shakespeare's *Hamlet.* Return by train to Copenhagen in time for a stroll along Strøget, the longest pedestrians-only street in Europe. Have dinner at a restaurant in Dragør. On the fifth day, visit Frilandsmuseet, a re-created village of farmsteads and rural cottages at Lyngby, a half-hour train ride from Copenhagen. Have lunch at the park. Return to Copenhagen and take our second walking tour, which covers Kongens Nytorv to Langelinie (see "Walking Tour 2," below). If time remains, tour the Carlsberg Brewery. Pay a final visit to the Tivoli to cap your adventure.

1 In & Around the Tivoli Gardens

✪ Tivoli Gardens. Vesterbrogade 3. ☎ **33-15-10-01.** Admission 11am–1pm 49 DKK ($6.15) adults, 25 DKK ($3.15) children under 14; 1–9:30pm 45 DKK ($5.65) adults, 20 DKK ($2.50) children; 9:30pm–midnight 20 DKK ($2.50) for all. Rides 20 DKK ($2.50) each. May to mid-Sept, daily 11am–midnight. Partial Christmastime opening from mid-November until Christmas Eve (reduced admission). Closed mid-Sept to Apr. Bus: 1, 16, or 29.

Since it opened in 1843, this 20-acre garden and amusement park in the center of Copenhagen has been a resounding success. It boasts thousands of flowers, a merry-go-round of tiny Viking ships, games of chance and skill (pinball arcades, slot machines, shooting galleries), and a Ferris wheel of hot-air balloons and cabin seats. There's even a playground.

An Arabian-style fantasy palace complete with towers and arches, houses more than two dozen restaurants in all price ranges, from a lakeside inn to a beer garden. Finer, pricier meals are to be had at Divan II, La Crevette, and Louise Nimb. Walk around the edge of the tiny lake, with its ducks, swans, and boats.

Tivoli's newest attraction, The Golden Tower, rises 19 stories high over the city's skyline, and is crowned with a golden cupola. Patrons are taken 190 feet straight up to enjoy a panoramic view over Copenhagen before being dropped back to earth at a blazing speed that's even faster than a natural free fall. The tower is set in elaborately themed Oriental surroundings, with exotic plants and colored tiles.

A parade of the red-uniformed Tivoli Boys Guard takes place on weekends at 6:30 and 8:30pm, and their regimental band gives concerts on Saturday at 3pm on the open-air stage. The oldest building at the Tivoli, the Chinese-style Pantomime Theater, stages performances in the evening.

For more specifics on nighttime happenings—fireworks, brass bands, orchestras, discos, variety acts—see "Copenhagen After Dark," below.

◐ Ny Carlsberg Glyptotek. Dantes Plads 7. ☎ **33-41-81-41.** Admission 30 DKK ($3.75) adults, free for children; free for all Wed and Sun. Tues–Sun 10am–4pm. Bus: 1, 2, 5, 6, 8, or 10.

The Glyptotek, behind the Tivoli, is one of the most important art museums in Scandinavia. Founded by the 19th-century art collector Carl Jacobsen (Mr. Carlsberg Beer himself), the museum devotes two floors each to its modern (mainly 19th century) and antiquities collections; in 1996, the excellent French masters' wing was added. The modern section has both French and Danish art, including works by Rodin and Impressionist painting including van Gogh's *Landscape from St. Rémy*. The antiquities department is separated from the modern section by a conservatory and houses Egyptian, Greek, and Roman art on the main floor, Etruscan, Greek, and Cypriot art on the lower floor. The Egyptian collection is outstanding; the most notable prize is a prehistoric rendering of a hippopotamus. Fine Greek originals (headless Apollo, Niobe's tragic children) and Roman copies of original Greek bronzes (4th-century Hercules) are also on display, as are busts of Roman nobles—Pompey, Virgil, Augustus, and Trajan. A favorite of ours is the Etruscan art display, with sarcophagi, a winged lion, bronzes, and pottery.

Constructed of white marble and granite, the French masters' wing is in the inner courtyard and can be reached only through the conservatory. There are works by Manet, Monet, Degas, and Renoir, as well as an impressive collection of French sculpture, such as Rodin's *Burghers of Calais,* and one of only three complete sets of Degas bronzes. The display features Cézanne's famous *Portrait of the Artist,* as well as about 35 paintings by former Copenhagen resident Gauguin.

Rådhus (Town Hall) and World Clock. Rådhuspladsen. ☎ **33-66-25-82.** Rådhus, 30 DKK ($3.75); clock, 10 DKK ($1.25) adults, 5 DKK (65¢) children. Guided tour: Rådhus, Mon–Fri 3pm, Sat 10am; tower, Mon–Sat noon. Bus: 1, 6, or 8.

Built in 1905, the Town Hall has impressive statues of Hans Christian Andersen and of Niels Bohr, the Nobel Prize–winning physicist. Jens Olsen's famous World Clock is on the ground floor and is open for viewing weekdays from 10am to 4pm and Saturday from 10am to 1pm. Frederik IX set the clock on December 15, 1955. The clockwork is so exact that it's calibrated to lose just 0.4 seconds in 300 years.

Climb the tower for an impressive view. To the east of the Rådhus is one of Copenhagen's most famous landmarks, the Lurblæserne (Lur Blower Column), the column topped by two Vikings blowing an ancient trumpet called a *lur.* It involves a bit of artistic license—the lur dates from the Bronze Age (around 1500 B.C.), and the Vikings lived some 1,000 years ago. But it's a fascinating sight just the same. City tours often begin here.

Louis Tussaud Wax Museum. H. C. Andersens Blvd. 22. ☎ **33-11-89-00.** Admission 65 DKK ($8.15) adults, 40 DKK ($5) students, 25 DKK ($3.15) children. Apr 29–Sept 13, daily 10am–11pm; Sept 14–Apr 28, daily 10am–6pm. Bus: 1, 2, 16, 28, 29, or 41.

A visit to the Louis Tussaud Wax Museum, so the publicity goes, is the closest some of us will ever get to meeting our heroes. It *is* a major Copenhagen attraction and it features more than 200 wax figures—everybody from Danish kings and queens to

Leonardo da Vinci to the Fab Four. Children can visit the Snow Queen's Castle, or watch Frankenstein and Dracula guard the monsters and vampires.

2 Amalienborg Palace & Environs

☉ Amalienborg Palace. Christian VIII's Palace. ☎ **33-12-21-86.** Admission 45 DKK ($5.65) adults, 40 DKK ($5) students and seniors, 5 DKK (65¢) children 5–12, free for children under 5. Jan–Apr, Oct–Dec 13, Tues–Sun 11am–4pm; May, Sept–Oct, Dec 26–30, daily 11am–4pm; June–Aug, daily 10am–4pm. Closed Dec 14–Dec 25. Bus: 1, 6, 9, or 10.

These four 18th-century French-style rococo mansions have been the home of the Danish royal family since 1794, when Christiansborg burned. They open onto one of the most attractive squares in Europe, Amalienborg. When the royal family is in residence, visitors flock to witness the changing of the guard at noon. A swallowtail flag signifies that the queen is in Copenhagen, not at her North Zealand summer home, Fredensborg Palace. The Royal Life Guard, in black bearskin busbies, leaves Rosenborg Castle at 11:30am and marches along Gothersgade, Nørre Voldgade, Frederiksborggade, Købmagergade, Østergade, Kongens Nytorv, Bredgade, Sankt Annæ Plads, and Amaliegade to Amalienborg. After the event, the guard, accompanied by a band, returns to Rosenborg Castle via Frederiksgade, Store Kongensgade, and Gothersgade. In 1994 some official and private rooms in Amalienborg opened to the public for the first time. The rooms, reconstructed to reflect the period 1863 to 1947, belonged to members of the reigning royal family, the Glücksborgs, who ascended the throne in 1863. The highlight is the period devoted to the long reign (1863–1906) of Christian IX (1818–1906) and Queen Louise (1817–98). The items in his study and her drawing room—gifts from their far-flung children—reflect their unofficial status as "parents-in-law to Europe." Both came from distant sides of the then-heirless royal family to create a true "love match." The author of the verses for their wedding song (a Danish tradition), in 1842, was none other than Hans Christian Andersen.

Christian and Louise gave their six children a simple but internationally oriented upbringing. One daughter, Alexandra, married Edward VII of England; another, Dagmar, wed Tsar Alexander III of Russia. The crown prince, who became Frederik VIII, married Louise of Sweden-Norway; another son became king of Greece, and yet another declined the throne of Bulgaria. In 1905 a grandson became king of Norway.

In the 1880s, members of the Danish royal family, numbering more than 50, got together each summer at Fredensborg Palace, north of Copenhagen. The children, now monarchs, brought Christian IX and Louise presents—works of art from the imperial workshops and from jewelers such as Fabergé—as well as souvenirs, embroideries, and handcrafts made by the grandchildren. All became treasures for the aging king and queen, and many are exhibited today.

Also open to the public are the studies of Frederik VIII and Christian X. Thanks to his marriage to Louise of Sweden-Norway, the liberal-minded Frederik VIII (1843–1912), who reigned from 1906 to 1912, had considerable wealth, and he furnished Amalienborg Palace sumptuously. The king's large study is decorated in lavish neo-Renaissance style.

The final period room in the museum is the study of Christian X (1870–1947), king from 1912 to 1947 and grandfather of Queen Margrethe II. He became a symbol of national resistance during the German occupation of Denmark during the Second World War. Along with the period rooms, a costume gallery and jewelry room are open to the public. The Amalienborg Museum rooms are one of two divisions of the Royal Danish Collections; the other is at Rosenborg Palace.

Copenhagen Attractions

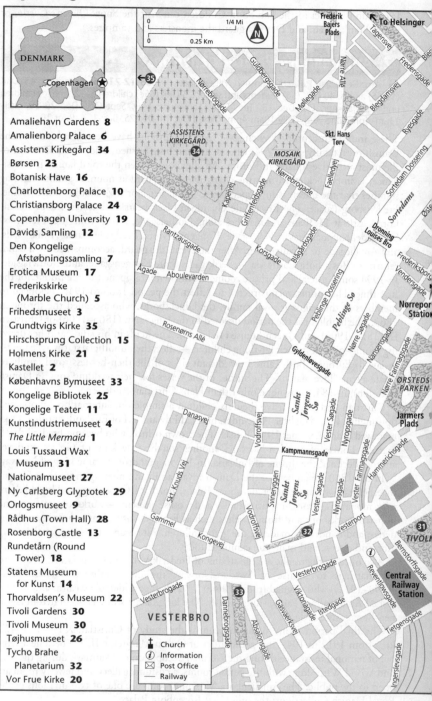

Amaliehavn Gardens **8**
Amalienborg Palace **6**
Assistens Kirkegård **34**
Børsen **23**
Botanisk Have **16**
Charlottenborg Palace **10**
Christiansborg Palace **24**
Copenhagen University **19**
Davids Samling **12**
Den Kongelige
  Afstøbningssamling **7**
Erotica Museum **17**
Frederikskirke
  (Marble Church) **5**
Frihedsmuseet **3**
Grundtvigs Kirke **35**
Hirschsprung Collection **15**
Holmens Kirke **21**
Kastellet **2**
Københavns Bymuseet **33**
Kongelige Bibliotek **25**
Kongelige Teater **11**
Kunstindustriemuseet **4**
The Little Mermaid **1**
Louis Tussaud Wax
  Museum **31**
Nationalmuseet **27**
Ny Carlsberg Glyptotek **29**
Orlogsmuseet **9**
Rådhus (Town Hall) **28**
Rosenborg Castle **13**
Rundetårn (Round
  Tower) **18**
Statens Museum
  for Kunst **14**
Thorvaldsen's Museum **22**
Tivoli Gardens **30**
Tivoli Museum **30**
Tøjhusmuseet **26**
Tycho Brahe
  Planetarium **32**
Vor Frue Kirke **20**

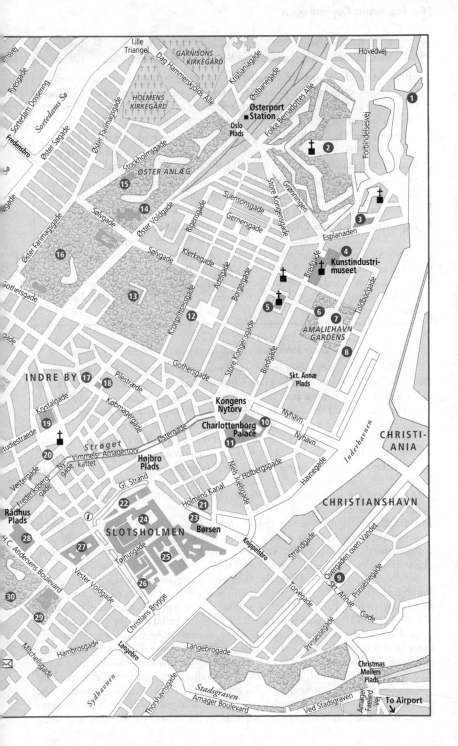

Lille Triangel

GARNISONS KIRKEGÅRD

Dag Hammerskjölds Alle

Hovedvej

Kristianiagade

Østbanegade

Folke Bernadottes Alle

Forbindelsesvej

HOLMENS KIRKEGÅRD

Øster Farimagsgade

Stockholmsgade

Østerport Station

Oslo Plads

①

② ✝

Store Kongensgade

Grønningen

③ ✝

Esplanaden

ØSTER ANLÆG

⑮

⑭

Sølvgade

Øster Voldgade

Rigensgade

Suensonsgade

Gernersgade

④ Kunstindustri-museet

Bredgade

Toldbodgade

⑯

Sølvgade

Klerkegade

Adelgade

Borgergade

✝ ⑤ ✝

⑥ ⑦

AMALIEHAVN GARDENS

⑬

⑫

Kronprinsessegade

Gothersgade

Store Kongensgade

Bredgade

⑧

INDRE BY ⑰ ⑱ Pilestræde

Skt. Annæ Plads

Krystalgade

Købmagergade

Kongens Nytorv

Nyhavn

CHRISTI-ANIA

⑲

Studiestræde

Strøget

Østergade

Charlottenborg Palace ⑩

⑪

Nyhavn

Inderhavnen

✝ ⑳

Vimmels-Amagertorv kaftet

Nyr gade

Højbro Plads

Niels Juelsgade

Holbergsgade

Havnegade

Vestergade

Frederiksberg gade

Gl. Strand

CHRISTIANSHAVN

Rådhus Plads

ⓘ

㉒

Holmens Kanal ㉑

Strandgade

Overgaden oven Vandet

Skt. Annæ Gade

Prinsessegade

H.C. Andersens Boulevard

㉘

㉔ SLOTSHOLMEN

㉓ Børsen

㉗

Tøjhusgade

㉕

Knippelsbro

Torvegade

⑨

㉚

Vester Voldgade

㉖

Christians Brygge

㉙

Prinsessegade

Mitchellsgade

Hambrosgade

Langebro

Langebrogade

Christmas Møllers Plads

✉

Sydhavnen

Thorshavnsgade

Stadsgraven

Amager Boulevard

Ved Stadsgraven

Amager Fælled Vej

To Airport ↓

✪ Frommer's Favorite Copenhagen Experiences

Sitting at an Outdoor Cafe. Because of Copenhagen's long gray winters, sitting outdoors and drinking beer or eating is a favorite, savored summer pastime. The best spot is at Nyhavn (New Harbor), beginning at Kongens Nytorv. Enjoy ice cream while admiring the tall ships moored in the canal.

Going to the Tivoli. This is the quintessential summer adventure, a tradition since 1843. It's an amusement park with a difference—even the merry-go-rounds are special, using a fleet of Viking ships instead of the usual horses.

Strolling Strøget. The Danish word *strøget* means "to stroll"—and that's exactly what shopping addicts do along this nearly three-quarter-mile stretch, from Rådhuspladsen to Kongens Nytorv.

Exploring Alternative Lifestyles. Not for everybody, but worth a look, is a trip to the Free City of Christiania, on the island of Christianshavn (take bus no. 8 from Rådhuspladsen). Since 1971 some 1,000 squatters have taken over 130 former army barracks (spread across 20 acres) and declared themselves a free city. You can shop, dine, and talk to the natives about the experimental community, which has its own doctors, clubs, and stores. It even flies its own flag. Exercise caution here, however.

Den Lille Havfrue (The Little Mermaid). Langelinie, on the harbor. Bus: 1, 6, or 9.

This is the one statue in Copenhagen *everybody* wants to see. The life-size bronze of *Den Lille Havfrue* was inspired by Hans Christian Andersen's *The Little Mermaid,* one of the world's most famous fairy tales. Edvard Eriksen's sculpture, unveiled in 1913, rests on rocks right off the shore. In spite of its small size, the statue is as important a symbol to Copenhageners as the Statue of Liberty is to New Yorkers.

The mermaid has fallen prey to vandals over the years. In the early 1900s, her arm was cut off and later recovered. She was decapitated on April 25, 1964, and the head was never returned. (The original mold exists, so missing body parts can be recast.) In January 1998, she lost her head again, and most of the city responded with sadness. "She is part of our heritage, like the Tivoli, the queen, and stuff like that," said local sculptor Christian Moerk.

Although not taking blame for the attack, the Radical Feminist Faction sent flyers to newspapers to protest "the woman-hating, sexually fixated male dreams" allegedly conjured by the statue's nudity. The head mysteriously turned up at a TV station, delivered by a masked figure. Welders restored it, making the seam invisible.

Nearby is the **Gefion Fountain** (Gefion Springvandet), sculpted by Anders Bundgaard. Gefion, a goddess in Scandinavian myth, plowed Zealand away from Sweden by turning her sons into oxen. Also in the area is **Kastellet** at Langelinie (☎ 33-11-22-33), a citadel constructed by King Frederik III in the 1660s. Some of Copenhagen's original ramparts surround the structure. The citadel was the capital's main fortress until the 18th century, when it fell into disuse. During the Nazi occupation of Copenhagen in the Second World War, the Germans made it their headquarters. Today the Danish military uses the buildings, and the beautiful grounds of Churchillparken that surround Kastellet are open to visitors. At the entrance to the park stands St. Alban's, the English church of Copenhagen. You can still see the double moats built as part of Copenhagen's defense in the wake of the Swedish siege of the capital on February 10, 1659. This ruined citadel can be explored daily from 6am to sunset. Admission is free.

Frihedsmuseet (Museum of Danish Resistance, 1940–45). Churchillparken. ☎ **33-13-77-14.** Admission 30 DKK ($3.75) adults, free for children under 16. May–Sept 15, Tues–Sat 10am–4pm, Sun 10am–5pm; Sept 16–Apr, Tues–Sat 11am–3pm, Sun 11am–4pm. Bus: 1, 6, or 9.

This museum displays the tools of espionage and sabotage that the Danes used to throw off the Nazi yoke in the Second World War. Beginning with peace marches in the early days of the war, the resistance movement grew into a skilled underground that eventually electrified and excited the Allied world. "Danes Fighting Germans!" blared the headlines.

A moment in history is graphically and dramatically preserved. The museum highlights the workings of the outlaw press, the equipment used in the wireless and illegal films, relics of torture and concentration camps, British propaganda leaflets dropped in the country, satirical caricatures of Hitler, information about Danish Jews and Danish Nazis, and the paralyzing nationwide strikes. An armed car, used against Danish Nazi informers and collaborators, is displayed on the grounds.

Kunstindustrimuseet (Museum of Decorative and Applied Art). Bredgade 68. ☎ **33-14-94-52.** Museum, 35 DKK ($4.40) adults, free for children under 16; library, free. Museum, Tues–Sun 1–4pm; library, Tues–Sat 10am–4pm. S-tog: Østerport. Bus: 1, 6, or 9.

This rococo building consists of four wings surrounding a garden, and was part of the Royal Frederik Hospital built from 1752 to 1757 under King Frederik V. It was restored in the early 1920s and adapted to house the museum's collections, which consist mostly of European decorative and applied art from the Middle Ages to the present, arranged in chronological order. Important collections include furniture, tapestries and other textiles, pottery, porcelain, glass, and silver. There are also collections of Chinese and Japanese art and handcrafts. The library contains some 65,000 books and periodicals that deal with arts and crafts, architecture, costumes, advertising, photography, and industrial design.

Davids Samling. Kronprinsessegade 30. ☎ **33-73-49-49.** Free admission. Tues–Sun 1–4pm. Bus: 1, 6, 9, 10, 19, 29, 31, 42, or 43.

Danish attorney C. L. David (1878–1960) established this museum shortly after the Second World War on the premises of his private house across from the park surrounding Rosenborg Castle. This privately funded museum is visited mainly because it has Scandinavia's largest collection of Islamic art. However, Samling didn't stop there in his collecting, as he had rather global taste, also accumulating an exquisite collection of French china from the 18th century along with centuries-old antiques and paintings, especially strong in English furniture. He was also an inveterate collector of Scandinavian ceramics and silver.

David's other major bequest to Denmark was his summer villa in the northern suburbs of Copenhagen at Marienborg, which is for the prime minister's use.

Impressions

There is nothing of Hamlet in their character.
                                    —R. H. Bruce Lockhart, *My Europe,* 1952
Copenhagen is the best-built city of the north.
                                    —William Coxe, *Travels,* 1792

3 Rosenborg Castle, Botanical Gardens & Environs

✪ Rosenborg Castle. Øster Voldgade 4A. ☎ **33-15-32-86.** Admission 50 DKK ($6.25) adults, 30 DKK ($3.80) students and seniors, 10 DKK ($1.25) children 5–12, free for children 4 and under. Palace and treasury (royal jewels), June–Aug, daily 10am–4pm; May and Sept to mid-Oct, daily 11am–3pm; mid-Oct to Apr, Tues, Fri, Sun 11am–2pm. S-tog: Nørreport. Bus: 5, 10, 14, 16, 31, 42, 43, 184, or 185.

Founded by Christian IV in the 17th century, this red-brick Renaissance-style castle houses everything from narwhal-tusk and ivory coronation chairs to Frederik VII's baby shoes. Most impressive are the dazzling crown jewels and regalia housed in the basement Treasury, where there's also a lavishly decorated coronation saddle from 1596. The Knights Hall (Room 21) boasts a coronation seat, three silver lions, and relics from the 1700s. Another important attraction is Room 3, a bedroom decorated with Asian lacquer art and a stucco ceiling in which founding father Christian IV died. The King's Garden (*Have*) surrounds the castle, and the Botanical Gardens are across the street.

Botanisk Have (Botanical Gardens). Gothersgade 128. ☎ **35-32-22-40.** Free admission. May–Sept, daily 8:30am–6pm; Oct–Apr, daily 8:30am–4pm. S-tog: Nørreport. Bus: 5, 7, 14, 16, 24, 40, or 43.

Planted from 1871 to 1874, the Botanical Gardens are at a lake that was once part of the city's defensive moat. Across from Rosenborg Castle, they contain hothouses growing tropical and subtropical plants. Special features include a cactus house and a palm house, all of which appear even more exotic so far north. An alpine garden contains mountain plants from all over the world.

✪ Statens Museum for Kunst (Royal Museum of Fine Arts). Sølvgade 48–50. ☎ **33-74-84-94.** Admission 30–50 DKK ($4.35–$7.25) adults, free for children under 16. (Note: Higher admission for special exhibitions only.) Tues and Thurs–Sun 10am–5pm, Wed 10am–8pm. Bus: 10, 14, 43, or 184.

The largest art museum in Denmark, the Royal Museum is well stocked with painting and sculpture from the 13th century to the present. There are Dutch golden age landscapes and marine paintings by Rubens and his school, plus portraits by Frans Hals and Rembrandt. Eckersberg, Købke, and Hansen represent the Danish golden age. French 20th-century art includes 20 works by Matisse. In the Royal Print Room are 300,000 drawings, prints, lithographs, and other works by such artists as Dürer, Rembrandt, Matisse, and Picasso. The museum is especially strong in artifacts unearthed from the Viking era. A sculpture garden is filled with classical and contemporary works.

A major expansion in 1998 added a concert hall, a Children's Art Museum, and a glass wing designed for temporary exhibits.

Den Hirschsprungske Samling (Hirschsprung Collection). Stockholmsgade 20. ☎ **35-42-03-36.** Admission 25 DKK ($3.15) adults, 15 DKK ($1.90) students, free for children under 16; 40 DKK ($5) during special exhibitions. Wed 11am–9pm, Thurs–Mon 11am–4pm. Bus: 10, 14, 40, 42, or 43.

This collection of Danish art from the 19th and early 20th centuries lies in Ostre Anlaeg, a park in the city center. Heinrich Hirschsprung (1836–1908), a tobacco merchant, created the collection and it has grown ever since. The emphasis is on the Danish golden age, with such artists as Eckersberg, Købke, and Lundbye, and on the Skagen painters—P. S. Krøyer and Anna and Michael Ancher. Some furnishings from the artists' homes are exhibited.

4 Christiansborg Palace & Environs

✪ Christiansborg Palace. Christiansborg Slotsplads. ☎ **33-92-64-92.** Royal Reception Rooms, 40 DKK ($5) adults, 10 DKK ($1.25) children; parliament, free; castle ruins, 20 DKK ($2.50) adults, 5 DKK (65¢) children. Reception rooms, guided tours June–Aug, daily 11am, 1pm, and 3pm; May and Sept, Tues–Sun 11am and 3pm; Oct–Apr, Tues, Thurs, Sun 11am and 3pm. Parliament, English-language tours daily 11am, 1pm, and 3pm. Ruins, May–Sept, Tues–Fri and Sun 9:30am–3:30pm. Closed Oct–Apr. Bus: 1, 2, 6, 8, 9, 42, or 43.

This granite-and-copper palace on Slotsholmen—a small island that has been the center of political power in Denmark for more than 800 years—houses the parliament, Supreme Court, prime minister's offices, and Royal Reception Rooms. A guide leads you through richly decorated rooms, including the Throne Room, Banqueting Hall, and Queen's Library. Before entering, you'll be asked to put on soft overshoes to protect the wood floors. Under the palace, visit the well-preserved ruins of the 1167 castle of Bishop Absalon, founder of Copenhagen. At **Kongelige Stalde & Kareter,** Christianborg Ridebane 12 (☎ **33-40-10-10**), you can see the royal stables and coaches. Elegantly clad in riding breeches and jackets, riders exercise the horses. Vehicles include regal coaches and "fairy-tale" carriages, along with a display of harnesses in use by the royal family since 1778. Admission is 10 DKK ($1.25) for adults, 5 DKK (65¢) for children. The site can be visited May to September, Friday to Sunday, from 2 to 4pm. During other months, hours are Saturday and Sunday from 2 to 4pm.

✪ Nationalmuseet (National Museum). Ny Vestergade 10. ☎ **33-13-44-11.** Admission 40 DKK ($5) adults, 30 DKK ($3.75) students, free for children under 16. Tues–Sun 10am–5pm. Closed Dec 24, 25, and 31. Bus: 1, 2, 5, 6, 8, 10, or 41.

This gigantic repository of anthropological artifacts ambitiously survey 10,000 years of history. The first of five area represented focuses on prehistory, the Middle Ages, and the Renaissance in Denmark. Collections date from the Stone Age and include Viking stones, helmets, and fragments of battle gear. Especially interesting are the *lur* (horn), a Bronze Age piece that's among the oldest musical instruments in Europe, and the world-famous "Sun Chariot," an elegant Bronze Age piece of pagan art. The next area is a study of the 18th-century royal palace in which the museum is housed. There's also the Royal Collection of Coins and Medals and the Collection of Egyptian and Classical Antiquities, which offers outstanding fragments of ancient civilizations such as Roman chalices depicting Homeric legends. Finally, in the ethnographic section, relics of Eskimo culture and the people of Greenland and Denmark are represented.

Erotica Museum. Købmagergade 24. ☎ **33-12-03-11.** Admission 65 DKK ($8.15). May–Sept, daily 10am–11pm; Oct–Apr, Mon–Fri 11am–8pm, Sat 10am–9pm, Sun 10am–8pm. S-tog: Nørreport. Those 16–18 must be accompanied by an adult. No one under 16 admitted.

This is perhaps the only museum in the world where you can learn about the sex lives of such famous people as Freud, Nietzsche, and Duke Ellington—assuming that you were interested in the first place. Founded by Ole Ege, a well-known Danish photographer of nudes, it's within walking distance of the Tivoli and the Central Railway Station. In addition to providing a glimpse into the sex lives of the famous, it presents a survey of erotica from around the world and through the ages. The exhibits range from tame to torrid—everything from Etruscan drawings and Chinese paintings to Greek vases depicting a lot of sexual activity. On display are remarkably lifelike naughty tableaux created by craftspeople from Tussaud's Wax Museum, as well as a collection of those dirty little postcards Americans tried to sneak through customs in the 1920s and 1930s.

As you ascend the floors of the museum, the exhibits get steamier and seamier. By the time you reach the fourth (top) floor, a dozen video monitors are showing erotic films, featuring everything from black-and-white underground films from the 1920s to today's XXX-rated releases in full-bodied color, with the emphasis on "bodied."

Tøjhusmuseet (Royal Arsenal Museum). Tøjhusgade 3. ☎ **33-11-60-37.** Admission 30 DKK ($3.75) adults, 5 DKK ($1.25) children 6–12, free for children under 6. Tues–Sun noon–4pm. Closed Jan 1, and Dec 24, 25, and 31. Bus: 1, 2, 5, 6, 8, 10, 28, 29, 30, 32, 33, 34, or 35.

This museum, housed in the former arsenal (erected from 1598 to 1604), features a fantastic display of weaponry and hunting devices. On the ground floor—the longest vaulted Renaissance hall in Europe—is the Cannon Hall, stocked with artillery from 1500 to the present. Above the Cannon Hall is the impressive Armory Hall, with one of the world's finest collections of small arms, colors, and armor.

Thorvaldsen's Museum. Porthusgade 2. ☎ **33-32-15-32.** Admission 20 DKK ($2.50) adults, free for children under 15; free to all Wed. Tues–Sun 10am–5pm. Bus: 1, 2, 5, 6, 8, 10, 28, 29, or 550S.

On Slotsholmen next to Christiansborg, this museum houses the greatest collection of the works of Bertel Thorvaldsen (1770–1844), the most significant name in neoclassical sculpture. Thorvaldsen's life personified the romanticism of the 18th and 19th centuries—he rose from semi-poverty to the pinnacle of success. The sculptor is famous for his classical works taken from mythology: Cupid and Psyche, Adonis, Jason, Hercules, Ganymede, and Mercury, all of which are on display here. The museum also contains Thorvaldsen's extensive, private collection, which includes everything from Egyptian relics of Ptolemy to contemporary paintings such as *Apollo Among the Thessalian Shepherds.* After many years of exile in Italy, Thorvaldsen returned in triumph to his native Copenhagen, where he died a national figure and was buried in the courtyard of his museum.

5 In the Old Town (Indre By)

Rundetårn (Round Tower). Købmagergade 52A. ☎ **33-73-03-73.** Admission 15 DKK ($1.90) adults, 5 DKK (65¢) children. Tower, June–Aug, Mon–Sat 10am–8pm, Sun noon–8pm; Sept–May, Mon–Sat 10am–5pm, Sun noon–5pm. Observatory, Oct 15–Mar 20, Tues–Wed 7–10pm. Closed Mar 21–Sept 25. Bus: 5, 7E, 14, 16, or 42.

This 17th-century public observatory, attached to a church, is visited by thousands who climb the spiral ramp (there are no steps) for a panoramic view of Copenhagen. The tower is one of the crowning architectural achievements of the Christian IV era. Peter the Great, in Denmark for a state visit, galloped up the ramp on horseback, preceded by his carriage-drawn tsarina. On the premises is a Bibliotekssalen (Library Hall), which holds changing exhibits on art, culture, history, and science.

Vor Frue Kirke (Copenhagen Cathedral). Nørregade. ☎ **33-14-41-28.** Free admission. Mon–Fri 9am–5pm. Bus: 5.

This Greek Renaissance-style church, built in the early 19th century near Copenhagen University, features Bertel Thorvaldsen's white marble neoclassical works, including *Christ and the Apostles.* Hans Christian Andersen's funeral took place here (in 1875), as did Sören Kierkegaard's (in 1855).

6 More Museums

Den Kongelige Afstøbningssamling. Vestindisk Pakhus, Toldbodgade 40. ☎ **33-78-84-94.** Admission 20 DKK ($2.50) adults, 13 DKK ($1.65) children; free to all Wed. Tues and Thurs–Sun 10am–5pm, Wed 10am–8pm. Bus: 1, 6, or 9.

The Royal Cast Collection is one of the largest and oldest cast collections in the world, comprising some 2,000 plaster casts modeled after famous sculptures from 4,000 years of Western culture. The best-known original works from antiquity and the Renaissance are now scattered all over the museums of the world, but here they make up a world of plaster—monumental Egyptian sphinxes, gold from Atreus' treasury, Venus de Milo, the Pergamon altar, and marble sculpture from the temples of the Acropolis in Athens, plus a large collection by leading European plaster workshops from 1870 to 1915.

Founded in 1895 as part of the Statens Museum for Kunst (Royal Museum of Fine Arts), the collection was in that building until the 1960s. In 1984 the collection was placed permanently in the Vestindisk Pakhus, a rebuilt warehouse overlooking the harbor, close to Amalienborg Palace.

Kongelige Bibliotek (Royal Library). Sørenkierkegaards Plads 1. ☎ **33-47-47-47.** Free admission. Mon–Fri 9am–7pm, Sat 10am–7pm. Bus: 1, 2, 5, 6, 8, or 9.

The Royal Library, which dates from the 1600s, is the largest library in Scandinavia. As a national library, Kongelige Bibliotek owns the world's most complete collection of works printed in Danish; some volumes go back as far as 1482. It reopened in the late fall of 1998 following a restoration. In a classic building with high-ceilinged reading rooms and columned hallways, it is a grand and impressive place for storing some 2 million volumes—everything from sagas of Viking journeys to America (yes, before Columbus "discovered" the already inhabited continent), and enough prints, maps, and manuscripts to keep the most intense scholar busy for several lifetimes. The library owns original manuscripts by such fabled Danish writers as Hans Christian Andersen and Karen Blixen (who wrote as Isak Dinesen).

While it was closed, a gargantuan granite annex, The Black Diamond, expanded the library all the way to the waterfront. The growth was necessary because of the vast output of Danish works since the Second World War. Likened to the Taj Mahal or Sydney's Opera House for its evocative and enigmatic appearance, the Black Diamond's progressive design suits its central location on Christians Brygge—by the harbor between the bridges Langebro and Knippelsbro. The origin of the building's name is easy to surmise: Its facade is covered with a myriad of dazzling, reflective black granite tiles from Zimbabwe (the granite itself was cut in Portugal and polished in Italy) and its exterior walls slant sharply toward the water. Apart from space for 200,000 books, the Black Diamond features a bookshop, a restaurant with a spectacular harborfront view, six reading rooms, a courtyard for exhibitions, and a concert hall. After viewing the interior of the library, you can wander through its formal gardens, past the fish pond and statue of philosopher Sören Kierkegaard (1813–55).

Orlogsmuseet (Royal Naval Museum). Overgaden Oven Vandet 58. ☎ **32-54-63-63.** Admission 30 DKK ($3.75) adults, 20 DKK ($2.50) children. Tues–Sun noon–4pm. Bus: 2, 8, 9, 28, 31, or 350S.

In Søkvasthuset, the former naval hospital, this museum opens onto Christianshavn canal. It traces the history of the navy, and because Denmark is a maritime nation, it almost becomes a saga of the country. More than 300 model ships, many from as early as the 1500s, are on display. The models served as prototypes for the ships, which were launched into the North Sea. Some models are fully "dressed," with working sails; others are merely cross-sections, with their frames outlined. You can see a vast array of other naval artifacts here, especially an intriguing collection of figureheads. Also look for navigational instruments, and even the propeller from the German U-boat that sank the *Lusitania* in 1915. Finally, there is a display of uniforms worn by Danish officers and sailors over the decades.

Tivoli Museum. Vesterbrogade 3. ☎ **33-15-10-01.** Admission 20 DKK ($2.50) adults, 10 DKK ($1.25) children. Apr 24–Sept 13, daily 11am–6pm; Sept 14–Apr 23, Tues–Sun 10am–4pm. S-tog to Central Station.

Some 150 years in the life of Europe's most famous amusement park are remembered in this offbeat museum. Models, films, 3-D displays, pictures, posters, and original artifacts cover everything from Marlene Dietrich to a flea circus that ran for 65 years. Children will delight in the rides of yesterday (some of them good enough to recycle today). Definitely come here if the Tivoli is closed during your visit.

7 The Churches of Copenhagen

For information on the Copenhagen Cathedral, refer to "In the Old Town (Indre By)," above.

Holmens Kirke. Holmens Kanal. ☎ **33-13-61-78.** Free admission. May 15–Sept 15, Mon–Fri 9am–2pm, Sat 9am–noon; Sept 16–May 14, Mon–Sat 9am–noon. Bus: 1, 2, 6, 8, 9, 10, 31, 37, or 43.

This royal chapel and naval church lies across the canal from Slotsholmen, next to the National Bank of Denmark. The structure was converted into a church for the royal navy in 1619, but its nave was originally built in 1562, when it was first used as an anchor forge. By 1641 the ever-changing church had become predominantly Dutch Renaissance, an architectural style maintained to this day. The "royal doorway" was brought here from Roskilde Cathedral in the 19th century. Inside, look for a baroque altar of unpainted oak and a carved pulpit by Abel Schrøder the Younger. Both artifacts date from the mid–seventeenth century. In the burial chamber are the tombs of some of Denmark's most important naval figures, including Admiral Niels Juel, who successfully fought off an attack by Swedes in 1677 in the epic Battle of Køge Bay. Peder Tordenskjold, who defeated Charles XII of Sweden during the Great Northern War in the early 1700s, is also entombed here. On a happier note, this is the church where Queen Margrethe II took her wedding vows in 1967.

Frederikskirke. Frederiksgade 4. ☎ **33-15-01-44.** Free admission to church; dome, 20 DKK ($2.50) adults, 10 DKK ($1.25) children. Church, Mon–Thurs 10am–5pm, Fri–Sun noon–5pm. Dome, June 15–Sept 1, daily 1–3pm; Oct–May, Sat–Sun 1–3pm. Bus: 1, 6, or 9.

This 200-year-old church, with its massive green copper dome—one of the largest in the world—is a short walk from Amalienborg Palace. Lined with valuable Norwegian marble, it's often called the Marmorkirken (marble church). After an unsuccessful start during the neoclassical revival of the 1750s, the church was finally completed in Roman baroque style in 1894. In many ways it's even more impressive than the Copenhagen Cathedral, not just for its dome, but for its rich, lush decorations and its facade decorated with statues of great figures in ecclesiastical history.

Vor Frelsers Kirken (Our Savior's Church). Skt. Annægade 29. ☎ **32-57-27-98.** Admission to tower, 20 DKK ($2.50) adults, 10 DKK ($1.25) children; church, free. Apr–Aug,

Mon–Sat 11am–4:30pm and Sun noon–4:30pm; Sept–Oct, Mon–Sat 11am–3:30pm and Sun noon–3:30pm; Nov–Mar, daily 11:30am–3:30pm. Bus: 1, 2, 5, 8, or 9.

This baroque church with an external tower staircase dates from 1696. Local legend maintains that when the encircling staircase was constructed going the wrong way, the architect climbed to the top, realized what he'd done, and then jumped to his death. The Gothic structure's green and gold tower is a Copenhagen landmark, dominating the Christianshavn area. Inside, view the splendid baroque altar, richly adorned with cherubs and other figures. There is also a lovely font and richly carved organ case. Climb 400 steps to the top, where you'll find a gilded figure of Christ standing on a globe, and a panoramic view of the city.

8 A Glimpse into the Past Outside Copenhagen

Frilandsmuseet (Open-Air Museum). Kongevejen 100. ☎ **33-13-44-11.** Admission 40 DKK ($5) adults, free for children under 16. Easter–Sept, Tues–Sun 10am–5pm; Oct 1–20, Tues–Sun 10am–4pm. Closed Oct 21–Easter. S-tog: Copenhagen Central Station to Sorgenfri (trains leave every 20 minutes). Bus: 184 or 194.

This reconstructed village in Lyngby, on the edge of Copenhagen, recaptures Denmark's rural character. The "museum" covers nearly 90 acres, a 2-mile walk around the compound, and includes a dozen re-created buildings—farmsteads, windmills, fishers' cottages. Exhibits include a half-timbered 18th-century farmstead from a tiny, windswept Danish island; a primitive longhouse from the remote Faeroe Islands; thatched fishermen's huts from Jutland; tower windmills, and a mid–nineteenth century potter's workshop.

On summer afternoons, organized activities are staged. On a recent visit, folk dancers in native costume performed, and there were demonstrations of lace making and loom weaving.

The park is about 9 miles from the Central Railroad Station. At the entry to the museum is an old-style restaurant.

9 Literary Landmarks

Admirers of **Hans Christian Andersen** may want to seek out the addresses where he lived in Copenhagen, including Nyhavn 18 and Nyhavn 20 (where he lived only briefly) and Nyhavn 67 (where he lived during the 1860s). He also lived for a time at Vingårdsstræde 6.

Assistens Kirkegård (Assistens Cemetery). Nørrebrogade/Kapelvej. Free admission. Mar–Apr and Sept–Oct, daily 8am–6pm; May–Aug, daily 8am–8pm; Nov–Feb, daily 8am–4pm. Bus: 5, 7E, or 16.

The largest cemetery in Copenhagen, dating from 1711, holds the tombs of Sören Kierkegaard, Hans Christian Andersen, and Martin Andersen Nexø, a famous novelist of the working class. The cemetery is now a public park.

Kobenhavns Bymuseet (Copenhagen City Museum). Vesterbrogade 59. ☎ **33-21-07-72.** Admission 20 DKK ($2.50) adults, 10 DKK ($1.25) children under 12. Wed–Mon 10am–4pm. Bus: 6, 16, 27, or 28.

The permanent exhibition here presents the history of Copenhagen in artifacts and pictures. A smaller separate department is devoted to Søren Kierkegaard (1813–55), the father of existentialism; you'll find exhibits of his drawings, letters, books, photographs, and personal belongings.

10 Architectural Highlights

Børsen (Stock Exchange). Børsgade. Bus: 1, 2, 5, 6, 8, or 9.

One of the most unusual buildings in Copenhagen, on Slotsholmen, must be viewed from the outside because it's not open to the public. Architects Hans and Lorenz Steenwinkel built the long, low Renaissance structure for Christian IV. The spire, 177 feet high, resembles a quartet of intertwined dragon tails. The Stock Exchange is no longer housed here; the building is now the headquarters of the Copenhagen Chamber of Commerce.

Grundtvigs Kirke (Grundtvig Church). På Bjerget, Bispebjerg. ☎ **35-81-54-42.** Free admission. Apr–Oct, daily 9am–4:45pm, Nov–Mar, daily 9am–4pm. Bus: 10, 16, 43, or 69.

This church, built from 1921 to 1940, was designed by Jensen Klint, who died before it was completed. About 6 million yellow bricks were used in its construction. The interior is 250 feet wide and 115 feet tall; the exterior resembles a huge organ. The church is a popular venue for concerts.

11 Of Artistic Interest

Arken Museum of Modern Art. Ishøj Strandpark, Skovvej 100. ☎ **43-54-02-22.** Admission 50 DKK ($6.25) adults, 20 DKK ($2.50) children. Tues and Thurs–Sun 10am–5pm, Wed 10am–9pm. Train: E or A to Ishøj Station, then bus no. 128.

Adjacent to a popular public beach in Ishøj, a suburb south of Copenhagen, this museum houses an extensive collection of modern art. The impressive structure was designed by the Danish architect Søren Robert Lund while he was a student at the Royal Academy of Fine Arts. Constructed of stark white concrete and steel, it opened in 1996. The lines evoke the hull of a beached ship. Lund designed both the structure and the interiors, including display space and furniture. In addition to gallery space, the museum contains a concert hall, sculpture courtyards, and a restaurant. Recent exhibitions have included an Emil Nolde retrospective.

12 Especially for Kids

Copenhagen is a wonderful place for children, and many adult attractions also appeal to youngsters. See the listings above for details on the following diversions.

If you're traveling with kids, the **Tivoli** is the obvious choice, as is *The Little Mermaid* at Langelinie. Try to see the changing of the queen's Royal Life Guard at **Amalienborg Palace,** including the entire parade to and from the royal residence. Kids also enjoy **Frilandsmuseet,** the open-air museum. Other attractions great for kids include the following.

Bakken Amusement Park. Dyrehavevej 62, Klampenborg. ☎ **39-63-73-00.** Free admission. Daily 1pm–midnight. Closed late Aug–late Mar. S-tog: Klampenborg train from Central Railroad Station to Klampenborg (about 20 minutes); then walk through the Deer Park or take a horse-drawn cab.

On the northern edge of Copenhagen, about 7½ miles from the city center, this amusement park was created 35 years before the Pilgrims landed at Plymouth Rock. It's a local favorite, featuring roller coasters, dancing, the tunnel of love, and a merry-go-round. Open-air restaurants are plentiful, as are snack bars and ice cream booths. Proceeds from the amusements support this unspoiled natural preserve. There are no cars—only bicycles and horse-drawn carriages.

Denmark's Aquarium. Strandvejen, in Charlottenlund Fort Park, Charlottenlund. ☎ **39-62-32-83.** Admission 60 DKK ($7.50) adults, 30 DKK ($3.75) children. Mar–Oct, daily 10am–6pm; Nov–Feb, Mon–Fri 10am–4pm, Sat–Sun 10am–5pm. S-tog: Line C to Charlottenlund. Bus: 6.

North of Copenhagen along the Øresund coast, this is one of the most extensive aquariums in Europe that boasts all four of the major marine groups in the world. This is also the oldest aquarium in Scandinavia, established in 1939. Hundreds of saltwater and freshwater species are on exhibit. Of special interest is the collection of piranhas, whose codfish feeding occurs every Wednesday and Saturday at 2pm—watch the schoolchildren squeal.

Experimentarium (Hands-On Science Center). Tuborg Havnevej 7, Hellerup. ☎ **39-27-33-33.** Admission 85 DKK ($10.65) adults, 60 DKK ($7.50) children 4–14, free for children under 4. Mon, Wed, Fri 9am–5pm; Tues 9am–9pm; Sat–Sun 11am–5pm. S-tog: Hellerup or Svanemøllen. Bus: 6 or 21.

Here's one museum where your children won't be scolded for touching the exhibits. Housed in the old mineral-water bottling hall of the Tuborg breweries, this museum encourages visitors to use all their senses as they participate in some 300 exhibitions and demonstrations on three themes: "Man," "Nature," and "The Interaction Between Man and Nature." Visitors hear what all the world's languages sound like, make a wind machine blow up to hurricane force, dance in an "inverted" disco, or visit a slimming machine. Families can work as a team to examine enzymes, make a camera from paper, or test perfume. Exhibitions change frequently.

Tycho Brahe Planetarium. Gammel Kongevej 10. ☎ **33-12-12-24.** Admission 15 DKK ($1.90) adults, 10 DKK ($1.25) children; Omnimax films 75 DKK ($9.40) adults, 56 DKK ($7) children. Daily 10:30am–9:30pm. Bus: 1 or 14.

A star projector re-creates the marvel of the night sky, with its planets, galaxies, star clusters, and comets, using the planetarium dome as a screen. Named after the famed Danish astronomer Tycho Brahe (1546–1601), the planetarium also stages Omnimax film productions. There's an information center and a restaurant.

Zoologisk Have (Copenhagen Zoo). Roskildevej 32, Frederiksberg. ☎ **36-30-25-55.** Admission 70 DKK ($8.75) adults, 35 DKK ($4.40) children. Daily 9am–6pm. S-tog: Valby. Bus: 6, 18, 28, 39, or 550S.

With more than 2,000 animals from Greenland to Africa, this zoo boasts spacious new habitats for reindeer and musk oxen as well as an open roaming area for lions. Take a ride up the small wooden Eiffel Tower, or walk across the street to the petting zoo. The zoo is mobbed on Sunday.

13 Copenhagen on Foot: Walking Tours

Walking Tour 1: The Old City

Start: Rådhuspladsen.

Finish: Tivoli Gardens.

Time: 1½ hours.

Best Time: Any sunny day.

Worst Times: Rush hours (weekdays 7:30 to 9am and 5 to 6:30pm).

Start at:

1. **Rådhuspladsen (Town Hall Square)**, in the center of Copenhagen. You can stop in at the Town Hall, but even more appealing is a bronze statue of Hans Christian Andersen. The spinner of fairy tales stands near a boulevard bearing his name. Also on this square is a statue of two *lur* (horn) players that has stood here since 1914.

   Bypassing the horn players, walk southeast along Vester Voldgade onto a narrow street on your left. This is:

2. **Lavendelstræde.** Many houses along here date from the late 18th century. At Lavendelstræde 1, Mozart's widow, Constanze, lived with her second husband, Georg Nikolaus Nissen, a Danish diplomat, from 1812 to 1820.

   The little street quickly becomes Slutterigade.

3. **Courthouses** rise on both sides of this short street, joined by elevated walkways. Built between 1805 and 1815, this was Copenhagen's fourth town hall. It now holds the city's major law courts. The main courthouse entrance is on Nytorv.

   Slutterigade leads to:

4. **Nytorv,** a famous square where you can admire fine 19th-century houses. Søren Kierkegaard, the noted philosopher (1813–55), lived in a house adjacent to the courthouse at the corner of Nytorv and Frederiksberggade. It's a private residence, however, and not open to visitors.

   Cross Nytorv, and veer slightly to your left until you reach Nygade, part of the famed:

5. **Strøget,** a traffic-free shopping street. It begins at Rådhuspladsen, where it's called Frederiksberggade. The major shopping street of Scandinavia, Strøget is a stroller's and shopper's delight, stretching three-quarters of a mile through the heart of Copenhagen.

   Nygade is one of the five streets that make up Strøget. Turn right and head northeast along the street. It quickly becomes winding and narrow Vimmelskaftet, and then turns into Amagertorv. Along Amagertorv on your left, you'll come across the:

6. **Helligåndskirken (Church of the Holy Ghost),** with its 15th-century abbey, Helligåndshuset. This is the oldest church in Copenhagen, founded at the beginning of the 15th century. Partially destroyed in 1728, it was reconstructed in 1880 in a neoclassical style. Some of the buildings on this street date from 1616. The sales rooms of the Royal Porcelain Factory are at Amagertorv 6.

   Next you'll come to Østergade, the last portion of Strøget. You'll see Illum's department store on your left.

   Østergade leads to:

7. **Kongens Nytorv,** Copenhagen's largest square. Many interesting buildings surround it, and there's an equestrian statue of Christian IV in the center. The statue is a bronze replica of a 1688 sculpture. (For more about this square, see "Walking Tour 2," below.)

   From Kongens Nytorv, follow Niels Juels Gade until you come to Laksegade. Turn right and follow this street until you reach the intersection with Nikolajgade. Turn right. This street leads to the:

8. **Nikolaj Church,** which dates from 1530. It was the scene of the thundering sermons of Hans Tausen, a father of the Danish Reformation.

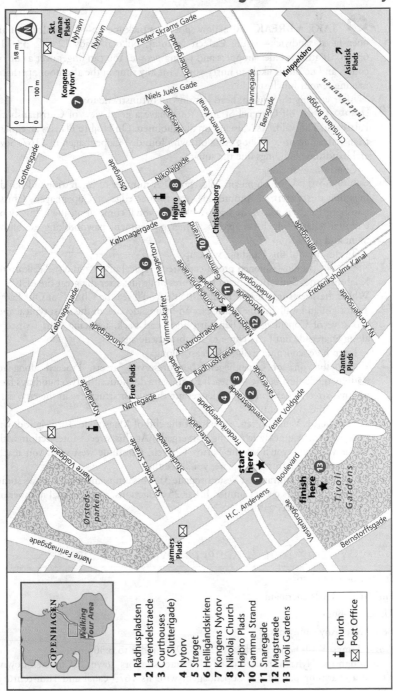

1/8 mi
100 m

Skt. Annae Plads

Nyhavn

Peder Skrams Gade

Holbergsgade

Nyhavn

Kongens Nytorv **7**

Niels Juels Gade

Havnegade

Knippelsbro

Asiatisk Plads

Inderhavnen

Christians Brygge

Børsgade

Holmens Kanal

Læderstraede

Gothersgade

Østergade

Nikolajgade

8

9 Højbro Plads

Christiansborg

Torvegade

Købmagergade

6

Amagertorv

10

Gammel Strand

11

Nybrogade

Vindebrogade

Frederiksholms Kanal

Ny Kongensgade

Skindergade

Købmagergade

Vimmelskaftet

Kompagnistraede

Snaregade

12

Nygade

Knabrostraede

Magstraede

Frue Plads

Krystalgade

Nørregade

Rådhusstraede

5

3

4

2

Farvergade

Vester Voldgade

Dantes Plads

start here 1

finish here

13

Tivoli Gardens

Boulevard

Vesterbrogade

Bernstorffsgade

H.C. Andersens

Ørsteds-parken

Jarmers Plads

Nørre Farimagsgade

Nørre Voldgade

Skt. Peders Straede

Studiestraede

Vestergade

Frederiksberggade

Lavendelstraede

COPENHAGEN

Walking Tour Area

1 Rådhuspladsen
2 Lavendelstraede
3 Courthouses (Slutterigade)
4 Nytorv
5 Strøget
6 Helligåndskirken
7 Kongens Nytorv
8 Nikolaj Church
9 Højbro Plads
10 Gammel Strand
11 Snaregade
12 Magstraede
13 Tivoli Gardens

✝ Church
⊠ Post Office

TAKE A BREAK   A mellow spot for a pick-me-up—a cool drink or an open-faced sandwich—is the **Cafeen Nikolaj,** Nikolaj Plads 12 (☎ **33-11-63-13**). It attracts older shoppers and young people. You can linger over a cup of coffee, and no one is likely to hurry you. Visit any time in the afternoon, perhaps making it your lunch stop.

After viewing the church, head left down Fortunstræde to:

9. **Højbro Plads,** off Gammel Strand. You'll have a good view of Christiansborg Palace and Thorvaldsen's Museum on Slotsholmen. On Højbro Plads is an equestrian statue honoring Bishop Absalon, who founded Copenhagen in 1167. Several handsome buildings line the square.

   Continue west along:

10. **Gammel Strand,** which means "old shore." A number of interesting old buildings line this waterfront promenade, the former edge of Copenhagen. Christiansborg Palace is across the way. At the end you'll come upon the Ministry of Cultural Affairs, which occupies a former government pawnbroking establishment and dates from 1730.

    To the right of this building, walk up:

11. **Snaregade,** an old-fashioned provincial street, typical of the old city. Walk up to Knabrostræde. Both streets boast structures built just after the great fire of 1795. Where the streets intersect at Knabrostræde, you'll see the Church of Our Lady. Turn right and walk for one block east on Snaregade, one of the most typical and evocative of Copenhagen. Then turn and head back, retracing your footsteps along Snaregade until you come to Knabrostræde again.

    From here, continue straight (or east) along:

12. **Magstræde,** one of Copenhagen's best-preserved streets. Proceed along to Rådhusstræde. Just before you reach Rådhusstræde, notice the two buildings facing that street. These private residences are the oldest structures in the city, dating from the 16th century.

    Walk across Vandkunsten, a square at the end of Magstræde. Turn right down Gasegade, then quickly left along Farvergade. At this street's intersection with Vester Voldgade, you'll see the Vartov Church. Continue west until you reach Rådhuspladsen. Across the square, you'll see the:

13. **Tivoli Gardens** (entrance at Vesterbrogade 3). This amusement park draws some 4.5 million visitors every summer. It has 25 attractions, and an equal number of restaurants and beer gardens.

Walking Tour 2: Kongens Nytorv to Langelinie

Start: Kongens Nytorv.

Finish: The Little Mermaid.

Time: 1½ hours.

Best Time: Any sunny day.

Worst Times: Rush hours (weekdays 7:30 to 9am and 5 to 6:30pm).

Although the Nyhavn quarter, once a boisterous sailors' town, has quieted down, it's still a charming part of old Copenhagen, with its 1673 canal and 18th-century houses.

Walking Tour: Kongens Nytorv to Langelinie

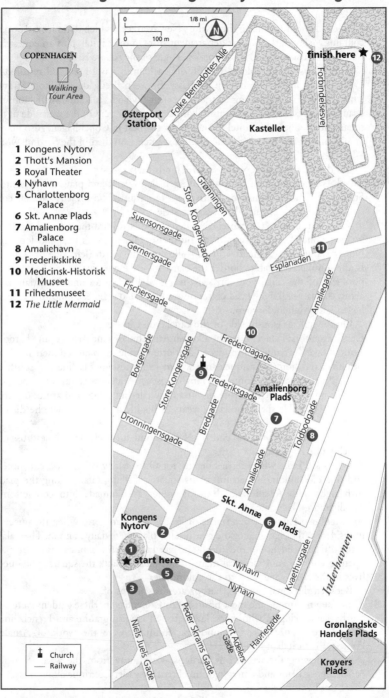

COPENHAGEN

Walking Tour Area

1 Kongens Nytorv
2 Thott's Mansion
3 Royal Theater
4 Nyhavn
5 Charlottenborg Palace
6 Skt. Annæ Plads
7 Amalienborg Palace
8 Amaliehavn
9 Frederikskirke
10 Medicinsk-Historisk Museet
11 Frihedsmuseet
12 The Little Mermaid

Østerport Station

Kastellet

finish here ★ 12

Store Kongensgade

Suensonsgade

Gernersgade

Fischersgade

Borgergade

Store Kongensgade

Dronningensgade

Folke Bernadottes Alle

Grønningen

Forbindelsesvej

Esplanaden

Amaliegade

Fredericiagade

10

9

Frederiksgade

Bredgade

Amalienborg Plads

7

8

Toldbodgade

Amaliegade

11

Kongens Nytorv

2

Skt. Annæ 6 Plads

1 ★ start here

4

5

Nyhavn

Nyhavn

3

Kvæsthusgade

Inderhavnen

Niels Juels Gade

Peder Skrams Gade

Cort Adelers Gade

Havnegade

Grønlandske Handels Plads

Krøyers Plads

✝ Church
— Railway

Begin at:

1. **Kongens Nytorv,** meaning the "King's New Market," which dates from 1680. It contains Magasin, the biggest department store in the capital, plus an equestrian statue of Christian IV. On the northeast side of the square is:

2. **Thott's Mansion,** completed in 1685 for a Danish naval hero and restored in 1760. It now houses the French Embassy. Between Bredgade and Store Strand-stræde, a little street angling to the right near Nyhavn, is Kanneworff House, a beautifully preserved private home that dates from 1782. On the west side of the square, at no. 34, is the Hotel d'Angleterre, the best in Copenhagen. Also here is an old anchor memorializing the Danish seamen who died in the Second World War.

On the southeast side of the square stands the:

3. **Royal Theater,** founded in 1748, where ballet, opera, and plays are presented. Statues of famous Danish dramatists are out front. The present theater, con-structed in 1874, is in neo-Renaissance style.

With your back to the Hotel d'Angleterre, walk toward the water along:

4. **Nyhavn,** once filled with maritime businesses and seamen's bars and lodgings. Nowadays, it's restaurant row. First, walk along the north (left) side of Nyhavn. In the summer, cafe tables border the canal, giving it a festive atmosphere. At the port end of the canal you can see the Naval Dockyards, and Christianshavn across the harbor. High-speed craft come and go all day here, connecting Copen-hagen with Malmö, Sweden.

On the quieter (south) side of the canal, you can see:

5. **Charlottenborg Palace,** now the Danish Academy of Fine Arts. A pure baroque work, it takes its name from Queen Charlotte Amalie, who moved there in 1700. Beautiful old homes, antiques shops, and more restaurants line the southern bank. Nyhavn was the home of Hans Christian Andersen at various times. He lived at no. 20, where he wrote his first fairy tales, in 1835, and at no. 67 from 1845 to 1864. He spent the last 2 years of his life at no. 18, where he died in 1875.

Walk back to the harbor end of Nyhavn and turn left onto Kvæsthusgade, which will take you to:

6. **Skt. Annæ Plads,** where ferries depart for Oslo. Many consulates, two hotels, and fine old buildings open onto this square. Walking inland along the plads, turn right onto Amaliegade. It leads under a colonnade into cobblestoned Amalienborg Plads, site of:

7. **Amalienborg Palace,** with a statue of Frederik V at its core. When the queen is in residence, the changing of the guard takes place here daily at noon. The palace is the official residence of the queen and her French prince, but sections of it are open to visitors. Four identical mansionlike palaces flank the square. The queen lives in the right wing, next to the colonnade.

Between the square and the harbor are the gardens of:

8. **Amaliehavn.** Among the most beautiful in Copenhagen, these gardens were laid out by Jean Delogne, who made lavish use of Danish granite and French lime-stone. The bronze pillars around the fountain were the work of Arnaldo Pomodoro, an Italian sculptor.

After viewing the waterfront gardens, walk away from the water, crossing Amalienborg Plads and emerging onto Frederiksgade. Continue along this short street until you reach:

9. **Frederikskirke** (no. 1), often called the Marmorkirken or "marble church." Construction began in 1740, but had to stop in 1770 because of the staggering

costs. The church wasn't completed until 1894—using Danish marble instead of more expensive Norwegian marble. The church was modeled on and intended to rival St. Peter's in Rome; indeed, it ended up with one of the largest church domes in Europe. Supported on a dozen towering piers, the dome has a diameter of 108 feet.

Facing the church, turn right and head north along Bredgade, passing at no. 22 the:

10. **Medicinsk-Historisk Museet (Medical History Museum).** The collection is gruesome, with aborted fetuses, dissected heads, and the like.

TAKE A BREAK   Before you approach *The Little Mermaid,* consider tea and a snack at **Café Lumskebugten,** Esplanaden 21 (☎ 33-15-60-29; see Chapter 3, "Introducing Copenhagen"). Dating from 1854, this cafe offers a cold plate served throughout the afternoon. There are five specialties: beef tartare, fish cakes with mustard sauce, marinated salmon, baked cod, and shrimp.

Bredgade ends at Esplanaden, which opens onto Churchillparken, a green belt bordering the water. Turn right and walk along Esplanaden until you come to the:

11. **Frihedsmuseet,** Churchillparken. The Danish Resistance museum commemorates the struggle against the Nazis from 1940 to 1945 (see listing above in "Amalienborg Palace & Environs").

After leaving the museum, walk toward the water along Langelinie where signs point the way to:

12. **The Little Mermaid.** Perched on rocks just off the harbor bank, *Den Lille Havfrue,* the most photographed statue in Scandinavia, dates from 1913. The bronze figure, by Edvard Eriksen, was modeled after the figure of prima ballerina Ellen Price. In time, this much-attacked and abused statue became the symbol of Copenhagen.

14 Organized Tours

BUS & BOAT TOURS   The boat and bus sightseeing tours in Copenhagen range from get-acquainted jaunts to in-depth excursions. Either of the following tours can be arranged through **Copenhagen Excursions** (☎ 32-54-06-06) or **Vikingbus** (☎ 31-57-26-00). Inexpensive bus tours depart from the *lur* (horn) blowers' statue at Town Hall Square, and boat trips leave from Gammel Strand (the fish market) or Nyhavn.

For orientation, hop on a bus for the **1½-hour City Tour,** which covers major scenic highlights like *The Little Mermaid,* Rosenborg Castle, and Amalienborg Palace. Monday through Friday, tours also visit the Carlsberg Brewery, which adds 1 hour to the time if you choose to continue.

Tours depart from Rådhuspladsen daily at 1pm from May 30 to September 13. They cost 130 DKK ($16.25) for adults, 65 DKK ($8.15) for children.

We heartily recommend the **City and Harbor Tour,** a 2½-hour trip by launch and bus that departs from Town Hall Square. The tour gives you a wonderful overview of the cityscape in relation to the sea. The boat tours the city's main canals, passing *The Little Mermaid* and the Old Fish Market. It operates May 30 to September 13, daily at 1pm. It costs 175 DKK ($21.90) for adults, 90 DKK ($11.25) for children.

Shakespeare buffs may be interested in an afternoon excursion to the castles of North Zealand. The 7-hour tour explores the area north of Copenhagen, including Kronborg (Hamlet's castle), a brief visit to Fredensborg, the queen's residence, and a stopover at Frederiksborg Castle and the National Historical Museum. Tours depart from Town Hall Square. They run May 2 to October 16, Wednesday, Saturday, and Sunday at 10:15am. The cost is 335 DKK ($41.90) for adults, half price for children.

For more information about these tours and the most convenient place to buy tickets in advance, call **Vikingbus** or **Copenhagen Excursions.**

GUIDED WALKS THROUGH COPENHAGEN   Staff members of the Copenhagen Tourist Information Office conduct 2-hour guided walking tours of the city Monday to Saturday at 10:30am, between May and September. The price is 80 DKK ($10) for adults, 25 DKK ($3.15) for children. For information, contact the **Copenhagen Tourist Information Center,** Bernstorffsgade 1 (☎ **33-25-38-44** or 32-97-14-40; www.woco.dk).

A VISIT TO COPENHAGEN'S MOST FAMOUS BREWERY   Carlsberg is the most famous beer in Denmark, and associated with many of the good times you're likely to have within that country. You can take a self-guided tour of the factory that turns out 3 million bottles of beer a day, walking around an observation gallery whose English-language signs explain the brewery process and why Carlsberg does it so well. The factory is open for visits Monday to Friday from 10am to 4pm. Entrance is free, and each visitor is given a quota of one free beer at the end of the tour, with the option of buying more at the pub that's on-site. The entrance to the factory is prefaced with a pair of sculpted elephants, each with armored regalia that includes a swastika. That doesn't mean the company was a Nazi sympathizer—Carlsberg used the symbol as part of its image long before Hitler. Take bus no. 6 from Rådhuspladsen to **Carlsberg Brewery,** Ny Carlsberg Vej 140 (☎ **33-27-13-14**).

15 Active Sports

BICYCLING   The absence of hills and the abundance of parks and wide avenues with bicycle lanes make cycling the best way to explore Copenhagen. Bike-rental shops and stands are scattered throughout the city. Two suggestions are **Københavns Cyker,** Reventlowsgade 11 (☎ **33-33-86-13**), and **Dan Wheel,** Colbjørnsensgade 3 (☎ **33-21-22-27**).

FITNESS   Form & Fitness, Øster Allé 42E (☎ **35-55-00-78**), offers a day pass for 75 DKK ($9.40). Aerobics, weights, and fitness machines are available Monday to Thursday from 6:30am to 9:30pm, Friday 6:30am to 8pm, Saturday and Sunday 8am to 5pm.

GOLF   Denmark's best-known golf course, and one of its most challenging, is at the **Rungsted Golf Klub,** Vestre Stationsvej 16 (☎ **45-86-34-14**). It's in the heart of Denmark's "Whisky Trail," a string of upper-crust homes and mansions known for their allure to retirees, about 13 miles north of Copenhagen. Golfers visit from around the world. Some degree of competence is required, so beginners and intermediate golfers might want to hold off. If you're an advanced golfer, call for information and to arrange a tee time. Greens fees run 375 and 425 DKK ($46.90 and $53.15) for a full day's use of the club's 18 holes. To play, you must present evidence of a 20 handicap on Saturday and Sunday, or 25 on weekdays. With advance notice, you can rent clubs for 250 DKK ($31.25). The course is closed between November and March. No carts are allowed on the ecologically fragile course.

JOGGING   The many parks (known to many locals as "green lungs") of Copenhagen provide endless routes for joggers. Our favorite, just west of the city center, circles Lakes Sortedams, St. Jorgens, and Peblinge. The paths that wind through the Frederiksborg gardens are also well suited for joggers.

SWIMMING   Swimming is a favorite Danish pastime. The **Frederiksborg Svømmehal,** Helgesvej 29 (☎ **38-14-04-04**), is open to the public Monday to Friday from 8am to 8pm, Saturday 8am to 2pm, Sunday 9:30am to 2:15pm. Tickets cost 30 DKK ($3.75). You can also try **Sundby Swimming-pool,** Sundbyvestervej 50 (☎ **32-58-55-68**); **Kildeskovshallen,** Adolphsvej 25 (☎ **39-68-28-22**); or **Vesterbro Swimming Baths,** Angelgade 4 (☎ **31-22-05-00**).

TENNIS   Visitors usually pay a large supplement to play tennis at hotels and clubs in Copenhagen. There's a high hourly rate, and courts must be reserved in advance. Indoor courts may be rented at the **Hotel Mercur,** Vester Farimagsgade 17 (☎ **33-12-57-11**); visitors pay 130 DKK ($16.25) for the first hour, 100 DKK ($12.50) for each additional hour. Another club is **Københavns Boldklub,** Peter Nagsvej 147 (☎ **38-71-41-80**).

16 The Shopping Scene

Copenhagen is in the vanguard of shopping in Europe, and much of the action takes place on **Strøget,** the pedestrian street in the heart of the capital. Strøget begins as Frederiksberggade, north of Rådhuspladsen, and winds to Østergade, which opens onto Kongens Nytorv. The jam-packed street is lined with stores selling everything from porcelain statues of *Youthful Boldness* to Greenland shrimp to Kay Bojesen's teak monkeys.

Between stops, relax with a drink at an outdoor cafe, or just sit on a bench and watch the crowds.

In two nearby walking areas—**Gråbødretorv** and **Fiolstræde**—you can browse through antiques shops and bookstores.

Bredgade, beginning at Kongens Nytorv, is the antiques district. Prices tend to be very high. **Læderstræde** is another shopping street that competes with Bredgade in antiques.

BEST BUYS   In a country famed for its designers and craftspeople, the best buys are in stainless steel, porcelain, china, glassware, toys—especially Kay Bojesen's wooden animals—functionally designed furniture, textiles, and jewelry (decorative, silver, and semiprecious stones).

STORE HOURS   In general, shopping hours are 9:30 or 10am to 5:30pm Monday to Thursday, until 7 or 8pm on Friday, and until 2pm on Saturday. Most shops are closed Sunday, except the kiosks and supermarket at the Central Railroad Station. Here you can purchase food until 10pm or midnight. The Central Railroad Station's bakery is open until 9pm, and one of the kiosks at Rådhuspladsen, which sells papers, film, and souvenirs, is open 24 hours.

SHIPPING IT HOME & RECOVERING VAT   Denmark imposes a 25% tax on goods and services, a "value-added tax" known in Denmark as *moms* (pronounced "mumps"). Tax-free exports are possible. Many stores will mail goods to your home so you can avoid paying the tax. If you want to take your purchases, look for shops displaying Danish tax-free shopping notices. Such shops offer tourists tax refunds for personal export. This refund applies to purchases of over 300 DKK ($37.50) for visitors from the United States and Canada—spent at the same store, but not necessarily all at once. For more information, see "Taxes" in "Fast Facts: Denmark," in Chapter 2, "Planning a Trip to Denmark." For answers to tax-refund questions, call **Global Refund** (☎ **32-52-55-66**).

SHOPPING A TO Z

AMBER

The Amber Specialist. Frederiksberggade 28. ☎ **33-11-88-03.** Bus: 28, 29, or 41.

The owners, known to customers as the "Amber Twins," deal in "the gold of the north." This petrified resin originated in the large coniferous forests that covered Denmark some 35 million years ago. The forests disappeared, but the amber remained, and is now used to create handsome jewelry.

ART GALLERIES & AUCTION HOUSES

Bruun Rasmussen Auctioneers of Fine Arts. Bredgade 33. ☎ **33-13-69-11.** Bus: 1, 6, 9, or 10.

Established shortly after the Second World War, this is Denmark's leading auction house. July is usually quiet, although the premises remain open for appraisals and purchases. The season begins in August, with an auction of paintings and fine art. Viewing time is allowed before auctions, which take place about once a month. There are also auctions of modern art, wine, coins, books, manuscripts, and antique weapons.

Galerie Asbaek. Bredgade 20. ☎ **33-15-40-04.** Bus: 1, 6, 9, 10, 28, 29, or 41.

This modern-art gallery has a permanent exhibit of the best local artists, along with changing shows by Scandinavian and foreign artists. There's a bookshop and a cafe that serves French-inspired Danish food. Graphics and posters are for sale.

Kunsthallens Kunstauktioner. Gothersgade 9. ☎ **33-32-52-00.** Bus: 1, 6, 9, or 10.

Established in 1926, this is Europe's leading dealer in the pan-European school of painting known as COBRA (an acronym for Copenhagen, Brussels, and Amsterdam, where the artists originated). These works, produced from 1948 to 1951, were an important precursor of abstract expressionism. The gallery holds 12 auctions yearly, 8 with modern art; the others concentrate on the 19th century.

BOOKS

Boghallen. Rådhuspladsen 37. ☎ **33-11-85-11.** Bus: 2, 8, or 30.

This big store at Town Hall Square carries many books in English, as well as a wide selection of travel related literature, including maps. It stocks books in English on Danish themes, such as the collected works of Hans Christian Andersen.

DEPARTMENT STORES

Illum. Østergade 52. ☎ **33-14-40-02.** Bus: 1, 6, 9, or 10.

One of Denmark's top department stores, Illum is on Strøget. Take time to browse through its vast store of Danish and Scandinavian design. There's a restaurant and a special export cash desk at street level.

✪ **Magasin.** Kongens Nytorv 13. ☎ **33-11-44-33.** Bus: 1, 6, 9, or 10.

An elegant department store, Magasin is the biggest in Scandinavia. It offers a complete assortment of Danish designer fashion, a large selection of glass and porcelain, and souvenirs. Goods are shipped abroad tax-free.

FASHIONS

Sweater Market. Frederiksberggade 15. ☎ **33-15-27-73.** Bus: 2, 8, or 30.

Take your pick from top-grade Scandinavian and Icelandic cardigans, pullovers, hats, scarves, and mittens, hand-knit in Denmark of 100% wool. There's also a large selection of Icelandic wool jackets and coats.

FLEA MARKETS

Det Blå Pakhus. Holmbladsgade 113. ☎ **32-95-17-07.** Bus: 5 or 37.

The motto of "The Blue Warehouse," Copenhagen's largest indoor marketplace with 325 booths, is that you can find "everything between heaven and earth here," and that's probably right; at the very least it includes secondhand furniture, antiques, carpets, and assorted bric-a-brac. It is open Saturday and Sunday from 10am to 5pm. The entrance fee is 10 DKK ($1.25).

GLASSWARE, PORCELAIN & CRYSTAL

Danborg. Holbergsgade 17. ☎ **33-32-93-94.** Bus: 1, 6, or 9.

Behind the Royal Theater, this shop offers a large selection of Flora Danica porcelain at reduced prices. It specializes in antique quality Georg Jensen objects, and you can sometimes save up to 50% on Georg Jensen estate silver. It also carries exquisite jewelry.

Holmegaards Glasværker. In the Royal Copenhagen retail center, Amagertorv 6 (Strøget). ☎ **33-12-44-77.** Bus: 1, 6, 8, 9, or 10.

This is Denmark's most famous and visible producer of glasswork, with a pedigree that extends back at least 200 years, and a series of elegant products that have graced the table settings of politicians and aristocrats for generations. Look for reissues of famous patterns of the past, including "Wellington," dedicated to English military hero, the Duke of Wellington, an 1859 pattern recently re-released to a small but select audience.

Rosenthal Studio-Haus. Frederiksberggade 21. ☎ **33-14-21-01.** Bus: 28, 29, or 41.

You'll find an array of ceramic works here, especially by well-known Danish artist Bjørn Wiinblad, whose figures we find whimsical and delightful. You can also get good buys on Orrefors crystal, including some stunning bowls. The sculptural reliefs, handmade in lead crystal, range from miniatures to giant animals in limited world editions of 199 pieces. They often depict the animals of the far north.

✪ Royal Copenhagen Porcelain. In the Royal Scandinavia retail center, Amagertorv 6 (Strøget). ☎ **33-13-71-81.** Bus: 1, 2, 6, 8, 28, 29, or 41 for the retail outlet; 1 or 14 for the factory.

Royal Copenhagen's trademark, three wavy blue lines, has come to symbolize quality in porcelain throughout the world. Founded in 1775, the factory was a royal possession before passing into private hands in 1868. Royal Copenhagen's Christmas plates—an annual release since 1908—are collectors' items. Most of the motifs depict the Danish countryside in winter. On the top floor is a huge selection of seconds, and unless you're an expert, you probably can't tell the difference.

In this location are various porcelain and silver retailers, as well as the Royal Copenhagen Antiques shop. It specializes in buying and selling antique Georg Jensen, Royal Copenhagen, Bing & Grøndahl porcelain, and Michelson Christmas spoons.

Anyone who's interested in the laborious processes whereby Denmark's most famous porcelain is made is welcome to tour the **Royal Copenhagen factory,** Smallegade 45 (☎ **38-14-48-48**). Set within a 15-minute drive east of Copenhagen's center, it's accessible with bus 1 or 14. You must call ahead to reserve a spot within one of the hour-long tours, priced at 25 DKK ($3.15) per person. They're conducted Monday to Friday at 9am, 10am, 11am, 1pm, and 2pm. There's a sales outlet on the premises, selling basically the same inventories that are available at the organization's more glamorous main showroom at Amagertorv 6.

HOME FURNISHINGS

☉ Illums Bolighus. Amagertorv 10 (Strøget). ☎ **33-14-19-41.** Bus: 28, 29, or 41.

A center for modern Scandinavian and Danish design, this is one of Europe's finest showcases for household furnishings and accessories. It stocks furniture, lamps, rugs, textiles, bedding, glassware, kitchenware, flatware, china, jewelry, and ceramics. The store also sells women's and men's clothes and accessories. There's a gift shop, too.

Lysberg, Hansen & Therp. Bredgade 3. ☎ **33-14-47-87.** Bus: 1, 6, 9, or 10.

This major interior-decorating center offers fabrics, carpets, and furniture. The model apartments are furnished in impeccable taste. The company manufactures its own furniture in traditional design and imports fabrics, usually from Germany or France. The gift shop has many hard-to-find creations.

☉ Paustian. Kalkbrænderiløbskaj 2. ☎ **39-16-65-65.** S-tog: Nordhavn.

Copenhagen's leading furniture showroom, in the somewhat distant industrial Nordhavn section, will ship anywhere in the world. The finest of Scandinavian design is on display, along with reproductions of the classics. There's a well-recommended adjoining restaurant.

JEWELRY

Hartmann's Selected Estate Silver & Jewelry. Bredgade 4. ☎ **33/33-09-63.** Bus: 1, 6, 9, or 10.

This shop buys secondhand silver and jewelry from old estates and sells them at reduced prices. Sometimes it's possible to purchase heirloom Georg Jensen estate silver. Ulrik Hartmann, the store's owner, launched his career as a 10-year-old trading at a local flea market. The shop is near Kongens Nytorv. While in the neighborhood, you can walk for hours, exploring the various auctioneering rooms, jewelry shops, and nearby art galleries.

Kaere Ven. 14–16 Bredgade. ☎ **33-11-43-15.** Bus: 1, 6, 9, or 10.

One of the city's oldest diamond dealers, in business for more than 100 years, this outlet claims to offer "prices from another century." That's a bit of an exaggeration but you can often find bargains here in antique jewelry, even old Georg Jensen silver. An array of rings, earrings, necklaces, and bracelets is sold, along with other items. A few items in the store are sold at 50% off competitive prices but you have to shop carefully for those and know what you're buying.

MUSIC

Axel Musik. In Scala Center (1st floor), Axeltorv 2. ☎ **33-14-05-50.** Bus: 1, 6, or 8.

One of the best-stocked music stores in the Danish capital, Axel also has a newer branch in the city's main railway station.

NEEDLEWORK

Eva Rosenstand A/S—Clara Wæver. Østergade 42. ☎ **33-13-29-40.** Bus: 1, 6, 9, or 10.

You'll find Danish-designed cross-stitch embroideries here. The materials are usually linen in medium or coarser grades, but cotton is also available. The admission-free needlework museum is the only one of its kind in Europe.

SHOPPING CENTERS

For excellent buys in Scandinavian merchandise, as well as tax-free goods, we recommend the **shopping center at the airport.** The prices cannot be higher than those downtown, and there's a VAT-refund office nearby.

Bolten's. Store Kongensgade 5/Gothersgade 8. ☎ **33-32-44-44.** Bus: 1, 6, or 9.

Near Kongens Nytorv and the Hotel d'Angleterre, the small-scale development incorporates private offices and apartments, a series of traffic-free interior courtyards filled with flowers, and a handful of shops, restaurants, and cafes. The half-dozen shops on the site usually sell private-label merchandise, including children's clothing, lacy undergarments, hats, and shoes. On the premises are two discos (the Kitsch and X-Ray Underground), a theater that stages comedy acts and satire, and scattered gallery space (some of it underground) for modern art. There's also a ticket kiosk where you can arrange bookings for cultural events throughout Copenhagen.

SILVER

✪ **Georg Jensen.** In the Royal Scandinavia retail center, Amagertorv 4 (Strøget). ☎ **33-11-40-80.** Bus: 1, 6, 8, 9, or 10.

Legendary Georg Jensen is known for its fine silver. For the connoisseur, there's no better address—the store displays the largest and best collection of Jensen holloware in Europe. Gold and silver jewelry in traditional and modern Danish designs are also featured.

VIKING JEWELRY

Museums Kopi Smykker. Frederiksberggade 2. ☎ **33-32-63-60.** Bus: 28, 29, or 41.

This shop sells museum jewelry reproductions, all copies of adornments found in Scandinavia, the Baltic region, Germany, Britain, and the Netherlands. The jewelry covers a wide range of periods, including the Bronze and the Iron Ages, although the hottest selling items are from the Viking era. It's cast and handcrafted at Vissenbjerg on the island of Funen. The jewelry—often copies of pieces on display in the National and other major museums—is made in bronze, sterling silver, and gold-plated sterling, and also comes in 8- and 14-karat gold.

17 Copenhagen After Dark

Danes really know how to party. A good night means a late night, and on warm weekends, hundreds of rowdy revelers crowd Strøget until sunrise. Merrymaking in Copenhagen is not just for the younger crowd; jazz clubs, traditional beer houses, and wine cellars are routinely packed with people of all ages. The city has a more serious cultural side as well, exemplified by excellent theater, opera, ballet, and one of the best circuses in Europe.

To find out what's happening at the time of your visit, pick up a free copy of *Copenhagen This Week* at the tourist information center. Ignore the "Copenhagen by Night" section, which usually focuses on women advertising themselves as companions for visiting males. The "Events Calendar" has a week-by-week roundup of the most interesting entertainment and sightseeing events.

TIVOLI GARDENS

In the center of the gardens, the large **open-air stage** books vaudeville acts (tumbling clowns, acrobats, aerialists) who perform daily at 7 and 10:30pm, and also on Saturday at 5pm. Spectators must enter through the turnstiles to get seats, but there's an unobstructed view from outside if you'd rather stand. Special arrangements with jazz, beat, and folklore groups are made during the season. Admission is free.

Near the Vesterbrogade 3 entrance, the 150-year-old outdoor **Pantomime Theater,** with a Chinese stage and peacock curtain, presents shows Tuesday to Sunday at 6:15 and 8:30pm. The repertory consists of 16 *commedia dell'arte* productions with the entertaining trio of Pierrot, Columbine, and Harlequin—authentic pantomimes that have been performed continuously in Copenhagen since 1844. Admission is free.

The modern **Tivolis Koncertsal** (concert hall) is a great place to hear talented artists led by equally famous conductors. Inaugurated in 1956, the concert hall can seat 2,000, and its season—which runs for more than 4 months, beginning in late April—has been called "the most extensive music festival in the world." Performances of everything from symphony to opera are presented Monday to Saturday at 7pm, and sometimes at 9pm, depending on the event. Good seats are available at prices ranging from 200 to 400 DKK ($25 to $50) when major artists are performing, but most performances are free. Tickets are sold at the main booking office on Vesterbrogade 3 (☎ 33-15-10-12).

Tivoli Glassalen (☎ 33-15-10-12) is housed in an octagonal gazebolike century-old building with a glass, gilt-capped canopy. Shows here are often comedic or satirical performances by Danish comedians in Danish, and they usually don't interest non-Danish audiences. But there are also musical revues. Call for the unpredictable schedule. Tickets cost 205 to 240 DKK ($25.65 to $30).

THE PERFORMING ARTS

For **discount seats** (sometimes as much as 50% off the regular price), go in person to a ticket kiosk across from the Nørreport train station, at the corner of Fiolstræde and Nørre Voldgade. Discount tickets are sold only on the day of the performance and may be purchased Monday to Friday from noon to 5pm, Saturday noon to 3pm.

○ **Det Kongelige Teater (Royal Theater).** Kongens Nytorv. ☎ 33-69-69-69. Tickets 60–600 DKK ($7.50–$75); half-price for seniors (over 66) and young people (under 26). Bus: 1, 6, 9, or 10.

A major winter cultural event in Copenhagen is a performance by the world-renowned **Royal Danish Ballet** or **Royal Danish Opera.** Because the arts are state subsidized, ticket prices are comparatively low. Some seats may be available at the box office the day before a performance. The season runs from August to May.

THE CLUB & MUSIC SCENE
JAZZ, ROCK & BLUES

Copenhagen JazzHouse. Niels Hemmingsensgade 10. ☎ 33-15-26-00. Cover 40–70 DKK ($5–$8.75) for live music. Bus: 10.

This place plays host to more non-Danish jazz artists (U.S., Britain, Germany, Africa) than just about any other jazz bar in town. Shows begin relatively early, at around 8:30pm, and usually finish reasonably early. Around midnight on Thursday, Friday, and Saturday, the venue shifts from a live concert hall into a disco. It's closed Monday; otherwise, the ever-changing schedule depends on the bands' agendas.

La Fontaine. Kompagnistræde 11. ☎ 33-11-60-98. Cover 45 DKK ($5.65) Fri–Sat only. Bus: 5 or 10.

This is the kind of place your parents might have considered a "dive," but it's the kind of dive that—if you meet the right conversational partner, or if you groove with the music—can be a lot of fun. Small, and cozy to the point of being cramped, it's a bordeaux-colored womb whose decor hasn't changed much since the 1950s. It's a bar Tuesday to Saturday from 8pm till 6 or even 8am. Sunday hours are 9pm to 1:30am. There's live music on Friday and Saturday, when free-form jazz artists hold court beginning at around 11:30pm.

Mojo Blues Bar. Løngangsstræde 21C. ☎ **33-11-64-53.** Cover 50 DKK ($6.25) Fri–Sat only. Bus: 2, 8, or 30.

Mojo is a candlelit drinking spot that offers blues music, mostly performed by Scandinavian groups. It's open daily from 8pm to 5am.

DANCE CLUBS

Baron & Baroness. Vesterbrogade 2E. ☎ **33-16-01-01.** Cover 50 DKK ($6.25) for disco. Bus: 250E or 350E.

A short walk from the Tivoli, this is a relatively upscale nightclub with faux-medieval decor. It attracts a crowd that's a bit more prosperous and mature than nearby competitors that cater to teenagers. It's really best for dancing, but dinner is available at about 150 to 250 DKK ($18.75 to $31.25). The bars are open nightly from 6pm till at least 3am; the restaurant, 6pm to 11pm. The disco, which is featured one floor above the street-level restaurant, plays only Thursday to Saturday, from 10pm till dawn. On nights when there's no disco, you'll find a solo musician.

Den Røde Pimpernel. H. C. Andersens Blvd. 7 (near Rådhuspladsen). ☎ **33-12-20-32.** Cover 50 DKK ($6.25) Fri–Sat only. Bus: 2, 8, or 30.

The lively, clublike atmosphere of "The Scarlet Pimpernel" makes it a good place for dancing. If you can withstand the scrutiny, you'll be admitted after being inspected through a peephole. A live band plays dance music. It's open Tuesday to Saturday from 9pm to 8am. A beer will set you back 30 DKK ($3.75), and mixed drinks cost 45 to 50 DKK ($5.65 to $6.25).

Enzo. Nørregade 41. ☎ **33-13-67-88.** Cover 60 DKK ($7.50). S-tog: Nørreport Station.

Few other nightclubs in Copenhagen offer as many bars. In this case, each has a different theme, ranging from plush intimate hideaways to more Spartan stand-up affairs where patrons compete elbow-to-elbow on how fast they can throw back a shot of liquor. Come here for an all-around introduction to Copenhagen's night owls, then gravitate to either the Couch Lounge (where cozy tuckaway sites are pre-reserved); the Cigar Lounge; a disco dance bar; a Water Bar (where, despite its name, you can still get a drink of whiskey); and the Shot Bar that boasts a comprehensive collection of tequilas, exotic rums, and vodkas. It's open to the public only on Friday and Saturday; the rest of the week it's reserved for private parties.

NASA. Gothersgade 8F, Bolthensgaard. ☎ **33-93-74-15.** Cover 100 DKK ($12.50) for nonmembers. Bus: 1, 6, or 9.

Its name has changed several times in the past decade, but even so, this is the most posh and prestigious of three nightclubs that occupy three floors of the same building. The late-night crowd of 25- to 40-year-olds includes many avid fans of whatever musical innovation has just emerged in London or Los Angeles. The decorative theme includes lots of white, lots of mirrors, and lots of artfully directed spotlights. Don't be surprised to see a room full of expensively, albeit casually dressed Danes chattering away in a cacophony of different languages. Technically, the site is a private club, but polite and presentable newcomers can usually gain access. It's open Thursday to Sunday from 10pm to 6am.

Rosie McGee's. Vesterbrogade 2A. ☎ **33-32-19-23.** Cover 40 DKK ($5) on disco nights only. Bus: 250E or 350E.

Across the boulevard from the Tivoli, this is a funky, American-style nightclub that caters to high-energy Generation X-ers. Lots of teeny-boppers come here to mingle, compare notes, and dance, dance, dance. The simple restaurant serves mostly Mexican food and frothy, foamy drinks. The bars and restaurant open nightly at 5:30pm, with disco featured every Thursday to Saturday from 11:30pm till dawn.

Rust. Guldbergsgade 8. ☎ **35-24-52-00.** Cover 20–40 DKK ($2.50–$5) Wed–Sat only. Bus: 5 or 6.

Rust sprawls over a one-story setting in the Nørrebro district. It combines a restaurant, several hopping bars, a dance floor, and a stage where live musicians perform every Tuesday at around 9pm. Meals are served Monday to Saturday from 5:30pm to around midnight, and things get going on the dance floor after 9:30pm. The setting is dark and shadowy. There are seats, but none so comfortable that you'll opt to remain in one place for too long. No one under 21 is admitted, and you'll spot very few people over 45. Rust is open from 5:30pm to at least 2am Monday to Saturday.

Subsonic. Skindergade 45. ☎ **33-13-26-25.** Cover 50 DKK ($6.25). Bus: 1 or 6.

Thanks to an armada of designers who developed it, this self-proclaimed "Design Disco" has an interior that's more artfully outfitted than that of any other competitor in Copenhagen. Expect lots of post-modern gloss, references to the California rave movement, an occasional emphasis on dance music of the 1980s, a small corner outfitted like a cozy beer hall, and a clientele that seems familiar with the music and ambience of some very hip clubs in Europe and the U.S. Part of its interior was copied directly from the waiting room of a 1970s Scandinavian airport, complete with the then-innovative streamlined design that's been associated with Denmark ever since. It's open Friday and Saturday from 11pm till at least 5:30am.

THE BAR SCENE
PUBS

Det Lille Apotek. Stor Kannikestraede 15. ☎ **33-12-56-06.** Bus: 2, 5, 8, or 30.

This is a good spot for English-speaking foreign students to meet their Danish contemporaries. The menu varies, but keep an eye out for the prawn cocktail and tenderloin, which are highly recommended. Main courses run about 88 to 128 DKK ($11 to $16), and a beer costs 16 to 32 DKK ($2 to $4). It's open daily from 11am to midnight; closed December 24 to 26.

Drop Inn. Kompagnistræde 34. ☎ **33-11-24-04.** Bus: 28, 29, or 41.

This is not a disco, but it does offer live, iconoclastic bands who perform for patrons in their late teens and twenties. The room combines antique and modern oil paintings and a long bar. It's open daily from 11pm to 5am. Beer starts at 20 DKK ($2.50).

✪ **Library Bar.** In the Hotel Plaza, Bernstorffsgade 4. ☎ **33-14-15-19.** Bus: 6.

Malcolm Forbes once rated this place one of the top five bars in the world. Surrounded by antique books and art, you can order everything from cappuccino to cocktails. The setting is the lobby level of the landmark Plaza, commissioned in 1913 by Frederik VIII. The bar, which attracts celebrities and royalty, was originally the hotel's ballroom. The oversized mural of George Washington and his men dates from 1910. It's open Monday to Saturday from 11:30am to 1am, Sunday 11:30am to midnight. Beer costs 35 DKK ($4.40); drinks are 55 DKK ($6.90) and up.

Nyhavn 17. Nyhavn 17. ☎ **33-12-54-19.** Bus: 1, 6, 27, or 29.

This cafe is the last of the honky-tonks that made up the former sailors' quarter. It's a short walk from the patrician Kongens Nytorv and the luxury Hotel d'Angleterre. In the summer you can sit outside. It's open Sunday to Thursday from 10am to 2am, Friday and Saturday until 4am.

The Queen's Pub. In the Kong Frederik Hotel, Vester Voldgade 25. ☎ **33-12-59-02.** Bus: 1, 2, 6, 8, or 28.

Cozy, traditional, and rich in Baltic history, this is the kind of bar where a businessperson can feel at home after a transatlantic flight. The older members of the staff have served every politician and journalist in Denmark. On the ground floor of one of Copenhagen's most legendary (and discreet) hotels, it's open daily from 11:30am to 11:45pm. Beer costs 25 to 38 DKK ($3.15 to $4.75); drinks begin at 55 DKK ($6.90).

A WINE BAR

Hvids Vinstue. Kongens Nytorv 19. ☎ **33-15-10-64.** Bus: 1, 6, 9, or 10.

Built in 1670, this old wine cellar is a dimly lit safe haven for an eclectic crowd. Many patrons—theater-goers, actors, dancers—come from the Royal Theater across the way. It's open daily from 10am to 1am, but closed Sunday in July and August.

GAY & LESBIAN CLUBS

See chapter 3 for a recommendation of the **Sebastian Bar & Café,** Copenhagen's most popular gay restaurant which has also has a cruisy bar.

Cosy Bar. Studiestraede 24. ☎ **33-12-74-27.** Bus: 6 or 29.

It runs a fine line between a crowd that favors leather, and what you'd expect from a working crew of men performing manual labor down by the harborfront. Popular and cruisy, it's open daily from 11pm till 8am, dispensing ample amounts of schnapps and suds during the course of a working night.

The Men's Bar. Teglårdsstræde 3. ☎ **33-12-73-03.** Bus: 2, 8, or 30.

This is the only leather bar in town, filled with an unusual collection of uniforms, leather, and Levi's. Open daily from 3pm to 2am.

Pan Society. Knabrostræde 3. ☎ **33-11-37-84.** Cover 55 DKK ($6.90) for dance club. Bus: 28, 29, or 41.

This nationwide organization was established in 1948 for the protection and advancement of gay and lesbian rights. Its headquarters is a 19th-century yellow building off the Strøget. A dance club occupies three floors, and a modern cafe is on the ground level. Every night is gay night, although a lot of straights come here for the music. The cafe is open daily from 8pm to 5am. The dance club is open Sunday and Wednesday 11pm to 3am, Thursday 10pm to 4am, Friday and Saturday 10pm to 5am.

SLM (Scandinavia Leather Men) Club. Studiestraede 14. ☎ **33-32-01-06.** Bus: 6 or 29.

Set amid the densest concentration of gay bars in Denmark, just around the corner from the also recommended Men's Bar, this is technically a private club that caters to men interested in the way other men look and act in leather. Non-members visiting from other countries, if they're dressed properly, can usually pay 40 DKK ($5) for a temporary membership that will get them past the doorman. It's open Friday and Saturday nights only, from 10pm till at least 4am, and usually later.

GAMBLING

Casino Copenhagen. In the SAS Scandinavia Hotel, Amager Blvd. 70. ☎ **33-96-59-65.** Cover 80 DKK ($10); free for guests at any of Copenhagen's SAS hotels. Bus: 5, 11, 30, or 34.

The country's first fully licensed casino has operated in this first-class hotel since 1990. It offers popular games such as roulette, baccarat, punto banco, and blackjack, as well as slot machines. It's open daily from 2pm to 4am.

18 Side Trips from Copenhagen

BEACHES

The closest beach to Copenhagen is **Bellevue** (S-tog: Klampenborg), but the water is not recommended for swimming. If you want to take a dip at a sandy beach, ride the train or drive to the beaches at North Zealand—**Gilleleje, Hornbæk, Liseleje,** and **Tisvildeleje.** Although these are family beaches, minimum bathing attire is worn. To reach them, take the train to Helsingør and continue by bus. Or make connections by train to Hillerød and switch to a local train; check at the railroad station for details. If you drive, you may want to check out the discos at the little beach resort towns that dot the north coast of Zealand.

DRAGØR

3 miles S of Copenhagen's Kastrup Airport

This old seafaring town on the island of Amager is filled with well-preserved 18th-century cottages with steep red-tile or thatched roofs. Many are under the protection of the National Trust.

Dragør (pronounced *Drah*-wer) was a busy port on the herring-rich Baltic Sea in the early Middle Ages; when fishing fell off, it became just another sleepy little waterfront village. After 1520, Amager Island and its villages—Dragør and Store Magleby—were inhabited by the Dutch. They brought along their own customs, Low German language, and agricultural expertise, especially their love of bulb flowers. In Copenhagen you still see wooden-shoed Amager selling hyacinths, tulips, daffodils, and lilies in the streets.

ESSENTIALS

GETTING THERE   Take bus no. 30, 33, or 73E from Rådhuspladsen (Town Hall Square) in Copenhagen. It's a 35-minute trip.

SEEING THE SIGHTS

Amager Museum. Hovedgaden 4–12, Store Magleby. ☎ **32-53-93-07.** Admission 20 DKK ($2.50) adults, 10 DKK ($1.25) children. Apr–Sept, Wed–Sun noon–4pm; Oct–Mar, Wed and Sun noon–4pm. Bus: 30, 33, or 350S.

This museum outside Dragør holds a rich trove of historic treasures. The exhibits reveal the affluence the Amager Dutch achieved, with rich textiles, fine embroidery, and carved silver buckles and buttons. The rooms of a Dutch house are especially interesting, showing how the people decorated their homes and lived in comfort.

Dragør Museum. Havnepladsen 2–4. ☎ **32-53-41-06.** Admission 20 DKK ($2.50) adults, 10 DKK ($1.25) children. May–Sept, Tues–Fri 2–5pm, Sat–Sun and holidays noon–6pm. Closed Oct–Apr. Bus: 30, 33, or 350S.

The exhibits at this harborfront museum show how the Amager Dutch lived from prehistoric times to the 20th century. Pictures and artifacts illustrate farming, goose breeding, seafaring, fishing, ship piloting, and ship salvage.

WHERE TO STAY & DINE

Hotel Dragør Kro. Kongvejen 23, DK-2791 Dragør. ☎ **32-53-01-87.** Fax 32-53-00-53. Reservations recommended. Main courses 100–195 DKK ($12.50–$24.40); 3-course fixed-price menu 115–230 DKK ($14.40–$28.75). AE, DC, MC, V. Winter, daily noon–9:30pm; summer, daily noon–10:30pm. Closed Dec 22–Jan 15. Bus: 30, 33, or 73E. DANISH/FRENCH.

This beautiful *kro* (inn) has one of the oldest continuously operated restaurants in Denmark. The building dates from 1650, and the inn was established in 1721, with

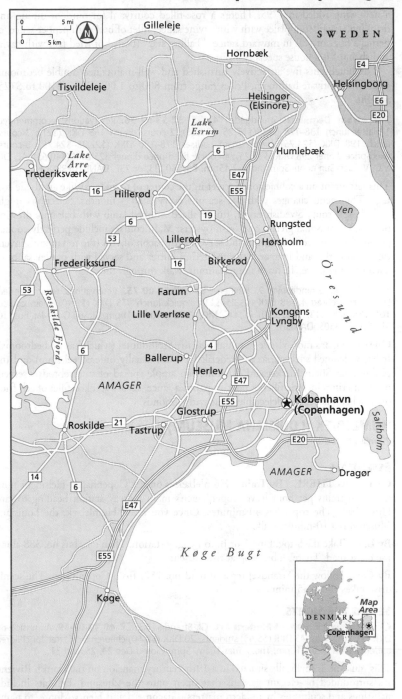

0   5 mi
0   5 km

Gilleleje

SWEDEN

Hornbæk

E4

Tisvildeleje

Helsingborg

E6

Helsingør
(Elsinore)

E20

*Lake
Esrum*

Humlebæk

6

*Lake
Arre*

E47

Frederiksværk

E55

Ven

16

Hillerød

19

6

Rungsted

53

Lillerød

Hørsholm

Frederikssund

16

Birkerød

Ö
r
e
s
u
n
d

53

Rosskilde Fjord

Farum

6

Lille Værløse

Kongens
Lyngby

4

Ballerup

Herlev

E47

AMAGER

E55

★ København
(Copenhagen)

Glostrup

Saltholm

Roskilde

21

Tastrup

E20

14

AMAGER

Dragør

6

E47

Køge Bugt

E55

Køge

*Map
Area*

DENMARK

Copenhagen

a new wing added in 1795. There's a rose-filled courtyard for outdoor dining and drinking. Try fillet of plaice with white-wine sauce, fillet of beef with pepper sauce, or perhaps fillet of veal in mustard sauce. "Falling star" (boiled or fried fish with caviar and shrimp) is a house specialty.

The hotel rents five attractively furnished and well-maintained double bedrooms, each with a private bathroom. Prices range from 800 to 1,000 DKK ($100 to $125) a night.

Restaurant Beghuset. Strandgade 14. ☎ **32-53-01-36.** Reservations recommended. 1-platter lunch 138–178 DKK ($17.25–$22.25); 2-course lunch 168 DKK ($21); 3-course lunch 198 DKK ($24.75); dinner main courses 178–198 DKK ($22.25–$24.75); 3-course fixed-price dinner 298 DKK ($37.25); 4-course fixed-price dinner 325 DKK ($40.65). AE, DC, MC, V. Tues–Sun noon–3pm and 6–9:45pm. Bus: 30, 33, or 73E. DANISH/FRENCH.

This restaurant on a cobblestoned street in the center of town looks like an idyllic cottage. The menu changes with the seasons every 2 to 3 months. Selections might include fish soup, Swedish caviar, thinly sliced smoked lamb with balsamic dressing on a bed of seasonal greens, and fresh oysters. Main courses include perfectly cooked guinea fowl braised in red wine and served with bacon of veal (the restaurant's invention) and herbs, and Dragør plaice roasted in butter and served with parsley sauce or bacon-thyme sauce. To reach the restaurant, walk through the cafe.

Strandhotel. Strandlinbyn 9, Havnen. ☎ **32-53-00-75.** Reservations recommended. Lunch smørrebrød 42–88 DKK ($5.25–$11); "quick lunch" 75 DKK ($9.40); main courses 105–188 DKK ($13.15–$23.50). AE, DC, MC, V. Daily 10am–10pm. Closed Oct–Mar. Bus: 30, 33, 73E, or 350S. DANISH.

One of Dragør's most visible restaurants is the Strandhotel (which has no bedrooms). It has welcomed such guests as Frederik III (who usually ordered eel soup) and the philosopher Sören Kierkegaard. At lunch an ample spread of smørrebrød is served; other offerings include fillet of pork in paprika sauce, savory smoked fillet of eel, fried or poached plaice, and delectable trout with almonds.

HUMLEBÆK (LOUISIANA MUSEUM)
20 miles N of Copenhagen

ESSENTIALS
GETTING THERE   By Train   Humlebæk is on the Copenhagen-Helsingør train line; two trains per hour leave Copenhagen's main railway station heading toward Humlebæk. The trip takes 40 minutes. Once you reach Humlebæk, the Louisiana Museum is a 10-minute walk.

By Bus   Take the S-tog, Line A or B, to Lyngby station. Then take bus no. 388 along the coast road. There's a bus stop at the museum.

By Car   Follow the Strandvej (coastal road no. 152) from Copenhagen. The scenic drive takes about 45 minutes.

SEEING THE SIGHTS
✪ **Louisiana Museum of Modern Art.** Gl. Strandvej 13. ☎ **49-19-07-19.** Admission 60 DKK ($7.50) adults, 45 DKK ($5.65) students, 20 DKK ($2.50) children 5–16, free for children under 5. Wed 10am–10pm, Thurs–Tues 10am–5pm. Closed Dec 24, 25, and 31.

This museum is idyllically situated in a 19th-century mansion on the Danish Riviera. It's surrounded by elegant gardens that open onto the Øresund. Exhibits include paintings and sculptures by modern masters (Giacometti and Henry Moore, to name two) as well as the best and most controversial works of modern art. Look especially for paintings by Carl-Henning Pedersen. The museum's name comes from the wives of the first owner of the estate, Alexander Brun—all three named Louise.

The museum has one of the largest exhibition spaces in Europe, and mounts major contemporary art shows. There is also a program of lectures, films, discussion with authors, and public debates. The concert series is known throughout Denmark. For children, there's the Børnehuset (children's house) and Søhaven (sea garden). The museum's cafe is on the famed terrace with Alexander Calder's playful sculptures.

WHERE TO DINE

Gamla Humlebæk Kro. Ny Strandvej 2A. ☎ **49-19-02-65**. Reservations recommended. Lunch main courses 45–115 DKK ($5.65–$14.40); dinner main courses 95–220 DKK ($11.90–$27.50). AE, CB, DC, DISC, MC, V. Daily 11:30am–9:30pm. DANISH.

This is the obvious luncheon choice for anyone visiting the Louisiana Museum, a short walk away. Built in 1722, the inn has a large dining room and three hideaway rooms. Selections include a range of open-faced sandwiches, deep-fried fillet of plaice with shrimp and mayonnaise sauce, Wiener schnitzel, medallions of veal with morel sauce, and herring with sherry sauce. The food is old-fashioned and satisfying.

HILLERØD

22 miles NW of Copenhagen

Hillerød offers some very interesting sights, including one of Scandinavia's most beautiful castles. The ideal time to visit Hillerød is for its summer Viking festival (see "A Special Event," below).

But there's always something of interest here, as Hillerød lies in the heart of North Zealand, surrounded by some of the most beautiful and extensive woodlands in Denmark.

The city's history goes back 4 centuries, although its status became really significant in 1602 when Christian IV began the construction of Frederiksborg Castle (see "Exploring the Town," below).

The wide forests around Hillerød remain as vestiges of the prehistoric North Zealand wilderness. To the south sprawls the woodlands of Store Dyrehave, and to the north stretch the forests of **Gribskov,** the second largest in the country. The forests today are still rich in game, notably the pale fawn-colored roe deer with no tail. Gribskov forest contains some 800 fallow deer distinguished by their white-speckled hide. The great philosopher, Sören Kierkegaard, regularly reveled in the tranquillity of these forests.

Leaflets outlining the best walks and trails to follow in Gribskov and Store Dyrehave are available at the tourist office (see "Visitor Information," below).

ESSENTIALS

GETTING THERE   By Train   The S-tog from Copenhagen arrives every 10 minutes throughout the day, taking 40 minutes. Trains also link Hillerød with Helsingør in the east, and there are also rail links with Gilleleje and Tisvildeleje.

By Bus   Hillerød also has good bus connections with the major towns of North Zealand: Bus 305 from Gilleleje, buses 306, 336, and 339 from Hornbæk, and buses 336 and 339 from Fredensborg.

By Car   Take Route 16 north from Copenhagen.

VISITOR INFORMATION   The **tourist office,** at Slotsgade 52 (☎ **48-24-26-26**), is open June to August, Monday to Saturday from 9am to 6pm; September to May, Monday to Saturday 9am to 4pm.

A SPECIAL EVENT   One of the most important Viking festivals in Scandinavia takes place every year near Hillerød. **Frederikssund** is a little town 8 miles southwest of Hillerød and 30 miles northwest of Copenhagen. It stages a 2-week ✪ **Viking festival** each summer where Nordic sagas are sometimes revived—and the record is set straight about who "discovered" America 5 centuries before Christopher Columbus. *Hamlet* is rarely performed anymore. Instead, a revolving series of plays, medieval and modern, concerning the Vikings, are what it's all about.

The festival begins in mid-June. The traditional play is performed nightly at 8pm, and a Viking banquet follows. Tickets for the festival are 100 DKK ($12.50) for adults, 25 DKK ($3.15) for children 5 to 12 (it's not suitable for children under 5). The dinner costs 130 DKK ($16.25) for adults, 75 DKK ($9.40) for children 5 to 12. Trains depart at 20-minute intervals from Copenhagen's Central Railroad Station for Frederikssund. Travel time is 50 minutes, and there are enough trains back to Copenhagen after the spectacle ends to allow commutes from the capital. From Frederikssund station, it's a 20-minute walk to the site of the pageant. For details, contact the Copenhagen tourist information office or phone the Frederikssund Tourist Office (☎ 47-31-06-85).

EXPLORING THE TOWN

✪ **Det Nationalhistoriske Museum på Frederiksborg.** In Frederiksborg Slot. ☎ **48-26-04-39.** Admission 45 DKK ($5.65) adults, 10 DKK ($1.25) children 6–15, free for children under 6. Nov–Mar, daily 11am–3pm; Apr and Oct, daily 10am–5pm. Bus: 701 from Hillerød Station.

This moated *slot* (castle), known as the Danish Versailles, is the major castle in Scandinavia, constructed on three islands in the castle lake. Like Kronborg, it was built in Dutch Renaissance style (red brick, copper roof, sandstone facade). The oldest parts date from 1560 and the reign of Frederik II. However, the main part of the castle was erected by his son, Christian IV, from 1600 to 1620. The castle was used by Danish monarchs for some 2 centuries. From 1671 to 1840 Danish kings were crowned in Christian IV's chapel, which is used to this day as a parish church. Since 1693 it has been a chapel for the knights of the Order of the Elephant and of the Grand Cross of Danneborg. Standing in the gallery is an old organ built by Esaias Compenius in 1610. Every Thursday from 1:30 to 2pm, the chapel organist plays for museum guests. In 1859 the castle was ravaged by fire, but it has been restored.

Since 1878 the Museum of National History has been housed at the castle. Founded by the brewer J.C. Jacobsen as a special department of the Carlsberg Foundation, it encompasses the Great Hall and the former Audience Chamber of Danish monarchs. The museum contains the most important collection of portraits and historical paintings in the country. The collection, organized on a chronological basis, illustrates Danish history from the 16th century until today. The modern collection covering the 20th century was added on the third floor in 1993.

To reach the castle, it's a 15-minute walk from the train station or a short taxi ride.

✪ **Frederiksborg Castle Garden.** Rendelæggerbakken 3. ☎ **42-26-02-62.** Free admission. May–Aug, daily 10am–9pm; Sept and Apr, daily 10am–7pm; Oct–Mar, daily 10am–5pm; Nov–Feb, daily 10am–4pm. Bus: 701 from Hillerød Station.

In the beginning of the 18th century, this baroque garden, laid out by Frederik IV north of the castle, became one of the finest in the country. The royal architect and landscape designer, Johan Cornelius Krieger, was responsible for its actual look.

The gardens were built around a central axis, creating continuity between building, garden, and the open land. Along the main axis, a cascade was built with water canals and fountains. Symmetrically surrounding the cascades were avenues, *bosquets* (thickets), and *parterres* (ornamental gardens arranged in patterns) sporting royal monograms. The parterre was planted with box hedges exactly as King Frederik had seen similar gardens arranged in France and Italy. The garden existed for 40 years, having enjoyed the patronage of three kings, Frederik IV, Christian VI, and Frederik V.

The last remains of the cascade were removed during the reign of Christian VII (1766–1808), presumably because the garden had grown out of style and become too expensive to maintain. In 1993, all that remained of the original baroque garden was the terraced ground, avenues in decay, and deformed box hedges.

Finally, the baroque garden was re-created when funds became available, and it was inaugurated on June 5, 1996. As many as 65,000 box plants and 166 pyramid-shaped yews have been planted in the parterre, and 375 limes and 7,000 hornbeam plants have been used to create the avenues and bosquets. The cascade floor consists of a quarter of a mile of dressed granite stones.

During the summer the gardens offer a venue for several recurring concerts, Maypole celebrations, and other cultural events.

Nordsjællandsk Folkemuseet (North Zealand Folk Museum). Helsingørsgade 65. ☎ **48-24-34-48.** Admission 15 DKK ($1.90) adults, free for children. Tues–Sun 11am–4pm. Closed Nov–Apr. Bus: 701.

Collections depict the rural history of North Zealand, with special emphasis on the preindustrialization era in Hillerød.

There are supplementary displays at **Sophienborg,** Sophienborg Allé (☎ **48-24-34-48**), an estate on the western outskirts of Hillerød. Sophienborg is easily reached by bus no. 734 from Hillerød station. From there, it's an 8-minute walk. By car, take either Frederiksværksgade or Herredsvejen, turn right at Tulstrupvej, and follow the signs to the Folkemuseet Sophienborg. It keeps the same hours as the folk museum, and admission is on the same ticket.

Four miles west of Hillerød, you'll find the **Aebelholt Klostermuseum,** Abelholt 4 (☎ **48-21-03-51**), the ruins of an Augustinian monastery founded in 1175. A museum on this site—housed in the ruins—exhibits human skeletons dating from medieval times and provides clues to diseases that were commonplace at the time. Healing methods used by these early monks are also revealed. You can wander through a medicinal garden adjoining the museum. From March 1 to April and in October, hours are Saturday and Sunday from 1 to 4pm. From May to August, hours are Tuesday to Sunday 10am to 4pm, and in September, Tuesday to Sunday 1 to 4pm. Closed otherwise. Admission is 15 DKK ($1.90) adults, free for children under 17.

WHERE TO DINE

Slotsherrens Kro. Frederiksborg Slot. ☎ **48-26-75-16.** Main courses 76–158 DKK ($9.50–$19.75); 2-course fixed-price menu 162 DKK ($20.25); lunch plate 76 DKK ($9.50); smørrebrød 32–68 DKK ($4–$8.50). DC, MC, V. Tues 10am–5pm, Wed–Mon 10am–9pm. Closed Dec–Mar. Bus: 701. DANISH.

Since the 1970s, this well-managed tavern has flourished here in what were formerly the stables for nearby Frederiksborg Castle. It's the most sought-after dining spot in town for anyone visiting the castle, partly because of its carefully crafted array of open-faced sandwiches. The place also serves grilled meats, salads, and platters of food and kill, which usually are a meal in themselves.

FREDENSBORG
6 miles W of Helsingør, 25 miles N of Copenhagen

On the southeast shore of Esrum Sø, the country's second largest lake, Fredensborg is visited mainly for its royal palace. Many visitors rush through just for the day, visiting the palace and then departing immediately. However, you can stay and dine in the area, and enjoy a number of other attractions as well (see below).

Naturally, the first inhabitants of the town were people who helped service the royal court. But over the years many others moved in, and today the town is a lively little place even when the Queen isn't in residence. To Denmark, it occupies a position somewhat similar to Windsor in England. The town is home to some 40 specialty shops, which can be enjoyed in a pedestrian street environment.

The palace is a major backdrop for events in the royal family's life—weddings, birthday parties, whatever. Here, heads of states from many other countries are received when they pay official visits, and foreign ambassadors present their credentials to the monarch.

ESSENTIALS

GETTING THERE   By Train & Bus   From Copenhagen's Central Railroad Station, frequent trains run to Fredensborg. Bus nos. 336 and 384 from Copenhagen's Central Railroad Station go to Fredensborg.

By Car   From Copenhagen, head north on the E55 toward Helsingør, turning west on Route 6.

VISITOR INFORMATION   The **Fredensborg Turistinformation,** Slotsgade 2 (☎ 48-48-21-00), is open Monday to Friday 10am to 4pm.

SEEING THE SIGHTS

✪ Fredensborg Slot. Slottet. ☎ **33-40-31-87.** Admission 30 DKK ($3.75) adults, 10 DKK ($1.25) children. Palace, July only, 1–5pm.

This is the summer residence of the Danish royal family. Founded in 1720, the present building dates from the end of the Great Northern War. Although the palace has been extended many times, it still retains its baroque, rococo, and classical features.

The palace was particularly celebrated during the reign of Christian IX, who assembled the greats of European royalty here in the days of Queen Victoria. When the queen is in residence, visitors assemble at noon to watch the changing of the guard. On Thursdays, except in July, the queen often appears to acknowledge a regimental band concert in her honor.

The palace was built for King Frederik IV by the Danish architect J.D. Krieger. Originally there was only the main building with a Cupola Hall. Over the years, the palace was extended with such additions as the Chancellery House and the Cavaliers Wing.

Frederik IX and Queen Ingrid began the tradition of spending several months of the year at Fredensborg Palace. They preferred spring and autumn. That tradition is still upheld today by Queen Margrethe and Prince Henrik.

Today the palace is hardly one of the impressive royal palaces of Europe, but it has its own charm, especially in the Domed Hall and the Garden Room.

The palace opens onto a 275-year-old baroque garden. There is a public part of the palace garden open all year. However, the private reserved royal garden is open only in July daily from 9am to 5pm. The orangery in the royal garden is also open in July daily from 1 to 4:30pm.

These are some of the largest and best preserved gardens in Denmark. Note how strictly symmetrical and geometrical the shapes are. The palace gardens were laid out in the 1720s by Frederik IV and J.C. Krieger, drawing on Italian designs for their inspiration. In the 1760s Frederik V redesigned the garden, adding elements from French baroque horticulture.

HELSINGØR (ELSINORE): IN SEARCH OF HAMLET

25 miles N of Copenhagen, 15 miles NE of Hillerød, 45 miles NE of Roskilde

Once you reach Helsingør, usually by train from Copenhagen, you'll be in the center of town and can cover all the major attractions on foot. Helsingør (Elsinore in English) is visited chiefly for "Hamlet's Castle." Aside from its literary associations, the town has a certain charm: a quiet market square, medieval lanes, and old half-timbered and brick buildings—remains of its once prosperous shipping industry.

In 1429 King Erik of Pomerania ruled that ships passing Helsingør had to pay a toll for sailing within local waters. The town quickly became a center for international shipping, bringing in a lot of revenue. King Erik also constructed the Castle of Krogen, later rebuilt by Christian IV as the Castle of Kronborg. For a while Helsingør prospered and grew so much that it was the second largest town in the country.

ESSENTIALS

GETTING THERE   By Train   There are frequent trains from Copenhagen, taking 50 minutes. Buses have been discontinued.

By Ferry   Ferries ply the waters of the narrow channel separating Helsingør (Denmark) from Helsingborg (Sweden) in less than 25 minutes per trek. They're operated by **Scandlines** (☎ **33-15-15-15**) around the clock, which charges 40 DKK ($5) each way for a pedestrian without a car, and 245 DKK ($30.65) each way for a car with up to five persons inside. Between 6am and 11pm, departures are every 20 minutes; between 11pm and 6am, departures are timed at intervals of between 40 and 80 minutes. The venue is simple and straightforward: You simply drive your car on board, and wait in your car in a line that might remind you of the Staten Island ferryboat. Border formalities during the crossing between Denmark and Sweden are perfunctory, and although you should carry a passport, it might not even be asked for.

By Car   Take E-4 north from Copenhagen.

VISITOR INFORMATION   The **tourist office,** at Havnepladsen 3 (☎ **49-21-13-33**), is open Monday to Friday from 9am to 5pm, Saturday from 10am to 1pm.

SEEING THE SIGHTS

✪ **Kronborg Slot.** Kronborg. ☎ **49-21-30-78.** Admission 40 DKK ($5) adults, 15 DKK ($1.90) children 6–14, free for children under 6. May–Sept, daily 10:30am–5pm; Apr and Oct, Tues–Sun 11am–4pm; Nov–Mar, Tues–Sun 11am–3pm. Closed Dec 25.

There is no evidence that Shakespeare ever saw this sandstone-and-copper Dutch Renaissance–style castle, full of intriguing secret passages and casemates (artillery compartments on ramparts), but he made it famous in *Hamlet*. If Hamlet had really lived, it would have been centuries before Kronborg was built (1574–1585). Over the years a number of famous productions of the Shakespearean play have been staged here. One great performance was Derek Jacobi's interpretation in 1979. In 1954 the parts of Hamlet and Ophelia were played by Richard Burton and Claire Bloom.

The castle, on a peninsula jutting out into Øresund, was restored in 1629 by Christian IV after it was gutted by fire. Other events in its history include looting, bombardment, occupation by Swedes, and use as a barracks (1785–1922). The facade is sandstone covered, and the entire castle is surrounded by a deep moat. You approach the castle via a wooden bridge and by going through Mørkeport, a gate dating from the 16th century. This leads you to the main courtyard of Kronborg. Instead of immediately entering the castle, you can walk around the moat to the waterfront where you can see a spectacular vista of the Swedish coast. At the platform—backed by massive bronze guns—Hamlet is said to have seen the ghost of his father, all shrouded in pea-soup fog.

The starkly furnished Great Hall is the largest in northern Europe. Originally 40 tapestries portraying 111 Danish kings were hung around this room on special occasions. They were commissioned by Frederik II and woven around 1585. Only seven remain at Kronborg, seven are in the Nationalmuseet in Copenhagen, and the rest have disappeared. The church with its original oak furnishings and the royal chambers are worth seeing. The bleak and austere atmosphere adds to the drama. Lying beneath the castle is Holger Danske, the mythological hero who is believed to assist Denmark whenever the country is threatened. Also on the premises is the **Danish Maritime Museum** (☎ 49-21-06-85), which explores the history of Danish shipping. Guided tours are given every half hour from October to April. In summer you can explore on your own. The castle is half a mile from the rail station.

Karmeliterklostret. Skt. Annagade 38. ☎ **49-21-17-74.** Admission 10 DKK ($1.25) adults, 5 DKK (65¢) children. Guided tours, mid-May to mid-Sept, daily at 2pm.

This well-preserved 15th-century former Carmelite monastery, at the intersection of Havnegade and Kronborgvej, is the best of its kind in Scandinavia. After the Reformation it became a hospital, but by 1630 it was a poorhouse.

Skt. Mariæ Church. Skt. Annagade 38. ☎ **49-21-17-74.** Free admission. May 15–Sept 14, daily 10am–3pm; Sept 15–May 14, daily 10am–2pm.

An addition to the Karmeliterklostret complete with late 15th-century frescoes, St. Mary's also contains the organ played by baroque composer Dietrich Buxtehude from 1660 to 1668 (still in use).

Skt. Olai's Kirke. Skt. Annagade 12. ☎ **49-21-04-43.** Free admission. May–Aug, Mon–Sat 10am–4pm; Sept–Apr, daily 10am–2pm.

Built between 1480 and 1559, this christening chapel is worth a visit. The interior of the church and the baptistry in particular are one of a kind. The spired church, near the intersection of Havnegade and Kronborgvej, is connected to the Carmelite cloisters.

Helsingør Bymuseet. Skt. Annagade 36. ☎ **49-21-00-98.** Admission 10 DKK ($1.25) adults, free for children. Daily noon–4pm.

Installed in part of the Carmelite monastery (see listing for Karmeliterklostret, above), this museum houses the town's historic archives and various exhibits. Of special interest are 15th-century items related to Helsingør's collection of duties in the sound. The exhibits present materials of the trades practiced in days gone by, including a printing house. There's also a collection of about 200 antique dolls and a fine scale model of the town in 1801. It's a short walk from the bus, train, and ferryboat station.

Marienlyst Slot. Marienlyst Allé 32. ☎ **49-28-37-91.** Admission 20 DKK ($2.50) adults, free for children. Daily noon–5pm.

Marienlyst was built from 1759 to 1763 in a neoclassical style by the French architect N.H. Jardin. The building was intended to be a royal summer home, but was never used as such. Up until 1953 it served as a private residence. Today it's a museum, with well-preserved interiors in the original Louis XVI style and a permanent collection of paintings from Helsingør, along with an exhibit of silverworks. Special exhibits are arranged upstairs in summer. The castle is surrounded by a fine park, and from the top of a steep slope behind the castle is a panoramic view of the sound.

Denmark's Tekniske Museet (Technical Museum of Denmark). Nodre Strandvej 23. ☎ **49-22-26-11.** Admission 25 DKK ($3.15) adults, 13 DKK ($1.65) children. Tues–Sun 10am–5pm.

This museum contains technical, industrial, scientific, and transportation exhibits, including the oldest Danish airplanes and trains, the world's first typewriter, and the world's first electromagnetic sound recorder (tape recorder). There's also an 1888 Danish automobile, the Hammelvognen. The museum is next door to the train station.

WHERE TO DINE

Typical Danish hot meals, such as *hakkebøf* (hamburger steak), *frikadeller* (Danish rissoles or meatballs), rib roast with red cabbage, cooked or fried flounder or herring, and *æggekage* (egg cake) with bacon, are served in the local restaurants. Helsingør has many fast-food places, too, and you won't want to miss the celebrated ice-cream wafers.

Anno 1880. Kongensgade 6. ☎ **49-21-54-80.** Reservations recommended. Main courses 162–188 DKK ($20.25–$23.50); fixed-price menu 275 DKK ($34.40). AE, DC, MC, V. Mon–Sat 11:30am–10pm. DANISH.

Set in a long, narrow, half-timbered building that originally functioned as a greengrocer's shop, this comfortable and traditional restaurant is owner-managed and always alert to the freshness of its ingredients. Within old-fashioned dining rooms, you'll enjoy seasonal meals that might include cream of clam soup with saffron; fillets of salmon, haddock, or plaice in butter sauce with herbs; fried steak with fried onions and boiled potatoes; and such desserts as a kirsch-flavored parfait.

Ophelia Restaurant. In the Hotel Hamlet, Bramstræde 5. ☎ **49-21-05-91.** Reservations recommended. Main courses 80–175 DKK ($10–$21.90). AE, DC, MC, V. Daily noon–9:30pm. Bus: 801 or 802. DANISH/FRENCH.

The Ophelia is one of the most appealing restaurants in town. In the elegantly rustic dining room, photos of various world *Hamlet* productions line the brick walls. Specialties of the house include Hamlet veal steak and richly caloric desserts. Lunches cost only half as much as dinner. Although not overly imaginative, the cookery is very competent, with dish after tasteful dish emerging from the kitchen.

Samos. Stengade 81 (at Færgaarden). ☎ **49-21-39-46.** Reservations recommended. Main courses 110–185 DKK ($13.75–$23.15); all-you-can-eat buffet dinner 115 DKK ($14.40).I MC, V. Daily noon–11pm. GREEK.

Situated near Helsingør Castle and the ferryboat terminal for passengers heading back to Copenhagen, this restaurant was inspired by a Greek island *taverna*. It's part of Færgaarden, the former 1770 Customs House that's now a complex of international restaurants and the most popular choice for dining in Helsingør. Amid a color scheme of Ionian blue and white and a decor of fishnets and murals of such monuments as the Acropolis, you can order heaping portions of moussaka, roast lamb, grilled fish, meatballs, and the honey-enriched dessert, baklava. The buffet offers more than 20 delightful items. Additional seating is available on a breezy outdoor pavilion overlooking the sea.

ROSKILDE

20 miles W of Copenhagen

Roskilde, once a great ecclesiastical seat, was Denmark's leading city until the mid–fifteenth century. Today the twin spires of Roskilde Cathedral stand out from the landscape like elegantly tapered beacons. These towers are the first landmark you see when approaching the city that celebrated its 1,000th anniversary in 1998.

Once the capital of Denmark, Roskilde is centuries past its peak, but it is no sleepy museum town, either. It's filled with a dynamic student community, boutique lined walking streets, several landmark and major sights, and a population of more than 52,000 people who call themselves Roskildenser.

Today Roskilde's cobbled streets and towering cathedral only hint at the power and mystery of its Viking past. Toward the end of the last millennium, the Vikings settled the area, drawn no doubt by its sinuous coastline where they could launch their ships. In 1957 divers in the Roskilde Fjord came upon shards of wood. Their discovery turned out to be bigger than anyone imagined. Here, sunk and preserved by mud, were five Viking ships that presumably had been put there to block the passage of enemy ships.

Archeologists began the painstaking job of building a watertight dam and draining that section of the fjord, while keeping the chunks and splinters of wood wet enough so as not to disintegrate. Splinter by splinter, they began reconstructing and reassembling the boats—a process that continues today. You can see their efforts on display at the **Viking Ship Museum** (see "Seeing the Sights," below), a modern museum that contains the five found ships.

Between 990 and the turn of the century, Roskilde's prominence grew, becoming the home of the royal residence. By the 11th century, a Catholic church and a Bishop's Seat resided at Roskilde, which remained Denmark's capital until the Reformation in 1536.

At that time, all the parish churches were abolished and the Catholic hierarchy disappeared. The government and the monarchy moved to Copenhagen. Nonetheless, at its peak, Roskilde's importance was expressed in its architecture. By 1150, it was surrounded by an embankment and a moat, inside of which stood 12 churches and a cathedral. In 1170 Bishop Absalon built a new church on the same site where Harald Bluetooth had erected his church 2 centuries before. Though it took 300 years in its construction, and was subsequently burned, destroyed, ravaged, and rebuilt, Absalon's cathedral laid the foundation for the existing Roskilde Cathedral, or Domkirche, which today is a UNESCO World Heritage site.

ESSENTIALS

GETTING THERE   By Train & Bus   Trains leave three times an hour from Copenhagen's Central Railroad Station for the 35-minute trip to Roskilde. Buses depart for Roskilde several times daily from Copenhagen's Central Railroad Station.

By Car   Take the E-21 express highway west from Copenhagen.

VISITOR INFORMATION   The **Roskilde-Egnens Turistbureau,** Gullandsstræde 15 (☎ **46-35-27-00**), provides pamphlets about the town and the surrounding area. The office is open April to June, Monday to Friday from 9am to 5pm and Saturday from 10am to 1pm; July and August, Monday to Friday from 9am to 6pm, Saturday from 9am to 3pm, and Sunday from 10am to 2pm; and September to March, Monday to Friday from 9am to 5pm, and Saturday from 10am to 1pm. While at the tourist office, inquire about a Roskilde card, which costs 110 DKK ($13.75) for adults or 55 DKK ($6.90) for children. The card admits you to the 10 major attractions in the area and is valid for 7 days from the date of issue. Without the card, it would cost 252 DKK ($31.50) to visit these same attractions.

A SPECIAL EVENT   The **Roskilde Festival** (☎ **46-35-27-00**), held outdoors July 1 to 4 on a large grassy field, attracts fans of rock music. To get information on the festival's dates and performances, call the above number or contact the Roskilde-Egnens Turistbureau (see "Visitor Information," above).

SEEING THE SIGHTS

✪ **Roskilde Domkirke.** Domkirkestræde 10. ☎ **46-35-27-00.** Admission 12 DKK ($1.50) adults, 6 DKK (75¢) children. Apr–Sept, Tues–Fri 9am–4:45pm, Sat 9am–noon, Sun 12:30–4:45pm; Oct–Mar, Tues–Fri 10am–3:45pm, Sat 11:30am–3:45pm, Sun 12:30–3:45pm. Bus: 602, 603, or 604.

This cathedral elevated Roskilde into the spiritual capital of Denmark and northern Europe. Today it rises out of a modest townscape like a mirage—a cathedral several times too big for the town surrounding it. Construction started in 1170 when Absalon was bishop of Roskilde. Work continued into the 13th century, and the building's original Romanesque features gave way to an early Gothic overlay. The twin towers weren't built until the 14th century.

Today the cathedral's beauty goes beyond a single architectural style, providing almost a crash course in Danish architecture. Although damaged by a fire in 1968, the cathedral has been restored, including its magnificent altarpiece.

The Domkirke is the final abode of 38 Danish monarchs whose tombs are here, ranging from the modest to the downright eccentric. Not surprisingly, the tomb of Christian IV, the builder king, who was instrumental in having constructed nearly all of Copenhagen's famous towers and castles, is in a grandiose chapel with a massive painting of himself in combat and a bronze likeness by the Danish sculptor Bertel Thorvaldsen. In humble contrast is the newest addition, from 1972, of the simple brick chapel of King Frederik IX, which stands outside the church. This octagonal chapel is decorated with hand-painted tiles designed by the architects Johannes and Inger Exner and Vilhelm Wohlert.

Other notable tombs include the white marble sarcophagus of Queen Margrethe I. In King Christian I's chapel, from the 15th century, there is a column marked with the heights of several kings. The tallest monarch was Christian I at 6 feet, 9 inches. This, no doubt, was an exaggeration as his skeleton measures only 6 feet, 2 inches. The late 18th and early 19th century chapel of King Frederik V is graced by a large, bright cupola. Note also the Gothic choir stalls, each richly and intricately carved with details from the *Old* and *New Testaments*.

The choir's gilded winged altar, made in Antwerp in the 1500s, was originally intended for Frederiksborg Castle. Pictures on the wings of the altar depict scenes from the life of Jesus, ranging from the Nativity to the Crucifixion. Following the fire, a new altar cloth was created by the renowned artisan Anna Thommesen.

The most charming aspect of the cathedral is its early 16th-century clock poised on the interior south wall above the entrance. A tiny St. George on horseback marks the hour by charging a dragon. The beast howls, the sound of which echoes through the cavernous church causing Peter Doever, "the Deafener," to sound the hour. A terrified Kirsten Kiemer, "the Chimer," shakes in fright but pulls herself together to strike the quarter hours.

✪ **Viking Ship Museum (Vikingeskibshallen).** Vindeboder 12, 4000 Roskilde. ☎ **46-30-02-00.** Admission 54 DKK ($6.75) adults, 30 DKK ($3.75) children 6–16, free for children under 6; family ticket 132 DKK ($16.50). May–Sept, daily 9am–5pm; Oct–Apr, daily 10am–4pm. Bus: 605.

Five vessels found in Roskilde Fjord, and painstakingly pieced together from countless pieces of wreckage, are on display here. It's presumed that the craft (dating from 1000–1050) were deliberately sunk about 12½ miles north of Roskilde at the narrowest section of the fjord to protect Roskilde from a sea attack. The discovery was relatively unprotected and unpublicized until 1962 when the Danish National Museum carried out a series of underwater excavations.

Also on display are a merchant cargo ship used by the Vikings, a small ferry or fishing boat, and a Danish Viking warship similar to the ones portrayed in the Bayeux Tapestry. Also discovered was a "longship," a Viking man-of-war that terrorized European coasts. You can buy copies of Viking jewelry in the museum gift shop, and there's a cafeteria.

To understand the attraction better, you can see a short film, *The Ships of the Vikings,* about excavating and preserving the ships and building and navigating Roar Ege, a Viking ship replica.

The Viking Ship Museum operates a museum harbor for its collection of Nordic vessels, including Roar Ege, plus another Viking ship replica, Helge Ask. Also moored here is the museum's restored sloop, Ruth. Opposite the Boat Yard are the workshops for old maritime crafts, such as rope- and sail-making and woodworking.

Roskilde Museum. Sankt Ols Gade 15–18. ☎ **46-36-60-44.** Admission 25 DKK ($3.15) adults, free for children under 12. Daily 11am–4pm. Closed Dec 24–25 and Dec 31–Jan 1. Bus: 601, 602, 603, or 605.

This museum, set in a former merchant's house 100 yards from the Town Square, features exhibits of the celebrated Hedebo embroidery, regional costumes, and antique toys. Displays also include an aurochs (extinct wild ox) skeleton, a unique Viking tomb, and many medieval finds from the town. The museum also has a grocer's courtyard, with the shop in operation.

Museet for Samtidskunst (Museum of Contemporary Art). Stændertorvet 3A. ☎ **46-36-88-74.** Admission 20 DKK ($2.50) adults, free for children. Tues–Fri 11am–5pm, Sat–Sun noon–4pm. Bus: 601, 602, 603, or 605.

Housed in a beautiful 18th-century palace, this museum of modern art has frequently changing exhibitions, along with performances, film shows, and modern dance and classical music concerts. It also houses a videotheque that presents programs featuring Danish and foreign artists. "The Palace Collections" (see below) are also here.

Palæsamlingerne (The Palace Collections). Stændertorvet 3E. ☎ **46-35-78-80.** Admission 25 DKK ($3.15) adults, free for children. May 15–Sept 14, daily 11am–4pm; off-season, Sat–Sun 2–4pm. Bus: 601, 602, 603, or 605.

After a visit to the Museet for Samtidskunst (see above), you can view the collections in Roskilde Palace at the same site. Most of these objets d'art and paintings date from the era of great prosperity Roskilde merchants enjoyed in the 1700s and 1800s. Here such local families as the Bruuns and the Borchs amassed a great deal of art and antiques, which you can see today.

MORE ATTRACTIONS

St. Jørgensbjerg quarter was originally a small fishing village, and a number of old, half-timbered houses, some with thatched roofs, remain. These houses cluster around **Skt. Jørgensbjerg Kirke,** Kirkegade, which stands on the top of a hill with a panoramic view of Roskilde Fjord. This is one of the oldest and best preserved stone buildings in Denmark. The nave and choir of the church date from the beginning of the 12th century, but the walled-up north door is even older, maybe from 1040. In the corners of the church and in the center of the nave are slender billets (ornamentations in Norman moldings), found only in wooden churches. A model of a medieval merchant vessel, or *kogge,* has been engraved in a wall. The church is open Monday to Friday, 10am to noon from June 22 to August 31 (closed otherwise). From Roskilde, take bus 605 toward Boserup.

The same bus will deliver you to **Skt. Ibs Kirke** ("The Church of St. James"), Skt. Ibs Vej, also in the north of Roskilde. Although no longer in use as a church, this ruin dates from around 1100. Abolished as a church in 1808, it was later a field hospital and a merchant's warehouse. Regrettably, the merchant destroyed the tower, the chancel, the porch, and the church vaults of this medieval relic, but spared the nave. From sunup to sundown, it is open for visits from April 4 to October 18 (closed otherwise).

NEARBY ATTRACTIONS

Lejre Research Center. Slagealléen 2, DK-4320 Lejre. ☎ **46-48-08-78.** Admission 60 DKK ($7.50) adults, 30 DKK ($3.75) children. Daily 10am–5pm. Closed mid-Sept to Apr. Take the train from Copenhagen to Lejre, then bus no. 233 to the center. From Roskilde, there are frequent buses to Lejre; then take bus no. 233.

Five miles west of Roskilde, this archaeological research center, Lejre Research Center, is the site of a reconstructed Iron Age community on 25 acres of woodland. The main feature is clay-walled and thatch houses built with tools just as they were some 2,000 years ago. Staffers re-create the physical working conditions as they thatch Iron Age huts, plow with "ards", weave, and make pottery by an open fire. They also sail in dugout canoes, grind corn with a stone, and bake in direct fire. Visitors can take part in these activities. Jutland black pottery is produced here, and handcrafts and books are for sale at the gift shop. There are tables where you can enjoy a picnic lunch.

Ledreborg Park Og Slot. Allé 2, DK-4320 Lejre. ☎ **46-48-00-38.** Admission 50 DKK ($6.25) adults, 25 DKK ($3.15) children 6–16, free for children under 6. Family ticket 130 DKK ($16.25). Mid-June to Aug, daily 11am–5pm; May 1 to mid-June and Sept, Sun 11am–5pm. Closed Oct–Apr. From Copenhagen's Central Railroad Station, take the direct train to Lejre, which leaves hourly and takes 35 minutes; from Lejre station, take the 3-minute bus (no. 233) ride to the castle and park. From Roskilde, there are frequent buses to Lejre, followed by the short bus ride.

A baroque manor house and French-English–style park 4½ miles southwest of Roskilde and 27 miles west of Copenhagen, Ledreborg is one of the best-preserved monuments in Denmark. A 33-room house with a landscaped garden and 217-acre park, this manor has been owned by one family, the Holstein-Ledreborgs, for eight generations. It was built by a minister to Christian IV, Johan Ludwig Holstein. Between 1741 and 1757 it was turned from a farmhouse into a baroque manor. Inside is a collection of antiques from the 17th and 18th centuries and a gallery of Danish paintings. It's approached by a 4-mile long *allée* of lime trees, some 2 centuries old. A nearby passage grave dates from the late Stone Age, approximately 3000 B.C.

The Tramway Museum. Skjoldenæsholm, Skjoldenæsvej 107. ☎ **57-52-88-33.** Admission 50 DKK ($6.25) adults, 25 DKK ($3.15) children. May 6–June 20 and Aug 3–Oct 22 Sat 1–5pm, Sun 10am–5pm. June 21–Aug 2 Sun and Tues–Thurs 10am–5pm, Sat 1–5pm. Take a train from Copenhagen to Borup, and then bus no. 249 from the station.

In Justrup, some 10 miles southwest of Roskilde, in a pleasant woodland area close to Glydenveshj, the summer season Tramway Museum with its collection of antique trams is situated on the highest point on Zealand, 416 feet above sea level. Board an old tram at the entrance and travel the 1,000 feet to the museum's main building.

WHERE TO DINE

Club 42 (Restaurant Den Hvide Fugl). Skomagergade 42. ☎ **46-35-17-64.** Reservations recommended. Main courses 100–200 DKK ($12.50–$25); 3-course fixed-price menu 200 DKK ($25). DC, MC, V. Daily 11am–10pm. DANISH/INTERNATIONAL.

Sandwiched between two similar houses in the heart of town, this brick-fronted building originally housed a blacksmith's shop 300 years ago, where most of the town's horses were fitted with shoes. In a long narrow interior with a greenhouse-style roof that can be opened during good weather, it offers a selection of open-faced sandwiches, pork ribs prepared in barbecue sauce or in garlic-onion sauce, fillet steak with red-wine sauce, a fish platter of the house served with butter sauce, and grilled pepper steak. This is one of the middle-bracket staples of Roskilde. Although the food is a bit standard, it is well prepared with tasty ingredients.

Raadhuskælderen. Stændertorvet, Fondens Bro 1. ☎ **46-36-01-00.** Reservations recommended. Lunch menu 128–188 DKK ($16–$23.50); main courses 142–280 DKK ($17.75–$35); fixed-price dinner 245 DKK ($30.65). AE, DC, MC, V. Mon–Sat 11am–10pm, Sun 11am–9pm. DANISH.

One of the oldest restaurants in Roskilde occupies the street level of a red-brick building erected in 1430, across the street from the town's cathedral. Although it's tempting to remain in the vaulted and arcaded interior (you have to descend only about four steps to reach it), there's also an outdoor terrace that's appealing during midsummer, especially because of its view of the cathedral. Menu items are carefully prepared using very fresh ingredients. Examples include lobster soup served with homemade bread; smoked salmon with a small portion of scrambled eggs; tournedos in red wine sauce; and pepper steak that's flambéed at your table. One particularly succulent main course is a *Raadhus teller* that's composed of paprika-dusted pork cutlets with noodles and herbs.

Restaurant Toppen. Bymarken 37. ☎ **46-36-04-12.** Reservations recommended. Main courses 62–117 DKK ($7.75–$14.65). DC, MC, V. Mon–Fri 3:30–10pm, Sat–Sun noon–10pm. Bus: 601. DANISH.

At the top of a 1961 water tower, 274 feet above sea level, Restaurant Toppen offers a panoramic view of the whole town, the surrounding country, and Roskilde Fjord—all from the dining room. Begin with a shrimp cocktail served with dill and lemon, accompanied by salad, bread, and butter. Main dishes include sirloin of pork à la Toppen with mushrooms and béarnaise sauce, with a baked potato and salad. For dessert, try the chef's nut cake with fruit sauce and sour cream. The cookery has much improved in recent months, and there is a finesse and consistency that wasn't here before. The restaurant lies a mile east of the town center between Vindingevej and Københavnsvej. The water tower doesn't revolve electronically, but some clients, in the words of the management, "get the feeling that it's turning only if they drink enough." There's a free elevator to the top.

You Paid What?

47,000 hotels, 700 airlines, 50 rental car companies. And a few million ways to save money.

Travelocity.com
A Sabre Company

Go Virtually Anywhere.

AOL Keyword: Travel

Will you have enough stories to tell your grandchildren?

Yahoo! Travel

Exploring the Danish Countryside

5

Denmark, a relatively flat country with good roads, is easy to explore on your own in several driving tours. To reach Bornholm from Copenhagen and Zealand, you'll need to rely on ferry connections. A new bridge links Funen and Zealand. Another bridge connects Funen and Jutland, which is linked to the mainland of Europe.

If you have time for only one destination outside Copenhagen, make it **Funen.** It's the most visited island, mainly because of its capital, Odense, the birthplace of Hans Christian Andersen. Some of northern Europe's best-preserved castles are here.

Denmark's western peninsula, **Jutland** (also called Jylland), is the only part of the country that's connected to the European mainland; its southern border touches Germany.

Bornholm, "the pearl of the Baltic," can be reached only by plane or boat. Inhabited since the Iron Age, the island is quite different from the rest of Denmark. A visit is a good choice if you're looking for something offbeat.

1 Funen

Funen ("Fyn" in Danish), the country's second-largest island, separates Zealand from the mainland peninsula, Jutland. It offers unique attractions, from a Viking ship to runic stones.

Hans Christian Andersen was born on Funen in the town of Odense. A visit to the storyteller's native island is a journey into a land of hop gardens and roadside orchards, busy harbors, market towns, castles, and stately manor houses.

Funen has some 700 miles of coastline, with wide sandy beaches in some parts; in others, woods and grass grow all the way to the water's edge. Steep cliffs provide sweeping views of the Baltic and the Kattegat.

Although ferries have plied the waters surrounding Denmark's islands and peninsulas since ancient times, the government has always regretted the lack of bridges. In 1934 the first plans were developed for a bridge over the 8-mile span of water known as the **Great Belt** (Storebaelt), the silt-bottomed channel that separates Zealand and Copenhagen from Funen and the rest of continental Europe. War, technical embarrassments, and lack of funding caused many delays. After the submission of 144 designs by engineers from around the world, construction began in 1988 on an intricately calibrated network of bridges and tunnels. Finally, in 1998 the bridge over the Storebaelt opened to motor traffic.

This driving tour of the island of Funen begins at Nyborg. You reach it by crossing the bridge from the town of **Korsør** on the island of Zealand. To reach Korsør from Copenhagen, take E20 heading south, then west to Korsør.

NYBORG: GATEWAY TO FUNEN
81 miles W of Copenhagen, 21 miles E of Odense

After crossing the bridge, you'll come to this old seaport and market town, a perfect place to explore before you head to Odense. Founded some 700 years ago, Nyborg is one of the oldest towns in Denmark. Its location in the middle of the trade route between Zealand and Jutland helped boost its importance. In medieval times, from about 1200 to 1413, Nyborg was the capital of Denmark. Medieval buildings and well-preserved ramparts are testaments to that era. The town square, the **Torvet**, was created in 1540, when a block of houses was demolished to make room for Christian III's tournaments.

In the summer, Denmark's oldest open-air theater, **Nyborg Voldspil**, is the setting for an annual musical or operetta under the light beeches on the old castle ramparts. Throughout the summer, classical music concerts featuring international soloists are performed in the castle's Great Hall. Inquire at the tourist office (see "Essentials," below) for further details.

ESSENTIALS
GETTING THERE　　Ferry service from Zealand has been eliminated. Drive across the bridge at Korsør and follow the directions into Nyborg.

If you're not driving, you can reach Nyborg by train or bus. Trains leave Copenhagen every hour, and there's frequent bus service. Trains arrive twice an hour from Odense.

VISITOR INFORMATION　　The **Nyborg Turistbureau** is at Torvet 9 (☎ **65-31-02-80**). It's open June 15 to August, Monday to Friday 9am to 5pm, Saturday 9am to 2pm; September to June 14, Monday to Friday 9am to 4pm, Saturday 9am to noon.

GETTING AROUND　　Buses cover the major arteries of town; a typical fare costs 10 DKK ($1.25). If you plan to visit several sights in and around town, consider a 24-hour pass costing 25 DKK ($3.15). Both individual tickets and the 24-hour passes are available directly from the bus driver of whichever bus you choose.

Thanks to the city administration, a network of coin-operated kiosks has been installed whereby you can deposit 20 DKK ($2.50) into a machine, and a bright yellow bicycle will be released from its moorings for rides about town. Whenever you return it, the 20 DKK ($2.50) will be returned to you automatically. Several of these kiosks lie at strategic intervals throughout Nyborg's core, but the most central and most visible is on the Norregade, just around the corner from the tourist office, at Torvet 9 (☎ **65-31-02-80**).

SEEING THE SIGHTS
Mads Lerches Gård (Nyborg Og Omegns Museet). Slotsgade 11. ☎ **65-31-02-07.** Admission 10 DKK ($1.25) adults, 5 DKK (65¢) children 6–14, free for children 5 and under. Mar–May and Sept–Oct, Tues–Sun 10am–3pm; June–Aug, daily 10am–4pm. Closed Nov–Feb. Bus: 1, 3, or 4.

This two-story structure is the finest and best-preserved half-timbered house in Nyborg. It was constructed in 1601 by Mads Lerche, the mayor. The 30 rooms contain exhibitions on local history.

Nyborg Slot. Slotspladsen. ☎ **65-31-02-07.** Admission 30 DKK ($3.75) adults, 15 DKK ($1.90) children 6–14. Mar–May and Sept–Oct, Tues–Sun 10am–3pm; June–Aug, daily 10am–4pm. Closed Nov–Feb. Bus: 1, 2, or 3.

Nyborg Castle, with its ramparts still intact, is the oldest royal seat (1170) in Scandinavia. King Erik Glipping signed Denmark's first constitution in this moated castle in 1282, and Nyborg Castle was the seat of the Danish parliament, the Danehof, until 1413. The present furnishings date primarily from the 17th century, when Nyborg was a resplendent Renaissance palace. It's directly north of the landmark Torvet (tower) in the town center.

Vor Frue Kirke. Adelgade. ☎ **65-31-16-08.** Free admission. June–Aug, Mon–Sat 9am–6pm, Sun 9am–1pm. Sept–May, Mon–Sat 9am–4pm, Sun 9am–1pm.

Dating from the late 14th and the early 15th century, the Church of Our Lady has a fine Gothic spire, three aisles, woodcarvings, old epitaphs, candelabra, and model ships. Nightly at 9:45, the Watchman's Bell from 1523 is rung, continuing a long-standing tradition. Opposite the church is the 12th-century **chapter house** of the Order of St. John (Korsbrødregård), with a fine vaulted cellar that's now a gift shop. The church is at the end of Kongegade in the town center.

WHERE TO STAY

○ **Hotel Hesselet.** Christianslundsvej 119, DK-5800 Nyborg. ☎ **65-31-30-29.** Fax 65-31-29-58. www.hesselet.dk. E-mail: hotel@hesselet.dk. 46 units. MINIBAR TV TEL. Mon–Thurs 1,490–1690 DKK ($186.25–$211.25) double; Fri–Sun 1,590 DKK ($198.75) double. All week long 2,200–2,700 DKK ($275–$337.50) suite. Rates include breakfast. AE, DC, MC, V. Free parking.

Set among beech trees, with a view across the Great Belt, this red-brick building with a pagoda roof is one of the most stylish hotels in Denmark. Completely refurbished in 1996, it offers spacious rooms, good-sized bathrooms, and firm beds. The Oriental carpets, leather couches, fireplace, tasteful library, and sunken living rooms create a glamorous aura.

Dining/Diversions: The hotel's gourmet restaurant, with a view of the Great Belt, is one of the finest on Funen. Main dishes might include sautéed breast of duck, served pink, with fennel or poached tenderloin of veal. The Tranque Bar is a chic rendezvous.

Amenities: Indoor swimming pool, sauna, solarium, two tennis courts, nearby golf.

WHERE TO DINE

The **Hotel Hesselet** (see "Where to Stay," above) has an excellent restaurant.

Danehofkroen. Slotsplads. ☎ **65-31-02-02.** Reservations recommended. Main courses 135–190 DKK ($16.90–$23.75); fixed-price menus 189–325 DKK ($23.65–$40.65). MC, V. Tues–Sun 12:30–9pm. Closed Oct–Mar. DANISH/FRENCH.

This restaurant was built in 1815 as a barracks for the soldiers who guarded the nearby castle. The Jensen family took over in 1993. The well-managed restaurant has two dining rooms outfitted in elegant country tavern style. Tasty menu items include fish soup with saffron, fried duck liver flavored with bacon and leeks, turbot with mushroom sauce, delectable veal fried with chanterelle mushrooms, and a dessert specialty of raspberry parfait with fresh melon.

Restaurant Østervemb. Mellengade 18. ☎ **65-30-10-70.** Reservations recommended. Lunch platters 48–200 DKK ($6–$25); dinner main courses 170–250 DKK ($21.25–$31.25). DC, MC, V. Mon–Sat noon–3pm and 5–9pm. DANISH/FRENCH.

The heart-warming fare here is the sort that might be offered to a hungry crew by a nourishing Danish aunt. You can order platters piled high with three preparations of herring, cold potato soup with bacon and chives, breast of Danish hen served with spinach and mushrooms, curried chicken salad with bacon, and slices of grilled beef tenderloin served with a fricassée of oyster mushrooms and tarragon-flavored glaze.

ODENSE: BIRTHPLACE OF HANS CHRISTIAN ANDERSEN

97 miles W of Copenhagen, 21 miles W of Nyborg, 27 miles NW of Svendborg

This ancient town, the third largest in Denmark, has changed greatly since Hans Christian Andersen walked its streets. However, it's still possible to discover a few unspoiled spots.

ESSENTIALS

GETTING THERE   From Nyborg, head west on E20 to Allerup and then follow Route 9 north to Odense. From Copenhagen, it's an easy 3-hour trip by train or bus. About 12 trains or buses a day leave Copenhagen's Central Railroad Station.

VISITOR INFORMATION   Odense Tourist Bureau is at Rådhuset Vestergade 2A (☎ 66-12-75-20; www.odenseturist.dk). It's open mid-June to August, Monday to Saturday from 9am to 7pm, Sunday 10am to 5pm; September to mid-June, Monday to Friday 9:30am to 4:30pm, Saturday 10am to 1pm.

Besides helping arrange excursions, the tourist bureau sells the **Odense Adventure Pass.** It gives you access to 13 of the city's museums, the Odense Zoo, six indoor swimming pools, and unlimited free travel on the city buses and DSB trains within the municipality. It also entitles you to discounts on river cruises and admission to the summer-only presentation of the city's Hans Christian Andersen plays (see "Seeing the Sights," below). Passes are valid for 1 or 2 days. A 1-day pass is 85 DKK ($10.65) for adults, 40 DKK ($5) for children under 14; 2-day passes cost 125 DKK ($15.65) and 60 DKK ($7.50).

GETTING AROUND   You can hop aboard a bus at various stops and buy your ticket once you're aboard. You can also rent a bike from **City Cykler,** Vesterbro 27 (☎ 66-13-97-83), for prices ranging from 50 to 150 DKK ($6.25 to $18.75) per day, depending on the type of cycle.

SEEING THE SIGHTS

Odense Tourist Bureau (see above) offers **2-hour walking tours** from mid-June through August. They leave every Tuesday, Wednesday, and Thursday at 11am from a meeting place behind the tourist office, and cover the town's major sights. Tours are given in English, and advance reservations are recommended. Tours cost 35 DKK ($4.40) per adult, 10 DKK ($1.25) per child.

Also at the tourist office, you can get information about the **Hans Christian Andersen plays,** presented every year from mid-July to mid-August. The plays are given on an outdoor stage in the Funen Village, where members of the audience stand (if it's raining or the ground is wet) or sit on the grass (often on blankets, if it's dry).

Even if you don't understand Danish, the visuals afford lots of entertainment value. The 90-minute plays begin every day at 4pm. They cost 60 DKK ($7.50) for adults, 35 DKK ($4.40) for children, and are usually mobbed with Andersen fans.

Carl Nielsen Museet. Claus Bergsgade 11. ☎ 66-14-88-14. Admission 30 DKK ($3.75) adults, 15 DKK ($1.90) children 5–14, free for children under 5. Tues–Sun 10am–4pm. Bus: 2.

Adjoining the Odense Concert Hall, this museum documents the life and work of composer Carl Nielsen and his wife, the sculptor Anne Marie Nielsen. Visitors hear excerpts of Nielsen's music while they look at the exhibits and biographical slide show. Parking is available outside the concert hall.

Danmarks Jernbanemuseum (Railway Museum). Dannebrogsgade 24. ☎ **66-13-66-30.** Admission 30 DKK ($3.75) adults, 10 DKK ($1.25) children. Daily 10am–4pm. Bus: 2.

The displays here—original locomotives and carriages that illustrate Denmark's railway history—include the first railroad, from 1847. One of the oldest locomotives in the collection is an 1869 "B-Machine." Also on display are three royal coaches, a double-decker carriage, and a model railway. The museum is next to the train station.

Funen Village/Den Fynske Landsby. Sejerskovvej 20. ☎ **66-14-88-14.** Admission 35 DKK ($4.40) adults, 15 DKK ($1.90) children. Apr–May and Sept–Oct, Tues–Sun 10am–5pm; June–Aug, daily 9:30am–7pm; Nov–Mar, Sun 11am–3pm. Bus: 21 or 22 from Flakhaven.

A big open-air regional culture museum, this is an archive of 18th- and 19th-century Funen life. It's in the Hunderup Woods, 1½ miles south of the town center. The old buildings—a toll house, weaver's shop, windmill, farmstead, jail, vicarage, village school, and brickworks—have been reassembled and authentically furnished. Plays and folk dances are staged at the Greek theater. You can also visit workshops and see a basket maker, spoon cutter, blacksmith, weaver, and others at work.

H. C. Andersens Barndomshjem (Andersen's Childhood Home). Munkemøllestraede 3. ☎ **66-14-88-14.** Admission 10 DKK ($1.25) adults, 5 DKK (65¢) children. July–Aug, daily 10am–5pm; Sept–June, daily 10am–3pm. Bus: 2.

This is Andersen's humble boyhood home, where the fairy-tale writer lived from age 2 to 14. From what is known of Andersen's childhood, his mother was a drunken, superstitious washerwoman, and he was a gawky boy, lumbering and graceless, the victim of his fellow urchins' cruel jabs. All is serene at the cottage today, however, and the "garden still blooms," as in *The Snow Queen.*

✪ H. C. Andersens Hus. Hans Jensensstraede 37–45. ☎ **66-14-88-14.** Admission 35 DKK ($4.40) adults, 15 DKK ($1.90) children 5–14, free for children under 5. June 16–Aug, daily 9am–7pm; Sept–June 15, daily 10am–4pm. Bus: 2.

The object of most Funen pilgrimages is the house and museum of Hans Christian Andersen. It's popular with both adults and children. You'll see his famous walking stick, top hat, and battered portmanteau, plus letters to his dear friend Jenny Lind and fellow writer Charles Dickens. In addition, hundreds of documents, manuscripts, and reprints of his books in dozens of languages are on display.

St. Canute's Cathedral. Klosterbakken 2. ☎ **66-12-61-23.** Free admission. May 15–30 and Sept 1–14, Mon–Sat 10am–5pm; Apr–May 14 and Sept 15–30, Mon–Sat 10am–4pm; June–Aug, Mon–Sat 10am–5pm, Sun and holidays noon–3pm; Oct–Mar, Mon–Fri 10am–4pm, Sat 10am–2pm. Bus: 21 or 22.

Despite its unimpressive facade, this is the most important Gothic-style building in Denmark. A popular feature of the 13th-century brick structure is the gold altar screen, an elegant triptych carved by Claus Berg in 1526 at Queen Christina's request. King Canute was killed by angry Jutland taxpayers in 1086 and canonized 15 years later. The church stands opposite the Town Hall.

NEARBY ATTRACTIONS

✪ Egeskov Castle. Egeskovgade 18, Kvaerndrup. ☎ **62-27-10-16.** Admission including castle, park, and maze 110 DKK ($13.75) adults; 60 DKK ($7.50) children 4–12; park, maze, museum 60 DKK ($7.50) adults; 30 DKK ($3.75) children 4–12. Both free for children under 4. May, Sept, park and castle daily 10am–5pm. June, Aug, park daily 10am–7pm; castle daily 10am–6pm. July, park daily 10am–8pm; castle daily 10am–6pm. Closed Oct–May. Train: From Odense or Svendborg every hour. Bus: 920 from Nyborg.

This 1554 Renaissance water castle, northeast of Fåborg at Kvaerndrup, is the most romantic and splendid of Denmark's fortified manors. The castle, which has magnificent gardens, was built on oak pillars in the middle of a moat or small lake. It's considered the best-preserved Renaissance castle of its type in Europe.

Every year some 200,000 visitors roam the 30-acre park and castle, located on the main road between Svendborg and Odense. There's a vintage automobile, horse carriage, and airplane museum on the grounds. Chamber music concerts are held in the Great Hall of the castle on 10 summer Sundays beginning in late June, starting at 5pm.

The most dramatic story in the castle's history is about an unfortunate maiden, Rigborg, who was seduced by a young nobleman and bore him a child out of wedlock. Banished to the castle, she was imprisoned by her father in a tower from 1599 to 1604.

Ladbyskibet. Vikingevej 123, Ladby. ☎ **65-32-16-67.** Admission 25 DKK ($3.15) adults, free for children under 15. Mar–May 14 and Sept 15–Oct, daily 10am–4pm; May 15–Sept 14, daily 10am–6pm; Nov–Feb, Wed–Sun 11am–3pm. Bus: 482 from Kerteminde, which is accessible by bus from Odense.

Ladby, 12 miles northeast of Odense, is the site of a 72-foot-long 10th-century Viking ship, discovered in 1935. The ship's remains are displayed in a burial mound along with replicas from the excavation (the originals are in the National Museum in Copenhagen). A skeleton of the pagan chieftain buried in this looted ship was never found, but the bones of his horses and dogs were.

SHOPPING

Inspiration Zinch, Vestergade 82-84 (☎ **66-12-96-93**), offers the widest selection of Danish design and handcrafts on the island of Funen. All the big names are here, from Royal Copenhagen to Georg Jensen but you will also come across younger, more modern designers. In the heart of the old town, opposite Hans Christian Andersen's house, you'll find a display of Danish crafts and Christmas decorations in a typical atmosphere of old Funen at **Klods Hans,** Hans Jensens Staede 34 (☎ **66-11-09-40**). A most interesting outlet is **Smykker,** 3 Klaregade (☎ **66-12-06-96**). It offers museum jewelry copies from the Bronze, Iron, and Viking ages—all made in gold, sterling silver, and bronze in the outlet's workshop. **College Art,** Grandts Passage 38 (☎ **66-11-35-45**), has assembled a unique collection of posters, lithographs, silk screens, original art, and cards. The best gallery for contemporary art is **Galleri Torso,** Vintapperstraede 57 (☎ **66-13-44-66**). Finally, if none of these shops has what you want, head for **Rosengårdcentret,** Munkerisvej and Ørbaekvej; it's Denmark's biggest shopping center, with more than 100 stores under one roof.

WHERE TO STAY

Hotel Ansgar. Østre Stationsvej 32, DK-5000 Odense. ☎ **66-11-96-93.** Fax 66-11-96-75. 44 units. TV TEL. June–Aug, 600 DKK ($75) double; Sept–May, 765 DKK ($95.65) double. Extra bed 150 DKK ($18.75). AE, DC, MC, V. Free parking. Bus: 31, 33, 35, or 36.

Built a century ago as an affiliate of a local church, this hotel dropped its religious connections many years ago. In the heart of town, behind a brick-and-stone facade, it boasts a modern interior. Double-glazed windows cut traffic noise considerably. The rooms are well furnished and vary in size from spacious to small. Likewise, bathrooms are medium sized or cramped. All rooms have a trouser press; in most units you'll also find a minibar. The hotel's reasonably priced restaurant serves Danish food. A particularly good value is the two-course fixed-price dinner for 95 DKK ($11.90). The hotel is a 5-minute walk from the train depot.

Odense Plaza Hotel. Østre Stationsvej 24, DK-5000 Odense. ☎ **800/233-1234** in the U.S., or 66-11-77-45. Fax 66-14-41-45. www.odenseplaza.dk. E-mail: infor@odenseplaza.dk. 68 units. MINIBAR TV TEL. July–Aug, 795 DKK ($99.40) double; 875 DKK ($109.40) suite. Sept–June, 1,250 DKK ($156.25) double; 1,550 DKK ($193.75) suite. Rates include breakfast. AE, DC, MC, V. Free parking. Bus: 31, 33, 35, or 36.

A quarter mile from the town center, Odense's classic hotel is one of its most alluring hostelries. It was built in 1915, and many guest rooms were renovated in 1997. The rooms evoke an English country home, and open onto scenic views. Some are quite spacious. Units for nonsmokers can be requested.

Dining/Diversions: The terrace overlooking a park and garden serves drinks. The dining room, with large picture windows opening onto the park, serves refined Danish and international cuisine.

Amenities: Room service, concierge.

Radisson SAS H. C. Andersen Hotel. Claus Bergs Gade 7, DK-5000 Odense. ☎ **800/333-3333** in the U.S., or 66-14-78-00. Fax 66-14-78-90. www.radisson.dk 145 units. MINI-BAR TV TEL. 700–1,135 DKK ($87.50–$141.90) double. Rates include breakfast. AE, DC, MC, V. Free parking. Bus: 4 or 5.

This brick hotel in the heart of the old city lies next to a former residence of Hans Christian Andersen. Decorated in 1960s Nordic modern, it is one of Funen's premier hotels. Most guests are businesspeople. Rooms vary in size from large to a bit cramped; the quietest open onto the interior. Bathrooms tend to be small, but have thoughtful extras such as makeup mirrors and hair dryers. Accommodations for nonsmokers can be requested, and some units are suitable for those with disabilities.

Dining/Diversions: Overlooking the market square, the hotel's formal restaurant is known for catering to special requests. It serves refined international and Danish cuisine and does so exceedingly well, using market-fresh ingredients. There are two cozy bars. On-site is one of Denmark's six casinos, where you can play blackjack, roulette, and baccarat.

Amenities: Sauna, solarium, room service, concierge.

WHERE TO DINE

Den Gamle Kro. Overgade 23. ☎ **66-12-14-33.** Reservations recommended. Main courses 169–258 DKK ($21.15–$32.25); fixed-price menus 238–328 DKK ($29.75–$41). AE, DC, MC, V. Mon–Sat 11am–10:30pm, Sun 11am–9:30pm. Bus: 2. DANISH/FRENCH.

At this well-preserved 1683 inn in the town center, two cozy dining rooms are furnished with antiques. It also offers a cellar-level bar lined with antique masonry, with the main dining at street level. The inn has long been known for its accomplished chefs who use the best ingredients. Two of the best menu items are trout fried in butter and herbs, served with creamed potatoes, asparagus, and parsley; and beef tenderloin with herbs and green vegetables.

✪ Marie Louise. Lottrups Gaard, Vestergade 70–72. ☎ **66-17-92-95.** Reservations recommended. Main courses 280–305 DKK ($35–$38.15); fixed-price menus 395–610 DKK ($49.40–$76.25). AE, DC, MC, V. Mon–Sat noon–2pm and 6–9:30pm. Closed July. Bus: 2. FRENCH.

A centrally located antique house painted yellow is the home of Odense's smallest, most exclusive restaurant. Its dining room is a white-walled re-creation of an old-fashioned country tavern, although closer inspection reveals a decidedly upscale slant. The polished staff serves well-planned dishes based on French recipes. Delectable specialties include salmon-and-dill mousse with shrimp sauce, platters of fresh fish, turbot in Riesling or champagne sauce, lobster in butter or Provençal sauce, and an array of toothsome desserts.

Under Lindetraeet. Ramsherred 2. ☎ **66-12-92-86.** Reservations required. Main courses 165–220 DKK ($20.65–$27.50); fixed-price lunch 198 DKK ($24.75); fixed-price dinner 355 DKK ($44.40). DC, MC, V. Mon–Sat 11am–11pm. Closed July 4–24. Bus: 2. DANISH/ INTERNATIONAL.

This 2½-century-old inn is across the street from Hans Christian Andersen's house. For more than a quarter-century it has been a landmark restaurant, with a menu based on fresh, high-quality ingredients. Skillfully prepared dishes include tender Danish lamb, fillet of plaice with butter sauce, escalope of veal in sherry sauce, fried herring with new potatoes, and an upscale version of *lobscouse,* the famed sailors' hash. In the summer, meals and light refreshments are served outside under linden trees. Artists often sit here to sketch Andersen's house.

SVENDBORG
27 miles S of Odense, 91 miles W of Copenhagen

This old port on Svendborg Sound has long been a popular boating center, and you can see yachts, ketches, and kayaks in the harbor. The town retains some of its medieval heritage, but many buildings have been torn down in the name of progress. Visitors find that Svendborg makes a good base for touring the Danish châteaux country and the South Funen archipelago.

Svendborg is a market town. On Sunday morning, visit the cobblestoned central plaza, where flowers and fish are sold. Wander through the many winding streets where brick and half-timbered buildings still stand. On **Ragergade** you'll see the old homes of early seafarers. **Møllergade,** a pedestrian thoroughfare with about 100 shops, is one of the oldest streets in town.

The German writer Bertolt Brecht lived at Skovsbo Strand west of Svendborg from 1933 to 1939, but he left at the outbreak of the Second World War. During this period he wrote *Mother Courage and Her Children.*

ESSENTIALS
GETTING THERE   From Odense, head south on Route 9 for 27 miles to the port of Svendborg. If you're not driving, you can take a train from Copenhagen to Odense, where you can get a connecting train to Svendborg.

VISITOR INFORMATION   Svendborg Tourist Office is at Centrumpladsen (☎ 62-21-09-80). It's open June 14 to August, Monday to Friday from 9am to 7pm, Saturday 9am to 3pm; January 2 to June 13 and September to December 22, Monday to Friday 9am to 5pm, Saturday 9:30am to 12:30pm. The office is closed December 23 to January 1.

SEEING THE SIGHTS
Viebaeltegård. Grubbemøllevej 13 (near Dronningemaen). ☎ **62-21-02-61.** Admission 20 DKK ($2.50) adults, free for children accompanied by an adult. May 1–Oct 24, Mon–Fri 10am–5pm; Oct 25–Apr, Mon–Fri 10am–4pm.

The headquarters of the Svendborg County Museum's four branches, Viebaeltegård is in the town center. The building, a former poorhouse and workhouse constructed in 1872, is the only one of its kind still existing in a Danish town. These social-welfare buildings, including the garden, now make up a historical monument. Inside, see displays from ancient times and the Middle Ages, including excavation finds from old Svendborg and South Funen. Available workshops include goldsmithing, pottery making, and printing. There's a big museum shop, and you can picnic in the garden.

Anne Hvides Gård. Fruestraede 3. ☎ **62-21-76-15.** Admission 20 DKK ($2.50) adults, free for children accompanied by an adult. June–Aug 31, daily 10am–5pm; off-season, by arrangement with the main office.

The oldest secular house in Svendborg, a branch of the County Museum, was built around 1558. It's a beautiful half-timbered structure with 18th- and 19th-century interiors and collections of Svendborg silver, glass, copper, brass, and faïence. It's in the center of the Torvet.

St. Nicolaj Church. Skt. Nicolajgade 2B. ☎ **62-21-12-96.** Free admission. May–Aug, daily 10am–4pm; Sept–Apr, daily 10am–noon.

Svendborg's oldest church is among a cluster of old houses off Kyseborgstraede, in the vicinity of Gerrits Plads. Built before 1200 in the Romanesque style and last restored in 1892, its red-brick walls and white vaulting complement the fine altarpiece and stained-glass windows.

St. Jørgen's Church. Strandvej 97. ☎ **62-21-14-73.** Free admission. Daily 8am–4pm.

The beauty of St. George's Church is exceeded only by that of the Church of St. Nicolaj (above). The core of the church is a Gothic longhouse with a three-sided chancel from the late 13th century. During restoration of the church in 1961, an archaeological dig of the floor disclosed traces of a wooden building. Note the glass mosaics.

WHERE TO STAY

Hotel Svendborg. Centrumpladsen 1, DK-5700 Svendborg. ☎ **62-21-17-00.** Fax 62-21-90-12. www.hotel-svendborg.dk. E-mail: booking@hotel-svendborg.dk. 87 units. MINIBAR TV TEL. June to mid-Aug, 750 DKK ($93.75) double; Mid-Aug to May, 895–995 DKK ($111.90–$124.40) double. Rates include breakfast. AE, DC, MC, V. Free parking. Bus: 200 or 204.

This stylish hotel offers the best accommodations in Svendborg. Built in the 1950s, it rises four floors above the commercial core of town. Except for five or six rooms that missed out on an overhaul in 1994 (and are priced accordingly), the comfortable accommodations have Scandinavian modern furniture and good bathrooms. On the premises is a restaurant that serves international food, and a cafe-bar with a glassed-in front terrace. There's also an on-site tanning facility.

Hotel Tre Roser. Fåborgvej 90, DK-5700 Svendborg. ☎ **62-21-64-26.** Fax 62-21-15-26. 70 units. TV TEL. 525 DKK ($65.65) double. AE, DC, MC, V. Free parking. Bus: 200 or 208.

This hotel, built in 1975, offers attractively furnished units that are comfortable but short on frills. The 58 rooms with kitchenettes cost the same as those without. About a mile's drive south of Svendborg, the hotel contains a bistro-style restaurant, sauna, billiard room, and facilities for table tennis. There's a big swimming pool and children's playground on the premises, plus a nearby golf course and bathing beach.

WHERE TO DINE

✪ **Restaurant Gaasen.** Kullinggade 1B. ☎ **62-22-92-11.** Reservations recommended. Main courses 150–230 DKK ($18.75–$28.75); fixed-price menu 395 DKK ($49.40). MC, V. Mon–Sat noon–2pm and 5:30–10pm. DANISH/SEAFOOD.

At the edge of the harbor in a former ironmonger's smithy, this is one of the most appealing and congenial restaurants in town. Its creative force derives from chef and owner Claus Holm, who invents many of the dishes that attract a steady stream of local business. This is clearly a labor of love. Three dishes of which he is most proud are grilled freshwater crabs with saffron-flavored bouillon and homemade lobster-stuffed ravioli; veal stuffed with black truffles and sweetbreads, served with Madeira sauce; and gray mullet with herbs, beurre blanc (white butter), and sautéed spinach. The establishment's name (which means "goose") comes from its location a few steps from the site where live poultry was bought and sold in the Middle Ages.

Svendborgsund. Havnpladsen 5A. ☎ **62-21-07-19.** Reservations recommended. Lunch smørrebrød 60–100 DKK ($7.50–$12.50); main courses 80–170 DKK ($10–$21.25). No credit cards. Daily 11am–midnight. DANISH/FRENCH.

A 5-minute walk south of the commercial center, this waterfront restaurant is the oldest in town. The stone house was built in the 1830s. From the windows or summer terrace, you can see the harbor and its ferries, trawlers, and yachts. The talented chef specializes in fresh fish and meat, including the very filling *biksemad* (meat, potatoes, and onions). The separate bar is popular with locals.

NEARBY ATTRACTIONS ON TÅSINGE

The largest island in the South Funen archipelago, Tåsinge has been connected to Funen by the Svendborg Sound Bridge since 1966. **Troense,** the "skipper town" of Tåsinge, is one of the best-preserved villages in Denmark. Many half-timbered houses still stand on Badstuen and on Grønnegade, which has been declared Denmark's prettiest street.

The island was the setting for the tragic story of forbidden love depicted in the film *Elvira Madigan.* After checking out of a hotel in Svendborg, Danish tightrope walker Elvira Madigan and her lover, Sixten Sparre, a Swedish lieutenant, crossed by ferry to Tåsinge, where they committed suicide. The Romeo and Juliet of Denmark were buried in the Landet Kirkegård, Elvira Madigansvej, at Landet in the middle of Tåsinge. Even today, many brides throw their wedding bouquets on the graves. The 100th anniversary of the lovers' death was widely observed throughout Scandinavia in 1989; many ballads were written to commemorate the date. The island is best explored by car—drive over the causeway bridge (following Route 9). You can also take local bus no. 200. The most important attraction, Valdemar's Slot (Castle), can be seen by taking the vintage steamer MS *Helge* (☎ **62-50-25-00** for information), which departs several times daily from the harbor at Svendborg. The steamer operates May 11 to September 8. A round-trip ticket costs 50 DKK ($6.25). Tickets are sold on board or at the Svendborg Tourist Office (see above).

Søfartssamlingerne I Troense. Strandgade 1, Troense. ☎ **62-22-52-32.** Admission 25 DKK ($3.15) adults, 15 DKK ($1.90) children and seniors. May–Sept, daily 10am–5pm; Oct–Apr, Mon–Fri 10am–5pm, Sat 9am–noon. Cross the causeway to Tåsinge, turn left and then left again, heading down Bregningevej toward the water; turn right at Troensevej and follow the signs to the old port of Troense and the old village school (now the museum) on Strandgade.

The Maritime Museum (a branch of the County Museum), housed in a 1790 school, traces nautical history from the early 19th century to the present. Displays include pictures of ships, panoramas, yachting models, and memorabilia of the China and East India trade routes. You'll see Staffordshire figures, Liverpool ware, Sunderland china, ropework art, and ships in bottles.

Valdemars Slot. Slotsalléen 100, Troense. ☎ **62-22-61-06.** Admission 50 DKK ($6.25) adults, 35 DKK ($4.40) children. Apr–May and Oct 1–18, Sat–Sun 10am–5pm; May–Sept, daily 10am–5pm. Closed Oct 19–Mar. Take the MS Helge from Svendborg harbor. By car, from Troense follow Slotsalléen to the castle.

This castle was built between 1639 and 1644 by order of Christian IV for his son, Valdemar Christian. In 1678 it was given to the naval hero Niels Juel after his third victory over the Swedes in a Køge Bay battle. The Juel family still owns the structure, which is in considerably better condition than when the admiral arrived. The enemy Swedes had occupied the estate, sent the copper roof home to make bullets, and stabled horses in the church. The castle is now a museum.

Valdemar's Castle Church, in the south wing, was cleaned up by Admiral Juel and consecrated in 1687. Two stories high, it's overarched by three star vaults and illuminated by Gothic windows.

WHERE TO STAY & DINE

Hotel Troense. Strandgade 5–7, Troense, DK-5700 Svendborg. ☎ **62-22-54-12.** Fax 62-22-78-12. www.hoteltroense.dk. 31 units, 28 with bathroom. TV. 710–725 DKK ($88.75–$90.65) double. Rates include breakfast. AE, DC, MC, V. Free parking. Bus: 200.

Since 1905 this establishment has been both a hotel and a restaurant. It was last renovated in 1993. Most rooms are in the main white-walled building, with several in comfortable but lackluster annexes nearby. Accommodations cost the same with or without bathrooms. In the nautically decorated restaurant, which is also open to the public, specialties include fillet of lemon sole; plaice stuffed with shrimp, asparagus, and mushrooms; and medallions of pork with cream-and-curry sauce. The restaurant is open daily for lunch and dinner.

Restaurant Slotskælderen. In Valdemars Slot, Slotsalléen, Troense, DK-5700 Svendborg. ☎ **62-22-59-00.** Restaurant, main courses 175–195 DKK ($21.90–$24.40); bistro, main courses 45–110 DKK ($5.65–$13.75). AE, MC, V. Apr–May and mid-Sept to Oct, daily 11am–5pm; June to mid-Sept, daily 11am–9pm. Closed Nov–Mar. DANISH/FRENCH.

Inside the thick stone walls of one of the region's most foreboding castles, this restaurant is divided into a simple Danish bistro and an upscale French restaurant. The bistro serves such dishes as schnitzels, lobscouse (hash), and roulades of beef with Danish beer and aquavit. The views over the tidal flats and sea are better from the restaurant, but most visitors prefer the informality and lower prices of the bistro.

If you'd like to stay overnight, five luxurious guest rooms (four with private bathrooms) and one suite are in a modern outbuilding of the historic castle. Doubles without bathroom cost 840 DKK ($105), doubles with bathroom are 940 DKK ($117.50), and the suite goes for 1,450 DKK ($181.25).

Nearby at Millinge

The epitome of Danish roadside lodging, the following 15th-century smugglers' inn has been converted into a premier hotel, the finest in Funen, just 40km (24 miles) from Odense and 42km (25 miles) from Svendborg.

✪ **Falsled Kro.** Assensvej 513, Falsled, DK-5642 Millinge. ☎ **62-68-11-11.** Fax 62-68-11-62. www.falsledkro.dk. E-mail: falsled@relaischateaux.fr. 19 units. TEL. 1,725–1,850 DKK ($215.65–$231.25) double; 2,300–2,650 DKK ($287.50–$331.25) suite. AE, DC, MC, V. Bus: 930.

This Relais & Châteaux property offers tradition and quality in its colony of thatched buildings clustered around a cobblestoned courtyard with a fountain. Each accommodation is elegantly furnished and comfortable. Some are in converted outbuildings, others in cottages across the road. Eleven rooms have a TV, and seven have minibars. A garden leads to the water and a yacht harbor. Amenities include room service, laundry, baby-sitting, luggage service, translation and guide service, fishing and bathing areas, helipad, and nearby tennis courts and horseback riding.

Dining at this *kro* (inn) may be the culinary highlight of your stay in Denmark, so be sure to make a reservation. The kitchen uses only fresh seasonal produce, much of it grown there. The preparations are inspired by French cuisine.

Some of this restaurant's most noted dishes are among the simplest, such as the succulent salmon, smoked on the premises. Other choices include scallop salad with basil sauce, fish-and-shellfish soup with sorrel, fiery lobster in the style of Tiger Lee (spiced with hot peppers), French duck liver with wild rice and sweet-corn relish, and saddle of rabbit or braised beef in red wine sauce. The owners breed quail locally and cook and serve them with a port wine sauce. The chef's seafood platter is a gift to put before Neptune. Try salmon grilled or flamed over fennel. Game dishes predominate in autumn. The kitchen also bakes its own bread and cakes. The wine list is well chosen.

The restaurant serves lunch daily from noon to 2:30pm and dinner Tuesday through Sunday from 6 to 9:30pm (closed Monday October through March). Main courses are about 275 to 370 DKK ($34.40 to $46.25); three- to five-course fixed-price menus are 440 to 760 DKK ($55 for $95) and 760 DKK ($95).

ACROSS THE WATER TO ÆRØ
18 miles S of Svendborg, 46 miles S of Odense, 110 miles SW of Copenhagen

Ærø, an island 22 miles long and 6 miles wide, has seaside and country hamlets linked by winding, sometimes single-lane roads, with thatched-roof farmhouses in pastures and cultivated fields. The island has both sand and pebble beaches good for bathing along the north and east coasts.

There are many good places to eat and sleep—cozy inns in the country, and comfortable little hotels in town. Try some of the local rye bread, which is the best in Denmark. With your *aquavit* (schnapps), ask for a dash of Riga balsam bitters, a tradition that started when Ærø sailors brought them back from Riga.

ESSENTIALS
GETTING THERE   The only way to reach Ærø is by ferry. Car ferries depart from Svendborg six times daily. The trip takes about an hour. It costs around 155 DKK ($19.40) for the average car, and a one-way passenger fare costs 70 DKK ($8.75). For a schedule, contact the tourist office or the ferry office at the harbor in Svendborg. Bookings are made through **Det Æroske Færgegrafikselskab Ærø** in Ærøskøbing (☎ **62-52-40-00**). Ferry service is also available on the west coast of Funen, at Fåborg (☎ **02-61-14-88**).

VISITOR INFORMATION   The **Ærøskøbing Turistbureau** is at Vestergade 1 (☎ **62-52-13-00;** www.aeroeturistbureau.dk). It's open June 15 to August, Monday to Saturday from 9am to 5pm; September to June 14, Monday to Friday 9am to 4pm, Saturday 9am to noon. **Marstal Turistbureau,** Havnegade 5 (☎ **62-53-19-60**), is open from mid-June to August, Monday to Friday 10am to 5pm, Saturday 10am to 3pm. In July, the peak month to visit Ærø, it is also open Sunday 10am to noon. Off-season hours are Monday to Friday 9am to 4pm.

GETTING AROUND   It's best to take a car on the ferry because there's limited **bus service** on Ærø. Call ☎ **62-53-10-10** in Ærøskøbing for bus information. Bus no. 990 runs every hour on the hour in the afternoon between Ærøskøbing, Marstal, and Søby. Morning service is limited. Tourist offices (see "Visitor Information," above) provide bus schedules, which change seasonally. Tickets, which cost 62 DKK ($7.75) for the day, can be bought on the bus. If you'd like to take a bus tour of the island, call **Jesper "Bus" Jensen** (☎ **62-58-13-13**). His bus holds 12 to 14 passengers, and costs 50 DKK ($6.25).

Ærø is one of the best islands in Denmark for **cycling** because of its low-lying terrain and scenic paths. Local tourist offices provide maps outlining routes for 15 DKK ($1.90). You can use these maps for bike rides but also for **walks.** Cycle trails around the coast are marked by numbers 90, 91, and 92. Bike rentals cost 50 DKK ($6.25) a day, and rentals in Ærøskøbing are available at the Ærøskøbing Vandrerhjem, Smedevejen 15 (☎ 62-52-10-44); at Marstal at Nørremark Cykelforretning, Møllevejen 77 (☎ 62-53-14-77), and at Søby Cykelforretning, Langebro 4A (☎ 62-58-18-42).

EXPLORING THE ISLAND

The neat little village of ✪ Ærøskøbing was a 13th-century market town that came to be known as a skippers' town in the 17th century. Called "a Lilliputian souvenir of the past," it has small gingerbread houses, intricately carved wooden doors, and cast-iron lamps. Few Scandinavian towns have retained their heritage as much as Ærøskøbing. In the heyday of the windjammer, nearly 100 commercial sailing ships made this their home port.

The ferry from Fåborg docks at **Søby,** in the northwest part of the island. Before you rush to Ærøskøbing, visit a mellow manorial property, **Søbygård.** Now in ruins, this manor house in the center of Søby is complete with a moat and dank dungeons. Photographers are fond of the local **church.** Its octagonal steeple dates from about 1200, and it has had many additions and alterations over the centuries. See, in particular, Claus Berg's triptych, a primitive rendition of the Crucifixion.

Marstal, a thriving little port on the east coast of Ærø, has had a reputation in sailors' circles since the days of the tall ships. The harbor, protected by a granite jetty, is still busy. It has a shipyard that produces steel and wooden vessels, an engine factory, a ferry terminal, and one of Denmark's biggest yacht basins. The street names attest to Marstal's seafaring background—Skonnertvej, Barkvej, and Galeasevej (Schooner, Bark, and Ketch roads); Danish naval heroes; and seven Ferry Lanes.

Visit the **seamen's church,** with the spire and illuminated clock, in the town center. Inside are ship models and an altarpiece that depicts Christ stilling the tempest at sea.

Twice a day a mail boat takes a limited number of passengers on a 45-minute trip to tiny **Birkholm Island** for swimming and exploration. There are no cars on Birkholm. Reservations on the mail boat can be made at the Marstal Tourist Office.

SEEING THE SIGHTS

Æroskøbling Kirke. Søndergade 43. ☎ 62-52-11-72. Free admission. Daily 8:30am–5pm.

Built between 1756 and 1758 to replace a rather dilapidated church from the Middle Ages, this reconstruction still maintains the original 13th-century font and the pulpit stem, donated by Duke Philip of Lyksborg in 1634, the year he bought Gråsten County on the island of Ærø. (The year before that, he had inherited the market town of Ærøskøbing and an estate in Voderup.) The altarpiece is a copy of Eckersberg's picture hanging in Vor Frue Kirke in Svendborg. The colors selected for the interior of the church, along with the floral motifs, were the creation of Elinar V. Jensen in connection with an extensive restoration project carried out in 1950.

Flaskeskibssamlingen. Smedegade 22. ☎ 62-52-29-51. Admission 25 DKK ($3.15) for adults, 10 DKK ($1.25) for children. Daily 10am–5pm.

The seafaring life is documented in this museum of Peter Jacobsen's ships in bottles, which represents his life's work. Upon his death in 1960 at the age of 84, this former cook, nicknamed "Bottle Peter," had crafted more than 1,600 bottled ships and some 150 model sailing vessels built to scale, earning him the reputation in Ærøskøbing of "the ancient mariner." The museum also has Ærøclocks, furniture, china, and carved works by sculptor H. C. Petersen.

Ærø Museum. Brogade 35 (at the corner of Nørregade). ☎ **62-52-29-50.** Admission 15 DKK ($1.90). June 13–Aug 23, Tues–Sun 10am–4pm; off-season, Tues–Sun 10am–1pm. Closed Aug 24–June 12.

This is the best museum on Ærø. In the old days it was inhabited by the bailiff, but today you'll find a rich collection of the island's past, including antiques and paintings from the mid-1800s.

WHERE TO STAY
In Ærøskøbing
Det Lille Hotel. Smedegade 33, DK-5970 Ærøskøbing. ☎ **62-52-23-00.** 6 units, none with bathroom. 480–550 DKK ($60–$68.75) double. Rates include breakfast. No credit cards. Free parking on street.

Lying 100 yards from the ferry and harbor, Det Lille Hotel was built in 1844 as a private home. Today it offers simple but cozy guest rooms. The hotel is also a good dining choice. It serves meals daily from 11:30am to 2pm and 6 to 9pm. Try asparagus soup, pork chops with vegetables, ham cutlets with mushrooms, beef steaks, fried chicken, or hash.

Hotel Ærøhus. Vestergade 38, DK-5970 Ærøskøbing. ☎ **62-52-10-03.** Fax 62-52-21-23. 70 units, 55 with bathroom. MINIBAR TV TEL. 530 DKK ($66.25) double without bathroom; 760 DKK ($95) double with bathroom. Rates include breakfast. AE, DC, MC, V. Closed Dec 24–Feb 1. Free parking.

This typical Danish inn is charming, with many traditional features, such as copper kettles hanging from the ceiling and warm lamps glowing. The guest rooms are traditional—in vaguely French boudoir style—although they've been modernized. You can also enjoy good Danish meals here. In the summer there's dining in the large garden. The hotel, a 3-minute walk from the harbor, offers live music on summer weekends.

In Marstal
Ærø Kongreshotel. Egehovedvej 4, DK-5960 Marstal. ☎ **62-53-33-20.** Fax 62-53-31-50. www.hotelaeroestrad.dk. 100 units. TV TEL. 675 DKK ($84.40) double; 975 DKK ($121.90) suite. Rates include breakfast. DC, MC, V. Closed Dec 18–Jan 2. Free parking. Bus: 990 to Marstal.

A 5-minute walk south of the center of town and a quarter mile from the beach, this hotel, opened in 1989, is the largest and most up-to-date on the island. Surrounded by sea grass and sweeping vistas, the rooms are first class, decorated in pastel colors, with all the amenities. The suites are twice the size of regular rooms. There's an excellent restaurant, Østersøen, and a bar.

WHERE TO DINE
Restaurant Mumm. Søndergade 12, Ærøskøbing. ☎ **62-52-12-12.** Main courses 115–180 DKK ($14.40–$22.50). AE, DC, MC, V. May and Sept, Tues–Sun 11:30am–2:30pm and 6–9:30pm; June–Aug, daily 11:30am–2:30pm and 6–9:30pm. Closed Oct–Apr. AMERICAN/INTERNATIONAL.

In a simple house whose foundation dates from 1780, this restaurant enjoys a reputation for well-prepared dishes. There are two dining rooms; the less formal offers a view into the busy kitchen. There's also a terrace in the garden in back, where umbrellas and candles usually adorn the tables. The restaurant offers an unusual combination of American- and Danish-style dishes (a former owner had been a chef at a Florida resort). There's a copious salad buffet, flavorful steaks, and an abundance of seafood, mostly from local waters. You might try fillet of plaice, grilled salmon with hollandaise sauce, sole in parsley-butter sauce, or various preparations of shrimp and snails.

2 Bornholm

95 miles E of Copenhagen

Surrounded by the Baltic Sea, astride the important shipping lanes that connect St. Petersburg with Copenhagen and the Atlantic, Bornholm sits only 23 miles off the coast of Sweden. It's 95 miles from Copenhagen and the rest of Denmark. Prized as a strategic military and trading outpost since the early Middle Ages, Bornholm has been the focus of bloody territorial disputes by the Danes, Germans, and Swedes. It's home to 45,000 year-round residents, and a vacation spot for an additional 450,000 during the balmy summer months. Besides tourism, which is growing rapidly, the economy relies on trade, fishing, herring processing, agriculture, and the manufacture of ceramics. Thanks to the island's deep veins of clay, ceramics has been an important industry since the 1700s.

Covering a terrain of granite and sandstone is a thin but rich layer of topsoil; the island's rock-studded surface consists of forests and moors. The unusual topography and surprisingly temperate autumn climate—a function of the Baltic waters—promote the verdant plant growth. Figs, mulberries, and lavish conifers create the third largest forest in Denmark (right in the center) grow on the island.

Don't expect to enjoy a holiday on Bornholm without some inconvenience. Boats from Copenhagen take 7 hours each way, and if you plan to visit in midsummer, reservations are essential. All ferries arrive at Rønne.

ESSENTIALS

GETTING THERE   The most popular route from Copenhagen is the 7-hour ferry ride. **Bornholmstraffiken** (☎ 33-13-18-66) ferries depart from the pier at Kvaesthusbroen near the center of Copenhagen every evening year-round at 11:30pm, with scheduled arrival at 6:30am. Between late June and mid-August, there's an additional departure at 8:30am every day except Wednesday. Passage costs 206 DKK ($25.75) per person each way, plus an optional supplement of 161 DKK ($20.15) for a private cabin. Transporting a car from Copenhagen costs about 424 DKK ($53) each way. **Bornholm Ferries,** Havnen, Rønne (☎ 56-95-18-66), take 2½ hours to cross from Ystad on the southern coast of Sweden. There are up to four departures daily. A car with a maximum of five passengers costs 430 DKK ($53.75) one-way. You can also travel from Sassnitz-Mukran (Rügen) in northern Germany to Rønne; the crossing takes 3½ hours, and there's tax-free shopping on board. From Germany, one-way passage for a car with a maximum of five passengers is 452 DKK ($56.50). Each ferry has a restaurant or bistro featuring a buffet with Danish and Bornholm specialties.

Maersk Airlines (☎ 32-31-45-45 in Copenhagen or 56-95-11-11 in Bornholm) has about eight flights a day from Copenhagen to Bornholm's airport, 3½ miles south of Rønne. Round-trip fares are 595 to 1,000 DKK ($74.40 to $125).

VISITOR INFORMATION   The **Bornholm Welcome Center** is at Kystvej 3, Rønne (☎ 56-95-95-00; www.bornholminfo.dk). It's open June through August daily 7am to 9pm; September through May, Monday to Friday 9am to 4pm, Saturday 11:30am to 2:30pm, closed on Sunday.

GETTING AROUND   **Hertz,** Snellamark 19, Rønne, adjacent to the ferry piers (☎ 800/654-3001 in the U.S., or 30-54-00-15), is the island's leading car-rental agency. The cheapest cars rent for 1,550 DKK ($193.75), for 3 days, which includes unlimited mileage, all insurance coverage, and the whopping government tax. **Avis** is at Snellamark 21, Rønne (☎ 800/331-2112 in the U.S., or 56-95-22-08).

During nice weather, bicycling around the island is almost as popular as driving. If you want to do as the Danes, rent a bike; the prices are pretty much the same

Bornholm

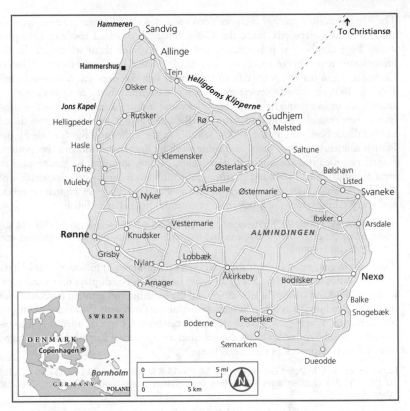

throughout the island—about 60 DKK ($7.50) a day. Bike-rental companies in Rønne include **Bornholms Cykleudleijning,** Nordre Kystveg 5 (☎ **56-95-13-59**).

EXPLORING THE ISLAND

Even if you have a car, you might want to bike the tour we've outlined below. Ask at any tourist office for a map of the island's 120-plus miles of bicycle trails, and divide this tour into several days, hitting the highlights at your own speed.

This tour begins at Rønne, but you could join at almost any point; the route goes counterclockwise around the island's periphery. Be aware that Bornholm's highways do not have route numbers. Some maps show the main east-west artery as Route 38, but local residents call it "the road to Nexø," also called Neksø. Consistent with local customs, this tour suggests that you follow the directional signs pointing to towns you'll eventually reach en route.

RØNNE

This is the island's capital and largest settlement, with 15,000 permanent residents.

SEEING THE SIGHTS

Hjorth's Fabrik (Bornholm Ceramic Museum). Krystalgade 5. ☎ **56-95-01-60.** Admission mid-Apr to mid-Oct, 30 DKK ($3.75) adults, 10 DKK ($1.25) children; mid-Oct to mid-Apr, 10 DKK ($1.45) adults, free for children. May–Oct, Tues–Sat 10am–5pm; Nov–Apr, Tues–Fri 1–5pm, Sat 10am–1pm.

The island's unusual geology includes deep veins of a clay that potters have appreciated for many generations. Since the 1700s, hundreds of island residents have produced large numbers of pots, plates, and cups, many of them whimsical, highly idiosyncratic reminders of another way of life. In 1858 a small-scale factory, Hjorth's Ceramics, began making pottery from the island's rich clay deposits. It survived until 1993. In 1995 the island's newest museum was established in the company's original factory. It's an intriguing hybrid of art gallery and industrial museum. You'll see the island's best examples of the dark brown, yellow, and gray pottery that was produced in abundance beginning in the 1700s, samples of the dishes and bowls made by the Hjorth company over the years, and some work by Bornholm's modern-day potters. Several ceramic artists maintain studios inside, casting, spinning, or glazing pots in view of visitors. Small-scale and charming, the museum is run by two descendants of the Hjorth family. The museum shop sells modern-day replicas of Hjorth ceramics, and many exhibits trace the production of ceramics from start to finish.

Bornholms Museum. Skt. Mortensgade 29. ☎ **56-95-07-35.** Admission 35 DKK ($4.40) adults, 5 DKK (65¢) children. Mid-Apr to mid-Oct, Mon–Sat 10am–5pm; mid-Oct to mid-Apr, Tues, Thurs, Sat 1–4pm.

This is the largest, most distinguished museum on Bornholm. It focuses on the island's unique position in the Baltic. Set in a former hospital, it has displays on archaeology, local traditions and costumes, ethnology, and the seafaring and agrarian traditions that made the island what it is today. Several rooms are outfitted with 19th-century antique furniture, toys, island-made silverware, and accessories. Of special interest is the collection of Bornholm-made clocks, copied from a shipment of English clocks salvaged from a Dutch shipwreck in the late 1700s.

Forsvarsmuseet. Kastellet Gallokken. ☎ **56-95-65-83.** Admission 20 DKK ($2.50) adults, 10 DKK ($1.25) children ages 6–12, free for children 5 and under. May–Oct, Tues–Sat 10am–4pm.

Housed within a citadel built around 1650 by the Danish king, this Defense Museum is in the southern part of town. With its massive round tower, this old castle is filled with weapons, maps, and models of fortifications. There is also a collection of antique armaments and military uniforms. In our view, the most interesting displays depict the Soviet aerial bombardment of Bornholm in 1945 and the subsequent Russian occupation of the island.

WHERE TO STAY

Best Western Hotel Fredensborg. Strandvejen 116, DK-3700 Rønne. ☎ **800/528-1234** in the U.S., or 56-95-44-44. Fax 56-95-03-14. www.hotelfredensborg.dk. E-mail: www.info@hotelfredensborg.dk. 73 units. TV TEL. 895–1,095 DKK ($111.90–$136.90) double; 1,100–6,500 DKK ($137.50–$812.50) suite. Rates include buffet breakfast. AE, DC, MC, V.

This is one of the few hotels on the island that remains open year-round. In a quiet forest, adjacent to a beach about a mile south of the Rønne harborfront, it was built during the 1960s. There's Danish modern furniture in the comfortable guest rooms; prices vary according to season and views of the water.

Dining: Two restaurants on the premises serve well-prepared food. The less formal, Fisken, is open only from April to late October, daily for lunch and dinner. The more formal restaurant, De 5 Ståuern F, serves lunch and dinner year-round. On warm summer evenings when the weather's clear, the hotel offers a barbecue on the terrace, with a view of the garden and the Baltic Sea. Every Thursday during the summer, a large fish buffet is featured.

Amenities: Sauna, tennis court, billiards, bike rentals.

Hotel Griffen. Krfedsen 1, DK-3700 Rønne. ☎ **56-95-51-11.** Fax 56-95-52-97. www.hotelgriffen.dk. E-mail: griffen@hotelgriffen.dk. 140 units. TV TEL. 745–1,075 DKK ($93.15–$134.40) double; 1,450 DKK ($181.25) suite. AE, DC, MC, V.

Near the heart of Rønne, a 5-minute walk from the beach, the town center, and an upscale marina, this hotel is the largest on Bornholm. Built in the 1970s, its buildings vaguely resemble 18th-century hip-roofed manor houses. Two of the four buildings contain only lodgings, and because of their isolation from dining, drinking, and convention facilities, they tend to be quiet and peaceful. Guest room furnishings are contemporary and minimalist, but with occasional touches of elegance enhanced by floor-to-ceiling windows and glass doors that afford views of the sea.

Dining/Diversions: Restaurant Viktoria is a rather formal venue with contemporary decor. It serves Danish cuisine, and meals average 78 to 250 DKK ($9.75 to $31.25). There's also a cocktail lounge.

Amenities: Room service, sauna, solarium, table tennis, indoor swimming pool.

WHERE TO DINE

✪ **De 5 Stâuerna.** In the Hotel Fredensborg, Strandvejen 116. ☎ **56-95-44-44.** Reservations recommended. Main courses 78–300 DKK ($9.75–$37.50); fish platter of the day 78 DKK ($9.75); fixed-price "menu degustation" 265 DKK ($33.15). AE, DC, MC, V. DANISH/INTERNATIONAL.

This is the best and most upscale restaurant in Rønne, with a clientele that tends to select it for celebratory meals of any ilk, including family gatherings during important rites of passage. Its name translates to "the five rooms," each of which is outfitted in a rustic country-Danish style, with white walls and light that's filtered through yellow-tinted windows. There's always a platter of the proposed fish of the day, which is invariably prepared in a simple, Danish-derived style, usually fried in butter and served with new potatoes in a way that Bornholmers have witnessed since their childhood. Other, more elaborate, options include Hereford beefsteak prepared Cordon Bleu style, with salted cured ham and Emmenthaler cheese; tournedos of beef flambéed in Calvados and served with apples and onions; an exotic sautéed fillet of ostrich with Mexican pimentos and peppers; marinated and minced beefsteak with chili; and a dish that we personally prefer more than almost anything else on the menu, Bornholm lamb served with a sauce concocted from rosemary, olive oil, and tarragon.

Rådhuskroen. Nørregade 2, Rønne. ☎ **56-95-00-69.** Reservations recommended on weekends. Main courses 78–144 DKK ($9.75–$18). AE, DC, MC, V. Daily noon–10pm. DANISH.

This is the most visible and, in its own way, most charming restaurant in Rønne. Set in the dark, intimate cellar of the Town Hall, a 140-year-old building, Rådhuskroen has a long history of feeding island residents in a cozy setting protected from midwinter winds. The well-trained staff serves such dishes as fillet of salmon in a fresh tomato "summer sauce" and two sizes of steak ("Mr. Beef" and "Mrs. Beef").

FROM RØNNE TO NEXØ

From Rønne, drive east along the island's modern highway, A38, following signs for Nexø. About 3 miles later, stop in **Nylars,** a town that's known as the site of the best-preserved of Bornholm's four round churches. The **Nylarskirke** (☎ **56-97-20-13**) was built around 1250. It rises prominently from the center of a community with no more than about 50 buildings. Frescoes inside depict Creation and the ejection of Adam and Eve from the Garden of Eden. It's open April to October 20, daily from 9am to 5pm. Admission is free.

Drive another 3 miles east until you reach **Åkirkeby,** the only inland settlement of any size. Its economy is based on farming and an animal-fodder factory (the Bovaerk Company). Small-scale and sleepy, this is Bornholm's oldest settlement—its town charter dates from 1346. It's also home to the island's oldest and largest church, the **Åkirke,** Torvet (☎ **56-97-41-03**), built around 1250. Although this church isn't as eccentric as some of the others, it's a sandstone-fronted monument built with defense in mind, as you'll note from the small windows. Notice the Romanesque baptismal font with runic inscriptions; it's believed they were carved by the master craftsman Sigraf on the island of Gotland. Other runic inscriptions appear on the cloverleaf-shaped arches. The church is open daily from 10am to 4pm; admission is 6 DKK (75¢).

From Åkirkeby, cut southeast for 2¾ miles, following the signs to **Pedersker,** a hamlet with three shops. (They close during the cold-weather months.) Four miles later you'll reach **Dueodde,** the name of both a raffish beachfront community and the entire region around the island's southern tip. The village marks the southern edge of a stretch of coastline that some people believe is Bornholm's finest beach. The best beaches on the island stretch north and east to the town of Balke, 3 miles beyond. The white sand grains are so fine that they were used for generations to fill hourglasses. The towns themselves are little more than backdrops for seasonal kiosks and a scattering of holiday homes. Most of the landscape is a virtual wilderness of pine and spruce trees, salt-tolerant shrubs, and sand dunes, some of which rise more than 40 feet above the sea.

The focal point of this southeastern coastline is the **Dueodde Fyr** (Lighthouse). It's the tallest on the island, built in 1962 to warn ships away from the extreme southern tip of the island. Weather permitting, you can climb to its top during daylight hours between May and October for a fee of 5 DKK (65¢), which you pay directly to the lighthouse keeper. For more information, call ☎ **56-48-80-42.**

From Dueodde, continue northeast along the coast, passing through the unpretentious fishing hamlets of **Snogebæk** and **Balke,** a sleepy midsummer resort area that's even sleepier in winter.

WHERE TO DINE ALONG THE WAY

Den Lille Havfrue. Hovedgaden 5, Snogebæk. ☎ **56-48-80-55.** Reservations recommended. Main courses 100–170 DKK ($12.50–$21.25). AE, DC, MC, V. Daily 11:30am–10pm. Closed Oct–Apr. DANISH.

Housed in a cozy modern building erected in the 1980s, this is one of the least pretentious but most reliable restaurants on the island. Its woodsy setting is accented with dozens of pottery pieces crafted by local artist Kirsten Kleman. The hard-working staff serves traditionally prepared fish and meat dishes, including salmon with lobster sauce (a perennial favorite), codfish with potatoes and onions, beefsteak and calf's liver, and broiled plaice with lemon and parsley-butter sauce. The menu includes an ample selection of soups, salads, and simple desserts.

FROM NEXØ TO ALLINGE

Nexø, with a year-round population of 3,900, is the island's largest fishing port. It's home to excellent replicas of the privately owned 17th- and 18th-century buildings that were considered architectural highlights of the island before the Second World War. In May 1945, several days after the rest of Denmark had been liberated from the Nazis, the Russians bombed Nexø heavily for 2 days. It had been a final holdout of Nazi soldiers during the closing days of the war. (Bornholm was also the last area of

Denmark to get rid of its Soviet "liberators," who didn't completely evacuate until 1946.)

The destruction of most of the town's 900 buildings and their restoration along original lines is the stuff of which legends are made. Because the region around Nexø is composed mostly of sandstone, much of the town's masonry is tawny, rather than the granite gray found elsewhere on the island.

One of the town's more eccentric monuments is the **Nexø Museum,** Havnen (☎ **56-49-25-56**). You'll see displays of fishing-related equipment that has sustained the local economy, and memorabilia of the author Martin Andersen (1869–1954). He was better known as Martin Andersen Nexø, the name he adopted to honor his native village. His novel, *Pelle the Conqueror,* which was set in Bornholm and later made into an acclaimed film, showed how Danish landowners in the early 20th century exploited Swedish newcomers to the island. The museum is open from May to October, daily 10am to 4pm. Admission is 15 DKK ($1.90).

After Nexø, the topography of the island gradually changes from sandstone to a more heavily forested area that has thin topsoil, deep veins of clay, and outcroppings of gray granite.

Continue 3½ miles north along the coastal road, following the signs to **Svaneke.** Denmark's easternmost settlement has fewer than 1,200 year-round residents. It bears some resemblance to eastern regions of the Baltic with which it has traded, and has many 17th- and 18th-century cottages along cobblestoned streets leading to the harbor. Many writers, sculptors, and painters are buying homes in Svaneke, an idyllic retreat from the urban life of Copenhagen. Svaneke is the most photogenic town on Bornholm; in 1975 it won the European Gold Medal for town preservation. Its most famous citizen was J. N. Madvig, an influential philologist who was born here in 1804.

From Svaneke, leave the Baltic coastline and head inland through the northern outskirts of the third largest forest in Denmark, the **Almindingen.** Dotted with creeks and ponds, and covered mostly with hardy conifers, it's known for its wildflowers— especially lilies-of-the-valley— and well-designated hiking trails. Head for **Østermarie,** a village of about 40 relatively nondescript buildings. Two miles northwest of Østermarie is the more culturally significant **Østerlars,** home to the largest of the island's distinctive round churches. The **Østerlarskirke** is at Gudhjemsveg 28 (☎ **56-49-82-64**). It's open from early April to mid-October, Monday to Saturday from 9am to 5pm. The entrance fee is 5 DKK (65¢) for adults, free for children. It was built around 1150 by the Vikings, who used rocks, boulders, and stone slabs. The church was dedicated to St. Laurence and later enlarged with chunky-looking buttresses; it was intended to serve in part as a fortress against raids by Baltic pirates. Inside are several wall paintings that date from around 1350, depicting scenes from the life of Jesus.

From Østerlars, drive 2 miles north, following the signs to **Gudhjem** ("God's Home"), a steeply inclined town that traded with the Hanseatic League during the Middle Ages. Most of its population died of the plague in 1653–54, but the town was repopulated some years later by Danish guerrilla fighters and sympathizers following territorial wars with Sweden. You'll find a town with many fig and mulberry trees and steep slopes that give it a vaguely Mediterranean flavor.

SEEING THE SIGHTS ALONG THE WAY IN GUDHJEM

Especially charming are Gudhjem's 18th-century half-timbered houses and the 19th-century smokehouses, known for their distinctive techniques of preserving herring with alderwood smoke. Its harbor, blasted out of the rocky shoreline in the 1850s, is the focal point for the town's 1,200 permanent residents.

Landsbrugs Museum (Bornholm Agricultural Museum). Melstedvej 25 (½ mile south of Gudhjem). ☎ **56-48-55-98.** Admission 30 DKK ($3.75) adults, 5 DKK (65¢) children. Mid-May to mid-Oct, Tues–Sun 10am–5pm. Closed mid-Oct to mid-May.

This museum is in a half-timbered, thatched-roof farmhouse built in 1796. It displays the kind of farm implements that were commonplace as recently as 1920. Also on view are a group of pigs, goats, cows, and barnyard fowl that are genetically similar to those bred on Bornholm a century ago.

Gudhjem Museum. Stationsvej 1. ☎ **56-48-54-62.** Admission 15 DKK ($1.90) adults, free for children under 16. Daily 10am–5pm. Closed mid-Sept to mid-May.

This museum is in Gudhjem's old train station, an early 20th-century building that closed in 1952 with the island's railways. Its exhibits honor the now-defunct rail lines that once crisscrossed the island. There are locomotives and other train-related memorabilia.

CONTINUING ON TO ALLINGE

Proceed west along the coastal road. Between Gudhjem and Allinge (9 miles), you'll enjoy dramatic vistas over granite cliffs and sometimes savage seascapes. The entire coastline is known as **Helligdoms Klipperne** ("Cliffs of Sanctuary"), for the survivors of the many ships that foundered along this granite coastline over the centuries.

Midway along the route, you'll see **Bornholms Kunstmuseet** (Art Museum of Bornholm), Helligdommen (☎ **56-48-43-86**). Opened in 1993, it contains the largest collection of works by Bornholm artists, including Olaf Rude and Oluf Høst. It's open from May to September, Tuesday to Sunday from 9am to 3pm. Admission is 25 DKK ($3.15), free for children under 16. From the rocky bluff where the museum sits, you can see the wind-tossed island of **Christiansø,** about 7 miles offshore. It's home to only about 120 year-round residents, most of whom make their living from the sea.

Continue driving northwest until you reach the twin communities of **Allinge** and **Sandvig.** Allinge's architecture is noticeably older than that of Sandvig. The 200- and 300-year-old half-timbered houses were built for the purveyors of the herring trade, and the smokehouses preserved the fish for later consumption or for export abroad. The newer town of Sandvig, to the northwest, flourished around the turn of the century, when many ferries connected it with Sweden. Sandvig became a stylish beach resort. The woods that surround the twin communities are known as the **Trolleskoe** ("Forest of Trolls"), home to wart-covered and phenomenally ugly magical creatures that delight in brewing trouble, mischief, and the endless fog that sweeps over this end of the island.

From Allinge, detour inland (southward) for about 2½ miles to reach **Olsker,** site of the **Olskirke** (Round Church of Ols), Lindesgordsvej (☎ **56-48-05-29**). Built in the 1100s, it's the smallest of the island's round churches, and was painstakingly restored in the early 1950s. Dedicated to St. Olav (Olav the Holy, king of Norway, who died in 1031), it looks something like a fortress—an image the original architects wanted very much to convey.

Now double back to Allinge and head north toward Sandvig, a distance of less than a mile. You'll soon see **Madsebakke,** a well-signposted open-air site that contains the largest collection of Bronze Age rock carvings in Denmark. There's no building, enclosed area, or even a curator. Simply follow the signs beside the main highway. The carvings include 11 depictions of high-prowed sailing ships of unknown origin. The carvings were made in a smooth, glacier-scoured piece of bedrock close to the side of the road.

From here, proceed just over a mile to the island's northernmost tip, **Hammeren,** for views that—depending on the weather—may extend all the way to Sweden. Here you'll see the island's oldest lighthouse, **Hammerfyr** (1871).

WHERE TO STAY IN SANDVIG

Strandhotellet. Strandpromenaden 7, DK-3770 Sandvig. ☎ **56-48-03-14.** Fax 56-48-02-09. 49 units. TV TEL. 750–950 DKK ($93.75–$118.75) double; 1,100–1,275 DKK ($137.50–$159.40) suite. AE, DC, MC, V. Closed Nov–Mar.

The foundations and part of the core of this historic hotel were built as stables in 1896; a decade later it became the largest, most stylish hotel on Bornholm. Today it's a reminder of a former way of life, when Sandvig was the main point of access from abroad. Nowadays Rønne has that role, and Sandvig is less commercial and more isolated than it was a century ago. A worthy detour for diners who drive from other parts of the island, the hotel offers three floors of Spartan accommodations with lots of exposed birch wood and (in most cases) sea views. The interior was modernized in 1991, making it suitable for a secluded getaway.

WHERE TO DINE IN SANDVIG

Strandhotellet Restaurant. Strandpromenaden 7, Sandvig. ☎ **56-48-03-14.** Lunch main courses 59 DKK ($7.40); dinner main courses 89–130 DKK ($11.15–$16.25). Daily noon–10pm. AE, DC, MC, V. Closed Nov–Mar. DANISH/SEAFOOD.

This hotel dining room was designed in the 1930s as a dance hall and supper club. Big windows overlook the sea, and you'll sense the care and attention to detail that's consistent with the Strandhotellet's role as a special dining destination on Bornholm. Choices include smoked fillet of wild salmon with tomato tapenade, a mixed platter of the daily catch, and medallions of beef with a ragoût of fresh vegetables and fresh mushrooms. The abundance of food and flavor make this a good value.

FROM ALLINGE & SANDVIG BACK TO RØNNE

Now turn south, following the signs pointing to Rønne. After about a mile you'll see the rocky crags of a semiruined fortress that Bornholmers cite as the most historically significant building on the island.

The ✪ **Hammershus Fortress** was begun in 1255 by the archbishop of Lund, Sweden. He planned for this massive fortress to reinforce his control of the island. Since then, Bornholm has passed from Swedish to German to Danish hands several times; it was a strategic powerhouse controlling what was then a vitally important sea lane. The decisive moment came in 1658, when the Danish national hero Jens Kofoed murdered the Swedish governor and sailed to Denmark to present the castle (and the rest of the island) to the king.

The fortress's dilapidated condition was caused by the regrettable actions of later builders, who used it as a rock quarry. It supplied the stone used in some of the buildings and streets (including Hovedvagten) of Rønne, as well as several structures on Christiansø, the tiny island 7 miles northeast of Bornholm. The systematic destruction of the fortress ended in 1822, when it was "redefined" as a Danish national treasure. Much of the work that restored the fortress to the eerily jagged condition you'll see today was completed in 1967. Interestingly, Hammershus escaped the fate of the second-most powerful fortress on the island, Lilleborg. Deep in the forest, Lilleborg was gradually stripped of its stones for other buildings after its medieval defenses became obsolete.

Some 2½ miles south of Hammershus, on the coastal road heading back to Rønne, is a geological oddity called **Jons Kapel** (Jon's Chapel). To see the rocky bluff and its marvelous panoramic view of the island's western coast, follow the signs for the mile hike from the highway. Ancient legend says this is where an agile but reclusive hermit, Brother Jon, preached to the seagulls and crashing surf below.

From here, continue driving south another 8 miles to Rønne, passing through the hamlet of **Hasle.**

3 Jutland

Dramatically different from the rest of Denmark, Jutland ("Jylland" in Danish) is a peninsula of heather-covered moors, fjords, farmland, lakes, and sand dunes. Besides its major tourist centers—Ribe in the south, Århus and Aalborg (Ålborg) in the north—it has countless old inns and undiscovered towns.

Jutland borders the North Sea, the Skagerrak, and the Kattegat. It extends 250 miles from the northern tip, Skagen, to the German border in the south. The North Sea washes up on many miles of sandy beaches, making this a favorite holiday place.

The meadows are filled with rich bird life and winding rivers; nature walks are a popular pastime. The heart of Jutland is mainly beech forest and lake land, sprinkled with modest-sized towns and light industry. Steep hills surround the deep fjords of the east coast. Gabled houses in the marshlands of South Jutland add to the peninsula's charm. Two of the most popular vacation islands are Rømø and Fanø, off the southwest coast. Here, many traditional homes of fishermen and ship captains have been preserved.

Our driving tour of Jutland begins at Ribe. If you're arriving in East Jutland from Copenhagen, take Route 32 west. From mainland Europe, take Route 11 from Tønder. Esbjerg is connected to Ribe by Route 24, which joins Route 11 south.

RIBE

20 miles S of Esbjerg, 186 miles W of Copenhagen

Ribe is a town of narrow cobblestoned lanes and crooked half-timbered houses. It became legendary because of the graceful—and endangered—storks that build their nests on top of its red-roofed medieval houses. Every year the residents of Denmark's oldest town ponder the question: Will the storks return in April?

This port was an important trading center during the Viking era (the 9th century) and became an episcopal seat in 948, when one of the first Christian churches in Denmark was established here. It was also the royal residence of the ruling Valdemars around 1200.

In medieval days, sea trade routes linked Ribe to England, Germany, Friesland, the Mediterranean, and other ports, but then the waters receded. Today marshes surround Ribe. The town watchman, armed with a lantern and staff, has made his rounds since the ancient custom was revived in 1936.

ESSENTIALS

GETTING THERE   If you're not driving, Ribe is easy to reach by train; there is hourly service from Copenhagen by way of Bramming. Train and bus schedules are available at the tourist office.

VISITOR INFORMATION   The **Ribe Turistbureau** is at Torvet 3 (☎ 75-42-15-00; www.ribetourist.dk). It's open June 15 to August, Monday to Saturday from 9am to 5:30pm, Sunday 10am to 2pm; April to June 14 and September to October, Monday to Friday 9am to 5pm, Saturday 10am to 1pm; November to March, Monday to Friday 9:30am to 4:30pm, Saturday 10am to 1pm.

SEEING THE SIGHTS

☯ Ribe Domkirke. Torvet (in the town center off Sønderportsgade). ☎ **75-42-06-19.** Admission 10 DKK ($1.25) adults, 3 DKK (40¢) children. May and Sept, daily 10am–5pm; June–Aug, daily 10am–6pm; Oct–Apr, Mon–Sat 11am–3pm, Sun 1–3pm.

This stone-and-brick cathedral, the little town's crowning achievement, was under construction from 1150 to 1175. Inspired by Rhineland architecture, it's a good example of Romanesque influence on Danish architecture, although it has Gothic arches. A century later a tower was added. Climb it if you want to see how the storks view Ribe. The legendary "Cat's Head Door" was once the principal entrance to the church, and the granite tympanum, *Removal from the Cross*, is the most significant piece of medieval sculpture in Denmark. Mosaics, stained glass, and frescoes in the eastern apse are by the artist Carl-Henning Pedersen.

Ribe Vikinger (Museum of the Viking Age and the Middle Ages in Ribe). Odins Plads. ☎ **75-42-22-22.** Admission 40 DKK ($5.80) adults, 15 DKK ($1.90) children. Apr–June 14 and Sept 15–Oct, daily 10am–4pm; June 15–Sept 14, daily 10am–5pm; Nov–Mar, Tues–Sun 10am–4pm.

Opened in 1995, this museum traces the story of Ribe. Beginning in A.D. 700, it depicts the Viking age and the medieval period. Archaeological finds are on display, along with such reconstructed scenes as a Viking-age marketplace, dating from around 800, and a church building site from around 1500.

Quedens Gaard. Overdammen 12. ☎ **75-42-00-55.** Admission 45 DKK ($5.65) adults, 15 DKK ($1.90) children. Mar–Apr and Sept–Oct, Tues–Sun 11am–3pm; June–Aug, daily 10am–5pm; Nov–Feb, Tues–Sun 11am–1pm.

In the rooms of an old merchant house, you can see how life was lived in Ribe "upstairs and downstairs." Different interiors from 1600 to 1900 are shown, along with an old kitchen. A collection of silver made by Ribe craftsmen is on display, along with artifacts illustrating the town's industrial development.

Ribe Kunstmuseet. Skt. Nicolai Gade 10. ☎ **75-42-03-62.** Admission 30 DKK ($4.35) adults, free for children under 16 and under. Feb–June 14 and Sept–Dec, Tues–Sat 1–4pm, Sun 11am–4pm; June 15–Aug, daily 11am–5pm. Closed Jan.

The Ribe Kunstmuseet displays an extensive collection of Danish art, including works of acclaimed artists like Eckersberg, Kobke, C. A. Jensen, Hammershøj, and Juel. Housed in a stately mid–19th century villa in a garden on the Ribe River, many paintings are from the golden age of Danish art. Exhibits change occasionally.

Det Gamle Rådhus (Town Hall Museum). Von Støckends Plads. ☎ **79-89-89-55.** Admission 15 DKK ($1.90) adults, 5 DKK children 7–14, free for children under 7. June–Aug, daily 1–3pm; May and Sept, Mon–Fri 1–3pm. Closed Oct–Apr.

In the oldest existing town hall in Denmark, built in 1496, the medieval Town Hall Museum houses Ribe's artifacts and archives. Included are a 16th-century executioner's sword, ceremonial swords, the town's money chest, antique tradesmen's signs, and a depiction of the "iron hand," still a symbol of police authority.

☯ St. Catharine's Church and Monastery. Skt. Catharine's Plads. ☎ **75-42-05-34.** Free admission to church; cloisters, 3 DKK (40¢) adults, 1 DKK (15¢) children under 14. May–Sept, daily 10am–noon and 2–5pm; Oct–Apr, daily 10am–noon and 2–4pm. Closed during church services.

The Black Friars, or Dominicans, came to Ribe in 1228 and began constructing a church and chapter house (the east wing of a monastery). Parts of the original edifice can still be seen, especially the southern wall. The present church, near Dagmarsgade, dates from the first half of the 15th century, and the tower is from 1617. Extensive restorations have made this one of the best-preserved abbeys in Scandinavia. Only the monks' stalls and the Romanesque font remain from the Middle Ages. The handsome pulpit dates from 1591, the altarpiece from 1650.

You can walk through the cloisters and see ship models and religious paintings hanging in the southern aisle. Tombstones of Ribe citizens from the Reformation and later are along the outer walls of the church.

A SIDE TRIP TO RØMØ

Rømø, the largest Danish island in the North Sea, is about 5½ miles long and 4 miles wide. It has a certain appeal because of its wild, windswept appearance. In the summer it attracts lots of tourists (especially Germans), possibly because of the nude sunbathing. In the off-season it's one of the sleepiest places in Europe, making it great for rest and relaxation.

To reach Rømø, take the 6-mile stone causeway from mainland Jutland. Or you can take a bus south from Ribe to Skaerbaek, then bus no. 29 across the tidal flats.

WHERE TO STAY

Weis' Stue (see "Where to Dine," below) also rents rooms.

✪ **Den Gamle Arrest.** Torvet 11, DK-6760 Ribe. ☎ **79/89-89-55.** 12 units, 3 with bathroom. 540–690 DKK ($67.50–$86.25) double without bathroom; 690–990 DKK ($86.25–$123.75) double with bathroom. Rates include breakfast. No credit cards.

One of the town's most charming hotels occupies a structure built in 1546 as the town jail. Set on the main square of Ribe, and constructed of the same russet-colored bricks that formed most of the town's important buildings, it functioned as a jail until 1989. The present owners transformed it into a cozy hotel. The guest rooms are snug, often with exposed brick and enough old-fashioned amenities to remind you of a gentrified version of the building's original function. There's a restaurant on the premises (see "Where to Dine," below).

✪ **Hotel Dagmar.** Torvet 1, DK-6760 Ribe. ☎ **75-42-00-33.** Fax 75-42-36-52. www.hoteldagmar.dk. E-mail: dagmar@hoteldagmar.dk. 50 units. MINIBAR TV TEL. 975–1,325 DKK ($121.90–$165.65) double. Rates include breakfast. AE, CB, DC, MC, V.

A Denmark legend, this historic 1581 building is the most glamorous address in the region. Converted from a private home in 1850, it's named after a medieval Danish queen. The guest rooms are comfortable and roomy, with lovely traditional furniture and state-of-the-art bathrooms. On Friday and Saturday nights (except in summer), there's music and dancing. The hotel has a restaurant (see "Where to Dine," below).

Hotel Fru Mathies. Saltgade 15, DK-67660 Ribe. ☎ **75-42-34-20.** 6 units, 4 with bathroom. MINIBAR TV. 590 DKK ($73.75) double with or without bathroom. AE, DC, MC, V.

Set behind a bright yellow stucco facade, a very short walk from the city's pedestrian zone, this hotel was named after its present guardian and supervisor. Fru (Mrs.) Inga Mathies. There's a shared TV/living room on the premises, and bedrooms are simple but cozy affairs, each with a radio and modest numbers of old-fashioned accessories. Breakfast is the only meal served.

Kalvslund Kro. Koldingvej 105 (at Kalvslund), DK-6760 Ribe. ☎ **75-43-70-12.** 5 units, none with bathroom. 300 DKK ($37.50) double. Rates include breakfast. No credit cards. May–Sept, daily 11am–10pm; other times of year by advance reservation only. Free parking. Bus: 57 or 921 from Ribe. 5½ miles north of Ribe on Rte. 52.

This 1865 inn offers comfortable rooms but few frills. The furniture, according to the management, "is old but not antique." The restaurant serves home-style cooking that is well prepared and presented. Full meals include such dishes as asparagus soup, Danish beef with sautéed onions, and pork cutlets.

WHERE TO DINE

Den Gamle Arrest. Torvet 11. ☎ **75-42-37-00.** Reservations recommended. Main courses 120–160 DKK ($15–$20). AE, DC, MC, V. June–Sept, daily noon–3pm and 6–9pm. Closed Oct–May. DANISH.

One of the newest restaurants in Ribe has one of the most unusual physical plants. This red-brick monument was built in the 1500s as the town's debtor's prison and jail. You can stroll in the red-brick courtyard that functioned for centuries as an exercise yard. Menu items include grilled fillets of salmon with spicy herb sauce, fillet of ox meat with fresh vegetables and red wine sauce, and roasted turkey with mango-flavored chutney sauce. Nothing overtaxes the chef's imagination, but the fare is good and tasty, the portions filling, and the ingredients fresh.

✪ **Restaurant Dagmar.** In the Hotel Dagmar, Torvet 1. ☎ **75-42-00-33.** Reservations required. Main courses 185–255 DKK ($23.15–$31.90); fixed-price lunch 98–185 DKK ($12.25–$23.15); fixed-price dinner 295–385 DKK ($36.90–$48.15). AE, CB, DC, MC, V. Daily noon–10pm. DANISH/INTERNATIONAL.

Opposite the cathedral and near the train station, the Hotel Dagmar's four dining rooms are a 19th-century dream of ornate furnishings and accessories. The international cuisine is the best in town, and it's impeccably served and complemented by a good wine list. Two fresh North Sea fish dishes of the day are usually offered. Among meat and poultry selections, try the fried quail stuffed with mushrooms on beurre blanc (white butter), or veal tenderloin with shallot mousse in port sauce. There's also a cozy cellar restaurant.

✪ **Restaurant Saelhunden.** Skibbroen 13, DK-6760 Ribe. ☎ **75-42-09-46.** Reservations recommended. Main courses 85–135 DKK ($10.65–$16.90). DC, MC, V. Apr–Oct, 11am–9:45pm (last food order); Nov–Mar, 11am–8:45pm (last food order). Beer served till midnight. DANISH/INTERNATIONAL.

One of the most evocative and cheerful restaurants in Ribe occupies a venerable but cozy brick building whose history goes back to 1634. Set beside the river that flows through Ribe, within full view of the craft that kept its commerce alive during its mercantile heyday, it has flourished as a restaurant since 1969. Today, you're likely to find an engaging staff deriving from every corner of Europe, and an antique format whose size is doubled during mild weather thanks to an outdoor terrace. Menu items include at least three kinds of steaks that include T-bone, French-style entrecôte, and something known as "English steak," that presumably gives British visitors access to the kinds of meat that is no longer legal in England. There are also fried fillets of plaice cooked in white wine with leeks; platters of meatballs or smoked salmon; and a local delicacy, smoked and fried dab, a flat fish not unlike flounder that flourishes in the local estuaries. The cookery is imaginative and versatile, using fresh, quality ingredients. No one will mind if you come here just for a beer or a simple snack. In summertime, it's one of the closest approximations in town to the kind of beer garden you might have expected in Hamburg.

Vaertshuset Saelhunden. Skibbroen 13. ☎ **75-42-09-46.** Main courses 55–105 DKK ($6.90–$13.15). DC, MC, V. Daily noon–9pm. DANISH.

This charming little restaurant stands amid stately trees near the edge of the town's narrow canal just north of the cathedral. The low-slung brick building dates from the 1600s, although in the 18th and 19th centuries it was the town's shoe factory. The dining room, the **Seals Room,** is decorated with many pictures and seal skins. Regional dishes include *skipperlavskovs* (beef, potatoes, and onions concocted into a hash) served with brown bread and a beetroot salad. Also featured are clear bouillon with meatballs, and fried fillet of plaice. The chef also specializes in ostrich, which is grown on a farm nearby. Here the bird is roasted and served with tomato sauce, potatoes, and sweet peas. For dessert, there is a homemade strawberry jelly served with thick cream and a home-made nougat and walnut ice cream. In summer you can sit in the cozy yard.

Weis' Stue. Torvet 2, DK-6760 Ribe. ☎ **75-42-07-00.** Reservations recommended. Main courses 85–175 DKK ($10.65–$21.90); 2-course fixed-price menu 125 DKK ($15.65). MC, V. Daily 11am–10pm. DANISH.

Small, charming, and rich with history, this brick-and-timber inn is on the market square next to the cathedral. Originally built in the 1500s, it was gradually enlarged over the centuries. The food in the ground-floor restaurant is plentiful and well prepared. You might try shrimp with mayonnaise, marinated herring with raw onions, smoked Green-land halibut with scrambled eggs, liver paste with mushrooms, sliced ham and Italian salad, fillet of beef with onions, and two cheeses with bread and butter.

The inn also has four upstairs guest rooms. They're cozy, but don't have private bathrooms. A double costs 460 DKK ($57.50), including breakfast.

FANØ

29 miles NW of Ribe, 176 miles W of Copenhagen

Nordby, where the ferry arrives, is a logical starting point for exploring the island of Fanø. Here you'll find heather-covered moors, windswept sand dunes, fir trees, wild deer, and bird sanctuaries. From Ribe, Fanø makes a great day's excursion (or a longer trip if there's time).

Fanø is a popular summer resort for the Danes, Germans, and English. **Sønderho,** on the southern tip, is our favorite spot. It's somewhat desolate, but that's its charm.

A summer highlight on Fanø is the **Fannikerdagene** festival, on the second week-end in July. It includes traditional dancing, costumes, and events connected with the days when sailing ships played a major part in community life.

If you miss the festival, try to be on Fanø on the third Sunday in July for **Sønderho Day.** The high point is a wedding procession that passes through the town to the square by the old mill. Attractions include traditional costumes and bridal dances.

ESSENTIALS

GETTING THERE   From Ribe, head north on Route 11 to Route 24. Follow Route 24 northwest to Esbjerg, where you can board a **Scandlines** ferry (☎ **75-13-45-00**). From May to October, ferries depart Esbjerg every 20 minutes during the day for the 12-minute crossing. In the winter, departures are during the day every 45 min-utes. A round-trip ticket costs 25 DKK ($3.15) for adults, 12 DKK ($1.50) for chil-dren. One car with five passengers travels for 280 DKK ($35) round-trip.

VISITOR INFORMATION   The **Fanø Turistbureau** is at Færgevej 1, Nordby (☎ 75-16-26-00; www.fanoturistbureau.dk). It's open Monday to Friday from 8:30am to 5:30pm, Saturday 9am to 1pm, Sunday 11am to 1pm. From June 6 to August 23, it's open until 6pm on weekdays, Saturday until 7pm, Sunday 9am to 5pm.

WHERE TO STAY & DINE

Fanø Krogaard. Langelinie 11, Nordby, DK-6720 Fanø. ☎ **75-16-20-52.** Fax 75-16-23-00. 9 units, 7 with bathroom. TV. 340 DKK ($49.30) double without bathroom; 595 DKK ($74.40) double with bathroom. Rates include breakfast. AE, DC, MC, V. Free parking.

This old-fashioned inn has welcomed wayfarers ever since it was constructed in 1624. Located 100 yards from the ferry dock, its rooms are simple but comfortable. The rooms without a bathroom are in the less popular century-old annex a short walk from the main building. The inn has some of the best food on the island; main dishes cost 47 to 135 DKK ($5.90 to $16.90). The restaurant is open daily from noon to 2pm and 5:30 to 9pm. There's also a popular bar, open daily from 8am to midnight, and an outdoor terrace that's used in the summer.

✪ **Sønderho Kro.** Kropladsen 11, Sønderho, DK-6720 Fanø. ☎ **75-16-40-09.** Fax 75-16-43-85. E-mail: sdrhokro@post6.tele.dk. 8 units. TEL. 780–1,190 DKK ($97.50–$148.75) double. Half board 325 DKK ($40.65) per person. AE, DC, MC, V. Free parking.

This is an unbeatable choice. The 1722 thatched-roof, ivy-covered inn, a National Trust House, nestles behind the sand dunes. Each room has a distinctive character, yet all suit the inn's traditional atmosphere. Antiques add a nice touch. The first-floor lounge offers views of the tidal flats. The dining room's cuisine is superb and plentiful; meals begin at 305 DKK ($38.15) for three courses. Sønderho Kro is 8 miles south of the Nordby ferry dock; a bus connects with ferry arrivals.

ÅRHUS

99 miles NE of Fanø, 109 miles W of Copenhagen

Jutland's capital and Denmark's second-largest city, Århus is a cultural center and university town with a lively port. You can enjoy the city's many restaurants, hotels, and nighttime amusements, and then use Århus as a base for excursions to Silkeborg, Ebeltoft, and the moated manors and castles to the north.

ESSENTIALS

GETTING THERE   When you return to the mainland from Fanø, head northeast on Route 30 to Grinsted. Here, follow Route 28 east until you connect with E45, near Vejle. Drive north on E45 to Århus. If you aren't driving, you can easily reach Århus by plane, train, or bus. **SAS** (☎ **70-10-20-00**) flies from Copenhagen to Århus. An airport bus from the airport to Århus's Central Station costs 50 DKK ($6.25). About a half-dozen trains a day leave Copenhagen for the 5-hour trip to Århus. Two buses a day leave Copenhagen for Århus. Travel time is 4 hours.

VISITOR INFORMATION   The **Tourist Århus** office is in the Rådhuset, Park Allé (☎ **89-40-67-00**). It is open mid-June to mid-September Monday to Friday 9:30am to 6pm, Saturday 9:30am to 5pm, Sunday 9:30am to 1pm; off-season Monday to Friday 10am to 5pm, Saturday 10am to 1pm.

GETTING AROUND   A regular bus ticket, valid for one ride, can be purchased on the rear platform of all city buses for 13 DKK ($1.65). You can buy a **tourist ticket** for 88 DKK ($11) at the tourist office or at newsstands (kiosks) throughout the city center. The 24-hour ticket covers an unlimited number of rides within the central city and includes a 2½-hour guided tour of Århus. The **Århus Pass** allows unlimited travel by public transportation and free admission to many museums and attractions. It also includes a 2½-hour guided tour. A 2-day pass costs 110 DKK ($13.75) for adults and 55 DKK ($6.90) for children; 1-week passes are 155 DKK ($19.40) and 75 DKK ($9.40). The Århus Pass is sold at the tourist office, many hotels, camping grounds, and kiosks throughout the city.

SEEING THE SIGHTS

For the best introduction to Århus, head for the town hall's tourist office, where a 2½-hour **sightseeing tour** leaves daily at 10am from June 24 to August 31. It costs 45 DKK ($5.65) per person and is free with the purchase of the Århus Pass (see "Getting Around," above).

Cathedral of St. Clemens (Århus Domkirke). Bispetorvet. ☎ **86-12-38-45.** Free admission. May–Sept, Mon–Sat 9:30am–4pm; Oct–Apr, Mon–Sat 10am–3pm. Bus: 3, 11, 54, or 56.

This late Gothic cathedral is the longest in Denmark, practically as deep as it is tall. The red-brick, copper-roofed structure has a 315-foot spire, begun in the early 13th century and completed in the 15th. Of chief interest are the Renaissance pulpit, 15th-century triptych, and 18th-century pipe organ.

After you see the cathedral, we suggest a visit to the nearby medieval **arcade,** Vestergade 3. It has half-timbered buildings, a rock garden, an aviary, and antique interiors.

✪ **Den Gamle By.** Viborgvej 2. ☎ **86-12-31-88.** Admission 60 DKK ($7.50) adults, 15 DKK ($1.90) children. Jan–Mar, daily 11am–3pm; June–Aug, daily 9am to 6pm; Sept–Oct and Apr–May, daily 10am–5pm; Nov–Dec, daily 10am–4pm. Bus: 3, 14, or 25.

Århus's top attraction, Den Gamle By displays more than 75 buildings representing Danish urban life from the 16th to the 19th century, re-created in a botanical garden. The open-air museum differs from similar attractions near Copenhagen and Odense, where the emphasis is on rural life. Visitors walk through the authentic-looking workshops of bookbinders, carpenters, hatters, and other craftspeople. There's also a pharmacy, a school, and even an old-fashioned post office. A popular attraction is the Burgomaster's House, a wealthy merchant's antique-stuffed, half-timbered home, built at the end of the 16th century. Be sure to see the textile collection and the Old Elsinore Theater, erected in the early 19th century. The museum also houses a collection of china, clocks, delftware, and silverware; inquire at the ticket office. Summer music programs are staged, and there's a restaurant, tea garden, bakery, and beer cellar.

Rådhuset (Town Hall). Rådhuspladsen. ☎ **89-40-20-00.** Guided tour 10 DKK ($1.25); admission to tower only 5 DKK (65¢). Guided tours Mon–Fri 11am; tower, noon and 4pm. Closed Sept–June 23. Bus: 3, 4, 5, or 14.

A crowning architectural achievement in the center of Århus, the Rådhuset was built between 1936 and 1941 to commemorate the 500th anniversary of the Århus charter. It's been the subject of controversy ever since. Arne Jacobsen was one of the designers of the modern marble-plated structure, with lots of airy space and plenty of glass. It can be seen only on a guided tour. An elevator (and 346 steps) runs to the top of the 197-foot tower, where a carillon occasionally rings. *Note:* The guided tour at 11am includes the tower. Otherwise, the tower can be visited only at noon and again at 4pm. The elevator and stairs are open three times a day: 11am, noon, and 4pm.

THE MANOR HOUSES OF EAST JUTLAND

Clausholm. Voldum, Hadsten. ☎ **86-49-16-55.** Admission (including guided tour) 60 DKK ($7.50) adults, 15 DKK ($1.90) children 13 and under. Daily 11am–5pm. Closed Sept–May 14. Bus: 221 from Randers.

Seventeenth century Clausholm is a splendid baroque palace, one of the earliest in Denmark. It was commissioned by Frederik IV's chancellor, whose adolescent daughter, Anna Sophie, eloped with the king. When Frederik died, his son by his first marriage banished the queen to Clausholm, where she lived with her court until her death in 1743.

The rooms are basically unaltered, but few of the original furnishings remain. The salons and ballroom feature elaborate stucco ceilings and decorated panels, and an excellent collection of Danish rococo and Empire furnishings has replaced the original pieces. The Queen's Chapel, where Anna Sophie and her court worshiped, is unchanged and contains the oldest organ in Denmark. In 1976 the Italian baroque gardens were reopened, complete with a symmetrically designed fountain system.

Clausholm is about 8 miles southeast of Randers and 19 miles north of Århus.

The Museums at Gammel Estrup. Jyllands Herregårdsmuseum, Randersvej 204, Auning. ☎ **86-48-30-01.** Admission 60 DKK ($7.50) adults, free for children under 14. Apr–Oct, daily 10am–5pm; May–Sept, Agricultural Museum Tues–Sun 10am–4pm and Manor House Museum Tues–Sun 11am–3pm. From Randers, take Route 16 east to Auning. Bus: 214.

Positioned 13 miles from Randers, and 24 miles from Århus, this is a compound of buildings that includes the **Jutland Manor House Museum,** complete with a great Hall, chapel, and richly decorated stucco ceilings; and the **Danish Agricultural Museum** which celebrates the role of Danish farming over the past thousand years. The entire compound dates from the 14th century, but the structures you see were extensively rebuilt and remodeled in the early 1600s. Expect a glimpse into medieval fortifications, baronial furnishings, the changing nature of tools and machines used during Danish plantings and harvests, and an enormous sense of pride in Denmark and its traditions.

✪ **Rosenholm Slot.** Hornslet. ☎ **86-99-40-10.** Admission 50 DKK ($6.25) adults, 20 DKK ($2.50) children 6–12, free for children under 6. May–June 19 and Sept, Sat–Sun 10am–5pm; June 20–Aug, daily 10am–5pm. Closed Oct–Apr. Bus: 119 or 121 from Århus.

On an islet 13 miles north of Århus and half a mile north of Hornslet, this moated Renaissance manor has been the Rosenkrantz family home for 4 centuries. The four-winged castle, encircled by about 35 acres of parkland, houses a Great Hall, as well as a large collection of Flemish woven and gilded leather tapestries, old paintings, Spanish furniture, a vaulted gallery walk, and pigskin-bound folios.

SHOPPING

Århus is the biggest shopping venue in Jutland, with some 400 specialty stores. They're tightly clustered within an area more than a half-mile square. The centerpiece of this district is Strøget, whose terminus is the Store Torv, dominated by the Århus Domkirke.

You might try a large-scale department store first, such as **Salling,** Søndergade 17 (☎ **86-12-18-00**), with some 30 specialty boutiques under one roof. **Magasin du Nord,** Immervad 2–8 (☎ **86-12-33-00**), is the largest department store in Scandinavia. The staff will assist foreign visitors with tax-free purchases.

"The greatest silversmith the world has ever seen" is a common description of **Georg Jensen,** Søndergade 1 (☎ **86-12-01-00**). A tradition since 1866, Georg Jensen is known for style and quality. The company produces unique silver and gold jewelry, elegant clocks and watches, and stainless steel cutlery, among other items. The biggest goldsmith outside Copenhagen, **Boye,** Søndergade 36 (☎ **86-19-21-22**), has been in business in Århus for more than 50 years. It offers an impressive selection of jewelry, much of it made in the company's workshops.

WHERE TO STAY

Low-cost accommodations in this lively university city are limited. Those on a modest budget should check with the tourist office in the Rådhuset (☎ **86-12-16-00**) for bookings in **private homes.** Prices begin at 175 DKK ($21.90) per person, single or double occupancy, but they could go higher depending on the home.

Hotel La Tour. Randersvej 139, DK-8200 Århus. ☎ **86-16-78-88.** Fax 86-16-79-95. 101 units. TV TEL. 695–895 DKK ($86.90–$111.90) double. Rates include breakfast. AE, DC, MC, V. Bus: 2, 3, or 11.

Since its construction in 1956, and its rebuilding in 1986, this hotel has followed a conscious policy of downgrading (yes, downgrading) its accommodations and facilities from a once lofty status to a decidedly middle-brow formula. The result is a hotel that's far from being the best in town—viewed, we imagine, as a great success by the management—that attracts hundreds of foreign visitors. The hotel, appropriately housed in an unimaginative 2-story building is 2¼ miles north of Århus center. It offers clean, simple bedrooms with small bathrooms and fewer of the facilities (such as the sauna and exercise room) that used to be part of its premises. There's a patio-style restaurant serving competently prepared Danish and international food, a bar, and a children's playroom (open May through September only).

⊙ **Hotel Royal.** Stove Torv 4, DK-8000 Århus. ☎ **86-12-00-11.** Fax 86-76-04-04. www.hotelroyal.dk. 102 units. MINIBAR TV TEL. 1,345–1,695 DKK ($168.15–$211.90) double; 2,900 DKK ($362.50) suite. Rates include breakfast. AE, DC, MC, V. Parking 90 DKK ($11.25). Bus: 56 or 58.

This is the most glamorous accommodation in town. The gilt date on its neo-baroque facade commemorates the hotel's establishment in 1838. There have been numerous additions and upgrades since. The Royal stands close to the city's symbol, its cathedral. A vintage elevator takes you to the guest rooms, many of them quite spacious. They're modernized, with good-size bathrooms. Beds are newly refurbished, with strong, durable mattresses, and accommodations are fitted with high-quality furniture, carpeting, and fabrics.

Dining/Diversions: The mezzanine greenhouse restaurant, the **Queen's Garden,** has an excellent chef who's always experimenting, and happily so. A meal might begin with salmon ravioli and "honey gravy," or halibut carpaccio. Follow up with grilled Norway lobster salad or truffle-flavored turbot on apple chutney with spinach sauce. Desserts are worth saving room for, especially the strawberry gazpacho with anise parfait. The hotel has the only casino in Århus—but it's definitely not Vegas.

Amenities: Sauna, car-rental desk, room service, dry cleaning and laundry, solarium.

Radisson SAS Scandinavia Hotel Århus. Margrethepladsen 1, DK-8000 Århus C. ☎ **800/333-3333** or 86-12-86-65. Fax 86-12-86-75. 233 units. MINIBAR TV TEL. June to mid-Aug and Fri–Sun year-round, 795–1,590 DKK ($99.40–$198.75) double; rest of year, 850–1,860 DKK ($106.25–$232.50) double. Year-round, from 2,025 DKK ($253.15) suite. Rates include breakfast. AE, DC, MC, V. Bus: 1, 2, 6, or 16.

This is one of the most modern and dynamic modern hotels in Denmark, and a city showplace that municipal authorities proudly show off to dignitaries visiting on trade missions from abroad. It was built in 1995 directly above the largest convention facilities in Jutland, and as such, maintains a closer contact with the dynamics of huge conventions and their planners than any other hotel in the region. Bedrooms occupy floors 4 to 11 of a glass-and-stone-sheathed tower that's visible from throughout the city. Lower floors contain check-in, dining, drinking, and convention facilities. Bedrooms are outfitted in plush upholsteries with bright colors. Each has a tasteful decor that's different from its immediate neighbor, incorporating Scandinavian, English, Japanese, or Chinese themes. Each has a trouser press, hair dryer, and large-windowed views over the city.

Dining/Diversions: There's a well-managed restaurant, Scenario, on the premises, and a very stylish modern bar whose decor is based on a series of sinuous curves, soft lighting, verdant plants, and carefully varnished paneling.

Amenities: Room service, health club and sauna.

Scandi Plaza. Banegårdsplads 14, DK-8100 Århus C. ☎ **87-32-01-00.** Fax 87-32-01-99. www.scandi-hotels.com. 168 units. 1,095–1,595 DKK ($136.90–$199.40) double; 1,995 DKK ($249.40) suite. Rates include breakfast. DC, MC, V. Bus: 3, 17, 56, or 58.

This dignified and traditional hotel (known until recently as the Ansgar) is convenient to the Town Hall and city center attractions. Completely renovated and vastly improved in 1997, it is part of an original hotel that opened in 1930. The hotel is now first-class, with tastefully decorated guest rooms, good beds, and modern bathrooms.

Dining: Café Brasserie Agnete & Havmanden offers lunch specialties with meats prepared by the hotel butcher. The more formal Restaurant Brazil features Latin-American barbecue, which may consist of five to seven kinds of meat, according to the season, prepared on a special barbecue and served at table on large skewers. Vegetables are stir-fried in a deep wok, and spicy relishes and sauces accompany the feast.

Amenities: Room service, concierge, Jacuzzi, sauna.

WHERE TO DINE

Kroen i Krogen. Banegårdspladsen 4. ☎ **86-19-24-39.** Lunch platters 15–130 DKK ($1.90–$16.25); dinner main courses 98–158 DKK ($12.25–$19.75); fixed-price menus 158–228 DKK ($19.75–$28.50). AE, DC, MC, V. Daily noon–10pm. DANISH.

"The inn in the corner" has built a loyal clientele since it was established across from the railway station in 1934. It's got a good, conventional Danish menu and one of the most unusual interiors in town—the walls are decorated with about two dozen panels depicting local artist Michael Fisker's interpretation of the history of Århus from the 14th to the mid–20th century. They were painted shortly after the World War II on the back of canvas coffee sacks because conventional art supplies weren't available.

You can order something as straightforward and simple as grilled sausages with black bread—a worthy foil for a glass of beer—or the house specialty, *kroens Anretning*, a platter with two kinds of herring, a fish fillet, a handful of shrimp, and a small steak with fried onions. Other items include a savory orange-marinated salmon, perfectly grilled rib-eye steak, and hazelnut cake. Between April and September, there are at least 50 additional seats on an outdoor terrace.

✪ **Le Canard.** Frederiksgade 74. ☎ **86-12-58-38.** Reservations recommended. Fixed-price menus 375–575 DKK ($46.90–$71.90). DC, MC, V. Mon–Sat 5pm–midnight (last order). FRENCH.

One of Århus's most appealing French restaurants sits in the heart of the city's pedestrian shopping zones. Within a conservatively contemporary black-and-white setting that's softened with bouquets of fresh flowers, the staff will propose a series of fixed-price menus that are cosmopolitan and sophisticated. A meal might begin with beef carpaccio served with pesto and baby greens; home-smoked salmon with quail eggs; or roasted scallops on a bed of arugula and peanut sauce. Main courses include breast of duck with raspberry sauce; rack of baby lamb with a mild mustard sauce; and Danish veal chops with tomato-and-basil sauce. Dessert might be a pear strudel with pear sorbet, served in a coconut shell.

✪ **Prins Ferdinand.** Viborgvej 2. ☎ **86-12-52-05.** Reservations recommended. Lunch main courses 135–225 DKK ($16.90–$28.15); dinner main courses 150–235 DKK ($18.75–$29.40); fixed-price lunch 195–225 DKK ($24.40–$28.15), fixed-price dinners 375–475 DKK ($46.90–$59.40). AE, DC, MC, V. Tues–Sat 11am–3pm and 6–9pm. Bus: 3. DANISH/INTERNATIONAL.

On the edge of Århus's historic center in a former tea salon, this is one of the city's finest restaurants. It was established in 1988 by Per Brun and his wife, Lotte Norrig, who create a version of modern Danish cuisine that has won favor with the region's business community. In two pink-toned dining rooms laden with flickering candles and flowers, you can order a platter of fresh smoked salmon served with tartare of salmon and pepper-cream sauce, turbot with Russian caviar and a drizzle of olive oil, sea devil with lobster prepared Thai style with lemongrass, or boneless pigeon stuffed with fresh goose liver served with a raspberry sauce. A dessert specialty is pears cooked with elderberries and served with vanilla ice cream, nougat, and almonds. The restaurant's array of dessert cheeses, the most unusual array in Jutland, includes esoteric local creations produced by small farmers.

✪ **Restaurant de 4 Arstider (Four Seasons).** Aboulevarden 47. ☎ **86-19-96-96.** Reservations required. Fixed-price menus 290–490 DKK ($36.25–$61.25). AE, DC, MC, V. Mon–Sat 11am–10pm. Closed July. Bus: 1, 2, 3, 6, 9, or 16. FRENCH.

The kitchen presents a carefully crafted cuisine based on the specialties of the season and presented as fixed price menus. In spring that means fresh asparagus (sometimes with foie gras), along with the catch of the day, perhaps red snapper in a zesty sauce. Succulent preparations of veal and lamb are always featured, and in the autumn there are game dishes. Because the menu is always changing, we can't recommend specific specialties, but over the years it's always been a heart-warming experience to arrive on the doorstep and discover the chef's surprises.

Teater Bodega. Skolegade 7. ☎ **86-12-19-17.** Reservations recommended. Lunch *smørrebrød* 30–79 DKK ($3.75–$9.90); main courses 79–165 DKK ($9.90–$20.65); 3-course fixed-price menu 208 DKK ($26). DC, MC, V. Mon–Sat 11am–11:30pm. Bus: 6. DANISH.

Originally established at a different address in 1907, Teater Bodega in 1951 moved across the street from both the Århus Dramatic Theater and the Århus Cathedral. It tries to provide an amusing dining ambience for theater and art lovers. The walls are covered with illustrations of theatrical costumes along with other thespian memorabilia. The food is solid and flavorful in the Danish country style. Various kinds of Danish hash, including *biksemad,* are served along with regular or large portions of Danish roast beef. There's also English and French beef, fried plaice, and flounder.

SILKEBORG
27 miles W of Århus, 174 miles W of Copenhagen

Silkeborg is in the midst of some of Denmark's most beautiful scenery. It's an ideal spot to explore **Himmelbjerget** (Sky Mountain), the highest peak in low-lying Denmark. *But be warned:* The "mountain" is less than 500 feet high.

ESSENTIALS
GETTING THERE   From Århus, follow Route 15 west to Silkeborg. If you aren't driving, there's frequent train service from Copenhagen by way of Fredericia.

VISITOR INFORMATION   The **Silkeborg Turistbureau** is at Godthåbsvej 4 (☎ 86-82-19-11; www.silkeborg.com). It's open June 15 to August, Monday to Friday 9am to 5pm, Saturday 9am to 3pm, Sunday 9:30am to 12:30pm; off-season, Monday to Friday 9am to 4pm, Saturday 9am to noon.

GETTING AROUND   Numerous bus routes service the city; all local buses depart from the bus stop on Fredensgade. There's no number to call for information. Tickets cost 11 DKK ($1.40) per individual ride, or 14 DKK ($1.75) if you need a transfer.

SEEING THE SIGHTS
The most intriguing way to see Sky Mountain and the surrounding countryside is aboard the paddle steamer *Hjejlen.* It has operated since 1861, and sails frequently in the summer. For schedules and more information, call **Hjejlen Co. Ltd.,** Havnen (☎ 86-82-07-66). A round-trip ticket costs 79 DKK ($9.90) for adults, half-price for children. Departures from Silkeborg Harbor are daily at 10am and 1:45pm from mid-June until mid-August.

❂ **Silkeborg Museum.** Hovedgaardsvej 7. ☎ **86-82-14-99.** Admission 20 DKK ($2.50) adults, 5 DKK (65¢) children 6–14, free for children 5 and under. May to mid-Oct, daily 10am–5pm; mid-Oct to Apr, Wed and Sat–Sun noon–4pm. Bus: 10.

This 18th-century manor by the Gudenå River, directly east of Torvet, houses the 2,200-year-old **Tollund Man,** discovered in a peat bog in 1950. His face is the least spoiled found to date. His body was so well preserved, in fact, that scientists were able to determine that his last meal was flax, barley, and oats. His head capped by fur, the Tollund Man was strangled by a plaited leather string, probably as part of a ritual sacrifice. Equally well preserved is the **Elling Woman,** who was found near the same spot. Scientists estimate that she was about 25 years old when she died in 210 B.C.

The museum also has a special exhibition of old Danish glass, a clogmaker's workshop, a collection of stone implements, antique jewelry, and artifacts from the ruins of Silkeborg Castle. In the handcraft and Iron Age markets, artisans use ancient techniques to create iron, jewelry, and various crafts.

WHERE TO STAY

Silkeborg Turistbureau (see "Visitor Information," above) can book you into nearby **private homes.** Prices begin at 175 DKK ($21.90) per person.

❂ **Best Western Hotel Louisiana.** Chr. 8, Vej 7, DK-8600 Silkeborg. ☎ **800/528-1234** in the U.S., or 86-82-18-99. Fax 86-80-32-69. www.louisianahotel.dk. E-mail: info@ louisianahotel.dk. 43 units. MINIBAR TV TEL. 1,125 DKK ($140.65) double; 1,450 DKK ($181.25) suite. Rates include breakfast. AE, DC, MC, V.

One of Silkeborg's best-established hotels was built in 1940 a few blocks south of the center of town. A massive renovation completed in 1998 brought its interior up to the standards of the most modern hotels in town. Part of the hotel's charm derives from its attentive staff, unusual modern art collection, and concern for the natural environment—the hotel donates a percentage of its receipts to environmental causes. The conservatively decorated guest rooms are a bit larger than you might expect. On the premises is a worthy steakhouse, the Angus, which serves dinner nightly from 5 to 10pm. Main courses run 130 to 180 DKK ($16.25 to $22.50).

Hotel Dania. Torvet 5, DK-8600 Silkeborg. ☎ **86-82-01-11.** Fax 86-80-20-04. www. hoteldania.dk. E-mail: info@hoteldania.dk. 47 units. TV TEL. 850–1,145 DKK ($106.25–$143.15) double. Rates include breakfast. AE, DC, MC, V. Free parking. Bus: 3.

On Silkeborg's main square, within a 5-minute walk of the railway station, this is the oldest hotel in town. Established in 1848, it underwent a radical upgrade and renovation in 1997. Antiques fill the corridors and reception lounge, but the guest rooms have been completely renovated in functional, modern style. Outdoor dining on the square is popular in the summer, and the Underhuset restaurant serves typical Danish food along with Scandinavian and French dishes. The hotel's dining room is one of the longest restaurants in Denmark: A corridor-like room with windows along one side, it stretches more than 150 feet, encompassing one end of the ground floor of two buildings.

Hotel Impala. Vestre Ringvej 53, DK-8600 Silkeborg. ☎ **86-82-03-00.** Fax 86-81-40-66. www.impala.dk. E-mail: impala@vip.cibercity.dk. 60 units. MINIBAR TV TEL. 1,070 DKK ($133.75) double. Rates include breakfast. AE, DC, MC, V.

One of the best hotels in the area, the Impala has streamlined rooms with angular Danish modern furniture and private balconies. Its gardens slope past an artificial pond to the highway. The rustic core was built as a farmhouse in 1890, and several modern chalet extensions were added in 1975 when it became a hotel. Twenty units overlook nearby Langsø Lake; the rest have a view of the hotel garden. Lunch and dinner are served daily in the upstairs dining room to hotel guests and the public. A full list of European wines is available.

WHERE TO DINE

Spiesehuset Christian VIII. Christian VIII Vej 54. ☎ **86-82-25-62.** Reservations required. Main courses 165–198 DKK ($20.65–$24.75); 3-course fish menu 328 DKK ($41); 4-course fixed-price menus 398–425 DKK ($49.75–$53.15). AE, DC, MC, V. Mon–Sat noon–3pm and 5:30–9:30pm. DANISH/FRENCH.

One of the best restaurants in Silkeborg, this establishment was founded about a decade ago in what was originally a private house built in the late 1700s. It seats only 30 people in a dining room painted in what the owners describe as the color of heaven (cerulean blue), accented with dramatic modern paintings. Delectable choices include lobster ravioli, carpaccio of marinated sole and salmon with saffron sauce, fillet of beef with truffle sauce, medallions of veal stuffed with a purée of wild duck and herbs, and tender rack of Danish lamb with garlic sauce. Service is attentive and professional.

EBELTOFT

60 miles E of Silkeborg, 33 miles NE of Århus, 209 miles W of Copenhagen

A well-preserved town of half-timbered buildings, Ebeltoft ("apple orchard") is the capital of the Mols hill country. This is a village of cobblestoned streets, hidden-away lanes, old inns, and ruddy-faced fishermen who carry on with the profession of their ancestors.

ESSENTIALS

GETTING THERE   From Silkeborg, head east on Route 15 through Århus and continue around the coast; then follow Route 21 south to Ebeltoft. There's no direct train service to Ebeltoft. From Copenhagen, take the train to Århus by way of Frederica; at Århus Central Station, board bus no. 123 for Ebeltoft.

VISITOR INFORMATION   The **Ebeltoft Turistbureau** is at Strandvejen 2 (☎ **86-34-14-00;** www.ebeltoftturist.dk). It's open June 15 to August, Monday to Saturday from 10am to 6pm, Sunday 11am to 4pm; September to June 14, Monday to Friday 9am to 4pm, Saturday 10am to 1pm.

SEEING THE SIGHTS

Fregatten *Jylland.* Strandvejen 4. ☎ **86-34-10-99.** Admission 60 DKK ($7.50) adults, 20 DKK ($2.50) children. Daily 10am–7pm.

The *Jylland* is the oldest man-of-war in Denmark (1860) and the world's longest wooden ship at 71 meters (13 meters wide). The frigate is moored in the harbor.

Det Gamle Rådhus. Torvet. ☎ **86-34-13-82.** Admission 20 DKK ($2.50) adults, 5 DKK (65¢) children. Apr–May, Tues–Sun, 11am–3pm; Sept–Oct, Tues–Sun, 11am–3pm; Nov–Mar, Sat–Sun, 11am–3pm.

The Town Hall looks like something erected just for kindergarten children to play in—a 1789 building, blackened halftimbering, a red-brick with timbered facade, and a bell tower. Its museum houses an ethnographic collection from Thailand and artifacts from the town's history. It's in the town center north of Strandvejen.

WHERE TO STAY & DINE

Hotel Ebeltoft Strand. Nordre Strandvej 3, DK-8400 Ebeltoft. ☎ **86-34-33-00.** Fax 86-34-46-36. E-mail: ebelstra@pip.dknet.dk. 72 units. MINIBAR TV TEL. Midsummer, 775 DKK ($96.90) double; rest of year, 1,085 DKK ($135.65) double. Rates include breakfast. AE, DC, MC, V. Free parking. Bus: 123 from Århus.

This centrally located two-story hotel was constructed in 1978 and most recently renovated in 1995. Each comfortable, well-furnished guest room has a balcony or terrace that overlooks Ebeltoft Bay. Facilities include tennis courts, horseback riding, an indoor swimming pool, and a sauna. The hotel also has a restaurant, bar, open fireplace, and playground. It's about a 5-minute drive from the ferry and a 15-minute drive from Tirstrup Airport.

Mols Kroen. Hovegaden 16, Femmøller Strand, DK-8400 Ebeltoft. ☎ **86-36-22-00.** Fax 86-36-23-00. www.molskroen.dk. E-mail: molskroen@adr.dk. 18 units. MINIBAR TV TEL. 1,280–1,680 DKK ($160–$210) double; 3,200 DKK ($400) suite. Rates include breakfast. AE, DC, V. Closed Dec 24–Jan 8. Free parking. Bus: 123 from Århus.

This hotel was vastly upgraded in 1998, and its prices rose dramatically, too. Nevertheless, it's one of the better places to stay in the area. Many rooms have terraces overlooking Mols Hills, and a fine white sandy beach is only 350 feet away. The *kro* (inn) is in the center of an area of summer houses mostly built in the 1920s and 1930s. The medium-sized guest rooms are now sleek, functional, and most comfortable, with freshly tiled bathrooms, generous towels, and new beds and mattresses. The hotel restaurant has a cozy, friendly ambience. Opt for a fish dish, especially oyster soup flavored with fresh herbs, or fried angler on spinach with baby vegetables. There's a vegetarian menu as well.

AALBORG
82 miles NW of Ebeltoft, 238 miles W of Copenhagen

The largest city in northern Jutland, Aalborg (Ålborg) is known worldwide for its aquavit. Although essentially a shipping town and commercial center, Aalborg makes a good base for sightseers, with its many hotels and attractions, more than 300 restaurants, and diverse nightlife.

History is a living reality in Aalborg. The city was founded 1,000 years ago when the Viking fleets assembled in these parts before setting off on their predatory expeditions. The city's historic atmosphere has been preserved in its old streets and alleys. Near the Church of Our Lady are many beautifully restored and reconstructed houses, some of which date from the 16th century.

Denmark's largest forest, **Rold,** where robber bandits once roamed, is just outside town. **Rebild National Park** is the site of the annual American Fourth of July celebration.

Not far from Aalborg, on the west coast of northern Jutland, some of the finest beaches in northern Europe stretch from Slettestrand to Skagen. The beach resort towns of **Blokhus** and **Løkken** are especially popular with Danes, Germans, and Swedes.

ESSENTIALS
GETTING THERE From Ebeltoft, follow Route 21 north until you reach the junction with Route 16. Drive west on Route 16 until you come to E45, which runs north to Aalborg. You can fly from Copenhagen to Aalborg; the **airport** (☎ **98-17-11-44**) is 4 miles from the city center. There is frequent train service from Copenhagen by way of Fredericia to Århus; there you can connect with a train to Aalborg, a 90-minute ride. Aalborg's bus station is the transportation center for northern Jutland, and is served from all directions. For all bus information in northern Jutland, call **Nordjyllands Trafikselskab** (☎ **98-11-11-11**).

VISITOR INFORMATION The **Aalborg Tourist Bureau** is at Østerågade 8 (☎ **98-12-60-22;** www.aalborg-turist.dk). It's open June to August, Monday to Friday 9am to 6pm, Saturday 9am to 5pm; September to May, Monday to Friday 9am to 4:30pm, Saturday 10am to 1pm.

GETTING AROUND   For bus information, call ☎ **98-11-11-11**. Most buses depart from Østerågade and Nytorv in the city center. A typical fare costs 12 DKK ($1.50), although you can buy a 24-hour tourist pass for 70 DKK ($8.75) and ride on all the city buses for a day. Information about bus routes is available from the *Aalborg Guide*, which is distributed free by the tourist office.

SEEING THE SIGHTS

The finest example of Renaissance domestic architecture in northern Europe is **Jens Bang's Stenhus**, Østerågade 9. The six-floor mansion was built in 1624 in glittering Renaissance style. It once belonged to a wealthy merchant, Jens Bang. The historic wine cellar, Duus Vinkjaelder, is the meeting place of the Guild of Christian IV. On the ground floor is an old apothecary shop. The mansion is privately owned and not open to the public. To get there, take bus no. 3, 5, 10, or 11.

Aalborgtårnet. Søndre Skovvej, at Skovbakken. ☎ **98-12-04-88**. Admission 20 DKK ($2.50) adults, 10 DKK ($1.25) children. June 17–Aug 11, daily 10am–7pm; May–June 16 and Aug 12–Sept 15, daily 10am–5pm. Closed Sept 16–Apr. Bus: 8 or 10.

This tower rises 325 feet above sea level, offering a perfect view—reachable by stair or elevator—of the city and the fjord.

Aalborg Zoologiske Have. Mølleparkvej 63. ☎ **96-31-29-29**. Admission 70 DKK ($8.75) adults, 35 DKK ($4.40) children, free for children under 12. Jan–Mar and Nov–Dec, daily 10am–3pm. Apr and Sept–Oct, daily 10am–5pm; May–Aug, daily 9am–7pm. Last ticket is sold 1 hour before closing. Bus: 1.

Set 2½ miles south of Aalborg, this is the second largest zoo in Scandinavia, where some 800 animal specimens from all over the world wander freely in surroundings designed to mirror an open African range. Apes and beasts of prey are kept under minimal restrictions. There's a good bistro, and snack bars here and there. The zoo is in Mølleparken, a large park with a lookout where you can see most of Aalborg and the Isle of Egholm. Look for Roda Reilinger's sculpture *Noah's Ark* near the lookout.

Nordjyllands Kunstmuseet (Museum of Modern and Contemporary Art). Kong Christians Allé 50. ☎ **98-13-80-88**. Admission 30 DKK ($3.75) adults, free for children. July–Aug, daily 10am–5pm; Sept–June, Tues–Sun 10am–5pm. Bus: 1, 4, 8, 10, or 11.

This building is a prime example of modern Scandinavian architecture. Built from 1968 to 1972, it was designed by Elissa and Alvar Aalto and Jean-Jacques Baruël as a showplace for 20th-century Danish and international art. It has changing exhibits, sculpture gardens, two auditoriums, a children's museum, an outdoor amphitheater, and a restaurant, the Museumscafeen.

WHERE TO STAY

✪ **Helnan Phønix Hotel.** Vesterbro 77, DK-9000 Aalborg. ☎ **98-12-00-11**. Fax 98-10-10-20. www.helnan.com/phoenix.htm. 201 units. MINIBAR TV TEL. July–Aug, 940 DKK ($117.50) double; 1,500 DKK ($187.50) suite. Sept–June 1,245 DKK ($155.65) double; 2,400 DKK ($300) suite. AE, DC, MC, V. Bus: 8, 10, or 11.

This is the oldest, largest, most prestigious hotel in Aalborg. The old-fashioned public rooms disguise how modern it is. It originated in 1783 on the town's main street as a private home. It became a hotel in 1853, and entered the modern age after three significant expansions, in the 1960s, '70s, and '80s. Today, it looks deceptively small from Aalborg's main street, and very imposing from the back, where you can see the modern wings. Guest rooms are outfitted with a combination of dark-grained furniture based on turn-of-the-century English models and light-grained Danish modern pieces.

   Dining/Diversions: The hotel's restaurant, Brigadieren, serves sophisticated Danish international cuisine. There's also a cocktail lounge.
   Amenities: Concierge, health club, solarium.

Hotel Hvide Hus. Vesterbro 2, DK-9000 Aalborg. ☎ **98-13-84-00.** Fax 98-13-51-22. www.hotelhvidehus.dk. 200 units. TV TEL. 1,095–1,295 DKK ($136.90–$161.90) double. Rates include breakfast. AE, DC, MC, V. Free parking. Bus: 1, 4, 8, 10, or 11.

The first-rate "White House Hotel" is in Kilde Park, about a 12-minute walk from the heart of Aalborg. Many international businesspeople have started staying here instead of at the traditional Hotel Helnan Phønix. In cooperation with well-known galleries, the hotel is decorated with works by some of Denmark's leading painters. The guest rooms are well furnished in fresh Scandinavian modern style; all have private balconies with a view of Aalborg. On the 15th floor is the Restaurant Kilden, which serves Danish and international specialties. Room service, laundry, and baby-sitting are available, and there is a sauna and a swimming pool.

Limsfordhotellet. Ved Stranden 14–16, DK-9000 Aalborg. ☎ **98-16-43-33.** Fax 98-16-17-47. E-mail: limhotel@pip.dknet.dk. 188 units. MINIBAR TV TEL. 895–1,250 DKK ($111.90–$156.25) double; 2,335 DKK ($291.90) suite. Rates include breakfast. AE, DC, MC, V. Closed Dec 24–26. Parking 40 DKK ($5). Bus: 1, 4, 40, or 46.

This most avant-garde hotel in town—a five-story yellow brick structure with huge expanses of glass in a streamlined Danish modern layout. In the center of town, a 3-minute walk east of the cathedral, the hotel opens onto the famous Limsjorden Canal. It's near Jomfru Anegade, a street packed with bars and restaurants. The public rooms are sparsely furnished with modern, streamlined furniture. Many of the comfortable guest rooms overlook the harbor. The medium-sized rooms have good-sized tile bathrooms. Mattresses are firm, and everything is maintained in state-of-the-art condition. The suites have Jacuzzis.
   Dining/Diversions: The hotel has a good restaurant that serves international and Danish regional dishes and is perfectly fine if you're staying at the hotel, but it's not worth a special trip. The piano bar in the reception area is open Monday to Saturday from 5pm to 1 or 2am. There's also a casino, open daily from 8pm to 4am, which charges an entrance fee of 40 DKK ($5.80) unless you're a hotel guest.
   Amenities: car-rental desk, room service, dry cleaning and laundry, solarium, fitness club.

WHERE TO DINE

Fyrtøjet. Jomfru Anegade 17. ☎ **98-13-73-77.** Reservations recommended. Main courses 60–120 DKK ($8.70–$17.40). AE, DC, MC, V. Mon–Sat 11:30am–midnight, Sun noon–11pm. Bus: 1, 3, 5, or 15. DANISH/INTERNATIONAL.

A cozy, small restaurant in the center of town, Fyrtøjet serves competent filling fare though it's not especially exciting We suggest a Danish specialty, the *almueplatte* (peasant's plate), with marinated herring, curry salad, two warm rissoles, cold potato salad and chives, and deep-fried Camembert cheese with black-currant jam. Other main dishes include stuffed plaice with shrimp, pepper steak, and breast of duck. In the summertime, enjoy your meal at outdoor tables.

Hos Boldt. Ved Stranden 7. ☎ **98-16-17-77.** Reservations recommended. Main courses 160–400 DKK ($20–$50); fixed-price menus 160–400 DKK ($20–$50). AE, DC, MC, V. Mon–Sat 5pm–midnight. Bus: 1, 4, 40, or 46. DANISH/FRENCH.

One of Aalborg's most likable restaurants was established in 1992 in a 19th-century building that had been a simple tavern for many years. The family-run business consists of two deliberately old-fashioned dining rooms filled with antique furniture and candles. Menu items change with the availability of the ingredients, but might include such perfectly prepared dishes as steamed turbot with julienne of leeks, consommé of veal with herbs and quail eggs, lobster bisque, a platter with various preparations of salmon, snails in herb-flavored cream sauce, rack of Danish lamb in rosemary-flavored wine sauce, and sea bass cooked in salt crust.

SKAGEN

65 miles NE of Aalborg, 303 miles W of Copenhagen

The "Land's End" of Denmark, Skagen (pronounced "skane") is the northernmost tip of Jutland. It has been compared to a bony finger pointing into the North Sea. Skagen is the country's second-biggest fishing port enlivened by a thriving artists' colony.

ESSENTIALS

GETTING THERE   By Car   Take E45 northeast to Frederikshavn. From there, head north on Route 40 to Skagen.

By Train   Several trains a day run from Copenhagen to Århus, where you connect with another train to Frederikshavn. From Frederikshavn there are 12 daily trains to Skagen.

VISITOR INFORMATION   The **Skagen Turistbureau** is at Skt. Laurentiivej 22 (☎ 98-44-13-77; www.skagen.turist.dk). It's open June 22 to August 11, daily from 9am to 7pm; June 1 to 21 and August 12 to 31, Monday to Saturday 9am to 5:30pm, Sunday 10am to 2pm; May and September, Monday to Friday 9am to 5:30pm, Saturday and Sunday 10am to 2pm; October to April, Monday to Friday 9am to 5:30pm, Saturday 10am to 1pm.

SEEING THE SIGHTS

If you walk to a point of land called **Grenener,** you'll be at the northernmost point of mainland Europe and can dip your toes into the Skagerrak and Kattegat seas. Another charming oasis to seek out is **Gammel Skagen,** a little seaside resort.

The most important attraction in the town is the **Skagens Museum,** Brøndumsvej 4 (☎ **98-44-64-44**). It houses the work of many local artists. You'll see paintings by P. S. Krøyer (1851–1909), Micheal Ancher (1849–1909), and Anna Ancher (1859–1935). Admission is 50 DKK ($6.25), free for children under 15. It's open May to September, daily from 10am to 6pm; April and October, Tuesday to Sunday 11am to 4pm; November to March, Wednesday to Friday 1 to 4pm, Saturday 11am to 4pm, and Sunday 11am to 3pm.

WHERE TO STAY

Color Hotel Skagen. Gammel Landevej 39, DK-9990 Skagen. ☎ **98-44-22-33.** Fax 98-44-21-34. www.skagenhotel.dk. E-mail: skagen@skagenhotel.dk. 153 units. TV TEL. 900–1,050 DKK ($112.50–$131.25) double; 1,000–1,300 DKK ($125–$162.50) suite; 3,500–8,000 DKK ($437.50–$1,000) apt per week. AE, CB, DC, MC, V. From Skagen, drive 1¼ miles southwest of town along Route 40.

Southwest of Skagen, beside the only road leading into town from the rest of Jutland, this sprawling, one-story hotel lies 1¼ miles from the sea. There, alone on sandy flatlands, it possesses an almost otherworldly sense of isolation. Unlike many of its competitors, which cater to families with children, this place appeals mostly to couples. Built in 1969, and enlarged and modernized in 1997, the hotel has an outdoor swimming pool, a bar, an appealing formal restaurant, and a sauna. The spacious, attractively furnished guest rooms have hardwood floors, padded armchairs, and big windows. Of the accommodations, 45 are listed as apartments and, as such, are rented only for 3 days at a time, although per week during the midsummer.

The Best of Norway   6

From snow-capped mountains to fjords warmed by the Gulf Stream, Norway is the "Land of the Midnight Sun." Although Norway is a modern, industrial nation, it is equally a world of remote towns and villages with a population devoted to outdoor activities. So you won't have to exhaust yourself making difficult decisions, we've searched out the best deals and once-in-a-lifetime experiences for this section. What follows is the best of the best.

1 The Best Travel Experiences

- **Enjoying Nature:** Norway is one of the last major countries of the world where you can experience nature on an exceptional level. The country extends 1,100 miles from south to north (approximately the distance from New York to Miami). Spread across it are 12,400 miles of fjords, narrows, and straits, which gave the country its name—Norway means "the way to the North." It's a land of contrasts, with soaring mountains, panoramic fjords, ice-blue glaciers, deep-green forests, fertile valleys, and rich pastures. The glowing red midnight sun reflects off snow-covered mountains, and the northern lights have fired the imagination of artists and craftspeople for centuries.
- **Experiencing Norway in a Nutshell:** One of Europe's great train rides, this 12-hour excursion is Norway's most exciting. The route encompasses two arms of the Sognefjord, and the section from Myrdal to Flåm—a drop of 2,000 feet—takes you past seemingly endless waterfalls. Tours leave from the Bergen train station. If you have limited time but want to see the country's most dramatic scenery, take this spectacular train trip. See chapter 9.
- **Visiting the North Cape:** For many, a trip to one of the northernmost inhabited areas of the world will be the journey of a lifetime. Accessible by ship, car, or air, the North Cape holds a fascination for travelers that outweighs its bleakness. Ship tours started in 1879 and, except in wartime, have gone to the Cape ever since. Hammerfest, the world's northernmost town of significant size, is an important port of call for North Cape steamers. See chapter 10.
- **Exploring the Fjord Country:** Norway's fjords are stunningly serene and majestic, some of the world's most awe-inspiring sights. The fjords are reason enough for a trip to Norway. Bergen

can be your gateway; two of the country's most famous fjords, the Hardanger-fjord and the Sognefjord, can easily be explored from there. You can go on your own or take an organized tour, which will probably include the dramatic Folge-fonn Glacier. Norway's longest fjord, the Sognefjord, can be crossed by express steamer to Gudvangen. See chapter 10.

- **Seeing the Midnight Sun at the Arctic Circle:** This is one of the major reasons visitors flock to Norway. The Arctic Circle marks the boundary of the midnight sun of the Arctic summer and the sunless winters of the north. The midnight sun can be seen from the middle of May until the end of July. The Arctic Circle cuts across Norway south of Bodø. Bus excursions from that city visit the circle. The adventurous few who arrive in the winter miss the midnight sun, but are treated to a spectacular display of the aurora borealis (northern lights), the flaming spectacle of the Arctic winter sky. In ancient times, when the aurora could be seen farther south, people thought it was an omen of disaster. See chapter 10.

2 The Best Scenic Towns & Villages

- **Fredrikstad:** Founded in 1567 at the mouth of the River Glomma, Fredrikstad preserved its Old Town, which had become a fortress by 1667. Today Fredrikstad (about 60 miles south of Oslo) offers a glimpse of what a Norwegian town looked like several hundred years ago. The old buildings in the historic district have been converted into studios for craftspeople and artisans, while maintaining their architectural integrity. After a visit here, you can drive along Oldtidsveien (the "highway of the ancients"), the most concentrated collection of archaeological monuments in Norway. See chapter 8.
- **Tønsberg:** On the western bank of the Oslofjord, this is Norway's oldest town. It was founded in A.D. 872, a year before King Harald Fairhair united parts of Norway. This Viking town became a royal coronation site. Its hill fortress is sometimes called "the Acropolis of Norway." Its ancient district, Nordbyen, is filled with well-preserved houses, and the folk museum houses a treasure trove of Viking-era artifacts. See chapter 8.
- **Bergen:** The gateway to Norway's fjord country, this town is even more scenic than the capital, Oslo. It was the capital of Norway for 6 centuries, and a major outpost of the medieval Hanseatic merchants. The town's biggest tourist event is the Bergen International Music Festival, but there are also many year-round attractions. Many visitors come to explore Bergen's museums (including Edvard Grieg's former home) as well as its varied environs—fjords galore, mountains, and waterfalls. See chapter 9.
- **Trondheim:** Norway's third-largest city traces its history to 997, when the Vikings flourished. Norway's kings are crowned at the ancient cathedral, Nidaros Domen; Scandinavia's largest medieval building, it was erected over the grave of St. Olaf (also spelled Olav), the Viking king. Trondheim is the popular stopover for travelers from Oslo to destinations north of the Arctic Circle. See chapter 10.
- **Bodø:** Lying 811 miles north of Oslo, this far northern seaport, the terminus of the Nordland railway, is the gateway to the Arctic Circle which lies just south of this breezy town. Another excellent place to observe the midnight sun from June 1 to July 13, Bodø is the capital of Nordland. From the center, you can also explore the environs, filled with glaciers and "bird islands." Bodø is also a gateway to the remote Lofoten Islands. See chapter 10.

3 The Best Active Vacations

- **Fishing:** The cold, clear waters of Norway's freshwater streams are renowned for their salmon and trout, and the storm-tossed seas off the coast have traditionally provided enough cod and mackerel to satisfy most of the nation's population. Serious anglers sometimes end up losing themselves in the majesty of the scenery. Tips on fishing in and around the Norwegian fjords are provided by the **Bergen Angling Association,** Fosswinckelsgata 37, Bergen (☎ 55-32-11-64), and the tourist information offices in Oslo and Bergen. Rural hotels throughout the nation can also give pointers to likely spots. For a truly unusual fishing experience, **Borton Overseas** (☎ 800/843-0602) can arrange treks and accommodations in old-fashioned fishermen's cottages in the isolated Lofoten Islands. The rustic-looking, fully renovated cottages are adjacent to the sea. Rentals are for 1 to 3 days, and include bed linens, maid service, boat rentals, and fishing equipment. The most popular seasons are March, when cod abounds, and June through August, when the scenery and weather are particularly appealing.
- **Hiking:** The woods (Marka) around Oslo are ideal for jogging or walking. There are thousands of miles of trails, hundreds of which are lit. If you don't want to leave the city, Frogner Park also has many paths. Any Norwegian regional tourist bureau can advise you about hiking and jogging. In Bergen, for example, you can take a funicular to Fløyen, and within minutes you'll be in a natural forest filled with trails. Longer, guided hikes (from 5 to 8 days) may be arranged through the **Norwegian Mountain Touring Association,** Stortingsgata, N-0125 Oslo 1 (☎ 22-82-28-22; www.dntoa.no).
- **Skiing:** This is the undisputed top winter sport in Norway, attracting top-notch skiers and neophytes from around the world. Norway is a pioneer in promoting skiing as a sport for persons with disabilities. Modern facilities comparable to those in Europe's alpine regions dot the landscape. If you're a serious skier, consider the best winter resorts, in Voss, Geilo, and Lillehammer (site of the 1994 Winter Olympics). See chapters 8 and 10.
- **Mountain Climbing:** Local tourist offices can offer advice. What we like best are guided hikes to the archaeological digs of the 8,000-year-old Stone Age settlements near the Hardangerjøkulen (Hardanger Glacier). The digs are about an hour's drive north of the mountain resort of Geilo. For information, contact the **Geilo Tourist Office** (☎ 32-09-13-00). See chapter 10.

4 The Best Festivals & Special Events

- **Bergen International Festival:** This European cultural highlight, which takes place in late May and early June, ranks in importance with the Edinburgh and Salzburg festivals. Major artists from all over the world descend on the small city to perform music, drama, opera, ballet, folkloric presentations, and more. The works of Bergen native Edvard Grieg dominate the festival, and daily concerts are held at his former home, Troldhaugen. Contemporary plays are also performed, but the major focus is on the works of Ibsen. See chapter 7.
- **Molde International Jazz Festival:** In this "city of roses," Norway's oldest jazz festival is held every summer, usually around mid-July. Some of the best jazz artists in the world wing in for this event. People stay up most of the night listening to music and drinking beer. Sometimes the best concerts are the impromptu jam sessions in smoky little clubs. See chapter 7.

- **Nobel Peace Prize Ceremony:** The most prestigious event on the Oslo cultural calendar, the ceremony takes place at Oslo City Hall on December 10. Even though it's only possible to attend by invitation, the event is broadcast around the world. See chapter 7.
- **Holmenkollen Ski Festival:** This large ski festival takes place in February at the Holmenkollen Ski Jump, on the outskirts of Oslo. The agenda is packed with everything from international ski-jumping competitions to Norway's largest cross-country race for amateurs. See chapter 7.

5 The Best Museums

- **Viking Ship Museum** (Oslo): Three stunning burial vessels from the Viking era were excavated on the shores of the Oslofjord and are now displayed in Bygdøy, Oslo's "museum island." The most spectacular is the *Oseberg,* from the 9th century, a 64-foot-long dragon ship with a wealth of ornaments. See chapter 8.
- **Edvard Munch Museum** (Oslo): Here you'll find the most significant collection of the work of Edvard Munch (1863–1944), Scandinavia's most noted artist. It was his gift to the city, and it's a staggering treasure trove: 1,100 paintings, 4,500 drawings, and about 18,000 prints. See chapter 8.
- **Norwegian Folk Museum** (Oslo): Some 140 original buildings from all over Norway were shipped here and reassembled on 35 acres at Bygdøy. Although Scandinavia is known for such open-air museums, this one is the best. The buildings range from a rare, stave church constructed around 1200 to one of the oldest wooden buildings still standing in Norway. Old-time Norwegian life is captured here as nowhere else. See chapter 8.
- **Vigelandsparken** (Oslo): This stunning park in western Oslo displays the lifetime work of Gustav Vigeland, the country's greatest sculptor. In the 75-acre Frogner Park, you can see more than 200 sculptures in granite, bronze, and iron. Including the "Angry Boy," his most celebrated work, and the most recognizable. See chapter 8.
- **Det Hanseatiske Museum** (Bergen): Depicting commercial life on the wharf in the early 18th century, this museum is housed in one of the city's best-preserved wooden buildings. German Hanseatic merchants lived in similar medieval houses near the harbor. See chapter 9.

6 The Best Buys

Most of the products mentioned below are available at better shops in Oslo and Bergen; see "Shopping" in chapters 8 and 9.

- **Knitwear:** Norwegian knitwear is eagerly sought by many visitors. Among the best buys are handknit or "half-handmade" garments. The latter, knit on electric looms, are so personalized and made in such small quantities that only an expert can tell that they aren't completely handmade. The tradition of women hand-knitting sweaters while rocking a cradle or tending a fire thrives in rural Norway, especially during the long winter.
- **Costumes:** Norway boasts more than 450 regional costumes, especially in the coastal communities. The original fishermen's sweater was knit of naturally colored wool (beige, brown, black, or off-white) in a deliberately large size, and then washed in hot water so that it shrank. The tightly woven sweater could then resist water. Modern versions of these sweaters are known for their nubbly texture, sophisticated patterns, and varying shades of single colors.

- **Crystal:** In Norway you can buy flawless crystal that's as clear as a Nordic iceberg. Norwegian tastes lean toward the clean, uncluttered look, stressing line, form, and harmony.
- **Ceramics:** In the 1960s and 1970s, Norway earned a reputation among potters and stoneware enthusiasts for its chunky, utilitarian pottery. The trend today is to emulate the fragile, more decorative designs popular in France, England, and Germany, so Norwegian ceramists are producing thinner, more delicate, and more ornate forms.

7 The Best Hotels

- **Grand Hotel** (Oslo; ☎ 800/223-5652 in the U.S., or 22-42-93-90): This is Norway's premier hotel, the last of Oslo's classic old-world palaces. It opened in 1874 and is still going strong. Ibsen and Munch were regular visitors. Constant renovations keep the hotel up-to-date and in great shape. The opulent suites house the Nobel Peace Prize winner every year. See chapter 8.
- **Bristol Hotel** (Oslo; ☎ 22-82-60-00): Inspired by Edwardian-era British taste, the interior design is the most lavish and ornate in Oslo. You enter a world of rich paneling, leather chairs, glittering chandeliers, and carved pillars. The most inviting area is the bar off the lobby, decorated in a library motif. The guest rooms boast painted classic furnishings and rich fabrics. See chapter 8.
- **Radisson SAS Hotel Norge** (Bergen; ☎ 800/333-3333 in the U.S., or 55-57-30-00): This grand hotel on Norway's west coast is sleek, modern, and cosmopolitan. The center of Bergen's major social events, the hotel is both traditional and handsomely up-to-date. It's also equipped with all the amenities guests expect in a deluxe hotel. The service is highly professional. See chapter 9.
- **Dr. Holms Hotel** (Geilo; ☎ 32-09-06-22): One of Norway's most famous resort hotels, this establishment was opened by Dr. Holms in 1909. It still stands for elegance, comfort, and tradition, all of which are especially evident during the winter ski season. After its face lift in 1989, the hotel offers beautifully furnished rooms with classic styling, and two completely new wings with a swimming complex. Famed musical artists often perform here. See chapter 10.
- **Radisson SAS Royal Garden Hotel** (Trondheim; ☎ 800/333-3333 or 73-80-30-00): The largest hotel in Norway's old medieval capital, this sleek steel-and-glass structure is a tasteful enclave of style and comfort. The glassed-in wings permit lots of natural light, and tasteful modern art and Scandinavian contemporary design create an inviting oasis. The hotel's dining room offers refined Norwegian and international fare in elegant surroundings; on weekends an orchestra provides music for dancing. See chapter 10.

8 The Best Restaurants

- **D'Artagnan** (Oslo; ☎ 22-41-50-62): Right off Karl Johans Gate (the main street), this restaurant is the domain of the Norwegian chef Freddie Nielson, inspired by the great French chefs Michel Guérard and Raymond Blanc. Such dishes as boned fillet of salmon with lobster-cream sauce and saffron-poached pike are reason enough to visit. See chapter 8.
- **Statholdergaarden** (Oslo; ☎ 22-41-88-00): Gourmets from all over Norway have flocked to this citadel of refined cuisine to sample chef Bent Stiansen's interpretation of modern Norwegian cooking. Stiansen is almost fanatically tuned to what's best in any season, and he serves some of the capital's finest dishes. He uses great imagination and widely varied ingredients—everything from Arctic char to

a rare vanilla bean imported from Thailand. See chapter 8.

- **Restaurant Julius Fritzner** (Oslo; ☎ 22-42-93-90): One of the most impressive dining establishments to make its debut in Norway in the mid-1990s, this restaurant in the Grand Hotel is still getting rave reviews. The chef uses only the finest Scandinavian ingredients in contemporary and traditional dishes; the emphasis is on enhancing and balancing flavors rather than creating surprises. See chapter 8.
- **Finnegaardstuene** (Bergen; ☎ 55-55-03-00): In a converted Hanseatic League warehouse, this Norwegian–French restaurant is one of the finest in western Norway. The cuisine revolves around only the freshest ingredients, especially fish. The kitchen uses classical French preparation methods to create such delectable items as lime-marinated turbot in caviar sauce or breast of duck in lime and fig sauce. See chapter 9.
- **Bryggen** (Trondheim; ☎ 73-52-02-30): This restaurant's excellent cuisine is a harmonious blend of Norwegian and French dishes. Menus change seasonally so that only the best and freshest ingredients are used. Ever had reindeer fillet salad with a cranberry vinaigrette? Here's your chance. Norwegian duck, when it appears on the menu, is a rare treat. See chapter 10.

Planning a Trip to Norway

This chapter contains many of the details you'll need to plan your trip to Norway. See Chapter 2, "Planning a Trip to Denmark," which includes information pertaining to Scandinavia as a whole.

1 The Regions in Brief

WESTERN NORWAY Western Norway is fabled for its fjords, saltwater arms of the sea that stretch inland. Many date from the end of the last Ice Age. Some fjords cut into mountain ranges as high as 3,300 feet. The longest fjord in western Norway is the Sognefjord, north of Bergen, which penetrates 110 miles inland. Other major fjords in the district are the Nordfjord, Geirangerfjord, and Hardangerfjord. The capital of the fjord district is **Bergen,** the largest city on the west coast. **Lofthus,** a collection of farms extending along the slopes of Sørfjorden, offers panoramic views of the fjord and the **Folgefonn Glacier.** Hiking is the primary activity in this region. The area north of the **Hardangerfjord** is a haven for hikers. Hardangervidda National Park is here, on Europe's largest high-mountain plateau, and is home to Norway's largest herd of wild reindeer. The town of **Voss,** birthplace of the American football great Knute Rockne, is surrounded by glaciers, fjords, rivers, and lakes.

CENTRAL NORWAY Fjords are also common in central Norway; the two largest are the Trondheimsfjord and Narnsfjord. It's not unusual for roads to pass waterfalls that cascade straight down into fjords. Many thick forests and snowcapped peaks fill central Norway. The town of **Geilo,** halfway between Bergen and Oslo, is one of Norway's most popular ski resorts. It boasts more than 80 miles of cross-country trails. **Trondheim,** central Norway's largest city, is home to Nidaros Domen, the 11th-century cathedral that was once the burial place for kings. **Røros** is a well-preserved 18th-century mining town. The medieval city of **Molde,** Norway's capital during the Second World War, plays host to one of Europe's largest jazz festivals. **Geiranger,** site of the Seven Sisters waterfall, is one of Norway's most popular resorts.

EASTERN NORWAY On the border with Sweden, eastern Norway is characterized by clear blue lakes, rolling hills, and green valleys. In some ways it's the most traditional part of the country. Because of its many fertile valleys, it was one of the earliest areas to be settled. Some of the biggest valleys are Valdres, Østerdal, Hallingdall, Numedal, and

Gudbrandsdalen. Campers and hikers enjoy the great forests of the Hedmark region, site of Norway's longest river, the Glomma (Gløma), which flows about 360 miles. The area has many ski resorts, notably **Lillehammer,** site of the 1994 Winter Olympics. Norway's most visited destination is the capital, **Oslo,** which rises from the shores of the Oslofjord. The city of **Frederikstad,** at the mouth of the Glomma, was once the marketplace for goods entering the country. Its 17th-century Kongsten Fort was designed to defend Norway from Sweden. **Tønsberg,** Norway's oldest town, dates to the 9th century. This area is also the site of the **Peer Gynt Road,** of Ibsen fame, and the mountainous region is home to numerous ski resorts.

SOUTHERN NORWAY   Southern Norway is sometimes referred to as "the Riviera" because of its unspoiled and uncrowded—but chilly—beaches. It's also a favorite port of call for the yachting crowd. **Stavanger,** the oil capital of Norway, is the largest southern city and also quite popular. There is much to explore in this Telemark region, which is filled with lakes and canals popular for summer canoeing and boating. **Skien,** birthplace of the playwright Henrik Ibsen (1828–1906), is primarily an industrial town. In Skien, you can board a lake steamer to travel through a series of canals. The southern part of **Kristiansand** links Norway with continental Europe. Close by is 6-mile **Hamresanden Beach,** one of the longest uninterrupted beaches in Europe. Along the western half of the district are more fjords, notably the Lysefjord, Sande-fjord, and Vindefjord.

NORTHERN NORWAY   The "Land of the Midnight Sun" is a region of craggy cliffs that descend to the sea and of deep, fertile valleys along the deserted moors. It has islands with few, if any, inhabitants, where life has remained relatively unchanged for generations. The capital of the Nordland region is **Bodø,** which lies just north of the Arctic Circle; it's a base for Arctic fishing trips and visits to the wild Glomfjord. Norway's second-largest glacier, **Svartisen,** is also in this region, as is the city of **Narvik,** a major Arctic port and the gateway to the **Lofoten Islands.** The islands, which have many fishing villages, make up one of the most beautiful areas of Norway. Visitors come here from all over the world for sport fishing and bird-watching.

TROMS   The main city in this region is **Tromsø,** from which polar explorations launch. A key attraction is the world's northernmost planetarium. Troms contains one of Norway's most impressive mountain ranges, the Lyngs Alps, which attract winter skiers and summer hikers. **Alta,** site of the Altafjord, is reputed to have the best salmon-fishing waters in the world.

FINNMARK   At the top of Norway is the Finnmark region, home of the Lapps (or Samis). Settlements here include **Kautokeino** (the Lapp town) and **Hammerfest,** the world's northernmost town. Most tourists come to Finnmark to see the **North Cape,** Europe's northernmost point and an ideal midnight sun viewing spot. **Vardø** is the only Norwegian mainland town in the Arctic climate zone. In the 17th century it was the site of more than 80 witch burnings. The town of **Kirkenes** lies 170 miles north of the Arctic Circle, close to the Russian border.

2 Visitor Information & Entry Requirements

VISITOR INFORMATION

In the **United States,** contact the **Norwegian Tourist Board,** 655 Third Ave., Suite 1810, New York, NY 10017 (☎ **212/885-9700**), at least 3 months in advance for maps, sightseeing pointers, ferry schedules, and other information.

In the **United Kingdom,** contact the **Norwegian Tourist Board,** a division of the Scandinavian Tourist Board, Charles House, 5–11 Lower Regent St., London SW1Y 4LX (☎ **020/7839-6255**).

Norway

The Norwegian Krone

For American Readers: At this writing, $1 = approximately 8.9 kroner (or 1 krone = 11¢); this was the exchange rate used to calculate the dollar values given in this edition, rounded to the nearest nickel.

For British Readers: At this writing, £1 = approximately 13 kroner (or 1 krone = 8 pence); this was the exchange rate used to calculate the pound values in the chart below.

Regarding the Euro: At press time, 1€ = 8 kroner (or 1 krone = .12€), although this will almost certainly change as Norway works through the role it wants to play within a united Europe with a shared European currency.

Note: International exchange rates fluctuate, so the figures in this chart may not be the same by the time of your trip to Norway. Use this table as a guideline.

NOK	US$	UK£	Euro	NOK	US$	UK£	Euro
1	0.11	0.08	0.12	75	8.25	6.00	9.00
2	0.22	0.16	0.24	100	11.00	8.00	12.00
3	0.33	0.24	0.36	125	13.75	10.00	15.00
4	0.44	0.32	0.48	150	16.50	12.00	18.00
5	0.55	0.40	0.60	175	19.25	14.00	21.00
6	0.66	0.48	0.72	200	22.00	16.00	24.00
7	0.77	0.56	0.84	225	24.75	18.00	27.00
8	0.88	0.64	0.96	250	27.50	20.00	30.00
9	0.99	0.72	1.08	275	30.25	22.00	33.00
10	1.10	0.8	1.20	300	33.00	24.00	36.00
15	1.65	1.20	1.80	350	38.50	28.00	42.00
20	2.20	1.60	2.40	400	44.00	32.00	48.00
25	2.75	2.00	3.00	500	55.00	40.00	60.00
50	5.50	4.00	6.00	1000	110.00	80.00	120.00

You might also try the tourist board's official Web site: **www.visitnorway.com**.

If you get in touch with a **travel agent,** make sure the agent is a member of the American Society of Travel Agents (ASTA). If a problem arises, you can complain to the Consumer Affairs Department of the society at 1101 King St., Alexandria, VA 22314 (☎ **703/789-2782**).

ENTRY REQUIREMENTS

Citizens of the United States, Canada, Ireland, Australia, and New Zealand, and British subjects, need a valid **passport** to enter Norway. You need to apply for a visa only if you want to stay more than 3 months. A British Visitor's Passport is also valid for holidays and some business trips of less than 3 months. The passport can include your spouse, and it's valid for 1 year. Apply in person at a main post office in the British Isles, and the passport will be issued that day.

Your current domestic **driver's license** is acceptable in Norway. An international driver's license is not required.

What Things Cost in Oslo	U.S.$
Taxi from Gardermoen Airport to the city center	55.50
Bus from Gardermoen Airport to the city center	10.55
Local telephone call	.40
Double room at the Grand Hotel (very expensive)	208.15
Double room at the Hotell Bondeheimen (moderate)	119.35
Double room at the Munch Hotel (inexpensive)	96.55
Lunch for one at the Primo Restaurant Ciaou-Ciaou (moderate)	28.00
Lunch for one at Mamma Rosa (inexpensive)	19.45
Dinner for one, without wine, at Blom (expensive)	42.75
Dinner for one, without wine, at Lipp (moderate)	33.30
Dinner for one, without wine, at Det Gamle Rådhus (inexpensive)	26.65
Pint of beer (draft Pilsner)	4.80
Coca-Cola (in a restaurant)	2.50
Cup of coffee	2.60
Admission to Viking Ship Museum	4.45
Movie ticket	8.00
Theater ticket (at National Theater)	16.65–24.40

3 Money

For a general discussion of changing money, using credit and charge cards, and other money matters, see "Money," in chapter 2.

CURRENCY   The Norwegian currency is the **krone** (plural: **kroner**), written as "NOK." There are 100 **øre** in 1 krone. Bank notes are issued in denominations of 50, 100, 200, 500, and 1,000 kroner. Coins are issued in denominations of 50 øre, 1 krone, and 5, 10, and 20 kroner.

4 When to Go

CLIMATE

In the summer, the average temperature in Norway ranges from 57°F to 65°F. In January, it hovers around 27°F, ideal for winter sports. The Gulf Stream warms the west coast, where winters tend to be temperate. Rainfall, however, is heavy.

Above the Arctic Circle, the sun shines night and day from mid-May until late July. For about 2 months every winter, the North Cape is plunged into darkness.

Norway's Average Daytime Temperatures (°F)

	Jan	Feb	Mar	Apr	May	June	July	Aug	Sept	Oct	Nov	Dec
Oslo	25	26	32	41	51	60	64	61	53	42	33	27
Bergen/Stavanger	35	35	38	41	40	55	59	58	54	47	42	38
Trondheim	27	27	31	38	47	53	58	57	50	42	35	31

THE MIDNIGHT SUN   In the summer, the sun never fully sets in northern Norway, and even in the south, the sun may set around 11pm and rise at 3am.

The best vantage points and dates for seeing the spectacle of the midnight sun are the **North Cape,** May 12 to August 1; **Hammerfest,** May 14 to July 30; **Tromsø,** May 19 to July 26; **Lofoten Islands,** May 23 to July 17; and **Harstad,** May 23 to July 22. All are accessible by public transportation. Keep in mind that although the sun shines at midnight, it's not as strong as at midday. Bring a warm jacket or sweater.

HOLIDAYS

Norway celebrates the following public holidays: New Year's Day (January 1), Maundy Thursday, Good Friday, Easter, Labor Day (May 1), Ascension Day (mid-May), Independence Day (May 17), Whitmonday (late May), Christmas (December 25), and Boxing Day (December 26).

Norway Calendar of Events

Specific dates are for 2001; others are approximate. Check with the local tourist office before making plans to attend a specific event, especially in 2002.

January
- **Northern Lights Festival,** Tromsø. Classical and contemporary music performances by musicians from Norway and abroad. Late January.

February
- **Kristiansund Opera Festival.** Featuring Kristiansund Opera's productions of opera and ballet, plus art exhibitions, concerts, and other events. Early February.

March
- ✪ **Holmenkollen Ski Festival,** Oslo. One of Europe's largest ski festivals, with World Cup Nordic skiing and biathlons, international ski-jumping competitions, and Norway's largest cross-country race for amateurs. Held at Holmenkollen Ski Jump on the outskirts of Oslo. To participate, attend, or request more information, contact Skiforeningen, Kongeveien 5, Holmenkollen, N-0390 Oslo 3 (☎ 22-92-32-00). March 11 to 13.
- **Narvik Winter Festival.** Sports events, carnivals, concerts, and opera performances highlight this festival dedicated to those who built the railway across northern Norway and Sweden. Second week of March to mid-April.
- **Birkebeiner Race,** Rena to Lillehammer. This historic international ski race, with thousands of participants, crosses the mountains between Rena and Lille-hammer, site of the 1994 Olympics. It's a 33-mile cross-country trek. March 21.

April
- **Voss Jazz Festival.** Three days of jazz and folk music performances by European and American artists. First week of April.

May
- **The Grete Waitz Run,** Oslo. A women's run through the streets of Oslo, with participation by the famous marathoner Grete Waitz. May 2.
- **The Viking Run,** Sognefjord. An international half-marathon is staged in the Sognefjord. Some participants extend their stay to participate in other sports, such as summer skiing, glacier climbing, biking, boating, or mountain climbing. Late May.
- ✪ **Bergen International Festival (Bergen Festspill).** A world-class music event, featuring artists from Norway and around the world. This is one of the largest annual musical events in Scandinavia. Held at various venues in Bergen. For

information, contact the Bergen International Festival, Slottsgaten 1, 4055, Dregen N-5835 Bergen (☎ **50-31-38-60**). May 21 to June 8.

June

- **Faerder Sailing Race.** Some 1,000 sailboats participate in this race, which ends in Borre, by the Oslofjord. First week of June.
- **North Cape March.** This trek from Honningsvåg to the North Cape is one of the world's toughest. The round-trip march is 42 miles. Mid-June.
- **Emigration Festival,** Stavanger. Commemoration of Norwegian immigration to North America, with exhibitions, concerts, theater, folklore. Mid-June.
- **Midsummer Night,** nationwide. Celebrations and bonfires all over Norway. June 23.
- **Emigration Festival,** Kvinesdal. Commemorates the Norwegian immigration to the United States. Late June to early July.

July

- **Kongsberg Jazz Festival.** International artists participate in one of the most important jazz festivals in Scandinavia, with open-air concerts. July 1 to 4.
- **Midnight Sun Marathon,** Tromsø. The marathon in northern Norway starts at midnight. July 4.
- **Mobil Bislett Games,** Oslo. International athletic competitions are staged in Oslo, with professional participants from all over the world. July 15.
- ✪ **Molde International Jazz Festival.** The "City of Roses" is the site of Norway's oldest jazz festival. It attracts international stars from both sides of the Atlantic every year. Held at venues in Molde for 6 days. For details, contact the Molde Jazz Festival, Box 271, N-6401 Molde (☎ **71-21-60-00**). Mid-July.
- **Norway Cup International Youth Soccer Tournament,** Oslo. The world's largest youth soccer tournament attracts 1,000 teams from around the world to Oslo. Last week of July.

August

- **Telemark Festival,** Bø. An international festival of folk music and folk dance takes place in the home of many famous fiddlers, dancers, and singers. July 30 to August 2.
- **Peer Gynt Festival,** Vinstra. Art exhibitions, evenings of music and song, parades in national costumes, and other events honor Ibsen's fictional character. July 31 to August 8.
- **Oslo Jazz Festival.** This annual festival features music from the earliest years of jazz (1920 to 1925), as well as classical concerts, opera, and ballet. First week of August.
- **Chamber Music Festival,** Oslo. Norwegian and foreign musicians perform at Oslo's Akershus Castle and Fortress, which dates from A.D. 1300. Second week of August.
- **World Cup Summer Ski Jumping,** Marikollen. Takes place in Marikollen, Raelingen, just outside the center of Oslo. Mid-August.

September

- **International Salmon Fishing Festival,** Suldal. Participants come from Norway and abroad to the Suldalslagen River outside Stavanger in western Norway. Dates vary.
- **Oslo Marathon.** This annual event draws some of Norway's best long-distance runners. Mid-September.

December

✪ **Nobel Peace Prize Ceremony,** Oslo. A major event on the Oslo calendar, attracting world attention. Held at Oslo City Hall on December 10. Attendance is by invitation only. For information, contact the Nobel Institute, Drammensveien 19, N-0255 Oslo 2 (☎ **22-44-36-80**).

5 The Active Vacation Planner

BICYCLING   Bikes can be rented in just about every town in Norway. Inquire at your hotel or the local tourist office. The Norwegian Mountain Touring Association (see "Hiking," below) provides inexpensive lodging for those who take overnight bike trips. For suggestions on tours, maps, and brochures, contact **Den Rustne Eike,** Vestbaneplassen 2, N-0458 Oslo (☎ **22-83-52-08**). The only large bike-rental firm in Oslo, it can arrange guided tours in the Oslo area and elsewhere in Norway. Tours last 3 hours to 14 days.

BIRD-WATCHING   Some of Europe's noteworthy bird sanctuaries are on islands off the Norwegian coast or on the mainland. Rocky and isolated, the sanctuaries offer ideal nesting places for millions of sea birds that vastly outnumber the local human population during certain seasons. Foremost among the sanctuaries are the **Lofoten Islands**—particularly two of the outermost islands, Vaerøy and Røst—and the island of Runde. A quarter-mile bridge (one of the longest in Norway) connects **Runde** to the coastline, a 2½-hour drive from Ålesund. Runde's year-round human population is about 150, and the colonies of puffins, cormorants, razor-billed auks, guillemots, gulls, and eider ducks number in the millions. Another noteworthy bird sanctuary is at **Fokstumyra,** a national park near Dombås.

The isolated island of **Lovund** is a 2-hour ferry ride from the town of Sandnesjøen, south of Bødo. Lovund ("the island of puffins") has a human population of fewer than 270 and a bird population in the hundreds of thousands. You can visit Lovund and the other famous Norwegian bird-watching sites on your own, or sign up for one of the organized bird-watching tours sponsored by such well-recommended companies as **Borton Overseas,** 1621 E. 79th St., Bloomington, MN 55425 (☎ **800/843-0602** or 612/883-0704).

Brochures and pamphlets are available from the tourist board **Destination Lofoten** (☎ **76-07-30-00**).

FISHING   Norway has long been famous for its salmon and trout fishing. The best months for salmon are June and July, and the season extends into August. Sea trout fishing takes place from June to September, and is best in August. The brown trout season varies with altitude.

Fishing in the ocean is free. To fish in lakes, rivers, or streams, anyone over 15 must have a fishing license. A license to fish in a lake costs from 25 to 50 NOK ($2.80 to $5.55); or in a river, 100 to 450 NOK ($11.10 to $49.95). National fishing licenses can be purchased at local post offices. For more information, contact the **Bergen Angling Association,** Fosswinckelsgata 37, Bergen (☎ **55-32-11-64**).

One company that arranges fishing tours in Norway is **Passage Tours of Scandinavia,** 239 Commercial Blvd., Fort Lauderdale, FL 33308 (☎ **800/548-5960** in the U.S., or 954/776-7070).

A U.S.-based company that can arrange fishing (as well as hunting) excursions anywhere within Norway and the rest of Scandinavia is **Five Stars of Scandinavia,** 13104 Thomas Rd., KPN, Gig Harbor, WA 98329 (☎ **800/722-4226**). For a truly unusual fishing experience, consider their ability to arrange rentals of old-fashioned fishermen's cottages in the isolated Lofoten Islands. The rustic-looking, fully renovated cottages each lie adjacent to the sea, and evoke 19th-century isolation in a way that you'll find either wondrous or terrifying, depending on your point of view. Five Stars will rent you a cottage for as short a period as 1 night, although we recommend a minimum stay of 3 nights to best appreciate this offbeat adventure. Rentals include bed linens.

One of the most qualified fishing outfitters in Bergen spends part of its time delivering food, tools, and spare parts to the thousands of fishermen who make their living in boats and isolated fjords along the western coast of Norway. **Camperlan,** P.O. Box 11, Strandkaien 2, N-5083 Bergen (☎ 55-32-34-72) and its president and founder, Captain Dag Varlo, will take between two and four passengers out for deep-sea fishing excursions in the teeming seas off the country's western coast. Although his boats go out in all seasons, midsummer is the most appealing, because of the extended daylight hours. Most avidly pursued are codfish, valued as a "good-eating" fish, and a local species known as saet, prized for its fighting properties as a gamefish. (They range anywhere from 3 to 22 pounds each.) A full-day's fishing excursion, with all equipment included, for up to six passengers, costs 6,000 NOK ($666). In midsummer, full-day excursions depart from Bergen's harbor, and are usually scheduled from 9am to around 5pm.

GOLF   Many golf clubs are open to foreign guests. Greens fees tend to be moderate. Clubs include the **Oslo Golf Klubb** (18 holes), at Bogstad, Oslo (☎ 22-50-44-02), and the **Bergen Golf Club** (9 holes), Aastvedt, Ovre Ervik, Bergen (☎ 55-18-20-77).

HIKING   The mountains and wilderness make hiking a favorite pastime. The **Norwegian Mountain Touring Association,** Stortingsgata, N-0125 Oslo 1 (☎ 22-82-28-22; www.dntoa.no), offers guided hikes that last 5 to 8 days. They cost 3,000 to 4,500 NOK ($333 to $499.50), including meals and lodging.

HORSEBACK RIDING   Many organizations offer horseback tours of Norway's wilderness, enabling visitors to see some of the more spectacular scenery. Tours can range from a few hours to a full week, and they're available all over the country. Luggage is transported by car. One tour organizer is **Borton Overseas,** 1621 E. 79th St., Bloomington, MN 55424 (☎ 800/843-0602 or 612/883-0704).

SAILING   Norway's long coast can be a challenge to any yachting enthusiast. The most tranquil havens are along the southern coast. To arrange rafting trips or boat trips, along with boat rentals and evening parasailing, call **SeaAction** at ☎ 90-58-43-00 or 33-33-69-93.

SCUBA DIVING   Excellent diving centers provide scuba-diving trips and instruction. Divers who enjoy harpooning often catch their own dinners, with many kinds of fish to choose from. The conditions for submarine photography are generally good, with underwater visibility of 30 to 100 feet. There are a number of shipwrecks along Norway's extensive coastline and fjords. Diving information is available from **Dykkernett** at ☎ 22-02-31-29; www.dykkernett.no.

SKIING   Norway's skiing terrain is world class. The optimum season is February and March (the first half of April also tends to be good). Two of the principal resorts, **Geilo** and **Voss,** lie on the Oslo–Bergen rail line. The most famous and easily accessible resort is **Lillehammer,** north of Oslo. In and around the Norwegian capital skiing is common; the famous ski jump, **Holmenkollen,** with its companion ski museum, is minutes from the heart of Oslo. Its yearly ski championship attracts ace skiers from all over Europe and North America every March.

Norwegian ski resorts are known for their informality, which is evident in the schools and the atmosphere. The emphasis is on simple pleasures, not the sophistication often found at alpine resorts. (Incidentally, the word *ski* is an Old Norse word, as is *slalom.*)

Tracing Your Norwegian Roots

If you're of Norwegian ancestry, you can get information on how to trace your family from the nearest Norwegian consulate. In Norway, contact the **Norwegian Emigration Center,** Strandkaien 31, N-4005 Stavanger (☎ **51-53-88-60**), for a catalog of information about Norwegian families who emigrated to the United States.

In the United States, the **Family History Library of the Church of Jesus Christ of Latter-day Saints,** 35 N. West Temple, Salt Lake City, UT 84150 (☎ **801/240-2331**), has extensive records of Norwegian families who emigrated to the United States and Canada. The library is open to the public without charge for genealogical research. Mormon churches in other cities have listings of materials available in Salt Lake City; for a small fee you can request pertinent microfilms, which you can view at a local church.

Much of Norwegian skiing is cross-country—perfect for the amateur—and there are lots of opportunities for downhill skiing. Other winter sports include curling, sleigh rides, and skating. All major centers have ski lifts, and renting equipment in Norway is much cheaper than in some luxury resorts.

Norway also offers summer skiing, both downhill and cross-country, at summer ski centers near glaciers. You can get more information from the **Galdhø-piggen Sommerskisenter,** N-2687 Bøverdalen (☎ **61-21-17-50**), and the **Stryn Sommerskisenter,** N-6880 Stryn (☎ **57-87-40-40**).

WHALE WATCHING In Norway you can catch a glimpse of 65-foot-long, 88,000-pound sperm whales, the largest toothed whales in the world. You can also see killer whales, harbor porpoises, minke whales, and white-beaked dolphins. Whale researchers conduct 6-hour whale-watching tours in the Arctic Ocean.

For information and bookings, contact **Passage Tours of Scandinavia,** 239 Commercial Blvd., Fort Lauderdale, FL 33308 (☎ **800/548-5960** or 954/776-7070). Whale watching in the Lofoten Islands can be arranged by **Borton Overseas,** 1621 E. 79th St., Bloomington, MN 55425 (☎ **800/843-0602** or 612/883-0704).

6 Health & Insurance

For a general discussion of health and insurance, see "Health & Insurance" in chapter 2.

Put your essential medicines in your carry-on luggage and bring enough of prescription medications to last through your stay. In Norway, pharmacists cannot legally honor a prescription written outside the country; if you need more of your medications, you'll have to see a doctor and have a new prescription written.

Norway's national health plan does not cover American or Canadian visitors. Medical expenses must be paid in cash. Medical costs are generally more reasonable than elsewhere in Western Europe.

7 Tips for Travelers with Special Needs

A number of resources and organizations in North America and Britain can assist travelers with special needs in trip planning. For details, see "Tips for Travelers with Special Needs" in chapter 2.

FOR TRAVELERS WITH DISABILITIES   Scandinavian countries have been in the vanguard of providing services for people with disabilities. In general, trains, airlines, ferries, and department stores and malls are accessible. For information about wheelchair access, ferry and air travel, parking, and other matters, contact the Norwegian Tourist Board (see "Visitor Information & Entry Requirements," above).

The **Norwegian Association of the Disabled,** Schweigaardsgt #12, 9217 Grænland, 0312 Oslo (☎ 22-17-02-55; www.nhf.no), provides useful information.

FOR GAY & LESBIAN TRAVELERS   Call **Gay/Lesbian Visitor Information,** St. Olavs Plass 2, N-0165 Oslo (☎ 22-11-05-09). An English-speaking representative will give you up-to-date information on gay and lesbian life in Oslo and let you know which clubs are currently in vogue. In Norway, gays and lesbians have the same legal status as heterosexuals, with the exception of adoption rights. Legislation passed in 1981 protects gays and lesbians from discrimination. In 1993, a law was passed recognizing the "partnerships" of homosexual couples—in essence, a recognition of same-sex marriages. The age of consent for both men and women in Norway is 16 years of age.

FOR SENIORS   People over 67 are entitled to 50% off the price of first- and second-class train tickets. Ask for the discount at the ticket office.

8 Getting There

BY PLANE

For a more complete discussion of plane travel options, see "Getting There," in chapter 2.

All transatlantic flights from North America land at Oslo's Fornebu Airport. **SAS** (☎ 800/221-2350 in the U.S.; www.flysas.com) flies nonstop daily from Newark to Oslo. The trip takes about 7½ hours. Most other SAS flights from North America go through Copenhagen. Flying time from Chicago is 10¾ hours; from Seattle, 11¾ hours, not including the layover in Copenhagen.

Prices for flights to Denmark (see chapter 2) are similar to those for flights to Oslo and Bergen. Transatlantic passengers on SAS are occasionally allowed to transfer to a Norwegian domestic flight from Oslo to Bergen for no additional charge.

If you fly to Norway on another airline, you'll be routed through a gateway city in Europe, and sometimes continue on a different airline. **British Airways** (☎ 800/AIRWAYS in the U.S.; www.british-airways.com), for example, has dozens of daily flights from many North American cities to London, and you can continue to Oslo. **Icelandair** (☎ 800/223-5500 in the U.S.; www.icelandair.com) can be an excellent choice, with connections through Reykjavik. **KLM** (☎ 800/347-7747 in the U.S.; www.nwa.com) serves Oslo through Amsterdam.

For passengers from the U.K., **British Airways** (☎ 0845/773-3377 in London) operates at least four daily nonstops to Oslo from London. **SAS** (☎ 020/8990-7122 in London) runs four daily flights from Heathrow to Oslo. Flying time from London to Oslo on any airline is around 2 hours.

BY CAR

If you're driving from the Continent, you must go through Sweden. From **Copenhagen,** take the E47/55 express highway north to Helsingør and catch the car ferry to Helsingborg, Sweden. From there, E6 runs to Oslo. From **Stockholm,** drive across Sweden on E18 to Oslo.

BY TRAIN

Copenhagen is the main rail hub for service between Scandinavia and the rest of Europe. There are three daily trains from Copenhagen to Oslo, seven from Copenhagen to Stockholm, and six from Copenhagen to Gothenburg. All connect with the Danish ferries operating either to Norway through Helsingør or Hirtshals, or to Sweden via Helsingør or Frederikshavn.

Most rail traffic from Sweden into Norway follows the main corridors between Stockholm and Oslo and between Gothenburg and Oslo.

For information on rail passes, please refer to "Getting There" in chapter 2.

BY SHIP & FERRY

FROM DENMARK   Three major ferries operate from Denmark to Norway. All operate year-round. Passage from Hirtshals to Kristiansand takes 5 hours on the Viking Line and can be booked in the United States through **EuroCruises,** 303 W. 13th St., New York, NY 10014 (☎ **800/688-3876** in the U.S., or 212/691-2099). The trip from Frederikshavn to Oslo takes 11 hours and can be reserved through the **Larvik Line,** Box 265, Skøyen, N-0212 Oslo 2 (☎ **22-52-55-00**). It departs twice daily year-round, and includes a night crossing. The third operates daily year-round from Copenhagen to Oslo overnight, and takes 16 hours. For reservations, contact **DFDS Seaways,** Cypress Creek Business Park, 6555 NW Ninth Ave., Fort Lauderdale, FL 33309-2049 (☎ **800/533-3755** in the U.S., or 305/491-7909).

FROM SWEDEN   From Strømstad, Sweden, in the summer, the daily crossing to Sandefjord, Norway, takes 2½ hours. Bookings can be made through **Scandi Line,** Tollbugata 5, N-3210 Sandefjord (☎ **33-42-10-00**).

FROM ENGLAND   The **Norwegian Coastal Voyages/Bergen Line,** 405 Fifth Ave., New York, NY 10017 (☎ **800/323-7436** in the U.S., or 212/986-2711), operates from Newcastle, England, to Stavanger and Bergen on the west coast of Norway.

BY CRUISE SHIP

Norway's fjords and mountain vistas are among the most spectacular panorama in the world. Many ship owners and cruise lines offer excursions along the Norwegian coast.

One of the most prominent lines is **Cunard** (☎ **800/528-6273** in the U.S. and Canada); its superliner flagship, the *QE2,* makes two annual visits to the fjords. Departing from Southampton, England, the ship calls at Oslo, Bergen, Trondheim, the offshore island of Spitzbergen, Stavanger, and the North Cape; en route it also stops at the most frequently visited fjords. Prices for the 5-day cruise include round-trip airfare to London on British Airways from 79 gateway cities throughout the world.

Cunard also maintains about half a dozen smaller ships; one of the most luxurious specializes in cruises through the Baltic Sea and along the coast of Norway. The *Vistafjord* offers cruises throughout the summer from Hamburg, Germany, that travel as far north as Norway's North Cape and as far east as St. Petersburg (formerly Leningrad), Russia. Cruises last 13 to 21 days and include round-trip airfare on British Airways from most cities along the eastern seaboard of North America. Transportation from the West Coast can be arranged for a reasonable supplement. Hotel or theater packages in London or side trips to almost anywhere else in Europe can be arranged through Cunard and British Airways at favorable discounts.

The Bergen Line offers much less expensive cruises aboard steamer ships that also carry mail and supplies to fjord communities. For more information, see "By Coastal Steamer" in "Getting Around," below and in Chapter 10, "Exploring the Norwegian Coast."

9 Getting Around

BY PLANE

The best way to get around Scandinavia is to take advantage of air passes that apply to the whole region. If you're traveling extensively in Europe, special European passes are available. For information on **SAS's Visit Scandinavia Fare,** see "Getting Around, By Plane," in chapter 2.

WITHIN NORWAY   Norway has excellent air service. In addition to SAS, two independent airways, Braathens and Wideroe Flyveselskap, provide quick and convenient ways to get around a large country with many hard-to-reach areas. All three airlines offer reduced rates available when booked outside Norway, known as "minifares."

BRAATHENS   The top-notch independent airline Braathens (☎ 67-12-20-70 in Oslo or 55-23-55-23 in Bergen; www.braathens.no) carries more passengers on domestic routes than any other airline in Norway. It has regularly scheduled flights inside Norway, linking major cities as well as more remote places not covered by other airlines. Its air routes directly link Oslo with all major Norwegian cities; it also offers frequent flights along the coast, from Oslo to Tromsø and to Longyearbyen on the island of Spitsbergen. (Braathens also operates charter flights throughout Europe and North Africa.)

You might also inquire about the **Northern Light Pass,** which provides discounts and is valid for 1 month between May and September. There are two sets of fares. Flights between airports in north Norway are short journeys, and the one-way fare for pass-holders is $85. Flights from south Norway to north Norway or vice versa count as long journeys, and the one-way fare is $240. The Visit Norway Pass is sold by airlines that have agreements with Braathens airlines. To buy one, call **Passage Tours of Scandinavia** (☎ 800/548-5960 in the U.S.) or **SAS** (☎ 800/221-2350 in the U.S.).

SAS   Regularly scheduled domestic flights on SAS (☎ 800/221-2350 in the U.S. or 81-00-33-00 in Oslo) crisscross Norway. They connect Bergen, Oslo, Trondheim, and Bodø. SAS also flies to the Arctic gateway of Tromsø; to Alta in Finnmark, the heart of Lapland; and to Kirkenes, near the Russian border. Transatlantic SAS passengers might also consider SAS's Visit Scandinavia Fare (see "Getting Around, By Plane," in chapter 2).

OTHER AIRLINES   Linked to the SAS reservations network, **Wideroe** specializes in STOL (short takeoff and landing) aircraft. It services rarely visited fishing communities on offshore islands, isolated fjord communities, and destinations north of the Arctic Circle. For more information or tickets, contact SAS or local travel agents in Norway.

BY TRAIN

Norway's network of electric and diesel-electric trains runs as far as Bodø, 62 miles north of the Arctic Circle. (Beyond that, visitors must take a coastal steamer, plane, or bus to Tromsø and the North Cape.) Recently upgraded express trains (the fastest in the country) crisscross the mountainous terrain between Oslo, Stavanger, Bergen, and Trondheim.

The most popular, and the most scenic, run covers the 300 miles between Oslo and Bergen. Visitors with limited time often choose this route for its fabled mountains, gorges, white-water rivers, and fjords. The trains often stop for passengers to enjoy breathtaking views.

Second-class travel on Norwegian trains is recommended. In fact, second class in Norway is as good as or better than first-class travel anywhere else in Europe, with reclining seats and lots of unexpected comforts. The one-way second-class fare from Oslo to Bergen is 555 NOK ($61.60), plus a mandatory seat reservation of 25 NOK ($2.80). Another popular run, from Oslo to Tronmdheim, costs 590 NOK ($65.50) one-way in second class.

One of the country's obviously scenic trips, from Bergen to Bodø, is not possible by train because of the terrain. Trains to Bodø leave from Oslo. Express trains are called *Expresstog,* and you have to read the fine print of a railway schedule to figure out whether an Expresstog is much faster than a conventional train.

On express and other major trains, you must reserve seats at the train's starting station. Sleepers are priced according to the number of berths in each compartment. Children 4 to 15 years of age and senior citizens pay 50% of the regular adult fare. Group and midweek tickets are also available.

There are special compartments for persons with disabilities on most medium- and long-distance trains. People in wheelchairs and others with physical handicaps, and their companions, may use the compartments. Some long-distance trains offer special playrooms ("Kiddie-Wagons") for children, complete with toys and educational items.

NORWAY RAIL PASS   A restricted rail pass applicable only to the state railway lines, the Norway Rail Pass is available for 7 or 14 consecutive days of unlimited rail travel in 1 month, or any 3 days of travel within 1 month. It's suitable for anyone who wants to cover the long distances that separate Norwegian cities. The costs are $181 for adults in first class or $139 in second class for any 3 days in 1 month; $224 in first class or $172 in second class for any 4 days in 1 month; and $250 in first class or $192 in second class for any 5 days in 1 month. Children 4 to 15 years of age pay half the adult fare. Those under 4 ride free.

OTHER SPECIAL TICKETS & DISCOUNTS   With a **Miniprice Ticket** you can travel in second class for 530 NOK ($58.85) one-way, but only on routes that take you more than 150km (93 miles) from your point of origin. No stopovers are allowed except for a change of trains. Tickets are valid only on selected trains, for boarding that begins during designated off-peak hours. You can buy Miniprice Tickets at any railway station in Norway.

Travelers over age 67 are entitled to a 50% discount, called an **Honnorrabatt,** on Norwegian train trips of more than 31 miles. Regardless of age, the spouse of someone over 67 can also receive the 50% discount.

BY BUS

Where the train or coastal steamer stops, passengers can usually continue on a scenic bus ride. Norway's bus system is excellent, linking remote villages along the fjords. Numerous all-inclusive motor-coach tours, often combined with steamer travel, leave from Bergen and Oslo in the summer. The train ends in Bodø; from there you can get a bus to Fauske (39 miles east). From Fauske, the Polar Express bus spans the entire distance along the Arctic Highway, through Finnmark (Lapland) to Kirkenes near the Russian border and back. The segment from Alta to Kirkenes is open only from June to October, but there's year-round service from Fauske to Alta. Passengers are guaranteed hotel accommodations along the way.

Buses have air-conditioning, toilets, adjustable seats, reading lights, and a telephone. Reservations are not accepted on most buses, and payment is made to the driver on board. Fares depend on the distance traveled. Children under 4 travel free, and children 4 to 16 and senior citizens pay half-price. For the Oslo–Sweden–Hammerfest "Express 2000," a 30-hour trip, reservations must be made in advance.

For more information about bus travel in Norway, contact **Norway Buss Ekspress AS,** Karl Johans Gate (☎ 22-33-01-90) in Oslo, or **Passage Tours of Scandinavia** (☎ 800/548-5960 in the U.S.).

BY CAR & FERRY

Dazzling scenery awaits you at nearly every turn. Some roads are less than perfect (often dirt or gravel), but passable. Most mountain roads are open by May 1; the so-called motoring season lasts from mid-May to the end of September. In western Norway hairpin curves are common, but if you're willing to settle for doing less than 150 miles a day, you needn't worry. The easiest and most convenient touring territory is in and around Oslo and south to Stavanger. However, you can drive to the North Cape.

Bringing a car into Norway is relatively uncomplicated. If you own the car you're driving, you must present your national driver's license, car registration, and proof that the car is insured. (This proof usually takes the form of a document known as a "Green Card," which customs agents will refer to specifically.) If you've rented a car in another country and want to drive it into Norway, be sure to verify at the time of rental that the registration and insurance documents are in order—they probably will be. Regardless of whether you own or rent the car you're about to drive into Norway, don't assume that your private North American insurance policy will automatically apply. Chances are good that it will, but in the event of an accident, you may have to cope with a burdensome amount of paperwork.

If you're driving through any of Norway's coastal areas, you'll probably have to traverse one or many of the country's famous fjords. Although more and more bridges are being built, Norway's network of privately run ferries is essential for transporting cars across hundreds of fjords and estuaries. Motorists should ask the tourist bureau for the free map "Norway by Car" and a timetable outlining the country's dozens of car ferry services. The cost for cars and passengers is low.

RENTALS   Avis, Budget, and Hertz offer well-serviced, well-maintained fleets of rental cars. Prices and terms tend to be more favorable for those who reserve vehicles in North America before their departure and who present evidence of membership in such organizations as AAA or AARP. The major competitors' prices tend to be roughly equivalent, except for promotional deals scheduled from time to time.

The prices quoted here include the 23% government tax. Rates are always best when you pay for them before you leave home. At **Budget** (☎ 800/527-0700 in the U.S. and Canada), the cheapest car is a cramped but peppy Volkswagen Polo that rents for $373 a week with unlimited mileage. This is more than the price for an equivalent car at **Hertz** (☎ 800/654-3001 in the U.S.), which charges $352 a week, with unlimited mileage, for its smallest car, a VW Polo. **Avis** (☎ 800/331-2112 in the U.S.) matches Hertz, charging around $375 for its cheapest car, also a VW Polo. Despite pressure from the telephone sales representative, it pays to ask questions before you commit to a prepaid reservation. Each company maintains an office at the Oslo airport, in the center of Oslo, and at airports and city centers elsewhere around the country.

Note: Remember that prices and the relative merits of each company can and will change during the lifetime of this edition, depending on promotions and other factors.

An alternative to the big three companies is a small but reliable outfit called **Kemwel** (☎ 800/678-0678 in the U.S.), based in Harrison, New York. As part of a special promotion, Kemwel sometimes offers discounts to some SAS passengers.

INSURANCE   Rates include nominal insurance coverage, which is probably enough for most drivers and most accidents. However, if you did not buy additional insurance and you have a mishap, your responsibility depends on the car-rental firm. At Budget, where insurance policies are the most favorable to the renter, the maximum amount you might be charged is 15,000 NOK ($1,665). At the other companies, without additional insurance you might be held responsible for the car's full value. Obviously, you need to learn what your liability would be in case of an accident. To avoid this responsibility, you might want to get an additional insurance policy (a collision-damage waiver) for about $21 a day. We usually find that buying additional insurance is well worth the expense, considering the unfamiliar driving conditions.

Note that when certain credit or charge cards are used to pay for a car rental, no additional insurance purchases are necessary. Although many readers have taken advantage of this cost-saving approach, the fine print of these insurance options must be individually verified directly with the card issuer.

No matter what type of insurance you choose, remember that driving after having consumed even a small amount of alcohol is punishable by heavy fines, imprisonment, or both.

BY COASTAL STEAMER

The fjords of western Norway are among the most beautiful sights in Europe. For a seagoing view, nothing beats the indomitable steamer ships that carry mail, supplies, and passengers. If you have the time and enjoy an offbeat adventure, you can book a 12-day, all-inclusive round-trip steamer trip from Bergen to Kirkenes (one of the northernmost ports). It covers some 2,500 miles of jagged, scenic coastline.

Because of the long distances, steamers are equipped with cabins similar to those on a transatlantic liner. Depending on the accommodations and the time of year, cabins cost $1,210 to $3,280 per person, double occupancy, for the 12-day round-trip excursion. Because sailings in June, July, and August are the most expensive, many visitors choose a spring or autumn trip. All meals are included in the price. Children under 12 receive a 25% discount on round-trip voyages. During special periods, travelers over age 67 may be eligible for discounts. Steamers make scheduled stops in hamlets and cities along the way, ranging from half an hour to half a day. Passengers who prefer to spend more time in selected cities usually choose port-to-port tickets, for which children under 12 receive a special rate. Be warned, however, that booking cabins on a port-to-port basis from May to August is often extremely difficult because of the popularity of these cruises. Cruises are available even in winter—the Norwegian coast is famous for remaining ice-free all year.

For reservations and information, contact the **Norwegian Coastal Voyages/Bergen Line,** 405 Park Ave., New York, NY 10022 (☎ **800/323-7436** in the U.S., 212/319-1300, or 800/666-2374 for brochures only).

10 Organized Tours

One of the best ways to see Norway's wilderness is by organized tour. The following are a few of the wide variety that's available. Check with your travel agent for other options or a custom-designed tour. All prices in this section are per person with double occupancy.

Norway's brisk waters are known for the abundance and quality of their salmon, with a season lasting only from June 15 to August 31. The best salmon-fishing tours are arranged in central Norway, especially along the Guala River, one of the country's best- known salmon-fishing rivers. Week-long fishing tours are offered in Trondheim by **Ursus Major** (☎ **99-22-49-60;** www.ursusmajor.no), costing 15,000 to 18,000 NOK ($1,665 to $1,998) per person, including meals and accommodations.

In July and August, 7-day **bike trips** run through the Lofoten Islands. They offer moderately rolling terrain, dramatic scenery, traditional *rorbuer* (fishing cottage) lodging, and hearty regional cuisine. Prices begin at $2,000. Tours are offered by **Backroads** (☎ 800/GO-ACTIVE).

Suggested Itineraries

If You Have 1 Week

Day 1   Fly to Oslo, check into your hotel, and relax. Few can fight jet lag on their first day in the Norwegian capital.

Day 2   After breakfast in Oslo, take the ferry to the Bygdøy peninsula to visit the *Kon-Tiki* Museum, the polar ship *Fram,* the Viking ships, and the Norwegian Folk Museum.

Day 3   In Oslo, visit Frogner Park to see the Vigeland sculptures and Edvard Munch paintings. You should have enough time to see the Henie–Onstad Foundation art center 7 miles from Oslo. Return in time to go to the Lookout Tower and ski jump at Holmenkollen, where you can dine and enjoy a panoramic view of Oslo.

Day 4   Head south for a day trip to some of the major towns along the Oslofjord. In the morning, drive to Fredrikstad on the Glomma River, and visit its Old Town as well as Norway Silver Designs, its handcraft center. Drive back to Moss and take a ferry across the fjord. From Horten on the west bank, drive south to Tønsberg, Norway's oldest town, and visit the Vestfold Folk Museum. Drive back to Oslo for dinner.

Day 5   Head west to Bergen by train on a 300-mile all-day trip. You go across the "rooftop of Norway," past the ski resorts of Geilo and Voss, before reaching Bergen.

Day 6   Explore Bergen's many attractions, such as Troldhaugen (Trolls' Hill), the summer villa of composer Edvard Grieg.

Day 7   Visit Ulvik, on the Hardangerfjord in the western fjord district, reached by public transportation from Bergen. Spend the night in the beautiful town, which typifies the fjord towns in this district.

If You Have 2 Weeks

Week 1   See "If You Have 1 Week," above.

Day 8   In Ulvik (see "Day 7," above), continue exploring the fjord district.

Day 9   Return to Bergen, and then fly to Trondheim.

Day 10   If it's summer, take a 13-hour train ride from Trondheim to Bodø on the *Midnight Sun Special.* Spend the night in Bodø, north of the Arctic Circle.

Day 11   From Bodø, fly to Tromsø, 250 miles north of the Arctic Circle (it doesn't have rail service). Stay overnight in Tromsø and see its limited, but interesting, attractions.

Day 12   Rent a car in Tromsø and head north for the last leg of the trip: a 280-mile run over the Arctic Highway. Spend the night in Alta. Travel is slow, because the road wraps around inlets and fjords.

Day 13   Continue driving north to Hammerfest, the world's northernmost town of any significant size. Stay overnight.

Day 14   From Hammerfest, take an excursion boat directly to the North Cape. Those with more time can drive to Honningsvåg, the world's northernmost village and the gateway to the North Cape. Buses leave its marketplace daily for the cape, a 22-mile run.

Return to Tromsø, where air connections can be made to Oslo and your return flight to North America or elsewhere.

Fast Facts: Norway

Area Code   The international country code for Norway is **47**. If you're calling from outside the country, the city code is **2** for Oslo and **5** for Bergen. Inside Norway, no area or city codes are needed. Phone numbers have eight digits.

Business Hours   Most **banks** are open Monday to Friday from 8:15am to 3:30pm (on Thursday to 5pm), and are closed Saturday and Sunday. The Felles-banken's Exchange at the Oslo Central Railway Station (☎ **22-41-26-11**) is open Monday to Friday from 8am to 11pm, Saturday 8am to 7pm, Sunday 8am to noon. The bank at Fornebu Airport is open daily from 7am to 10:30pm, and there's another bank at Gardermoen Airport, open Monday to Saturday from 6:30 am to 8pm, and Sunday from 7am to 8pm. Most **businesses** are open Monday to Friday from 9am to 4pm. **Stores** are generally open Monday to Friday from 9am to 5pm (many stay open on Thursday until 6 or 7pm) and Saturday 9am to 1 or 2pm. Sunday closings are observed.

Customs   With certain food exceptions, personal effects intended for your own use can be brought into Norway. If you take them with you when you leave, you can bring in cameras, binoculars, radios, portable TVs, and the like, as well as fishing and camping equipment. Visitors of all nationalities can bring in 400 cigarettes, or 500 grams of tobacco, and 200 sheets of cigarette paper, or 50 cigars, and 1 liter of spirits or 1 liter of wine. Upon leaving, you can take with you up to 25,000 NOK ($2,775) in Norwegian currency.

Dentists   For emergency dental services, ask your hotel or host for the nearest dentist. Most Norwegian dentists speak English.

Doctors   If you become ill or injured while in Norway, your hotel can refer you to a local doctor, nearly all of whom speak English. If you don't stay at a hotel, call ☎ **113,** the national 24-hour emergency medical number.

Drugstores   Drugstores, called *apotek,* are open during normal business hours.

Electricity   Norway uses 220 volts, 30 to 50 cycles, A.C., and standard continental two-pin plugs. Transformers and adapters will be needed with Canadian and American equipment. Always inquire at your hotel before plugging in any electrical equipment.

Embassies & Consulates   In case you lose your passport or have some other emergency, contact your embassy in Oslo. The Embassy of the **United States** is at Drammensveien 18, N-0255 Oslo 2 (☎ **22-44-85-50**); **United Kingdom,** Thomas Heftyes Gate 8, N-0264 Oslo 2 (☎ **23-13-27-00**); and **Canada,** Oscarsgate 20, N-0244 Oslo 3 (☎ **22-99-53-00**). Visitors from Ireland and New Zealand should contact the British Embassy. Australians should contact the Canadian Embassy. There is a British consulate in Bergen at Carl Konowsgate 34 (☎ **55-94-47-00**).

Emergencies   Throughout Norway, call ☎ **112** for the **police,** ☎ **110** to report a **fire,** or ☎ **113** to request an **ambulance.**

Laundry & Dry Cleaning   Most hotels provide these services. There are coin-operated launderettes and dry cleaners in most Norwegian cities.

Liquor Laws   Most restaurants, pubs, and bars in Norway are licensed to serve liquor, wine, and beer. The drinking age is 18 for beer and wine and 20 for liquor.

Mail   Airmail letters or postcards to the United States and Canada cost 6 NOK (65¢) for up to 20 grams (seven-tenths of an ounce). Airmail letters take 7 to 10 days to reach North America. The principal post office in Norway is Oslo Central Post Office, Dronningensgate 15, N-0101 Oslo. Mailboxes are vibrant red, embossed with the trumpet symbol of the postal service. They're found on walls, at chest level, throughout cities and towns. Stamps can be bought at the post office, at magazine kiosks, or at some stores. For more information, call ☎ **23-14-78-02.**

Only the post office can weigh, evaluate, and inform you of the options for delivery time and regulations for sending parcels. Shipments to places outside Norway require a declaration on a printed form stating the contents and value of the package.

Maps   Many tourist offices supply free maps of their district. You can also contact the Norwegian Automobile Club, Storgata 2, N-0155 Oslo 1 (☎ **22-34-14-00**), which offers free or inexpensive road maps. Most visitors find it quicker and more convenient to buy a detailed road map; this is the best approach for anyone who plans to tour extensively outside the major cities. Some of Norway's most reliable maps are published by Cappelen.

Police   Dial ☎ **112** nationwide.

Radio & TV   Radio and television broadcasts are in Norwegian. However, Norwegian National Radio (NRK) has news summaries in English several times weekly.

Rest Rooms   All terminals, big city squares, and the like have public lavatories. In small towns and villages, head for the marketplace. Hygiene standards are usually adequate. If you patronize the toilets in a privately run establishment (such as a cafe), it's polite to buy at least a small pastry or coffee.

Taxes   Norway imposes a 20% value-added tax (VAT) on most goods and services, which is figured into your final bill. If you buy goods in any store bearing the tax-free sign, you're entitled to a cash refund of up to 18.7% on purchases costing over 308 NOK ($34.20). Ask the shop assistant for a tax-free shopping check, and show your passport to indicate that you're not a resident of Scandinavia. You may not use the articles purchased before leaving Norway, and they must be taken out of the country within 3 months of purchase. Complete the information requested on the back of the check you're given at the store; at your point of departure, report to an area marked by the tax-free sign, not at customs. Your refund check will be exchanged there in kroner for the amount due you. Refunds are available at airports, ferry and cruise-ship terminals, borders, and train stations.

Telephone & Telegrams   Direct-dial long-distance calls can be made to the United States and Canada from most phones in Norway by dialing ☎ **00** (double zero), then the country code (**1** for the U.S. and Canada), followed by the area code and phone number. Check at your hotel's front desk before you place a call. Norwegian coins of 1 NOK (10¢), 5 NOK (55¢), and 10 NOK ($1.10) are used in pay phones.

Telegrams can be sent from private or public phones by dialing ☎ **0138.**

Time   Norway operates on Central European Time—1 hour ahead of Greenwich Mean Time and 6 hours ahead of Eastern Standard Time. (For example: at noon Eastern Standard Time—say, in New York City—it's 6pm in Norway.)

Norway goes on summer time—1 hour earlier—from the end of March until around the end of September.

Tipping   Hotels add a 10% to 15% service charge to your bill, which is sufficient unless someone has performed a special service. Most bellhops get at least 10 NOK ($1.10) per suitcase. Nearly all restaurants add a service charge of up to 15% to your bill. Barbers and hairdressers usually aren't tipped, but toilet attendants and hat-check people expect at least 3 NOK (35¢). Don't tip theater ushers. Taxi drivers don't expect tips unless they handle heavy luggage.

Water   Tap water is generally safe to drink throughout Norway. Never drink from a mountain stream, fjord, or river, regardless of how clean it might appear.

Oslo 8

One of the oldest Scandinavian capitals, Oslo has never been on the mainstream European tourist circuit. Many have the impression that it's lean on historic and cultural sights. In fact, it offers enough sights and activities to fill at least 3 or 4 busy days. It's also the starting point for many easy excursions along the Oslofjord or to nearby towns and villages.

In the '90s Oslo grew surprisingly—from what even the Scandinavians considered a backwater to one of the glittering cities of Europe. Restaurants, nightclubs, cafes, shopping complexes, and other places have opened. A Nordic joie de vivre permeates the city. The only problem is that Oslo is one of the most expensive cities in Europe. Proceed with caution if you're on a strict budget.

Oslo was founded in the mid–11th century by a Viking king, and became the capital around 1300 under Haakon V. In the course of its history, the city burned down several times; it was destroyed by fire in 1824. The master builder, Christian IV, king of Denmark and Norway, ordered the town rebuilt near the Akershus Castle. He named the new town Christiania (after himself), and that was its official name until 1924, when the city reverted to its former name.

In 1814 Norway separated from Denmark and united with Sweden, a union that lasted until 1905. During that period the Royal Palace, the House of Parliament, the old university, the National Theater, and the National Gallery were built.

After the Second World War, Oslo grew to 175 square miles. Today it's one of the 10 largest world capitals in area. Oslo is also one of the most heavily forested cities, with fewer than half a million inhabitants.

One final point: Oslovians love nature. They devote much time to pursuits in the forests and on the fjords. It takes only half an hour by tram to go from the Royal Palace to the 390-foot Tryvann Observation Tower, where you can enjoy a view over Oslo Marka, the giant forest. The Krogskogen forest was the setting for many Norwegian folk tales about princesses, kings, penniless heroes, and the inevitable forest trolls. From this observation tower in the summer, you can look down on hundreds of sailboats, motorboats, and windsurfers among the numerous islands of the Oslo archipelago.

1   Orientation

ARRIVING

BY PLANE   Since the recent closing of a small-scale, relatively outmoded airport named Fornebu, Oslo has coped with all of its air traffic being funneled into the **Oslo International Airport** in Gardermoen (☎ **67-59-70-00**), about 31 miles east of downtown Oslo, a 45-minute drive from the center. Through this much-upgraded airport arrive all domestic and international flights coming into Oslo, including aircraft belonging to SAS, British Airways, and Icelandair.

There's frequent bus service, departing at intervals of between 15 and 30 minutes throughout the day, into downtown Oslo. It's maintained by both SAS (whose buses deliver passengers to the Central Railway station and to most of the SAS hotels within Oslo) and the **Norwegian Bus Express** (☎ **81-54-44-44**), whose buses head for the main railway station. Both companies charge 95 NOK ($10.55) per person, each way. There's also a high-speed railway service between Gardermoen and Oslo's main railway station, requiring transit time of only 20 minutes, priced at 120 NOK ($13.30) per person each way. If you want to take a taxi, be prepared for a lethally high charge of around 500 NOK ($55.50) for up to four passengers plus their luggage. If you need a "maxi-taxi," a minivan that's suitable for between 5 and 15 passengers, plus their luggage, you'll be assessed 800 NOK ($88.80).

BY TRAIN   Trains from the Continent, Sweden, and Denmark arrive at **Oslo Sentralstasjon,** Jernbanetorget 1 (☎ **81-50-08-88** for train information). It's at the beginning of Karl Johans Gate, in the center of the city. The station is open daily from 7am to 11pm. From the Central Station, trains leave for Bergen, Stavanger, Trondheim, Bodø, and all other rail links in Norway. You can also take trams to all major parts of Oslo. Lockers and a luggage office are available at the station, where you can also exchange money.

BY CAR   If you're driving from mainland Europe, the fastest way to reach Oslo is to take the car ferry from Frederikshavn, Denmark. From Frederikshavn, car ferries run to several towns near Oslo, and to Gothenburg, Sweden. You can also take a car ferry from Copenhagen to several points in western Sweden, or from Helsingør, Denmark, to Helsingborg, Sweden. Highway E6 runs the length of Sweden's western coast from Malmö through Helsingborg and Gothenburg, right up to Oslo. If you're driving from Stockholm to Oslo, take E3 west to Örebro, where it connects with E18 to Oslo. Once you near the outskirts of Oslo from any direction, follow the signs into the Sentrum.

BY FERRY   Ferries from Europe arrive at the Oslo port, a 15-minute walk (or a short taxi ride) from the center. From Denmark, Scandinavia's link with the Continent, ferries depart for Oslo from Copenhagen, Hirtshals, and Frederikshavn.

From Strømstad, Sweden, in the summer, the daily crossing to Sandefjord, Norway, takes 2½ hours; from Sandefjord, it's an easy drive or train ride north to Oslo.

VISITOR INFORMATION

Assistance and information for visitors are available at the **Tourist Information Office,** Vestbaneplassen 1, N-0250 Oslo (☎ **22-83-00-50**). Free maps, brochures, sightseeing tickets, and guide services are available. The office is open in June daily from 9am to 7pm; July and August daily 9am to 7pm; May and September Monday to Saturday 9am to 4pm; October to April, Monday to Friday 9am to 4pm.

The information office at the **Oslo Sentralstasjon** (Central Station), Jernbanetorget 1, is open daily from 8am to 11pm. There's no phone.

CITY LAYOUT

MAIN ARTERIES & STREETS   Oslo is at the mouth of the 60-mile-long Oslofjord. Opening onto the harbor is **Rådhusplassen** (City Hall Square), dominated by the modern City Hall, a major attraction. Guided bus tours leave from this point, and the launches that cruise the fjords depart from the pier facing the municipal building. You can catch Bygdøy-bound ferries from the quay at Rådhusplassen. On a promontory to the east is **Akershus Castle.**

Karl Johans Gate, Oslo's main street (especially for shopping and strolling), is north of City Hall Square. This boulevard begins at Oslo Sentralstasjon (Central Station) and stretches all the way to the 19th-century Royal Palace at the western end.

A short walk from the palace is the famed **Students' Grove** (Studenter Lunden), where seemingly everybody gathers on summer days to socialize. The University of Oslo is nearby. Dominating this center is the National Theater, guarded by statues of Ibsen and Bjørnson, the two greatest names in Norwegian theater. South of the theater, near the harbor, is **Stortingsgaten,** another shop-filled street.

The main city square is **Stortorvet,** although it's no longer the center of city life, which has shifted to Karl Johans Gate.

At a subway stop near the National Theater, you can catch an electric train to **Tryvannstårnet,** the loftiest lookout in Scandinavia, and to the **Holmenkollen Ski Jump.**

FINDING AN ADDRESS   Street numbers begin on the southern end of streets running north-south and on the eastern end of streets running east-west. Odd numbers are on one side of the street, and even numbers on the other. Some large buildings hold several establishments, so different addresses are designated with A, B, and C.

STREET MAPS   Maps of Oslo are distributed free at the tourist office (see above). For extensive exploring, especially of some back streets, you may need a more detailed map. Opt for a pocket-sized map with a street index that can be opened and folded like a wallet. Such maps are sold at most newsstands in the central city. If you can't find one, go to the city's most central bookstore, **Tanum Karl Johan,** Karl Johans Gate 43 (☎ **22-41-11-00**).

Neighborhoods in Brief

Oslo is made for walking—in fact, you can walk from the Central Station all the way to the Royal Palace (Slottet) in a straight line. Except for excursions to the museum-loaded Bygdøy peninsula and the Holmenkollen Ski Jump, most attractions can be covered on foot.

Oslo is not neatly divided into separate neighborhoods or districts. It consists mainly of **central Oslo,** with the Central Station to the east of the city center and the Royal Palace to the west. Karl Johans Gate, the principal street, connects these two points. Central Oslo is the heart of the city—the most crowded and traffic congested, but also the most convenient place to stay. It's not a real neighborhood but the core of the city, as Piccadilly Circus is to London. Most Oslo hotels and restaurants are here as are almost 50 museums and galleries—enough to fill many a rainy day. The most interesting include Akershus Castle, the Historical Museum, and the National Gallery.

The streets Drammensveien and Frognerveien lead northwest to Frogner Park (Frognerparken), whose main entrance is on Kirkeveien. This historical area is the site of the Vigeland Sculpture Park, which displays some masterpieces of Gustav Vigeland (1869–1943).

The **Old Town** (or Gamlebyen) lies south of the Parliament Building (the Stortinget) and Karl Johans Gate. This section contains some of the city's old-fashioned restaurants, along with the Norwegian Resistance Museum and the Old Town Hall.

Aker Brygge is Oslo's newest neighborhood, an excellent place for dining and diversions, but not for hotels. It emerged near the mouth of the Oslofjord in the old wharf area formerly used for shipbuilding yards. Fueled by oil wealth, steel-and-glass buildings now rise from what had been a relatively dilapidated section. Some of the best shops, theaters, restaurants, and cultural attractions are here, along with apartments for such well-heeled owners as Diana Ross.

The main attractions in **eastern Oslo** are the Botanisk Hage (Botanic Garden), the Zoological Museum, and the Munch Museum in Tøyen—little more is worth seeing there.

The **West End** is a chic residential area graced with some of the city's finest hotels and restaurants. It's a more tranquil setting than the center, which we prefer, and only 15 minutes away by public transportation.

Further west—4 miles by car but better reached by car ferry—is the **Bygdøy** peninsula. Here you'll find such attractions as the Norwegian Folk Museum, the Viking ships, the polar ship *Fram* Museum, and the *Kon-Tiki* Museum. Break up your sightseeing venture with a meal here but plan to stay elsewhere.

The suburb of Frogner begins a half-mile west of Oslo center and stretches for a mile or so. There's a good hotel and restaurant here.

Many Oslo neighborhoods lie along the **Oslofjord,** which stretches more than 60 miles north from the Skagerrak to Oslo, and is filled with basins dotted with islands. (There are 40 islands in the immediate Oslo archipelago.)

Nearly all visitors want to see **Holmenkollen,** a wooded range of hills northwest of the city rising to about 1,740 feet. You can reach it in 35 minutes by electric train from the city center.

Marka, Oslo's forest, is a sprawling recreation area that offers hiking, bicycle riding, skiing, fishing, wild berry picking, jogging trails, and more. It contains 343 lakes, 310 miles of ski trails, 387 miles of trails and roads, 11 sports chalets, and 24 ski jumps and alpine slopes.

2 Getting Around

BY PUBLIC TRANSPORTATION

Oslo has an efficient citywide network of buses, trams (streetcars), and subways. Buses and electric trains take passengers to the suburbs; from mid-April to October, ferries to Bygdøy depart from the harbor in front of the Oslo Rådhuset (City Hall).

DISCOUNT PASSES The **Oslo Card (Oslo-Kortet)** can help you become acquainted with the city at a fraction of the usual price. It allows free travel on public transportation, free admission to museums and other top sights, discounts on sightseeing buses and boats, a rebate on your car rental, and special treats in restaurants. You can purchase the card at hotels, fine stores, and tourist information offices, from travel agents, and in the branches of Sparebanken Oslo Akershus. Adults pay 180 NOK ($20) for a 1-day card, 290 NOK ($32.20) for 2 days, and 410 NOK ($45.50) for 3 days. Children's cards cost 60 NOK ($6.65), 80 NOK ($8.90), and 110 NOK ($12.20).

The 24-hour **Tourist Ticket (Turistkort)** lets you travel anywhere in Oslo by bus, tram, subway, local railway, or boat, including the Bygdøy ferries in the summer. The

Tourist Ticket costs 45 NOK ($5) for adults, half price for children 4 to 15; children under 4 travel free. The ticket will be stamped when it's used for the first time and is good for the next 24 hours.

BY BUS, TRAM & SUBWAY   Jernbanetorget is Oslo's major **bus and tram** terminal stop. Most buses and trams passing through the heart of town stop at Wessels Plass, next to the Parliament, or at Stortorget, the main marketplace. Many also stop at the National Theater or University Square on Karl Johans Gate, as well as Oslo's suburbs.

The **subway (T-banen)** has four branch lines to the east. The Western Suburban route (including Holmenkollen) has four lines to the residential sections and recreation grounds west and north of the city. Subways and trains leave from near the National Theater on Karl Johans Gate.

For schedule and fare information, call **Trafikanten** (☎ 22-17-70-30). Automated machines cancel tickets. Drivers sell single-trip tickets for 20 NOK ($2.20); children travel for half-fare. An eight-coupon Maxi card costs 120 NOK ($13.30), half-price for children. Maxi cards can be used for unlimited transfers for 1 hour from the time the ticket was stamped.

BY TAXI

If you need a taxi, call ☎ 22-38-80-90, 24 hours a day. Reserve at least an hour in advance.

The approximate fare from Oslo International Airport to the center of Oslo is 500 NOK ($55.50). All taxis have meters, and Norwegian cab drivers are generally honest. When a cab is available, a roof light goes on. Taxis can be hailed on the street, provided they're more than 100 yards from a taxi rank. The worst time to hail a taxi is Monday to Friday from 8:30 to 10am and 3 to 5pm, and Saturday 8:30 to 10am.

BY CAR

Driving is not a practical way to get around Oslo because parking is limited. The efficient network of public transportation makes a private car unnecessary. You can reach even the most isolated areas by public transportation.

Among the multistory parking lots in the city center the best is **Vestre Vika Bilpark,** Dronning Mauds Gate (☎ 22-83-35-35). The cost of parking a car in a public garage is 25 NOK ($2.80) per hour or 130 NOK ($14.45) for 24 hours. Illegally parked cars are towed away. For car problems, call the **NAF Alarm Center** (☎ 22-34-16-00), 24 hours a day.

BY FERRY

Beginning in mid-April, ferries depart for Bygdøy from Pier 3 in front of the Oslo Rådhuset. For schedules, call **Båtservice** (☎ 22-20-07-15). The ferry or bus to Bygdøy is a good choice, because parking there is limited. Other ferries leave for various parts of the Oslofjord. Inquire at the **Tourist Information Office,** Vestbaneplassen 1 (☎ 22-83-00-50).

BY BICYCLE

Den Rustne Eike, Vestbaneplassen 2 (☎ 22-83-52-08), rents bikes at moderate rates, complete with free maps of interesting routes in Oslo and its environs. The cost is 85 to 135 NOK ($9.45 to $15) per day or 465 to 835 NOK ($51.60 to $92.70) per week, with a 1,000 NOK ($111) deposit required. Helmets are included, and a child seat is available for about 50 NOK ($5.55). It's open May to October, daily from 10am to 6:30pm; in the off-season, Monday to Friday from 10am to 6pm.

Fast Facts: Oslo

American Express   American Express Reisebyrå, Karl Johans Gate 33 (☎ 22-98-37-00), is open Monday to Friday from 9am to 6pm, Saturday 10am to 3pm.

Area Code   The country code for Norway is **47.** If you're calling from outside the country, the city code for Oslo is **2.** Inside Norway, no area or city codes are needed. Telephone numbers have eight digits.

Baby-sitters   Hotels can often enlist the help of a housekeeper for "child-minding." Give at least a day's notice, two if you can. You can also contact the tourist office (see "Visitor Information," above), which keeps a list of available sitters on file.

Bookstores   Oslo has many bookstores. The most central and one of the best stocked is **Tanum Karl Johan,** Karl Johans Gate 43 (☎ 22-41-11-00).

Currency Exchange   **Banks** will exchange most foreign currencies or cash traveler's checks. Bring your passport for identification. If banks are closed, try automated machines at the Oslo Sentralstasjon to exchange currency. You can also exchange currency at the **Bureau de Change** at the main Oslo post office, Dronningensgatan 15 (☎ 23-14-78-02).

Dentists   In an emergency, contact the **Tøyen Senter,** Kolstadgate 16 (☎ 22-67-78-00), which is open daily from 11am to 2pm and 7 to 10pm. If you can wait, volume 1B of the telephone directory lists private dentists under *Tannleger,* (literally "tooth doctors"). There's rarely a language barrier.

Doctors   Some larger hotels have arrangements with doctors in case a guest becomes ill, or try the 24-hour **Oslo Kommunale Legavakten,** Storgata 40 (☎ 22-11-70-70). A privately funded alternative is **Oslo Akutten,** Nedre Vollgate 8 (☎ 22-41-24-40). For more routine medical assistance, you can contact the biggest hospital in Oslo, **Ullaval,** Kirkeveien 166 (☎ 22-11-80-80). To consult a private doctor (nearly all of whom speak English), check the telephone directory or ask at your hotel for a recommendation.

Drugstores   A 24-hour pharmacy is **Jernbanetorvets Apotek,** Jernbanetorget 4A (☎ 22-41-24-82).

Embassies & Consulates   See "Fast Facts: Norway," in Chapter 7, "Planning a Trip to Norway."

Emergencies   Dial the Oslo **police** at ☎ **112;** report a **fire** to ☎ **110;** call an **ambulance** at ☎ **113.**

Eyeglass Repair   **Ulf Jacobsen Optiker,** Karl Johans Gate 20 (☎ 22-42-85-14), is a big supplier. Most contact lenses are in stock, too. Unusual prescriptions take about 2 days. Hours are Monday and Wednesday to Friday from 9am to 5pm, Tuesday 9am to 6pm, Saturday 10am to 2pm.

Internet Access   You can tap in free at the Rådhuset, the City Hall on Rådhusplassen (☎ 22-86-16-00). For opening hours, refer to "Seeing the Sights," below. There is also free service at the library (see below) where you must sign up for slots.

Laundry & Dry Cleaning   Washing and drying can usually be completed in an hour. You must have your coins ready to put in the machines. Dry cleaning is extremely expensive in Oslo, and many establishments take more than a week to return clothing. Try **Oslo American Rens,** Griniveien 1 (☎ 22-50-57-41), which promises 24-hour service.

Libraries   The Oslo municipal library, **Diechmann Library,** Henrik Ibsens Gate 1 (☎ **22-03-29-00**), is the largest in Norway. It has many English-language volumes, a children's department, and a music department. It's open Monday to Friday from 10am to 8pm (to 6pm in summer), Saturday 9am to 2pm.

Lost Property   The **Lost and Found Office,** Hittegodskontoret, Grøland-sleiret 44 (☎ **22-66-98-65**), is open May 15 to September 15, Monday to Friday from 8:15am to 1:45pm; September 16 to May 14, Monday to Friday 8:15am to 3pm.

Luggage Storage & Lockers   Facilities for luggage storage are available at the **Oslo Sentralstasjon,** Jernbanetorget 1 (☎ **81-50-08-88**). It's open daily from 7am to 11pm. Lockers cost 25 to 40 NOK ($2.80 to $4.45) per day, depending on size.

Newspapers & Magazines   English-language newspapers and magazines are sold—at least in the summer months—at newsstands (kiosks) throughout Oslo. International editions, including the *International Herald Tribune* and *USA Today* are always available, as are the European editions of *Time* and *Newsweek.*

Photographic Needs   Try **Preeus Photo,** Karl Johans Gate 33 (☎ **22-42-98-04**), for supplies, including black-and-white and color film. Film can be developed in 1 hour. It's open Monday to Friday from 9am to 5pm, Saturday 10am to 3pm.

Police   Dial ☎ **112.**

Post Office   The **Oslo General Post Office** is at Dronningensgatan 15 (☎ **23-14-78-02** for information). Enter at the corner of Prinsensgate. It's open Monday to Friday from 8am to 6pm, Saturday 9am to 3pm; closed Sunday and public holidays. You can arrange for mail to be sent to the main post office c/o General Delivery. The address is Poste Restante, P.O. Box 1181-Sentrum, Dronningensgatan 15, N-0101 Oslo, Norway. You must show your passport to collect it.

Radio & TV   The most important broadcaster is the Norwegian government, which owns and controls programming on the NRK station. Oslo receives many broadcasts from other countries, including BBC programs from London. Radio Norway International broadcasts on MHz frequency.

Rest Rooms   Clean public toilets can be found throughout the city center, in parks, and at all bus, rail, and air terminals. For a detailed list, contact the Tourist Information Office.

Safety   Of the four Scandinavian capitals, Oslo is widely considered the safest. However, don't be lulled into a false sense of security. Oslovians no longer leave their doors unlocked. Be careful, and don't carry your wallet visibly exposed or sling your purse over your shoulder.

Taxes   Oslo has no special city taxes. You pay the same value-added tax throughout the country (see "Fast Facts: Norway," in chapter 7).

Taxis   See "Getting Around," above.

Transit Information   For information about tram and bus travel, call **Trafikanten** (☎ **22-17-70-30**), located in front of the Central Station. For information about train travel, go to the Central Station or call ☎ **23-15-00-00.**

Weather   See the temperature chart in "When to Go," in chapter 7.

3 Accommodations

By the standards of many U.S. and Canadian cities, hotels in Oslo are very expensive. If the prices make you want to cancel your trip, read on. Oslovian hotels lose most of their business travelers, and their main revenue source, during the peak tourist months in midsummer. Even though the city is filled with visitors, many hotels slash their prices. July is always a month for discounts. Some hotels' discounts begin June 21. Regular pricing usually resumes in mid-August. For exact dates of discounts, which often change from year to year, check with the hotel.

Hotels also slash prices on weekends—usually Friday and Saturday, and sometimes Sunday. Again, hotels often change their policies, so it's best to check when you make your reservations. Don't always expect a discount—a quickly arranged conference could lead hotels to increase their prices.

The most economy-minded tourists can cut costs by staying at one of the old-fashioned hotels that offer a number of rooms without private bathrooms. Sometimes a room has a shower but no toilet. In most cases, corridor toilets and bathrooms are plentiful. Even the rooms without bathrooms usually have a sink with hot and cold running water.

HOTEL RESERVATIONS   The worst months for finding a place to stay in Oslo are May, June, September, and October, when many business conferences are held. July and August are better, even though that's the peak time of the summer tourist invasion.

If you happen to arrive in Oslo without a reservation, head for the Oslo Tourist Information Office (see above), which will book you into a room in your price category. The minimum stay is 2 days. Don't try to phone—the service is strictly for walk-ins who need a room on the night of their arrival.

Note: Rates quoted below include the service charge and tax. Breakfast—usually a generous Norwegian buffet—is almost always included. Unless otherwise indicated, all our recommended accommodations come with bathrooms.

CENTRAL OSLO
VERY EXPENSIVE

✪ **Grand Hotel.** Karl Johans Gate 31, N-0159 Oslo. ☎ **800/223-5652** in the U.S., or 22-21-20-00. Fax 23-21-21-00. www.grand-hotel.no. E-mail: admin@grand-hotel.no. 289 units. A/C MINIBAR TV TEL. Summer, 1,190 NOK ($132.10) double; 2,050–10,000 NOK ($227.55–$1,110) suite. Fall, winter, spring, 1,875 NOK ($208.15) double; 2,675–10,000 NOK ($296.95–$1,110) suite. Rates include buffet breakfast. AE, DC, MC, V. Parking 145 NOK ($16.10). T-banen: Stortinget.

Norway's leading hostelry is on the wide boulevard that leads to the Royal Palace. The stone-walled hotel with its mansard gables and copper tower has been an integral part of Oslo life since 1874. Famous guests have included Arctic explorer Roald Amundsen, Edvard Munch, Gen. Dwight Eisenhower, Charlie Chaplin, Henry Ford, and Henrik Ibsen, who was especially fond of the place. More recent guests have included Helmut Kohl, Elton John, and Michael Jackson.

Dramatically renovated in 1996, the guest rooms are in the 19th-century core or one of the tasteful modern additions. Newer rooms contain plush facilities and electronic amenities, and the older ones have been completely modernized. Some accommodations have air-conditioning, and all have good beds with firm mattresses, double-glazed windows, and trouser presses. Most of the old-fashioned bathrooms are done in marble or tile and have hair dryers. An eight-story extension contains larger, brighter doubles, but many guests prefer the old-fashioned accommodations in the older section.

Dining/Diversions: The hotel has several restaurants that serve international and Scandinavian food. The Palmen, the Julius Fritzner, and the Grand Café offer live entertainment. The Grand Café is the most famous in Oslo. The Etoile Bar is an informal meeting place next to the swimming pool. The Bonanza, in the cellar, is a throbbing nightclub.

Amenities: A "solve-everything" concierge, room service, laundry, guide services, message desk, express checkout, safe-deposit boxes, business services center; indoor swimming pool, sauna, solarium, boutiques, and car-rental desk.

✪ Hotel Continental. Stortingsgaten 24–26, N-0117 Oslo 1. ☎ **22-82-40-00.** Fax 22-42-96-89. www.hotel-continental.no. 159 units. A/C MINIBAR TV TEL. Sun–Thurs 1,880 NOK ($208.70) double; Fri–Sat 1,160 NOK ($128.75) double. All week long, 3,150 NOK ($349.65) suite. Rates include breakfast. AE, DC, MC, V. Parking 140 NOK ($15.55). T-banen: Stortinget.

One of the leading hotels of Europe, the Continental is rich in tradition and quality, although not the great classic the Grand is. Built in 1900, it's right in the city center between the Royal Palace and City Hall, and has been owned by the same family for four generations. Personal service is a hallmark. The stylish guest rooms are furnished in light Nordic tones with many amenities. All have blackout draperies, classic furnishings, good beds with frequently renewed mattresses, and trouser presses. Bathrooms are tiled or marble, with hair dryers and makeup mirrors. Guest rooms that open onto the courtyard are more tranquil, and units for nonsmokers are available.

Dining: The gourmet restaurant Annen Etage is one of the finest in Norway. The Lipp is moderately priced, with an excellent grill menu, and the Theatercafeen is northern Europe's only Viennese cafe. Breakfast is served at Carolines.

Amenities: Room service, baby-sitting, laundry, private underground garage, newsstand, perfumery, and men's hairdresser.

EXPENSIVE

✪ Bristol Hotel. Kristian IV's Gate 7, N-0164 Oslo 1. ☎ **22-82-60-00.** Fax 22-82-60-01. www.bristol.no. E-mail: booking@bristol.no. 252 units. A/C MINIBAR TV TEL. 1,000–1,750 NOK ($111–$194.25) double; 2,800–4,000 NOK ($310.80–$444) suite. Children under 15 stay free in parents' room. Rates include breakfast. AE, DC, MC, V. Parking 130 NOK ($14.45). T-banen: Stortinget.

In the heart of the city, on a side street north of Karl Johans Gate, this 1920s-era hotel is warm, inviting, and luxurious. The Moorish-inspired lobby, with its Winter Garden and Library Bar, sets an elegant tone. The comfortable guest rooms have special character. Most are furnished in light Nordic pastels, with excellent beds and many amenities, such as tile or marble bathrooms with hair dryers. Some units are set aside for nonsmokers.

Dining/Diversions: The Bristol has several drinking and dining options, including the intimate Bristol Grill, which features seafood and red meat grilled over charcoal. The Bristol Night Spot is a dine-and-dance restaurant, with live bands and a welcoming bar. The Bristol Lounge serves drinks.

Amenities: Room service, laundry and dry cleaning, baby-sitting, salon.

Clarion Hotel Royal Christiania. Biskop Gunnerus Gate 3, N-0106 Oslo. ☎ **23-10-80-00.** Fax 23-10-80-80. www.royalchristiania.no. E-mail: royalchristiania.no. 503 units. MINIBAR TV TEL. Mon–Thurs 1,895 NOK ($210.35) double; 2,195 NOK ($243.65) suite. Fri–Sun 1,080 NOK ($119.90) double; 1,380 NOK ($153.20) suite. Rates include breakfast. AE, DC, MC, V. Parking 135 NOK ($15). Bus: 30, 31, or 41.

This is the second-largest hotel in Norway, a soaring 14-story tower built to house athletes and administrators during the 1952 Winter Olympics. It was radically upgraded in 1990, with the addition of two nine-story wings, and in 1999 it was enlarged again.

Oslo Accommodations

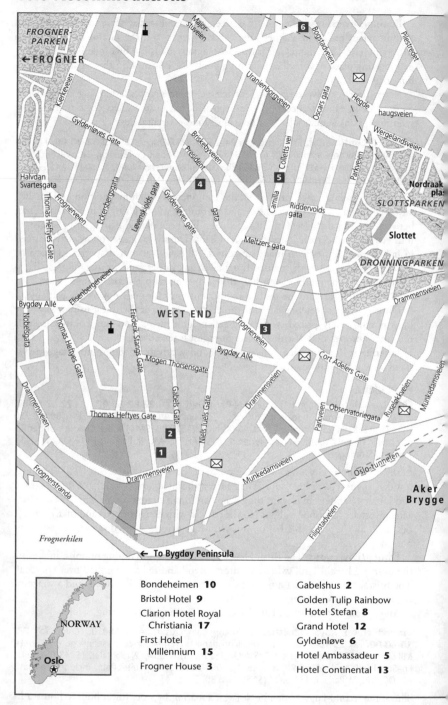

Bondeheimen **10**
Bristol Hotel **9**
Clarion Hotel Royal
  Christiania **17**
First Hotel
  Millennium **15**
Frogner House **3**

Gabelshus **2**
Golden Tulip Rainbow
  Hotel Stefan **8**
Grand Hotel **12**
Gyldenløve **6**
Hotel Ambassadeur **5**
Hotel Continental **13**

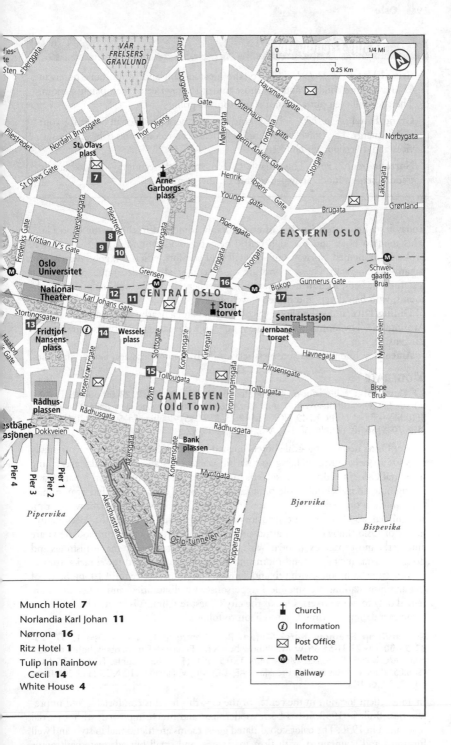

Munch Hotel **7**
Norlandia Karl Johan **11**
Nørrona **16**
Ritz Hotel **1**
Tulip Inn Rainbow
    Cecil **14**
White House **4**

† Church
ⓘ Information
⊠ Post Office
– – Ⓜ Metro
— Railway

ⓕ   Family-Friendly Hotels

Bristol Hotel *(see p. 191)*   One of the most elegant and comfortable hotels in Oslo welcomes children and lets those under 15 stay free in their parents' room. The chef will even put a "junior steak" on the grill.

Grand Hotel *(see p. 190)*   The Grand's indoor pool provides an outlet for your child's energy. The "solve-everything" concierge can recommend baby-sitting services and diversions for children.

Norrøna *(see p. 196)*   This reliable choice attracts the economy-minded family trade. There's a moderately priced cafe on the premises.

Today it's a luxury hotel that is often favorably compared to the nearby Oslo Plaza. This modern hotel and the high-traffic neighborhood around it don't in any way evoke old-fashioned Norway, but you will find comfort, efficiency, good design, and a hard-working staff. Guest rooms are quiet, conservatively decorated, and blandly tasteful. The beds, with firm mattresses, are excellent, as are the well-maintained bathrooms, with hair dryers and heated towel racks.

Dining/Diversions: The hotel has a lobby bar and a nearby cafe and snack bar, the Atrium Café. The more formal dining venue is a well-managed Norwegian restaurant, Lingens.

Amenities: Room service, business services, baby-sitting, massage, laundry facilities.

MODERATE

✪ **First Hotel Millennium.** Tollbugate 25, N-0157 Oslo. ☎ **23-00-30-00.** Fax 23-00-30-30. www.firsthotels.com. E-mail: per.sorenson@firsthotels.no. 114 units. MINIBAR TV TEL. Mon–Thurs 1,349–1,749 NOK ($149.75–$194.15) double; Fri–Sun 799–1,409 NOK ($88.70–$156.40) double. AE, DC, MC, V. Tram: 30, 42.

One of Oslo's newest large-scale hotels opened late in 1998 within what was originally a 1930s art-deco office building. It's within walking distance of virtually everything in central Oslo, including the Akershus fortress and the shops of the Karl Johans Gate. Rising nine floors behind a pale pink facade, it's noted for a stylish kind of minimalism, which in the bedrooms translates into ochre-colored walls with dark wood trim, streamlined wooden furniture, and lots of comfort. This is one of the "personality" hotels of Oslo, known for its atmosphere and character. The accommodations are among the most spacious in town, with many art deco touches in the furnishings and designs. Extras include second room phones, hair dryers, heated towel racks, trouser presses, large bathrooms with tub and shower, and room service until 10pm. Some of the accommodations are suitable for persons with disabilities, and other units are rented only to nonsmokers. One of the city's finest restaurants is located here. See our recommendation of Primo Ciaou-Ciaou to follow.

Golden Tulip Rainbow Hotel Stefan. Rosenkrantzgate 1, N-0189 Oslo 1. ☎ **23-31-55-00.** Fax 23-31-55-55. www.rainbow-hotels.no. E-mail: stefan@rainbow/hotels.no. 139 units. A/C MINIBAR TV TEL. Mon–Thurs 1,015 NOK ($112.65) double; Fri–Sat 775 NOK ($86.05) double. Rates include breakfast. AE, DC, MC, V. Parking 110 NOK ($12.20) Tram: 10, 11, 17, or 18.

In an excellent location in the center of the city, this hotel is comfortable and unpretentious. Built in 1952, it has been modernized and much improved, with a partial renovation in 1996. The color-coordinated guest rooms are traditional in style and well furnished and maintained, with firm mattresses, and small but adequate bathrooms with hair dryers. Two guest rooms offer facilities for people with disabilities. From May until September 1, weekend rates are granted only to those who make reservations less than 48 hours before arrival. At lunch, guests can enjoy selections from a Norwegian cold-table buffet (see "Dining," below).

Hotell Bondeheimen. Rosenkrantzgate 8 (entrance on Kristian IV's Gate), N-0159 Oslo 1. ☎ **800/528-1234** in the U.S., or 22-42-95-30. Fax 22-41-94-37. www.bondeheimen.com. E-mail: booking@bondeheimen.com. 81 units. MINIBAR TV TEL. Mon–Thurs 1,195 NOK ($149.40) double; Fri–Sun 795 NOK ($99.40) double. Rates include breakfast. AE, DC, MC, V. Parking 125 NOK ($13.90). Tram: 7 or 11.

In the city center, a short block from the Students' Grove at Karl Johans Gate, the Bondeheimen was built in 1913. A cooperative of farmers and students established it to provide inexpensive accommodations when they visited Oslo from the countryside. Although small, the compact rooms are comfortably furnished, often with Norwegian pine pieces; accommodations for nonsmokers are offered. The hotel was renovated in 1995. The beds are good, and the bathrooms, although small and mostly without tubs, contain hair dryers and heated floors. An inexpensive Kaffistova (coffee shop and cafeteria) is on the premises, and guests get a 10% discount. Homemade and traditional Norwegian food is the specialty, and the hotel runs its own bakery. The hotel shop, Heimen Husflid, sells Norwegian crafts and regional clothing.

Norlandia Karl Johan. Karl Johans Gate 33, N-0162 Oslo. ☎ **23-16-17-00.** Fax 22-42-05-19. www.norlandia.no. E-mail: service@norlandia.karljohan.no. 111 units. MINIBAR TV TEL. Mon–Thurs 1,450 NOK ($160.95) double; 1,650 NOK ($183.15) suite. Fri–Sun 890 NOK ($98.80) double; 1,190 NOK ($132.10) suite. Rates include breakfast. AE, DC, MC, V. Parking 110 NOK ($12.20) in nearby public garage. T-banen: Stortinget.

For the past century or so, an old-fashioned aura hung above this gray stone hotel, the former Karl Johan. Now, a recent renovation has made it brighter, more inviting, and a lot less dim compared to it neighbor across the street, the prestigious (yet still far better) Grand Hotel. Filled with Norwegian folk art, it welcomes you to a reception area filled with mirrors and marble, along with rugs from Asia and antiques (or reproductions at least). The medium-sized bedrooms have a classic decor with excellent fabrics, good beds, trouser presses, double glazing on the windows to cut down on the noise outside, and tiny but marble-clad bathrooms with hair dryers. The best units open onto the front, and contain French windows with a panorama of the central city. About fifty percent of the accommodations are reserved for nonsmokers. Don't expect a lot of amenities here, except room service. There is a bar and restaurant serving continental food at lunch and dinner.

Tulip Inn Rainbow Cecil. Stortingsgate 8 (entrance on Rosenkrantzgate); N-0130 Oslo. ☎ **23-31-48-00.** Fax 23-31-48-50. www.rainbow-hotels.no. E-mail: cecil@rainbow-hotels.no. 112 units. MINIBAR TV TEL. Mon–Thurs 1,075 NOK ($119.35) double; Fri–Sat 725 NOK ($80.50) double. AE, DC, MC, V. Parking 140 NOK ($15.55). T-banen: Stortinget.

Following a fire in the mid-1980s, when an older building on this centrally located site was destroyed, this contemporary hotel was built. Thanks to the eccentrically shaped site, only four rooms on each of the eight floors overlook the street (the sometimes rowdy, at least late at night, Rosenkrantzgate). The others look out over a quiet inner courtyard. Expect relatively simple styling with none of the trappings of more expensive nearby competitors—there's no health club, sauna, or full-fledged room service. The well-maintained rooms are cozy and not overly large, with firm mattresses; bathrooms are small, however. On site is a simple restaurant serving breakfast and an abbreviated buffet-style lunch daily from 11:15am to 1pm, costing 45 NOK ($5) per person.

INEXPENSIVE

Munch Hotel. Munchsgaten 5, N-0130 Oslo 1. ☎ **23-21-96-00.** Fax 23-21-96-01. www.rainbow-hotels.no. E-mail: munch@rainbow-hotels.no. 180 units. MINIBAR TV TEL. Mon–Thurs 920 NOK ($102.10) double; Fri–Sun 690 NOK ($76.60) double. Rates include breakfast. AE, DC, MC, V. Parking 130 NOK ($14.45). T-banen: Stortinget. Tram: 7 or 11. Bus: 37.

This hotel is somewhat like a bed-and-breakfast, and just 5 minutes north of Karl Johans Gate. Built in 1983, the solid, nine-floor hotel offers comfortably furnished, well-maintained guest rooms, decorated with reproductions of Edvard Munch's paintings. Although not overly large, the rooms are cozy and comfortable, with firm mattresses. The bathrooms are tiny. If you don't plan to spend a lot of time in your room, this is an adequate choice, charging a fair price for what it offers. There's no bar or restaurant, but the neighborhood has plenty.

Norrøna. Grensen 19, N-0159 Oslo 1. ☎ **23-31-80-00.** Fax 23-31-80-01. www.rainbow-hotels.no. E-mail: hoteln@online.no. 93 units. A/C TV TEL. 790–1,020 NOK ($98.75–$127.50) double. Rates include breakfast. AE, DC, MC, V. Parking 140 NOK ($17.50). T-banen: Stortinget. Tram: 1 or 7. Bus: 17.

In the heart of Oslo's old section, occupying the upper floors of a modernized building, this hotel is ideal for families. Convenient to both sightseeing and shopping, it offers well-equipped rooms, with good beds, furnished in Scandinavian modern style. A few have private balconies. Many rooms are large enough for families of three or four, although bathrooms have only minimal space. There's a reasonably priced cafeteria, and the lounge is homey and informal.

WEST END
EXPENSIVE

Hotel Ambassadeur. Camilla Colletts Vei 15, N-0258 Oslo. ☎ **23-27-23-00.** Fax 22-44-47-91. www.bestwestern.com/no/ambassadeur. E-mail: post@hotelambassadeur.no. 41 units. MINIBAR TV TEL. Mon–Thurs 1,375 NOK ($152.65) double; 1,750 NOK ($218.75) suite. Fri–Sun 910 NOK ($101) double; 1,350 NOK ($149.85) suite. Rates include breakfast. AE, DC, MC, V. Free parking. Bus: 21.

One of the most consistently reliable hotels in Oslo was built around 1890 as an apartment house. Near the Royal Palace, in an upscale residential neighborhood, it boasts a well-upholstered salon with tapestries and antiques. The theme-decorated guest rooms were renovated between 1994 and 1998. They have double-glazed windows, good beds, and trouser presses. The small, tiled bathrooms have hair dryers and heated towel racks. Suites are more elaborate. There's no restaurant, sauna, or health club on the premises, but there is a basement-level bar.

MODERATE

Gabelshus. Gabels Gate 16, N-0272 Oslo 2. ☎ **23-27-65-00.** Fax 23-27-65-60. www.gabelshus.no. E-mail: gabelshus.hotel@os.enitel.no. 43 units. TV TEL. July and Fri–Sun year-round, 935 NOK ($116.90) double; rest of year, 1,295 NOK ($161.90) double . Rates include breakfast. AE, DC, MC, V. Free parking. Tram: 10.

On a quiet, tree-lined street, this 1912 building has been a small hotel since 1945. Discreetly conservative, it looks like an English manor house, laced with climbing ivy. The public rooms are filled with antiques, art, burnished copper, and working fireplaces. Guest rooms are decorated with tasteful colors and textiles, and some have terraces. You have a choice of Scandinavian modern furniture or traditional styling. The accommodations are well maintained and equipped with double-glazed windows and good beds. Bathrooms are small but immaculate, with hair dryers and decent towels. It's a brisk 15-minute walk from the city center.

Gyldenløve (Golden Lion). Bogstadveien 20, N-0355 Oslo 3. ☎ **22-60-10-90.** Fax 22-60-33-90. www.rainbow-hotels.no. E-mail: gyldenloeve@rainbow-hotels.no. 168 units. MINI-BAR TV TEL. 925 NOK ($115.65) double. Rates include breakfast. AE, DC, MC, V. Parking 90 NOK ($10). Tram: 11, 13, or 19.

This once-dowdy *hospits* (an inexpensive hotel, but better than a youth hostel), built in 1937, was radically upgraded in 1992 and incorporated into the well-recommended Rainbow chain of Norwegian hotels. It's 10 minutes on foot from the Royal Palace, on a tree-lined street known for its exclusive boutiques. The guest rooms have Scandinavian modern styling and firm beds, but small bathrooms. There's a cozy bar on the premises; breakfast is the only meal served.

Ritz Hotel. Frederick Stangs Gate 3, N-0272 Oslo 2. ☎ **22-44-39-60.** Fax 22-92-61-60. www.ritz.no. E-mail: ritzhotel@os.enitel.no. 48 units. TV TEL. Mon–Thurs 1,130 NOK ($125.45) double; Fri–Sun 800 NOK ($88.80) double. Rates include breakfast. AE, DC, MC, V. Free parking. Tram: 10.

In a prosperous residential neighborhood on Oslo's western outskirts, this hotel was built in 1915; it shares ownership and management with the Gabelshus (above). The rooms are well maintained and comfortable. Most were updated recently, with wall-to-wall carpeting, double-glazed windows, and good, firm mattresses. Bathrooms are tiled and a bit small. Some of the accommodations have French doors that lead to tiny balconies, and some are for nonsmokers. Although drinks are served in the rooms, guests looking for a restaurant are usually directed to the dining room at the nearby Gabelshus.

INEXPENSIVE

White House. President Harbitzgate 18, N-0259 Oslo 2. ☎ **22-44-19-60.** Fax 22-55-04-30. www.hotel-whitehouse.com. 21 units. MINIBAR TV TEL. Mon–Thurs 1,095 NOK ($121.55) double; Fri–Sun 795 NOK ($88.25) double. Rates include breakfast. AE, DC, MC, V. Free parking. Tram: 1.

One of the smallest hotels in Oslo, the White House was built around 1900 as a private home. It lies in the forested residential district of Breskeby, a short walk from the rear of the Royal Palace. Set on a steeply sloping lot, it has been greatly modernized. The hotel attracts a loyal repeat clientele that includes rock stars and businesspeople, all of whom appreciate its small scale and intimacy. The rooms are simply furnished but comfortable, with firm beds, great housekeeping, and snug but adequate bathrooms. The in-house restaurant, Den Lelle Sondue, has an outdoor wooden deck.

AT FROGNER

Frogner House. Skovveien 8, Frogner, N-0257 Oslo. ☎ **22-56-00-56.** Fax 22-56-05-00. www.frognerhouse.com. E-mail: mail@frognerhouse.com. 60 units. MINIBAR TV TEL. Sun–Thurs 1,515 NOK ($168.15) double; Fri–Sat 1025 NOK ($113.80) double. AE, DC, MC, V. Tram: 12.

In 1992, a turn-of-the-century red-brick apartment house was transformed into this stylish, upscale hotel. In the affluent Oslo suburb of Frogner, about a half-mile west of the city's commercial core, it's outfitted in conservative but cozy English style, with lots of lace curtains, a scattering of antiques, and soft cheerful colors. This hotel has built its reputation by catering to international business travelers, many involved in shipping and real estate. This is an upscale bed-and-breakfast, loaded with attentive service and comforts, but most amenities must be arranged through outside suppliers by the reception staff.

4 Dining

You can now "dine around the world" without leaving the city of Oslo. The biggest concentration of restaurants is at Aker Brygge. The former shipbuilding yard on the harborfront is now the smartest dining and shopping complex in Norway.

Not all restaurants in Oslo are new. Some have long been associated with artists and writers—the Grand Café, for example, was the stomping ground of Henrik Ibsen and Edvard Munch. Blom is also a traditional favorite.

The influx of foreigners in recent years has led to the growth of Mexican, Turkish, Moroccan, Chinese, Greek, and other international restaurants. Among European cuisines, French and Italian are the most popular. Many restaurants offer American-style food.

At nearly all restaurants recommended below, a 15% service charge and the 20% value-added tax are included in the bill. No further tipping is required, although it's customary to leave some small change if the service has been satisfactory.

Wine and beer can be lethal to your final bill, so be careful.

CENTRAL OSLO
VERY EXPENSIVE

✪ **D'Artagnan.** Øvre Slottsgate 16. ☎ **23-10-01-60.** Reservations required. Main courses 250–285 NOK ($27.75–$31.65) ; 5-course fixed-price menu 645 NOK ($71.60). AE,CB, DC, MC, V. Mon–Sat 6pm–1am. Closed Dec 22–Jan 3. Bus: 27, 29, 30, 41, or 61. FRENCH.

Named after one of the Three Musketeers, a childhood hero of owner Freddie Nielson, D'Artagnan is one of Oslo's most elegant restaurants. Like a private club, it has a discreet brass plaque out front. On the ground floor of the same building is a more visible (and less expensive) restaurant, Touch of France.

You'll probably peruse the menu in the second-floor cocktail bar before climbing the stairs to the third-floor dining room, adorned with flowers and candles. Menu items change with the seasons, and might include a salad of king crab from Finnmark with avocados and grapefruit segments, foie gras of duck with caramelized port wine sauce, steamed fillet of catfish with shallots and basil sauce, and grilled breast of honey-glazed duck with raspberry vinaigrette. One of the most unusual dishes is pieces of wild lamb from the mountains of central Norway, served with herb-flavored mustard sauce. An unusual treat is the dessert cart laden with jars of fruit preserved in liqueurs. These are served with velvety-smooth ice creams and sorbets—a real taste treat.

✪ **Restaurant Julius Fritzner.** In the Grand Hotel, Karl Johans Gate 31. ☎ **22-42-93-90.** Reservations recommended. Main courses 250–300 NOK ($27.75–$33.30) ; 3-course fixed-price menu 450 NOK ($49.95), 4-course fixed-price menu 530 NOK ($58.85), 6-course fixed-price menu 595 NOK ($66.05). AE, DC, MC, V. Mon–Sat 5–10:30pm. Closed July–Aug 5. T-banen: Stortinget. NORWEGIAN/CONTINENTAL.

This is one of the best and most impressive restaurants in Oslo. It opened in 1995 to rave reviews and the accolades keep coming. It's one floor above street level in Norway's most prestigious hotel. The venue is appropriately conservative, with a battalion of impeccably trained waiters who maintain their humor and personal touch despite the sophisticated setting. The dishes, all made with the finest Scandinavian ingredients, change with the season and the chef's inspiration. Examples include pan-fried turbot, lobster and caviar sauce, crispy fried cod with sautéed vegetables, poached halibut with vermouth sauce, fillet of veal with crispy fried sweetbreads, and roast saddle of lamb with rosemary. Desserts, which are delicious and occasionally theatrical, include a terrine of chocolate with a compote of peaches and sorbet flavored with basil and cinnamon. The restaurant, incidentally, is named after the controversial entrepreneur who established the Grand Hotel in 1874.

EXPENSIVE

Babette's Gjestehus. Rådhuspassasjen, Roald Amundsensgate 6. ☎ **22-41-64-64.** Reservations recommended. Main courses 230–265 NOK ($25.55–$29.40). AE, DC, MC, V. Mon–Sat 4–10:30pm, Sun 5–10:30pm. T-banen: Centrum. SCANDINAVIAN.

Named for the heroine of the film *Babette's Feast*—which almost every Scandinavian has seen at least once—this restaurant is decorated in the style of a turn-of-the-century Norwegian home. Walls are blue, antiques are genuine, curtains are lace, and there's a scattering of old paintings. Menu items are authentic as well, with such time-tested favorites as fillets of reindeer with lingonberries, steamed brill with mustard sauce and stewed tomatoes, breast of pheasant with mushroom sauce, and pan-fried breast of duck with creamed cabbage. The masterful chefs use seasonal products to produce reliable, good-tasting food all year.

Blom. Karl Johans Gate 41B. ☎ **22-42-73-00.** Reservations required. Main courses 235–308 NOK ($26.10–$34.20); fixed-price lunch 285 NOK ($31.65); fixed-price dinner 385 NOK ($42.75). AE, DC, MC, V. Mon–Fri 11am–2:30pm and 5pm–12:30am, Sat 3pm–12:30am. T-banen: Stortinget. NORWEGIAN/INTERNATIONAL.

A cultural and architectural landmark, this symbol of early 20th-century bohemian life has been painstakingly restored to its original glory. Cultural giants, including Charles Chaplin, Edvard Grieg, Henrik Ibsen, Edvard Munch, and Gustav Vigeland, dined here, and they're commemorated with plaques.

The food is tasty and well prepared. At dinner, full meals might include marinated fillet of reindeer with morel cream sauce, lamb cutlet with lamb medallions in Dijon mustard and rosemary sauce, beef tenderloin with red wine and onions, and a host of delectable fresh fish dishes. The wine list is one of the most complete in Oslo. A smörgåsbord is priced on a per-portion basis, unless you select from an array of open-faced sandwiches. When we prepared the first edition of this guide, this restaurant was the best in Oslo. Although it's still going strong, Blom no longer enjoys such a lofty position.

MODERATE

Bristol Grill. In the Bristol Hotel, Kristian IV's Gate 7. ☎ **22-82-60-20.** Reservations required. Main courses 235–265 NOK ($26.10–$29.40); 4-course fixed-price menu 498 NOK ($55.30). AE, DC, MC, V. Mon–Sat 11:30am–11:15pm, Sun 3–11:15pm. T-banen: Stortinget. FRENCH/INTERNATIONAL.

This is the premier dining room of one Oslo's most prestigious hotels. You'll find old-world courtliness, formal service without a lot of flash or frenzy, and elegant decor. A good appetizer is mousse of pheasant Périgord. Main courses include baked codfish with warm potato salad, marinated and grilled breast of salmon in port wine butter sauce, grilled fillet of sole with sautéed spinach, and a succulent grilled fillet of pork. The food is always reliable, with first-class ingredients deftly handled.

Grand Café. In the Grand Hotel, Karl Johans Gate 31. ☎ **23-21-20-00.** Reservations recommended. Main courses 175–275 NOK ($19.45–$30.55). AE, DC, MC, V. Mon–Sat 11am–midnight, Sun noon–11pm. T-banen: Stortinget. NORWEGIAN.

This traditional cafe is an Oslo legend. A large mural on one wall depicts Ibsen (a fan of whale steaks), Edvard Munch, and many other patrons. A postcard sold at the reception desk identifies the mural's subjects.

Oslo Dining

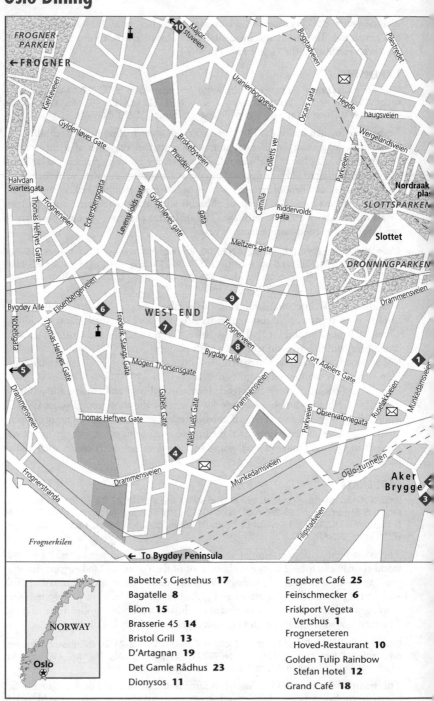

Babette's Gjestehus **17**
Bagatelle **8**
Blom **15**
Brasserie 45 **14**
Bristol Grill **13**
D'Artagnan **19**
Det Gamle Rådhus **23**
Dionysos **11**

Engebret Café **25**
Feinschmecker **6**
Friskport Vegeta
  Vertshus **1**
Frognerseteren
  Hoved-Restaurant **10**
Golden Tulip Rainbow
  Stefan Hotel **12**
Grand Café **18**

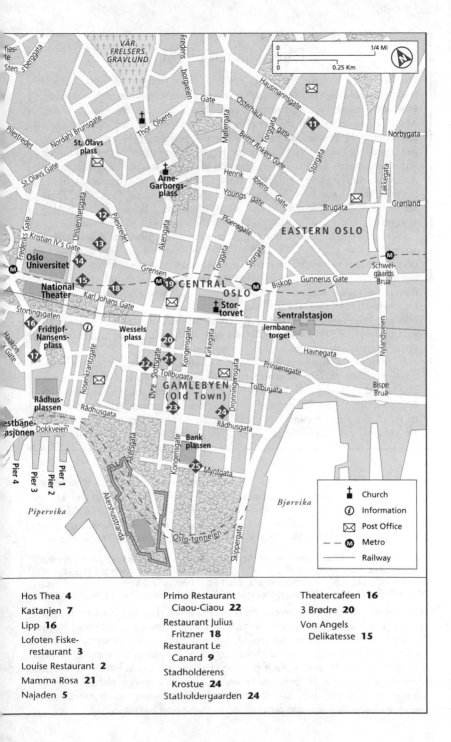

Hos Thea **4**
Kastanjen **7**
Lipp **16**
Lofoten Fiske-
  restaurant **3**
Louise Restaurant **2**
Mamma Rosa **21**
Najaden **5**

Primo Restaurant
  Ciaou-Ciaou **22**
Restaurant Julius
  Fritzner **18**
Restaurant Le
  Canard **9**
Stadholderens
  Krostue **24**
Statholdergaarden **24**

Theatercafeen **16**
3 Brødre **20**
Von Angels
  Delikatesse **15**

Dining Secrets of Oslo

One of Oslovians' favorite pastimes is visiting **Aker Brygge**. Formerly a dilapidated shipbuilding yard, the futuristic complex now combines more shopping, entertainment, and dining diversions in one area than anywhere else in Norway. Many people, some with children, come here to check out the restaurants and cafes, watch the people, and listen to the music playing in the bars. Part of the fun is strolling through the complex and picking a restaurant. Norwegian food is served along with a representative selection of foreign food offerings, including American. An especially good choice is the Louise Restaurant (see above). In the summer, visitors and locals fill the outdoor tables overlooking the harbor. There are also many nightlife options (see "Oslo After Dark," below). To reach Aker Brygge, take bus no. 27 or walk down from the center west of the Rådhus.

Not as formal as Louise, but a local favorite is the **Albertine Café & Bar,** Stranden 3, Aker Brygge (☎ 22-83-00-60), an informal place on the wharf's edge, offering a panoramic view over the harbor and Akershus fortress. Consistently, this place serves some of the freshest and tastiest oysters in Oslo. You can drop in for just a hamburger or a full Norwegian seafood dinner. It's an easy place for singles to meet others in that condition.

A good choice for the makings of a picnic is **Von Angels Delikatesse,** Karl Johans Gate 41B (☎ 22-42-73-22). It's open Monday to Friday from 10am to 8pm, Saturday 10am to 5pm.

In front of the Rådhuset, you can join Oslovians for a special picnic treat. From 7 to 8am, **shrimp fishermen** pull their boats into the harbor after having caught and cooked a fresh batch of shrimp during their night at sea. You can order shrimp in a bag (it comes in two sizes). Seafood fanciers take their shrimp to the dock's edge, remove the shells, and feast. The fishermen usually stick around until they've sold the last batch, saving just enough for their families.

You can order everything from a napoleon with coffee to a full meal with fried stingray or reindeer steaks. Sandwiches are available for 75 NOK ($8.30) and up. The atmosphere and tradition here are sometimes more compelling than the cuisine. The menu, nonetheless, relies on Norwegian country traditions (after all, how many places still serve elk stew?). If you like solid, honest flavors, this is the place to be seen.

Golden Tulip Rainbow Stefan Hotel. Rosenkrantzgate 1. ☎ **23-31-55-00.** Reservations recommended. Main courses 150–200 NOK ($16.65–$22.20); lunch smörgåsbord 185 NOK ($20.55). AE, DC, MC, V. Smörgåsbord, Mon–Fri 11:30am–2:30pm, Sat noon–2:30pm; Thurs–Fri 4:30–10:30pm. À la carte, Mon–Sat 4:30–10:30pm. Tram: 7 or 11. NORWEGIAN.

This bustling, unpretentious restaurant is better known than the hotel it's in. Local business people come for the city's best smörgåsbord, laden with traditional Norwegian foods that includes cucumber salad, fish and meat salads, sausages, meatballs, potato salad, smoked fish, assorted cheeses, and breads. During the evening, you can order from a rich à la carte menu if you don't feel like waiting in line, plate in hand. Selections from the à la carte menu include "Stefan's special platter"—an old-fashioned but flavorful dish that incorporates slices of reindeer, moose meat, and ox tongue, with lingonberries and potatoes, on the same heaping plate.

Lipp. In the Hotel Continental, Stortingsgaten 24. ☎ **22-82-40-60.** Reservations recommended. Main courses 158–245 NOK ($17.55–$27.20). AE, DC, MC, V. Daily 12:30pm–3am. T-banen: Stortinget. INTERNATIONAL.

Stylish and lighthearted, this restored brasserie is the Oslovian version of Paris in the 1920s. Painted a canary yellow, it employs a staff traditionally dressed, bistro style, in black vests. Each day a special dish is offered of which the chef is justly proud. On our last visit it was roasted grouse served with a wild mushroom pie with crisp bacon. The menu changes about every 5 weeks, and it is seasonally adjusted, using the finest of produce from land and field, not to mention river and lake. You might face a delectable salmon in a white wine sauce, or else reindeer (not Santa's) in a mushroom sauce. Lighter fare is also offered as well for those watching their weight—perhaps an array of freshly made salads or grilled fish dishes. Succulent pastas are also regularly featured.

Primo Restaurant Ciaou-Ciaou. In the First Hotel Millennium, Tollbugate 25. ☎ **23-00-30-00.** Reservations recommended. Pastas 125–130 NOK ($13.90–$14.45); main courses 185–220 NOK ($20.55–$24.40). AE, DC, MC, V. Mon–Sat 11:30am–10:30pm. Tram: 30, 42. MEDITERRANEAN/NORWEGIAN.

The food here is a cut above what you'd expect in the average hotel dining room. Norwegian ingredients get inspiration from the Italian and Spanish chefs who use them, resulting in dishes with a bit more verve than you might have expected in this Nordic clime. Try baked swordfish with a piquant tomato sauce, homemade pâté of venison served with marinated olives, fillet of beef braised with broccoli and mushrooms with a spicy *salsa de pepperoni*, and succulent preparations of Norwegian lamb. There's also bar here, with a staff that mixes a medley of American libations.

Theatercafeen. In the Hotel Continental, Stortingsgaten 24. ☎ **22-82-40-50.** Reservations recommended. Main courses 160–365 NOK ($17.75–$40.50). AE, DC, MC, V. Mon–Sat 11am–midnight, Sun 3–10pm. T-banen: Stortinget. INTERNATIONAL.

The last of the grand Viennese cafes in the north of Europe, this long-standing favorite was founded a century ago to rival the Grand Café. Each has its devotees, although we like this one better because of its Viennese *schmaltz*. Seranaded by piano and a duet of violins, the style might have pleased the Habsburg emperor Franz-Josef had he ever ventured this far north. It attracts present-day *boulevardiers* and businesspeople. With soft lighting, antique bronzes, cut-glass lighting fixtures, and art-nouveau mirrors, it is the type of place that encourages lingering. Menu items are well prepared and traditional, and are adjusted accordingly to get the best flavors out of each new season. That might mean fresh asparagus and spring lamb, or in the autumn, breast of wild goose and other game dishes. The fish dishes are particularly well prepared, including a recently sampled casserole of mussels. You can also enjoy such traditional Norwegian fare as reindeer with wild mushrooms or Norwegian fjord salmon.

INEXPENSIVE

Brasserie 45. Karl Johans Gate 45. ☎ **22-41-34-00.** Reservations recommended. Main courses 89–179 NOK ($9.90–$19.85). AE, DC, MC, V. Mon–Thurs noon–midnight, Fri–Sat noon–1am, Sun 2:30pm–11pm. T-banen: Centrum. CONTINENTAL.

Airy and stylish, this second-story bistro overlooks the biggest fountain along downtown Oslo's showplace promenade. The uniformed staff bears steaming platters of ambitious, imaginative cuisine, including especially flavorful versions of fried catfish with lemon-garlic sauce; fried chicken in spicy, tomato-based sweet-and-sour sauce; pork schnitzels with béarnaise sauce and shrimp; and tartare of salmon with dill-enriched boiled potatoes. For dessert, try chocolate terrine with cloudberry sorbet.

① Family-Friendly Restaurants

Mamma Rosa *(see p. 205)*   The best place to fill up on 15 kinds of pizzas or a pasta dish, each a meal in itself.

Najaden *(see p. 207)*   As if being in the Norwegian Maritime Museum weren't enough for kids, they can also enjoy an elaborate summer lunch buffet for half-price—they must be under 12.

OLD TOWN (GAMLEBYEN)
VERY EXPENSIVE

✪ Statholdergaarden. Rådhusgata 11. ☎ **22-41-88-00.** Reservations recommended. Main courses 260–330 NOK ($28.85–$36.65); 4-course fixed-price menu 650 NOK ($72.15); 6-course fixed-price menu 760 NOK ($84.35). AE, DC, MC, V. Mon–Sat 6pm–midnight. Tram: 11, 15, or 18. NOUVELLE NORWEGIAN.

One of Oslo's most historic restaurant settings (the building dates to 1640) has one of its most successful chefs, Bent Stiansen, whose unique interpretation of Norwegian nouvelle cuisine have attracted the admiration of gastronomes throughout the country. At this century-old restaurant, menu items change frequently, according to what's in season. Examples include grilled crayfish served with scallop and salmon tartare, and thyme-infused codfish with crabmeat mousse and two sauces (a simple white wine sauce and another based on a rare vanilla bean imported from Thailand). One of our all-time favorite dishes is lightly fried Arctic char with sautéed savoy cabbage and lime *beurre blanc* (white butter). Also appealing are roasted rack of lamb with sage sauce, platters of French cheeses, and cloudberry crêpes. Don't confuse this upscale and prestigious site with the less expensive bistro Statholderens Krostue (see below), which occupies the building's vaulted cellar.

✪ Statholderens Krostue. Rådhusgata 11. ☎ **22-41-88-00.** Main courses 230–330 NOK ($25.55–$36.65); fixed-price menu 400 NOK ($44.40). AE, DC, MC, V. Tues–Sat 11:30am–10pm. Tram: 11, 15, 18. SWEDISH/DANISH.

This relatively uncomplicated cellar-level bistro is associated with Statholdergaarden, one of Oslo's most prestigious restaurants (see above). Unlike its more sophisticated sibling, it's open for lunch as well as dinner, and features relatively uncomplicated food that's mostly based on traditional Swedish and Danish recipes. The cuisine provides many original and, most of the time, happy combinations of ingredients. Beneath the vaulted Renaissance-era ceiling, you can order *frikadeller* (meatballs), minced veal patties in creamy dill sauce, steak with fried onions, fried eel with potato and herb dumplings, and grilled salmon with saffron-flavored noodles. Lunch specialties include platters piled high with Danish or Norwegian ham, herring, boiled eggs, and vegetables, and a selection of smørrebrød (Danish open-faced sandwiches).

MODERATE

3 Brødre. Øvre Slottsgate 14. ☎ **23-10-06-70.** Main courses 190–200 NOK ($21.10–$22.20). AE, DC, MC, V. Kaelleren, Mon–Sat 5–11pm; street-level bar, Mon–Sat 11am–11pm; piano bar, Mon–Sat 8:30pm–4am. Bus: 27, 29, or 30. NORWEGIAN.

"Three Brothers" is named after the glove manufacturers who once occupied this building. This is a longtime favorite drawing more locals than visitors. Habitues know of its fresh food, which is well prepared with hearty portions and reasonable prices. You might begin with Norwegian salmon tartare or snails, followed by an almond-and-garlic gratinée. The most popular appetizer is a selection of fresh mussels poached with leeks, parsley, garlic, and cream. For a main course, try the fried catfish with prawns, mussels, red peppers, and capers, or beefsteak with béarnaise sauce. The entire street level houses the bustling bar. Upstairs is a piano bar. A large beer costs 48 NOK ($5.35). Lighter meals, such as snacks and sandwiches ranging in price from 62 to 75 NOK ($6.90 to $8.30), are available on the outside dining terrace in the summer.

INEXPENSIVE

Engebret Café. Bankplassen 1. ☎ **22-33-66-94.** Reservations recommended. Main courses 205–295 NOK ($22.75–$32.75); smørbrød 55–95 NOK ($6.10–$10.55). AE, DC, MC, V. Mon–Sat noon–11pm. Bus: 27, 29, or 30. NORWEGIAN.

A favorite since 1857, this restaurant is directly north of Akershus Castle in two landmark buildings. It has an old-fashioned atmosphere and good food, served in a former bohemian literati haunt. During lunch, a tempting selection of open-faced sandwiches is available. The evening menu is more elaborate; you might begin with a terrine of game with blackberry port-wine sauce, or Engebret's fish soup. Main dishes include red wild boar with whortleberry sauce, Norwegian reindeer, salmon Christiania, or Engebret's big fish pot. For dessert, try the cloudberry parfait.

Friskport Vegeta Vertshus. Munkedamsveien 3B. ☎ **22-83-42-32.** Soups and salads 35 NOK ($3.90); buffet 125 NOK ($13.90). AE, DC, MC, V. Daily 11am–10pm. Bus: 27. VEGETARIAN.

Since 1938 this basement cafeteria near the Rådhus has been Oslo's major vegetarian restaurant. It's a stronghold of social activism and news of countercultural activities. At street level is a cafe with a buffet of 25 salad dishes and many hot dishes, along with bread, butter, cheese, and coffee. A new smoke-free bar downstairs serves a special student buffet for 112 NOK ($12.45) Tuesday to Saturday. The kitchen is also proud of its pizza. You can order juices, mineral water, soft drinks, or nonalcoholic wine. To go to the buffet once, a small plate costs 68 NOK ($7.55), a large plate, 78 NOK ($8.65).

Det Gamle Rådhus (Old Town Hall). Nedre Slottsgate 1. ☎ **22-42-01-07.** Reservations recommended. Main courses 120–220 NOK ($13.30–$24.40); open-faced sandwiches 48–65 NOK ($5.35–$7.20). AE, DC, MC, V. Mon–Fri 11am–3pm; Mon–Sat 4–11pm. Kroen Bar, Mon–Sat 4pm–midnight. Bus: 27, 29, 30, 41, or 61. NORWEGIAN.

The oldest restaurant in Oslo, Det Gamle Rådhus is in Oslo's former Town Hall (1641). In the spacious dining room, a full array of open-faced sandwiches is served on weekdays only. À la carte dinner selections can be made from a varied menu that includes fresh fish, game, and Norwegian specialties. Although it sounds like a culinary turn-off, the house specialty is quite delectable. It's lutefisk, a Scandinavian specialty made from dried fish that has been soaked in lye, and then poached in broth. If you want to sample a dish that Ibsen might have enjoyed, check this one out.

Mamma Rosa. Øvre Slottsgate 12. ☎ **22-42-01-30.** Main courses 86–210 NOK ($9.55–$23.30); pizzas from 97 NOK ($10.75). DC, MC, V. Mon–Sat noon–11:30pm, Sun 1–10:30pm. T-banen: Stortinget. ITALIAN.

Established by two Tuscan brothers, this trattoria enjoys popularity that's a good indication of Norwegians' changing tastes. The second-floor dining room is decorated in "reproduction rococo." You can order 15 kinds of pizza, fried scampi and squid, rigatoni, pasta Mamma Rosa (three kinds of pasta with three sauces), grilled steaks, and gelato. Frankly, some of the dishes have lost a bit of flavor on the trip this far north, but Mamma Rosa is nonetheless a marvelous change of taste and texture.

AKER BRYGGE

✪ **Lofoten Fiskerestaurant.** Stranden 75, Aker Brygge. ☎ **22-83-08-08.** Reservations recommended. Main courses 200–270 NOK ($22.20–$29.95); fixed-price lunch 380 NOK

($47.50); fixed-price dinner 470 NOK ($58.75). AE, DC, MC, V. Mon–Sat 11am–11pm, Sun noon–10pm. SEAFOOD.

Near one of the most distant corners of the Aker Brygge dining complex, on the ground floor with views over the harbor, this is one of the city's most appealing seafood restaurants. The interior sports nautical accessories that might remind you of an upscale yacht. In good weather, tables are set up on an outdoor terrace lined with flowering plants. Menu items change according to the available catch, with few choices for meat-eaters. The fish is plentiful, served in generous portions, and very fresh. Examples include fillet of trout poached in white wine and served with tomato-enriched *beurre blanc* (white butter) sauce; grilled halibut with assorted shellfish and coconut-flavored risotto; and grilled fillet of tuna with garlicky potato cakes, Parmesan cheese, and red-pepper cream sauce. Look for culinary inspirations from Italy and France, and ample use of such Mediterranean preparations as pesto.

Louise Restaurant. Stranden 3, Aker Brygge. ☎ **22-83-00-60.** Reservations recommended. Main courses 176–260 NOK ($19.55–$28.85). AE, DC, MC, V. Mon–Sat 11am–11pm, Sun 11am–10pm. Bus: 27. NORWEGIAN.

Named for a 19th-century Norwegian steamboat, Louise Restaurant is considered the best restaurant in the Aker Brygge complex. The chef prepares such tasty specialties as braised hare with Brussels sprouts and stewed mushrooms and cranberries, and a "cold symphony" of shrimp, salmon, hare, roast beef, potato salad, and cheese. A house specialty, also a complete meal, is the Brygge Tallerken—fried horsemeat with stewed mushrooms.

EASTERN OSLO

Dionysos. Calmeyersgate 11. ☎ **22-60-78-64.** Reservations recommended. Main courses 110–168 NOK ($12.20–$18.65). AE, MC, V. Daily 3–11pm. Tram: 1, 2, or 11. GREEK.

This restaurant, which resembles a family-oriented *taverna* in Greece, serves specialties that include dishes from Cyprus, Crete, Thessalonika, and the Peloponnese. The exuberant Greek waiters serve up *gastra manis* (a northern Greek dish made with ox meat, eggplant, pepperoni, vegetables, and potatoes), moussaka, souvlaki, and a wide selection of kebabs. Recorded bouzouki music is played from 7pm to midnight.

WEST END
VERY EXPENSIVE

✪ **Bagatelle.** Bygdøy Allé 3. ☎ **22-44-63-97.** Reservations required. Main courses 300–350 NOK ($33.30–$38.85); 3-course fixed-price menu 550 NOK ($61.05); 5-course fish menu 850 NOK ($94.35); 7-course fixed-price menu 950 NOK ($105.45). AE, DC, MC, V. Mon–Sat 6–10:30pm. Bus: 30, 31, 45, 72, or 73. FRENCH.

This contemporary, informal restaurant is widely regarded as one of Oslo's premier dining choices. Owner-chef Eyvind Hellstrøm serves light, modern cuisine, using market-fresh ingredients. Seafood is the star here, and the menu changes daily. You can begin with a selection of warm or cold appetizers including carpaccio of scallops in oyster sauce. Fish entrees include smoked catch of the day, steamed halibut with caviar cream sauce, and sole steamed in seaweed. Other main dishes are saddle of reindeer with pears and pepper sauce, loin of veal with sage, and herb-roasted Norwegian rack of lamb for two.

EXPENSIVE

✪ **Feinschmecker.** Balchensgate 5. ☎ **22-44-17-77.** Reservations recommended. Main courses 260–385 NOK ($28.85–$42.75); fixed-price menus 555–595 NOK ($61.60–$66.05). AE, DC, MC, V. Mon–Sat 4:30–10:30pm. Closed 3 weeks in July. Tram: 12 or 19 to Ilesberg. SCANDINAVIAN.

One of the most prestigious restaurants in Olso will entertain you with the same style and verve it produced for King Harald and his queen, Sonya, during their recent visit. The dining room's antique furniture and small-paned windows evoke old-time style despite the building's modernity. Menu items change frequently; the roster of staples includes grilled scallops with crispy potatoes and celeriac purée; sautéed ocean crayfish tails with apple cider, wild rice, and sun-dried tomatoes; and grilled monkfish with sautéed mushrooms and morel-enriched cream sauce. A particularly sought-after main course is rack of Norwegian lamb, and a dessert that has been preeminent here since the place was established in the late 1980s is a gratin of raspberries. One of our local friends, a savvy food critic, has proclaimed this the best restaurant in Oslo. We're not prepared to go that far, but it ranks at the top.

MODERATE

Hos Thea. Gabelsgate 11 (entrance on Drammensveien). ☎ **22-44-68-74.** Reservations recommended. Main courses 195–230 NOK ($21.65–$25.55). AE, DC, MC, V. Daily 4:30–10:30pm. Tram: 10 or 13. SCANDINAVIAN.

This stylish, well-managed restaurant attracts a loyal crowd of people active in the media and the arts. The wait staff and chefs share duties, so the person who prepares your meal is likely to carry it to your table as well. Depending on the staff's mood and the season, the superbly prepared menu items might include medallions of veal served with beurre blanc (white butter) and carrots, breast of duck with red wine sauce, whitefish fillets with saffron sauce, and venison with a sauce of mixed Nordic berries. The century-old building, once a private home, is in a West End neighborhood about 2 miles south of Oslo's commercial center.

Kastanjen. Bygdøy Allé 18. ☎ **22-43-44-67.** Reservations required. Main courses 235–255 NOK ($26.10–$28.30); 3-course fixed-price menu 395–595 NOK ($43.85–$66.05); 4-course fixed-price menu 465 NOK ($51.60); 5-course fixed-price menu 535 NOK ($59.40); 6-course fixed-price menu 595 NOK ($66.05). AE, DC, MC, V. Mon–Sat 6–11pm. Closed July. Tram: 30. NORWEGIAN.

Named for the chestnut trees that line the street, this restaurant is in a residential area, near several embassies. The decor, illuminated by candlelight, is modern and unpretentious. The menu changes monthly, and fixed-price menus change daily. Six or seven dishes every night may be ordered as appetizers or main courses; a good choice is salmon with crayfish. There are one or two luxurious main-dish selections, but most are moderately priced. Monkfish is sautéed and served with a crayfish sauce, or you might order reindeer, which is sautéed, baked, and served with reindeer gravy and red currants.

AT BYGDØY

Najaden. Bygdøynesveien 37. ☎ **22-43-81-80.** Reservations recommended. Main courses 145–198 NOK ($16.10–$22); lunch buffet (summer only, 11am–3pm) 185 NOK ($20.55), half-price for children under 12. AE, DC, MC, V. May 16–Oct 14, daily 11am–7pm; Oct 15–May 15, Mon–Wed and Sat 11am–4pm, Thurs–Fri 11am–7pm. Bus: 30. Ferry: Bygdøy. NORWEGIAN.

In the Norwegian Maritime Museum, this restaurant (the name translates as "mermaid") overlooks a room of sculptures removed from 19th-century clipper ships. The popular summer lunch buffet offers an elaborate array of freshly prepared fish and meat dishes; the rest of the year, lunch is à la carte. You don't get a lot of culinary excitement, but the food is fresh and served in generous portions—and the location is unbeatable when you're sightseeing on Bygdøy.

HOLMENKOLLEN

Frognerseteren Hoved-Restaurant. Holmenkollveien 200. ☎ **22-14-05-50.** Reservations recommended. Open-faced sandwiches 45–70 NOK ($5–$7.75); main courses 195–260 NOK ($21.65–$28.85); fixed-price menu 300 NOK ($33.30). DC, MC, V. Restaurant, Tues–Fri noon–3pm, Mon–Sat 5–10pm, Sun 1–8pm; cafe, daily 11am–10pm. T-banen: 15 to Frognerseteren. NORWEGIAN.

On a mountain ledge, this lodge offers a panoramic view of Oslo and the fjord. The restaurant is a historic monument, built by entrepreneur Thomas Heftey in 1896. Prices in the cafe are about 15% lower than those in the dining room, and there's a breezy outdoor terrace for snacks and beer. The chef specializes in delectable game dishes, including pheasant pâté with Cumberland sauce, medallions of reindeer, and fillet of elk sautéed in honey and nuts. You can also order poached, marinated, or smoked Norwegian salmon. The chef's specialty is a scrumptious apple cake.

The restaurant is a 40-minute ride on the T-banen to the Frognerseteren stop some 1,600 feet above sea level, or it's 1,000 feet downhill from the Holmenkollen railway stop.

AT FROGNER

Restaurant Le Canard. President Harbitzgate 4. ☎ **22-54-34-10.** Reservations recommended. Main courses 295–380 NOK ($32.75–$42.20); 3-course fixed-price menu 495 NOK ($54.95); 5-course fixed-price menu 765 NOK ($84.90); 7-course fixed-price menu 925 NOK ($102.70). AE, CB, DC, DISC, MC, V. Mon–Thurs 5–10:30pm, Fri–Sat 6–10pm. FRENCH/CONTINENTAL.

The mansion that contains this prestigious restaurant is almost as interesting as the cuisine. Designed in the 1880s by a noted Jewish architect named Lowzow, it contains many religious symbols. Look for the Star of David in some of the stained-glass windows, and representations of the Lion of Judah here and there throughout. Everyone from the Queen of Norway to British comedian John Cleese has dined on the first-class cuisine. A meal might include grilled lobster with sautéed chanterelles and watercress sauce, carpaccio of smoked scallops, or baked artichokes with creamy mussel and lobster sauce. One enduringly popular meat dish is roasted duck with fig and foie gras sauce. Guinea fowl is stuffed with foie gras and served with a sauce of Banyuls (a sweet French red wine). The food here is always impeccable. The restaurant is in the suburb of Frogner, about a mile west of the center of Oslo.

5 Seeing the Sights

Some would be happy to come to Oslo just for the views of the harborfront city and the Oslofjord. Panoramas are a major attraction, especially the one from Tryvannstårnet, a 390-foot observation tower atop 1,900-foot-high Tryvann Hill in the outlying area. Many other attractions are worthy of your time and exploration, too. The beautiful surroundings make these sights even more appealing.

Suggested Itineraries

If You Have 1 Day

Arm yourself with a bag of freshly cooked shrimp (see the sidebar "Dining Secrets of Oslo," above) and take a ferry to the Bygdøy peninsula. Explore the Viking ships, the polar ship *Fram* Museum, the *Kon-Tiki* Museum, the Norwegian Maritime Museum, and the Norwegian Folk Museum. In the late afternoon, go to Frogner Park to admire the Vigeland sculptures.

If You Have 2 Days
On your first day, follow the itinerary above. On your second day, take a walking tour (see below), have lunch in a Norwegian restaurant, and explore the Edvard Munch Museum in the afternoon. In the summer, visit the Students' Grove, near the National Theater, for some beer and fresh air.

If You Have 3 Days
For your first 2 days, follow the suggestions above. On Day 3, take another walking tour (see below), eating lunch along the way. Explore Akershus Castle and the adjoining Norwegian Resistance Museum in the afternoon. By late afternoon, visit the lofty lookout tower at Tryvannstårnet and see the Skimuseet at Holmenkollen, taking in a panoramic view of the area. Have dinner at Holmenkollen.

If You Have 4 or 5 Days
For the first 3 days, follow the itinerary above. On Day 4, head south on an excursion to the Oslofjord country, with stopovers at the Old Town at Fredrikstad; Tønsberg, Norway's oldest town; and Sandefjord, an old whaling town. Head back to Oslo for the night.

On Day 5, see the rest of Oslo's major sights, such as the National Gallery, the Historical Museum, and the Henie-Onstad Art Center (7 miles from Oslo), a major museum of modern art.

IN CENTRAL OSLO

Oslo Domkirke (Oslo Cathedral). Stortorvet 1. ☎ **23-31-46-10.** Free admission. Daily 10am–4pm. T-banen: Stortinget. Bus: 17.

Oslo's 17th-century cathedral at Stortorvet (the marketplace) was restored in 1950, when Hugo Louis Mohr completed its modern tempera ceiling decorations.

The cathedral contains works by 20th-century Norwegian artists, including bronze doors by Dagfin Werenskiold. Try to view the pulpit and altar, which date from the cathedral's earliest days. There are stained-glass windows by Emanuel Vigeland (not to be confused with the sculptor, Gustav) in the choir and Borgar Hauglid in the transepts. The organ is five stories tall. A bilingual service (in Norwegian and English) is conducted on Wednesday at noon, and an organ recital is presented on summer Saturdays at noon.

Rådhuset (City Hall). Rådhusplassen. ☎ **22-86-16-00.** May–Sept, 25 NOK ($2.80) adults, 15 NOK ($1.65) children; Oct–Apr, free admission. May–Sept, Mon–Sat 9am–5pm, Sun noon–5pm; Oct–Apr, Mon–Sat 9am–4pm, Sun noon–4pm. Guided tours, Mon–Fri at 10am, noon, and 2pm. Bus: 30, 31, 32, 45, or 81.

The modern City Hall, inaugurated in 1950, must be seen to be judged. It has been called everything from "aggressively ugly" to "the pride of Norway." Its simple brick exterior with double towers houses, among other things, the stunning 85-by-43-foot wall painted by Henrik Sørensen, and the mural *Life* by Edvard Munch. Tapestries, frescoes, sculpture, and woodcarvings by Dagfin Werenskiold are also on display. Guided tours in English are available. In the courtyard you can see the astronomical clock and Dyre Vaa's swan fountain.

Stortinget (Parliament). Karl Johans Gate 22. ☎ **23-31-35-96.** Free admission. Guided tours in English, Mon–Fri 10am, 11:30am, and 1pm; Sept 15–Dec 15, Sat 11am and 12:30pm. T-banen: Stortinget. Tram: 13, 15, or 19.

Constructed from 1861 to 1866, the Parliament, in the center of the city, was richly decorated by contemporary Norwegian artists. The style is neo-Romanesque. The public is admitted only on guided tours.

Oslo Attractions

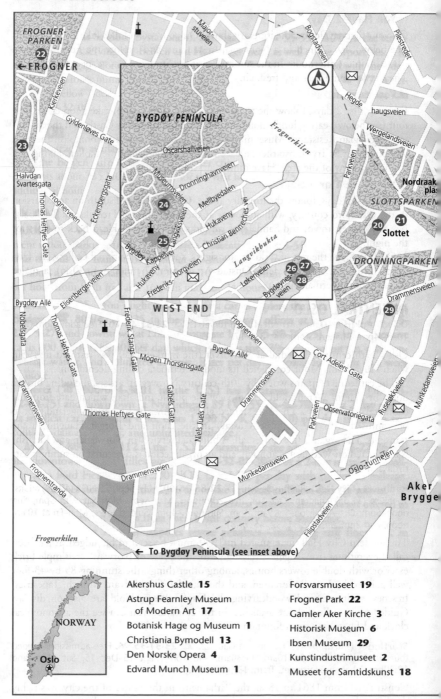

Key to map labels:

FROGNER-PARKEN **22**
←FROGNER
23
Halvdan Svartesgata
BYGDØY PENINSULA
Oscarshallveien
24
25
WEST END
Bygdøy Allé
26 **27**
28
29
Nordraak plas
SLOTTSPARKEN
20 **21** Slottet
DRONNINGPARKEN
Aker Brygge

← To Bygdøy Peninsula (see inset above)

NORWAY

Oslo

Akershus Castle **15**
Astrup Fearnley Museum
  of Modern Art **17**
Botanisk Hage og Museum **1**
Christiania Bymodell **13**
Den Norske Opera **4**
Edvard Munch Museum **1**

Forsvarsmuseet **19**
Frogner Park **22**
Gamler Aker Kirche **3**
Historisk Museum **6**
Ibsen Museum **29**
Kunstindustrimuseet **2**
Museet for Samtidskunst **18**

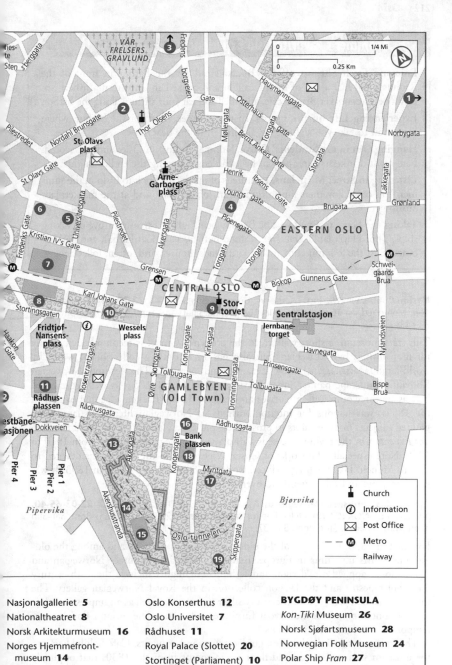

Nasjonalgalleriet **5**

Nationaltheatret **8**

Norsk Arkitekturmuseum **16**

Norges Hjemmefront-
museum **14**

Oslo Bymuseum **23**

Oslo Domkirke **9**

Oslo Konserthus **12**

Oslo Universitet **7**

Rådhuset **11**

Royal Palace (Slottet) **20**

Stortinget (Parliament) **10**

Slottsparken **21**

Vigelandsparken **22**

BYGDØY PENINSULA

Kon-Tiki Museum **26**

Norsk Sjøfartsmuseum **28**

Norwegian Folk Museum **24**

Polar Ship *Fram* **27**

Vikingskiphuset **25**

✪ Frommer's Favorite Oslo Experiences

Enjoying Fresh Shrimp off the Boats. Head for the harbor in front of the Rådhuset and buy a bag of freshly caught and cooked shrimp from a fisherman. Buy a beer at an Aker Brygge cafe, and shell and eat your shrimp along the harbor.

Experiencing Life on the Fjords. In the summer, head for the harbor, where boats wait to take you sightseeing, fishing, or to the beach.

Hanging Out in the Students' Grove. Summer is short in Oslo, and it's savored. Late-night drinkers sit in open-air beer gardens, enjoying the endless nights.

Listening to Street Musicians. Hundreds of musicians flock to Oslo in the summer. You can enjoy their music along Karl Johans Gate and at the marketplace Stortorget.

Taking the Ferry to Bygdøy. The Bygdøy peninsula is a treasure trove of Viking ships, Thor Heyerdahl's *Kon-Tiki,* seafood buffets, a sailboat harbor, and bathing beaches. At the folk museum are old farmsteads, houses, and, often, folk dancing.

Nasjonalgalleriet (National Gallery). Universitetsgata 13. ☎ **22-20-04-04.** Free admission. Mon, Wed, Fri 10am–6pm; Thurs 10am–8pm; Sat 10am–4pm; Sun 11am–4pm. Tram: 7 or 11.

This state museum, a short walk from the Students' Grove, is recommended chiefly for its paintings by Norwegians but also has an intriguing collection of works by world-famous artists, including Cézanne and Matisse. The leading Norwegian Romantic landscape painter Johan Christian Dahl (1788–1857) is well represented here as are three outstanding Norwegian Realists. Harriet Backer, a leading painter in the 1880s, was famous for interior portraits of Norwegian life; Christian Krohg painted subjects from seafarers to prostitutes; and Erik Werenskiold is noted for *Peasant Funeral.* On the main staircase is a display of Norwegian sculpture from 1910 to 1945. Note especially the works of Gustav Vigeland and the two rooms devoted to Edvard Munch. His much-reproduced work *The Scream* was painted in 1893. It was stolen in 1994 and subsequently recovered.

Kunstindustrimuseet (Museum of Applied Art). St. Olavs Gate 1. ☎ **22-03-65-40.** Admission 65 NOK ($7.20) adults, free for children under 12. Tues–Fri 11am–3pm, Sat–Sun noon–4pm. T-banen: Stortinget. Bus: 37.

Founded in 1876, this is one of the oldest museums in Norway and among the oldest applied-arts museums in Europe. Extensive collections embrace Norwegian and international applied art, design, and fashion. Highlights include the 13th-century Baldishol tapestry and the fashion collection in the Royal Norwegian gallery. The museum displays pieces of 18th-century silver and glass, as well as an impressive selection of contemporary Scandinavian furniture and crafts. The ground floor houses temporary craft and design exhibits.

The museum schedules lectures, guided tours, and concerts. Café Solliløkken and the museum shop on the ground floor are in rooms from the 1830s that originally were in a small country house.

Museet for Samtidskunst (Museum of Contemporary Art). Bankplassen 4. ☎ **22-86-22-10.** Free admission. Tues–Wed and Fri 10am–5pm, Thurs 10am–8pm, Sat–Sun 11am–4pm. Tram: 10, 12, 13, 15, or 19. Bus: 60.

Opened in 1990, this collection of works acquired by the state after the Second World War presents an array of international and Norwegian contemporary art. Once grouped together in the National Gallery, it has more room to "breathe" in its new home. Exhibits change frequently.

Astrup Fearnley Museum of Modern Art. Dronningensgatan 4. ☎ **22-93-60-60.** Admission 40 NOK ($4.45) adults; 20 NOK ($2.20) children, students, and seniors. Tues–Wed and Fri noon–4pm, Thurs noon–7pm, Sat–Sun noon–5pm. T-banen: Stortinget. Tram: 10, 12, 13, 15, or 19. Bus: 60.

A 5- to 10-minute walk from the Oslo City Hall, this museum was created by some of Norway's leading architects and designers and showcases postwar art. The changing exhibits are often drawn from the museum's permanent collection. Here, you might see works by Francis Bacon, Lucian Freud, Gerhard Richter, or less familiar Norwegians, including Arne Ekeland, Knut Rose, or Bjørn Carlsen.

Historisk Museum (University Museum of Cultural Heritage). Frederiksgate 2 (near Karl Johans Gate). ☎ **22-85-99-12.** Free admission. May 15–Sept 14, Tues–Sun 10am–4pm; Sept 15–May 14, Tues–Sun 11am–4pm. Tram: 7, 8, 11, or 17.

Devoted to enthnography, antiquities, and numismatics, this museum, operated by the University of Oslo, houses an interesting collection of prehistoric objects on the ground floor. Viking artifacts and a display of gold and silver from the 2nd through the 13th century are in the Treasure House. In the medieval hall, look for the reddish Ringerike Alstad Stone, which was carved in relief, and the Dynna Stone, an 11th-century runic stone honoring the handiest maiden in Hadeland. There's also a rich collection of ecclesiastical art in a series of portals from stave churches.

Akershus Castle. Festnings-Plassen. ☎ **22-41-25-21.** Admission 30 NOK ($3.35) adults, 10 NOK ($1.10) children, family ticket 70 NOK ($7.75). May–Sept 15, Mon–Sat 10am–4pm, Sun 12:30–4pm. Closed Sept 16–Apr 14. Tram: 10 or 12. Bus: 60.

One of the oldest historical monuments in Oslo, Akershus Castle was built in 1300 by Haakon V Magnusson. It was a fortress and a royal residence for several centuries. A fire in 1527 devastated the northern wing, and the castle was rebuilt and transformed into a royal Renaissance palace under the Danish-Norwegian king, Christian IV. Now the government uses it for state occasions. English-speaking guided tours are offered Monday to Saturday at 11am, 1pm, and 3pm, and on Sunday at 1 and 3pm.

Norges Hjemmefrontmuseum (Norwegian Resistance Museum). Akershus Fortress. ☎ **23-09-31-38.** Admission 25 NOK ($2.80) adults, 10 NOK ($1.10) children. Apr 15–June 14 and Sept, Mon–Sat 10am–4pm, Sun 11am–4pm; June 15–Aug, Mon–Sat 10am–5pm, Sun 11am–5pm; Oct–Apr 14, Mon–Sat 10am–3pm, Sun 11am–4pm. Tram: 10, 12, 15, or 19.

From underground printing presses to radio transmitters, from the German attack in 1940 to the liberation in 1945, this museum documents Norway's Second World War resistance activities. Outside is a monument dedicated to Norwegian patriots, many of whom were executed by the Nazis at this spot.

Forsvarsmuseet (Armed Forces Museum). Akershus Fortress, Bygning 62. ☎ **23-09-35-82.** Free admission. June–Aug, Mon–Fri 10am–6pm, Sat–Sun 11am–4pm; Sept–May, Mon–Fri 10am–3pm, Sat–Sun 11am–4pm. Tram: 1, 2, or 10.

While you're in the area, you can also explore this museum, which documents Norwegian military history from the dawn of the Viking Age to the 1950s. Guns, tanks, bombs, and planes are all here, from fighter planes to German tanks left over from the Second World War. The weapons and modern artillery are housed in a 19th-century military arsenal. The museum has a cafeteria.

IN FROGNER PARK

✪ Vigelandsparken. Frogner Park, Nobelsgate 32. ☎ **22-54-25-30.** Free admission to park; museum, 30 NOK ($3.35) adults, 15 NOK ($1.65) children. Park, daily 24 hours.

Museum: May–Sept, Tues–Sat 10am–6pm, Sun noon–7pm; Oct–Apr, Tues–Sat noon–4pm, Sun noon–6pm. Tram: 12 or 15. Bus: 20, 45, or 81. Tram: 12 or 15.

The lifetime work of Gustav Vigeland, Norway's greatest sculptor, is on display in the 75-acre Frogner Park. More than 200 sculptures in granite, bronze, and iron are here. Notice his four granite columns, symbolizing the fight between humanity and evil (a dragon, the embodiment of evil, embraces a woman). The angry boy is the most photographed statue in the park. The most celebrated work is the 52-foot monolith composed of 121 colossal figures, all carved into one piece of stone.

Nearby, the **Vigeland Museum,** Nobelsgate 32 (☎ **22-54-25-30**), is the sculptor's former studio. It contains more of his works, sketches, and woodcuts. It is open Tuesday to Saturday 10am to 6pm, Sunday noon to 7pm. Admission is 30 NOK ($3.35) for adults, 15 NOK ($1.65) for children.

ON BYGDØY

Located south of the city, the peninsula is reached by commuter ferry (summer only) leaving from Pier 3, facing the Rådhuset (Town Hall). Departures during the day are every 40 minutes, and a one-way fare costs 18 NOK ($2.35). The no. 30 bus from the National Theater also runs to Bygdøy. The museums lie only a short walk from the bus stops on Bygdøy.

☉ Vikingskiphuset (Viking Ship Museum, University Museum of Cultural Heritage). Huk Aveny 35, Bygdøy. ☎ **22-43-83-79.** Admission 40 NOK ($4.45) adults, 20 NOK ($2.20) children. Apr, daily 11am–4pm; May–Aug, daily 9am–6pm; Sept, daily 11am–5pm; Oct, daily 11am–6pm; Nov–Mar, daily 11am–3pm. Ferry: From Pier 3 facing the Rådhuset (summer only). Bus: 30 from the National Theater.

Displayed here are three Viking burial vessels that were excavated on the shores of the Oslofjord and preserved in clay. The most spectacular find is the 9th-century *Oseberg,* discovered near Norway's oldest town. The richly ornamented 64-foot dragon ship is the burial chamber of a Viking queen and her slave.

The *Gokstad* find is an outstanding example of Viking vessels because it's so well preserved. The smaller *Tune* ship was never restored. Look for the *Oseberg's* animal-head post and four-wheeled cart, and the elegantly carved sleigh used by Viking royalty.

Polar Ship *Fram* (Frammuseet). Bygdøynesveien. ☎ **22-43-83-70.** Admission 25 NOK ($2.80) adults, 15 NOK ($1.65) children. Mar–Apr, Mon–Fri 11am–3:45pm, Sat–Sun 11am–3:45pm; May 1–15 and Sept, daily 10am–4:45pm; May 16–Aug, daily 9am–5:45pm; Oct–Nov, Mon–Fri 11am–2:45pm, Sat–Sun 11am–3:45pm; Dec–Feb, Sat–Sun 11am–3:45pm. Ferry: From Pier 3 facing the Rådhuset (summer only). Bus: 30 from the National Theater.

This museum contains the sturdy polar exploration ship *Fram,* which Fridtjof Nansen sailed across the Arctic (1893–96). The vessel was later used by the famed Norwegian explorer Roald Amundsen, the first man to reach the South Pole (1911).

***Kon-Tiki* Museum.** Bygdøynesveien 36. ☎ **23-08-67-67.** Admission 30 NOK ($3.35) adults, 15 NOK ($1.65) children, family ticket 70 NOK ($7.75). Apr–May and Sept, daily 10:30am–5pm; June–Aug, daily 9:30am–5:45pm; Oct–Mar, daily 10:30am–4pm. Ferry: From Pier 3 facing the Rådhuset (summer only). Bus: 30 from the National Theater.

Kon-Tiki is a world-famous balsa-log raft. In 1947, the young Norwegian scientist Thor Heyerdahl and five comrades sailed it from Callao, Peru, to Raroia, Polynesia (4,300 miles). Besides the raft, there are other exhibits from Heyerdahl's subsequent visits to Easter Island. They include casts of stone giants and small originals, a facsimile of the whale shark, and an Easter Island family cave, with a collection of sacred lava figurines hoarded in secret underground passages by the island's inhabitants. The museum also houses the original papyrus *Ra II,* in which Heyerdahl crossed the Atlantic in 1970.

Norsk Sjøfartsmuseum (Norwegian Maritime Museum). Bygdøynesveien 37. ☎ 22-43-82-40. Admission to museum and boat hall 30 NOK ($3.35) adults, 20 NOK ($2.20) children. May–Sept, daily 10am–7pm; Oct–Apr, Mon and Fri–Sat 10:30am–4pm, Tues–Thurs 10:30am–7pm. Ferry: From Pier 3 facing the Rådhuset (summer only). Bus: 30 from the National Theater.

This museum chronicles the maritime history and culture of Norway, complete with a ship's deck with helm and chart house. There's also a three-deck section of the passenger steamer *Sandnaes.*

The Boat Hall features a fine collection of original small craft. The fully restored polar vessel *Gjoa,* used by Roald Amundsen in his search for the Northwest Passage, is also on display. The three-masted schooner *Svanen* (Swan) is moored at the museum. Built in Svendborg, Denmark, in 1916, it sailed under the Norwegian and Swedish flags. The ship now belongs to the museum and is used as a training vessel and school ship for young people.

✪ **Norwegian Folk Museum.** Museumsveien 10. ☎ 22-12-37-00. Admission 70 NOK ($7.75) adults, 20 NOK ($2.20) children under 17. Jan 1–May 14 and Sept 15–Dec 31, Fri–Sat 11am–3pm, Sun 11am–4pm; May 15–June 14 and Sept 1–Sept 14, daily 10am–5pm; June 15–Aug 31, daily 10am–6pm. Ferry: From Pier 3 facing the Rådhuset (summer only). Bus: 30 from the National Theater.

From all over Norway, 140 original buildings have been transported and reassembled on 35 acres on the Bygdøy peninsula. This open-air folk museum, one of the oldest of its kind, includes a number of medieval buildings. The Raulandstua is one of the oldest wooden dwellings still standing in Norway, and a stave church dates from about 1200. The rural buildings are grouped together by region of origin, and the urban houses are laid out in the form of an old town.

Inside, the museum's 225,000 exhibits capture every imaginable facet of Norwegian life, past and present. Furniture, household utensils, clothing, woven fabrics, and tapestries are on display, along with fine examples of rose painting and woodcarving. Farming implements and logging gear pay tribute to the development of agriculture and forestry. Also look for the outstanding exhibit on Norway's Lapp population.

NEAR OSLO

Tryvannstårnet (Lookout Tower). Voksenkollen. ☎ 22-14-67-11. Admission 35 NOK ($3.90) adults, 20 NOK ($2.20) children. May and Sept, daily 10am–5pm; June, daily 10am–7pm; July, daily 9am–8pm; Aug, daily 9am–8pm; Oct–Apr, Mon–Sun 10am–4pm. T-banen: Frognerseteren SST Line 1 from near the National Theater to Voksenkollen (30-minute ride), then an uphill 15-minute walk.

The loftiest lookout tower in Scandinavia offers a view of the Oslofjord with Sweden to the east. The gallery is approximately 1,900 feet above sea level.

A walk down the hill returns you to Frognerseteren (see "Dining," above). Another 20-minute walk down the hill takes you to the Holmenkollen Ski Jump, where the 1952 Olympic competitions took place. It's also the site of Norway's winter sports highlight, the Holmenkollen Ski Festival.

✪ **Henie-Onstad Kunstsenter (Henie-Onstad Art Center).** Høkvikodden, Baerum. ☎ 67-80-48-80. Admission 60 NOK ($6.65) adults, 30 NOK ($3.35) ages 15–25, free for children 14 and under. June–Aug, Mon 11am–5pm, Tues–Fri 9am–9pm, Sat–Sun 11am–7pm; Sept–May, Tues 9am–9pm, Sat–Mon 11am–5pm. Bus: 151, 152, 251, or 261.

Former skating champion and movie star Sonja Henie and her husband, shipping tycoon Niels Onstad, opened this museum to display their art collection. On a handsome site beside the Oslofjord, 7 miles west of Oslo, it's an especially good 20th-century collection. There are some 1,800 works by Munch, Picasso, Matisse, Léger, Bonnard, and Miró. Henie's contributions can be seen in her Trophy Room. She won three Olympic gold medals—she was the star at the 1936 competition—and 10 world championships. In all, she garnered 600 trophies and medals.

Besides the permanent collection, there are plays, concerts, films, and special exhibits. An open-air theater-in-the-round is used in the summer for folklore programs, jazz concerts, and song recitals. On the premises is a top-notch, partly self-service, grill restaurant, the Piruetten.

Skimuseet (Ski Museum). Kongeveien 5, Holmenkollen. ☎ **22-92-32-00.** Admission (museum and ski jump) 60 NOK ($6.65) adults, 30 NOK ($3.35) children. May and Sept, daily 10am–5pm; June, daily 9am–8pm; July–Aug, daily 9am–10pm; Oct–Apr, daily 10am–4pm. T-banen: Holmenkollen SST Line 15 from near the National Theater to Voksenkollen (30-minute ride), then an uphill 15-minute walk.

At Holmenkollen, an elevator takes visitors up the jump tower for a view of Oslo and the fjord. At the base of the ski jump, the Ski Museum (Skimuseet) displays a wide range of exhibits. They include a 4,000-year-old pictograph from Rødøy in Nordland, which documents skiing's thousand-year history. The oldest ski in the museum dates from around A.D. 600. The museum has exhibits on Nansen's and Amundsen's polar expeditions, plus skis and historical items from various parts of Norway, including the first "modern" skis, from about 1870.

PARKS & GARDENS

Marka, the thick forest that surrounds Oslo, is a giant pleasure park, and there are others. You can take a tram marked "Holmenkollen" from the city center to Oslo-marka, a forested pleasure and recreational area. Locals go here for summer hikes in the forest and for skiing in winter. The area is dotted with about two dozen *hytter* (mountain huts) where you can seek refuge from the weather if needed. **Norske Turistforening,** Storgate 3 (☎ **22-82-28-22**), sells maps with the hiking paths and roads of the Oslomarka clearly delineated. Open Monday to Friday 10am to 4pm, Saturday 10am to 2pm.

Botanisk Hage og Museum (Botanical Gardens). Trondheimsvn 23B. ☎ **22-85-17-00.** Free admission. Apr–Sept, Mon–Fri 7am–8pm, Sat–Sun 10am–8pm; Oct–Mar, Mon–Fri 7am–5pm, Wed until 8pm, Sat–Sun 10am–5pm. Bus: 20.

At Tøyen, near the Munch Museum, this is an oasis in the heart of Oslo. It's home to many exotic plants, including cacti, orchids, and palms. More than 1,000 mountain plants can be viewed in the rock garden, which has waterfalls. There's also a museum in the park, with a botanical art exhibit.

Slottsparken. Drammensveien 1. Free admission. Daily dawn–dusk. T-banen: Nationaltheateret.

The park surrounding the Royal Palace (Slottet) is open to the public year-round. The changing of the guard takes place daily at 1:30pm. When the king is in residence, the Royal Guard band plays Monday through Friday during the changing of the guard.

The palace was constructed from 1825 to 1848. Some first-time visitors are surprised at how open and relatively unguarded it is, without walls or rails. You can walk through the grounds, but can't go inside unless you have an invitation from the king. The statue at the front of the castle (at the end of Karl Johans Gate) is of Karl XIV Johan himself, who ruled Norway and Sweden. He ordered the palace constructed, but died before it was finished.

The Man Behind *The Scream*

Scandinavia's greatest artist, Edvard Munch (1863–1944), was a pioneer in the expressionist movement. *The Scream,* painted in 1893, is his best-known painting. He grew up in Oslo (then called Christiania) and was often ill. Early memories of illness, death, and grief in his family had a tremendous impact on his later works. His father's death may have contributed to the loneliness and melancholy of one of his most famous works, *Night* (1890).

By the early 1890s, Munch had achieved fame (though slight in comparision with his renown today). He was at the center of a *succès de scandale* in Munich in 1892, when his art was interpreted as "anarchistic provocation." A major exhibit was closed in protest.

Munch went to Berlin, entering a world of literati, artists, and intellectuals. He met August Strindberg, and they discussed the philosophy of Nietzsche, symbolism, psychology, and occultism. The discussions clearly influenced his work. His growing outlook was revealed to the world in an 1893 show in Berlin, where several paintings had death as their theme. *Death in a Sickroom* created quite a stir.

In 1896 Munch moved to Paris, where he made exquisite color lithographs and his first woodcuts. By the turn of the century he was painting in a larger format and incorporating some of the art nouveau aesthetics of the time. *Red Virginia Creeper and Melancholy* reflects the new influences.

A nervous disorder sent him to a sanitarium, and he had a turbulent love affair with a wealthy bohemian nicknamed "Tulla." The affair ended in 1902 when a revolver permanently injured a finger on Munch's left hand. He became obsessed with the shooting incident, and poured out his contempt for "Tulla" in such works as *Death of Murat* (1907).

Prominent people asked Munch to paint their portraits, and he obliged. The group portrait of Dr. Linde's sons (1904) is a masterpiece of modern portraiture. Munch became increasingly alcoholic, and in 1906 painted *Self-Portrait with a Bottle of Wine.*

From 1909 until his death, Munch lived in Norway. In his later years he retreated into isolation, surrounded only by his paintings, which he called "my children." The older Munch placed more emphasis on the monumental and the picturesque, as in landscapes or people in harmony with nature.

In 1940 he decided to leave his huge collection of paintings to the city of Oslo upon his death. Today the Munch Museum provides the best introduction to this strange and enigmatic artist.

OF ARTISTIC INTEREST

Aula (Great Hall). University of Oslo, Karl Johans Gate 47. ☎ **22-85-98-55.** Free admission. Daily 24 hours. T-banen: Stortinget.

Admirers of the work of Edvard Munch will want to see the Great Hall of the university, where Scandinavia's greatest artist painted murals. Until it moved to larger headquarters at the City Hall, this used to be the site of the Nobel Prize award ceremony.

✪ **Edvard Munch Museum.** Tøyengate 53. ☎ **23-24-14-00.** Admission 60 NOK ($7.50) adults, 30 NOK ($3.75) children. June to mid-Sept, daily 10am–6pm; mid-Sept to May, Tues–Wed and Fri–Sat 10am–4pm, Thurs and Sun 10am–6pm. T-banen: Tøyen. Bus: 20.

Devoted exclusively to the works of Edvard Munch (1863–1944), Scandinavia's leading painter, this collection was his gift to the city. It traces his work from early realism to latter-day expressionism. The collection comprises 1,100 paintings, some 4,500 drawings, around 18,000 prints, numerous graphic plates, six sculptures, and important documentary material. The exhibits change periodically.

LITERARY LANDMARKS

"Walking Tour 2," below, follows in the footsteps of Ibsen.

Ibsen Museum. Arbinsgate 1. ☎ **22-55-20-09.** Admission 40 NOK ($4.45) adults, 10 NOK ($1.10) children. Tues–Sun noon–3pm; guided tour in English at noon, 1pm, and 2pm. T-banen: Nationaltheatret.

In 1994 Oslo opened a museum to honor its most famous writer. Ibsen lived in an apartment within walking distance of the National Theater from 1895 until his death in 1906. Here he wrote two of his most famous plays, *John Gabriel Borkman* and *When We Dead Awaken.* The museum curators have tried to re-create the apartment (a longtime exhibit at the Norwegian Folk Museum) as authentically as possible. The study, for example, has Ibsen's original furniture, and the entire apartment is decorated as though Ibsen still lived in it. The attraction has been called "a living museum," and regularly scheduled talks on play writing and the theater, recitations, and theatrical performances are planned.

Oslo Bymuseum (City Museum). Frognerveien 67. ☎ **23-28-41-70.** Admission 30 NOK ($3.35) adults, 15 NOK ($1.65) children. June–Aug, Tues–Fri 10am–6pm, Sat–Sun 11am–5pm; Sept–May, Tues–Fri 10am–4pm, Sat–Sun 11am–4pm. Bus: 20, 45, or 81. Tram: 12 or 15.

Housed in the 1790 Frogner Manor at Frogner Park, site of the Vigeland sculptures, this museum surveys the history of Oslo. It also contains mementos of Henrik Ibsen, such as the chair and marble-topped table where he sat at the Grand Café. Four glasses from which he drank are engraved with his name.

ARCHITECTURAL HIGHLIGHTS

Those interested in modern architecture should head to **Vaterland,** in East Oslo. One of Oslo's major development sites, launched in the 1980s, this "city within a city" includes a 9,000-seat hall for musical and sporting events, an art gallery, a train station, and large conference facilities.

Those interested in recycling old districts will want to explore **Aker Brygge,** along the harbor. The "Fisherman's Wharf of Oslo" opened in 1986 in what had been shipbuilding yards. It's a modern complex of shops, nightspots, restaurants, delis, wine bars, and ice-cream parlors. Take bus no. 27 or walk west from the Rådhus.

Norsk Arkitekturmuseum (Norwegian Museum of Architecture). Kongensgate 4. ☎ **22-42-40-80.** Free admission. Mon–Fri 11am–4pm, Sat–Sun noon–4pm. Tram: 10, 12, or 13. Bus: 60.

Near Akershus Castle and the Oslo City Hall, right in the center of the city, this museum presents changing exhibits. Most are examples of Norwegian architecture from this century. In 1996 it gained a new permanent exhibit that delineates Norway's architectural history. Temporary exhibits change frequently.

Christiania Bymodell. Høymagasinet, Akershus Festning. ☎ **22-33-31-47.** Admission 30 NOK ($3.35) adults, 15 NOK ($1.65) children. Tues–Sun noon–5pm. Closed Sept–May. Tram: 10 or 12.

Norway's capital was called Oslo, then Christiania, and then Oslo again. This architectural model of the city of Christiania in 1838 is part of a multimedia program that traces the city's history from its foundation in 1624 until 1840.

Gamle Aker Kirke (Old Aker Church). Akersbakken 26. ☎ 22-69-35-82. Free admission. Mon–Sat noon–2pm. Bus: 37. T-banen: Bjerregårdsgaten.

Constructed in 1100, this is the oldest stone church in Scandinavia that's still in use by a parish. Guided tours in English are conducted year-round. There are occasional church concerts, and Masses on Sunday at 9 and 11am.

6 Especially for Kids

Oslo rivals Copenhagen when it comes to attractions suitable for both children and grown-ups. The top thrill of a trip to the fjord is seeing the excavated **Viking burial ships** on the Bygdøy peninsula and the **Norwegian Maritime Museum** and Boat Hall.

Other sights already discussed will be of special interest to children. They include the polar exploration ship *Fram*, which took Nansen and Amundsen on their ventures to the North and South Poles; the balsa-log raft *Kon-Tiki*, in which Thor Heyerdahl and his comrades made their historic journey across the Pacific; the lookout tower, ski jump, and Ski Museum at **Holmenkollen;** the **folk museum,** depicting life in Norway since the Middle Ages; and the ancient fortress on the Oslofjord, **Akershus Castle.**

Barnekunst Museum (International Children's Art Museum). Lille Frøens vei 4. ☎ 22-46-85-73. Admission 40 NOK ($4.45) adults, 20 NOK ($2.20) children. Jan 20–June 25 and Sept 10–Dec 15, Tues–Thurs 9:30am–2pm, Sun 11am–4pm; June 26–Aug 15, Tues–Thurs and Sun 11am–4pm. Closed Dec 16–Jan 19 and Aug 16–Sept 9. T-banen: Frøen.

The collection in this unique museum consists of children's drawings, paintings, ceramics, sculpture, tapestries, and handcrafts from more than 30 countries, some of which would have pleased Picasso. There's also a children's workshop devoted to painting, drawing, music, and dance.

Norgesparken Tusenfryd. Vinterbro by E6/E18/Mossevelen. ☎ 64-97-66-99. All-day ticket 190 NOK ($21.10) adults, 165 NOK ($18.30) children. June–Sept 19, daily 10:30am–7pm. Closed Sept 20–May. Bus: Shuttle service from Oslo's Central Station daily 10am–1pm (every 30 minutes), 3, 4, and 5pm; final return shortly after park closes. Fare: 30 NOK ($3.75) adults, 20 NOK ($2.20) children.

This is the largest amusement park in Norway, conceived as a smaller version of Copenhagen's Tivoli. It includes a number of simple restaurants, a roller coaster with a loop and corkscrew, an amphitheater with all-day entertainment by performers such as musicians and clowns, and many games of skill or chance. The park is 12 miles south of the Central Station.

7 Oslo on Foot: Walking Tours

Walking Tour 1: Historic Oslo

Start: Aker Brygge.

Finish: Royal Palace.

Time: 2½ hours.

Best Time: Any day when it's not raining.

Worst Times: Rush hours (weekdays 7 to 9am and 5 to 7pm).

Start at:

1. **Aker Brygge,** on the harbor to the west of the Rådhuset. This steel-and-glass complex is a rebuilt district of shops and restaurants that was developed from Oslo's old shipbuilding grounds. It has a fine view of Akershus Castle.

   Head east along Rådhusplassen, looking at the:

2. **Rådhuset,** on your left. The Oslo City Hall, built in 1950, is decorated with artwork by Norwegian artists.

   Climb the steps at the east end of the square and a small hill to see the:

3. **Statue of Franklin D. Roosevelt.** Eleanor Roosevelt flew to Oslo to dedicate the statue.

   This area is the heart of the 17th-century Renaissance city. Take Rådhusgata east to:

4. **Christiania Torv,** a traffic hub. The yellow house on your left, the Young Artists Association, was once the home of the dreaded executioner. His fee depended on the type of execution performed.

   ☕ **TAKE A BREAK**   To the right of the Young Artists Association is **Kafé Celsius,** Rådhusgatan 19 (☎ 22-42-45-39), Oslo's oldest residential house. Today it's a charming arts-oriented cafe that serves tasty food. Sandwich prices start at 70 NOK ($7.75). You can also order pasta salads and such dishes as ratatouille or tortellini. On cold days there's a fire in the fireplace. It's open Sunday, Tuesday, and Wednesday from 11:30am to 12:30am, Thursday to Saturday 11:30am to 1:30am.

   Continue along Rådhusgata, turning right onto Nedre Slottsgate. Walk to the end of the street. At Myntgata, turn right and pass through a gate. You are now on the greater grounds of Akershus Castle. The first building on the right is the:

5. **Norwegian Resistance Museum.** It has displays on events related to the Nazi occupation of Norway from 1940 to 1945. Also at the site is:

6. **Akershus Castle and Fortress,** dating from 1300 but rebuilt in the 17th century. Take a guided tour of the fortress and walk its ramparts. Pause on the grounds to look at the:

7. **Execution Site,** in front of the Norwegian Resistance Museum. Here the Nazis shot prisoners, often Norwegian freedom fighters. There's a memorial to the resistance movement, and you'll have a good view of the harbor in the distance.

   Cross the drawbridge to the east, right before Kongens Gate, and continue through the castle grounds to the:

8. **National Monument to the German Occupation,** commemorating Norway's suffering at the hands of the Nazis.

   After seeing the monument, turn left (north) into:

9. **Grev Wedels Plass,** the site of Den Gamle Logen (Freemason's Lodge). In 1850, Ibsen wrote poems here. At no. 9 and Dronningensgatan 4 is the Astrup Fearnley Museum of Modern Art, with changing exhibits of Norwegian and foreign art from the postwar period.

   Head north along Kirkegata until you reach:

10. **Bankplassen,** site of the old Bank of Norway. Today it's the Museum of Contemporary Art (Bankplassen 4), with the state collection of international and Norwegian modern art acquired since the Second World War. This square was once Oslo's social center. Ibsen staged his first play here in 1851 (at a theater that burned down in 1877).

    From Bankplassen, turn right onto Revierstredet and left onto Dronningensgatan. At one time the waterfront came up to this point. Go right at the Central

Walking Tour: Historic Oslo

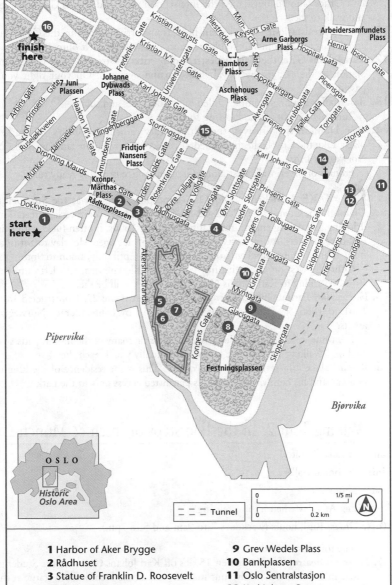

1 Harbor of Aker Brygge
2 Rådhuset
3 Statue of Franklin D. Roosevelt
4 Christiania Torv
5 Norwegian Resistance Museum
6 Akershus Castle and Fortress
7 Execution Site
8 National Monument to the German Occupation
9 Grev Wedels Plass
10 Bankplassen
11 Oslo Sentralstasjon
12 Karl Johans Gate
13 Basarhallene
14 Oslo Domkirke
15 Norwegian Parliament (Stortinget)
16 Royal Palace (Slottet)

Post Office onto Tollbugata. At the intersection with Fred Olsens Gate, turn left and walk to the:

11. Oslo Sentralstasjon, the city's rail hub. Trains arrive here from the Continent and depart for all points linked by train in Norway. Turn left onto:

12. Karl Johans Gate, the main pedestrian-only street. It stretches from the Central Station in the east to the Royal Palace in the west end. On your right you'll pass the:

13. Basarhallene, a huge complex filled with boutiques and shops.

Turn right at Kirkegata, heading for the:

14. Oslo Domkirke, Stortorvet, the 17th-century cathedral at Oslo's old marketplace. Like the City Hall, the cathedral is decorated with outstanding works by Norwegian artists.

From Stortorvet, walk west along Grensen. You're probably ready to:

☕ **TAKE A BREAK**   Old Oslo atmosphere lives on at the **Stortorvets Gjaestgiveri,** Grensen 1 (☎ 22-42-88-63), on a busy commercial street. This drinking and dining emporium, dating from the 1600s, is often filled with spirited beer drinkers. A beer costs 48 NOK ($5.35). It's open Monday to Saturday from 10am to 9pm, Sunday (from November to April only) noon to 9pm.

Continue west on Grensen until you reach Lille Grensen. Cut left onto this street, returning to Karl Johans Gate. On your left will be the:

15. Norwegian Parliament (Stortinget), Karl Johans Gate 22. Constructed from 1861 to 1866, it's richly decorated with works by contemporary Norwegian artists.

Continue west along Karl Johans Gate, passing many of the monuments covered on "Walking Tour 2" (see below). Eventually you'll reach the:

16. Royal Palace (Slottet), Drammensveien 1. This is the residence of the king of Norway and his family. The public is permitted access only to the park.

Walking Tour 2: In the Footsteps of Ibsen & Munch

Start: National Theater.

Finish: National Gallery.

Time: 2 hours.

Best Time: Any day when it's not raining.

Worst Times: Rush hours (weekdays 7 to 9am and 5 to 7pm).

The tour begins at the:

1. Nationaltheatret, Stortingsgaten 15. It's off Karl Johans Gate near the Students' Grove in Oslo's center. Study your map in front of the Henrik Ibsen statue at the theater, where many of his plays were first performed and are still presented. The Norwegian National Theater, inaugurated in 1899, is one of the most beautiful in Europe. Phone (☎ 22-00-14-00) for information.

Facing the statue of Ibsen, continue up Stortingsgaten toward the Royal Palace (Slottet). Cut left at the next intersection and walk along Ruselokkveien. The Vika Shopping Terraces, an unattractive row of modern storefronts tacked onto an elegant 1880 Victorian terrace, used to be among Oslo's grandest apartments. During the Second World War it was the Nazi headquarters.

Walking Tour: In the Footsteps of Ibsen & Munch

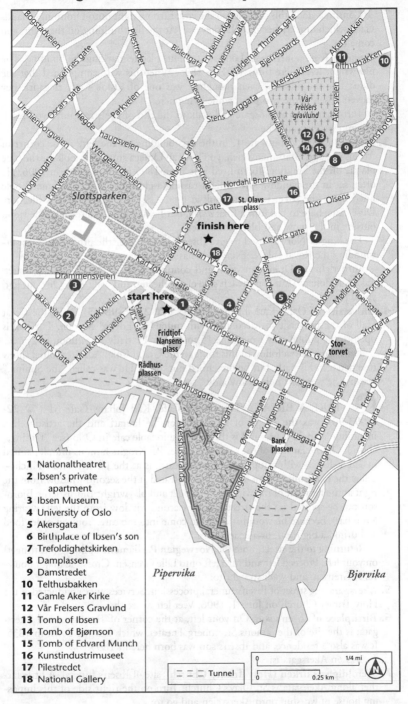

1 Nationaltheatret
2 Ibsen's private
apartment
3 Ibsen Museum
4 University of Oslo
5 Akersgata
6 Birthplace of Ibsen's son
7 Trefoldighetskirken
8 Damplassen
9 Damstredet
10 Telthusbakken
11 Gamle Aker Kirke
12 Vår Frelsers Gravlund
13 Tomb of Ibsen
14 Tomb of Bjørnson
15 Tomb of Edvard Munch
16 Kunstindustrimuseet
17 Pilestredet
18 National Gallery

= = = Tunnel

0   1/4 mi
0   0.25 km

Continue along this complex to the end, turning right onto Dronnings Mauds Gate, which quickly becomes Lokkeveien. At the first building on the right, you come to:

2. **Ibsen's private apartment.** Look for the blue plaque marking the building. The playwright lived here from 1891 to 1895. When his wife complained that she didn't like the address, even though it was one of Oslo's most elegant, they moved. Ibsen wrote two plays while living here.

Turn right onto Arbinsgate and walk to the end of the street until you reach Drammensveien and the:

3. **Ibsen Museum,** Arbinsgate 1. In the first building on the left, at the corner of Arbinsgate and Drammensveien, you'll see an Omega store, but look for the blue plaque on the building. Ibsen lived here from 1895 until his death in 1906. He often sat in the window, with a light casting a glow over his white hair. People lined up in the street below to look at him. The great Italian actress Eleanora Duse came here to bid him a final *adieu,* but he was too ill to see her. She stood outside in the snow and blew him kisses.

The king of Norway used to give Ibsen a key to enter the private gardens surrounding the Royal Palace. Everybody has that privilege today.

Turn right on Drammensveien and continue back to the National Theater. Take Karl Johans Gate, on the left side of the theater, and walk east. On your left, you'll pass the:

4. **University of Oslo,** Karl Johans Gate 47 (☎ 22-85-98-55). Aula, the Great Hall of the university, is decorated with murals by Edvard Munch. The hall is open to the public only from June 15 to August 15, daily from noon to 2pm.

Twice a day Ibsen followed this route to the Grand Café. Admirers often threw rose petals in his path, but he pretended not to see. He was called "the Sphinx," because he wouldn't talk to anybody.

☕ **TAKE A BREAK** The **Grand Café,** Karl Johans Gate 31 (☎ 22-42-93-90), was the center of social life for the literati and the artistic elite, including Munch. It was and is the most fashionable cafe in Oslo (see "Dining," above). On the far wall of the cafe you can see Per Krogh's famous mural, painted in 1928. Ibsen, with a top hat and gray beard, is at the far left, and Munch—called the handsomest man in Norway—is seated at the second window from the right at the far right of the window. The poet and playwright Bjørnstjerne Bjørnson can be spotted on the street outside (second window from the left, wearing a top hat), because he wouldn't deign to come into the cafe. You can order food and drink, a big meal, or a snack.

Returning to the street, note the **Norwegian Parliament** building (Stortinget) on your left. Proceed left and turn left onto Lille Grensen. Cross the major boulevard, Grensen, and walk straight to:

5. **Akersgata,** the street of Ibsen's funeral procession. Services were conducted at the Holy Trinity Church on June 1, 1906. Veer left to see the:

6. **Birthplace of Ibsen's son.** On your left, at the corner of Teatergata and Akersgata, is the site of the famous Strømberg Theater, which burned down in 1835. It was also a residence, and Ibsen's son was born here in 1859.

Also on Akersgata is:

7. **Trefoldighetskirken (Holy Trinity Church),** site of Ibsen's funeral. A little farther along Akersgata is St. Olav's Church. Turn on the right side of this imposing house of worship onto Akersveien and go to:

8. Damplassen, a small square—one of the most charming in Oslo—that doesn't appear on most maps. Norway's greatest poet, Henrik Wergeland, lived in the pink house on this square from 1839 to 1841.

Take a right at the square and head down:

9. Damstredet, a typical old Oslo street, with antique wooden houses mainly occupied by artists.

Damstredet winds downhill to Fredensborgveien. Here a left turn and a short walk will take you to Maridalsveien, a busy but dull thoroughfare. As you walk north along this street, on the west side look for a large unmarked gateway with wide stone steps inside. Climb to the top, follow a little pathway, and go past gardens and flower beds. Pass a set of brick apartment buildings on the left, and proceed to:

10. Telthusbakken, a little street where you'll see a whole row of early Oslo wooden houses. Look right in the far distance at the green building where Munch used to live. Telthusbakken leads to Akersveien. On your left you can see the:

11. Gamle Aker Kirke (Old Aker Church). Enter at Akersbakken, where Akersveien and Akersbakken intersect. Built in 1100, this is the oldest stone parish church in Scandinavia that's still in use. It stands on a green hill with an old graveyard around it, inside a stone wall.

A short block from the church along Akersbakken (veer left outside the front of the church and go around a corner), you'll come to the north entrance of:

12. Vår Frelsers Gravlund (Our Savior's Cemetery), the city's expansive burial ground. In a section designated as the "Ground of Honor" are the graves of famous Norwegians, including Munch, Ibsen, and Bjørnson. Signs don't point the way, but it's easy to see a tall obelisk. This is the:

13. Tomb of Ibsen. His wife, Susanna, whom he called "the cat," is buried to the playwright's left. She died in 1914. The hammer on the obelisk symbolizes his work *The Miner,* indicating how he "dug deep" into the soul of Norway.

To the right of Ibsen's tomb is the:

14. Tomb of Bjørnson. The literary figure Bjørnstjerne Bjørnson (1832–1910) once raised money to send Ibsen to Italy. Before the birth of their children, Ibsen and Bjørnson agreed that one would have a son and the other a daughter, and that they would marry each other. Miraculously, Ibsen had a son, Bjørnson a daughter, and they did just that. Bjørnson wrote the national anthem, and his tomb is draped in a stone representation of a Norwegian flag.

To the far right of Bjørnson's tomb is the:

15. Tomb of Edvard Munch. Scandinavia's greatest painter has an unadorned tomb. If you're visiting on a snowy day, it will be buried, because the marker lies close to the ground. Munch died during the darkest days of the Nazi occupation. His sister turned down a request from the German command to give Munch a state funeral, feeling that it would be inappropriate.

On the west side of the cemetery you'll come to Ullevålsveien. Turn left on this busy street and head south toward the center of Oslo. You'll soon see St. Olav's Church, this time on your left. Stay on the right (west) side of the street. Ullevålsveien intersects with St. Olavs Gate at the:

16. Kunstindustrimuseet (Museum of Applied Art), St. Olavs Gate 1. Even if you don't have time to visit the museum, you may want to go inside to the cafe.

After visiting the museum, continue along St. Olavs Gate to:

17. Pilestredet. Look to the immediate right at no. 30. A wall plaque on the decaying building commemorates the fact that Munch lived here from 1868 to 1875. In this building he painted, among other masterpieces, *The Sick Child.* He moved here when he was 5, and many of his "memory paintings" were of the interior. When demolition teams started to raze the building in the early 1990s, a counterculture group of activists known as "The Blitz Group" illegally took over the premises to prevent its destruction. On its brick wall side, his master-piece *The Scream* was re-created in spray paint. The protesters are still in control of the city-owned building, and they are viewed as squatters on very valuable land. It's suspected that if a more conservative government comes into power, officials will toss out the case, throw out the activists, and demolish the building. For the moment, however, they remain in control.

At Pilestredet, turn left. One block later, turn right onto Universitetsgata, heading south toward Karl Johans Gate. You'll pass a number of architecturally interesting buildings, and will eventually arrive at the:

18. National Gallery, Universitetsgata 13. The state museum has a large collection of Norwegian and foreign art. Two rooms are devoted to masterpieces by Munch.

8 Organized Tours

CRUISES AROUND THE FJORD   Båtservice Sightseeing, Rådhusbrygge 3, Rådhusplassen (☎ 22-20-07-15), offers a 50-minute boat tour. You'll see the harbor and the city, including the ancient fortress of Akershus and the islands in the inner part of the Oslofjord. Cruises depart from Pier 3 in front of the Oslo Rådhuset (City Hall). They run from mid-May to late August, daily on the hour from 11am to 8pm during the high season, less frequently at the beginning and end of the season. Tick-ets are 85 NOK ($9.45) for adults, 40 NOK ($4.45) for children.

If you have more time, take a 2-hour cruise through the maze of islands and nar-row sounds in the Oslofjord. From May to September, they leave daily at 10:30am and 1pm, 3:30pm, and 5:45pm; the cost is 155 NOK ($17.20) for adults, 75 NOK ($8.30) for children. Refreshments are available on board. The 2-hour fjord cruise with lunch runs from May to mid-September. It leaves daily at 10:30am and costs 310 NOK ($34.40) for adults, 155 NOK ($17.20) for children. Lunch is served at Lanter-nen Restaurant after the cruise.

The 2-hour evening fjord cruise includes a seafood buffet, also at the Lanternen. It's offered from late June to August, daily at 3:30 and 5:45pm. Prices are 495 NOK ($54.95) for adults, 225 NOK ($25) for children.

CITY TOURS   H. M. Kristiansens Automobilbyrå, Hegdehaugsveien 4 (☎ 22-20-82-06), has been showing visitors around Oslo for more than a century. Both of their bus tours are offered daily year-round. The 3-hour "Oslo Highlights" tour is offered at 10am and 1:30pm. It costs 235 NOK ($26.10) for adults, 120 NOK ($13.30) for children. The 2-hour "Oslo Panorama" tour costs 155 NOK ($17.20) for adults, 85 NOK ($9.45) for children. It departs at 10am and 5:30pm. The starting point is the Norway information center, Vestbaneplassen 1; arrive 15 minutes before departure. Tours are conducted in English by trained guides.

9 Active Sports

From spring to fall, the Oslofjord is a center of swimming, sailing, windsurfing, and angling. Daily excursions are arranged by motor launch at the harbor. Suburban for-est areas await hikers, bicyclists, and anglers in the summer. In the winter, the area is ideal for cross-country skiing (on marked trails that are illuminated at night), down-hill or slalom skiing, tobogganing, skating, and more. Safaris by Land Rover are arranged year-round.

BATHS   The most central municipal bath is **Vestkantbadet,** Sommerrogate 1 (☎ 22-44-07-26), which offers a Finnish sauna and Roman baths. Admission is 100 NOK ($11.10). The baths are reserved for men on Monday, Wednesday, and Friday from noon to 4pm, and for women on Tuesday and Thursday from noon to 9pm and Saturday 9:30am to 3pm. Prices for massages are start at 290 NOK ($32.20) for 30 minutes. If you book a massage, you can use the baths free. This municipal bath is near the American Embassy, about a mile north of Oslo's center. It's primarily a winter destination, and closed in July.

    Frognerbadet, Middelthunsgate 28 (☎ 22-44-74-29), in Frogner Park, is an open-air pool near the Vigeland sculptures. The entrance fee is 50 NOK ($5.55) for adults, 25 NOK ($2.80) for children. It's open mid-May to mid-August, Monday to Friday from 7am to 7pm, Saturday and Sunday 11am to 5pm. Take tram no. 2 from the National Theater.

BEACHES   Avoid the polluted inner-harbor area. The nearest and most popular beach is at **Hovedøya,** which is also the site of a 12th-century Cistercian monastery erected by English monks. Swimming is from a rocky shore. From Oslo's central station, local trains run frequently throughout the day to Sandvika. Also try **Drøbak,** 24 miles south of Oslo (take bus no. 541).

    Oslovian beach devotees say **Gressholmen** and **Langøyene,** a 15-minute ride from Vippetangen, have the finest beaches in the vicinity. Nudism is practiced at beaches on the south side of Langøyene.

    The closest clean beaches are those west of the Bygdøy peninsula, including **Huk** (where there's nude bathing) and **Paradisbukta.** Bygdøy can be reached by bus no. 30 from the National Theater. There are also beaches at **Langåra,** 10 miles west of Oslo. Take the local train to Sandvika and make ferry connections from there.

    You can reach a number of beaches on the east side of the fjord by taking bus no. 75B from Jernbanetorget in East Oslo. Buses leave about every hour on weekends. It's a 12-minute ride to **Ulvøya,** the closest beach and one of the best and safest for children. Nudists prefer **Standskogen.**

GYMS   Male and female weight lifters call **Harald's Gym,** Hausmannsgate 6 (☎ 22-20-34-96), the most professional gym in Oslo. Many champion bodybuilders have trained here, and its facilities are the most comprehensive in Norway. Nonmembers pay 50 NOK ($6.50) for a day pass. It's open Monday to Friday from 9am to 9pm, Saturday 11am to 5pm, Sunday noon to 5pm.

JOGGING   Marka, the forest that surrounds Oslo, has hundreds of trails. The easiest and most accessible are at Frogner Park. You can also jog or hike the trails along the Aker River, a scenic route. A great adventure is to take the Sognsvann train to the end of the line, where you can jog along the fast-flowing Sognsvann stream. **Norske Turistforening,** Storgata 28 (☎ 22-82-28-00), sells maps outlining jogging trails around the capital, and the staff can give you advice about routes.

SKATING   Oslo is home to numerous skating rinks. **Grünerhallen,** Seilduksgate 30 (☎ 22-35-55-52), admits the public for pleasure skating. For a 2-hour session, the price is 20 NOK ($2.20) for adults, 5 NOK (55¢) for children. Skate rentals cost 10 to 20 NOK ($1.10 to $2.20). Grünerhallen is open October to March; days and hours are erratic because it's used primarily for hockey, so call in advance. Other skating rinks include **Narvisen,** Spikersuppa, near Karl Johans Gate (☎ 22 33 30 33), open October to March.

SKIING   A 15-minute tram or bus ride from central Oslo to Holmenkollen will take you to Oslo's winter wonderland, **Marka,** a 1,612-mile ski-track network. Many ski schools and instructors are available in the winter. You can even take a sleigh ride.

Other activities include dogsled rides, snowshoe trekking, and Marka forest safaris. There are 14 slalom slopes to choose from, along with ski jumps in all shapes and sizes, including the famous one at Holmenkollen. For information and updates on ski conditions, you can call Skiforeningen, Kongeveien 5 (☎ 22-92-32-00). The tourist office can give you details about the venues for many of these activities.

TENNIS   The municipal courts at **Frogner Park** are usually fully booked for the season by the locals, but ask at the kiosk about cancellations.

Njårdhallen, Sørkedalsceien 106 (☎ 22-14-15-93), offers indoor tennis Monday to Thursday from 7am to 10pm, Friday to Sunday 7am to 8pm. Book your court well in advance. During nice weather, you might prefer outdoor tennis at **Njårds Tennis,** Jenns Messveien 1 (☎ 22-14-67-74), a cluster of courts that are generally open whenever weather and daylight permit.

10 Shopping

THE SHOPPING SCENE

Oslo has many **traffic-free streets** for strollers and shoppers. The heart of this district is the **Stortorvet,** where more than two dozen shops sell everything from handcrafts to enameled silver jewelry. At the marketplace on Strøget, you can stop for a glass of beer at an open-air restaurant in fair weather. Many stores are clustered along **Karl Johans Gate** and the streets branching off it.

BEST BUYS   Look for bargains on sportswear, silver and enamelware, traditional handcrafts, pewter, glass by Hadeland Glassverk (founded in 1762), teak furniture, and stainless steel.

SHIPPING GOODS & RECOVERING VAT   Norway imposes a 20% value-added tax (VAT), but there are ways to avoid paying it. See "Taxes" in "Fast Facts: Norway," in chapter 7. Special tax-free exports are possible; many stores will mail goods home to you, which makes paying and recovering tax unnecessary.

SHOPPING HOURS   Most stores are open Monday to Friday from 9am to 5pm, Saturday 9am to 3pm. Department stores and shopping malls keep different hours—in general, Monday to Friday 9am to 8pm, Saturday 9am to 6pm. Many shops stay open late on Thursday and on the first Saturday of the month. Shoppers call this *super lørdag* ("super Saturday"). During the holiday season, stores are open on Sunday.

SHOPPING A TO Z
ARTS & CRAFTS

Baerum Verk. Verksgata 15, Baerum Verk. ☎ 67-13-00-18. Bus: 143 or 153.

For a unique adventure you can head outside of town to a restored iron works site dating from 1610. Here are more than 65 different shops selling handcrafts and other items, including jewelry and woolens, plus there are exhibitions and six restaurants to choose from. If time remains, visit the iron works museum on site and see a smelting production dating back to the 17th century.

✪ **Den Norske Husfliden.** Møllergata 4. ☎ 22-42-10-75. T-banen: Stortinget.

Near the marketplace and the cathedral, Husfliden is the display and retail center for the Norwegian Association of Home Arts and Crafts, founded in 1891. Today it's almost eight times larger than any of its competitors, offering an unparalleled opportunity to see the finest Norwegian design in ceramics, glassware, clothing, furniture, and woodworking. It also carries souvenirs, gifts, textiles, rugs, knotted Rya rugs, embroidery, and wrought iron. Goods are shipped all over the world.

⭘ **Norway Designs.** Stortingsgaten 28. ☎ **23-11-45-10.** Tram: 2, 8, or 9.

This is the only store in Norway that came into being as the result of a crafts exhibit. Shortly before it was established in 1957, an exposition of Norwegian crafts went to Chicago and New York, and it attracted a lot of attention. The upscale merchandise here—crystal, pewter, jewelry, and knitwear—emerged from the innovative designs of that exposition. The store's distinguished owner, Mr. Westlund, refuses to display or sell what he refers to as "touristic junk."

Books

Damms Antikvariat. Tollbugata 25. ☎ **22-41-04-02.** T-banen: Stortinget.

This shop, established in 1843, specializes in old and rare books, atlases, maps, and nautical prints.

Tanum Karl Johan. Karl Johans Gate 43. ☎ **22-41-11-00.** T-banen: Stortinget.

A fine bookstore in the center of town, this is the largest and most comprehensive in Oslo. It offers a vast selection, including many English titles.

Department Stores

Glasmagasinet. Stortorvet 9. ☎ **22-42-53-05.** T-banen: Stortinget. Bus: 7, 8, 11, 37, or 92.

Claiming that smaller boutiques tend to charge more, locals usually head for this big department store, which specializes in unusual home and kitchen accessories. It's the largest outlet in Norway for the Hadelands Glassverk (Glassworks); there's also a coffee shop and a restaurant.

⭘ **Steen & Strøm.** Kongensgate 23. ☎ **22-00-40-00.** T-banen: Stortinget.

The largest department store in Norway, Steen & Strøm specializes in Nordic items. Look for hand-knit sweaters and caps, hand-painted wooden dishes reflecting traditional Norwegian art, and pewter dinner plates made from old molds. There's a souvenir shop on the ground floor.

Folk Costumes

Heimen Husflid. Rosenkrantzgate 8. ☎ **22-41-40-50.** T-banen: Stortinget. Tram: 7, 8, or 11.

This leading purveyor of modern and traditional Norwegian handcrafts and apparel carries antique and reproduction folk costumes. More than three dozen different *bunads* (styles) include different regions of Norway, both north and south. Handknit sweaters in traditional Norwegian patterns are a special item, as are pewter and brass goods. It's about a block from Karl Johans Gate.

Glass

Hadeland Glassverk. Jevnaker. ☎ **61-31-64-00.** Museum admission 30 NOK ($3.35) adults, 15 NOK ($1.65) children 7–15, free for children under 7. Bus: Hønefoss/Jevnaker bus from Jernbanetorget, leaving on the hour.

The most famous name in Norwegian glass dates from 1762. You can see glass being blown and shaped, and visit a glass museum and gallery with changing exhibits. You can also buy Hadeland's complete collection and discounted "seconds." There's a restaurant on the premises. From June 15 to August 15, the museum is open daily from 9am to 7pm, shops daily 10am to 8pm. The rest of the year, the museum is open daily 9am to 3pm, shops daily from 10am to 7pm. The complex can easily be reached by public transportation; it's a 90-minute ride east of Oslo.

JEWELRY, ENAMELWARE & SILVER
✪ **David-Andersen.** Karl Johans Gate 20. ☎ **22-41-69-55.** T-banen: Stortinget.

This outstanding jeweler, established more than a century ago, sells enameled demitasse spoons and sterling silver bracelets with enamel. They're available in many stunning colors, such as turquoise and dark blue. Multicolored butterfly pins are also popular in gold-plated sterling silver with enamel. David-Andersen's collection of Saga silver was inspired by Norwegian folklore and Viking designs, combined with the pristine beauty of today's design. The store also offers an exquisite collection of pewter items.

MUSIC
Norsk Musikforlag. Karl Johans Gate 39A. ☎ **22-17-34-70.** T-banen: Stortinget.

This centrally located store's selection of CDs, records, and tapes is the best in Oslo.

PEWTER
Heyerdahl. Roald Amundsens Gate. ☎ **22-41-59-18.** T-banen: Nationaltheatret.

Between the City Hall and Karl Johans Gate, this store offers an intriguing selection of silver and gold Viking jewelry. There are also articles in pewter and other materials, including Viking vessels, drinking horns, and cheese slicers. It has an array of trolls, as well as one of Oslo's largest collections of gold and silver jewelry.

SHOPPING MALLS
Oslo has three large shopping arcades: Oslo City and Galleri Oslo, both near the Central Station, and Aker Brygge, at the west side of the harbor, a short walk from the Rådhuset.

   Oslo City, Stenersgate 1, opposite the Central Station, is the biggest shopping center in Norway—loaded with shops and restaurants.

   Also near the Central Station, **Galleri Oslo,** at Vaterland, has been called Europe's longest indoor shopping street. Businesses are open daily until midnight, including Sunday. A walkway connects Galleri Oslo to the Central Station.

   Aker Brygge is a unique shopping venue by the Oslofjord. It carries a wide variety of merchandise, and the complex also includes restaurants, theaters, cinemas, and cafes.

SOUVENIRS & GIFTS
William Schmidt. Karl Johans Gate 41. ☎ **22-42-02-88.** T-banen: Stortinget.

Established in 1853, William Schmidt is a leading purveyor of unique souvenirs. It carries pewter items (from Viking ships to beer goblets), Norwegian dolls in national costumes, woodcarvings—the troll collection is the best in Oslo—and sealskin items, such as moccasins and handbags. The shop specializes in hand-knit cardigans, pullovers, gloves, and caps. Sweaters are made from mothproofed 100% Norwegian wool.

SWEATERS
Oslo Sweater Shop. In the Radisson SAS Scandinavia Hotel, Tullins Gate 5. ☎ **22-11-29-22.** T-banen: Stortinget.

Some 5,000 handcrafted sweaters are in stock here, close to the Royal Palace. Try them on before you buy. The store has branches at the Oslo Cruise Terminal, Skur 35 (☎ **22-41-87-71**), and the Royal Christiania Hotel, Biskop Gunnerus Gate 3 (☎ **22-42-42-25**).

11 Oslo After Dark

Oslo has a bustling nightlife. Midnight is no longer the curfew hour. The city boasts more than 100 night cafes, clubs, and restaurants, 35 of which stay open until 4am.

   Autumn and winter are the seasons for cabaret, theater, and concerts. There are four cabarets and nine theater stages. Oslo is also a favorite destination of international performing artists in classical, pop, rock, and jazz music.

For movie lovers, Oslo has a lot to offer. The city has one of the most extensive selections in Europe, with 30 screens and five large film complexes. Films are shown in their original languages, with subtitles.

THE ENTERTAINMENT SCENE

The best way to find out what's happening is to pick up a copy of *What's On in Oslo,* detailing concerts and theaters and other useful information.

Oslo doesn't have agents who specialize in discount tickets, but it does have an exceptional number of free events. *What's On in Oslo* lists free happenings as well as the latest exhibits at art galleries, which can be a delightful place to spend the early part of an evening.

Tickets to the theater, ballet, and opera are sold at box offices and at **Billettsen-tralen,** Karl Johans Gate 35 (☎ 81-53-31-33). Tickets to most sporting and cultural events in Oslo can be purchased by computer at any post office in the city. The same postal clerk who sells you stamps can also sell you a voucher for a ticket to the ballet, the theater, or a hockey game.

The world-famous **Oslo Philharmonic** performs regularly under the leadership of Mariss Janson. There are no Oslo performances between June 20 and the middle of August.

If you visit Oslo in the winter season, you might be able to see its thriving opera and ballet company, **Den Norske Opera.** Plays given at the **Nationaltheatret** (where Ibsen is regularly featured) are in Norwegian. Those who know Ibsen in their own language sometimes enjoy hearing the original version of his plays.

THE PERFORMING ARTS
CLASSICAL MUSIC

✪ **Oslo Konserthus.** Munkedamsveien 14. ☎ 23-11-31-11. Tickets 200–700 NOK ($22.20–$77.70). Box office Mon–Fri 10am–5pm, Sat 11am–2pm. T-banen: Stortinget.

Two blocks from the National Theater, this is the home of the widely acclaimed Oslo Philharmonic. Performances are given autumn to spring, on Thursday and Friday. Guest companies from around the world often appear on other nights. The hall is closed from June 20 until the mid-August, except for occasional performances by folkloric groups.

THEATER

Nationaltheatret (National Theater). Johanne Dybwads Plass 1. ☎ 81-50-08-11. Tickets 150–220 NOK ($16.65–$24.40) adults, 85–170 NOK ($9.45–$18.85) for students and seniors. Box office Mon–Fri 8:30am–7:30pm, Sat 11am–6pm. T-banen: Nationaltheatret. Tram: 12, 13, or 19.

This theater at the upper end of the Students' Grove opens in August, so it may be of interest to off-season drama lovers who want to hear Ibsen and Bjørnson in the original. Avant-garde productions go up at the **Amfiscenen,** in the same building. There are no performances in July and August. Guest companies often perform plays in English.

OPERA & DANCE

✪ **Den Norske Opera (Norwegian National Opera).** Storgaten 23. ☎ 23-31-50-00. Tickets 170–320 NOK ($18.85–$35.50), except for galas. Box office Mon–Sat 10am–6pm, to 7:30pm on performance nights. Bus: 56, 62, or 66.

The Norwegian opera and ballet troupes make up Den Norske Opera. The 1931 building, originally a movie theater, was dedicated to the Norwegian National Opera in 1959. It's also the leading venue for ballet—the companies alternate performances. About 20 different operas and operettas are staged every year. There are no performances from mid-June to August. Unlike those for some European opera companies, tickets are generally available to nonsubscribers; seats can be reserved in advance and paid for with a credit card.

SUMMER CULTURAL ENTERTAINMENT

Det Norske Folkloreshowet (Norwegian Folklore Show) performs from July to early September at the Oslo Konserthus, Munkedamsveien 15 (☎ 23-11-31-11 for reservations). The 1-hour performances are on Monday and Thursday at 8:30pm. Tickets cost 160 NOK ($17.75) for adults, 90 to 110 NOK ($10 to $12.20) for children (T-banen: Stortinget).

The ensemble at the **Norwegian Folk Museum,** on Bygdøy, often presents folkdance performances at the open-air theater in the summer. See *What's On in Oslo* for details. Most shows are given on Sunday afternoon. Admission to the museum includes admission to the dance performance. Take the ferry from Pier 3 near the Rådhuset.

SPECIAL & FREE EVENTS

Oslo has many free events, including summer jazz concerts at the National Theater. In front of the theater, along the Students' Grove, you'll see street entertainers, including singers, clowns, musicians, and jugglers.

Concerts are presented in the chapel of **Akershus Castle & Fortress,** Akershus Command, on Sunday at 2pm. During the summer, promenade music, parades, drill marches, exhibits, and theatrical performances are also presented on the castle grounds.

In August the **Chamber Music Festival** at Akershus Castle & Fortress presents concerts by Norwegian and foreign musicians.

The **Oslo Jazz Festival,** also in August, includes not only old-time jazz, but also classical concerts, opera, and ballet performances.

FILMS

American and British films are shown in English, with Norwegian subtitles. Tickets are sold for specific performances only. Many theaters have showings nightly at 5pm, 7pm, and 9pm, but really big films are usually shown only once in an evening, generally at 7:30pm.

Two of the city's biggest theaters are the **Colosseum,** on Freitjoj Nansens vei 6 (T-banen: Majorstua), and **Filmteatret,** Stortingsgaten 16 (T-banen: Nationaltheatret). Most tickets cost 90 NOK ($10) for adults, half-price for children; at Monday and Thursday matinees the cost is 50 NOK ($5.55) for adults, 30 NOK ($3.35) for children. For information about all films presented in Oslo call ☎ 82-03-00-01.

THE CLUB & MUSIC SCENE

One of the most all-encompassing restaurant and nightlife complexes in Oslo is **The Restaurant Huset,** Universitatsgata 26 (☎ 22-41-36-33), a warehouse-like building formerly known as the Dixie, with a labyrinth of hallways, dance areas, and bars. In the cellar, you'll find the **New Orleans Restaurant** (☎ 22-42-44-20), devoted to the gumbos and filés you'd expect in Louisiana. Main courses, most of which are inspired by the cuisine of the Mississippi Delta, cost 60 to 210 NOK ($6.65 to $23.30). It's open daily from 5 to 11pm. Upstairs, and under the same management, is the **Barock Disco** (☎ 22-42-44-20). Three bars encircle a common dance floor with a 20-something clientele. Barock is open Thursday to Sunday from 10pm to 3:30am. Beers cost 42 NOK ($4.65) each, and entrance on disco nights costs 60 to 100 NOK ($6.65 to $11.10) per person.

In the same complex, with a somewhat more sedate clientele, is **John's Bar** (☎ 22-11-37-09), open Wednesday to Sunday 10pm till 3am. Restaurant Huset's other major venue is recommended only for those who understand rapid-fire Norwegian. **Dizzie's Cabaret Theater** (☎ 22-33-36-56) serves supper to an audience that enjoys the all-Norwegian satire and comedy acts. Theater presentations and ticket prices vary, and advance reservations are recommended. Tram: 5, 6, or 7.

DANCE CLUBS & DISCOS

Smuget. Rosenkrantzgate 22. ☎ 22-42-52-62. Cover 50–70 NOK ($5.55–$7.75) . T-banen: Stortinget.

This is the most talked-about nightlife emporium in Oslo, with long lines, especially on weekends. It's behind the Grand Hotel in a 19th-century building that was a district post office. There's an active dance floor with disco music, and a stage where live bands (sometimes two a night on weekends) perform. The clientele includes artists, writers, rock stars, and a cross section of the capital's night owls. The complex is open every night except Sunday. A restaurant serves Thai, Chinese, Norwegian, Italian, and American food from 8pm to 3am; live music plays from 11pm to 3am; and there's disco music from 10pm till very late. Half-liters of beer cost 46 NOK ($5.10); main courses run 50 to 175 NOK ($5.55 to $19.45).

A SUPPER CLUB

Bristol Night Spot. In the Bristol Hotel, Kristian IV's Gate 7. ☎ 22-82-60-30. Cover 60 NOK ($6.65). T-banen: Stortinget.

The entrance to this cellar nightclub is visible from the sidewalk near the hotel's main entrance. A popular dance bar with an intimately lit restaurant, a dance floor, and a cellar tavern, this has become one of the most popular places in Oslo. Conservative dress is suggested. A dance band starts playing at 8pm. Main dishes include poached salmon with butter-cream sauce, chateaubriand with béarnaise sauce, fillet of veal Oscar with asparagus, and mixed grill. Cocktails include a Norwegian bomb called Fjellbekk (mountain stream), made with aquavit, vodka, lime juice, and Sprite. Meals begin at 250 NOK ($27.75), drinks at 65 NOK ($7.20). It's open Monday to Saturday 9pm to 3am. Reservations are recommended.

JAZZ & ROCK

Herr Nilsen. C.J. Hambros Plass 5. ☎ 22-33-54-05. Cover 50–60 NOK ($5.55–$6.65) Wed and Sat. T-banen: Stortinget.

This is a conventional pub on most evenings, with recorded jazz. On Wednesday at 9pm and Saturday at 4pm and 11pm, live jazz is played to an appreciative audience. Expect everything from progressive jazz to Dixieland or blues. The rest of the time, entrance is free. Beer, depending on the time of the evening, costs 36 to 42 NOK ($4 to $4.65). It's open Monday to Saturday 10am to 3am, Sunday noon to 3am.

Rockefeller Music Hall. Torggata 16. ☎ 22-20-32-32. Tickets cost 60–300 NOK ($6.65–$33.30), depending on act. T-banen: Stortinget.

With a capacity of 1,200 patrons, this concert hall and club is one of the largest establishments of its kind in Oslo. It's one floor above street level in a 1910 building, formerly a public bath. Live concerts feature everything from reggae to rock to jazz. When no concert is scheduled, films are shown on a wide screen. Simple foods, such as pasta and sandwiches, are available in the cafe. Most of the crowd is in the 18 to 37 age bracket. It's usually open Sunday to Thursday 8pm to 2:30am, Friday and Saturday 9pm to 3:30am. Show time is about an hour after the doors open.

THE BAR SCENE
PUBS & BARS
Etoile Bar. In the Grand Hotel, Karl Johans Gate 31. ☎ **22-42-93-90.** T-banen: Stortinget.

This elegant bar with a Far Eastern motif is attached to Norway's most famous hotel, the Grand. You might see members of Parliament from across the street. The "Star Bar" has views of historic Oslo. Out-of-town businesspeople mingle at night with a young spirited Oslo crowd. To reach the bar, you take a special elevator to the right of the hotel entrance. Beers cost 48 NOK ($5.35), stronger drinks from 60 NOK ($6.65). The bar is open Monday to Saturday from 7pm to 12:30am.

✪ Library Bar. In the Bristol Hotel, Kristian IV's Gate 7. ☎ **22-82-60-22.** T-banen: Stortinget.

In a lobby that evokes the Edwardian era, this is a perfect spot for people-watching. You'll be sheltered behind racks of leather-bound books, which you can remove and read. It's like being in a well-furnished private club. There's live piano music at lunchtime, when you can order from a selection of open-faced sandwiches for 40 to 80 NOK ($4.45 to $8.90). Specialty cocktails have such coy names as "Take Me Home" and "Norwegian Kiss." It's open daily from 10am to 11:30pm; alcohol service starts at 1pm. A beer will cost you 49 NOK ($5.45); mixed drinks begin at 80 NOK ($8.90).

Limelight. In the Grand Hotel, Karl Johans Gate 31. ☎ **22-42-93-90.** T-banen: Stortinget.

Steeped in the atmosphere of the theater, this fashionable bar next door to the Oslo Nye Teater is a favorite rendezvous for drinks before or after a show. It's open daily from 6pm to midnight. Beer and mixed drinks cost 60 NOK ($6.65) and up.

NIGHT CAFES
Café Lorry. Parkveien 12. ☎ **22-69-69-04.** Tram: 11.

This cafe prides itself on stocking more kinds of beer (204) than any other nightclub in Scandinavia. It boasts an extensive selection of imports, but most are made in Norway, and many are so esoteric they're known only to the cognoscenti. Ask a staff member for a recommendation. One of the most expensive beers is Lone Star. Lots of patrons sing spontaneously and sudsily at the piano. The serious drinking begins after 5pm. Beer costs 46 to 50 NOK ($5.10 to $5.55). It's open Monday to Saturday from 11am to 2:30am, Sunday 11am to 2am.

GAY & LESBIAN BARS
Gay and lesbian nightlife is more limited than in Copenhagen or Stockholm, but there is some—two gay bars in a city of 500,000. Pick up a copy of *Blick* for 30 NOK ($3.35) available at most newsstands within the central city. Otherwsise call Gay/Lesbian Visitor Information (☎ **22-11-05-09**), Monday to Friday 9am to 4pm.

Club Spartacus. Pilestredet 9. ☎ **22-41-52-04.** Cover 50 NOK ($5.55).T-banen: Nationaltheatret.

Since "Spartacus" is used as a secret code word around the world indicating a gay bar, you'll know you've arrived at the right place as you approach this disco. It is one of only two men's bars in the Norwegian capital. As such it's usually a lively, hot place, and young men predominate, although there's also a fair share of older and wealthier guys hoping to make contact with that mythical Viking god. The place is primarily for drinking, talking, and flirting. Don't waste any time looking for the old "Club Castro" which appears in all gay guides around the world. Club Castro has moved and is now Club Spartacus, although these same guides will continue to list the Club Castro until the next millenniumat least. Open Tuesday to Sunday 10pm to 3:30am.

London. C. J. Hambros Plass 5. ☎ **22-70-87-00.** T-banen: Stortinget.

This place is smaller than it's only other competitor (Club Spartacus, see above), but it's undeniably more popular. Expect all kinds of gay men, from a roster of guys in suits and ties to an occasional leather master who comes in with denim and/or a full regalia of cowhides. The cellar here evokes a woodsy-looking British pub, the upstairs something that's a bit more cutting edge and high-tech. The age level here ranges from 18 to 80. It's open Tuesday to Sunday from 5pm till at least 2am. No cover.

12 Side Trips from Oslo

The Oslo area offers a variety of 1-day excursions that are manageable by boat, car, or bus. Except for boat tours of the Oslofjord (see "Organized Tours," above), getting around is a do-it-yourself activity.

   Fredrikstad is in Østfold on the east bank of the Oslofjord. A day trip can be combined with a visit to the port of **Tønsberg** on the west bank by crossing on the ferry from Moss to Horten, then heading south.

   The summer resort and ski center of **Lillehammer,** to the north, was the site of the 1994 Olympics.

FREDRIKSTAD
60 miles S of Oslo

In recent years Fredrikstad has become a major tourist center, thanks to its Old Town and 17th-century fortress. Across the river on the west is a modern industrial section; although a bridge links the areas, the best way to reach the Old Town is by ferry, which costs 5 NOK (55¢). The departure point is about 4 blocks from the Fredrikstad railroad station. Follow the crowd out the main door of the station, make an obvious left turn, and continue down to the bank of the river. You can also travel between the two areas by bus (no. 360 or 362), although most pedestrians prefer the ferry.

ESSENTIALS
GETTING THERE   By Train   Trains from Oslo's Central Station depart for Fredrikstad about every 2 hours. The trip takes about 30 minutes from central Oslo.

By Bus   There is frequent bus service daily from Oslo to Fredrikstad.

By Car   Take Highway E6 south from Oslo heading toward Moss. Continue past Moss until you reach the junction at Route 110, and follow the signs south to Fredrikstad.

VISITOR INFORMATION   The **Fredrikstad Turistkontor** is on Turistsenteret, Østre Brohode, Gamle Fredrikstad (☎ **69-32-03-30**). It's open June to September, Monday to Friday from 9am to 7pm, Saturday 10am to 7pm; October to May, Monday to Friday 9am to 4pm.

SEEING THE SIGHTS
Fredrikstad was founded in 1567 as a marketplace at the mouth of the River Glomma. **Gamlebyen** (the Old Town) became a fortress in 1663 and continued in that role until 1903, boasting some 200 guns in its heyday. It still serves as a military camp. The main guardroom and the old prison contain the headquarters and most of the exhibition space of the **Fredrikstad Museum,** Gamleslaveri (☎ **69-32-09-01**). It's open May to September, Monday to Friday from noon to 5pm, Saturday 11am to 5pm, and Sunday noon to 5pm; closed October to April. Admission is 30 NOK ($3.35) for adults, 10 NOK ($1.10) for children.

   Outside the gates of the Old Town is **Kongsten Fort,** on what was first called Gallows Hill, an execution site. When Fredrikstad Fortress was built, it was provisionally fortified in 1677, and became known as Svenskeskremme (Swede Scarer). Today's Kongsten Fort was built there, with 20 cannons, underground chambers, passages, and countermines.

Since Fredrikstad's heyday as a trading port and merchant base, the Old Town has attracted craftspeople and artisans, many of whom create their wares in historic houses and barns. Many of these glassblowers, ceramic artists, and silversmiths don't display or sell their products at their studios, but leave that to local shops. One of the best emporiums is **Plus,** Kirkegatan 28 (☎ **69-32-06-78**). It's open Monday to Friday from 10am to 4:30pm, Saturday 10am to 2pm, Sunday 1 to 3pm.

After leaving Fredrikstad, drive along the **Oldtidsveien** ("highway of the ancients"), Norway's most concentrated collection of archaeological monuments. It lies along Route 110 between Fredrikstad and Skjeberg. The ancient monuments include 3,000-year-old rock carvings at Begby, Hornes, and Solberg, and 2,000-year-old burial grounds with stone circles at Hunn.

Other attractions include **Tomta** (☎ **69-34-83-26**), the birthplace (in 1872) of explorer Roald Amundsen, at Borge, in Hvisten. A museum and monument are dedicated to him. They're between Fredrikstad and Sarpsborg, off E6. Tomta is open May to August, Friday to Sunday from 10am to 3pm; September to April, by appointment only. Admission is 25 NOK ($2.80) for adults, 10 NOK ($1.10) for children.

WHERE TO DINE

Balaklava Guestgiveri. Faergeportgate 78. ☎ **69-32-30-40.** Reservations recommended. Main courses 105–365 NOK ($11.65–$40.50). AE, DC, MC, V. Daily noon–10:30pm. Bus: Gamlebyen from the center. NORWEGIAN.

For tradition and atmosphere, this restaurant has no competition in the Old Town. It was built in 1803 as the home of the village priest in a style known in North America as "carpenter Gothic." Today, simple but flavorful meals are served in the cellar, near a massive fireplace. There's access to an outdoor courtyard. The well-prepared fare includes baked salmon with dill sauce, fillet of sole with lemon-butter sauce, fish-and-clam casserole with herbs, and an assortment of fresh game dishes.

Majorstuen. Vollportgatan 73. ☎ **69-32-15-55.** Main courses 130–199 NOK ($14.45–$22.10); pizzas (for 1–4 people) 140–170 NOK ($15.55–$18.85). AE, DC, MC, V. Sun–Thurs noon–10pm, Fri–Sat noon–11pm. INTERNATIONAL.

In an 18th-century house at the edge of the Old Town, this restaurant has a large dining room, a pub, and a warm-weather outdoor terrace. The food is unpretentious but plentiful. Among the most popular dishes are pizzas, fillet of beef served with vegetables and salad, Wiener schnitzel, fish platters, and marinated whale steak in black peppercorn sauce. Majorstuen is the only restaurant in the region that offers whale steak year-round.

TØNSBERG

64 miles S of Oslo

Bordering the western bank of the Oslofjord, Tønsberg is Norway's oldest town. It consists of a historic area, filled with old clapboard-sided houses, and the commercial center, where the marketplace is. The 40-square-mile town has some 32,000 residents.

Tønsberg was founded a year before King Harald Fairhair united parts of the country in 872, and the Viking town became a royal coronation site. Svend Foyn, who invented modern whaling and seal hunting, was born here.

ESSENTIALS

GETTING THERE   By Train   Trains depart for Tønsberg from Oslo's main railway station at intervals of between 60 and 90 minutes between around 6am and

11:30pm every day, requiring a travel time of about 90 minutes and a fare of 145 NOK ($16.10) each way. The railway station is in the town center, thanks to the fact that the island on which Tønsberg sits is connected to the mainland with a bridge. For information and schedules, call ☎ 22-17-70-30.

There is no NOR bus service from Oslo.

By Car   Take Route 18 south from Oslo via Drammen.

VISITOR INFORMATION   Tønsberg **Tourist Information** is at Nedre Langgate 36B, N-3100 Tønsberg (☎ 33-31-02-20). It's open in July daily 10am to 8pm; August to June, Monday to Friday 8:30am to 4pm. A little tourist kiosk on the island of Tjøme provides information in July, daily from 11am to 5pm.

SEEING THE SIGHTS

Slottsfjellet, a huge hill fortress near the train station, is touted as "the Acropolis of Norway." It has only some meager ruins, and people mostly visit for the view from the 1888 lookout tower, **Slottsfjelltårnet** (☎ 33-31-18-72). It's open May 18 to June 23, Monday to Friday from 10am to 3pm; June 24 to August 18, daily 11am to 6pm; August 19 to September 15, Saturday and Sunday noon to 5pm; September 16 to 29, Saturday and Sunday noon to 3pm. Admission is 10 NOK ($1.10) for adults, 5 NOK (55¢) for children.

Nordbyen is the old, scenic part of town, with well-preserved houses. **Haugar** cemetery, at Møllebakken, is in the center of town. It contains the Viking graves of King Harald's sons, Olav and Sigrød.

Sem Church, Hageveien 32 (☎ 33-36-93-99), the oldest church in Vestfold, was built of stone in the Romanesque style around 1100. It's open Tuesday to Friday from 9am to 2pm; inquire at the vestry. Admission is free.

Another attraction is **Fjerdingen,** a street of charming restored houses near the mountain farmstead. Tønsberg was also a Hanseatic town during the Middle Ages, and some houses have been redone in typical Hanseatic style—wooden buildings constructed along the wharfs as warehouses to receive shipments of goods among fellow Hanseatic League members.

Vestfold Folk Museum, Frammannsveien 30 (☎ 33-31-29-19), contains many Viking and whaling treasures. One of the chief sights is the skeleton of a blue whale, the largest mammal the world has ever known. They sometimes weigh 150 tons. There's also a real Viking ship, the *Klastad* from Tjolling, built about A.D. 800.

In the rural section of the museum, visit the **Vestfold Farm,** which includes a 1600 house from Hynne, a timbered barn from Bøen, and a storehouse from Fadum (with the characteristic apron, or platform). The Heierstadloft (about 1350) is the oldest preserved timbered building in Vestfold, and there's a smithy with a charcoal shed, a grain-drying house, and a mountain farmstead.

At the museum, you can have lunch at a real mountain farmstead. A typical meal includes *rømmergrøt* (porridge made with sour cream) and other farm foods. The area is perfect for a picnic.

Admission is 20 NOK ($2.60) for adults, 5 NOK (65¢) for children. It's open mid-May to mid-September, Monday to Saturday from 10am to 5pm, Sunday and holidays noon to 5pm; closed from mid-September to mid-May.

WHERE TO DINE

Fregatten. Storgaten 17. ☎ **33-31-47-76.** Main courses 200–220 NOK ($22.20–$24.40). AE, DC, MC, V. Mon–Sat 5–10pm. INTERNATIONAL.

In the Hotel Maritim building (in the town center), Fregatten is one of the best restaurants in Tønsberg. Main courses include fillet of reindeer with mushroom sauce and fillet of tenderloin with paprika sauce and fresh vegetables. Fresh fish is often prepared with shrimp-and-lobster sauce. It's a 10-minute walk east of the train station.

LILLEHAMMER

105 miles N of Oslo, 226 miles S of Trondheim

Surrounded by mountains, Lillehammer is a favorite resort for Europeans. The town, at the head of Lake Mjøsa, became internationally famous when it hosted the 1994 Winter Olympics.

ESSENTIALS

GETTING THERE   By Train   From Oslo, express trains take about 2 hours, 20 minutes, and local trains about 3 hours. Depending on the time of year, there are five to eight trains per day. Call ☎ 81-50-08-88 for information.

By Bus   Bus trips between Oslo and Lillehammer take about 2½ hours, and depart two or three times a day.

By Car   Head north from Oslo along E6.

VISITOR INFORMATION   The **Lillehammer Tourist Office** is at Lilletorget 1 (☎ 61-25-92-99). From mid-June to mid-August it is open Monday to Saturday 9am to 7pm. Off-season hours are Monday to Friday 9am to 4pm.

SEEING THE SIGHTS

During the peak summer season, usually June 20 to August 20, the tourist bureau schedules several excursions. They include a trip to the **Maihaugen Open-Air Museum (Sandvig Collections)** and one on **Lake Mjøsa** aboard the *White Swan of Lake Mjøsa,* an 1850s paddle steamer. Ask the tourist bureau (see "Visitor Information," above) for a list of activities.

Hunderfossen Family Park. Fåberg. ☎ **61-27-72-22.** Admission 145 NOK ($16.10) adults, 75 NOK ($8.30) seniors, 135 NOK ($15) children 3–14, free for children under 3. May–Sept, daily 10am–8pm. Closed Oct–Apr. Bus: Hunderfossen from Lillehammer.

Here you'll find an interesting presentation of the most popular Norwegian fairy tales, more than 50 activities for children and adults, and lots of space just to roam around. There is a merry-go-round and Ferris wheel, as well as carnival booths, a cafeteria, and a swimming pool. A 40-foot troll at the gate welcomes visitors. The park is 7½ miles north of Lillehammer on E6.

Lillehammer Art Museum. Stortorget. ☎ **61-26-94-44.** Admission 40 NOK ($4.45) adults, 20 NOK ($2.20) students and seniors, free for children under 12. June 17–Sept 2, Mon–Wed 11am–4pm, Thurs–Sun 11am–5pm; Sept 3–June 16, Tues–Sun 11am–4pm.

This museum, in the center of town, displays one of Norway's largest collections of national art. The pieces date from the 1830s to the present. Opened in the winter of 1992, it was one of the major cultural venues during the 1994 Olympics.

✪ **Maihaugen Open-Air Museum (Sandvig Collections).** Maihaugveien 1. ☎ **61-28-89-00.** Admission 70 NOK ($7.75) adults, 30 NOK ($3.35) children 7–15, free for children under 7. June–Aug, daily 9am–6pm; May and Sept, daily 10am–5pm; Oct–Apr (indoor museum only), Tues–Sun 11am–4pm. Bus: Route 007.

This museum consists of 150 buildings, from manor farms to the cottage of the poorest yeoman worker. There are more than 40,000 exhibits. The houses reassembled here and furnished in 17th- to 18th-century style came from all over the Gudbrandsdal (Gudbrands Valley). Of particular interest is the Garmo Stave Church, built in 1200. The 37 old workshops range from gunsmithing to wood engraving. A large exhibit covers Norwegian history from 10,000 B.C. to the present. The city's concert hall is also at the museum. The two cafeterias serve Norwegian food. The museum is about half a mile (10 minutes on foot) from the town center.

Museum of Norwegian Vehicle History. Lilletorget 7. ☎ **61-25-61-65.** Admission 30 NOK ($3.35) adults; 15 NOK ($1.65) children 7–14, free for children under 7. June 15–Aug 20, daily 10am–6pm; Aug 21–June 14, Mon–Fri 11am–3pm, Sat–Sun 11am–4pm.

Norway's only vehicle museum shows the development of transportation from the first sledges and wagons to the car of today. It's east of the town center; from the bus stop, head out on Elvegata.

OUTDOOR ACTIVITIES

The **Hafjell Alpine Center,** the main venue for Olympic alpine competitions in 1994, is about 9 miles from the center of Lillehammer. It has seven lifts and 12 miles of alpine slopes. Lillehammer is also the starting point for 250 miles of prepared tracks, 3 miles of which are illuminated. The ski center has three lifts and 2 miles of alpine slopes.

Lillehammer gears up in December for its winter sports season. In addition to the ski center, there's an admission-free **skating rink.** It's open in the winter Monday to Friday from 11am to 9pm, Sunday 11am to 5pm. In the winter there are also festivals, folklore nights, and ski races.

SKIING   Lillehammer has a 307-foot slope for professionals and a smaller jump for the less experienced. The lifts take skiers 1,500 feet above sea level up the slalom slope, and more than 250 miles of marked skiing trails are packed by machines. The Lillehammer Ski School offers daily classes, and several cross-country tours are held weekly. Ask at the tourist office (see "Visitor Information," above) for details.

SPORTS FACILITIES   The **Olympiaparken** or Olympic Park (☎ 61-21-14-00) is a legacy of the 1994 Winter Games. Many sports, including gymnastics, can be performed here. For example, **Håkons Hall** (☎ 61-25-21-00), the main venue for Olympic ice hockey, is a multipurpose arena for indoor sports. It has squash courts and an indoor mountaineering wall. A guide shows visitors around the hall. Admission is 50 NOK ($5.55), free for children under 10. The hall is open May 19 to September 15, daily from 10am to 7pm; off-season, daily 11am to 4pm.

In the upper part of the park, the **Birkebeineren Nordic Center** has areas for cross-country skiing, a ski lodge, and a cafeteria. The **Kanthaugen Freestyle Facility** is one of the most compact facilities of its type in the world, with hills for aerials, moguls, and "ballet." Skiing instruction is offered on the ballet hill. The **Lysgårdsbakkene** ski-jumping facilities, centrally located in the park, have a jumping hill tower and a chair lift. The lift operates from mid-June to mid-August, daily 10am to 7pm, depending on the weather. Admission is 20 NOK ($2.20) for adults, 15 NOK ($1.65) for children under 12. Ask at the tourist office (see "Visitor Information," above) for information about any of these facilities or others nearby.

The most recent addition to the park is the **Norwegian Olympic Museum** (☎ 61-25-21-00). It's intended to capture the experience of the Lillehammer Games, and to explore the history of the Olympic spirit. Exhibitions are presented with captions in English. Admission to the museum is 50 NOK ($5.55). A double ticket, for 80 NOK ($8.90), also allows admission to the Maihaugen Open-Air Museum.

9

Bergen

In western Norway the landscape takes on an awesome beauty, with iridescent glaciers, deep fjords that slash into rugged, snowcapped mountains, roaring waterfalls, and secluded valleys that lie at the end of twisting roads. From Bergen the most beautiful fjords to visit are the Hardanger (best at blossom time, May and early June), to the south; the Sogne, Norway's longest fjord, immediately to the north; and the Nordfjord, north of that. A popular excursion on the Nordfjord takes visitors from Loen to Olden along rivers and lakes to the Brixdal Glacier.

On the Hardangerfjord you can stop over at a resort such as Ulvik or Lofthus. From many vantage points, it's possible to see the Folgefonn Glacier, Norway's second-largest ice field. It spans more than 100 square miles. Other stopover suggestions include the summer resorts (and winter ski centers) of Voss and Geilo. For resorts in the fjord district, see Chapter 10, "Exploring the Norwegian Coast."

Bergen, with its many attractions; its good hotels, boarding houses, and restaurants; and its excellent boat, rail, and coach connections, makes the best center in the fjord district. It's an ancient city that looms large in Viking sagas. Until the 14th century, it was the seat of the medieval kingdom of Norway. The Hanseatic merchants established a major trading post that lasted until the 18th century.

Bergen has survived many disasters, including several fires and the explosion of a Nazi ship during the Second World War. It's a town with important traditions in shipping, banking, and insurance, and its modern industries are expanding rapidly.

1 Orientation

ARRIVING

BY PLANE   Planes to and from larger cities such as Copenhagen and London land at the **Bergen Airport** in Flesland, 12 miles south of the city. Dozens of direct or nonstop flights go to just about every medium-sized city in Norway on such airlines as **SAS** (☎ 67-59-60-50) and **Braathens SAFE** (☎ 55-99-82-50).

Frequent **airport bus** service connects the airport to the Radisson SAS Royal Hotel, Braathens SAFE's office at the Hotel Norge, and the city bus station. Departures are every 20 minutes Monday to Friday and every 30 minutes Saturday and Sunday. The one-way fare is 40 NOK ($4.45).

BY TRAIN   Day and night trains arrive from Oslo and stations en route. For information, call ☎ **55-96-60-00.** Travel time from Oslo to Bergen is 6 to 8½ hours.

BY BUS   Express buses travel to Bergen from Oslo, Trondheim, Ålesund, and the Nordfjord area. The trip from Oslo takes 11 hours.

BY CAR   A toll is charged on all vehicles driven into the city center Monday to Friday from 6am to 10pm. A single ticket costs 10 NOK ($1.10); a book of 20 tickets, 90 NOK ($10).

The trip from Oslo to Bergen is a mountain drive filled with dramatic scenery. Because mountains split the country, there's no direct road. The southern route, E76, goes through mountain passes until the junction with Route 47; then head north to Kinsarvik and make the ferry crossing to E16 leading west to Bergen. The northern route is Highway 7, through the resort of Geilo, to the junction with Route 47; then head south to Kinsarvik. Take the ferry, and then go west on E16.

Visitors with a lot of time may spend 2 or 3 days driving from Oslo to Bergen. Fjords and snowcapped peaks line the way, and you can photograph waterfalls, fjord villages, and perhaps ancient stave churches.

To reduce driving time, motorists can use a tunnel—almost 7 miles, the longest in northern Europe—that goes between Flåm (see chapter 10) and Gudvangen. From Gudvangen, follow E16 southwest to Bergen.

VISITOR INFORMATION

The **Bergen Tourist Office,** Bryggen 7 (☎ **55-32-14-80**), provides information, maps, and brochures about Bergen and the rest of the region. It's open June to August, daily from 8:30am to 10pm; May and September, daily 9am to 8pm; October to April, Monday to Saturday 9am to 4pm. The Bergen Tourist Office can also help you find a place to stay (see "Accommodations," below), exchange foreign currency, and cash traveler's checks when banks are closed. You can also buy tickets for city sight-seeing or for tours of the fjords.

CITY LAYOUT

Bergen is squeezed between mountain ranges and bounded by water. The center of the city lies between the harbor, **Bryggen** (see "The Top Attractions," below), the railway station, and the main square, **Torgalmenningen.**

Like Rome, Bergen is said to have grown up around seven hills. For the best overall view, take the funicular to **Fløien** (see "Seeing the Sights," below). The northern section of the city is **Sandviken,** which is filled with old warehouses. The area south of central Bergen has recently been developed at an incredible rate.

In the center of Bergen, walk on cobblestoned streets as you explore the quayside with its medieval houses and the open-air fish market. The center has colonnaded shops and cafes, and in **Gamle Bergen,** you can step back to the early 19th century.

2 Getting Around

The **Bergen Card** entitles you to free bus transportation and (usually) free museum entrance throughout Bergen, plus discounts on car rentals, parking, and some cultural and leisure activities. It's a good value. Ask for it at Tourist office (see "Visitor Information," above). A 24-hour card costs 150 NOK ($16.65) for adults, 60 NOK ($6.65) for children 3 to 15. A 48-hour card is 230 NOK ($25.55) or 100 NOK ($11.10). Children under 3 generally travel or enter free.

BY BUS

The **Central Bus Station** (Bystasjonen), Strømgaten 8 (☎ 55-55-90-70), is the terminal for all buses serving the Bergen and Hardanger areas, as well as the airport bus. The station has luggage storage, shops, and a restaurant. City buses are marked with their destination and route number. For **bus information** in the Bergen area, call ☎ **177.** A network of yellow-sided city buses serves the city center only. For information, call ☎ **55-59-32-00.**

BY TAXI

Taxis are readily available at the airport. To request one, call ☎ **55-99-70-00.** A ride from the Bergen Airport to the city center costs 235 NOK ($26.10). Sightseeing by taxi costs about 325 NOK ($36.10) for the first hour and 275 NOK ($30.55) for each additional hour.

BY CAR

PARKING   Visitors can park on most streets in the city center after 5pm. For convenient indoor parking, try the **Bygarasjen Busstation** (☎ **55-56-88-70**), a large garage near the bus and train stations, about a 5-minute walk from the city center. It's open 24 hours a day and charges 10 NOK ($1.10) per hour from 7am to 5pm, 7 NOK (80¢) per hour from 5pm to 7am. You can park for 24 hours for 70 NOK ($7.75).

RENTAL CARS   You might want to rent a car to explore the area for a day or two. **Budget** (☎ **800/472-3325** in the U.S.) maintains offices at the airport (☎ **55-22-75-27**) and downtown at Lodin Leppsgate 1 (☎ **55-90-26-15**). Its least expensive car is 800 NOK ($88.80) per day, which includes the 23% government tax, collision-damage waiver, and unlimited mileage. Rates per day are lower for rentals of a week or more.

Hertz (☎ **800/654-3001** in the U.S.) has locations at the airport (☎ **55-22-60-75**) and downtown at Nygårdsgate 89 (☎ **55-96-40-70**). For a 2-day rental, its smallest car, a Renault Clio, costs 1,190 NOK ($132.10) per day, including tax, collision-damage waiver, and unlimited mileage.

Avis (☎ **800/331-2112** in the U.S.) has branches at the airport (☎ **55-22-76-18**) and downtown at Lars Hillesgate 20 (☎ **55-32-01-30**). For a 2-day rental, its smallest car, a Ford Fiesta, costs 1,200 NOK ($133.20) per day with unlimited mileage. The price does not include the 23% tax or the optional collision-damage waiver.

Of course, rates are subject to change. The lowest rates are almost always offered to those who reserve their cars from their home country before they leave.

Remember that Norway imposes severe penalties—including stiff fines and, in some cases, imprisonment—on anyone who drinks and drives.

BY FERRY

You can take a ferry across the harbor Monday to Friday from 7am to 4:15pm; they don't run on Saturday or Sunday. One-way fares are 9 NOK ($1) for adults, 5 NOK (55¢) for children. Ferries arrive and depart from either side of the harbor at Dreggekaien and Munkebryggen. For information, call ☎ **55-14-01-29.**

BY COASTAL STEAMER

Bergen is the cruise capital of Norway, home to a flotilla of well-engineered ships that carry passengers, cars, and vast amounts of freight up and down the coast. At least 10 of the boats begin and end their itineraries in Bergen and make about 30 stops en route before landing 5 to 6 days later at Kirkenes, far north of the Arctic Circle, near the

Russian border. You can book a berth on any of one of these ships for short- or long-haul transits, and do a quick bit of sightseeing while the ship docks in various ports.

Depending on the season and the category of berth you select, a full 11-day round-trip excursion from Bergen to Kirkenes and back costs $895 to $4,000 per person, double occupancy. It's best to book these cruises through the New York City office of the Bergen Line (☎ 800/323-7436 or 212/319-1300). The line owns some of the ships and acts as a sales agent for the others. If you're already in Norway, talk to any travel agent. You can make arrangements through Bergen-based **Cruise Spesialisten,** Veiten 2B, N-5020 Bergen (☎ 55-23-07-90). It has brochures and lots of information concerning the crop of newly built Norwegian cruise ships. They include *Nord Norge* (launched in 1997); *Polarys* (1996); *Nordkapp* (1996); *Nordlys* (1994); *Richard With* (1993); *Kong Harald* (1993); and the older but stalwart *Narvik* (1982), *Midnatt Sol* (1982), and *Lofoten* (1964).

Other routes head south from Bergen to Stavanger and other ports, and tours go to some of the fjords to the south. For information and reservations, contact the Bergen Line, Cruise Spesialisten (see above), or a local operator. They include **Flaggruten** (☎ 55-23-87-00), and **H.S.D.** (☎ 55-23-87-90). The firms share offices at P.O. Box 2005, Nordnes, N-5024 Bergen. Both outfits are also associated with the flotilla of express boats (☎ 55-23-40-15) that travel from Bergen up the length of the world's longest fjord, the Sognefjord. Faster than many hydrofoils, they go to the inner reaches of the fjord. They stop frequently en route to pick up cargo and passengers, and are worthy vehicles for sightseeing expeditions. Many of them dock at Bergen's inner harbor, near the Stradkaiterminalen.

Fast Facts: Bergen

Area Code   The country code for Norway is **47.** If you're calling from outside the country, the city code for Bergen is **5.** Inside Norway, no area or city codes are needed. Phone numbers have eight digits.

Banking   Bergen has dozens of banks. The most visible is **Den Norske Bank,** Torg Almenning 2 (☎ 55-21-10-00). Branches of many of its competitors can be found near the Radisson-SAS Hotel Norge, on Rådstuplass.

Bookstores   One of the best, with a wide range of books in English, is **Melvaer Libris,** in the Galleriet, Torgalmenningen 8 (☎ 55-96-28-10). It's open Monday to Friday from 9am to 8pm, Saturday 9am to 6pm.

Business Hours   Most **banks** are open Monday to Friday from 8:15am to 3:30pm, and Thursday until 6pm. Most **businesses** are open Monday to Friday from 9am to 4pm. **Shops** are generally open Monday to Wednesday and Friday from 9am to 4:30pm, Thursday 9am to 7pm (sometimes also on Friday until 7pm), Saturday 9am to 2pm.

Currency Exchange   There's a currency exchange at the Bergen Airport. In town, you can exchange money at several banks. When the banks are closed, you can exchange money at the tourist office (see "Visitor Information," above).

Dentists   Emergency care only is available at **Bergen Legevakt,** Lars Hillesgate 30 (☎ 55-32-11-20), daily from 4 to 9pm.

Doctors   For medical assistance, call **Bergen Legevakt,** Lars Hillesgate 30 (☎ 55-32-11-20), daily from 4 to 9pm. If it's not an emergency, your hotel can make an appointment with an English-speaking doctor.

Drugstores   One convenient pharmacy is **Apoteket Nordstjernen,** at the Central Bus Station (☎ 55-31-68-84). It's open Monday to Saturday from 8am to midnight, Sunday 9:30am to midnight.

Embassies & Consulates   Most foreign nationals will have to contact their embassies in Oslo if they have a problem; only the **United Kingdom** maintains a consulate in Bergen, at Carl Konowsgate 34–35 (☎ 55-94-47-05).

Emergencies   For the **police,** dial ☎ **112;** to report a **fire,** call ☎ **110;** for an **ambulance,** dial ☎ **113.**

Eyeglass Repair   A good optician is **Optiker Svabø,** Strandgaten 18 (☎ **55-31-69-51**).

Hairdressers & Barbers   One of the best in town is **Prikken Frisørsalong,** Strandkaien 2B (☎ 55-32-31-51). It's open Monday to Friday 9am to 5pm, Saturday 9am to 3pm.

Hospitals   A medical center, **Accident Clinic,** is open around the clock. It's at Lars Hillesgate 30 (☎ 55-32-11-20). There is a general hospital, but you can't go directly there; you must go through the Accident Clinic or call **Sykebesøksformidling** (Sick Call Help) at ☎ **55-32-40-60.**

Laundry   Try **Jarlens Vaskoteque,** Lille Øvregate 17 (☎ 55-32-55-04). It's near the Hotel Victoria in a little alley about 50 yards northeast of the 17th-century Korskirken church, off Kong Oscars Gate. It's open Monday to Friday from 10am to 8pm, Saturday 9am to 3pm.

Libraries   The **Bergen Public Library,** Strømgaten (☎ 55-56-85-60), is open in July and August on Tuesday, Wednesday, and Friday from 9am to 3pm, Monday and Thursday 9am to 7pm, Saturday 9am to 1pm; the rest of the year, Monday to Friday 9am to 8pm, Saturday 9am to 2pm.

Lost Property   Various agencies recover lost objects. For assistance, contact the local police station or **Tourist Information** (☎ 55-32-14-80).

Luggage Storage & Lockers   Rental lockers and luggage storage are available at the **Jernbanestasjonen** (railway station), Strømgaten 1, which is open daily from 7am to 11:50pm. The cost is 20 NOK ($2.20) per day.

Photographic Needs   Go to **Foto Knutsen,** in the Galleriet, Torgalmenningen 8 (☎ 55-31-16-78). It's open Monday to Friday 8:30am to 8pm, Saturday 9am to 4pm.

Police   Call ☎ **112.**

Post Office   The main post office is on Småstrandgaten (☎ 55-54-15-00), 1 block from Torget. It's open Monday to Friday 8am to 6pm, Saturday 9am to 3pm. If you want to receive your mail c/o General Delivery, the address is Poste Restante, N-5002 Bergen. You'll need your passport to pick it up.

Shoe Repairs   Try **Mr. Minit Sko & Nøkkelservice,** in the Galleriet, Torgalmenningen 8 (☎ 55-96-06-40). It's open Monday to Friday from 9am to 8pm, Saturday 9am to 4pm.

Taxes   Bergen adds no city taxes to the national value-added tax.

Telephone   Public telephones take 1 NOK (15¢) coins. Local calls cost 2 to 3 NOK (20¢ to 35¢). To call abroad, dial ☎ **00;** to call collect, dial ☎ **115.**

3 Accommodations

Easily found at Bryggen 7, the **Bergen Tourist Office** (see "Visitor Information," above) books guests into hotels and secures accommodations in private homes. More than 30 families take in guests during the summer. The booking service costs 15 to 30 NOK ($1.65 to $3.35), and prospective guests also pay a deposit that's deducted from the final bill. Double rooms in **private homes** usually cost 290 to 330 NOK ($32.20 to $36.65), with no service charge. Breakfast is not served.

The rates quoted for the hotels below include service and tax. Many expensive accommodations lower their rates considerably on weekends and in midsummer. We've mentioned it when these reductions are available, but the situation is fluid, and it's best to check on the spot. All our recommended accommodations come with private bathrooms unless otherwise indicated.

EXPENSIVE

Clarion Admiral Hotel. Christian Sundts Gate 9, N-5004 Bergen. ☎ **55-23-64-00.** Fax 55-23-64-64. www.admiral.no. E-mail: post@admiral.no. 205 units. MINIBAR TV TEL. Mon–Thurs 1,575 NOK ($174.85) double; 2,500–4000 NOK ($277.50–$444) suite. Fri–Sun 950 NOK ($105.45) double; 1,550–2,550 NOK ($172.05–$283.05) suite. AE, DC, MC, V. Bus: 2, 4, or 11.

When it was built in 1906, this building was one of the largest warehouses in Bergen, with six sprawling floors peppered with massive trusses and beams. In 1987, it became a comfortable, tastefully appointed hotel, and in 1998, it was enlarged and renovated into the bustling establishment you'll see today. Rooms are a bit smaller than you might hope—with small bathrooms to match—but comfortable, with excellent beds. Many rooms lack water views, but the ones that do open onto flower-bedecked balconies with the best harbor views in town.

Dining/Diversions: The restaurant, Emily, offers fixed-price menus at lunch and dinner for 210 NOK ($23.30). They're especially appealing at dinner (nightly from 6 to 10pm), when the hot platters follow an all-you-can-eat buffet. There's also a bar.

Amenities: Room service (noon to 11pm).

First Hotel Marin. Rosenkrantzgaten 8, N-5003 Bergen. ☎ **53-05-15-00.** Fax 53-05-15-01. 122 units. MINIBAR TV TEL. 1,348–1,548 NOK ($149.65–$171.85) double; 2,045 NOK ($227) suite. AE, DC, MC, V. Bus: 1, 5, or 9.

In the heart of Bergen, this first-class hotel is new and elegant, catering to an equal mix of business and leisure clients. The bedrooms are moderate to spacious in size, and each is handsomely furnished in functional, stylish Nordic modern, with tiled bathrooms that are immaculately kept. For Bergen, the hotel offers a large number of suites—34 deluxe ones in all—the best of which are a trio of penthouse units with a view so panoramic it encompasses all seven mountains surrounding Bergen. Many accommodations are reserved for nonsmokers, and the finest units are in front, overlooking the harbor.

Dining: A coffee shop, La Strada, is busy all day, but for topnotch cuisine, reserve a table in the main restaurant where continental chefs provide a savory Mediterranean cuisine nightly.

Amenities: Room service, laundry, concierge, Turkish bath, sauna, solarium, and fitness center.

⊕ **Radisson SAS Hotel Norge.** Nedre Ole Bulls Plass 4, N-5807 Bergen. ☎ **800/ 333-3333** in the U.S., or 55-57-30-00. Fax 55-57-30-01. www.radissonsas.com. E-mail: salesbgo@radissonsas.com. 345 units. A/C MINIBAR TV TEL. May–Sept, 1,895 NOK ($210.35) double; 2,000–5,000 NOK ($222–$555) suite. Oct–Apr, 1,795 NOK ($199.25) double; 2,500 NOK ($277.50) suite. Rates include breakfast. Children under 18 stay free in parents' room. DC, MC, V. Parking 150 NOK ($16.65); reserve with room. Bus: 2, 3, or 4.

In the city center, near Torgalmenningen, the Norge has been a Bergen tradition since 1885; it continues to be a favorite of visiting celebrities. The current building opened in 1962 and in 1997 the lobby was upgraded. Rooms are better than ever after a refurbishment, with double-glazed windows, bedside controls, firm mattresses, and ample bathrooms with hair dryers and trouser presses (and some with bathtubs big enough for two). Ninth-floor units open onto private balconies overlooking the flower-ringed borders of a nearby park. Non-smoking and wheelchair-accessible rooms are available.

Dining/Diversions: Ole Bull is an informal place for lunch and à la carte dinners. The best service and the best cuisine, both Norwegian and international, are in the Grillen. The American Bar is a piano bar, and Bull's Eye is an English pub. The Night Spot, in the cellar, is a leading nightlife venue.

Amenities: Room service, laundry (Monday to Friday), baby-sitting, swimming pool, solarium, sauna, Jacuzzi, gym, library, garage.

✪ **Radisson SAS Royal Hotel.** Bryggen, N-5835 Bergen. ☎ **800/333-3333** in the U.S., or 55-54-30-00. Fax 55-32-48-08. www.radissonsas.com. E-mail: salesbgo@radissonsas.com. 273 units. A/C MINIBAR TV TEL. May–Sept, 1,895 NOK ($210.35) double; Oct–Apr, 1,795 NOK ($199.25) double. Year-round, 2,200–3,500 NOK ($244.20–$388.50) suite. Rates include breakfast. AE, DC, MC, V. Parking 100 NOK ($11.10). Bus: 1, 5, or 9.

Opened in 1982, this hotel was built on the fire-ravaged site of old warehouses that had stood here since 1170. It's contemporary, with the finest services and amenities in Bergen. The guest rooms are beautifully maintained, with lithographs and comfortable, upholstered furniture. Newly renovated guest rooms have trouser presses, good mattresses, and bedside lighting. Although the bathrooms are small, they have hair dryers and phones. Some rooms are reserved for nonsmokers; some are designed for guests with disabilities.

Dining/Diversions: There's a cocktail lounge, a gourmet restaurant, Statsraaden, and the Café Royal. The hotel has a nightclub, Engelen, and a pub, Madame Felle, named after a lusty matron who ran a sailors' tavern on these premises during the 19th century. The pub's outdoor terrace (Madame Felle's Promenade) does a thriving business in the summer.

Amenities: Room service (8am to 11pm), laundry, baby-sitting, business service center, secretarial service, indoor swimming pool, sauna, and health club.

MODERATE

✪ **Augustin Hotel.** Carl Sundts gate 24, N-5004 Bergen. ☎ **55-30-40-40.** Fax 55-30-40-10. www.augustin.no. 87 units. MINIBAR TV TEL. 750–1,490 NOK ($83.25–$165.40) double. AE, DC, MC, V. Bus: 2 or 4.

The Augustin has one of the best locations in Bergen—right in the harborfront shopping district—with front rooms that have terrific harbor views. Constructed in 1909 in the Jugend or art nouveau style, Augustin has been in the same family for four generations. In 1995 it more than doubled in size by adding a new wing, with new modern rooms (equipped with all the modern trimmings) designed by award-winning Bergen architect Aud Hunskår. More traditional rooms remain in the old section. Bathrooms in both sections have both showers and tubs, along with a hairdryer and trouser press. The hotel is decorated with lots of art, many pieces from well-known contemporary Norwegian artists. Special accommodations are available for non-smokers, wheelchair users, and allergy sufferers.

One of the city's oldest taverns, the Altona, used to stand on the site of the hotel since 1600, and the tavern became known as the gathering spot for artists and musicians in west Norway. That nostalgic memory is evoked in the hotel's wine cellar, which is open to the public. The ground-floor restaurant, Kjøbmandsstuen (The Merchant's Room) has an intimate and rustic atmosphere, serving a varied menu of fish specialties and grill dishes.

Best Western Hotell Hordaheimen. Christian Sundts Gate 18, N-5004 Bergen. ☎ **55-23-23-20.** Fax 55-23-49-50. 64 units. MINIBAR TV TEL. May 15–Sept 15, Mon–Thurs 1,390 NOK ($154.30) double; Fri–Sun 790 NOK ($87.70) double. Sept 16–May 14, Mon–Thurs 1,170 NOK ($129.85) double; Fri–Sun 790 NOK ($87.70) double. Year-round, 1,290–1,490 NOK ($143.20–$165.40) suite. Rates include breakfast. AE, DC, MC, V. Bus: 1, 5, or 9.

This hotel near the harbor has long been a base for young people from nearby districts. It's operated by the Bondeungdomslaget i Bergen, an association that sponsors cultural and folklore programs. School and civic groups sometimes reserve nearly all the rooms. The hotel was built at the turn-of-the-century and renovated in stages between 1989 and 1995. Lars Kinsarvik, an internationally known designer, created the furniture in the late 19th century. Although Laura Ashley designs are widely featured in the hotel's literature, they are few in number. Some accommodations for nonsmokers are available, and some units are suitable for those with disabilities. The small, simple guest rooms are immaculate, with good beds and tiny bathrooms.

Grand Hotel Terminus. Zander Kaaesgate 6, N-5001 Bergen. ☎ **55-31-16-55.** Fax 55-21-25-01. E-mail: dhh@atm.no. 130 units. TV TEL. 1,460 NOK ($162.05) double. Rates include breakfast. AE, DC, MC, V. Parking 100 NOK ($11.10). Bus: 2 or 4.

A Bergen landmark since 1928, this hotel, located between the bus and railroad stations, offers quality and tradition. If explorer Roald Amundsen checked in today, as he once did, he would find the downstairs familiar. Once a Lutheran temperance hotel, it was most recently updated in 1994. The guest rooms have been modernized and furnished attractively in light Nordic pastels; all are equipped with such extras as radios, firm mattresses, and hair dryers in the average-size tiled bathrooms. The in-house restaurant, the Terminus Café, is known for its good value and Norwegian buffets. Guests gather in the lounge after dinner for cocktails and coffee.

✪ Quality Edvard Grieg Hotel and Suites. Sandsliåsen 50, N-5049 Sandsli. ☎ **55-98-00-00.** Fax 55-98-01-50. 153 units. MINIBAR TV TEL. Mon–Fri 1,550 NOK ($172.05) suite for 2; Sat–Sun 1,050 NOK ($116.55) suite for 2. Rates include breakfast. AE, DC, MC, V. Free parking. Bus: 30 from the Bergen bus station.

Opened in 1987, this modern, all-suite hotel—Norway's first—lies 12 miles south of Bergen and 3 miles from the airport. Luxuriously appointed suites are amply sized, with good beds in the rather small sleeping quarters, and a separate lounge. Extras include trouser presses and ironing boards. The bathrooms are excellent, with lots of shelf space and hair dryers. Some accommodations for nonsmokers are available, as are units for persons with disabilities. Three suites are wheelchair accessible. Monday to Friday, guests can dine in the intimate and expensive Mozart Restaurant, or can enjoy Norwegian and international food in the H. C. Andersen Restaurant. The lobby bar is cozy, and patrons can also dance at the Amitra nightclub. Free airport transfers are arranged for arriving and departing guests Monday to Friday from 7am to 10pm. The sixth-floor fitness center has a gym, sauna, and decent-sized pool with panoramic views.

Rosenkrantz. Rosenkrantzgate 7, N-5003 Bergen. ☎ **55-31-30-14-00.** Fax 55-31-14-76. E-mail: rosenkrantz@rainbow-hotels.no. 129 units. MINIBAR TV TEL. May 15–Sept 15, 1,250 NOK ($138.75) double. Sept 16–May 14, Sun–Thurs 1,400 NOK ($155.40) double; Fri–Sat 750 NOK ($83.25) double. Rates include breakfast. AE, DC, MC, V. Parking 100 NOK ($11.10) in adjacent covered garage. Bus: 1, 5, or 9.

This 1921 hotel, near Bryggen in the city center, is a simple, unpretentious choice. The lobby leads to a comfortable dining room and bar. The rooms are pleasantly furnished; modern amenities include hair dryers in the small bathrooms. Half the rooms are reserved for nonsmokers. Facilities include a TV lounge, a piano bar, a restaurant (Harmoni), and a nightclub (Rubinen) with live music.

Victoria Hotel. Kong Oscars Gate 29, N-5017 Bergen. ☎ **800/528-1234** in the U.S., or 55-31-50-30. Fax 55-32-81-78. www.victoriahotel.no. E-mail:mail@victoriahotel.no. 43 units. MINIBAR TV TEL. Mid-May to mid-Sept, 1,395 NOK ($154.85) double. Mid-Sept to mid-May, Mon–Thurs 940 NOK ($104.35) double; Fri–Sun 750 NOK ($83.25) double. Rates include breakfast. AE, DC, MC, V. Parking 120 NOK ($13.30). Bus: 2 or 4.

Between the harbor and the railway station, this hotel, constructed around 1912 and completely rebuilt in 1985, is a longtime favorite, offering comfort and tradition. The guest rooms are medium-sized and well furnished; half are reserved for nonsmokers. The hotel is especially proud of its art collection, primarily contemporary paintings by Norwegian artists that decorate the public areas and guest rooms. The hotel has one of only two Japanese restaurants in Bergen. There's also a breakfast room and a lounge with an open fireplace.

INEXPENSIVE

Anker Hotel. Vestre Torggate 5–7, N-5015 Bergen. ☎ **55-21-00-00.** Fax 55-21-00-01. www.bergen-guide.com/hotels.asp?id=2. 33 units. TV TEL. 650–998 NOK ($72.15–$110.80) double. Extra bed 200 NOK ($22.20). AE. DC, MC, V. Bus: 2 or 3.

One of the newest of the small hotels of Bergen, this is a cozy, family-run place known for its good rates in spite of its central location. All the medium-sized bedrooms are well furnished with comfortable mattresses and small but well-maintained bathrooms (with shower only). Children under 3 stay free in their parents' room. On site is a restaurant and pub, serving a good selection of British beers serving and moderately priced Norwegian meals. The best bet is a daily special along with the freshly made soup of the day. Live dance music is presented on the weekends in the pub, which gets quite lively by 9pm.

Hotel Ambassadeur. Vestre Torvgate 9, N-5015 Bergen. ☎ **55-90-08-90.** Fax 55-90-05-84. www.bergen-guide.com/hotels.asp?id=1. 33 units. TV TEL. 760–850 NOK ($84.35–$94.35) double. AE, MC, V. Bus: 1 or 9.

This is a small and reasonably priced hotel, housed in a 19th-century building in the town center, within walking distance of good shopping and many of the town's major attractions. It's a favorite among business travelers, young couples, and single travelers but, according to management, not recommended for families with children. (It is not suited for persons with disabilities, either.) Rooms tend to be small but are comfortably furnished—functional more than stylish. Bathrooms are a bit cramped but contain showers. Only breakfast is served. On site is a pub, Forballpuben, attracting a regular crowd of drinkers ranging in age from 20 to 45. There is also a disco on site, Trøkkeriet, luring the 18- to 20-year-old Bergener.

Hotel Dreggen. Sandbrugaten 3, N-5003 Bergen. ☎ **55-31-61-55.** Fax 55-31-54-23. www.bergen-guide.com/hotels.asp?id=10. 31 units. TV TEL. 700–900 NOK ($77.70–$99.90) double. AE, DC, MC, V. Bus: 2 or 5.

Reasonable prices and an accommodating staff make this a family favorite. Located in the heart of Bergen, this hotel is walking distance from the embarkation point for the fjords. Rather dull architecturally from the outside, it improves considerably once you enter the seven-story structure. Bedrooms are medium in size and have been recently renewed, with fresh linens, good mattresses, and spic-and-span though small bathrooms with showers.

Hotel Park. Harald Hårfagresgaten 35 and Allegaten 20, N-5007 Bergen. ☎ **55-54-44-00.** Fax 55-54-44-44. www.parkhotel.no. E-mail: booking@parkhotel.no. 40 units. TV TEL. 950 NOK ($105.45) double. Rates include breakfast. AE, V. Free parking. Bus: 11.

This converted 1890 townhouse is in an attractive university area near Grieghall and Nygård Park. The rooms are traditionally furnished, often with antiques. Accommodations vary in size but all have good beds and adequate bathrooms. In the summer, a neighboring building (furnished in the same style) accommodates overflow guests. A delicious Norwegian breakfast is served in the dining room; later in the day sandwiches, small hot dishes, and wine and beer are available there. In the summer, reserve well in advance. The Park is a 10-minute walk from the train and bus stations.

✪ **Steens Hotel.** 22 Parkveien, N-5007 Bergen. ☎ and fax **55-31-40-50.** 20 units, 16 with bathroom. TV TEL. 650–840 NOK ($72.15–$93.25) double. Extra bed 150 NOK ($16.65). Rates include Norwegian breakfast. AE, MC, V. Bus: 1 or 5.

This is a stylish 1890 house that has been successfully converted to receive guests. Owned and operated by the same family since 1950, Steens offers great accommodations at most reasonable prices. The bedrooms are moderate in size and comfortable, and the bathrooms, though small, are beautifully maintained. The interior has plenty of atmosphere in the public rooms, although the bedrooms are modern. The best rooms are in front and open onto a park. Within a short walk are the bus and railway stations, and shops and attractions in the center of town. All doubles have a private bathroom; a few singles are rented without bathroom for 620 NOK ($68.80) per night. Throughout the day coffee and light meals are served.

4 Dining

EXPENSIVE

Banco Rotto. Vågsalmenningen 14–22. ☎ **55-32-75-20.** Reservations required. Lunch platters 60–110 NOK ($6.65–$12.20); main courses 162–229 NOK ($18–$25.40). AE, DC, MC, V. Restaurant, Fri–Sat 8pm–2am; pub, Mon–Sat 6pm–1am. Bus: 1, 5, or 9. NORWEGIAN.

One of Bergen's most unusual restaurants is in a fortresslike former bank constructed in 1875. Dinners are elaborate, including such dishes as grilled fillet of beef with pepper sauce. Classic dishes get a modern spin.

The building also contains a pub with a separate entrance, a luxurious bar, and a dance floor where live bands perform every Friday and Saturday beginning at 10pm. Prices for drinks in the bar start at 62 NOK ($6.90). Diners dance free; nondiners pay 60 to 80 NOK ($6.65 to $8.90).

✪ **Finnegaardstuene.** Rosenkrantzgate 6. ☎ **55-55-03-00.** Reservations recommended. Main courses 220–275 NOK ($24.40–$30.55); fixed-price menu 520 NOK ($57.70). AE, DC, MC, V. Mon–Sat 4:30–11pm. Closed 1 week at Easter, Dec 22–Jan 8. Bus: 5, 21. NORWEGIAN/ FRENCH.

The foundations of this popular restaurant were laid around 1400, when Hanseatic League merchants used it as a warehouse. Today, some of the woodwork dates from the 1700s, and four small-scale dining rooms create a cozy atmosphere. The chefs have created magic in sleepy Bergen. The menu is well thought out, with carefully prepared dishes. It revolves around Norwegian ingredients, especially fresh fish, and classical French methods of preparation. The menu changes with the season and the inspiration of the chef. It might include platters of crayfish served with fillets of French foie gras in a cider and foie gras sauce; lime-marinated turbot with caviar sauce; gratin of monkfish with sea scallops; fillets of venison with juniper berry sauce; and breast of duck with lime and fig sauce. An appropriate and satisfying dessert is berries from the Norwegian tundra, especially lingonberries and cloudberries.

⭐ **Fiskekroen.** Zacchariasbrygge 50. ☎ **55-55-96-60.** Reservations required. Main courses 230–260 NOK ($25.55–$28.85). AE, DC, MC, V. May–Aug, Mon–Sat noon–11pm, Sun 1–10pm; Sept–Apr, Mon–Sat 4–11pm. Bus: 1, 5, or 9. FISH/GAME.

One of the smallest (36 seats) and most exclusive restaurants in Bergen, this dining room occupies rustically elegant premises in the historic Zacchariasbrygge harborfront complex. There's a panoramic view of the harbor and a menagerie of stuffed animals. Menu specialties, which change with the seasons, might include a delectable combination of salmon, wolffish, and anglerfish in lobster sauce; fried fillet of reindeer with green-pepper gravy; halibut poached in white sauce; and several preparations of venison.

⭐ **To Kokker.** Enhjørninggården. ☎ **55-32-28-16.** Reservations required. Main courses 210–275 NOK ($23.30–$30.55). AE, DC, MC, V. Mon–Sat 5–10pm. Bus: 1, 5, or 9. CONTINENTAL/ NORWEGIAN.

To Kokker ("Two Cooks") is a favorite with celebrities, including Britain's Prince Andrew and a bevy of French starlets. Savvy local foodies increasingly gravitate here for the chef's well-considered juxtaposition of flavors and textures. Menu items include such time-tested favorites as lobster soup; whitebait roe with chopped onions, sour cream, and fresh-baked bread; reindeer with lingonberry sauce; and fillet of lamb with mustard sauce and pommes Provençal. The 1703 building is adjacent to the oldest piers and wharves in Bergen. The dining room, one floor above street level, has scarlet walls, old paintings, and a solid staff that works competently under pressure, albeit without a lot of flair.

MODERATE

Holberg-Stuen. Torgalmenningen 6. ☎ **55-31-80-15.** Reservations recommended. Main courses 175–200 NOK ($19.45–$22.20). AE, DC, MC, V. Mon–Sat 11am–11pm, Sun 1–10:30pm. Bus: 1, 5, or 9. NORWEGIAN.

One floor above street level, this restaurant was established in 1927 midway between the harborfront and Ole Bulls Plass. It was named in honor of the 18th-century writer Ludvig Holberg. He divided his time between Bergen and Copenhagen, and both cities ferociously claim him as part of their cultural heritage. The setting is much like a tavern, with beamed ceilings, an open log fire, and lots of exposed wood. The well-prepared dishes include fish fillets in white-wine sauce with prawns, mushrooms, and asparagus; and a variety of meats, some of them grilled. This is a longtime favorite; you come here for old-fashioned flavors, not trendy experiments.

Wessel-Stuen. Engen 14. ☎ **55-90-08-20.** Reservations recommended. Main courses 179–290 NOK ($19.85–$32.20); fixed-price menu 85–120 NOK ($9.45–$13.30). AE, DC, MC, V. Mon–Sat 11:30am–11pm, Sun 11:30am–10pm. Bus: 2, 3, or 4. NORWEGIAN.

This restaurant (named for the 18th-century humorist Johan Herman Wessel) has all the trappings of an 18th-century wine cellar. It's decorated in old tavern style with beamed ceilings, and its adjoining pub is a famous meeting place for locals. Meals are likely to include such dishes as grilled fillet of catfish with coriander and lime, grilled tournedos with forest mushroom sauce, and breast of duck with honey-blackberry sauce. The daily steak special is one of the most popular dishes in town. The chefs can be experimental at times, but they are also soundly grounded in the classics.

INEXPENSIVE

Bryggeloftet and Stuene. Bryggen 11. ☎ **55-31-06-30.** Reservations recommended. Main courses 130–159 NOK ($14.45–$17.65); lunch smørbrød 65–79 NOK ($7.20–$8.75). AE, DC, MC, V. Mon–Sat 11am–11:30pm, Sun 1–11:30pm. Bus: 1, 5, or 9. NORWEGIAN.

The Bryggeloftet and Stuene is the best established restaurant along the harborfront. At street level, the Stuene has low-beamed ceilings, carved banquettes, and 19th-century murals of old Bergen, along with dozens of clipper-ship models. For a more formal meal, head upstairs to the Bryggeloftet, with its high ceilings and wood paneling. Dinner in either section might include fried porbeagle (a form of whitefish) served with shrimp, mussels, and white-wine sauce; roast reindeer with cream sauce; or pepper steak with a salad. Several different preparations of salmon and herring are featured, along with roast pork with Norwegian sour cabbage. This is a quintessential Norwegian place—come here if you're seeking authentic flavors.

5 Seeing the Sights

SUGGESTED ITINERARIES

IF YOU HAVE 1 DAY   See the top attractions of Bergen, including the old Hanseatic Bryggen, with its nearby museums. Explore the shops and artisans' workshops along the harbor, and, to end the day, take the funicular to Fløien for a panoramic view.

IF YOU HAVE 2 DAYS   On your first day, follow the suggestions for Day 1. On your second day, head for the Bergen area, which you can reach by public transportation. Visit Troldhaugen, Edvard Grieg's former home. In the afternoon, journey to Ole Bull's Villa, 16 miles south of Bergen.

IF YOU HAVE 3 DAYS   For your first 2 days, follow the suggestions above. On the third day, take the 12-hour "Norway in a Nutshell" tour (see "Side Trips from Bergen," below).

IF YOU HAVE 4 OR 5 DAYS   On the first 3 days, follow the itinerary above. On Day 4, explore the Hardangerfjord and the Folgefonn Glacier by round-trip bus from Bergen (see "Side Trips from Bergen," below). On the fifth day, explore the Sognefjord by express steamer, going by bus through Voss, and returning by train to Bergen (see "Side Trips from Bergen," below).

THE TOP ATTRACTIONS

In addition to the sights below, take a stroll around ✪ **Bryggen.** This row of Hanseatic timbered houses, rebuilt along the waterfront after a disastrous fire in 1702, is what remains of medieval Bergen. The northern half burned to the ground in 1955. Bryggen has been incorporated into UNESCO's World Heritage List as one of the most significant cultural and historical re-creations of a medieval settlement, skillfully blending with the surroundings of modern Bergen. It's a center for arts and crafts, where painters, weavers, and craftspeople have their workshops. Some workshops are open to the public.

Bergen Aquarium. Nordnesbakken 4. ☎ **55-55-71-71.** Admission 80 NOK ($8.90) adults, 50 NOK ($5.55) children. May–Sept, daily 9am–8pm; Oct–Apr, daily 10am–6pm. Bus: 11 from the fish market.

A 15-minute walk from the city center, this aquarium is one of the largest and finest in Scandinavia. The exceptional marine life includes seals, penguins, lobsters, and piranhas. In the outer hall you can get the feel of the fish—dip your hand into the shallow pool of unpolluted water pumped up from a depth of 400 feet in the fjord outside. Nine glass tanks, each containing about 62,500 gallons of water, ring the hall. Downstairs, a wide range of marine life in 42 small aquariums demonstrates many colorful forms of sea life and illustrates evolutionary development. A popular attraction is seal and penguin feeding time. In the summer, they eat daily at 11am, 2pm, and 6pm; in the winter, daily at noon and 4pm.

Impressions

Reaching Bergen we fail to find it particularly attractive. Everything is fishy. You eat fish and drink fish and smell fish and breathe fish.
    —Lilian Leland, *Traveling Alone: A Woman's Journey Round the World,* 1890

Bergen Art Museum. Rasmus Meyers Allé 3–7 and Lars Hillesgate 10. ☎ **55-56-80-00.** Admission 35–50 NOK ($3.90–$5.55) adults, free for children. May15–Sept 15, daily 11am–5pm; Sept 16–May 14, Tues–Sun 11am–5pm. Bus: 1, 5, or 9.

In the center of the city, this museum displays works by Norwegian and international artists. It has three galleries: the Bergen Billedgalleri, the Stenersen Collection, and the Rasmus Meyers Collection. Picasso, Braque, Miró, and Kandinsky are represented here, and the Stenersen Collection has one of Europe's finest assemblages of the works of Paul Klee. In the Rasmus Meyers Collection, you can see some of Edvard Munch's most important works. In the Bergen Billedgalleri are excellent examples of paintings from some of Norway's leading "old masters," including Munch, I. C. Dahl, Lars Hertervig, Christian Krohg, and Harriet Backer.

Bryggens Museum. Bryggen. ☎ **55-58-80-10.** Admission 30 NOK ($3.35) adults, free for children. May–Aug, daily 10am–5pm; Sept–Apr, Mon–Fri 11am–3pm, Sat noon–3pm, Sun noon–4pm. Bus: 20, 21, 22, 23, 50, 70, 71, 80, and 90.

This museum displays artifacts unearthed during extensive archaeological excavations of Bryggen from 1955 to 1972. Exhibits include remains of the oldest buildings in Bergen (from the 12th century) in their original settings. You can also see runic inscriptions and changing exhibits. The museum illustrates the daily and cultural life of Bergen in the Middle Ages.

❂ Det Hanseatiske Museum. Finnegårdsgaten 1A, Bryggen. ☎ **55-31-41-89.** May–Sept, admission 40 NOK ($4.45) adults; Oct–Apr, admission 25 NOK ($2.80) adults; free for children. June–Aug, daily 9am–5pm; Sept–May, daily 11am–2pm. Bus: 1, 5, or 9.

In one of the best-preserved wooden buildings at Bryggen, this museum illustrates Bergen's commercial life on the wharf centuries ago. German merchants, representatives of the Hanseatic League centered in Lübeck, lived in these medieval houses built in long rows up from the harbor. With dried cod, grain, and salt as articles of exchange, fishers from northern Norway met German merchants during the busy summer season. The museum is furnished with authentic articles dating from 1704.

Fløibanen. Vetrlidsalm 23A. ☎ **55-31-48-00.** Round-trip 40 NOK ($4.45) adults, 20 NOK ($2.20) children. May 25–Aug, Mon–Fri 7:30am–midnight, Sat 8am–midnight, Sun 9am–midnight; Sept–May 24, Mon–Thurs 8am–11pm, Fri 8am–11:30pm, Sat 8am–11:30pm, Sun 9am–11pm. Bus: 6.

A short walk from the fish market is the station where the funicular heads up to Fløien, the most famous of Bergen's seven hills. The view of the city, the neighboring hills, and the harbor from 1,050 feet is worth every øre.

Gamle Bergen. Elsesro and Sandviken. ☎ **55-25-78-50.** Admission 40 NOK ($4.45) adults, 20 NOK ($2.20) children and students. Houses, mid-May to Aug only, guided tours daily on the hour 10am–4pm. Park and restaurant, daily noon–6pm. Bus: 1 or 9 from the city center (every 10 minutes).

This collection of houses from the 18th and 19th centuries is set in a park. The Old Town is complete with streets, an open square, and narrow alleyways. Some of the interiors are exceptional, including a merchant's living room in the typical style of the

Bergen Attractions

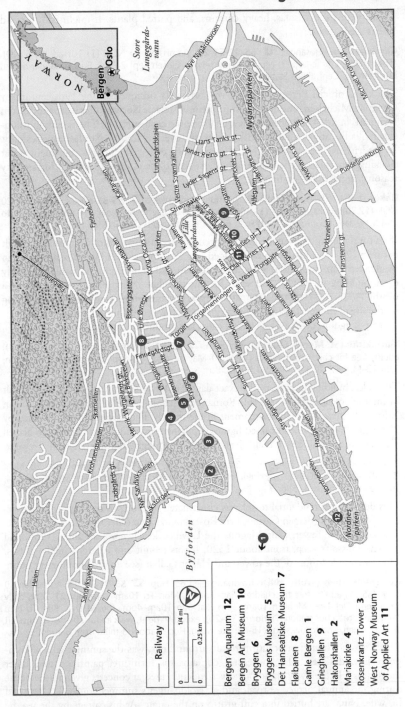

Railway

1/4 mi
0.25 km

Bergen Aquarium **12**
Bergen Art Museum **10**
Bryggen **6**
Bryggens Museum **5**
Det Hanseatiske Museum **7**
Fløibanen **8**
Gamle Bergen **1**
Grieghallen **9**
Hakonshallen **2**
Mariakirke **4**
Rosenkrantz Tower **3**
West Norway Museum
of Applied Art **11**

1870s, with padded sofas, heavy curtains, and potted plants. It might call to mind Ibsen's *Doll's House*.

Gamlehaugen. Fjøsanger. ☎ **55-92-51-20.** Admission 10 NOK ($1.10) adults, 5 NOK (55¢) children. June–Sept 1, Mon–Fri 10am–1pm. Closed Sept 2–May. Bus: Fjøsanger-bound bus from the Central Bus Station.

The king's official Bergen residence was originally occupied in the 19th century by Christian Michelsen, one of the first prime ministers of Norway after it separated from Denmark in 1814. It's open for just a short time each summer. The rambling wood-sided villa lies about 6 miles south of the city, overlooking the Nordåsvannet estuary. Its gardens are open to the public all year. Don't expect the hoopla you might see at Buckingham Palace—the venue is understated, discreet, and (probably for security reasons) aggressively mysterious.

Håkonshallen (Håkon's Hall). Bergenhus, Bradbenken. ☎ **55-31-60-67.** Admission 20 NOK ($2.20) adults, 10 NOK ($1.10) children. Mid-May to Aug, daily 10am–4pm; Sept to mid-May, daily noon–3pm, Thurs until 6pm. Closed various days in May.

If you walk along the water from Bryggen, you come upon the Håkonshallen, built between 1247 and 1261. It was damaged in a 1944 fire caused by the explosion of an overloaded Nazi munitions ship, and later restored. The explosion damaged nearly every building in Bergen, and sent the ship's anchor flying almost to the top of a nearby mountain. Håkonshallen is the largest and most imposing building remaining on the site of the royal residence of Bergen, which was the political center of the 13th-century kingdom of Norway. Guided tours are conducted hourly.

Mariakirke (St. Mary's Church). Dreggen. ☎ **55-31-59-60.** Admission 10 NOK ($1.10) adults, free for children; free to all Sept 10–May 17. May 18–Sept 9, Mon–Fri 11am–4pm; Sept 10–May 17, Tues–Fri noon–1:30pm. Bus: 5, 9, 20, 21, or 22.

The oldest building in Bergen (the exact date is unknown, but it could have been built in the mid–twelfth century) is this Romanesque church, one of the most beautiful in Norway. Its altar is the oldest ornament in the church. The baroque pulpit, donated by Hanseatic merchants, bears carved figures depicting everything from Chastity to Naked Truth. Church music concerts are given from May through August several nights a week.

Rosenkrantz Tower. Bergenhus, Bradbenken. ☎ **55-31-43-80.** Admission 20 NOK ($2.20) adults, 10 NOK ($1.10) children. May 15–Aug 31, daily 10am–4pm; Sept 1–May 14, Sun noon–3pm. Bus: 1, 5, or 9.

This defense and residential tower was constructed in the 13th century by the governor of Bergenhus (Bergen Castle), Erik Rosenkrantz. Two older structures were incorporated into the tower: King Magnus the Lawmender's keep, from about 1260, and Jørgen Hanssøn's keep, from about 1520. It was rebuilt and enlarged in the 1560s. There are guided tours of the tower and Håkonshallen (see above) about every hour.

✪ Troldhaugen (Trolls' Hill). Troldhaugveien 65, Hop. ☎ **55-91-17-91.** Admission 50 NOK ($5.55) adults, free for children. Jan–Apr 20, Mon–Fri 10am–2pm; Apr 21–Sept, daily 9am–6pm; Oct–Nov, Mon–Fri 10am–2pm, Sat–Sun 10am–4pm. Closed Dec. Bus: To Hop from the Bergen bus station (Platforms 18–20); exit, turn right, walk about 200 yards, turn left at Hopsvegen, and follow signs (15-minute walk). Hop is about 3 miles from Bergen.

This Victorian house, in beautiful rural surroundings, was the summer villa of composer Edvard Grieg. The house still contains his furniture, paintings, and other mementos. His Steinway grand piano is frequently used at concerts given in the house during the annual Bergen festival, and at Troldhaugen's summer concerts. Grieg and his wife, Nina, are buried in a cliff grotto on the estate. At his cottage by the sea, he composed many of his famous works.

Vestlandske Kunstindustrimuseum (West Norway Museum of Applied Art). Permanenten, Nordahl Bruns Gt. 9. ☎ **55/32-5108.** Admission 35 NOK ($3.90). May 15–Sept 14, Tues–Sun 1am–4pm; Sept 15–May 14, Tues–Sun noon–4pm. Bus 1, 5, or 9.

In the center of Bergen, this unique (for Norway) museum has one of the largest collections of Chinese applied art outside China. Its main attraction is a series of huge marble Buddhist temple sculptures created over a range of centuries. The collection also includes applied art from 1500 to the present day, with special attention paid to the Bergen silversmiths of the 17th and 18th centuries, who were celebrated for their heavy but elaborate baroque designs. Their collection of tankards, for example, is stunning. Most of them are embossed with flora motifs and others are inlaid with silver coins.

IN NEARBY LYSØEN

To reach the island of Lysøen, 16 miles south of Bergen, drive or take a bus (from Platform 20 at the Bergen bus station, marked FANA-OS-MILDE) to Sørestraumen on Road 553. Take the Ole Bull ferry across the channel from Sørestraumen, Buena Kai. The round-trip fare is 30 NOK ($3.35) for adults, 15 NOK ($1.65) for children. When the museum and villa are open, ferry schedules coincide with the site's hours, and boats depart for the mainland at hourly intervals. The last boat leaves a few minutes after the museum closes.

Museet Lysøen/Ole Bull's Villa. Lysøen. ☎ **56-30-90-77.** Admission 25 NOK ($2.80) adults, 10 NOK ($1.10) children. Guided tours, early May–Sept Mon–Sat noon–4pm, Sun 11am–5pm. Closed Oct–early May. Transportation: See "Organized Tours," below.

This villa and concert hall were built in 1872–73 for the world-famous violin virtuoso and Norwegian national hero, Ole Bull. The building, now a national monument, is preserved as it was when the musician died in 1880. Eight miles of trails built by Bull meander around the island.

ORGANIZED TOURS

For information about and tickets to tours, contact **Tourist Information,** Bryggen 7 (☎ 55-32-14-80).

The most popular and most highly recommended tour of Bergen is the 3-hour city bus tour. It departs daily at 10am and covers the major attractions, including Troldhaugen and "Old Bergen." It operates May to September and costs 230 NOK ($25.55) for adults, 100 NOK ($11.10) for children.

6 Outdoor Activities

FISHING   In the region around Bergen, anyone can fish in the sea without restrictions. If you plan to fish in fresh water (ponds, streams, and most of the best salmon and trout rivers), you'll need a permit. These are sold at any post office. You'll also need the permission of the owner of the land on either side of the stream. Information and fishing permits, which cost 95 to 150 NOK ($10.55 to $16.65), are available from **Bergen Sportsfiskere** (Bergen Angling Association), Fosswinckelsgate 37 (☎ 55-32-11-64). It's open Monday to Friday from 9am to 2pm.

GOLF   The **Åstvelt Golf Course** (☎ 55-18-20-77) has nine holes and is open to nonmembers; call in advance. It's a 15-minute drive north of Bergen on E16. You can also take the Åsane bus from the central station in Bergen. Greens fees are 180 NOK ($20).

SWIMMING   The **Sentralbadet,** Theatersgaten 37 (☎ 55-56-95-70) has a heated saltwater indoor pool. An open-air pool whose season is limited to the fleeting Nordic summer is at **Nordnes Sjøbad,** Nordnes (☎ 55-90-21-70). For hours, check with the tourist office. At either pool, adults pay 20 NOK ($2.20), children 15 NOK ($1.65).

TENNIS   Paradis Sports Senter, Highway R1, Paradis (☎ 55-91-26-00), lies 4 miles south of Bergen. The club has five indoor courts, four squash courts, four badminton courts, a health club and gym, and a solarium. It's open Monday to Friday from 9am to 10pm, Saturday 10am to 6pm, Sunday noon to 9pm.

WALKING   Only 10 minutes away from town by the funicular, several roads and footpaths lead to **Mount Fløien,** an unspoiled wood and mountain terrace with lakes and rivers.

The **Bergen Touring Club,** Tverrgaten 4–6 (☎ 55-32-22-30), arranges walking tours farther afield and supplies information on huts and mountain routes all over Norway. It also provides maps and advice on where to hike. The office is open Monday to Friday 10am to 4pm (until 6pm on Thursday).

7 Shopping

Shoppers who live outside Scandinavia and spend more than 300 NOK ($33.30) in a tax-free tourist shop can receive a refund of 10% to 15% of the purchase price when they leave Norway. See "Taxes" in "Fast Facts: Norway," in Chapter 7, "Planning a Trip to Norway."

THE SHOPPING SCENE

Bargain hunters head to the **Marketplace (Torget).** Many local handcrafts from the western fjord district, including rugs and handmade tablecloths, are displayed. This is one of the few places in Norway where bargaining is welcomed. The market keeps no set hours, but is best visited between 8am and noon. Take bus no. 1, 5, or 9.

HOURS   Stores are generally open Monday to Friday from 9am to 4pm (until 6pm Thursday and sometimes Friday), Saturday 9am to 1 or 3pm. Shopping centers outside the city are open Monday to Friday from 10am to 8pm, Saturday 9am to 4pm. Some food stores stay open until 8pm Monday to Friday and 6pm on Saturday.

SHOPPING A TO Z
DEPARTMENT STORE

Sundt & Co. Torgalmenningen. ☎ 55-32-31-00.

Many Bergeners remember this leading department store from childhood shopping expeditions with their parents. The store now faces stiff competition from such newer emporiums as Galleriet (see "Shopping Mall," below).

FASHION

Kløverhuset. Strandgaten 13–15. ☎ 55-31-37-90.

Next to the fish market on the harbor, this four-story shopping center has been Bergen's largest fashion store since 1923. Besides the latest in modern design, it also offers bargains, such as moderately priced and attractively designed knit sweaters, gloves, and Lapp jackets. The special gift shop is open only in the summer.

Viking Design. Strandkaien 2A. ☎ 55-31-05-20.

Opposite the Flower Market, this shop has the most unusual knitwear in Bergen—many of the its designs have even won prizes. In addition to fashion, there is also a selection of quality pewter produced in Bergen, along with a selection of intriguing Norwegian gifts and souvenirs. Items purchased can be shipped abroad.

Shopping Tour

Norway has a centuries-old tradition of crafts, which undoubtedly developed to help people pass the time during the cold, dark winters when farm families were more or less housebound for many months. Some of the major crafts were woodcarving, weaving, and embroidery, and these skills live on today at many local artists and crafts centers. Some of the best areas include Hardanger (around the Hardanger-fjord, near Bergen); and Song (just north of the Sognefjord, also near Bergen); and Telemark (the district around Skien, within a day's drive from Oslo). For a true, behind-the-scenes look at Norway **Five Stars of Scandinavia,** 13104 Thomas Rd., KPN, Gig Harbor, WA 98329 (☎ **800/722-4126**), will set up a self-drive, self-guided tour, factoring in everything they know about local artisans which you can then visit on your own wheels.

HANDCRAFTS

In and around **Bryggen Brukskunst,** the restored Old Town near the wharf, many craftspeople have taken over old houses and ply ancient Norwegian trades. Crafts boutiques often display Bergen souvenirs, many based on designs 300 to 1,500 years old. For example, we purchased a reproduction of a Romanesque-style cruciform pilgrim's badge. Other attractive items are likely to include sheepskin-lined booties and exquisitely styled hand-woven wool dresses.

Prydkunst-Hjertholm. Olav Kyrres Gate 7. ☎ **55-31-70-27.**

The leading outlet for glassware and ceramics purchases much of its merchandise directly from the artisans' studios. The quality goods include glass, ceramics, pewter, wood, and textiles. Gift articles and souvenirs are also available.

JEWELRY

Juhls' Silver Gallery. Bryggen. ☎ **55-32-47-40.**

Next to the SAS Royal Hotel, along the harborfront, Juhls' displays the town's most unusual selection of quality jewelry. The designers take for their inspiration the constantly changing weather of the far north, and, in their words, provide "a cultural oasis in a desert of snow."

SHOPPING MALL

Galleriet. Torgalmenningen 8. ☎ **55-32-45-50.**

This is the most important shopping complex in the Bergen area, with 70 stores offering tax-free shopping. Close to the fish market, it displays a wide array of merchandise and features summer sales and special exhibitions. It has several fast-food establishments, too.

8 Bergen After Dark

THE PERFORMING ARTS

Grieghallen. Lars Hillesgate 3A. ☎ **55-21-61-50.** Tickets 90–300 NOK ($10–$33.30). Closed July. Bus: 2, 3, or 4.

The modern Grieg Hall, which opened in 1978, is Bergen's monumental showcase for music, drama, and a host of other cultural events. The stage is large enough for an entire grand opera production, and the main foyer comfortably seats 1,500 guests for lunch or dinner. Snack bars provide drinks and light snacks throughout the performances. The upper floors house the offices of the Philharmonic Orchestra.

The Bergen Symphony Orchestra, founded in 1765, performs here from August to May, often on Thursday at 7:30pm and Saturday at 12:30pm. Its repertoire consists of classical and contemporary music, as well as visiting opera productions. International conductors and soloists perform.

Den National Scene. Engen 1. ☎ **55-54-97-10.** Tickets 180–280 NOK ($20–$31.10). Bus: 2, 3, or 4.

September to June is the season for Norway's oldest theater, founded in the mid–19th century. It stages classical Norwegian and international drama, contemporary plays, and musical drama, as well as visiting productions of opera and ballet.

SUMMER CULTURAL ENTERTAINMENT

Bergen Folklore. Bryggens Museum, Bryggen. ☎ **55-31-95-50.** Tickets 95 NOK ($10.55) adults, free for children. Bus: 1, 5, or 9.

The Bergen Folklore dancing troupe performs from June to August on Tuesday and Thursday at 9pm. The program, which lasts about an hour, consists of traditional folk dances and music from rural Norway. Tickets are on sale at Tourist Office (see "Visitor Information," above) and at the door.

FILMS

Bergen has two large movie theaters, **Konsertpaleet,** Neumannsgate 3 (☎ **55-56-90-83**), and **Forum,** in Danmarkplass (☎ **55-29-80-70**), that show all films in their original versions. The earliest performance is at 11am, the latest at 11pm. Tickets usually cost 60 NOK ($6.65).

THE CLUB & MUSIC SCENE

Engelen. In the Radisson SAS Royal Hotel, Bryggen. ☎ **55-54-30-00.** Cover 50 NOK ($5.55), free to hotel guests. Bus: 1, 5, or 9.

This is one of Bergen's more elegant discos. Wednesday to Friday night, an older, sedate crowd gathers to enjoy the music and ambience. On Saturday, beware—the atmosphere changes drastically with the arrival of noisy, fun-seeking 20-somethings. Light meals are available. Drink prices begin at 65 NOK ($7.20), 49 NOK ($5.45) for a beer. It's open Wednesday to Saturday from 9pm to 3am.

Maxime. Ole Bulls Plass. ☎ **55-30-71-20.** Cover 50 NOK ($5.55) for the disco. Bus: 2, 3, or 4.

One of Bergen's most reliable drinking venues caters to men and women who are unattached (or trying to be). In a prominent location near the Hotel Norge, it boasts three bar areas. Sandwiches and platters of food are served every day from noon to around 9:30pm, making it a well-known lunchtime spot. The bars are open Monday to Saturday from 7pm to 1am, Sunday 3pm to 1am. Less popular, but a viable alternative on Saturday night, is the cellar-level disco. It's open Thursday to Saturday 11pm to 2:30am. Regardless of where you drink it, a large beer costs 46 NOK ($5.10).

Rick's Café. Veiten 3. ☎ **55-35-31-31.** No cover. Bus: 1, 5, or 9. No one under 24 permitted.

This is something of a labyrinth, with rooms devoted to the after-dark pursuit of cabaret and comedy (there's a small stage for small-scale acts); some serious drinking (on cold winter's nights, things can get rather sudsy); or a general, friendly pick-up (no doubt encouraged by the bar's potent cocktails). It's open Wednesday to Saturday from 5pm till around 2am, depending on business.

Rubinen. Rosenkrantzgate 7. ☎ **55-31-74-70.** Cover 50 NOK ($5.55). Bus: 2, 3, or 4.

Rubinen is one of Bergen's most popular nightclubs, attracting an over-35 crowd of mostly married couples. It plays all kinds of music, including country-western and rock. Drinks cost about 50 NOK ($5.55). It's open Wednesday to Saturday from 10pm to 3am, with live music nightly.

THE BAR SCENE
The English Pub. Ole Bulls Plass. ☎ **55-30-71-39.** Bus: 2, 3, or 4.

This is one of the most authentic duplications of a merrie Olde English pub in Norway, with battered paneling, a pool table, much-used dartboards, foaming mugs of beer, and a clientele composed of equal parts local office workers and nearby residents. It's open Monday to Thursday from 7pm to 2am, Friday to Sunday from 3pm till 2am.

Kontoret Pub. In the Hotel Norge, Ole Bulls Plass 8–10. ☎ **55-90-07-60.** Bus: 2, 3, or 4.

The most frequented pub in the city center, the Kontoret is next to the Dickens restaurant and pub. Drinkers can wander freely between the two places, which are connected and also accessible through exterior doors. In the Kontoret Pub you can order the same food served at Dickens, although most people seem to come here to drink. The local brew is called Hansa; a half-liter of draft beer is 48 NOK ($5.35). It's open Sunday to Thursday from 4pm to 1am, Friday and Saturday 4pm to 3am.

Zacchariasbrygge Pub. Zacchariasbrygge 50. ☎ **55-55-96-40.** Bus: 2, 3, or 4.

On the harborfront of Old Bergen, in the same oxblood-colored former warehouse as the restaurant Fiskekroen (see "Dining," above), this is one of Bergen's most popular, and sometimes noisiest, pubs. Piano music and a live singer accompany copious quantities of flowing suds. A half-pint of lager goes for 46 NOK ($5.10), and French and Italian wines by the glass cost about the same. There's additional, quieter seating upstairs. Open Monday to Friday from noon to 12:30am, Saturday noon to 12:30am, Sunday 1pm to 12:30am.

A GAY CAFE
Café Fincken. Nygårdsgaten 2A. ☎ **55-32-13-16.** Bus: 2, 3, or 4.

This cafe and bar serves refreshments, wine, and beer. It's open Monday to Saturday from noon to 2am, Sunday 3pm to 2am. The clientele is mostly gay and lesbian. There's a new art exhibition every month.

9 Side Trips from Bergen

Norway's longest and deepest fjord, the **Sognefjord,** is a geologic and panoramic marvel. The terrain soars upward from the watery depths of the North Atlantic, and many waterfalls punctuate its edges with spray. The best way to view it involves a full-day jaunt that's possible only between May 18 and September 15. It combines self-guided travel by boat, bus, and rail. Begin by heading to the Bergen harborfront (the Strandkaien), where you'll board a ferry for the 4½-hour ride to the fjordside hamlet of Gudvangen. A bus carries participants on to the town of Voss (see Chapter 10, "Exploring the Norwegian Coast"). In Voss, after exploring the town, you can board a train to carry you back to Bergen. Many schedule permutations are possible, but one that's particularly convenient involves leaving Bergen at 8:30am and returning at 5:15pm. The combined round-trip fare is 550 NOK ($61.05). Details on this and on several other explorations by public transport are available from Tourist Office (see "Visitor Information," above).

NORWAY IN A NUTSHELL   This 12-hour tour has been cited as the most scenically captivating 1-day tour of Norway. Its breadth and diversity of landscapes encapsulates the majesty of the country's fjords and mountains.

Several different transit options operate throughout the day. The one most aggressively recommended by Bergen's Tourist Office runs from June to August only. It starts at 8:30am at **Bergen's** railway station. After a 2-hour train ride, you disembark in the mountaintop hamlet of **Myrdal,** where you sightsee for about 40 minutes. In Myrdal, you board a cog railway for one of the world's most dramatically inclined train rides. The trip down to the village of **Flåm,** a drop of 2,900 feet, takes an hour and passes roaring streams and seemingly endless waterfalls.

After a 2-hour stopover in Flåm, where you can have lunch or take a brief hike, you board a fjord steamer for a ride along the Sognefjord. You reach the fjordside town of Gudvangen after a 2-hour ride. After 30 minutes in Gudvangen, you board a bus for the 75-minute ride to Voss. There you spend 30 minutes before boarding a train for the 75-minute ride back to Bergen. Arrival is scheduled for 8:18pm.

Expect only a rushed overview of each town for there is more scenery than you can digest in a 12-hour day. The round-trip fare, excluding meals, is 560 NOK ($62.15) for adults, 280 NOK ($31.10) for children under 12. There are discounts for holders of Eurail or Scanrail passes. For more information, contact Bergen's **Tourist Office** (☎ **55-32-14-80**).

10

Exploring the Norwegian Coast

The west coast of Norway is the heart of the fjord country (see map, page 165). Fjords are narrow arms of the sea that snake inland. It took 3 million years to form the furrows and fissures that give the Norwegian coast its distinctive look. At some points the fjords become so narrow that a boat can hardly wedge between the mountainsides.

Bergen is the best departure point for trips to the fjords. To the south lies the famous Hardangerfjord, and to the north, the Sognefjord, cutting 111 miles inland. We'll begin our journey in Bergen, heading north by coastal steamer.

1 By Coastal Steamer

Coastal steamers are elegantly appointed ships that travel along the Norwegian coast from Bergen to Kirkenes, carrying passengers and cargo to 34 ports. A total of 11 ships make the journey year-round. Along the route, the ships sail through Norway's more obscure fjords, revealing breathtaking scenery and numerous opportunities for adventure. At points along the way, passengers have the opportunity to take sightseeing trips to the surrounding mountains and glaciers, and excursions on smaller vessels.

The chief cruise operator is the **Norwegian Coastal Voyage/Bergen Line,** 405 Park Ave., New York, NY 10022 (☎ **800/323-7436** or 212/319-1300). Various packages are available. Tours may be booked heading north from Bergen, south from Kirkenes, or round-trip. The 7-day one-way northbound journey costs $636 to $2,865 per person, including meals and taxes. The 12-day one-way voyage from Bergen to Kirkenes is $643 to $2,370 per person. For information on these and other trips, including air-cruise packages from the United States, contact the Bergen Line.

We'll focus on two of the most popular and interesting ports of call along the coastal steamer route.

HAMMERFEST
1,438 miles N of Bergen, 90 miles N of Alta, 1,364 miles N of Oslo

The Hammerfest area stretches from Måsøy, near the North Cape, to Loppa in the south. The wide region includes the rugged coasts along the Arctic Sea. The regional capital, Hammerfest, often serves as a base for exploring the North Cape.

Hammerfest is a major traffic hub, and in the summer there's a wide choice of boat and bus excursions. The tourist office can tell you what's available.

ESSENTIALS

GETTING THERE　If you don't take the coastal steamer, you can drive, although it's a long trek. From Oslo, take E6 north until you reach the junction with Route 94 west. Hammerfest is at the end of Route 94. During the summer, there are three buses a week from Oslo. Travel time is 29 hours. SAS has daily flights from Oslo and Bergen to Alta, where you can catch a bus to Hammerfest (April to September only). For bus information, call **Finnmark Fylkesrederi** (☎ 78-40-70-00).

VISITOR INFORMATION　The **Hammerfest Tourist Office,** Strandgate (☎ 78-41-21-85), in the town center, is open daily from 8am to 6pm.

SEEING THE SIGHTS

This is the world's northernmost town of significant size, and a port of call for North Cape coastal steamers. Destroyed during the Second World War by the retreating Nazis, it has long since been rebuilt. Lapps from nearby camps often come into town to shop. Count yourself lucky if they bring their reindeer.

The port is ice free year-round, and shipping and exporting fish is a major industry. The sun doesn't set from May 12 to August 1—and doesn't rise from November 21 to January 23.

For a panoramic view over the town, take a zigzag walk up the 80-yard **Salen** "mountain." Atop Salen is a 20-foot-tall square tower, with walls built of gray and blue stones. The old tower was torn down during the war, but restored in 1984.

Why not take time to do as 150,000 others have and join the **Royal and Ancient Polar Bear Society** (☎ 78-41-31-00) here? Apply in person while you're in Hammerfest. Membership costs 150 NOK ($16.65) annually, and the money is used to protect endangered Arctic animals through conservation programs. The society's building is filled with stuffed specimens of Arctic animals. There's a small museum devoted to the hunting heyday of Hammerfest, which lasted from 1910 to 1950, when eagles, Arctic foxes, and polar bears were trapped by the English, and then German officers during the war. It's in the basement of the Town Hall, on Rådhusplassen. The center is open only June to August, Monday to Friday from 10am to 5pm, Saturday and Sunday 9am to 5pm.

Gjenreisningsmuseet, Söröygatan (☎ 78-42-26-40), opened adjacent to the Rica Hotel in 1998. This small museum commemorates the cold bleak years after World War II, when local residents, deprived of most of their buildings, livelihoods, and creature comforts, heroically rebuilt Finnmark and North Norway in the wake of Nazi devastation. Entrance is 12 NOK ($1.35) per person, and it is open June to September, daily 9am to 5pm; off-season, daily noon to 4 pm.

CRUISES TO THE NORTH CAPE　The first tour ships arrived in 1879, and they've been coming ever since. **FFR** (☎ 78-40-70-00) operates 8- to 9-hour cruises from Hammerfest to the North Cape and back, including meals, shore bus, and guide. The cost is 900 NOK ($99.90) per person, 600 NOK ($66.60) for children 4 to 16, free for children under 4. Tours are scheduled from June 6 to August 6. Boats leave Hammerfest at 7pm and arrive at 9:10pm in Honningsvåg (see below), where a bus takes you to the North Cape. Buses return sometime after midnight (hardly a problem, since it's still daylight). Boats usually return to Hammerfest by about 3:40am.

WHERE TO STAY

Rica Hotel Hammerfest. Sørøygata 15, N-9600 Hammerfest. ☎ **78-41-13-33.** Fax 78-41-13-11.　80 units. TV TEL. July–Aug, Mon–Thurs 850–1,195 NOK ($94.35–$132.65) double; Mon–Thurs 1,295 NOK ($143.75) suite. Sept–June, Mon–Thurs 1,195 NOK ($132.65) double; Mon–Thurs 1,295 NOK ($143.75) suite. Year-round, Fri–Sun 850 NOK ($94.35) double and suite. AE, DC, MC, V. Bus: 1 or 2.

This is the largest hotel in town and the preferred place to stay in the area. It's in the town center, opening directly onto the waterfront. Built in the mid-1970s on steeply sloping land, the hotel was completely redecorated in 1989 and has been regularly spruced up since then. The small, modern guest rooms are decorated with Nordic-inspired pastels, but the look is strictly functional. The plumbing has been upgraded, but bathrooms tend to be small.

WHERE TO DINE

✪ **Odd's Mat og Vinhus.** Strandgata 24. ☎ **78-41-37-66.** Reservations recommended. Main courses 120–270 NOK ($13.30–$29.95). AE, DC, MC, V. Mon–Thurs 1–11pm, Fri 1pm–1am, Sat 6pm–1am. Bus: 1, 5, or 9. NORTHERN NORWEGIAN.

Since it opened in 1992, this rustic restaurant has become famous thanks to a survey by a Trondheim radio station that voted it the best restaurant in Norway. It's adjacent to the town's largest pier, overlooking the harbor. Inside, every effort has been made to simulate the wild splendor of Finnmark (northern Norway), with the use of roughly textured wood, stone, and many yards of natural hemp knotted into ropes that form curtains. A kitchen opens to the dining room.

The recipes and ingredients are almost completely derived from northern Norway, with an emphasis on fish and game. You might try fillet of carp, partially sun-dried, then boiled and served with mustard sauce and bacon fat; or freshly killed grouse prepared "like beef," with a game-laced cream sauce. To start, fillet of reindeer is served, raw and chopped, like a tartare, or smoked and thinly sliced, like a carpaccio.

Rica Hotel Restaurant. In the Rica Hotel Hammerfest, Sørøygata 15. ☎ **78-41-13-33.** Main courses 155–245 NOK ($17.20–$27.20). AE, DC, MC, V. Daily 11am–11pm. Bus: 1 or 2. NORWEGIAN/INTERNATIONAL.

This dining room in the cellar of the Rica Hotel Hammerfest opens onto the harborfront. Specialties include pepper steak and fillet of reindeer. It also serves delicious dishes based on the day's catch from the fjord, as well as some international selections, including Mexican and Chinese cuisine. The Rica Bar and Disco, also in the cellar of the hotel, is open Monday to Thursday from 5pm to 1am, Friday and Saturday 5pm to 3:30am. Admission is 55 NOK ($6.10) on Friday and Saturday night; other nights, it's free. The minimum age is 20, and beer costs 45 NOK ($5) per half liter.

HONNINGSVÅG

81 miles NE of Hammerfest, 1,519 miles NE of Bergen

The world's northernmost village, the gateway to the North Cape, is a completely modern fishing harbor. Only the chapel withstood the German destruction of 1944. It's some 50 miles nearer to the North Pole than Hammerfest, on the Alta–Hammerfest bus route.

Honningsvåg is on the southern side of the island of Magerøy, connected to the North Cape by a 22-mile-long road.

ESSENTIALS

GETTING THERE   If you don't take the coastal steamer, you can reach Honningsvåg by car. From Oslo (a very long trip—about 30 hours during the period from June to September), take E6 north to the junction with Route 95 north. That route leads to Honningsvåg, with one ferry crossing. SAS flies from Oslo or Bergen to Alta; there you can catch a bus to Hammerfest (April to September only), where you change to another bus to Honningsvåg. For bus information, call **Finnmark Fylkesrederi** (☎ 78-40-70-00).

VISITOR INFORMATION   The **Honningsvåg Tourist Office,** in the Nordkapphuset (☎ 78-47-25-99), can give you information on sightseeing boat trips, museums, walks, and deep-sea fishing. The office is open June to August, Monday to Friday from 8:30am to 6pm, Saturday and Sunday noon to 6pm; September to May, Monday to Friday 8:30am to 4pm.

A SPECIAL EVENT   The **North Cape Festival,** held for 1 week in mid-June each year, presents a wide display of local culture. During the festival, participants in the **North Cape March** trek from Honningsvåg to the North Cape and back, a total of around 44 miles.

SEEING THE SIGHTS

Nordkapphallen. Nordkapp. ☎ 78-47-22-33. Admission 175 NOK ($19.45) adults, 50 NOK ($5.55) children, 350 NOK ($38.85) family. Apr 1–May 17, daily 2–5pm; May 18– June 5, daily noon–1am; June 6–10, daily noon–2am; June 11–Aug 11, daily 9am–2am; Aug 12–20, daily 9am–midnight; Aug 21–Sept 9, daily noon–5pm; Sept 10–30, daily 2–5pm. Closed Oct–Mar.

This visitors' center has a video presentation and museum exhibits. Downstairs you'll find a super-videograph and a cave with a panoramic window facing the Arctic Ocean. On the way to the cave, you'll see several scenes from the history of the North Cape. A monument commemorates the visit of King Oscar (king of Norway and Sweden) to the Cape in 1873, and another exhibit commemorates the arrival of King Chulalongkorn of Siam (now Thailand) who came for a look at the Cape in 1907; Chulalongkorn was the son of the king in the musical *The King and I.* There's also a monument marking the terminus of the "Midnight Sun Road." Although the admission price is steep, the views from inside are incredible and unforgettable. Call before you visit because opening hours and days are subject to change without notice.

Nordkappmuseet. In the Nordkapphuset, Fergeveien 4. ☎ 78-47-28-33. Admission 25 NOK ($2.80) adults, 5 NOK (55¢) children, free for children under 6. June 15–Aug 15, Mon–Sat 11am–8pm, Sun 1–8pm; Aug 16–June 14, Mon–Fri 12:30–4pm.

This museum has displays about the cultural history of the North Cape, fishery artifacts, and an exhibit that details the effects of the Second World War on the North Cape. The museum lies at the harbor and town center, a 3-minute walk from the coastal steamer and the North Cape Hotel.

WHERE TO STAY

North Cape Hotel. Nordkappgata 2–4, N-9750 Honningsvåg. ☎ 78-47-23-33. Fax 78-47-33-79. 163 units. TV TEL. June–Aug, 850–1,260 NOK ($94.35–$139.85) double; 1,400–1,800 NOK ($155.40–$199.80) suite. Sept–May, 900 NOK ($99.90) double; 950–1,550 NOK ($105.45–$172.05) suite. AE, DC, MC, V.

The world's northernmost hotel, 21 miles from the North Cape, is in the central zone, near the quay. Early reservations are strongly advised. This five-story yellow-fronted 1956 building has been enlarged and considerably upgraded in the 1990s. The guest rooms, which have views of the harbor, are functionally furnished with modern but plain pieces. The rooms and bathrooms are a bit small, but the beds are good. In this part of the world, you'll happily settle for a roof over your head. Restaurant Carolina is one of the best in town. The hotel also runs an unpretentious grill and offers disco action on Friday and Saturday nights.

WHERE TO DINE

Restaurant Carolina. In the North Cape Hotel, Nordkappgata 2–4. ☎ 78-47-23-33. Reservations recommended. Main courses 160–185 NOK ($17.75–$20.55). AE, DC, MC, V. Summer, daily 5:30–11:30pm; off-season, daily 6pm–9pm. NORWEGIAN.

In the cellar of the North Cape Hotel, this place is at its most elegant in the winter, when the tour groups are gone. During the summer, the smörgåsbord is in the dining room and à la carte dinners are served in the less formal Bistro. The cuisine is competently prepared but never exciting; most of the ingredients are shipped in. In the evening music begins at 8pm, and the place is very popular with locals. It's decorated with old-fashioned photographs of Honningsvåg.

A TRIP TO THE NORTH CAPE

The ✪ **Nordkapp (North Cape)** symbolizes the "top of Europe." (Knivskjellodden actually extends about 1,500 yards farther north, but it is inaccessible.) In prehistoric times the North Cape Horn was a Sami place of sacrifice. The North Cape's name used to be Knyskanes, but in 1553 it was named "North Cape" by the Lord Richard Chancellor of England, who was searching for a sea passage to China. The road to the North Cape is open to traffic from May 1 to October 20.

The first tour ships arrived in 1879. They anchored in Hornvika Bay, and the visitors had to climb 307 yards up to the plateau. After the road from Honningsvåg opened in 1956, the flow of tourists turned into a flood. In summer, buses to the North Cape leave daily from outside the tourist office at Fergeveien 4 at Honningsvåg, stop briefly at the ferry terminal across from the Sifi Sommerhotell, and then continue to the visitors' center at the North Cape. The one-way passage from any point along the route is 60 NOK ($6.65) adults, 30 NOK ($3.35) children. For more information, call **FFR** (☎ **78-47-58-50**).

On the road to the Cape is a Lapp encampment. It's a bit contrived, but visitors do have an opportunity to go inside one of the tents, and they come away with an idea of how nomadic Lapps used to live.

2 The Fjords

For visitors who'd like to explore the fjords on a driving tour, we begin our tour in Bergen. From Bergen, head east on Route 7 to Ulvik.

ULVIK

93 miles E of Bergen

Ulvik is a rarity—an unspoiled resort. It lies like a fist at the end of an arm of the Hardangerfjord, and is surrounded in the summer by misty peaks and fruit farms. The village's 1858 church is attractively decorated in the style of the region. It's open June to August, daily from 9am to 5pm. Concerts are presented here.

ESSENTIALS

GETTING THERE   If you're not driving, you can reach Ulvik by train or bus from Bergen or Oslo. From either city, take a train to Voss, where you can catch a bus for the 25-mile (45-minute) ride to Ulvik. Buses run from Voss daily, five times in the summer, three in the winter. In Ulvik the bus stops in front of the Ulvik church in the town center. There's no formal bus station.

VISITOR INFORMATION   Contact the **Ulvik Tourist Office,** in the town center (☎ **56-52-63-60**). It's open May 15 to September 15, Monday to Saturday from 8:30am to 5pm, Sunday 1 to 5pm; September 16 to May 14, Monday to Friday 8:30am to 1:30pm. It can arrange excursions, from trips on fjord steamers to bus tours of the Osa mountains.

SEEING THE SIGHTS

A number of do-it-yourself excursions begin at Ulvik; see the tourist office for details. They change seasonally and depend on the weather. You can explore the Eidfjord district, which is the northern tip of the Hardangerfjord and a paradise for hikers. It's

Frommer's Favorite Offbeat Adventures

- **Dogsledding:** Traveling over the frozen tundra or through snow-laced forests at the speed of a dog can be one of the great experiences of the Nordic world. You can be a passenger, bundled aboard a sled, or a driver urging on a team of huskies. A Norway-based outfitter who specializes in the experience, usually as part of midwinter camping trips under a canopy of stars, is **Canyon Huskies,** Stengelsen, N-9518lta, Norway (☎ 78-43-33-06; www.canyonhuskies.no). Tours last 1 to 10 days and are conducted by owner Roger Dahl. They run between December and May, and involve overnight stays in mountain cabins, which usually contain five to six bunk beds each. Negotiate with these folks directly, or contact U.S.-based outfitter **Borton Overseas** (☎ 800/843-0602; www.bortonoverseas.com).

- **Observing Musk Oxen:** A remnant of the last Ice Age, the musk ox had become nearly extinct by the 1930s. Between 1932 and 1953, musk oxen were shipped from Greenland to the Dovrefjell (a national park that's about an hour's train ride south of Trondheim), where about 60 still roam. On a safari, you can observe this thriving herd—take along some binoculars. The park, another remnant of the last Ice Age, is Europe's most bountiful wildflower mountain. As part of your treks throughout the region, you can also observe the purest herd of original mountain reindeer in Norway. Accommodations in or near the park can be arranged through **Borton Overseas** (☎ 800/843-0602; www.bortonoverseas.com). Hotel staff members are adept at indicating the locations where the animal herds were last sighted, and where they're most likely to be.

- **Rafting:** Norway's abundant snow and rainfall and its steep topography feed dozens of roaring whitewater streams. Experience these torrents firsthand as part of whitewater treks downriver. One of Norway's most respected river outfitters is **Norwegian Wildlife and Rafting AS,** Randswerk, N-2680 Vågå (☎ 61-23-87-27; www.nwr.no). Based in Central Norway, about a

home to some 1,000 people and the continent's largest herd of wild reindeer. Mountain trout attract anglers to the area.

The district contains nearly one-quarter of ✪ **Hardangervidda National Park,** on the largest high-mountain plateau in Europe. Some 20,000 wild reindeer live there. Well-marked hiking trails connect a series of 15 tourist huts.

Several canyons, including the renowned **Måbø Valley,** lead down from the plateau to the fjords. Here you'll see the famous 550-foot Voringfoss waterfall; the Valurefoss in Hjømo Valley has a free fall of almost 800 feet. Part of the 1,000-year-old road across Norway, traversing the Måbø Valley, has been restored for hardy hikers. The Måbø Valley, like the neighboring Hjømo Valley, is part of the previously mentioned Hardangervidda National Park.

After exploring the area around Eidfjord, you can drive south along the fjord banks to Kinsarvik, another major region of tourist interest. The main village of **Kinsarvik** stands on a glacier-formed ridge at the mouth of the Kinso River, which flows into four magnificent waterfalls as it drops from the plateau to Husedalen on its way to the sea. Since early times, Kinsarvik has been the marketplace for the region.

Kinsarvik was Hardanger's principal timber port in the 17th and early 18th centuries. When the export of timber was transferred to Bergen in 1750, Kinsarvik

90-minute drive north of Lillehammer, it employs a part-time staff of 30 and a flotilla of devices suitable for helping you float, meander, or shoot down the whitewater streams of Norway. Whatever conveyance you can imagine (paddle boards, kayaks, canoes, or inflatable rafts), this company can provide. Trips last 1 to 8 days.

- **Trekking the Fjords:** Two respected U.S.–based outfitters, **Borton Overseas** (☎ 800/843-0602; www.bortonoverseas.com) and **Five Stars of Scandinavia** (☎ 800/722-4126; 5stars-of-scandinavia.com), offer 7- and 8-day treks through Norway designed to acquaint you with the country's heritage and its thousands of scenic wonders. Amid the cliffs and waterfalls of the fjords, you can participate in point-to-point guided treks that average around 15 miles per day. En route, you'll visit wooden churches, mountain hamlets, and, in some cases, snow fields and slow-moving glaciers. Depending on your budget and your tastes, overnight accommodations range from first-class hotels to simple mountain huts favored by rock climbers and many trekkers.

- **Bicycling in the Lofoten Islands:** Some of the weirdest and most isolated tundra and lichen-covered rock formations in Norway lie within the Lofoten archipelago, north of the Arctic Circle. Ecologists claim that one of the best and least invasive ways to experience the wildlife here is on a bicycle.

  Berkeley, California-based **Backroads Travel** (☎ 800/GO-ACTIVE; www.backroads.com) conducts 6-day hiking and biking (they refer to them as "multi-sport") tours of the isolated archipelago at least twice a year, during July and August, with an emphasis on ecology and natural beauty. Washington state-based **Five Stars of Scandinavia** (☎ 800/722-4126; 5stars-of-scandinavia. com) offers comparable tours and tend to be cheaper than Backroads. Both operators house their participants in simple mountain huts and lodges, and make frequent trips across bodies of water by bridge, tunnel, and ferryboat.

developed a shipbuilding industry that continued until 1870, when the village became a center for wood carving. Today one of its principal industries is a pewter factory.

The plot of grass that slopes to a stony beach near the Kinsarvik ferry terminal is **Skiperstod,** site of a boathouse for naval longships from about 900 until 1350.

Borstova, the building on the fjord side of the green facing the church, was constructed partly from the timbers of St. Olav's Guildhall, the meeting place of the local guild until 1680. It's now a council chamber and social center.

Kinsarvik Church, said to have been constructed by Scottish master builders at the end of the 12th century, is one of the oldest stone churches in Norway. The interior was restored in 1961 to its pre-Reformation condition. It has a 17th-century pulpit painted by Peter Reimers, a painted and carved altarpiece, and medieval frescoes.

The stone **column** (*minnestein*) on the green commemorates the local men who fought in the wars that led to the end of Norway's union with Denmark in 1814.

The **Tillegg i Tekst (Hardanger Recreation Park),** in the middle of Kinsarvik, is open on weekends from May to mid-June and in September, and daily from mid-June through August.

About 9 miles from Kinsarvik en route to Eidfjord, off Highway 7, is the **Bu Museum,** Ringøy (☎ 53-66-69-00). It has three old houses containing furniture and domestic and craft equipment. The basement of an old farmhouse is filled with artifacts dating from the Stone Age to modern times. The museum also has a collection of national costumes from the Hardanger area. It's open June 1 to August 10, daily from 11am to 4pm, and by request the rest of the year. Admission is 50 NOK ($6.50) for adults, 30 NOK ($3.90) for seniors and students, and free for children.

WHERE TO STAY & DINE
Moderate
Rica Brakanes Hotel. N-5730 Ulvik. ☎ **56-52-61-05.** Fax 56-52-64-10. E-mail: brakanes. hotel@hl.telia.no. 144 units. TV TEL. 1,370–1,420 NOK ($152.05–$157.60) double. Rates include breakfast. AE, DC, MC, V. Free parking.

There's a famous view of the Hardangerfjord and the surrounding forest from this well-recommended hotel. It's near the town center, at the edge of the fjord. The original building, from the 1860s, burned during a Second World War bombing raid and was reconstructed in 1952. Today all that remains of the original building is one small dining room. The rest of the hotel is airy, sunny, and comfortable. The guest rooms are small but well maintained, with good beds and sparkling-clean bathrooms. Its facilities include a sauna, solarium, swimming pool, fitness center, and tennis courts. In the summer, plane rides over the fjords can be arranged, and windsurfing and boat rentals are available.

The hotel has two lounges. The Fjord Lounge is an elegant, sedate room offering panoramic views of the fjord, and the Vaskariet Pub (the Laundry Pub) is in the hotel's former laundry room. It attracts a younger crowd.

Inexpensive
Ulvik Fjord Pensjonat. N-5730 Ulvik. ☎ **56-52-61-70.** Fax 56-52-61-60. www. ulvikfjordpensjonat.no. E-mail: post@ulvikfjordpensjonat.no. 20 units, 17 with bathroom. TEL. 620 NOK ($68.80) double without bathroom; 780 NOK ($86.60) double with bathroom. Rates include breakfast. V. Closed Oct–Apr. Free parking.

Ulvik Fjord Pensjonat, constructed in two stages, in 1946 and 1977, is one of the finest guest houses along the Hardangerfjord. The rooms are spacious and pleasantly furnished in regional Norwegian style. You'll be welcomed by the Hammer family, who won the Norwegian Hospitality Prize in 1989. A sauna and solarium are available for guests' use. A dinner of delicious fjord cooking costs 160 NOK ($17.75).

Ulvik Hotel. N-5730 Ulvik. ☎ **56-52-62-00.** Fax 56-52-66-41. 57 units. TEL. 1,090 NOK ($121) double. Rates include breakfast. AE, DC, MC, V. Free parking.

Updated in 1996, the guest rooms are modern and comfortable, with good beds and well-maintained bathrooms. More than half the units overlook the fjord. A dining room serves excellent Norwegian food; the shrimp and salmon are the most popular items on the menu. The hotel is on the fjord in the town center.

VOSS
25 miles W of Ulvik, 63 miles E of Bergen

Between two fjords, Voss is a famous year-round resort, also known for its folklore. It was the birthplace of the American football hero Knute Rockne. Maybe the trolls don't strike fear in the hearts of farm children anymore, but they're still called out of hiding to give visitors a little fun.

Voss is a natural base for exploring the two largest fjords in Norway, the **Sognefjord** to the north and the **Hardangerfjord** to the south. In and around Voss are glaciers, mountains, fjords, waterfalls, orchards, rivers, and lakes.

ESSENTIALS

GETTING THERE   From Ulvik, take Highway 20 to Route 13; then follow Route 13 northwest to Voss. If you're not driving, there's frequent train service from Bergen (travel time is 1¼ hours) and Oslo (5½ hours). There are six daily buses from Bergen (1¾ hours) and one bus a day from Oslo (9 hours).

VISITOR INFORMATION   The **Voss Information** is at Hestavangen 10 (☎ 56-52-08-00). It's open June to August, Monday to Saturday from 9am to 7pm, Sunday 2 to 7pm; September to May, Monday to Friday 9am to 4pm.

SEEING THE SIGHTS

St. Olav's Cross, Skulegata, is near the Voss Cinema. It's the oldest historic relic in Voss, believed to have been raised when the townspeople adopted Christianity in 1023.

A ride on the **Hangursbanen cable car** (☎ 56-51-12-12) will be a memorable part of your visit. It offers panoramic views of Voss and its environs. The mountain-top restaurant serves refreshments and meals. The hardy take the cable car up, and then spend the rest of the afternoon strolling down the mountain. A round-trip ride costs 50 NOK ($5.55) for adults, 25 NOK ($2.80) for children 8 to 16, free for children under 8. Entrance to the cable car is on a hillside, a 10-minute walk north of the town center. It's open in summer and winter, but closes during the often gray and rainy months of May and September to December.

Finnesloftet. Finne. ☎ **56-51-11-00.** Admission 30 NOK ($3.35) adults, 15 NOK ($1.65) children. Daily 10:30am–4:30pm. Closed Aug 16–June 14.

This is one of the oldest timbered houses in Norway, dating from the mid–13th century. It's located about a mile west of Voss and is a 15-minute walk west from the train station.

Vangskyrkje. Vangsgata 3. ☎ **56-51-22-78.** Admission 10 NOK ($1.10) adults, 5 NOK (55¢) children, free for children under 7. Daily 10am–4pm. Closed Sept–May.

This 1277 church with a timbered tower contains a striking Renaissance pulpit, a stone altar and triptych, fine woodcarvings, and a painted ceiling. It's in the center of Voss, a 5-minute walk east from the train station. Call in advance if you would like to reserve an English-speaking guide.

Voss Folkemuseum. Mølster. ☎ **56-51-15-11.** Admission 30 NOK ($3.35) adults, free for children. May and Sept, daily 10am–5pm; June–Aug, daily 10am–7pm; Oct–Apr, Mon–Fri 10am–3pm, Sun noon–3pm.

Half a mile north of Voss on a hillside overlooking the town, this museum consists of more than a dozen farmhouses and other buildings dating from the 1500s to around 1870. They were not moved here, but were built on this site by two farm families.

SKIING

Voss continually adds to its facilities, and is definitely in the race to overtake Geilo and Lillehammer as Norway's most popular winter playground. Its chair lifts, ski lifts, and aerial cableway carry passengers up 2,625 feet.

The town offers what it calls a "ski circus." Beginners take the Hangursbanen cable car; one ski lift (3,000 feet long) goes from Traastolen to the top of Slettafjell (with a wide choice of downhill runs); the Bavallen lift is for the slalom slopes; and the down-hill runs are at Lonehorgi.

Lessons at the **Ski School** (☎ 56-51-00-32 in winter or 56-51-34-36 in summer), at the end of the cable-car run, are moderately priced. The tourist office and hotels can arrange bookings. All equipment is available for rent.

Children over 7 are allowed on the slopes. A special branch of the Ski School handles these youngsters. Baby-sitting is available for children under 7.

WHERE TO STAY
Moderate

Fleischers Hotel. Evangerveiten 13, N-5700 Voss. ☎ **56-52-05-00.** Fax 56-51-22-89. www.fleischers.no. 90 units. MINIBAR TV TEL. 1,290 NOK ($143.20) double; 700–1,000 NOK ($77.70–$111) apt. Rates include breakfast. AE, DC, MC, V. Free parking.

On the lakefront beside the Voss train station, Fleischers Hotel couldn't be more convenient. The gracious 1889 frame hotel has a modern wing with 30 units, all with private showers, toilets, and terraces overlooking the lake. In the older part of the hotel, the rooms are old-fashioned and more spacious. The hotel has a dining room, billiard room, sauna, solarium, and two bars. The restaurant serves an à la carte menu; main courses cost 180 to 250 NOK ($20 to $27.75). In the summer, a buffet is served for 225 NOK ($25).

Hotel Jarl. Voss Sentrum, N-5700 Voss. ☎ **56-51-19-33.** Fax 56-51-37-69. 78 units. MINIBAR TV TEL. 980 NOK ($108.80) double; 1,480 NOK ($164.30) suite. Rates include breakfast. AE, DC, MC, V. Free parking.

In this centrally located hotel are comfortably modern singles, doubles, and suites. Guest rooms and bathrooms are a bit small, but the beds are firm. Built in 1972, the hotel was enlarged and renovated in 1996. Facilities include attractive public rooms, an indoor swimming pool, a solarium, a sauna bath, an English pub, a games room, and a popular nightclub (the Knight's Club). You can take your meals in the pleasant dining room or the intimate bistro and bar.

Park Hotel Vossevangen. Uttrågate, N-5701 Voss. ☎ **56-51-13-22.** Fax 56-51-00-39. 131 units. MINIBAR TV TEL. 1,050 NOK ($116.55) double. Rates include breakfast. AE, DC, MC, V. Free parking.

The product of a 1990 merger, this hotel consists of two sections (originally the Park Hotel and the Vossevangen Hotel), joined by a covered passageway. The guest rooms are attractively furnished. The hotel is family-owned and houses the best restaurant in town, the Elysée (see "Where to Dine," below). Facilities include the Café Stationen, the Pentagon Dance Bar, the Stallen Pub, and the Pianissimo Bar. It's in the town center, about 100 yards from the train station.

Inexpensive

Kringsjå Pension. Strengjarhaujen 6, N-5700 Voss. ☎ **56-51-16-27.** Fax 56-51-63-30. www. kringsja.no. 18 units, 14 with bathroom. 700 NOK ($77.70) double. Rates include breakfast. AE, DC, MC, V. Free parking.

This pleasant three-story guest house is in the center of Voss; some parts were built in the 1930s, others much more recently. The public rooms are spacious and airy, and the guest rooms are simply, comfortably furnished, with good beds but small bathrooms. Breakfast is served daily, and other meals are sometimes available. Prices are the same for units with or without bathrooms. The hall bathrooms are well maintained.

Nøring Pensjonat. Uttrågate 41, N-5700 Voss. ☎ **56-51-12-11.** Fax 56-51-12-23. 21 units, 9 with bathroom. 600 NOK ($66.60) double without bathroom; 750 NOK ($83.25) double with bathroom. Rates include breakfast. AE, DC, MC, V. Free parking.

The Nøring is a first-class pension built in 1949 near the river, about a 10-minute walk from the town center. It provides clean, functional accommodations, which are small but comfortable, with firm mattresses. Half of the rooms face the mountains. The boarding house serves good, hearty breakfasts, plus light meals (with beer or wine) at lunch and dinner. The lounge opens onto a terrace.

WHERE TO DINE
Moderate
Elysée. In the Park Hotel Vossevangen, Uttrågate. ☎ **56-51-13-22.** Reservations recommended. Main courses 165–225 NOK ($18.30–$25); lunch smörgåsbord 160 NOK ($17.75); fixed-price dinner 235 NOK ($26.10). AE, DC, MC, V. Sun–Thurs 1–10:30pm, Fri–Sat 1–11pm. FRENCH/NORWEGIAN.

The decor of this prestigious restaurant includes trompe l'oeil murals based on a modern interpretation of the Parthenon. It features such dishes as baked sea scorpion, fillet of lamb marinated in honey, and a daily game dish. Homemade ice cream with berries and vanilla sauce makes a smooth dessert. The food here is satisfying and based on fresh ingredients. You leave feeling you've had an adequate meal, substantial and hearty. There's an extensive wine list.

Fleischers Restaurant. Evangerveiten 13. ☎ **56-52-05-00.** Reservations recommended. Lunch smörgåsbord 230 NOK ($25.55); fixed-price dinner 190–260 NOK ($21.10–$28.85); summer buffet 250 NOK ($27.75). AE, DC, MC, V. Mon–Sat 1–10:30pm, Sun 1–9:45pm. NORWEGIAN.

The dining room of this landmark hotel, a few steps from the Voss train station, hasn't been altered since the hotel opened over a century ago. Long the leading restaurant in the Voss area, the Victorian-style Fleischers remains the traditionalists' favorite. Its lunchtime smörgåsbord is a lavish array of all-you-can-eat Norwegian delicacies. Specialties include smoked salmon and fillet of beef, lamb, pork, and veal. This is authentic cuisine that would have pleased Ibsen—a real "taste of Norway." What you don't get is dash and culinary sophistication.

Inexpensive
Vangen Café. Vangen Super-Market, Vangsgata. ☎ **56-51-12-05.** Smørbrød 28–38 NOK ($3.10–$4.20); dagens menu (daily specials) 75–95 NOK ($8.30–$10.55). No credit cards. Mon–Fri 10:30am–6pm, Sat 10:30am–4pm, Sun noon–6pm. NORWEGIAN.

The least expensive cafeteria-style outlet in Voss is one floor above street level over a small souvenir shop and food market. It's in the center of town, a 5-minute walk south of the train station. Soft drinks and fruit juices are sold, but no alcohol. The *dagens menu* is the best food value in town.

VOSS AFTER DARK
Fleischers Top Spot Nightclub. In Fleischers Hotel, Evangerveiten 13. ☎ **56-52-05-00.** Cover 60 NOK ($6.65) Fri–Sat only (no cover for hotel guests).

In the cellar of Fleischers Hotel (see "Where to Stay," above) you'll find this well-established nightspot. Dance bands play nightly for an older crowd that's dressed up a bit. Many people come here just to drink—beer costs 46 NOK ($5.10). The club is open Monday to Thursday from 9:30pm to 1am, Friday and Saturday until 3am.

A SIDE TRIP TO THE SOGNEFJORD
If you have a car and time to spare, you may want to visit the Sognefjord district, around the largest of the Norwegian fjords. From Voss the northern route leads to **Vik.** The scenery is beautiful, and the road runs for miles across a desolate tableland at 3,000 feet above sea level. On a summer day the lakes appear green, and there's snow on the distant slopes.

In Vik, try to see the stave church, one of the most attractive in Norway. Then take the road to Vangsnes, where you can make ferry connections across the Sognefjord to Balestrand or Dragsvik. On the other side, take Route 5 north. The steep highway runs through rolling countryside with waterfalls to Viksdalen, about 40 miles from Dragsvik.

BALESTRAND
56 miles N of Voss, 130 miles NE of Bergen

Long known for its arts and crafts, Balestrand lies on the northern rim of the Sogne-fjord, at the junction of the Vetlefjord, the Esefjord, and the Fjaerlandsfjord.

ESSENTIALS
GETTING THERE From Voss, continue driving north on Route 13 to Vangsnes and board a car ferry for the short crossing northwest to Balestrand. You can also take a train from Bergen or Oslo to Voss or Flåm, and then make bus and ferry connections north to Balestrand. Bus and ferry schedules are available at the Voss tourist office (☎ 56-52-08-00) and the Flåm tourist office (☎ 57-63-21-06). From Bergen there are daily express boats to Balestrand; the trip takes 3½ hours.

VISITOR INFORMATION The **Tourist Office** (☎ 57-69-16-17 in winter or 57-69-12-55 in summer) is in the town center. From June to August, it's open daily from 8:30am to 10pm; May and September, daily 9am to 8pm; October to April, Monday to Saturday 9am to 4pm.

SEEING THE SIGHTS
The staff at the tourist office can help you plan a tour of the area and put you in touch with local craftspeople. Pick up a list of excursions and buy tickets for one of the scheduled 1½-day tours—for example, a taxi plane across the **Jostedal Glacier.**

Kaiser Wilhelm II, a frequent visitor to Balestrand, presented the district with two statues of old Norse heroes, King Bele and Fridtjof the Bold. They stand in the center of town. Another sight is the English church of **St. Olav,** a tiny wooden building that dates from 1897.

You can explore the area by setting out in nearly any direction on scenic country lanes with little traffic or a wide choice of marked trails and upland farm tracks. The tourist office sells a touring map. There's good sea fishing, as well as lake and river trout fishing. Fishing tackle, rowboats, and bicycles can all be rented in the area.

WHERE TO STAY
Moderate
Kviknes Hotel. Balholm, N-5850 Balestrand. ☎ **57-69-42-00.** Fax 57-69-42-01. www. kviknes.no. E-mail: booking@kviknes.no. 210 units. TV TEL. 1,290 NOK ($143.20) double; 1,970 NOK ($218.65) suite. Rates include breakfast. AE, DC, MC, V. Closed Oct–Apr. Free parking.

Built in 1913 as a summer retreat for Europeans, this hotel was much enlarged in 1970. At its core it's an elaborately detailed building with balconies opening onto the edge of the fjord. All but a few of the guest rooms have fjord views. They vary widely in size and style. The most popular units are those in the original structure, with old-fashioned Norwegian style, flowery fabrics, good beds, and spacious bathrooms. Some of these accommodations are furnished with antiques. The less personal rooms are in the annex, where bland Nordic style prevails. Bathrooms tend to be very small. Many of the accommodations are set aside for nonsmokers, and others are wheelchair accessible. The hotel has a large dining room, several lounges, and a dance club. An extensive buffet is served every night; lunches are less elaborate, with brasserie-style meals. Sports such as waterskiing, windsurfing, and fjord fishing can be arranged, as can helicopter flights to the Jostedal Glacier. Facilities include a whirlpool, sauna, and solarium.

Inexpensive
Dragsvik Fjord Hotel. Dragsvik, N-5850 Balestrand. ☎ **57-69-12-93.** Fax 57-69-13-83. www.dragsvik.no. E-mail: mail@dragsvik.no. 19 units. TEL. Feb–May and Sept–Oct, 720 NOK

($79.90) double; June–Aug, 775 NOK ($86.05) double. Rates include breakfast. AE, MC, V. Closed Nov–Jan. Free parking.

About half a mile from Balestrand and 300 yards from the ferry quay at Dragsvik, this hotel is a bargain. Doubles in the new wing have the most up-to-date plumbing. The units are comfortable, though small. They're well maintained, with good mattresses, but bathrooms are tiny. The large dining room offers a panoramic view of the Fjaerlandsfjord. The hotel has a private swimming area. You can also rent bicycles, rowboats, and motorboats.

Midtnes Pensjonat. N-5850 Balestrand. ☎ **57-69-11-33.** Fax 57-69-15-84. www. midtnes.no. 34 units. 650–750 NOK ($72.15–$83.25) double. Rates include breakfast. No credit cards. Free parking.

This well-run, reasonably priced boarding house, in the center of Balestrand next to the English church, is family-owned and managed. The rooms are pleasantly furnished, and most open onto the Sognefjord. The rooms aren't terribly spacious, but housekeeping is good and the mattresses are firm. There's a private pier with rowboats. The boarding house offers good food and the dining room has a view of the fjord.

FROM BALESTRAND TO FLÅM

From Balestrand, take Route 55 east along the Sognefjord, crossing the fjord by ferry at Dragsvik and by bridge at Sogndal. At Sogndal, drive east to Kaupanger, where you'll cross the Ardalsfjord by ferry, and head south to Revsnes. In Revsnes, pick up Route 11 heading southeast. Drive east until you connect with a secondary road heading southwest through Kvigno and Aurland. From Aurland, take Route 601 southwest to Flåm. The whole trip takes 2 to 3 hours, depending on weather and road conditions.

FLÅM

60 miles SE of Balestrand, 103 miles E of Bergen

Flåm (pronounced "Flawm") lies on the Aurlandsfjord, a tip of the more famous Sognefjord. In the village you can visit the old church (1667), with painted walls done in typical Norwegian country style.

ESSENTIALS

GETTING THERE   If you're not driving, the best and most exciting approach to Flåm is aboard the ❍ **electric train from Myrdal,** which connects with trains from Bergen and Oslo. The electric train follows a 12-mile route overlooking a 2,900-foot drop, stopping occasionally for passengers to photograph spectacular waterfalls. The trip takes 50 minutes. In winter about four or five trains a day make the run to Flåm. In summer, depending on business, service begins at 7:40am and runs throughout the day. Tickets must be purchased in advance. The one-way fare from Myrdal to Flåm is 115 NOK ($12.75).

Bus travel is less convenient. One **bus** a day Monday to Saturday runs between Aurland and Flåm. The trip takes 30 minutes.

From May to September, two **ferries** per day cross the fjord between Aurland and Flåm. The trip takes 30 minutes.

Flåm can also be reached by high-speed **express boats** from Bergen, Balestrand (see above), and Leikanger. The boats carry passengers only. In Bergen, call **Fylkesbaatana** (☎ **55-32-40-15**); the one-way trip costs 550 NOK ($61.05).

VISITOR INFORMATION   The **tourist office** (☎ **57-63-21-06**) is near the railroad station. It's open May to September, daily from 8:30am to 8:30pm.

SEEING THE SIGHTS

Flåm is an excellent starting point for car or boat excursions to other well-known centers on the Sognefjord, Europe's longest and deepest fjord. Worth exploring are two of the wildest and most beautiful fingers of the Sognefjord: the Nærøyfjord and the Aurlandfjord. Ask at the tourist office about a summer-only cruise from Flåm to both fjords. From Flåm by boat, you can disembark in Gudvangen or Aurland and continue by bus. Alternatively, you can return to Flåm by train.

There are also a number of easy walks in the Flåm district. A map with detailed information is available from the tourist office.

WHERE TO STAY

Heimly Pension. N-5743 Flåm. ☎ **57-63-23-00.** Fax 57-63-23-40. www.heimly.no. E-mail: post@heimly.no. 26 units. 550–870 NOK ($61.05–$96.55) double. Rates include breakfast. AE, DC, MC, V. Free parking. Closed Dec 24–Jan 2.

At the edge of the fjord, this simple lodge was built in the 1950s as a family-run pension. It later housed the clients of a nearby ski school. Designed in the style of an A-frame chalet, it offers a ground-floor lounge, guest rooms with views over the fjord on the two upper floors, and a separate pub and restaurant in an annex across the road. Like a small-scale resort, the lodge offers such sports as tennis, badminton, swimming, waterskiing, fishing, and boating.

GEILO

68 miles SE of Flåm, 149 miles E of Bergen, 149 miles W of Oslo

One of Norway's best-known ski resorts is also an attractive summer resort. Geilo lies some 2,600 feet above sea level in the Hol mountain district. Although it's not strictly in the fjord country, it's included here because it's a "gateway" there en route from Oslo to Bergen.

The Geilo area boasts 81 miles of marked cross-country skiing tracks.

ESSENTIALS

GETTING THERE From Flåm, return to Aurland to connect with Route 50. It runs southeast through the towns of Steine, Storestølen, Hovet, and Hagafoss. In Hagafoss, connect with Route 7 going southwest into Geilo.

If you're not driving, you can reach Geilo by plane, train, or bus. **Sun Air** (☎ **23-11-17-60**) has two flights a week in summer and four flights a week in winter from Oslo. The trip takes 30 minutes. Planes arrive at Dagali Airport, 16 miles from Geilo. From Dagali, the taxi fare to Geilo is 50 NOK ($5.55). Trains from Oslo or Bergen run four times a day and take 4 hours. The bus runs from Oslo's Central Station, but the train is preferable because Geilo is on the main line between Bergen and Oslo.

VISITOR INFORMATION The **Turistinformasjonen** office is at Vesleslåtteveien 13 in the town center (☎ **32-09-59-00**). It's open June to August, daily from 9am to 9pm; September to May, Monday to Friday 9am to 4pm, Saturday 9am to 1pm. The town doesn't use street addresses, but everything is easy to find.

SEEING THE SIGHTS

The main ski season is January to March. The **Ski School** has more than two dozen instructors, known for their patience with amateurs. Other fun activities include sleigh rides, curling, and skating at the **Geilo Stadium.**

From Geilo you can visit the historical museum in **Hol,** 6 miles northeast, to see 16th-century wood carvings and a 12th-century stave church. Another destination is the ancient Viking burial ground at **Fekjo.** The tourist office can supply maps and help you plan day-long excursions.

The chair lift ride is great for dramatic scenery of the mountain plateau and fjords. The lift terminal is a short walk from the railway station.

WHERE TO STAY
Very Expensive
✪ **Dr. Holms Hotel.** N-3580 Geilo. ☎ **32-09-57-00.** Fax 32-09-16-20. www.drholms.no. E-mail: post@drholms.no. 127 units. MINIBAR TV TEL. May–Aug, 970 NOK ($107.65) double; Sept–Apr, 1,940–2,500 NOK ($215.35–$277.50) double. Year-round, 500 NOK ($55.50) supplement for suite. Rates include breakfast. Rates may be higher during Christmas and New Year's. AE, DC, MC, V. Free parking.

One of the most famous resort hotels in Norway, this is the finest place to stay in the area. Here, near the railroad station, you get elegance, comfort, and traditional styling. Dr. J. C. Holms opened the hotel in 1909, and there have been many changes since, including the addition of two wings and a swimming complex. The most recent facelift took place in 1999. Original works of art decorate the hotel. Guest rooms are beautifully furnished in traditional style and offer many amenities including good beds, ample bathrooms, and TVs with satellite and video channels.

Dining/Diversions: Musicians perform in the main lounge. There are three bars—including the Skiers' Bar, the après-ski favorite—and a 400-seat dining room.

Amenities: Room service (daily 7:30am–10pm), baby-sitting, laundry, swimming pool, gym, sauna, library, conservatory, conference center, heated lockers for ski equipment storage.

Moderate
Bardøla Hoyfjellshotel. N-3580 Geilo. ☎ **32-09-04-00.** Fax 32-09-45-01. www.bardoela. no. 100 units, some with shower only. MINIBAR TV TEL. May–Aug, 900 NOK ($99.90) double. Rates include breakfast. Sept–Apr, 1,240–1,980 NOK ($137.65–$219.80) double. Rates include half board. Year-round, 500 NOK ($55.50) supplement for suite. Rates higher during Christmas and New Year's. AE, DC, MC, V. Free parking.

In tranquil surroundings about a mile east of the train station lies this well-run hotel. Built in the 1930s, it's been expanded and renovated many times. It attracts many guests in summer and winter, partly because it has a higher proportion of suites than any other hotel in the region. Each year the hotel renovates five rooms and five suites. Many of the traditionally styled guest rooms are generous in size. All have good, firm mattresses and ample bathrooms with plenty of towels. The hotel has an indoor swimming pool, Jacuzzi, and sun-tanning salon. An outdoor pool and two tennis courts are open in summer. In winter, guests stay here on the half-board plan, which includes breakfast and lunch or dinner; it's the way to go.

Norlandia Geilo Hotell. Gamleveien 2, Box 113, N-3580 Geilo. ☎ **32-09-05-11.** Fax 32-09-17-30. www.norlandia.no. E-mail: booking@geilohotel.com. 72 units. MINIBAR TV TEL. 2,020–2,220 NOK ($224.20–$246.40) double. Rates include full board. AE, DC, MC, V. Free parking.

In the center of the resort, a short walk from the train station, the Geilo was the town's first hotel. The oldest part dates from 1880. The guest rooms are attractive and warmly furnished. Most of the medium-sized rooms have a sitting area. Mattresses are firm; bathrooms are a bit small but ample for your stuff, with decent-sized towels. The nearest ski lift is only 200 yards away. There's room service, and facilities include a sauna, whirlpool, and two bars. In 1994 the cozy restaurant was upgraded in charming 19th-century Nordic style.

Quality Hotel Vestlia. N-3580 Geilo. ☎ **32-09-06-11.** Fax 32-09-16-89. 75 units. MINIBAR TV TEL. May–Aug, 1,350 NOK ($149.85) double; Sept–Apr, 1,680–2,238 NOK ($186.50–$248.40) double. Rates include half board. AE, DC, MC, V. Free parking.

This isn't a fancy hotel, but it keeps guests coming back. It's half a mile east of the train station, 200 yards from the ski lifts and cross-country slopes. Built in the 1960s, the hotel was completely renovated in the early 1990s, with all the bathrooms renewed in 1999. The regular guest rooms are furnished in an attractive ski-chalet style with lots of wood; some large family rooms, with four beds, cost the same as regular rooms. About half the accommodations are in comfortable annexes scattered about the grounds. In addition to its obvious allure to skiers, the hotel is a good summer choice—guests can go hiking, boating, or horseback riding. Facilities include a swimming pool, sauna, and solarium, plus two restaurants (one featuring Norwegian buffets). Live dance music is provided almost every evening year-round except Sunday.

WHERE TO DINE
Most visitors to Geilo eat at their hotels.

Café Alpin. Geiloveien. ☎ **32-09-03-84.** Main courses 90–125 NOK ($10–$13.90). MC, V. Mon–Sat 9am–8pm, Sun 10am–8pm. NORWEGIAN.

On the second floor above the bank, this cafe is the best low-cost dining choice in town. It's good for coffee, sandwiches, or hot meals. The cafeteria serves hot but rather standard fare starting at noon. If creamed fish soup is on the menu, try it. For main dishes, you might like such Norwegian specialties as chopped reindeer meat cakes with mixed vegetables, or cured herring with sliced beets, raw onions, and boiled potatoes. For dessert, a tempting selection of Norwegian pastries is offered.

3 Trondheim to Narvik

To explore the northern Norwegian coast by car, begin your tour in Trondheim.

TRONDHEIM
425 miles N of Bergen, 343 miles NW of Oslo

Founded by the Viking king Olaf I Tryggvason in the 10th century, Trondheim is Norway's third-largest city. Scenic and pleasant, it's an active university center. The city lies on the south bay of the Trondheim Fjord, at the mouth of the Nidelven River.

Noted for its timbered architecture, Trondheim retains much of its medieval past, notably the Gothic-style Nidaros Cathedral. Until the early 1200s Trondheim was the capital of Norway. Pilgrims came from all over Europe to worship at the shrine of Olav, who was canonized in 1031. With the Reformation, however, the city's fortunes declined.

ESSENTIALS
GETTING THERE Flights to Trondheim land at **Vaernes Airport** (☎ **74-84-30-00**), 20 miles from town. Service is available from **SAS** (☎ **74-84-34-50**) and **Braathens SAFE** (☎ **74-84-32-00**). Buses to the city center take about 30 minutes. There are two trains a day from Stockholm (travel time is 12 hours) and three trains a day from Oslo (7 hours). One bus a day arrives from Bergen; the trip takes 15 hours. Contact **Norway Buss Ekspress** (☎ **22-33-01-90**) for information. The coastal steamer (see "By Coastal Steamer," above) from Bergen to Kirkenes calls at Trondheim.

VISITOR INFORMATION Contact the **Trondheim Tourist Office,** Munkegaten 19 (☎ **73-80-76-60;** www.trondheim.com), near the marketplace. The staff can make hotel reservations or arrange for rooms in a private home. Double rooms in private homes cost from 350 NOK ($38.85); the service fee is 50 NOK ($5.55), which is deducted at checkout time. The tourist office is open September 4 to May 14 Monday to Friday 9am to 4pm; May 15 to June 4 and August 21 to September 3 Monday to Friday 8:30am to 6pm, Saturday and Sunday 10am to 4pm; June 5 to June 25 and August 7 to August 20 Monday to Friday 8:30am to 8pm, and Saturday and Sunday 10am to 6pm; and June 26 to August 6 Monday to Saturday 8:30am to 10pm and Saturday and Sunday 10am to 8pm.

GETTING AROUND You can travel all over Trondheim and to outlying areas on city buses operated by **Trondheim Trafikkselskap (TT),** Dronningens Gate (☎ 73-88-44-44). Tickets for **single rides** are sold on buses for 18 NOK ($2) for adults, 9 NOK ($1) for children 4 to 16; children under 4 travel free. If you don't have exact change, you'll get a credit slip from the driver, which can be redeemed at the TT office or on a later trip. A **day card** for 24 hours of unlimited rides costs 40 NOK ($4.45) per person.

SEEING THE SIGHTS

Museum of Natural History and Archaeology. At the Norwegian University of Science and Technology, Erling Skakkes Gate 47. ☎ 73-59-21-45. Admission 25 NOK ($2.80) adults, 10 NOK ($1.10) children. May–Aug, Mon–Fri 10am–5pm, Sat–Sun 11am–5pm; Sept–Apr, Tues–Fri 10am–3pm, Sat–Sun 11am–4pm. Bus: 63.

The collections and exhibits at this university museum cover natural history, archaeology, and the social history of central Norway from prehistoric times to the Middle Ages. Special features include a diorama display of birds, archaeological displays, collections of church art, and a small ethnographic exhibit. One exhibit shows the most important habitats of central Norway and central Scandinavia. The exhibit also reveals how people have used and exploited nature through history.

✪ **Nidaros Cathedral.** Bispegaten 5. ☎ **73-53-91-60.** Admission (cathedral and museum) 35 NOK ($3.90) adults, 20 NOK ($2.20) children. Cathedral, May–June 19 and Aug 20–Sept 14, Mon–Sat 9am–3pm, Sun 1–4pm; June 20–Aug 19, Mon–Sat 9am–6pm, Sun 1–4pm; Sept 15–Apr, Mon–Sat noon–4pm, Sun 1–3pm. Bus: 2, 5, 6, 7, or 9.

Dating from the 11th century, this cathedral is one of the major ecclesiastical buildings in Scandinavia. It's in the town center, near the Rådhus. The burial place of the medieval Norwegian kings, it was also the site of the coronation of Haakon VII in 1905, an event that marked the beginning of modern Norway.

A classical European cathedral representing different architectural styles, including Gothic and Romanesque, it features an intricate rose window on the west front. Gustav Vigeland carved the gargoyles and grotesques for the head tower and northern transept. The 12th-century Archbishop's Palace, Erkebispegården, is behind the cathedral.

A small museum inside the cathedral displays the crown jewels of Norway.

Ringve Museum. Lade Allé 60 (2 miles from the center of town at Ringve Manor). ☎ 73-92-24-11. Admission 70 NOK ($7.75) adults, 25 NOK ($2.80) children, 40 NOK ($4.45) students, 140 NOK ($15.55) family. Guided tours, May 20–June, daily at 11am, noon, 12:30pm, and 2:30pm; July–Aug 10, daily at 11am and 12:30, 2:30, and 4:30pm; Aug 11–31, daily at 11am, 12:20pm, and 2:30pm; Sept, daily at noon and 2pm; Oct–May 19, Sun at 1:30pm. Bus: 3 or 4.

This museum can be viewed only on guided tours. At specified times, concerts are given on carefully preserved antique instruments, including an impressive collection of spinets, harpsichords, clavichords, pianofortes, and string and wind instruments. Also on the premises is an old kro (inn) that serves waffles, light refreshments, and coffee. The mansion was the birthplace of Admiral Tordenskiold, the Norwegian sea hero.

Stiftsgården. Munkegaten 23. ☎ **73-84-28-80.** Admission 40 NOK ($4.45) adults, 20 NOK ($2.20) children, 100 NOK ($11.10) family. Guided tours every hour on the hour. Tues–Sat 10am–5pm, Sun noon–5pm. Closed Sept–late June. Bus: 2, 5, 6, 7, or 9.

This buttercup-yellow royal palace near the marketplace was built as a private home by a rich merchant's widow in the 1770s, when Trondheim began to regain its prosperity. It's the largest wooden building in northern Europe, with 144 rooms encompassing approximately 12,000 square feet. The exterior walls were notched together, log-cabin style, then sheathed with wooden exterior panels. The unpretentious furnishings represent an amalgam of design styles.

Trøndelag Folk Museum. Sverresborg Allé. ☎ **73-89-01-00.** Admission 70 NOK ($7.75) adults, 25 NOK ($2.80) children. June–Aug, daily 11am–6pm; off-season, Tues–Sat 11am–3pm, Sun noon–4pm. Bus: 8 or 9.

One of Norway's major folk-culture museums, this complex is filled with farmhouses and cottages. With churches and town buildings, they represent aspects of everyday life in the region over the past 3 centuries. The proudest possession is Norway's northernmost stave church. The museum is surrounded by a nature park with animals. It also has a ski museum, with a lively introduction to the region's long skiing tradition, and demonstrations of old handcrafts. A restaurant (see "Where to Dine," below) in a 1739 building serves traditional Norwegian dishes.

Tyholttårnet. Otto Nielsens Vei 4, Blussuvoll. ☎ **73-87-35-00.** Admission 30 NOK ($3.35) adults, 20 NOK ($2.20) children. Mon–Sat 11am–11:30pm, Sun and holidays noon–11:30pm. Bus: 20 or 60 (ask the driver to tell you when to get off).

This 400-foot concrete tower, built in 1985 to relay radio signals along the coast, is the tallest structure in central Norway. The tower, 3 miles east of Trondheim, offers a sweeping view over the entire area. There's a revolving restaurant near the top (see "Where to Dine," below). You can go to the viewing gallery even if you don't patronize the restaurant; admission to the tower is free for diners.

ORGANIZED TOURS

From June to August, a 2-hour **bus tour** departs from the marketplace daily at noon. It costs 130 NOK ($14.45) for adults, 65 NOK ($7.20) for children. The highlight is a guided tour of the cathedral, but the price does not include admission.

There are also daily boat trips from May 22 to August 31. They leave Ravnkloa for **Munkholmen Island** (Monks Island) every hour on the hour from 10am to 5pm. In ancient times the island was an execution site. In the 11th-century Benedictine monks constructed a monastery, one of the first two in Scandinavia. In 1658 it was turned into a prison fort. You can take a guided tour of the island's historic fortress. Lunch is not included in the fare but is available at Munkholmen. The boat fare is 35 NOK ($3.90) for adults, 19 NOK ($2.10) for children. A guided tour of the fortress costs 15 NOK ($1.65) for adults, 10 NOK ($1.10) for children. Bookings can be made at the Lilletorget Hotel (☎ 73-52-05-24).

EXPLORING NEARBY ISLANDS

You can reach the islands of **Hitra** (Ansnes) and **Frøya** (Sistranda) by fast steamer from Trondheim Monday to Saturday. For more information, ask at the tourist information office in Trondheim.

Hitra is one of Norway's largest islands, with an array of forests, wooded hills, well-stocked lakes, weathered rocks, and small fjords. The island is also known for its large herds of red deer. Other attractions include the **Dolm Church** and **Dolmen town,** a miniature community designed and built by a Dolmoy crofter and fisherman. After you reach Hitra, you might want to visit neighboring Frøya by ferry.

WHERE TO STAY
Many hotels offer special summer prices from mid-June to the end of August. The rest of the year, hotels offer weekend discounts if you stay 2 nights.

Expensive
Clareon Grand Olav Hotel. Kjøpmannsgaten 48, N-7001 Trondheim. ☎ **73-53-53-10.** Fax 73-53-57-20. www.grandolav.no. 112 units. A/C MINIBAR TV TEL. 975–1,595 NOK ($108.25–$177.05) double; 2,000–4,000 NOK ($222–$444) suite. Rates include breakfast. AE, DC, MC, V. Parking 100 NOK ($11.10). Bus: 54.

This six-story hotel is the most stylish in Trondheim. It was designed in 1989 by the architect of the nearby Radisson SAS Royal Garden Hotel, a close competitor. The hotel (which became the Clareon Grand in 1998) is adjacent to a building complex that includes elegant boutiques and Trondheim's largest concert hall. Its modern interior is plush and imaginative; guest rooms are decorated in one of 27 different styles. They have good beds and ample bathrooms, with state-of-the-art plumbing.

Dining/Diversions: There's a lobby-level bar, the Fiolinen; an upscale restaurant, the Scenario'n; and a pub. The informal Torgcafé is an atrium restaurant that serves snacks and drinks.

Amenities: Room service, laundry, baby-sitting, salon, and massage.

✪ **Radisson SAS Royal Garden Hotel.** Kjøpmannsgaten 73, N-7010 Trondheim. ☎ **800/333-3333** in the U.S., or 73-80-30-00. Fax 73-80-30-50. www.radissonsas.com. 298 units. A/C MINIBAR TV TEL. 990–1,795 NOK ($109.90–$199.25) double; from 3,500 NOK ($388.50) suite. Children under 15 stay free in parents' room. Rates include buffet breakfast. AE, CB, DC, MC, V. Parking 130 NOK ($14.45). Bus: 54.

This architecturally innovative hotel lies at the northwestern edge of the Old Town, southwest of the train station. Opened in 1984, it has a soaring lobby atrium and public rooms that are lavishly furnished and plant-filled. The comfortable guest rooms, all designed as doubles, attract an international business trade and many tour groups in the summer. Mirrored walls and classic appointments characterize the ample rooms, which have firm mattresses and double-glazed windows. The marble bathrooms are medium sized with hair dryers.

Dining/Diversions: There's piano music in the evening at the bar on an indoor terrace. The elegant restaurants—Cicignon, with live dance music, and the more formal and expensive Prins Olav Grill—both offer views of the harbor. The Royal Garden Bistro is more informal.

Amenities: Room service, laundry, baby-sitting, sauna, health club, whirlpool, solarium, indoor swimming pool, and boutiques.

Moderate
Britannia Hotel. Dronningens Gate 5, N-7001 Trondheim. ☎ **73-53-53-53.** Fax 73-51-29-00. www.britannia.no. 175 units. MINIBAR TV TEL. Midsummer, 810 NOK ($89.90) double. Rest of year, Sun–Thurs 1,350 NOK ($149.85) double; Fri–Sat 850 NOK ($94.35) double. Year-round, 2,000–2,500 NOK ($222–$277.50) suite. Rates include breakfast. AE, DC, MC, V. Parking 95 NOK ($10.55). Bus: 2, 5, 6, 7, or 9.

This turn-of-the-century lodging is Trondheim's traditional hotel, with many of its original details intact. The ornate Palm Garden (Palmehave), with its art nouveau winter garden, fountain, and piano, captures the grand spirit. The renovated guest rooms have wooden floors. The most tranquil rooms, which front the courtyard, are also the smallest. Most accommodations are medium sized with excellent beds, tiled bathrooms and hair dryers. Dining choices include the Hjoernet Bar and Brasserie for light meals and snacks, and the Jonathan, an intimate restaurant with an impressive wine list that serves grilled main dishes. The Queen's Pub is a traditional English watering hole, and there's a stylish piano bar.

Scandic Hotel Residence. Munkegaten 26, N-7011 Trondheim. ☎ **800/528-1234** in the U.S., or 73-52-83-80. Fax 73-52-64-60. E-mail: residence@scandic-hotels.com. 66 units. MINIBAR TV TEL. Sun–Thurs 1345 NOK ($149.30) double; Fri–Sat 825 NOK ($91.60) double. Rates include breakfast. AE, DC, MC, V. Parking 50 NOK ($5.55). Bus: 2, 5, 6, 7, or 9.

On the market square opposite the Royal Palace, the Hotel Residence, built in 1915 in Jugend (art nouveau) style, has recently been renovated. Accommodations are tastefully decorated, and the units in front open onto the marketplace. The generously sized guest rooms have triple-glazed windows, safes, and good beds. The big marble bathrooms offer great shelf space, hair dryers, and, in some cases, bidets. Much of the hotel's ground floor is given over to the Café Amsterdam, a trio of rustically decorated rooms reminiscent of a Dutch tavern, with an area for drinking and separate areas for well-prepared platters and snacks. A separate entrance from the street opens into a casual pub, the Jørgen B. (named after the region's most famous brewer).

Inexpensive

Gildevagen Hotell. Søndre Gate 22B, N-7010 Trondheim. ☎ **73-87-01-30.** Fax 73-52-38-98. www.rainbow.hotels.no. E-mail: gildevagen@online.no. 81 units. MINIBAR TV TEL. 1,195 NOK ($132.65) double. AE, CB, DC, MC, V. Parking 50 NOK ($5.55).

Locals often cite this hotel as offering good value. Built in the late 19th century, it has been renovated many times, most recently in 1994. It's a short walk uphill from the harbor, near the Old Town's famous bridge and the train station. The guest rooms are generally quite large; 33 are reserved for nonsmokers. Beds are good, and rooms come in a variety of sizes, from snug to spacious. Bathrooms are small. A new wing with 25 modern rooms was in the works at press time. A big Norwegian "cold table" breakfast is served in an old-fashioned dining room; no other meals are offered.

Singsaker Sommerhotell. Rogertsgate 1, N-7016 Trondheim. ☎ **73-89-31-00.** Fax 73-89-32-00. www.singsaker-smmerhotell.com. 106 units, 16 with bathroom. TEL. 540 NOK ($59.95) double without bathroom, 640 NOK ($71.05) double with bathroom; 720 NOK ($79.90) triple without bathroom, 840 NOK ($93.25) triple with bathroom; 155 NOK ($17.20) per person in dormitory room. Rates include breakfast. AE, DC, MC, V. Closed Aug 20–May 15. Bus: 63.

This student residence hall is also a choice bargain hotel in summer. It's about a 10-minute walk from the center of Trondheim. The small rooms are cozy, and all have wash basins. The least expensive rooms are no-frills dormitory style. The dining room serves good, wholesome breakfasts. In the evening, young people gather around the open fireplace or play billiards or other games.

Trondheim Hotell. Kongensgate 15, N-7013 Trondheim. ☎ **73-50-50-50.** Fax 73-51-60-58. www.rainbow-hotels.no. E-mail: trondheim.hotell@online.no. 131 units. MINIBAR TV TEL. 1,195 NOK ($132.65) double. Rates include breakfast. AE, DC, MC, V. Parking 110 NOK ($12.20). Bus: Bus from airport stops here.

This hotel, near the market square, offers medium-size guest rooms with upholstered classic bentwood furniture. Many have an extra foldaway bed. Some rooms are suitable for persons with disabilities, and others are reserved for nonsmokers. The beds are good, and the bathrooms, though small, are amply supplied with such amenities as trouser presses and hair dryers. Constructed in 1913, it was renovated and expanded in 1990. There's a self-service laundry, and an upscale cafe that serves light international meals. The nearby Monte Cristo Disco admits hotel guests free.

WHERE TO DINE

Try a local specialty, *vafler med øst* (waffle and cheese), sold at most cafeterias and restaurants.

Expensive

❂ **Bryggen.** Øvre Bakklandet 66. ☎ **73-52-02-30.** Reservations recommended. Main courses 220–290 NOK ($24.40–$32.20); 3-course fixed-price menu 440 NOK ($48.85); 5-course fixed-price dinner 590 NOK ($65.50). AE, DC, MC, V. Mon–Sat 6pm–11pm. Bus: 1, 5, or 9. NORWEGIAN/FRENCH.

One of the most atmospheric restaurants in Trondheim is in a 1749 warehouse with a heavily trussed brick interior. It's on the verdant banks of the Nidelven River, a few steps from the town's oldest bridge, the Gamle Bybro. The restaurant is a 10-minute walk from the town center. The menu varies with the season. It might include fish-and-shellfish soup, suprême of Norwegian duck, medaillons of reindeer in juniper-berry cream sauce, or poached fresh fish of the day. You'll find the staff devoted and professional, and justifiably proud of the interesting cuisine. There's an extensive wine list and an impressive selection of cognac and cigars.

Jonathan's. In the Brittania Hotel, Dronningens Gate 5. ☎ **73-53-53-53.** Reservations required. Main courses 185–245 NOK ($20.55–$27.20). AE, DC, MC, V. Mon–Sat 3–11pm. Bus: 2, 5, 6, 7, or 9. NORWEGIAN/FRENCH.

One of the best hotel restaurants in town, Jonathan's is designed like a Mediterranean wine cellar, with antiques, a big open fireplace, and waiters colorfully dressed as troubadours. The beautifully prepared food relies on high-quality ingredients. Dinner might include canapés of shrimp, smoked salmon, and local caviar, followed by grilled salmon garnished with shellfish and fresh vegetables, or a grilled steak—perhaps a veal schnitzel.

Monte Cristo. Prinsensgaten 38. ☎ **73-52-18-80.** Reservations recommended on weekends. Main courses 160–230 NOK ($17.75–$25.55). AE, DC, MC, V. Mon–Sat 7–11:30pm. Bus: 2, 5, 6, 7, or 9. NORWEGIAN/INTERNATIONAL.

The region's busiest and most popular supper club, the Monte Cristo lies within the thick walls of an 1832 private house. The club serves simple but delightfully flavorful, expertly prepared food, not the usual dull nightclub fare. It also books the leading traditional dance bands of Norway and Sweden. Menu choices include fillet of monkfish in sour-cream sauce, barbecued spareribs in spicy Cajun sauce, and fillet of Norwegian lamb. The disco upstairs attracts a younger group for live music Tuesday to Saturday from 9pm to 3am. Entrance is free for diners, 80 NOK ($8.90) for others.

Restaurant Egon Tårnet (Tårnrestauranten Galaksen). Otto Nielsens Vei 4, Blussuvoll. ☎ **73-51-31-66.** Reservations recommended on weekends. Main courses 210–255 NOK ($23.30–$28.30). AE, DC, MC, V. Mon–Sat 11:30am–10pm, Sun noon–6pm. Bus: 20 or 60. NORWEGIAN/INTERNATIONAL.

This restaurant is near the top of the region's tallest building (listed under "Seeing the Sights," above). The restaurant's floor makes one full revolution per hour, allowing sweeping views of the surrounding mountains and coastline. Specialties include cold, thinly sliced, marinated salmon; fillet of reindeer in juniper-berry game sauce; and fresh fillet of monkfish in a sauce of crème fraîche with soya. Although it's at a tourist attraction, the restaurant maintains high standards. Chefs are making greater efforts to create lighter but still flavorful cuisine. Diners who visit the observation platform are reimbursed for the elevator ride.

Moderate

❂ **Havfruen Fiskerestaurant.** Kjøpmannsgaten 7. ☎ **73-87-40-70.** Reservations required. Main courses 180–280 NOK ($20–$31.10). AE, DC, MC, V. Mon–Fri 4–10:30pm, Sat 6–10:30pm. Bus: 2, 5, 6, 7, or 9. SEAFOOD.

The better of the two fish restaurants in Trondheim, Havfruen Fiskerestaurant is in a memorable setting. The 1680 warehouse is near the Nidelven River and the town's most famous bridge, so naturally it's decorated in a nautical style. The staff seems to enjoy evaluating and offering advice about the daily harvest of fish. The menu changes each season, based on local fish migration patterns. Staples include fried and peppered sea wolf served with ragoût of mushrooms, poached halibut (a summer favorite) in crabmeat sauce, and grilled fillet of salmon in dill-flavored cream sauce.

✪ **Tavern På Sverresborg.** Sverresborg Allé, at Trøndelag Folk Museum. ☎ **73-52-09-32.** Reservations recommended. Snack-style main dishes 75 NOK ($8.30); main courses 110–220 NOK ($12.20–$24.40). MC, V. Mon–Fri 4pm–midnight, Sat 2pm–midnight, Sun noon–midnight. Bus: 8 or 9. NORWEGIAN.

No restaurant in town offers more authentic Norwegian cuisine than this historic eatery, 3 miles south of Trondheim's commercial center. Built as a private merchant's house in 1739, and later transformed into a clapboard-sided tavern, it's one of the few wooden buildings of its age in this area. Cramped and cozy, it's the town's most vivid reminder of the past, with wide-plank flooring and antique rustic accessories. There's an emphasis on 18th- and 19th-century recipes. Try *blandet spekemat,* served with flatbrød; it consists of thinly sliced smoked ham, diced meat, slices of salami, smoked mutton, and garnishes of lettuce and tomato. Other comparably priced items include *rømmergrøt* (sour-cream porridge), *finnbiff* (reindeer meat), omelets, herring, and meatballs.

TRONDHEIM AFTER DARK

Monte Cristo (see "Where to Dine," above) has a disco.

Frekken. Dronningensgaten 12. ☎ **73-51-45-22.**

Set in the heart of Trondheim, and catering to a crowd of drinkers and dancers ages 20 to 40, this is one of the more visible discos in town. Containing separate areas devoted to a pub, a disco, and a piano bar. It's open Thursday to Sunday from 9:30pm to around 3am, charging an entrance of 50 NOK ($5.55).

FROM TRONDHEIM TO BODØ

On the long trek north on E6, the first town of any size is **Steinkjer.** It's a military base for "boot campers." Another 218 miles along is **Mo i Rana,** whose poetic name ("Mo on the Ranafjord") is more romantic than it is. It's a center for iron and steel production. Nineteen miles north of the town lies **Svartisen** ("Black Ice"), a glacier.

Fifty miles north of Mo i Rana toward the Arctic Circle, you'll come to the **Polarsirkelsenteret,** on E6. It offers a multiscreen show depicting the highlights of Norway. Many people send cards and letters from here with a special postmark from the Arctic Circle. There's also a cafeteria and gift shop on the grounds. The center is at N-8242 Polarsirkelen (☎ **75-16-60-66**). It's open in May and June, daily from 10am to 8pm; July to September, daily 9am to 8pm. Admission is 50 NOK ($5.55).

Continue north to Fauske, and then follow Route 80 west along the Skjerstadfjord. Depending on weather conditions, you should reach Bodø in under an hour.

BODØ

466 miles N of Trondheim, 889 miles N of Bergen, 811 miles N of Oslo

This seaport, the terminus of the Nordland railway, lies just north of the Arctic Circle. Visitors flock to Bodø, the capital of Nordland, for a glimpse of the midnight sun, which shines brightly from June 1 to July 13. But don't expect a clear view of it—many nights are rainy or hazy. From December 19 to January 9, Bodø gets no sunlight at all.

From Bodø you can take excursions in many directions to glaciers and bird islands; perhaps the most important are to the Lofoten Islands (see below).

ESSENTIALS

GETTING THERE   If you're not driving or traveling by coastal steamer, you can reach Bodø from major cities throughout Norway, usually with connections through either Trondheim or Oslo, on **SAS** (☎ 75-54-47-00) or Braathens (☎ 75-54-27-00). The airport lies less than a mile southwest of the city center, and is accessed by a bus (it's marked "Centrums Bussen") that departs at 20-minute intervals every Monday to Friday. Passengers arriving on a Saturday or Sunday hire one of the many taxis waiting at the arrivals gate. Bodø is at the end of the Nordland rail line.

Two **trains** a day leave Trondheim for Bodø. The trip takes 10 hours, 20 minutes.

For **bus** information, contact **Saltens Bilruter** in Bodø (☎ 75-50-90-10). Fauske is a transportation hub along the E6 highway to the north and Route 80 west to Bodø. From Fauske there are two buses a day to Bodø. The trip takes an hour and 10 minutes. If you take the train from Stockholm to Narvik (north of Bodø), you can make bus connections to Fauske and Bodø, a total trip of 5 hours.

VISITOR INFORMATION   The **tourist office, called Destination Bodø,** is at Sjøgaten 21, N-8000 Bodø (☎ 75-54-80-00), in the town center. It's open mid-June to mid-August, daily from 9am to 8:30pm; mid-August to mid-June, Monday to Friday 9am to 4pm.

SEEING THE SIGHTS

Bodin Kirke. Gamle Riksvei 68. ☎ 75-54-80-00. Free admission. June–Aug, Mon–Fri 10am–3pm. Closed Sept–May. Bus: 23 from the station.

Dating from 1240, this church is 2 miles east of the town center. It has a baroque altar-piece. This is the most famous church in the district, and one of the few in the north from the Middle Ages. Local residents are proud of it, despite its simplicity.

Bodø Domkirke. Torv Gate 12. ☎ 75-52-17-50. Free admission. May–Sept, daily 9am–3pm. Closed Oct–Apr.

Completed in 1956, this is the most notable building constructed since German bombers leveled Bodø on May 27, 1940. It features tufted rugs depicting ecclesiastical themes, wall hangings, and a stained-glass window that captures the northern lights. A memorial outside honors those killed in the war with the inscription NO ONE MENTIONED, NO ONE FORGOTTEN. There's also an outstanding spire that stands separate from the main building.

Nordlandmuseet (Nordland Museum). Prinsengate 116. ☎ 75-52-16-40. Admission 30 NOK ($3.35), 15 NOK ($1.65) for children under 15. Mon–Fri 9am–3pm, Sat 10am–3pm, Sun noon–3pm.

In the town center, the main building of this museum is one of the oldest structures in Bodø. Here you'll find, among other exhibits, artifacts recalling the saga of local fishermen and artifacts from the Lapp culture. There's also a "dry" aquarium, along with silver treasure dating from the Viking era.

ACTIVE SPORTS

If you'd like to go horseback riding under the midnight sun, **Bodø Hestecenter,** Soloya Gård (☎ 75-51-41-48), about 9 miles southwest of Bodø, rents horses. Buses go there Monday to Friday morning and evening and Saturday morning. For more information, ask at the Bodø Tourist Office. The cost is 100 NOK ($11.10) for a 45-minute ride.

Svømmehallen, Sivert Nielsens Gate 63 (☎ 75-55-75-20), is Bodø's largest and busiest indoor swimming pool. It's open September to May, Tuesday to Friday from

10am to 8pm, Saturday and Sunday 10am to 3pm; June to August, Monday, Wednesday, and Friday 10am to 2pm, Tuesday and Thursday 3 to 8pm (closed Saturday and Sunday). Admission is 40 NOK ($4.45) for adults, 20 NOK ($2.20) for children under 18.

EXPLORING A SPECTACULAR LANDSCAPE

THE MAELSTROM   From Bodø, you can take a bus to the mighty maelstrom, the ✪ **Saltstraumen Eddy,** 20 miles south of the city. The variation between high- and low-tide levels pushes immense volumes of water through narrow fjords, creating huge whirlpools known as "kettles." When the eddies and the surrounding land vibrate, they produce an odd yelling sound. Saltstraumen is nearly 2 miles long and only about 500 feet wide, with billions of gallons of water pressing through at speeds of about 10 knots. It's best to go in the morning when it's most dramatic. Buses from Bodø run five times a day Monday to Saturday, twice on Sunday. The cost is 150 NOK ($16.65) for adults round-trip, half-price for children. A round-trip taxi excursion costs 500 NOK ($55.50) for two passengers.

VISITING A GLACIER   One of Norway's major tourist attractions, **Svartisen** is second in size in the country only to the Jostedal Glacier. This ice plateau 330 feet above sea level covers 150 square miles of high mountains and narrow fjords. About 100 miles from Bodø, the glacier can be reached by car, although a boat crossing over the Svartisenfjord is more exciting. Tours to the glacier on the Helgeland Express, a combination bus-and-ferry excursion, are offered from Bodø several times in the summer (usually every second Saturday in July and August). The cost is 350 NOK ($38.85) for adults, 170 NOK ($18.85) for children under 16. The tours leave Bodø at 1pm and return around 8pm. You can go ashore to examine the Engaglacier and see the nearby visitor center (☎ 75-75-00-11). The local tourist office, or the local tour operator **Nordtrafikk** (☎ 75-72-12-00), can provide more information and make reservations. Depending on ice conditions, the visitor center may be able to arrange boat transportation across a narrow but icy channel so you can have a closer look at the ice floe.

WHERE TO STAY

The Bodø Tourist Office (see above) can help you book a room in a hotel.

Expensive

Diplomat Hotel. Sjøgata 23, N-8001 Bodø. ☎ **75-52-70-00.** Fax 75-54-70-55. E-mail: hotel@diplomat-hotel.no. 103 units. MINIBAR TV TEL. Mid-June to Aug 5, 800 NOK ($88.80) double. Aug 6 to mid-June, Mon–Thurs 1,400 NOK ($155.40) double; Fri–Sun 720 NOK ($79.90) double. Year-round, 1,800–2,500 NOK ($199.80–$277.50) suite. Rates include breakfast. AE, DC, MC, V. Free parking.

Located at the harbor and offering a view of Vestfjorden, this is one of Bodø's best hotels, built in 1986 and enlarged in 1990. Most of the somberly furnished rooms have large writing desks. Only moderate in size, rooms are comfortable and well maintained, with good beds and rather small bathrooms. The hotel has two popular restaurants (see "Where to Dine," below).

✪ **Radisson SAS Royal Hotel.** Storgaten 2, N-8000 Bodø. ☎ **800/333-3333** in the U.S., or 75-52-41-00. Fax 75-52-74-93. 190 units. MINIBAR TV TEL. June–Aug, 840 NOK ($93.25) double; 1,600 NOK ($177.60) suite. Sept–May, 1,550 NOK ($172.05) double; 2,000 NOK ($222) suite. Rates include breakfast. AE, DC, MC, V. Free parking.

By far the finest hotel in the area, this glistening structure has several bars and dining facilities. A complete renovation of the exterior, the public rooms, and all guest rooms was complete in September 2000. The guest rooms are furnished in sleek contemporary style. They're good-sized and decorated in a number of motifs, including Japanese, Nordic, Chinese, and British. Amenities include trouser presses and small shower/bathtubs with hair dryers in the medium-size bathrooms. The Royal is on the main street at the harborfront.

Dining/Diversions: The Top 13 is a panoramic bar. Other options for a drink or snack include the Pizzakjeller'n, the Baquette'n, the Royal Café, and the Sjøsiden.

Amenities: Room service (during meal hours), express laundry service, secretarial services, sauna, solarium, fitness center.

Moderate

Bodø Hotell. Professor Schyttesgate 5, N-8001 Bodø. ☎ 75-52-69-00. Fax 75-52-57-78. 31 units. TV TEL. June 20–Aug 15 and Fri–Sat year-round, 660 NOK ($73.25) double; rest of year, Sun–Thurs 860 NOK ($95.45) double. Year-round, 800–1,000 NOK ($88.80–$111) suite. Rates include breakfast. AE, DC, MC, V. Closed Dec 20–Jan 3. Free parking.

Opened in 1987, this hotel quickly became known for its good value. In the town center 2½ blocks from the harbor, it has a helpful staff and modern rooms, with satellite TV and good beds. Bathrooms are small, but they are kept sparkling clean. The hotel also offers rooms for nonsmokers and persons with disabilities. The hotel operates Cuisine Imperiale, a Mongolian eatery, open Monday to Saturday from 11am to 4pm, that serves Southeast Asian dishes.

Inexpensive

Norrøna. Storgaten 4, N-8000 Bodø. ☎ 75-52-41-18. Fax 75-52-33-88. 99 units. TV TEL. 600–710 NOK ($66.60–$78.80) double. Rates include breakfast. AE, DC, MC, V. No parking.

The Norrøna is run by the nearby Radisson SAS Royal Hotel, which uses it primarily as a bed-and-breakfast. Its prime location is one of its chief advantages. The functional modern building stands in the center of Bodø. The comfortable, simply furnished guest rooms, though small and plain, are comfortable. Guests enjoy the same privileges as patrons of the more expensive Radisson SAS Royal Hotel. The hotel operates a British-style pub, Piccadilly.

Shama Sentrum Hotel. Storgaten 39, N-8001 Bodø. ☎ 75-52-48-88. Fax 75-52-58-90. www.sentrum-hotel.no. 19 units. TV TEL. 590–750 NOK ($65.50–$83.25) double. Rates include breakfast. AE, DC, V. Free parking.

The rooms in this boarding house near the harbor are efficiently furnished and comfortable, if a bit small, and have firm mattresses on the beds. Bathrooms are very small. The Centrum is known for its unpretentious cellar restaurant, Shama, which is open daily from 3 to 10:30pm.

WHERE TO DINE

China Garden. Storgata 60. ☎ 75-52-71-25. Reservations recommended. Main courses 112–160 NOK ($12.45–$17.75); fixed-price menu 175 NOK ($19.45). AE, MC, V. Sun–Thurs 2–10:45pm, Fri–Sat 2pm–midnight. CANTONESE.

This well-managed restaurant, run by emigrants from Hong Kong, is one of the only Asian restaurants in town. It serves sophisticated, flavorful Chinese food. The red-and-gold restaurant, behind large signs with Chinese calligraphic symbols, is quite popular. Three favorite dishes are sweet-and-sour prawns, sweet-and-sour pork, and sweet-and-sour pork served with black beans and garlic. Although it doesn't rank with Oslo's better Chinese restaurants, China Garden is a welcome change of pace this far north.

Diplomat Hotel Restaurants. Sjøgata 23. ☎ 75-52-70-00. Main courses 155–225 NOK ($17.20–$25); daily lunch plates 120–160 NOK ($13.30–$17.75); lunch buffet 195 NOK ($21.65). AE, DC, MC, V. Daily 7am–midnight. NORWEGIAN/INTERNATIONAL.

Although the Diplomat is best known for its well-maintained accommodations, it also runs two restaurants (the Spisestuen and Blix) that serve some of the best food in town. Usually the Spisestuen serves lunch and the Blix dinner, but the arrangement changes depending on the number of bus tours and cruise ships expected. Wherever the meal is served, you're likely to be joined by local residents, especially at lunch. Choices include lasagne, steak, fillets of reindeer, fish soup, and fresh local fish. You don't get palate-tantalizing excitement here, but the solid, reliable fare uses some of the freshest ingredients that reach the far north.

Sjøsiden (Sea Side). In the Radisson SAS Royal Hotel, Storgaten 2. ☎ **75-52-41-00.** Reservations recommended. Main courses 135–250 NOK ($15–$27.75); summer seafood buffet 190 NOK ($21.10). AE, DC, MC, V. Mon–Fri 11am–2pm; Mon–Sat 6–10:30pm. SEAFOOD/INTERNATIONAL/NORWEGIAN.

This waterfront spot has the best summer seafood buffet in town. It's served from late June to late August and consists of local seafood dishes, including fried squid, smoked halibut, fresh shrimp, coalfish, and cod—all are quite delectable. A variety of sauces go with the fish, as well as fish soup prepared in the style of northern Norway. To finish, there's a selection of desserts. At any time of the year, you can order cream of wild mushroom soup or a seafood appetizer that includes an entire fjord crab garnished with shrimp. Specialties are grilled fillet of reindeer and grilled monkfish.

LOFOTEN ISLANDS

174 miles N of Bodø, 886 miles NE of Bergen, 777 miles N of Oslo

The island kingdom of Lofoten, one of the most beautiful regions of Norway, lies 123 miles north of the Arctic Circle. Its population of 35,000 spreads over large and small islands. Many visitors come just to fish, but the area offers abundant bird life and flora. The midnight sun shines from mid-May to the end of July.

The Lofoten Islands stretch from Vågan in the east to Røst and Skomvaer in the southwest. The steep Lofoten mountain peaks—often called the Lofotwall—shelter farmland and deep fjords from the elements.

The Gulf Stream contributes to the seasonal Lofoten fishing, Lofotfisket. Beyond Lofoten, and especially in the Vestfjord, Arctic Sea codfish spawn; huge harvesting operations are carried out between January and April.

The first inhabitants of the Lofoten Islands were nomads who hunted and fished, but excavations show that agriculture existed here at least 4,000 years ago. The Vikings pursued farming, fishing, and trading; examples of Viking housing sites can be seen on Vestbågøya, where more than 1,000 burial mounds have been found.

Harsh treatment of local residents by the Nazis during the Second World War played a major part in the creation of the famous Norwegian resistance movement. Allied forces that landed here to harass the German iron-ore boats sailing from Narvik withdrew in June 1940. They evacuated as many Lofoten residents as they could to Scotland for the duration of the war.

Today the Lofotens have modern towns with shops, hotels, restaurants, and public transportation.

ESSENTIALS

Svolvær is the largest town on the archipelago's largest island.

GETTING THERE From Bodø, drive east on Route 80 to Fauske. Take E6 north to Ulvsvåg, and head southwest on Route 81 toward the town of Skutvik. From Skutvik, take the 2-hour ferry to Svolvær. For ferry information and reservations, contact **Ofotens og Vesterålens Dampskibsselskab A/S,** Box 375, N-8451 Stokmarknes (☎ **76-96-76-00**).

You can fly to Svolvær on **Widerøe Airline,** which has seven flights a day from Bodø. For information, call ☎ **75-50-48-00** in Bodø or **76-07-00-99** in Svolvær.

You can also read the Lofotens by using a combination of rail, bus, and ferry. Many visitors take a train to Bodø, and then transfer to a bus that crosses from Bodø to Svolvær on a ferry. Most bus departures from Bodø are timed to coincide with the arrival of trains from Oslo, Bergen, and other points. Buses also take passengers from elsewhere in Norway to Ulvsvåg, then on to Skutvik, where you can board a ferry to Svolvær. For information on train-bus-ferry connections, contact **Destination Bodø Office** (☎ **75-54-80-00**).

The coastal steamer (see "By Coastal Steamer," above) calls at Stamsund and Svolvær. The steamer departs from Bodø at 3pm daily.

VISITOR INFORMATION   Contact **Destination Lofoten,** Box 210, N-8301 Svolvær (☎ **76-07-30-00**), near the ferry docks in a big red building. It's open July to mid-August, daily from 9am to 9pm; mid-June to June 30 and mid-August to August 31, daily 9am to 8pm; September to mid-June, Monday to Friday 8am to 4pm.

GETTING AROUND   At the Tourist office at Svolvær you can pick up a free pamphlet, "Lofoten Info-Guide," with information about all ferries and buses throughout the archipelago. All inhabited islands are linked by ferry, and buses service the four major islands, including Svolvær.

SEEING THE SIGHTS

Outdoor activities include mountain climbing, diving, canoeing, rambling through the countryside, bird-watching (see "Røst & Vaerøy: World-Class Bird-Watching," below), whale watching, sailing, riding, downhill and cross-country skiing, and ice fishing.

There are handcraft shops at Svolvær, Leknes, Sørvågen, and Vaerøy.

You can also find examples of a special old-fashioned method of knitting—needle binding, which dates to Viking times. The **Glass Cabin** at Vikten, near Napp, is northern Norway's only such studio. It's open to the public and offers products of top quality and original design.

Many artists visit the islands, and there are galleries at Svolvær, Oersnes, Stamsund, and Leknes. Local and international artists are represented. The North Norway Artists' Center is in Svolvær.

The fishing village of **Nusfjord** has been cited by UNESCO for its well-preserved historic buildings, especially traditional *rorbuer* (fishing cottages).

Lofoten Museum. Kabelvåg. ☎ **76-07-82-23.** Admission 40 NOK ($4.45) adults, 15 NOK ($1.65) children. June 1–14 and Aug 16–31, daily 9am–6pm; June 15–Aug 15, daily 9am–9pm; Sept–May, Mon–Fri 9am–3pm.

The regional museum depicts past life in the islands. Excavations are under way at the site of an old trading post, Vagar, Europe's northernmost town in the Middle Ages. The museum is on the outskirts of Kabelvåg, 3 miles from Svolvær.

Skaftnes Section. Sennesvik. ☎ **76-08-00-43.** Admission 35 NOK ($3.90) adults, 15 NOK ($1.65) children. June–Aug, Tues–Fri 11am–4pm, Sun 1–6pm; Sept–May, by appointment only.

Skaftnes is a small fishing community where visitors can explore the main house and a boathouse that date to the 1860s. Other buildings, including a blacksmith shop, re-create an earlier period when local people relied almost entirely on the sea for their livelihood. This village is at Sennesvik, on the main road (Route 837) 5 miles from Leknes and 10 miles from Stamsund. Skaftnes is now operated by the Vestvågøy Museum (see below).

Vestvågøy Museum. Fygleveien 109. ☎ **76-08-00-43.** Admission 35 NOK ($3.90) adults, 15 NOK ($1.65) children. Mon–Fri 11am–4pm, Sun noon–3pm. Closed Sept–May.

This museum has exhibits depicting the lifestyle of the Lofoten fisherman-farmer. It's on the main road at Fygle, 1 mile from Leknes and 9 miles from Stamsund.

Røst & Vaerøy: World-Class Bird-Watching

Mountains speckled with birds range from Andøy in the north all the way to the southern tip of Lofoten. Many different types of seabird can be seen during nesting season. The most famous nesting cliffs are at Røst and Vaerøy, remote islands that can be reached by steamer, plane, or helicopter.

On the flat island of **Røstlandet,** the main attraction is the bird sanctuary, made up of approximately 1,000 little offshore islands. The highly prized eider duck is found here. Locals provide small nesting shelters for the ducks and collect eiderdown after the ducklings hatch. Cormorants and sea gulls nest on the steep cliffs. Puffins nest at the end of narrow tunnels in the grassy hills, and auks and sea eagles nest high up on ledges.

Vaerøy's **Mount Mostadfjell** is the nesting place for more than 1.5 million seabirds, including sea eagles, auks, puffins, guillemots, kittiwakes, cormorants, and others that breed from May to August.

North Vaerøy Church, with its onion-shaped dome, was brought here from Vagån in 1799. The altarpiece, from around 1400, is a late medieval English alabaster relief. It depicts the Annunciation, the Three Magi, the Resurrection, and the Ascension.

For information about these islands, contact Destination Lofoten or the ferry company, **Ofotens og Verterålens Dampskibsselskab A/S,** Box 375, N-8451 Stokmarknes (☎ **76-96-76-00**).

Where to Stay & Dine

Destination Lofoten (see "Visitor Information," above) publishes an accommodations guide to the islands.

In addition to hotels, guest houses, and campsites, the Lofoten Islands offer lodging in old traditional fishing cottages known as rorbuer. The larger (often two stories), usually more modern version is a sjøhus (sea house). The traditional *rorbu* was built on the edge of the water, often on piles, with room for 10 bunks, a kitchen, and an entrance hall used as a work and storage room. Many rorbuer today are still simple and unpretentious, but some have electricity, a wood stove, a kitchenette with a sink, and running water. Others have been outfitted with separate bedrooms, private showers, and toilets. **Backroads** (☎ **800/462-2848**) is the best and most convenient outfitter or try Destination Lofoten.

In Stamsund

Stamsund Lofoten. N-8340 Stamsund. ☎ **76-08-93-00.** Fax 76-08-97-26. www. stamsund.no. 28 units. TV TEL. 710 NOK ($78.80) double. Rates include breakfast. AE, DC, MC, V. Free parking.

This hotel in the heart of town offers a view of the harbor. The small guest rooms are simply furnished but have good beds, and many have TVs. On the premises is a bar and a restaurant that serves standard Norwegian fare.

In Svolvær

Royal Hotel Lofoten. Sivert Nelsen Gate, N-8300 Svolvær. ☎ **76-07-12-00.** Fax 76-07-08-50. 48 units. MINIBAR TV TEL. 1,095 NOK ($121.55) double; 1,200 NOK ($133.20) suite. Rates include breakfast. AE, DC, MC, V. Free parking.

About half the well-furnished rooms at this 1975 hotel overlook the sea. It's in the town center, near the express steamer quay. The look is rather functional, but maintenance is good. Beds have firm mattresses, and the bathrooms, though cramped, are sparkling clean. On the premises are a bar and a lively disco. Restaurant Lofoten specializes in fish and steak; main courses run 180 to 250 NOK ($20 to $27.75).

Vestfjord Hotel. Box 386, N-8301 Svolvær. ☎ **76-07-08-70.** Fax 76-07-08-54. 63 units. TV TEL. June–Aug 1 and Sun–Thurs year-round, 1,095 NOK ($121.55) double; Aug 2–May, Fri–Sat 650 NOK ($72.15) double. Year-round, 1,430 NOK ($158.75) suite. Rates include breakfast. AE, DC, MC, V. Free parking.

This building was a former warehouse that stored marine supplies and fish. After extensive remodeling in the late 1980s, it reopened as this well-managed hotel. The guest rooms are functional but comfortable; most contain a minibar, and many overlook the sea. Beds are good and mattresses firm. The bathrooms are tiny, with hardly enough room to store your stuff. You may have to ask the maid to bring more of the skimpy towels. Facilities include a lobby bar and a pleasant restaurant that specializes in fish and steaks. It serves sustaining fare—nothing remarkable.

NARVIK
187 miles NE of Bodø, 1,022 miles NE of Bergen, 919 miles N of Oslo

This ice-free seaport on the Ofotfjord is in Nordland *fylke* (country), 250 miles north of the Arctic Circle. Narvik, founded in 1903 when the Ofoten (not to be confused with "Lofoten") railway line was completed, boasts Europe's most modern shipping harbor for iron ore. It's the northernmost electrified railway line in the world. It covers a magnificent scenic route, through precipitous mountain terrain and tunnels, over ridges, and across tall stone embankments.

Only 6½ miles from Narvik, Straumsnes station is the last permanent habitation as you go east. The last Norwegian station, Bjørnfjell, is well above the timber line and about 3 hours from Kiruna, Sweden, some 87 miles north of the Arctic Circle. You can catch a train at Kiruna to Stockholm. A road connects Kiruna and Narvik.

ESSENTIALS
GETTING THERE   From the Lofoten Islands, take the ferry to Skutvik. Take Route 81 northeast to the junction with E6, and then take E6 north to Bognes. Cross the Tysfjord by ferry. Continue north on E6 to Narvik.

The **train** from Stockholm to Narvik takes 21 to 24 hours. There are also two buses a day from Fauske/Bodø (5 hours).

VISITOR INFORMATION   The **Narvik Tourist Office** is at Konensgate 66 (☎ **76-94-33-09**). It's open daily from 9am to 4pm.

SEEING THE SIGHTS
To get a good look at Narvik, take the **Gondolbanen cable car** (☎ **76-96-04-94**), whose departure point is directly behind the Norlandia Narvik Hotel, a 10-minute walk from the town center. The car operates from March to October, and the round-trip fare is 80 NOK ($8.90) for adults, 50 NOK ($5.55) for children 6 to 15 (5 and under free). In just 13 minutes it takes you to an altitude of 2,100 feet, at the top of Fagernesfjell. You can see the impressive panorama of the town and its surroundings. From mid-February to mid-June, and in August and September, the cable operates Monday to Friday from 1 to 9pm and every Saturday and Sunday from 10am to 5pm. From mid-June to the end of July it operates daily from noon to 1am. It is closed otherwise.

The **midnight sun** shines from May 27 to July 19.

Nordland Røde Kors Krigsminnemuseum (War Museum). ☎ **76-94-44-26.** Admission 30 NOK ($3.35) adults, 10 NOK ($1.10) children. Mar–June 7, daily 11am–3pm; June 8–Aug 20, Mon–Sat 10am–10pm, Sun 11am–5pm; Aug 21–Sept, daily 11am–3pm. Closed Oct–Feb.

Near Torghallen in the town center, this is one of the most important sights in town. Most of Narvik was destroyed by the Germans, who occupied it until the end of the Second World War. Following Hitler's attack on Denmark and Norway, a bitter battle for Narvik and its iron ore raged for 2 months. German forces fought troops from France, Poland, and Norway, and a considerable British flotilla at sea. Events of that era are depicted, as well as experiences of the civilian population and foreign POWs.

Ofoten Museum. Administrasjonsveien 3. ☎ **76-96-00-50.** Admission 25 NOK ($2.80) adults, 5 NOK (55¢) children. July, Mon–Fri 11am–3pm, Sat–Sun noon–3pm; Aug–June, Mon–Fri 10am–4pm.

In the town center, this museum preserves the cultural history of the area. The Ofoten Museum has artifacts tracing the oldest human settlements in the area. They go back to the Stone Age, which is revealed in rock carvings. Other exhibits (including a scraper for animal skins and a flint-and-tinder box) show how the people lived and worked in the area. Most of the display is from the 20th century, beginning when the rail line was under construction.

WHERE TO STAY

These hotels are among the few buildings in Narvik that survived the World War II.

Moderate

Grand Royal. Kongensgate 64, N-8501 Narvik. ☎ **76-97-70-00.** Fax 76-94-55-31. 119 units. MINIBAR TV TEL. Sun–Thurs 920–1,350 NOK ($102.10–$149.85) double; Fri–Sat 750 NOK ($83.25) double. Year-round, 1,090–1,650 NOK ($121–$183.15) suite. Rates include breakfast. AE, DC, MC, V. Free parking. Bus: 14, 15, 16, or 17.

This hotel is the largest and best equipped in Narvik. It opens onto the main street in the town center, between the train station and the harbor. Built in the 1920s, it has seen many enlargements since. It's called the Grand Royal because the late King Olav was a frequent visitor. Portraits of him adorn some of the public rooms. The comfortable, good-sized rooms are traditionally furnished and among the most tasteful in the area. Beds are good, and the well-equipped, medium-sized bathrooms are the best in town. The finest restaurant in town is also here (see "Where to Dine," below). The recently redecorated lobby bar is one of the best cocktail bars in northern Norway.

Inexpensive

Nordst Jernen Hotel. Kongensgate 26, N-8500 Narvik. ☎ **76-94-41-20.** Fax 76-94-75-06. 25 units. TV TEL. 695 NOK ($77.15) double. Rates include breakfast. DC, MC, V. Free parking. Bus: 14 or 16.

In the town center, south of the bus station, the Nordst Jernen has long been known as one of the best hotel values in the area. Guest rooms are decorated in pastels to off-set the winter gloom. Rooms vary in size, but all are comfortable and well maintained, with firm mattresses. Bathrooms are small.

WHERE TO DINE

Royal Blue. In the Grand Royal Hotel, Kongensgate 64. ☎ **76-97-70-00.** Reservations recommended. Main courses 100–265 NOK ($11.10–$29.40). AE, DC, MC, V. Daily 11am–11pm. Bus: 14, 15, 16, or 17. NORWEGIAN.

The best restaurant in the region is decorated appropriately in strong royal blues. It's the preferred choice of visiting dignitaries, including the king. Service is polite and the food delectable. Specialties include thinly sliced, sauna-smoked ham with asparagus, cured salmon with crème fraîche, reindeer curry with Brussels sprouts and apricots, and large beefsteaks. It's on the lobby level of the Grand Royal (see "Where to Stay," above). The menu changes seasonally.

The Best of Sweden

11

In the towns and cities of Scandinavia's largest country, you can let yourself be dazzled by the contemporary or wander back to a bygone era—the choice is yours. From the castles and palaces in the south to the barren tundra of Lapland, we have combed this vast land of forests, lakes, and glacier-ringed mountains to bring you the best.

1 The Best Travel Experiences

- **Soaking Up Local Culture:** Home to a great cultural tradition, Sweden is acclaimed for its symphony orchestras, theater, ballet (including the renowned Swedish Cullberg Ballet), and opera companies. During the long days of summer, open-air concerts are staged all over the country (local tourist offices can provide details). Many concerts, especially those featuring folk dancing and regional music, are free.

- **Touring the Stockholm Archipelago:** The capital lies in a bucolic setting with more than 24,000 islands (if you count big rocks jutting out of the water). Boats leave frequently in summer from Stockholm's harbor, taking you to Vaxholm and other scenic islands, where you'll typically find interesting shops and restaurants. See chapter 14.

- **Seeing the Country from the Water:** Passengers glide through Sweden's scenic heartland, between Stockholm and Gothenburg, on a Götä Canal Cruise. The route takes you along three of the country's largest lakes and through 58 carefully calibrated locks. The cruise, available between mid-May and mid-September, offers a glimpse of the best of Sweden in a nutshell. See chapter 17.

- **Exploring the Land of the Midnight Sun:** Above the Arctic Circle, the summer sun never dips below the horizon. You have endless hours to enjoy the beauty of the region and the activities that go with it, from hiking to white-water rafting. After shopping for distinctive wooden and silver handcrafts, you can dine on fillet of reindeer served with cloudberries. You can even pan for gold in Lannavaara, with real-life pioneers, or climb rocks and glaciers in Sarek National Park. See chapter 17.

2 The Best Scenic Towns & Villages

- **Sigtuna:** Sweden's oldest town, founded at the beginning of the 11th century, stands on the shores of Lake Mälaren northwest of

Stockholm. Walk its High Street, believed to be the oldest street in Sweden. Traces of Sigtuna's Viking and early Christian heritage can be seen throughout the town. See chapter 14.

- **Uppsala:** Swedens's major university city lies northwest of Stockholm. Gamla (Old) Uppsala, nearby, is especially intriguing. It's built on the site of Viking burial grounds where humans and animals were sacrificed. See chapter 14.

- **Lund:** This town, 11 miles northeast of Malmö, rivals Uppsala as a university town. It, too, is ancient—Canute the Great founded it in 1020. Centuries-old buildings, winding passages, and cobblestoned streets fill Lund; a major attraction is its ancient cathedral, one of the finest expressions of Romanesque architecture in northern Europe. See chapter 16.

- **Jokkmokk:** Just north of the Arctic Circle, this is the best center for absorbing Lapp (or Sami) culture. In early February, the Lapps hold their famous "Great Winter Market" here, a tradition that goes back 4 centuries. You can visit a museum devoted to Sami culture, and then go salmon fishing in the town's central lake. See chapter 17.

- **Rättvik:** This great resort borders Lake Siljan in the heart of Dalarna, a province known for its regional painting, handcrafts, and folk dancing. Timbered houses characterize Dalarna's old-style architecture, and on a summer night you can listen to fiddlers, whose music evokes the past. See chapter 17.

- **Visby:** On the island of Gotland, this was once a great medieval European city and Viking stronghold. For 8 days in August, during Medieval Week, the sleepy Hanseatic town awakens. The annual festival features fire-eaters, belly dancers, and jousting tournaments. Filled with the ruins of 13th- and 14th-century churches and memories of a more prosperous period, Visby is intriguing in any season. See chapter 17.

3 The Best Active Vacations

- **Fishing:** Sweden offers some of the world's best fishing in pristine lakes and streams. You can even fish in downtown Stockholm! Many varieties of fresh- and saltwater fish are available in Sweden's waters.

- **Golfing:** Many Swedes are obsessed with golf. Most courses are open to the public, from the periphery of Stockholm to Björkliden (above the Arctic Circle), where enthusiasts play under the midnight sun. One unusual course is the "Green Zone," on the Swedish-Finnish border. You tee off in Sweden and sink your putt in Finland! Players cross the border four times during one round. See chapter 17.

- **Hiking:** The Kungsleden ("King's Trail") might provide the hike of a lifetime. It takes you through the mountains of Lapland, including Kebnekaise, at 6,965 feet the highest mountain in Sweden. This 500km trail cuts through the mountains of Abisko National Park to Riksgränsen on the Norwegian frontier. For more information about this adventure, contact the **Svenska Turistförening** (Swedish Tourist Club), P.O. Box 25, Amiralitetshuset 1, Flagmansvägen 8, S101 20 Stockholm (☎ **08/463-21-00**). See chapter 17.

- **Skiing:** In Lapland you can enjoy downhill and cross-country skiing year round. One of Sweden's main downhill skiing areas is in Øre in Jämtland. Serious skiers head for the Kebnekaise mountain station, where skiing can be combined with dogsledding and other sports. Other leading resorts are Idre Fjäll, south of Gällivåre, and Sälen in Dalarna. See chapter 17.

- **White-Water Rafting:** Sweden has some of Europe's best white-water rafting. Trips run the gamut from a short, comfortable rides along lazy rivers to fast descents down whitewater rapids. In Dalarna the best white-water rafting is on the moderately difficult Västerdalälven River rapids. An organization in western Dalarna will rent, with or without a guide, watercraft suitable for between one and eight occupants, including inflatable rafts, kayaks, canoes, and river boards. Most excursions last a half-day, include access to a foaming stretch of river, plus a barbecued picnic, some local sightseeing, and a soak in a communal hot tub. For more information, contact **Kajaktiv, A.B.,** Lissförsvägen 11, S-78044 Dala-Floda (☎ **0241/22361**). If you're looking for something easier and less dramatic, a nearby competitor conducts relatively easy downriver treks in paddle boats or on rafts constructed from clusters of lashed-together timbers. Excursions leave from a point 3 miles south of Höljes in northern Värmland. For more information, contact **Branäs Sport,** Branäs Fritidsanläggin, S-680 20 Sysslebäck (☎ **564/352-09**).

4 The Best Festivals & Special Events

- **Walpurgis Eve:** One of Europe's great celebrations to welcome spring takes place in Sweden on April 30. Bonfires, songs, lively festivals, and all sorts of antics herald the demise of winter. The best—and rowdiest—celebrations are at the university cities of Umeå, Lund, Uppsala, Stockholm, and Gothenburg.
- **Stockholm Waterfestival:** In August, much of the city turns out for a weeklong festival along the waterfront. It's entertainment galore—everything from concerts to fireworks. Stockholm goes wild before the chilly months arrive. Theoretically, the concept behind the festival is water preservation, but it offers a great opportunity to have a good time. See chapter 12.
- **Drottningholm Court Theater** (Drottningholm): In May, Sweden's cultural highlight is a series of 30 opera and ballet performances presented at this theater, which dates from 1766. The theater's original stage machinery and settings are still used. Drottningholm Palace (the "Versailles of Sweden") is on an island in Lake Mälaren, about 7 miles from Stockholm. See chapter 14.
- **Falun Folkmusik Festival:** This annual gathering of folk musicians from around the world at the town of Falun is one of Scandinavia's major musical events. Folkloric groups—many of them internationally famous—perform. Concerts, films, lectures, and seminars round out the events, which usually last for 4 days in July. See chapter 17.
- **Medieval Week** (Gotland): On the island of Gotland, Swedes celebrate the Middle Ages for about a week every August. Visby, especially, swarms with people in medieval garb. Many of them—from the blacksmith to the cobbler—tend market stalls as in olden days. Musicians play the hurdy-gurdy or the fiddle, and jesters play the fool. A program of some 100 medieval events, from tournaments to a nightly king procession, is scheduled in Visby. See chapter 17.

5 The Best Museums

- **Royal Warship *Vasa*** (Stockholm): In the Djurgården, this 17th-century man-of-war—now a museum—is a popular tourist attraction, and deservedly so. The *Vasa* is the world's oldest known complete ship. It capsized and sank on its maiden voyage in 1628 before horrified onlookers. The ship was salvaged in

1961 and has been carefully restored; 97% of its 700 original sculptures were retrieved. See chapter 14.

- **National Museum** (Stockholm): One of the oldest museums in the world (it celebrated its 200th birthday in 1992) houses Sweden's treasure trove of rare paintings and sculpture. From Rembrandt to Rubens, from Bellini to van Gogh, a panoply of European art unfolds before your eyes. Artifacts include everything from porcelain to antiques. See chapter 14.
- **Millesgården** (Lidingö, outside Stockholm): Sweden's foremost sculptor, Carl Milles (1875–1955), lived here and created a sculpture garden by the sea. Milles relied heavily on mythological themes in his work, and many of his best-known pieces are displayed in what's now a museum. See chapter 14.
- **Göteborgs Konstmuseum** (Gothenburg): This is the city's leading art museum, a repository of modern painting that's strong on French Impressionism. Modern artists such as Picasso and Edvard Munch are also represented, as are sculptures by Milles. See chapter 15.
- **Ájtte** (Jokkmokk): In Lapp country, this is the best repository of artifacts of the Sami people. Integrating nature with culture, the museum is the largest of its kind in the world. It depicts how the Lapps lived and struggled for survival in a harsh terrain, and shows the houses they lived in and the animals and weapons needed for their livelihood. See chapter 17.

6 The Best Offbeat Experiences

- **Log-Rafting on the Klarälven River:** You can enjoy a lazy trip down the river, winding through beautiful, unspoiled valleys among high mountains, with sandy beaches where you can occasionally swim. There's excellent fishing for pike and grayling. You travel through northern Värmland at a speed of 1¼ mph from the mouth of the Vingängssjön Lake in the north to Edebäck in the south. It takes 6 days to cover the 68 miles. Overnight accommodations are on the moored raft or ashore. Each raft can accommodate two to five people, and the trips are available from May to August. Contact **Sverigeflotten,** Transtrand 20, S-680 63 Likenäs (☎ 564/402-27).
- **Exploring the Orsa "Outback" by Horse and Covered Wagon:** In the province of Dalarna (central Sweden), you can rent a horse and covered wagon (with space for up to five) for a 3- or 5-day trek across the forest and tundra of the Orsa "outback," an almost unpopulated area of wild beauty. For more information, contact **Häst och Vagn,** Torsmo 1646, S-794 91 Orsa (☎ 2505/530-14). See chapter 17.
- **Playing Golf by the Light of the Midnight Sun:** In a land where the Lapps and reindeer still lead a nomadic life, you can play at the Björkliden Arctic Golf Course, some 150 miles north of the Arctic Circle (near the hamlet of Björkliden, 60 miles west of Kiruna). The nine-hole course is open between late June and mid-August only. For information, contact the Björkliden Arctic Golf Club at ☎ 0980/64100. The rest of the year, contact its affiliate, the Stockholm-based Bromma Golf Course, Kvarnbacksvägen 303, 16874 Bromma, Stockholm (☎ 08/289-430). See chapter 17.
- **Seeing Lapland on a Safari:** On this tour you can explore the last wilderness of Europe and record your impressions on film. You can see Swedish Lapland up close, and become acquainted with the Sami people's rich culture. Highlights include visits to old churches and village settlements (usually along a lake), and seeing reindeer. The outdoors outfitter **Borton Overseas** (☎ 800/843-0602) offers tours from March to October. See chapter 17.

7 The Best Buys

- **Glass:** In the deep woods of Småland, Swedish glasswork has helped set the world standard. Glass has been a local tradition since King Gustav Vasa invited Venetian glass blowers to come to Sweden in the 16th century. The first glass was melted here in 1556. The oldest name in Swedish glass, Kosta, was founded in 1742 and is now part of the Orrefors group, the best-known manufacturer. Fifteen major glassworks in Småland, which encompasses Växjö and Kalmar, are open to visitors. Glass is sold at department stores and specialty outlets throughout Sweden.
- **Handcrafts:** Designers create a wide variety of objects, often in wood, but also in pewter, enamel, tapestry, brass, and even reindeer skins and antlers. Many handcrafts are based on Viking designs, and most objects are in the traditional Lapp (or Sami) style. Shoppers eagerly seek wall textiles, leatherwork, handwoven carpets, and embroidered items. Swedish cutlery and china are valued for their quality and craftsmanship. Stockholm has the widest selection of shops, and Gothenburg and other towns have specialty outlets.
- **Swedish Design:** Good design and craftsmanship are the hallmarks of Swedish housewares—swinging metal CD racks, wooden chickens on rockers, tea wagons, and more. One of the best places to find products of Swedish design is in the constantly changing display at **DesignTorget,** in the Kulturhuset in the center of Stockholm. It's open daily year-round.

8 The Best Hotels

- **Grand Hotel** (Stockholm; ☎ 800/223-5652 in the U.S., or 08/679-35-00): Opposite the Royal Palace, this is the most prestigious hotel in Sweden. Well-known guests have included Sarah Bernhardt and many Nobel Prize winners. It dates from 1874 and is continuously renovated to keep it in excellent condition. The rooms are luxuriously decorated, and the bathrooms are Italian marble with heated floors. See chapter 13.
- **Lady Hamilton Hotel** (Stockholm; ☎ 08/23-46-80): This is one of Old Town's stellar properties. It's made up of three buildings that have been artfully connected and provide sumptuously furnished accommodations for those who prefer an old-fashioned atmosphere. Even the sauna is luxurious! See chapter 13.
- **Victory Hotel** (Stockholm; ☎ 08/506-400-00): In the Old Town, this small but stylish hotel was built in 1642. It's famous for the treasure once buried here, part of which can be seen at the Stockholm City Museum. The well-furnished guest rooms typically have exposed beams and pine floors. On a small rooftop terrace, tables are arranged around a fountain. See chapter 13.
- **Radisson SAS Park Avenue Hotel** (Gothenburg; ☎ 800/221-2350 in the U.S., or 031/758-40-00): Since it opened in 1950, Gothenburg's premier hotel has played host to everybody from the Beatles to David Rockefeller. On the attractive main boulevard, near the cultural center, it's a cosmopolitan hotel with a fresh and contemporary aura. The best double rooms are quite spacious and sleek; about a quarter of the guest rooms have balconies. See chapter 15.
- **Radisson SAS Scandinavia Hotel** (Gothenburg; ☎ 800/221-2350 in the U.S., or 031/80-60-00): Fashioned in marble and glass with bay windows, this hotel, with innovative styling and beautiful architecture, is more than just a typical chain hotel. Balconies overlook a vast atrium with eye-catching elevators and trees. Amenities include everything from a gym and sauna to a well-equipped health club; the gourmet dining room has a bar. See chapter 15.

9 The Best Restaurants

- **Operakällaren** (Stockholm; ☎ 08/676-58-00): This historic monument, part of the Royal Opera Complex, dates from 1787. The chef is a culinary adviser to the king and queen. This is the best place to sample Sweden's legendary smörgåsbord—a groaning table of delectable dishes with an emphasis on fresh fish. All the northern delicacies, from smoked eel or reindeer to Swedish red caviar and grouse, appear on the menu. See chapter 13.
- **Paul & Norbert** (Stockholm; ☎ 08/663-81-83): With only eight tables, this exclusive restaurant on the fashionable Strandvägen is in a patrician residence that dates from 1873. The most innovative restaurant in Stockholm, it's the culinary domain of German owners Paul Beck and Norbert Lang. The Swedish game served here in the winter (such as pigeon with Calvados sauce) is without equal in the country. Always count on something tempting and unusual—perhaps sautéed sweetbreads in nettle sauce. See chapter 13.
- **Wedholms Fisk** (Stockholm; ☎ 08/611-78-74): This classic Swedish restaurant serves some of the capital's finest local food, skillfully prepared with a French touch. Traditional and haute cuisine dishes have been modernized. Each dish seems guaranteed to ignite your enthusiasm, although nothing is showy or ostentatious. The fresh ingredients retain their natural flavor. See chapter 13.
- **Gripsholms Värdshus Restaurant** (Mariefred; ☎ 0159/34750): If you're seeking traditional Swedish food with French overtones, this is the best dining choice on the periphery of the capital. Local game dishes, including wild grouse, are featured in autumn, and marinated salmon with mild mustard sauce is a year-round favorite. Tastings in the wine cellar can be arranged. See chapter 14.
- **Sjömagasinet** (Klippan, outside Gothenburg; ☎ 031/773-59-20). By far the most interesting restaurant in town, this is one of the finest seafood places on the west coast of Sweden. In a converted warehouse, it serves an array of fresh fish in wonderful concoctions, and the sauces and preparations never diminish the flavor of the seafood. Pot-au-feu of fish and shellfish with chive-flavored crème fraîche is worth the trek out of town. See chapter 15.

Planning a Trip to Sweden 12

This chapter gives you many of the details you need to plan your trip to Sweden. Also see Chapter 2, "Planning a Trip to Denmark," which discusses travel to Scandinavia as a whole.

1 The Regions in Brief

GÖTALAND   The southern part of Sweden takes its name from the ancient Goths. Some historians believe they settled in this region, which is similar in climate and architecture to parts of northern Europe, especially Germany. This is the most populated part of Sweden, comprising eight provinces—Östergötland, Småland (the kingdom of glass), Västergötland, Skåne, Dalsland, Bohuslän, Halland, and Blekinge—plus the islands of Öland and Gotland. The Göta Canal cuts through this district. **Gothenburg** is the most important port in the west, and **Stockholm,** the capital, the chief port in the east. Aside from Stockholm, **Skåne,** the châteaux district, is the most heavily visited area. It's often compared to the Danish countryside. Many seaside resorts are on both the west and east coasts.

SVEALAND   The central region encompasses the folkloric province of **Dalarna** (Dalecarlia in English) and **Värmland** (immortalized in the novels of Selma Lagerlöf). These districts are the ones most frequented by visitors. Other provinces include Västmanland, Uppland, Södermanland, and Nårke. Ancient Svealand is often called the cultural heart of Sweden. Some 20,000 islands lie along its eastern coast.

NORRLAND   Northern Sweden makes up Norrland, which lies above the 61st parallel and includes about 50% of the landmass. It's inhabited by only about 15% of the population, including Lapps and Finns. Norrland consists of 24 provinces, of which **Lapland** is the most popular with tourists. It's a land of thick forests, fast-flowing (and cold) rivers, and towering mountain peaks. Lapland, the home of the Lapp reindeer herds, consists of tundra. **Kiruna** is one of Norrland's most important cities because of its iron-ore deposits. Many bodies of water in Norrland freeze for months every year.

2 Visitor Information & Entry Requirements

VISITOR INFORMATION
In the **United States,** contact the **Scandinavian Tourist Board,** 655 Third Ave., 18th floor, New York, NY 10017 (☎ 212/885-9700), at

least 3 months in advance for maps, sightseeing information, ferry schedules, and other advice and tips.

In the United Kingdom, contact the **Swedish Travel & Tourism Council,** 11 Montague Pl., London W1H 2AL (☎ **020/7870-5600**).

You can also try the Web site **www.visit-sweden.com.**

If you use a **travel agent,** make sure the agent is a member of the American Society of Travel Agents (ASTA; www.astanet.com). If a problem arises, you can complain to the Consumer Affairs Department of the society at 1101 King St., Suite 200, Alexandria, VA 22314 (☎ **703/739-8739**).

ENTRY REQUIREMENTS

American, Canadian, Irish, Australian, and New Zealand citizens, and British subjects, need only a valid **passport** to enter Sweden. You need a visa only if you want to stay more than 3 months. A British Visitor's Passport is also valid, for a holiday or some business trips of less than 3 months. The passport can include your spouse, and it's valid for 1 year. Apply in person at a main post office in the British Isles, and the passport will be issued that day.

Your current domestic **driver's license** is acceptable in Sweden. An international driver's license is not required.

3 Money

For a general discussion of changing money, using credit and charge cards, and other matters, see "Money," in chapter 2.

CURRENCY   Sweden's basic unit of currency is the **krona** (plural: **kronor**), written **SEK.** (Denmark and Norway also use kroner, but note the different spelling.) There are 100 **öre** in 1 krona. Bank notes are issued in denominations of 20, 50, 100, 500, 1,000, and 10,000 SEK. Silver coins are issued in denominations of 50 öre and 1 and 5 SEK.

4 When to Go

CLIMATE

It's hard to generalize about Sweden's climate. Influenced by the Gulf Stream, temperatures vary considerably from the fields of Skåne to the wilderness of Lapland. The upper tenth of Sweden lies north of the Arctic Circle.

The country as a whole has many sunny summer days, but it's not super-hot. July is the warmest month, with temperatures in Stockholm and Gothenburg averaging around 64°F. February is the coldest month, when the temperature in Stockholm averages around 26°F, and Gothenburg is a few degrees warmer.

It's not always true that the farther north you go, the cooler it becomes. During the summer, the northern parts of the country (Halsingland to northern Lapland) may suddenly have the warmest weather and bluest skies. Swedes claim the weather forecasts on television and in the newspapers are 99% reliable.

Sweden's Average Daytime Temperatures (°F)

	Jan	Feb	Mar	Apr	May	June	July	Aug	Sept	Oct	Nov	Dec
Stockholm	27	26	31	40	50	59	64	62	54	45	37	32
Karesuando	6	5	12	23	39	54	59	51	44	31	9	5
Karlstad	33	30	28	37	53	63	62	59	54	41	29	26
Lund	38	36	34	43	57	63	64	61	57	47	37	37

Sweden

The Swedish Krona

For American Readers At this writing, $1 = approximately 9 kronor (or 1 krona = 11 U.S. cents); this was the rate of exchange used to calculate the dollar values giving in this edition (rounded to the nearest nickel).

For British Readers At this writing, £1 = approximately 12.60 kronor (or 1 krona = approximately 8 pence); this was the rate of exchange used to calculate the pound values in the table below.

About the Euro At press time one Euro (€) was worth approximately 8.1 kronor, although this will almost certainly change as Sweden resolves the links it wishes to maintain with the shared European currency.

Note: International exchange rates fluctuate, so the figures in this chart may not be the same by the time of your trip to Sweden. Use this table only as a rough guideline.

SEK	U.S.$	U.K.£	Euro	SEK	U.S.$	U.K.£	Euro
1	0.11	0.08	0.12	75	8.33	6.00	9.23
2	0.22	0.16	0.25	100	11.10	8.00	12.30
3	0.33	0.24	0.37	125	13.88	10.00	15.38
4	0.44	0.32	0.49	150	16.65	12.00	18.45
5	0.56	0.40	0.62	175	19.43	14.00	21.53
6	0.67	0.48	0.74	200	22.20	16.00	24.60
7	0.78	0.56	0.86	225	24.98	18.00	27.68
8	0.89	0.64	0.98	250	27.75	20.00	30.75
9	1.00	0.72	1.11	275	30.53	22.00	33.83
10	1.11	0.80	1.23	300	33.30	24.00	36.90
15	1.67	1.20	1.85	350	38.85	28.00	43.05
20	2.22	1.60	2.46	400	44.40	32.00	49.20
25	2.78	2.00	3.08	500	55.50	40.00	61.50
50	5.55	4.00	6.15	1000	111.00	80.00	123.00

THE MIDNIGHT SUN In the summer, the sun never fully sets in northern Sweden; even in the south, daylight may last until 11pm—and then the sun rises around 3am.

The best vantage points and dates for seeing the thrilling spectacle of the midnight sun are **Björkliden,** May 26 to July 19; **Abisko,** June 12 to July 4; **Kiruna,** May 31 to July 14; and **Gällivare,** June 2 to July 12. All are accessible by public transportation.

Remember that although the sun shines brightly late at night, it's not as strong as at midday. Bring a warm jacket or sweater.

HOLIDAYS

Sweden celebrates the following public holidays: New Year's Day (January 1); Epiphany (January 6); Good Friday; Easter Sunday; Easter Monday; Labor Day (May 1); Ascension Day (mid-May); Whitsunday (late May); Whitmonday; Midsummer Day (June 21); All Saints' Day (November 1); and Christmas Eve, Christmas Day, and Boxing Day (December 24, 25, and 26). Inquire at a tourist bureau for the dates of the holidays that vary.

What Things Cost in Stockholm	U.S. $
Taxi from the airport to the city center	38.50
Basic bus or subway fare	1.75
Local telephone call	.30
Double room at the Grand Hotel (very expensive)	351.45
Double room at the Adlon Hotell & Kontor (moderate)	170.00
Double room at the Hotell Kom (inexpensive)	102.85
Lunch for one at Eriks Bakfica (moderate)	31.90
Lunch for one at Cattelin Restaurant (inexpensive)	7.15
Dinner for one, without wine, at Operakällaren (very expensive)	52.80
Dinner for one, without wine, at Prinsens (moderate)	37.20
Dinner for one, without wine, at Tennstopet (inexpensive)	22.00
Pint of beer (draft Pilsner) in a bar	4.30
Coca-Cola in a cafe	3.50
Cup of coffee in a cafe	3.10
Admission to Drottningholm Palace	5.50
Movie ticket	10.50
Budget theater ticket	12.10

Sweden Calendar of Events

The dates given here are approximate. Be sure to check with the tourist office before you make plans to attend a specific event.

April

○ **Walpurgis Eve,** nationwide. Celebrations with bonfires, songs, and speeches welcome spring. The revelry is especially lively among university students at Uppsala, Lund, Stockholm, Gothenburg, and Umeå. April 30.

May

○ **Drottningholm Court Theater.** Some 30 opera and ballet performances, from baroque to early romantic, are presented in a unique 1766 theater, with original decorative paintings and stage mechanisms.

Call ☎ **08/660-82-24** for tickets. Take the T-bana to Brommaplan, then bus no. 301 or 323. A steamboat runs in the summer; call ☎ **08/411-7023** for information. Late May to late September.

June

• **Midsummer,** nationwide. Swedes celebrate Midsummer Eve all over the country. Maypole dances to the sound of the fiddle and accordion are typical festive events. Dalarna observes the most traditional celebrations. June 21 to 23.

July

○ **Falun Folkmusik Festival.** International musicians gather to participate in and attend concerts, seminars, lectures, exhibitions, and films on folk music. Held at various venues. Contact the Falun Tourist Office, Trotzgatan 10–12 S-791 83 Falun (☎ **023/830-50**), for more information. Mid-July.

- **Around Gotland Race,** Sandhamm. The biggest and most exciting open-water Scandinavian sailing race starts and finishes at Sandhamn, in the Stockholm archipelago. About 450 boats, mainly from Nordic countries, take part. Two days in mid-July.
- **Rättviksdansen (International Festival of Folk Dance and Music),** Rättvik. Every other year for some 25 years, around 1,000 folk dancers and musicians from all over the world have gathered to participate. Last week in July.

August

✪ **Medieval Week,** Gotland. Events held throughout the island of Gotland include tours, concerts, medieval plays, and other festivities. For more information, contact the Tourist Office, Hamngatan 4, S-621 25 Visby (☎ **0498/20-17-00**). August 4 to 11.

✪ **Stockholm Waterfestival.** A more recent tradition, begun in 1989, this week-long festival takes place around the city's shores. There are fireworks, competitions, and concerts, plus lots of information about the care and preservation of water. A $150,000 award is given to an individual or organization that has made an outstanding contribution to water preservation. August 4 to 18.

- **Minnesota Day,** Utvandra Hus, Växjö, Småland. Swedish-American relations are celebrated at the House of Emigrants, with speeches, music, singing, and dancing. The climax is the election of the Swedish-American of the year. Call ☎ **0470/414-10** for information. Second Sunday in August.

December

✪ **Nobel Day,** Stockholm. The king, members of the royal family, and invited guests attend the ceremony for Nobel Prize winners in literature, physics, chemistry, medicine, physiology, and economics. A banquet at City Hall follows. Held at the Concert Hall in Stockholm, December 10. Attendance is by invitation only.

- **Lucia, the Festival of Lights,** nationwide. To celebrate the shortest day and longest night of the year, young girls called "Lucias" appear in restaurants, offices, schools, and factories. They wear floor-length white gowns and special headdresses, and each holds a lighted candle. Their escorts are "star boys"—young men in white, with wizard hats covered in gold stars, holding wands topped with large golden stars. One "Lucia" is eventually crowned queen. In olden days, Lucia was known as "Little Christmas." December 13.

5　The Active Vacation Planner

BIKING　Much of Sweden is flat, which makes it ideal for cycling tours. Bicycles can be rented all over the country, and country hotels sometimes make them available free. A typical rental is 200 SEK ($22) a day. For more detailed information, contact the **Svenska Turistförening** (Swedish Touring Club), P.O. Box 25, Amiralitetshuset 1, Flagmansvägen 8, S101 20 Stockholm (☎ **08-463-21-00**).

FISHING　In Stockholm, within view of the king's palace, you can cast a line for some of the finest salmon in the world. Ever since Queen Christina issued a decree in 1636, anyone can fish in waters adjoining the palace. Throughout the country, fishing is an everyday affair; an estimated one-third of Swedes are anglers.

To fish elsewhere in Sweden, you need a license; the cost varies from region to region. Any local tourist office can give you information. Pike, pike-perch, eel, and perch are found in the heartland and the south of the country.

GOLF   After Scotland, Sweden may have more golf enthusiasts than any other country in Europe. There are about 300 courses, and they're rarely crowded. Visitors are often granted local membership cards. Many golfers fly from Stockholm to Boden (in the far north) in the summer to play by the light of the midnight sun. For information on courses, contact the **Svenska Golfförbundet,** Solkraftsvägen 25, Stockholm S-135 70 (☎ **08/622-15-00**).

HIKING   Sarek, in the far north, is one of Europe's last real wilderness areas. Swedes come here to hike in the mountains, pick mushrooms, gather berries, and fish.

The **Svenska Turistförening** (Swedish Touring Club), P.O. Box 25, Amiralitetshuset 1, Flagmansvägen 8, S101 20 Stockholm (☎ **08/463-21-00**; www.stfturist.se), organizing accommodations in the area in mountain huts with 10 to 30 beds. The staff knows the northern part of Sweden very well, and can advise you about marked tracks, rowboats, the best excursions, the problems you're likely to encounter, communications, and transportation. The company also sells trail and mountain maps.

HORSEBACK RIDING   Many overnight horseback pack trips go to such wilderness areas as the forests of Värmland or Norrbotten, where reindeer and musk oxen roam. The most popular overnight trips start just north of the city of Karlstad in Värmland. A typical horseback trip begins in the lakeside village of Torsby and follows a forested trail up a mountain. Travelers spend an average of 4 hours a day on horseback, and eat meals cooked over an open fire. There are also covered-wagon trips with overnight stops.

In northern Sweden, two popular starting points are Funäsdalen, close to the Norwegian border, and Ammarnäs, not far from the Arctic Circle. Trips begin in June. Local tourist offices can provide information.

Sweden also has many riding stables and riding schools. Ask at local tourist offices. One of the most popular excursions is a pony trek through the region around Sweden's highest mountain, Kebnekaise.

RAFTING   White-water rafting and river rafting are the two major forms of this sport enjoyed in Sweden. Throughout the country, there are short and multiple-day white-water trips. In Värmland, contact **Branäs Sport AB,** Branäs Fritidsanläggnin, P.O. Box 28, S-680 60 Syssleback (☎ **564/352-09**).

River rafting on a slow-moving river in Sweden's heartland is much tamer. Many Swedes build their own log rafts. Adventurers can sleep in tents and cook over a campfire. Bring plenty of mosquito repellent in the summer. For information, contact **Kukkolaforsen-Turist & Konferens,** P.O. Box 184, S-593 91 Haparanda (☎ **922/310-00**).

SAILING & CANOEING   Canoes and sailboats can be rented all over the country; you can get information from the local tourist office. Hotels near watersports areas often rent canoes.

SWIMMING   If you don't mind swimming in rather cool water, Sweden has one of the world's longest coastlines, plus some 100,000 lakes. The best bathing beaches are on the west coast. The islands of Öland and Gotland have popular summer seaside resorts. Beaches in Sweden are generally open to the public, and nude bathing is allowed on designated beaches. Topless bathing is prevalent everywhere. If a Swedish lake is suitable for swimming, it's always signposted.

WALKING & JOGGING   Sweden is ideal for either activity. Local tourist offices can provide details and sometimes even supply you with free maps of the best trails or jogging paths. In Stockholm, hotel reception desks can often tell you the best places to go jogging nearby.

6 Health & Insurance

For a general discussion of health and insurance concerns, see "Health & Insurance" in chapter 2.

Put your essential medicines in your carry-on luggage and bring enough prescription medications to last through your stay. In Sweden, pharmacists cannot legally honor a prescription written outside the country; if you need more of your medications, you have to see a doctor and have a new prescription written.

Sweden's national health-care program does not cover American or Canadian visitors. Medical expenses must be paid in cash. Medical costs in Sweden are generally more reasonable than elsewhere in Western Europe.

7 Tips for Travelers with Special Needs

A number of resources and organizations in North America and Britain can assist travelers with special needs in trip planning. For details, see "Tips for Travelers with Special Needs," in chapter 2.

FOR TRAVELERS WITH DISABILITIES   Scandinavian countries have been in the vanguard of providing services for people with disabilities. In general, trains, airlines, ferries, and department stores and malls are accessible. For information about wheelchair access, ferry and air travel, parking, and other matters, contact the Scandinavian Tourist Board (see "Visitor Information & Entry Requirements," above).

About 2 million people in Sweden have a disability, and the country is especially conscious of special needs. Contact **Svenska Turistförening** or STF (Swedish Touring Club), P.O. Box 25, S-101 20 Stockholm (☎ 08/463-22-70; www.stfturist.se), for information, including data about youth hostels with special rooms for those with disabilities.

FOR GAY & LESBIAN TRAVELERS   Although it's not as openly liberal as Denmark (which legally recognizes same-sex marriages), Sweden has enacted an antidiscrimination law. Many gay and lesbian organizations in Stockholm welcome visitors from abroad.

Foremost among these is the **Federation for Gay and Lesbian Rights (RFSL),** Sveavägen 57 (Box 45090), S-104 30 Stockholm (☎ 08/736-02-12). It's open Monday to Friday from 9am to 5pm. Established in 1950, the group's headquarters are on the upper floors of the biggest gay nightlife center in Stockholm (see "The Capital of Gay Scandinavia" in Chapter 14, "Exploring Stockholm"). The federation holds a Wednesday 3pm meeting for gay men over 60 and a twice-monthly meeting of "Golden Ladies" (yes, they use the English expression) for lesbians over 50, plus a Monday-night youth session for those 18 to 21. It also operates a volunteer-staffed **Gay Switchboard** (☎ 08/736-02-12); call daily from 8 to 11pm for information. The nonprofit **Rosa Rummet Bookstore** (☎ 08/736-02-15), on the same premises, specializes in gay and lesbian literature and information. It's open Monday to Friday from noon to 9pm, Saturday and Sunday noon to 3pm. The biggest event of the year is **Gay Pride Week,** usually held the first week in August. Call or write the RSFL for information.

FOR SENIORS   Visitors over age 65 can get 30% off first- and second-class train travel on the Swedish State Railways Monday through Thursday and Saturday. In Stockholm, there are discounts on transportation and on concert, theater, and opera tickets.

8 Getting There

BY PLANE

See "Getting There," in chapter 2.

Travelers from the U.S. East Coast usually choose **SAS** (☎ **800/221-2350** in the U.S.; www.flysas.com) or **TWA** (☎ **800/221-2000** in the U.S.; www.twa.com). They fly from the New York–Newark area to Stockholm every day. Their major competitor is **American Airlines** (☎ **800/443-7300** in the U.S.; www.americanair.com). It offers daily flights to Stockholm from Chicago, and excellent connections through Chicago from its vast North American network. Between November and March (excluding the Christmas holidays), American sometimes offers round-trip fares for as low as $500 for weekday departures from Chicago. There's a supplemental charge of $49 for travel on a Friday, Saturday, or Sunday. This fare, which is subject to change, is usually matched by SAS. It requires a stay abroad of 7 to 60 days, and has several other restrictions. Travelers from Seattle usually fly SAS to Copenhagen, and then connect on one of the airline's frequent flights to Stockholm. **Delta** (☎ **800/241-4141** in the U.S.; www.delta.com) offers daily nonstop flights to Stockholm from JFK in New York, usually at prices comparable to those offered by SAS, TWA, and American.

Other airlines fly to gateway European cities, with connections to Stockholm. **British Airways** (☎ **800/247-9297** in the U.S. or 0845/773-3377 in the U.K.; www.british-airways.com), for example, flies from almost 20 North American cities to London (Heathrow), and then connects with about four flights to Stockholm. **Delta, Northwest** (☎ **800/325-1999** in the U.S.; www.nwa.com), and **TWA** also serve London frequently, and flights to Stockholm from there are available on SAS or British Airways. Finally, **Icelandair** (☎ **800/223-5500** in the U.S. or 020/7874-1000 in the U.K.; www.icelandair.com) is an excellent choice for travel to Stockholm through its hub in Reykjavik.

Travelers from Britain can fly SAS from Heathrow to Stockholm on any of five daily nonstop flights. Flying time is about 2½ hours each way. SAS serves Stockholm daily from Manchester, making a brief stop in Copenhagen. Flight time from Manchester to Stockholm is about 3½ hours.

BY CAR

The ferry routes from England to Denmark and from Denmark to Sweden are the most traveled (see "Getting There," in chapter 2), but there are better choices from the Continent.

FROM GERMANY   Drive to Travemünde, in northern Germany, and catch the ferry to Trelleborg, Sweden, a short drive south of Malmö. The trip takes 7½ hours. This route saves many hours by avoiding Denmark. If you want to visit Denmark before Sweden, you can take the 3-hour car ferry from Travemünde to Gedser in southern Denmark. From Gedser, the E64 and the E4 express highways head north to Copenhagen. After a visit, you can take a car ferry from Copenhagen to Malmö.

FROM NORWAY   From Oslo, E18 goes east via Karlstad all the way to Stockholm. This is a long but scenic drive, so plan on a 2-day drive with an overnight stop.

FROM DENMARK   The most popular way of reaching Sweden from Denmark is to drive across the new $3 billion Øresund Fixed Link, a bridge and a tunnel, plus an artificial island spanning the icy Øresund Sound between Copenhagen and Malmö. The bridge provides road and rail connections between the Scandinavia peninsula and the rest of Europe and is the final link in the centuries-old dream of connecting the continent from its northern tip to its southern toe. In other words, you can now drive all the way in either direction without taking a boat, ferry, or hydrofoil. Car ferries run frequently from Copenhagen to Malmö, and from Helsingør in North Zealand to Helsingborg on Sweden's west coast. To reach Stockholm from Malmö, take E6 north along the coast toward Helsingborg. In the Helsingborg area, turn northeast at the junction with E4 and continue across southern Sweden. Part of this highway is a four-lane express motorway, and part is a smaller national highway.

BY TRAIN

Copenhagen is the main rail hub between Scandinavia and the rest of Europe. There are seven daily trains from Copenhagen to Stockholm and six from Copenhagen to Gothenburg. All connect with the Danish ferries that operate to Sweden via Helsingør or Frederikshavn (see "Getting There," in chapter 2).

There are at least three trains a day from Oslo to Stockholm. Travel time is about 6½ hours. There are three trains a day from Oslo to Gothenburg. Travel time is about 4 hours.

RAIL PASSES FOR NORTH AMERICAN TRAVELERS

If you plan to travel extensively on the European and/or British railroads, it would be worthwhile for you to secure the latest edition of the *Thomas Cook European Timetable of Railroads*. It's available exclusively in North America from **Forsyth Travel Library,** 226 Westchester Ave., White Plains, NY 10604 (☎ **800/FORSYTH;** www. forsyth. com), at a cost of $27.95, plus $4.95 priority shipping in the States.

SCANRAIL PASS If your visit to Europe will be primarily in Scandinavia, the Scan-rail pass may be better and cheaper for you than the Eurailpass. This pass allows its owner a designated number of days of free rail travel within a larger time block. (Presumably, this allows for days devoted to sightseeing scattered among days of rail transfers between cities or sites of interest.) For example, you could choose a total of any 5 days of unlimited rail travel during a 2-month period, 10 days of rail travel within a 2-month period, or 1 month of unlimited rail travel. The pass, which is valid on all lines of the state railways of Denmark, Finland, Norway, and Sweden, offers discounts or free travel on some (but not all) of the region's ferry lines as well. The pass can be purchased only in North America, at any office of **Rail Europe** (☎ **800/361-RAIL;** www.raileurope.com) or at **Scanam World Tours,** 933 Highway 23, Pompton Plains, NJ 07444 (☎ **800/545-2204;** www.scanamtours.com).

Depending on whether you choose first- or second-class rail transport, 5 days out of 2 months ranges from $200 to $270, 10 days out of 2 months costs from $310 to $420, and 21 days of consecutive travel goes from $360 to $486. There are 20% discounts off these prices for senior citizens and students.

EURAILPASS If you're going to be traveling extensively in Europe, the **Eurailpass** might be a good bet. It's valid for first-class rail travel in 17 European countries. With one ticket, you travel whenever and wherever you please—more than 100,000 rail miles are at your disposal. Here's how it works: The pass is sold only in North America. A Eurailpass good for 15 days costs $554, a pass for 21 days is $718, a 1-month pass costs $890, a 2-month pass is $1,260, and a 3-month pass goes for $1,558. Children under 4 travel free if they don't occupy a seat (otherwise, they're charged half fare); children under 12 are charged half fare. If you're under 26, you can purchase a **Eurail Youthpass,** which entitles you to unlimited second-class travel for 15 days for $388, 21 days for $499, 1 month for $623, or 2 months for $882, or 3 months for $1,089. Travelers considering purchasing a 15-day or 1-month pass should estimate rail distance before deciding if such a pass is worthwhile. To take full advantage of the tickets for 15 days or a month, you'd have to spend a great deal of time on the train.

Eurailpass holders are entitled to substantial reductions on certain buses and ferries as well. Travel agents in all towns, and railway agents in such major cities as New York, Montréal, and Los Angeles, sell all these tickets. A Eurailpass is available at the North American offices of CIT Travel Service, the French National Railroads, the German Federal Railroads, and the Swiss Federal Railways.

Eurail Saverpass is a money-saving ticket that offers discounted 15-day travel for groups of three or more people traveling together between April and September, or two people traveling together between October and March. The price of a Saverpass, valid all over Europe for first-class only, is $715 for 15 days, $928 for 21 days, and $1,150 for 1 month, $1,630 for 2 months, $2,013 for 3 months. Even more freedom is offered by the **Saver Flexipass,** which is similar to the Eurail Saverpass, with the exception that you are not confined to consecutive day travel. For travel over any 10 days in 2 months, the fare is $556; any 15 days over 2 months, the fare is $732.

Eurail Flexipass allows greater flexibility in European travel. It's valid in first class and offers the same privileges as the Eurailpass. However, it provides a number of individual travel days that can be used over a much longer period of consecutive days. Using this pass makes it possible to stay longer in one city and yet not lose a single day of travel. There are two Flexipasses: 10 days of travel within 2 months for $654 and 15 days of travel within 2 months for $862.

With many of the same qualifications and restrictions as the Eurail Flexipass is a **Eurail Youth Flexipass.** Sold only to travelers under age 26, it allows 10 days of travel within 2 months for $458, and 15 days of travel within 2 months for $599.

RAIL PASSES FOR BRITISH TRAVELERS

Thousands of trains run from Britain to the Continent every month, and at least some of them are routed directly across or under the Channel, through France or Belgium and Germany to Copenhagen. For example, a train leaves London's Victoria Station daily at 9am, arriving the next day in Copenhagen at 8:25am. Another train leaves London's Victoria Station at 8:45pm, arriving the next day in Copenhagen at 8:20pm. Both go via Dover–Ostende. Once you're in Copenhagen, you can make good rail connections to Norway, Finland, and Sweden. Because of the time and distances involved, many passengers prefer to rent a couchette (sleeping berth), which costs around £18 ($30.60) per person. Designed like padded benches stacked bunk-style one atop another, they're usually clustered six to a compartment.

If you plan to do a lot of exploring, you might prefer one of three rail passes designed for unlimited train travel within a designated region during a predetermined number of days. These passes are sold only in Britain and several other European countries.

An **InterRail Pass** is available to passengers of any nationality, but only if they're under age 26 and can prove residency in a European or North African country (Morocco, Algeria, and Tunisia) for at least 6 months before purchasing the pass. It allows unlimited travel through all of Europe except Albania and the republics composing the former Soviet Union. Prices are complicated and vary depending on the countries you want to include. For pricing purposes, Europe is divided into eight zones, and the cost depends on the number of zones you include. The most expensive option, priced at £195 ($331.50), allows 1 month of unlimited travel in all seven zones (BritRail staff refers to this as a "global"). The least expensive option, priced at £113 ($192.10), allows 15 days of travel within only one zone.

Passengers aged 26 and over can buy an InterRail 26-Plus Pass, which covers Finland, Denmark, Sweden, and Norway. Second-class travel with the pass in 1 zone costs £179 ($304.30) for 22 days. For one calendar month, the cost is £235 ($399.50) in 2 zones, £269 ($457.30) in 3 zones, or £309 ($525.30) for all zones. The same residency requirements apply to this pass that apply to the InterRail Pass described above.

For information on the purchase of individual rail tickets or any of the above mentioned passes, contact **British Rail International,** Victoria Station, London (☎ **0990/848-848,** or 0845/748-4950 for information). Tickets and passes are also available at any of the larger railway stations as well as selected travel agencies throughout Britain and the rest of Europe.

BY SHIP & FERRY

FROM DENMARK From Copenhagen, you can go to Malmö, Sweden, by **hydrofoil** (known locally as the "Flyvebadene"; call ☎ 33-12-80-88 in Copenhagen for information). This is the fastest way for pedestrians to travel from Copenhagen to Sweden. (The hydrofoil doesn't transport cars.) Travel time is 45 minutes each way. A one-way ticket from Copenhagen to Malmö costs 35 DKK ($4.40). A business-class ticket without restrictions costs 80 DKK ($10). Hydrofoils depart from a terminal directly on Copenhagen's waterfront, at the corner of Havnegade and Nyhavn. Departures are daily every hour on the hour from 6am to 9pm and 11pm to 1am. Between 9 and 11pm, hydrofoils depart every half-hour in both directions. In midsummer, it's a good idea to reserve passage in advance (there's no extra charge).

Another boat route—this one by ferry—is the brief trip between Helsingør, a short drive north of Copenhagen, and Helsingborg, Sweden, just across the narrow channel that separates the countries. The 25-minute trip on a conventional ferry (not a catamaran) begins at 20- to 40-minute intervals, 24 hours a day. Operated by **Scandlines** (☎ **32-53-15-85** in Copenhagen), it's one of the most popular ferry routes in Europe. Round-trip passage costs 510 SEK ($56.10) for a car with up to nine passengers; the ticket is valid for up to 2 months. Round-trip passage on the same day costs 245 to 345 SEK ($26.95 to $37.95) for a car and up to five passengers. Pedestrians pay 40 SEK ($4.40) round-trip, regardless of their return date.

FROM ENGLAND Two English ports, Harwich (year-round) and Newcastle upon Tyne (summer only), offer ferry service to Sweden. Harwich to Gothenburg takes 23 to 25 hours; Newcastle to Gothenburg, 27 hours. Boats on both routes offer overnight accommodations and the option of transporting cars. Prices are lower for passengers who book in advance through the company's U.S. agent. For details, call **DFDS Seaways,** Cypress Creek Business Park, 6555 NW Ninth Ave., Suite 207, Fort Lauderdale, FL 33309 (☎ **800/533-3755** in the U.S. or 020/7616-1400 in the U.K.; www.scansea.com).

9 Getting Around

BY PLANE

The best way to get around Scandinavia is to take advantage of air passes that apply to the whole region. If you're traveling extensively in Europe, special European passes are available. For information on **SAS's Visit Scandinavia Pass,** see "Getting Around, By Plane," in chapter 2.

WITHIN SWEDEN For transatlantic flights from North America, Copenhagen and Stockholm are the major gateways for Scandinavia's best-known airline, **SAS.** For flights from other parts of Europe, the airport at Gothenburg supplements those at Stockholm and Copenhagen by funneling traffic into the Swedish heartland. Through **LIN Airlines (Linjeflyg),** SAS has access to small and medium-sized airports throughout Sweden, including such remote but scenic outposts as Kiruna, in Lapland. Among the larger Swedish cities SAS serves are Malmö, capital of the châteaux country; Karlstad, center of the verdant and folklore-rich district of Värmland; and Kalmar, a good base for exploring the glassworks district.

During the summer, SAS offers some promotional "minifares," which cut the price of a round-trip ticket nearly in half. Children under 12 travel free during the summer (at reduced fares other times), and up to two children 12 to 17 can travel with a parent at significantly reduced rates. Airfares tend to be lowest in July, with promotions almost as attractive during most of June and August. A minimum 3-night stopover is required, and it must include a Friday or Saturday night. Always ask the airline or travel agency about special promotions and restrictions.

Travelers under 26 can take advantage of SAS's special **standby fares,** and seniors (over 65) can apply for additional discounts, depending on the destination.

BY TRAIN

The Swedish word for train is *tåg,* and the national system is the Statens Järnvägar, the Swedish State Railways.

Swedish trains follow tight schedules. Trains leave Malmö, Helsingborg, and Gothenburg for Stockholm every hour throughout the day, Monday to Friday. There are trains every hour, or every other hour, to and from most big Swedish towns. On *expresståg* runs, seats must be reserved.

Children under 12 travel free when accompanied by an adult, and those up to age 18 are eligible for discounts.

BY BUS

Rail lines cover only some of Sweden's vast distances. Where the train tracks end, a bus usually serves as the link with remote villages. Buses are usually equipped with toilets, adjustable seats, reading lights, and a telephone. Fares depend on the distance traveled; for example, the one-way fare for the 326-mile trip from Stockholm to Gothenburg is 315 SEK ($34.65). **Swebus** (☎ 08/655-90-00), the country's largest bus company, provides information at the bus or railway stations in most cities. For travelers who don't buy a special rail pass (such as Eurail or ScanRail), bus travel between cities can sometimes be cheaper than traveling the same distances by rail. It's a lot less convenient and frequent, however—except in the far north, where there isn't any alternative.

BY CAR FERRY

Considering that Sweden has some 100,000 lakes and one of the world's longest coastlines, ferries play a surprisingly small part in the transportation network.

After the car ferry crossings from northern Germany and Denmark, the most popular route is from the mainland to the island of Gotland, in the Baltic. Service is available from Oskarshamn and Nynäshamn (call ☎ 08/20-10-20 for more information). The famous "white boats" of the Waxholm Steamship Company (☎ 08/679-58-30) also travel to many destinations in the Stockholm archipelago.

BY CAR

Sweden maintains an excellent network of roads and highways, particularly in the southern provinces and the central lake district. Major highways in the far north are kept clear of snow by heavy equipment that's in place just about year-round. If you rent a car, you'll be given the appropriate legal documents, including proof of adequate insurance (in the form of a "Green Card") as specified by your car-rental agreement. Current driver's licenses from Canada, the U.K., New Zealand, Australia, and the United States are acceptable in Sweden.

RENTALS   The major U.S.-based car-rental firms are represented at airports and in urban centers throughout Sweden. The companies' rates are aggressively competitive, with periodic sales promotions. Before you leave North America, phone around to find the lowest available rates. Membership in AAA or another auto club might get you a moderate discount. You may be able to avoid a supplemental airport tax by picking your car up at a central location rather than at the airport.

A word about drop-off charges: Some travelers prefer to begin and end their trip to Sweden at different points, perhaps landing in Stockholm and departing by ferry elsewhere. For an additional fee, car-rental companies allow you to drop off your car elsewhere—but only if you inform them when you first pick up the car. Otherwise, you might be in for an unpleasant surprise at the end of your trip.

The 25% government tax is not included in the rates below. All include unlimited mileage.

Avis (☎ **800/331-1084** in the U.S. and Canada; www.avis.com) offers a wide variety of cars. If you pay before you leave North America, the least expensive, a VW Polo, rents for around $191 a week. Avis's most expensive car, a Swedish-made Saab 903, goes for around $374 a week.

If you pay before your departure from the United States, **Hertz** (☎ **800/654-3001** in the U.S. and Canada) offers a Ford Fiesta for $245 a week.

Budget (☎ **800/527-0700** in the U.S. and Canada; www.budgetrentacar.com) charges $246 a week for its cheapest car, a VW polo, and $305 for the somewhat roomier Ford Mondeo. Many people upgrade to an Opel Vectra, at $355. For families with lots of luggage or camping equipment, Budget also offers a Vectra station wagon for about $517. These prices are for rentals paid for in North America before your departure. Any change in pickup date or type of vehicle costs an additional $25. Drop-offs can be made at any Budget office in Sweden for about $30 extra. Dropping off outside of Sweden—if allowed at all—is more expensive.

INSURANCE   The car-rental companies include a basic amount of liability insurance in their rates. Nevertheless, most renters feel more comfortable arranging for additional insurance to protect them from financial liability in the event of theft or damage to the car. A collision-damage waiver (CDW) is an optional insurance policy you can buy when you sign a rental agreement. For a fee of around $10 a day or more (depending on the value of the car), the rental agency eliminates all but a token amount of your financial responsibility for collision damage in case of an accident. If you don't have a CDW and you have an accident, you usually have to pay the full cost of repairing the vehicle. Exact figures, penalties, and deductibles vary between companies.

Some credit- and charge-card companies (including American Express, Master-Card, Visa, and Diners Club) reimburse card users for the deductible in the event of an accident. Because of that, many renters waive the cost of the extra CDW. Although the card issuers usually reimburse the renter for the damages (several weeks after the accident), payments are sometimes delayed until certain legal and insurance-related documents are filed. Unless a particular card has a high line of credit, some renters involved in an accident might have to pay a large amount of cash on the spot. If you have any doubt, purchase the CDW, if only for your own peace of mind.

10 Organized Tours

The country's regions, especially Dalarna and Lapland, offer such a variety of sights and activities that it may be preferable to take an organized tour. The following tours are a small sample of what's available. Contact your travel agent to learn about tours of interest to you or to design a special one for you.

ScanAm World Tours (☎ **800/545-2204;** www.scandinaviantravel.com) offers a tour of the Dalarna folklore region by rail. "Mora and the Folklore District" includes round-trip train fare from Stockholm to Mora and 2 nights at the Hotel Siljan. The 3-day tour is available May to September; prices start at $275 per person. The company also offers a "Kalmar and the Swedish Glass District" rail tour, from May to September. The 3-day excursion includes round-trip train fare from Stockholm to Kalmar and 2 nights at the Kalmarsund Hotel. Prices start at $285 per person. **Scantours, Inc.** (☎ **800/223-7226;** www.scantours.com), offers a 3-day tour of Sweden's folklore district. Participants travel from Oslo to Stockholm in a car with an English-speaking driver-guide. Along the way, it stops in Arvika, Mora, and Lake Siljan. "Kingdom of Folklore" tours include accommodations in first-class hotels and breakfast. Itineraries can be altered.

"Gotland Island and the City of Roses," offered by ScanAm World Tours (see above), is a cruise on the Gotland Line from Stockholm to Nynäshamn or from Oskarshamn to Visby, including 2 nights at the Visby Hotel. The 4-day cruise is available May to September.

For the more adventurous, Sweden's rugged north offers endless opportunities to achieve an adrenaline rush. On the "Midnight Sun Skiing" package offered by **Passage Tours** (☎ **800/548-5960;** www.passagetours.com), you can ski in shorts. Offered from May to June, the tour has additional options, including a reindeer sleigh safari and Stockholm lodging packages. This company also offers hiking tours that include a trip through the mountains, with wonderful panoramic views.

Suggested Itineraries

If You Have 1 Week

Day 1 Settle into Stockholm and relieve your jet lag. If you're feeling up to it, take a walking tour of Gamla Stan (the old town). Select a favorite restaurant to return to for dinner, but only after a pre-dinner stroll along the harbor.

Days 2 and 3 Explore Stockholm's attractions, including the raised royal flagship *Vasa.* Reserve one morning or afternoon for a boat trip through the archipelago and another for exploring Drottningholm Palace, on an island in Lake Mälaren.

Day 4 Take a day trip north. Visit Sweden's oldest town, Sigtuna, on the shores of Lake Mälaren, and nearby Skokloster Castle, which houses one of the most interesting baroque museums in Europe. Then it's on to the university city of Uppsala and to the neighboring Gamla (Old) Uppsala to see Viking burial mounds.

Day 5 Begin a fast 3-day excursion through the most interesting folkloric provinces, Dalarna and Värmland. In the mining town of Falun, visit the Falun Copper Mine and the home of Carl Larsson, the famous Swedish painter. Spend the night here or in one of the smaller Lake Siljan resort towns, such as Tällberg, Rättvik, Mora, or Leksand.

Day 6 Visit the Lake Siljan towns just mentioned. Glacial Lake Siljan, ringed by lush forests, is one of the most beautiful in Europe. Take a boat tour from Rättvik. On its outskirts, you can visit Gammelgården, an old farmstead, for a glimpse into the past. Stay overnight in one of the lakeside villages or towns.

Day 7 From Falun, Route 60 heads south to Karlstad. You'll pass through the heart of Selma Lagerlöf country (Sweden's most famous novelist). Have lunch at Filipstad, the birthplace of John Ericsson, who designed the U.S. Civil War ironclad ship *Monitor.* Spend the night in Karlstad.

If You Have 2 Weeks

Days 1–7 Spend the first week as described above.

Day 8 Spend another night in Karlstad, exploring its attractions and branching out into the area, including Rottneros Manor.

Day 9   In the morning, head south along the eastern shore of Lake Vänern. After lunch in charming lakeside Lidköping, head for Gothenburg, Sweden's second-largest city.

Day 10   Explore Gothenburg and make a side trip to Kungälv or Marstrand, a former royal resort.

Days 11–13   From Gothenburg, take the Göta Canal excursion, which covers the 350 miles to Stockholm. As you pass through 58 locks, you'll have a chance to see the essence of Sweden.

Day 14   Arrive in Stockholm and prepare for your return flight.

Fast Facts: Sweden

Area Code   The international country code for Sweden is **46.** The local city (area) codes are given for all phone numbers in the Sweden chapters.

Business Hours   Generally, **banks** are open Monday to Friday from 9:30am to 3pm. In some larger cities, banks stay open on Thursday or Friday until 5:30 or 6pm. Most **offices** are open Monday to Friday 8:30 or 9am to 5pm (sometimes to 3 or 4pm in the summer). On Saturday, offices and factories are closed, or open for only a half-day. Most **stores and shops** are open Monday to Friday 9:30am to 6pm, Saturday 9:30am to somewhere between 1 and 4pm. Once a week, usually on Monday or Friday, some larger stores are open until 7pm (during July and August, to 6pm).

Camera & Film   Cameras (especially the famed Hasselblad), film, projectors, and enlarging equipment are good values in Sweden. Practically all the world's brands are for sale. Photographic shops give excellent service, often developing and printing film in 1 day.

Customs   The government allows visitors aged 16 and older to bring in 200 cigarettes or 50 cigars duty-free. If you're over 21, you are also allowed 1 liter of liquor, 2 liters of wine, gifts totaling 600 SEK ($66), and a "reasonable" amount of perfume. There's no limit on the amount of currency you can bring in or take out.

Dentists   In an emergency, ask your hotel or host for the location of the nearest dentist. Nearly all dentists in Sweden speak English.

Doctors   Hotel desks can usually refer you to a local doctor. Nearly all doctors speak English. If you need emergency treatment, your hotel should be able to direct you to the nearest facility. In case of an accident or injury away from the hotel, dial ☎ **90-000** to call the police.

Drug Laws   Sweden imposes severe penalties for the possession, use, purchase, sale, or manufacture of illegal drugs. Penalties are usually based on quantity. Possession of a "small" amount of hard or soft drugs can lead to a heavy fine and deportation. Possession of a "large" amount of drugs can result in imprisonment for 3 months to 15 years.

Drugstores   Called *apotek* in Swedish, drugstores are generally open Monday to Friday from 9am to 6pm, Saturday 9am to 1pm. In larger cities, one drugstore in every neighborhood stays open until 7am. All drugstores post the names and addresses of the *nattapotek* (as they're called) in their windows.

Electricity   Sweden uses 220 volts AC and standard continental two-pin plugs. You'll need a transformer (sometimes erroneously called a converter), which you can buy at a hardware store. Before using any American-made appliance, always ask at your hotel desk.

Embassies & Consulates   All embassies are in Stockholm. The Embassy of the
United States is at Strandvägen 101, S-115 89 Stockholm (☎ **08/783-53-00**);
United Kingdom, Skarpögatan 6–8, S-115 27 Stockholm (☎ **08/671-30-00**);
Canada, Tegelbacken 4, S-101 23 Stockholm (☎ **08/453-30-00**); **Australia,**
Sergels Torg 12, S-103 27 Stockholm (☎ **08/613-29-00**). **New Zealand** does
not maintain an embassy in Sweden.

Emergencies   Call ☎ **90-000** from anywhere in Sweden if you need an ambulance, the police, or the fire department (*brandlarm*).

Language   The national language is Swedish, a Germanic tongue, and there are
many regional dialects. Some minority groups speak Norwegian and Finnish.
English is a required course in school and is commonly spoken, even in the hin-
terlands, especially among young people.

Liquor Laws   Most restaurants, pubs, and bars in Sweden are licensed to serve
liquor, wine, and beer. Some places are licensed only for wine and beer. Wine,
liquor, and export beer can be purchased only through the government-
controlled monopoly, Systembolaget. Branch stores, throughout the country, are
usually open Monday to Friday from 9am to 6pm. The minimum age for buying alcoholic beverages is 21.

Mail   Post offices are usually open Monday to Friday from 9am to 6pm, Saturday 9am to noon. Sending a postcard or letter to North America costs 8 SEK
(90¢) by airmail. Letters less than 20 grams ($\frac{7}{10}$ of an ounce) cost the same.
Mailboxes carry a yellow post horn on a blue background. You can also buy
stamps in most tobacco shops and stationers.

Maps   Many tourist offices supply free maps of their districts, and you can also
contact a Swedish automobile club. Bookstores throughout Sweden sell detailed
maps of the country and of major cities. The most reliable country maps are published by Hallweg. The best and most detailed city maps are by Falk, which sells
a particularly good and properly indexed map to Stockholm.

Newspapers & Magazines   In big cities (such as Stockholm and Gothenburg),
English-language newspapers, including the latest editions of the *International
Herald Tribune* and *USA Today,* are usually available. American newspapers are
not commonly available, but in Stockholm and Gothenburg you can buy London newspapers, such as *The Times.* Kiosks and newsstands in major cities carry
the European editions of *Time* and *Newsweek.*

Police   In an emergency, dial ☎ **90-000** anywhere in the country.

Radio & TV   In the summer, Radio Stockholm broadcasts a program for English-
speaking tourists, "T-T-T-Tourist Time," on 103.3 MHz (FM) from 6 to 7pm
daily. Swedish radio transmits P1 on 92.4 MHz (FM) and P2 on 96.2 MHz (FM)
in the Stockholm area. P3 is transmitted on 103.3 MHz (102.9 MHz in southern
Stockholm), a wavelength shared by Radio Stockholm and local programs.

The two most important TV channels, STV1 and STV2, are nonprofit. There
are three major privately operated stations—Channel 4, TV3, and TV5—and
several minor stations.

Rest Rooms   The word for toilet in Swedish is *toalett*, and public facilities are
in department stores, rail and air terminals, and subway (T-bana) stations.
They're also along some of the major streets, parks, and squares. Signs read
DAMER or D for women, HERRAR or H for men. Often the toilet is marked WC.
Most toilets are free, although a few have attendants who offer towels and soap.

In an emergency, you can use the toilets in most hotels and restaurants, although in principle they're reserved for customers.

Shoe Repairs   Shoe-repair shops rarely accommodate you while you wait. In summer, especially in July, many shops close, but the larger stores in the center of Stockholm have repair departments. If all you need is a new heel, look for *klackbar* in the stores or shoe departments of department stores. They'll make repairs while you wait.

Taxes   Sweden imposes a "value-added tax," called *moms,* on most goods and services. Visitors from North America can beat the tax by shopping in stores with the yellow-and-blue tax-free shopping sign. There are more than 15,000 in Sweden. To get a refund, your purchase must cost at least 200 SEK ($22). Get a tax-refund voucher before you leave the store. Tax refunds range from 16% to 18%, depending on the amount purchased. Moms begins at 19% on food items, but is 25% for most goods and services. The tax is part of the purchase price. You'll get your moms back, minus a small service charge, at your point of departure from the country (wherever you go through customs). Two requirements: You cannot use your purchase in Sweden, and it must be taken out of the country within 1 month after purchase. For more information, phone ☎ 024/74-17-41.

Telephone, Telex & Fax   Instructions in English are posted in public phone boxes, found on street corners. Very few phones are coin operated; most require a phone card, sold at most newspaper stands and tobacco shops. You can send a telegram by phoning ☎ 00-21 anytime. Avoid placing long-distance calls from your hotel, where the charge may be doubled or tripled.

Time   Sweden is on Central European Time—Greenwich Mean Time plus 1 hour, or Eastern Standard Time plus 6 hours. The clocks are advanced 1 hour in summer.

Tipping   Hotels include a 15% service charge in the bill. Restaurants, depending on their class, add 13% to 15%. Taxi drivers are customarily tipped 8% of the fare, and cloakroom attendants usually get 6 SEK (65¢).

Water   Tap water is generally safe to drink all over Sweden. Don't drink water from lakes, rivers, or streams, no matter how clear.

Introducing Stockholm

Stockholm, a city of 1.5 million people, stands on 14 islands in Lake Mälaren. It marks the beginning of an archipelago of 24,000 islands, skerries, and islets stretching all the way to the Baltic Sea. Stockholm is a city of bridges and islands, towers and steeples, cobblestoned squares and broad boulevards, Renaissance splendor, and steel-and-glass skyscrapers. Access to nature is just a short distance away. You can even go fishing in the downtown waterways, thanks to a 17th-century decree signed by Queen Christina.

Although the city was founded more than 7 centuries ago, it did not become the official capital of Sweden until the middle of the 17th century. Today it's the capital of a modern welfare state. The medieval walls of the Old Town (Gamla Stan) no longer stand, but the winding streets have been preserved.

1 Orientation

ARRIVING

BY PLANE You'll arrive at **Stockholm Arlanda Airport** (☎ 08/ 797-61-00 for flight information), about 28 miles north of the city on the E4 highway. A long covered walkway connects the international and domestic terminals.

A bus outside the terminal building takes you to the City Terminal, on Klarabergsviadukten in Stockholm, for 60 SEK ($6.60). The trip takes about 40 minutes.

A taxi to or from the airport is expensive, costing 350 to 400 SEK ($38.50 to $44) or more. *Travelers beware:* Smaller taxi companies may charge up to 650 SEK ($71.50) for the same ride. Be sure to ask in advance what the price is to your destination. For the name of a reputable company, see "Getting Around," below.

BY TRAIN Trains arrive at Stockholm's **Centralstationen** (Central Station) on Vasagatan, in the city center (☎ 020/75-75-75 in Sweden or 08/696-75-09 from abroad). There you can make connections to Stockholm's subway, the T-bana. Follow the tunnelbana sign.

BY BUS Buses also arrive at the Centralstationen city terminal, where you can catch the T-bana (subway). For bus information or reservations, check with the **ticket offices** at the station (☎ 08/440-85-70).

BY CAR Getting into Stockholm by car is relatively easy. The major national expressway from the south, E4, joins the national expressway

E3, from the west, and leads into the heart of the city. Stay on the highway until you see the turnoff for Central Stockholm (or Centrum).

Parking in Stockholm is extremely difficult unless your hotel has a garage, which is unlikely. Call in advance and find out what the parking situation is. If you're driving into the city, you can often park long enough to unload your luggage and ask a member of the hotel staff to direct you to the nearest garage.

BY FERRY   Large ships, including those of the **Silja Line,** Kungsgatan 2 (☎ 08/ 22-21-40), and the **Viking Line,** Centralstationen (☎ 08/452-40-00), arrive at berths near the junction of Södermalm and the entrance to Gamla Stan. This neighborhood is Stadsgården, and the avenue that runs along the adjacent waterfront is Stadsgårdshamnen. The Slussen T-bana stop, right at the berths, is a 3-minute walk from the Old Town. Holders of a valid Eurailpass receive discounts on Silja ferries to Helsinki and Turku.

Ferries from Gotland (whose capital is Visby) dock at Nynäshamn, south of Stockholm. Take a Nynäshamn-bound bus from the Central Station in Stockholm or the SL commuter train to reach the ferry terminal at Nynäshamn.

VISITOR INFORMATION

The **Tourist Center** is at Sweden House, Hamngatan 27, off Kungsträdgården (Box 7542), S-103 93 Stockholm (☎ 08/789-24-95 or 08/789-24-90). It's open June to August, Monday to Friday from 9am to 7pm, Saturday and Sunday 9am to 5pm; September to May, Monday to Friday 9am to 6pm, Saturday and Sunday 10am to 3pm. Maps and other free materials are available.

Kulturhuset, Sergels Torg 3 (☎ 08/508-31-400), distributes information about cultural activities and organizations throughout Sweden and Europe. The largest organization of its kind in Sweden, it was built in 1974 by the city of Stockholm as a showcase for Swedish and international art and theater. There are no permanent exhibits; display spaces hold a changing array of paintings, sculpture, photographs, and live performance groups. Inside are a snack bar, a library (which has newspapers in several languages), a reading room, and a collection of recordings. Admission is 30 SEK ($3.30) for adults, 20 SEK ($2.20) children 12 to 18, free for children under 12. It's open Tuesday to Thursday 11am to 7pm, Friday 11am to 6pm, Saturday 11am to 4pm, and Sunday noon to 4pm.

CITY LAYOUT

MAIN STREETS & ARTERIES   Stockholm's major streets are in the neighborhood of Norrmalm, north of Gamla Stan or Old Town. They are **Kungsgatan** (the main shopping street), **Birger Jarlsgatan,** and **Strandvägen** (which leads to Djurgården). **Stureplan,** which lies at the junction of Kungsgatan and Birger Jarlsgatan, is the commercial hub of the city.

About 4 blocks east of Stureplan is **Hötorget City,** a landmark of modern urban planning, which includes five 18-story skyscrapers. Its main, traffic-free artery is **Sergelgatan,** a 3-block shopper's promenade that leads to the modern sculptures in the center of Sergels Torg.

About 9 blocks south of Stureplan, at **Gustav Adolfs Torg,** are the Royal Dramatic Theater and the Royal Opera House.

A block east of the flaming torches of the opera house is the verdant north-to-south stretch of **Kungsträdgården.** Part avenue, part public park, it serves as a popular gathering place for students and a resting perch for shoppers.

Three blocks to the southeast, on a famous promontory, are the landmark Grand Hotel and the National Museum.

Most visitors to Stockholm arrive at the SAS Airport Bus Terminal, the Central Station, or Stockholm's Central (Public) Bus Station. They're in the heart of the city, on the harborfront, about 7 blocks due west of the opera house. **Kungsholmen** (King's Island) lies across a narrow canal from the rest of the city, a short walk west from the Central Station. It's visited chiefly by those who want to tour Stockholm's elegant Stadshuset (City Hall).

South of **Gamla Stan** (Old Town), and separated from it by a narrow but much-navigated stretch of water, is **Södermalm,** the city's southern district. Quieter than its northern counterpart, it's an important residential area.

To the east of Gamla Stan, on a large, forested island surrounded by complicated waterways, is **Djurgården** (Deer Park). The summer pleasure ground of Stockholm is the site of many of its most popular attractions (see "Neighborhoods in Brief," below).

FINDING AN ADDRESS Even numbers are on one side of the street, odd numbers on the other. Buildings go in numerical order, often with A, B, or C after the number.

MAPS Free maps of Stockholm are available at the tourist office. If you want to explore the narrow old streets of Gamla Stan, you'll need a more detailed map. The best, published by **Falk,** is a pocket-size map with a street index that can be opened and folded like a wallet. It's sold at most newsstands in central Stockholm and at major bookstores, including **Akademibokhandeln,** Mäster Samuelsgatan 32 (☎ **08/613-61-00**).

Neighborhoods in Brief

On 14 major islands in an archipelago, the city naturally has many neighborhoods. Those of interest to the average visitor lie in central Stockholm.

GAMLA STAN (OLD TOWN) The "cradle" of Stockholm lies at the entrance to Lake Mälaren on the Baltic. Its oldest city wall dates from the 13th century. The Old Town and the Vasa are the city's most popular attractions. Gamla Stan has only a few hotels, but dozens of restaurants. Its major shopping street is Västerlånggatan, and many little artisans' galleries and antiques stores abound on its small lanes. The main square, and the heart of the ancient city, is Stortorget.

LANGHOLMEN Queen Christina donated Langholmen, meaning "long island" to the city of Stockholm in 1647, and for many years it was a bleak prison site on a rocky terrain. Female prisoners planted thousands of trees and today the island is a "green lung," a virtual park that's perfect for a fine leafy stroll that's linked by bridge to the center of Stockholm. Even the prison has been transformed to a most unusual hotel with a fine restaurant.

NORRMALM North of Gamla Stan, this is the cultural and commercial heart of modern Stockholm, with a good concentration of moderately priced hotels. Once a city suburb, now it virtually *is* the city. If you come by train, you arrive at Central Station on Vasagatan in Norrmalm. The major pedestrian shopping street is Drottninggatan, which starts at the bridge to the Old Town.

The most famous park in Stockholm, Kungsträdgården (King's Garden), is in Norrmalm. In the summer this park is a major rendezvous point. Norrmalm also embraces the important squares of Sergels Torg and Hötorget (a modern shopping complex).

VASASTADEN As Norrmalm pushed north, this new district was created. It's split by the main arteries S:t Eriksgatan, Sveavägen, and Odengatan. The area around S:t Eriksplan is called "the Off-Broadway of Stockholm" because it has so many theaters. Increasingly, this district has attracted fashionable restaurants and bars and become a popular residential area for young Stockholmers in such fields as journalism, television, and advertising.

KUNGSHOLMEN   Once known as "Grey Friars Farm," today Kungsholmen (King's Island), to the west of Gamla Stan, is the site of City Hall. Established by Charles XI in the 17th century as a zone for industry and artisans, the island has been gentrified. One of its major arteries is Fleminggatan. Along Norrmälarstrand, old Baltic cutters tie up to the banks. The headquarters of Stockholm's newspapers are at Marieberg on the southwestern tip of the island.

SÖDERMALM   South of Gamla Stan, Södermalm (where Greta Garbo was born) is the largest and most populated district of Stockholm. Once synonymous with poverty, today the working-class area is becoming more fashionable, especially with artists, writers, and young people. If you don't come here to stay in one of the moderately priced hotels or to dine in one of its restaurants, you may want to take the Katarina elevator, at Södermalmstorg, Slussen, for a good view of Stockholm and its harbor. Admission is 10 SEK ($1.10), free for ages 6 and under.

ÖSTERMALM   In central Stockholm, east of Birger Jarlsgatan, the main artery, lies Östermalm. In the Middle Ages the royal family kept horses, and even armies, here. Today it's the site of the Army Museum. It has wide, straight streets, and one of the city's biggest parks, Humlegården, dating from the 17th century.

DJURGÅRDEN   To the east of Gamla Stan (Old Town) is Djurgården (Deer Park), a lake-encircled forested island that's the city's summer recreation area. Here you can visit the open-air folk museums of Skansen, the *Vasa* man-of-war, Gröna Lunds Tivoli (Stockholm's version of Copenhagen's pleasure garden), the Waldemarsudde estate and gardens of the "painting prince" Eugen, and the Nordic Museum. The fastest way to get here is over the bridge at Strandvägen and Narvavägen.

2 Getting Around

BY PUBLIC TRANSPORTATION

You can travel throughout Stockholm county by bus, local train, subway (T-bana), and trams, going from Singö in the north to Nynäshamn in the south. The routes are divided into zones, and one ticket is valid for all types of public transportation in the same zone within 1 hour of being stamped.

REGULAR FARES   The basic fare for public transportation (subway, tram, streetcar, or bus) is 16 SEK ($1.75). Purchase a ticket for a tram or streetcar at the tollbooth on the subway platform. On buses you pay the driver. To travel in most of Stockholm, all the way to the borders of the inner city, requires two tickets. The maximum ride, to the outermost suburbs, requires five tickets. You can transfer free (or double back and return to your starting point) within 1 hour of your departure. Day passes can be purchased at the SL Center (see "Transit Information" under "Fast Facts," below).

SPECIAL DISCOUNT TICKETS   Your best transportation bet is a **tourist season ticket.** A 1-day card costs 70 SEK ($7.70) and is valid for 24 hours of unlimited travel by T-bana, bus, and commuter train within Stockholm. It also includes passage on the ferry to Djurgården. Most visitors will probably prefer the 3-day card for 135 SEK ($14.85), valid for 72 hours in Stockholm and the adjacent county. The 3-day card is also valid for admission to the Skansen museum, the Kaknäs tower, and Gröna Lunds Tivoli. A card for a child 8 to 17 costs 70 to 80 SEK ($7.70 to $8.80), and kids under 8 travel free with an adult. Tickets are available at tourist information offices, in subway stations, and from most news vendors. Call ☎ 08/689-10-00 for more information.

Subway Art in Stockholm

In 1950 Stockholm decided to commission artists to decorate the city's subway stations. Some of the country's finest artists were asked to participate, and their work is now in some 100 stations, all the way from the center of Stockholm to the suburbs. The 173-mile-long art exhibit is popularly called "the longest and deepest art gallery in the world."

Stockholmskortet (Stockholm Card) is a discount card that allows unlimited travel by bus (except airport buses), subway, and local trains throughout the city and county of Stockholm. Admission to 70 attractions is included in the package. You can also take a sightseeing tour with City Sightseeing, getting on and off as often as you please. Tours are available daily mid-June to mid-August. The card is good for a 50% discount on a boat trip to the Royal Palace of Drottningholm.

You can buy the card at several places in the city, including the Tourist Center in Sweden House, HotellCentralen, the Central Station, the tourist information desk in City Hall (summer only), the Kaknäs TV tower, SL-Center Sergels Torg (subway entrance level), and Pressbyrån newsstands. The cards are stamped with the date and time at the first use. A 24-hour card costs 199 SEK ($21.90) for adults, 25 SEK ($2.75) for children 7 to 17.

BY T-BANA (SUBWAY)   Subway entrances are marked with a blue T on a white background. Tickets are bought on the platform. For information about schedules, routes, and fares, phone ☎ **08/686-10-00.**

BY BUS   Where the subway line ends, the bus begins. If the subway doesn't reach an area, a bus will. Many visitors ride the bus to Djurgården (although you can walk), where the T-bana doesn't go. If you're staying long enough to warrant it, you can buy the *SL Stockholmskartan* booklet (10 SEK/$1.30) at the Tourist Center at Sweden House, Hamngatan 27, off Kungsträdgården (☎ **08/789-24-95**), for a list of bus routes.

BY CAR

In general, you can park in marked spaces Monday to Friday from 8am to 6pm, but these spaces are hard to come by. Consider leaving your car in a parking garage—there are several in the city center and on the outskirts—and using public transportation. Parking exceptions or rules for specific areas are indicated on signs in the area. At Djurgården, parking is always prohibited, and from April to mid-September, it's closed to traffic Friday to Sunday.

BY TAXI

Taxis in Stockholm are the most expensive in the world. The meter starts at 28 SEK ($3.10), and a short ride can easily cost 80 SEK ($8.80). You can hail those that display the sign LEDIG, or you can order one by phone. **Taxi Stockholm** (☎ **08/15-00-00** or 08/15-04-00) is a large, reputable company.

BY FERRY

Ferries from Skeppsbron on Gamla Stan (near the bridge to Södermalm) can take you to Djurgården if you don't want to walk or go by bus. They leave every 20 minutes Monday to Saturday, and about every 15 minutes on Sunday, from 9am to 6pm. They cost 20 SEK ($2.20) for adults, 10 SEK ($1.10) for senior citizens and children 7 to 12, free for children under 7.

BY BICYCLE

The best place to go cycling is on Djurgården. You can rent bicycles from **Skepp o Hoj,** Djurgårdsbron (☎ 08/660-57-57), for about 150 SEK ($16.50) per day. It's open May to August, daily from 9am to 9pm.

Fast Facts: Stockholm

American Express   The office is at Norrlandsgatan 21 (☎ 08/411-05-40). It's open Monday to Friday from 9am to 6pm (until 5pm in winter), Saturday 10am to 3pm (until 1pm in winter).

Area Code   The international country code for Sweden is **46;** the city code for Stockholm is **08.** If you're calling Stockholm from abroad, drop the zero.

Baby-sitters   Stockholm hotels maintain lists of competent women who baby-sit. Nearly all of them speak English. There is no official agency. Your hotel reception desk can assist you.

Bookstores   For a good selection of English-language books, including maps and touring guides, try **Akademibokhandeln,** Mäster Samuelsgatan 32 (☎ 08/613-61-00). It's open Monday to Friday from 9:30am to 6pm, Saturday 10am to 4pm.

Car Rentals   See "Getting Around," in Chapter 12, "Planning a Trip to Sweden." In Stockholm, some of the big companies include **Avis,** Ringvägen 90 (☎ 08/644-99-80), and **Hertz,** Vasagatan 24 (☎ 08/24-07-20).

Currency Exchange   The currency-exchange office at the Central Station, **Forex** (☎ 08/411-67-34), is open daily from 7am to 9pm. It's approved by the Bank of Sweden and the Swedish tourist authorities, offers some of the best exchange rates in town, and takes some of the lowest commissions for cashing traveler's checks. Several other offices are scattered throughout the city.

Dentists   In an emergency, go to Sct. Eriks Hospital, Fleminggatan 22 (☎ 08/654-11-17), open daily from 8am to 8pm.

Doctors   For 24-hour emergency medical care, check with Medical Care Information (☎ 08/672-10-00). There's also a private clinic, City Akuten, Apelberg Sq. 481, 4th floor (☎ 08/412-29-61).

Drugstores   C. W. Scheele, Klarabergsgatan 64 (☎ 08/454-81-00), is open 24 hours a day.

Embassies & Consulates   See "Fast Facts: Sweden," in chapter 12.

Emergencies   Call ☎ **112** for the police, ambulance service, or the fire department.

Eyeglasses   **Nordiska Kompaniet (NK),** Hamngatan 18–20 (☎ 08/762-80-00), a leading department store, has a registered optician on duty at its ground-floor Service Center. The optician performs vision tests, stocks a large selection of frames, and makes emergency repairs.

Hospitals   Call Medical Care Information (☎ 08/672-21-00), 24 hours a day, and an English-speaking operator can direct you to the nearest hospital.

Internet Access   One of the most central places for receiving e-mail or checking messages is **Café Nine,** Odengatan 44 (☎ 08/673-67-97; E-mail: info@ninestudios.com). It charges only 1 krone (10¢) per minute, and is open Monday to Friday 10am to 1am and Saturday and Sunday 11am to 1am.

Impressions

It [Stockholm] is not a city at all. It is ridiculous of it to think of itself as a city. It is simply a rather large village, set in the middle of some forests and some lakes. You wonder what it thinks it is doing there, looking so important.
    —Ingmar Bergman, in an interview with James Baldwin, 1960

Laundry & Dry Cleaning   The system of coin-operated launderettes is pretty much outmoded in Sweden. **City Kemtvatt,** Drottningsholmsvägen 9 (☎ 08/654-95-34), offers same-day delivery of dry cleaning and laundry (by the kilo, or 2.2 pounds) brought in before 10am. It's open Monday to Friday from 7am to 6pm, Saturday 10am to 2pm. The cost for doing laundry is 55 SEK ($6.05) per kilo.

Libraries   The **Stockholms Stadsbibliotek,** Sveavägen 73 (☎ 08/508-31-100), is the biggest municipal library in Sweden, with 2.5 million books (many in English) and audiovisual materials. It also subscribes to 1,500 newspapers and periodicals (many in English). It's open Monday to Thursday from 10am to 8:30pm, Friday 10am to 6pm, Saturday and Sunday noon to 4pm.

Lost Property   If you've lost something on the train, go to the Lost and Found office in the Central Station, lower concourse (☎ 08/762-25-50). There's another office at the police station at Bergsgatan 39 (☎ 08/401-07-88). The Stockholm Transit Company (SL) keeps its recovered articles at the Rådmansgatan T-bana station (☎ 08/736-07-80).

Luggage Storage & Lockers   Facilities are available at the Central Station on Vasagatan, lower concourse (☎ 08/762-25-50). You can also rent lockers at the ferry stations at Värtan and Tegelvikshamnen, at the Viking Line terminal, and at the Central Station.

Photographic Needs   Stockholm has many photo shops. One of the most centrally located is the **Kodak Image Center,** Hamngatan 16 (☎ 08/21-40-42). It's open Monday to Friday 8am to 6pm, Saturday 10am to 2pm.

Police   Call ☎ **112** in an emergency.

Post Office   The main post office, at Vasagatan 28–34 (☎ 08/781-20-00), is open Monday to Friday from 8am to 6pm, Saturday 9am to 1pm. General delivery mail can be sent to Poste Restante, [c/o] Postens Huyudkontor (Main Post Office), Vasagatan 28–34, S-10 430 Stockholm, Sweden.

Radio & TV   Sweden has two TV channels and three national radio stations, plus a local station for Stockholm, broadcasting on 103.3 MHz (FM). Many hotels get English-language TV programs broadcast from England, and many of the more expensive hotels have 24-hour CNN news broadcasts in English.

Rest Rooms   Public facilities are in the Central Station, all subway stations, and department stores, and along some major streets, parks, and squares. In an emergency, you can also use the toilets in most hotels and restaurants, although in principle they're reserved for patrons.

Shoe Repair   The shoe-repair place in the basement of **Nordiska Kompaniet (NK),** Hamngatan 18–20 (☎ 08/762-80-00), a leading department store, may also be able to repair broken luggage.

Taxis   See "Getting Around," above.

Telephone, Telex & Fax   Instructions in English are posted in public phone boxes, which can be found on street corners. Very few phones in Sweden are coin operated; most require a phone card, which you can buy at most newspaper stands and tobacco shops. You can send a telegram by phoning ☎ **00-21** anytime.

Post offices throughout Stockholm offer phone, fax, and telegram services. All but the smallest boarding houses in Stockholm have fax services.

Transit Information   For information on all services, including buses, subways (Tunnelbana), and suburban trains (*pendeltåg*), call ☎ **08/689-10-00.** The SL Center, on the lower level of Sergels Torg, provides transportation information. It also sells a map of the city's system, including suburban trains, and day and discount passes for public transportation. It's open in summer, Monday to Thursday from 9am to 6pm, Friday 9am to 5:30pm, Saturday 9am to 4pm, Sunday 10am to 3pm; the rest of the year, Monday to Friday 9am to 5pm.

3 Accommodations

By the standards of many U.S. and Canadian cities, hotels in Stockholm are very expensive. If the prices make you want to cancel your trip, read on. Dozens of hotels offer reduced rates on weekends all year and daily from around mid-June to mid-August. For further information, inquire at a travel agency or the Tourist Center (see "Visitor Information," above). In the summer, it's best to make reservations in advance just to be on the safe side.

Most medium-priced hotels are in Norrmalm, north of the Old Town, and many of the least expensive lodgings are near the Central Station. There are comparably priced inexpensive accommodations within 10 to 20 minutes of the city, easily reached by subway, streetcar, or bus. We'll suggest a few hotels in the Old Town, but they're limited and more expensive.

Note: In most cases a service charge ranging from 10% to 15% is added to the bill, plus the inevitable 21% *moms* (value-added tax). Unless otherwise indicated, all our recommended accommodations come with a private bathroom.

BOOKING SERVICES   HotellCentralen, Vasagatan (☎ **08/789-24-56**), on the lower level of the Central Station, is the city's official housing bureau. It can arrange accommodations in hotels, pensions (boarding houses), and youth hostels, but not in private homes. There's a 40 SEK ($4.40) service fee. It's open June to August, daily from 7am to 9pm; May and September, daily 8am to 7pm; October to April, daily 9am to 6pm. Credit and charge cards are accepted.

The least expensive accommodations in Stockholm are rooms in private homes. The best way to book one is to go to the **Hotell Tjänst AB,** Vasagatan 15–17 (☎ **08/ 10-44-37** or 08/10-44-57; fax 08/21-37-16); it's open Monday to Friday, 9am to noon and 1 to 5pm. As you leave the Central Station, turn left on Vasagatan and walk to this address, which is on the fourth floor of an older building. Mr. Gustavsson and his staff will book you into a private room, without breakfast, for 450 SEK ($49.50) in a double, including the reservation fee. From June 15 to August 15, the agency can also book you into Stockholm's major hotels at a big discount.

This service is usually available only in person. The agency maintains a long "secret" list of private addresses, and Mr. Gustavsson doesn't answer letters requesting reservations. The hours listed above are firm and advanced booking is rarely accepted, but if you're going to arrive in Stockholm on a weekend, call or fax the office and Mr. Gustavsson might bend the rules.

NORRMALM (CENTER OF STOCKHOLM)
VERY EXPENSIVE

⭘ **Grand Hotel.** Södra Blasieholmshamnen 8, S-103 27 Stockholm. ☎ **800/223-5652** in the U.S. and Canada, or 08/679-35-00. Fax 08/611-86-86. www.grandhotel.se. E-mail: hotel.grand@grandhotel.se. 320 units. MINIBAR TV TEL. 3,195–3,995 SEK ($351.45–$439.45) double; from 4,895 SEK ($538.45) suite. Rates include breakfast. AE, DC, MC, V. Parking 340 SEK ($37.40). T-bana: Kungsträdgården. Bus: 46, 55, 62, or 76.

Opposite the Royal Palace, this hotel—a bastion of elite hospitality since 1874—is the finest in Sweden. The most recent restoration was in 1996, but its old-world style has always been maintained. Guest rooms come in all shapes and sizes, all elegantly appointed with traditional styling, all with excellent mattresses. Some feature an air-cooling system. The bathrooms are decorated with Italian marble and tiles and have heated floors and hair dryers. The priciest rooms overlook the water. The hotel's ballroom is an exact copy of Louis XIV's Hall of Mirrors at Versailles.

Dining/Diversions: The Grand Veranda specializes in traditional food served from a buffet, and the Franska Matsalen is the gourmet restaurant. The Cadier Bar is one of the most sophisticated spots in Stockholm.

Amenities: Room service (24 hours), same-day laundry and dry cleaning, concierge, house doctor, shoeshine service, valet parking, limousine service, sauna, hairstylist, newsstand, florist, gift shop, fitness center.

EXPENSIVE

Berns' Hotel. Näckströmsgatan 8, S-111 47 Stockholm. ☎ **08/614-07-00.** Fax 08/566-32-201. www.berns.se. E-mail: hotel.berns@bernshotel.se. 68 units. A/C MINIBAR TV TEL. 2,495–2,995 SEK ($274.45–$329.45) double; 3,795–5,500 SEK ($417.45–$605) suite. Rates include breakfast. AE, DC, MC, V. Parking 300 SEK ($33). T-bana: Östermalmstorg.

During its 19th-century heyday, this was the most elegant hotel in Sweden, with an ornate Gilded Age interior that was the setting for many a legendary rendezvous. In 1989, following years of neglect, it was rebuilt in the original style, and the restaurant facilities were upgraded. Although the dining and drinking areas are usually crowded with young disco-lovers and bar patrons, the guest rooms are soundproofed and comfortably isolated from the activities downstairs. Each room has a satellite TV, CD player, and a good-size bathroom sheathed in Italian marble. Bathrooms are small but have hair dryers, phones, and makeup mirrors. Some units are reserved for nonsmokers, and others are accessible to those in wheelchairs.

Dining/Diversions: The Red Room is the setting and namesake of Strindberg's novel *Röda Rummet*. The hotel also has a bar.

Amenities: Baby-sitting, dry cleaning and laundry service, car-rental desk, access to a nearby health club.

Hotell Diplomat. Strandvagen 7C, Östermalm, S-104-40 Stockholm. ☎ **08/663-5800.** Fax 08/783-6634. 128 units. MINIBAR TV TEL. Mon–Thurs 2,495 SEK ($274.45) double; Fri–Sun 1,395–2,495 SEK ($153.45–$274.45) double. All week long 3,295–3,495 SEK ($362.45–$384.45) suite. AE, DC, MC, V. Rates include breakfast. No parking. T-bana: Storeplan.

Well-managed, discreet, and solid, this hotel is a dignified and conservative operation that knows how to handle business clients and corporate conventions. Built in 1911, it retains hints of its original art nouveau styling. Public areas are more streamlined. The guest room amenities, such as TVs and minibars, are concealed in well-crafted furniture or built-in cupboards. Many rooms contain bay windows overlooking the harbor; most of the less expensive accommodations face a quiet inner courtyard. Rooms range in size from cramped singles to spacious doubles with sitting areas. All have good beds and average-sized bathrooms, with tiled vanities, bidets, good towels, and both mounted and hand-held showers. At least once, take the circular stairs for views over the hotel's antique stained-glass windows.

Dining: The Tea Room restaurant has a decor inspired by colonial Asia and views over Stockholm's harbor. A bar on the second floor resembles a posh men's club.

Amenities: Sauna, meeting rooms, room service (7am to midnight).

Lydmar Hotel. Sturegatan 10, S-114 36 Stockholm. ☎ **08/566-11-300.** Fax 08/566-11-301. www.lydmar.se. E-mail: info@lydmar.se. 63 units. MINIBAR TV TEL. 2,200–3,750 SEK ($242–$412.50) double; 7,500 SEK ($825) junior suite. Rates include buffet breakfast. AE, DC, MC, V. Parking 250 SEK ($27.50). T-bana: Östermalmstorg. Bus: 41, 46, 56, or 91.

Opposite the garden of the King's Library, in what looks like an office building, the Lydmar opened in 1930 (as the Eden Terrace). The guest rooms are cozy and traditionally furnished, and come in many shapes and sizes. Although the rooms aren't large, they are exceptionally well maintained. Mattresses are firm, and bathrooms are well appointed. The hotel has a large dining room and a rooftop terrace where guests can enjoy drinks in the summer. In recent years, the Matsalen restaurant has become ever-so-chic.

Dining/Diversions: The relatively formal Matsalen has interesting dishes such as mussels with chorizo, fish soup with *rouille* (garlic-flavored mayonnaise), or the scrumptious pan-fried scallops with citrus risotto. The lobby restaurant is a more casual brasserie with monthly art exhibits and live music several nights a week. There's also a popular lobby bar, with live jazz and soul music.

Amenities: Room service, laundry, baby-sitting (will assist with arrangements), access to nearby health club (with reduced fee).

Scandic Hotel Sergel Plaza. Brunkebergstorg 9, S-103 27 Stockholm. ☎ **800/THE-OMNI** in the U.S., or 08/22-66-00. Fax 08/21-50-70. www.scandic-hotels.se. E-mail: sergel. plaza.hotel@scandic-hotels.se. 418 units. A/C TV TEL. 2,200–3,200 SEK ($242–$352) double; from 7,000 SEK ($770) suite. Rates include breakfast. AE, DC, MC, V. Parking 210 SEK ($23.10). T-bana: Centralen. Bus: 47, 52, or 69.

This hotel opened in 1984 at the entrance to Drottninggatan, the main shopping street. Designed as living quarters for parliament members, it has been so improved that today it's one of the city's leading hotels. The elegant decor includes 18th-century artwork and antiques. The beautifully decorated guest rooms are done in modern but traditional style. All units contain firm mattresses and double-glazed windows. The average-size tiled bathrooms have hair dryers. Maintenance is first rate, and some accommodations are for nonsmokers and wheelchair users. A special executive floor offers enhanced amenities and several electronic extras.

Dining/Diversions: The Anna Rella, the gourmet restaurant, offers Swedish and international specialties. There's also a lobby and piano bar.

Amenities: Concierge, room service (24 hours), laundry, baby-sitting, saunas, solariums, Jacuzzis.

MODERATE

Adlon Hotell & Kontor. Vasagatan 42, S-111 20 Stockholm. ☎ **08/402-65-00.** Fax 08/20-86-10. www.adlon.se. E-mail: hotel@adlon.se. 78 units. TV TEL. 1,550–2,800 SEK ($170.50–$308) double. Rates include breakfast. AE, DC, MC, V. Parking 250 SEK ($27.50) in garage 1 block away. T-bana: Centralen.

This 1890s building was redesigned by brothers Axel and Hjalmar Jumlin in the 1920s. Upgraded and improved many times since, it lies near the Central Station (and the subway) and is convenient to buses to and from Arlanda Airport. All the rather small rooms have been renovated and are comfortably furnished; 70% of them are designated for nonsmokers. The small bathrooms have hair dryers.

ℹ️ Family-Friendly Hotels

AF *Chapman* (see p. 331)   Although there are no family rooms, kids delight in staying in a stateroom (with two to eight beds) aboard an authentic three-masted schooner.

Hotel Tegnérlunden (see p. 329)   Twenty big, airy rooms are ideal for families on a budget.

Sheraton Stockholm & Towers (see p. 328)   This well-run chain has always pampered children. The spacious rooms can be comfortably shared with parents.

Castle Hotel. Riddargatan 14, S-114 35 Stockholm. ☎ 08/679-57-00. Fax 08/611-20-22. www.castle-hotel.se. E-mail: receptionen@castle-hotel.se. 49 units. TV TEL. 875–1,700 SEK ($96.25–$187) double; 2,400 SEK ($264) suite. Rates include breakfast. AE, DC, MC, V. Parking 300 SEK ($33). T-bana: Östermalmstorg.

In an expensive neighborhood a short walk east of the center, this 1920 building was originally an apartment building. In the late 1980s it was renovated as a hotel. The good-sized guest rooms have gilded accents and art deco accessories. Discounts are offered on some weekends.

Elite Hotel Stockholm Plaza. Birger Jarlsgatan 29, S-103 95 Stockholm. ☎ 08/566-22-000. Fax 08/566-22-020. www.elite.se. E-mail: info@stoplaza.elite.se. 151 units. TV TEL. 1,290–2,095 SEK ($141.90–$230.45) double; 2,495–3,495 SEK ($274.45–$384.45) suite. Rates include breakfast. AE, DC, MC, V. Parking 220 SEK ($24.20). T-bana: Hötorget or Östermalmstorg.

Built on a triangular lot that might remind some visitors of New York's Flatiron Building, this first-class hotel is a well-run and inviting choice in the city center. Since its construction a century ago, the building has had many uses—a run-down rooming house, private apartments, offices—until 1984, when it was radically upgraded and renovated into a hotel. The light, fresh guest rooms have firm beds, tiled bathrooms, and hair dryers. The elegant restaurant, the Plaza Grill, serves French and Swedish specialties. Below the restaurant is a stylish disco—the Penny Lane—that plays music from the 1960s and '70s and reserves entry for mature, reasonably well-dressed guests. The disco is open Wednesday to Saturday from 8:30pm to 2am. Admission is free for hotel guests, 75 SEK ($8.25) for others.

Esplanade Hotel. Strandvägen 7A, S-114 56 Stockholm. ☎ 08/663-07-40. Fax 08/662-59-92. www.hotelesplanade.se. E-mail: hotel@esplanadesto.se. 34 units. TV TEL. 1,495–1,995 SEK ($164.45–$219.45) double. Rates include breakfast. AE, DC, MC, V. Parking 200 SEK ($22). T-bana: Östermalmstorg. Bus: 47 or 69.

This informal hotel, next to the more expensive Diplomat, attracts representatives from the nearby embassies and others who like its comfortable charm and traditional atmosphere. Constructed in 1910, it became a family-style hotel in 1954. Many of the rooms, furnished in old-fashioned style, have minibars. Single rooms are minuscule. Most doubles have double-glazed windows, trouser presses, extra-long beds, and well-kept, decent-sized tile bathrooms. Four rooms have a water view, and the English lounge features a balcony with a view of Djurgården. Only breakfast is served.

Kung Carl Hotel. Birger Jarlsgatan 21, S-11145 Stockholm. ☎ 08/463-50-00. Fax 08/463-50-50. www.hkchotels.se. E-mail: kungcarl@hkchotels.se. 110 units. MINIBAR TV TEL. 1,850–2,450 SEK ($203.50–$269.50) double; 4,000 SEK ($440) suite. Rates include breakfast. AE, DC, MC, V. Parking 200 SEK ($22). T-bana: Östermalmstorg.

Stockholm Accommodations

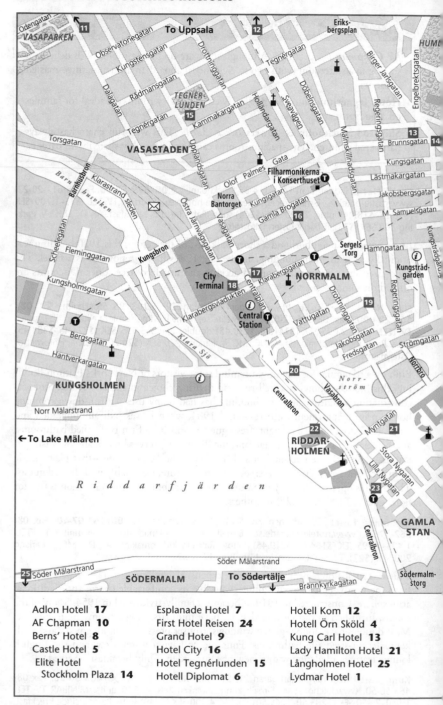

Adlon Hotell **17**

AF Chapman **10**

Berns' Hotel **8**

Castle Hotel **5**

Elite Hotel
   Stockholm Plaza **14**

Esplanade Hotel **7**

First Hotel Reisen **24**

Grand Hotel **9**

Hotel City **16**

Hotel Tegnérlunden **15**

Hotell Diplomat **6**

Hotell Kom **12**

Hotell Örn Sköld **4**

Kung Carl Hotel **13**

Lady Hamilton Hotel **21**

Långholmen Hotel **25**

Lydmar Hotel **1**

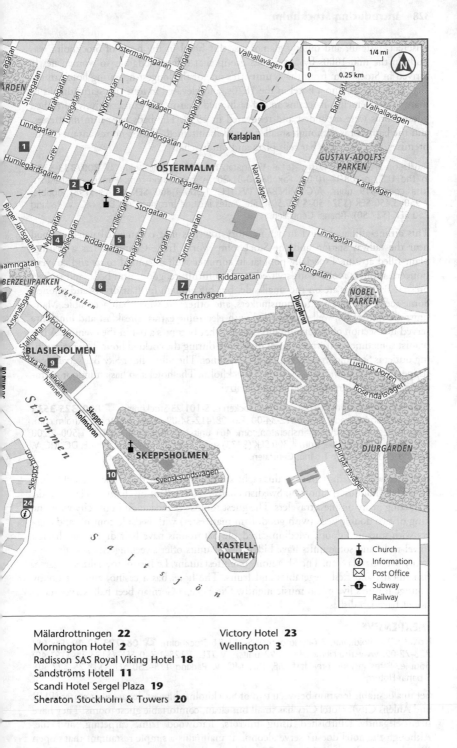

Mälardrottningen **22**
Mornington Hotel **2**
Radisson SAS Royal Viking Hotel **18**
Sandströms Hotell **11**
Scandi Hotel Sergel Plaza **19**
Sheraton Stockholm & Towers **20**

Victory Hotel **23**
Wellington **3**

Discreet, tasteful, and quietly glamorous, this hotel in the heart of Stockholm was built in the mid-1800s by a religious group that offered lodgings to women newly arrived in Stockholm from the country. It's one of the longest-operating hotels in the city. Transformed into a hotel in the 1870s, and elevated to four-star status thanks to many improvements, it retains an old-fashioned charm. The conservatively furnished guest rooms were expanded and renovated in 1998. The beds have firm mattresses, and the bathrooms, although small, are well maintained. There's no restaurant on the premises, but the lobby bar sells pizza and sandwiches.

Radisson SAS Royal Viking Hotel. Vasagatan 1, S-101 23 Stockholm. ☎ **800/333-3333** in the U.S., or 08/14-10-00. Fax 08/10-81-80. www.radisson.com. E-mail: guest@stozs. rdsas.com. 319 units. A/C MINIBAR TV TEL. 1,300–1,800 SEK ($143–$198) double; 2,950–3,450 SEK ($324.50–$379.50) suite. Rates include breakfast. AE, DC, MC, V. Parking 250 SEK ($27.50). T-bana: Centralen.

This airline-affiliated hotel in a nine-story tower is in a commercial neighborhood near the railway station and the Stockholm World Trade Center. It has a soaring, plant-filled atrium. Especially popular in summer with organized tours and conventioneers, it offers rooms with stylized modern furniture, good, firm beds, and trouser presses. Bathrooms are on the small side, but big enough for hair dryers and phones. Some rooms are set aside for nonsmokers, and others are wheelchair accessible. Many units are minisuites, well accessorized with electronic extras. Breakfast and lunch are served in a section of the atrium lobby, near what becomes a bar in the evening. A live pianist sometimes performs at brief interludes during the cocktail hour. The main dining outlet is Stockholm Fisk, which serves dinner. The ninth-floor Sky Bar serves light suppers and has a sweeping view over Stockholm. The hotel also has an indoor swimming pool with sauna, solarium, and Jacuzzi.

Sheraton Stockholm & Towers. Tegelbacken 6, S-101 23 Stockholm. ☎ **800/325-3535** in the U.S. and Canada, or 08/412-34-00. Fax 08/412-34-09. www.sheratonstockholm.com. E-mail: sheraton-stockholm@ittsheraton.com. 461 units. A/C MINIBAR TV TEL. 1,500–2,200 SEK ($165–$242) double; from 4,300 SEK ($473) suite. Rates include breakfast. AE, DC, MC, V. Parking 200 SEK ($22). T-bana: Centralen.

Sheathed with Swedish granite, this eight-story hostelry is within view of Stockholm's City Hall (Rådhuset). Short on Swedish charm, it's excellent by chain hotel standards, attracting many business travelers. The guest rooms are the largest in the city with one king or two double beds (with good, firm mattresses) with bedside controls and closets with mirrored doors. Medium-sized tile bathrooms have hair dryers and heated towel racks and some units have bidets. Most units offer sweeping views of the city, many over Gamla Stan. The Sheraton's main restaurant, Le Bistro, specializes in game, fish, meats, and fresh vegetables and fruits. The hotel has a casino, and the Lobby Lounge features live piano music nightly. Die Ecke, a German beer hall, serves traditional Bavarian dishes.

INEXPENSIVE

Hotel City. Slöjdgatan 7 (at Hötorget), S-111 81 Stockholm. ☎ **08/723-72-00.** Fax 08/ 723-72-09. www.rica.cityhotel.se. 292 units. TV TEL. 1,125–1,740 SEK ($123.75–$191.40) double. Rates include breakfast. AE, DC, MC, V. Parking 175–250 SEK ($19.25–$27.50). T-bana: Hötorget.

Set in a desirable location between two of Stockholm's biggest department stores (PUB and Åhléns City), Hotel City has small but clean, comfortable guest rooms. They have been elegantly refurbished using mirrors, hardwood trim, carpeting, and tile. Although the hotel doesn't serve alcohol, it maintains a simple restaurant that's open Monday to Friday from 11am to 3pm. There's also a sauna.

Hotell Kom. 17 Döbelnsgatan, S-11140 Stockholm. ☎ **08/412-23-00.** Fax 08/412-23-10. E-mail: dxmling@komhotell.se. 90 units. MINIBAR TV TEL. Mon–Thurs 1,450–1,550 SEK ($159.50–$170.50) double; Fri–Sun 965 SEK ($106.15) double. Rates include breakfast. AE, DC, MC, V. Parking 120 SEK ($13.20). T-bana: Rådmansgatan.

Don't expect too much at this former youth hostel—people stay here mainly for the price. But Hotell Kom was upgrades to a hotel over 20 years ago and is certainly appropriate for extended stays. Each unit has a small kitchenette, creating an apartment-like ambience. It's in a residential neighborhood scattered with stores and private apartments. The rooms are clean and decent, with reasonably comfortable beds, and rather small but immaculate bathrooms. There's an exercise room and health club on the premises, and a solarium. Only breakfast is served.

Hotell Örn Sköld. Nybrogatan 6, S-11434 Stockholm. ☎ **08/667-02-85.** Fax 08/ 667-69-91. 27 units. MINIBAR TV TEL. 1,175–1,275 SEK ($129.25–$140.25) double. 300 SEK ($33) discount on selected weekends (Fri–Sat). Rates include breakfast. AE, MC, V. Parking 100 SEK ($11) in nearby public garage. T-bana: Östermalmstorg.

The five-story building that contains this hotel was built in 1910, and today the nearby Royal Dramatic Theater uses most of it for prop storage and staff housing. The hotel is on the floor above street level. High-ceilinged rooms have simple, contemporary furnishings, and more expensive units are big enough to hold extra beds if necessary.

Hotel Tegnérlunden. Tegnérlunden 8, S-113 59 Stockholm. ☎ **08/5454-5550.** Fax 08/ 5454-5551. E-mail: info.tegener@swedenhotels.se. 103 units. TV TEL. 990–1,460 SEK ($108.90–$160.60) double; 1,795 SEK ($197.45) junior suite. Rates include breakfast. AE, DC, MC, V. Parking 140 SEK ($15.40) in nearby garage. Bus: 47, 53, or 69.

In a 19th-century building at the edge of a city park, this hotel has a few public rooms, a lobby, and a bar. The best feature is the tasteful, functionally furnished rooms. They're blissfully quiet, especially those opening onto the rear. The rooms vary in size and shape, and those we inspected were well maintained. The hotel offers comfort but not a lot of style. The bathrooms are small but beautifully kept. There's also a sauna.

Mornington Hotel. Nybrogatan 53, S-102 44 Stockholm. ☎ **800/528-1234** in the U.S. and Canada, or 08/663-12-40. Fax 08/662-21-79. www.morningtonhotel.com. E-mail: mornington.hotel-sth@wmhotels.se. 141 units. TV TEL. June 26–Aug 9, 800 SEK ($88) double; Aug 10–June 25, 1,595–1,770 SEK ($175.45–$194.70) double. Year-round, 3,250 SEK ($357.50) suite. Rates include breakfast. AE, DC, MC, V. Closed Dec 23–26. Parking 150 SEK ($16.50). T-bana: Östermalmstorg. Bus: 49, 54, or 62.

Proud of its image as an English-inspired hotel, this efficient modern establishment has a concrete exterior brightened with rows of flower boxes. It was built in 1956 and has been renovated several times, most recently in 1997. Most rooms have standard decor, and many are quite small. The lobby contains a small rock garden. The hotel offers rooms for nonsmokers and guests with disabilities, and its sauna and Turkish bath are free. Restaurant Eleonora serves international and Swedish cuisine, and there's a Library Bar.

Wellington. Storgatan 6, S-11451 Stockholm. ☎ **08/667-09-10.** Fax 08/667-12-54. www.wellington.se. E-mail: info.wellington@swedenhotels.se. 60 units. TV TEL. Summer and Fri–Sat year-round, 1,245 SEK ($136.95) double; rest of year, 1,895 SEK ($208.45) double. Rates include breakfast. AE, DC, MC, V. Parking 165 SEK ($18.15). T-bana: Östermalmstorg.

A longtime favorite with frugal travelers, the Wellington sounds like something you'd find in London. Built in the late 1950s, it maintains some English decorative touches and lies in a quiet but convenient neighborhood about a half-mile east of Stockholm's commercial core. The public rooms are filled with engravings of English hunting scenes and leather-covered chairs. Some of the small but stylish guest rooms overlook a flower-filled courtyard. Some rooms on higher floors have panoramic views. Beds are firm, and the small bathrooms are well equipped, including hair dryers. Two floors are reserved for nonsmokers. The hotel has an excellent sauna. The fare in the breakfast room is good (no other meals are served).

ON GAMLA STAN (OLD TOWN)
EXPENSIVE

First Hotel Reisen. Skeppsbron 12–14, S-111 30 Stockholm. ☎ **08/22-32-60.** Fax 08/ 20-15-59. www.firsthotels.com. E-mail: info@firsthotels.se. 144 units. MINIBAR TV TEL. 2,299–2,899 SEK ($252.90–$318.90) double; 3,800-4,800 SEK ($418–$528) suite. Rates include breakfast. AE, DC, MC, V. Parking 275 SEK ($30.25). Bus: 43, 46, 55, 59, or 76.

Just three alleyways from the Royal Palace, this hotel faces the water. Dating from the 17th century, the three-building structure attractively combines the old and the new. The rooms are comfortably furnished in a stylish modern fashion inspired by traditional designs. Beds are frequently renewed, and the bathrooms are excellent, with such amenities as massaging shower heads, scales, marble floors, heated towel racks, and phones. Some suites have Jacuzzis. Some units for nonsmokers are available, and the top-floor accommodations open onto small balconies.

Dining/Diversions: The hotel's specialty restaurant, Ciao Ciao, serves refined international and Italian cuisine, and the Clipper Club specializes in grills. There's also a Library Bar and Clipper Club Pianobar, with live entertainment Monday to Saturday.

Amenities: Room service (7am to 11pm), laundry, guide services in summer, indoor pool, sauna.

✪ Lady Hamilton Hotel. Storkyrkobrinken 5, S-111 28 Stockholm. ☎ **08/23-46-80.** Fax 08/411-11-48. www.lady-hamilton.se. E-mail: info@lady-hamilton.se. 34 units, some with shower only. MINIBAR TV TEL. 1,590–2,570 SEK ($174.90–$282.70) double. Rates include breakfast. AE, DC, MC, V. Parking: 250 SEK ($27.50). T-bana: Gamla Stan. Bus: 48.

This hotel, consisting of three connected buildings, stands on a quiet street surrounded by antiques shops and restaurants—a very desirable location indeed. Dozens of antiques are scattered among the well-furnished guest rooms. Most rooms have beamed ceilings. The beds (queen or double) are of high quality. Bathrooms are tiled but vary in size from spacious to cramped. All have heated towel racks, heated floors, and hair dryers. Top-floor rooms have skylights and memorable views over the old town. Some rooms for nonsmokers are available. You'll get a sense of the 1470 origins of this hotel when you use the luxurious sauna, which encompasses the stone-rimmed well that formerly supplied the building's water. The ornate staircase wraps around a large model of a clipper ship suspended from the ceiling.

Amenities: Coffee shop (no restaurant), car rental desk, bar, business center, laundry and dry cleaning, massage.

✪ Victory Hotel. Lilla Nygatan 3–5, S-111 28 Stockholm. ☎ **08/506-400-00.** Fax 08/ 20-21-77. www.victory-hotel.se. E-mail: info@victory-hotel.se. 48 units, some with shower only. A/C MINIBAR TV TEL. 1,750–2,750 SEK ($192.50–$302.50) double; 3,590–4,890 SEK ($394.90–$537.90) suite. Rates include breakfast. AE, DC, MC, V. T-bana: Gamla Stan. Bus: 48.

A small but stylish hotel, the Victory offers warm, inviting rooms, each named after a prominent sea captain. They sport a pleasing combination of exposed wood, antiques, and 19th-century memorabilia. Many rooms are smoke-free, and the beds are comfortable, with firm mattresses. The average-sized bathrooms are tiled and have heated floors and towel racks, hair dryers, robes, and phones. Only the suites have tubs. The hotel rests on the foundations of a 1382 fortified tower. In the 1700s the building's owners buried a massive silver treasure under the basement floor—you can see it in the Stockholm City Museum. There's a shiny brass elevator, but from the stairs you'll see one of Sweden's largest collections of 18th-century nautical needlepoint, much of it created by the sailors during their long voyages.

Dining: The Restaurant Leijontornet specializes in fish, fowl, and game. A bistro, the Lohe Room, serves Swedish home cooking in a cozy, informal atmosphere.

Amenities: Room service (7am to 11pm), same-day laundry and dry cleaning, travel and concierge desk, safe-deposit boxes, saunas.

MODERATE

Mälardrottningen. Riddarholmen, S-11128 Stockholm. ☎ **08/545-187-80.** Fax 08/24-36-76. www.malardrottningen.se. E-mail: receptionen@malardrottningen.se. 60 units. A/C TV TEL. Mon–Thurs 1,020–1,460 SEK ($112.20–$160.60) double; Fri–Sun 860–1,360 SEK ($94.60–$149.60) double. Rates include breakfast. AE, DC, MC, V. Parking 15 SEK ($1.65) per hour. T-bana: Gamla Stan.

During its heyday, this was the most famous motor yacht in the world, the subject of gossip columns everywhere, thanks to the complicated friendships that developed among the passengers and, in some cases, the crew. Built in 1924 by millionaire C.K.G. Billings, it was the largest (240 feet) motor yacht in the world, and was later acquired by the Woolworth heiress, Barbara Hutton. The below-deck space originally contained only seven suites. The yacht was converted into a hotel in the early 1980s, and permanently moored beside a satellite island of Stockholm's Old Town. The cabins are now cramped and somewhat claustrophobic. Most have bunk-style twin beds. Considering the hotel's conversation-piece status, and its location close to everything in the Old Town, it might be worth an overnight stay. There's a sauna, and a lounge and TV room that are separated with a glass panel from the gleaming brass of what used to be the engine room. The hotel contains small conference facilities, and a restaurant and bar (see "Where to Dine," below).

ON LANGHOLMEN

Långholmen Hotel. Kronohåktet, S-101 72 Stockholm. ☎ **08/668-05-00.** Fax 08/720-85-75. www.langholmen.com. E-mail: hotel@langholmen.com. 102 units. TV TEL. Sun–Thurs 1,255 SEK ($138.05) double; Fri–Sat 925 SEK ($101.75) double. Extra bed 205 SEK ($22.55) per person. AE, MC, V. Rates include breakfast. T-bana: Hornstul. Bus: 4, 40, and 66.

In 1724 it was a state penitentiary on the little island of Langholmen detaining women charged with "loose living." The last prisoner was released in 1972 and today it's a newly restored and reasonably priced accommodation which, in addition to comfortable but small rooms, also houses a museum of Sweden's prison history and one of the best restaurants in the country. Accommodations were carved from some 200 cells, creating cramped but most serviceable rooms equipped with such modern amenities as phones, radios, and cable TVs, even small showers and toilets. And every guest, the hotel contends, receives his or her very own room key.

Ten of the bedrooms are suitable for persons with disabilities, and 91 are reserved for nonsmokers. This is one of the best hotels in Stockholm for the single visitor on a budget, as 89 rooms are rented only to solo travelers. Just 13 rooms are large enough to accommodate two persons. Instead of a prison induction area, you get the hotel's reception area and a 24-hour snack bar.

ON SKEPPSHOLMEN

AF Chapman. Västra Brobänken, Skeppsholmen, S-111 49 Stockholm. ☎ **08/679-50-15.** Fax 08/611-98-75. www.stfchapman.com. E-mail: info@chapman.stfturist.se. 136 beds in 33 cabins, none with bathroom. Members, 145 SEK ($15.95) per adult, 65 SEK ($7.15) per child; nonmembers, 190 SEK ($20.90) per adult, 95 SEK ($10.45) per child. MC, V. Closed Dec 16–Apr 1. Bus: 65.

Moored off Skeppsholmen, this authentic three-masted schooner has been converted into a youth hostel. Staterooms have two, four, six, or eight beds; there are no single cabins. Each section—one for men, one for women—has showers and washrooms. Personal lockers are available. The gangplank goes up at 2am, with no exceptions, and there's a 5-day maximum stay. The rooms are closed from 11am to 3pm. No cigarette smoking is allowed. A summer cafe operates on the ship's deck. Breakfast, at an extra charge, is available in the self-service coffee bar and dining room. International Youth Hostel Association cards can be obtained at the AF *Chapman.*

4   Dining

Food is expensive in Stockholm, especially with the 21% "value-added tax" included in the bill. Those on a budget can stick to self-service cafeterias. At all restaurants other than cafeterias, a 12% to 15% service charge is added to the bill to cover the tip. Wine and beer can be lethal to your final bill, so proceed carefully. For good value, try ordering the *dagens ratt* (daily special), if available.

One tip to save you a little inconvenience: Don't rush into a bar for a martini. "Bars" are self-service cafeterias, and the strongest drink many of them offer is apple cider.

NORMMALM (CENTER OF STOCKHOLM)
VERY EXPENSIVE

✪ **Operakällaren.** Operahuset, Kungsträdgården. ☎ **08/676-58-00.** Reservations required. Main courses 300–400 SEK ($33–$44); 3-course fixed-price menu 480 SEK ($52.80); 4-course fixed-price menu 800 SEK ($88); 7-course menu dégustation 1,250 SEK ($137.50). AE, DC, MC, V. Daily 5–10pm. Closed July. T-bana: Kungsträdgården. FRENCH/SWEDISH.

Opposite the Royal Palace, this is the most famous and unashamedly luxurious restaurant in Sweden. Its elegant decor and style are reminiscent of a royal court banquet at the turn of the century. The service and house specialties are impeccable. Many come here for the elaborate fixed-price menus; others prefer the classic Swedish dishes or the modern French ones. A house specialty that's worth the trip is the platter of northern delicacies, with everything from smoked eel to smoked reindeer, along with Swedish red caviar. Salmon and game, including grouse from the northern forests, are prepared in various ways. There's a cigar room, too.

✪ **Paul & Norbert.** Strandvägen 9. ☎ **08/663-81-83.** Reservations required. Main courses 150–295 SEK ($16.50–$32.45); 8-course *grand menu de frivolité* 1,300 SEK ($143). AE, DC, MC, V. Mid-Aug to June, Tues–Fri noon–3pm; Mon–Sat 5:30–10:30pm. July to mid-Aug, Mon–Sat 5:30–10:30pm. Closed Dec 24–Jan 6. T-bana: Östermalmstorg. CONTINENTAL.

In a patrician residence dating from 1873, adjacent to the Hotell Diplomat, this is the finest and most innovative restaurant in Stockholm. Seating only 30 people, it has vaguely art deco decor, beamed ceilings, and dark paneling. Owners Paul Beck and Norbert Lang worked in many top European restaurants before opening this establishment. To start, they prepare a tantalizing terrine of scallops in saffron sauce. The foie gras is the finest in town. Perfectly prepared main dishes include sauté ed medallion of fjord salmon, scallops, and scampi in lobster sauce; crisp breast of duck with caramelized orange sauce; and juniper-stuffed noisettes of reindeer immersed in caraway sauce with portabella.

EXPENSIVE

✪ **Franska Matsalen (French Dining Room).** In the Grand Hotel, Södra Blasieholmshamnen 8. ☎ **08/679-35-84.** Reservations required. Main courses 225–430 SEK ($24.75–$47.30); 5-course fixed-price menu 695–1,200 SEK ($76.45–$132). AE, DC, MC, V. Mon–Fri 6–11pm. T-bana: Kungsträdgården. Bus: 46, 55, 62, or 76. FRENCH.

Widely acclaimed as one of the greatest restaurants in Stockholm, this elegant establishment is on the street level of the city's finest hotel. The dining room is appointed with polished mahogany, ormolu, and gilt accents under an ornate plaster ceiling. Tables on the enclosed veranda overlook the Royal Palace and the Old Town. Begin with a cannelloni of foie gras with flap mushrooms (*cèpes*), or perhaps mousseline of scallops with Sevruga caviar. Main dishes include seared sweetbreads served with artichokes, *langoustines* (prawns) and frog's legs with broad beans, and veal tartare with caviar. Fresh Swedish salmon is also featured. The chefs—highly trained professionals working with the finest ingredients—have pleased some of Europe's more demanding palates.

○ **Restaurangen.** Oxtorgsgatan 14. ☎ **08/220-952.** Reservations recommended. 3-course fixed-price menu 200 SEK ($22); 5-course fixed-price menu 300 SEK ($33); 7-course fixed-price menu 400 SEK ($44). AE, DC, MC, V. Mon–Fri 11:30am–2pm; Mon–Sat 5–11pm. T-bana: Hörtorget. INTERNATIONAL.

Come here for a high-ceilinged decor whose angularity might remind you of an SAS airport lounge, and for combinations of cuisine that many cosmopolitan Swedes have found absolutely fascinating. Owner and chef Malker Andersson divides his menu into "fields of flavor" as defined by unexpected categories. These include, among others, lemon-flavored themes or coriander-flavored themes, which can be consumed in any order you prefer. If you want a "taste of the lemon," for example, it might appear to flavor fresh asparagus and new potatoes. Freshly chopped coriander is used to flavor a delectable shellfish ceviche. The chef roams the world and doesn't try to duplicate classical international dishes but to take the flavor of one country and combine its traditional dish with the time-honored dish of another country. An amazing and very tasty example of this is tacos from Mexico combined with foie gras of France and caviar from Russia. Since none of the portions are overly large, some diners interpret a meal here like something akin to a series of tapas, each permeated with flavors that linger on your palate after you consume them.

○ **Wedholms Fisk.** Nybrokajen 17. ☎ **08/611-78-74.** Reservations required. Lunch main courses 110–260 SEK ($12.10–$28.60); dinner main courses 255–450 SEK ($28.05–$49.50). AE, DC, MC, V. Mon–Sat 5–11pm. Closed July. T-bana: Östermalmstorg. SWEDISH/FRENCH.

This is one of the classic—and one of the best—restaurants in Stockholm. It has no curtains in the windows and no carpets, but the display of modern paintings by Swedish artists is riveting. You might begin with marinated herring with garlic and *bleak* (a freshwater fish) roe, or tartare of salmon with salmon roe. The chef has reason to be proud of such dishes as perch poached with clams and saffron sauce; prawns marinated in herbs and served with Dijon hollandaise; and grilled fillet of sole with Beaujolais sauce. For dessert, try the homemade vanilla ice cream with cloudberries. The cuisine is both innovative and traditional—for example, chevre mousse accompanies simple tomato salad. On the other hand, the menu features grandmother's favorite: cream stewed potatoes.

MODERATE

Akvarium. Kungsträdgården. ☎ **08/100-626.** Reservations recommended. Fixed-price lunches 55–110 SEK ($6.05–$12.10); main courses 150–175 SEK ($16.50–$19.25). AE, DC, MC, V. Mon–Fri 11:30am–2:30pm and 5pm–midnight, Sat–Sun 11:30am–midnight. T-bana: Kungsträdgården. SEAFOOD/CONTINENTAL.

Don't expect bubbling fish tanks in this stylish restaurant: Its name derives from its former incarnation as a seafood restaurant, not from any current accessories. Amid lime-green and lemon-yellow walls, and lots of stainless steel, you'll find a bustling open kitchen, a bar dotted with colored lamps, and a big veranda. Menu items include

Stockholm Dining

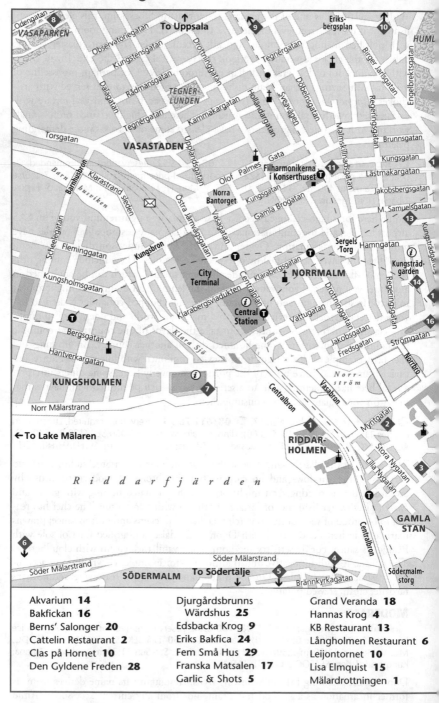

Akvarium **14**
Bakfickan **16**
Berns' Salonger **20**
Cattelin Restaurant **2**
Clas på Hornet **10**
Den Gyldene Freden **28**
Djurgårdsbrunns
 Wärdshus **25**
Edsbacka Krog **9**
Eriks Bakfica **24**
Fem Små Hus **29**
Franska Matsalen **17**
Garlic & Shots **5**
Grand Veranda **18**
Hannas Krog **4**
KB Restaurant **13**
Långholmen Restaurant **6**
Leijontornet **10**
Lisa Elmquist **15**
Mälardrottningen **1**

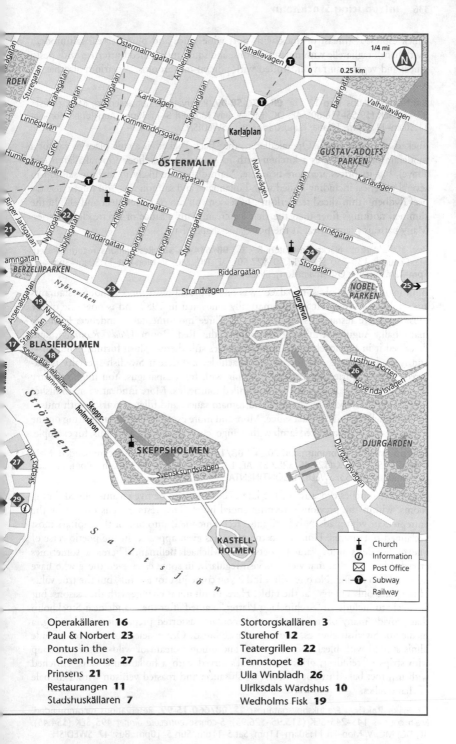

Map labels and streets:

0 1/4 mi
0 0.25 km

Östermalmsgatan
Valhallavägen
Artillerigatan
Skeppargatan
Banérgatan
Valhallavägen
RDEN
Sturegatan
Brahegatan
Turegatan
Nybrogatan
Karlavägen
Kommendörsgatan
Karlaplan
Linnégatan
Grev
Humlegårdsgatan
ÖSTERMALM
Linnégatan
GUSTAV-ADOLFS-PARKEN
Narvavägen
Banérgatan
Karlavägen
Birger Jarlsgatan
Nybrogatan
Sibyllegatan
Artillerigatan
Storgatan
Skeppargatan
Greygatan
Svärmansgatan
Riddargatan
Linnégatan
Storgatan
amngatan
BERZELIIPARKEN
Riddargatan
Arsenalsgatan
Nybroviken
Nybrokajen
Strandvägen
Djurgbron
NOBEL-PARKEN
BLASIEHOLMEN
Stallgatan
Södra Blasieholms-hamnen
Lusthus norten
Rosendalsvägen
Strömmen
Skepps-holmsbron
SKEPPSHOLMEN
Svensksundsvägen
DJURGÅRDEN
Djurgårdsvägen
Skeppsbron
Saltsjön
KASTELL-HOLMEN

Legend:

- † Church
- ⓘ Information
- ⊠ Post Office
- -Ⓣ Subway
- Railway

Operakällaren **16**	Stortorgskallären **3**
Paul & Norbert **23**	Sturehof **12**
Pontus in the Green House **27**	Teatergrillen **22**
Prinsens **21**	Tennstopet **8**
Restaurangen **11**	Ulla Winbladh **26**
Stadshuskällaren **7**	Ulriksdals Wardshus **10**
	Wedholms Fisk **19**

"duck espresso" (breast of duck with port wine sauce and plums); veal saltimbocca (with ham); tagliatelle with mussels, clams, and squid ink; grilled butterfish with pesto sauce; and vegetarian ravioli, stuffed with porcini mushrooms. Akvarium also has an appealing bar.

Bakfickan. Jakobs Torg 12. ☎ **08/676-58-09.** Reservations not accepted. Main courses 87–169 SEK ($9.55–$18.60). AE, DC, MC, V. July, Mon–Fri 5–11:30pm; Aug–June, Mon–Sat 11:30am–11:30pm. T-bana: Kungsträdgården. SWEDISH.

Tucked away behind the Operakällaren, the "Back Pocket" is a chic place to eat for a moderate price. It shares a kitchen with its glamorous neighbor Operakällaren (see above), but its prices are more bearable. Main dishes are likely to include salmon in several varieties, including boiled with hollandaise and salmon roe. You might also try beef Rydberg (thin-sliced tenderloin). In season you can order reindeer and elk. In the summer, nothing's finer than the rich ice cream with a sauce of Arctic cloudberries. Many patrons prefer to eat at the horseshoe-shaped bar.

Berns' Salonger. Näckströmsgatan 8. ☎ **08/614-05-50.** Reservations recommended. Main courses 130–250 SEK ($14.30–$27.50). AE, DC, MC, V. Mon–Sat 11:30am–3pm and 5pm–1am. T-bana: Östermalmstorg. SWEDISH.

Built in 1860, this "pleasure palace" was one of Stockholm's most famous restaurants and nighttime venues. It was dramatically renovated in 1989 and is now one of the most attractive restaurants in the capital. Three monumental chandeliers light the main hall. August Strindberg frequented the Red Room (*Röda Rummet*), and described it in his novel of the same name. It's still there—plush furniture and all—and is used by guests at Berns' Hotel. Each day a different Swedish specialty is featured, including fried fillet of suckling pig with fresh asparagus. You might also try calves' liver with garlic and bacon, or grilled tournedos. More innovative main dishes include cuttlefish with black pasta and tomato sauce, and fillet of ostrich with mushroom cannelloni and Marsala sauce. More and more exotic dishes are appearing on the menu—tandoori-marinated lamb with mango, curry sauce, and couscous, for example.

Clas på Hornet. Surbrunnsgatan 20. ☎ **08/16-51-30.** Reservations recommended. Main courses 195–255 SEK ($21.45–$28.05). AE, DC, MC, V. Mon–Fri 11:30am–10pm, Sat–Sun 5–10pm. Bus: 46, 53. SWEDISH/CONTINENTAL.

Decorative touches evocative of the late 1700s adorn these five cream-colored dining rooms, within the previously recommended hotel. This restaurant is owned by the entrepreneur who made Nils Emil (also recommended) into one of the capital's most acclaimed restaurants. Homage to the place has even appeared in the poetic verse of one of Sweden's most valued poets, Carl Michael Bellman. There's a sometimes crowded bar area that many clients visit regularly, in some cases even those who have no interest in dining. No one will mind if you come just for a drink, but the true value of the place only emerges at the table. Here, menu items change with the seasons, but are likely to include an "Archipelago Platter," named after the islands near Stockholm that provide many of its ingredients. It contains assorted preparations of herring, a medley of Swedish cheeses, and homemade bread. Other delectable choices include blinis stuffed with bleak roe, trout roe, and onions; cream of wild-mushroom soup with strips of reindeer; grilled char that's served with a hollandaise sauce enriched with fish roe; baked turbot in horseradish sauce; and roasted venison with a timbale of chanterelles.

✪ **Eriks Bakfica.** Fredrikshovsgatan 4. ☎ **08/660-15-99.** Reservations recommended. Main courses 145–245 SEK ($15.95–$26.95); 5-course *entrecôte dinner* 495 SEK ($54.45). AE, DC, MC, V. Mon–Fri 11:30am–11pm, Sat 5–11pm, Sun 5–10pm. Bus: 47. SWEDISH.

Although other restaurants in Stockholm bear the name Eriks, this one is relatively inexpensive and offers particularly good value. Established in 1979, it features a handful of Swedish dishes from the tradition of *husmanskost* (wholesome home cooking). A favorite opener is toast Skagen, with shrimp, dill-flavored mayonnaise, spices, and bleak roe. There's also a daily choice of herring appetizers. Try the tantalizing "archipelago stew," a ragoût of fish prepared with tomatoes and served with garlic mayonnaise. Marinated salmon is served with hollandaise sauce. You might also try Eriks cheeseburger with the special secret sauce, but you have to ask for it—the secret specialty is not on the menu.

Grand Veranda. In the Grand Hotel, Södra Blasieholmshamnen 8. ☎ **08/679-35-00.** Reservations required. Main courses 135–225 SEK ($14.85–$24.75); Swedish buffet 245 SEK ($26.95). AE, DC, MC, V. Mon–Sat 11am–3pm; daily 6–9:30pm. T-bana: Kungsträdgården. Bus: 46, 55, 62, or 76. SWEDISH.

On the ground floor of Stockholm's most prestigious hotel, and fronted with enormous sheets of glass, this restaurant opens onto a stunning view of the harbor and the Royal Palace. The Veranda is famous for its daily buffets, which occasionally feature a medley of shellfish, including all the shrimp and lobster you can eat. Try such à la carte dishes as fillet of reindeer marinated in red wine or braised wild duck and deep-fried root vegetables served with an apple-cider sauce. Here is your chance to sample the offerings of the most famous hotel in Sweden, to enjoy wonderful food, and to have one of the best views in town—all for a reasonable price.

KB Restaurant. Smålandsgatan 7. ☎ **08/679-60-32.** Reservations recommended. Main courses 195–310 SEK ($21.45–$34.10); fixed-price lunch 265–325 SEK ($29.15–$35.75); fixed-price dinner 365–470 SEK ($40.15–$51.70). AE, DC, MC, V. Mon–Fri 11:30am–11:30pm, Sat 5–11:30pm. Closed June 23–Aug 7. T-bana: Östermalmstorg. SWEDISH/CONTINENTAL.

A traditional artists' rendezvous in the center of town, KB Restaurant features good Swedish food as well as continental dishes. Fish dishes are especially recommended. You might begin with salmon trout roe and Russian caviar, followed by boiled turbot or lamb roast with stuffed zucchini in thyme-flavored bouillon. Dishes usually come with aromatic, freshly baked sourdough bread. Desserts include sorbets with fresh fruits and berries, and a heavenly lime soufflé with orange-blossom honey. There's also a relaxed and informal bar.

Lisa Elmquist. Östermalms Saluhall, Nybrogatan 31. ☎ **08/553-404-10.** Reservations recommended. Main courses 100–350 SEK ($11–$38.50). AE, DC, MC, V. Mon–Thurs 10am–6pm, Fri 10am–6:30pm, Sat 10am–4pm. T-bana: Östermalmstorg. SEAFOOD.

Under the soaring roof, amid the food stalls of Stockholm's produce market (the Östermalms Saluhall), you'll find this likable cafe and oyster bar. It's owned by one of the city's largest fish distributors, so its menu varies with the catch. Some patrons come here for shrimp with bread and butter for 85 to 115 SEK ($9.35 to $12.65). Typical dishes include fish soup, salmon cutlets, and sautéed fillet of lemon sole. It's not the most refined cuisine in town—it's an authentic "taste of Sweden," done exceedingly well. The establishment looks like a pleasant bistro under the tent at a country fair.

Prinsens. Mäster Samuelsgatan 4. ☎ **08/611-13-31.** Reservations recommended. Fixed-price lunch 99–250 SEK ($10.90–$27.50); main courses 169–245 SEK ($18.60–$26.95). AE, DC, MC, V. Mon–Fri 11:30am–10:30pm, Sat 1–10:30pm, Sun 5–9:30pm. T-bana: Östermalmstorg. SWEDISH.

A 2-minute walk from Stureplan, this artists' haunt has become increasingly popular with foreign visitors. It has been serving people since 1897. Seating is on two levels, and in summer some tables are outside. The fresh, flavorful cuisine is basically Swedish food prepared in a conservative French style. It includes such traditional Swedish dishes as veal patty with homemade lingonberry preserves, sautéed fjord salmon, and roulades of beef. For dessert, try the homemade vanilla ice cream. Later in the evening, the restaurant becomes something of a drinking club.

Sturehof. Stureplan 2. ☎ **08/440-57-30.** Main courses 100–350 SEK ($11–$38.50). AE, DC, MC, V. Mon–Fri 11am–2am, Sat noon–2am, Sun 1pm–2am. T-bana: Östermalmstorg. SWEDISH.

This seafood restaurant in the center of town was founded in 1897. Tasty and carefully prepared specialties include Swedish or Canadian lobsters and oysters, fried plaice, boiled salmon with hollandaise, and fresh shrimp. A daily changing menu of genuine Swedish *husmanskost* (home cooking) is a bargain. Sample, for example, boiled salted veal tongue or potato and beet soup with sour cream. Try the famous *sotare* (grilled small Baltic herring served with boiled potatoes) if you want to sample a local favorite. Many locals come here to make an entire meal from the various types of herring—everything from tomato herring to curry herring.

Teatergrillen. Nybrogatan 3. ☎ **08/611-70-44.** Reservations recommended. Main courses 160–300 SEK ($17.60–$33). AE, DC, MC, V. Mon–Fri 11:30am–1pm, Sat 1pm–1am; Mon–Fri 5–11:30pm. Closed July. T-bana: Östermalmstorg. Bus: 46. SWEDISH/FRENCH.

This restaurant decorated with theater memorabilia is near the Royal Dramatic Theater on Nybroplan, where Ingmar Bergman was once arrested for a tax investigation. Lunch offerings include typical Swedish fare cooked grandmother's style, and a daily specialty—perhaps sautéed fish in tarragon sauce with rice or pork schnitzel with thyme-flavored fried potatoes. At dinner the cuisine is considerably more refined, with the likes of halibut with chanterelles in curry sauce or pike-perch with mussels in citrus-flavored tomato broth. A classic is the Swedish beefsteak with red onion. The chefs are becoming more innovative, offering such appetizers as deep-fried chicken in peanut sauce with coriander and mint salad. Marinated duck appears with pickled shiitake mushrooms and soba noodles. The dessert chef creates daring experiments—everything from mango yogurt ice cream to cashew dumplings. The Teatergrillen shares its kitchen with the century-old Restaurant Riche, a nightclub and dining emporium whose entrance is on the far side of the building.

ON GAMLA STAN (OLD TOWN)
VERY EXPENSIVE

Leijontornet. In the Victory Hotel, Lilla Nygatan 5. ☎ **08/14-23-55.** Reservations required. Main courses 145–315 SEK ($15.95–$34.65); fixed-price dinner 420 SEK ($46.20). AE, DC, MC, V. Mon–Sat 6pm–midnight. Closed July, bank holidays. T-bana: Gamla Stan. SWEDISH/INTERNATIONAL.

This is one of the Old Town's most stylish restaurants, noted for its fine food and the quality of its service. From the small street-level bar, patrons descend into the intimately lit cellar (the hotel was built around a medieval defense tower). To reach the restaurant, you have to negotiate a labyrinth of brick passageways through the Victory.

You might begin with grilled marinated calamari with eggplant and paprika cream, salad with roast deer and curry dressing, or perhaps a potato crêpe with bleak roe vinaigrette and fried herring. Main courses include roast lamb with moussaka and basil; grilled salmon with tomato, spinach, and lime *taglierini* (a pasta similar to tagliatelle); and risotto with pumpkin and flap mushrooms (*cèpes*). Dishes often arrive looking like works of art, and they incorporate some of the country's finest produce.

✪ **Pontus in the Green House.** Österlånggatan 17. ☎ **08/23-85-00.** Reservations recommended. Main courses 350–500 SEK ($38.50–$55); 8-course fixed-price menu 985 SEK

ⓘ Family-Friendly Restaurants

Djurgårdsbrunns Wärdshus *(see p. 341)*   At this restaurant in the royal Deer Park, about 2 miles east of the center, families can dine inexpensively in a cafeteria or enjoy more elaborate food in the formal 19th-century inn.

Lisa Elmquist *(see p. 337)*   Because this restaurant is in the produce market, Östermalms Saluhall, having lunch here with the family is a colorful adventure. One particular favorite is shrimp with bread and butter. Families can dine under a tent, which suggests a country fair setting.

Solliden   Near the top of the Skansen compound, a Williamsburg-type park dating from 1891, Solliden (☎ **08/662-93-03**) is a cluster of restaurants in a sprawling building. The array of dining facilities makes the dining emporium attractive to families. Solliden offers a lunch smörgåsbord.

($108.35). AE, DC, MC, V. Mon–Fri 11:30am–3pm and 6–11pm, Sat noon–4pm and 5:30–11pm. T-bana: Gamla Stan. FRENCH/SWEDISH/ASIAN.

Set within a building whose foundations date to the 16th century, this is a well-orchestrated and elegant restaurant that has attracted some of the most powerful figures in modern Stockholm. Your dining experience will begin with a drink or apéritif in the ground-floor bar and cocktail lounge, where a staff member will explain the menu and record your choices. You'll then be ushered upstairs to a gold-and-green dining room with high arched windows and an undeniable sense of respect for food and its presentation. The chef here, Pontus Frithiof, was inspired by some of the grand francophile chefs of England, Marco Pierre White and Gordon Ramsay, as shown by dishes that include garlic-sautéed turbot with sweetbreads; tender veal tongue with Jerusalem artichokes; steamed turbot with horseradish, prawns, and brown butter; and citrus-glazed Challonais duck breast that's served with foie gras, shiitake mushrooms, spring onions, and teriyaki sauce. In our view, his herring with vinegar-and-onion marmalade is the old town's tastiest. It's worth the trek across town to sample the creamy Roquefort made from the first milk the nursing cows produce. After tasting this cheese, you'll never go back—except with regret—to that store-bought stuff again.

EXPENSIVE

Den Gyldene Freden. Österlånggatan 51. ☎ **08/24-97-60.** Reservations recommended. Main courses 110–265 SEK ($12.10–$29.15). AE, DC, MC, V. Mon–Fri 6–11pm, Sat 1–11pm. Closed July 2–Aug 2. T-bana: Gamla Stan. SWEDISH.

"Golden Peace" is said to be Stockholm's oldest tavern. The restaurant opened in 1722 in a structure built the year before. The Swedish Academy owns the building, and members frequent the place on Thursday night. The cozy dining rooms are named for Swedish historical figures who were patrons. Today it's popular with artists, lawyers, and poets. You get good traditional Swedish cooking, especially fresh Baltic fish and game from the forests. Herring is a favorite appetizer. More imaginative appetizers include a creamy soup of artichokes and Jerusalem artichokes with a dollop of caviar, and an especially intriguing consommé of oxtail with tiny ravioli stuffed with quail breast. Notable main courses are fried breast of wild duck in Calvados sauce, and roast of reindeer in juniper-berry sauce. A particular delight is homemade duck sausage with three kinds of mushrooms in black pepper sauce. Want something different for dessert? How about warm rose hip soup with vanilla ice cream? Of course, if you order that, you'd be denying yourself the "symphony" of lingonberries or the longtime favorite: Stockholm's best chocolate cake.

Fem Små Hus. Nygränd 10. ☎ **08/10-87-75.** Reservations required. Main courses 195–245 SEK ($21.45–$26.95). AE, DC, MC, V. Sun–Mon 5–11pm, Tues–Sat 5pm–midnight. T-bana: Gamla Stan. SWEDISH/FRENCH.

This historic restaurant, with cellars that date from the 17th century, is furnished like a private castle, with European antiques and oil paintings. The nine rooms in the labyrinthine interior hold candlelit tables. You can order assorted herring, slices of fresh salmon in Chablis, braised scallops with saffron sauce, terrine of duckling with goose liver and truffles, fillet of beef with herb sauce, and sorbets with seasonal fruits and berries. The best ingredients from Sweden's forests and shores appear on the menu. The cuisine and staff are worthy of the restaurant's hallowed reputation.

MODERATE

Mälardrottningen. Riddarholmen. ☎ **08/545-187-80.** Reservations recommended. Main courses 105–225 SEK ($11.55–$24.75). AE, DC, MC, V. Mon–Fri 11am–2pm and 3–10pm, Sat 5–10pm. T-bana: Gamla Stan. INTERNATIONAL.

This is one of the most upscale floating restaurants in Sweden. It occupies the show-place deck of a motor yacht, built by industrialist C. K. G. Billings in 1924, that's now a hotel (see "Where to Stay," above). Admittedly, a lot of its allure derives from its novelty, but the food is well prepared, with some of the flair associated with the ship's heyday. Menu items change with the seasons, but might include imaginative offerings such as salmon-fillet spring roll with pepper-garlic vinaigrette; pear-and-goat-cheese salad with thyme-flavored honey; and skewered scampi served with Parmesan cheese and chutney made from pesto and bananas. One of the least expensive main courses—appropriate for foggy days beside the harborfront—is a heaping portion of marinated mussels in white wine and butter sauce, served with French fries. More formal dishes include a parfait of chicken livers with an apricot and oregano brioche; cream of chanterelle soup with a pumpkin- and sage-flavored gnocchi; and prosciutto-wrapped tiger prawns; grilled Dublin Bay prawns with a fennel-flavored butter sauce; and fried fillets of pike-perch with crisp-fried paella, red peppers, and lobster sauce.

Stortorgskällaren. Stortorget 7. ☎ **08/10-55-33.** Reservations required. Main courses 150–220 SEK ($16.50–$24.20); 3-course fixed-price dinner 216 SEK ($23.75). AE, DC, MC, V. Mon–Fri 11am–11pm, Sat noon–11pm, Sun noon–10pm. T-bana: Gamla Stan. SWEDISH.

In the winter, this restaurant occupies medieval wine cellars whose vaulted ceilings date from the 15th century. Old walls and chandeliers complement plush carpeting and subtle lighting. In summer, seating is on the outdoor terrace, beside a charming square opposite the Stock Exchange, or in the street-level dining room (in bad weather).

The menu changes often. You might begin with pâté of wild game with blackberry chutney and pickled carrots, or cured salmon and white bleak roe served with crème fraîche and onions. There's also fried salmon with mushroom sauce. Another specialty is a casserole of Baltic fish seasoned with saffron. After you've sampled some of these dishes, you'll know why Stockholmers have long cited this restaurant as one of their most reliable. You don't get fireworks, but you do get a cheerful atmosphere, lots of flavor, and a hearty menu.

INEXPENSIVE

✪ **Cattelin Restaurant.** Storkyrkobrinken 9. ☎ **08/20-18-18.** Reservations recommended. Main courses 95–195 SEK ($10.45–$21.45); dagens (daily) menu 65 SEK ($7.15). AE, DC, MC, V. Mon–Fri 11am–10pm, Sat–Sun noon–10pm. T-bana: Gamla Stan. SWEDISH.

This restaurant on a historic street opened in 1897 and continues to serve fish and meat in a boisterous, convivial setting. Don't expect genteel service—the clattering of china can sometimes be almost deafening, but few of the regular patrons seem to mind. First-rate menu choices include various preparations of beef, salmon, trout, veal, and chicken, which frequently make up the daily specials, often preferred by lunch patrons. This restaurant has survived wars, disasters, and changing food tastes, so it must be doing something right. It remains a sentimental favorite—and not just for the memories. In a city where people have been known to faint when presented with their dining tabs, it has always been a good, reasonably priced choice. We can't say that Greta Garbo actually dined here, but we spotted her one wintry day staring in the window. When we motioned for her to come in to join us, she fled into the snowy night. The fixed-price lunch is served only Monday to Friday from 11am to 2pm.

ON KUNGSHOLMEN

✪ **Stadshuskällaren.** Stadshuset. ☎ **08/650-54-54.** Main courses 170–225 SEK ($18.70–$24.75); 2-course fixed-price lunch 300 SEK ($33); 3-course fixed-price dinner 360 SEK ($39.60). AE, DC, MC, V. Skänken, Mon–Fri 11am–2pm. Stora Matsalen, Mon–Fri 11:30am–11pm, Sat 2–11pm. T-bana: Rådhuset. Bus: 48 or 62. SWEDISH/INTERNATIONAL.

Two dignified restaurants are in the basement of the City Hall, near the harbor (the entrance has a beautiful carved wooden doorway). The interior is divided into two sections, the Skänken, which serves lunch only, and the Stora Matsalen. Here is where chefs prepare the annual banquet for the Nobel Prize winners, and you can actually sample a Nobel menu. Dining here is like taking a culinary trip through Sweden. To go truly local, you'll want to try the elk or reindeer dishes (in season). Swedish salmon is our all-time favorite, and here it's prepared with consummate skill. Lately the chefs have become more imaginative, preparing such dishes as marinated fillet of chicken breasts with avocado pesto (yes, avocado pesto), or perhaps almond-fried catfish with olives and mushrooms. Our vote for the finest dish offered on recent Nobel menus goes to roast pigeon breast with cèpe and pigeon meat ragoût, flavored with tart raspberry vinegar and accompanied by onion and potato compote.

ON DJURGÅRDEN

The royal Deer Park, Djurgården, lies about 2 miles east of Stockholm's center.

Djurgårdsbrunns Wärdshus. Djurgårdsbrunnsvägen 68. ☎ **08/667-90-95.** Main courses 166–200 SEK ($18.25–$22). AE, DC, MC, V. Summer, daily 11:30am–9pm; off-season, Mon–Fri 11:30am–3pm, Sat–Sun 11:30am–5pm. Bus: 69. SWEDISH.

This establishment occupies a cluster of antique and modern buildings. Although there's a simple cafeteria on the premises, most diners prefer the more formal restaurant, an intimate place in a 19th-century inn. Menu choices include grilled salmon with morel-butter sauce, noisettes of venison with fresh vegetables, roast beef with horseradish, and fried trout with almonds. It's not trendy, but you get honest, flavorful cooking. Ingredients are well chosen, recipes time-tested, and prices quite fair.

Ulla Winbladh. Rosendalsvägen 8. ☎ **08/663-05-71.** Reservations required. Main courses 95–270 SEK ($10.45–$29.70). AE, DC, MC, V. Mon 11:30am–10pm, Tues–Fri 11:30am–11pm, Sat 1pm–11pm, Sun 1pm–10pm. Bus: 47. SWEDISH.

Since it opened in 1994, this restaurant has enjoyed an explosion of publicity, which has impressed even the most jaded of Stockholm's restaurant aficionados. It's in a white stone structure, built as part of Stockholm's International Exposition of 1897. There's a large dining room decorated with works by Swedish artists, and a summer-only outdoor terrace laced with flowering plants. The menu focuses on conservative Swedish cuisine, all impeccably prepared. (Patrons who agree with this assessment include members of the Swedish royal family and a bevy of well-known TV, theater, and art-world personalities.) In 1996 the king presented a medal to chef Emel Ahalen for his

Perfect Picnics

Fast-food eateries and fresh-food markets abound in Stockholm, especially in the center of the city, around Hötorget. **Hötorgs Hallen** is a fresh food market where you can buy the makings of an elegant picnic. Recently arrived immigrants sell many Turkish food products, including stuffed pita bread.

For the most elegant fare of all, go to **Östermalms Hallen,** at the corner of Humlegårdsgatan and Nybrogatan, east of the center. Stall after stall sells picnic fare, including fresh shrimp and precooked items that will be wrapped carefully to go.

With your picnic fixings in hand, head for **Skansen** or the wooded peninsula of **Djurgården.** If you like to picnic with lots of people around, go to **Kungsträdgården,** "the summer living room of Stockholm," in the center of town.

proficiency in preparing Swedish cuisine. Menu choices include tender steak with artichokes and a perfectly prepared rack of Swedish lamb flavored with bacon. Fish selections might be platters of herring (marinated and fried), whitefish or pike-perch in white-wine sauce, divine turbot with saffron sauce, the inevitable salmon with dill sauce, and others that vary with the season.

NEAR VASAPARKEN

Tennstopet (Pewter Tankard). Dalagatan 50. ☎ **08/32-25-18.** Reservations recommended. Main courses 82–240 SEK ($9–$26.40); 2-course fixed-price menu 200 SEK ($22). AE, DC, MC, V. Mon–Fri 4pm–1am, Sat–Sun 1pm–1am. T-bana: Odenplan. Bus: 54. SWEDISH.

A well-known pub and restaurant, Tennstopet is in the northern part of town, near the Hotel Oden. It's the oldest pub in Sweden, adjacent to a classic dining room. Main dishes might include a ragout of fish and shellfish, salmon schnitzel, and plank steak. At lunch, you can dine on pork chops, vegetables, bread, butter, and coffee. Or just order a draft beer, toss some darts, and admire the setting. This is the type of food that accompanies heavy drinking—it's good, hearty, and filling, but nothing more. The place prides itself on serving genuine English pints.

AT SÖDERMALM

Garlic & Shots. Folkungagatan 84. ☎ **08/640-84-46.** Reservations recommended. Main courses 85–190 SEK ($9.35–$20.90). MC, V. Daily 5–11pm. T-bana: Medborgarplatsen.

This theme restaurant follows two strong, overriding ideas: Everyone needs a shot of garlic every day, and everything tastes better if it's doctored with a dose of the Mediterranean's most potent ingredient. The no-frills setting is artfully Spartan, with bare wooden tables that have hosted an unexpectedly large number of rock stars. Expect garlic in just about everything, from soup (try garlic-ginger with clam) to such main courses as beefsteak covered with fried minced garlic and Transylvania-style vampire steak, drenched in horseradish-tomato-and-garlic sauce. Dessert might be a slice of garlic-laced cheese or garlic-honey ice cream garnished with honey-marinated cloves of garlic. An appropriate foil for all these flavors? Garlic ale or garlic beer, if you're up to it.

Hannas Krog. Skånegatan 80. ☎ **08/643-82-25.** Reservations recommended. Main courses 98–189 SEK ($10.80–$20.80). AE, DC, MC, V. Mon–Fri 11:30am–3pm; daily 5pm–midnight. T-bana: Medborgarplatsen. INTERNATIONAL.

One of the most appealing neighborhood restaurants in Södermalm is this bustling bistro. In its own way, it's fashionable. The decor, with such artfully rustic touches as a collection of cuckoo clocks, might remind you of a Swedish version of a British pub. Hannas Krog serves a medley of food with inspirations from around the world. You might begin with a slice of pie made with Swedish cheddar cheese, then move on to marinated and baked salmon wrapped in Italian pancetta ham, Provençal-style lamb, or grilled butterfish with tiger prawns wrapped in wontons and served with crayfish consommé. Trendy Stockholmers, who used to avoid Södermalm like the plague, are increasingly showing up for the good fare, excellent service, and inviting ambience.

ON LANGHOLMEN

Långholmen Restaurant. Kronohäktet. ☎ **08/720-85-50.** Reservations recommended. Main courses 158–250 SEK ($17.40–$27.50). AE, DC, MC, V. Mon–Fri 11:30am–5pm and 5–11pm, Sat noon–midnight, Sun noon–8pm. T-bana: Hornstul. Bus: 4, 40, and 66. INTERNATIONAL.

This premier dining venue is housed within the Långholmen Hotel, the former state penitentiary turned hotel. From the windows of the old-fashioned dining room, you can still see the high brick walls and the paraphernalia of what caused a lot of inmates a great deal of mental distress—small doors with heavy bolts, bars on the windows. Ironically, within the establishment's new venue, these mementos are showcased, rather than concealed—even the paintings, many in gentle pastels, reflect the workhouse drudgery that used to prevail here. Come here for an unusual insight into the hardships of the 19th century, and menu items that change with the seasons. Examples include a carpaccio of shellfish; smoked breast of duck with a walnut-cranberry vinaigrette; a combination of lobster and turbot stewed with vegetables in a shellfish bouillon; and tournedos of venison with juniperberries, smoked ham, pepper sauce, and Swedish potatoes. This is hardly prison food—in fact, the most dedicated devotees of the restaurant hail it as one of the finest in Stockholm. There is a dedication here to pleasing your palates and using only the freshest and best of ingredients available in the market on any given day.

AT SOLNA

✪ Ulriksdals Wärdshus. Ulriksdals Royal Park, S-170 79 Solna. ☎ **08/85-08-15.** Reservations required. Main courses 280–350 SEK ($30.80–$38.50); smörgåsbord 250 SEK ($27.50); fixed-price menus 375–500 SEK ($41.25–$55). AE, DC, MC, V. Mon–Fri noon–10pm, Sat 12:30–10pm, Sun 12:30–6:30pm. Closed Dec 24–26. Take Sveavägen toward Arlanda Airport (Exit E18), 3 miles north of Stockholm. SWEDISH.

This out-of-town establishment serves the best smörgåsbord in Sweden. On the grounds of Ulriksdal's Royal Palace on Edviken Bay, you can dine in the all-glass Queen Silvia Pavilion, which opens onto gardens owned by the king and queen. The smörgåsbord, featuring 86 delicacies (both shellfish and meat), is accompanied by beer or aquavit. Most people eat the smörgåsbord in five courses, beginning with herring (20 varieties). They follow with salmon and then meat dishes, including *frikadeller* (meatballs) or perhaps reindeer, then a choice of cheese, and finally dessert. Some dishes are based on old farm-style recipes, including "Lansson's Temptation," which blends anchovies, heavy-cream potatoes, and onions. Over the Christmas season, the almost-doubled buffet is lavishly decorated in a seasonal theme, and costs 450 SEK ($49.50) per person.

AT SOLLENTUNA

Edsbacka Krog. Sollentunavägen 220, Sollentuna. ☎ **08/96-33-00.** Reservations recommended. Main courses 255–360 SEK ($28.05–$39.60); fixed-price menus 575–1,295 SEK ($63.25–$142.45). AE, DC, MC, V. Mon 5:30pm–midnight, Tues–Fri 11:30am–2:30pm and 5:30pm–midnight, Sat 2pm–midnight. T-bana: Sollentuna. SWEDISH/FRENCH.

In a historic, thick-walled building from 1626, this was the first licensed inn in Stockholm. Ten minutes by taxi from the town center, you'll find dining rooms with an upscale country atmosphere. Menu items include combinations you're not likely to find in many other restaurants. Examples include whitebait roe with marinated halibut and avocado; boiled lobster in vegetable terrine; scallops with smoked cod in duck liver sauce; terrine of duck liver served with fried sweetbreads; and a platter that combines oxtail and beef tongue with duck liver and duck liver sauce. Chef Christer Lindström's dishes attract visitors from around the district. He is dedicated to his cuisine, offering a judicious combination of sturdy continental cooking with immaculate taste.

Exploring Stockholm 14

In every season, Stockholm is loaded with interesting sights and activities for people of all ages—from the *Vasa* Ship Museum to the changing of the guard at the Royal Palace to the Gröna Lunds Tivoli amusement park. Even just window-shopping for beautifully designed crafts can be an enjoyable way to spend an afternoon. After dark, Stockholm is one of the livelier cities in northern Europe.

Suggested Itineraries

If You Have 1 Day

Take a ferry to Djurgården and visit the *Vasa* Ship Museum, Stockholm's most famous attraction, and explore the open-air Skansen folk museum. In the afternoon, take our walking tour (see below) of Gamla Stan (Old Town) and have dinner there.

If You Have 2 Days

On your first day, follow the suggestions above. On Day 2, get up early and visit the Kaknästornet television tower for a panoramic view of the city and its archipelago. Go to the Museum of Nordic History for a review of 5 centuries of life in Sweden. After lunch, visit the Millesgården of Lidingö, the sculpture garden and former home of Carl Milles, Sweden's most famous sculptor.

If You Have 3 Days

For the first 2 days follow the itinerary above. On the third morning, take our second walking tour (see below). At noon (1pm on Sunday), return to Gamla Stan to see the changing of the guard at the Royal Palace. The French-inspired building has been the residence of Swedish kings for more than 700 years. In winter, if your visit doesn't coincide with the changing of the guard, you can visit Kungsträdgården Park in the center of the city and enjoy the ice-skating (the Swedes are superb at this). Schedule a visit to Stockholm's renowned city hall. In the afternoon, visit the National Museum.

If You Have 4 or 5 Days

For Days 1 to 3, follow the suggestions above. On Day 4, take one of the many available tours of the Stockholm archipelago. Return to Stockholm and spend the evening at the Gröna Lunds Tivoli amusement park on Djurgården.

For your last day, visit Drottningholm Palace and its 18th-century theater. In the afternoon go to Uppsala, which is easily reached by public transportation (see "Side Trips from Stockholm," below).

1 On Gamla Stan & Neighboring Islands

✪ **Kungliga Slottet (Royal Palace) & Museums.** Kungliga Husgerådskammaren. ☎ **08/402-61-32** for Royal Apartments & Treasury, 08/402-61-34 for the Skattkammaren, 08/666-44-75 for Royal Armory, or 08/402-61-30 for Museum of Antiquities. Royal Apartments, 50 SEK ($5.50) adults, 25 SEK ($2.75) students, free for children under 7; Royal Armory, 50 SEK ($5.50) adults, 30 SEK ($3.30) seniors and students, 15 SEK ($1.65) children, free for children under 7; Museum of Antiquities, 50 SEK ($5.50) adults, 25 SEK ($2.75) seniors and students, free for children under 7; Treasury, 50 SEK ($5.50) adults, 25 SEK ($2.75) seniors and students, free for children under 7. Combination ticket to all parts of palace 100 SEK ($11) adults, 70 SEK ($7.70) students and children. Apartments and Treasury, Sept–June, Tues–Sun noon–3pm; July–Aug, daily 10am–4pm; closed during government receptions. Royal Armory, Sept–Apr, Tues–Sun 11am–4pm; May–Aug, daily 11am–4pm. Museum of Antiquities, May–Aug, daily 10am–4pm; Sept–Apr, daily noon–3pm. T-bana: Gamla Stan. Bus: 43, 46, 59, or 76.

Kungliga Slottet is one of the few official residences of a European monarch that's open to the public. Although the king and queen prefer to live at Drottningholm, this massive 608-room showcase remains their official address. Severe, dignified, even cold-looking on the outside, it has a lavish interior designed in the Italian baroque style and built between 1691 and 1754.

Visitors may walk through the Council Chamber, where the king and his ministers meet several times a year. The **State Apartments,** with magnificent baroque ceilings and fine tapestries, the **Bernadotte Apartment,** and the **Guest Apartment** are on view. They're beautifully furnished in Swedish rococo, Louis XVI, and Empire style.

The **Skattkammaren,** or Treasury, in the cellar, is worth a visit. It exhibits one of the most celebrated collections of crown jewels in Europe. You'll see a dozen crowns, scepters, and orbs, along with antique jewelry. Be sure to see the **Royal Armory,** Slottsbacken 3, also in the cellar. Kings used to ride in these elegant gilded coaches. You'll also see coronation costumes from the 16th century, weapons, and armor.

Gustav III's collection of sculpture from the days of the Roman Empire can be viewed in the **Antikmuseum** (Museum of Antiquities).

Changing of the Royal Guard: In summer you can watch the parade of the military guard daily. In winter it takes place on Wednesday and Sunday; on the other days there's no parade, but you can see the changing of the guard. The parade route on Monday through Saturday begins at Sergels Torg and proceeds along Hamngatan, Kungsträdgårdsgatan, Strömgatan, Gustav Adolfs Torg, Norrbro, Skeppsbron, and Slottsbacken. On Sunday the guard departs from the Army Museum, going along Riddargatan, Artillerigatan, Strandvägen, Hamngatan, Kungsträdgårdsgatan, Strömgatan, Gustav Adolfs Torg, Norrbro, Skeppsbron, and Slottsbacken. For information on the time of the march, ask at the Tourist Center in Sweden House. The changing of the guard takes place at noon Monday to Saturday and at 1pm on Sunday in front of the Royal Palace.

Riddarholm Church. Riddarholmen. ☎ **08/402-61-30.** Admission 20 SEK ($2.20) adults, 10 SEK ($1.10) students and children. May–Aug, daily 10am–4pm; Sept, Sat–Sun noon–3pm. Closed Oct–Apr. T-bana: Gamla Stan.

The second-oldest church in Stockholm is on the tiny island of Riddarholmen, next to Gamla Stan. It was founded in the 13th century as a Franciscan monastery. Almost all the royal heads of state are entombed here (except Christina, who is buried in Rome).

✪ Frommer's Favorite Stockholm Experiences

Exploring Skansen.   Butter churning or folk dancing, there's always something to intrigue people of all ages here. Wander at leisure through the world's oldest open-air museum (which covers about 75 acres of parkland), getting a glimpse of Swedish life in the long-ago countryside.

Strolling Through Gamla Stan at Night.   To walk the narrow cobblestoned alleys of the Old Town after dark, with special lighting, is like going back in time. It takes little imagination to envision what everyday life must have been like in this "city between the bridges."

Taking the Baths.   Both men and women are fond of roasting themselves on wooden platforms like chickens on a grill, and then plunging into a shower of Arctic-chilled water. After this experience, bathers emerge light-hearted and light-headed into the fresh air, fortified for an evening of revelry.

Watching the Summer Dawn.   In midsummer at 3am, you can get out of bed, as many Swedes do, sit on a balcony, and watch the eerie blue sky—pure, crystal, exquisite. Gradually it's bathed in peach, as the early dawn of a "too-short" summer day approaches. Swedes don't like to miss a minute of summer, even if they have to get up early to enjoy it.

There are three principal royal chapels, including one—the Bernadotte wing—that belongs to the present ruling family. Karl XIV Johan, the first king of the Bernadotte dynasty, is buried here in a large marble sarcophagus.

Stockholms Medeltidsmuseum (Museum of Medieval Stockholm). Strömparterren, Norrbro. ☎ **08/508-31-790.** Admission 40 SEK ($4.40) adults, 5 SEK (55¢) children. July–Aug, Tues–Thurs 11am–6pm, Fri–Mon 11am–4pm; Sept–June, Tues and Thurs–Sun 11am–4pm, Wed 11am–6pm. Bus: 43.

Built around archaeological excavations, this museum traces the city's founding and development during the Middle Ages. Exhibits include parts of the old city wall that date to 1530, which were discovered from 1978 to 1980. In essence, the museum opens a window on the Middle Ages. Objects tell you about children's games, women's work, monastic life, and other activities. The museum also houses the *Riddarsholm* ship (circa 1520), which was excavated in 1930, with some of its leather goods, ceramics, and nautical artifacts well preserved.

Östasiatiskamuseet (Museum of Far Eastern Antiquities). Skeppsholmen. ☎ **08/ 519-55-750.** Admission 50 SEK ($5.50) adults, free for children under 16. Tues noon–8pm, Wed–Sun noon–5pm. T-bana: Kungsträdgården. Bus: 65 to Karl XII Torg; 7-minute walk.

The permanent collection at this small, intimate museum consists of archaeological objects, fine arts, and handcrafts from China, Japan, Korea, and India. The collection is one of the finest and most important of its kind outside Asia. Among the outstanding displays are Chinese Neolithic painted pottery, bronze ritual vessels, archaic jades, wood carvings, ivory, lacquerwork, and enamelware. You might see Chinese glass, Buddhist sculpture, Chinese painting and calligraphy, T'ang tomb pottery figurines, Sung classical stoneware (such as celadon and temmoku), Ming blue-and-white wares, and Ch'ing porcelain made for the Chinese and European markets. The building was erected from 1699 to 1700 as stables for Charles (Karl) XII's bodyguard.

2 On Norrmalm

○ **Hallwylska Museet (Hallwyl Museum).** Hamngatan 4. ☎ **08/519-55-599.** Guided tours 60 SEK ($6.60) adults, 25 SEK ($2.75) students, free for children under 7. Guided tours in English July–Aug, daily on the hour starting at 1pm; Sept–June, Sun starting at 1pm. Tues–Sun 1–3pm.T-bana: Kungsträdgården.

Sweden has never seen a collector to compare with Countess Wilhelmina von Hallwyl. She spent nearly three-quarters of a century collecting "things," most of them rare and valuable. She carefully catalogued them and left them to the state upon her death. Today the most eccentric of Stockholm's museums is in a turn-of-the-century residence of great splendor. The house is a fine example of the skilled craftsmanship of its day.

The catalog of this passionate collector came to 78 volumes, so you can imagine the amount of decorative art on display. Open to the public since 1938, the collection includes priceless paintings, rare tapestries, silver, armor, weapons, antique musical instruments, glassware, even umbrellas and buttons (but only the finest ones). The aristocratic Hallwyl family occupied this town house from 1898 to 1930. One of the three daughters became a sculptor and studied with the great Carl Milles. On the tour, you learn historical tidbits. This house had a modern bathroom even before the royal palace. Ask about summer evening concerts presented in the central courtyard.

Kaknästornet (Kaknäs Television Tower). Mörkakroken. ☎ **08/789-24-35.** Admission 25 SEK ($2.75) adults, 15 SEK ($1.65) children 7–15, free for children under 7. May–Aug, daily 9am–10pm; Sept–Apr, daily 10am–9pm. Closed Dec 24–25. Bus: 69.

In the northern district of Djurgården stands the tallest man-made structure in Scandinavia—a 508-foot radio and television tower. Two elevators run to an observation platform, where you can see everything from the cobblestoned streets of Gamla Stan (Old Town) to the city's modern concrete-and-glass structures and the archipelago beyond. A moderately priced restaurant that serves classic Swedish cuisine is at the top of the tower.

○ **Nationalmuseum (National Museum of Art).** Södra Blasieholmshamnen. ☎ **08/519-54-300.** Admission 75 SEK ($8.25) adults, 60 SEK ($6.60) seniors and students, free for children under 16. Tues 11am–8pm, Wed–Sun 11am–5pm. T-bana: Kungsträdgården. Bus: 46, 62, 65, or 76.

At the tip of a peninsula, a short walk from the Royal Opera House and the Grand Hotel, is Sweden's state treasure house of paintings and sculpture. Founded in 1792, it's one of the oldest museums in the world. Its collections include a wide assortment of masterpieces by such artists as Rembrandt and Rubens (*Sacrifices to Venus*).

The first floor focuses on applied arts (silverware, handcrafts, porcelain, Empire furnishings, and the like). First-time visitors, if pressed for time, may want to head directly to the second floor. Here, among the paintings from northern Europe, is Lucas Cranach's most amusing *Venus and Cupid.* Also displayed is a rare collection of Russian icons, most of them—such as *St. George and the Dragon*—from the Moscow School of the mid–16th century.

The museum shows an exceptional number of excellent paintings by such masters as Perugino (*St. Sebastian*), Ribera (his oft-rendered *Martyrdom of Bartolomé*), El Greco (*Peter and Paul*), Giovanni Bellini (*Portrait of Christ*), Lotto (*Portrait of a Man*), and Poussin (*Bacchus*). The gallery contains some outstanding Flemish works, notably Rubens's *Bacchanal at Andros* and *Worship of Venus,* and Jan Brueghel's *Jesus Preaching from the Boat.*

Perhaps the most important room in the museum has one whole wall featuring the works of Rembrandt—*Portrait of an Old Man, Portrait of an Old Woman,* and

Kitchen Maid (one of the most famous works in Stockholm). Here also is *The Oath of the Batavians.*

In yet another room is Watteau's *Lesson in Love,* and another room is noted for its Venetian works by Guardi and Canaletto, as well as English portraits by Gainsborough and Reynolds.

Modern works include Manet's *Parisienne;* Degas's dancers; Rodin's nude male (*Copper Age*) and his bust of Victor Hugo; van Gogh's *Light Movements in Green;* landscapes by Cézanne, Gauguin, and Pissarro; and paintings by Renoir, notably *La Grenouillère.*

Moderna Museet (Museum of Modern Art). Skeppsholmen. ☎ **08/519-55-200.** Admission 60 SEK ($6.60) adults, 40 SEK ($4.40) seniors and students, free for children under 17. Tues–Thurs 11am–10pm, Fri–Sun 11am–6pm. T-bana: Kungsträdgården. Bus: 65.

This building, designed by renowned Spanish architect Rafael Moneo, opened on Valentine's Day 1998. The museum (which had been on Birger Jarlsgatan) focuses on contemporary works, including kinetic sculptures, by Swedish and international artists. Highlights include a small but good collection of cubist art by Picasso, Braque, and Léger; Matisse's *Apollo* découpage; the famous *Enigma of William Tell* by Salvador Dalí; and works by Brancusi, Max Ernst, Giacometti, and Arp, among others. There's also a collection of pop art—Robert Rauschenberg (*Monogram*), Claes Oldenburg, and Andy Warhol. Among 1960s works by prominent New York artists are Oldenburg's 12-foot-high *Geometric Mouse; Fox Trot,* an early Warhol; and *Total Totality All,* a large sculpture by Louise Nevelson.

Museum activities include a children's workshop, concerts, films, discussions, and theater. There's also a cafe and pub.

Historiska Museet (Museum of National Antiquities). Narvavägen 13–17. ☎ **08/519-556-00.** Admission 60 SEK ($6.60) adults, 50 SEK ($5.50) seniors and students, 35 SEK ($3.85) children 7–15, free for children under 7, 140 SEK ($15.40) family. Apr–Sept, Tues–Sun 11am–5pm; Oct–Mar, Tues–Wed and Fri–Sun 11am–5pm, Thurs 11am–8pm. T-bana: Karlaplan or Östermalmstorg. Bus: 44, 47, or 54.

If you're interested in Swedish history, especially the Viking era, this museum is the nation's finest repository of relics. Many have been unearthed from ancient burial sites. The collection of artifacts ranges from prehistoric to medieval times, including Viking stone inscriptions and coins minted in the 10th century. In 1994, in the presence of King Carl XVI Gustaf and Queen Silvia, a Gold Room was inaugurated. It features Viking silver and gold jewelry, large ornate charms, elaborate bracelet designs found nowhere else in the world, and a unique neck collar from Färjestaden. The valuable treasury is underground, along long corridors and behind solid security doors.

3 On Djurgården

The forested island of Djurgården (Deer Park) lies about 2 miles to the east of Gamla Stan (Old Town).

✪ **Vasamuseet (Royal Warship Vasa).** Galärvarvsvägen, Djurgården. ☎ **08/666-48-00.** Admission 60 SEK ($6.60) adults, 40 SEK ($4.40) seniors and students, 10 SEK ($1.10) children 7–15, free for children under 7. June 10–Aug 20, daily 9:30am–7pm; Aug 21–June 9, Wed 10am–8pm, Thurs–Tues 10am–5pm. Closed Jan 1, May 1, Dec 24–26 and 31. Bus: 44 or 47. Ferry from Slussen year-round, from Nybroplan in summer only.

This 17th-century man-of-war is the top attraction in Scandinavia—and for good reason. Housed near Skansen in a museum specially constructed for it, the *Vasa* is the world's oldest identified and complete ship.

Stockholm Attractions

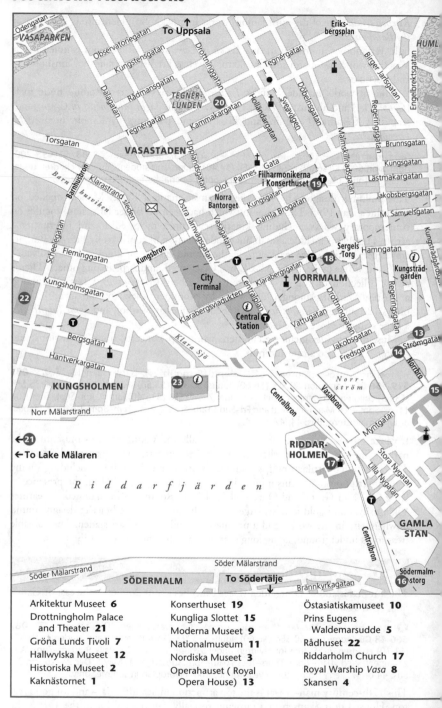

Arkitektur Museet **6**

Drottningholm Palace and Theater **21**

Gröna Lunds Tivoli **7**

Hallwylska Museet **12**

Historiska Museet **2**

Kaknästornet **1**

Konserthuset **19**

Kungliga Slottet **15**

Moderna Museet **9**

Nationalmuseum **11**

Nordiska Museet **3**

Operahauset (Royal Opera House) **13**

Östasiatiskamuseet **10**

Prins Eugens Waldemarsudde **5**

Rådhuset **22**

Riddarholm Church **17**

Royal Warship *Vasa* **8**

Skansen **4**

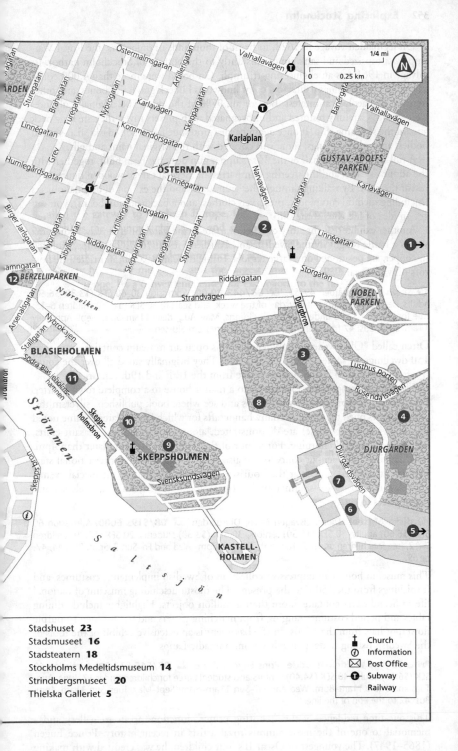

Stadshuset **23**
Stadsmuseet **16**
Stadsteatern **18**
Stockholms Medeltidsmuseum **14**
Strindbergsmuseet **20**
Thielska Galleriet **5**

† Church
ⓘ Information
✉ Post Office
🔵T Subway
— Railway

On its maiden voyage in 1628, in front of thousands of onlookers, the Royal Warship *Vasa* capsized and sank almost instantly to the bottom of Stockholm harbor. Its salvage in 1961 was an engineering triumph. On board were more than 4,000 coins, carpenter's tools, sailor's pants (in a color known as Lübeck gray), fish bones, and other items of archaeological interest. Best of all, 97% of the ship's 700 original sculptures were found. Carefully restored and impregnated with preservatives, they are now back aboard the stunning ship. It once again carries grotesque faces, lion masks, fish-shaped bodies, and other carvings, some still covered with the original paint and gilt.

A full-scale model of half of the *Vasa*'s upper gun deck has been built, together with the admiral's cabin and the steering compartment. Several carved wooden figures represent the crew. By walking through the "gun deck" and the exhibit of original objects (including medical equipment, preserved clothes, and a backgammon board), you can get an idea of life aboard the ship.

Another exhibit tells the story of naval warfare in the *Vasa*'s brief heyday. A diorama shows a battle fought by the Swedish and Polish navies in 1627. The ships, sculpted in copper, are positioned on a large cupola. Inside the cupola a film illustrates the horrors of war at sea.

✪ **Skansen.** Djurgården 49–51. ☎ **08/442-80-00.** Admission 30–60 SEK ($3.30–$6.60) adults, depending on time of day, day of the week, and season; 10 SEK ($1.10) children 6–15; free for children 5 and under. Historic buildings, May–Aug, daily 11am–5pm; Sept–Apr, daily 11am–3pm. Bus: 47 from central Stockholm. Ferry from Slussen.

Often called "Old Sweden in a Nutshell," this open-air museum contains more than 150 dwellings on some 75 acres of parkland. They originally stood all over the country, from Lapland to Skåne, and most are from the 18th and 19th centuries.

The exhibits range from a windmill to a manor house to a complete town quarter. Browsers can explore the old workshops and see where book publishers, silversmiths, and druggists plied their trades. Many handcrafts for which Swedes later became noted (glassblowing, for example) are demonstrated, along with traditional peasant crafts, such as weaving and churning. For a tour of the buildings, arrive no later than 4pm. Folk dancing and open-air concerts are also featured. In summer, international stars perform at Skansen. Check at the Tourist Center for information on special events. There's much to do on summer nights (see "Stockholm After Dark," below), and many places to eat.

Nordiska Museet. Djurgårdsvägen 6–16, Djurgården. ☎ **08/5195-6000.** Admission 60 SEK ($6.60) adults, 50 SEK ($5.50) seniors, 30 SEK ($3.30) students, 20 SEK ($2.20) children 7–12, free for children under 7. Tues and Thurs 2–8pm, Wed and Fri–Sun 2–5pm. Bus: 44, 47, or 69.

This museum houses an impressive collection of Swedish implements, costumes, and furnishings from the 1500s to the present. The most outstanding museum of national life in Scandinavia contains more than a million objects. Highlights include dining tables and period costumes ranging from matching garters and ties for men to purple flowerpot hats from the 1890s. In the basement is an extensive exhibit of the tools of the Swedish fishing trade, plus relics from nomadic Lapps.

Prins Eugens Waldemarsudde. Prins Eugens Väg 6. ☎ **08/545-837-00.** Admission 60 SEK ($6.60) adults, 40 SEK ($4.40) seniors and students, free for children under 17. June–Aug, Tues and Thurs 11am–8pm, Wed and Fri–Sun 11am–5pm; Sept–May, Tues–Sun 11am–4pm. Bus: 47 to the end of the line.

This one-time residence of the "painting prince" functions as an art gallery and a memorial to one of the most famous royal artists in recent history, Prince Eugen (1865–1947). The youngest of Oscar II's four children, he was credited with making innovative contributions to the techniques of Swedish landscape painting. He specialized in depictions of his favorite regions in central Sweden. Among his most publicly visible works are the murals on the inner walls of the City Hall.

Built between 1903 and 1904, and set directly on the water, the house is surrounded by a flower and sculpture garden. Eugen's private collection of paintings, which includes works by Edvard Munch, Carl Larsson, and Anders Zorn, is one of the most rewarding aspects of the residence. The house and its contents were willed to the Swedish government after the prince's death, and opened to the public in 1948.

The house and art gallery are furnished as the prince left them. While at Waldemarsudde, see the **Old Mill,** built in the 1780s.

Thielska Galleriet (Thiel Gallery). Sjötullsbacken 6–8, Djurgården. ☎ **08/662-58-84.** Admission 50 SEK ($5.50) adults, 30 SEK ($3.30) seniors and students, free for children under 12. Mon–Sat noon–4pm, Sun 1–4pm. Bus: 69.

At the tip of Djurgården, this gallery houses one of Sweden's major art collections. Many feel it surpasses the Prins Eugens Waldemarsudde collection. The sculptures and canvases here were acquired by Ernst Thiel, a financier and banker who eventually went bankrupt. The Swedish government acquired the collection in 1924.

Some big names in Scandinavian art are here, including Norway's Edvard Munch and Sweden's Anders Zorn (see his nude *In Dreams*). Gustav Fjaestad's furniture is also displayed. You'll also see a portrait of Nietzsche, whom Thiel greatly admired. Works by Manet, Rodin, and Toulouse-Lautrec, among others, round out the collection. Thiel is buried on the grounds beneath Rodin's statue *Shadow.*

4 On Kungsholmen

Stadshuset (Stockholm City Hall). Hantverksgatan 1. ☎ **08/508-290-59.** Admission 50 SEK ($5.50) adults, free for children under 12. Tower, May–Sept, daily 10am–4pm. City Hall tours (subject to change), June–Sept, daily at 10am, 11am, noon, and 2pm; Oct–Apr, daily at 10am and noon. T-bana: Centralen or Rådhuset. Bus: 3 or 62.

Built in the "National Romantic Style," the Stockholm City Hall (Stadhuset), on the island of Kungsholmen, is one of the finest examples of modern architecture in Europe. Designed by Ragnar Ostberg, it was completed in 1923. A lofty square tower 348 feet high dominates the red-brick structure. It bears three gilt crowns, the symbol of Sweden, and the national coat-of-arms. There are two courts: the open civic court and the interior covered court. The Blue Hall is used for banquets and other festive occasions, including the Nobel Prize banquet. About 18 million pieces of gold and colored-glass mosaics cover the walls, and the southern gallery contains murals by Prince Eugen, the painter prince. The 101 City Council members meet in the council chamber.

5 On Södermalm

Stadsmuseet (Stockholm City Museum). Ryssgården, Slussen. ☎ **08/508-31-600.** Admission 40 SEK ($4.40) adults, free for children under 17. June–Aug, Tues–Wed and Fri–Sun 11am–5pm, Thurs 5–7pm; Sept–May, Tues–Wed and Fri–Sun 11am–5pm, Thurs 11am–9pm. T-bana: Slussen. Bus: 43 or 46.

Housed in a building dating from 1684, the Stadsmuseet depicts the history of Stockholm and its citizens. Exhibits portray life in the industrial city throughout the past few centuries. Daily at 1pm, a 30-minute slide show in English describes Stockholm from the 16th century to the present.

6 Near Stockholm

❂ Drottningholm Palace and Theater. Ekerö, Drottningholm. ☎ **08/402-62-80.** Palace, 50 SEK ($5.50) adults, 25 SEK ($2.75) students and persons under 26; theater, guided tour 50 SEK ($5.50) adults, 20 SEK ($2.20) students and persons under 26; Chinese Pavilion, 50 SEK ($5.50) adults, 25 SEK ($2.75) students and persons under 26. All free for children under 16. Palace, Oct–Apr, Sat–Sun noon–3:30pm; May–Aug, daily 10am–4:30pm; Sept, daily noon–3:30pm. Theater, guided tours in English, May, daily 12:30pm, 1:30pm, 2:30pm, 3:30pm, and 4:15pm; June–Aug, daily 11:30am, 12:30pm, 1:30pm, 2:30pm, 3:30pm, and 4:15pm; Sept, daily 1:30pm, 2:30pm, 3:30pm. Chinese Pavilion, Apr and Oct, daily 1–3:30pm; May–Aug, daily 11am–4:30pm; Sept, daily noon–3:30pm. T-bana: Brommaplan, then bus no. 301 or 323 to Drottningholm. Ferry from the dock near City Hall.

Conceived as the centerpiece of Sweden's royal court, this regal complex of stately buildings sits on an island in Lake Mälaren. Dubbed the "Versailles of Sweden," Drottningholm (Queen's Island) lies about 7 miles west of Stockholm. The palace, loaded with courtly art and furnishings, sits amid fountains and parks, and still functions as one of the royal family's official residences.

On the grounds is one of the most perfectly preserved 18th-century theaters in the world, **Drottningholm Court Theater** (☎ 08/759-04-06). Between June and August, 30 performances are staged. Devoted almost exclusively to 18th-century opera, it seats only 450 for one of the most unusual entertainment experiences in Sweden. Many performances sell out far in advance to season-ticket holders. The theater can be visited only as part of a guided tour, which focuses on the original sets and stage mechanisms.

For tickets to the evening performances, which cost 150 to 545 SEK ($16.50 to $59.95), call ☎ **08/660-82-25.**

❂ Millesgården. Carl Milles Väg 2, Lidingö. ☎ **08/446-75-90.** Admission 70 SEK ($7.70) adults, 50 SEK ($5.50) seniors and students, 20 SEK ($2.20) children 7–16, free for children under 7. May–Sept, daily 10am–5pm; Oct–Apr, Tues–Sun noon–4pm. T-bana: Ropsten, then bus to Torsviks Torg or train to Norsvik.

On the island of Lidingö, northeast of Stockholm, is Carl Milles's former villa and sculpture garden beside the sea, now a museum. Many of his best-known works, including *Hand of God*, are displayed here (some are copies), as are works of other artists. Milles (1875–1955), who relied heavily on mythological themes, was Sweden's most famous sculptor.

7 A Literary Landmark

Strindbergsmuseet (Strindberg Museum). Drottninggatan 85. ☎ **08/411-53-54.** Admission 35 SEK ($3.85) adults, 25 SEK ($2.75) students, free for children. Tues noon–7pm (June–Aug 11am–4pm), Fri 11am–4pm, Sat–Sun noon–4pm. T-bana: Rådmansgatan.

This building, popularly known as "The Blue Tower," is where August Strindberg, the dramatist and novelist, spent his last 4 years (1908–12). It contains a library; three furnished rooms; and books, articles, and letters representing the last 20 years of his life. Of special interest to those familiar with Strindberg's plays is the fact that he furnished his rooms like stage sets from his plays, with color schemes as he visualized them. The dining room contains sculptures, casts of busts, and masks representing people and events that were important to him.

8 Architectural Highlights

Arkitektur Museet (Museum of Architecture). Skeppsholmen. ☎ **08/587-27-000.** Admission 60 SEK ($6.60) adults, 30 SEK ($3.30) students and seniors. Tues–Thurs 11am–8pm, Fri–Sun 11am–6pm; archive and library, Tues 4–8pm, Wed–Fri noon–4pm. Bus: 65.

Founded in 1962 in a building designed by the Spanish architect Rafael Moneo, this museum illustrates the art of architecture combined with social planning. It displays copies of rooms, buildings, places, and cities from different eras, covering 1,000 years of Swedish architecture. The history of the buildings is presented in chronological sections. The collection consists of some 2 million sketches, drawings, and documents, plus a half-million photographs and about 1,000 architectural models. The library alone has some 25,000 volumes, most donated by Swedish architects. The library is dedicated to the memory of the Swedish diplomat Raoul Wallenberg, known for his humanitarian efforts in Hungary in 1944 and 1945. Less well known is that Wallenberg was a trained architect. His few existing drawings, mainly from his student days in the United States, are in the museum's archives.

9 Especially for Kids

The open-air park, Skansen, on Djurgården, contains **Lill-Skansen,** "Little Skansen." There's a petting zoo with lots of child-friendly animals, including pigs, goats, and horses. Lill-Skansen offers a break from the dizzying (and often tantrum-inducing) excitement frequently generated by commercial amusement parks. A miniature train ride through the park (see above) is about as wild as it gets. Lill-Skansen is open daily in summer from 10:30am to 4pm.

Kids can spend a day or several at Skansen and not get bored. Before going to Skansen, stop off at the **Vasa Museum,** which many youngsters find an epic adventure. The evening can be capped by a visit to **Gröna Lunds Tivoli** (see "Stockholm After Dark," below), also on Djurgården.

10 Stockholm on Foot: Walking Tours

Walking Tour 1: Gamla Stan (Old Town)

Start: Gustav Adolfs Torg.

Finish: Slussplan.

Time: 3 hours.

Best Time: Any day when it's not raining.

Worst Times: Rush hours (weekdays 8 to 9:30am and 5:30 to 7pm).

Begin at:

    1. Gustav Adolfs Torg, facing the Royal Palace, with the Royal Opera on your left. Gustavus III, patron of the arts, was assassinated at a masked ball at the Royal Opera in 1792.

Walk across Norrbro (North Bridge), heading toward the Royal Palace. On your right you'll pass the:

2. **Swedish Parliament (Riksplan),** at Helgeandsholmen. The Parliament building dates from 1897, when its foundation stone was laid. It can be visited only on guided tours.

Along the bridge on your left are stairs leading to the:

3. **Medeltidsmuseet (Museum of Medieval Stockholm),** Strömparterren, with objects and artifacts from medieval Stockholm, including the Riddarholmship and parts of the old city wall.

☕ **TAKE A BREAK**   One of Stockholm's hidden cafes, **Café Strömparterren,** Helgeandsholmen (☎ **08/21-95-45),** is also centrally located—next door to the Medeltidsmuseet. Many Stockholmers come here for a morning cup of coffee and a stunning view of the waterfront. Later they can fish for salmon—everybody can—in front of the Royal Palace, a right that has existed since Queen Christina's day. In the summer, tables are outside; the interior is built into the walls under Norrbro.

After leaving the museum, turn to the right and walk back to the bridge and cross it to Slottskajen. Here, directly in front of the Royal Palace, make a right turn and head to Mynttorget. You'll see the **Kanslihuset,** a government office building erected in the 1930s. The neoclassical columned facade remains from the Royal Mint of 1790.

Continue straight along Myntgatan until you reach Riddarhustorget. On your right is the:

4. **Riddarhuset,** the 17th-century House of Nobles, where the Swedish aristocracy met during the Parliament of the Four Estates (1665–68).

Continue straight across Riddarholmsbron (bridge) until you come to the little island of:

5. **Riddarholmen,** called "the island of the knights." It's closely linked to the Old Town; its chief landmark, which you'll see immediately, is the Riddarholmskyrkan (church), with its cast-iron spire. Founded as an abbey in the 13th century, it has been the burial place of Swedish kings for 4 centuries.

Walk along the right side of the church until you reach Birger Jarls Torg. From there, take 1-block-long Wrangelska Backen to the water. Then go left and walk along Södra Riddarholmshamnen.

Veer left by the railroad tracks, climb some steps, and go along Hebbes Trappor until you return to Riddarholmskyrkan. From here, cross over Riddarholmsbron and return to Riddarhustorget.

Cross Stora Nygatan and take the next right onto Storkyrkobrinken, passing the landmark Cattelin Restaurant on your right. Continue along this street, past the Lady Hamilton Hotel. Turn right onto Trångsund, which leads to:

6. **Stortorget (Great Square),** where you'll find park benches for resting. This plaza was the site of the Stockholm Blood Bath of 1520, when Christian II of Denmark beheaded 80 Swedish noblemen and displayed a "pyramid" of their heads in the square. The Börsen on this square is the Swedish Stock Exchange (1776). This is where the Swedish Academy meets every year to choose the Nobel Prize winners in literature.

At the northeast corner of the square, take Källargränd north to view the entrance to the:

Walking Tour: Gamla Stan (Old Town)

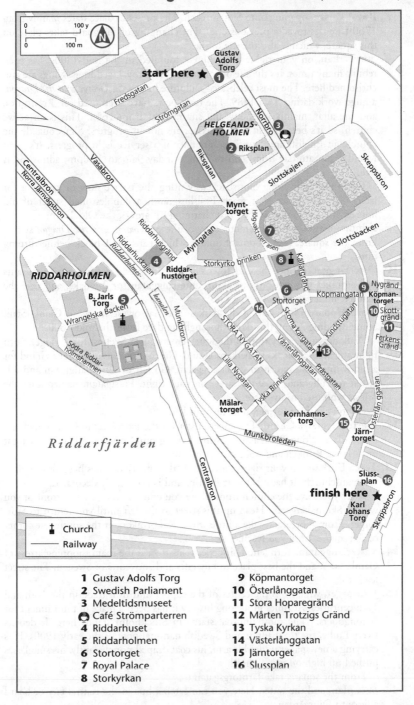

1 Gustav Adolfs Torg
2 Swedish Parliament
3 Medeltidsmuseet
   Café Strömparterren
4 Riddarhuset
5 Riddarholmen
6 Stortorget
7 Royal Palace
8 Storkyrkan
9 Köpmantorget
10 Österlånggatan
11 Stora Hoparegränd
12 Mårten Trotzigs Gränd
13 Tyska Kyrkan
14 Västerlånggatan
15 Järntorget
16 Slussplan

7. **Royal Palace,** opening onto Slottsbacken. The present palace dates mainly from 1760 (fire destroyed a previous one). The changing of the guard takes place on this square, which is also the site of the:
8. **Storkyrkan,** on your right. This church, founded in the mid-1200s, has been rebuilt many times. It's the site of coronations and royal weddings. Kings are also christened here. The most celebrated sculpture here is *St. George and the Dragon,* a huge work dating from 1489. The royal pews have been used for 3 centuries, and the altar, mainly in ebony and silver, dates from 1652. This is an active church, so it's best to visit when services are not in progress. Signs outside the church, in English and Swedish, announce if a service is in progress. It's open Monday to Saturday from 9am to 7pm, Sunday 9am to 5:30pm; admission is free.

   Continue right along Slottsbacken, visiting the palace now or saving it for later. Go right when you reach Bollshusgränd, a cobblestoned street of old houses. It leads to one of the most charming squares of the Old Town:
9. **Köpmantorget,** with its famous copy of the *St. George and the Dragon* statue. From the square, take Köpmanbrinken, which runs for 1 block before turning into:
10. **Österlånggatan,** once the Old Town's harbor street, and site of many restaurants and antiques shops. Continue along Österlånggatan for 2 blocks, and take the first left under an arch, leading into:
11. **Stora Hoparegränd,** one of the darkest and narrowest streets in Gamla Stan. Some buildings along this dank thoroughfare date from the mid-1600s.

   Walk down the alley toward the water, emerging at Skeppsbron (bridge). Turn right and walk 2 blocks to Ferkens Gränd. Go right again up Ferkens Gränd for a block until you return to Österlånggatan. Go left on Österlånggatan and follow it to Tullgränd. Take the street on your right, Prästgatan, named after the priests who used to live here.

   As you climb this street, note on your left:
12. **Mårten Trotzigs Gränd.** The street of steps is the narrowest in Gamla Stan.

   Continue along Prästgatan, passing a playground on your right. Turn right onto Tyska Brinken and walk to the church:
13. **Tyska Kyrkan,** on your right. Since the 17th century this has been Stockholm's German church. It has a baroque interior and is exquisitely decorated.

   After you leave the church from where you entered, the street in front of you will be Skomakargatan. Head up this street to the left until you return to Stortorget. From Stortorget, take a little street, Kåkbrinken, at the southwest corner of the square, until you reach:
14. **Västerlånggatan.** Turn left. This pedestrian street is the main shopping artery of Gamla Stan, and the best place to buy gifts and souvenirs of Sweden. The street leads to:
15. **Järntorget,** which was the center of the copper and iron trade in the 16th and 17th centuries. At times in its long history it has been a place of punishment for "wrongdoers." The most unusual statue in Stockholm stands here. It depicts Evert Taube, the troubadour and Swedish national poet of the early 1900s. He's carrying a newspaper under his arm, his coat draped nonchalantly, his sunglasses pushed up high on his forehead.

   From the square, take Järntorgsgatan to:
16. **Slussplan,** and the water. Here you can catch a bus to the central city or board a ferry to Djurgården.

Walking Tour 2: Along the Harbor

Start: Stadshuset.

Finish: Museum of Architecture.

Time: 3 hours.

Best Time: Any day when it's not raining.

Worst Times: Rush hours (weekdays 8 to 9:30am and 5:30 to 7pm).

Start at the:

1. **Stadshuset (Stockholm City Hall),** Hantverkargatan 1, on Kungsholmen. This island has some of the loveliest and most varied waterfront walks in the city. It took 12 years, 8 million bricks, and 19 million gilded mosaic tiles to erect City Hall, which can be visited on a guided tour. Go inside the courtyard on your own and admire the architecture.

   After exploring the building, exit and turn right. Walk across Stadshusbron (City Hall Bridge) to Norrmalm. You'll see the Sheraton Stockholm & Towers coming up on your left, and on your right the Stadshuscafeet, where sight-seeing boats depart on canal cruises in summer. Walk past the boats and go under an underpass (watch out for fast-riding bicyclists).

   Continue along the canal until you reach Tegelbacken, a waterfront square. At the entrance to the Vasabron (bridge), cross the street and continue along Freds-gatan. Veer right at the intersection with Malmtorgsgatan, hugging the canal. This will take you to Rosenbad, a little triangular park.

   At Strömgatan, along the canal, the building on your right is the:

2. **Swedish Parliament (Riksplan),** which you can visit on a guided tour. Upon your arrival at:

3. **Gustav Adolfs Torg,** you'll have a panoramic view of the Royal Palace across the canal and of the Royal Opera straight ahead. This is one of Stockholm's most famous squares, and the most scenic.

   Strömgatan, which briefly comes to an end at Gustav Adolfs Torg, resumes at the corner of the Opera House, site of the Operakällaren, for many years the finest restaurant in Stockholm. Continue until you reach the southern end of the:

4. **Kungsträdgården,** the summer living room of Stockholm. These royal gardens, established in the 1500s as a pleasure garden for the court, reach from Hamn-gatan on the north side down to the water. They are now open to all, and have cafes, open-air restaurants, and refreshment kiosks.

   ☕ **TAKE A BREAK** The **Café Victoria,** Kungsträdgården (☎ 08/ 10-10-85), has attracted crowds since the late 1800s. It's an ideal spot for a refresh-ing drink or snack. It's open Monday to Saturday from 11:30am to 3am, Sunday noon to 11pm. (See "Stockholm After Dark," below, for more information.)

   Continue along the waterfront, past Strömbron, a bridge leading to Gamla Stan. After a block you'll come to Södra Blasieholmshamnen, site of the:

5. **Grand Hotel,** at no. 8. For decades this has been Stockholm's most prestigious address, attracting Nobel Prize winners, most visiting dignitaries, and movie stars. On your right, many sightseeing boats depart for summer tours of the Stockholm archipelago. From this vantage point, you have a good view of the Royal Palace and Gamla Stan.

   Continue south along this street until you reach the:

Walking Tour: Along the Harbor

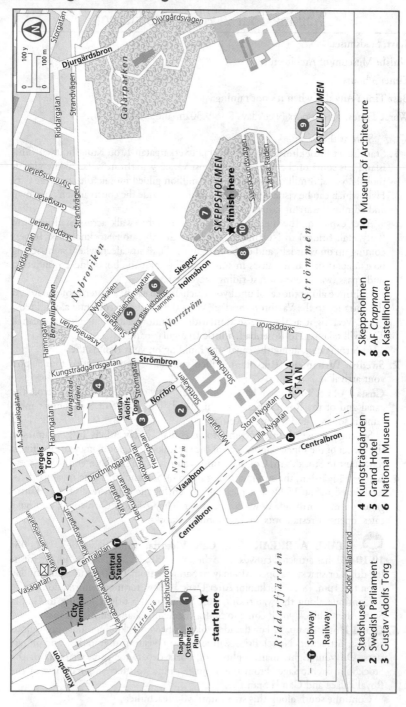

1 Stadshuset
2 Swedish Parliament
3 Gustav Adolfs Torg

4 Kungsträdgården
5 Grand Hotel
6 National Museum

7 Skeppsholmen
8 AF Chapman
9 Kastellholmen

10 Museum of Architecture

6. **National Museum,** Södra Blasieholmshamnen. This is the repository of the state's art treasures—everything from Renoir to Rembrandt.

Cross the Skeppsholmsbron (bridge) leading to the little island of:

7. **Skeppsholmen,** home to a number of attractions, such as the *AF Chapman* and the Museum of Architecture. After crossing the bridge, turn right and follow Västra Brobänken. On your right you'll pass the:

8. **AF** *Chapman,* a "tall ship" with fully rigged masts that sailed the seas under three different flags. It was permanently anchored in 1949 and became a youth hostel.

Turn left onto Flaggmansvägen. Continue along Holmamiralens Torg, passing the Nordiska Institute on your right. Cut right toward the water at Södra Brobänken. Turn right and cross the bridge leading to the small island of:

9. **Kastellholmen,** one of the most charming, and least visited, islands in Stockholm. Follow the water, going around Kastellholmskajen. Circle around and turn left at the end of Kastelleton. Walk back along Örlogsvägen, which runs through the center of the small island.

Cross the Kastellholmsbron (bridge) and return to Skeppsholmen. This time go straight along Amiralsvägen, turning left onto Långa Raden. Cut right and continue to walk along Långa Raden. The first building on your left is the:

10. **Museum of Architecture,** which has slides and thousands of architectural drawings and sketches from the last 100 years.

11 Organized Tours

CITY TOURS   The quickest and most convenient way to see the highlights of Stockholm is to take one of the bus tours that leave from Karl XII Torg, near the Kungsträdgården.

Stockholm Sightseeing, Skeppsbron 22 (☎ **08/587-140-20**), offers a variety of tours, mostly in the summer. The 3-hour "Royal Stockholm" tour visits the Royal Palace or the Treasury and the *Vasa* Museum, with daily departures mid-April to mid-October from Gustav Adolfs Torg, by the Royal Opera House. They cost 240 SEK ($26.40). The quickest, cheapest tour—but also the most superficial—is the 1-hour "City Tour," for 130 SEK ($14.30). It leaves daily year-round from Gustav Adolfs Torg. "Under the Bridges" takes 2 hours and goes through two locks and two bodies of water. Departures are from Stromkajen (near the Grand Hotel), daily from mid-April to mid-September. The cost is 140 SEK ($15.40). The 1-hour "Sightseeing Anno 1935" explores the Stockholm harbor in an open-topped wooden boat, with a captain in period uniform. The tour costs 110 SEK ($12.10). Daily departures, early July to mid-August, are from the statue of Gustavus III by the Royal Palace.

OLD TOWN STROLLS   Authorized guides lead 1½-hour walking tours of the medieval lanes of Gamla Stan (Old Town). Walks depart from the Royal Opera House at Gustav Adolfs Torg, daily from June to mid-August. They cost 75 SEK ($8.25). Tickets and departure times are available from **Stockholm Sightseeing,** Skeppsbron 22 (☎ **08/587-140-20**).

CANAL CRUISES   **Stockholm Sightseeing** (☎ **08/587-140-20**) offers the "Royal Canal Tour" daily from May to September, every 30 minutes. Tours cost 90 SEK ($9.90) for adults, 45 SEK ($4.95) for children. The tour goes around the canals of Djurgården.

12 Spectator Sports

Soccer and ice hockey are the most popular spectator sports in Sweden, and Stockholm is the home of world-class teams. The most important sports venue in the capital, the Stockholm Globe Arena (Globen), is less than 4 miles south of central Stockholm. Built in 1989, it's believed to be the biggest round building in the world, with a seating capacity of 16,000. It stages political rallies, motorcycle competitions, sales conventions, basketball games, tennis, ice hockey, and rock concerts. The ticket office (☎ 08/600-34-00) also sells tickets for most of Stockholm's soccer games, which are played in an open-air stadium nearby. It's open Monday to Friday from 9am to 4pm. The Globen complex lies in the suburb of Johnneshov (T-bana: Globen).

Another popular sport is trotting races, with the associated gambling. They usually take place on Wednesday at 6:30pm and occasionally on Saturday at 12:30pm, summer and winter. (Slippery snow and ice on the racecourse sometimes lead to unpredictable results.) Admission to Solvalla Stadium (☎ 08/635-90-00), about 4 miles north of the city center, is 20 SEK ($2.20). From Stockholm, take the bus marked SOLVALLA.

For schedules and ticket information, inquire at your hotel or the tourist office, or buy a copy of Stockholm This Week from a newspaper kiosk.

13 Outdoor Activities

GOLF   For those who want to play golf at the "top of Europe," there is the Bromma Golf Course, Kvarnbacksvägen 303, 16874 Bromma (☎ 08/289-430), lying 3 miles west of the center of Stockholm. It's a nine-hole golf course with well-maintained greens; greens fees are 130 SEK ($14.30); rental clubs are available.

HORSEBACK RIDING (VIKING STYLE)   You can ride small, gentle Iceland horses at the Haninge Iceland Horse Center in Hemfosa, 23 miles south of Stockholm (☎ 08/500-481-81). The cost is 400 SEK ($44) per person for 2½ hours, including a picnic lunch. Besides walking, galloping, trotting, and cantering, the horses have another gait, the tölt. The equine speedwalk has no English translation.

SAUNA & SWIMMING   Vilda Vanadis (☎ 08/30-12-11) is a combination sauna, outdoor heated pool, and children's paddling pool. It's at Vanadislunden, near the northern terminus of Sveavägen, within easy walking distance of the Oden Hotel and the city center. This is really an adventure park, with a variety of attractions. There's also a sauna and a restaurant. The entrance fee is 60 SEK ($6.60), and once you're inside, the attractions are free. It's open from early May to the end of August, daily from 10am to 6pm.

TENNIS, SQUASH & WEIGHT LIFTING   At the Royal Tennis Hall, Lidingövägen 75 (☎ 08/459-15-00 for reservations), you can play racquet sports, lift weights, and enjoy a sauna and solarium. The center has 16 indoor courts, five outdoor clay courts, and eight squash courts. Tennis courts cost 170 to 200 SEK ($18.70 to $22) per hour; squash courts, 70 to 95 SEK ($7.70 to $10.45) for a 30-minute session. Use of the weight room costs 30 SEK ($3.30). The center is open Monday to Thursday from 7am to 11pm, Friday 7am to 9pm, Saturday and Sunday 8am to 9pm.

14 Shopping

THE SHOPPING SCENE

Stockholm is filled with shop after shop displaying dazzling merchandise—often at dazzling prices. In the land of supertaxes and superwelfare, Sweden's noted craftspeople are well paid for their skill, which translates into high prices.

Bargain shoppers: Proceed with caution. There are some good buys, but they take a lot of searching. If you're a casual shopper, you might want to confine your purchases to handsome souvenirs and gifts.

Swedish glass is world famous. The wooden items are outstanding, and many people love the functional furniture in blond pine or birch. Other items to look for include children's playsuits, silver necklaces, reindeer gloves, hand-woven neckties and skirts, sweaters and mittens in Nordic patterns, clogs, and colorful handcrafts from the provinces. The most famous souvenir is the Dala horse from Dalarna.

TAXES & REFUNDS   Sweden imposes the value-added tax, *moms,* on all products and services. When buying larger and more expensive items, you can avoid moms if you spend more than 200 SEK ($22). Give the store your name, address, and passport number, and ask for a "Tax-Free Check." Don't unwrap your purchase until after you've left Sweden. The customs official will want to see both the Tax-Free Check and your purchase. You'll be given a cash refund, minus a small commission, on the spot. If you're departing by plane, hold on to your luggage until after you've received your refund, and then you can pack your purchase in your bag and check it (or carry the purchase with you, if it's not too big). At the **Tourist Center,** Hamngatan 27 (☎ 08/ 789-24-95), you can pick up a pamphlet about tax-free shopping in Sweden. Additional information is available by phone; call ☎ 0410/613-01. (For more information, see "Taxes" in "Fast Facts: Sweden," in chapter 12.)

SHOPPING STREETS & DISTRICTS   Everybody's favorite shopping area in Stockholm is **Gamla Stan** (Old Town). It's near the Royal Palace—even the queen has been seen shopping here. The main street for browsing is **Västerlånggatan.** Many antiques stores are there, but don't expect low prices.

In the summer, **Skansen** is an interesting area to explore. Many craftspeople display their goods there. There are gift shops (some sell "Skansen glass"), as well as individuals who offer their handmade goods on temporary stands.

In the **Sergels Torg** area, the main shopping street is **Hamngatan.** There you'll find the famous shopping center Gallerian, at the corner of Hamngatan and Sergels Torg, and bordering Kungsträdgården at Sweden House. Big department stores, such as NK and Åhléns City, are nearby.

Other major shopping districts include the **Kungsgatan** area, which stretches from Hötorget to the intersection of Kungsgatan and Vasagatan, and **Hötorget,** home to the PUB department store. **Drottninggatan** is one long pedestrian mall, flanked with shops. Many side streets off it are also filled with shops.

SHOPPING HOURS   Shops are open Monday to Friday from 10am to 6pm, Saturday from 10am to somewhere between 1 and 4pm. Once a week, usually on Monday or Friday, some larger stores are open from 9:30am to 7pm (during July and August, to 6pm).

SHOPPING A TO Z
ART GALLERIES
Galerie Nordenhake. Fredsgatan 12. ☎ **08/211-892.** T-bana: Centralen.

Some aspects of this prestigious, high-profile gallery might remind you of a SoHo loft. Pale Nordic light streams into some of the minimalist display areas through arched 19th-century windows.

AUCTIONS
Stockholms Auktionsverket (Stockholm Auction Chambers). In Gallerian, Hamngatan 37. ☎ **08/453-67-00.** T-bana: Kungsträdgården.

The oldest auction company in the world (1674) holds auctions 3 days a week from noon to "whenever." You can view the merchandise on Friday from 11am to 5pm and Saturday 10am to 4pm. An estimated 150,000 lots a year are auctioned—everything from ceramics to Picassos.

BOOKS & MAPS

Akademibokhandeln. Mäster Samuelsgatan 32. ☎ **08/613-61-00.** T-bana: Hötorget.

The biggest bookstore in Sweden carries more than 100,000 titles. A wide range of fiction and nonfiction is available in English. Many travel-related materials, such as maps, are also sold.

Sverige Bokhandeln (Sweden Bookshop). Sweden House (Sverigehuset), 2nd floor. Kungsträdgården. ☎ **08/789-21-31.** T-bana: Kungsträdgården.

Whatever's available in English about Sweden can be found at this bookstore above the Tourist Center. The store sells many rare items, including records of Swedish music.

CERAMICS

Blås & Knåda. Hornsgatan 26. ☎ **08/642-77-67.** T-bana: Slussen.

This store sells the best products made by members of a cooperative of 50 Swedish ceramic artists and glassmakers. Prices begin at 160 SEK ($17.60) for a single teacup, and rise to as much as 35,000 SEK ($3,850) for museum-quality pieces.

Keramiskt Centrum Gustavsberg. Värmdö Island (13 miles east of Stockholm). ☎ **08/ 570-356-58.** Bus: 422 or 440.

Bone china, stoneware dinner services, and other fine table and decorative ware are made at the Gustavsberg Ceramics Center. A museum at the center displays historic pieces such as *parian* (a type of unglazed porcelain) statues based on the work of the famous Danish sculptor Torvaldsen and other artists. You'll also see hand-painted vases, Toby jugs, majolica, and willowware, examples of Pyro (the first ovenware), royal dinner services, and sculptures by modern artists.

Visitors can watch potters at work and see artists hand-painting designs. You can even decorate a mug or plate yourself. A shop at the center sells Gustavsberg ware, including seconds.

DEPARTMENT STORES

Åhléns City. Klarabergsgatan 50. ☎ **08/676-60-00.** T-bana: Centralen.

In the center of Stockholm, the largest department store in Sweden has a gift shop, a restaurant, and a famous food department. Also seek out the fine collection of home textiles, and Orrefors and Kosta Boda crystal ware. The pewter with genuine Swedish ornaments makes a fine gift item.

Nordiska Kompanient (NK). Hamngatan 18–20. ☎ **08/762-80-00.** T-bana: Kungsträdgården.

NK has been a high-quality department store since 1902. It displays most of the big names in Swedish glass, including Orrefors (see the Nordic Light collection) and Kosta. Thousands of handcrafted Swedish items can be found in the basement. Stainless steel, also a good buy in Sweden, is profusely displayed. It's open Monday to Friday from 10am to 7pm, Saturday 10am to 5pm, Sunday noon to 5pm.

PUB. Hötorget 13. ☎ **08/23-99-15.** T-bana: Hötorget.

Greta Garbo worked in the millinery department here from 1920 to 1922. It's one of the most popular department stores in Stockholm; the boutiques and departments generally sell mid-range clothing and good-quality housewares, but not the international designer names of the more prestigious (and more expensive) NK. Massive and bustling, with an emphasis on traditional and conservative Swedish clothing, it offers just about anything you'd need to stock a Scandinavian home. There's also a restaurant.

FLEA MARKET

Loppmarknaden i Skärholmen (Skärholmen Shopping Center). Skärholmen. ☎ 08/710-00-60. Bus: 13 or 23 to Skärholmen (20 minutes).

At the biggest flea market in northern Europe, you might find a pleasing item from an attic in Värmland. You might indeed find *anything*. Try to go on Saturday or Sunday (the earlier the better), when the market is at its peak. Admission is 10 SEK ($1.10) for adults, free for children.

GEMS & MINERALS

Geocity. Tysta Marigången 5, Tegelbacken. ☎ 08/411-11-40. T-bana: Centralen.

Geocity offers exotic mineral crystals, jewelry, Scandinavian gems, Baltic amber, and lapidary equipment. The staff includes two certified gemologists who will cut and set any gem you select and do appraisals. The inventory holds stones from Scandinavia and around the world, including Greenland, Madagascar, Siberia, and South America.

GIFTS & SOUVENIRS

Slottsbodarna (Royal Gift Shop). Royal Palace south wing, Slottsbacken. ☎ 08/402-61-48. T-bana: Gamla Stan.

This unusual outlet sells products related to or copied from the collections in the Royal Palace. Items are re-created in silver, gold, brass, pewter, textiles, and glass. Every item is made in Sweden.

GLASS & CRYSTAL

Rosenthal Studio-Haus. Birger Jarlsgatan 6. ☎ 08/611-66-01. T-bana: Östermalmstorg.

This is the largest outlet in Sweden for delicate German-made Rosenthal porcelain. You'll find mostly modern patterns of crystal, porcelain, glass, and upscale stainless steel.

✪ Svenskt Glas. Karlavägen 61. ☎ 08/679-79-09. T-bana: Östermalmstorg.

Royal families patronize this establishment, which features Swedish-made glass at every price level. You'll see Orrefors and Kosta Boda stemware, candlesticks, flower-shaped bowls in full lead crystal, bar sets, vases, wineglasses, pitchers, and perfume bottles. Worldwide shipping is available.

HANDCRAFTS & GIFTS

Brinken Konsthantverk. Storkyrkobrinken 1. ☎ 08/411-59-54. T-bana: Gamla Stan.

On the lower floor of a building near the Royal Palace in the Old Town, this elegant purveyor of gift items will ship handcrafted brass, pewter, wrought iron, or crystal anywhere in the world. About 95% of the articles are made in Scandinavia.

✪ DesignTorget. In the Kulturhuset, Sergels Torg 3. ☎ 08/508-31-520. T-bana: Centralen.

In 1994, the government-owned Kulturhuset (Swedish Culture House) reacted to declining attendance by inviting one of Stockholm's most influential designers and decorators, Jerry Hellström, to organize an avant-garde art gallery. Swedes modestly refer to it as a "shop." In a large room in the cellar, you'll find a display of handcrafts created by 150 to 200 mostly Swedish craftspeople. The work must be approved by a jury of connoisseurs before being offered for sale. The merchandise includes some of the best pottery, furniture, textiles, clothing, pewter, and crystal in Sweden, for 25 to 20,000 SEK ($2.75 to $2,200) per object. The most expensive object in the gallery, at the time of this writing, was a magnificently proportioned bathtub assembled from glued and laminated strips of wood. Almost as impressive were a series of ergonomically designed computer workstations. The organization maintains a branch in southern Stockholm, **DesignTorget Mode,** Götgatan 31 (☎ 08/462-35-20). It stocks clothing for men, women, and children, and furniture, with less emphasis on ceramics and handcrafts.

Duka. Kungsgatan 41. ☎ **08/20-60-41.** T-bana: Hötorget.

A large selection of crystal, porcelain, and gifts is available in this shop near the Konserthuset (Concert Hall). It offers tax-free shopping and shipping.

Gunnarssons Träfigurer. Drottninggatan 77. ☎ **08/21-67-17.** T-bana: Rådmansgatan.

This is one of the city's most interesting collections of Swedish carved wooden figures. All are by Urban Gunnarsson, a second-generation master carver. They include Second World War figures, such as Winston Churchill, and U.S. presidents from Franklin D. Roosevelt to Bill Clinton. There's also a host of mythical and historical European personalities. Prices range from 300 to 800 SEK ($33 to $88); larger pieces cost up to 2,000 SEK ($220). The carvings are usually made from linden or basswood.

Konsthantverkarna. Mäster Samuelsgatan 2. ☎ **08/611-96-60.** T-bana: Östermalmstorg.

This store has an unusual selection of some of the best Swedish handcrafts, created by a group of artisans. All pieces must pass scrutiny by a strict jury before they're offered for sale. Choose from glass, sculpture, ceramics, wall textiles, clothes, jewelry, silver, brass, and wood and leather work. Each item is handmade and original. Ask about the tax-free service.

Svensk Hemslojd (Society for Swedish Handcrafts). Sveavägen 44. ☎ **08/23-21-15.** T-bana: Hötorget.

Svensk Hemslojd offers a wide selection of glass, pottery, gifts, and wooden and metal handcrafts by some of Sweden's best artisans. There's a display of hand-woven carpets, upholstery fabrics, hand-painted materials, tapestries, lace, and embroidered items. You'll also find beautiful yarns for weaving and embroidery.

HOME FURNISHINGS

Nordiska Galleriet. Nybrogatan 11. ☎ **08/442-83-60.** T-bana: Östermalmstorg.

This store features the finest in European furniture design, including the best from Scandinavia. Two floors hold the latest contemporary furniture. The store can arrange shipment.

✪ **Svenskt Tenn.** Strandvägen 5. ☎ **08/670-16-00.** T-bana: Östermalmstorg.

Along "embassy row," Swedish Pewter (its English name) has been Sweden's most prominent store for home furnishings since 1924. Pewter is no longer king, and the shop now sells Scandinavia's best selection of furniture, printed textiles, lamps, glassware, china, and gifts. The inventory is stylish, and although there aren't a lot of bargains, it's an excellent place to see the newest trends in Scandinavian design. It carries an exclusive collection of Josef Frank's hand-printed designs on linen and cotton. It will pack, insure, and ship your purchases anywhere in the world.

LINENS

Solgården. Karlavägen 58. ☎ **08/663-9360.** T-bana: Rådmansgatan.

For the dwindling few who really care about luxury linens and elegant homeware, such as lace and embroideries, this shop is the finest of its kind in Scandinavia. It was conceived by its owner, Marianne von Kantzow Ridderstad, as a tribute to Gustav III, the king who is said to have launched the neoclassical style in Sweden. Ridderstad designed her shop like a country house with rough-hewn wood and whimsical furnishings. Each of her linens is virtually a work of art. The tablecloths are heirloom pieces. You're told to cherish the work for its originality as much as for its loveliness.

MARKETS

Östermalms Saluhall. Nybrogatan 31. No central phone. T-bana: Östermalmstorg.

One of the most colorful indoor markets in Scandinavia features cheese, meat, vegetable, and fish merchants who supply food for much of the area. You may want to have a snack or a meal at one of the restaurants.

SHOPPING MALLS

Gallerian Arcade. Hamngatan 37. No phone. T-bana: Kungsträdgården.

A short walk from Sweden House at Kunådgården, this modern two-story shopping complex is, to many, the best shopping destination in Sweden. Merchandise in most of the individually managed stores is designed to appeal to local shoppers, not the tourist market—although in summer that changes a bit as more souvenir and gift items appear.

○ **Sturegallerian.** Stureplan. ☎ **08/611-46-06.** T-bana: Östermalmstorg.

In the center of Stockholm, this mall has a dazzling array of merchandise, both foreign and domestic, in some 50 specialty shops. Summer brings out more displays of Swedish souvenirs and gift items. There are also restaurants and cafes. Sturegallerian opened in 1989 and a year later was named "Shopping Center of the Year in Europe" by the International Council of Shopping Centers.

TEXTILES

Handarbetets Vänner. Djurgårdsslatten 82–84. ☎ **08/667-10-26.** Bus: 47.

This is one of the oldest and most prestigious textile houses in Stockholm. It also sells art weaving and embroidery items.

JOBS. Stora Nygatan 19. ☎ **08/20-98-16.** T-bana: Gamla Stan.

Hand-painted fabrics from the JOBS family workshops in Dalarna are prized for their quality and the beauty of their design. Patterns are inspired by the all-too-short Swedish summer and by rural traditions. If you plan to be in Dalarna, you might enjoy visiting the **JOBS factory,** Västanvik 201, Leksand, (☎ **0247/122-22**). Other items include tablecloths, handbags, and children's clothing.

TOYS

Bulleribock (Toys). Sveavägen 104. ☎ **08/673-61-21.** T-bana: Rådmansgatan.

Since it opened in the 1960s, this store has carried only traditional, noncomputerized toys made of wood, metal, or paper (no plastics). There are no commando-tactic war games that pacifist parents find objectionable. Many of these charming playthings are suitable for children up to age 10. "As many as possible" are made in Sweden, with wood from Swedish forests.

15 Stockholm After Dark

Djurgården is the favorite spot for indoor and outdoor events on a summer evening. Although the more sophisticated might find it corny, Djurgården is the best bet in the early evening. Afterward, you can make the rounds of jazz and disco clubs, some of which stay open until 3 or 4 in the morning.

Pick up a copy of *Stockholm This Week,* distributed at the Tourist Center at Sweden House (see chapter 12) to see what's on.

THE PERFORMING ARTS

The major opera, theater, and concert seasons begin in the fall, except for special summer festival performances. Most major opera and theatrical performances are funded by the state, which keeps ticket prices reasonable.

CONCERT HALLS

Berwaldhallen (Berwald Concert Hall). Strandvägen 69. ☎ **08/784-18-00.** Tickets 50–355 SEK ($5.50–$39.05). T-bana: Karaplan.

This hexagonal concert hall is Swedish Radio's big music studio. The Radio Symphonic Orchestra performs here, and other musical programs include lieder and chamber music recitals. The hall has excellent acoustics. The box office is open Monday to Friday from 11am to 6pm and 2 hours before every concert.

○ **Filharmonikerna i Konserthuset (Concert Hall).** Hötorget 8. ☎ **08/10-21-10** or 08/457-02-11. Tickets 110–400 SEK ($12.10–$44). T-bana: Hötorget.

Home of the Stockholm Philharmonic Orchestra, this is the principal place to hear classical music in Sweden. The Nobel Prizes are awarded here. Constructed in 1920, the building houses two concert halls. One seats 1,600 and is better suited to major orchestras; the other, seating 450, is suitable for chamber music groups. Besides local orchestras, the hall features visiting ensembles, such as the Chicago Symphony Orchestra. Some series sell out in advance to subscription-ticket holders; for others, visitors can readily get tickets. Sales begin 2 weeks before a concert and continue until it begins. Concerts usually start at 7:30pm, with occasional lunchtime (noon) or "happy hour" (5:30pm) concerts. Most performances are broadcast on Stockholm's main classical music station, 107.5 FM. The box office is open Monday to Friday from 10am to 6pm, Saturday 10am to 1pm. The concert hall is closed in July and early August.

OPERA & BALLET

○ **Drottningholm Court Theater.** Drottningholm. ☎ **08/660-82-25.** Tickets 150–545 SEK ($16.50–$59.95). T-bana: Brommaplan, then bus no. 301 or 323. Boat from the City Hall in Stockholm.

Founded by Gustavus III in 1766, this unique theater is on an island in Lake Mälaren, 7 miles from Stockholm. It stages operas and ballets with full 18th-century regalia, period costumes, and wigs. Its machinery and 30 or more complete theater sets are intact and in use. The theater, a short walk from the royal residence, seats only 450, which makes it difficult to get tickets. Eighteenth-century music performed on antique instruments is a perennial favorite. The season is May to September. Most performances begin at 7:30pm and last 2½ to 4 hours. You can order tickets in advance by phone with an American Express card.

○ **Operahauset (Royal Opera House).** Gustav Adolfs Torg. ☎ **08/24-82-40.** Tickets 100–400 SEK ($11–$44); 10%–30% senior and student discounts. T-bana: Kungsträdgården.

Founded in 1773 by Gustavus III (who was later assassinated here at a masked ball), the Opera House is the home of the Royal Swedish Opera and the Royal Swedish Ballet. The building dates from 1898. Performances are usually Monday to Saturday at 7:30pm (closed mid-June to August). The box office is open Monday to Friday from noon to 6pm (until 7:30pm on performance nights), Saturday noon to 3pm.

THEATER

The theater season begins in mid-August and lasts until mid-June.

Kungliga Dramatiska Teatern (Royal Dramatic Theater). Nybroplan.
☎ **08/667-06-80.** Tickets 100–300 SEK ($11–$33); student discount available. T-bana: Östermalmstorg.

Greta Garbo got her start in acting here, and Ingmar Bergman stages two productions a year. The theater presents the latest experimental plays and the classics—in Swedish only. The theater is open all year (with a slight slowdown in July), and performances are scheduled Tuesday to Saturday at 7pm and Sunday at 4pm. The box office is open Monday to Saturday from 10am to 6pm.

Oscars Teatern. Kungsgatan 63. ☎ **08/20-50-00.** Tickets 240–375 SEK ($26.40–$41.25). T-bana: Hötorget.

Oscars is the flagship of Stockholm's musical entertainment world. It's been the home of classic operetta and musical theater since the turn of the century. Known for its extravagant staging of traditional operettas, it was one of the first theaters in Europe to produce such hits as *Cats* in Swedish. The box office is open Monday to Saturday from 9am to 5pm.

LOCAL CULTURE & ENTERTAINMENT

Skansen. Djurgården 49–51. ☎ **08/442-80-00.** Admission 30–60 SEK ($3.30–$6.60) adults, 10 SEK ($1.10) children 6–15, free for children 5 and under. Bus: 44 or 47. Ferry from Nybroplan.

Skansen arranges traditional seasonal festivities, special events, autumn market days, and a Christmas Fair. In summer there are concerts, sing-alongs, and guest performances. Folk dancing performances are staged from June to August, Monday to Saturday at 7pm and Sunday at 2:30 and 4pm. From June to August, outdoor dancing is presented with live music Monday to Friday from 8:30 to 11:30pm.

AN AMUSEMENT PARK

Gröna Lunds Tivoli. Djurgården. ☎ **08/587-501-00.** Admission 45 SEK ($4.95), free for children under 13. Bus: 44 or 47. Ferry from Nybroplan.

Unlike its Copenhagen namesake, this is an amusement park, not a fantasyland. For those who like Coney Island–type amusements, it can be a nighttime adventure. One of the big thrills is to go up to the revolving tower for an after-dark view. The park is open daily from the end of April to August, usually from noon to 11pm or midnight. Call for exact hours.

THE CLUB & MUSIC SCENE
A HISTORIC NIGHTCLUB

✪ **Café Opera.** Operahauset, Kungsträdgården. ☎ **08/676-58-07.** Cover 80 SEK ($8.80) after 10pm. T-bana: Kungsträdgården.

By day a bistro, brasserie, and tearoom, Café Opera becomes one of the most crowded nightclubs in Stockholm in the evening. Visitors have the best chance of getting in around noon, when a *dagens* (daily) lunch is offered for 120 SEK ($13.20). A stairway near the entrance leads to one of the Opera House's most beautiful corners, the club-like Operabaren (Opera Bar). It's likely to be as crowded as the cafe. The bar is a monumental but historically charming place to have a drink; beer costs 53 SEK ($5.85). After 10pm, there is less emphasis on food and more on disco activities. Open Monday to Saturday from 11:30am to 3am, Sunday 1pm to 3am. At night, long lines form outside. Don't confuse this establishment with the opera's main (and far more expensive) dining room, the Operakällaren.

The Capital of Gay Scandinavia

Copenhagen thrived for many years as a refreshingly raunchy city with few inhibitions and fewer restrictions on alternative sexuality. Beginning in the mid-1990s, Stockholm witnessed an eruption of new gay bars, discos, and roaming nightclubs. Copenhagen's more imperial and, in many ways, more staid competition made the Danes' legendary permissiveness look a bit weak. Today, thanks partly to the huge influence of London's gay subcultures, no other city in Scandinavia offers gay-friendly nightlife options as broad and diverse as Stockholm's. Some of the new gay bars and clubs maintain fixed hours and addresses. Others, configured as roving parties, constantly change addresses. The acknowledged king of the gay underground is Swedish-born entrepreneur Ulrik Bermsio, who has been compared to the legendary Steve Rubell of Studio 54 fame. Listings for his entertainment venues—and those promoted by his less visible competitors—appear regularly in *QX*, a gay magazine published in Swedish and English. It's available at news kiosks throughout Stockholm. You can also check out the magazine's Web site (www.qx.se). And don't overlook the comprehensive Web site (www.rfsl.se) maintained by RSFL, a Swedish organization devoted to equal rights for gays.

Permanent bars and clubs: The Disco, Torsgatan 1 (☎ 08/22-51-70; T-bana: Centralen), and its attractively permissive restaurant, Las Vegas, are open every Wednesday, Friday, and Saturday at 7pm. The music shuts down at 3am. Unless you opt to dine here before your dancefest, you'll pay 60 SEK ($6.60) to enter. The high-energy venue is styled after discos in New York and Los Angeles. Fridays are the most fun.

Looking for a non-confrontational bar peopled with regular guys who happen to be gay? Consider a round or two at **Sidetrack,** Wollmar Yxkullsgatan 7 (☎ 08/641-1688; T-bana: Mariatorget). Small, and committed to shunning trendiness, it's named after the founder's favorite gay bar in Chicago. It's open every night from 6pm to 1am. Tuesday seems to be something of a gay Stockholm institution. Other nights are fine, too—something like a Swedish version of a bar and lounge at the local bowling alley, where everyone happens to be into same-sex encounters.

To find a Viking, or Viking wannabe, in leather, head for **SLM (Scandinavian Leather Men),** Wollmar Yxkullsgatan 18 (☎ 08/643-3100; T-bana: Mariatorget).

DANCE CLUBS & DISCOS

The Daily News. In Sweden House (Sverigehuset), at Kungsträdgården. ☎ 08/21-56-55. Cover 60–90 SEK ($6.60–$9.90). T-bana: Kungsträdgården.

One of the capital's most enduring entertainment emporiums, this place has flourished through dozens of changes over the years. Currently there's a disco and a pub in the cellar, a somewhat smaller dance floor and a bar on the street level, and a street-level restaurant that serves platters of Swedish and international food. On weekends, there's sometimes a line. Platters of food begin at around 70 SEK ($7.70), full dinners at around 200 SEK ($22). Beer costs about 40 SEK ($4.40). The place is open every night from 11pm to between 4 and 5am.

Göta Källare. In the Medborgplatsen subway station, Södermalm. ☎ 08/642-08-28. Cover 70 SEK ($7.70) before 9:30pm, 90 SEK ($9.90) after 9:30pm. T-bana: Medborgplatsen.

Technically, this is a private club. If you look hot, wear just a hint (or even a lot) of cowhide or rawhide, or happen to have spent the past 6 months felling timber in Montana, you stand a good chance of getting in. Wednesday and Friday from 10pm to 2am, the place functions as Stockholm's premier leather bar. You'll find lots of masculine-looking men on the street level and a handful of toys and restrictive accoutrements in the cellar-level dungeon. On Saturday from 10pm to 2am, a DJ spins highly danceable music. It's closed on other nights.

If you need a caffeine fix and a slice of chocolate cake before all that leather and latex, you might want to drop into Stockholm's most appealing, best-managed gay cafe, **Chokladkoppen,** Stortorget (☎ 08/203170; T-bana: Gamla Stan). Open daily from 11am to 11pm, it specializes in sandwiches, "gorgeous" pastries, and all manner of chocolate confections that appeal even to straight people. The staff is charming, and the clientele more gay than not.

Our remaining selections involve venues that cater to a gay crowd only on specific nights of the week. They're subject to change according to the outrageous whims of fashion and scheduling concerns. Examples include **Häcktet ("The Jail"),** Hornsgatan 82 (no phone; T-bana: Mariatorget). Most of the week, its clientele is supposedly straight. Every Wednesday and Friday from 7pm till around 1am, the place promotes itself to a gay clientele, with a high percentage of lesbians. Disco music energizes a too-small dance floor; otherwise, people just drink. There's no cover charge. In the summer, a barbecue pit in the courtyard does an active business.

Then there's **Patricia,** Stadsgårdskajen 152 (☎ 08/743-0570; T-bana: Slussen). It's straight most of the week, and avowedly gay every Sunday between 7pm and 5am. Sprawling and labyrinthine, with three bars and a good sound system, it attracts gay folk from all walks of life and income levels. It's most crowded on Sundays during the summer, much less so in the winter. There's a restaurant on the premises.

Lesbians appreciate the freedom afforded by a roving party held at a series of rented catering halls throughout Stockholm. **The Bitch Girl Club** takes place on the second Saturday of every month. The usual admission price is 75 SEK ($8.25). For information, consult *QX* magazine or either of the Web sites mentioned above.

Stockholm's largest and most successful supper-club-style dance hall has a reputation for successful matchmaking. Large, echoing, and paneled with lots of wood in *faux-Español* style, it has a terrace that surrounds an enormous tree. The restaurant serves platters of food priced at 80 to 200 SEK ($8.80 to $22). Menu items include tournedos, fish, chicken, and veal. Expect an atmosphere that recalls the old days at Roseland in New York City and a crowd of people over 45. The live orchestra (which performs *Strangers in the Night* a bit too frequently) plays every night. The place opens every night at 8:30pm.

ROCK & JAZZ CLUBS

Fasching. Kungsgatan 63. ☎ **08/21-62-67.** Cover 90–200 SEK ($9.90–$22). T-bana: Centralen.

This is the country's premier venue for live jazz. Its roster of artists might remind you of a Who's Who of the entertainment industry. It originated around the turn of the century as a cafe that served drinks to patrons of a nearby theater. Today the smoke-filled premises attract a considerably less sedate crowd. Doors open at 8pm Friday and Saturday (6pm Monday to Thursday), with the main act beginning at 9pm (8pm Monday to Thursday). On Friday and Saturday between midnight and 4am, the site transforms into a salsa or soul club, depending on the whim of the management. Patrons already in don't pay extra; post-midnight stragglers pay 60 SEK ($6.60) each. At the restaurant, main courses cost about 100 SEK ($11).

Hard Rock Cafe. Sveavägen 75. ☎ **08/16-03-50.** No cover. T-bana: Rådmansgaten.

The Swedish branch of this chain is fun and gregarious. Sometimes an American, British, or Scandinavian rock band presents a live concert; otherwise, rock blasts from the sound system. Club sandwiches, hamburgers, T-bone steaks, and barbecued spareribs are available. Burgers cost 95 SEK ($10.45), steaks are 150 to 192 SEK ($16.50 to $21.10), and a beer goes for 39 SEK ($4.30). It's open Sunday to Thursday from 11am to 1am, Friday and Saturday 11am to 3am.

Pub Engelen/Nightclub Kolingen. Kornhamnstorg 59B. ☎ **08/20-10-92.** Cover 40–60 SEK ($4.40–$6.60) after 9pm. T-bana: Gamla Stan.

The Engelen Pub, the Restaurant Engelen, and the Nightclub Kolingen (in the 15th-century cellar) share this address. The restaurant, which serves some of the best steaks in town, is open Sunday to Thursday from 5 to 11:30pm, Friday and Saturday 5pm to 1:30am. Prices for platters of bar food run 80 to 200 SEK ($8.80 to $22). Live performances, usually soul, funk, and rock by Swedish groups, take over the pub daily from 8:30pm to midnight. The pub is open Tuesday to Thursday from 4pm to 1am, Friday and Saturday 4pm to 2am, Sunday 5pm to 1am. Beer begins at 34 SEK ($3.75), and items on the bar menu cost 30 to 70 SEK ($3.30 to $7.70). The Nightclub Kolingen is a disco nightly from 10pm to about 3am. It charges the same food and drink prices as the pub, and you must be at least 23 to enter.

Stampen. Stora Nygatan 5. ☎ **08/20-57-93.** Cover 100 SEK ($11). T-bana: Gamla Stan.

This pub attracts crowds of jazz lovers in their 30s and 40s. Guests crowd in to enjoy live Dixieland, New Orleans, mainstream, and swing music from the 1920s, '30s, and '40s. On Tuesday, it's rock 'n' roll from the 1950s and 1960s. A menagerie of stuffed animals and lots of old, whimsical antiques are suspended from the high ceiling. It's open Monday to Wednesday from 8pm to 1am, Thursday to Saturday 8pm to 2am. In summer, an outdoor veranda is open when the weather permits. The club has two stages, and there's dancing downstairs almost every night.

THE BAR SCENE

Akvarium. Kungsträdgården. ☎ **08/100-626.** No cover. T-bana: Kungsträdgården.

Most of the business at this hip and bustling place derives from its restaurant, but you can still enjoy the bar, which seems to have a social energy of its own. Clients tend to be attractive and hip. American-style martinis are among the most popular drinks. The bar is open daily from 11:30am to midnight.

Cadier Bar. In the Grand Hotel, Södra Blasieholmshamnen 8. ☎ **08/679-35-00.** No cover. T-bana: Kungsträdgården.

From the bar of this deluxe hotel—one of the most famous in Europe—you'll have a view of the harbor and the Royal Palace. It's one of the most sophisticated places in Stockholm. Light meals—open-faced sandwiches and smoked salmon—are served all day in the extension overlooking the waterfront. Drinks run 96 to 120 SEK ($10.55 to $13.20); imported beer is 45 SEK ($4.95). The bar is named for the hotel's builder.

It's open Monday to Saturday from noon to 2am, Sunday noon to 12:30am; a piano player performs Monday to Saturday from 9:30pm to 1:30am.

Café Victoria. Kungsträdgården. ☎ **08/10-10-85.** No cover. T-bana: Kungsträdgården.

The most central cafe in Stockholm becomes crowded after 9pm in winter (7pm in summer). It attracts a varied crowd. Many patrons come just to drink, but you can have lunch or dinner in an interior section beyond the lively bar area. Light snacks cost 80 to 130 SEK ($8.80 to $14.30); main dishes are 120 to 230 SEK ($13.20 to $25.30). A bottle of beer will set you back 46 SEK ($5.05). It's open Monday to Saturday from noon to 3am, Sunday 1pm to 3am.

Gondolen. 13 Stadtsgården. ☎ **08/641-70-90.** No cover. T-bana: Slussen.

You might find Gondolen's architecture as impressive as the view. Part of the structure is suspended beneath a pedestrian footbridge that soars above the narrow channel separating the island of Gamla Stan from the island of Södermalm. The engineering triumph was executed in 1935. The elevator hauls customers (without charge) up the equivalent of 11 stories to the '40s-style restaurant. The view encompasses Lake Malar, the open sea, and huge areas of downtown Stockholm. You'll pay 75 SEK ($8.25) for a whisky with soda. It is open Monday to Friday 11:30am to 1am, Saturday 1pm to 1am.

Sturehof. Stureplan 2. ☎ **08/440-57-30.** No cover. T-bana: Östermalmstorg.

Since 1897, this pub and restaurant has been one of Stockholm's major drinking and dining venues. In the exact center of the city, it has been engulfed in urban restoration and is now in a covered arcade with other restaurants and shops. It remains a pleasant refuge from the city's congestion, and is popular as both an after-work bar and a restaurant. It's open daily from 11am to 1am. Beer costs 46 SEK ($5.05).

Tiger Bar/Havana Bar. 18 Kungsgatan. ☎ **08/244-700.** Cover 50 SEK ($5.50) Wed, 60 SEK ($6.60) Thurs, 100 SEK ($11) Fri–Sat. T-bana: Östermalmstorg.

One of the most talked-about bars in Stockholm attracts a bevy of supermodels and TV actors from all over. The street-level Tiger Bar has black leather upholstery and an atmosphere of postmodern cool. The basement-level Havana Bar channels pre-Castro Cuba with *faux* palms and garish colors. On both levels, everybody's favorite drink seems to be the Russian-inspired *caprinoshka,* concocted from vodka and limes. You might hear anything from recorded disco (every Friday and Saturday beginning at midnight) to live salsa and merengue (every Wednesday from 9pm to 5am). The place is open Thursday from 7pm to 3am, Friday and Saturday 7pm to 4am. Incidentally, no one will object if you light up a cigar.

16 Side Trips from Stockholm

Some of Sweden's best-known attractions are clustered around Lake Mälaren. Centuries-old villages and castles revive the pomp and glory of the 16th-century Vasa dynasty.

You can spend a very busy day exploring Sigtuna, Skokloster Castle, Uppsala, and Gamla (Old) Uppsala, and stay overnight in Sigtuna or Uppsala. Other easy day trips are to Gripsholm Castle in Mariefred, or Tullgarn Palace.

A popular boat excursion leaves from Klara Mälarstrand Pier, near Stockholm's Town Hall and the T-Bana Centralen station, at 9:45am. It goes along the beautiful waterway Mälaren and the Fyris River to Sigtuna, where it makes a 2-hour stop. The boat arrives in Uppsala at 5pm. Visit the cathedral and other interesting sights, dine, and return on the train, a 45-minute trip. Trains run every hour until 11pm. The one-way boat fare from the pier to Sigtuna is around 75 SEK ($8.25), and the one-way overland fare (which combines train and bus transfer) costs 50 SEK ($5.50).

SIGTUNA

28 miles NW of Stockholm

Founded at the beginning of the 11th century, Sigtuna, on the shores of Lake Mälaren, is Sweden's oldest town. **High Street (Stora Gatan),** with its low-timbered buildings, is thought to be the oldest street in Sweden that follows its original route. Traces of Sigtuna's Viking and early Christian heritage can be seen throughout the town.

ESSENTIALS

GETTING THERE   From Stockholm's train station, take a 45-minute train ride to Märsta. Trains depart at 30-minute intervals throughout the day and evening. In Märsta, transfer to a bus (it will be marked either "Sigtuna no. 575" or "Sigtuna no. 570") for an additional 20-minute ride on to Sigtuna. In the summer, boats run to Sigtuna from Klara Mälarstrand Pier in Stockholm and from Uppsala.

VISITOR INFORMATION   For information contact the Sigtuna Tourist Info office at ☎ 08/529-500-20.

SEEING THE SIGHTS

Sigtuna has many church ruins, mostly from the 12th century. Chief among them is **S:t Per's,** Sweden's first cathedral. The 13th-century **Monastery of St. Maria** is open to the public daily. The well-preserved **Town Hall** dates from the 18th century.

Wander the narrow streets and, if you have time, visit the **Sigtuna Museum,** Storagatan (☎ 08/592-510-18). The archaeological museum contains artifacts, found in the surrounding area, that date to the early medieval period. You'll see gold rings, runic inscriptions, and coins, as well as objects from Russia and Byzantium. Admission is 20 SEK ($2.20), free for children under 17. It's open June to August daily noon to 4pm; September to May Tuesday to Sunday noon to 4pm.

One reason for the town's resurgence is the **Sigtuna Foundation,** a Lutheran retreat and cultural center founded near the turn of the century and often frequented by writers. Although there are no exhibits here, the foundation is intellectually alluring, and its two chapels and rose garden are a source of pride and tranquility. The superb library is composed of mostly Swedish- and, to a lesser extent, German-language texts, plus a clipping file that chronicles the course of Sweden and the world's theological history. It's open to the public daily free of charge from 1 to 3pm.

WHERE TO STAY & DINE

Sigtuna Foundation. Manfred Björkquists Allé 2–4, S-193 31 Sigtuna. ☎ 08/592-589-00. Fax 08/592-589-99. E-mail: bokninken@sigtunastiftelsen.se. 55 units. 880 SEK ($96.80) double. Rates include breakfast. MC, V. Free parking. Bus: 570 or 575.

A stay at this massive building might provide one of your most memorable stopovers in Sweden. Intended as a center where sociological and philosophical viewpoints can be aired, the 1917 structure is more a way of life than a hotel. Over the years, guest lecturers have included the Dalai Lama, various Indian gurus, and many of postwar Europe's leading theologians. The establishment functions as both a conference center and a guesthouse. There's no proselytizing, although there might be opportunities to share experiences. There are secluded courtyards, lush rose and herb gardens, and fountains. Recently all the guest rooms were refurbished in bland modern style, and modern bathrooms were added. To guarantee a room, be sure to make arrangements in advance. The foundation is less than a mile from the town center.

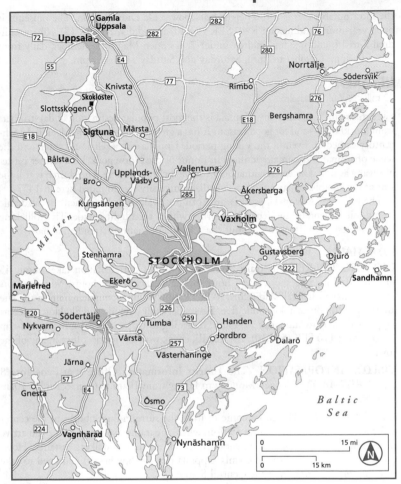

En Route from Sigtuna to Uppsala
Skokloster Castle

From Stockholm, take the train to Bålsta, then bus no. 894.

The splendid 17th-century castle **Skokloster,** S-746 96 Sklokloster (☎ 018/38-60-77), is one of the most interesting baroque museums in Europe. It's next to Lake Mälaren, 40 miles from Stockholm and 31 miles from Uppsala. With original interiors, the castle is noted for its extensive collections of paintings, furniture, applied art, tapestries, arms, and books.

Admission is 65 SEK ($7.15) for adults, 50 SEK ($5.50) for seniors, 30 SEK ($3.30) for students and children. Guided tours in English are offered May to August, daily on the hour from 11am to 4pm; in September, Monday to Friday at 1pm and Saturday and Sunday at 1, 2, and 3pm. It's closed from October to April.

Skokloster Motor Museum (☎ 018/38-61-06), on the palace grounds, houses the largest collection of vintage automobiles and motorcycles in the country. One of the most notable cars is a 1905 eight-horsepower De Dion Bouton. The museum is open year-round. Admission is 40 SEK ($4.40) for adults, 10 SEK ($1.10) for children 7 to 14, and free for children under 7. It's open May to September, daily from 11am to 5pm; October to April, Saturday and Sunday 11am to 5pm.

UPPSALA

42 miles NW of Stockholm

Sweden's major university city, Uppsala is the most popular destination of day-trippers from Stockholm—and for good reason. It has a great university and a celebrated 15th-century cathedral. Even in the Viking period, Uppsala was a religious center, and the scene of animal and human sacrifices in honor of the Norse gods. It's a former center of royalty as well. Queen Christina occasionally held court here. The church is still the seat of the archbishop, and the first Swedish university was founded here in 1477.

The best time to visit Uppsala is on April 30, Walpurgis Eve, when the academic community celebrates the rebirth of spring with a torchlight parade. The rollicking festivities last until dawn throughout the 13 student "nations" (residential halls).

ESSENTIALS

GETTING THERE   The **train** from Stockholm's Central Station takes about 45 minutes. Trains leave about every hour during peak daylight hours. Some visitors spend the day in Uppsala and return to Stockholm on the commuter train in the late afternoon. Eurailpass holders ride free. **Boats** between Uppsala and Skokloster depart Uppsala Tuesday to Sunday at 11:45am, returning to Uppsala at 5:30pm. Round-trip passage costs 110 SEK ($12.10). For details, check with the tourist office in any of the towns.

VISITOR INFORMATION   The **Tourist Information Office** is at Fyris Torg 8 (☎ 018/27-48-00). It's open Monday to Friday from 10am to 6pm, Saturday 10am to 3pm.

GETTING AROUND   Buses come in from the surrounding suburbs to the center of Uppsala arriving at the Central Station, where the trains also arrive. Once you arrive in the center of Uppsala, all the major attractions are in easy walking distance. However, if you're going to explore Gamla Uppsala (see the box below) you need to take bus 2 or 24, departing from the Central Station.

SEEING THE SIGHTS

Carolina Rediviva (University Library). Drottninggatan. ☎ **018/471-39-00.** Admission 20 SEK ($2.20) adults, free children under 12. Exhibit room, June 18–Aug 17, Mon–Fri 9am–5pm, Sat 10am–4pm, Sun 11am–4pm; June 2–17 and Aug 18–Sept 15, Sun 1–3:30pm. Closed Sept 16–June 1. Bus: 6, 7, or 22.

At the end of Drottninggatan is the Carolina Rediviva, with more than 5 million volumes and 40,000 manuscripts, including many rare works from the Middle Ages. The manuscript that interests most visitors is in the exhibit room. It's the *Codex Argenteus* (Silver Bible), translated into Gothic in the middle of the 3rd century and copied in about A.D. 525. It's the only book extant in old Gothic script. Also worth seeing is *Carta Marina*, the earliest map (1539), a fairly accurate map of Sweden and its neighboring countries.

Linnaeus Garden & Museum. Svartbäcksgatan 27. ☎ **018/13-65-40** for the museum, or 018/10-94-90 for the garden. Museum 25 SEK ($2.75) adults, free for children. For gardens, donation suggested, free for children. Museum, June–Aug, Tues–Sun noon–4pm. Closed Sept–May. Gardens, May–Aug, daily 9am–9pm; Sept, daily 9am–7pm. Closed Oct–Apr. Walk straight from the train station to Kungsgatan, turn right, and walk about 10 minutes.

Swedish botanist Carl von Linné, known as Carolus Linnaeus, developed a classification system for the world's plants and flowers. His garden and former home are on the spot where Uppsala University's botanical garden was restored by Linnaeus in the style of a miniature baroque garden. Linnaeus, who arranged the plants according to his "sexual classification system," left detailed sketches and descriptions of the garden, which have been faithfully followed.

Linnaeus was a professor of theoretical medicine, including botany, pharmacology, and zoology, at Uppsala University. You can visit his house, which has been restored to its original design, and an art gallery that exhibits the works of contemporary local artists.

✪ Uppsala Domkyrka. Domkyrkoplan 2. ☎ **018/18-72-01.** Free admission to cathedral; museum, 20 SEK ($2.20) adults, 15 SEK ($1.65) seniors and students, 10 SEK ($1.10) children 7–15, free for children under 7. Cathedral, daily 8am–6pm. Museum, Apr–Aug, daily 10am–5pm; Sept–Mar, Sun Sat 10am–5pm, Sun 12:30–5pm. Bus: 1.

The largest cathedral in Scandinavia, this twin-spired Gothic structure stands nearly 400 feet tall. Founded in the 13th century, it was severely damaged in 1702 in a disastrous fire, then was restored near the turn of the 20th century. Among the regal figures buried in the crypt is Gustavus Vasa. The remains of St. Erik, patron saint of Sweden, are entombed in a silver shrine. The botanist Linnaeus and the philosopher-theologian Swedenborg are also buried here. A small museum displays ecclesiastical relics.

Museum Gustavianum. Akademigatan 3. ☎ **018/471-75-71.** Admission 40 SEK ($4.40) adults, 20 SEK ($2.20) students, free children under 12. Mid–May to mid-Sept, daily 11am–4pm (until 9pm Thurs); off-season, Wed–Sun 11am–4pm (until 9pm Thurs). Bus: 1, 2, 51, 53.

Gustavianum is Uppsala University's oldest preserved building. Here you can see a number of attractions, including an Anatomical Theatre, the Augsburg Art Cabinet, and an exhibition about the history of the university itself. The museum also includes archeological exhibitions, from Swedish prehistory to the Middle Ages. Some of the rarer pieces are from the Mediterranean and the Nile Valley, including the sarcophagus of a priest, Khonsumes, from the 21st dynasty. In the historical exhibition on the ground floor you can see everything from student lecture notes from the first term in 1477, the year the university was founded, to the development of the institution over the years as a seat of learning.

WHERE TO STAY

Diakonistiftelsen Samariterhemmet. Samaritegränd 2, S-753 19 Uppsala. ☎ **018/10-34-00.** Fax 018/10-83-75. 25 units, 12 with bathroom. 670 SEK ($73.70) double without bathroom; 770 SEK ($84.70) double with bathroom. Rates include breakfast. MC, V.

One of the best bargains in town, this large guesthouse, run by a Christian charity, has spotlessly maintained rooms with comfortable beds. You can use a kitchenette with a refrigerator, and there's a TV lounge. Most of the units evoke an Ivy League dormitory. Smoking is not permitted.

First Hotel Linné. Skolgatan 45, S-75332 Uppsala. ☎ **018/10-20-00.** Fax 018/13-75-97. www.firsthotels.se. E-mail: linne@firsthotels.se. 116 units. MINIBAR TV TEL. Sun–Thurs 1,449–1,549 SEK ($159.40–$170.40) double; from 1,569–1,749 SEK ($172.60–$192.40) suite. Fri–Sat 799–849 SEK ($87.90–$93.40) double; from 899–999 SEK ($98.90–$109.90) suite. Rates include breakfast. AE, DC, MC, V. Parking 30 SEK ($3.30).

At the edge of Linnaeus Garden, this is one of the best-managed hotels in town. You'll probably be able to see Linnaeus's lovely garden from your window. The rooms feature modern furniture and plumbing, and each unit has a refrigerator or minibar that you stock yourself. It's a good value; one drawback is that the less expensive doubles are a bit cramped. One floor, with 36 rooms, is reserved for nonsmokers. The hotel has a bar and a sauna.

○ Gamla Uppsala

About 15 centuries ago, "Old Uppsala" was the capital of the Svea kingdom. In its midst was a grove set aside for human and animal sacrifices. Viking burial mounds dating from the 6th century are believed to contain the pyres of three kings.

Nearby, on the site of the old pagan temple, is a 12th-century **parish church,** once badly damaged by fire and never properly restored. Indeed, some people describe it as a stave church that turned to stone. Before Uppsala Cathedral was built, Swedish kings were crowned here.

Across from the church is the **Stiftelsen Upplandsmuseet,** Sankt Eriksgränd 6 (☎ 018/16-91-00). The open-air museum with reassembled buildings depicts peasant life in Uppland. It's open from mid-May through August, daily from noon to 5pm. Tours are conducted Monday to Friday at 1 and 2pm, Saturday and Sunday every hour on the hour from noon to 4pm. Admission is free.

Gamla Uppsala, about 3 miles north of the commercial heart of Uppsala, is easily accessible by bus no. 2 or 24, which leaves frequently from the Central Station.

Radisson SAS Hotel Gillet. Dragarbrunnsgatan 23, S-751 42 Uppsala. ☎ **018/15-53-60.** Fax 018/15-33-80. www.radissonsas.com. E-mail: sales@rdsas.com. 160 units. TV TEL. 900–1,850 SEK ($99–$203.50) double; 2,000–3,500 SEK ($220–$385) suite. Rates include breakfast. AE, DC, MC, V. Parking 95 SEK ($10.45). Bus: 801.

This attractively designed first-class hotel, built in 1972, offers well-furnished rooms, a breakfast room, cozy cocktail bar and lounge, swimming pool, and sauna. The medium-sized rooms have good beds, modern furnishings, and excellent housekeeping. With its two restaurants, the hotel is also one of Uppsala's major dining venues. The East West Bistro serves dinner Monday to Saturday; the more upscale Gillet Restaurant offers lunch and dinner Monday to Saturday.

Scandic Hotel Uplandia. Dragarbrunnsgatan 32, S-751 40 Uppsala. ☎ **800/528-1234** in the U.S., or 018/10-21-60. Fax 018/69-61-32. www.scandic-hotels.com. 133 units. MINIBAR TV TEL. 1,395–1,580 SEK ($153.45–$173.80) double. Rates include breakfast. AE, DC, MC, V.

Located next to the bus terminal, this is the best hotel in town. It was constructed in two stages, in the 1960s and early 1980s, in two connected buildings of three to six floors each. During the final enlargement, all rooms in the older section were brought up to modern standards. Bathrooms were completely overhauled in 1996. The hotel offers comfortably furnished rooms with such extras as trouser presses. There's a sauna on the premises.

On the lobby level is an elegant cocktail lounge, plus a spacious restaurant. Full meals might include a mousse of shrimp and salmon, noisettes of veal, Alsatian sauerkraut, or a vegetarian platter.

WHERE TO DINE

Domtrappkällaren. Sankt Eriksgränd 15. ☎ **018/13-09-55.** Reservations recommended. Main courses 145–230 SEK ($15.95–$25.30). AE, DC, MC, V. Mon–Sat 11:30am–11pm, Sun 5–9pm. Closed Dec 24–26. Bus: 1. SWEDISH.

No other restaurant in Uppsala can compete with this one for charm and atmosphere. It was built in the town center on the ruins of 12th-century cathedral buildings. The vaulted ceilings and copies of Jacobean paintings in the main dining room complement the low-ceilinged, sun-flooded intimacy of the upper floors. On request, you can dine in a narrow room where unruly students were imprisoned in the Middle Ages or in one that served as a classroom in the 17th century. The restaurant serves delectable salmon and reindeer and specializes in game. Salads are often exotic—one includes breast of pigeon with roasted nuts.

Restaurant Flustret. Svandammen. ☎ **018/13-01-14.** Reservations recommended. Main courses 120–150 SEK ($13.20–$16.50). AE, DC, MC, V. Mon–Fri 11am–2pm and 4–9pm, Sat–Sun 11am–10pm. Bus: 24. FRENCH.

In a riverside setting near the castle, this recently constructed pavilion is an exact replica of its predecessor, a demolished Victorian building. Its spacious ground-floor dining room serves tasty meals, which might include lobster soup, salmon "boathouse style," veal steak Oscar, pheasant Véronique, and bananas flambé. A disco on the second floor is open Saturday from 9pm to 2am. Admission is free before 9pm, 60 SEK ($6.60) after 9pm.

Restaurant Odinsborg. Near the burial grounds, Gamla Uppsala. ☎ **018/323-525.** Main courses 110–180 SEK ($12.10–$19.80); Sun smörgåsbord 205 SEK ($22.55). AE, DC, MC, V. Daily noon–6pm. SWEDISH.

In a century-old former private house, this restaurant serves strictly old-fashioned Swedish food. The culinary highlight in the Viking-theme dining room is the Sunday smörgåsbord. A traditional roster of foods you might expect at a Swedish family celebration is laboriously prepared and laid out. The rest of the week, menu items include traditional preparations of fried herring, marinated salmon, smoked eel, whitefish with a dill-flavored butter sauce. You might also try roasted lamb, chicken fillets, or steak. Street addresses aren't used in Gamla Uppsala, but the restaurant is easy to spot.

GRIPSHOLM CASTLE

Gripsholm Castle is 42 miles southwest of Stockholm. By **car,** follow E20 south; you can drive right to the castle parking lot. The Eskilstuna **bus** runs to the center of Mariefred, as do the boats. **Boats** leave mid-May to September at 10am from Klara Mälarstrand Pier. The castle is a 10-minute walk from the center of Mariefred.

On an island in Lake Mälaren, ✪ **Gripsholm Castle** (☎ **0159/101-94**) is one of the best-preserved castles in Sweden. The fortress, built by Gustavus Vasa in the late 1530s, is near Mariefred, an idyllic small town known for its vintage narrow-gauge railroad.

During the reign of the 18th-century actor-king Gustavus III, a theater was built at Gripsholm, but the castle's outstanding feature is its large collection of portrait paintings.

Even though Gripsholm was last occupied by royalty (Charles XV) in 1864, it's still a royal castle. It's open May to August, daily from 10am to 4pm; September, Tuesday to Sunday 10am to 3pm; October to April, Saturday and Sunday noon to 3pm. Admission is 50 SEK ($5.50) for adults, 25 SEK ($2.75) ages 7 to 15. Ages 6 and under free.

WHERE TO STAY

✪ **Gripsholms Värdshus & Hotel.** Kyrkogatan 1, S-647 23 Mariefred. ☎ **0159/34750.** Fax 0159/34777. www.gripsholms-vardshus.se. 45 units. A/C MINIBAR TV TEL. 1,690–1,960 SEK ($185.90–$215.60) double; 500–2,500 SEK ($55–$275) supplement for suite, depending on the unit and the season. Rates include breakfast. AE, DC, MC, V.

Built as an inn in 1609 (it's one of the oldest in Sweden), this building was restored and reopened in 1989. It's now the most stylish and charming hotel in the region. It's a few steps from the village church, in the center of Mariefred, a 10-minute walk from the castle. Each guest room is individually decorated and furnished with a mixture of antiques and contemporary pieces. Amenities include such thoughtful extras as a hair dryer and heated bathroom floors and towel racks.

Dining: The hotel has the best restaurant in the region (see "Where to Dine," below). The pub keeps the same hours as the restaurant and serves ample platters of homemade Swedish food.

Amenities: Room service, massage, laundry, solarium, recreation center, sauna, copper tub for ice baths, billiard room.

WHERE TO DINE

✪ Gripsholms Värdshus Restaurant. Kyrkogatan 1. ☎ **0159/34750.** Reservations recommended. Main courses 195–235 SEK ($21.45–$25.85); 2-course fixed-price lunch 210 SEK ($23.10). AE, DC, MC, V. Midsummer, daily noon–10pm. Rest of year, Mon–Fri noon–2pm, Sat noon–4pm; Mon–Sat 6–10pm. FRENCH/SWEDISH.

This elegantly appointed restaurant serves traditional Swedish food, local game dishes, and international cuisine. The main dining room has a veranda that opens onto Gripsholm Bay. The menu changes every season, but is likely to include baked saddle of venison with herbs and mushroom pastry, grilled halibut accompanied by red paprika cream and basil ratatouille, or lamb cutlets smothered in Dijon mustard and shallots. For dessert, try the raspberry mousse parfait. Tastings in the wine cellar can be arranged.

TULLGARN PALACE

Tullgarn Palace is 37 miles south of Stockholm. By **car,** take E4 south about 37 miles and turn right at the sign directing you to Tullgarns Slott, near Vagnhärad. It's another quarter mile to the palace. Getting here by public transportation is extremely inconvenient and not worth the trouble. You first have to take a train to Södertälje Södra (about 20 minutes), and then wait for a bus to Trosa, which lies 4½ miles south of the castle. From Trosa, you have to take a taxi the rest of the way. You could spend all morning just trying to get to the castle, so we recommend skipping it unless you have private transportation or endless amounts of time.

The royal palace of Tullgarn, in Vagnhärad (☎ **08/551-720-11**), occupies a panoramic setting on a bay of the Baltic Sea. It was the favorite of Gustavus V (1858–1950), the great-grandfather of Sweden's present king. Construction began in 1719, and the well-kept interiors date from the late 18th century.

Admission is 50 SEK ($5.50) for adults, 25 SEK ($2.75) for students and children. The palace is open to the public on weekends from early May to early September. Guided tours leave the main entrance every hour from 11am to 4pm.

WHERE TO DINE

Tullgarns Värdshus. In Tullgarn Palace, Vagnhärad. ☎ **08/551-720-26.** Main courses 150–197 SEK ($16.50–$21.65). MC, V. May 15–Sept 8, Mon–Fri noon–2:30pm and 5–7pm, Sat–Sun noon–7pm. Closed Sept 9–May 14. SWEDISH/FRENCH.

This inn, in a wing of Tullgarn Palace, offers three-course lunches or dinners. You can sample such dishes as salted salmon with creamed potatoes (an old Swedish specialty), or perhaps pâté of wild boar. You can also order breast of wild duck with chicken liver mousse, or poached fillet of salmon with chive-flavored butter sauce.

Or you can order a picnic lunch and eat in the royal park. Picnics of cold chicken or roast beef, with beer or coffee (in a take-out container), or a cup of coffee with a sandwich, can be ordered at the inn daily from 11am to 5pm.

SANDHAMN, VAXHOLM & THE ARCHIPELAGO OF STOCKHOLM

Stockholm is in what the Swedes call a "garden of skerries," an archipelago of more than 24,000 islands (including some rocks jutting out of the water). The islands nearest the city have become part of the suburbs, thickly populated and connected to the mainland by car ferries or bridges. Many others are wild and largely deserted, attracting boaters for picnics and swimming. Summer homes dot some of the islands. July is the peak vacation month, when yachts crowd the waters.

You can see the islands by taking a boat trip from Stockholm harbor. If you'd like to stop at a resort island, consider **Sandhamn,** where you'll find shops and restaurants. It takes about an hour to explore the entire island on foot. The beaches at the eastern tip are the best in the archipelago. **Vaxholm,** a bathing resort known as "the gateway to the northern archipelago," also makes a pleasant stop. Artists and writers have traditionally been drawn to Vaxholm, and some hold exhibits during the summer, when the tourist influx quadruples the population. The west harbor and the main sea route north are filled with pleasure craft.

ESSENTIALS

GETTING THERE   Throughout the year (but more often in the summer), boats operated by several companies depart from in front of the Grand Hotel at Södra Blasieholmshamnen. Most of them say Vaxholm, and boats usually continue to Sandhamn after a stop in Vaxholm. Be sure to ask before boarding.

The trip from Stockholm through the archipelago to Sandhamn takes 3½ hours each way and costs 95 SEK ($10.45) one-way. The ferry trip to Vaxholm from Stockholm takes less than 40 minutes and costs 60 SEK ($6.60) one-way. There are no car ferries. If you plan lots of travel around the archipelago, consider buying an **Inter-Skerries Card** for 300 SEK ($33). The card allows 16 days of unlimited travel anywhere within the Stockholm archipelago for much less than the cost of individual tickets.

Vaxholm-bound boats depart every hour during the summer (about five times a day in winter) from the Strömkagen, the piers outside the Grand Hotel. For information, call the steamship company **Vaxholmes Belaget** (☎ 08/679-5830).

Buses to Vaxholm (nos. 670, 671, 672, and 673) often—but not always—go on to Sandhamn. They depart from the Central Station daily (unless bitter weather prevents it) every 30 minutes beginning at 6am. The last bus from Vaxholm leaves at 1am. A round-trip fare is 100 SEK ($11).

ORGANIZED TOURS

Strömma Kanal Steamship (☎ 08/541-314-80) offers a guided cruise in English to Sandhamn. Ships sail through canals and bays. Tours depart June to August at 10am and last 8 hours. The "Canal Cruise to Sandhamn" begins at 185 SEK ($20.35); it's free for children under 12. The company also offers the "Thousand Island Cruise" through the Stockholm archipelago. The 11-hour guided tour includes lunch, dinner, and stopovers on four islands. Tours are available in July and August.

WHERE TO STAY

Vaxholm Hotel. Hamngatan 2, S-185 00 Vaxholm. ☎ **08/541-301-50.** Fax 08/541-313-76. www.vaxholmhotel.se. E-mail: info@vaxholmhotel.se. 32 units. TV TEL. 930–1,240 SEK ($102.30–$136.40) double. Rates include breakfast. AE, DC, MC, V. Closed Dec 24–Jan 1. Free parking.

Built in 1902, this stone hotel, painted bright yellow, is at the pier where the ferries from Stockholm dock. It offers modern but rather bland guest rooms. Its disco is open in the summer, Friday and Saturday from 9pm to 2am. The cover charge is 80 SEK ($8.80). An informal pub, Kabyssen, is at street level. One floor above is the Vaxholm Hotel Restaurant (see "Where to Dine," below).

WHERE TO DINE
In Vaxholm
Vaxholm Hotel Restaurant. Hamngatan 2. ☎ **08/541-301-50.** Reservations required in summer. Main courses 87–245 SEK ($9.55–$26.95). AE, DC, MC, V. Summer, daily noon–11pm; off-season, daily noon–9pm. Closed Dec 24–Jan 1. SEAFOOD.

This is the best place to dine in Vaxholm. It overlooks the water from the second floor of the hotel. The chef says his specialties are "fish, fish, fish." The uncompromising house specialty—and the best buy—is a platter of pan-fried Swedish herring served with mashed potatoes. You can also order a number of other dishes, notably smoked reindeer with horseradish, tender tournedos stuffed with herbs and served with a mustard sauce, or poached fillet of sole with white wine sauce. Summer desserts use locally grown berries and fruits, including rhubarb pie, elderberry sorbet, and lingonberries (often with almond flan).

In Sandhamn
Sandhamns Värdshus. Harbourfront. ☎ **08/571-53-051.** Reservations required Sat–Sun. Main courses 145–239 SEK ($15.95–$26.30); 3-course fixed-price menu 260 SEK ($28.60). AE, DC, MC, V. Sun–Thurs noon–9pm, Fri–Sat noon–10:30pm. SWEDISH.

The islanders' favorite restaurant was established in 1672. It offers a view of the moored boats at the harborfront. You can always get a good and reasonably priced meal here by selecting a fish dish or the local choice—steak with red onions.

Gothenburg 15

Called the gateway to northern Europe, Gothenburg (Göteborg in Swedish) is the country's chief port and second-largest city. Swedes often say that Gothenburg is a friendlier town than Stockholm. Canals, parks, and flower gardens enhance its appeal.

The city has many museums, and the largest amusement park in northern Europe. It's a convenient center for excursions to the fishing villages and holiday resorts to the north of the city.

A walk down "The Avenue" is a Gothenburg tradition. This is Kungsportsavenyn, called *Avenyn* (Avenue), with its many outdoor cafes where you can watch the passing parade. Start at Parkgatan, at the foot of The Avenue. Gothenburg's pedestrian street is heated by underground pipes in the winter so that the snow melts quickly.

Gustavus Adolphus II granted Gothenburg's charter in 1621. The port contains a shipyard—Cityvarvet—and a manufacturer of platforms for oil rigs (Götaverken/Arendal). The city is also the home of Volvo, the car manufacturer (whose plant is about a 15-minute drive from the city center), and of the Hasselblad space camera. Spanning the Göta River, Ålvsborg Bridge (the longest suspension bridge in Sweden) is almost 3,000 feet long and built high enough to allow ocean liners to pass underneath.

1 Orientation

ARRIVING

BY PLANE Many residents of Sweden's west coast consider Copenhagen's airport to be more convenient than Stockholm's. **SAS** (☎ 800/221-2350 in the U.S.; www.flysas.com) operates 8 to 10 daily flights from Copenhagen to Gothenburg between 7:30am and 11:05pm. (Most of them are nonstop.) SAS also operates 10 to 20 daily flights between Stockholm and Gothenburg, beginning about 7am and continuing until early evening.

Planes arrive at **Landvetter Airport** (☎ 031/94-10-00), 16 miles east of Gothenburg. An airport bus (Flygbuss) departs every 30 minutes for the half-hour ride to the city's central bus terminal, just behind Gothenburg's main railway station. Buses run daily between 5am and 11:30pm. A one way trip costs 50 SEK ($5.50).

BY TRAIN The **Oslo-Copenhagen express train** runs via Gothenburg and Helsingborg, connecting two Scandinavian capitals. North-south trains run frequently between Gothenburg and Helsingborg and

Malmö in the south. The most traveled rail route is between Gothenburg and Stockholm, with trains leaving hourly in both directions; the trip takes 4 hours, 40 minutes.

Trains arrive at the Central Station, on one side of Drottningtorget. The station has a currency-exchange bureau and an office of the Swedish National Railroad Authority (SJ), which sells rail and bus tickets for connections to nearby areas.

BY BUS   There are several buses from Gothenburg to Helsingborg and Malmö (and vice versa) daily. Trip time from Gothenburg to Helsingborg is 3½ hours; Gothenburg to Malmö, 4½ hours. Several daily buses connect Stockholm and Gothenburg. The trip takes 7 to 8 hours. If you plan to travel by public land transportation, we recommend taking the train—it's cheaper and faster. Gothenburg's bus station is behind the railway station, at Nils Ericson Gate. For information in Gothenburg, call **Swebus,** Sweden's largest bus company (☎ 031/10-38-00).

BY FERRY   The **Stena Line** (☎ 031/704-00-00; www.stenaline.se) has six crossings a day in summer from North Jutland (a 3-hour trip); call for information on departure times, which vary seasonally. The vessels have excellent dining rooms.

Stena offers twice-weekly ferry service between Harwich (England) and Gothenburg. The trip generally takes 24 hours. From June to mid-August, there's also service from Newcastle upon Tyne (England) to Gothenburg once a week, also taking 24 hours. This service is operated by **Scandinavian Seaways** (☎ 031/65-06-50 for information; www.dfdsseaways.se). There's no railpass discount on the England-Sweden crossings.

BY CAR   From either Malmö or Helsingborg, the two major west coast "gateways" to Sweden, take E6 north. Gothenburg is 173 miles north of Malmö and 141 miles north of Helsingborg. From Stockholm, take E4 west to Jonköping and continue on Route 40 the rest of the way via Borås to Gothenburg, a total distance of 292 miles.

VISITOR INFORMATION

The **Gothenburg Tourist Office** is located at Kungsportsplatsen 2 (☎ 031/ 10-07-40; www.goteborg.com). It's open June to August, daily 9am to 6pm; September to May, Monday to Friday 9am to 6pm, Saturday 10am to 2pm.

CITY LAYOUT

Gothenburg's design, with its network of streets separated by canals, is reminiscent of Amsterdam's—not surprisingly, because it was laid out by Dutch architects in the 17th century. Its wealth of parks and open spaces has given it a reputation as Sweden's greenest city.

Some of the old canals have now been filled in, but you can explore the major remaining waterway and the busy harbor—the most important in Sweden—by taking one of the city's famous Paddan sightseeing boats. *Paddan* is the Swedish word for "toad," and the allusion is to the boats' squat shape, which enables them to navigate under the many low bridges. A Paddan service takes you from the point of embarkation, Drottningtorget (near the Central Station), to the Liseberg amusement park. The amusement park is the most popular visitor attraction in the area, with some 3 million visitors annually.

The best place to start sightseeing on foot is Kungsportsavenyn (The Avenyn, or The Avenue), a wide, tree-lined boulevard with many sidewalk cafes. The Avenyn leads to Götaplatsen, a square that's the city's artistic and historic center. Its centerpiece is a huge bronze fountain with a statue of the sea god Poseidon sculpted by Carl Milles.

Gothenburg's old and commercial section lies on either side of the central canal. At the central canal is Gustav Adolfs Torg, dominated by a statue of Gustav himself. Facing the canal is the **Börshuset** (Stock Exchange building). On the western side is the

Rådhuset (Town Hall), originally constructed in 1672. Around the corner, moving toward the river, is the **Kronhuset** (off Kronhusgatan). The 17th-century Dutch-designed building is the oldest in Gothenburg.

Gothenburg is dominated by its harbor, which is best viewed from one of the Paddan boats. The major attraction here is the **Maritime Center** (see "Seeing the Sights," below). The shipyards, whose spidery forms look as though they were constructed from an Erector set, are dominated by the IBM building and other industries. An overhead walkway connects part of the harbor to the shopping mall of Nordstan.

2 Getting Around

Visitors usually find that the cheapest way to explore Gothenburg (except on foot) is to buy a **Göteborgskortet** (Gothenburg Card). Available at hotels, newspaper kiosks, and the city's tourist office, it entitles you to unlimited travel on local trams, buses, and ferries. The card also covers certain sightseeing tours; either free or discounted admission to the city's major museums and sightseeing attractions; discounts at some shops; free parking in some centrally located parking lots; and several other extras, which usually make the card worthwhile. A ticket valid for 24 hours costs 90 SEK ($9.90) for adults, 60 SEK ($6.60) for children; a 48-hour ticket is 180 SEK ($19.80) for adults and 90 SEK ($9.90) for children; and a 72-hour ticket goes for 270 SEK ($29.70) for adults and 135 SEK ($14.85) for children.

BY PUBLIC TRANSPORTATION (TRAM)   A single tram ticket costs 20 SEK ($2.20); a 24-hour travel pass is 60 SEK ($6.60). If you don't have an advance ticket, board the first car of the tram and buy one from the driver. One-way tram tickets are stamped by the driver who sells them to you. Previously purchased tickets must be stamped in the automatic machine as soon as you board the tram.

BY TAXI   Taxis are not as plentiful as you might like. However, you can always find one by going to the Central Station. To call a taxi, dial ☎ **031/27-27-27.** A taxi ride within the city limits now costs 155 to 275 SEK ($17.05 to $30.25). With the Gothenburg Card, you get a 10% reduction.

BY CAR   Because of parking problems, a car is not a practical vehicle for touring Gothenburg. However, the city has good public transportation. You might need a car to tour the surrounding area, but public transportation is available to many sights. **Avis** (☎ **031/80-57-80**) has a rental office at the Central Station and another at the airport (☎ **031/94-60-30**). **Hertz** has an office at in the center of town at Spannmålsgatan 16 (☎ **031/80-37-30**) and one at the airport (☎ **031/94-60-20**). Compare rates and make sure you understand the insurance coverage before you sign a contract.

Fast Facts: Gothenburg

Area Code   The international country code for Sweden is **46;** the city code for Gothenburg is **031** (if you're calling Gothenburg from abroad, drop the zero).

Bookstores   The biggest and most central is **Akademi Bokhandeln,** Norra Hamngatan 32 (☎ **031/61-70-80**).

Business Hours   Generally, shops are open Monday to Friday 9am to 6pm, and Saturday 9am to 2pm; banks, Monday to Friday 9:30am to 3pm; and offices, Monday to Friday 9am to 5pm.

Currency Exchange   Currency can be exchanged at **Forex,** in the Central Station (☎ **031/15-65-16**). There's also a currency-exchange desk at Landvetter Airport, open daily from 8am to 9pm.

Dentists   Call the referral agency **Akuttandkliniken** (☎ **031/80-78-00**) Monday to Friday from 7am to 8pm, Saturday and Sunday 9am to 8pm.

Doctors   If it's not an emergency, your hotel can call a local doctor and arrange an appointment. In an emergency, go to **City Akuten,** Drottninggatan 45 (☎ **031/10-10-10**).

Drugstores   A good pharmacy is **Apoteket Vasen,** Götgatan 12, Nordstan (☎ **031/80-44-10**), open daily 8am to 10pm.

Embassies & Consulates   There is no U.S. consulate in Gothenburg. Citizens of the U.S., Australia, Ireland, and New Zealand must contact their embassy in Stockholm. The **British Consulate,** at Götgatan 15 (☎ **031/13-13-27**), is open Monday to Friday 9am to 1pm and 2 to 4pm.

Emergencies   For nearly all emergencies (fire, police, medical), call ☎ **112.**

Eyeglasses   Go to **Wasa Optik,** Vasaplatsen 7 (☎ **031/711-05-35**). It's open Monday to Friday 9am to 6pm.

Hairdressers & Barbers   A good one is **Salong Noblesse,** Södra Larmgatan 6 (☎ **031/711-71-30**). It's open Monday to Friday 9am to 7pm, Saturday 9am to 3pm.

Internet Access   The city library, **Stadsbibliotek,** Götaplatsen (☎ **031/ 61-65-00**), has free internet access. Open Monday to Thursday 10am to 8pm, Friday 10am to 6pm, and Saturday and Sunday 11am to 4pm. There's also an internet cafe, with at least a dozen internet terminals, at **Game Station,** Kungstorget 1 (☎ **031/711-05-95**).

Laundry & Dry Cleaning   Laundries are hard to find. There's one at **Käärralund Camping,** Olbersgatan (☎ **031/25-27-61**). For dry cleaning, go to **Express Kem,** Drottninggatan 57 (☎ **031/711-22-22**).

Liquor Laws   You must be 18 to consume alcohol in a restaurant, but 20 to purchase alcohol in liquor stores. No alcohol can be served before noon. Most pubs stop serving liquor at 3am, except some nightclubs with a license to stay open later. State-owned liquor shops known as **Systembolag** sell liquor, but only Monday to Friday 9am to 6pm.

Lost Property   Go to the police station (see "Police," below).

Luggage Storage & Lockers   You can store luggage and rent lockers at the **Central Station** (☎ **031/10-44-64**). It's open Monday to Saturday 8am to 8pm.

Photographic Needs   An excellent store is **Arkadens Fotoexpert,** Arkaden 9 (☎ **031/80-20-70**). It's open Monday to Friday 10am to 6pm, Saturday 10am to 2pm.

Police   The main police station is **Polismyndigheten,** Skånegatan 5 (☎ **031/ 61-80-00**).

Post Office   The main post office is at **Drottningtorget 10** (☎ **031/ 62-33-36**), next to the Central Station. It's open Monday to Saturday 10am to 4am.

Radio & TV   Gothenburg has Swedish-language TV broadcasts on TV1, TV2, TV3, and TV4, and receives foreign channels such as Super Sky and BBC broadcasts from London. National radio stations include P1, P2, P3, and P4; Radio Gothenburg broadcasts on 101.9 MHz (FM).

Shoe Repair Try **Norrdvan's Klackbar,** Nyagatan (☎ 031/215-91-02). Repairs are made while you wait.

Taxes Gothenburg imposes no special city taxes other than the value-added tax (*moms*), which applies nationwide.

Telegrams, Telex & Fax To send such communications, go to the post office recommended above.

Transit Information For tram and bus information, call ☎ 031/80-12-35; for train information, call ☎ 031/10-44-45.

3 Accommodations

Reservations are important, but if you need a place to stay on the spur of the moment, try the **Gothenburg Tourist Office,** at Kungsportsplatsen 2 (☎ 031/10-07-40; www.goteborg.com). It lists the city's hotels and boarding houses, and reserves rooms in private homes. Reservations can also be made in advance, by letter or phone. The tourist office charges a booking fee of 60 SEK ($6.60). Double rooms in private homes start at 475 SEK ($52.25). Breakfast is always extra.

The hotels listed below as "Expensive" actually become "Moderate" in price on Friday and Saturday and during the middle of the summer.

EXPENSIVE

Hotel Gothia Towers. Mässans Gata 24, S-402 26 Göteborg. ☎ **031/75-08-800.** Fax 031/18-98-04. www.hotel-gothia.se. E-mail: hotelbok@hotel-gothia.se. 292 units. MINIBAR TV TEL. Mon–Thurs 1,690–1,795 SEK ($185.90–$197.45) double; Fri–Sun 1,140–1,320 SEK ($125.40–$145.20) double. All week long 3,500–4,600 SEK ($385–$506) suite. AE, DC, MC, V. Tram: 4 or 5.

This well-respected four-star hotel, which rises 18 mirror-plated stories above Sweden's largest convention center, was the tallest building in Gothenburg until it was surpassed in the late 1990s by a taller competitor. It opened in 1985 and was renovated in the mid-1990s. The brisk, friendly format places it among Scandinavia's best business-oriented hotels. Rooms are comfortable, contemporary, and tasteful. Touches of wood, particularly the hardwood floors, take the edge off any sense of cookie-cutter standardization. Bathrooms are spacious, with steaming hot water. Rooms on the top three floors are more plush, with enhanced amenities and services. A covered passageway runs directly to the convention center, the largest in Sweden.

Dining/Diversions: The "18th Floor Restaurant" serves lunch and dinner daily. The panoramic pub next door has big-windowed aerial views over the city.

Amenities: Room service (7am to 11pm), sauna, health club, business center, laundry service, and a concierge to arrange virtually anything in and around Gothenburg.

☉ Radisson SAS Park Avenue Hotel. Kungsportsavenyn 36–38, S-400 16 Göteborg. ☎ **800/333-3333** in the U.S., or 031/758-40-00. Fax 031/758-40-01. www.radissonsas. com. E-mail: sales@gotzh.radissonsas.com. 318 units. MINIBAR TV TEL. June 19–Aug 16, 1,455 SEK ($160.05) double; 3,150 SEK ($346.50) suite. Aug 17–June 18, 1,435–2,225 SEK ($157.85–$244.75) double; 3,215 SEK ($353.65) suite. Rates include breakfast. AE, CB, DC, MC, V. Parking 250 SEK ($27.50). Tram: 1, 4, 5, or 6. Bus: 40.

Constructed in 1950 and renovated in 1992, this Radisson property stands on Gothenburg's major boulevard. Everyone from Henry Kissinger to the Beatles, David Rockefeller to the Rolling Stones, has stayed here. The hotel has 10 floors, with attractively designed bedrooms. Upper-floor units enjoy excellent views of the city. The rooms are equipped with work desks, cable TV, and trouser presses. Bathrooms are a bit tiny but equipped with robes and hair dryers; maintenance is high.

Dining/Diversions: The Parkbaren serves lunch, dinner, and light meals throughout the day. The hotel's gourmet dining room, Belle Avenue, is one of the best known in Gothenburg. It specializes in game and fresh fish from the Atlantic. The hotel's famous nightclub, Park Lane, is recommended separately (see "Gothenburg After Dark," below).

Amenities: Room service, SAS Euroclass check-in, valet parking, same-day laundry and dry cleaning; the hotel also maintains a garage, beauty salon, sauna, solarium, newsstand, business service center, Royal Club with separate breakfast lounge.

✪ **Radisson SAS Scandinavia Hotel.** Södra Hamngatan 59–65, S-401 24 Göteborg. ☎ **800/221-2350** in the U.S., or 031/80-60-00. Fax 031/15-98-88. www.radissonsas.com. 344 units. A/C MINIBAR TV TEL. 1,890–2,125 SEK ($207.90–$233.75) double; 2,800–4,800 SEK ($308–$528) suite. Rates include breakfast. AE, DC, MC, V. Parking 215 SEK ($23.65). Tram: 1, 2, 3, 4, 5, or 7. Bus: 40.

This unusual deluxe hotel surrounds a large atrium, which seems like a tree-lined city square indoors. Opposite the railroad station, it's one of the best-run and -equipped hotels in Sweden. Opened in 1986, the hotel offers the finest rooms in town; they're large, with good beds, and luxuriously appointed. Some are suitable for people with disabilities. Bathrooms are small but have hair dryers. The fifth floor of the hotel contains the exclusive concierge rooms with extended service and speedier check-ins. These upgraded accommodations are most often booked by the business community.

Dining/Diversions: The atrium lobby is a restaurant, called Frascati, which serves international cuisine. There's also a piano bar and a small casino in the lobby, open Monday to Saturday 7pm to 1am.

Amenities: Room service (24 hours), laundry, baby-sitting, health club, large swimming pool, Jacuzzi, saunas, solariums, indoor garage.

MODERATE

✪ **Hotel Best Western Eggers.** Drottningtorget, S-401 25 Göteborg. ☎ **800/528-1234** in the U.S. and Canada, or 031/80-60-70. Fax 031/15-42-43. E-mail: hotel.eggers@mailbox. swipnet.se. 79 units. TV TEL. June 29–Aug 6 and Fri–Sat year-round, 925–1,255 SEK ($101.75–$138.05) double; rest of year, 1,640–1,890 SEK ($180.40–$207.90) double. Rates include breakfast. AE, DC, MC, V. Parking 110 SEK ($12.10). Tram: 1, 2, 3, 4, 5, 6, 7, 8, or 9. Bus: 40.

The second-oldest hotel in Gothenburg was built in 1859, predating the Swedish use of the word to describe a building with rooms for travelers. Many emigrants to the New World spent their last night in the old country at the Hotel Eggers, and during the Second World War, the Germans and the Allies met here for secret negotiations. Today it's just as good as or better than ever, with stained-glass windows, ornate staircases, and wood paneling. Rooms vary in size, but they are all individually furnished and beautifully appointed, often with large bathrooms. Only the superior doubles have hair dryers. In the hotel dining room, gilt leather tapestry and polished mahogany evoke the 19th century.

Hotel Onyxen. Sten Sturegatan 23, S-412 52 Göteborg. ☎ **031/81-08-45.** Fax 0321/16-56-72. www.hotelonyxen.com. 34 units. TV TEL. July–Aug and Fri–Sat year-round, 850 SEK ($93.50) double; rest of year, 1,190–1,240 SEK ($130.90–$136.40) double. Extra bed 200 SEK ($22). Rates include breakfast. AE, DC, MC, V. Tram: 4, 5.

Clean, decent, and family-managed, this hotel was originally built around 1900 as a many-balconied apartment house. In the 1980s, its interior was extensively reconfigured into a streamlined and efficiently decorated hotel. Bedrooms have high ceilings, with comfortable beds, and in most cases, a color scheme of white and pale blue. Bathrooms are small but well maintained. There's a residents' pub and cocktail lounge near the lobby, but the only meal served is breakfast.

Hotel Opera. Norra Hamngatan 38, S-411 06 Göteborg. ☎ **031/80-50-80.** Fax 031/ 80-58-17. www.hotelopera.se. 146 units. TV TEL. June 26–Aug 9 and Fri–Sat year-round, 850 SEK ($93.50) double; rest of year, 1,050–1,200 SEK ($115.50–$132) double. Rates include breakfast. AE, DC, MC, V. Parking 115 SEK ($12.65). Tram: 1, 4, 5, 6, 7, 8, or 9.

In 1994, the Hotel Ekoxen joined forces (and facilities) with another hotel to become the Hotel Opera. It's an up-to-date, well-run hotel that often attracts business travelers, although summer visitors gravitate to it as well. Both buildings date from the late 19th century but were upgraded in the 1990s. All rooms are individually designed and tastefully furnished, with firm mattresses. Amenities include such conveniences as trouser presses. The hotel also offers a sauna and Jacuzzi.

Novotel Göteborg. Klippan 1, S-414 51 Göteborg. ☎ **800/221-4542** in the U.S., or 031/ 14-90-00. Fax 031/42-22-32. www.novotel.com. E-mail: hotel.got@novotel.se. 152 units. A/C TV TEL. June 26–Aug 10 and Fri–Sat year-round, 700 SEK ($77) double; 1,190 SEK ($130.90) suite. Rest of year, 1,440 SEK ($158.40) double; 1,790 SEK ($196.90) suite. Rates include breakfast. AE, DC, MC, V. Free parking. From Gothenburg, follow the signs on E20 to Frederikshavn, then the signs to Kiel; exit at Klippan, where signs direct you to the hotel. Tram: 3 or 9. Bus: 91 or 92.

This converted harborfront brewery 2½ miles west of the center is a stylish hotel run by the French hotel conglomerate Accor. Each plushly carpeted room offers panoramic views of the industrial landscape. The room style is Swedish modern, with many built-in pieces, good-sized closets, and firm sofa beds. Bathrooms tend to be small but they do have hair dryers. When it was completed in the 1980s, it was one of the most unusual restorations of a 19th-century building in Sweden. There's a well-accessorized sauna, and laundry facilities are available.

The hotel restaurant, Carnegie Kaj (open until midnight), serves well-prepared food with a French accent. In the summer, snacks and light meals are served on the terrace. The Carnegie Porter Pub is named after the beer that was produced on this site for 160 years.

Panorama Hotel. Eklandagatan 5153, S-400 22 Göteborg. ☎ **800/528-1234** in the U.S. and Canada, or 031/767-70-00. Fax 031/767-70-70. www.panorama.se. E-mail: info@ panorama.se. 338 units, some with shower only. TV TEL. June 20–Aug 10 and Fri–Sat year-round, 890 SEK ($97.90) double; 1,260 SEK ($138.60) suite. Rest of year, 1,490 SEK ($163.90) double; 1,600 SEK ($176) suite. Rates include breakfast. AE, DC, MC, V. Free parking. Closed Dec 21–Jan 7. Tram: 4 or 5. Bus: 40 or 51.

Spacious and dramatic, this 13-story hotel is a 10-minute walk west of the center of town. One of the tallest buildings in Gothenburg, the Panorama is a major hotel that gets surprisingly little publicity. The plant-filled lobby has a skylight, piano bar, and balcony-level restaurant. The bedrooms have stylish furnishings and soft lighting. Amenities include wood floors and double-glazed windows. Bathrooms tend to be small, mostly without tubs. The finest accommodations are found on floors 7 through 13. Only the bathrooms in the superior rooms contain hair dryers. On the premises are a whirlpool, sauna, and solarium.

INEXPENSIVE

Hotel Örgryte. Danska Vägen 68–70, S-416 59 Göteborg. ☎ **031/707-89-00.** Fax 031/ 707-89-99. www.hotelorgryte.se. E-mail: info@hotelorgryte.se. 70 units. TV TEL. Sun–Thurs 1,200–1,290 SEK ($132–$141.90) double; Fri–Sat 700 SEK ($77) double. All week long 1,470–1,670 SEK ($161.70–$183.70) suite. Rates include breakfast. AE, DC, MC, V. Parking 85 SEK ($9.35). Bus: 60 or 62.

Named after the leafy residential district of Örgryte, it lies a mile east of the commercial core of Gothenburg. It was originally built around 1960, and renovated many times since, most recently in the mid-1990s. Rooms were upgraded and outfitted with pastel-colored upholsteries and streamlined, uncomplicated furniture that makes use of birch-veneer woods. Rooms are medium-sized, often big enough to contain a sitting area; mattresses are firm but a bit thin, and bathrooms are rather cramped. Both the exterior and the public areas are clean but not particularly inspired in their design, but overall, the place provides decent, safe accommodations at a relatively reasonable price. On the premises is a restaurant that serves full-meal platters for 75 SEK ($8.25) at lunchtime and 100 SEK ($11) at dinner.

Hotell Royal. Drottninggatan 67, S-411 07 Göteborg. ☎ **031/700-11-70.** Fax 031/700-11-79. www.hotel-royal.com. E-mail: info@hotel-royal.com. 81 units. TV TEL. June 22–Aug 14 and Fri–Sat year-round, 760–910 SEK ($83.60–$100.10) double; 1,200 SEK ($132) suite. Rest of year, 1,200–1,300 SEK ($132–$143) double; 1,695 SEK ($186.45) suite. Rates include buffet breakfast. AE, CB, DC, MC, V. Parking 130 SEK ($14.30) depending on the size of the car. Tram: 1, 2, 3, 4, 5, or 6. Bus: 60.

Founded in 1852, the oldest hotel in Gothenburg still in use is about a quarter mile from the railroad station. All major bus and tram lines pass close by. It's decorated in a typical 19th-century style, with wrought-iron banisters and heavy cast-bronze lamps at the stairs. In the reception area is a unique hand-painted glass ceiling. The rooms are individually designed and modernized, with firm mattresses and ample bathrooms. The breakfast buffet included in the price is generous. The hotel serves a light evening meal, and sandwiches are always available.

Hotel Winn. Gamla Tingstadsgatan 1, S-402 76 Göteborg. ☎ **031/750-1900.** Fax 031/51-21-00. www.winnhotel.com. E-mail: info@winnhotel.com. 121 units. MINIBAR TV TEL. June 15–Aug 15 and Fri–Sat year-round, 840 SEK ($92.40) double; rest of year, 1,140 SEK ($125.40) double. Rates include breakfast. AE, DC, MC, V. Free parking. Bus: 40.

Named after the mythical explorer who circumnavigated the globe in 80 days, this four-story hotel is about 2 miles north of Gothenburg's ferryboat terminal. Functional and modern, its bedrooms are more comfortable than you might have imagined from the uninspired exterior. Each is outfitted in pastel shades, with many amenities. There's a bar, Broken Dreams, frequented by business travelers, and a restaurant (the Hotel Winn Restaurant) serves regional and continental food. Facilities include a swimming pool, sauna, and solarium.

✪ Tidbloms Hotel. Olskroksgatan 23, S-416 66 Göteborg. ☎ **031/707-50-00.** Fax 031/707-50-99. www.tidbloms.com. E-mail: info.tidbloms@swedenhotels.se. 42 units. MINIBAR TV TEL. Sun–Thurs 1,140–1,460 SEK ($125.40–$160.60) double; Fri–Sat 890 SEK ($97.90) double. Rates include breakfast. AE, DC, MC, V. Free parking. Tram: 1, 3, or 6.

Set 2 miles east of Gothenburg's center, in a residential neighborhood filled with other Victorian buildings, this hotel was built in 1897 as a dormitory for Scottish craftsmen imported to work at the nearby lumber mill. Nevertheless, its builders graced it with a conical tower, fancy brickwork, and other architectural adornments that remain in place today. After stints as a warehouse, a delicatessen, and a low-rent hotel, the building was upgraded in 1987 into a cozy, charming, and well-accessorized hotel. Guest rooms have good, firm beds, ample bathrooms, and wooden floors—and have more flair and character than you'll find at many larger, more anonymous hotels in Gothenburg's center. On the premises is a restaurant, which is recommended separately in "Where to Dine," below, and a sauna whose wall paintings and recordings of waves and sea birds were inspired by the sights and sounds of the archipelago. The hotel also offers convention facilities for business meetings and reunions. The most dramatic of these spaces lies under the tower's soaring cone-shaped roof.

4 Dining

EXPENSIVE

Bistro Mannerström. Archivgatan 7. ☎ **031/16-03-33.** Reservations recommended. Main courses 250–300 SEK ($27.50–$33); fixed-price menus 245–270 SEK ($26.95–$29.70). AE, DC, MC, V. Mon–Sat 5–11pm. Closed July. Tram: 4 or 5. SWEDISH.

This place is appealing partly because of the way it celebrates old-fashioned Swedish wholesomeness and old-fashioned Swedish *husmanskost* (home cooking), albeit with a sophisticated and often upscale flair. Despite the high standards it attains, it modestly defines itself as a simple neighborhood restaurant. You'll be seated within one or two white-walled dining rooms whose only color derives from the varnished light-grained woods that permeate the place with a feeling like that of the early 1900s. Menu items are considerably more elegant, and might include poached halibut with a turbot and scallop mousseline; broiled cutlets of turbot with glazed carrots, salsify, and a sauce concocted from red wine, butter, lemon, and rosemary; or breast of wild Swedish duck served with a confit of bacon-flavored purée of potatoes served in a cabbage shell. You might also try fillet of veal with truffle-flavored potatoes and Jerusalem artichokes or grilled and cured brisket of beef with chanterelles, bacon, and spring onions. Expect a clientele of entrepreneurs and corporate leaders, many of whom mingle business with their meals.

Fiskekrogen. Lilla Torget 1. ☎ **031/10-10-05.** Reservations recommended. Main courses 225–325 SEK ($24.75–$35.75); vegetarian menu 395 SEK ($43.45); small menu 595 SEK ($65.45); big menu 795 SEK ($87.45). AE, DC, MC, V. Mon–Fri 11:30am–2pm and 5:30–11pm, Sat 1–11pm. Tram: 2 or 5. SEAFOOD.

One of the most appealing seafood restaurants in Gothenburg occupies a building across the canal from the Stadtsmuseum, in a handsome, internationally modern setting whose sea-green and dark-blue color scheme reflects the colors of the ocean. Fiskekrogen prides itself on a medley of fresh seafood that's artfully displayed and prepared with a zest that earns many loyal customers throughout the city. One of the most appealing aspects of the place is a richly accessorized seafood bar, from which heaping platters of oysters, lobster, crayfish, clams, and mussels are presented, usually with a flourish, at the table. More conventional seafood dishes include poached tournedos of cod with beetroot marmalade and a horseradish-butter sauce; and grilled halibut with a ragoût of baby scallops, bacon, onions, mushrooms, and Zinfandel.

Restaurang Räkan/Yellow Submarine. Lorensbergsgatan 16. ☎ **031/16-98-39.** Reservations recommended. Main courses 175–265 SEK ($19.25–$29.15). AE, DC, MC, V. Tram: 1, 4, 5, or 6. Bus: 40. SEAFOOD.

This is one of Gothenburg's best seafood restaurants. It naturally has a nautical decor with buoy lamps, wooden-plank tables typical of the Swedish west coast, and a shallow-bottomed re-creation of a Swedish lake. Your seafood platter arrives on a battery-powered boat with you directing the controls. You can order various combinations of crayfish (in season), along with prawns, poached sole, mussels, lobster, fillet of gray sole, and fresh crabs. If you don't want fish, a choice of chicken and beef dishes is available. Attached to the restaurant is a popular pub, Yellow Submarine, named for the Beatles song by the same name.

✪ Restaurant 28+. Götabergsgaten 28. ☎ **031/20-21-61.** Reservations recommended. Fixed-price menus 655–755 SEK ($72.05–$83.05); main courses 245–325 SEK ($26.95–$35.75). AE, DC, MC, V. Mon–Wed 6–10pm, Thurs–Sat 6–11pm. Bus: 40. Tram: 1, 4, 5, or 6. INTERNATIONAL.

Cozy, intimate, and reeking of Old-World charm, this is a chic and stylish restaurant whose trio of dining rooms are lit with flickering candles and capped with soaring masonry ceiling vaults. It's one of the city's hippest culinary venues, featuring main courses that include cooked crayfish with a fennel-flavored *nage;* smoked fillet of char in a red wine and butter sauce; grilled breast of pigeon, or saddle of reindeer with Jerusalem artichokes and blackberry vinaigrette. We have consistently found that the finest—and most imaginative—cuisine in Gothenburg is served here. The items taste fabulously fresh, and the food is handled faultlessly in the kitchen and delicately seasoned. The service is the city's best, and the sommelier will offer expert guidance, although you'll feel that the tax on wine is so high that you're putting someone's kid through college. The most demanding palates in Gothenburg go here and come away satisfied.

✪ **Sjömagasinet.** Klippans Kulturreservat. ☎ **031/775-59-20.** Reservations recommended. Main courses 270–345 SEK ($29.70–$37.95); 1-course fixed-price lunch 105 SEK ($11.55); 3-course fixed-price dinner 410–545 SEK ($45.10–$59.95). AE, DC, MC, V. Mon–Fri 11:30am–11pm, Sat 5–11pm, Sun 2–9pm. From the town center, head west on E3, following the signs to Frederikshavn, and then to Kiel; exit at Klippan and then follow the signs for the Novotel. Tram: 3 or 9. SEAFOOD.

By far the most interesting and intriguing restaurant in town, Sjömagasinet is located near the Novotel in the western suburb of Klippan, about 2½ miles from the center. The building, erected in 1775, was originally a warehouse. It contains a bar in cozy English colonial style, and another bar in the eyrie.

Very fresh seafood is served here, evidenced in the shrimp-stuffed crêpes with dill, shellfish with curry sauce, baked fillet of beef and lobster, poached fillet of sole with crayfish, and turbot béarnaise. Two very special dishes are the pot-au-feu of fish and shellfish, served with a chive-flavored crème fraîche and poached fillet of halibut with warm cabbage salad and potato salad.

MODERATE

A Hereford Beefstouw. Linnégatan. ☎ **031/775-04-41.** Reservations recommended. Main courses 115–285 SEK ($12.65–$31.35); salad bar as a main course 80 SEK ($8.80). AE, DC, MC, V. Mon–Fri 11:30am–2pm and 5–10pm, Sat 4–11pm, Sun 3–9pm. Tram: 1, 3, 4, 9. STEAKS.

This is the most appealing and best-recommended steakhouse in Gothenburg, with a reputation for well-prepared Australian beef, and a salad bar that's the most varied and copious in town. One of the three separate dining rooms is smoke-free, and all have thick-topped wooden tables, lots of varnished pine, and touches of African oak. The only sauces available to accompany your beef are béarnaise-butter sauce, parsley butter sauce, and garlic butter sauce. The management believes in allowing the flavor of the meat to come through, unmasked by more elaborate seasonings. The largest platter is a 500-gram (17½ ounce) T-bone steak, a portion so large that we advise you to finish it at your own risk. Other platters, such as fillet steaks, veal sirloins, or tenderloins, are more reasonably sized. A full list of wines and beers can accompany your meal.

Brasserie Lipp. Kungsportsavenyn 8. ☎ **031/711-50-58.** Reservations required. Main courses 155–198 SEK ($17.05–$21.80); daily platters 85 SEK ($9.35). AE, DC, MC, V. Daily 11:30am–11:30pm. Tram: 1, 4, 5, or 6. Bus: 40. SWEDISH/FRENCH.

Located on Gothenburg's busiest avenue, this brasserie was established in 1987, inspired by the legendary Left Bank bistro in Paris, with palate adjustments for Swedish tastes. Its good food is a combination of French and Swedish—for example, escargots in garlic-butter sauce, Lipp's Skagen toast (piled high with shrimp), Swedish entrecôte of beef with Dijon mustard sauce, grilled halibut with garlic-tomato sauce, carpaccio of beef, and Thai chicken. There's also *choucroute garnie* (sauerkraut with sausage and pork, the most famous dish served at its Paris namesake) and many different kinds of fish, most caught in the waters near Gothenburg.

La Gondola. Kungsportsavenyn 4. ☎ **031/711-68-28.** Reservations recommended. Main courses 85–210 SEK ($9.35–$23.10); *dagens* (daily) lunch 70–80 SEK ($7.70–$8.80). AE, DC, MC, V. Daily 11:30am–11pm. Tram: 1, 4, 5, or 6. Bus: 38 or 75. ITALIAN.

This restaurant evokes Venice with its striped poles, sidewalk awnings, and summer outdoor cafe. It makes the best pizzas in town and does a lively business. There's also an elaborate menu with many classic Italian dishes. The spaghetti Gondola is very good, and the saltimbocca ("jump in your mouth") alla romana, a veal-and-ham dish, is tasty. You might also try one of the grilled specialties including a tender, juicy steak. The minestrone is freshly made and filling, and a velvet-smooth ice cream is served. Every day there's a different lunch special and an à la carte dinner.

Lilla London. Avenyn/Vasagatan 41. ☎ **031/18-40-62.** Reservations recommended. Main courses 100–210 SEK ($11–$23.10). AE, DC, MC, V. Daily 5pm–midnight. Tram: 1, 4, 5, or 6. Bus: 40. SWEDISH/FRENCH.

The quiet, publike atmosphere is a local favorite. The restaurant, down a flight of steps, is dark and attractively designed, with illuminated paintings of clipper ships and nautical accents. Full meals might include grilled chicken with morels, beef and lamb fillet in a mustard-flavored cream sauce, fillet mignon, or broiled salmon with fresh asparagus. This is a good, standard fare, nothing more, prepared with fresh ingredients and selling for a fair price. Less expensive light meals are also available. The pub sells about 10 different kinds of beer.

Restaurang Gillestugan. Järntorget 6. ☎ **031/24-00-50.** Reservations recommended. Main courses 82–185 SEK ($9–$20.35); fixed-price menus 250–275 SEK ($27.50–$30.25). AE, DC, MC, V. Daily 11:30am–2pm and 5–11:30pm; bar, Sun–Thurs 11am–1am, Fri–Sat 11am–3am. Entertainment 9–11pm. Tram: 1, 3, 4, and 9. SWEDISH/INTERNATIONAL.

Local entrepreneurs put a new spin on one of Gothenburg's most nostalgic restaurants, the Gillestugan (ca. 1918), in the mid-1990s. They transformed the antique-looking establishment into the city's busiest and most creative cabaret and supper club—though the street-level bar, the Tullen Pub, remains. Throughout most of the day, you can drop in for a meal and a drink and be entertained only by whomever you happen to be dining with and the good-natured, hard-working staff.

But one floor above street level, every evening from 9 to 11pm, a revolving series of musical, theatrical, or poetic events takes over the small stage. Recent examples have included folk singers whose repertoire is in both Swedish and English, and an Elvis impersonator whose act has drawn rave reviews from local residents who insist he's better than the real thing. Some of the entertainment involves Swedish-language satire, so phone in advance to avoid any production that's simply too esoteric.

If you do opt to attend, food is well prepared and served in generous portions, and there's no cover charge for the entertainment. Menu items include salmon tartare with horseradish sauce and fried onions; a mushroom and apple terrine with air-dried ham and spicy oil; and fillet of lamb with tomato and feta-cheese sauce, and baked, sliced, and fried potatoes.

INEXPENSIVE

Froken Olssons Café. Östra Larmgatan 14. ☎ **031/13-81-93.** Coffee 16 SEK ($1.75); *dagens* (daily) menu 58 SEK ($6.40); hot pies with salad 50 SEK ($5.50); sandwiches 20–50 SEK ($2.20–$5.50). MC, V. Mon–Thurs 9am–10pm, Fri 9am–1am. Tram: 1, 4, 5, or 6. Bus: 40. SWEDISH.

Perfect Picnics

Go to Saluhallen, Kungstorget, for the makings of an elegant picnic. Built in 1888, this is the city's colorful indoor market. Shops sell meat, fruit, vegetables, and delicatessen products. You can buy, for example, quail and all sorts of game, including moose and reindeer, and even lamb from Iceland. The produce (including exotic fruit) comes from all over the world. Bread, coffee, olives, and pâtés are also sold. There are, in addition, four restaurants and one coffee bar in the building. Much of the food is already cooked and can be packaged for you to take out. The hall is open Monday to Thursday 9am to 6pm, Friday 8am to 6pm, and Saturday 8am to 1pm. Take tram no. 1, 4, 5, or 6 to Kungsportsplatsen.

Take your picnic basket to any of Gothenburg's major parks (see "Parks & Gardens," in "Seeing the Sights," below). Trädgårdsföreningen, across from the Central Station, is especially pleasant, although there's a 10 SEK ($1.10) entrance fee.

Less than 2 blocks from The Avenyn, this is a traditional favorite with Gothenburgers. It tends to be crowded and noisy at lunchtime. Even though there's a large interior, the seating overflows onto an outdoor terrace in summer. At night, hot pies with a salad are featured, and you can also order baguette sandwiches filled with such ingredients as shrimp or ham and cheese. Light beer is served, but no wine or liquor. Basically, it's light cafe dining, with homemade soups and such main courses as entrecôte.

Solrosen (Sunflower). Kaponjärgatan 4. ☎ **031/711-66-97.** Main courses 50–110 SEK ($5.50–$12.10). AE, DC, MC, V. Mon–Fri 11:30am–1am, Sat 2pm–1am. Tram: 1, 3, or 4. VEGETARIAN.

In the Haga district, a low-rise neighborhood of 18th-century and early 19th-century buildings, this is the best vegetarian restaurant in Gothenburg. You serve yourself at the counter, with an all-you-can-eat salad bar that accompanies the main dishes. There's unlimited coffee and second helpings. Beer and wine are available.

Tapas Bar & Brasserie. Kungsgatan 8. ☎ **031/711-3077.** Reservations recommended on weekends. Main courses 60–130 SEK ($6.60–$14.30). AE, MC, V. Daily 5–11pm. Bar, daily 5pm–1am. Tram: 1, 4, or 5. INTERNATIONAL.

Many of the clients who drop in here don't ever move on to a table, remaining instead at a bar that can get busy with the singles crowd as the night progresses. But if you do get hungry, the blue-and-white dining room will present a relatively inexpensive and unpretentious roster of well-prepared dishes that include a tomato and onion salad garnished with shrimp and scallops; sea bass in teriyaki sauce; chicken breast with chili sauce; and well-prepared steaks.

✪ **Tidbloms Restaurang.** Olskroksgatan 23. ☎ **031/707-50-00.** Main courses 149–199 SEK ($16.40–$21.90); fixed-price menus 80–190 SEK ($8.80–$20.90). AE, DC, MC, V. Mon–Fri 11:30am–1:30pm and 6–10pm, Sat 4–10pm, Sun 1–8pm. Tram: 1, 3, or 6. INTERNATIONAL.

Set near the lobby of the recommended Tidbloms Hotel, this restaurant is particularly charming, thanks to the staff that works hard to keep things personalized. In the wood-paneled dining room, you can order well-seasoned dishes that include cream of chanterelle soup; seafood medley on toast; African-style beef in a piquant peanut sauce; salmon in a saffron-flavored cream sauce; and a combination of pork and beef prepared Provençal style with red wine and Lyonnaise potatoes.

5 Seeing the Sights

SUGGESTED ITINERARIES

IF YOU HAVE 1 DAY   Enjoy a cup of coffee at one of the cafes along The Avenyn in the center of Gothenburg; then take the classical Paddan boat ride, traveling through the moat and canal out to the harbor and the giant docks. Return for a stroll along The Avenyn, and then take one of the summertime vintage trams to see part of the city ashore. Go to Liseberg amusement park in the evening. Winter visitors can explore some of Gothenburg's numerous museums, including the Röhsska Museum of Arts and Crafts, the Göteborg Maritime Center, and the East India House.

IF YOU HAVE 2 DAYS   On the first day, follow the suggestions above. On Day 2, take a boat trip to Elfsborg Fortress, leaving from Stenpiren in the Gothenburg harbor, and continuing under the Älvsborg Bridge to Elfsborg. In the afternoon, visit the Göteborgs Konstmuseum and the Botanical Garden.

IF YOU HAVE 3 DAYS   For the first 2 days, follow the itinerary suggested above. On Day 3, get up early to visit the fish auction at the harbor (it begins at 7am), then go to the nearby Feskekörka (Fish Church). Take tram no. 6 to Guldhedens Våttentorn (water tower) for a panoramic view of Gothenburg. Go to Götaplatsen to see the famed Poseidon fountain by Carl Milles. In the afternoon, visit the Röhsska Museum of Arts and Crafts and stroll through the rose-filled Trädgårdsföreningen, across from the Central Station.

IF YOU HAVE 4 OR 5 DAYS   For Days 1 to 3, follow the itinerary suggested above. On Day 4, take an excursion to Marstrand, north of the city. On Day 5, visit Nordstan, the biggest shopping center in Scandinavia. Spend the rest of the day exploring the southern archipelago, which you can do free with your Gothenburg Card (see "Getting Around," above). The MS *Styrsö* and the steamboat *Bohuslän* depart from Skeppsbron/Stenpiren for trips around the archipelago.

THE TOP ATTRACTIONS

For a quick orientation to Gothenburg, visit the 400-foot-tall **Guldhedens Våttentorn** (water tower), Syster Estrids Gata (☎ **031/82-00-09**); take tram no. 6 or 7 from the center of the city, about a 10-minute ride. The elevator ride up the tower is free, and there's a cafeteria/snack bar on top. The tower is open May to September daily noon to 10pm.

Early risers can visit the daily fish auction at the harbor, the largest fishing port in Scandinavia. The entertaining sale begins at 7am sharp. You can also visit the Feskekörka (Fish Church), on Rosenlundsgatan, which is in the fish market. The Feskekörka is not a church at all—rather, its architectural outline evokes one. It's open Tuesday to Friday 9am to 5pm, Saturday 9am to 1pm.

For a look at Gothenburg, the traditional starting point is the cultural center, Götaplatsen. Its Poseidon fountain is the work of Carl Milles, one of Sweden's most important sculptors. The big trio of buildings here is the Concert Hall, the municipally owned theater, and the Göteborgs Konstmuseum.

Göteborgs Konstmuseum. Götaplatsen. ☎ **031/61-29-80.** Admission 45 SEK ($4.95) adults, 15 SEK ($1.65) children 7–16, free for children under 7. May–Aug, Mon–Fri 11am–4pm, Sat Sun 11am 5pm; Sept–Apr, Tues and Thurs–Fri 11am–4pm, Wed 11am–9pm, Sat–Sun 11am–5pm. Tram: 4 or 5. Bus: 40.

Göteborgs Konstmuseum is the city's leading art museum of Gothenburg, with a good collection of modern artworks, notably by the French Impressionists. Bonnard,

Cézanne, van Gogh, and Picasso are represented, along with sculptures by Milles and Rodin. The gallery is noted for its collection of the works of 19th- and 20th-century Scandinavian artists (Zorn and Larsson of Dalarna, Edvard Munch and Christian Krohg of Norway). Old masters, including Rembrandt and Rubens, are also represented. The modern section includes works by Francis Bacon and Henry Moore.

Liseberg Park. Korsvägen. ☎ **031/40-01-00,** or 031/40-02-20 for daily programs and times. Admission 45 SEK ($4.95) adults, free for children under 7. June–Aug, Mon–Fri 3–11pm, Sat 11am–midnight, Sun 11am–10pm; Sept–Nov, Fri 5–11pm, Sat 11am–midnight, Sun 11am–10pm. Tram: 4 or 5 from the city.

With 3 million visitors a year, Liseberg Park is the number-one tourist attraction in Sweden. Since 1923 it has been the largest amusement park in Scandinavia. For dining, nightlife, and entertainment in general, Gothenburgers head for this pleasure garden of fountains, pavilions, and flowers. The festively lit park comes alive with music, artists, dances, dozens of rides, and open-air vaudeville shows on seven stages. The park's complicated daily schedule is announced yearly. It's generally open on some days in April, daily from May through August, and weekends in September.

Röhsska Museum of Arts and Crafts. Vasagatan 37–39. ☎ **031/61-38-50.** Admission 25 SEK ($2.75) adults, 5 SEK (55¢) children 7–16, free for children under 7. May–Aug, Mon–Fri noon–4pm, Sat–Sun noon–5pm; Sept–Apr, Tues noon–9pm, Wed–Fri noon–4pm, Sat–Sun noon–5pm. Closed Aug 15–Sept 21. Tram: 1, 4, 5, 6, or 8. Bus: 40.

This museum houses a large collection of European furnishings, china, glass, and pottery, and Asian artifacts. It mounts permanent and temporary exhibits of modern handcrafts and industrial design. Among the exhibits are books, silver, and Chinese and Japanese art. The museum presents lecture series and guided tours.

Göteborg Maritime Center. Packhujkajem 8. ☎ **031/10-59-50.** Admission 70 SEK ($5.50) adults, 25 SEK ($2.75) children 7–15, free for children under 7. July, daily 10am–9pm; May–June and Aug, daily 10am–6pm; Mar–Apr and Sept–Nov, daily 10am–4pm. Closed Dec–Feb. Tram: 5 to Lilla Bommen.

Located on the harbor, this museum is partly aboard the destroyer *Småland,* which is equipped with guns and torpedoes. In authentic settings, you can see lightships, steamships, and tugboats, among other watercraft. There are cafes at the center and on the quay.

East India House (Museum of Gothenburg). Norra Hamngatan 12. ☎ **031/61-27-70.** Admission 40 SEK ($4.40) adults, 10 SEK ($1.10) children 7–14, free for children under 7. June–Aug, daily 11am–4pm; Sept–May, Tues–Sun 11am–4pm. Tram: 1 or 9. Bus: 40, 58, or 60 to Brunnsparken.

This museum focuses on the history of Gothenburg and its environs—archaeological, cultural, technical, and medical. It has an array of interesting permanent exhibits, including displays from the Viking era and unique artifacts found in the area.

Stadsbibliotek. Götaplatsen. ☎ **031/61-65-00.** Free admission. Mon–Fri 10am–8pm, Sat–Sun 11am–5pm. Tram: 1, 4, 5, or 6. Bus: 40.

Toward the end of The Avenyn is the public library, on the left at Götaplatsen. This is the city's main library, the home of some 450,000 volumes in 50 languages, and a cafe. The library also has a listening room with recorded music, and a reading room with more than 100 foreign daily newspapers. One hall features continuously changing exhibits.

Gothenburg Attractions

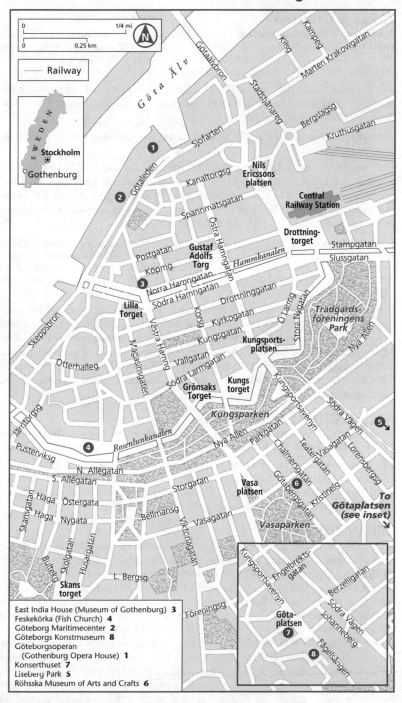

Railway

Sweden
★ Stockholm
○ Gothenburg

Göta Älv

Götaälvbron

Götaleden

Sjofarten

Kanaltorgsg

Spannmatsgatan

Nils Ericssons platsen

Central Railway Station

Stadstjänareg

Bergslagsg

Kruthusgatan

Kltsg

Kampeg

Marten Krakowgatan

Postgatan

Gustaf Adolfs Torg

Köpmg

Östra Hamngatan

Hammkanalen

Drottning-torget

Stampgatan

Slussgatan

Norra Hamngatan

Södra Hamngatan

Drottninggatan

Kyrkogatan

Store Nygatan

Ö. Larmg

Trädgards-föreningens Park

Nya Allén

Lilla Torget

Korsg

Kungsgatan

Vallgatan

Kungsports-platsen

Södra Larmgatan

Kungs torget

Grönsaks Torget

Kungsparken

Kungsportsavenyn

Södra Vägen

Skeppsbron

Otterhalleg

Macasinsgatan

Västra Hamng

Jämtorgsg

Rosenlunkanalen

Nya Allén

Parkgatan

Chalmersgatan

Teatergatan

Vasagatan

Lorensbergg

Pusterviksg

N. Allégatan

S. Allégatan

Storgatan

Vasa platsen

Göteborgsgatan

Kristinelg

To Götaplatsen (see inset)

Skansgatan

Haga

Östergata

Haga

Nygata

Bellmansg

Vasagatan

Vasaparken

Viktoriagatan

Skolgatan

Husargatan

Bultekg

L. Bergsg

Skans torget

Föreningsg

Kungsportsavenyn

Engelbrekts-gatan

Berzeligatan

Götaplatsen ❼

Södra Vägen

Johanneberg

Fågelsången

❽

East India House (Museum of Gothenburg) **3**
Feskekörka (Fish Church) **4**
Göteborg Maritimecenter **2**
Göteborgs Konstmuseum **8**
Göteborgsoperan
  (Gothenburg Opera House) **1**
Konserthuset **7**
Liseberg Park **5**
Röhsska Museum of Arts and Crafts **6**

PARKS & GARDENS

Botaniska Trädgården (Botanical Garden). Carl Skottsbergsgata 22. ☎ **031/ 741-11-00.** Free admission to garden; greenhouses, 20 SEK ($2.20) adults, free for children under 17. Garden, daily 9am–sunset. Greenhouses, May–Aug, daily 10am–5pm; Sept–Apr, daily 10am–4pm. Tram: 1, 2, or 7.

The Botanical Garden lies opposite Slottsskogen Park in southern Gothenburg. It features trees and shrubs from Asia, rock gardens, orchids, and greenhouses. The rhododendrons bloom in May and June.

Slottsskogen. Near Linnéplatsen. ☎ **031/61-18-90.** Free admission. Daily 24 hours. Tram: 1 or 2 to Linnéplatsen.

At 274 acres, this is the largest park in Gothenburg. Laid out in 1874 in a naturally wooded area, today it has beautiful walks, animal enclosures, a saltwater pool, bird ponds, and an aviary. The children's zoo is open May to August. A variety of events and entertainment take place here in the summer. There's an outdoor cafe at the zoo, and restaurants at Villa Bel Park and Björngårdsvillan.

Trädgårdsföreningen. Entrances on Slussgatan (across from the Central Station) and Södra Vägen. ☎ **031/61-18-83.** Park, 15 SEK ($1.65) adults, free for children under 17, free for everyone Sept–Apr; Palm House, 20 SEK ($2.20) adults and children; Butterfly House, 35 SEK ($3.85) adults, 10 SEK ($1.10) children. May–Aug, daily 7am–9pm; Sept–Apr, daily 7am–7:30pm.

Across the canal from the Central Station, this park boasts a large rosarium that flourishes with about 10,000 rose bushes of 4,000 different species. The park's centerpiece is the Palm House, a greenhouse maintained at subtropical temperatures even in the depths of winter. The Butterfly House contains winged insects of great beauty that flutter through a simulation of a natural habitat. The city of Gothenburg sometimes hosts exhibits, concerts (occasionally during the lunch hour), and children's theater pieces in the park.

ARCHITECTURAL HIGHLIGHTS

Drottning Kristinas Jaktslott (Queen Christina's Hunting Lodge). Ötterhallegatan 16. ☎ **031/13-34-26.** Free admission. Daily 11am–4pm. Tram: 2, 3, 4, or 7 to Lilla Torget.

The oldest dwelling in Gothenburg, the hunting lodge was saved from demolition in 1971 by the Ötterhallen Historical Preservation Society and the Historical Museum. Today you can visit this 17th-century hunting lodge and enjoy coffee and waffles in its old-world atmosphere. Waffles cost 30 SEK ($3.30) and up.

ORGANIZED TOURS

A sightseeing boat trip along the canals and out into the harbor will show you the old parts of central Gothenburg and take you under 20 bridges and out into the harbor. ✪ **Paddan Sightseeing Boats** (☎ **031/60-96-70**) offers 55-minute tours May to September 15, daily 10am to 5pm; September 12 to October 6, daily noon to 3pm. They leave from the terminal at Kungsportsplatsen in the city center. The fare is 75 SEK ($8.25) for adults, 50 SEK ($5.50) for children 4 to 15, and free for kids under 4. A family ticket for (two adults and two children) costs 195 SEK ($21.45).

Nya Elfsborg (☎ **031/10-07-40**) is docked in the 17th-century fortress at the harbor's mouth. This boat takes you from Lilla Bommen on a 90-minute tour through the harbor to and around Elfsborg Fortress, built in the 17th century to protect the Göta Älv estuary and the western entrance to Sweden. It still bears traces of hard-fought sea battles against the Danes. Carvings on the prison walls tell tales of the threats and hopes of the 19th-century lifetime prisoners. A guide will be waiting for you at the cafeteria, museum, and souvenir shop. There are five departures a day from mid-May to the end of August. The fare is 75 SEK ($8.25) for adults, 45 SEK ($4.95) for children.

MS *Poseidon* is available for an evening cruise of the archipelago. For information about available tours, check with the tourist office (see "Visitor Information," above), or **Bohus Line** (☎ 031/13-30-37), which provides excursion packages, brochures, tickets, and timetables. The tour costs 325 SEK ($35.75) for adults and 170 SEK ($18.70) children 6 to 12. The 4-hour trip departs at 7pm.

For a guided 90-minute **bus tour** of Gothenburg, go to the tourist office (see "Visitor Information," above) or call ☎ 031/60-96-70 for details. City tours are offered daily from May to September. The fare is 125 SEK ($13.75) for adults, 85 SEK ($9.35) for children. Tours last 1½ hours. A combined 2-hour bus and boat tour, costs 225 SEK ($24.75) for adults, 110 SEK ($12.10) for children.

6 Especially for Kids

At **Liseberg Park** (see "The Top Attractions," above), every day is children's day. The Liseberg Cirkus is a fun fair, and there are always actors in animal costumes to play with children. The pony merry-go-round, children's boats, and a fun-on-wheels ride are all free for tots.

Your children might want to stay at the amusement park's hotel, in the city center, a short walk from the park. **Hotel Liseberg Heden,** Sten Sturegatan S-411 38 Göteborg (☎ 031/750-69-109; fax 031/750-69-30; www.liseberg.se), offers discounted summer rates. They include breakfast and coupons for free admission to the amusement park and many of its rides and shows. Between May and September, the discounted rate for double rooms is 850 SEK ($93.50). From October to April, doubles cost 840 SEK ($92.40) Friday through Sunday, and 1,190 SEK ($130.90) Monday through Thursday. The hotel accepts major credit cards (American Express, Diners Club, MasterCard, Visa). It was built in the 1930s as an army barracks and later functioned as a youth hostel. Today, after tons of improvements, it's a first-class, very comfortable hotel. To reach the 172-room hotel, take tram no. 4 or 5 to Berzeliegatan.

Naturhistoriska Museet I Göteborg, Slottsskogen (☎ 031/775-24-00), displays stuffed animals from all over the world, including Sweden's only stuffed blue whale. It's open Tuesday to Friday 9am to 6pm, and Saturday and Sunday 11am to 5pm. Admission is 40 SEK ($4.40) for adults, 10 SEK ($1.10) for ages 7 to 20, and free for children under 7. To reach the museum, you can use tram lines 1, 2, or 6, or bus lines 51 or 54 to Linnéplatsen.

There's also a children's zoo at Slottsskogen from May to August (see "Parks & Gardens," above).

7 Shopping

THE SHOPPING SCENE
Many residents of Copenhagen and Helsingør come to Gothenburg just for the day to buy Swedish merchandise. You can, too, but you should shop at the stores bearing the yellow-and-blue tax-free shopping sign. These stores are scattered throughout Gothenburg. If your purchases in one of these stores total more than 200 SEK ($22), you're entitled to a tax refund. You must pay the tax along with the purchase price, but then ask for a tax-refund voucher before leaving the store. You'll get a tax refund, minus a small service charge, when you clear customs as you leave Sweden. You're not permitted to use your purchase in Sweden, and you must take it out of the country within 1 month of purchase.

MAJOR SHOPPING DISTRICTS Nordstan, with its 150 shops and stores, restaurants, hotel, pâtisseries, coffee shops, banks, travel agencies, and the post office, is the largest shopping mall in Scandinavia (call the main tourist office for more information). You can find almost anything, ranging from exclusive clothing boutiques to outlets for the major confectionery chains to bookshops. There's also a tourist information center. Most shops here are open Monday to Friday 9:30am to 7pm, and Saturday 9:30am to 4pm.

Kungsgatan and **Fredsgatan** make up Sweden's longest pedestrian mall (2 miles in length). The selection of shops is big and varied. Near these two streets, you'll also find some smaller shopping centers, including Arkaden, Citypassagen, and Kompassen.

At **Grönsakstorget** and **Kungstorget,** you'll see flowers, fruits, handcrafts, and jewelry, among other items, arranged on little trolleys. They're right in the city center, a throwback perhaps to the Middle Ages.

The oft-mentioned **Avenyn,** with its many restaurants and cafes, also has a number of stores selling merchandise of interest to visitors.

Kronhusbodarna, Kronhusgatan 1D (☎ **031/711-08-32**), one of the city's architectural showpieces, was originally built in the 1650s; it's the oldest non-ecclesiastical building in town. In the 1660s, it was pressed into service as the meeting place for the Swedish Parliament, which convened hastily to welcome a visit from Charles X Gustav during his wars with Denmark. For many years, the building functioned as a military warehouse and repair center, stockpiling sailcloth and armaments. Today its echoing interior accommodates a number of small-scale and rather sleepy studios for glass-blowers, watchmakers, potters, and coppersmiths. Some sell their goods to passersby. You can visit the studios, if the artisans happen to show up. Take tram no. 1 or 7 to Brunnsparken.

SHOPPING A TO Z
DEPARTMENT STORES
Bohusslöjds. Kungsportsavenyn 25. ☎ **031/16-00-72.** Bus: 40.

This store has one of the best collections of Swedish handcrafts in Gothenburg. Amid a light-grained birch decor, you'll find wrought-iron chandeliers, unusual wallpaper, and fabric by the yard. Other items, ideal as gifts or souvenirs, include hand-woven rugs, pine and birch bowls, and assorted knickknacks.

C. J. Josephssons Glas & Porslin. Korsgatan 12. ☎ **031/17-56-15.** Tram: 1, 2, 3, 4, 5, or 7. Bus: 60.

This store has been selling Swedish glass since 1866 and has established an enviable reputation. The selection of Orrefors crystal and porcelain is stunning. It carries signed original pieces by such well-known designers as Bertil Vallien and Goran Warff. There's a tourist tax-free shopping service, plus full shipping service.

Nordiska Kompaniet (NK). Östra Hamngatan 42. ☎ **031/710-10-00.** Bus: 40.

Since this is a leading department store, shoppers are likely to come here first. The store stocks typical Swedish and Scandinavian articles. It carries more than 200,000 items, ranging from Kosta Boda "sculpture" crystal, Orrefors crystal in all types and shapes, Rorstrand high-fired earthenware and fine porcelain, stainless steel, pewter items, dolls in national costume, leather purses, Dalarna horses, Finnish carpeting, books about Sweden, Swedish records, and much, much more. The store's packing specialists will ship your purchases home. There's another NK in Stockholm (see "Shopping," in Chapter 14, "Exploring Stockholm").

FASHION

Gillblad's. Kungsgatan 44. ☎ **031/10-88-46.** Tram: 1, 2, or 3.

This fashion outlet is known for its high-quality, well-made clothing for men and women. It's especially noted for men's and women's business suits. The inventory is tasteful, and not too flashy, which is just the way many of its long-standing clients like it.

Hennes & Mauritz. Kungsgatan 55–57. ☎ **031/711-00-11.** Tram: 1, 2, or 3.

Established in the 1940s, this is a well-established women's clothing store that keeps an eye on cutting-edge fashion capitals in other parts of the world. The store and spirit here are trendy, with an emphasis on what might make a woman look as appealing and youthful as possible for a very cool night out on the town. Despite their immediate sense of international flair, garments are less expensive than you might have thought, with lots of cost-conscious bargains. The same outfit maintains a menswear store a few storefronts away at no. 61 up the street at Kungsgatan 61 (☎ **031/711-00-32**).

Ströms. Kungsgatan 27–29. ☎ **031/17-71-00.** Tram: 1, 2, or 3.

This is the most visible men's clothing emporium in Gothenburg, with a history that stretches back to 1886. Scattered over two floors of retail space, you'll find garments that range from the very formal to the very casual, and boutique-inspired subdivisions with ready-to-wear garments from Europe's leading fashion houses. It also sells women's and children's clothing, but most of its fame and reputation derives from its appeal to men.

HANDCRAFTS

Aside from some of the markets and streets already mentioned, the following establishments also specialize in handcrafts.

Lerverk. Västra Hamngatan 24 26. ☎ **031/13-13-49.** Tram: 1, 2, 3, 4, or 7 to Grönsakstorget.

This is a permanent exhibit center for 30 potters and glassmaking craftspeople.

8 Gothenburg After Dark

If Swedish dinner theater interests you, see **Restaurang Gillestugan** under "Dining," above.

To the Gothenburgers, there's nothing more exciting than sitting outdoors at a cafe along The Avenyn enjoying the short-lived summer. Residents also like to take the whole family to the **Liseberg Park** (see "The Top Attractions," above). Although clubs are open in the summer, they're not well patronized until the cool weather sets in.

For a listing of entertainment events scheduled at the time of your visit, check the newspapers or inquire at the tourist office.

THE PERFORMING ARTS
THEATER

The Gothenburg Card (see "Getting Around," above) allows you to buy two tickets for the price of one. Call the particular theater or the tourist office for program information. Performances are also announced in the newspapers.

Folkteatern. Olof Palmes Plats (byat Järntorget). ☎ **031/60-75-75.** Tickets 80 110 SEK ($8.80–$12.10). Tram: 1, 3, 4, or 9.

This theater stages productions of Swedish plays or foreign plays translated into Swedish. The season is from September to May, and performances are Tuesday to Friday at 7pm and Saturday at 6pm.

Stadsteatern. Götaplatsen. ☎ **031/61-50-50.** Tickets 120–160 SEK ($13.20–$17.60). Bus: 40.

This is one of Gothenburg's major theaters, but the plays are performed in Swedish only. Ibsen translated into Swedish can be a bit hard to take, but a musical might still be enjoyable. The season runs from September to May. Performances are usually Tuesday to Friday at 7pm, Saturday at 6pm, and Sunday at 3pm.

OPERA & BALLET

Göteborgsoperan (Gothenburg Opera House). Packhuskajen. ☎ **031/10-80-00,** or 031/13-13-00 for ticket information. Ticket prices depend on the event.

The Swedish king opened this elegant new opera house in 1994. It features theater, opera, operettas, musicals, and ballet performances. It's situated right on a dock (a short walk from the Central Station), with views overlooking the water, and there are five bars and a cafe in the lobby. The main entrance (on Östra Hamngatan) leads to a foyer with a view of the harbor; here you'll find the box office and cloakroom. Big productions can be staged on a full scale. You'll have to check to see what performances may be scheduled at the time of your visit.

CLASSICAL MUSIC

Konserthuset. Götaplatsen. ☎ **031/61-53-10.** Tickets usually 150–450 SEK ($16.50–$49.50), but could range lower or higher depending on the performance. Bus: 40.

In the very center of Gothenburg, this is the major performance hall for classical music. In season (September to June), top world-class performers appear.

THE CLUB & MUSIC SCENE
NIGHTCLUBS

Bubbles. Avenyn 8. ☎ **031/10-58-20.** No cover. Tram: 1, 4, 5, or 6.

In stark contrast to the sprawling size of the Trädgoårn (see below), this nightclub and cocktail lounge is small-scale and intimate. Outfitted in pale colors, and attracting a clientele over 30, it's the most popular late-night venue in Gothenburg, sometimes attracting workers from restaurants around town, who relax and chitchat here after a hard night's work in the restaurant trade. There's a small dance floor, but most visitors ignore it in favor of dialogues at the bar instead. Open daily 8pm to 5am.

Oakley's Country Club. Tredje Långgatan 16. ☎ **031/42-60-80.** No cover. Reservations recommended. Tram: 1, 3, 4, or 9.

This restaurant with the eye-catching scarlet facade opened in a former fire station in 1998. It's a tongue-in-cheek parody of what you might have expected in the Nevada deserts. At midday, it looks something like an upscale luncheonette in a state west of the Rocky Mountains, with service by female students from a nearby ballet academy dressed as Gold Rush–era can-can ingenues.

From 9pm on, live entertainment heats things up a bit, thanks to reincarnations of Dale Evans about to break into song, can-can dancers belting out excerpts from *Annie Get Your Gun,* and a scantily clad trapeze artist who advises the menfolk in the audience how best to lasso a bedmate, a bride, or both. The campy atmosphere highlights this completely unexpected interpretation of the American vernacular style that you might never, ever have expected east of the Atlantic. Menu items, incidentally, include sophisticated interpretations of new American cuisine—chili-roasted crayfish, Mississippi alligator ribs, Caesar salads studded with crayfish, Annie's blackened salmon, Buffalo Bill's rib-eye steak, and "our own" version of spare ribs. One particularly elegant room specializes in cigars and brandies that can be enjoyed by men and any cowgirl wannabe who wants to experiment with them. Main courses cost 129 to 198 SEK ($14.20 to $21.80), and the club is open daily 11am to 2pm and 6 to 11pm.

Park Lane Nightclub. In the Radisson SAS Park Avenue Hotel, Kungsportsavenyn 36–38. ☎ **031/20-60-58.** Cover 60–80 SEK ($6.60–$8.80); no cover for hotel guests. Tram: 1, 4, 5, or 6. Bus: 40.

The leading nightclub on Sweden's west coast, this dinner-dance room sometimes features international stars. Past performers have included Marlene Dietrich, Eartha Kitt, and Prince. The dance floor is usually packed. Light suppers, such as crab salad or toasted sandwiches, are served. Beer begins at 50 SEK ($5.50). It's open Wednesday to Sunday 11pm to 3am.

Trädgoårn. Allegaten 8. ☎ **031/10-20-80.** Cover charge for disco 80–100 SEK ($8.80–$11); 2-course dinner and access to cabaret show 520 SEK ($57.20); main courses in restaurant 175–235 SEK ($19.25–$25.85). Restaurant, Mon–Fri 11:30am–3:30pm and Tues–Sat 6–10:30pm; cabaret, Wed–Sat beginning at 8pm; disco, Fri–Sat 11pm–5pm. Tram: 1, 3, or 5.

This is the largest and most comprehensive nightspot in Gothenburg, with a cavernous two-story interior that echoes on weekends with the simultaneous sounds of a restaurant, a cabaret, and a disco. No one under 25 is admitted to a venue that's cosmopolitan and urbane, and has at one time or another welcomed virtually every nightclubber in town.

A DANCE CLUB

Valand. Vasagatan 41. ☎ **031/18-30-93.** Cover 80–100 SEK ($8.80–$11) for disco. Tram: 1, 4, 5, or 6. Bus: 40.

This combination restaurant and disco, one floor above street level in the center of town, is the biggest and most famous in Gothenburg. As you enter, there's a restaurant on your left and a large bar and dance floor on your right. There's also a small-stakes casino with blackjack and roulette. You must be 23 to enter. The club is open Thursday to Saturday, 8pm to 3am. For more memorable food, head for Lilla London, one floor below (see "Dining," above).

GAY GOTHENBURG

Greta. Drottningsgaten 35. ☎ **031/13-69-49.** Reservations recommended Fri–Sat. Cover 60 SEK ($6.60). AE, MC, V. Daily 4pm–3am. Tram: 1, 2, or 3.

Named in honor of Greta Garbo, whose memorabilia adorns the walls here, this is the leading gay bar and restaurant in Gothenburg, with a clientele that includes all ages, and all types, of gay men and lesbians. Two animated bars rock and roll in ways that are completely independent from the on-site restaurant. Decor is a mixture of the kitschy old-fashioned and new wave, juxtaposed in ways that are almost as interesting as the clientele. Menu items change at least every season, but might include fish and lime soup; lamb fillet with mushrooms in a red wine sauce; breast of duck with potato croquettes; and a creamy chicken stew baked in phyllo pastry. Main courses run 90 to 150 SEK ($9.90 to $16.50). Every Friday and Saturday nights, the place is transformed into a disco, from 10pm till 3am.

Leche. Vallgaten 30. No phone. Cover 60 SEK ($6.60). Tram: 1, 3, or 4.

It's tiny and it's open only one night a week, but during that brief interlude, it reigns as the premier women's bar of Gothenburg, attracting lesbians of all ages from miles around the city limits. Other nights of the week, gay women tend to congregate at Greta (see above). Open only Saturday 8pm to 3am.

16 | Skåne (Including Helsingborg and Malmö)

In Sweden's southernmost corner, the province of Skåne offers varied scenery, large forests, and many waterways. The sea and the ample, uncrowded beaches are always within reach. Many of the larger towns have a continental aura, because of the nearness of Denmark and the rest of Europe.

Denmark and the rest of Europe are now easier to reach than ever before. In 2000, Øresund Fixed Link between Denmark and Sweden was completed and opened to the public. A new artificial island was constructed halfway across the Øresund to connect 2 miles of immersed railway and motorway tunnels and a 4.8-mile bridge. Bridging the divide between Copenhagen and Malmö, this link will benefit culture, education, and research between the two countries, as well as business and transportation. With 3 million people living within a 31-mile radius of the link, the region has the largest population concentration in the Nordic area.

Skåne's major urban cities are Malmö, Helsingborg, and the university and cathedral city of Lund. Many summer visitors also seek out the little villages and undiscovered coastal towns.

The topography of the area encapsulates almost every type of Nordic scenery, except fjords and snowcapped Lapp mountains. For decades, poets, authors, and painters have found it inspirational. The tip of the Scandinavian peninsula was where Selma Lagerlöf's *The Wonderful Adventures of Nils* began. The story of the hero, a boy who travels on the back of a wild goose, has been translated into all major languages.

The first settlers were deer hunters and fishers who moved from southern Europe as the Ice Age ended and the glaciers melted. Over thousands of years, their ancestors—from the Stone Age right to the Viking Age and the early beginnings of Christianity—left many traces. There are no fewer than 300 small medieval parish churches in the province, and all are still in use. Castles and mansions, many constructed 400 or 500 years ago, dot the landscape.

Skåne once belonged to Denmark, but since 1658, it has firmly been part of the Swedish kingdom. The famous Swedish smörgåsbords are served in the province. Skåne is known as the "Swedish Riviera." For swimming and sunbathing, there are many beaches along its coast.

Skåne is associated with young Nils's wild goose, but the webfooted, flat-billed, large-bodied bird is actually tame, never traveling far from home. Until November 10, that is. Then Scanians celebrate their (almost) sacred bird with a gargantuan dinner, enjoyed by all but the bird.

Skåne is easy to reach. You have a wide choice of conventional flights, either to Malmö's Sturup Airport, or to the Copenhagen airport, from which there are frequent Hovercraft connections directly to the center of Malmö. Hovercraft also run between the Copenhagen airport and downtown Copenhagen and Malmö; every 15 or 20 minutes—day or night—connections are possible by car ferry from Helsingør, Denmark, to Helsingborg, Sweden.

If you're traveling by car, there are ferry routes from Denmark, Germany, and Poland.

Our driving tour of Skåne begins at Båstad. If you're coming south from Gothenburg, our last stopover, you can take the E6. If you're motoring from Malmö, follow the E6 north to the Båstad turnoff. The resort lies 4 miles off this main road.

1 Båstad

111 miles SW of Gothenburg, 65 miles N of Malmö

Jutting out on a peninsula, surrounded by hills and a beautiful landscape, Båstad is the most fashionable international seaside resort in Sweden.

All the famous international tennis stars have played on the courts at Båstad, which hosts the annual Swedish Open. Swedish players, inspired by the playing of Björn Borg, do much of their training here. There are more than 50 courts in the district, in addition to the renowned Drivan Sports Centre. Tennis was played here as early as the 1880s and became firmly established in the 1920s. King Gustaf V took part in these championships from 1930 to 1945, under the pseudonym of "Mr. G," and Ludvig Nobel guaranteed financial backing for international tournaments.

Golf has established itself as much as tennis, and the Bjäre peninsula offers a choice of five courses. In 1929 Nobel purchased land at Boarp for Båstad's first golf course. The bay provides opportunities for regattas and different kinds of boating. Windsurfing is popular, as is skin diving. In summer, sea bathing is also popular along the coast.

The Bjäre peninsula, a traditional farming area, is known for its early potatoes, which are in demand all over Sweden. They appear on the midsummer table with a selection of pickled herring.

ESSENTIALS

GETTING THERE   From Gothenburg by car, continue southwest along the E6 until you see the turnoff for Båstad. If you're not driving, you'll find speedy trains running frequently throughout the day between Gothenburg and Malmö, with a stopover at Båstad. Six buses a day also make the 1-hour trip from Helsingborg.

VISITOR INFORMATION   For tourist information, **Båstad Turism,** Köpmangatan 1, Stortorget (☎ **0431/750-45;** www.bastad.se), is open June 20 to August 7, Sunday to Friday 10am to 6pm, Saturday 10am to 4pm; off-season, Monday to Saturday 10am to 2pm. You can book private rooms here—rates start at 150 SEK ($16.50) per person—or rent bikes for 60 SEK ($6.60) per day. The staff can also provide information about booking tennis courts, renting sports equipment, or reserving a round of golf.

GETTING AROUND   You don't need to rely on buses once you're in Båstad, as you can walk around the center of town in about 30 minutes. To reach the harbor and the beach, follow Tennisvägen off Köpmansgatan through a residential district until you come to Strandpromenaden. To your immediate west, you'll see a number of old bathhouses now converted to restaurants and bars. If you don't have a car, you'll need a bus to reach the Bjäre peninsula. From Båstad, bus no. 525 leaves every other hour Monday to Saturday only, and runs through the center of the peninsula. If it's a Sunday, you'll have to rely on a taxi. Call ☎ **0431/696-66** for service.

EXPLORING THE AREA

The most interesting sights are not in Båstad itself but on the Bjåre peninsula (see below). However, before leaving the resort, you may want to call on **Mariakyrkan,** Köpmansgatan (☎ **0431/78706**). One of Skåne's landmark churches, Saint Mary's was built between 1450 and 1500. Its tower was restored in 1986, and the entire interior renewed in 1967. It holds many treasures, including a sculpture of Saint Mary and Christ from about 1460 (found in the sanctuary). The altarpiece is from 1775, but the crucifix is medieval. The trumpet-angel above the altar is from about the same time as the altarpiece. The pulpit is from 1836, its hourglass from 1791. In the northern nave is a church clock from 1802 and fresco paintings. The church is open daily from 9am to 4pm.

Båstad is noted for one of southern Sweden's principal attractions, the ✪ **Norrvikens Trädgårdar (Norrviken Gardens),** Kattvik (☎ **0431/723-70**), 1½ miles west of the resort's center. Founded in 1906 by Rudolf Abelin, these gardens have been expanded and maintained according to his plans, embracing a number of styles. One garden is in Italian baroque style, with a pond framed by pyramidal-shaped boxwood hedges and tall cypresses. The Renaissance Garden is reminiscent of the tapestry art of 15th-century Italy, with its boxwood patterns, and the flower garden, with bulb flowers competing with annuals. There are also a Japanese Garden, an Oriental Terrace, a Rhododendron Dell, a Romantic Garden, and a Water Garden.

At Villa Abelin, designed by the garden's founder, wisteria climbs on the wall and is in bloom twice a year. The villa houses shops, exhibits, and information facilities. There are also a restaurant and cafeteria on the grounds.

The gardens may be viewed from May 1 to September 6, daily 10am to 5pm. Admission is 45 SEK ($4.95) for adults, 30 SEK ($3.30) for children under 12.

THE BJÅRE PENINSULA

After exploring the gardens, you may want to turn your attention to the ✪ **Bjåre Peninsula.** It's the highlight of the entire region because of its widely varied scenery, ranging from farm fields to cliff formations. Before exploring in depth, it's best to pick up a detailed map from the Båstad tourist office (see "Visitor Information," above).

The peninsula is devoted to sports, including windsurfing, tennis, golf, hiking, and mountain biking. It has white sandy beaches reaching down to the sea, riding paths, and cycle roads set aside for these activities. You can play golf at five different 18-hole courses, starting in early spring. The Båstad tourist office can supply information.

If you don't have a car, you can take bus. no. 525, which leaves Båstad every hour Monday to Saturday. It traverses the center of the peninsula.

The **Skaneleden walking trail** runs the entire perimeter of the peninsula and is also great for cycling. However, the terrain is quite hilly in places, so you need to be in fabulous shape.

On the peninsula's western coast is the sleepy village of **Torekov,** a short drive from Kattvik. Here you'll find a beach and pier where early-morning swimmers can be seen walking down to the sea in bathing gowns and sandals.

From Torekov, you can set out to explore **Hallands Väderö,** an island off Sweden's west coast. Old wooden fishing boats make the 15-minute crossing on the hour from June to August. From September to May, departures are every 2 hours. The cost is 70 SEK ($7.70) round-trip. The last departure is at 4:30pm daily. For more information, call **Bokningstelefon Halmstead** (☎ **035/10-50-70**).

Skåne

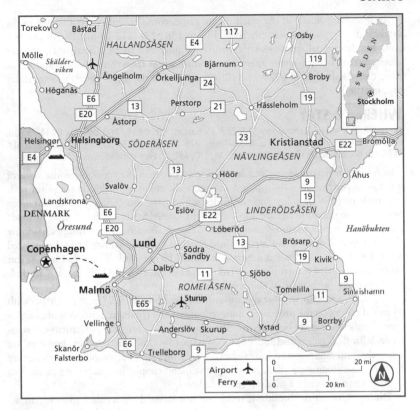

The Bjåre peninsula has one of Sweden's few remaining **seal colonies.** "Seal safaris" come here to view (but not disturb) these animals. In addition to seals, the island is noted for its rich bird life, including guillemots, cormorants, eiders, and gulls.

OUTDOOR ACTIVITIES

GOLF   The region around Båstad is home to five separate golf courses. Two of them allow nonmembers to use the course during short-term visits to the region. To reach the **Båstad Golf Club,** Boarp, S-26921 Båstad (☎ 0431/731-36), follow the signs to Boarp and drive 2½ miles south of town. To reach the **Bjåre Golf Club,** Solomonhög 3086, S-269 93 Båstad (☎ 0431/36-10-53), follow the signs to Förslöv, 6 miles east of Båstad). Both charge greens fees of 235 to 350 SEK ($25.85 to $38.50) for 18 holes, depending on the season, and both have pro shops that rent clubs. Advance reservations for tee-off times are essential.

TENNIS   Båstad is irretrievably linked to the game of tennis, which it celebrates with fervor thanks to its role as the long-time home of the Swedish Open tennis tournament. There are 14 outdoor courts (available only between April and September) and 6 indoor courts (available year-round) at the **Drivan Tennis Center,** Drivangårdens Vandrarhem (☎ 0431/685 00). About a half-mile north of Båstad's town center, it employs a corps of tennis professionals and teachers, who give 60-minute lessons for 250 SEK ($27.50) per hour. Indoor and outdoor courts rent for 80 to 110 SEK ($8.80 to $12.10) per hour, depending on the time of day or night you arrive, and whether the courts need to be illuminated.

To immerse yourself in the spirit of the game, consider renting a bunk bed in the establishment's youth hostel, priced at 110 to 130 SEK ($12.10 to $14.30) per person. The functional, barracks-style bedrooms hold two to four occupants, and are often the temporary home of members of tennis teams from throughout Scandinavia. Originally established in 1929, this club built most of the tennis courts you see today around 1980.

WHERE TO STAY

Hotel Buena Vista. Tarravägen 5, S-269 35 Båstad. ☎ **0431/760-00.** Fax 0431/79100. www.buena.se. 30 units. TV TEL. Mon–Thurs 975 SEK ($107.25) double; Fri–Sun 895 SEK ($98.45) double. Rates include breakfast. AE, DC, MC, V. Free parking. Bus: 226.

The most historic and glamorous hotel in town occupies the venerable white walls of a mansion perched on a hilltop, a 3-minute walk uphill from the center of town. It was built in 1906 by John Francis Andersson, a late 19th-century immigrant from Småland who moved to Britain and then to the United States. In the process, he made a respectable income as the general contractor for the construction of bridges spanning the Thames and many of the streams and rivers of the New World. Later, he invested $5,000 with a then-unknown automaker named Henry Ford. When that investment evolved into a massive fortune, he opted to retire in Sweden, and built this elegant Italianate mansion with some of the profits.

Today, it's a site for small-scale conventions, wedding parties (there's a chapel with a vaulted ceiling on the premises), honeymooners, and regular tourists as well as sightseers. Public areas have been restored to some of their original Edwardian-era opulence, with dark colors and lots of varnished hardwoods. Guest rooms, however, are relatively contemporary, and in many cases, are a bit cramped, although mattresses are first-rate. Bathrooms are tiled, relatively small, and simple, in many ways equivalent to what you'd expect in a modern roadside hotel.

Dining: Other than breakfast, meals are not served here regularly, but on an as-needed, catered basis. Dinner for groups of two to several hundred people can be arranged with advance notice. It costs 150 to 400 SEK ($19.20 to $51.20) per person, depending on what you order.

Amenities: Room service (breakfast only), concierge.

Hotel-Pension Enehall. Stationsterrassen 10, S-26900 Båstad. ☎ **0431/750-15.** Fax 0431/724-09. www.enehall.se. E-mail: enehall@enehall.se. 40 units. TV TEL. 660–800 SEK ($72.60–$88) double. Half board 480 SEK ($52.80) per person. Rates include breakfast. AE, DC, MC, V. Free parking. Bus: 513.

On a slope of Hallandsåsen mountain only a few minutes' walk from the sea, this cozy, intimate place caters mainly to Swedish families and some occasional Danes and Germans. There are many personal touches, and the rooms, although small, are adequately equipped with good beds and small bathrooms. The food is tasty, and the service polite and efficient.

Hotel Riviera. Rivieravägen, S-269-39 Båstad. ☎ **0431/369-050.** Fax 0431/761-00. www.hotelriviera.nu. E-mail: hotel.riviera@bastad.mail.telia.com. 50 units. TV TEL. 720 SEK ($79.20) double. Rates include breakfast. MC, V. Closed Sept–Apr. Free parking. Bus: 513.

A favorite venue for conferences, this is one of the better hotels in the area. It takes on a somewhat festive air in summer. By the sea, half a mile from the railroad station and 2 miles east of the town center, it offers views from many of its modern rooms and its 300-seat restaurant. Rooms and bathrooms are small, but comfortably furnished, with good beds and excellent housekeeping. Everything is functionally furnished, but in good taste. Many guests sit out in the gardens or on the terrace, while others prefer to play on the tennis courts. There's a large, cozy bar, and a summer cafe on a sun-filled loggia. The excellent kitchen serves a combination of Scandinavian and international food. Dinners with dancing to a live band are often scheduled in season.

Hotel Skansen. Kyrkogatan 2, S-269 21 Båstad. ☎ **0431/720-50.** Fax 0431/700-85. www.hotelskansen.se. 52 units. TV MINIBAR TEL. 830 SEK ($91.30) double. Rates include breakfast. AE, DC, MC, V. Free parking. Bus: 513; 5-minute walk.

Although it isn't as expensive as some of the other hotels within the chain that controls it, the Hotel Skansen is associated with some of Sweden's most opulent and prestigious lodgings, including the Grand Hotel in Stockholm. It's also the most visible tennis venue in Sweden—its eight tennis courts are the home every year to the annual Swedish Open. As such, it has housed, usually more than once, the most famous tennis stars in Sweden, including Björn Borg, Anders Järryd, and Henrik Holm. Built as a grain warehouse in 1877, it's a few minutes' walk from the marina and 50 yards from the beach. The hotel incorporates its original building (which is today listed as a Swedish national monument) with four more recent structures that surround eight tennis courts, some of which are equipped with stadiums for the above-mentioned tennis competitions. The interior has a beamed roof, pillars, and views over the sea. Renovated in 1997, guest rooms are airy, elegant, and traditionally outfitted with conservative furniture, including good beds, and ample private bathrooms.

Dining: The in-house restaurant is open only from June to mid-September. Set within the oldest of the hotel's five buildings and outfitted in autumn tones of yellow and brown, it serves Swedish and international cuisine. The rest of the year, meals are served only to guests who make special arrangements. A cafe operates year-round and has seating in the courtyard during warm weather.

Amenities: Beach facilities, conference facilities, eight tennis courts, and a health club, sauna, and solarium within a 4-minute walk.

WHERE TO DINE

The hotels listed above all have good restaurants, although you should call in advance for a reservation. If you're just passing through, consider dropping in at the **Solbackens Café & Wåffelbruk,** Italienska vägen (☎ **0431/702-00**). If the weather is fair, opt for a table on the terrace overlooking the water. This cafe is locally famous, and has been known for serving Swedish waffles and other delights since 1907.

Centrecourten. Köpmansgatan 70b. ☎ **0431/75275.** Reservations recommended. Pizzas 55–70 SEK ($6.05–$7.70); main courses 85–140 SEK ($9.35–$15.40). AE, M, V. Mon–Thurs 4–10pm, Fri 4–11:30pm, Sat noon–10:30pm, Sun noon–10pm. SWEDISH/INTERNATIONAL.

In a town as obsessed with tennis as Båstad, you'd expect at least one restaurant to be outfitted in a tennis-lovers theme. In this case, it consists of a cozy and small-scale dining room with photos of such stars as Bjorn Borg, a scattering of trophies, and old-fashioned tennis memorabilia. Menu items include fresh fish, including mussels and lemon sole, and cod, breast of duck with bacon-flavored purée of potatoes, and brisket of beef with chanterelles and shallots. The ingredients are fresh and the flavors are often enticing, especially in the seafood selections.

Persson & Co. Köpmansgatan 75. ☎ **0431/75005.** Reservations recommended. Main courses 100–135 SEK ($11–$14.85). V. Wed–Sun 5–10pm. Bar stays open till 1am. SWEDISH.

Set close to both the bus station and Båstad's largest food market, this restaurant is known for its active bar area that's favored by the young-at-heart and the restless, a woodsy decor that might remind you of an English pub, and gargantuan portions. Menu items include a salmon tartare with capers and horseradish; at least three kinds of steaks; grilled halibut with a garlic-tomato sauce; and roasted fillet of reindeer on a bed of wild mushrooms. Even if your taste buds don't always scream out hysterical praise here, the flavor combinations are most satisfying, and we like the chef's reliance on local ingredients whenever they are available to him.

BÅSTAD AFTER DARK

One of the most appealing places to hang out in Båstad include the bar at the already-recommended Persson & Co. Restaurant (see above). Here, according to a well-seasoned staff member, "it's not unlikely that you might form some kind of companionship bond with one of the locals." It's liveliest every Wednesday to Sunday from around 10pm till the 1am closing. Another choice is **Pepe's Bodega,** Warmbadhuset Hamnen (☎ **0431/369169**), where there's spicy food, colorful cocktails, and a spirited atmosphere. It's open Wednesday to Sunday, from 5pm till 11pm for food, and till 1am for drinks.

2 Helsingborg

143 miles S of Gothenburg, 347 miles SW of Stockholm, 39 miles N of Malmö

At the narrowest point of the Øresund (Öresund in Swedish), 3 miles across the water that separates Sweden and Denmark, is this industrial city and major port. Many people who travel from Copenhagen to visit Kronborg Castle (in Helsingør, Denmark) take a 25-minute ferry ride across the sound (leaving every 20 minutes) for a look at Sweden.

What they see isn't "Sweden," but a modern city with an ancient history. Helsingborg and Helsingør jointly controlled shipping along the sound in the Middle Ages. Helsingborg is mentioned in the 10th-century *Nial-Saga,* and documents show that there was a town here in 1085. The city now has more than 100,000 inhabitants and the second-busiest harbor in the country. This is the home of Sweden's first pedestrian streets, and it has long shore promenades along the sound.

Helsingborg (Hålsingborg) recently rebuilt large, vacant-looking sections of its inner city into one of the most innovative urban centers in Sweden. The centerpiece of these restorations lies beside the harbor, and includes an all-glass building, the Knutpunkten, on Järnvägsgatan. It contains the railroad, bus, and ferryboat terminals, an array of shops similar to a North American mall, and a heliport. Many visitors say that the railroad station, which is flooded with sunlight, is the cleanest, brightest, and most memorable they've ever seen. In addition, many dozens of trees and shrubs have transformed the center into something like a verdant park, with trees between the lanes of traffic.

ESSENTIALS

GETTING THERE From Malmö, drive north on the E6. The trip takes 1 hour. From Gothenburg, drive south on the E6 for 2½ hours. From Stockholm, take the E4 south for 7½ hours until you reach Helsingborg. If you're not driving, there are many other ways to reach Helsingborg.

Ferries from Helsingør, Denmark, leave the Danish harbor every 20 minutes day or night (trip time is 25 minutes). For information about ferryboats in Helsingborg, call ☎ **042/18-61-00;** for information on the Danish side, call ☎ **33-15-15-15.** Pedestrians pay 23 SEK ($2.55) each way or 40 SEK ($4.40) round-trip. The regular round-trip cost of the ferryboat price for a car with up to five passengers is 510 SEK ($56.10) Sunday to Wednesday, 445 SEK ($48.95) Thursday to Saturday. A round-trip journey commencing and ending on the same day costs 345 SEK ($37.95).

Ångelholm–Helsingborg airport lies 30 minutes from the center of the city, with regular connections to Stockholm's Arlanda airport. There are between seven and nine SAS flights per day from Stockholm's Arlanda airport (flying time is 1 hour). For SAS reservations, call ☎ 0431/55-80-10.

Trains run hourly during the day between Helsingborg and Malmö. The trip takes 50 minutes. Trains both arrive from and return to Stockholm twice a day. It's a 7-hour trip. Trains between Gothenburg and Helsingborg depart and arrive twice a day (trip time is 2½ hours). Call ☎ 020/75-75-75 for information.

Three buses a day link Malmö and Helsingborg. Two leave in the morning, and one in the afternoon. The trip takes 1 hour, 10 minutes. Buses leave twice a day for the 3¼-hour trip from Gothenburg. Buses to and from Stockholm leave once a day (trip time is 10 hours).

VISITOR INFORMATION   The tourist office, **Helsingborg Turistbyrå,** Knutpunkten (☎ 042/10-43-50; www.helsingborg.se), is open May to September 15, Monday to Friday 9am to 8pm, and Saturday and Sunday 9am to 5pm; September 16 to April, Monday to Friday 9am to 6pm, and Saturday 10am to 2pm.

GETTING AROUND   Most of Helsingborg's sights are within walking distance. But if your legs are tired and the weather less than perfect, you can always take a city bus, numbered 1 to 7. Most buses on their way north pass the Town Hall. Those heading south go by Knutpunkten. Tickets are valid for transfer to another city bus line as long as you transfer within 3 hours from the time the ticket was stamped. Tickets bought on board cost 14 SEK ($1.55). For information, call ☎ 020/61-61-61.

SEEING THE SIGHTS

Built in 1897, the **Town Hall (Rådhuset),** Drottninggatan 7 (☎ 042/10-50-00), has handsome stained-glass windows depicting scenes from the town's history. Two memorial stones, presented by the Danes and the Norwegians to the Swedes for their assistance during the Second World War, stand outside. There is also a sculpture relief representing the arrival of Danish refugees.

In the main town square, the Stortorget, is a monument commemorating General Stenbock's victory at the Battle of Helsingborg (1710) between Sweden and Denmark.

Fredriksdal Open-Air Museum and Botanical Garden. Hävertgatan (at Fredriksdal). ☎ 042/104-540. Admission 30 SEK ($3.30) adults, free for children 9 and under. Park, June–Aug, daily 10am–8pm; Sept–May, daily 11am–4pm. Manor, June–Sept, daily 11am–5pm; Oct–May, daily 10am–3pm. Bus: 2, 3, or 250.

This is among the largest and most complete open-air museums in Sweden, covering some 70 acres of rolling land. (Skansen, in Stockholm, is larger, but few others are.) The park, a 20-minute walk east of the town center, was built around a manor house constructed in 1787. The rose garden contains about 450 different types of varieties, all part of one of Sweden's most remarkable botanical gardens. The open-air theater, part of the complex, was established in 1927. You can also wander through the French Park and the English Park.

Kärnan (The Keep). Kärngränden (off the Stortorget). ☎ 042/105-991. Admission 15 SEK ($1.65) adults, 5 SEK (55¢) children. Apr–May, Tues–Sun 9am–4pm; June–Aug, Tues–Sun 10am–7pm; Sept, daily 9am–3pm; Oct–Mar, daily 10am–2pm. Bus: 1 or 6.

One of the most important medieval monuments in Sweden, and the symbol of Helsingborg, this monument rises from the crest of a rocky ridge in the town center. A 100-foot-tall square tower with mysterious origins in the 11th century, it adopted its present form in the 1300s. Its name translates as "the core," and it was so labeled because it was originally conceived as the most central tower (and prison) of the once-mighty Helsingborg Castle. The thickness of its walls (about 14 feet) makes it the most solidly constructed building in the region. An object of bloody fighting between the Swedes and the Danes for generations, the castle and its fortifications were demolished in 1679. Of the once-mighty fortress, only Kärnan (which was restored and rebuilt in 1894) remains.

The easiest way to reach Kärnan is to board the elevator, which departs from the *terrasen* (terrace) of the town's main street, the Stortorget. For 10 SEK ($1.10) per person, you'll be carried up the rocky hillside to the base of the tower. Many visitors, however, avoid the elevator, preferring instead to climb a winding set of flower-flanked steps as part of their exploration of the city. Once inside the tower, an additional 147 steps lie between you and one of the most sweeping views in the district.

Mariakyrkan (Church of St. Mary). Södra Storgaten. ☎ **042/37-28-30.** Free admission. June–Aug, Mon–Sat 8am–6pm, Sun 9am–6pm; Sept–May, Mon–Sat 8am–4pm, Sun 9am–4pm. Bus: 1 or 6.

A short walk from the harbor, this 13th-century church was substantially rebuilt in the 15th century in a Danish Gothic style, evoking a basilica. The facade is plain, but the interior is striking, especially the medieval altarpiece and its intricately carved pulpit. If the sun is shining, the modern stained-glass windows are jewel-like.

Sofiero Slott. Sofierovägen. ☎ **042/137-400.** Admission 50 SEK ($5.50) adults, 10 SEK ($1.10) children. Daily 10am–6pm. Closed Oct to mid-Apr. Bus: 219 or 221.

One of the most famous buildings in southern Sweden, lying 3 miles north of Helsingborg, this was constructed in 1864–65 as the summer residence of King Oscar II and his wife, Sofia. In 1905 it was bequeathed to their grandson, Gustav Adolph, and his wife, Margareta, who enlarged the site and created some of the most memorable gardens in the country. Their interests supposedly sparked a nationwide interest in landscape architecture that's stronger than ever throughout Sweden today. After his coronation, King Gustav Adolph spent his last days here, eventually bequeathing Sofiero as a gift to the city of Helsingborg in 1973. In 1993 many of the original gardens were re-created in memory of their designer, Queen Margareta. Today the most-visited sites include the 1865 castle, which contains a cafe and restaurant; the rose garden; and the Rhododendron Ravine. It holds an estimated 10,000 rhododendrons, which are in their full glory in early June.

SHOPPING

Northwest Scania (English for Skåne) can also be called the pottery district of Sweden. The region's first Scanian pottery factory was founded in 1748 in Bosarp, 9¼ miles east of Helsingborg. The city of **Helsingborg** got its first factory in 1768 and another began manufacturing in 1832. Since then, the traditional pottery industry has been developed and revitalized, making the area famous far beyond the borders of Sweden.

At a point 4½ miles south of Helsingborg, you can visit **Raus Stenkarlsfabrik,** ½ mile east of Råå (look for signs along Landskronavagen). One of the leading potteries of the area, it is open May to December, Monday to Friday 10am to 6pm, Saturday 10am to 4pm; off-season, January to April, Saturday from 10am to 4pm. Call ☎ **042/26-01-30** for more information.

In Gantofta, about 6¼ miles southeast of Helsingborg, lies **Jie-Keramik** (☎ **042/990-31**). It's one of Scandinavia's leading manufacturers of hand-painted decorative ceramics, wall reliefs, wall clocks, figures, and other such items. You can visit the factory shop or patronize a cafe on-site. From Helsingborg, drive south to Råå, and then follow the signs to Gantofta. You can also take bus no. 209 from Knutpunkten in the center of Helsingborg. From June to August, the outlet is open Monday to Friday 8am to 6pm, Saturday 8am to 4pm, and Sunday 11am to 5pm. Off-season hours are Monday to Friday 10am to 5pm, Saturday 10am to 4pm, and Sunday noon to 4pm.

Höganäs, 12½ miles north of Helsingborg, is home to two famous stoneware factories. **Höganäs Saltglaserat** (☎ 042/33-83-33), has been manufacturing salt-glazed stoneware since 1835. The classic piece is the salt-glazed Höganäs jars with an anchor symbol. Everything is made by hand and fired in coal-burning circular kilns from the turn of the century. The shop here is within the factory, so you can see the throwers in action and go inside the old kilns. Hours are Monday to Friday, 9am to 4pm; from June to August and during December, it's also open Saturday 10am to 1pm.

The other outlet, **Höganäs Keramik** (☎ 042/33-20-75) is Scandinavia's largest stoneware manufacturer. In the Factory Shop, inaugurated in 1994, flawed goods from both Höganäs Keramik and Boda Nova are on sale at bargain prices. This outlet is open May to August, Monday to Friday 9am to 6pm, Saturday and Sunday 10am to 5pm. Off-season hours are Monday to Friday 10am to 6pm, Saturday 10am to 4pm, and Sunday 11am to 4pm.

Motorists can also visit **Gröna Gården,** Välluvsvågen 34, in Påarp (☎ 42/22-71-70), southeast of Helsingborg. Head toward Malmö, but exit at Barslov toward Påarp-Välluv. The outlet offers many beautiful handcrafts in ceramic, glass, birch bark, forged metal, and wood. Hand-woven fabrics, baskets, candles, wooden toys, and handmade jewelry are just some of the merchandise also on sale. Hours are Tuesday to Friday 1 to 6pm, Saturday 10am to 1pm. In November and December, it's also open Sunday 1 to 4pm.

In the center of Helsingborg, you'll find a number of shopping possibilities, including **Väla Centrum,** which is one of the largest shopping centers in Scandinavia. To reach it, follow Hälsovågen and Ångelholmsvägen north about 3½ miles (it's signposted) or else take bus no. 202 from Knutpunkten. Seemingly everything is here under one roof, including two large department stores and some 42 specialty shops, selling everything from shoes and clothing to tropical fish.

The best bookstore in town is **Bokman,** Järnvägsgatan 3 (☎ 042/13-75-75), with many English-language editions. The best center for class glass is **Duka Carl Anders,** Södergatan 22 (☎ 042/24-27-00), which carries the works of such prestigious manufacturers as Kosta Boda and Orrefors.

WHERE TO STAY
EXPENSIVE

Radisson/SAS Grand Hotel Helsingborg. Stortorget 8–12, Box 1104, S-251 11 Helsingborg. ☎ **800/333-3333** in the U.S., or 042/38-04-00. Fax 042/38-04-04. www.radissonsas.com. 117 units. MINIBAR TV TEL. Mid-June to Aug and Fri–Sun year-round, 790–900 SEK ($86.90–$99) double; 1,090–1,900 SEK ($119.90–$209) suite. Rest of year, 1,400–1,600 SEK ($154–$176) double; 1,800–2,700 SEK ($198–$297) suite. Rates include breakfast. AE, DC, MC, V. Parking 115 SEK ($12.65). Bus: 7B or 1A.

Helsingborg's grandest hotel, an imposing brick-fronted monument built in 1926, underwent a radical upgrade in 1996. It's now one of the most visible Swedish hotels in the Radisson/SAS chain, and one of the most appealing hotels in southern Sweden. It combines high-ceilinged, richly paneled public areas and spacious, well-accessorized guest rooms with elaborate ceiling moldings, many of the decorative accessories of the Old World, and lots of modern comforts and conveniences. The newly renovated rooms have good mattresses and ample bathrooms, with hair dryers. Some rooms are equipped with facilities for people with disabilities; there are also nonsmoking rooms.

Dining/Diversions: The Grand Séparée serves Scandinavian delicacies as classical music plays. The Granderiet offers exotic and spicy international dishes. The hotel's bar, Bakfickan, serves drinks and pub food: salads, pastas, and burgers.

Amenities: Conference facilities, room service, exercise room with sauna and solarium, concierge.

MODERATE

Hotel Helsingborg. Stortorget 20, S-252 23 Helsingborg. ☎ **042/12-09-45.** Fax 042/21-54-61. www.hkchotels.se. E-mail: info.hotelhelsingborg@swedenhotels.se. 56 units. TV TEL. 995–1,225 SEK ($109.45–$134.75) double; 1,100–1,600 SEK ($121–$176) suite. Rates include breakfast. AE, DC, MC, V. Parking 90 SEK ($9.90). Bus: 7A, 7B, 1A, or 1B.

Of the three hotels that lie along this grand avenue, this one is closest to the city's medieval tourist attraction, the Kärnan. It has a heroic neoclassical frieze and three copper-sheathed towers, and occupies four floors of what used to be a bank headquarters, dating from 1901. The high-ceilinged rooms are pleasantly modernized and flooded with sunlight. They retain a certain Jugendstil (art nouveau) look, with strong colors and many decorative touches. All rooms were upgraded and renovated in the early 1990s, with good beds and small, though perfectly functional, bathrooms. There's a lobby bar and a breakfast room. The lobby bar serves simple platters of light food and sandwiches 24 hours a day. A sauna is on the premises, along with boutiques at street level.

Hotel Mollberg. Stortorget 18, S-251 10 Helsingborg. ☎ **800/528-1234** in the U.S., or 042/12-02-70. Fax 042/14-96-18. www.hotelmollberg.se. 100 units. MINIBAR TV TEL. 790–1,290 SEK ($86.90–$141.90) double. Rates include breakfast. AE, DC, MC, V. Parking 85 SEK ($9.35). Bus: 7A, 7B, 1A or 1B.

Hotel Mollberg is often called "Sweden's oldest continuously operated hotel and restaurant." Although a tavern has stood on this site since the 14th century, most of the building was constructed in 1802 by the establishment's namesake, Peter Mollberg. Its elaborate wedding-cake exterior and high-ceilinged interior have long been its hallmarks. A major renovation was carried out in 1986, with several minor restorations throughout the 1990s. Its first-class rooms are equipped with color TVs, good beds, trouser presses, and hair dryers, among other amenities. Rates include use of the solarium and sauna. The Mollberg has a dining room and a cocktail lounge. The Mollberg Brasserie serves light cuisine Monday to Saturday from noon to 11pm.

Hotel Nouveau. Gasverksgatan 11. S-250 02 Helsingborg. ☎ **042/18-53-90.** Fax 042/14-08-85. www.nouveauhotel.se. 79 units. TV TEL. Mid-June to mid-Aug and Fri–Sat year-round, 800 SEK ($88) double; rest of year, 1,295 SEK ($142.45) double. AE, DC, MC, V. Free parking. Bus: 7A or 1A.

Once a somewhat nondescript and outmoded hotel from the 1960s, the Hotel Nouveau was radically reconfigured and upgraded in 1996. The result is a tastefully decorated brick building of ochre with touches of marble. The decor throughout draws on upscale models from England and France, and includes chintz curtains, varnished mahogany, often with wood inlays, and warm colors inspired by autumn. Rooms are nice and cozy, not overly large but well maintained, with tasteful fabrics, good beds, frequently renewed linen, and small but adequate bathrooms. A fresh flower is often placed on your pillow at night, a thoughtful touch. The hotel has conference facilities, a worthwhile restaurant, and a well-trained staff with a good sense of humor.

✪ **Marina Plaza.** Kungstorget 6, S-251 Helsingborg. ☎ **800/528-1234** in the U.S., or 042/19-21-00. Fax 042/14-96-16. www.marinaplaza.elite.se. 190 units. MINIBAR TV TEL. 790–1,295 SEK ($86.90–$142.45) double; 1,995–2,700 SEK ($219.45–$297) suite. Mid-summer discounts available. AE, DC, MC, V. Free parking. Bus: 41, 42, 43, or 44.

This is Helsingborg's most innovative and most talked-about hotel. It's adjacent to the city's transportation hub, the Knutpunkten. The atrium-style lobby overflows with trees, flowers, rock gardens, and fountains. Guest rooms line the inner walls of the hotel's atrium and have, as you might expect, a color scheme of marine blue with nautical accessories. Beds have firm mattresses, and the adequate bathrooms are equipped with hair dryers. The hotel contains two restaurants, the upscale Hamnkrogen and less formal Sailor's Pub, where Italian food is offered. A piano provides evening entertainment near the lobby's popular bar. There is also an aptly titled disco, the Marina Nightclub. The hotel also maintains a health club with a sauna and solarium.

Scandic Partner Hotel Horisont. Gustav Adolfs Gate 47, S-250 02 Helsingborg. ☎ **042/ 49-52-100.** Fax 042/49-52-111. www.scandic-hotels.com. E-mail: horisont@scandic-hotels. com. 170 units. TV TEL. 710–1,473 SEK ($78.10–$162.05) double. Rates include breakfast. AE, DC, MC, V. Free parking. Bus: 7B or 1B.

Near a park at the edge of the town's commercial center, this hotel with the futuristic facade was erected in 1985. The guest rooms are comfortably conservative, with plush upholstery, soundproof windows, and comfortable mattresses. The bathrooms are adequate in size and well maintained. On the premises are an attractive bar lined with brick and touches of brass, and a high-ceilinged formal restaurant. There's a center with saunas, whirlpools, and solariums. The hotel is about half a mile south of the ferryboat terminal.

INEXPENSIVE

Hotel Högvakten. Stortorget 14, PO Box 1074, SE-251 10 Helsingborg. ☎ **042/ 12-03-90.** Fax 042/12-00-95. www.hotelhogvakten.com. 41 units. TV TEL. Mid-June to mid-Aug and Fri–Sun year-round, 675 SEK ($74.25) double; rest of year, 1,045 SEK ($114.95) double. Rates include breakfast. AE, DC, MC, V. Free parking. Bus: 7A, 7B, 1A, or 1B.

A 5-minute walk from the ferryboat terminal for boats headed across the straits to Denmark, this hotel was built as a private town house in 1914. Its well-designed interior underwent a radical renovation in 1996. The decor included lots of autumn-inspired colors, comfortable, well-upholstered furnishings in public areas and bedrooms. The recently refurbished rooms are bright, and fresh, and generally quite spacious. Bathrooms are extremely well maintained in state-of-the-art condition. Only breakfast is served, but a member of the polite, attentive staff can direct you to restaurants—many within easy walking distance from the hotel.

Hotell Linnéa. Prästgatan 4, S-252 24 Helsingborg. ☎ **042/21-46-60.** Fax 042/14 16 55. www.hotel-linnea.se. E-mail: linnea@hotel-linnea.se. 19 units. TV TEL. July–Aug and Fri–Sat year-round, 565–695 SEK ($62.15–$76.45) double; rest of year, 895 SEK ($98.45) double. Rates include breakfast. AE, DC, MC, V. Parking 90 SEK ($9.90). Bus: 7A, 7B.

Conveniently located a few yards from where ferries from Denmark pull in, this is a pleasant, small-scale hotel that occupies a pink-fronted, Italianate house, circa 1897. The scale and detailing might remind you of something in a historic neighborhood of New Orleans. Guest rooms are appealingly outfitted, with comfortable beds and high-quality furnishings that include tasteful reproductions of 19th-century antiques. Bathrooms are small but adequate. Only breakfast is served, but many reliable dining choices are close by.

Hotell Viking. Fågelsångsgatan 1, S-252 20 Helsingborg. ☎ **042/14-44-20.** Fax 042/ 18-43-20. www.hotellviking.se. E-mail: hotel.vlking@helsingborg.se. 41 units. MINIBAR TV TEL. Mid-June to July and Fri–Sun year-round, 765 SEK ($84.15) double; rest of year, 1,095 SEK ($120.45) double. Rates include breakfast. AE, DC, MC, V. Free parking. Bus: 7A, 7B, 1A, or 1B.

In the center of town, less than 2 blocks north of the Drottninggatan, this hotel looks more historic, more cozy, and a bit more artfully cluttered, than many of its more formal and streamlined competitors. It was built during the late 19th century as a row of shops, usually where the owners lived upstairs from their businesses. Today, after a radical remodeling in the mid-1990s, you'll find a carefully preserved sense of history; a pale color scheme of grays, beiges, and ochres; and a hands-on management style by the resident owners. Guest rooms are cozy, neat, and functional, with exceptionally firm mattresses. Bathrooms are a bit small, but adequately supplied with hair dryers and trouser presses. Breakfast is the only meal served. A staff member can usually direct you to any of about 30 nearby restaurants.

WHERE TO DINE

Anna Kock. Järnvägsgatan 23. ☎ **042/18-13-00.** Reservations recommended at lunch, required at dinner. Main courses 85–195 SEK ($9.35–$21.45); lunch platters 60 SEK ($6.60); 2-course fixed-price dinner 185 SEK ($20.35). AE, DC, MC, V. Tues–Fri 11am–2pm and 5:30–10pm, Sat noon–10:30pm. Bus: 3, 5, 7, 9, or 12. SWEDISH.

Decorated with the kind of antique knickknacks you might find in a Swedish farmstead, and modern Swedish watercolors, this cozy restaurant contains only 11 well-manicured tables. Opened in 1989, it was named after "Anna the Cook," a locally famous chef to the region's early 20th-century bourgeoisie and aunt of the present owners, Claes and Sussan Andren. Menu items reflect the best of both modern and old-fashioned culinary techniques. Your meal might include Anna's pickled herring served with a Dutch bleu cheese sauce, fillet of reindeer on a bed of morels and lingonberry sauce, breast of wild duck with kumquat sauce and rhubarb chutney, fried fillet of lemon sole with vermouth sauce and whitebait roe, or sautéed eggplant on a bed of mushrooms with pasta and tomato sauce. Lunches are simpler and less expensive than the carefully executed dinners that are the norm here.

Elinor. Kullagatan 53. ☎ **042/12-23-30.** Reservations required. Main courses 195–265 SEK ($21.45–$29.15); fixed-price lunch 230 SEK ($25.30); fixed-price dinner 300–400 SEK ($33–$44). AE, DC, MC, V. Mon–Sat 11:30am–2:30pm and 6–10:30pm. Closed July and lunch in early Aug. Bus: 1 or 6. SWEDISH/CONTINENTAL.

One of the best restaurants in town, Elinor is in a modest 1920s house on a pleasant walkway in the town center. There's a small bar for apéritifs and a well-upholstered dining room outfitted in soft pastels. The menu depends on seasonal changes. Though less influenced by nouvelle cuisine than it was in the past years, the restaurant offers well-prepared and often tantalizing dishes, such as marinated herring with Swedish caviar and an onion and sour-cream sauce; fillet of reindeer with fresh morels; a ragoût of shrimp with chanterelles; and unusual preparations, based on the seasons, of crayfish, lobster, turbot, salmon, trout, pheasant, duck, and partridge. Desserts often showcase such semi-wild fruits as lingonberries, cloudberries, and blueberries. Plans are in the works for a less expensive wine bar annex.

☼ Oscar's Trapp. Terasstrapporna. ☎ **042/14-60-44.** Reservations recommended. Fixed-price menu 535 SEK ($58.85). AE, DC, MC, V. Mon–Sat 6–10pm. Closed July. Bus: 7A, 7B, 1 or 6. FRENCH/CONTINENTAL.

This appealingly upscale restaurant sits directly at the base of Helsingborg's symbol and most visible tower, the Kärnan, which was originally designated as a jail. It's small and choice, with windows that overlook a view of the sea and no reminders of its once-punitive former functions. It serves impeccably prepared fixed-price menus, which are composed every day based on market ingredients and traditional French recipes. Menu items might include carpaccio of tuna in a truffle vinaigrette; terrine of foie gras with sliced apples; or a delectable roasted rack of venison on a cake of parsley root and carrots, served with a lingonberry sauce. Don't confuse Oscar's Trapp with its more bustling competitor, Restaurant Oscar (see below).

✪ **Restaurant Oscar.** Sundstorget 7. ☎ **042/21-25-21.** Reservations recommended. Main courses 86–130 SEK ($9.45–$14.30); fixed-price lunch 79–210 SEK ($8.70–$23.10); fixed-price dinner 114–250 SEK ($12.55–$27.50). AE, DC, MC, V. Mon–Fri 11:30am–2pm; Mon–Sat 7:30–11pm. Bus: 7A, 7B, 1, or 6. SEAFOOD/GAME.

Overlooking a large parking lot near the ferryboat piers, in the center of town, this is Helsingborg's best-known and most frequently recommended seafood restaurant. Decorated like an upscale tavern, it contains nautical antiques that many diners find very appealing. Seafood is impeccably fresh, with a wide array of choices that range from the savory but unpretentious (fillet of cod fried in butter with capers, garlic, and boiled potatoes) to the rather grand (butterflied fillet of sole flambéed tableside with brandy and served with a ragoût of shrimp in lobster sauce). Other options include a worthwhile version of Marseilles bouillabaisse, which must be ordered a full day in advance, and a succulent version of Baltic-style fish stew, which is usually available anytime. Also look for poached fillet of sole with a Chablis sauce and whitebait roe, and in the autumn and winter, a roster of well-prepared venison dishes. Before or after your meal, check out the proudly displayed carcass of an 11-pound lobster—a zoological oddity that might remind you of a prop from a grade-B horror flick—that was caught long ago in offshore waters.

HELSINGBORG AFTER DARK

Helsingborg has had its own symphony orchestra since 1912. In 1932, its **Concert Hall (Konserthuset)** opened at Drottinggatan 19 (☎ **042/17-65-00**). One of the finest examples of 1930s Swedish functionalism, the hall is today the venue for performances by the 50-member orchestra. The season opens in the middle of August with a 10-day **Festspel,** a festival with a different theme every year. Tickets are available at the 1817 **Helsingborg Stadsteater (City Theater),** Karl Johans gata (☎ **042/ 10-68-10**). The theater is one of the most modern in Europe. Performances, of course, are in Swedish.

In the summer, when sunset is relatively late in the evening, sitting in cafes and watching the city go by is a popular pastime. An ideal place for this, open long after the sun finally sets, is the **Ångfärjestationen,** Kungsgatan 1 (☎ **042/18-71-71**). It has an outdoor cafe, and indoor versions of pubs, restaurants, and a disco that rocks and rolls every Wednesday to Saturday 7pm to 2am year-round, regardless of the time of year or the length of the day.

Something akin to a German Biergarten is **Dag & Natt,** Nordhamn (☎ **042/ 13-53-53**). The cocktail bar, a restaurant, a mini-casino (with small-stakes roulette tables), and a disco keep things hopping. It also offers a sweeping view over the straits between Sweden and Denmark. During the summer, the area's space expands into a colorful tent with temporary tables set up just for beer drinkers.

Somewhat more attuned to hipsters, with a decor that includes crystal chandeliers and lots of original paintings (which are often rotated with works by other artists), is **Marina Nightclub,** Kungstorget 6, in the Marina Plaza hotel (☎ **042/19-21-00**). You must be able to prove that you're over 23. It's open only Friday and Saturday from 11pm till around 5am.

A cozy, English-inspired pub that draws a busy and sometimes convivial crowd is **Telegrafen,** Norra Storgatan 14 (☎ **042/18-14-50**). Live music is sometimes presented on either of the two levels devoted to drinking, dialoguing, and—in some cases—flirting.

Jazz enthusiasts might enjoy an evening at one of the largest jazz venues in Sweden, **Jazzklubben,** Nedre Långvinkelsgatan 22 (☎ 042/18-49-00). Keynote nights are Wednesday, Friday, and Saturday, when live Dixieland, blues, Celtic ballads, and progressive jazz are featured beginning at around 8:30pm. Most other nights, based on a schedule that varies with the season and the whims of the staff, the place functions as a conventional bar.

3 Malmö

177 miles S of Gothenburg, 384 miles SW of Stockholm

Sweden's third-largest city, a busy port across the Øresund sound from Copenhagen, is the capital of Skåne. A good base for exploring the ancient castles and manor nearby, Malmö is an old city, dating from the 13th century.

From early days, Malmö (pronounced Mahl-*mer*) has prospered because of its location on a sheltered bay. In the 16th century, when it was the second-largest city in Denmark, it vied with Copenhagen for economic and cultural leadership. Reminders of that age are Malmöhus Castle (see below), the Town Hall, and the Stortorget, plus several homes of rich burghers. Malmö has been a Swedish city since the end of a bloody war in 1658, when the Treaty of Roskilde awarded Sweden the province of Skåne.

ESSENTIALS

GETTING THERE   Motorists coming from Copenhagen can take the new Øresund Bridge. From Helsingborg, motorists can drive southeast along the motorway 110, directly into the center of Malmö. Malmö's airport (☎ 040/613-11-00) is at Sturup, 19 miles southeast of the city, which receives flights from London and from cities within Sweden, including Gothenburg (50 minutes) and Stockholm (1 hour). Two airlines that serve the airport are **Malmö Aviation** (☎ 040/660-29-00) and SAS (☎ 040/635-7200). The airport's major international link to the world is Copenhagen Kastrup Airport, near Copenhagen, to which Malmö is connected by Hovercraft service.

The **Stockholm–Copenhagen express train** (☎ 040/202-000) has a branch service that serves Malmö. Service is frequent between Gothenburg and Malmö (a 3½-hour trip). From Helsingborg to Malmö (45-minute trip), trains leave hourly. From Stockholm, travel takes 4½ hours aboard the high-speed X-2000 train, 6 to 7 hours aboard slower trains. Two buses daily make the 4½-hour run from Gothenburg to Malmö. For bus information, call **Swebus** (☎ 0900/020-200).

Malmö and Copenhagen are linked by the Flygbåtana (hydrofoil), with hourly service year-round from 5am to midnight. The ride takes 45 minutes. Call ☎ 040/10-39-30 for information. The one-way fare is 80 SEK ($8.80).

VISITOR INFORMATION   The **Malmö Tourist Office,** Central Station, Skeppsbron 2 (☎ 040/30-01-50; www.malmo.se), is open Monday to Friday 9am to 5pm, Saturday 10am to 2pm.

GETTING AROUND   It's easy to walk around the city center, although you may need to rely on public transport if you're branching out to sights on the periphery. An individual bus ticket costs 12 SEK ($1.30) and is valid for 1 hour. You can also purchase a 100 SEK ($11) magnetic card, which offers a slight reduction on the fare discount and can be used by several passengers at the same time. Both types of tickets are sold on the bus.

SEEING THE SIGHTS

The **Malmö Card,** which is available from the Malmö Tourist Office (see "Visitor Information," above) entitles visitors to free admission to most of the city's museums. It also includes free parking, free bus travel within the city limits, and discounts in selected shops and restaurants. A card that's valid for 1 day costs 125 SEK ($13.75); for 2 days, 150 SEK ($16.50); for 3 days, 175 SEK ($19.25).

In the center of the square stands an equestrian statue of Carl X Gustav, commemorating the return of Skåne to Sweden from Denmark in 1658. There are occasional tours of the interior; check with the tourist office (see "Visitor Information," above).

Nearby lies **Lilla Torg,** Malmö's most charming square, with many fine half-timbered buildings dating from the 16th to the 18th centuries. It looks like a film set. In addition to its fountains and cafes, many handcrafts shops are also here in what used to be marshland. For many centuries, this was Malmö's bustling open-air marketplace. However, in the 20th century a covered market replaced the open-air booths and stalls. Today, a modern market building also houses a number of restaurants. In summer, there are a lot of jewelry stalls.

Four major attractions are under the direction of **Malmö Museer (☎ 040/341-000).** Heading the list is **Malmöhus Castle,** on Malmöhusvägen. It was founded in the 15th century by Eric of Pomerania, and rebuilt by Christian III in the 16th century. It was also a prison—the Earl of Bothwell, third husband of Mary, Queen of Scots, was incarcerated here from 1568 to 1573. The castle now houses the City Museum, the Natural History Museum, the Aquarium and Tropicarium, and the Art Museum. The Art Museum's collection of old Scandinavian masters is especially noted for its works by artists from southern Sweden, such as Carl Fredrik Hill (1849–1911), one of Sweden's best landscape painters and a forerunner of European modernism. Most interesting is the large collection of Russian oil paintings from around 1900— the largest collection outside Russia. It also houses some modern art and good samples of Swedish furniture and textiles. The lyrical sketches in the foyer are by Carl Larsson, one of Sweden's best-known artists. West of Stortorget, the castle can be easily reached on foot.

Also in the group, across the street from the castle, is **Kommendanthuset,** Malmöhusvägen, a military museum, and a piece of history in its own right. **Teknik-Och Sjöfartsmuseet** (Museum of Technology and Shipping), on Malmöhusvägen, is near the Kommendanthuset. You can see exhibits of ancient means of communication, as well as the submarine U-3. Technical history can be followed from the steam engine to the jet. The children's department even has a pirate ship, and in summer an old-fashioned tramway is in operation. The **Vagnmusset (Carriage Museum),** housed in the former military horse stable at Drottningtorget, displays carriages since the 18th century, coaches, and cycles.

A 1-day ticket good for all the Malmö Museer properties costs 40 SEK ($4.40) for adults, 10 SEK ($1.10) for children 7 to 16, if visited on the same day. The museums are open daily from noon to 4pm.

Malmö's **S:t Petri (St. Peter's Church),** on Göran Olsgatan (☎ 040/35-90-40), lies a block east of the Rådhus. Dark and a bit foreboding on the outside, it is light and airy within. This Gothic church originated in the 14th century, when Malmö was under the control of the Hanseatic League. It was modeled on Marienkirche, a famous church in Lübeck, Germany. Other than the slender pillars and supporting ogive (diagonal) vaulting, the church's most stunning feature is its 15th-century Krämarkapellet (tradesmen's chapel) from the 1400s. Amazingly, the original artwork remains. During the Reformation, the decoration was viewed as "redundant," and the chapel was sealed off—in effect protecting its paintings from the reformers' overzeal-ous "restoration." Look for the New Testament figures on the vaulted ceiling; they are quite impressive, and surrounded by decorative foliage. Look also for a tall retable from 1611 and an exquisitely carved black limestone and sandstone pulpit from 1599. The pulpit and the octagonal baptismal font from 1601 were the work of master craftsman Daniel Tommisen. The church is open Monday to Friday 8am to 6pm, Sat-urday 9am to 6pm, and Sunday 10am to 6pm. Admission is free.

A final attraction, ✪ **Rooseum,** Gasverksgatan 22 (☎ **040/121-716**), is one of the country's outstanding art museums. It's installed in a former electricity generating sta-tion built at the turn of the century. In 1988 it was converted into this elegant museum, the brainchild of art collector Fredrik Ross (1951–1991). He set out to showcase modern art movements through a series of thematic exhibitions and shows. Although strongest on Nordic art, the exhibitions are international. Hours are Tues-day to Sunday 11am to 5pm (until 8pm Thursday), and admission is 40 SEK ($4.40).

A NEARBY ATTRACTION

Svaneholm, between Malmö and Ystad, was established in 1530 as a fortress, and later partially converted into an Italian-style palace. Today it houses a museum of paintings, furnishings, and tools dating primarily from the 18th and 19th centuries.

Admission to the castle is 30 SEK ($3.30) for adults, 10 SEK ($1.10) for children. It's open April to June and September to December, Wednesday to Sunday, from 11am to 4pm. In July and August, it's open Tuesday to Sunday 11am to 5pm. The cas-tle is completely closed from January to March. There is a restaurant on-site (☎ **0411/450-40**) serving regional specialties. For more information about the cas-tle, write to Svaneholm Museum, S-274 00 Skurup (☎ **0411/400-12**).

Reaching Svaneholm is difficult by public transportation; a train from Malmö stops at Skurup, but it's a 2-mile walk from there. Many visitors opt to go by taxi the rest of the way.

SHOPPING

Malmö's main pedestrian shopping street is **Södergatan,** which runs south of Stor-torget toward the canal. Nearby, at the 16th-century Lilla Torg, a charming 16th-century antique square, you can visit the **Form Design Centre** (☎ **040/10-36-10**). It combines a museum-like exhibition space with boutiques selling upscale handcrafts, including Swedish textiles-by-the-yard, wood carvings, and all manner of other crafts.

At **Röda Tråden,** Adelgatan 5 (☎ **040/23-70-46**), you'll find clothes by the well-known designer Maria Haid, plus handcrafts and souvenirs. You'll also see unique ceramics, studio-designed glass, bronze and silver jewelry, and decorative tiles. On the top floor is an art gallery.

A well-respected name in glassware and crystal is **Silverbergs i Malmö,** Baltzars-gatan 31 (☎ **040/740-80**). This famous store reliably ships its stunning collection of glassware, crystal, furniture, and gifts all over the world. Established in 1927, **Juvel-erare Hugo Nilsson,** Södra Tullgatan 2 (☎ **040/12-65-92**), features some of the most famous names in Danish jewelry making, including Georg Jensen, Rauff, and Ole Lynggaard. Jewelry by Finnish designers such as Lapponia is also sold.

You'll find an unusual collection of Nordic arts and crafts at **Älgamark,** Ö. Rön-nholmsvägen 4 (☎ **040/97-49-60**). It carries Viking jewelry (replicas in pewter, bronze, silver, and gold), along with handcrafts from Swedish Lapland. Traditional pendants, bracelets, and knives are also for sale.

One of Sweden's leading furriers is **Mattssons Päls,** Norra Vallgatan 98 (☎ **040/ 12-55-33**). Saga mink coats and jackets are the most luxurious buys, but Mattssons has a full range of fine furs at prices lower than you'll see in the United States. In the boutique are fur-lined poplins and accessories, all tax free for tourists. The store is 5 minutes on foot from the Central Station and the Copenhagen boats.

Finally, if you haven't found what you're looking for in the specialty shops, try **Hansa Companiet,** Stora Nygatan 50 (☎ **040/77-000**). It's a shopping complex with more than 40 shops, cafes, and restaurants. The latest fashions and items for the home are among the many specialties featured here. However, most foreign visitors come by to check out its selection of Swedish souvenirs and handcrafts.

WHERE TO STAY
EXPENSIVE

⚙ **Hotel Noble House.** Gustav Adolfs Torg 47, S-211 39 Malmö. ☎ **040/664-30-00.** Fax 040/664-30-50. www.hkchotels.se. E-mail: noblehouse@hkchotels.se. 130 units. MINIBAR TV TEL. June 24–Aug 15 and Fri–Sat year-round, 995 SEK ($109.45) double; rest of year, 1,495 SEK ($164.45) double. Year-round, 1,850 SEK ($203.50) suite. Rates include breakfast. AE, DC, MC, V. Closed Dec 22–26. Parking 95 SEK ($10.45). Bus: 10, 11, 17, or 20.

One of the most modern and up-to-date hotels in town—and certainly the most glamorous—is named after the best-selling novel by James Clavell (the former owner was a great devotee of the writings of Clavell). The comfortable pastel-colored rooms are decorated with copies of early 20th-century Swedish paintings. Because of the four-story hotel's convenient location in the town center, its quietest rooms face the interior courtyard. Mattresses are changed as often as the need arises, and the standard hotel-sized bathrooms have an abundance of towels.

Dining/Diversions: The hotel has a restaurant and bar, which serves international and Swedish cuisine.

Amenities: An excellent concierge, room service, conference center, laundry service, and a solarium.

Radisson SAS Hotel. Östergatan 10, S-211 Malmö. ☎ **800/333-3333** or 040/698-40-00. Fax 040/698-40-01 www.radissonsas.com. 224 units. MINIBAR TV TEL. June 5–Aug 5, Mon–Thurs, 1,090 SEK ($119.90) double; Aug 6–June 4, Mon–Thurs 1,780 SEK ($195.80) double; year-round, Fri–Sun 980 SEK ($107.80) double. Year-round, from 2,700 SEK ($297) suite. Rates include breakfast. AE, DC, MC, V. Parking 80 SEK ($8.80). Bus: 14 or 17.

The Radisson SAS contains tastefully decorated rooms, with elegant bathrooms and such amenities as VCRs, hair dryers, trouser presses and radios. Built in 1988, the seven-story hotel was designed to accommodate people with disabilities. Although it's affiliated with Scandinavia's most visible airline, SAS, some visitors consider this hotel bland, anonymous, and somewhat sterile.

Dining/Diversions: A restaurant, Thott's, serves Scandinavian and continental cuisine in a half-timbered house from the mid–16th century. There's also a bar.

Amenities: Baby-sitting, laundry, heated parking garage, sauna, business center, room service.

Scandic Hotel Triangeln. Triangeln 2, S-200 10 Malmö. ☎ **040/693-47-00.** Fax 040/693-47-11. www.scandic-hotels.com. 214 units. A/C MINIBAR TV TEL. June 24–Aug 7 and Fri–Sat year-round, 910 SEK ($100.10) double; rest of year, 1,704 SEK ($187.45) double. Year-round, 2,300–4,100 SEK ($253–$451) suite. Rates include breakfast. AE, DC, MC, V. Parking 90 SEK ($9.90). Bus: 14 or 17.

Malmö's most visible international luxury hotel rises 20 stories from a position in the commercial heart of town. Built in 1989, it boasts sweeping views from almost all its bedrooms. The top three floors contain only suites and a well-engineered health club. Many of the guests are business travelers, often attending one of the dozens of conventions that attract participants from throughout Europe. The rooms are tastefully and comfortably appointed, with light colors, many electronic amenities, and firm mattresses. The bathrooms are more than adequate and well supplied.

Dining/Diversions: One floor above lobby level is a restaurant that serves well-prepared but uncomplicated lunches. In the evening, it becomes a stylish international restaurant, called Figaro, where the prices are more expensive and the ambience more formal and unhurried. There's also a lobby bar-bistro.

Amenities: Laundry, dry cleaning, a fitness center with its own sauna and solarium, concierge, limited room service.

MODERATE

Elite Hotel Savoy. Norra Vallgatan 62, S-201 80 Malmö. ☎ **040/702-30.** Fax 040/ 97-85-51. www.savoy.elite.se. 109 units. MINIBAR TV TEL. June 19–Aug 9 and Fri–Sat year-round, 895 SEK ($98.45) double; rest of year, 1,350 SEK ($148.50) double. Year-round, 2,490 SEK ($273.90) suite. Rates include breakfast. AE, DC, MC, V. Parking 125 SEK ($13.75). Bus: 14 or 17.

This hotel has figured prominently in Malmö history; famous guests have included Dag Hammarskjöld, Liv Ullmann, Alan Alda, and Johnny ("Tarzan") Weissmuller. It boasts some of the most plushly decorated accommodations in Sweden. Rooms contain champagne-colored upholstery, cabriole-legged or Chippendale-style furniture, excellent beds, and all the extras of a deluxe hotel. Well-maintained bathrooms come in a wide variety of sizes, with hair dryers. In the hotel restaurant, you can order from an international menu, perhaps stopping for a before-dinner beer in the British-style pub, the Bishop's Arms.

Hotell Baltzar. Södergatan 20, S-211 24 Malmö. ☎ **040/665-5700.** Fax 040/665-5710. www.baltzarhotel.se. 41 units. MINIBAR TV TEL. Mon–Thurs 1,080–1,600 SEK ($118.80–$176) double; Fri–Sun 830–1,350 SEK ($91.30–$148.50) double. Rates include breakfast. AE, DC, MC, V. Parking 110 SEK ($12.10) per night. Bus: 10.

Around 1900, an entrepreneur who had made a fortune selling chocolate moved into a private home whose turrets, towers, and fanciful ornamentation resembled a stone-carved confection. Several decades later, when it became an elegant and prestigious hotel, it expanded into one of the neighboring buildings. Today, you'll find a hotel with many charming corners and cubbyholes. Grace notes include frescoed ceilings, substantial-looking antiques, and elaborate draperies in some of the public areas. The comfortable, high-ceilinged guest rooms have been upgraded, with furnishings (including good beds) and parquet floors that would suit a prosperous private home. The medium-sized bathrooms are impeccably maintained. The location on an all-pedestrian street keeps things relatively quiet inside. Breakfast is the only meal served, but room service (sandwiches, salads and drinks only) is available 24 hours a day.

Rica City Hotel. Stortorget 15 S-211 22 Malmö. ☎ **040/660-95-50.** Fax 040/660-95-59. www.malmocityhotels.se. 80 units. TV TEL. Mon–Thurs 1,370–1,410 SEK ($150.70–$155.10) double; Fri–Sun 800–900 SEK ($88–$99) double. Rates include breakfast. AE, DC, MC, V. Parking 60 SEK ($6.60). Bus: 14 or 17.

Built in 1912, the hotel lies on Malmö's main square, facing the Town Hall, a short walk from the railway station and the ferryboat terminals for Copenhagen-bound ships. In 1992 the guest rooms were rebuilt in a tasteful modern format. The hotel is owned by the Salvation Army, which strictly forbids the consumption of alcohol on the premises. It's also part of a hotel chain (City Hotels) that operates four other Swedish hotels. The rooms are larger than you might have expected, with good mattresses. Bathrooms tend to be cramped, but are well maintained. There's a sauna and solarium in the hotel's cellar. There's no restaurant (and certainly no bar) on the premises, but about a dozen restaurants are within walking distance.

Scandic Hotel Kramer. Stortorget 7, S-201 21 Malmö. ☎ **040/20-88-00.** Fax 040/
12-69-41. www.scandic-hotels.com. E-mail: kramer@scandic-hotels.com. 113 units. TV TEL.
900–1,695 SEK ($99–$186.45) double. Rates include breakfast. AE, DC, MC, V. Parking 150
SEK ($16.50). Bus: 14, 17, or 20.

At the side of the town's main square, this château-like twin-towered building is one
of Malmö's landmark hotels. Built in 1875, it was renovated at the height of the art
deco era. Between 1992 and 1994 the rooms were redecorated again with an old-
fashioned sense of nostalgia, vaguely reminiscent of staterooms on a pre–Second
World War ocean liner. Each has a firm mattress, a marble bathroom with dark paneling, curved walls, and kitschy, 1930s-style accessories. On the premises is Kramer's
British Pub, an Anglophilic watering hole that serves whiskies, beers, and platters of
food every day from 4pm to 1am.

Theaterhotellet. Rönngatan 3, S-211 47 Malmö. ☎ **040/665-58-00.** Fax 040/665-58-10.
www.teaterhotellet.se. 45 units. TV TEL. Mon–Thurs 1,200 SEK ($132) double; Fri–Sun 750
SEK ($82.50) double. Rates include breakfast. AE, DC, MC, V. Free parking. Bus: 11.

The only negative aspect to this hotel is its banal-looking 1960s-era facade, which is
no uglier than hundreds of other contemporaneous Scandinavian buildings, but isn't
particularly inviting or pleasing. Inside, however, you'll find a cozy, tasteful, and colorful establishment that attracts many repeat clients. Appealing touches include
tawny-colored marble floors, lots of elegant hardwood paneling, lacquered walls in
tones of amber and beige, and spots of vibrant colors in the guest rooms (especially
jewel tones of red and green) that perk up even the grayest of Swedish winter days.
Rooms were renovated in 1996 with new furniture and mattresses, plus new bathrooms with tubs. About a half-mile south of the railway station, the hotel is near a verdant park and the Stadtstheater. Only breakfast is served, but you can usually get
someone to bring you a sandwich and coffee.

INEXPENSIVE

Elite Hotel Residens. Adelgatan 7, S-211 22 Malmö. ☎ **040/611-25-30.** Fax 040/
30-09-60. www.elite.se. 70 units. TV TEL. June to mid-Aug and Fri–Sat year-round, 750 SEK
($82.50) double; rest of year, 1,200 SEK ($132) double. Rates include breakfast. AE, DC,
MC, V. Free parking. Bus: 14 or 17.

In 1987, a team of local investors enlarged the white-sided premises of a historic 1517
inn with the addition of a new brick-and-stone structure. The interconnected structures provide solid, comfortable, and upscale lodgings near the railroad station. Business travelers appreciate its many convention facilities. Except for specialized corners
where an effort was made to duplicate a woodsy-looking men's club in London, many
of the public areas are outfitted in a glossy, modern setup with lots of mirrors, touches
of chrome, and polished marble floors. Guest rooms are more traditionally outfitted
and larger than you might have expected. They have hardwood floors or wall-to-wall
carpeting, good beds, well-upholstered furnishings, and, in some cases, Oriental carpets. The medium-size bathrooms are equipped with hair dryers and trouser presses.
Windows are large and double-insulated against noise from the urban landscape outside. There's a bar on the premises, and a stylishly decorated lobby restaurant, but it's
open only for lunch.

Hotell Royal. Norra Vallgatan 94, S-211 22 Malmö. ☎ **040/664-2500.** Fax 040/12-77-12.
www.hotellroyal.com. E-mail: inforoyal@swedenhotels.se. 30 units. TV TEL. July and Fri–Sat
year-round, 795–895 SEK ($87.45–$98.45) double; rest of year, 995–1,195 SEK
($109.45–$131.45) double. AE, DC, MC, V. Free parking on street 6pm–9am; otherwise, 12
SEK ($1.30) per hour 9am–6pm. Bus: 14 or 17.

This hotel, adjacent to a canal in the historic core of Malmö, is composed of three antique buildings. The most visible is a stately early 20th-century neoclassical town house; the oldest (which was closed for restoration at this writing) dates from the 1500s. Bedrooms are rather small but inviting. The mattresses are good and most units have a minibar. Bathrooms are a bit cramped. The owners, the hard-working Kilström brothers, maintain a small conference center, and work hard to keep their hotel ship-shape. Breakfast is the only meal served.

WHERE TO DINE
EXPENSIVE

✪ Årstiderna I Kockska Huset. Frans Suellsgatan 3. ☎ **040/23-09-10.** Reservations recommended. Main courses 150–265 SEK ($16.50–$29.15); fixed-price lunch 140–260 SEK ($15.40–$28.60); fixed-price dinner 295–450 SEK ($32.45–$49.50). AE, DC, MC, V. Mon–Fri 11:30am–midnight, Sat 5pm–1am. Bus: 14 or 17. SWEDISH/INTERNATIONAL.

One of the most prestigious restaurants in Malmö lies on a "perpetually shadowed" medieval street. It was built in the 1480s as the home and political headquarters of the Danish-appointed governor of Malmö, Jürgen Kock. In its own richly Gothic way, it's the most unusual restaurant setting in town, with vaulted brick ceilings, severe-looking medieval detailing, and a deliberate lack of other kinds of adornment. Owners Marie and Wilhelm Pieplow have created an environment where the prime ministers of Sweden and Finland, as well as dozens of politicians, artists, and actors, have dined exceedingly well. Menu items change with the seasons; the establishment's name, Årstiderna, translates from the Swedish as "The Four Seasons." Likely to be featured are fried monkfish with parsley butter, salmon roe, and Norwegian lobster; orange-glazed wild duck with flap mushrooms and honey-rosemary sauce; fillet of venison in an herb crust with chanterelle mushrooms and juniper-berry sauce; Swedish beefsteak with red wine and potato gratin; and a chocolate terrine with cloudberry sorbet and a compôte of blackberries.

✪ Johan P. Saluhallen, Landbygatan. ☎ **040/97-18-18.** Reservations recommended. Main courses 170–225 SEK ($18.70–$24.75); 2-course fixed-price menu 210 SEK ($23.10); 3-course fixed-price menu 245 SEK ($26.95); 4-course fixed-price menu 495 SEK ($54.45); 5-course fixed-price menu 525 SEK ($57.75). AE, MC, V. Mon–Thurs 11:30am–10:30pm, Fri 7–11pm, Sat 11:30am–5pm. Bus: 14 or 17. FISH/SEAFOOD.

Some of the most appealing seafood in Malmö is prepared and served in this artfully simple, mostly white dining room that has managed to suppress any advertisements of brand-name products. The result is an almost pristine setting where the freshness of the seafood is the main draw. Menu items are prepared fresh every day, based on whatever is available at the nearby Saluhallen (marketplace). Examples include an award-winning version of fish soup that's inspired by the traditions of Provence; a leek and potato vichyssoise served with fresh mussels and a timbale of pike; baked monkfish with mustard-flavored spaetzle, served with dried ham and braised cabbage in a tomato-flavored broth; and an old-fashioned version of chicken dumplings with mushroom risotto and sweet-and-sour tomato sauce. Dessert might include a mousse made with bitter white chocolate, served with dark-chocolate madeleines and coffee sauce.

✪ Restaurant Kramer Gastronomie. In the Scandic Hotel Kramer, Stortorget 7. ☎ **040/20-88-06.** Reservations recommended. Main courses 155–240 SEK ($17.05–$26.40); 3-course fixed-price menu 285 SEK ($31.35); 7-course fixed price menu 595 SEK ($65.45). AE, DC, MC, V. Mon–Fri 5–11pm, Sat 6–11pm. Bar open till 1am. Bus: 10. CONTINENTAL.

Accessed through the lobby of the also-recommended hotel, this restaurant serves the best food of any hotel dining room in Malmö. There's an upscale, woodsy-looking bar that's separated from the brown and off-white dining room with a leaded glass divider, and an attention to cuisine that brings a conservative, not particularly flashy clientele back again and again. The composition of the fixed-price menus changes every week, and it's relatively common for a group of business partners to spend 3 hours at table sampling the seven-course *menu dégustation*. The food is faultlessly fresh and handled beautifully by the kitchen staff that believes in delicate seasonings and perfectly cooked dishes. The chef is dedicated to his job, personally shopping for market-fresh ingredients to inspire his imaginationMenu items include shots of shellfish bouillon served with parmesan chips and coriander salsa; scallops with grilled tuna and bacon; blackened fillet of beef with pecorino cheese, lemon wedges, arugula, and a sauce made with a reduction of *court bouillon* and red wine; and char-grilled halibut with glazed turnips, truffle butter, and dill oil. Pastas here are upscale and esoteric, including a version with spinach, crayfish, fried fillet of sole, and dill sauce.

MODERATE

Centiliter & Gram. Stortorget 17. ☎ **40/12-18-12.** Reservations recommended. Main courses 135–205 SEK ($14.85–$22.55). AE, DC, MC, V. Mon–Sat 11:30am–2pm; Mon–Wed 4:30pm–midnight, Thurs 4:30pm–1am, Fri–Sat 4:30pm–3am. Bus: 10. CONTINENTAL.

This is one of Malmö's hottest restaurants, with a hipster clientele that includes lots of well-known painters and football (soccer) stars, as well as enough media and P.R. people to change the public opinions of Sweden. It occupies an artfully minimalist gray-and-mauve-colored space whose focal point is a central, rectangular-shaped bar. Here, flirtation games continue until late into the night, long after virtually everybody else has lost his or her interest in food. Menu items change with the seasons, and with whatever food fad happens to be in vogue in London, Stockholm, or Paris at the time. Stellar examples include a parcel of Italian goat cheese baked in phyllo pastry with a tomato and basil sauce; black mussels with white wine and cream sauce, and served with a tomato *bruschetta;* deliberately undercooked (i.e., "pink") duck breast with teriyaki sauce and an orange and mango-flavored chutney; and grilled halibut and scallops with a spicy Thai red curry, coconut milk, and jasmine-flavored rice. The establishment's name, incidentally, derives from wine (which is measured in centiliters) and food (which is measured in grams).

Lemongrass. Grunbodgatan 9. ☎ **40/30-69-79.** Reservations recommended. Main courses 106–196 SEK ($11.65–$21.55); 7-course fixed-price menu 355 SEK ($39.05). AE, MC, V. Mon–Thurs 6pm–midnight, Fri–Sat 6pm–1am. Bus: 6 or 10. ASIAN.

Lemongrass is set in one large, Spartan room that's devoid of the artsy clutter of many Asian restaurants. Instead, on pale gray walls, you'll find clusters of exotic-looking orchids, as well as tufted bunches of the lemongrass for which it was named. There's a bar where you can wait for your table, if you have to, and a menu that contains food items from Japan (including sushi), China, and Thailand. A staff member will help you coordinate a meal from disparate culinary styles in ways that you might have expected only in Los Angeles, London, or New York.

Min Brors Krog (My Brother's Restaurant). S:t Pauli Kyrkogata 11. ☎ **040/305-303.** Reservations recommended. Main courses 95–165 SEK ($10.45–$18.15); 3-course fixed-price menu 198–225 SEK ($21.80–$24.75). AE, DC, MC, V. Sun–Wed 6–10pm, Thurs–Sat 6–11pm. Closed Jan. Bus: 11. CONTINENTAL.

The owner of this place has a sister, and the name by which she recommended it to her friends (My Brother's Restaurant) eventually became the establishment's legal moniker. It's more self-consciously "New Age" than the other restaurants within this section, a fact that may or may not appeal to you. What you'll get is a compact dining room outfitted in monochromes of gray and white with brightly patterned tablecloths. The food is consistently good and very fresh, and the dishes here have many local fans. Dishes are perfectly executed and well flavored. Menu items change with the whims of the chef, but might include duck consommé, oven-fried duck breast served with red wine and herb sauce; reindeer with juniperberry and herb sauce; and a chocolate mousse served with raspberry sorbet. A separate bar welcomes cigar smokers.

Rådhuskällern. Kyrkogatan 5. ☎ **040/790-20.** Reservations recommended. Main courses 160–210 SEK ($17.60–$23.10); 1-course lunch 75 SEK ($8.25). AE, DC, MC, V. Mon–Fri 11:30am–2pm and 6–11pm, Sat 5–11pm. Bus: 14 or 17. SWEDISH.

This is the most atmospheric place in Malmö, located in the cellar of the Town Hall. Even if you don't eat here, at least drop in for a drink in the pub or lounge. The severe exterior and labyrinth of underground vaults were built in 1546; the dark-vaulted dining room was used for centuries to store gold, wine, furniture, and food. Menu staples include halibut with lobster sauce, plank steak, fillet of veal, pepper steak, and roast duck; and there's always an array of daily specials. Although the fare is first-rate here, it never overexcites the palate.

Wallman's Salonger. Generalsgatan 1. ☎ **040/74945.** Reservations recommended. Main courses 200–250 SEK ($22–$27.50); 3-course fixed-price menu 399 SEK ($43.90). AE, DC, MC, V. Wed–Sat 7pm–2am. Closed May to mid-Aug. CONTINENTAL.

Large enough for 400 diners at a time, and painted a heady shade of Bordeaux, this is the most entertaining restaurant in Malmö—with a most entertaining staff. At one end of the restaurant is stage upon which members of the wait staff—each a candidate for a job in the theater—will sing, dance, and generally, wonderfully amuse you. Your meal will consist of a flavorful but not particularly spectacular assortment of steaks, soups, salads, seafood, veal, and/or pork dishes, but since most clients are gyrating on the dance floor before 11pm anyway, no one especially cares.

INEXPENSIVE

Anno 1900. Norra Bultoftavagen 7. ☎ **040/18-47-47.** Reservations recommended. Main courses 120–190 SEK ($13.20–$20.90); fixed-price lunch 100 SEK ($11). AE, DC, MC, V. Mon–Fri 11:15am–2pm; Tues–Fri 6–11pm. Bus: 14 or 17. SWEDISH.

The name of this place gives a hint about its decor: lots of antique woodwork and accessories from the heyday of the Industrial Revolution. There's a garden in back that's open during warm weather, if you want a break from turn-of-the-century fussiness. Menu items derive from tried-and-true classics: old-fashioned versions of cauliflower soup, halibut with horseradish sauce, chicken dumplings with noodles, roasted beef, steaks, *frikadeller* (meatballs), and fried herring. If you have a Swedish grandmother, bring her here—she'll feel right at home.

Casa Mia. Södergatan 12. ☎ **040/23-05-00.** Reservations recommended. Pastas and pizzas 90–198 SEK ($9.90–$21.80); 1-course *dagens* (daily) menu 89–110 SEK ($9.80–$12.10). AE, DC, MC, V. Mon–Sat noon–11:30pm, Sun noon–10pm. Bus: 14 or 17. ITALIAN.

Venetian gondola moorings ornament the front terrace of this Nordic version of a neighborhood trattoria. Troubadours stroll from table to crowded table singing Neapolitan ballads, and your waiter is likely to address you in Italian. You might begin with a steaming bowl of *stracciatella alla romana* (egg-and-chicken soup) or the fish soup of the house, then move on to penne with shrimp, basil, cream, and tomatoes, or spaghetti with seafood. Later you can dig into *saltimbocca alla romana* (veal with ham), a portion of grilled scampi, escalope of veal stuffed with goose liver, or an array of grilled meats with aromatic herbs. There are more than 15 types of pizza on the menu, and pastries are offered for dessert. Okay, it's not as good as the food served in a typical trattoria in northern Italy, but the cuisine is a refreshing change of pace.

Restaurant B & B (Butik och Bar). Saluhallen, Landbygatan 52. ☎ **040/12-71-20.** Reservations recommended. Main courses 98–160 SEK ($10.80–$17.60); fixed-price lunch 65 SEK ($7.15). AE, DC, MC, V. Mon–Sat noon–10:30pm. Bus: 14 or 17. SWEDISH/INTERNATIONAL.

This well-managed, relatively inexpensive bistro is in a corner of the Saluhallen (food market), which provides the fresh ingredients that go into each menu item. In a simple, old-fashioned setting, with glowing hardwood floors, pristine white walls, and a scattering of antiques that evokes the Sweden of long ago, you'll find flavorful, unpretentious food. It's international cuisine, with occasional emphasis on Swedish staples known to every grandmother, including creamy fish soup in the Swedish style. Most of the other dishes are more exotic, including New Orleans versions of jambalaya, Cajun-inspired tagliatelle with blackened chicken and fiery sauces, teriyaki pork, roasted chicken with tiger prawns, and pasta with a salmon-flavored vodka sauce.

MALMÖ AFTER DARK

For serious nighttime pursuits, many locals—especially young people—head for easily reached Copenhagen. However, there are several local amusements, the best of which is previewed below. See "Copenhagen After Dark," in Chapter 4, "Exploring Copenhagen."

From May to September, locals head for **Folkets Park (People's Park),** Amiralsgatan 35 (☎ **040/709-90**). It consists of sprawling amusement grounds and pleasure gardens. The dancing pavilions, vaudeville performances, and open-air concerts also draw big crowds. There's even a reptile center. Children will find a playhouse, plus a small zoo and a puppet theater. Restaurants dot the grounds. Open daily from 3pm to midnight in summer, daily noon to 6pm in winter. Admission is usually free; however, for some performances it's 50 to 110 SEK ($5.50 to $12.10). Take bus no. 11, 13, or 17 from Gustav Adolfs Torg.

Dancing is the rage at the creatively designed **Nightclub Etage,** Stortorget 6 (☎ **040/23-20-60**). Initially conceived as an upscale bar and restaurant in the late 1980s, this nightspot lowered its prices and began marketing to a mass audience a few years later—and it hasn't seemed to suffer as a result of the change. To get there, climb a circular staircase from an enclosed courtyard in the town's main square. Bars open and close regularly on other floors, but the establishment's heart and soul is on the third floor, where a futuristic restaurant serves simple platters of food for 60 to 110 SEK ($6.60 to $12.10). The disco is just a few steps away. The complex is open Monday and Thursday through Saturday from 9pm to at least 3am, depending on the crowd. Cover for the disco is 50 to 90 SEK ($5.50 to $9.90).

The Swedes pronounce the club's name as "Plush," although it's spelled **Plysch.** Lying at Lillatorget 1 (☎ **040/12-76-70**), this place is open only on Friday and Saturday nights from 8pm to 3am, charging a cover charge of 50 SEK ($5.50); it attracts a 30-plus crowd. When this nightclub and cocktail bar was developed, its owners did everything they could to appoint it like a well-upholstered private apartment. The result is a labyrinth of medium-sized rooms, each personalized and intimate with bars are positioned here and there within the maze. Love often blooms at **Restaurang Stadt,** Hamburgsgatan 3 (☎ **040/12-22-21**). At Malmö's equivalent of New York's Roseland, romantic dancing, sometimes check to check, is the norm. Patrons tend to be over 35, and they enjoy recorded music of the style that might remind you of a 1960s variety show. There's a restaurant on the premises that serves platters of traditional Swedish food every Tuesday to Saturday between 8 and 11:30pm. Main courses cost 100 to 165 SEK ($11 to $18.15). Music and bar activities are scheduled as follows: The bar is open for music and dancing Monday to Wednesday 7pm to 1am, Thursday 8pm to 2am, and Friday and Saturday 8pm to 3am. The cover charge is 70 SEK ($7.70).

The largest nightclub in Malmö, five-floor **Club Privée,** Malmborgsgatan 7 (☎ 040/97-46-66), attracts a devoted clientele that seems to revolve their calendars around the limited number of nights the place is open. Near the Gustav Adolfs Torg in the center of town, it has a decor that replicates an English pub, lots of Chesterfield sofas, and a clientele of mostly twentysomethings on Friday and Saturday. There's a bar, and different musical ambiences on each of the establishment's five floors. You'll pay 42 SEK ($4.60) for a large beer. It's open only on Friday and Saturday nights from 11pm to 5am. The cover charge is 60 to 70 SEK ($6.60 to $7.70).

Nostalgic for Britain? The best replica of a British pub is the **Bishop's Arms,** Norra Vallgatan 62 (☎ 040/702-30), in the Savoy Hotel. Some of the best and coldest beer in town is served here, and there's always a congenial crowd.

Culturally, the **Malmö Symphony Orchestra** is renowned across Europe. It performs at the Konserthus, Föreningsgatan 35 (☎ 040/34-35-00), and the Musikhögskolan Ystadvägen 25 (☎ 040/19-22-00). The tourist office distributes programs of cultural events.

4 Lund

11 miles NE of Malmö, 187 miles S of Gothenburg, 374 miles SW of Stockholm

The city was probably founded in 1020 by Canute the Great, ruler of the United Kingdom of England and Denmark, when this part of Sweden was a Danish possession. The city really made its mark when its cathedral was consecrated in 1145. The city's 1,000-year anniversary was celebrated in 1990, since archaeological excavations show that a stave church was built here in 990. Lund quickly became a center of religion, politics, culture, and commerce for all of Scandinavia.

The city town has winding passageways, centuries-old buildings, and the richness of a university town. Lund University, founded in 1666, plays an active role in town municipal life.

The most exciting time to be in Lund, as in Uppsala, is on Walpurgis Eve, April 30, when student revelries signal the advent of spring. A visit to Lund at any time is a pleasure.

ESSENTIALS

GETTING THERE   From Gothenburg, drive south along the E6; Malmö and Lund are 20 minutes apart on an express highway. If you're not driving, trains run hourly from Malmö, a 15-minute ride. Buses leave Malmö hourly for the 30-minute trip.

VISITOR INFORMATION   The tourist information office, **Lunds Turistbyrå,** is at Kyrkogatan 11 (☎ 046/35-50-40; www.lund.se). It's open June to August, Monday to Friday 10am to 6pm, and Saturday and Sunday 10am to 2pm; September to May, Monday to Friday 10am to 5pm, and Saturday 10am to 2pm.

GETTING AROUND   All the major sights are within a 10-minute walk of each other, so exploring Lund on foot is the only way to go.

SEEING THE SIGHTS

Botaniska Trädgården (Botanical Gardens). Östra Vallgatan 20. ☎ **046/222-73-20.** Free admission. Gardens, daily 6am–8pm; greenhouses, daily noon–3pm. Bus: 1, 2, 3, 4, 5, 6, or 7.

A block east of the cathedral, these gardens contain some 7,500 specimens of plants gathered from all over the world. On a hot summer day, this is the city's most pleasant place to be. Clusters of students congregate here, stretching out beneath the trees, and families often picnic on the grounds. Serious horticulturists will want to visit when the greenhouses are open.

✪ **Domkyrkan (Cathedral of Lund).** Kyrkogatan. ☎ **046/35-87-00.** Free admission. Mon–Sat 8am–6pm, Sun 9am–6pm. Bus: 1, 2, 3, 4, 5, 6 or 7.

With this ancient cathedral, Romanesque architecture in Scandinavia reached its height. The church's eastern exterior is one of the finest expressions of Romanesque architecture in northern Europe. The sandstone interior has sculptural details similar in quality and character to those in Lombardy and other parts of Italy. There is also a crypt with a high altar dedicated in 1123, and intricately carved choir stalls from about 1375.

A partly reconstructed 14th-century astronomical clock not only tells the time and the date, but stages a splashy tournament from the Middle Ages—complete with clashing knights and the blare of trumpets. That's not all: The Three Wise Men come out to pay homage to the Virgin and Child. To see all this, time your visit so you're in the cathedral when the clock strikes noon (1pm on Sunday) or 3pm.

Drottens Museum (Medieval Museum). Kattesund 6. ☎ **046/14-13-28.** Admission 10 SEK ($1.10) adults, free for children. Tues–Fri 9am–4pm, Sat–Sun noon–4pm. Bus: 1, 2, 3, 4, 5, 6, 7.

During the excavations for an inner-city office building, workers discovered the remnants of one of Sweden's earliest churches—a now-ruined Romanesque building that was built about 1,000 years ago. Recognizing the remnants as historically and aesthetically valuable, civic leaders ordered the construction of a series of large windows in the new building, allowing pedestrians on the sidewalk outside to see the ruins from above. Visitors can walk among the ruins, viewing an exhibition of mannequins dressed in medieval garb in scenes of everyday life. Also on display are some of the skeletons unearthed at the excavation site.

Historiska Museet. Kraftstorg 1. ☎ **046/222-79-44.** Admission 35 SEK ($3.85) adults, 15 SEK ($1.65) children 7–18, free for children under 7. Tues–Fri 11am–4pm. Bus: 1, 2, 3, 4, 5, 6, or 7.

Founded in 1805, this is the second-largest museum of archaeology in Sweden. Collections trace the development of the people of Skåne from antiquity to the Middle Ages. One of the skeletons on display is that of a young man, one of the oldest finds of a human body in northern Europe, dating from around 7000 B.C. Most collections from the Bronze Age came from tombs. During excavations in eastern Skåne, a large grave field turned up jewelry and weapons, which are on display. Church art dominates the medieval exhibition.

Kulturen (Museum of Cultural History). Tegnérsplatsen. ☎ **046/35-04-00.** Admission 40 SEK ($4.40) adults, free for children. Apr 15–Sept, daily 11am–5pm; Oct–Apr 14, Tues–Sun noon–4pm. Bus: 1, 2, 3, 4, 5, 6, or 7.

After leaving Domkyrkan (the Cathedral of Lund), walk across the university grounds to Adelgatan, which the local citizens consider their most charming street. Here you'll find Kulturen, another open-air museum. It contains reassembled, sod-roofed farms and manor houses, a carriage museum, ceramics, peasant costumes, Viking artifacts, and old handcrafts. The wooden church was moved to this site from the glassworks district.

WHERE TO STAY

The tourist office (see "Visitor Information," above) can help put you up in private homes for as little as 175 SEK ($19.25) per person per night.

✪ **Grand Hotel.** Bantorget 1, S-221 04 Lund. ☎ **046/28-06-100.** Fax 046/28-06-150. www.grand.lundia.se. E-mail: info@grandilund.se. 84 units. MINIBAR TV TEL. June 7–Aug 8 and Fri–Sat year-round, 1,295–1,495 SEK ($142.45–$164.45) double; 2,900 SEK ($319) suite. Aug 9–June 6, 1,895–2,095 SEK ($208.45–$230.45) double; 3,900 SEK ($429) suite. Rates include breakfast. AE, CB, DC, V. Parking 100 SEK ($11). Bus: 1, 2, 3, 4, 5, 6, or 7.

This château-style hotel, the most prestigious in town, overlooks the fountains and flowers of a city park. The marble lobby is grand. Rooms in the hotel's conical corner tower are the most desirable. All the guest rooms are decorated in old-fashioned style. They have cable TV and very firm, frequently renewed mattresses. The bathrooms are moderate in size, with hair dryers. The elegant restaurant offers fixed-price meals beginning at 200 SEK ($22).

Hotel Concordia. Stålbrogatan 1, S-222-24 Lund. ☎ **046/13-50-50.** Fax 046/13-74-22. www.concordia.se. E-mail: info@concordia.se. 50 units. TV TEL. Sun–Thurs 1,495 SEK ($164.45) double; Fri–Sat 795 SEK ($87.45) double. All week long 1,500 SEK ($165) suite. Rates include breakfast. AE, DC, MC, V. Parking 50 SEK ($5.50). Bus: 1, 2, 3, 4, 5, 6, or 7.

Next door to the brick house where August Strindberg lived in 1897, this charming, ornate building was constructed in 1882 as a private home. It served as a student hotel for some time and was then upgraded to a pleasant hotel. The modernized rooms are moderate in size and sedate, with good beds; a few are reserved for nonsmokers. The bathrooms are a bit small, but equipped with hair dryers. Housekeeping here is among the finest in town. On the premises is a sauna. The hotel is a 5-minute walk south of the railroad station.

Hotel Djingis Khan. Margarethevägen 7, S 222 40 Lund. ☎ **800/528-1234** in the U.S., or 046/14-00-60. Fax 046/14-36-26. www.bestwestern.com. 55 units. TV TEL. Sun–Thurs 1,295 SEK ($142.45) double; Fri–Sat 800 SEK ($88) double. Rates include breakfast. AE, DC, MC, V. Closed July. Free parking. Bus: 3 or 93.

Within a 15-minute walk north of the town center, this hotel was originally built in the 1970s as employee housing for a local hospital. It became a pleasant, well-managed hotel in the early 1990s. Two of its wings still contain private apartments, but it's mostly made up of attractively modern guest rooms outfitted in a conservatively comfortable style. They have good beds and small but adequate bathrooms. Public areas contain lots of English-inspired dark paneling, Chesterfield sofas, and an ambience that might remind you of a private men's club in London.

The hotel's name, incidentally, comes from the most famous satirical comedy (*Ghenghis Khan*) ever produced in Lund. It was written in the 1950s by Hasse Alfredsson, and this hotel was named in its honor.

Hotel Lundia. Knut den Stores Gata 2, S-221 04. ☎ **046/280-65-00.** Fax 046/280-65-10. www.lundia.se. E-mail: hotel@lundia.se. 97 units. MINIBAR TV TEL. Late June to early Aug and Fri–Sat year-round, 995 SEK ($109.45) double; rest of year, 1,375–1,795 SEK ($151.25–$197.45) double. Year-round, 2,100–3,595 SEK ($231–395.45) suite. Rates include breakfast. AE, MC, V. Closed Dec 22–26. Parking 100 SEK ($11). Bus: 1, 2, 3, 4, 5, 6, or 7.

Under the same management as the Grand Hotel (see above), this is the most pleasantly situated and one of the most modern hotels in town. The interior has winding staircases, white marble sheathing, and big windows. Guest rooms have adequately sized tile bathrooms, clothes presses, and refrigerators, and are designed with Scandinavian fabrics and unusual lithographs. Most units are moderate in size; singles are a bit cramped. Guests interested in a formal meal usually head for the dining room at the Grand, about a block away. Hotel Lundia has a brasserie (see "Where to Dine," below). On the premises are a casino and a stylish nightclub.

✪ Scandic Hotel Star. Glimmervägen 5, PO Box 11026, SE-220 11 Lund. ☎ **046/211-20-00.** Fax 046/211-50-00. www.scandic-hotels.com. 196 units. TV TEL. Mid-June to mid-Aug and Fri–Sat year round, 720 SEK ($79.20) double; rest of year, 1,445 SEK ($158.95) double. Year-round, 2,380–2,800 SEK ($261.80–$308) suite. AE, DC, MC, V. Free parking. Bus: 3 or 7.

This hotel, a 20-minute walk from the town center, is the most comfortable in Lund. Built in 1991, it attracts lots of business conventions, as well as most of the rock stars and movie actors known throughout Sweden. Each of the hotel's double rooms is configured as a mini-suite, with a separate sitting area and traditional, conservative furnishings that would fit into a well-appointed upper-middle-class Swedish home. The public areas are more international and contemporary than the bedrooms, and have lots of potted or hanging plants, wicker furnishing, and varnished wood. The "relaxation center" has an exercise area, swimming pool, sauna, and solarium. The restaurant is open daily except Sunday for lunch and dinner. There's also a well-upholstered bar area, which serves burgers and sandwiches every day, and is especially busy on Sunday when the hotel's more formal dining room is closed.

WHERE TO DINE

Anna's Restaurant. Lilla Fiskaregatan 11. ☎ **046/13-04-24.** Reservations recommended. Main courses 110–185 SEK ($12.10–$20.35). AE, DC, MC, V. Mon–Sat 10am–11pm, Sun 10am–5pm. SWEDISH.

Some of the regular clients of this place compare it to a small, informal, and convivial tavern, the kind that's particularly appealing on cold winter nights. Set on two floors, one of which has a prominent and popular bar, it segues throughout the day from roles that swing from a simple bistro to a more elaborate restaurant as the evening progresses. Good-tasting menu items include dishes such as grilled salmon with lemon-butter and dill sauce, venison in port wine glaze, lobster soup, and savory steaks. In summer, consider a table on the outside terrace.

Brasserie Lundia. In the Hotel Lundia, Knut den Stores Gata 2. ☎ **046/12-41-40.** Reservations required Fri–Sat. Main courses 98–175 SEK ($10.80–$19.25). AE, DC, MC, V. Mon–Fri 11am–midnight, Sat noon–10pm, Sun 4–11pm. Bus: 1, 2, 3, 4, 5, 6, or 7. SWEDISH.

This brasserie is the only restaurant in Lund with its own in-house bakery. At lunch, when it's one of the most popular cafeterias in town, it serves crisp salads, open-faced sandwiches, and hot dishes as part of the full cafeteria meals. At night, it's an à la carte restaurant with waitress service, serving steak tartare, fettuccine with salmon, tagliatelle bolognese, grilled fillet mignon, grilled pork cutlet with pepper sauce, deep-fried Camembert, and seven kinds of alcohol-rich after-dinner coffees. Although no one ever accused the kitchen staff of being overly experimental here, what you get isn't bad. Everything is well prepared, and there's good, relaxed service. It has an inviting decor with wood and russet-colored marble tables.

Gloria's Bar and Restaurant. S:t Petri Kyrkogata 9. ☎ **046/15-19-85.** Reservations recommended. Main courses 89–159 SEK ($9.80–$17.50). AE, MC, V. Mon–Fri 11:30am–10:30pm, Sat 12:30–11pm, Sun 1–10pm. Bus: 1, 2, 3, 4, 5, 6, or 7. AMERICAN.

The success of this American-inspired sports and western bar would gladden the heart of any U.S.-born ideologue. On two floors of an old-fashioned building in the historic center of town, it has a crowded and likable bar in the cellar and an even larger bar upstairs. Scattered throughout the premises are photographs and posters of American sports heroes, baseball and football memorabilia, and Wild West artifacts. Draft beer costs 42 SEK ($5.40) for a foaming mug. The restaurant serves copious portions of such rib-stickers as hamburgers, steaks, and an array of Cajun-inspired dishes. The staff wears jeans, cowboy boots, and shirts emblazoned with Gloria's logo. Live music is performed between 9:30pm and 1am each Wednesday. Thursday is rock night.

Ø **Bar.** Mårtenstorget 9. ☎ **046/211-22-88.** Reservations recommended. Main courses 100–195 SEK ($11–$21.45). AE, DC, MC, V. Daily 11:30am–midnight; bar until 1 or 2am. INTERNATIONAL.

One of the most interesting restaurants in Lund defines itself as a "laboratory for chefs" because of the experimental nature of a menu that changes virtually every week. The venue looks like it might have been designed by a Milanese post-modernist, with blue and ash white walls and a strictly minimalist kind of angularity. It's usually mobbed every night both with diners and with clients of the convivial bar area. Here, you're likely to meet students from the university *and* their professors, all animated in dialogue. Menu items include fillet of elk with thyme sauce, served with apple and potato muffins; grilled halibut served with lemon oil, horseradish, and house-made pasta; and lime-flavored clam chowder with Vietnamese spring rolls.

Staket. Stora Södergatan 6. ☎ **046/211-93-67.** Reservations recommended. Main courses 135–155 SEK ($14.85–$17.05). AE, DC, MC, V. Mon–Thurs noon–10:30pm, Fri–Sat noon–11:30pm, Sun noon–10pm. Bus: 1, 2, 3, 4, 5, 6, or 7. SWEDISH/CONTINENTAL.

An old tavern that serves good food in an unspoiled atmosphere, this establishment occupies the cellar and street level of a 15th-century building. The step-gabled brick facade is a historic landmark. Menu items include crabmeat cocktail, lobster or goulasch soup, white fillet of pork, tournedos of beef, a mixed grill, marinated salmon, pickled herring, baked potatoes with black curry, and whitefish toast. Although both dining rooms are equally appealing, fondues (a ritual whereby skewers of meat are cooked at your table in pots of heated oil) are served only in the cellar.

LUND AFTER DARK

Most dance clubs in Lund tend to operate only on weekends, when the clientele mostly includes university students. Examples include **Tetner's Restaurant,** Sandgatan 2 (☎ **046/131-333**), which opens a dance floor in the cellar every Saturday from 9pm till 2am. There's also a dance floor in the basement of the also-recommended **Gloria's Restaurant,** every Friday and Saturday beginning at 10:30pm. Entrance is free. A final dance choice, also open only Friday and Saturday, is the **Palladium,** Stora Södergatan 13 (☎ **046/211-66-60**). Entrance is free to a place that resembles a somewhat beery pub with a college-age clientele every other night of the week.

Lundia Nightcafé. Knut den Stores Gata 2. ☎ **046/280-65-22.** Cover 50 SEK ($5.50). Bus: 1, 2, 3, 4, 5, 6, or 7.

In the cellar of the Hotel Lundia (see "Where to Stay," above) are a small-stakes casino (blackjack and roulette), two bars, a dance floor, and a modern cellar popular with students. Residents of the Hotel Lundia and guests and clients of diners from the Brasserie Lundia enter free, but everyone else pays the cover. Draft beer costs 45 SEK ($4.95). It's open from 11pm to 3am.

EASY EXCURSIONS

You may want to make a side trip to **Dalby Church,** 5-240 12 Dalby (☎ **046/ 20-00-65**), 8 miles east of Lund. The starkly beautiful, well-preserved 11th-century former bishop's church built of stone is the oldest in Scandinavia. Be sure to visit its crypt. The church is open daily 9am to 4pm. Several buses (nos. 158 and 161) a day run between Lund center and Dalby.

About a 30-minute drive northeast of Lund (off Route 23) is the **Castle of Bosjök-loster,** Höör by Ringsjön (☎ **0413/250-48**). Once a Benedictine convent founded around 1080, it was closed during the Reformation in the 16th century. The spectacular Great Courtyard contains thousands of flowers and exotic shrubs, terraces, and a park with animals and birds. In the vaulted refectory and the Stone Hall, native arts and crafts, jewelry, and other Swedish goods are displayed. You can picnic on the grounds or enjoy a lunch at a simple restaurant in the garden, for around 100 SEK ($11).

The entire complex is open daily from May 1 to September 30 8am to 8pm; the museum and exhibition hall inside the castle, daily 10am to 6pm. Admission is 40 SEK ($4.40) for adults, 25 SEK ($2.75) for senior citizens and students, 12 SEK ($1.30) for children 6 to 16, free for children under 6. In the park stands a 1,000-year-old oak tree. The castle lies 28 miles from Malmö and 18 miles from Lund. From Lund, there's a train link to Höör; after that, take bus no. R02 to Bösjokloster on Route 23, 3 miles south to Höör.

5 Ystad

34 miles E of Malmö, 28 miles W of Simrishamn

Ystad makes a good base for exploring the castles and manors of Skåne. An important port during the Middle Ages, Ystad retains its ancient look, with about 300 half-timbered houses, mazes of narrow lanes, and even a watchman who sounds the hours of the night in the tower of St. Mary's Church.

ESSENTIALS

GETTING THERE   From Malmö, drive east on route 65. If you're not driving, there are good rail connections. Monday through Friday, trains run roughly on the hour between Malmö and Ystad. The trip takes 1 hour. On Saturday there are four daily trains from Malmö, and on Sunday six trains. Three daily buses make the 1-hour trip Monday through Saturday from Malmö to Ystad. On Sunday, there's only one bus.

VISITOR INFORMATION   The tourist bureau, **Ystads Turistbyrå,** S:t Knuts Torg, (☎ **0411/577681;** www.ystad.se), is at the bus station in the same building as the art museum (Konstmuseum). It's open mid-June to mid-August, Monday to Saturday 9am to 7pm, and Sunday 1 to 7pm; off-season, Monday to Friday 9am to 5pm.

SEEING THE SIGHTS

The focal point of the town is **S:t Maria Kyrka,** Stortorget (☎ **0411/69-20-0**), which dates to the early 1200s. Each successive century brought new additions and changes. Regrettably, many of its richest decorative features were deemed unfashionable and removed in the 1880s because of changing tastes. (However, some of the more interesting ones were brought back in a restoration program 4 decades later.) The chancel with the ambulatory is late Gothic, and the church spire dates from 1688. Inside, look for the baptismal chapel, with a richly carved German altar from the 15th century. The font came from Lübeck, Germany, in 1617, and the iron candelabra is a very early one, from the 1300s. The early 17th-century baroque pulpit is also worth a look. The church is open June to mid-September only, daily 10am to 6pm. There is no admission fee.

The **Museum of Modern Art (Ystads Konstmuseum),** S:t Knuts Torg (☎ **0411/ 577-285**) in central Ystad, includes a small military museum. Permanent exhibits feature mainly art from Denmark and Skåne from the past 100 years. Admission is 20 SEK

($2.20). The Ystad Tourist Office is in the same building as the museum. The museum is open Tuesday to Friday noon to 5pm; Saturday and Sunday noon to 4pm.

The only museum in Sweden in a medieval monastic house is the **City Museum in the Grey Friars Monastery (Stadsmuséet i Gråbrödraklostret)**, S:t Petri Kykoplan (☎ 0411/577-286). Constructed in 1267, the building is a monument from the Danish era in the town of Ystad. Various antiquities in the museum trace the area's history. The museum is open year-round Monday to Friday noon to 5pm, and Saturday to Sunday noon to 4pm. The admission fee is 20 SEK ($2.20).

WHERE TO STAY

Hotel Continental. Hamngatan 13 S-271 00 Ystad. ☎ 0411/137-00. Fax 0411/125-70. www.hotelcontinental-ystad.se. 52 units. TV TEL. June 21–Aug 4 and Fri–Sat year-round, 950 SEK ($104.50) double; rest of year, 1,090–1,200 SEK ($119.90–$132) double. AE, DC, MC, V. Parking 20 SEK ($2.20).

Although it has modern appointments, this may be Skåne's oldest hotel, dating from 1829. The rooms are furnished in tasteful Italian-inspired decor and have a number of modern amenities, including comfortable mattresses. The bathrooms are well proportioned. A restoration added marble sheathing to the lobby and a glint of crystal chandeliers. The classically decorated dining room offers efficient and courteous service, and standard food, a combination of Swedish and continental. The hotel owners take a personal interest in the welfare of their guests. It's opposite the train station and close to the ferry terminal.

Hotel Tornväktaren. S:t Östergatan 33, S-271-34 Ystad. ☎ 0411/784-80. Fax 0411/729-27. 9 units. TV TEL. 695 SEK ($76.45) double. Rates includes breakfast. AE, MC, V. Free parking.

Much of the charm of this simple bed-and-breakfast hotel derives from its hardworking owner, Ms. Inger Larsson. Her home is a turn-of-the-century stone-built structure with a garden and red trim, 10 minutes on foot from the railway station. Rooms are outfitted in pale pastels with lots of homey touches that include frilly curtains, wall-to-wall carpeting, and lace doilies covering painted wooden furniture. Units with and without bathrooms rent for the same price. Other than a filling morning breakfast, no meals are served.

Ystads Saltsjöbad. Saltsjöbadsgatan 6, S-271 39 Ystad. ☎ 0411/136-30. Fax 0411/55-58-35. www.ystadssaltsjöbad.se. E-mail: info@ystadssaltsjöbad.se. 108 units. TV TEL. June 19–Aug 31, 990–1,090 SEK ($108.90–$119.90) double; Sept–June 18, 1,230–1,670 SEK ($135.30–$183.70) double. Year-round, Mon–Thurs 2,070–2,300 SEK ($227.70–$253) suite; Fri–Sun 1,390–1,790 SEK ($152.90–$196.90) suite. AE, DC, MC, V. Closed Dec 23–Jan 6. Free parking.

Beautifully situated on 10 acres of forested land beside the sea, this hotel is close to Sweden's southernmost tip. It was built in 1897 by one of the most famous opera stars of his day, Swedish-born Solomon Smith. Designed as a haven for the gilded-age aristocracy of northern Europe, it consists of three connected four-story buildings with big-windowed corridors, set close to the sands of an expansive beach. The guest rooms are comfortably furnished in turn-of-the-century style. About half of them were refurbished in the mid-1990s.

The clientele changes throughout the year. In the summer, the hotel caters to beachgoers; in the winter, it's often filled with corporate conventions. The neighborhood provides good opportunities for healthful pastimes such as tennis and golf. There's a heated indoor pool with a water slide and a sauna. The hotel's Apotheket Restaurant serves good international cuisine and features a dance band several nights a week. There's also a cocktail bar and two cafes (one open only in the summer).

WHERE TO DINE

Lottas Restaurang. Stortorget 11. ☎ **0411/788-00.** Reservations recommended. Main courses 130–175 SEK ($14.30–$19.25). AE, DC, MC, V. Mon–Sat 5–10:30pm. SWEDISH.

Fans praise it as one of the most popular and bustling restaurants in town; its detractors avoid it because of slow service by a small staff that sometimes seems impossibly overworked. Everyone awards high marks, however, for the well-prepared cuisine. It's served in a brick dining room within a century-old building that once functioned as a private home. The menu runs to conservative, old-timey Swedish cuisine, which might include fried and creamed fillet of cod with dill-flavored boiled potatoes, pork schnitzels with asparagus and béarnaise sauce, tenderloin of pork with mushrooms in cream sauce, and marinated breast of chicken with roasted potatoes. For dessert, try warm chocolate cake with ice cream.

Rådhuskällaren Ystad. Stortorget. ☎ **0411/185-10.** Main courses 85–150 SEK ($9.35–$16.50). AE, DC, MC, V. Mon–Sat 11:30am–2:30pm. SWEDISH.

One of the most reliable lunchtime restaurants in Ystad occupies a series of vaulted cellars that were built as part of a monastery in the 1500s. Several hundred years later, the Rådhus (Town Hall) was reconstructed after a disastrous fire above the monastery's cellars. Today, amid small tables and romantic candlelight, you can enjoy such good-tasting dishes as shellfish soup with saffron, beef fillet stuffed with lobster, marinated and grilled tenderloin steak, grilled angler-fish with basil-cream sauce, saddle of lamb with fresh herbs, and roast reindeer with mushrooms and game sauce.

✪ Restaurant Bruggeriet. Långgatan 20. ☎ **0411/69-9999.** Reservations recommended. Main courses 136–186 SEK ($14.95–$20.45). AE, DC, MC, V. Mon–Sat 11:30am–10:30pm, Sun 12:30–10pm. SWEDISH/INTERNATIONAL.

This novel Ystad restaurant was originally built in 1749 as a warehouse for malt. In 1996, a team of local entrepreneurs installed a series of large copper vats and transformed the site into a pleasant, cozy restaurant and brewery. Today, they specialize in two "tastes" of beer that's marketed under the brand name Ysta Färsköl, which comes in lager and dark versions. Depending on their size, they sell for 25 to 50 SEK ($3.20 to $6.40) per mug. Food items served here seem carefully calibrated to taste best when consumed with either of the two beers. Examples include fried herring marinated in mustard and sour cream and served with mashed potatoes; grilled salmon with red wine sauce; marinated and baked Swedish lamb with garlic and herbs; tenderloin steak with brandy sauce; and a succulent version of barbecued ribs you might have expected in New Orleans.

Sandskogens Vardshus. Saltsjøvagen, Sandskogen. ☎ **0411/147-60.** Reservations recommended. Main courses 100–200 SEK ($11–$22); fixed-price lunch 85 SEK ($9.35); fixed-price dinner 195 SEK ($21.45). AE, DC, MC, V. Tues–Sun 11:30am–10pm. Closed Jan–Feb. SWEDISH.

Set about a mile east of Ystad's center, this structure was originally built in 1899 as a summer home for the town's major. It was converted to a restaurant in the 1930s, and ever since, it has provided local diners with well-prepared Swedish specialties that include marinated mussels; toast with whitebait roe, sour cream, and onions; fried brill with caramelized butter sauce; turbot with shrimp and Swedish caviar; gratin of lobster with lemon sole; and lingonberry or cloudberry parfait (in season).

6 Simrishamn

391 miles S of Stockholm, 59 miles E of Malmö, 25 miles E of Ystad

One of the most idyllic towns along the Skåne coastline, Simrishamn features old half-timbered buildings, courtyards, and gardens. This seaport is the jumping-off point to the Danish island of Bornholm.

ESSENTIALS

GETTING THERE   From Ystad, our last stopover, continue east along Route 10. If you're not driving, four trains a day—three on weekends—make the 45-minute trip between Malmö and Simrishamn. Nine buses a day arrive from Kristianstad (four a day on weekends), and 10 buses a day from Ystad (3 on weekends). From Lund, there are eight daily buses. Tickets can be purchased on board the bus.

VISITOR INFORMATION   For information about hotels, boardinghouses, summer cottages, and apartments, check with the tourist bureau. **Simrishamns Kommun Turistbyrå,** Tullhusgatan 2 (☎ **0414/160-60;** www.turistbyra.simrishamn.se), is open June to August, Monday to Friday 9am to 8pm, Saturday 11am to 8pm, and Sunday 12:30 to 8pm; September to May, Monday to Friday 9am to 5pm.

SEEING THE SIGHTS

Other than the charming little town itself, there isn't much to see after you've walked through the historic core. (The major attractions are nearby; see below.) The old town is a maze of fondant-colored tiny cottages that in some ways evoke a movie set. The chief attraction here is **S:t Nicolai Kirke,** Storgatan (☎ **0414/41-24-80**). It's open daily 9am to 4pm, charging no admission.

Originally constructed as a fisherman's chapel in the 12th-century, the church literally dominates the town. It's built of chunky sandstone blocks, with a brick porch and step gables. Over the years, there have been many additions. A nave was added in the 1300s, and the vault dates from the 1400s. Inside, look for the flamboyantly painted pulpit from the 1620s. The pews and votive ships on display are much later—from the 1800s. Outside you'll see two sculptures, both by Carl Milles. He called them *The Sisters* and *Angel with Trumpet.*

NEARBY ATTRACTIONS

Backakra. S-270 20 Loderup. ☎ **0411/52-66-11.** Admission 30 SEK ($3.30) adults, 15 SEK ($1.65) children. June 8–Aug 16, daily noon–5pm; May 16–June 7 and Aug 17–Sept 20, Sat–Sun noon–5pm. Closed Sept 21–May 15.

Located off the coastal road between Ystad and Simrishamn is the farm that Dag Hammarskjöld, the late United Nations secretary-general, purchased in 1957 and intended to make his home. Although he died in a plane crash before he could live there, the old farm has been restored according to his instructions. The rooms are filled with gifts to Mr. Hammarskjöld—everything from a Nepalese dagger to a lithograph by Picasso.

The site is 19 miles southwest of Simrishamn, and can be reached by the bus from Simrishamn marked ystad. Likewise, a bus from Ystad, marked simrishamn, also goes by the site. Scheduling your return might be difficult because of infrequent service—check in advance.

Other than the caretakers, the site is unoccupied most of the year, with the exception of any of the 18 members of the Swedish Academy, whose benefits and honors include use of the house for meditation and writing whenever they want.

✪ **Glimmingehus.** Hammenhög. ☎ **0414/18-620.** Admission 50 SEK ($5.50) adults, free for children. Daily 10am–4pm. Closed Nov–Mar.

Located 6 miles southwest of Simrishamn, this bleak castle was built between 1499 and 1505. It's the best-preserved medieval keep in Scandinavia, but the somewhat Gothic, step-gabled building is unfurnished. Visitors can order snacks or afternoon tea at a cafe on the premises. June through August, a guided tour in English leaves at 2pm every day. Lots of events take place in summer, including theatrical presentations, lectures, medieval meals with entertainment, even a medieval festival in August.

⚪ **Kivik Tomb.** Bredaror. No phone. Admission 15 SEK ($1.65). Daily 10am–6pm. Closed Sept–Apr.

Discovered in 1748, Sweden's most notable Bronze Age relic is north of Simrishamn along the coast of Kivik. In a 1931 excavation, tomb furniture, bronze fragments, and some grave carvings were uncovered. A total of eight floodlit runic slabs depict pictures of horses, a sleigh, and what appears to be a fun-loving troupe of dancing seals. Kivik has long been recognized as one of the most amazing monuments of the Bronze Age. You can reach the site by car.

WHERE TO STAY

Hotel Kockska Gården. Storgatan 25, S-272 31 Simrishamn. ☎ **0414/41-17-55.** Fax 0414/117-55. 18 units. TV TEL. 700 SEK ($77) double. AE, MC, V. Free parking.

Like an unspoiled black-and-white half-timbered coaching inn, this hotel is built around a large medieval courtyard in the town center. Its lounge combines the old and new, with a stone fireplace contrasting with balloon lamps. The guest rooms have been modernized, and the furnishings are up-to-date with tastefully coordinated colors and good beds. Bathrooms tend to be small. The only meal served is breakfast.

Hotel Svea. Strandvägen 3, S-272 31 Simrishamn. ☎ **0414/41-17-20.** Fax 0414/143-41. www.hotelsvea-simrishamn.com. E-mail: receptionen@hotelsvea-simrishamn.com. 59 units. TV TEL. Mid-June to mid-Aug and Fri–Sun year-round, 890 SEK ($97.90) double; 1,050 SEK ($115.50) suite. Rest of year, 990 SEK ($108.90) double; 1,250 SEK ($137.50) suite. AE, DC, MC, V. Free parking.

Painted pale yellow, with a red tile roof that matches those of older buildings nearby, this is the best-recommended hotel in town, and site of a fine restaurant (Restaurant Svea, see below). Although much of what you'll see today was rebuilt and radically renovated in 1986, the origins of this waterfront hotel in the town center date from around 1900. Many of its well-appointed, conservatively comfortable rooms overlook the harbor; all rooms have good beds and medium-size bathrooms. The hotel's only suite, the Prince Eugen, is named after a member of the royal family of Sweden who stayed here shortly after the hotel was built.

WHERE TO DINE

Restaurant Svea. In the Hotel Svea. Strandvägen 3. ☎ **0414/41-17-20.** Reservations recommended. Fixed-price lunch 100 SEK ($11); main courses 105–195 SEK ($11.55–$21.45). AE, DC, MC, V. Mon–Fri noon–2pm; Mon–Sat 6–9:30pm. Closed Dec 21–Jan 8. SWEDISH/INTERNATIONAL.

The best restaurant in town lies within the pale yellow walls of the recommended Hotel Svea. Within a modern, mostly beige room whose windows overlook the harbor, the kitchen focuses on very fresh fish pulled from local waters. However, the kitchen also turns out beef, pork, chicken, and some exotic meats, such as grilled fillet of ostrich (that the chef added to the menu, mainly as a conversational oddity). Other menu items include strips of smoked duck breast in lemon sauce; a platter of artfully arranged herring prepared at least three different ways; fillet of fried sole with white wine or tartar sauce; fish of the day prepared au gratin with shrimp and lobster sauce; medallions of pork with béarnaise sauce; and a succulent fillet of beef with salsa-style tomato sauce.

17

Exploring the Swedish Countryside

After seeing Stockholm, visitors often face a difficult decision about what else to do. Sweden is a large country, and most travelers have limited time. In this chapter we'll focus on several interesting possibilities, including an excursion on the **Göta Canal,** one of Scandinavia's major attractions. Another trip is to **Dalarna.** More than any other, this folkloric province is quintessential Sweden. Besides the traditional customs, handcrafts, and festive costumes, the region is important artistically. Two of Sweden's most famous painters came from Dalarna: Anders Zorn and Carl Larsson.

We'll also take a ferry to **Gotland,** Sweden's holiday island, which is known for its cliff formations and wide, sandy beaches. Inhabited since 5000 B.C., Gotland is Scandinavia's most intriguing island. Visby is the capital.

For the more adventurous, **Swedish Lapland** is an alluring destination. Home of the once-nomadic Lapps (or Sami, as they prefer to be known), it is one of Europe's last great open spaces. As golden eagles soar above snowcapped crags, you can "listen to the silence." Skiers flock to the area, but the summer miracle of the midnight sun shining above the Arctic Circle attracts the most visitors. This area is so vast (some 620 miles from north to south) that we've highlighted only a few destinations. Swedish Lapland is also a great place for summer sports—canoeing, river rafting, salmon fishing, hiking, and climbing. Local tourist offices can put you in touch with outfitters who arrange offbeat adventures.

1 The Göta Canal

The 4-day Göta Canal cruise, one of Sweden's major attractions, is a fascinating summer boat trip. It covers 350 miles from Gothenburg (Göteborg) in the west to Stockholm in the east (or vice versa); the cruise includes four or five stops, and you sleep onboard. The Göta Canal consists of a series of man-made canals, lakes, and rivers connected by 58 locks. The highest is more than 300 feet above sea level.

The canal, begun in the early 19th century, was designed to transport goods across Sweden, avoiding the expensive tolls levied by Denmark on ships entering and leaving the Baltic Sea. Soon after the canal opened, however, Denmark waived the tolls, and the railway between Stockholm and Gothenburg was completed. Both options allowed cheaper and faster shipment of goods across Sweden, so the canal became more of a tourist attraction than a means of transportation.

Boats from Gothenburg head east along the Göta Älv River. About 30 minutes out-side Gothenburg, passengers can view the 14th-century **Bohus Fortress.** It played a leading role in the battles waged by Sweden, Norway, and Denmark. Bohus Castle and Fortress (Bohus Fästning) was built by order of Norway's Haakon V on Norwegian territory. After the territory was ceded to Sweden in 1658, Bohus Fortress was used as a prison. Most of the boats will stop here (but not necessarily all), so you can climb the tower—"Father's Hat"—for a panoramic view. Farther down the river, the boat passes the town of **Kungälv** (known to the Vikings as Konghälla). Its traditions date back 1,000 years.

As the boat proceeds east on the Göta's clear water, the landscape becomes wilder. About 5 hours into the journey, you reach the town of **Trollhättan,** home of one of Europe's largest power stations. The once-renowned Trollhättan Falls can be seen at their full capacity only in July. The rest of the year, they're almost dry. Today a series of underground channels diverts most of the water to the power station.

After passing through a series of locks, boats enter **Lake Vänern,** Sweden's largest lake, with a surface area of more than 2,100 square miles. The trip across takes about 8 hours. Along the way, you'll pass **Lidköping,** home of the famous Rörstrand porce-lain. Lidköping received its charter in 1446. North of Lidköping, on the island of Kållandsö, stands **Läckö Slott,** a castle dating from 1298. Originally home of the bishops of Skara, the castle was given to King Gustavus Vasa in 1528, and later pre-sented to Sweden's great military hero General Jacob de la Gardie.

Once across Lake Vänern, boats return to the canal. A series of locks, including the canal's oldest (at Forsvik), carries the steamers to Sweden's second-largest lake, **Lake Vättern.** It's famous for its beauty and translucent water. At some points, visibility reaches a depth of 50 feet.

On the eastern shore of Lake Vättern sits the medieval town of **Vadstena,** the most important stop on the Göta Canal trip. It has old, narrow streets and frame buildings. The town is known throughout Sweden for its delicate handmade lace, which you can see by walking along Stora Gatan, the main street. Also of interest is the **Klosterkyrkan** (Abbey Church). Built between the mid–14th and the 15th century to specifications outlined by its founder, St. Birgitta (Bridget) of Sweden, the Gothic church is rich in medieval art. Parts of the abbey date from 1250; the building shel-tered the nuns of St. Birgitta's order until they were expelled in 1595.

Another important sight is **Vadstena Castle.** Construction began in 1545 under Gus-tavus Vasa, king of Sweden, but was not completed until 1620. This splendid Renaissance castle, erected during a period of national expansion, dominates the town from its posi-tion on the lake, just behind the old courthouse in the southern part of town.

Boats bound for Stockholm leave Lake Vättern and pass through two small lakes, Boren and Roxen. South of Lake Roxen is the university town of **Linköping,** site of a battle between Roman Catholic King Sigismund of Poland and Duke Charles of Södermanland (later Charles IX). Charles won the battle and made Linköping part of Sweden, rather than a province of Rome. In the town's main square stands the Folkung Fountain, one of sculptor Carl Milles's most popular works. Northwest of the main square is the cathedral, a not-always-harmonious blend of Romanesque and Gothic architecture.

From Linköping, boats enter Lake Roxen and continue northeast by canal to **Slät-baken,** a fjord that stretches to the sea. The route continues along the coast to Stockholm.

The **Göta Canal Steamship Company,** offers turn-of-the-century steamers, includ-ing its 1874 *Juno,* which claims to be the world's oldest passenger vessel that offered overnight accommodations. The line also operates the 1912 *Wilhelm Tham* and the newer—that is, 1931—*Diana.* Officers, staff, and crew are Swedish. Passengers walk, jog, or bike along the canal path, and there are organized shore excursions at many stops along the way.

For bookings, contact **Scantours** (☎ 800/223-7226; www.scantours.com). The 4-day cruises range from $775 to $1,325 per person double occupancy; 6-day cruises from $1,225 to $1,650. Discounts are given for early reservations.

2 Dalarna

This province offers everything from maypole dancing and fiddle music to folk costumes and handcrafts (including the Dala horse). Dalarna means "valleys," and you'll sometimes see it referred to as "Dalecarlia," the Anglicized form of the name.

Lake Siljan, the most beautiful lake in Europe, is ringed with resort villages and towns. Leksand, Rättvik, and Mora attract summer visitors with sports, folklore, and a week of music. In the winter, people come here to ski.

From June 23 to June 26, the Dalecarlians celebrate midsummer with maypole dancing. They go through the forest gathering birch boughs and nosegays of wild-flowers to cover the maypole. Then the pole is raised and they dance around it until dawn, a good old respectable pagan custom.

FALUN
303 miles NE of Gothenburg, 142 miles NW of Stockholm

Our driving tour of the region begins in Falun, the old capital of Dalarna; it lies on both sides of the Falu River. The town is noted for its copper mines; copper revenue has supported many Swedish kings. Just 6½ miles northeast, you can visit the home of the famed Swedish painter Carl Larsson.

ESSENTIALS
GETTING THERE From Stockholm, take the E18 expressway northwest to the junction with Route 70. Take Route 70 to the junction with Route 60, where you head northwest. The train takes 3 hours from Stockholm, 6 hours from Gothenburg.

Swebus (☎ 0200/21818 in Sweden only) express buses run between Stockholm and Falun once or twice daily, depending on the season. From Gothenburg, local buses arrive twice every day. A second bus company that services Falun is **Masexpressen** (☎ 08/107766), which operates additional buses into Falun from Stockholm and other points within Sweden.

VISITOR INFORMATION The **Falun Tourist Office,** Trotzgatan 10–12 (☎ 023/830-50; www.welcome.falun.se), is open from mid-August to mid-June Monday to Friday from 9am to 6pm, and Saturday from 10am to 2pm. During summer, from mid-June to mid-August, it's open Monday to Friday from 9am to 9pm, Saturday from 10am to 5pm, and Sunday from 11am to 5pm.

A SPECIAL EVENT The 4-day **Falun Folkmusik Festival,** celebrated annually in July, attracts hundreds of folk musicians from around the world in one of Scandinavia's major musical events. In addition to concerts, there are films, lectures, and seminars. For information, contact the Falun Tourist Office (see address and phone above).

SEEING THE SIGHTS
You might go first to the market square, Stora Torget, to see the **Kristine Church** (☎ 023/279-10). The copper-roofed structure dates from the mid–17th century, the tower from 1865. From June to August, it's open daily from 10am to 6pm. The rest of the year, it's open daily from 10am to 4pm. Admission is free.

Dalarna

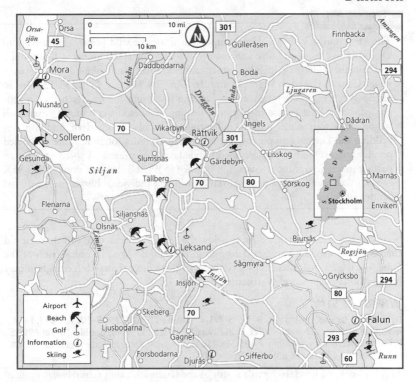

Falun is the site of **Lugnet** (☎ 023/83500), one of Sweden's largest sports complexes. The Bjursberget ski resort is 12½ miles away.

Carl Larsson-gården. Carl Larssons Väg 12, Sundborn. ☎ 023/600-53, or 023/600-69 for off-season reservations. Admission 70 SEK ($7.70) adults, 30 SEK ($3.30) children 7–15, free for children under 7. May–Sept, daily 10am–5pm; Oct–Apr, by appointment only. Bus: 64 from Falun.

The small village of Sundborn is the site of Lilla Hyttnas, Carl Larsson's home (now known as Carl Larsson-gården). Larsson became Sweden's most admired artist during his lifetime (1853–1919). However, when his erstwhile friend August Strindberg published a vicious attack on Larsson, the artist took a knife and stalked the playwright through the streets of Stockholm. Larsson's watercolor paintings have made his house known throughout Sweden. In the United States, reproductions of Larsson's watercolors, mainly of his wife, Karin, and their children, appear frequently on prints, calendars, and greeting cards. There are guided tours throughout the day, and English-language tours are sometimes available.

Bus no. 64 leaves from the Falun bus station several times a day. It's a 20-minute trip to Sundborn, 5 minutes from Carl Larsson-gården. Sundborn is a 2½-hour train ride from Stockholm.

Falun Copper Mine (Falu Koppargruva). Gruvplatsen. ☎ 023/158-25. Guided tour 60 SEK ($6.60) adults, 30 SEK ($3.30) children under 18. May–Aug, daily 10am–4:30pm; Mar–Apr and Sept–Nov 15, Sat–Sun 12:30–4:30pm. Closed Nov 16–Feb.

This mine in the town center was the world's largest producer of copper during the 17th century. It supplied the raw material for the roof of Versailles. The mine tour

Happy Trails

The Orsa "outback" is an almost unpopulated area of wild beauty. From May to October you can rent a horse and covered wagon (with space for up to five people) and tour the region's beautiful summer pastures, small forest lakes, and panoramic views. Contact **Häst och Vagn** (Torsmo 1646, S-794 91 Orsa; ☎ **2505/530-14**) to arrange your 3- or 6-day trek across Dalarna forest and tundra. Each tour is self-guided, but a brief course in care and feeding of horses is conducted first. Each wagon sleeps four adults plus an indeterminate number of children, and contains bedding and kitchen equipment. No more than 10 miles (often less) are scheduled per day and overnights are scheduled beside lakes and streams. A 6-day trek for all participants (without food) costs 4,900 SEK ($539); a 3-day trek costs 3,100 SEK ($341). Year-round, the same organization will rent individual horses for use on the tundra, on a per-day basis.

---

begins with an elevator trip 180 feet below the surface. Guides take you through old chambers and winding passages dating from the Middle Ages. In one section of the mine, you'll see a shaft divided by a timber wall that's more than 650 feet high; it may be the world's tallest wooden structure.

WHERE TO STAY

First Hotel Grand. Trotzgatan 9–11, S-791 71 Falun. ☎ **023/7948-80.** Fax 023/14143. www.firsthotels.se. 152 units. TV TEL. Sun–Thurs 1,249 SEK ($137.40) double; Fri–Sat 699 SEK ($76.90) double. All week long 2,195 SEK ($241.45) suite. Rates include breakfast. AE, DC, MC, V. Parking 80 SEK ($8.80). Bus: 701 or 704.

This buff-colored hotel 100 yards south of the landmark Falun Church was built in the late 19th century, with a modern addition constructed in 1974. The complex was renovated in 2000 and the guest rooms, in tasteful modern, are among the best deco-rated in town. All have good beds and ample-size bathrooms. There is a gym and health club in an area immediately adjacent to the lobby.

LEKSAND

30 miles W of Falun, 166 miles NW of Stockholm

Leksands Noret, as it's called, is a doorway to Lake Siljan. No less an authority than Hans Christian Andersen found the setting idyllic. In its present form, Leksand dates to the turn of the century, when it was reconstructed following a fire that had razed the community. A settlement has existed on this site since pagan times.

Many of the province's old traditions flourish here. Women don traditional dress for church on Sunday, and in June and July the long "church boats" from Viking times may cross the lake carrying parishioners to services. These boats compete in a race on the first Sunday in July. Since the Second World War, a miracle play, *The Road to Heaven,* has been presented in open-air performances. It provides insight into Dalarna's customs and folklore. The play runs for 10 days at the end of July.

ESSENTIALS

GETTING THERE   From Falun, head north on Route 80 to Bjursås, and then go west on a secondary road toward Sågmyra. Follow the signs to Leksand.

You can fly from Stockholm on **Skyways** (☎ **0250/301-75**). From **Dala-Airport** (☎ **0243/645-00**) in Borlänge, 31 miles south, there is frequent bus and train ser-vice to Leksand. Car rentals are available at the airport.

The train from Stockholm to Mora stops in Leksand. Travel time is 3½ hours. For reservations and information, call ☎ 020/75-75-75.

Another way to reach Leksand is by boat. The *Gustaf Wasa* (☎ 010/252-32-92) leaves Mora for Leksand (via Rättvik) every Monday at 3pm, and takes about 2 hours. The round-trip fare is 120 SEK ($13.20), free for children 12 and under. All trips depart Leksand during the day, and tickets are sold on board.

VISITOR INFORMATION   The **Leksands Turistbyrå** is at Norsgatan 23 (☎ 0247/803-00; www.stab.se). It's open June 15 to August 10, Monday to Friday from 9am to 8pm, Saturday 10am to 8pm, and Sunday 11am to 8pm; August 11 to 18, Monday to Friday 9am to 6pm, Saturday 10am to 6pm, and Sunday 11am to 6pm; August 19 to June 14, Monday to Friday 9am to 5pm, and Saturday 10am to 1pm.

A SPECIAL EVENT   Sweden's biggest music festival, **Music at Lake Siljan,** takes place during the first week of July. Some 100 concerts feature a wide range of music at venues in Leksand and Rättvik. Folk music, "the meeting of the fiddlers," predominates. For information, contact Music at Lake Siljan, Box 28, S-795 21 Rättvik (☎ 0248/102-90).

SEEING THE SIGHTS

Leksand's **parish church** (Leksands Kyrka) is in the town center, on Norsgatan, near the lake (☎ 0247/807-00). Founded in the 13th century, it assumed its present form in 1715 and is one of the largest rural churches in Sweden. During renovations in 1971, a burial site was found that dates to the period when the Vikings were being converted to Christianity. The church is open for worship throughout the year, but guided tours (in Swedish and English) are offered only from mid-June to early August. Tours are scheduled Monday to Saturday from 10am to 1pm and 2 to 5pm, Sunday 1 to 5pm. Admission to the church is free; the tour costs 50 SEK ($5.50) per person.

Nearby, also on Norsgatan, is an open-air museum, **Hembygdsgårdar** (☎ 0247/802-45). The cluster of 18th- and 19th-century buildings (which are part of the museum's collections) features depictions by that period's peasants of Christ and his Apostles in Dalarna dress. The museum is open only from mid-June to mid-August, Tuesday to Friday from 10am to 4pm, Saturday and Sunday noon to 5pm. Admission is 20 SEK ($2.20) for adults, free for children.

An athletic and health-conscious town, Leksand has ample opportunity for **outdoor sports.** There are downhill skiing facilities at the popular resort **Granberget,** about 13 miles to the southwest. The town's tourist office can provide information on swimming, cross-country skiing, curling, ice-skating, tennis, and boat rides on Lake Siljan. All are available in or near the town center, depending on the season and weather.

WHERE TO STAY

During the summer, you might find it fun to rent a *stuga* (log cabin) with four beds for 2,200 SEK ($242) a week. The **Leksands Turistbyrå,** Box 52, S-793 22 Leksand (☎ 0247/803-00), can book you into one. You can also inquire about renting a room in a private home.

Masesgården. Grytnäs 61, S-793 92 Leksand. ☎ **0247/122-31.** Fax 0247/122-51. www.masesgarden.se. E-mail: info@masesgarden.se. 34 units, 23 with bathroom. 4,150 SEK ($456.50) per person per week in double without bathroom; 4,750 SEK ($522.50) per person per week in double with bathroom. Rates include all meals and 30 hours of supervised sports activities. AE, DC, MC, V. Free parking.

This is one of the most sports-and-fitness-conscious hotels in Sweden. It has a reputation for educating guests about new eating and exercise habits, and a philosophy of preventing disease and depression through proper diet and exercise. Most people spend a week, participating in supervised aerobic and sports regimes, not indulging in conventional spa-style pampering. Beside a sea inlet, with a view of Leksand across the fjord, it's a sprawling compound of low-slung buildings. Guest rooms are soothing and more plush than you might have imagined.

The daily program includes lectures that stress the link between a healthy body and a healthy soul (astrological reincarnation and modern lifestyles is a favorite), and physical disciplines such as tai chi. Theme weeks concentrate on individual subjects, such as meditation and modern yoga, and Reiki healing through applied massage. Other activities include aerobics, sometimes in a swimming pool, and weight training. Classes are conducted in Swedish, but most staff members speak English. This is not a holiday for the faint-hearted. Be prepared to sweat and re-evaluate your lifestyle, in ways that might not always be completely comfortable.

Dining: The fresh vegetarian food is served buffet-style. At the communal meals, wait-staff members are "enablers" rather than employees. There's lots of chitchat and lots of socializing among the like-minded, often New Age–oriented guests.

Moskogen Motel. Insjövägen 50, S-793 00 Leksand. ☎ **0247/146-00.** Fax 0247/144-30. 52 units, all with shower only. TV TEL. 820 SEK ($90.20) double; 1,050 SEK ($115.50) suite. Rates include breakfast. DC, MC, V. Free parking. Bus: 58.

The motel and red wooden huts at this "self-service holiday village" make a good base for excursions around the Lake Siljan area. The rooms are well furnished and comfortable, with good beds. Each unit has a tiny kitchen. A restaurant on the premises serves light lunches and dinners. Facilities include a Jacuzzi, sauna, solarium, gym room, an outdoor pool, and tennis courts. The Moskogen is a mile west of the railway station.

WHERE TO DINE

Bosporen. Torget 1. ☎ **0247/132-80.** Main courses 70–200 SEK ($7.70–$22). AE, DC, MC, V. Daily 11am–11pm. SWEDISH/TURKISH.

This restaurant, 400 yards west of the railroad station, maintains longer, more reliable hours than any other place in town. Its Istanbul-derived name comes from the Turkish-born owners. The chefs are equally at home in the Swedish and Turkish kitchens. Shish kebabs and Turkish salads are featured, but you can also order fried Baltic herring, sautéed trout, fresh salmon, or plank steak. The cooking is fair and even a bit exotic in a town not renowned for its restaurants.

RÄTTVIK

13 miles NE of Leksand, 171 miles NW of Stockholm

Rättvik is one of the most popular resorts on Lake Siljan and has some of the best hotels in the district. Summer tours of the lake begin here. Culture and tradition are associated with Rättvik—you might find peasant costumes, folk dancing, Dalarna paintings, arts and crafts, "church boats," and fiddle music. There's an expression: "If you meet two men from Rättvik, three of them will be fiddlers." The old style of architecture is still prevalent, and there are many timber houses. Carpenters and painters from Rättvik are known for their craftsmanship.

ESSENTIALS

GETTING THERE From Leksand, head north on Route 70. The train from Stockholm to Mora stops in Leksand, where you can catch another train for the short trip to Rättvik. Train information in Stockholm is available at the **Central Station** (☎ **020/75-75-75**). Buses to Rättvik from outlying areas operate Friday to Sunday, but once in town you shouldn't need bus transportation. For information, call **Swebus** (☎ **0200/21818** in Sweden only).

VISITOR INFORMATION   The **Rättvik Tourist Office** is in the train station (☎ **0248/702-00**). It's open June 15 to August 10, Monday to Friday from 9am to 8pm, Saturday 10am to 8pm, and Sunday 11am to 8pm; August 11 to 18, Monday to Friday 9am to 6pm, Saturday 10am to 6pm, and Sunday 11am to 6pm; August 18 to June 14, Monday to Friday 9am to 5pm, and Saturday 10am to 1pm.

SEEING THE SIGHTS

In central Sweden, it's sometimes hard to get an overview of the forests. For an antidote—a sweeping view that stretches for many miles—drive 3 miles east of town along the road leading to Falun. Here, soaring more than 80 feet skyward, is a red-sided wooden tower, the **Vidablick,** in Hantverksbyn (☎ **0248/302-50**). There's no elevator, and the stairs are steep. Admission is 20 SEK ($2.20) for adults, 5 SEK (55¢) for children. On the premises are a coffee shop and a souvenir stand. The complex is open only from June to August 15, daily from 10am to 5pm.

One mile from the village is **Gammelgården** (☎ **0248/514-45**), an antique farmstead whose pastures and architecture evoke the 19th century. Phone ahead, because hours are erratic; it's open when a farm resident is able to conduct a tour. With enough notice, visits can be arranged throughout the year. The likely schedule between mid-June and mid-August is daily from 1 to 5pm. Admission is 20 SEK ($2.20).

You can also visit an artists' village established by the Swedish artist Sören Erikson. It's at **Rättviks Hantverksby,** Gårdebyn (☎ **0248/302-50**).

WHERE TO STAY

Expensive

Hotel Lerdalshöjden. S-795 00 Rättvik. ☎ **0248/511-50.** Fax 0248/511-77. 95 units. TV TEL. 853 SEK ($93.85) double; 1,400 SEK ($154) suite. Rates include breakfast. DC, MC, V. Free parking. Bus: 58 or 70.

Near the top of a hill overlooking Rättvik, a 10-minute walk north of the lake, this building is a stylish renovation of a turn-of-the-century hotel. The only remaining part of the original is the Lerdalshöjden Restaurant (see "Where to Dine," below). The guest rooms are well furnished and maintained. They have modern accessories and amenities, including firm mattresses and good-sized bathrooms. The hotel has a sauna with a view over the lake, plus an exercise room.

Inexpensive

Hotel Gärdebygården. S-795 00 Rättvik. ☎ **0248/30250.** Fax 0248/30660. E-mail: vidablick@hantverksbyn.se. 87 units. TV TEL. 795 SEK ($87.45) double. Rates include breakfast. MC, V. Free parking. Bus: 58 or 70.

This hotel, off Storgaten in the town center, is a very good value. It opened in 1906 and was renovated in 1995. Within a short walk of the lake, the hotel has expanded into a trio of outlying buildings. The comfortable rooms are sedately outfitted, with conservative furniture and good firm beds, but the bathrooms are very small. Some units have a view of the lake. The big breakfast is almost like a Swedish smörgåsbord. Some nights are devoted to communal singalongs. Cross-country ski trails and jogging paths are a short distance away.

WHERE TO DINE

Lerdalshöjden. In the Lerdalshöjden Hotel. ☎ **0248/511-50.** Reservations recommended. Main courses 135–210 SEK ($14.85 $23.10). DC, MC, V. Daily noon–2pm and 6–9pm. Closed Aug 16 June 14. SWEDISH.

This summer-only restaurant is the only original section remaining in the turn-of-the-century hotel. It has long been a favorite with lake-district locals. They like its traditional, tasty Swedish home-style cooking, including fresh fish and beef dishes. Try steak tartare with bleak (a freshwater fish) roe, or fried ptarmigan with red-currant sauce.

If a hungry visitor arrives off-season, he or she is often referred to the **Green Hotel** (☎ 0248/247-50250), signposted from the center of town and lying about a half mile away. This traditional hotel dates from the 1600s when it first opened as an inn. It's also a good bet for accommodations in rooms that date primarily from construction in the 1960s. With breakfast and dinner included, charges year-round range from 1,350 to 1,690 SEK ($148.50 to $185.90).

MORA

28 miles W of Rättvik, 204 miles NW of Stockholm

In Upper Dalarna, between Lake Orsa and Lake Siljan, the provincial town of Mora is our final major stop in the province. Summer travelers find this business and residential center a good base for exploring the district.

Mora was the village where Gustavus Vasa finally rallied the peasants in Sweden's 16th-century war against Danish rule. Every year in March the 50-mile Vasa Race, a major ski event, commemorates the uprising.

ESSENTIALS

GETTING THERE   From Rättvik, continue around Lake Siljan on Route 70.

You can fly from Stockholm on **Skyways Air** (☎ 08/595-13-500) from Sunday to Friday. Flight time is 40 minutes. The airport (☎ 0250/301-75) is about 4 miles from the town center; taxis meet arriving flights.

There's also direct daily rail service from Stockholm, which takes 4 hours. On weekends, buses leave from Stockholm's Central Station for the 4-hour, 15-minute trip. Contact **Swebus Vasatrafik** (☎ 020/656-565).

The *Gustaf Wasa* (☎ 010/252-32-92; see "Essentials" under "Leksand," above) travels between Mora and Leksand. The boat departs from Leksand in the afternoon and leaves Mora at 3pm on Monday. The round-trip cost is 120 SEK ($13.20) for adults and 60 SEK ($6.60) for children.

VISITOR INFORMATION   Contact the **Mora Turistbyrå,** Angbåtskajen (☎ 0250/265-50). It's open June 15 to August 10, Monday to Friday from 9am to 8pm, Saturday 10am to 8pm, and Sunday 11am to 8pm; August 11 to 18, Monday to Friday 9am to 6pm, Saturday 10am to 6pm, and Sunday 11am to 6pm; August 19 to June 14, Monday to Friday 9am to 5pm, and Saturday 10am to 1pm.

SEEING THE SIGHTS

Mora is home to a **Santa complex** (☎ 0250/212-00), with a house and a factory. Visitors can meet Santa and see his favorite helpers making and gift-wrapping presents for children all over the world. Children can enroll in "Santa School" and participate in troll and treasure hunts.

Mora was the hometown of **Anders Zorn** (1860–1920), Sweden's most famous painter. The town's top sights are all associated with him. The first, **Lisselby,** is an area near the Zorn Museum made up of old houses now used as arts and crafts studios and boutiques. At **Balder-Lisselby,** a craft center, you can watch handcrafts being made Monday to Saturday between 9am and 6pm, except at lunchtime.

Zornmuseet (Zorn Museum). Vasagatan 36. ☎ **0250/165-60.** Admission 35 SEK ($3.85) adults, 2 SEK (20¢) children. Mid-May to Aug, Mon–Sat 9am–5pm, Sun 11am–5pm; Sept to mid-May, Mon–Sat noon–5pm, Sun 1–5pm.

This museum displays a wide array of the artist's works, including *Midnight.* You'll also see paintings from his private collection by Prince Eugen and by Carl Larsson, also of Dalarna. Works by major foreign artists (sculptures by Kai Nielsen of Denmark and etchings by Rembrandt) are also exhibited, as well as rural art and handcrafts from Dalarna.

Zorngården. Vasagatan 36. ☎ **0250/165-60.** Admission 45 SEK ($4.95) adults, 15 SEK ($1.65) children. Mid-May to mid-Sept, Mon–Sat 10am–4pm, Sun 11am–4pm; mid-Sept to mid-May, Mon–Sat noon–3pm, Sun 1–4pm. Full guided tours of the house at noon, 1pm, 2pm, 3pm.

The artist's former home, adjoining the museum, has been left just as it was when Mrs. Anders Zorn died in 1942. Its chief attraction, aside from the paintings on display, is the Great Hall on the top floor. Zorn designed it himself.

SHOPPING IN NEARBY NUSNÄS

In Nusnäs, about 6 miles southeast of Mora, you can watch the famous wooden **Dalarna horse** (*dalahäst*), one of Sweden's most popular souvenirs, being made at **Nils Olsson Hemslöjd** (☎ **0250/372-00**). You're free to walk around the workshops and watch the craftspeople at work, and the finished products can be purchased at a shop on the premises. It also sells wooden shoes and other craft items.

The crafts store is open June to mid-August, Monday to Friday from 8am to 6pm, Saturday and Sunday 9am to 5pm; mid-August to May, Monday to Friday 8am to 5pm, Saturday 10am to 2pm. To find Nusnäs, take the signposted main road east from Mora, turning off to the right at Farnas. From Mora, bus no. 108 also runs to Nusnäs.

WHERE TO STAY

First Resort Mora. Strandgatan 12, S-792 00 Mora. ☎ **800/528-1234** in the U.S. and Canada, or 0250/717-50. Fax 0250/189-81. www.firsthotels.com. 141 units. MINIBAR TV TEL. 1,048–1,389 SEK ($115.30–$152.80) double. Rates include breakfast. AE, DC, MC, V. Parking 90 SEK ($9.90) in the garage, free outdoors.

The Mora is in the center of town across from the lakefront, a minute's walk from the tourist bureau. Renovations over the years have added sun terraces and glassed-in verandas. The interior is tastefully decorated with bright colors. All accommodations have comfortable furniture, including good beds and ample bathrooms. The minibars don't contain alcoholic beverages. On the premises is an indoor pool, along with several dining facilities. The best is the Terrassen (see "Where to Dine," below). On Friday and Saturday, the hotel's disco charges 70 SEK ($7.70) admission for visitors, but is free for hotel guests.

WHERE TO DINE

Terrassen. In the First Resort Mora, Strandgatan 12. ☎ **0250/717-50.** Reservations recommended. Main courses 175–300 SEK ($19.25–$33). AE, DC, MC, V. Mon–Sat 11:30am–11pm. SWEDISH.

One of the finest dining rooms in the area, this is a good bet for a meal even if you aren't staying at the hotel. Fresh produce is used whenever possible, and fresh fish and Swedish beef dishes are featured. You might begin with herring or a freshly made salad. Service is polite and efficient.

FROM MORA BACK TO STOCKHOLM

From Mora, take Route 70. In Enköping, pick up E18, which takes you to Stockholm.

3 Gotland (Visby)

136 miles S of Stockholm, 93 miles S of Nynäshamn, 55 miles E of the Swedish mainland

In the middle of the Baltic Sea sits the ancient home of the Goths, the island of Gotland. Swedes go to the country's most popular tourist island for sunny holidays by the sea; North Americans tend to be more interested in the old walled city of Visby. With its cliffs, rock formations, bathing beaches, and rolling countryside, Gotland is rich territory. Buses cover the island, which is about 75 miles long and 35 miles wide, as do organized tours from Visby, the capital.

In the 12th and 13th centuries, the walled city of Visby rose to the zenith of its power. It was the seat of the powerful Hanseatic merchants and the trade center of northern Europe. Seventeen churches were built during its heyday. Step-gabled stone houses were erected, and the townspeople lived in relative luxury. Visby was eventually ransacked by the Danes, however, and the city declined. After Visby was recognized as a treasure house of medieval art and became the number-one spot in Scandinavia for experiencing the charm of the Middle Ages, it became a major tourist attraction.

ESSENTIALS

GETTING THERE SAS (☎ 800/221-2350 in the U.S., or 020/727-000; www.flysas.com) flies to Gotland from Stockholm three times a day. Flights take about 30 minutes. There is bus service between Visby and the airport.

The boat to Gotland leaves from Nynäshamn; by bus from Stockholm, it's about a 1-hour ride. The car ferry to Visby leaves at midnight and takes about 5 hours. In summer there are also daytime trips. You can make reservations through your travel agent or directly with the ferry service, **Destination Gotland** (☎ 0498/201-020 in Stockholm), for a cabin, car space, or both. Book deck space if you plan to travel on a weekend.

VISITOR INFORMATION More than one agency is available within Visby to help you get the most out of your visit to Gotland. The official government-sponsored Gotland Tourist Office is at Hamngatan 4 (☎ 0498/20-17-00). It's open daily, year-round, from 8am to noon and from 12:30 to 4:15pm. Also useful is a privately owned travel agency, **Gotlands Turist Service** located at Östervåg 1 (☎ 0498/24-70-65). This group can arrange organized tours for groups, and can in many instances be helpful at providing tourist-related information about the island. From May to August, it's open Monday to Friday from 7am to 7pm; Saturday and Sunday from 7am to 6pm; the rest of the year, it's open Monday to Friday from 8am to 5pm, Saturday and Sunday from 10am to 4pm.

A SPECIAL EVENT During the annual **Medieval Week** in August, for 8 days Visby becomes a Hanseatic town again. At the harbor, Strandgatan swarms with people in medieval dress, many of them tending market stalls. You meet the blacksmith, barber, cobbler, and trader. Musicians play the hurdy-gurdy, the fiddle, and the flute, and jesters play the fool. Toward nightfall, a kingly procession comes into the square. More than 100 such events take place during the festival, along with medieval mystery plays, masses, choral and instrumental music, jousting tournaments, and displays of horses. There are archery competitions, fire-eaters, belly dancers, and walking tours of the medieval town.

SEEING THE SIGHTS
IN VISBY

This town is meant for walking. It can easily be explored on foot, and you may want to take one of the organized tours that are offered in season. Because so many sights, particularly the ruins of the 13th- and 14th-century churches, are better appreciated with some background, we recommend the tour. Ask at the tourist bureau (see "Visitor Information," above).

In town, you can walk about, observing houses from the Middle Ages, ruined fortifications, and churches. Notable among these is the **Burmeisterska Huset,** the home of the leading German merchant (burmeister), at Strandgatan 9.

You can walk down to the old **Hanseatic harbor** (not the harbor in use today) and stroll through the **Botanical Gardens,** which have earned Visby the title "City of Roses." You'll pass two of the most famous towers in the old wall. In the **Maiden's Tower,** a peasant girl was buried alive for helping a Danish king. The **Powder Tower** is the oldest fortification in Visby. Later you'll see **Gallow Hill,** a medieval hanging station in use until the mid-1800s.

At the height of its power and glory, little Visby boasted 16 churches. Only one, **Domkyrkan** (Cathedral of St. Mary), at Kyrkberget, is in use today. It was dedicated in 1225 and built with funds collected by German merchant ships. Pope Clement VI (in Avignon) gave his permission to build the "Swertingska chapel" in 1349. The church was damaged in serious fires in 1400, 1586, 1610, and 1744. It became a cathedral in 1572. The only original fixture left is a sandstone font from the 1200s. Visby's primary landmark is the church's towers. The tower at the western front is square; two slimmer ones appear on the east. In the interior, one of the curiosities is the frieze of grotesque angels' faces beneath the pulpit. Hours are Monday to Friday and Sunday from 8am to 9pm, Saturday 8am to 6:30pm. Admission is free. For more information, call ☎ **0498/206-800** daily from 10am to noon.

Also of interest are the ruins of the **Dominican Monastery of St. Nicholas,** just down the road from Domkyrkan (same phone for information). The church's rose window, cut from a single big stone, is more than 10 feet in diameter. Work began on the monastery in 1230, but it was destroyed by Lübeck forces in 1525.

Another sightseeing sojourn you can do on your own is to **Gotlands Fornsal,** the Historical Museum of Gotland, Strandgatan 14 (☎ **0498/29-27-00**). It's on a medieval street noted for its step-gabled houses. The museum contains some of the most interesting artifacts discovered on Gotland, including carved stones dating to A.D. 400, art from medieval and later periods, and furniture and household items. It's open May 15 to August, daily from 11am to 6pm; September to May 14, Tuesday to Sunday noon to 4pm. Admission is 40 SEK ($4.40) for adults, free for children under 17.

EXPLORING THE ISLAND

Tours of the island leave from the tourist bureau. They're different every day, but always include the **Lummelunda Grottan,** Lummelunds Bruk (☎ **0498/27-30-50**). It's a cave with stalactite and stalagmite formations, fossil remains, and subterranean waters. Visits on your own cost 45 SEK ($4.95) for adults, 30 SEK ($3.30) for children 5 to 15, free for children under 5.

Lummelunda is a karst cave—formed of limestone bedrock by a subterranean stream. The explored part of the stream cave stretches for 2.6 miles, and there's more that has not yet been investigated. Part of the cave with some of the biggest and most beautiful chambers is open to visitors. It's 8 miles north of Visby along Route 149. A bus departs from Österport Visby (the port in town) June 19 to August 14, daily at 2pm. The cave is only open May to June 25, daily from 9am to 4pm; June 26 to August 14, daily 9am to 6pm; August 15 to September 14, daily 9am to 4pm.

ISLAND TOURS   Ask at the **Turistbyrå** (see above) about what island tours are scheduled during your visit in summer only. These tours, if offered, are the best way to get a quick overview of Gotland. The price may be as low as 50 SEK ($5.50) or as high as 360 SEK ($39.60), but the lower end of the scale tends to be more likely.

An 11 hour bus tour of northern Gotland and Fårö takes you to the port of Färösund for the 10-minute ferry ride over the strait. On the excursion around Fårö (Sheep Island), you can see dwarf forests and moors.

Returning to Gotland, the bus takes you to the open-air cultural history museum at **Bunge,** which documents the old peasant culture. That's followed by a tour of the

Blase limestone museum in Fleringe, which has two restored turn-of-the-century lime kilns.

Another tour takes you to the southern tip of the island to see the legendary "old man of **Hoburgen**," a rock formation known as a chalk stack. The tour includes the Iron Age village of **Gervide** as well as two 17th-century farms. The bus travels along the windswept shoreline of the west coast.

A DRIVING TOUR From Visby, drive north on Route 149, heading toward the fishing port of **Lickershamn.** Look for a narrow trail along the cliffs. This path leads you to a rock that juts into the water. Known as the *Maiden,* this promontory offers some of the best views on Gotland.

From Lickershamn, continue along Route 149, passing through the towns of **Ire** and **Kappelshamn.** From Kappelshamn, follow Route 149 south to the junction with Route 148 in **Lärbro,** and then go north on Route 148 to **Fårösund.** The village sits on the shores of the Fårösund, the mile-wide channel separating the small island of **Fårö** (Sheep Island) from Gotland. You can take a ferry to Fårö, which has superb beaches.

From Fårösund, take Route 148 back to Lärbro. A few miles past Lärbro, take Route 146 southwest toward **Slite.** Follow it down the coast to **Aurungs,** and then go west on a secondary road heading toward **Siggur.** In Siggur, follow signs south to the village of **Dalhem.** The most remarkable sight in Dalhem is the village church, just outside town. Its wall paintings and stained glass are the finest on Gotland. Train buffs might enjoy visiting the Railway Museum in the old train station.

From Dalhem, continue south on the road that brought you to town. Head toward **Roma.** Look for the ruins of Roma Abbey, a Cistercian monastery destroyed during the Protestant Reformation.

Head west from Roma on a secondary road toward Route 140, which runs along Gotland's west coast. You'll pass through the villages of **Bander** and **Sojvide** before you reach Route 140. Follow it south to Burgsvik, a popular port and resort town. Just east of **Burgsvik,** visit the small hamlet of **Öja.** Its church boasts a triumphal cross dating from the 13th century.

After visiting Öja, return to Burgsvik and head south, passing through the villages of **Bottarvegården** and **Vamlingbo.** At the southern tip of Gotland you'll find **Hoburgen,** with its towering lighthouse. Along with the lighthouse, you'll see cliffs, many with strange rock formations, and a series of caves.

Return to Burgsvik and get back on Route 140. Turn off after **Fidenäs,** following Route 142 toward **Hemse.** Outside Hemse, take Route 144 to **Ljugarn,** a small port and resort town on Gotland's east coast. You can visit the small customs museum. Just south of Ljugarn, on a secondary road, is a series of Bronze Age stone sculptures. The seven rock formations, depicting ancient ships, are the largest group of stone-settings on the island.

Follow Route 143 northwest from Ljugarn and return to Visby. Moving rather quickly, you could do this tour in 2 hours or so, or you could spend all day, depending on where you wanted to stop and how long you wanted to spend at a particular place. The best place for a rest or a snack is the little summer resort of Ljugarn, which is filled with bars and snack shops that are open only June to September. These places sell beer, ice cream, sandwiches, pizzas, and the like.

SHOPPING

The most memorable goods are produced on the island, usually by individual crafts-people working on highly detailed, small-scale productions. You can find the fruits of their labor at any of the following shops.

Yllet, S:t Hansgatan 19 (☎ **0498/21-40-44**), carries clothing made from wool produced by thousands of local sheep. It comes in the form of sweaters, scarves, hats, gloves, coats, and winterwear for men, women, and children. Colors tend to be natural and soft, usually deriving from the untinted, unbleached fibers produced by the sheep.

Don't overlook the gift shop at the island's historical museum, **Gotlands Fornsal,** Strandgatan 14 (☎ **0498/29-27-00**). Reproductions of some of the museum's art are for sale, as well as handcrafts and textiles made on the island.

Most of Gotland's dozens of independent artists work out of their houses or have studios. They produce ceramics, textiles, woodcarvings, and metalwork. The good-quality merchandise is usually marketed by cooperatives. These loosely organized networks publicize and display articles by artists whose work is judged by a panel. Objects are displayed and can be purchased at two places: **Galerie & Butik Gotland Konsthantverkare,** Hästgatan (☎ **0498/21-03-49**), and **Galerie Kvinnfolki,** Donnersplats 2 (☎ **0498/21-00-51**). Kvinnfolki limits its merchandise to items crafted by women—jars of marmalade made from local berries, textiles, children's clothing, and a line of cosmetics made from all-natural oils, emollients, and pigments.

WHERE TO STAY

For all its attractions, Visby doesn't have enough hotels. Because accommodations are packed in summer, you need to reserve in advance. If at all possible, try to telephone for reservations from Stockholm. If you arrive without reservations, contact the **Gotland Resort** (☎ **0498/20-12-60**). The English-speaking staff will try to arrange for rooms in a hotel or private home in or near Visby. The average rate for an accommodation in a private home is 500 SEK ($55) per person per night.

✪ **Hotell St Clemens.** Smedjegatan 3, S-621 55 Visby. ☎ **0498/21-90-00.** Fax 0498/27-94-43. www.clemenshotell.se. E-mail: info@clemenshotell.se. 32 units. TV TEL. 840–980 SEK ($107.50–$125.45) double. Extra bed 180 SEK ($19.80). Rates include breakfast. DC, MC, V. Free parking.

This 18th-century building in the town center has been transformed into a well-run little hotel. A comfortable, cozy atmosphere permeates the place, a series of five antique buildings connected by two pleasant gardens. It's decorated tastefully in modern style. It's open all year, and the staff is helpful and efficient. In spite of the hotel's age, all of its rooms have modern shower/toilet facilities with adequate shelf space. No two rooms are identical—the smallest single is in the shoemaker's old house, with a view over church ruins, and there's a four-bed unit with a sloping ceiling that overlooks the Botanical Gardens. Even the old stable has rooms especially for guests with allergies. In these rooms the toilets are wheelchair accessible. Breakfast (a generous buffet) is the only meal served.

Hotell Solhem. Solhemsgatan 3, S-621 46 Visby. ☎ **0498/27-90-70.** Fax 0498/21-95-23. www.strandhotel.net/solhem. E-mail: solhem@strandhotel.net. 94 units. TV TEL. 895–1,240 SEK ($98.45–$136.40) double. Rates include breakfast. Closed Sat–Sun Jan–Feb. AE, DC, MC, V. Free parking.

One of the newest, most recently renovated hotels in Visby overlooks the harbor from a hilly slope a few blocks south of the center. It was built in 1987 and doubled in size in 1998, when an addition opened. Guest rooms are comfortable, cozy, and warm, with simple but tasteful furniture and good mattresses; the bathrooms are small. There's a breakfast room and a sauna, but no restaurant.

Strand Hotel. Strandgatan 34, S-621 56 Visby. ☎ **800/528-1234** in the U.S., or 0498/25-88-00. Fax 0498/27-81-11. www.strandhotel.net. E-mail: strand.hotel@gotlandica.se. 112 units. TV TEL. 1,290–1,390 SEK ($141.90–$152.90) double. Rates include breakfast. AE, MC, V. Free parking.

This popular four-story hotel, a Best Western, was built in 1982 on the waterfront a short walk from the harbor. Groups of people are always congregating in the lobby, and the comfortable rooms are decorated in a tasteful modern style. Mattresses are renewed as the need arises, and the bathrooms are well maintained, with up-to-date plumbing. Breakfast is the only meal served. Facilities include a sauna and an indoor pool.

✪ **Wisby Hotell.** Strandgatan 6, S-621 21 Visby. ☎ **0498/25-75-00.** Fax 0498/21-13-20. www.wisbyhotell.se. E-mail: info@wisbyhotell.se. 133 units. MINIBAR TV TEL. July and Fri–Sat year-round, 960–1,470 SEK ($105.60–$161.70) double; rest of year, 1,410 SEK ($155.10) double. Year-round, 1,950 SEK ($214.50) suite. Rates include breakfast. AE, DC, MC, V. Free parking.

This 1855 hotel (yes, it's spelled with a *w*) was radically restored and upgraded in the early 1990s. It's now the best and most glamorous hotel on the island, with a conscientious staff. Set close to the harborfront in the town center, its historic core includes medieval foundations. Radiating outward from the core are newer additions that span several centuries. Guest rooms are conservatively elegant, and some have reproductions of 18th-century furniture. Housekeeping is excellent, mattresses firm, and bathrooms, although small, are adequate. The feature that makes it the finest place to stay in the off-season is a Winter Garden—a bold combination of steel, glass, and Gotland sandstone. You can relax in a leather armchair with a drink and admire the greenery and the changing Nordic light. On the premises are a restaurant, a bistro, and two bars. There's room service daily from 7am to 11pm; saunas, massage, and baby-sitting services are also available.

WHERE TO DINE

Burmeister. Strandgatan 6, Visby. ☎ **0498/21-03-73.** Reservations required. Main courses 140–200 SEK ($15.40–$22); pizzas 85–110 SEK ($9.35–$12.10). AE, DC, MC, V. Daily noon–4pm and 6–10:30pm. Disco, mid-June to mid-Aug, Tues–Wed 10pm–2am; year-round, Fri–Sat 10pm–2am. ITALIAN.

This large summer-only restaurant in the town center offers dining indoors or under shady fruit trees in the garden of a 16th-century house. Diners can look out on the surrounding medieval buildings from many tables. The cuisine is rather standard, never achieving any glory, but not disappointing either. The place is often incredibly crowded in summer, and long lines form—they must be doing something right. Pizza is the most popular menu choice. After 10pm the restaurant becomes a disco on certain nights; the cover charge is 80 SEK ($8.80).

Gutekällaren. Stortorget 3, Visby. ☎ **0498/21-00-43.** Main courses 105–195 SEK ($11.55–$21.45). AE, DC, MC, V. Daily 6–11pm. SWEDISH.

This restaurant and bar, in the town center, was built as a tavern in the early 1600s, probably on older foundations. It was enlarged in 1789 and today is one of the oldest buildings (if not *the* oldest) in Visby. It offers fresh fish and meat dishes and some vegetarian specialties. You might begin with a fish soup with lobster and shrimp, and follow with fillet of sole Waleska or roast lamb chops. The dessert specialty in summer is a parfait of local berries. This is solid, reliable fare, prepared with fresh ingredients. The aura is sober—a contrast to the fun-loving island—but once the dining is out of the way, the place livens up considerably.

Munkkällaren. Lilla Torggränd 2, Visby. ☎ **0498/27-14-00.** Reservations required in summer. Main courses 90–168 SEK ($9.90–$18.50). AE, DC, MC, V. Daily 6–11pm; pubs, daily 6pm–2am. SWEDISH/INTERNATIONAL.

You'll recognize this restaurant in the center of Visby by its brown wooden facade. The dining room, which is only a few steps from the street, is sheathed in white stone, and parts of it date from 1100. The restaurant is one of the best in town. In summer, the management opens the doors to two more pubs in the compound. Glasses of beer cost 45 SEK ($4.95). The main pub, Munken, offers platters of *husmanskost* (Swedish home cooking), including *frikadeller* (meatballs). In the restaurant you might begin with escargots in creamy garlic sauce or toast with Swedish caviar. Specialties include shellfish stew, salmon-stuffed sole with spinach and saffron sauce, and venison in port wine sauce. Live music is often performed in the courtyard, beginning at around 8pm. After the live music stops on Saturday and Sunday, a disco opens every night from 11pm to 2am. Admission to the disco is 60 SEK ($6.60).

VISBY AFTER DARK

There's less emphasis on bar-hopping and nocturnal flirting on Gotland than you might want. A lot more energy is expended on stargazing, wave watching, and ecology. But there is some nightlife.

The island's premier draw for people over 40 who enjoy dancing "very tight" (that is, ballroom style) is Saturday night at the **Borgen Bar,** Hästgatan 24 (☎ **0498/ 24-79-55**). The recorded music ranges from the Big Band era to more modern supper-club selections. There's also a restaurant.

A more hipster alternative where dancers are less inclined to wrap themselves in each other's arms is the **Munkkällaren** (see "Where to Dine," above). **Gutckällaren** (see "Where to Dine," above) attracts high-energy dancers aged 35 and under. If you happen to be a bit older, you can still hang out at the bar, soaking up aquavit and local color.

4 Swedish Lapland

Swedish Lapland—"Norrland," to the Swedes—is the last wilderness of Europe. The vast northern land of the midnight sun has crystal-blue lakes, majestic mountains, glaciers, waterfalls, rushing rivers, and forests. Norrland covers roughly half the area of Sweden (one-quarter of which lies north of the Arctic Circle).

The sun doesn't set for 6 weeks in June and July, and brilliant colors illuminate the sky. In spring and autumn, many visitors come here to see the northern lights.

Swedish Lapland is a paradise for hikers and campers (if you don't mind the mosquitoes in the summer). Before you go, get in touch with the **Svenska Turistförening** (Swedish Touring Club), P.O. Box 25, Amiralitetshuset 1, Flagmansvägen 8, S101 20 Stockholm (☎ **08-463-21-00**). It maintains mountain hotels, and has built bridges and marked hiking routes. The touring club has a number of boats in Lapland that visitors can use for tours of lakes. There are hundreds of miles of marked hiking and skiing tracks. March, April, and even May are recommended for skiing. Some 90 mountain hotels or Lapp-type huts (called *fjällstugor* and *kåtor*) are available, with beds and bedding, cooking utensils, and firewood. Huts can be used for only 1 or 2 nights. The club also sponsors mountain stations (*fjällstationer*).

You must be in good physical condition and have suitable equipment before you set out because most of the area is uninhabited. Neophytes are advised to join one of the hiking or conducted tours offered by the Swedish Touring Club. Contact the club for more details.

Contact the outdoors outfitter **Borton Overseas** (☎ 800/843-0602; www.bortonoverseas.com) to arrange a safari tour of the Swedish Lapland from March to October. Highlights include visits to old churches and village settlements (usually along a lake), and seeing reindeer.

LULEÅ

578 miles N of Stockholm

Our driving tour begins in Luleå, a port city on Sweden's east coast at the northern end of the Gulf of Bothnia, 70 miles south of the Arctic Circle. It's often called the "gateway to Lapland." Founded by Gustavus Adolphus in 1621, it's the largest town in Norrbotten, and from its piers boats depart for some 300 offshore islets and skerries (rocky islets) known for their flora and fauna.

Luleå has a surprisingly mild climate—its average annual temperature is only 3° to 5° lower than that of Malmö, on Sweden's southern tip. Still, the harbor is frozen over until May. In the summer it's a port for shipping iron ore.

The settlement, which was once ravaged by Russian Cossacks, has an interesting history. Fire has destroyed most of the Old Town. Establishing a city this far north was laden with difficulties; development didn't really take hold until after 1940. The state-owned ironworks has led to a dramatic growth in population. Today, the population is 70,000, and the city is livelier when the students from the University of Luleå are there in winter. Most foreigners (except businesspeople) see it only in summer.

ESSENTIALS

GETTING THERE   From Stockholm, **SAS** (☎ **800/221-2350** in the U.S., or 020/727-000; www.flysas.com) runs 12 flights each weekday and 10 on Saturday and Sunday. The trip takes 1¼ hours. From Gothenburg, there are 11 flights each weekday, 7 on Saturday and Sunday. Trip time is 2¼ hours.

Six trains daily make the 15-hour trip from Stockholm, and six trains daily make the 19-hour trip from Gothenburg. Trains from Stockholm to Kiruna usually deposit passengers at the railway junction at Boden, 6 miles northwest of Luleå. Three connecting trains a day go between Boden and Luleå. Passengers from Gothenburg to Luleå also transfer in Boden.

A bus runs between Stockholm and Luleå on Friday and Sunday. The trip takes 14 hours. For more information, call **Swebus** (☎ **020/640-640** in Sweden only).

VISITOR INFORMATION   The **Luleå Tourist Office** is at Storgatan 43B, S-972 31 Luleå (☎ **0920/29-35-00**). It's open in summer, Monday to Friday from 9am to 7pm, Saturday and Sunday 10am to 4pm; off-season, Monday to Friday 10am to 6pm, Saturday 10am to 2pm.

SEEING THE SIGHTS

Gammelstad is 6 miles north of the city center. Gathered around its 15th-century church, the largest of its kind in Norrland, are 30 old houses and the largest "church village" in Sweden. It consists of more than 450 small church cottages. These cottages are used today as they were in the past—as overnight lodgings for parishioners during important religious festivals.

Gammelstad Bay was part of a navigable channel into Luleå, but sailing stopped when the city moved in 1649. (The city actually transferred its locale to be more accessible to harbor traffic). The bay has become shallow and is now a wetland area. In this region, just 3 miles north of the city center, ornithologists have counted 285 species of birds during the spring migration. The area is classified as a nature reserve, but the public has access to it. Signposted tracks lead to the bird-watching tower and barbecue fireplaces.

Norrbottens Museum, Storgatan 2 (☎ **0920/24-35-00**), close to the city center at Hermelin Park, offers a comprehensive look at Norrbotten's history. Exhibits show how people lived in the northern regions over the centuries. The museum has perhaps the world's most complete collection of Lapp artifacts. Admission is free. It's open

Monday to Friday from 10am to 4pm, Saturday and Sunday noon to 4pm. Take bus no. 1, 2, 4, 5, 8, or 9.

WHERE TO STAY & DINE

Max Hotel. Storgatan 59, S-951 31 Luleå. ☎ **0920/22-02-20.** Fax 0920/20-10-90. TV TEL. Mon–Thurs 1,275 SEK ($140.25) double; Fri–Sun 680 SEK ($74.80) double. AE, DC, MC, V. Closed June 30–Aug 8. Parking 85 SEK ($9.35). Bus: 1, 2, 4, 5, 8, or 9.

The bus from the airport stops in front of the Max, on Luleå's main street. Designed tastefully, with clean lines and Nordic furniture, the Max offers comfortable accommodations with good beds and ample-size bathrooms in a much-restored older hotel. Free coffee, tea, and hot chocolate are offered day and night in the lobby. There's an in-house sauna. Guests are usually directed to the drinking and dining facilities at one of the other hotels nearby. The hotel is closed in the summer.

Radisson SAS Hotel Luleå. Storgatan 17, S-971 28 Luleå. ☎ **800/221-2350** in the U.S., or 0920/940-00. Fax 0920/20-10-12. www.radissonsas.com. 211 units. TV TEL. Mon–Thurs 1,395–1,595 SEK ($153.45–$175.45) double; Fri–Sun 890 SEK ($97.90) double. All week 2,995 SEK ($329.45) suite. Rates include breakfast. AE, DC, MC, V. Parking 95 SEK ($10.45). Bus: 1, 2, 4, 5, 8, or 9.

Holiday on Ice

Since the late 1980s, the most unusual, and least permanent, hotel in Sweden has returned early every winter to the frozen steppes near the iron mines of Jukkasjärvi, 125 miles north of the Arctic Circle. The architect Yngve Bergqvist, financed by a group of friends who developed the concept over bottles of vodka in an overheated sauna, uses jackhammers, bulldozers, and chain saws to fashion a 14-room hotel out of 4,000 tons of densely packed snow and ice.

The basic design is that of an igloo, but with endless whimsical sculptural detail. Like Conrad Hilton's worst nightmare, the resulting "hotel" buckles, collapses, and finally vanishes during the spring thaw. During the long, frigid darkness of north Sweden's midwinter, it attracts a steady stream of engineers, theatrical designers, sociologists, and the merely curious. They avail themselves of dogsled and snowmobile rides, cross-country skiing, and shimmering views of the aurora borealis. On the premises are an enormous reception hall, a multimedia theater, two saunas, and an ice chapel that's used for simple meditation, weddings, and baptisms.

Available for occupancy (temperatures permitting) between mid-December and sometime in March, the hotel resembles a cross between an Arabian casbah and a medieval cathedral. Minarets are formed by dribbling water (for about a week) onto what eventually becomes a slender, soaring pillar of ice. Domes are formed igloo-style out of ice blocks arranged in a circle. Reception halls boast rambling vaults supported by futuristic-looking columns of translucent ice. Fanciful sculptures heighten the surreal atmosphere. Some are angled to amplify the weak midwinter daylight, which filters through panes of (what else?) chain-sawed ice.

Purists quickly embrace the structure as the perfect marriage of architecture and environment; sensualists usually admire it hastily before heading off to warmer climes and more conventional hotels.

Built in 1979 and most recently renovated in 1990, this hotel has six stories, two of which are buried underground. It lies on Luleå's main street in the town center. Guest rooms are comfortable but blandly international in style and decor. The hotel has an indoor swimming pool, a solarium, saunas, and billiard tables.

Hotel Luleå's restaurant, the Cook's Inn, specializes in charcoal-grilled meats. The Cleo disco, in the cellar, is open Thursday to Saturday from 9pm to 3am, year-round. The admission fee is 80 SEK ($8.80). Its most popular nights are Thursday and Saturday, when a live dance band is featured.

Scandic Stadshotellet Luleå. Storgatan 15, S-951 31 Luleå. ☎ **0920/67-000.** Fax 0920/ 670-92. www.scandic-hotels.se. 135 units. TV TEL. Mon–Thurs 1,561–1,726 SEK ($171.70–$189.85) double; 2,400 SEK ($264) suite. Fri–Sun 940 SEK ($103.40) double; 2,400 SEK ($264) suite. Rates include breakfast. AE, DC, MC, V. Parking 80 SEK ($8.80). Bus: 1, 2, 4, 5, 8, or 9.

The stately, ornate brick-and-stone building is the oldest (1900), grandest, and most traditional hotel in town. It's in the center of the city, next to the waterfront. The modernized public area has kept a few old-fashioned details from the original building. Guest rooms are comfortable and well furnished. There's a lounge, a bar, and a restaurant.

Almost everyone who shows up asks the same question: "Is it comfortable?" Not particularly, but a stay will probably enhance your appreciation for the comforts of conventional housing. Upon arrival, guests are issued thermal jumpsuits of "beaver nylon." The air-lock cuffs are designed to help the wearer survive temperatures as low as –8°F. Beds are fashioned from blocks of chiseled ice, lavishly draped, Eskimo-style, with reindeer skins. Guests keep warm with insulated body bags developed for use during walks on the moon. Other than a temporary escape into the sauna, be prepared for big chills— room temperatures remain cold enough to keep the walls from melting. Some claim the exposure bolsters your immune system when you return to your usual environment.

The interior decor is what you'd expect. Most rooms resemble a setting from a scary 1950s sci-fi flick, sometimes with an icy version of a pair of skin-draped Adirondack chairs pulled up to the surreal glow of an electric fireplace that emits light but—rather distressingly—no heat. Throughout, there's an endearing decorative reliance on bas-reliefs and curios the artisans have chiseled into the ice.

There's lots of standing up at the long countertop crafted from ice that doubles as a bar. What should you drink? Swedish vodka, of course, dyed a frigid shade of blue and served in cups crafted from ice. Vodka never gets any colder than this.

For information and reservations, contact **The Ice Hotel,** Jukkas AB, Marknadsvägen 63, S-981 91 Jukkasjärvi, Sweden (☎ **980/668-00;** fax 980/668-90). Doubles cost 1,700 SEK ($187) per day, including breakfast. Heated cabins near the ice palace are available for 1,480 to 1,680 SEK ($162.80 to $184.80) a night for a double.

FROM LULEÅ TO JOKKMOKK

From Luleå, take Route 97 northwest. Thirty minutes into the trip, you can stop at **Boden.** Founded in 1809, this is Sweden's oldest garrison town. After losing Finland to Russia, Sweden built this fortress to protect its interior from a Russian invasion. Visit the **Garnisonsmuseet** (Garrison Museum), which has exhibits on military history, as well as many uniforms and weapons used throughout Sweden's history. It is open June to September daily 11am to 4pm, charging 10 SEK ($1.30) for admission. Not on a street plan, it lies at the southwest edge of town.

After visiting Boden, continue along Route 97 to Jokkmokk.

JOKKMOKK

123 miles NW of Luleå, 740 miles N of Stockholm

This community on the Luleå River, just north of the Arctic Circle, has been a Lapp (Sami) trading and cultural center since the 17th century. With a population of 3,400 hearty souls, Jokkmokk (which means "bend in the river") is the largest settlement in the *kommun* (community). Bus routes link Jokkmokk with other villages in the area.

ESSENTIALS

GETTING THERE　If you're not driving, you can reach Luleå, 123 miles away, by plane; from there you must take a bus. The one scheduled bus a day to Jokkmokk is timed to meet the plane's arrival. There is one train a day from Stockholm to Jokkmokk, with a change of trains in Östersund. The train ride from Stockholm could be 8 or 9 hours, but everything depends on your connection when you change trains. There are seasonal variations here, and it's a pretty complicated schedule. Trains heading to Kiruna do not stop here.

VISITOR INFORMATION　The **Jokkmokk Turistbyrå** is at Stortorget 4 (☎ **0971/121-40**). It's open mid-June to mid-August, daily from 8am to 5pm; mid-August to mid-June, Monday to Friday 8:30am to 4pm.

SEEING THE SIGHTS

The Lapps (Sami) have an ✪ **annual market** here in early February, when they sell their handcrafts. The "Great Winter Market" is a tradition that dates back 400 years. Held on the first Thursday, Friday, Saturday, and Sunday of February, it attracts some 30,000 buyers. People come to the market not so much for buying and selling, but for the special experience of the place. If you're planning a subzero visit during this time of the year, you need to make hotel reservations a year in advance.

There's **salmon fishing** in the town's central lake, and in the summer locals sometimes take a dip in the river, but we suggest that you watch from the sidelines because of the water temperature. Jokkmokk is one of the coldest places in Sweden in winter, with temperatures plunging below –30°F for days at a time.

Karl IX decreed that the winter meeting place of the Jokkmokk Sami would be the site of a market and church. The first church, built in 1607, was known as the **Lapp Church.** Because of the cold weather, the church had to inter corpses in wall vaults until the spring thaw permitted burial in the ground.

A nearby hill, known as **Storknabben,** has a cafe. From there, if the weather is clear, you can see the midnight sun for about 20 days in midsummer.

Jokkmokk is the center of Sami culture in this area, and an important establishment is the national Swedish Mountain and Sami Museum, ✪ **Ájtte,** Kyrkogatan (☎ **0971/170-70**), in the center of town. Its exhibits reflect nature and life in the Swedish mountain region, especially the Sami culture. The museum is one of the largest of its kind, integrating nature and culture. There's also a restaurant and a gift shop. Museum admission is 40 SEK ($4.40) for adults, free for children under 17. The museum is open year-round. In the summer, hours are Monday to Friday from 9am to 7pm, Saturday and Sunday 11am to 6pm; in the off-season, it closes at 4pm.

WHERE TO STAY & DINE

Hotell Gästis. Harrevägen 1, S-96 231 Jokkmokk. ☎ **0971/100-12.** Fax 0971/100-44. 20 units. TV TEL. 500–795 SEK ($55–$87.45) double. Rates include breakfast. AE, DC, MC, V. Free parking.

Dating from 1932, this landmark hotel is in the exact center of town, about 200 yards from the railroad station. In some respects, it has the qualities of a frontier-country hotel. Run by the Åkerlund family, the hotel offers well-maintained guest rooms with modern furnishings, good beds, and small bathrooms. The sauna is free for hotel guests. The restaurant has won many awards and offers well-prepared dishes, including what the Swedes call *husmanskost* (good home cooking) and continental dishes. There's also entertainment and dancing once a week.

The Lapps (Sami) in Sweden

The Lapps (Sami) have inhabited this area since ancient times, and 15,000 to 17,000 live in Sweden today. Some 2,500 still lead the nomadic life of their ancestors, herding reindeer and wearing multicolored costumes. The area of Lapp settlement (known as Sapmi) extends over the entire Scandinavian Arctic region. It stretches along the mountain districts on both sides of the Swedish-Norwegian border, down to the northernmost part of Dalarna.

Many Lapps maintain links to their ancient culture, but others have completely assimilated. Their language belongs to the Finno-Ugric group. As with all Arctic people, oral—not written—literature has played the most prominent role. Among Lapps, the oral tradition takes the form of *yoiking*, a type of singing. Governments once tried to suppress this, but now yoiking is enjoying a renaissance. Much Lapp literature has been published in northern Sami, which is spoken by approximately 75% of Lapps. One classic work is Johan Turi's *Tale of the Lapps*, first published in 1910.

Handcrafts are important in the Lapp economy. Several designers have developed new forms of decorative art, producing a revival of the handcraft tradition.

Many members of the community feel that the term "Lapp" has negative connotations; it's gradually being replaced by the indigenous minority's name for itself, *sábme*, or other dialect variations. *Sami* seems to be the most favored English translation of Lapp, and the word is becoming more common.

A SIDE TRIP TO KVIKKJOKK

One of the most beautiful resorts in Lapland, this mountain village is the gateway to ✪ **Sarek National Park,** the largest wilderness area in Europe. Kvikkjokk is 80 miles west of Jokkmokk and 689 miles north of Stockholm. The park is virtually inaccessible, almost entirely without tracks, huts, or bridges. Nevertheless, the most adventurous visitors go to see the fascinating flora and fauna.

The national park, between the Stora and Lilla Luleälv rivers, covers an area of 750 square miles, with about 100 glaciers and 87 mountains rising more than 5,900 feet (eight are over 6,500 feet). The most visited valley, ✪ **Rapadel,** opens onto Lake Laidaure. In the winter, sled dogs pull people through this valley.

The park includes remains of 17th-century silver mines. Kvikkjokk was a silver-ore center in the 17th century, and many historical relics from that period can be seen in the area today. In 1909 Sweden established this nature reserve in the wilderness to preserve it for future generations. To walk through the entire park would take at least a week; most visitors stay only a day or two. Explore only with an experienced guide. Hotels in the area can put you in touch with a guide.

Kvikkjokk, at the end of Route 805, is the starting or finishing point for many hikers using the **Kungsleden** (King's Trail). One- or 2-day outings can be made in various directions. A local guide can also lead you on an interesting boat trip; inquire at Kvikkjokk Fjällstation (see "Where to Stay," below). The boat will take you to a fascinating delta where the Tarra and Karnajokk rivers meet. The area is also good for canoeing.

From Jokkmokk, drive north on Route 45. After passing the town of Vaikijaur, turn west on a secondary road, following the signs to Klubbudden. Continue west on this road, passing through the towns of Tjåmotis, Njavve, and Arrenjarka until you reach Kvikkjokk.

If you're not driving, you can reach Kvikkjokk by taking a train to Jokkmokk (see "Getting There," above), then a bus. Two buses a day run between Jokkmokk and Kvikkjokk, but they don't always connect with train arrivals from Stockholm.

WHERE TO STAY

Kvikkjokk Fjällstation. S-962 02 Kvikkjokk. ☎ **0971/210-22.** 18 units, none with bathroom. 200 SEK ($22) per person. AE, MC, V. Closed Sept 15–Mar 15. Free parking.

Established by the Swedish Touring Club in 1907, this mountain chalet gained an annex in the 1960s. It offers no-frills accommodations for hikers, hill-walkers, and rock climbers. It's also the headquarters for a network of guides who operate canoeing and hiking trips into the vast wilderness areas that fan out on all sides. Accommodations are functional and woodsy. There are eight double rooms, eight four-bed rooms, and two cabins with four beds each. There's a sauna, a simple restaurant, and access to canoe rentals and a variety of guided tours that depart at frequent intervals. The chalet is open only in summer. For information about the Kvikkmokk Fjällstation out of season, call the tourist information office in Jokkmokk (80 miles away) at ☎ **0971/121-40.**

FROM JOKKMOKK TO KIRUNA

After visiting Kvikkjokk, return to Jokkmokk and then head north on Route 45 toward Gällivare. Along the way, you'll pass **Muddus National Park.** You can enter from the town of **Saite.** Although not as dramatic as Sarek (see "A Side Trip to Kvikkjokk," above), this park, established in 1942, is worth a visit. Its 121,000 acres are home to bears, moose, otters, wolverines, and many bird species. The Muddusjokk River flows through the park and over a panoramic 140-foot waterfall. Trails cross the park; they're well marked and lead visitors to the most interesting sights.

Continue along Route 45 through Gällivare, toward Svappavaara. In Svappavaara, take E10 northwest to Kiruna.

KIRUNA

120 miles N of Jokkmokk, 818 miles N of Stockholm

Covering more than 3,000 square miles, Kiruna is the largest (in terms of geography) city in the world. Its extensive boundaries incorporate both Kebnekaise Mountain and Lake Torneträsk.

The northernmost town in Sweden, Kiruna lies at about the same latitude as Greenland. The midnight sun can be seen here from mid-May to mid-July.

ESSENTIALS

GETTING THERE   You can fly to Kiruna on **SAS** (☎ **800/221-2350** in the U.S., or 020/727-000; www.flysas.com); there are three daily flights from Stockholm. Travel time is 1 hour, 35 minutes. Two or three trains a day make the 16-hour trip from Stockholm to Gällivare (a major rail junction). Three trains a day run between Gällivare and Kiruna; the trip takes 1½ hours. There's also daily bus service between Gällivare and Kiruna. Contact **Länstrafiken** (☎ **0926/756-80**).

VISITOR INFORMATION   The **Kiruna Turistbyrå** is at Lars Janssons Vagen 17 (☎ **0980/188-80**). It's open June 15 to August 20, daily from 9am to 6pm; August 21 to June 14, Monday to Friday 9am to 4pm.

SEEING THE SIGHTS

Fifty miles from the commercial center of town, **Kebnekaise Mountain** rises 6,965 feet above sea level. It's the highest mountain in Sweden. Take a bus to **Aroksjokk**

Tee Off at Midnight

Because of their Lapland locale, the following two golf courses are a player's dream: exquisite scenery coupled with the possibility of playing any time the mood hits—day or night.

About 60 west of Kiruna, near the hamlet of Björkliden, is the world's northern-most golf course (and one of the most panoramic), the Björkliden Arctic Golf Course. Set on the tundra against a backdrop of snow-capped peaks, green valleys, and crystal lakes, the nine-hole, par-35 course offers many challenges because of its narrow fairways, small greens, and tricky winds. For details between late June and mid-August (the only time the course is open), contact the Björkliden Arctic Golf Club at ☎ 0980/64100. The rest of the year, contact its affiliate, the Stockholm-based Bromma Golf Course, Kvarnbacksvägen 303, 16874 Bromma, Stockholm (☎ 08/289-430).

The unique **Tornio Golf Club** (popularly called "Green Zone") allows you to play nine holes in one country (Finland) and the remaining nine in Sweden. Located 140 kilometers north of Oulu on the Finnish/Swedish border, the par-73 course is named for the Torino River, which runs through the course. For information, contact the Green Zone Golf Course at Narantie (☎ 0698/431711). Believe it or not, dedicated Finnish and Swedish golfers play in the snow—and in the darkness (except for artificial lighting) during the colder months. This course closes only in January.

---

village, where a motorboat will take you to the Lapp village of **Nikkaluokta**. From there, it's 13 miles on foot, including a short boat trip, to Kebnekaise. Lapp families can put you up overnight and arrange hikes or boating trips. The Swedish Touring Club has a mountain station at Kebnekaise, and the station guide can arrange group hikes to the summit. The ascent takes about 4 hours.

The town of Kiruna, which emerged at the turn of the century, owes its location to nearby deposits of iron ore. Guided tours of the mines are offered year-round, but only to people over 9 years old. Visitors are taken through an underground network of tunnels and chambers. For details on the tours, contact **LKAB Mining Company,** LKAB, S-981 86 Kiruna (☎ 0980/710-16).

Southeast of the railroad station, the tower of the **Stadshus** (☎ 0980/70-496) dominates Kiruna. Inside there's an art collection and some Sami handcraft exhibits. It's open June to August, Monday to Friday from 9am to 6pm, Saturday and Sunday 10am to 6pm; September to May, Monday to Friday 9am to 5pm.

A short walk up the road takes you to the **Kiruna Kyrka** (☎ 0980/101-40). This church was constructed in 1912 to resemble a stylized Sami hut—it's an origami-like design of rafters and wood beams. The church is open in July daily from 9am to 5pm, and the rest of the summer daily 8am to 10pm.

You can also visit **Hjalmar Lundbohmsgården** (☎ 0980/701-10), the official city museum. It's in a manor house built in 1899 by the city's founder, Hjalmar Lund-bohm, the owner of most of the region's iron mines. Many of the museum's exhibits deal with the city's origins in the late 19th century, the economic conditions that made its growth possible, and the personality of the entrepreneur who persuaded thousands of Swedes to move north to work in the mines. It's open June to August, daily from 10am to 6pm; in the off-season, phone ahead for hours, which could be any day in the afternoon. Admission is 30 SEK ($3.30) for adults, free for children.

About 2½ miles north of Kiruna along the E10 highway is a showcase of Lapp arti-facts, **Mattarahkka** (☎ 0980/191-91). It's a log house capped proudly with the red, blue, yellow, and green Sami flag. The site includes workshops where visitors can watch traditional Sami products (knives, leather knapsacks, hats, gloves, and tunics) being made. Many of the items are for sale. The center has a simple cafe. The site is open in summer, daily from 10am to 6pm; off-season, Monday to Friday noon to 6pm.

WHERE TO STAY & DINE
Moderate
Scandic Hotel Ferrum. Lars Janssongatan 15, S-981 21 Kiruna. ☎ **0980/39-86-00.** Fax 0980/39-86-11. E-mail: ferrum@scandic-hotels.com. 170 units. TV TEL. June 17–Aug 14, 790 SEK ($86.90) double. Aug 15–June 16, Sun–Thurs 1,574 SEK ($173.15) double; Fri–Sat 790 SEK ($86.90) double. Rates include breakfast. AE, DC, MC, V. Closed Dec 23–26. Parking 75 SEK ($8.25).

Run by the Scandic chain, this hotel is named after the iron ore (*ferrum*) for which Kiruna is famous. The six-story hotel, built in 1967, is one of the tallest buildings in town—functional and standard in design, it's one of your best bets for lodging and food. It has two well-run restaurants, Reenstiern and Mommas, a steakhouse, as well as a cocktail bar and a small casino. The modern guest rooms are comfortably furnished, with excellent beds. Rooms for people with disabilities and for guests with allergies are available. The hotel's top floor has conference rooms, a sauna, a solarium, and an exercise room.

Inexpensive
Hotel Kebne. Konduktogrsatan 7, S-981 34 Kiruna. ☎ **0980/123-80.** Fax 0980/681-81. 54 units. TV TEL. June 15–Aug 15, 595 SEK ($65.45) double. Aug 16–June 14, Sun–Thurs 1,075 SEK ($118.25) double; Fri–Sat 595 SEK ($65.45) double. Rates include breakfast. AE, DC, MC, V. Free parking.

Next to the police station on the main road through Kiruna, this hotel consists of two separate buildings. They were constructed around 1911 but radically renovated in the 1980s. The modern, comfortable guest rooms are decorated in bland international style. Room service is available until 11pm, and airport buses stop at the door.

The hotel also operates one of the best restaurants in Kiruna. Open only for breakfast and dinner, it offers a two-course fixed-price menu for 99 SEK ($12.65), which some visitors tout as the best evening bargain in town. Dinner is served Monday to Thursday from 5 to 11pm.

ABISKO
55 miles NW of Kiruna, 911 miles N of Stockholm

A resort north of the Arctic Circle is a curiosity. Abisko, a resort on the southern shore of Lake Torneträsk, has a scenic valley, a lake, and an island. An elevator takes passengers to Mount Nuolja (Njulla). Nearby is Abisko National Park, which contains remarkable flora, including orchids.

ESSENTIALS
GETTING THERE   From Kiruna, continue northwest on E10. You can take the train to Kiruna (see above), then a train or bus. Several buses a day run from Kiruna to Abisko, with continuing service to Narvik, Norway. Contact **Länstrafiken** (☎ **0926/756-80**).

VISITOR INFORMATION   Contact the tourist office in Kiruna (see "Visitor Information" under "Kiruna," above).

EXPLORING THE AREA

✪ **Abisko National Park** (☎ 0980/40-200), established in 1903, is around the Abiskojokk River, which flows into Lake Torneträsk. This is a typical alpine valley with a rich variety of flora and fauna. The highest mountain is Slåttatjåkka, 3,900 feet above sea level. Njulla Mountain (3,800 feet) has a cable car. *Abisko* is a Lapp word meaning "ocean forest." The park's proximity to the Atlantic gives it a maritime character, with milder winters and cooler summers than the continentally influenced areas east of the Scandes, or Caledonian Mountains.

In the area is the smaller **Vadvetjåkka National Park.** Established in 1920, it lies northwest of Lake Torneträsk, extending to the Norwegian border. It's made up of mountain precipices and large tracts of bog and delta. It also has rich flora and impressive brook ravines. The highest mountain is Vadvetjåkka, with a southern peak at 3,650 feet above sea level.

Abisko is more easily accessible than Vadvetjåkka. Three sides of Vadvetjåkka Park are bounded by water (which is difficult to wade through), and the fourth side is rough terrain with treacherously slippery slope bogs and steep precipices that are susceptible to rock slides. This park was once inhabited, and then abandoned.

Abisko is one of the best centers for watching the **midnight sun,** which you can see from June 13 to July 4. It's also the start of the longest marked trail in the world, the Kungsleden. You'll also see a reconstruction of a Lapp encampment at the resort.

The ✪ **Kungsleden (Royal Trail)** runs about 210 miles from Abisko to Hemavan. It's marked, and mountain huts are spaced a day's hike apart. Most of the stops are at what Swedes call *kåtors.* You can hike the trail on your own, and no special permits are needed. Lodgings are available on a first-come, first-served basis. Call the **Swedish Touring Club** (☎ 08/463-21-00) for more information and a trail map. *Note:* Since you'll cook your own food, be sure to clean up before leaving. At certain points the trail crosses lakes and rivers, where boats can be found for that purpose. The trail follows the Lapps' old nomadic paths. Travelers with less time or energy can explore a smaller segment of the trail.

WHERE TO STAY & DINE

Abisko Touriststation. S-98107 Abisko. ☎ 0980/402-00. Fax 0980/401-40. www. stfabisko.com. E-mail: info@abisko.stfturist.se. 77 units, 3 with bathroom; 56 cabin apts. 770 SEK ($84.70) double without bathroom; 910–1,030 SEK ($100.10–$113.30) double with bathroom. Room rates include breakfast. Cabin apt (without meals) 975 SEK ($107.25) per night or 5,425 SEK ($596.75) per week for up to 6 occupants. AE, MC, V. Free parking.

Owned by the Swedish Touring Club since 1910, this big, modern hotel stands about 500 yards from the bus station. It offers accommodations in the main building and the annex, and 28 cabins with two apartments each. Each cabin unit has a kitchen and private bathroom. From the hotel you can see the lake and the mountains. The helpful staff can provide information about excursions. The rooms are basic but reasonably comfortable, and some offer exceptional views. Abisko Touristation has a plain restaurant serving standard Swedish cuisine.

ENDING YOUR DRIVING TOUR

Abisko is close to the Norwegian border. To cross into Norway, take E10 west across the border toward Narvik. To return to Stockholm, follow E10 east toward the coast, and then head south on E4 to the capital.

18

The Best of Finland

Finland offers visitors an embarrassment of riches, everything from sophisticated Helsinki to magnificent islands and lakes, wilderness adventures, reindeer safaris, dogsledding, and more. To help you decide how best to spend your time in Finland, we've compiled a list of our favorite experiences and discoveries. In the following pages, you'll find the kind of candid advice we'd give our close friends.

1 The Best Travel Experiences

- **Taking a Finnish Sauna:** With some 1.6 million saunas in Finland—roughly one for every three citizens—there's a sauna waiting for you here in the country that virtually invented this steamy bath. Ideally, your sauna experience should be in a log cabin with windows and a view of the lake. Naturally, you'd be joined by friends with whom you'd share beer cooled in a frigid lake and sausages roasted on heat-retaining stones. After a sauna, the ideal way to cool off is to go for a swim in a cold lake. In winter, when the lake is frozen over, a hole is sometimes cut through the ice so that the really keen can take a dip. Visitors can enjoy saunas at most hotels, motels, holiday villages, and camping sites.
- **Exploring Europe's Last Frontier:** Located in Scandinavia's far north—its northern tier traversed by the Arctic Circle—Finnish Lapland seems like a forgotten corner of the world. Its indigenous peoples, the Sami, have managed to preserve their distinctive identity and are an integral part of Lapland and its culture. One of the greatest travel experiences in Europe is the opportunity to explore this land and enjoy a reindeer sled drive. Lapland is both a summer and a winter destination. In the winter darkness, you can experience the northern lights in all their glory, go dogsledding behind a team of huskies, float in a frozen fjord in a space-age survival suit, take a snowmobile safari (with an overnight stay in a log cabin), go skiing, or even celebrate Christmas in Lapland. Dozens of such tours are available through **Nordique Tours/Norvista,** a subdivision of Picasso Travel, 5250 West Century Blvd., Suite 626, Los Angeles, CA 90045 (☎ **800/ 995-7997** or 310/645-7527; www.nordiquetours.com).
- **Traversing the Finnish Waterworld:** From the coastal islands to the Saimaa lake district, from the tens of thousands of other lakes to the sleepy rivers of the west coast, Finland is one vast

waterworld. Adventures range from daring the giddy, frothing rapids of the midlands to paddling the deserted streams or swift currents and cascades of Lapland. You can explore Finland's vast bodies of water in many types of boats; there are even wooden boat cruises on both rivers and lakes that end with a sauna in the wilds. Every major town in Finland has canoe-rental outfitters, and local tourist offices can offer advice on touring the local waters.

- **Wandering Finnish Forests:** Finland has been called 1 huge forest with 5 million people hiding in it. In fact, nearly four-fifths of the country's total land area is forested, which is remarkable in a world where so many trees have been cut down elsewhere. The Finnish people enjoy a strong and ongoing relationship with their forests and have carefully preserved vast tracts of precious natural areas with rare flora and fauna. To walk in these woods and to pick wild berries and mushrooms (nonpoisonous only, please) is one of their favorite pastimes—and can quickly be enjoyed by the foreign visitor as well.

- **Discovering Finnish Design & Architecture:** Finnish buildings are among the world's newest—more than 90% have been erected since 1920—but their avant-garde design has stunned the world and spread the fame of such architects as Alvar Aalto. In Helsinki you can see the neoclassical Senate Square, Eliel Saarinen's controversial railway station (dating from 1914), and the Temppeliaukio Church, which has been hollowed out from rock with only its dome showing. The Gallen-Kallela Museum, built on a rocky peninsula, was designed by the artist to display his works, ranging from paintings to sculpture and furniture. While in Helsinki, you can also visit the University of Industrial Arts—the largest of its kind in Scandinavia—to learn about current exhibits of Finnish design. All the other major cities of Finland are filled with daring and innovative architecture and design, including Hvitträsk, a turn-of-the-century studio designed by a trio of architects as a lab experiment for their aesthetic principles.

2 The Best Scenic Towns & Villages

- **Turku:** Finland's most charming, evocative, and atmospheric town developed around an ancient trading post. Its castle played a prominent role in Finnish (as well as Scandinavian) history. The national capital until 1812, Turku today is an important cultural center, with two universities. It's also a good base for short cruises of the Turku Archipelago.

- **Savonlinna:** The commercial and cultural center of the eastern Savo region, one of Finland's most ancient provinces, this town is the center of Lake Saimaa traffic. It's also a spa. Home to the fabled Savonlinna Opera Festival, it has a history dating back to 1475 when Olavinlinna Castle was founded as a fortress on the eastern border of Sweden and Finland. Filled with attractions, including museums and art galleries, it's also a good center for exploring one the most scenic parts of Finland—often by boat.

- **Lappeenranta:** Founded in 1649 by Queen Christina of Sweden, this town lies at the southernmost edge of Lake Saimaa. It covers a large area stretching from the lake to the Russian border. The commercial and cultural center of South Karelia, it's a spa town and the gateway to the Saimaa Canal. It's filled with attractions, including Finland's oldest Orthodox church and several museums, plus fortified walls dating from the 18th century. It's also a good base for lots of excursions, including visa-free day tours to Vyborg in Russia.

- **Rauma:** Founded in 1442, and known for its old wooden buildings (dating mostly from the 18th and 19th centuries) and lacemaking, Rauma contains the best-preserved area of historic structures in Scandinavia. UNESCO has declared its Old Town to be a World Heritage Site. You can visit museums, churches, and the houses of craftspeople, including lace shops.

- **Porvoo:** Situated 30 miles northeast of Helsinki (at the mouth of the River Porvoo), this was an important trading center in the Middle Ages. Porvoo has been especially loved by poets and artists, including some of Finland's greatest. Old Porvoo, with its lanes and wooden houses—the oldest of which date from the 16th century—is well worth exploring. You can visit the home of the painter Albert Edelfelt, south of town, as well as the home of the Finnish national poet, Johan Ludwig Runeberg, which has been restored to its original condition. See chapter 20.

3 The Best Active Vacations

For additional sporting and adventure travel information, please see "The Active Vacation Planner" in chapter 19.

- **Bicycling:** Thousands of miles of narrow paths and captivating gravel tracks lead to towns where broad highways are flanked by well-maintained bicycle routes. Wherever you ride in Finland, you'll find many opportunities to enjoy the great outdoors to the fullest; local tourist offices can provide maps of the best trails. The town of Kuopio, for example, has established a network of well-signposted paths, and the local bicycling association has created special off-road routes outside the town proper, ranging from 6 to 18½ miles.

- **Canoeing:** Choose from among a large variety of waterscapes: coastal waters dotted with thousands of islands, rivers flowing to the sea, or lakes in the Greater Saimaa region. The best coastal areas are the archipelago along the southwest coast, the coast of Uusimaa province, and the Åland Islands. A popular region for canoeing is the lake district; here the lakes are linked in long chains by short channels with strong currents. Together the lakes form a network of routes extending for thousands of miles.

- **Fishing:** For those who are skilled, Finland offers the chance to fish year-round. Fishermen here divide their calendar not into months, but according to the fish in season. Sea trout become plentiful as the rivers rise in March and April. May and June are the golden months for pike, which become ravenous, especially after spawning. Midsummer, when the rapids are at their best, marks the season for Lapland grayling and pike-perch. Also in midsummer, salmon fishermen prepare for the high point of their year when the shiny, silver-flanged ranger of the deep, the salmon, arrive at their home rivers to spawn. Autumn brings sea trout inshore, along with the "Flying Dutchman of the Deep"—pike that stalk the shoals of herring. Even in winter, Finnish fishermen drill through the ice to catch perch, pike, and trout. Ice fishermen angle for burbot during the dark winter nights, since its roe is regarded as the choicest of caviars.

- **Hiking:** Hiking is a popular form of recreation in heavily forested Finland, which is full of places to wander. Lapland holds its own special appeal, but you can ramble for a day or more even in southern Finland. Outside Helsinki, for example, there are numerous rambling trails in Nuuksio National Park. The provinces of middle Finland have a network of hiking trails—a total of some 185 miles.

- **Skiing:** The ski season in Finland is longest in Lapland, from October until mid-May. However, the days are quite dark in early winter, and in the period preceding and following the winter solstice, the sun doesn't rise above the horizon north of the Arctic Circle. In northern Finland, south of Lapland, there's good skiing for more than 5 hours a day in natural light even when the days are short. Numerous ski trails are lit artificially when winter is at its darkest. The peak holiday ski season is just before spring, when there's lots of daylight and sunshine. In southern Finland skiing conditions are ideal in January and February, in central Finland the best months are December to March, and in northern Finland it's December to April. Finland's ski trails are varied, with beautiful forest scenery and ample climbs and descents. Lakes and fields are ideal for beginners.

4 The Best Festivals & Special Events

- **Savonlinna Opera Festival** (Savonlinna): Dating back to 1912, this annual event takes place in July; there are usually classic operas, supplemented by Finnish works. Every year from early July to early August the festival stages three or four of its own productions and hosts visiting opera companies from abroad. See chapter 19.
- **Helsinki Festival:** Beginning in mid-August, international artists come to Helsinki to perform chamber music and recitals, or present visual arts exhibits, dance programs, film screenings, and theatrical performances in the theater, as well as opera, jazz, pop, and rock concerts—and lots more. See chapter 19.
- **Tar Skiing Race** (Oulu): This cross-country ski race was established more than a century ago, and has been held almost continuously since then. In March hundreds of participants from around the world show up to compete on the 47-mile racecourse. See chapter 19.
- **Midnight Sun Film Festival** (Sodankylä): Held each June, this is the world's northernmost film festival, featuring works by well-known directors as well as new names in the industry. See chapter 19.
- **Kuopio Dance & Musical Festival** (Kuopio): This is Scandinavia's oldest drama festival, held in late June and the first week of July; distinguished performers and troupes from all over the world come to participate. There's a different theme each year. See chapter 19.

5 The Best Museums

- **Sara Hildén Art Museum** (Tampere; ☎ 03/214-3134): This lakeside museum, founded in 1962 with a bequest from collector Sara Hildén, offers one of Scandinavia's finest changing exhibits of modern art. Over the years the permanent collection has been greatly expanded, and today includes works by many renowned artists, especially from the 20th century.
- **Ainola** (Järvenpää, outside Helsinki): This was the home of Finland's famous composer, Jean Sibelius, who lived here for more than half a century until his death in 1957. Along with his wife, Aino (for whom the house is named), he's buried on the property. Situated 24 miles from Helsinki, Ainola is filled with Sibelius memorabilia. See chapter 20.
- **Seurasaari Open-Air Museum** (Seurasaari): This museum is on an island off the coast of Helsinki (now a national park). Here some 100 authentically furnished and decorated houses have been reassembled—everything from a 1600s church to an "aboriginal" sauna. If you don't have the opportunity to explore Finland in depth, these buildings will help you understand something of Finnish life past and present. On summer evenings, folk dances are presented here to the tunes of a fiddler. See chapter 20.
- **Mannerheim Museum** (Helsinki): This was the home of Baron Carl Gustaf Mannerheim, marshal of Finland and president of the republic from 1944 to

1946. It has been turned into a museum filled with memorabilia, including his swords, medals, and uniforms along with his collection of antiques and furnishings. The house remains as it was when he died in 1951. See chapter 20.

- **Gallen-Kallela Museum** (Espoo): On a wooded peninsula, this museum honors the Finnish artist Akseli Gallen-Kallela (1865–1931), who is known mainly for his paintings, especially those from the *Kalevala* (Land of Heroes), the Finnish national epic. Often compared to Homer's *Iliad* and *Odyssey,* the *Kalevala* was first published in 1835, but in a later edition was illustrated by Gallen-Kallela. See chapter 20.

6 The Best Offbeat Experiences

- **Camping in the Woods:** Join the Finns as they enjoy the great outdoors in the summer. There are about 350 campsites with some 6,300 camp cabins and holiday cottages. Most have washing and cooking facilities, as well as canteens (where you can buy food and miscellaneous supplies). If you have an international camping card (FICC), you don't need a Finnish camping card. Regional tourist offices can provide information about campsites, or write to the **Camping Department** of the **Finnish Travel Association,** Atomitie 5, F-00370 Helsinki (☎ **09/622-6280**). Camping cards (international or Finnish) may be purchased at the campsite for about $15. In North America, the card is available from **Family Campers and RVers Association,** 4804 Transit Rd., Bldg. 2, Depew, NY 14043 (☎ or fax **716/668-6242;** www.forv.org). Finnish Camping Cards are available from the Camping Department office above.

- **Experiencing a Finnish Farm:** Despite its role as an industrialized nation, Finland's roots extend deep into the soil, with a hardy group of farmers who are adept at coaxing crops out of the often-frozen earth. Several hundred English-speaking farmers have opened their homes to temporary guests, offering a first-hand view of how the country grows such flavorful produce and vegetables.

   A well-respected travel expert, **Lomarengas Finnish Country Holidays,** Hämeentie 105D, F-00550 Helsinki (☎ **09/57-66-33-50**) compiles an annual booklet with description, map locations, and photographs of scenic farms, antique and modern cottages, and log cabins. Depending on the accommodation, there's a minimum rental of between 1 and 3 days. Prices for rooms within farms range from $29 to $41 per person per day, double occupancy, which includes bed linens and breakfast. Rentals of cabins and cottages, suitable for between two and eight occupants, range from $340 to $840 per week, depending on the accommodation and the season. It's easiest to reach your holiday destination by car, but if you're traveling by train or bus, you can be met. Bookings can be arranged through the organization's North American agent, **Union Tours,** 245 Fifth Avenue, Suite 1101, New York, NY 10016 (☎ **212/683-9500**).

- **Panning for Gold:** In the Lemmenjoki region (near Inari), in Finnish Lapland, there are all-day gold-panning trips along the River Lemmenjoki between mid-June and mid-September. A motorboat will take you a distance of 15½ miles, and then you'll disembark and walk 2¼ miles to the gold-panning site. Participants are shown how to wash gold by sluicing and panning. On the return trip you'll stop at Ravadas waterfall, one of the most spectacular sights in northern Finland. For more information, contact **Lemmenjoki Cabins,** Ahkun Tupa, FIN-99885 (☎ **016/673-435**). Lemmenjoki Cabins is 28 miles southwest of the village of Inari. Its dozen cabins, each with kitchens, lie on both sides of the Lemmenjoki River, and you must use a rowboat to cross over to the other side to reach them. It's very rustic. They rent for 230 FIM ($35.40) per day double occupancy. Technically, they can be used in winter, but no one does, as it's simply too cold.

- **Seeing the Seals:** Excursions are scheduled between mid-April and mid-August, enabling you to spend a day with the seals. You'll depart from Vaasa in a partly covered fishing boat and will be taken through the protected waters that are favored by seals. There are also lots of opportunities to observe and photograph sea birds. An outdoor lunch will be arranged on a small island. For more information and reservations, contact **Botnia Tourist,** Senaatikatu 1, FIN-65100 Vaasa (☎ **06/325-1125;** www.botniatourist.com).

- **Taking a Snowmobile Safari:** From the first week of January until mid-April you can take a 6-day/5-night snowmobile safari; you fly from Helsinki to Ivalo in the north of Finland and back again. At the Saarisellkä Skiing Resort, you first get snowmobile driving lessons and then have the opportunity to go snowmobile trekking through varying winter landscapes. Overnights are sometimes arranged in wilderness huts; safari outfits and all meals are provided. For more information, contact **Nordique Tours/Norvista,** a subdivision of Picasso Travel, 5250 West Century Blvd., Suite 626, Los Angeles, CA 90045 (☎ **800/995-7997** or 310/645-7527; www.nordiquetours.com).

7 The Best Buys

- **Clothing & Textiles:** There's everything from cottons and linens (often in stunning modern fashions such as those by Marimekko) to warm stoles and shawls. Collectors also seek out *ryijy* rugs and *raanu* wall hangings. Many of these goods are displayed and sold at shops along the Esplanade in Helsinki.

- **Glass & Ceramics:** Finland offers a wide variety in stunning designs, ranging from practical everyday items at moderate prices to one-of-a-kind objects designed by well-known Finnish artisans. The best-known factory names (and the best quality) to look for are Arabia for china, or Nuutajärvi, Iittala, and Riihimäki for glass. Their products are displayed in shops throughout the country. Showrooms for both Arabia and Iittala are on the Esplanade in Helsinki. Many Finnish glassworks can be visited; contact local tourist offices for further information.

- **Jewelry:** Although Finland is not often associated with jewelry making, it has some rare items for sale—especially from the *Kalevala* series based on centuries-old Finnish ornaments. Modern designers working in gold or silver produce many bold and innovative pieces of jewelry as well, sometimes as settings for Finnish semiprecious stones, or combined wood and silver. Lapponia jewelry—sold all over the country—is one example of modern Finnish design.

- **Wines & Spirits:** Vodka and liqueurs made from local berries are popular, especially the rare cloudberry, the Arctic bramble, and the cranberry. Alcohol is sold at retail through the outlets of Alko, the State Alcohol Company.

8 The Best Hotels

- **Hamburger Börs** (Turku; ☎ **02/337-381**): This is the leading hotel in Finland's ancient capital, situated by the market square in the center of town. Built a century ago, it has been enlarged and improved countless times over the years. Possessed of both a regional aura and a refined patina, it functions as a lively social hub—with five different restaurants. There's even a nightclub, featuring the best local entertainment in town.

- **Rantasipi Pohjanhovi** (Rovaniemi; ☎ 016/333-11): This hotel, the largest in northern Scandinavia, stretches along the bank of the Kemijoki River and offers quick access to the waterfalls. A tunnel links the four-story main structure to additional accommodations across the street. With a cosmopolitan aura, the Pohjanhovi is known for its cuisine. Some rooms have black walls for guests who have trouble sleeping at the time of the midnight sun.
- **Scandic Hotel Rosendahl** (Tampere; ☎ 03/244-1111): This hotel is set in a forest at the edge of Lake Pyhäjärvi, about 1½ miles south of town. Built in 1977, it was completely updated and renovated in the early 1990s. An attentive staff keeps the building and facilities in tip-top shape from the open lobby to the beautifully furnished accommodations.
- **Hotel Kämp** (Helsinki; ☎ 09/5761-1999): One of the most luxurious hotels in the north of Europe, the Kämp brings five-star comforts to the Finnish capital. It was born in 1887 but has been dramatically and beautifully restored. A great deal of Finnish history took place under its roof, and the politics, a blend of east and west, continue to thrive on its dramatic premises. See chapter 20.
- **Palace Hotel** (Helsinki; ☎ 09/134-561): On the south harbor, this glamorous hotel—known for its scenic 10th-floor dining room—is the city's finest. The accommodations are spacious, with sleek Finnish styling such as dark-wood paneling and built-in furniture. The Palace offers the highest level of personal service, and amenities include three saunas on the 11th floor. See chapter 20.
- **Scandic Hotel Kalastajatorppa** (Helsinki; ☎ 09/45-811): Set in a bucolic parkland on the sea, this is a tranquil and luxurious choice. Comprising three buildings with two restaurants, plus two modern glass wings linked by tunnels, it's a cozy, snug retreat—ideal on a cold winter's day but also enjoyable in summer, when its sports amenities, including a beach with watersports equipment, are put to full use. See chapter 20.

9 The Best Restaurants

- **Restaurant Julia** (in the Scandic Hotel Julia, Turku; ☎ 02/2651-311): Regional gastronomes often cite Julia as one of Finland's finest restaurants. Against a backdrop of belle époque memorabilia and an open fireplace, Julia prepares only the freshest of Finnish foods, but with French culinary techniques. The atmosphere is warm and cozy, as you enjoy such dishes as grilled salmon with ribbons of a tartar of marinated Baltic herring. The menu changes seasonally to take advantage of the best available ingredients.
- **Restaurant Oppipoika** (in the Hotel Oppipoika, Rovaniemi; ☎ 016/338-81-11): In Finnish Lapland, one of the north's finest restaurants seeks to introduce and promote Lappish cuisine. Of course, this generally means fresh fish such as salmon, but other favorites include reindeer pepper steak.
- **Havis Amanda** (Helsinki; ☎ 09/666-882): Known for its fine seafood, this upscale tavern was established in 1973. Most of its saltwater fish comes from Finnish coastal waters, while its freshwater fish—everything from Baltic crayfish to brook trout—is from Finnish lakes. The restaurant has a beautiful atmosphere and some of the finest service in Helsinki. See chapter 20.
- **Olivo** (in the Scandic Hotel Continental; Helsinki; ☎ 09/40-551). Finland's most sumptuous Mediterranean cuisine is served in a relaxed, friendly, and bright atmosphere in this modern hotel. The menu is diverse, ranging from Italy to Morocco, from Turkey to the Middle East, and it also features a well-chosen

assortment of wines. The bracingly fresh quality of the produce astonishes and delights the palate. See chapter 20.

- **Restaurant Palace** (Helsinki; ☎ **09/134-561**): In one of the city's best hotels, this restaurant, a stellar choice since 1952, also provides Helsinki's most scenic dining—a panoramic view of the harbor. A refined Finnish-French cuisine is served. Dishes are delectable, prepared only with the highest quality ingredients. Finnish salmon is the perennial favorite. The chef's fillet and tongue of reindeer is the best in town. See chapter 20.

19

Planning a Trip to Finland

This chapter provides many of the details you need to know for planning your trip to Finland. See also Chapter 2, "Planning a Trip to Denmark," since much information about Scandinavia as a whole was discussed there.

1 The Regions in Brief

HELSINKI & THE SOUTHERN COAST   The capital city and its environs comprise the most industrialized area of the country, with the densest population. More than 25% of Finland's people live here. **Helsinki** is the capital of the country's government, entertainment, and culture; it's also a crossroads between Western and Eastern Europe. The eastern and central areas of the south are characterized by fertile farmland, crisscrossed by many rivers. This is the agriculture belt. The western land in the south has many shallow lakes and ridges. **Porvoo,** 30 miles northeast of Helsinki, was founded by the Swedes in 1346. It was the site of the first Finnish Diet, when the country became a Grand Duchy. **Kotka** is home to the Langinkoski Imperial Fishing Lodge, used by Tsar Alexander III, and later a favorite play spot for his granddaughter Anastasia.

TURKU & THE ÅLAND ISLANDS   The city of **Turku,** Finland's oldest city and former capital, is on the west coast. Its location on the Gulf of Bothnia, combined with a mild climate (its port remains ice free year-round), have made this city an important center for trade and commerce. **Naantali,** 12 miles northwest of Turku, is one of the finest examples of a medieval Finnish town. It developed around the convent and monastery of St. Birgitta and was a favorite spa for Russians tired of St. Petersburg. At the entrance to the Gulf of Bothnia lie the **Åland Islands** (about 6,500 in number)—only 75 miles from Stockholm. Only about 80 of the islands are inhabited, and all of their residents speak Swedish. The only significant town in the Ålands is **Mariehamn,** a fishing and tourist community founded in 1861.

THE LAKE REGION   Central Finland is home to thousands of lakes created millions of years ago by glaciers. This region is an important tourist area, with many resorts along the lakeshores. In this region you'll find **Tampere,** Finland's second-largest city. Although an industrial city, Tampere's location on an isthmus nestled between two lakes provides an enchanting backdrop for this young, vibrant city. **Lahti,** Finland's most "American" city, lies on the shores of Lake Vesijärvi, the

Finland

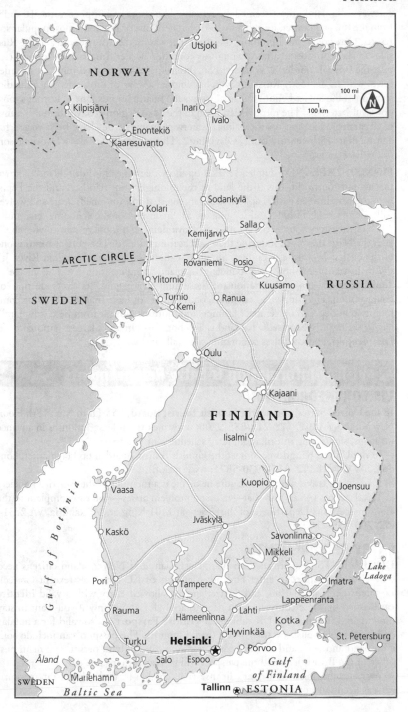

gateway to Finland's most scenic lake systems. The resort of **Lappeenranta,** 10 miles from the Russian border, founded in 1649, has been one of Finland's most popular spa resorts. Here you'll find Linnoitus, a fortress that was used by the Swedes and the Russians to stave off hostile attacks along this contested border. **Imatra,** in the southeast near the Russian border, is as close to St. Petersburg as it is to Helsinki. This border town, with its distinctly Russian flavor, has enjoyed a wave of prosperity since the dissolution of the Soviet Union. Outside town is the Imatra Rapids, one of Europe's most powerful waterfalls. The most visited town in the Lake Region is **Savonlinna.** Because of its strategic location on the Saimaa waterway, many battles have been waged for control of its 15th-century castle, Olavinlinna. This spa town was also a favorite resort of the Russian tsars.

FINNISH LAPLAND   Lapland makes up more than one-third of Finland. Known throughout the world, this is the land of the midnight sun, reindeer, and the Lapps with their traditional garb. Lapland is largely forested and untamed; bears and wolves still rule the land. Fishing and logging are the mainstays of the economy. Five miles south of the Arctic Circle, the capital city, **Rovaniemi,** is a modern new town, rebuilt after the Nazis destroyed it during their retreat from Finland. The port of **Kemi** is one of the busiest in northern Europe. Situated at the mouth of the Kemijoki River, it's the main transit method for products of Lapland's logging industry. The village of **Tankavaara** is a major destination for those hunting for gold. Its rivers are ripe for gold panning. The Lapp village of **Inari,** on the shores of Lake Inari, is a thriving community that depends on reindeer farming and tourism. Not far from here is Finland's largest ski resort—**Saariselk.** Lapland is also home to Finland's largest national park, **Lemmenjoki,** and countless panoramic waterfalls and swift rivers.

2 Visitor Information & Entry Requirements

VISITOR INFORMATION

In the United States, contact the **Finnish Tourist Board,** 655 Third Ave., 18th Floor, New York, NY 10017 (☎ 212/885-9700; www.mek.fi), at least 3 months in advance for maps, sightseeing information, ferry schedules, or whatever.

In the United Kingdom, contact the Finnish Tourist Board at 66 Haymarket, London, SW1Y 4RF (☎ 0171/930-5871; www.mek.fi).

If you use a **travel agent,** make sure he or she is a member of the American Society of Travel Agents (ASTA), so that—in case a problem arises—you can complain to the Consumer Affairs Department of the society at 1101 King St., Alexandria, VA 22314 (☎ 703/739-2782).

ENTRY REQUIREMENTS

DOCUMENTS   American, Canadian, Australian, and New Zealand citizens need only a valid **passport** to enter Finland. Members of EU countries (except Greece), Liechtenstein, San Marino, and Switzerland are allowed entry with a valid **identity card** issued by those countries. You need to apply for a visa only if you want to stay more than 3 months. For UK subjects, a **Visitor's Passport** is also valid for a holiday or even for some business trips of less than 3 months. The passport can include both a husband and wife, and it's valid for 1 year. You can apply in person at a main post office in the British Isles and the passport will be issued that same day.

Your current domestic **driver's license** is acceptable in Finland. An international driver's license is not required.

The Finnish Markka

For American Readers At this writing, 1 U.S. dollar was worth approximately 6.5 markka (or 1 markka = approximately 15¢), and this was the rate of exchange used to calculate the dollar values given throughout this edition, rounded to the nearest nickel.

For British Readers Also at this writing, 1 British pound equaled approximately 9.9 markka (or 1 markka = 10 pence), the rate used to calculate the pound values in the table below.

About the Euro At press time, 1 Euro (€) was worth approximately 5.95 markka, although this will almost certainly change as Finland works through the role it wants to play within a united Europe with a shared European currency.

Note: International exchange rates fluctuate, so the figures in this chart may not be the same by the time of your trip to Finland. Use this table as a guideline.

FIM	US$	UK£	Euro	FIM	US$	UK£	Euro
1	0.150	.10	0.17	75	11.55	7.5	12.6
2	0.31	0.20	0.34	100	15.40	10.00	16.80
3	0.46	0.30	0.50	125	19.25	12.50	21.00
4	0.62	0.40	0.67	150	23.10	15.00	25.20
5	0.77	0.50	0.84	175	26.95	17.50	29.40
6	0.92	0.60	1.01	200	30.80	20.00	33.60
7	1.08	0.70	1.18	225	34.65	22.50	37.80
8	1.23	0.80	1.34	250	38.50	25.00	42.00
9	1.39	0.90	1.51	275	42.35	27.50	46.20
10	1.54	1.00	1.68	300	46.20	30.00	50.40
15	2.31	1.50	2.52	350	53.90	35.00	58.80
20	3.08	2.00	3.36	400	61.60	40.00	67.20
25	3.85	2.50	4.20	500	77.00	50.00	84.00
50	7.70	5.00	8.40	1000	154.00	100.00	168.00

CUSTOMS All personal effects, including cameras and a reasonable amount of film (or other items intended for your own use) can be brought in duty-free. Gifts costing up to 1,100 FIM ($169.40) may also be brought in duty-free. You can bring in 200 cigarettes or 250gm of other manufactured tobacco. You can also bring in 15 liters of beer, 2 liters of wine, and 1 liter of spirits *or* 2 liters of beer and 2 liters of wine. You must be over the age of 20 to bring in alcohol and over 18 to bring in beer and wine. There are no restrictions on the amount of Finnish currency that can be taken in or out of the country.

3 Money

See "Money" in chapter 2 for a general discussion of changing currency, using credit and charge cards, and other matters.

CURRENCY The Finnish unit of currency is the **markka** (plural: **markkaa**), which is divided into 100 **pennia** (abbreviation: "p"). Banknotes are issued in denominations of 20, 50, 100, 500, and 1,000 markkaa, and coins circulate in denominations of 10p and 50p, as well as 1 and 10 markkaa.

Many international banks abbreviate the Finnish markka as **FIM,** which we use in this book.

What Things Cost in Helsinki	U.S.$
Taxi from the airport to the city center	20.80
Single ticket on a tram or bus	1.55
Local telephone call	.40
Double room at the Ramada Presidentti Hotel (expensive)	192.50
Double room at the Martta Hotelli (moderate)	87.80
Double room at the Hotel Arthur (inexpensive)	73.90
Lunch for one, without wine, at Kellarikrouvi (moderate)	23.10
Lunch for one, without wine, at Restaurant Kappeli (inexpensive)	15.40
Dinner for one, without wine, at Havis Amanda (expensive)	40.00
Dinner for one, without wine, at Bellevue (moderate)	33.00
Dinner for one, without wine, at Kynsilaukka Garlic Restaurant (inexpensive)	20.00
Pint of beer (draft Pilsner) in a pub	6.00
Coca-Cola at a cafe	3.00
Cup of coffee at a cafe	3.00
Admission to Mannerheim Museum	6.15
Movie ticket	8.50
Opera ticket	7.70–77.00

4 When to Go

CLIMATE

Spring arrives in May and the summers are short. A standing joke is that in Helsinki, summer lasts from Tuesday to Thursday. July is the warmest month, with temperatures averaging around 59°F. The coldest months are January and February, when the Finnish climate has been compared to that of New England. Snow arrives in southern Finland in December; it arrives in northern Finland in October. In Lapland, snow generally lasts until late April.

Finland's Average Daytime Temperatures (°F)

	Jan	Feb	Mar	Apr	May	June	July	Aug	Sept	Oct	Nov	Dec
Helsinki	26	27	33	44	57	66	69	66	57	48	39	31
Tampere	24	24	32	44	57	66	72	68	58	45	36	29
Jyväskylä	20	22	32	42	58	67	69	65	54	43	32	24
Ivalo	17	17	26	27	47	60	67	62	50	37	28	21

THE MIDNIGHT SUN In Lapland the midnight sun and mosquitoes offer the visitor an unforgettable experience.

The following places and dates are the best for seeing the midnight sun in Finland: **Utsjoki,** May 17 to July 28; **Ivalo,** May 23 to July 22; **Sodankyl,** May 30 to July 5; on the **Arctic Circle** and **Rovaniemi,** June 6 to July 7; **Kuusamo,** June 13 to July 1; and **Kemi,** June 19 to June 25. Helsinki has almost 20 hours of daylight during the summer months.

HOLIDAYS

The following holidays are observed in Finland: January 1 (New Year's Day); Epiphany (January 6); Good Friday, Easter Monday; May 1 (Labor Day); Ascension Day (mid-May); Whitmonday (late May); Midsummer Eve and Midsummer Day (Friday and Saturday of the weekend closest to June 24); All Saints' Day (November 6); December 6 (Independence Day); and December 25 and 26 (Christmas and Boxing Days).

Finland Calendar of Events

The dates given in this calendar can vary from year to year. Check with the Finnish Tourist Office for the exact dates and contact information (see "Visitor Information & Entry Requirements," above).

February
- **Finlandia Ski Race,** Hämeenlinna-Lahti. With almost 50 miles of cross-country skiing, this mass event is part of the Euroloppet and Worldloppet competitions. Late February.

March
- ✪ **Tar Skiing Race,** Oulu. This cross-country ski race has taken place each year, without interruption, since it was first established more than a century ago. Following a course that stretches more than 47 miles—and with hundreds of participants—it's the oldest long-distance cross-country ski race in the world. Early to mid-March.

April
- **Walpurgis Eve Celebration.** After a long, cold winter, most Helsinki residents turn out to celebrate the arrival of spring. Celebrations are held at Market Square, followed by May Day parades and other activities the next morning. April 30.

May
- **May Day.** Parades and other celebrations of the arrival of spring. May 1.
- **Women's 10km.** A 6-mile foot race for women. For more detailed information on this event, contact any office of the Finnish Tourist Board (☎ **212/885-9700** in the U.S.). Late May.

June
- ✪ **Kuopio Dance and Music Festival.** This international dance event takes a different theme every year, such as Dances in Japan, the Middle East, and North Africa. Last week in June to first week in July.
- ✪ **Midnight Sun Film Festival,** Sodankylää. The world's northernmost film festival features nostalgic releases from the great film masters—mainly European—but also new names in the film world. For more information, call ☎ **016/ 614-524.** Dates vary.

July
- ✪ **Savonlinna Opera Festival.** One of Europe's most important and best-known music festivals, it's part of a cultural tradition established in 1912. Traditionally, dozens of performances are held in the island fortress of Olavinlinna Castle in July. Internationally renowned artists perform in a variety of works, including at least one Finnish opera. For details and complete information, contact the

Savonlinna Opera Festival, Olavinkatu 27, FIN-57130 Savonlinna (☎ 015/ 47-67-50). Early July to early August.

- **Kaustinen Folk Music Festival.** The biggest international folk festival in Scandinavia. July 17 to 25.

August

- **Turku Music Festival.** A wide range of music is presented from the Renaissance and the baroque period (played on the original instruments) to modern, light music. Second week of August.
- **Helsinki Marathon.** This event attracts both Finnish and foreign runners of varying abilities. Mid-August.
- ✪ **Helsinki Festival.** A major Scandinavian musical event, the Helsinki Festival presents orchestral concerts by outstanding soloists and ensembles, chamber music and recitals, exhibitions, ballet, theater, and opera performances, along with jazz, pop, and rock concerts. For complete information about the program, contact the Helsinki Festival, Rauhankatu 7, FIN-00170 Helsinki (☎ 09/ 135-45-22). Mid-August to early September.

October

- **The Baltic Herring Market.** Since the 1700s, there has been an annual herring market along the quays of Market Square in early October. Prizes and blue ribbons go to the tastiest herring. Fishers continue the centuries-old tradition of bringing their catch into the city and selling it from their boats. First week in October.

5 The Active Vacation Planner

ADVENTURE TOURS   Summer and winter are both great periods for a holiday in Finland. Apart from the midnight sun and the Northern Lights, Finland has much to offer the adventurer. For information about adventure vacation packages, summer or winter, in Lapland, we recommend **Lapland Travel,** Koskikatu 1, PL-8156 Rovaniemi (☎ 016/312-622).

BICYCLING   In Finland, you can either rent a bike and cycle on your own or join one of dozens of cycling tours. One 6-day/5-night tour in the Åland Islands, for example, takes you along an excellent road network, past low hills and shimmering water. For bookings, contact **Alandsresor,** P.O. Box 62, FIN-22101 Mariehamn (☎ 018/ 280-40; www.alandsresor.fi). Some hotels, holiday villages, camping sites—even tourist information offices—rent bicycles. More information is available from the **Cycling Union of Finland,** Radikatu 20, FIN-00093 Helsinki (fax 09/278-6585).

CANOEING   The Finnish Canoe Federation arranges guided canoe tours along the country's most scenic waterscapes. Clubs rent canoes for the tours; one- and two-seat kayaks or canoes are available, and charts of the coastal waters are provided. For more information, contact the **Finnish Canoe Federation,** Olympiastadion, Eteläakaarre, FIN-00250 Helsinki (☎ 09/494-965).

FISHING   Finland has more than 6,000 professional fishers and about 1.5 million people fishing for recreation. For foreign visitors who'd like to fish for recreation, the usual methods permitted are summer and winter angling, and fishing with lure and fly.

In Finland most fishing waters are privately owned; cities and private companies also own fishing waters. The National Board of Forestry administers state fishing waters, mainly in northern and eastern Finland.

Foreign visitors must buy a general fishing license if they intend to do recreational fishing in Finland (a separate license is needed for the Åland Islands). You can get a general fishing license from postal bank offices and post offices; it costs 33 FIM ($6.25) per person and is valid for 1 week; a year's license costs 150 FIM ($28.50).

Transmarine (☎ 305/674-7853) offers a 7-day package, "Fishing on the Tainion-virta River." Essentially, you fish on your own, but the package includes accommodations, a fishing license, and use of a boat. These tours are priced from $500. The same company offers a package that includes a 7-day stay in a cottage on one of the many lakes in the Lahti area. The package includes a car, and may feature alternating days of canoeing and biking tours along the local rivers. It's ideal for those who prefer to move around without benefit of a guide. Prices begin at $700 and include equipment.

GOLF   There are 95 golf courses in Finland, and 66,000 members of the **Finnish Golf Union,** the organization that keeps tabs on the locations and attributes of every golf course in Finland. The best courses are in Helsinki and include Tali Manor, 4 miles from the center, and the Espoo Golf Course. Information about golf courses   and their pars, entry requirements, and greens fees is available from the Finnish Golf Union at Radiokatu 20, FIN-00240 Helsinki (☎ 09/3481-2244; www.golfpiste.com).

HIKING   Finland is an ideal country for hiking. The northern wilderness boasts the highest *fells* (rolling and barren hills), clear streams, and lots of open country. Eastern Finland's forested hills and vast woodlands conceal many lakes and deep gullies. Western Finland's low, cultivated plain is cut by fertile river valleys leading to the Gulf of Bothnia. Central Finland is known for its thousands of lakes and rolling woodlands, and the south of Finland, even though densely populated, has many forests suitable for hiking. Hiking maps can be ordered from **Karttakeskkus (Map Centre),** P.O. Box 85, FIN-00521 Helsinki (☎ 020/445-144). A special brochure on hiking is available from the Finnish Tourist Board abroad.

SKIING   Skiing conditions in Finland are among the best in the world. The season is long and the trails are good. The best skiing season in northern Finland is March and April, when there may be up to 16 hours of sunshine daily. But the early winter—*kaamos,* the season when the sun doesn't appear at all—has its own attractions for visitors who want to experience something different.

Finland is about 700 miles long, with distinct differences at each end. The south consists of gently rolling hills, with no elevations exceeding 3 feet, but the farther north one goes, the more deeply forested and mountainous the country becomes. The highest hills are in Lapland.

The slopes of Finnish ski resorts are maintained in excellent condition. Skiing instruction—both cross-country and downhill—is available at most resorts, and equipment can be rented on the spot.

Long-distance ski races are becoming increasingly popular, and the long trails, ranging from 25 to 55 miles, attract more and more participants from all over the world every year. As many as 15,000 skiers take part in the biggest event—the Finlandia Ski Race. A fair number of resorts organize guided ski treks. They take a few days, and overnight accommodations are arranged along the trail in farmhouses or, in Lapland, in wilderness huts or shelters.

6 Health & Insurance

For a general discussion of health and insurance concerns, see Chapter 2, "Planning a Trip to Denmark."

Finland's national health plan does not cover U.S. or Canadian visitors. Any medical expenses that arise must be paid in cash. (Medical costs in Finland, however, are generally more reasonable than elsewhere in Western Europe.) British and other EU citizens can ask their insurer for an E111 form, which will cover emergencies in Finland and all other EU countries.

7 Tips for Travelers with Special Needs

There are a number of resources and organizations in both North America and Britain to assist travelers with special needs in planning their trip to Finland. For details, see "Tips for Travelers with Special Needs" in chapter 2.

FOR TRAVELERS WITH DISABILITIES   Like its Scandinavian neighbors, Finland has been in the vanguard of providing services for people with disabilities. In general, trains, airlines, ferries, and department stores and malls are accessible. For information about wheelchair access, ferry and air travel, parking, and other matters, your best bet is to contact the Finnish Tourist Board (see "Visitor Information & Entry Requirements," above).

In Finland, you may obtain general information from the **Association of the Physically Challenged (Invalidiliitto Ry),** Kumpulantie 1A, FIN-00520 Helsinki (☎ **09/613-191**).

FOR GAY & LESBIAN TRAVELERS   Helsinging seudun SETA ry, Hietalah-denkatu 2B (☎ **09/612-32-33**), is a good source of information about gay life in the capital and Finland as a whole. The office is open Monday to Tuesday noon to 4pm, Wednesday noon to 6pm, Thursday noon to 4pm, and Friday noon to 2pm.

FOR SENIORS   In Finland, passengers age 65 and over are entitled to a 50% reduction on many Finnair flights. The domestic route system is divided into blue, black, and red flights; seniors cannot get reductions on blue flights since they are in the greatest demand. For the others, any generally accepted document of identification suffices for this purpose. The passenger's date of birth must be inserted in the "Fare Basis" column.

By showing their passport as proof of age, visitors over age 65 may buy regular railway tickets (either one-way or round-trip) at a 50% reduction.

FOR FAMILIES   On Finnair flights, one parent pays the full one-way or round-trip adult fare, the spouse pays 75% of the fare, children 12 to 23 are charged 50%, and children 2 to 11 are charged 25% of the fare. One child under 2 may be carried free.

On the Finnish national rail system, a maximum of four children age 6 and under can travel free with one adult. A 50% reduction is granted for children 6 to 16.

8 Getting There

BY PLANE

With more flights to Helsinki from more parts of the world (including Europe, Asia, and North America) than any other airline, **Finnair** (☎ **800/950-5000** in the U.S.; www.finnair.com) is the only airline flying nonstop from North America to Finland (an 8-hour trip). From New York, Finnair flies to Helsinki every day. The airline also maintains twice-weekly nonstop service to Helsinki throughout the year from Miami.

Midsummer round-trip fares from New York to Helsinki range from $984 to $3,780 (plus about $50 tax) for those who book their passage 21 days in advance and agree to remain abroad for 7 to 60 days. These prices are substantially lower in winter, and also lower during Finnair's frequent promotional sales. **Finnair**

(☎ 020/ 7408-1222 in London; www.finnair.com) also offers more frequent service to Helsinki from several airports in Britain; there are three or four daily nonstop flights from either Heathrow or Stanstead Airport, and one or two daily flights from Manchester. Flight time from London to Helsinki is 2 hours, 50 minutes; from Manchester, it's 3 hours, 40 minutes.

Several other airlines fly from all parts of the world to gateway European cities and then connect to Helsinki. Foremost among these is **British Airways (BA)** (☎ 800/247-9297 in the U.S. or 0345/222-111 in London; www.britishairways.com), which offers hundreds of daily flights into the U.K. from all over the world. From London's Heathrow, BA offers one or two daily nonstop flights to Helsinki, depending on the day of the week.

BY CAR
FROM WESTERN SCANDINAVIA The quickest routes to Finland are the E3 or E4 to Stockholm and the year-round 14- to 16-hour ferry from there to Helsinki.

FROM GERMANY From Travemünde there's a year-round high-speed car-ferry that takes 22 hours to reach Helsinki.

FROM DENMARK Take the car-ferry from Helsingør to Helsingborg in Sweden or the Øresund ridge from Copenhagen to Malmö, and then drive to Stockholm and catch the car ferry to Helsinki or Turku.

BY TRAIN
There's a rail and ferryboat link between London and Helsinki that goes via Ostende (Belgium), Cologne, Hamburg, and Stockholm. If you've taken the ferry from Stockholm and are arriving at Turku, on the west coast of Finland, you can catch one of the seven daily trains (including the high-speed Pendolino) that take you across southern Finland to Helsinki. The trip takes 2¼ hours. Rail connections are also possible from London to Hook of Holland (the Netherlands), Bremen, Hamburg, and Stockholm. However, each of these itineraries takes about 50 hours, plus a 2-hour stopover in Stockholm. It's possible to reserve sleepers and couchettes, but do so as far in advance as possible. Helsinki is also linked by rail to the major cities of Finland.

RAIL PASSES FOR NORTH AMERICAN TRAVELERS
If you plan to travel extensively on the European or British railroads, it would be worthwhile for you to secure the latest edition of the *Thomas Cook European Timetable of Railroads*. It's available exclusively in North America from **Forsyth Travel Library,** 226 Westchester Ave., White Plains, NY 10604 (☎ 800/FORSYTH in the U.S.; www.forsyth.com), at a cost of $27.95, plus $4.95 priority shipping in the States and $2 (U.S.) for airmail shipments to Canada.

SCANRAIL PASS If your visit to Europe will be primarily in Scandinavia, the Scanrail pass may be better and cheaper for you than the Eurailpass. This pass allows its owner a designated number of days of free rail travel within a larger time block. (Presumably, this allows for days devoted to sightseeing scattered among days of rail transfers between cities or sites of interest.) For example, you could choose a total of any 5 days of unlimited rail travel during a 15-day period, 10 days of rail travel within a 1-month period, or 1 month of unlimited rail travel. The pass, which is valid on all lines of the state railways of Denmark, Finland, Norway, and Sweden, offers discounts or free travel on some (but not all) of the region's ferryboat lines as well. The pass can be purchased only in North America, at any office of **RailEurope** (☎ 800/361-RAIL; www.raileurope.com) or at **ScanAm World Tours,** 933 Highway 23, Pompton Plains, NJ 07444 (☎ 800/ 545-2204; www.scanamtours.com).

Depending on whether you choose first- or second-class rail transport, 5 days' travel out of 1 month ranges from $166 to $250. There are 50% discounts off these prices for children ages 6 to 12.

EURAILPASS   If you're going to be traveling extensively in Europe, the **Eurailpass** might be a good bet. It's valid for first-class rail travel in 17 European countries. With one ticket, you travel whenever and wherever you please—more than 100,000 rail miles are at your disposal. Here's how it works: The pass is sold only in North America. A Eurailpass good for 15 days costs $554, a pass for 21 days is $718, a 1-month pass costs $890, a 2-month pass is $1,260, and a 3-month pass goes for $1,558. Children under 4 travel free if they don't occupy a seat (otherwise, they're charged half fare); children under 12 are charged half fare. If you're under 26, you can purchase a **Eurail Youthpass,** which entitles you to unlimited second-class travel for 15 days for $388, 1 month for $623, or 2 months for $882. Travelers considering purchasing a 15-day or 1-month pass should estimate rail distance before deciding if such a pass is worthwhile. To take full advantage of the tickets for 15 days or a month, you'd have to spend a great deal of time on the train. Eurailpass holders are entitled to substantial reductions on certain buses and ferries as well. Travel agents in all towns, and railway agents in such major cities as New York, Montréal, and Los Angeles, sell all these tickets. A Eurailpass is available at the North American offices of CIT Travel Service, the French National Railroads, the German Federal Railroads, and the Swiss Federal Railways.

Eurail Saverpass is a money-saving ticket that offers discounted 15-day travel for groups of three or more people traveling together between April and September, or two people traveling together between October and March. The price of the pass, valid all over Europe for first-class only, is $715 for 15 days, $928 for 21 days, and $1,150 for 1 month. Even more freedom is offered by the **Saver Flexipass,** which is similar to the Eurail Saverpass, except you are not confined to consecutive-day travel. For travel over any 10 days in 2 months, the fare is $556; any 15 days in 2 months, the fare is $732.

Eurail Flexipass allows greater flexibility in European travel. It's valid in first-class and offers the same privileges as the Eurailpass. However, it provides a number of individual travel days that can be used over a much longer period of consecutive days. Using this pass makes it possible to stay longer in one city and yet not lose a single day of travel. There are two Flexipasses: 10 days of travel within 2 months for $654 and 15 days of travel within 2 months for $862.

With many of the same qualifications and restrictions as the previously described Flexipass is a **Eurail Youth Flexipass.** Sold only to travelers under age 26, it allows 10 days of travel within 2 months for $458 and 15 days of travel within 2 months for $599.

RAIL PASSES FOR BRITISH TRAVELERS

Thousands of trains run from Britain to the Continent every month, and at least some of them are routed directly across or under the Channel, through France or Belgium and Germany to Copenhagen. For example, a train leaves London's Waterloo Station daily at 6:14am, arriving in Copenhagen at 9:59pm. The trip takes 15 hours and goes via Brussels and then makes stops in Cologne and Hamburg for a total of three train changes. Once you're in Copenhagen, you can make good rail connections to Norway, Finland, and Sweden. Because of the time and distances involved, many passengers prefer to rent a couchette (sleeping berth), which costs around £18 ($30.60) per person. Designed like padded benches stacked bunk-style one atop another, they're usually clustered six to a compartment.

If you plan to do a lot of exploring, you might prefer one of three rail passes designed for unlimited train travel within a designated region during a predetermined number of days. These passes are sold in Britain and several other European countries.

An **InterRail Pass** is available to passengers of any nationality, but only if they're under age 26 and can prove residency in a European or North African country (Morocco, Algeria, and Tunisia) for at least 6 months before purchasing the pass. It allows unlimited travel through all of Europe except Albania and the republics comprising the former Soviet Union. Prices are complicated and vary depending on the countries you want to include. For pricing purposes, Europe is divided into seven zones and the cost depends on the number of zones you include. The most expensive option, priced at £219 ($372.30), allows 1 month of unlimited travel in all seven zones (BritRail staff refers to this as a "global"). The least expensive option, priced at £129 ($219.30), allows 22 days of travel within only one zone.

Passengers aged 26 and over can buy an **InterRail 26-Plus Pass,** suitable for travel through Denmark, Finland, Norway, and Sweden. However, many other European countries, including France, Belgium, Switzerland, and most of Europe's southwestern tier (Spain, Portugal, and Italy), do not honor this pass. Travel with the pass costs £179 ($304.30) for 22 days or £309 ($525.30) for 1 month. The same residency requirements apply to this pass that apply to the InterRail Pass described above.

For information on buying individual rail tickets or any of the above-mentioned passes, contact **RailEurope,** Victoria Station, London (☎ **0990/848-848** for information). Tickets and passes are also available at any of the larger railway stations as well as selected travel agencies throughout Britain and the rest of Europe.

BY BUS

Although there are international bus links to Finland, this is the least convenient mode of transportation. One of the most popular is a bus connection from Stockholm—it includes a sea crossing to Turku, with continuing land service to Helsinki.

It's also possible to take coaches from Gothenburg going cross-country to Stockholm and to the ferry dock beyond, with land travel resuming after Turku on the same bus all the way to Helsinki.

For information about international bus connections and reservations, contact **Oy Matkahuolto Ab,** Simonkatu 3, FIN-00101 Helsinki (☎ **9600-4000**).

BY SHIP/FERRY

FROM SWEDEN   Frequent ferries run between Sweden and Finland, especially between Stockholm and Helsinki. Service is on either the Viking or Silja Line. Each company also operates a twice-daily service from Stockholm to Turku on Finland's west coast.

FROM GERMANY   The Silja Line also maintains regular passenger service from June 5 to September 15 between Travemünde (Germany) and Helsinki. You can get information about the **Silja Line** at Mannerheimintie 2, FIN-00101 Helsinki (☎ **09/ 180-41**). Information on the **Viking Line** is available at Mastokatu 1, FIN-00160 (☎ **09/123-51**).

PACKAGE TOURS

The best tours of Finland are offered by **Finnair** (☎ **800/950 5000** in the U.S.; www.finnair.com), including its most popular, the **Midnight Sun Flight** (Helsinki–Rovaniemi–Helsinki). This tour is offered daily in June and July. Any Finnair office around the world can provide information about tours for exploring Finland.

If you'd like to see as much as possible of Finland's highlights in the shortest possible time, consider one of the **Friendly Finland Tours,** lasting 3 to 6 days. It's offered at various times between June and August. This tour is operated by the **Finland Travel Bureau,** Kaivokatu 10A, PB 319, FIN-00101 Helsinki (☎ **09/182-61;** www.smt.fi). Bookings can be made through any travel agent.

9   Getting Around

BY PLANE

Finnair (☎ **800/950-5000** in the U.S.), along with its domestic subsidiaries, Karair and Finnaviation, offers reasonably priced air transportation to virtually every settlement of any size in Finland, including some that are not accessible by any other means. Its routes cover the length and breadth of the country with at least 100 flights a day.

If you plan to travel extensively throughout Scandinavia or into the Baltic countries, then consider the **Finnair Nordic Air Pass.** It is available only from May 1 through September 30, and you must have a transatlantic plane ticket to be eligible. A maximum of 10 passes and a minimum of 4 entitle you to huge discounts on flights within Finland, Denmark, Sweden, and the Baltic countries. Prices range from $85 to $170 for one-way flights. Call **Finnair** (☎ **800/950-5000**) or **Norvista** (☎ **800/ 677-6454**) for more information.

BY TRAIN

Finland has its own **Finnrailpass** for use on the country's elaborate network of railroads. It's a "flexipass," entitling the holder to unlimited travel for any 3, 5, or 10 days within a 1-month period on all passenger trains of the VR Ltd. Finnish Railways. Travel days may be used either consecutively or nonconsecutively. Prices are as follows: any 3 days in 1 month, $124 in second class, $186 in first class; any 5 days in 1 month, $166 in second class, $250 in first class; and any 10 days in 1 month, $224 in second class, $336 in first class. Travelers over 65 and children 6 to 16 are charged half the full fare (it may be necessary to show proof of age); children 5 and under ride free.

Second-class trains in Finland are comparable to first-class trains in many other countries. The Finnrailpass should be purchased before you enter Finland; sometimes it's available at border stations at the frontier.

Because the Finnish trains tend to be crowded, you should reserve a seat in advance—in fact, seat reservations are obligatory on all express trains marked "IC" or "EP" on the timetable. The charge for seat reservations, which depends on the class and the length of the journey, ranges from 20 to 200 FIM ($3.10 to $30.80).

For more information, contact **VR Ltd. Finnish Railways,** P.O. Box 488, Vilhonkatu 13, FIN-00101 Helsinki (☎ **09/707-4086**). In the United States, contact **RailEurope, Inc.,** 226–230 Westchester Ave., White Plains, NY 10604 (☎ **800/ 848-7245** or 800/4EURAIL; www.raileurope.com). For other railway information, call ☎ **09/707-57-06** in Helsinki, Monday to Friday 8:30am to 4:30pm.

BY BUS

Finland has an extensive bus network operated by private companies. Information on bus travel is available at the **Helsinki Bus Station,** just west of the post office between Salomonkatu and Simonkatu (☎ **09/02-00-40-10**). Tickets can be purchased on board or at the bus station. Ask about a "Coach Holiday Ticket," allowing travel up to 621 miles during any 2-week period. These discount tickets can be purchased in Finland at a cost of $66 (U.S.).

BY TAXI IN FINNISH CITIES

Service on most forms of public transportation ends around midnight throughout Finland, forcing night owls to drive themselves (unwise if you've been drinking) or to rely on the battalions of taxis (*taksi*) that line up at taxi stands in every Finnish town. In Helsinki, taxi stands are strategically situated throughout the downtown area, and it's usually less expensive to wait in line at a stand until one arrives. If you decide to call a taxi—they can be found under "Taksiasemat" in the local yellow pages—you have to pay the charges that accumulate on the meter from the moment the driver first receives the call, not from where he or she picks you up. In Helsinki there's a base charge of between 22 and 35 FIM ($3.40 and $5.40), depending on the time of day or night; after that there's an additional flat rate of around 5 FIM (75¢) for every kilometer you travel. Taxi prices in provincial Finnish cities are usually, but not always, a bit lower.

BY CAR

Because of the far-flung scattering of Finland's attractions and the relative infrequency of its trains and long-distance buses, touring the country by car is the best way to savor its sights and charms, especially during the summer months. Bear in mind that driving conditions can be very bad during the long winter months. Snow tires are compulsory in winter. Studded tires are not required, but they are allowed from November 1 until the first Sunday after Easter, and at other times if justified by weather conditions. All car-rental companies supply winter tires during the appropriate seasons as part of their standard equipment.

If you plan to rent a car, you get the best rates if you reserve one through a car-rental company before you leave North America.

Foreigners bringing a motor vehicle into Finland must have a driver's license and a clearly visible sign attached to the vehicle showing its nation of origin. This rule is enforced at the border. Your home driver's license will be honored; an international driver's license is not required.

RENTALS   Avis (☎ 800/331-1084 in the U.S. and Canada), **Budget** (☎ 800/527-0700 in the U.S. and Canada), and **Hertz** (☎ 800/654-3131 in the U.S. and Canada) are represented in Finland. Each company maintains 22 to 24 locations in Finland, usually in town centers or at airports, and sometimes in surprisingly obscure settings. For those who want to begin and end their tour of Finland in different cities, a drop-off within Finland can be arranged for a modest surcharge. A drop-off outside Finland, however, if allowed at all, is much more expensive—the surcharge could range from 2,000 to 4,000 FIM ($308 to $616), plus additional charges for each kilometer driven. Because of the horrendous costs of one-way international car rentals originating in Finland, most visitors rent cars separately in each country they visit.

Most companies provide child seats, rooftop racks, and ski racks, usually for a nominal one-time fee of between $10 and $12 per item. The charge to rent a luxury car begins at around $403 (U.S.) a week, plus the 22% Finnish tax.

If you plan to do a lot of touring, you'll find that a weekly rental with unlimited mileage is your best bet. All three companies offer a prepaid plan that requires you to complete the paperwork and make an advance payment within a reasonable time before you leave home. The main advantage of prepayment is that it "locks in" a specified net rental price in dollars before you actually use the car; this could save you about $100 a week over what you'd have to pay if you wait until you arrive in Finland.

All three companies offer small, cost-efficient cars that might be able to seat four passengers. However, we recommend these subcompact cars for no more than two passengers plus luggage. Rentals range from 1,987 FIM ($306) at Avis to 2,551 FIM ($392.85) at Budget per week, with unlimited mileage; Hertz's cheapest car, quoted at 2,916 FIM ($449.05) per week, makes a comparison difficult since it includes the whopping 22% government tax in its rates. Both Budget and Avis consider the 22% government tax as a supplemental charge that's added to your bill.

INSURANCE   Collision-damage waiver insurance (CDW) is available at each of the three companies usually for 80 FIM ($12.30) a day, depending on the value of your car. This coverage eliminates your financial responsibility in case of an accident. If you don't have a CDW and you have an accident, you'll probably have to pay for some or all of the damage to the car, even if it's not your fault. Some credit- and charge-card companies (including American Express, MasterCard, Visa, and Diners Club) reimburse their cardholders for the deductible in the event of an accident, but only after your private car insurance has paid the damages (your future premiums at home might be raised if you submit a substantial claim for damage to a rental car abroad). Although the card issuers reimburse the renter for the cost of some or all of the damages (usually several weeks after the accident), payments have occasionally been delayed pending completion of all the paperwork. Unless you have a large line of credit on your card, you might be obliged to pay a large sum of cash on the spot if you have an accident. To avoid any misunderstanding, some car-rental companies offer their clients the choice of automatically including the CDW as part of the total rental price. In any event, it's always a good idea to ask your insurance and credit-card companies about the extent of your coverage beforehand, and check with the rental companies about your liabilities when you reserve your car.

DRIVING RULES   Finns drive on the right side of the road, as in the U.S. and Europe. Speed limits are strictly enforced. It's illegal to drive a motor vehicle under the influence of alcohol (blood alcohol may not exceed 0.5%), and the penalties for doing so are severe.

FLY & DRIVE   Government taxes, insurance coverage, and the high cost of gasoline (petrol) can make the use of a rented vehicle in Finland more expensive than you might have assumed. One way to reduce these costs is to arrange for your fly-drive trip through **Finnair** (☎ 800/950-5000). When you book your flight, the airline may be able to arrange a lower car-rental price through Budget, Hertz, or Avis than you could have gotten on your own.

BY FERRY & LAKE STEAMER

Finland's nearly 188,000 lakes form Europe's largest inland waterway. Although railroads and highways now link most Finnish towns and villages, the romantic old steamers (and their modern counterparts) give both Finns and visitors a relaxing way to enjoy the inland archipelago areas of Finland in summer.

The excursion trips of most vessels last from just a couple of hours to a full day. In some cases you can travel from one lakeside town to another. There are even a couple of car ferries that cross some of the biggest lakes, reducing travel time significantly from the time required to drive around the lake. Unlike highway ferries, which are few in number today but can be used at no charge, the car ferries charge a fare for both cars and passengers. Information on all lake traffic schedules and fares is available from local tourist offices.

10   Organized Tours

Given its vastness and often-difficult driving conditions during the long winter months, Finland is the one Scandinavian country where an organized tour makes sense. Even for those who enjoy the outdoors, it may be best to enter Finland's true wilderness areas with a guide.

There's no better way to discover the natural beauty of Finland's lake region than by cruising its waters. **Norvista** offers an excursion trip on Finland's largest lake, Lake Saimaa. Beginning in Helsinki, the tour's first stop is the medieval town of Porvoo. Other stops include the fishing lodge in Langinlipslo and a brief visit to the monastery of Valamo. Lunch and dinner are served on board, and nights are spent in a hotel in town. The excursion lasts 3 days and begins at $495. For information, call ☎ **800/ 526-4927,** or 212/818-1198 in New York. This tour is available only during the summer months. From December through April, you might try the "Arctic Icebreaker Safari" offered by **Union Tours** (☎ **800/451-9511,** or 212/683-9500 in New York). It's a 3-day cruise on the *Sampo*, with 2 nights at a first-class hotel. Prices begin at $560 and include the voyage, accommodations, breakfast, lunch, and a ride in a reindeer sleigh.

Norvista also has a "Sample Icebreaker," which includes an icebreaker cruise, a reindeer drive, a 2-day ski and snowmobile safari, and even a visit to Santa. These tours cost $1,495, and include all transfers, accommodations, full board, and equipment. One of the more popular tours is the "Northern Lights"—2 days of husky-sledding, a half day of ice fishing, and a full-day reindeer safari. These tours, which cost $999, include the flight from Helsinki to Kittilla, all accommodations, full board, and equipment.

Intourist (☎ **800/556-5305**) offers a "Snowmobile Adventure to the Arctic Ocean." From February 15 to April 20, guides escort participants through Finland's snowfields. The tours include 2 nights in a hotel and 2 nights in a cabin in the wilderness, full board, equipment, and sauna.

Intourist also offers a "Dogsled Safari to the Lapp Fells." Guides take participants through northwestern Lapland. The 7-day tour covers approximately 12 to 21 miles per day. Prices include all equipment and full board. Another great adventure trip is Intourist's canoeing tour of northern Karelia. Canoers paddle through the Lieksa region in eastern Finland. The 7-day tours are available from June to September. Call to determine rates for specific itineraries.

For those who yearn for relaxation—not action—consider a Finnish spa. **Great Spas of the World** (☎ **800/SPA-TIME** or 212/889-8170; www.greatspas.com) sponsors a 7-day jaunt to the Levitunturi Hotel and Spa in Lapland. Its "Arctic Spa Holiday" includes 1 night in Helsinki and 5 at the spa. Available activities vary according to the season. This excursion is offered year-round. Great Spas of the World also sponsors trips to the Katinkulta Holiday Resort and Spa. "Winter Holiday" includes 1 night in Helsinki and 5 nights at the resort. The cost includes all spa and fitness programs. Among the available activities are snowmobile safaris, skiing, and dogsled excursions. Call for rates.

Suggested Itineraries

If You Have 1 Week

Although traveling by car is the best way to see sights and charms, most people rely on trains and airplanes more often in Finland than they might elsewhere in Europe. Nevertheless, we've outlined a weeklong, 317-mile driving tour through the country's "southern triangle."

Days 1–3   Spend your first day in Helsinki recovering from your flight. On Day 2, see the major sights, including the Finnish National Gallery, the National Museum of

Finland, and the Mannerheim Museum. On Day 3, explore the nearby islands of the Baltic, such as Suomenlinna, or take a steamer to Porvoo, Finland's second-oldest town.

Day 4　Drive from Helsinki to Hämeenlinna, a distance of 61 miles. Take E79 past forest-covered hills and meadows, which eventually give way to open country dotted with lakes. About 20 miles south of Hämeenlinna you can visit Riihimaki, which has a Glass Museum (Suomen Lasimuseo) and a glass shop. By afternoon you'll be in Hämeenlinna, Finland's oldest inland town, founded in 1639, and the birthplace of composer Jean Sibelius. You can also explore a castle on the shores of Lake Vanajavesi. Hämeenlinna is the starting point for many Silja Line cruise boats that go to Tampere. However, if you're pressed for time, you may want to just stay overnight in Hämeenlinna and then continue the tour.

Day 5　Leave Hämeenlinna and drive along E79 for 50 miles to Tampere. Folk dances and open-air concerts are performed in Hämeenpuisto Park in summer, and the city boasts one of the most famous summer theaters in the world. Many lake tours start from here. Spend the night in Tampere.

Day 6　Head for Turku on the west coast. Leaving Tampere, it's only 10 miles to Nokia, famous for its rapids in the Nokia River. Continue southwest on Route 41 for 33 miles until you reach Vammala. The road continues to Huittinen, only 56 miles from Turku. Plan to spend the night in Turku, Finland's oldest city, visiting its many attractions.

Day 7　From Turku, you could return directly to Helsinki on E3. This 103-mile drive can be broken by a stop at Salo, a lively town 33 miles from Turku. About 6 miles past Salo, you might want to stop at the Muurla Glass Factory. Spend the night in Helsinki.

If You Have 2 Weeks

Days 1–7　Spend the first week as suggested above.

Day 8　Spend a full day in Helsinki getting to know the city better.

Day 9　From Helsinki, head northeast to Lappeenranta, one of Finland's most charming provincial towns, 137 miles from Helsinki and only 10 miles from the Russian border, for a full day of sightseeing in Finland's glorious lake district.

Day 10　From Lappeenranta, continue northeast to the historic city of Imatra, favored by the tsars and site of the famous Imatra Rapids.

Days 11–12　From Lappeenranta, go to Savonlinna for 2 nights. During the first day, explore the land attractions, such as Olavinlinna Castle, the Marketplace, and the art center of Retretti; the next, take the lake steamer.

Day 13　Go to Kuopio, in the north lake district, for a day of sightseeing.

Day 14　Drive to Joensuu, the major town in northern Karelia, for a day's sightseeing in this richly folkloric province; Finland was obliged to cede half of this province to the Soviet Union during the Second World War.

Fast Facts: Finland

American Express　The Helsinki branch is at Kanavaranta 9 (☎ **09/613-20-400**). It's open Monday to Friday from 9am to 5pm. Whenever it's closed, you can call an active 24-hour-a-day toll-free information line about lost or stolen credit cards or travelers checks by dialing ☎ **0800/114-646.** That number is valid only within Finland.

Area Code　The international country code for Finland is **358.** The local city (area) codes are given for all phone numbers in the Finland chapters of this book.

Business Hours   Most **banks** are open Monday to Friday from 9:15am to 4:15pm. You can also exchange money at the railway station in Helsinki daily from 8am to 9pm, and at the airport daily from 6:30am to 11pm.

The hours for **stores and shops** vary. Most are open Monday to Friday from 9am to 6pm and Saturday from 9am to 3pm. Nearly everything is closed on Sunday. There are **R-kiosks**—which sell candy, tobacco, toiletries, cosmetics, and souvenirs—all over Helsinki and elsewhere; they're open Monday to Saturday 8am to 9pm and Sunday from 9 or 10am to 9pm.

Customs   See "Visitor Information & Entry Requirements," above.

Drug Laws   Drug offenses are divided into two categories: normal drug offenses and aggravated drug offenses. Normal drug offenses include the possession of a small amount of marijuana (which carries a maximum penalty of 2 years in prison and a minimum penalty of a fine for Finns and possible deportation for non-Finns). Aggravated drug offenses entail the ownership, sale, or dealing in dangerous drugs, including cocaine and heroin. This offense always carries a prison term of 1 to 10 years. Penalties for smuggling drugs across the Finnish border are even more severe.

Drugstores   Medicines are sold at pharmacies (*apteekki* in Finnish). Chemists (*kemikaalipauppa*) sell cosmetics only. Some pharmacies are open 24 hours, and all display notices giving the address of the nearest one on night duty.

Electricity   Finland operates on 220 volts AC. Plugs are usually the continental size with rounded pins. Always ask at your hotel desk before plugging in any electrical appliance. Without an appropriate transformer or adapter, you'll probably destroy the internal mechanism of your appliance or blow out one of the hotel's fuses.

Embassies & Consulates   The Embassy of the **United States** is at Itäinen Puistotie 14A, FIN-00140 Helsinki (☎ **09/171-931**); the Embassy of the **United Kingdom** is at Itäinen Puistotie 17, FIN-00140 Helsinki (☎ **09/2286-5100**); and the Embassy of **Canada** is at Pohjoisesplanadi 25B, FIN-00100 Helsinki (☎ **09/171-141**). Travelers from Australia and New Zealand should contact the British Embassy.

If you're planning to visit Russia after Finland and need information about visas, the **Russian Embassy** is at Tehtaankatu 1B, FIN-00140 Helsinki (☎ **09/661-876**). However, it's better to make all your travel arrangements to Russia before you leave home.

Emergencies   In Helsinki, dial ☎ **112;** for the police, call ☎ **100-22.**

Language   The Finns speak a language that, from the perspective of grammar and linguistics, is radically different from Swedish and Danish. Finnish is as difficult to learn as Chinese, and a source of endless frustration to newcomers. More than 90% of Finns speak Finnish, and the remaining population speaks mostly Swedish. Officially, Finland is a bilingual country, as you'll quickly see from maps and street signs in Helsinki (the street names are usually given in both languages).

The use of English, however, is amazingly common throughout Finland, especially among young people. In all major hotels, restaurants, and nightclubs, English is spoken almost without exception. The best phrase book is the *Berlitz Finnish for Travellers,* with 1,200 phrases and 2,000 useful words, as well as the corresponding pronunciations.

Liquor Laws   Alcohol can be bought at retail from **Alko,** the state liquor-monopoly shops. They're open Monday to Thursday 10am to 5pm, Friday 10am to 6pm, and Saturday 9am to 3pm; they're closed on Sunday and on May 1 and September 30. Alcoholic drinks can also be purchased at hotels, restaurants, and nightclubs. Some establishments, incidentally, are licensed only for beer (or beer and wine). Only beer can be served from 9 to 11am. In Helsinki most licensed establishments stay open until midnight or 1am (until 11pm in some cities).

You must be at least 20 years of age to buy hard liquor at the Alko shops; 18- and 19-year-olds can buy beer, wine, or other beverages that contain less than 22% alcohol.

Mail   Airmail letters take about 7 to 10 days to reach North America; surface mail—sent by boat—takes 1 to 2 months. Parcels are weighed and registered at the post office, which may ask you to declare the value and contents of the package on a preprinted form. Stamps are sold at post offices in all towns and cities, at most hotels, sometimes at news kiosks, and often by shopkeepers who offer the service for customers' convenience. In Finland, mailboxes are bright yellow with a trumpet embossed on them. Airmail letters to North America cost 6.30 FIM (95¢) and postcards to North America cost 3.40 FIM (50¢); to the rest of Europe, the cost is 3.20 FIM (50¢). For postal information, call ☎ 09/9800-7100.

Maps   The National Board of Survey publishes *Road Map of Finland* (GT 1:200,000), an accurate, detailed road and touring map; and *Motoring Road Map* (1:800,000), a new edition of the *Motoring Road Map of Finland,* appearing annually, and the only map with complete information on road surfaces. These maps are the most important ones, although the board also publishes numerous touring maps. They're for sale at major bookstores in Helsinki (see "Fast Facts: Helsinki," in Chapter 20, "Helsinki").

Newspapers & Magazines   English-language newspapers, including the *International Herald Tribune* and *USA Today,* are available at the larger bookstores, the railway station, and many kiosks in central Helsinki and other cities.

Police   Dial ☎ 112 in Helsinki. In smaller towns, ask the operator to connect you with the nearest police station.

Radio & TV   "Northern Report," a program in English, is broadcast at 558 kHz on the AM dial in Helsinki daily at 9:30am, 9:35pm, and midnight. There's also a special Saturday-morning program from 10:30 to 11:30am. A news summary in English is given on the domestic FM networks 1 and 4 daily at 10:55pm. Radio Finland international programs at 100.8 MHz (FM) in Helsinki are presented daily at 5:30, 7:35, 9:30, 11, and 11:30am, at 1:30, 2, 3, 4, 5:05, and 9:35pm, and at midnight, as well as on 94.0 MHz (FM) in Helsinki at 10:30pm. For information and a free publication, *Radio Finland,* about radio programs in foreign languages, call ☎ 09/1480-5830 in Helsinki.

Rest Rooms   Most public rest rooms are in terminals (air, bus, and rail). Hotels usually have very clean toilets, as do the better restaurants and clubs. Most toilets have symbols to designate men or women. Otherwise, *naisille* is for women and *miehille* is for men.

Safety   Finland is one of the safest countries in Europe, although with the arrival of desperately poor immigrants from former Communist lands to the south, the situation is not as tranquil or as safe as before.

Taxes   A 22% sales tax is added to most retail purchases in Finland. However, anyone residing outside the EU, Norway, and Finland can shop tax free in Finland, saving 12% to 16% on purchases costing more than 250 FIM ($38.50).

Look for the TAX-FREE FOR TOURISTS sticker that indicates which shops participate in this program. These shops give you a voucher covering the tax, which you can cash when you leave the country—even if you bought the items with a credit or charge card. The voucher and your purchases must be presented at your point of departure from the country, and you are then reimbursed for the amount of the tax. You're not permitted to use these tax-free purchases within Finland. Your refund can be collected at an airport, ferry port, or highway border point.

Telephone, Telex & Fax   To make **international calls** from Finland by direct dialing, first dial the international prefix of 990, 994, or 999, then the country code, then the area code (without the general prefix 0), and finally the local number. For information on long-distance calls and tariffs, call ☎ **9800-8353.**

To place calls to Finland, dial whatever code is needed in your country to reach the international lines (for example, in the United States, dial **011** for international long distance), then the country code for Finland (**358**), then the area code (without the Finnish long-distance prefix 0), and finally the local number.

To make long-distance calls within Finland, dial 0 to reach the long-distance lines (the choice of carrier is at random), the area code, and the local number. (Note that all area codes in this guide are given with the prefix 0.) For phone number information, dial ☎ **02-02-02.** Besides phone booths and hotels, calls can be made from local post and telephone offices.

You can send faxes and telex messages from your hotel (at an additional charge).

Time   Finnish standard time is 2 hours ahead of Greenwich Mean Time (GMT) and 7 hours ahead of U.S. Eastern Standard Time (when it's midnight in New York, it's 7am in Finland). While Finland is on "summer time" (from March 28 to September 26), it is 3 hours ahead of GMT.

Tipping   It's standard for **hotels and restaurants** to add a service charge of 15%, and usually no further tipping is necessary. In restaurants, it's customary to leave just small change. **Taxi drivers** don't expect a tip. However, it's appropriate to tip **doormen** at least 6 FIM (90¢), and **bellhops** usually get 6 FIM (90¢) per bag (in most Finnish provincial hotels, guests normally carry their own luggage to their room). At railway stations, **porters** are usually tipped 6 FIM (90¢) per bag. Hairdressers and barbers don't expect tips. **Coat check charges** are usually posted; there's no need for additional tipping unless you want to.

20 Helsinki

Helsinki may stand at the doorway to Russia, but its cultural links are firmly in Scandinavia. It was originally founded in 1550 on orders of the Swedish king Gustavus Vasa, halfway between Stockholm and St. Petersburg, and is still known to the Swedes as "Helsingfors."

Surrounded by water on three sides and fringed by islands, Helsinki grew up around a natural harbor overlooking the Gulf of Finland. A city of wide streets, squares, and parks, adorned with sculpture, Helsinki was one of the world's first planned municipalities, and is noted for its 19th-century neoclassical architecture. Because the city is relatively compact, most of it can be explored on foot.

From the capital of an autonomous Grand Duchy of Russia, Helsinki was transformed in 1917 (the year of the Russian Revolution) into the capital of the newly independent Finland. Today it's not only a center of government but the nation's intellectual capital, with a major university and many cultural and scientific institutions. Although Helsinki is also a business and industrial center (most major Finnish firms have their headquarters here), and the hub of Finland's transportation networks, the city is relatively free of pollution.

With a population of about half a million, Helsinki enjoys a certain urban sophistication—although the locals still refer to it as "a big village." Helsinki's residents are some of the best educated, best clothed, best fed, and best housed on earth.

1 Orientation

ARRIVING

BY PLANE The **Helsinki-Vantaa Airport** (☎ **09/82-771**) is 12 miles north of the center of town, about a 30-minute bus ride. Special buses to the airport leave from the City Terminal at Asemaukio 3, and stop at the Air Terminal at Töölönkatu 21 (near the Hotel Inter-Continental) at 15- to 30-minute intervals every day between 5am and midnight. Tickets cost 27 FIM ($4.15) each way. Another slightly less expensive, but less comfortable, option is taking public bus no. 615, which departs from Railway Square (Platform 12) two or three times an hour between 5:30am and 10:20pm. The price is 15 FIM ($2.30) each way.

A conventional taxi ride from the airport to the center of Helsinki costs about 130 to 150 FIM ($20 to $23.10) each way; you'll be assured of a private car shared only by members of your immediate party. A slightly cheaper alternative is to hire a special yellow taxi (☎ 09/2200-2500) at the airport terminal, which might be shared by up to four separate travelers; the cost is 60 FIM ($9.25) per person.

On your departure, note that the airport requires passengers on domestic flights within Finland to check in 30 minutes before flight time. Passengers on flights to other points in Europe usually must check in between 45 and 60 minutes before takeoff, and passengers bound for any of the former regions of the Soviet Union or anywhere in North America usually need to check in between 1 and 2 hours in advance.

BY TRAIN   The **Helsinki Railway Station** is on Kaivokatu (☎ 09/0307-20900 for train information). See "Getting Around" in Chapter 19, "Planning a Trip to Finland," for more information. The station has luggage-storage lockers costing 10 FIM ($1.55). The lost-luggage department is open daily from 6:30am to 10pm.

BY BUS   The **Helsinki Bus Station** does not have a street address, but it's located between Salomonkatu and Simonkatu in the city center (☎ 9600-40000). See "Getting Around" in chapter 19 for more information. If you're arriving from Stockholm, you can take the ferry to Turku on the west coast. At Turku, you can board 1 of about 20 daily buses that make the 2½-hour run to Helsinki.

BY CAR   Helsinki is connected by road to all Finnish cities. If you arrive at the port of Turku on a car ferry from Sweden, you can take the E18 express highway east to Helsinki. See "Getting Around," below, and in chapter 19 for information about car rentals.

BY FERRY   Ferries from Germany and Sweden operated by the **Viking Line** and **Silja Line** arrive at and depart from terminals on the island of Katajanokka, which is just east of Market Square (Kauppatori). The ferry terminals are within easy walking distance from downtown; you can also take tram no. 2 or 4 or a taxi. For tickets and information, contact **Silja Line,** Mannerheimintie 2 (☎ 09/180-41), or **Viking Line,** Mastokatu 1 (☎ 09/123-51).

VISITOR INFORMATION

Helsinki City Tourist Office, Pohjoisesplanadi 19, FIN-00100 Helsinki (☎ 09/ 169-3757), is open May 2 to September 30, Monday to Friday 9am to 7pm and Saturday and Sunday 9am to 3pm; off-season, Monday to Friday 9am to 5pm and Saturday 9am to 3pm. **TourExpert,** a service at the Helsinki Tourist Office, is your best bet for booking tours once you reach Helsinki. The tourist office also sells tickets to events and air, bus, and cruise tickets, and the money-saving **Helsinki Card.** Hotel packages and guide bookings are also available through this office.

CITY LAYOUT

MAIN ARTERIES & STREETS   Helsinki is a peninsula city, skirted by islands and skerries. The main artery is the wide and handsome **Mannerheimintie,** named in honor of the former field marshal. East of Mannerheimintie, opening onto Kaivokatu, is the Helsinki Railway Station. Toward the harbor is **Senaatintori,** crowned by the landmark cathedral. Designed by Carl Ludwig Engel, this "Senate Square" also includes the government and university buildings.

Continuing east is a bridge crossing over a tiny island —**Katajanokka**—dominated by the Eastern Orthodox cathedral. Back across the bridge, sticking close to the harbor, past the President's Palace, is the most colorful square in Helsinki, the **Kauppatori (Market Square)**—see it early in the morning when it's most lively. From the pier here, it's possible to catch boats for **Suomenlinna,** fortified islands that guard the sea lanes to Helsinki. The sea fortress celebrated its 250th anniversary in 1998.

The great promenade street of Helsinki—**Esplanadi** (Esplanade)—begins west of Market Square. Directly north of the Esplanade and running parallel to it is **Aleksanterinkatu,** the principal shopping street.

FINDING AN ADDRESS   Street numbers always begin on the south end of north-south streets and on the eastern end of streets running east-west. All odd numbers are on one side of the street and all even numbers on the opposite side. In some cases, where a large building houses several establishments, there might be an A or B attached to the number.

MAPS   The best city map of Helsinki is called **Falk Plan.** Containing a highly detailed and alphabetized street index, it can easily be carried in your pocket. Falk Plan maps are sold at nearly all bookstores and many news kiosks in the central city, including the major bookstore of Helsinki, **Academic,** Pohjoisesplanadi 39 (☎ **09/121-41**).

Neighborhoods in Brief

Helsinki is divided roughly into districts.

THE CENTER   The historic core stretches from Senaatintori (Senate Square) to Esplanadi. Senate Square is dominated by the Lutheran cathedral at its center, and Esplanadi itself is an avenue lined with trees. At one end of Esplanadi, the wide Mannerheimintie, extending for 3 miles, is the main road from the city center to the expanding suburbs. The section south of Esplanadi is one of the wealthiest in the capital, lined with embassies and elegant houses, rising into Kaivopuisto Park.

NORTH OF CENTER   If you'd like to escape the congestion in the center of town, especially around the rail terminus, you can follow the main artery, Manerheimintie, north. This section of Helsinki lies between Sibelius Park in the west and a lake, Töölönlahti, in the east. It has more a residential feel than does the area in the center and several fine restaurants are located here. Those driving cars into Helsinki prefer this section.

KRUUNUNHAKA & HAKANEIMI   The district of Kruununhaka is one of the oldest. Helsinki was founded in 1550 at the mouth of the Vantaa River, but was relocated in 1640 on the peninsula of Vironniemi in what's known as Kruununhaka today. This section, along with neighboring Hakaniemi, encompasses the remaining buildings from 17th-century Helsinki. The waters of Kaisaniemenlahti divide the districts of Hakaniemi and Kruununhaka.

THE ISLANDS   Helsinki also includes several islands, some of which are known as "tourist islands," including **Korkeasaari,** site of the Helsinki Zoo. The main islands are linked by convenient ferries and water taxis.

Called the "fortress of Finland" and the "Gibraltar of the North," **Suomenlinna** consists of five main islands, all interconnected, and is the site of many museums. You can spend a day here exploring the old fortifications. **Seurasaari,** another island, has a bathing beach and recreation area, as well as a national park and the largest open-air museum in Finland. One of the islands, tiny Kustaanmiekka, is the site of a longtime favorite restaurant (Walhalla) where you might want to enjoy lunch while exploring the Suomenlinna fortress and museums.

ESPOO   Many workers in Helsinki treat Espoo as a bedroom suburb. Actually, since 1972, when it received its charter, it has been the second-largest city of Finland, with a population of nearly 200,000.

TAPIOLA   Another "suburb city," Tapiola was founded in 1951, providing homes for some 16,000 residents. This "model city" greatly influenced housing developments around the world with its varied housing, which ranges from multistory condo units to more luxurious one-family villas. The great Finnish architect, Alvar Aalto, was one of its planners.

2 Getting Around

Helsinki has an efficient transportation network, which includes buses, trams, subway (metro), ferries, and taxis.

BY PUBLIC TRANSPORTATION

DISCOUNT PASSES   Visitors to Helsinki can purchase the **Helsinki Card,** which offers unlimited travel on the city's public buses, trams, subway, and ferries, and a free guided sight-seeing tour by bus (in summer daily, off-season on Sunday), as well as free entry to about 50 museums and other sights in Helsinki. The Helsinki Card is available for 1-, 2-, or 3-day periods. The price of the card for adults is 130 FIM ($20) for 1 day, 165 FIM ($25.40) for 2 days, and 195 FIM ($30.05) for 3 days. A card for children costs 55 FIM ($8.45) for 1 day, 65 FIM ($10) for 2 days, and 75 FIM ($11.55) for 3 days. The cards can be bought at 50 sales points in the Helsinki area, including the Helsinki City Tourist Office, the Hotel Booking Center (see "Accommodations," later in this chapter), travel agencies, and hotels. For further information, check with any Finnish Tourist Board worldwide or the **Helsinki City Tourist Office,** Pohjoisesplanadi 19 (☎ 09/169-3757).

You can also buy a **Tourist Ticket** for travel over a 1-, 3-, or 5-day period. This ticket lets you travel as much as you like within the city limits on all forms of public transportation except regional buses. A 1-day ticket costs 25 FIM ($3.85) for adults, 12.50 FIM ($1.95) for children 7 to 16; a 2-day ticket, 50 FIM ($7.70) for adults, 25 FIM ($3.85) for children 7 to 16; and a 5-day ticket, 75 FIM ($11.55) for adults, 37.50 FIM ($5.80) for children 7 to 16. Children under 7 travel free. Tickets can be purchased at many places throughout Helsinki, including the Helsinki City Tourist Office and transportation service depots, such as the Railway Square Metro Station, open Monday to Thursday 7:30am to 6pm and Friday 7:30am to 4pm.

BY METRO/BUS/TRAIN   The **City Transport Office** is at the Rautatientori metro station (☎ 09/472-2454), open Monday to Thursday 7:30am to 6pm and Friday 7:30am to 4pm. The transportation system operates daily from 5:30am to 1:35am. A single ticket with transfer costs 10 FIM ($1.55) for adults, 5 FIM (75¢) for children; a tram ticket is 8 FIM ($1.25), with no right of transfer. It's cheaper to buy a multitrip ticket, allowing 10 individual trips for 75 FIM ($11.55) for adults, 25 FIM ($3.85) for children. Transfers are allowed for single and multitrip tickets within 1 hour of the time stamped on the ticket.

BY FERRY   Ferries depart from the end of Eteläesplanadi (no terminal) heading for the offshore islands of Suomenlinna and Korkeasaari (Zoo).

BY TAXI

You can order taxis by telephone (☎ 09/700-700), find them at taxi ranks, or hail them on the street. All taxis have an illuminated yellow sign: taksi/taxi. The basic fare costs 22 to 35 FIM ($3.40 to $5.40) and rises on a per-kilometer basis, as indicated on the meter. Surcharges are imposed in the evening (6 to 10pm) and on Saturday after 2pm. There's also a surcharge at night from 10pm to 6am and on Sunday.

A taxi from the Helsinki-Vantaa Airport to the center of Helsinki costs 130 to 150 FIM ($20 to $23.10), and the ride generally takes 30 to 40 minutes. Call ☎ 09/700-800. An airport taxi shuttle service is available for individual travelers to any point in the greater Helsinki area, costing a flat rate of 60 FIM ($9.25). The van is shared by a maximum of eight passengers. Call ☎ **09/2200-2500** at any time.

BY CAR

Driving around Helsinki by car is not recommended because parking is limited. Either walk or take public transportation. However, touring the environs by car is ideal.

CAR RENTALS   The major car-rental companies maintain offices at the Helsinki airport (where airport surcharges apply to car pickups) and in the center of town. Most new visitors prefer to take a taxi to their hotel, and then rent a car after becoming oriented to the city. (This system also avoids parking fees.) **Avis Rent-a-Car** is at Pohjoinen Rautatiekatu 17 (☎ **09/441-155**), **Budget Rent-a-Car** is at Malminkatu 24 (☎ **09/686-6500**), and **Hertz** is at Mannerheimintie 44 (☎ **09/555-2300**).

PARKING   Helsinki has several multistory parking garages, including two centrally located facilities that almost always have an available space: **City-Paikoitus,** Keskuskatu (no numbered address) (☎ **09/6869-6851**), and **Parking Eliel,** adjacent to the railway station (☎ **09/6869-6850**).

BY BICYCLE

You can rent a bicycle from **Kimmo Suontakanen,** Mannerheimintie 13 (☎ **09/ 850-22850**), at rates that range from 90 to 180 FIM ($13.85 to $27.70) per day, depending on the type of bicycle you rent. A deposit of 100 FIM ($15.40) is required, or presentation of your passport. Otherwise, ask at your hotel for addresses within your immediate neighborhood.

Fast Facts: Helsinki

American Express   Its Helsinki branch is at Kanavaranta 9 (☎ **09/ 613-20-400**), open Monday to Friday from 9am to 5pm. Whenever it's closed, you can call an active 24-hour-a-day toll-free information line about lost or stolen credit cards or travelers checks by dialing ☎ **0800/114-646.** That number is valid only within Finland.

Area Code   The country code for Finland is **358;** the city code for Helsinki is **9.**

Baby-Sitters   Every hotel in Finland has a list of employees, such as maids, who, with advance notice, can baby-sit your child. Most speak English. The rate in Helsinki is about 35 FIM ($5.40) per hour, per child, perhaps less in certain provincial towns. Although hotels are the main procurers of baby-sitters throughout Helsinki, there are other possible alternatives. During daytime hours, if you're a devoted shopper, the well-respected **Stockmann Department Store,** Aleksanterinkatu 52 (☎ **09/1211**) offers a free child-minding service every Monday to Friday 10am to 7pm and Saturday 9am to 6pm.

Bookstores   The most famous bookstore in Finland—and the best stocked, with thousands of English titles—is Helsinki's **Academic Bookstore,** Pohjoisesplanadi 39 (☎ **09/121-41**).

Business Hours   Most **banks** are open Monday to Friday 9:15am to 4:15pm. Most **businesses and shops** are open Monday to Friday 9am to 5pm and Saturday 9am to 2pm. Larger stores are usually open until 7pm Monday to Friday and as late as 6pm on Saturdays. With a few exceptions (noted below) nearly everything is closed on Sunday. Many shops in the center of Helsinki are open until 8pm on certain nights, especially Monday and Friday. Shops in the Station Tunnel are generally open Monday to Saturday 10am to 10pm and Sunday noon to 10pm.

Selling candy, tobacco, toiletries, cosmetics, and souvenirs all over Helsinki and elsewhere, **R-kiosks** are open Monday to Saturday 8am to 9pm and Sunday 9 or 10am to 9pm.

Currency Exchange   You can exchange dollars for FIM at most banks and (if the amount is large enough) often in your hotel; however, you're likely to get less FIM at hotels than at banks. You can also exchange money at the railway station Monday to Friday 9am to 6pm; and at the airport daily, 6am to 11pm.

Dentists   Go to the **Ympyrätalo Dental Clinic,** Siltasaarenkatu 18A (☎ 09/709-6611), open Monday to Friday 8am to 8pm and Saturday 9am to 1pm.

Doctors   To summon a physician in an emergency, dial ☎ **112.** For private medical advice, dial ☎ **09/4711.**

Drugstores   Pharmacies dispensing medicines are known as *apteekki.* The **Yliopiston Apteekki,** Mannerheimintie 96 (☎ **09/415-778**), is open 24 hours daily.

Embassies & Consulates   The Embassy of the **United States** is at Itäinen Puisotie 14A (☎ **09/171-931**); the Embassy of **Canada,** at Pohjoiesplanadi 25B (☎ **09/171-141**); and the Embassy of the **United Kingdom,** at Itäinen Puistotie 17 (☎ **09/2286-5100**). Citizens of Australia and New Zealand should go to the British Embassy.

Emergencies   Dial ☎ **112** for medical help, an ambulance, police, or in case of fire.

Eyeglasses   One of the most conveniently situated and best recommended opticians—where you can get new glasses or contact lenses in about a day—is the optical department at **Stockmann Department Store,** Aleksanterinkatu 52 (☎ **09/1211;** Tram: 3b). One floor above street level, it's open Monday to Friday 9am to 8pm and Saturday 9am to 6pm.

Hairdressers & Barbers   Salon Alex/Salon Alexandra, Urgönkatu 23A (☎ **09/612-2700**), is a well-managed association of semi-independent hairdressers who specialize in cutting and styling men's (at Salon Alex) and women's (at Salon Alexandra) hair. Your fellow clients are likely to include some of Finland's most visible fashion models. Unless you prefer a specific hairdresser, an advance appointment is usually not necessary.

Hospitals   An emergency hospital for foreigners is the **Helsinki University Central Hospital,** Meilahti Hospital (for both medical and surgical care), at Haartmaninkatu 4 (☎ **09/4711**).

Internet Access   Opposite the train station, **Sonero,** Kaivokatu 2, gives you the first 15 minutes of access to the Internet free. Open Monday to Friday 9am to 7pm, Saturday 10am to 4pm.

Laundry   At the laundry **Exprès Pikapesula,** Laivurinrinne 2 (☎ **09/639-524**), clothes brought in early in the morning can be ready by the 5:30pm closing time.

Liquor Laws   The legal age for drinking beer and hard liquor throughout Finland is 18. Many nightclubs and discos, however, admit only "well-dressed" (and nonrowdy) patrons, and sometimes insist that they appear to be 24 or older. Age limits (or even the appearance of age limits), however, usually don't apply to pubs. Laws against drunken driving are rigidly enforced in Helsinki.

Lost Property   The **Lost Property Office** is at Päijänteentie 12A (☎ 09/ 189-3180), open year-round, Monday to Tuesday and Thursday to Friday 8am to 4:15pm, and Wednesday 8am to 5:30pm.

Luggage Storage & Lockers   These facilities are at the Central Station on Kaivokatu. The staff offers both lockers with keys and an employee-staffed area where you get a ticket for your luggage. The charge is 10 FIM ($1.55) per bag. The service operates daily from 6:30am to 10pm.

Mail   For post office information, call ☎ 09/195-51-17. The main post office in Helsinki is at Mannerheimintie 1A, open Monday to Friday 9am to 5pm. If you don't know your address in Helsinki, have your mail sent to you at FIN-00100 *Poste Restante* (general delivery) in care of the main post office. At this Poste Restante, you can pick up mail (after presenting your passport) Monday to Saturday 8am to 10pm and Sunday 11am to 10pm. You can buy stamps at the railway station post office Monday to Friday 7am to 9pm, Saturday 9am to 6pm, and Sunday 11am to 9pm. Yellow stamp machines outside post offices take 5 FIM (75¢) coins.

Photographic Needs   One of the most reliable chains in Helsinki, with three centrally located branches, is **Helios,** open Monday to Friday 9am to 6pm and Saturday 10am to 2pm. It takes only an hour to develop prints. Look for its outlets in the Central Station (☎ 09/657-627), at Mannerheimintie 69 (☎ 09/ 241-9682), or at Mannerheimintie 14 (☎ 09/680-1400).

Police   In an emergency, dial ☎ 112. Otherwise, dial ☎ 100-22 for information about the precinct nearest you. One central precinct is at the Helsinki Central Station (☎ 09/189-4160).

Radio & TV   Radio Finland (☎ 09/14-801) broadcasts news in English every day on the national YLE-3 network at 9:55pm. The external service of the Finnish Broadcasting Company has daily programs in English which can be heard on 103.7 MHz (FM) Monday to Friday at 7:30, 9:30, 11, and 11:30am, and 1:30, 3, 4, 5, and 9:30pm, midnight, and 2am. **Radio One** features a BBC World Service News daily at noon (in winter, broadcasts are at 11am). Helsinki has two TV channels. Programs from abroad, such as those from the United States and Britain, are broadcast in their original languages, with Finnish subtitles.

Rest Rooms   There's a centrally located public toilet at Sofiankatu 2. Otherwise, many locals use cafe toilets (where one should at least order a cup of coffee or a soft drink), or they make use of the facilities at transit terminals.

Taxes   Throughout Finland there's a value-added tax of between 6% and 22% on all goods and services. Most hotels carry a surcharge of 6%, but nearly everything else a foreign visitor is likely to buy in Finland is taxed at 22%.

Telephones, Telegrams, Telex & Fax   For **information** and number inquiries, dial ☎ 118 in Helsinki. If you're thinking about calling home (providing you're not calling collect) and want to know the cost, dial ☎ 0800/9-0999.

Direct-dialed **long-distance calls** (intercity calls) can be made from public pay phones located throughout the city that take 1 FIM or 5 FIM (15¢ or 75¢) coins; the routing numbers and rates are listed in the phone directory. Direct-dialed calls to other countries can also be made from these pay phones, or from the **Tele-Service** office, Mannerheimintie 11B. The Tele-Service office also handles other long-distance calls, telegrams, and telex; it's open daily from 9am to 9pm, but it offers 24-hour service by phone (☎ 020/211). If you call from your hotel, your phone charge might be doubled or tripled.

For local calls within the city of Helsinki, you don't need to dial the area code (**09**).

You can send faxes from most hotels. If your hotel does not have a fax machine, go to one of the larger hotels and ask someone on the staff to send your fax. You'll be billed for the transmission, and probably a surcharge, too.

Transit Information   See "Orientation," above.

Weather   Summers in Helsinki are often sunny, but the weather is rarely uncomfortably hot. The best weather is in July, when the highest temperature is usually about 69°F. Midsummer nights in Helsinki are greatly extended (at this time Lapland is bathed in the midnight sun). In winter, temperatures hover between 21° and 27°F, but it's not true that polar bears roam the streets.

3 Accommodations

There's a big choice of accommodations in Helsinki. The trick is to find something that suits your budget. As elsewhere in Scandinavia, Finland isn't cheap. Your best bet with hotels is to plan as far in advance as possible and to take advantage of any discounts that might be offered. Even an expensive hotel sometimes offers a few moderately priced rooms, but they are usually booked quickly and are difficult for the average visitor to get. In Helsinki, peak rates are charged in the winter because most of the major hotels depend on business travelers to fill their rooms.

Note: Taxes are included in the rates given here, and many hotels also include breakfast. Unless otherwise indicated, all our recommended accommodations below come with a private bathroom.

A ROOM IN A HURRY   Hotellikeskus (Hotel Booking Center), Rautatieasema (☎ **09/2288-1400**), in the heart of the city at the railway station (beside Platform 4), is open year-round, Monday to Friday 9am to 5pm. You tell them the price you're willing to pay and an English-speaking employee will make a reservation for you and give you a map and instructions for reaching your lodgings. Hotellikeskus charges a booking fee of 15 FIM ($2.30).

IN THE CITY CENTER
VERY EXPENSIVE

✪ **Hotel Kämp.** Pohjoisesplanadi 29, F-00100 Helsinki. ☎ **800/325-3859** or 09/576-111. Fax 09/576-1122. www.hotelkamp.fi. E-mail: hotelkamp@luxurycollection.com. 179 units. A/C MINIBAR TV TEL. 1,900 FIM ($292.60) double; 2,250–6,000 FIM ($346.50–$924) suite. Weekend packages available. AE, DC, MC, V. Parking 190 FIM ($29.25). Tram: 1, 7.

Finland's most opulent hotel resulted from a recent renovation of what many Finns remembered as the most luxurious belle-époque palace in the days before World War II. It reopened with fanfare, immediately attracting a bevy of politicians (including the President of Finland), writers, and rock stars, each lending his or her cachet to what is already a household name within Helsinki. Originally built in 1887, with a newer wing added in the 1960s, and a radical upgrade shortly before its "rebirth" in 1999, it rises floors adjacent to the city's most prestigious boulevard. Public areas are appropriately opulent, a combination of turn-of-the-century grandeur and conservatively traditional decors, with lots of glistening hardwoods and polished stone. Bedrooms are large, lavishly outfitted with elaborate curtains, and reproductions of furniture from the early 19th century. Service, as you'd expect, is superb.

Dining/Diversions: The hotel's most elaborate restaurant, Restaurant Kämp, is recommended separately. There's also a less formal brasserie, C.K.'s, where a simpler menu at less dramatic prices is available daily for breakfast, lunch, and dinner. Plush paneling and deep sofas evoke a private, clubby feel in the hotel bar.

Amenities: The health club here is more opulent than any other in town. There's 24-hour room service, a concierge trained to get virtually anything, and laundry/valet service.

🔾 **Palace Hotel.** Eteläranta 10, FIN-00130 Helsinki. ☎ **09/134-561.** Fax 09/654-786. www.palacehotel.fi. E-mail: reception@palacehotel.fi. 44 units. A/C MINIBAR TV TEL. July and Fri–Sun year-round, 860 FIM ($132.45) double; 1,450–3,500 FIM ($223.30–$539) suite. Rest of year, 1,300–1,800 FIM ($200.20–$277.20) double; 3,000 FIM ($462) suite. Rates include breakfast. AE, DC, MC, V. Parking 70 FIM ($10.80). Tram: 3B or 3T.

Overlooking the Presidential Palace, just a few steps from Market Square, this gem of a hotel was built in 1952 and subsequently renovated to high standards of glamour (most recently in 1996). The hotel offers bedrooms overlooking the harbor. All rooms are decorated with an elegant but restrained taste, and the most expensive ones have balconies. Most units have sitting areas; all have good-size tiled bathrooms, with hair dryers. The best units also come with double basins, robes, and bidets.

Dining: The specialty dining room, Restaurant Palace, is one of the best in Finland, offering a panoramic view from the 10th floor. Ristorante La Vista, on the second floor, serves some of the freshest Italian food in the capital.

Amenities: Room service (24 hours), pressing and valet service, 4-hour laundry service, dry cleaning, 24-hour news service, complimentary 5 o'clock tea, telex and fax service, TV lounge with terrace, garage, two saunas on the 11th floor (with open-air terraces and one heated with logs), safety-deposit boxes, currency exchange, tour and car-rental desks, and barbershop.

EXPENSIVE

Ramada Presidentti Hotel. Eteläinen Rautatiekatu 4, FIN-00100 Helsinki. ☎ **800/ 272-6232** in the U.S., or 09/69-11. Fax 09/694-78-86. www.ramadahotels.com. 505 units. A/C MINIBAR TV TEL. Mon–Thurs 1,050–1,250 FIM ($161.70–$192.50) double; Fri–Sun 590–690 FIM ($90.85–$106.25) double. All week long 3,500–4,500 FIM ($539–$693) suite. Rates include buffet breakfast. AE, DC, MC, V. Parking 120 FIM ($18.50). Tram: 3B or 3T.

Built in 1980 and renovated in 1997, this hotel stands in the commercial center of Helsinki, close to Finlandia Hall, Parliament House, and the railway station. It's a granite-and-copper structure with lots of drinking and dining facilities. The guest rooms are warm, comfortable, modern, and filled with such conveniences as trouser presses. The windows are triple-glazed. Beds have firm mattresses, but the bathrooms are small. Nevertheless, they have hand-held showers, makeup mirrors, adequate shelf space, hair dryers, and heated towel racks. Airport taxis depart from here directly for the airport.

Dining/Diversions: The hotel's largest, and most visible, restaurant is the Brasserie President, which offers a two-tiered price scale, one focusing on simple bistro-style platters, another emphasizing upscale gourmet food in the continental tradition. There's also a separate restaurant adjacent to the hotel's Casino Ray. Bars include the Hype Club, in the cellar, open Friday and Saturday from 10pm to 4am, that specializes in tropical drinks and music videos, and a lively, refreshingly flashy bar in the lobby, the Oasis, where business meetings tend to segue into social events. Coffee, tea, and inexpensive lunches are served in the Cafe Maria.

Amenities: Room service (7am to midnight), laundry service, swimming pool, and three saunas.

Rivoli Jardin. Kasarmikatu 40, F-00130 Helsinki. ☎ **09/681-500.** Fax 09/656-988. www.rivoli.fi. E-mail: rivoli.jardin@rivoli.fi. 54 units. A/C TV TEL. 1,090 FIM ($167.85) double; 1,900 FIM ($292.60) suite. Rate includes breakfast. AE, DC, MV, V. Free parking. Tram: 10.

Custom-built as a hotel in 1984, in a neighborhood that's convenient to everything in central Helsinki, this is a small-scale, well-managed, and stylish address that lodges lots of business travelers. You'll register in a stone-and-marble-sheathed lobby that's accented with tapestries. Guest rooms, although a bit smaller than you might have thought, are comfortable, monochromatically outfitted in pale colors, and have either wall-to-wall carpeting or hand-woven Oriental rugs scattered over hardwood floors. Bathrooms are attractively tiled, usually with walk-in showers but no bathtubs. All have hair dryers.

Dining/Diversions: A hideaway bar serves sandwiches and drinks. Breakfast, the only meal served, is available in a greenhouse-inspired winter garden.

Amenities: Room service (24 hours; drinks and sandwiches only), sauna (no exercise facilities).

Scandic Hotel Marski. Mannerheimintie 10, FIN-00100 Helsinki. ☎ **09/68-061.** Fax 09/42-377. www.scandi-hotels.com. E-mail: marski@scandic-hotels.com. 289 units. MINIBAR TV TEL. Sun–Thurs 1,300–1,400 FIM ($200.20–$215.60) double; Fri–Sat 590–690 FIM ($90.85–$106.25) double. All week long 2,600 FIM ($400.40) suite. Rates include breakfast. AE, DC, MC, V. Parking 100 FIM ($15.40). Tram: 3B, 3T, or 6.

Despite its somewhat forbidding appearance (resembling a bulky and anonymous-looking office building), this hotel is one of the best in Helsinki, conveniently located in the city's commercial core. Originally built in 1962 and renovated in 1996, it offers comfortable rooms outfitted with unusual textures, modern furniture, good beds, neutral colors, and trouser presses. If possible, opt for 1 of the 67 guest rooms in the hotel's extension; they are roomier and better decorated with dark wood furnishings, adequate work space, and print fabrics. Bathrooms throughout tend to be small but have good towels, hair dryers, and tubs for the most part. About 10 rooms boast a private sauna.

Dining/Diversions: The basement-level Marski Kellari is a worthwhile bistro serving generous portions of rib-sticking food in a womblike, cellar ambience. The Cafe Chin-Chin mingles the functions of a cafe and a bar. And the Irish bar Mulligan's evokes more Celtic nostalgia than you're likely to find in County Cork.

Amenities: Room service, laundry service, message service, warm garage, three saunas, nonsmoking floor, and 13 rooms for guests with allergies.

Sokos Hotel Klaus Kurki. Bulevardi 2, FIN-00120 Helsinki. ☎ **09/618-911.** Fax 09/6189-1234. www.sokoshotels.fi. 134 units. MINIBAR TV TEL. June 15–Aug 15 and selected weekends (Fri–Sat only), 600 FIM ($92.40) double; from 1,400 FIM ($215.60) suite. Rest of year, 1,165 FIM ($179.40) double; from 1,400 FIM ($215.60) suite. Rates include breakfast. AE, DC, MC, V. Free parking on street. Tram: 3B, 3T, 6, or 10.

Opposite the Swedish Theater and a short walk from Stockmann Department Store, this 1912 brick building, constructed in the Romantic Jugend style, was originally a lodging for hardware buyers. The hotel was named after a near-mythical Finnish hero who fought both the Swedes and the Russians. All the bedrooms were renovated in 2000 and most of them are handsomely decorated, often with Finnish rugs, French poster art, and Tiffany-style lamps. Tiled bathrooms are a bit small but contain hair dryers with heated towel racks. All but nine rooms contain tub baths; all have shower stalls. Although a suitable choice, our major complaint is that the hotel appears understaffed and service needs a vast improvement.

Dining: There are three separate dining areas associated with this hotel. They include the relatively formal Bulevardi Kaksi for dinner only; the Memphis Bistro, open for lunch and dinner, and outfitted with jazz memorabilia; and an Italian bistro and takeaway joint, Tony's Deli, that's accessible directly from the street.

Helsinki Accommodations

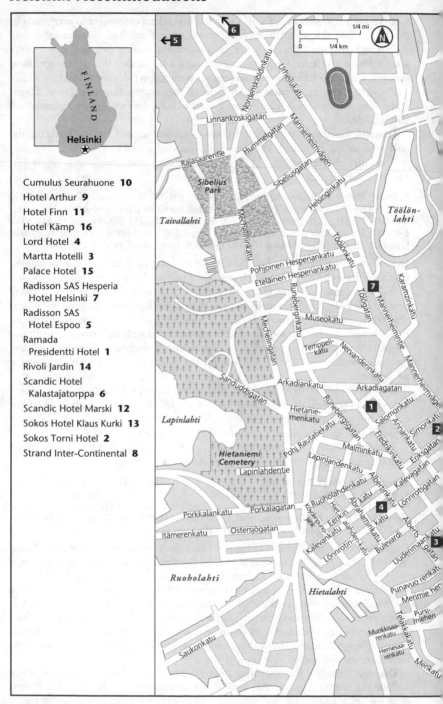

Cumulus Seurahuone **10**

Hotel Arthur **9**

Hotel Finn **11**

Hotel Kämp **16**

Lord Hotel **4**

Martta Hotelli **3**

Palace Hotel **15**

Radisson SAS Hesperia
Hotel Helsinki **7**

Radisson SAS
Hotel Espoo **5**

Ramada
Presidentti Hotel **1**

Rivoli Jardin **14**

Scandic Hotel
Kalastajatorppa **6**

Scandic Hotel Marski **12**

Sokos Hotel Klaus Kurki **13**

Sokos Torni Hotel **2**

Strand Inter-Continental **8**

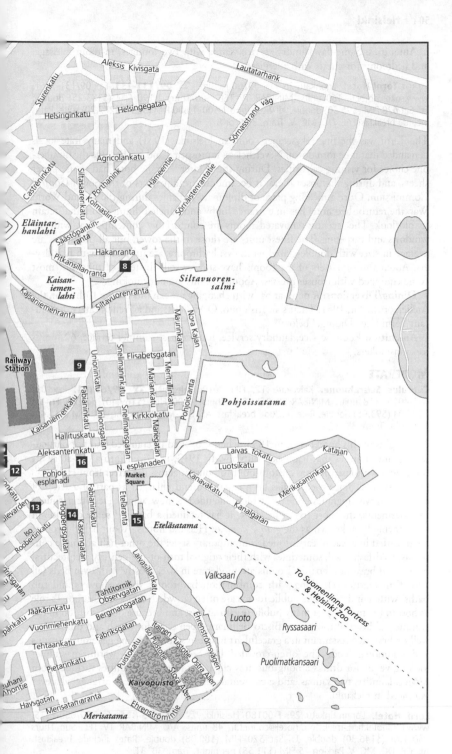

Amenities: Same-day laundry service, sauna with two lounges, in-room massage, and bedrooms for guests with allergies.

Sokos Torni Hotel. Yrjönkatu 26, FIN-00100 Helsinki. ☎ **09/131-131.** Fax 09/131-1361. www.sokos.hotel.fi. 160 units. MINIBAR TV TEL. Sun–Thurs 1,190 FIM ($183.25) double; Fri–Sat 620 FIM ($95.50) double. All week long 1,500–1,800 FIM ($231–$277.20) suite. Rates include breakfast. AE, DC, MC, V. Tram: 3, 4, or 8.

The Torni was the first "skyscraper" built in Helsinki (1931) and many irate locals demanded that it be torn down. Nevertheless, it prospered and has become the number-one choice for visiting celebrities. During the Winter War the hotel had to use paper sheets, and during the postwar era, it became the headquarters of the Soviet Control Commission. Once a meeting place of diplomats and spies during the Second World War, the refurbished hotel has an entrance lobby and paneled dining room that retain its old look. The recently renovated rooms are comfortably contemporary, with big windows and carpeting. The finest units are those in the tower, but all the rooms are average in size, with double-glazed windows; bathrooms are fully tiled with hair dryers. About three-quarters of the rooms have shower stalls instead of tubs, but most come equipped with trouser presses. About 65 units are nonsmoking.

Dining/Diversions: A popular bar with changing art exhibits on the 13th floor, the Atelier, opened in 1951. There's an Irish pub, O'Malley's, and a French eatery, Restaurant Torni (see "Dining," below).

Amenities: Room service, laundry service, four saunas, summer terrace, 62 rooms for nonsmokers.

MODERATE

Cumulus Seurahuone. Kaivokatu 12. FIN 00100. Helsinki. ☎ **09/69141.** Fax 09/691-4010. 118 units. MINIBAR TV TEL. Sun–Thurs 1,100 FIM ($169.40) double; Fri–Sat 610 FIM ($93.95) double. Rates include breakfast. AE, DC, MC, V. Parking 100 FIM ($15.40) per night. Tram: 3B. 3T, 4.

The origins of this hotel began in 1833, when it opened in cramped and not particularly grand premises that it quickly outgrew. In 1913, it moved into a five-story art nouveau townhouse that was custom-built to house it across the street from Helsinki's railway station. Since then, it has been expanded and enlarged as part of a series of comprehensive upgrades, one of which included a new wing. Despite frequent improvements, the most recent in 1994, it has retained a battered sense of pride in once having been known as the *grande dame* of Helsinki hotels. About half the rooms are outfitted in a warm, earth-toned contemporary style; the other half are more consciously old-fashioned, sometimes with their original turn-of-the-century architectural details and brass headboards. Rooms are moderate in size, mostly with twin beds (all with firm mattresses), along with combination bathrooms (both showers and tub baths) with hair dryers. The public rooms are often crowded, thanks to this hotel's role as host to the meetings of many public organizations, and because of its position in the commercial heart of town. The Bistro Bellmani, open daily for lunch and dinner, is a well-orchestrated restaurant in a graceful art nouveau setting, serving generous portions and traditional food. The often-crowded Bar Socis provides a warm, masculine-looking venue for drinks among business clients or friends. Amenities include room service, laundry, two saunas, and a car-rental desk; an alert staff can arrange whatever you need in Helsinki.

Lord Hotel. Lonnrotinkatu 29. F-00180 Helsinki. ☎ **09/615-815.** Fax 09/680-1315. www.lordhotel.fi. E-mail: lord.hotel@co.inet.fi. 48 units. A/C MINIBAR TV TEL. Sun–Thurs 950 FIM ($146.30) double; Fri–Sat 520 FIM ($80.08) double. Rates include breakfast. AE, CB, DC, MC, V. Parking 75 FIM ($11.55) per night. Tram: 3B, 3T.

This hotel consists of two interconnected buildings. The older and more interesting was built in 1903 as a student center and dormitory for the local university. Bedrooms are in the annex, an angular but comfortable building erected around 1990. Many aspects of the older building evoke a mock-medieval fortress, thanks to heavy ceiling beams, crenellations, and art nouveau touches. The staff is polite and hardworking, maintaining stylish rooms that boast hardwood floors, pastel-colored upholsteries, lots of storage space, and either queen-size or twin beds. All have blackout curtains, generous work space, and easy chairs. Bathrooms are small but tiled, mostly without tubs, but all have hair dryers. About 18 have whirlpool tubs and are the most desirable. The hotel contains two charming restaurants, the more upscale of which is Lord à la Carte, a gourmet place that's open Monday to Saturday for both lunch and dinner. The less formal one is Lord's Creole Kitchen, open Monday to Saturday for dinner only; it pays homage to the fiery flavors and smooth textures of the Cajun cuisine of New Orleans. Both restaurants have their own bars. The hotel also has two saunas.

Martta Hotelli. Uudenmaankatu 24, FIN-00120 Helsinki. ☎ **09/618-7400.** Fax 09/618-7401. www.marttahotelli.fi. E-mail: info@marttahotelli.fi. 45 units. TV TEL. Mid-June to mid-Aug and Fri–Sat year-round, 500 FIM ($77) double; rest of year, 720 FIM ($110.90) double. Year-round, 750–850 FIM ($115.50–$130.90) suite. Rates include breakfast. AE, DC, MC, V. Closed mid-summer and Christmas. Free parking. Tram: 3T.

Half a mile north of the main train station, in a quiet residential area, this cozy little hotel is owned by a women's organization (formerly a radical feminist group that supported Finland's educational advancement and was opposed by the tsarist government). Since the group has now achieved all its goals, it runs a home economics educational program. The hotel was built in the late 1950s on land bequeathed by a wealthy donor, and it was most recently renovated in 1995. It's strictly functional but comfortable. Both men and women are accepted. The small bedrooms have a no-nonsense Finnish design, but the bathrooms adequate. The restaurant on the upper floor serves breakfast and lunch. At night, room service is available. Facilities include a sauna and a free covered parking area.

INEXPENSIVE

Hotel Arthur. Vuorikatu 19, FIN-00100 Helsinki. ☎ **09/173-441.** Fax 09/626-880. www.hotelarthur.fi. E-mail: reception@hotelarthur.fi. 143 units. TV TEL. June 15–Aug 18 and some weekends (Fri–Sun) in winter, 500–600 FIM ($77–$92.40) double; rest of year, 595–695 FIM ($91.65–$107.05) double. Year-round, 800–895 FIM ($107.80–$137.85) suite. Rates include breakfast. Additional bed 100 FIM ($15.40). AE, DC, MC, V. Parking 60 FIM ($9.25). Tram: 1, 2, 3, 6, or 7.

A large and well-maintained establishment, the Arthur is owned and operated by the YMCA. It was built at the turn of the century and a newer wing added in 1950. The neighborhood is quiet, even though it's only a 4-minute walk from the main train station. The rooms are decorated in a functional, modern style, offering cleanliness and comfort instead of soul and character. Thirty of the rooms have a minibar. Mattresses are a bit thin, and both bedrooms and bathrooms are a bit cramped—stay here for economy reasons, although it's well maintained. There's an inexpensive restaurant on the premises that serves a lunch buffet.

Hotel Finn. Kalevankatu 3B, FIN-00100 Helsinki. ☎ **09/684-4360.** Fax 09/6844-3610. 27 units, 18 with bathroom. TV TEL. 360 FIM ($55.45) double without bathroom; 450 FIM ($69.30) double with bathroom. AE, DC, MC, V. Free parking overnight; 12 FIM ($1.85) per hour 8am–5pm. Tram: 3, 4, 7, or 10.

This is a clean and functional one-star hotel, built shortly after the Second World War and partially renovated in 1996. It occupies the top two floors (fifth and sixth) of a centrally located office building. It prides itself on being the cheapest hotel in Helsinki, and accommodates a scattering of summer tourists, dockworkers from northern and western Finland, and a handful of businesspeople from the Baltics. Rooms are small and just slightly better than the average college dorm lodgings, but the price is right. The mattresses a bit lean. Breakfast is the only meal served; there's no bar or sauna.

NORTH OF CENTER

Radisson SAS Hesperia Hotel Helsinki. Mannerheimintie 50, FIN-00260 Helsinki. ☎ **800/333-3333** in the U.S., or 09/43-101. Fax 09/431-0995. www.radissonsas.com. 383 units. A/C MINIBAR TV TEL. Summer and Fri–Sun year-round, 550–1,100 FIM ($84.70–$169.40) double; rest of year, 1,100–1,490 FIM ($169.40–$229.45) double. Year-round, 2,250–4,300 FIM ($346.50–$662.20) suite. Rates include breakfast. AE, DC, MC, V. Parking 90 FIM ($13.85). Tram: 3B or 3T.

Partially constructed of Carrara marble, and set behind a landscaped swath of garden beside one of the city's most prominent boulevards, this establishment is one of the leading hotels of Finland. Built in 1972 and renovated 20 years later, it's favored by business travelers who appreciate its uncluttered contemporary design. The bedrooms are comfortably furnished with conservatively upscale furniture and are well maintained. Textured wallpaper, safes, and fine carpeting add to the allure of the place, although many of the rooms are a bit small. Bathrooms, either in tile and marble, are first rate with hair dryers (about three-fourths of them, however, have shower stalls instead of tubs). Two floors are nonsmoking.

Dining/Diversions: The best dining is at a French-style Fransmanni, which is open for lunch and dinner every day until 1am. In summer, the restaurant lowers both prices and degree of formality. Next to Fransmanni is the Hesperia Nightclub.

Amenities: Room service, laundry, baby-sitting, massage, four saunas, swimming pool, gym, barbershop, hairdresser, solarium, and gift shop.

✪ **Strand Inter-Continental.** John Stenbergin Ranta 4, FIN-00530 Helsinki. ☎ **800/327-0200** in the U.S., or 09/39-351. Fax 09/3935-3255. www.interconti.com. E-mail: strand@interconti.com. 200 units. June 17–Sept 2, 880–900 FIM ($135.50–$138.60) double. Rest of year (winter), 1,660–1,770 FIM ($255.65–$272.60) double. Selected weekends (Fri–Sat only), 750 FIM ($115.50) double. Year-round, 2,800–6,000 FIM ($431.20–$924) suite. Rates include breakfast. AE, DC, MC, V. Parking 80 FIM ($12.30). Tram: 3T, 6, or 7.

The Strand is one of our preferred modern hotels here. Set at the edge of the water behind a bay-windowed facade of beige and brown brick, it has the most dramatic atrium in the capital, festooned with plants and with glass elevators rising to the top. The octagonal shape is repeated throughout the hotel's design. The rooms were designed by some of Finland's best talent and decorated with local designs, including weaving and Finnish parquet floors. Marble from Lapland was used extensively. Half the well-furnished bedrooms provide views of the harbor. Some rooms are equipped for people with disabilities and others are reserved for nonsmokers. The good-size units have such extras as electronic locks and three phones, and the medium-size bathrooms also have phones, robes, toiletries, hair dryers, heated floors, and even heated towel racks.

Dining/Diversions: The Pamir Restaurant is one of the best fish and game restaurants in Helsinki. Guests can enjoy breakfast or late-night salad buffets in the Atrium Plaza Restaurant or drinks in the Atrium Lounge and Bar.

Amenities: Room service (24 hours), laundry and valet, tour and guest-relations desk, key-card door lock, twice-daily maid service, four saunas, swimming pool, business center, movie channels, and gift shop.

WEST OF THE CENTER

✪ Scandic Hotel Kalastajatorppa. Kalastajatorpantie 1, FIN-00330 Helsinki. ☎ 09/
458-11. Fax 09/458-1668. www.scandic-hotels.com. 335 units. A/C MINIBAR TV TEL.
June 10–Aug 2 and Fri–Sat year-round, 500 FIM ($77) double; rest of year, 1,200 FIM
($184.80) double. Year-round, 1,600–3,600 FIM ($246.40–$554.40) suite. Rates include
breakfast. AE, DC, MC, V. Free parking outside, 60 FIM ($9.25) inside. Tram: 4.

Translated from the Finnish, the tongue-twisting name of this hotel means "cottage
of the fisherman." It's certainly no cottage, but it is close to the water, and just 3 miles
northwest of the city center. Located on a ridge of land between two arms of the sea,
this pair of marble- and granite-faced buildings was designed to blend in as closely as
possible with the surrounding landscape of birch and pines. The core of the hotel
dates from 1937, and the newer sections contain some of the most modern convention facilities in Finland. The bedrooms are in either the main building or a seashore
annex that provides panoramic views of the water. The medium-sized bedrooms were
renovated and upgraded after the hotel's acquisition by the Scandic chain in 1998.
Outfitted with wood paneling and hardwood floors, units are tasteful, understated,
and comfortable with firm mattresses and adequate size bathrooms with hair dryers.
On the premises is the state guesthouse where President Ronald Reagan rested en
route to a summit meeting in Moscow. President George Bush and former German
prime minister Helmut Kohl have also stayed here. In March 1997, President Bill
Clinton conducted a well-publicized meeting here with Russian President Boris
Yeltsin.

   Dining/Diversions: The Round Room is a full-fledged restaurant, and the Fiskis
Bar & Cafe is an informal place for light meals and drinks. The Red Room is a leading Helsinki nightclub. The Terrace summer restaurant offers grilled food and views
of the sea. The most elegant of the dining facilities is the stylish à la carte restaurant,
Meritorppa (Castle by the Sea), specializing in a continental cuisine with an emphasis
on game from Finnish forests and seafood.

   Amenities: Laundry room, and message service are provided, and guided walks
can be arranged. The hotel has a business center, hairdresser, gift shop, and two
heated parking garages. To keep you in shape, there is a gym, two indoor swimming
pools, five saunas (sometimes overheated guests dive directly into the sea), and a private
beach.

ESPOO

Radisson SAS Hotel Espoo. Otaranta 2, FIN-02150 Espoo. ☎ 09/435-80. Fax 09/
466-693. www.radissonsas.com. 206 units. MINIBAR TV TEL. July and Fri–Sat year-round,
570 FIM ($87.80) double; 810 FIM ($124.75) suite. Rest of year, 700 FIM ($107.80) double;
1,000 FIM ($154) suite. Rates include breakfast and morning sauna. AE, DC, MC, V. Free
parking. Bus: 102 (from Platform 51 at the Helsinki Bus Station).

About 6 miles west of the center of Helsinki, this four-story hotel offers a soothing,
somewhat isolated setting at the edge of the water surrounded by pinewood forests.
The area is the "Silicon Valley" of Finland, with the Helsinki University of Technology,
research institutes, and technological enterprises nearby. With views over the water,
guest rooms are moderate in size, with attractively built-in furniture, double-glazed
windows, twin beds with firm mattresses, adequate and well-lit work space, and trouser
presses. Most of the bathrooms lack tubs (shower stalls instead), but have spotless
maintenance. Some accommodations are suitable for those who have allergies, and
others are nonsmoking. On the premises are a restaurant, three saunas, and a swimming pool.

4 Dining

Many restaurants bring variety to their menus with typically Finnish dishes, particularly those offering a Scandinavian smörgåsbord. There are restaurants to suit every purse and taste in Helsinki, as well as an increasing number of ethnic restaurants.

IN THE CITY CENTER
VERY EXPENSIVE

۞ Restaurant Kämp. In the Hotel Kämp, Pohjoisesplanadi 29. ☎ **09/576-111.** Reservations recommended. Main courses 154–295 FIM ($23.70–$45.45); fixed-price lunch 215–275 FIM ($33.10–$42.35); fixed-price dinner 480 FIM ($73.90). AE, DC, MC, V. Mon–Fri noon–2:30pm; Mon–Sat 7–10:30pm. Tram: 1, 7. CONTINENTAL/INTERNATIONAL.

Helsinki's most opulent restaurant, and one of its newest, occupies a belle-époque dining room whose soaring columns and glittering accessories evoke the grandest moments of the late 19th century. With room for only 56 diners at a time, it features a menu that changes every month or so, emphasizing a mix of upscale Finnish dishes and the best aspects of pan-European, postmodern cuisine. Stellar examples include hot blinis with seasonal fish roe and garnish; a consommé of forest mushrooms with a profiterole of veal kidneys; and an old-fashioned version of traditional Finnish *vorschmack* (savory hash) with pickled vegetables and sour cream. Baked salmon *à la Kämp* manages to stuff a salmon with mashed potatoes and onions and accompany it with a roe-enhanced sour cream sauce. A delectable marinated rack of lamb with herb-dried tomatoes and spiced polenta is appropriate for cold days along the Baltic. Dessert might be an old-fashioned *tarte tatin* with Calvados-flavored ice cream and vanilla sauce.

Note that within the same hotel, adjacent to the lobby, is a well-managed brasserie, C.K.'s, whose prices are about 40% less than those at this gastronomic citadel. C.K.'s specializes in fresh meats, fish, and vegetarian dishes, serving them every day of the week from 7am to 11pm.

۞ Restaurant Palace. In the Palace Hotel, Eteläranta 10. ☎ **09/134-561.** Reservations required. 2-course fixed-price menu 285 FIM ($43.90); 3-course fixed-price menu 365 FIM ($56.20); 4-course fixed-price menu 435 FIM ($67). AE, DC, MC, V. July, Mon–Fri 7pm–1am; Aug–June, Mon–Fri 11am–1am. Tram: 3B. Bus: 16. FINNISH/FRENCH.

With a panoramic view of the harbor from the 10th floor of the Palace Hotel, the most acclaimed restaurant in Helsinki has been offering exquisite cuisine, combined with excellent service and a unique ambience, since 1952. The design hasn't been changed since it was created by Viljo Rewell a half-century ago. (Rewell was Finland's second most famous architect at that time, competing with Aalto.) It has wood paneling, a live pianist, large windows, and—to a trained eye—an excellent postwar Finnish design. Its wine cellar is one of the best in the country, having won many awards. Fixed-price menus at lunch supplant à la carte meals. You might begin with poached asparagus with smoked ham or celery-and-Parmesan soup. Fish dishes include grilled rolls of perch fillet with parsley sauce and warm smoked salmon with creamed morels. Other specialties include fillet and tongue of reindeer with rowanberry mousse and duck flavored with honey and a raspberry-vinegar sauce.

EXPENSIVE

۞ Alexander Nevski. Pohjoisesplanadi 17. ☎ **09/639-610.** Reservations required. Main courses 180–200 FIM ($27.70–$30.80); 3-course fixed-price lunch 100–120 FIM ($15.40–$18.50); menu Romanov 290–320 FIM ($44.65–$49.30). AE, DC, MC, V. July, daily 6pm–midnight; Aug–June, Mon–Fri 11am–midnight, Sat noon–midnight, Sun 6pm–midnight. Tram: 1, 2, 3T, or 4. RUSSIAN.

At the southern corner of Market Square, this is the finest Russian restaurant in Finland. Set in a 200-year-old building, the restaurant is named for the 12th-century Russian military hero. It has large beveled mirror panels in pastel frames, Lapland marble floors, stained-glass windows emblazoned with Romanov double-headed eagles, and *faux-marbre* columns. The cuisine blends the best of imperial tsarist cooking with the best Russian regional (peasant) dishes. While you dine, you're treated to live Russian musicians performing at the piano or perhaps the violin. Gypsy songs fill the air. Begin with borscht, one of several kinds of blinis, Russian-style crayfish soup with caviar and sour cream, or a julienne of forest mushrooms marinated in sour cream. There's also smoked salmon with parsley-studded risotto, roasted pike-perch with champagne sauce, rabbit braised in a clay pot with cream sauce and sour cabbage, and fried wild duck with cranberries and fennel. Sturgeon and salmon prepared in the traditional Russian way, grilled fillet of lamb Caucasian-style, or breast of willow grouse in a goose liver sauce are equally and deservedly popular.

✪ Havis Amanda. Unioninkatu 23. ☎ **09/666-882.** Reservations required. Main courses 120–150 FIM ($18.50–$23.10); 2-course fixed-price lunch 89–130 FIM ($13.70–$20); 4-course fixed-price dinner 305–330 FIM ($46.95–$50.80). AE, DC, MC, V. May 15–Sept 15, daily noon–midnight; Sept 16–May 14, Mon–Sat noon–midnight. Tram: 1, 2, 3T, or 4. Bus: 16. FINNISH/SEAFOOD.

Named after the heroic female statue (the *Havis Amanda*) that stands a few steps from its entrance, this upscale tavern is the finest seafood restaurant in Helsinki. Located in a cellar, its booths and banquettes are tucked away between pillars, columns, and walls for maximum dining privacy. Established in 1973, the restaurant prides itself on serving seafood primarily from Finland (don't expect North Atlantic lobster, Alaskan crabmeat, or tropical grouper). Depending on the season, menu choices might include a starter-sized platter of Finnish fish roe, Baltic crayfish (boiled Louisiana style and consumed with ice-cold beer), ceviche of whitefish and king crab, whitefish "glow-fried" beside the gentle coals of a log fire and served with Lapp cheese and Madeira sauce, poached fillet of perch with white wine and crayfish sauce, grilled perch with chanterelle sauce, or charcoal-grilled slices of salmon with morel-flavored cream sauce. The service is impeccable.

Restaurant Savoy. Eteläesplanadi. ☎ **09/684-40210.** Reservations required. Main courses 196–245 FIM ($30.20–$37.75); 3-course fixed-price menu 350 FIM ($53.90). AE, CB, DC, DISC, MC, V. June–Aug, Mon–Fri 11am–10:30pm; Sept–May, Mon–Fri 11am–3pm and 6–10:30pm. Tram: 3B. FINNISH/INTERNATIONAL.

In an office building near the harbor, this restaurant's decor exemplifies the quintessence of Finnish modernism. In 1937 Finland's greatest architect, Alvar Aalto, designed every detail of the place, even the lighting fixtures. The restaurant, a national monument, has largely adhered to the original design. Few other restaurants in Finland celebrate the memory and tastes of the nation's greatest national hero, Marshal Mannerheim, as devotedly as this one does. In addition to his favorite drink, which he consumed in large quantities here during the ravages of the Second World War, it also declares its *vorschmack*—with justification—as the best in town, and authentic to the tastes of the general himself. What should you order if you want to emulate his behavior? Try a Marskin Ryyppy (a schnapps made with vodka, aquavit, dry vermouth, and dry gin, stirred together and served icy cold), and *vorschmack,* a stew concocted from minced beef, lamb, and Baltic herring that's simmered for 2 days and served with baked potatoes and sour cream. Other specialties include a terrine of venison with cranberry sauce, fish-and-seafood soup flavored with saffron, poached fillet of pike-perch with crayfish and caviar sauce, sautéed fillet of turbot with a red-onion sauce, fried fillet of reindeer, and fried breast of duck.

MODERATE

Bellevue. Rahapajankatu 3. ☎ **09/179-560.** Reservations required. Main courses 100–200 FIM ($15.40–$30.80); fixed-price lunch 120 FIM ($18.50). AE, DC, MC, V. Mon–Fri 11am–midnight, Sat–Sun 5pm–midnight. Tram: 4. RUSSIAN.

In the heart of Helsinki, next to the Uspenski Orthodox cathedral, the Bellevue has been an enduring favorite since 1917 because of its good cooking and moderate prices. Actually the restaurant has operated since 1913, but in a different location. You can dine in a long corridor-like main room or in one of the smaller, cozier side rooms. Herring, still served Russian style, is always a good appetizer, or perhaps blinis and caviar. The chicken Kiev is a recommended main dish, as is the tantalizing roasted snow grouse, as well as cabbage rolls with wild mushrooms served in a stoneware crock. For dessert, a flaming baba cake is carried through the main dining room; one longtime patron likened its presentation to "a wake for Tsar Nicholas II." Russian wine is served.

Kartano Ravintola. Simonkatu 6. ☎ **09/586-0710.** Reservations recommended. Main courses 85–130 FIM ($13.10–$20). AE, DC, MC, V. Mon–Fri 11am–midnight, Sat 4pm–midnight, Sun 4–10pm. Tram: 4, 7, and 10. FINNISH.

This restaurant takes the preparation of its Finnish menu so seriously that some of its fans consider it almost a symbol of national pride. You'll dine within one of two birch-paneled dining rooms that are accessorized with tones of red and blue, and feast on menu items whose ingredients mostly derive from nearby lakes and forests. The cookery doesn't rate rave reviews, but it is substantial and satisfying nonetheless. Examples include roasted fillet of reindeer with forest mushrooms and red wine sauce; grilled pike-perch with garlic-flavored mayonnaise and horseradish-enhanced potatoes; fillet of veal with Finnish mushrooms and red wine sauce; carpaccio of venison; and a "cappuccino" of Finnish chanterelles. Thanks to is location in the heart of Helsinki's commercial center, the place bustles at lunchtime, but is somewhat calmer and more sedate at dinner.

Kellarikrouvi. Pohjoinen Makasiinikatu 6. ☎ **09/179-021.** Reservations recommended for dinner. Main courses 48–140 FIM ($7.40–$21.55); fixed-price lunch (11am–2pm) 75–150 FIM ($11.55–$23.10); fixed-price dinner 170–270 FIM ($26.20–$41.60). AE, DC, MC, V. Mon–Fri 11am–midnight, Sat 4pm–midnight, Sun (upstairs section only) 2pm–midnight. Tram: 3B. FINNISH/INTERNATIONAL.

This restaurant, built in 1901, was originally a storage cellar for potatoes and firewood for the apartment house above it. Fuel was winched upstairs to fend off the brutal winter cold. Since 1965 it has been a cozy restaurant, the first in Finland to serve beer from a keg. Enjoy it at the street-level bar (where you can also dine if you like) before descending a steep staircase to the vaulted labyrinth of the cellar. Here, depending on which room within the vast piece you opt for, the ambience can be noisy and animated—especially on weekends—or relatively subdued. Your dinner might begin with a terrine of perch followed by pork cutlets with a potato-and-cheese gratin, grilled kidneys in a mustard-cream sauce, reindeer steak with game sauce and roasted potatoes, or fried cubed salmon with root vegetables and whisky sauce. Dessert might consist of a Bavarian-style cream puff stuffed with cloudberries. The cuisine is inspired and adroit, combining local Finnish culinary techniques with innovative touches from the international schools of cooking.

König. Mikonkatu 4. ☎ **09/6844-0713.** Reservations required. Main courses 80–135 FIM ($12.30–$20.80). AE, DC, MC, V. Mon–Sat noon–midnight. Tram: 3B or 3T. SCANDINAVIAN.

Established in 1892, this restaurant is Helsinki's most traditional, situated in the cellar of what was once one of Finland's four largest banks. The great architect Eliel Saarinen redesigned the restaurant along the lines of the internationally modern style that would later sweep the world. In 1996 the restaurant was renovated, taking care to preserve Saarinen's aesthetic vision. Here, in what was at the time a private dining room, Marshal Mannerheim and his generals gathered for food and strategy talks during the darkest days of the Second World War. The restaurant has hosted all of Finland's presidents and many of its greatest artists and composers, including Jean Sibelius. Dishes might include pike-perch Waleska, smoked whitefish à la König, fillet of reindeer with Madeira sauce, fillet steak with mushrooms and red wine sauce, fillet de boeuf à la patronne, and a seasonal variety of fish. The fare has varied little over the years, and if the greats of yesterday were to miraculously return, they wouldn't be surprised by the offerings on the menu. "If we've always done it right," a waiter confided, "why change it?"

Kosmos Restaurant. Kalevankatu 3. ☎ **09/647-255.** Reservations recommended. Main courses 72–124 FIM ($11.10–$19.10); fixed-price lunch 98 FIM ($15.10). AE, DC, MC, V. Mon–Fri 11:30am–midnight, Sat 4pm–midnight. Tram: 3B, 3T or 4. Bus: 17 or 18. FINNISH.

Near the center of Helsinki's main street, Mannerheimintie, this restaurant is known throughout Finland as a gathering place for artists, writers, and television personalities. The decor is 1930s and simple, and the menu specialties include grilled whitefish, smoked eel, fried Baltic herring, mutton chops with a creamy herb sauce, and chicken in cherry sauce. Light meals, such as open tartar sandwiches, vorschmack with duchesse potatoes, and borscht, are also available. (Vorschmack, made with chopped mutton, herring, and anchovies, is served with salted cucumbers and beets.) If you want traditional Finnish cuisine, without a lot of innovative continental touches, this is your eating house. We liked the comments of one habitué; "I come here at least once or twice a week. The kitchen staff never causes me grief." In the summertime, you can order "deep-fried" strawberries for dessert; pears drenched with a chocolate-cream sauce are also delicious. The special lunch is served until 3pm.

Ravintola Rivoli. Albertinkatu 38. ☎ **09/643-455.** Reservations recommended. Main courses 100–154 FIM ($15.40–$23.70). AE, DC, MC, V. Mon–Fri 11am–midnight, Sat 5pm–midnight. Closed Sat June–July and bank holidays. Tram: 6. Bus: 14. FRENCH/FINNISH.

The dining room is an art nouveau fantasy set in a labyrinthine dining room with upholstered banquettes. One of its subdivisions is named "Fish Rivoli," and from its separate menu you can order some of the finest seafood dishes in the city. In both dining rooms, you can enjoy such fare as fillet of perch with herb butter and grilled salmon with mustard sauce. At lunchtime, special *husmanskost* cookery is offered, a reference to "grandmother's style," featuring such old-fashioned, good-tasting dishes as onion soup and grilled rainbow trout. The management also operates an adjoining pizzeria.

Ravintola Sipuli. Kanavaranta 3. ☎ **09/179-900.** Reservations recommended. Main courses 110–160 FIM ($16.95–$24.65). AE, DC, MC, V. Mon–Fri noon–2pm and 6–11pm. Tram: 2, 4. FINNISH/CONTINENTAL.

Set within five rooms of what was originally built in the 19th century as a warehouse, this restaurant takes its name, Sipuli (which translates as "onion"), from the gilded onion-shaped domes of the Russian Orthodox Uspenski Cathedral, which rises majestically a short distance away. While renovating the premises for its new role as a restaurant, a team of architects thoughtfully added a skylight that allows upward-angled views of the cathedral. This, coupled with redbrick walls, intricate paneling, and thick beams, creates coziness and charm. As with every visit, we fall under the bewitching spell of the chef who is an expert at creating robust flavors. He always uses the finest of ingredients from stream and field, and Finnish products when available. Cooked with precision and a certain enthusiasm are such dishes as snails flavored with sherry

Helsinki Dining

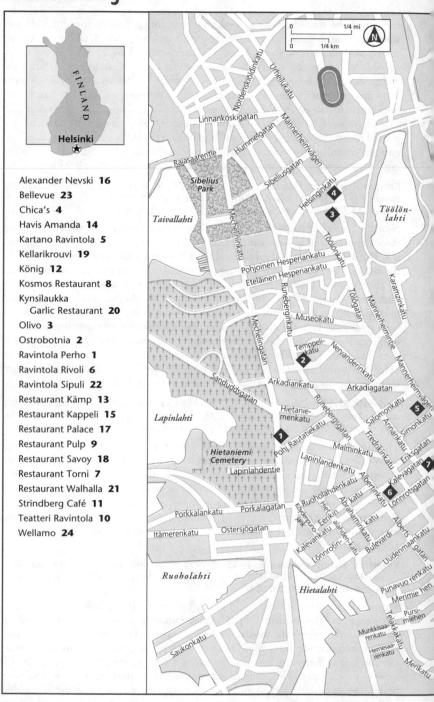

Alexander Nevski **16**

Bellevue **23**

Chica's **4**

Havis Amanda **14**

Kartano Ravintola **5**

Kellarikrouvi **19**

König **12**

Kosmos Restaurant **8**

Kynsilaukka
  Garlic Restaurant **20**

Olivo **3**

Ostrobotnia **2**

Ravintola Perho **1**

Ravintola Rivoli **6**

Ravintola Sipuli **22**

Restaurant Kämp **13**

Restaurant Kappeli **15**

Restaurant Palace **17**

Restaurant Pulp **9**

Restaurant Savoy **18**

Restaurant Torni **7**

Restaurant Walhalla **21**

Strindberg Café **11**

Teatteri Ravintola **10**

Wellamo **24**

and served with a Gorgonzola sauce. This is surprisingly good and filled with flavor—but not for the faint-hearted. He can really do something special with such main courses as smoked fillet of pike-perch served with a salmon mousse. From Lapland he imports reindeer meat in season that has been carefully butchered and shaped as noisettes. It comes with a richly flavored game sauce.

✪ **Restaurant Pulp.** In the Sanoma Media House, Mannerheiminaukio 3. ☎ **09/684-4290.** Reservations recommended. Lunch main courses 45–85 FIM ($6.95–$13.10); dinner main courses 95–155 FIM ($14.65–$23.85). AE, DC, MC, V. Mon–Fri 11am–3pm; Tues–Sat 5–11pm. Bar, daily 11am–1am. Tram: 1, 7. FINNISH/INTERNATIONAL.

One of the most exciting new restaurants of Helsinki occupies the entrance level of the glass headquarters of Sanoma Media, the organization that produces at least three of Finland's most respected newspapers. Expect the likely onslaught of media types, conducting interviews, or just hobnobbing at the bar. Here, fancy cocktails, priced at around 45 FIM ($6.95) each, might include a Ricky Martin, made with lime-flavored vodka, apple liqueur, and apple juice. Meals are consumed within a formal dining room whose views extend out toward the railway station. The options, which change seasonally, are always so enticing—thrilling, in fact—that you could simply close your eyes and pick at random. Lunches are more businesslike and efficient than dinners, focusing on an array of soups, salads such as teriyaki chicken, pastas, entrecote of beef with pepper sauce; and such fish as pike-perch with saffron-enhanced beurre blanc. Dinners include such vegetarian fare as bollito with spinach-stuffed ravioli, served with a pepper-flavored cream sauce; salmon with sorrel sauce and artichoke cakes; codfish with tuna, miso, scallops and a "soya foam"; slow-cooked tandoori of lamb with sweetbreads and cardamon sauce; and breast of duck with an orange glaze. There's live music, usually jazz, presented here every Friday and Saturday night.

Restaurant Torni. In the Sokos Torni Hotel, Kalevankatu 5. ☎ **09/131-131.** Reservations recommended. Main courses 87–148 FIM ($13.40–$22.80); 4-course fixed-price menu 315 FIM ($48.50). AE, DC, MC, V. Mon–Fri 11am–midnight, Sat 5pm–midnight. Tram: 3, 4, or 10. FINNISH.

The Sokos Torni Hotel (see "Accommodations," above) throws all its culinary energies into this showcase of Finnish cuisine. In a pastel-colored art nouveau dining room on the hotel's street level, a crew of formally dressed waiters serves specialties from the forests and streams of Finland. Examples include baked snow grouse with game sauce, breast of wild duck with port wine and ginger sauce, and "glow-fried" (that is, gently heated) trout served with honey-flavored fennel sauce. The refined cuisine is prepared with admirable products from all over the country. Here you are served a true "taste of Finland."

Teatteri Ravintola. In the Svenska Teather, Pohjoisesplandi 2. ☎ **09/681-11-36.** Main courses 60–120 FIM ($9.25–$18.50); 3-course fixed-price menus 185–195 FIM ($28.50–$30.05). AE, DC, MC, V. Food service, Mon–Thurs 11am–11pm, Fri–Sat 11am–midnight, Sun 1–10pm. Bar service, Mon–Sat 11am–4am, Sun 1pm–1am. Tram: 1, 7, 1. INTERNATIONAL.

Management of this very popular, sprawling complex of bars, nightclubs, and restaurants compares it to "a Caribbean cruise ship, in that we've got almost everything, and we're almost never closed." There's a deli and takeaway service near the entrance (open daily from 9am) and a well-managed restaurant whose menu includes the cuisines of Cuba, Asia, India, and Italy, with frequent changes and reinventions. Also on the premises are two bars: The Teatteri Bar attracts deal-making business folk relaxing after work. The more animated of the two, the Clock Bar, sports a blazing fireplace and lots of recorded rhythm and blues. One flight above street level, there's a nightclub (Clubbi Teatteri) where a 35-to-50 crowd dances the night away. It's open nightly from 10:30pm. Entrance is usually free, except for Friday and Saturday nights, when there's a cover charge of 40 FIM ($6.15).

⚙ **Wellamo.** Vyäkatu 9. ☎ **09/663-139.** Reservations recommended. Main courses 60–102 FIM ($9.25–$15.70); fixed-price menu 110–275 FIM ($16.95–$42.35). AE, MC, V. Tues–Fri 11am–2pm and 5–11pm, Sat 5–11pm, Sun 1–10pm. Tram: 4. FINNISH/FRENCH/RUSSIAN.

Established near Finland's foreign ministry, on a quiet residential island (Katajanokka Island) that's central to the rest of town, this is a charming, well-managed restaurant with a loyal clientele who sometimes travel across other neighborhoods of Helsinki to reach it. Paneled and darkly outfitted in warmly textured shades of brown, it features flickering candles and a revolving series of for-sale paintings by local artists. Menu items include selections from Russia, Finland, and France, and as such, represent more exoticism than that offered at many of its competitors. Examples include lamb soup; snails à la Bourguignonne; goat-cheese salad; mussels Provençal with aïoli and chips; whitefish à la Russe; Siberian ravioli *pelmens* (Siberian Ravioli) stuffed with minced lamb, herbs, mushrooms, and sour cream; and a sauté of rabbit, elk, and mutton "in the style of the Finnish hunters." Sweetbreads with gorgonzola sauce is another popular choice, as is Georgian-style chicken served with fried cheese, rice pilaf, and *smetana* (sour cream) sauce. During the evening hours, you're likely to hear the sounds of a live pianist.

INEXPENSIVE

Kynsilaukka Garlic Restaurant. Frederikkatu 22. ☎ **09/651-939.** Reservations recommended. Main courses 42–190 FIM ($6.45–$29.25); fixed-price lunch 80 FIM ($12.30). AE, DC, MC, V. Mon–Fri 11am–11:15pm, Sat–Sun noon–11:15pm. Tram: 3B, 3T. INTERNATIONAL.

Its name translates from medieval Finnish as "garlic," and that's exactly what you're likely to get at this restaurant that prides itself on its use of more than 20 pounds of Spanish garlic every day. It's used in every imaginable foodstuff, a fact that's deeply appreciated by a clientele who seems to strongly believe that garlic fights disease and might possibly even ward off vampires. You'll dine within a pair of cozy and consciously rustic dining rooms, perhaps preceding your meal with a garlic martini (chilled gin, shaken not stirred, and served with a clove of vermouth-marinated garlic), or a pint of garlic-flavored beer (the staff claims they add the garlic secretly). The cuisine is not for the faint-hearted, but garlic aficionados flock here. Menu items are influenced by the cuisine of Russia more than anywhere else, as in the example of grilled gratin of vegetables with garlic and *smetana* (sour cream). Other examples include pike balls in garlic-flavored cream sauce; a fish stew modeled on a Provençal bouillabaisse; cream of garlic soup; chicken casseroles; fillet steak with garlic and red wine sauce; and brochettes of seafood. Desserts include cloudberry crepes with ice cream, which can be rendered more or less garlicky depending on the degree to which you add the omnipresent condiment: garlic marmalade.

Ostrobotnia. Dagmarinkatu 2. ☎ **09/408-602.** Reservations recommended. Main courses 45–95 FIM ($6.95–$14.65); pizzas 38–58 FIM ($5.85–$8.95); fixed-price menu 125–135 FIM ($19.25–$20.80). AE, DC, MC, V. Mon–Fri 11am–4am, Sat–Sun 2pm–4am. Tram: 4, 7, or 10. FINNISH/INTERNATIONAL.

In a residential neighborhood several blocks west of the Inter-Continental and the Finnair Bus Terminal, this restaurant prides itself on both its cuisine and its collection of 19th-century Finnish paintings that line the walls. There's a popular and interesting bar with an outdoor terrace, which you'll see as you enter. You can enjoy such specialties as fresh fish, sautéed reindeer, grilled chicken with garlic potatoes on a hot iron grill, and fried Baltic herring. There's also a wide range of pizzas. The chef is well known for his homemade Finnish bread, served with a homemade cheese pâté. Virtually every night of the week the late-night bar attracts lots of actors and musicians, and on Friday and Sunday between 11pm and 4am, there's live "Finnish style" dance music, including the tango, a dance that's all the rage in Finland today. Admission on those nights is free, but a large beer costs 22 to 24 FIM ($3.40 to $3.70).

Restaurant Kappeli. Eteläesplanadi 1. ☎ **09/179-242.** Reservations recommended. Main courses 58–120 FIM ($8.95–$18.50). AE, DC, MC, V. Daily 9am–1am. Closed Dec 24–25. Tram: 3B. Bus: 16. INTERNATIONAL.

This famous restaurant and drinking complex is a Victorian Gothic fantasy, situated like an oversize gazebo in the middle of Esplanade Park, near the harbor. Originally built in 1837 as a rendezvous for artists and "high-society gentlemen" (Sibelius had a favorite table), it was closed for many years until its restoration in 1976. There are five different dining areas, one of them a summertime-only outdoor terrace. Long lines sometimes form here in the evening, and the place goes through wild mood swings throughout the day and night, everything from sedate to rowdy. Doormen and bouncers keep the crowd in order later in the evening. In the oldest section, the cafe, most patrons order sandwiches, pastries, or coffee. The middle section is the main restaurant, Runeberg, where white-linen tablecloths, lots of elbow room, and formal service are the hallmarks. Well-prepared main dishes, inexpensive by Finnish standards, include chateaubriand, pepper steak, entrecôte, fried salmon with red wine and pepper sauce, and whitefish.

Strindberg Café. Pohjoisesplanadi 33. ☎ **09/681-20-30.** Main courses in upstairs restaurant 78–128 FIM ($12–$19.70); sandwiches and pastries in street-level cafe 25–40 FIM ($3.85–$6.15). AE, DC, MC, V. Mon–Sat 11am–1am. Tram: 1, 7, and 10. CONTINENTAL.

Named after one of Sweden's greatest playwrights, a short walk from the Swedish Theater, this is a warm and convivial rendezvous point with a street-level cafe, and an upstairs "Library Bar" whose shelves are lined with books. The heart and soul of the place, however, is within the upstairs dining room, where a conservatively modern setting acts as a foil for dishes that include a savory version of Finnish *vorschmack* (hash); grilled Baltic herring in herb sauce; grilled fillet of salmon with hollandaise; and a sumptuous pike-perch with dill sauce.

NORTH OF CENTER
EXPENSIVE

✪ **Olivo.** In the Hotel Inter-Continental, Mannerheimintie 46. ☎ **09/40-551.** Reservations recommended. Main courses 80–140 FIM ($12.30–$21.55); fixed-price menu 235 FIM ($36.20). AE, DC, MC, V. Mon–Fri 11:30am–11:30pm, Sat noon–11:30pm, Sun noon–10:30pm. Tram: 4, 7, or 10. MEDITERRANEAN.

In 1998, the culinary experts at one of Helsinki's most sophisticated modern hotels threw out their long-time roster of prestigious but dull restaurants and focused all their attention, and their enormous resources, on this well-appointed charmer. Set on the hotel's lobby level, it specializes in cuisine from around the edges of the Mediterranean, and does so within a cutting-edge, sand-colored decor that includes lots of exposed wood and a cheerful emphasis on southern climes. You'll find some succulent salads and pastas (black tagliatelle with squid ink, tomatoes, garlic, and shellfish) inspired by the traditions of Italy. There's also *saltimbocca* (veal with ham). But aficionados of the Mediterranean world usually opt—at least here—for a medley of Moroccan, Mideastern, and North African dishes that, as a whole, contribute to one

---

Perfect Picnics

To buy all the foods you want for a picnic, head for the delicatessen on the street level of **Stockmann Department Store,** Aleksanterinkatu 52 (☎ 09/1211). (See "Shopping," below, for more information.) At this deli, display cases are filled with gourmet food worthy of the great capitals of Europe, with an East-Nordic twist, however. You'll find several types of smoked or marinated carp, whitefish, perch, or salmon along with marinated terrines of reindeer, and per-haps cloudberry or lingonberry preserves (sold in small jars), which can be thickly spread on fresh-baked herb bread. You'll also find little bottles of wine and Arc-tic liqueurs to enliven your picnic. The deli is open Monday to Friday 9am to 9pm and Saturday 9am to 6pm. Tram: 3B, 3T, 4, 6, or 10.

With your picnic basket, you can head for the **national park** on the island of Seurasaari, the best spot in Helsinki for a family outing.

---

of the most exotic and sophisticated menus in Helsinki. Examples include *mezze,* a platter of Turkish delicacies that includes stuffed vine leaves and hummus; lemon-marinated salmon with tabouleh salad; grilled jumbo prawns wrapped in bacon and served with shellfish and tomato sauce; Moroccan-style braised lamb served in a tagine (clay pot) with harissa (very spicy) sauce; and crispy Moorish duck breast with olives, dates, almonds, and couscous, served with a spinach salad. A vague hint of Finland appears in such dishes as warm carpaccio of reindeer with Parmesan cheese, but other-wise, the venue is based purely on olive oil and Mediterranean traditions.

INEXPENSIVE

Chica's. Mannerheimintie 68. ☎ **09/493-591.** Reservations recommended for dinner. Main courses 70–100 FIM ($10.80–$15.40). AE, DC, MC, V. Mon–Tues 11am–11pm, Wed–Fri 11am–1am, Sat noon–1am, Sun 1–11pm. Tram: 3B or 3T. TEX-MEX.

This is the least expensive and most popular of the limited number of Mexican restau-rants in Helsinki. We'll be frank: The food served here is not the equal of even a mid-dling good Mexican place in the American Southwest, but it comes as a welcome respite when you've had too many herring balls in cream sauce. The decor evokes the colors of the Mexican desert, accented with fiesta shades of green, yellow, and blue, and there's lots of exposed wood and a bar with comfortable sofas, which is worth vis-iting for a margarita even if you don't plan to have dinner afterward. Menu choices include seven kinds of fajitas, enchiladas, stuffed chilis, and a barbecue platter that everyone seems to like. The place was founded by an entrepreneurial Finn after visit-ing New Mexico and Arizona, so it has a distinctive American touch. The beer of choice is Coors, something of a novelty here.

Ravintola Perho. Mechelininkatu 7. ☎ **09/580-7866.** Reservations not accepted. Main courses 58–95 FIM ($8.95–$14.65). AE, DC, MC, V. Sept–June, Mon–Fri 11am–midnight, Sat–Sun noon–midnight; July–Aug, Mon–Sat 11am–5pm. Tram: 8. FINNISH/CONTINENTAL.

Owned and managed by the Helsinki Culinary School, this is the only restaurant of its kind in Finland. Completely staffed by students and trainees, it offers a comfort-able modern setting and a cuisine that's professionally supervised (though not neces-sarily prepared) by the teaching staff. Diners can choose either large or small portions of virtually any dish, so it's possible to sample combinations not available elsewhere. Menu items include tuna salads; "Finnish pasta," served with salmon, cream, and herbs; and fillet of reindeer with black-currant sauce. Many diners find the experience and the youthful enthusiasm of the staff charming. However, the cuisine depends on the culinary lesson for the day. On any number of occasions, we've found it excellent and always a pleasant surprise.

THE ISLANDS

Restaurant Walhalla. Kustaanmiekka Island, Suomenlinna. ☎ 09/668-552. Reservations not required. Main courses 110–155 FIM ($16.95–$23.85). AE, DC, MC, V. Daily noon–midnight. Closed Sept 11–Apr 30. Bus: Water bus to Kustaanmiekka. FINNISH.

On the fortified island many historians view as the cradle of modern Finland, this restaurant provides a sunny, cheerful, and historic insight into Finnish cuisine and culture. Open only in summertime, it requires access by ferryboats, which depart from Helsinki's harborfront, adjacent to the *Havis Amanda* statue, at intervals between every 30 and 60 minutes, depending on the time of day, daily from 9am to 11pm. The return trip to the center of Helsinki occurs at equivalent intervals daily between 9:30am and 11:30pm. Round-trip fares are 23 FIM ($3.55) per person. Once you land on Kustaamiekka Island, walk for about 5 minutes to a series of brick-and-granite vaults in the center of the Viapori fortress. There's a simple cafeteria on the premises, but the preferred spot is on a panoramic terrace with waiter service and water views. (The menu focuses on traditional Finnish specialties such as salmon soup, fillet of reindeer, fried snow grouse, and different preparations of salmon, lamb, pike-perch, and duck.) The cooking is competent in every way and the ingredients first-rate, although the setting competes with the food offerings.

5 Seeing the Sights

Helsinki is filled with many interesting activities, from exploring museums to enjoying a Finnish sauna, to taking a summer cruise through the archipelago, or even sampling a Finnish smörgåsbord. If your time is limited, though, be sure to visit the Mannerheim Museum, the home of Sibelius, the Seurasaari Open-Air Museum, and the Suomenlinna Fortress. For those with more time and money, Helsinki offers a number of specialty shops. For an overview of Finnish products, stop in at Stockmann, Helsinki's largest department store (see "Shoping," below).

Suggested Itineraries

If You Have 1 Day

Start your morning by visiting Market Square and, following in the footsteps of the late president, Lyndon B. Johnson, have coffee and a Karelian meat pie. The market opens at 7am. See the Presidential Palace and Uspenski Cathedral, and visit Senate Square and Eliel Saarinen's Central Railway Station. Before it's too late, stop by Stockmann Department Store or walk along Pohjoisesplanadi for a look at modern Finnish design in the store windows.

If You Have 2 Days

For your first day, follow the suggestions above. On Day 2, visit the Mannerheim Museum, housed in the home of Baron Carl Gustaf Mannerheim, Finland's former field marshal and president. Go to the Olympic Stadium to see the controversial nude statue of the famous runner Paavo Nurmi, and visit Finlandia Hall, Helsinki's main concert hall, designed by Alvar Aalto. Go to the National Museum and stroll through Sibelius Park, with its monument to the famous composer.

If You Have 3 Days

On the first 2 days, follow the itinerary suggested above. On Day 3, visit some of the attractions in the archipelago, including the Seurasaari Open-Air Museum and Suomenlinna Fortress.

If You Have 4 or 5 Days

For your first 3 days, follow the recommendations given above. On Day 4, head north on an excursion to visit the home of Jean Sibelius (Ainola) in Järvenpää. Explore the nearby town of Hämeenlinna and see his birthplace.

On Day 5, take a 1-day excursion to Porvoo, Finland's second-oldest town, 30 miles northeast of Helsinki. Dating back to 1346, the old town features charming red wooden buildings along the Porvoo River and cobblestoned streets.

IN THE CITY CENTER

Eduskuntatalo (Finnish Parliament). Mannerheimintie 30. ☎ **09/4321.** Free admission. Tours given Sat at 11am and noon; July–Aug, also Mon–Fri at 2pm. Tram: 3B or 3T.

Near the post office, this building of pink Finnish granite (built in 1931) houses the 200 members of the one-chamber parliament (40% of whose members are women). The building looks austere on the outside, but it's much warmer inside. Members meet in a domed interior (Parliament Hall), decorated with sculpture by Wäinö Aaltonen. The architect, J. S. Sirén, who wanted to celebrate the new republic, chose a modernized neoclassic style.

Finnish National Gallery. Kaivokatu 2. ☎ **09/173-361.** Admission 15–25 FIM ($2.30–$3.85) adults, 10 FIM ($1.55) students and seniors, free for children under 18. Special exhibits, 20–45 FIM ($3.10–$6.95). Tues and Fri 9am–6pm, Wed–Thurs 9am–8pm, Sat–Sun 11am–5pm. Tram: 3 or 6.

Finland's largest selection of sculpture, painting, and graphic art is displayed at this museum. The Finnish National Gallery is host to three independent museums: the **Museum of Finnish Art,** the **Kiasma (Museum of Contemporary Art),** and the **Sinebrychoff Art Museum (Museum of Foreign Art).** The first museum is housed in the Ateneum building across from the railway station. More than a century old, it was designed by Theodore Höijer. The Museum of Finnish Art has the largest collection of Finnish artists, from the mid-1700s to 1960, as well as the works of some 19th- and 20th-century foreign artists. For visiting times to the other museums, see below.

Helsinki City Museum. Sofiankatu 4 (by Senate Sq.). ☎ **09/1691.** Admission 20 FIM ($3.10), free for children under 18, free for everyone on Thurs. Mon–Fri 9am–5pm, Sat–Sun 11am–5pm. Tram: 1, 2, 3B, 3T, 4, 7A or 7B.

The history of Helsinki from its founding up to modern times is presented from various viewpoints. Exhibits trace the growth of the city, the people moving in or out, and different aspects of Helsinki life.

Kiasma (Museum of Contemporary Art). Mannerheiminaukio 2. ☎ **09/1733-6501.** Admission 40 FIM ($6.15) adults, free for those under 18. Tues 9am–5pm, Wed–Sun 10am–10pm. Tram: 3B or 3T.

Part of the Finnish National Gallery (see above), this is Helsinki's newest museum, having opened in 1998. An American architect, Steven Hall, designed the stunning building, which is ideally lit for displaying modern art. The collection exhibits post-1960 Finnish and international art. Look for changing exhibitions here. Based on the word *chiasma,* for crossovers in genetics and rhetoric, the name for the new museum suggests Finland's special ability to achieve crossovers between the worlds of fine art and high technology. The 14,400-square-foot structure houses Finland's finest

Helsinki Attractions

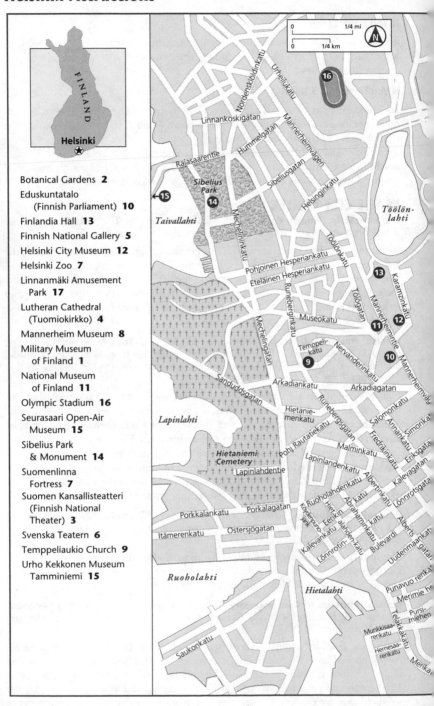

Botanical Gardens **2**

Eduskuntatalo
(Finnish Parliament) **10**

Finlandia Hall **13**

Finnish National Gallery **5**

Helsinki City Museum **12**

Helsinki Zoo **7**

Linnanmäki Amusement
Park **17**

Lutheran Cathedral
(Tuomiokirkko) **4**

Mannerheim Museum **8**

Military Museum
of Finland **1**

National Museum
of Finland **11**

Olympic Stadium **16**

Seurasaari Open-Air
Museum **15**

Sibelius Park
& Monument **14**

Suomenlinna
Fortress **7**

Suomen Kansallisteatteri
(Finnish National
Theater) **3**

Svenska Teatern **6**

Temppeliaukio Church **9**

Urho Kekkonen Museum
Tamminiemi **15**

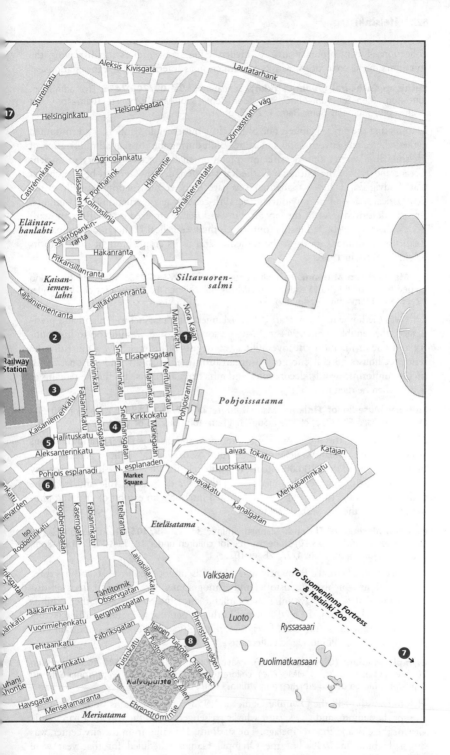

Aleksis Kivisgata
Lautatarhank
Sturenkatu
Helsinginkatu
Helsingegatan
Sörnasstrand väg
Castréninkatu
Agricolankatu
Porthaninik
Hämeentie
Siltasaarenkatu
Kolmaslinja
Sörnäisterrantatie
Säästöpankin-
ranta
Eläintar-
hanlahti
Hakanranta
Pitkänsillanranta
Kaisani-
emen-
lahti
Siltavuorenranta
*Siltavuoren-
salmi*
Kaisaniemenranta
Nora Kajan
Maurinkatu
2
Elisabetsgatan
Snellmaninkatu
Meritullinkatu
Mariankatu
1
Unioninkatu
*Railway
Station*
3
Fabianinkatu
Snellmansgatan
Kirkkokatu
Pohjoissatama
Kaisaniemenkatu
Unionsgatan
Mariegatan
Pohjoisranta
4
Hallituskatu
Laivas tokatu
Katajan
5
Aleksanterinkatu
Luotsikatu
Pohjois esplanadi
N. esplanaden
Kanavakatu
Merikasaminkatu
6
katu
Market
Square
Hogbergsgatan
Kasemgatan
Fabianinkatu
Etelaranta
Kanalgatan
varden
Iso
Roobertinkatu
Eteläsatama
sgatan
Laivasillankatu
Valksaari
*To Suomenlinna Fortress
& Helsinki Zoo*
Tähtitornik
Observgatan
Luoto
Jääkärinkatu
Bergmansgatan
Vuorimiehenkatu
Fabriksgatan
Ryssasaari
Tehtaankatu
Itainen Puistotie
Ostra Alen
Ehrenströmsvägen
8
Puistokatu
Iso Puistotie
Store Allen
uhani
hontie
Pietarinkatu
7
Havsgatan
Kaivopuisto
Puolimatkansaari
Merisatamaranta
Ehrenströmintie
Merisatama

17

521

collection of contemporary art. A "mediatheque" concentrates on displaying the museum's media collections. Kiosks also function as Internet and intranet stations.

Lutheran Cathedral (Tuomiokirkko). Senaatintori. ☎ **09/709-2455.** Free admission. June–Aug, Mon–Sat 9am–6pm, Sun noon–8pm; Sept–May, Mon–Fri 10am–4pm, Sat 10am–6pm, Sun noon–6pm. Tram: 1, 2, 3B, or 3T.

Dominating the city's skyline is one of the city's most visible symbols, a green-domed cathedral erected between 1830 and 1852. Built during the Russian administration of Helsinki in a severe, almost stark interpretation that reflected the glory of ancient Greece and Rome, the Lutheran Cathedral was designed by German-born architect Carl Ludvig Engel. It was inaugurated as part of the reconstruction—usually in the neoclassical style—of the city during the 19th-century reconstruction of Helsinki. (A fire had destroyed most of the city after it was forcibly annexed by the Russian czar.) Today, the rites celebrated inside conform to the Evangelical Lutheran denomination. Extensive renovations, both to the cathedral and to its crypt, brought it back to its original beauty in 1998.

✪ Mannerheim Museum. Kallionlinnantie 14. ☎ **09/635-443.** Admission (including guided tour) 40 FIM ($6.15) adults, 30 FIM ($4.60) children 12–16, free for children under 12. Fri–Sun 11am–5pm. Tram: 3B or 3T.

This was the home of Baron Carl Gustaf Mannerheim, marshal of Finland and president of the republic from 1944 to 1946—a sort of George Washington to his country and one of the most effective military strategists of his era. Now a museum, the residence houses his collection of European furniture, Asian art, and personal items, such as uniforms, swords, decorations, and gifts from admirers. The house remains as it was when he died in 1951.

Military Museum of Finland. Maurinkatu 1. ☎ **09/1812-6381.** Admission 20 FIM ($3.10) adults, 5 FIM (75¢) children. Sun–Fri 11am–4pm. Bus: 16 or 18.

Founded in 1929, this museum records, preserves, and displays material and traditions associated with Finland's defense forces and with general military history. The museum has more than 200,000 items, but only relatively few can be displayed at any one time. Highlights include objects from the days of Swedish rule and from the period between the two world wars. Of special interest is an exhibit of gripping photographs from the war years 1939 to 1945.

National Museum of Finland. Mannerheimintie 34. ☎ **09/405-01.** Admission 25 FIM ($3.85) adults, 20 FIM ($3.10) students, free for children under 18. Tues–Wed 11am–8pm, Thur–Sun 11am–6pm. Tram: 4, 7A, 7B, or 10.

Designed in the National Romantic style, this museum opened in 1916 and has three major sections—prehistoric, historic, and ethnographic. Archaeological finds on display reveal that people have inhabited Finland since the Stone Age. Other exhibits include church art from the medieval and Lutheran periods, folk-culture artifacts, folk costumes and textiles, furniture, foreign ethnographic collections, an important coin collection, and the Finno-Ugric collections.

Olympic Stadium (Olympiastadion). Paavo Nurmi tie 1. ☎ **09/440-363.** Admission 10 FIM ($1.55) adults, 5 FIM (75¢) children under 16. Mon–Fri 9am–8pm, Sat–Sun 9am–4pm. Closed during athletic competitions. Tram: 3B, 3T, 4, or 10.

Helsinki was host to the Olympic Games in 1952; a tower remains from its impressive sports stadium, and an elevator whisks passengers up to the top for a panoramic view of the city and the archipelago. The stadium, 1¼ miles from the city center, was originally built in 1938, but the Olympic Games scheduled for that year were cancelled when the Second World War broke out. The seating capacity of the stadium is 40,000, larger than any other arena in the country. The stadium was closed and rebuilt between 1992 and 1994, and today it conforms to the highest standards of a venue for mass-market sports. Outside the stadium is a statue by Wäinö Aaltonen of the great athlete Paavo Nurmi, "The Flying Finn." The runner is depicted in full stride and is completely nude, which caused considerable controversy when it was unveiled in 1952.

Sinebrychoff Art Museum (Museum of Foreign Art). Sinebrychoff, Bulevardi 40. ☎ 09/173-361. Admission 15 FIM ($2.30) adults, 10 FIM ($1.55) children under 18. Special exhibits 20–45 FIM ($3.10–$6.95). Mon and Thurs–Fri 9am–6pm, Wed 9am–8pm, Sat–Sun 11am–5pm. Tram: 6.

Part of the Finnish National Gallery (see above), this museum was built in 1842 and still displays its original furnishings. It houses an extensive collection of foreign paintings from the 14th to the 19th centuries and has a stunning collection of foreign miniatures. The collection originated from the wealthy Sinebrychoff dynasty, a family of Russians who owned a local brewery and occupied this yellow-and-white neo-Renaissance mansion built in 1840. They were great collectors of antiques, their taste leaning toward the opulent in furnishings. Their art collection was wide ranging, especially noted for its Dutch and Swedish portraits of the 17th and 18th centuries. There is also a stunning collection of porcelain. Outdoor concerts in summer are often staged in their formerly private park surrounding the estate.

Temppeliaukio Church. Lutherinkatu 3. ☎ 09/498-698. Free admission. Mon–Tues and Thurs–Fri 10am–8pm, Wed 10am–7pm, Sat 10am–6pm, Sun noon–1:45pm and 3:15–5:45pm. Closed during special events and Tues Sept–May. Tram: 3B or 3T.

Built into solid rock and consecrated in 1969, this church, called the "rock church," is about 2 blocks west of the National Museum in the Töölö residential district west of Mannerheimintie. Only the roof is visible from outside. It was designed by two architect brothers, Tuomo and Timo Suomalainen. They chose a rocky outcrop rising some 40 feet above street level. The interior walls were blasted from bedrock. Because of its superb acoustics, the church is often used as a concert hall. English-language services are conducted every Sunday at 2pm. Tourists are welcome.

Urho Kekkonen Museum Tamminiemi. Seurassarrentie 15. ☎ 09/480-684. Admission 20 FIM ($3.10) adults, free for children under 18. June–Aug, daily 11am–5pm; Sept–May, Tues–Sun 11am–5pm. Bus: 24 from Erottaja bus stop, adjacent to the Swedish Theater and Stockmann Department Store.

This site celebrates the accomplishments of Urho Kekkonen (1900–1986), who served longer as president of Finland (from 1956 to 1982, during some of the trickiest days of the Cold War) than anyone else. Built in 1904 in the Jugendstil (art nouveau) style, it's a not particularly large house whose official functions were replaced with a larger structure in 1995 in another part of Helsinki. As a sign of respect for their president, who was the eldest son of a foreman in the logging industry in an isolated region of northeast Finland, the Finnish parliament allowed the then-ailing Kekkonen to remain a resident here until his death in 1986. Today, the site is a testimonial to the survival of Finland against the Soviet menace, and a testimonial to the man who helped make that happen. Of particular interest is a view of the most famous sauna in Finland. A log-sided, old-fashioned building with a wood-fired stove, it hosted several pivotal diplomatic meetings, including some with Nikita Khrushchev. (As the Finns say, who can possibly remain hostile in the blazing heat of a sauna?) The sauna can be visited only between June and August. Finnish-language tours depart at 30-minute

---

⊘ Frommer's Favorite Helsinki Experiences

Enjoying a Finnish Sauna. Regardless of where you've bathed before, you haven't been cleansed to the core until you've experienced a Finnish sauna. Whether used for giving birth to babies or entertaining Russian ambassadors, the sauna is often looked upon with almost religious awe.

Hearing a Sibelius Concert. To listen to the work of Finland's greatest composer, Jean Sibelius, is a moving experience. This sensitive, vulnerable artist achieved a universal melodic language. In his lifetime Sibelius and his music became the symbol of Finland, a nation striving for independence and recognition.

Partaking of a Finnish Smörgåsbord. Feast on the harvest of the sea, Baltic herring in a tangy marinade, followed by lightly salted fish and roe, smoked and other cold fish dishes. Then try smoked reindeer meat for a touch of Lapland (flavored with lingonberries) and, for a finale, a selection of Finnish desserts, including fresh Arctic berries.

Cruising the Archipelago. Since Helsinki is the capital of a country of 188,000 lakes, it, too, is best seen from the water. On a warm summer day, take a cruise through the archipelago; you'll pass innumerable little islands and navigate around many peninsulas.

---

intervals throughout opening hours; an English-language tour is conducted every day at 1:30pm. Otherwise, you can borrow an English-language cassette and player for a self-guided tour.

NEAR HELSINKI

⊘ **Ainola.** Ainolantie, in Järvenpää. ☎ **09/287-322.** Admission 20 FIM ($3.10) adults, 5 FIM (75¢) children. June–Aug, Tues–Sun 11am–5pm; May and Sept, Wed–Sun 11am–5pm. Closed Oct–Apr. Bus: From Platform 1 of the Helsinki Bus Station, follow the Helsinki–Hyryla–Järvenpää route, to where the road forks at a sign saying AINOLA, then a 4-min. walk to the home. Train: Järvenpää station.

Few countries seem as proud of a native composer as Finns are of Jean Sibelius, who lived here for more than half a century. He named the house after his wife, Aino (sister of the artist Eero Järnefelt), and lived here from 1904 until his death in 1957; he and his wife are buried on the property. Avant-garde at the time of its construction, the house was designed by Lars Sonck, who also designed the summer residence of the president of Finland. The wooden interior of Ainola is lined with books and some surprisingly modern-looking furniture. Järvenpää is 24 miles from Helsinki.

Gallen-Kallela Museum. Tarvaspää, Gallen-Kallelantie 27, Espoo. ☎ **09/541-3388.** Admission 35 FIM ($5.40) adults, 20 FIM ($3.10) children 7–16, free for children under 7. May 15–Aug, Mon–Thurs 10am–8pm, Fri–Sun 10am–5pm; Sept–May 14, Tues–Sat 10am–4pm, Sun 10am–5pm. Tram: 4 to Munkkiniemi; then take bus no. 33 to Tarvo or walk about 1½ miles along the seaside (bus no. 33 runs Mon–Sat 9:20–11am and 1–3pm).

On a wooded peninsula in a suburb of Helsinki, this museum is dedicated to the great Finnish artist Akseli Gallen-Kallela (1865–1931), who built the studio between 1911 and 1913, calling it his "castle in the air." A restless, fanciful personality, Gallen-Kallela has a reputation based mainly on his paintings, especially those from the *Kalevala* (Land of Heroes). This Finnish national epic, first published in 1835, and often compared to Homer's *Iliad* and *Odyssey,* was in later editions illustrated by the artist. He wanted to illustrate all the cantos, but managed only a small part, which rank among the masterpieces of Finnish art. The museum houses a large collection of his paintings, graphics, posters, and industrial design products. Beside the museum is a cafe in a wooden villa dating from the 1850s.

ON NEARBY ISLANDS
ON SEURASAARI

✪ Seurasaari Open-Air Museum. Seurasaari Island. ☎ **09/40-501.** Admission 20 FIM ($3.10), free for children under 18. May 15–31 and Sept 1–15, Mon–Fri 9am–3pm and Sat–Sun 11am–5pm; June 1–Aug 30, Thurs–Tue 11am–5pm, Wed 11am–7pm. Closed Sept 16–May 14. Bus: 24 from the Erottaja bus stop, near Stockmann Department Store, to the island. The 3-mile ride takes about 15 min., and costs 10 FIM ($1.55) each way.

One of the largest collections of historic buildings in Finland, each moved here from somewhere else, lies on the island of Seurassari, a national park. Representing the tastes and evolution of Finnish architecture through the centuries, the collection includes a 17th-century church, an 18th-century gentleman's manor house, and dozens of oddly diverse farm buildings, each erected with a specific function in mind. There's also an old-fashioned "aboriginal" sauna, a kind of smokehouse that takes hours to heat.

The fire and verve associated with this collection of historic, freestanding buildings are most visible during the summer months, when you can visit the interiors, and when an unpretentious restaurant serves coffee, drinks, and platters of food. Although the buildings are locked during the winter months, you can still view the exteriors, and explore on foot the park that surrounds them. A stroll through this place in the wintertime is not as far-fetched an idea as you might think; the park is favored by strollers and joggers even during snowfalls.

ON SUSISAARI & KUSTAANMIEKKA

✪ Suomenlinna Fortress is known as the "Gibraltar of the North." This 18th-century fortress (☎ **09/684-1800**) lies in the Baltic's archipelago on five interconnected islands that guard the maritime approaches to Helsinki. With their walks and gardens, cafes, restaurants, and old frame buildings, the islands are one of the most interesting outings from Helsinki. Originally built in the mid–18th century when

---

❷ Did You Know?

- Helsinki is famed for its architects, but it was a German, Carl Ludvig Engel, who laid out the present inner city.
- Two brothers designed Temppeliauko Church from solid rock; it occupies nearly a whole block, but from the street only the dome is visible.
- The *Havis Amanda* fountain scandalized the city when it was placed in Market Square in 1908, but now it's Helsinki's symbol.
- The major boulevard, Esplanadi, was once a political dividing line—Finns walked on the south side and Swedes on the north.
- Wäinö Aaltonen caused an uproar in 1952 when his statue of Paavo Nurmi, the champion runner of the 1920s, was unveiled—he had depicted Nurmi fully nude.

The Building of Finland

Finland's architectural heritage before the 20th century incorporates Swedish, Russian, and Viking motifs into buildings that often seem to arise from the human subconscious as interpreted by Scandinavian mythology. More than in any other nation, Finland's identity is intimately associated with its postwar architecture.

The architectural landscape of Finland is relatively young—more than 90% of the country's structures were built after 1920. Part of this is because of Finland's ongoing struggle to survive during the many years it swung back and forth between the orbits of the often-violent regimes of Sweden and Russia. Much of the destruction during the 20th century was initiated by Nazi Germany, to a somewhat lesser degree by the Soviet Union. In some cases, however (as occurred in such "lost" provinces as Karelia, which was painfully ceded to the Soviets after World War II), it was the Finns themselves who burned their buildings.

At least some of the impetus for postwar rebuilding came from the government's passage of the "Arava System," which, in an attempt to honor the sacrifices of Finns during the war, offered state-subsidized loans to construct houses. So many utilitarian objects were created and so many homes built between 1940 and 1958 that Finns refer to this period as "The Age of Heroic Materialism." Everything from armaments to medicine to construction materials were marshaled into programs designed for the good (and the survival) of the Finnish nation.

In many cases the signature of the individual architect could rarely be discerned in the typical private home. Throughout Finland, many dwellings were designed as a simple cube, warmed with a centrally located stove (often wood-burning) and capped with a steeply pitched roof that sheltered a high attic suitable for conversion into additional bedrooms.

Finland was a part of Sweden, the fortress was named "Sveaborg" by the Swedes, and later became known by the Finns and Russians (who assumed control in 1808) as "Viapori." After Finland became an independent country in 1917, the fortress acquired its present name, Suomenlinna, which means "the fortress of Finland." It served as a working part of the nation's defenses until 1973.

Today the main attraction is that part of the fortress on Susisaari and Kustaanmiekka Islands, which are now joined together as one land body. Specifically, the sights include a small, well-preserved fort on Kustaanmiekka, with defense walls and tunnels, and another, larger fortress on Susisaari, which includes a number of parks, squares, and gardens.

You can take a **ferry** from Market Square to Suomenlinna year-round beginning at 6:20am daily. The boats run about once an hour, and the last one returns from the island at 1:45am. The round-trip ferry ride costs 28 FIM ($4.30) for adults and 12 FIM ($1.85) for children.

The island has no "streets," but individual attractions are signposted. During the peak summer months (June to September), Suomenlinna maintains two information kiosks, one at Market Square (by the departure point for the Suomenlinna ferryboat) and a second on the island itself (near Tykistolahti Bay). The latter kiosk serves as the starting point for **guided tours**—offered in English—of the fortress with a focus on its

Alvar Aalto (1898–1976), an architect whose comfortably minimalist and sometimes eccentric designs are now intertwined with the Finnish aesthetic, became an important visionary in the postwar rebuilding of Finland. His work was already well known to connoisseurs, thanks to his designs for the Finnish Pavilions at the Paris World's Fair of 1937 and the New York World's Fair of 1939.

A noteworthy (and pragmatic) moment in Aalto's career included designing a series of standardized wood-sided homes partially prefabricated in a Finnish lumberyard. By 1943, during an unexpected lull in the hostilities of World War II, 14 two-family homes designed by Aalto were completed, launching him into a postwar career that shifted his focus from classicism to functionalism and that continued at a fast pace throughout the 1950s and 1960s.

Since then, Aalto has been referred to as "a vitalist to whom nothing human was alien." Bold but tasteful, he developed the Finnish preference for exposed wood and free forms into undemonstrative, functional, and nurturing buildings that are noteworthy for their cost-effectiveness, comfort, and sense of style. Important commissions often incorporated fieldstone and red brick, poured concrete, and, later, large expanses of white stone, marble, or plaster. Noteworthy buildings include such monuments as the Säynätsalo Town Hall (completed in 1952); the Sunila pulp mill, which included a new town (Kotka) to house its workers; some of the buildings on the campus of the University of Jväskylä (completed in 1966); the main building of Helsinki University in Otaniemi (built between 1955 and 1964); and Finlandia Hall, Helsinki's main symphonic concert hall, completed in 1971. Other commissions included hospitals, libraries (such as the one at Viipuri), and private homes, some filled with the distinctive laminated wood furniture for which he and his wife, Aino (who died in 1949), eventually became world famous.

military history. Tours are scheduled between June and September, daily at 12:30 and 2:30pm, and cost 25 FIM ($3.85) for adults and 10 FIM ($1.55) for children. on an as-needed basis and priced at 360 FIM ($55.45) for between 1 and 16 participants.

The Museums of Suomenlinna

A number of minor museums on either Susisaari or the connected island of Kustaanmiekka can be explored if you have the time.

Coastal Artillery Museum. Kustaanmiekka. ☎ **09/1814-5295.** Admission 10 FIM ($1.55) adults, 5 FIM (75¢) children. May 11–Aug, daily 10am–5pm; Sept, daily 11am–3pm; Apr 4–May 10 and Oct 1–23, Sat–Sun 11am–3pm. Closed Oct 24–Apr 3.

Set within the thick walls and vaulted ceilings of an area of the Suomenlinna fortress originally built to store gunpowder, this museum contains exhibits that show how Finland defended itself from foreign aggression during World War I and II. Opened in 1948, the museum traces the stages in the defense of Finnish shores from prehistoric times to the present. The weapons for defending the coastline now include missiles, motorized artillery, and turret guns. Also on display is equipment for directing fire, range finders, and a marine surveillance camera. Newer technology is represented by close-range missiles and a laser range finder.

Impressions

I became aware at once of the translucent, transparent, pure, elusive, clean, and clinical quality of Helsinki. I began to hate the almost paralyzing perfection of modern buildings, equipment, accommodation, accessories, service.

—James Kirkup, *One Man's Russia,* 1968

Ehrensvärd Museum. Susisaari. ☎ **09/684-1850.** Admission 10 FIM ($1.55) adults, 5 FIM (75¢) children 7–16, free for children under 7. Mar 1–May 3, Sat–Sun 11am–4:30pm; May 4–Aug 30, daily 10am–5pm; Sept, daily 10am–4:30pm; Oct, Sat–Sun 11am–4:30pm. Closed Nov–Feb.

This historical museum includes a model ship collection and officers' quarters from the 18th century, as well as displays based on Suomenlinna's military history. The museum bears the name of Augustin Ehrensvärd, who supervised construction of the fortress and whose tomb is on Susisaari.

Submarine Vesikko. Susisaari. ☎ **09/1814-5295.** Admission 10 FIM ($1.55) adults, 5 FIM (75¢) children. May 9–Aug 30, daily 10am–4:45pm; Aug 31–Sept 27, daily 11am–3pm. Closed Sept 28–May 8.

The submarine *Vesikko* was built in Turku and launched in 1933. Germany had ordered the submarine built for experimental purposes, but Finland bought it in 1936. The submarine, which was used during the Second World War, torpedoed the 4,100-ton Russian ship *Vyborg.* The Paris Peace Treaty of 1947 forbade Finland to have submarines, so all except the *Vesikko* were scrapped. The *Vesikko* was opened as a museum in 1973.

ON KORKEASAARI

Helsinki Zoo. Korkeasaari Island. ☎ **09/169-591.** Admission by waterbus, 40 FIM ($6.15) adults, 20 FIM ($3.10) children; by bridge, 25 FIM ($3.85) adults, 15 FIM ($2.30) children. The Helsinki Card (see "Getting Around," above) covers admission to the zoo as well as free rides on the ferry and waterbus. Mar–Apr, daily 10am–6pm; May–Sept, daily 10am–8pm; Oct–Feb, daily 10am–4pm. Waterbus: From Market Square and Hakaniemenranta in front of the Merihotelli. Bus: 16 (year-round) to Kulosaari, then walk less than a mile via Mustikkamaa Island to the zoo; or 11 (summer only) from the Herttoniemi subway station.

An interesting collection of northern European animals, including a herd of wild forest reindeer, wolverines, northern owl species, and many other mammals and birds from Europe and Asia, can be found here.

PARKS & GARDENS

Botanical Gardens. University of Helsinki, Unioninkatu 44. ☎ **09/708-4041.** Admission 20 FIM ($3.10) adults, 10 FIM ($1.55) children, free for children under 7. May–Sept, daily 7am–8pm; Oct–Apr, daily 7am–6pm.

These gardens, a 5-minute walk from the Central Station, feature shrubs and flowers, herbs, ornamentals, Finnish wildflowers, and indigenous trees and bushes. The greenhouses here reopened in 1998 after extensive renovations, making them better than ever. However, unlike the rest of the gardens, they are closed on Monday.

Pihlajasaari Recreational Park. ☎ **09/630-065.** Admission 20 FIM ($3.10) adults, 10 FIM ($1.55) seniors and children. Daily 24 hours. Motorboat leaves from the end of Laivurinkatu May to mid-Oct, daily at 9am, 9:30am, and then at hourly intervals until 8:30pm, depending on weather.

Walking Tour: Central Helsinki

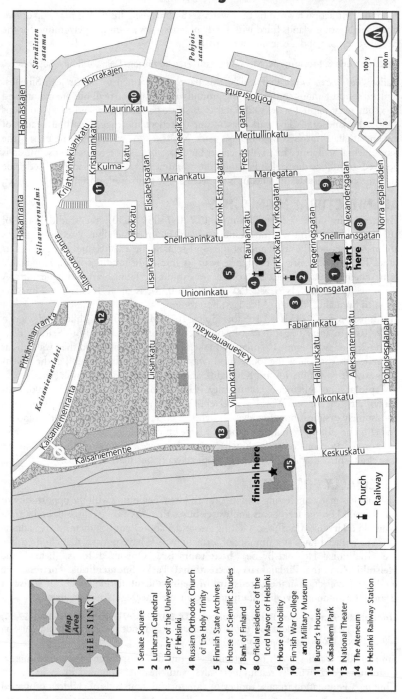

1 Senate Square
2 Lutheran Cathedral
3 Library of the University of Helsinki
4 Russian Orthodox Church of the Holy Trinity
5 Finnish State Archives
6 House of Scientific Studies
7 Bank of Finland
8 Official residence of the Lord Mayor of Helsinki
9 House of Nobility
10 Finnish War College and Military Museum
11 Burger's House
12 Kaisaniemi Park
13 National Theater
14 The Ateneum
15 Helsinki Railway Station

529

A popular attraction favored by bird-watchers and joggers, this park is made up of two small neighboring islands filled with sandy beaches—it's a summer playground for the city. A restaurant and a cafe are in the park.

Sibelius Park & Monument. Mechelininkatu. Free admission. Daily 24 hours. Bus: 24.

Called *Sibeliuksen puisto* in Finnish, this park was planned to honor Jean Sibelius, Finland's most famous composer. The grounds are not manicured, but are maintained in a somewhat natural state. Old birch trees shade park benches, and rocky outcrops divide the landscape. The park was meant to reflect the rugged natural beauty of Finland itself, as inspired by Sibelius's work *Finlandia*. At one side of the park is the monumental sculpture, Eila Hiltunen's tribute to Sibelius, the genius whose music is believed to embody the soul of Finland. The monument was unveiled in 1967, a decade after the composer's death; Sibelius is depicted at the peak of his powers and his career.

ARCHITECTURAL HIGHLIGHTS

Hvittrask, in Luoma, Kirrkkonummi (☎ 09/4050-9630), the studio home of architects Eliel Saarinen, Armas Lindgren, and Herman Gesellius, was built of logs and natural stone and ranks among the most remarkable architectural creations of its time. The artistic unity of the house with its forest surroundings was a remarkable achievement. Today it's used as a center for exhibits of Finnish art and handcrafts. A first-rate restaurant, **Hvittrask** (☎ 09/29-76-033), is open Tuesday to Thursday noon to 8pm and Friday to Monday noon to 6pm.

Admission is 20 FIM ($3.10) for adults, 10 FIM ($1.55) for children. It's open daily 10am to 7pm. To get here, take bus no. 166 from the Central Bus Station, Platform 62, then walk about 1¼ miles. Or take the train to Luoma, and then walk about 1¼ miles. By car, follow the Jorvas motorway about 12¼ miles, turn off at the Kivenlahti exit, drive 3 miles toward Kauklahti, and then follow the Hvittrask signs.

Tapiola, a notable model community, is in Espoo, 6 miles west of Helsinki. This garden city, of the pre–World War II era, is filled with parks, splashing fountains, handsomely designed homes and apartments, shopping centers, playgrounds, schools, and churches. In the center of Tapiola is a large office building with a self-service cafeteria on top (a good choice for lunch). To reach Tapiola, go to stop no. 52 or no. 53 near the Central Station. From either stop, take any bus marked tapiola.

ESPECIALLY FOR KIDS

Helsinki has many interesting activities for children, beginning with the opportunity to travel around on the **ferryboats** and **water buses** that link the city's islands and attractions. The Helsinki Card (see "Getting Around," above) entitles them to free admittance or reduced rates at a number of attractions. We have noticed that children like the "Traditional Helsinki by Sea" **boat tours** (see "Organized Tours," below), the **Helsinki Zoo,** the **Pihlajasaari Recreational Park, Suomenlinna Fortress,** the model-ship collection in the **Ehrensvärd Museum,** the submarine *Vesikko* on **Susisaari Island,** the outdoor **Olympic Stadium,** and many other sights and excursions.

Linnanmäki Amusement Park. Linnanmüki. ☎ 09/773-991. Admission 15 FIM ($2.30) adults, 10 FIM ($1.55) children 6–16, free for children 5 and under. Mon–Fri 4–10pm, Sat–Sun 1–9 or 10pm. Closed Sept–Apr. Tram: 3B or 3T.

Linnanmäki, 2 miles north of Helsinki, is a fun fair of splashing fountains, merry-go-rounds, Ferris wheels, restaurants, cafes, and theaters. Founded in 1950 by the Children's Foundation to raise money to care for the thousands of children orphaned by World War II, Linnanmäki is still raising money for a new generation of children. The amusement park has 34 different rides.

Walking Tour: Central Helsinki

Start: Senate Square.

Finish: Helsinki Railway Station.

Time: Allow 3 hours, not including museum and shopping stops.

Best Times: Any day it's not raining.

Worst Times: Rush hours (Monday to Friday between 8 and 9:30am and 5 and 6:30pm), because of the heavy traffic.

The tour begins at:

1. **Senate Square,** at the base of the monument to the Russian tsar Alexander II, erected in his honor shortly after the annexation of Finland. Helsinki's most historic and beautiful square was designed in the early 1800s at the height of the Russian Empire's fascination with the architectural glories of ancient Greece and Rome. The designer was Berlin-born Carl Ludvig Engel, who had created other public buildings in St. Petersburg. The:

2. **Lutheran Cathedral** stands on the north side of the square. Capped with triplicate statues of saints, it has four small cupolas ringing its central dome.

    As you face the cathedral, the Senate, capped by a low dome and graced by six Corinthian columns, is on your right. Opposite the cathedral, on the south side of the square, stand the ocher facade and Ionic columns of a house from 1762 that was redesigned by Engel.

    Leaving the square, ascend the steeply inclined Unioninkatu, skirting the right-hand (western) edge of the square. The street was dedicated to the tsar in 1819 and, because of its difficult terrain, considered extremely expensive at the time of its construction. The elegantly graceful building opposite the western facade of the cathedral is the:

3. **Library of the University of Helsinki.** Some critics consider this the most beautiful of the many buildings created by Engel. Admire its rhythmically repetitive Corinthian pilasters and columns before continuing uphill. At the northwestern corner of the cathedral's rear side rises the spire of the:

4. **Russian Orthodox Church of the Holy Trinity,** with an ocher-colored facade. Designed by Engel in 1827, it has an artfully skewed Orthodox double cross placed above its doorway.

    After passing Kirkkokatu, turn right (east) onto Rauhankatu. The statue of the young girl, set onto a porphyry base near the corner, is named *Dawn* and the gray-fronted modern building serving as the statue's backdrop contains the printing presses and engravers' shops for banknotes issued by the Bank of Finland.

    Continue east on the same street, passing an ornately neoclassical building with a trio of wise women set on its pediment. This is the storage space for the:

5. **Finnish State Archives,** originally designed in 1890. As they grew, they were greatly expanded with annexes and underground vaults.

    At the corner of Snellmaninkatu, turn right. The russet-fronted temple with four Corinthian columns and a single acanthus leaf at the pinnacle of its pediment is the:

6. **House of Scientific Studies,** erected in 1891. Just below its heraldic plaques is a heroic frieze cast in solid bronze, paying homage to the generosity of Alexander II, who promised to retain the internal laws and religion of Finland after its 1809 annexation. For many years the frieze was the largest bronze casting in Finland.

Across Snellmaninkatu is a somber gray building set above a steep embankment—the central headquarters of the:

7. **Bank of Finland,** designed by a Russian-German architect, Bohnsted, in 1892. In front of the bank stands a statue of the Finnish statesman J. V. Snellman, the patriot whose life was devoted to raising the Finnish language to the same legal status as Swedish. Snellman was also responsible for making the Finnish markka the official currency of the country, thereby replacing the Russian ruble.

Continue to walk downhill along Snellmaninkatu, skirting the eastern edge of the cathedral's outbuildings. Shortly you'll reenter Senate Square. Proceed to the bottom of the square and turn left onto Aleksanterinkatu. At no. 14 on that street, behind a russet-colored 1823 facade, is the:

8. **Official residence of the Lord Mayor of Helsinki,** standing next door to the Theater Museum at Aleksanterinkatu 12.

Continue walking east along Aleksanterinkatu. In a short time, you'll enter a small gate dotted with a handful of birch trees. Behind the trees rises the neo-Venetian facade of the:

9. **House of the Nobility,** completed in 1861 as a private club and the reunion hall of the Finnish and Russian aristocracy.

Walk along Aleksanterinkatu, crossing Mariankatu, and continue toward the harbor. Some of the buildings along here are among the oldest in Helsinki, dating from the 1760s. At the waterfront, turn left onto Meritullintori, skirting the edge of the harbor. A sweeping vista of the Russian Orthodox Uspenski Kathedralen (cathedral) comes into view.

At this point the street changes its name to Pohjoisranta and continues to follow the harborfront. Continue along this street to the third intersection, Maneeskikatu, where the quay will widen into a formal park ringed with art nouveau buildings, some of the finest in Helsinki. Facing the park, notice on your left the redbrick neo-Victorian building, the:

10. **Finnish War College and Military Museum,** Liisankatu, originally constructed as a barracks in the 1880s. Turn left onto Liisankatu, heading west. Completed in 1813, the street honored the Russian tsarina Elisabeth (*Liisa* is the Finnish version of *Elisabeth*).

Take the second right, turning uphill onto Meritullinkatu. Cross (but don't turn onto) Kulmakatu. At this point, Meritullinkatu becomes a pedestrians-only walkway for residents of the surrounding apartment buildings. At the dead end, turn left and negotiate a narrow, elevated sidewalk high above the street running below (Kristianinkatu). One block later, cross (but don't turn onto) Kulmakatu. A few paces later, at Kristininkatu 12, you'll see the simple stone foundation and ocher-colored clapboards of the:

11. **Burger's House,** Helsinki's oldest remaining wooden house, dating from the early 1800s and now accommodating a small museum.

A few steps later, Kristianinkatu dead-ends at a pedestrians-only sidewalk, Oikokatu. Go right (downhill), descending two narrow flights of concrete stairs heading toward the lake. At the bottom you emerge onto a busy avenue, Siltavuorenranta; turn left and notice the stylish bulk of the Hotel Strand Inter-Continental rising across the water. Walk along the curving embankment for a while, coming to the tramway and car traffic hub of Unioninkatu, which you should cross. You'll then enter:

12. **Kaisaniemi Park ("The Company Keeping Park"),** beloved by residents of Helsinki. Until the 1830s, this tract of waterfront land was only a marshy

bogland until it was drained and opened as Helsinki's first park. The park contains the Botanical Gardens of the University of Helsinki, which date from 1833.

Walk through the park, flanking the water on your right, and then follow the natural left-bending southward curve of the park's main path. (Don't cross any of the railroad tracks.) After exiting from the park, your path becomes Lantinen Teatterikuja, in a neighborhood of art nouveau apartment buildings. Follow the street for a block through the theatrical headquarters of Finland. On your left stands the:

13. National Theater, vaguely reminiscent of the opera house in Vienna. Note the decorative sculptures on its facade, especially the representation of bears. The theater was designed by the architect Tarjanne in 1902. Across the square, immediately opposite the National Theater, is:

14. The Ateneum, or Finnish National Gallery, designed by Hoijer and completed in 1887. Its interior contains the best art museum in Finland. On the western side of the square (to your right as you face the Ateneum) is one of the most famous public buildings in Europe, the:

15. Helsinki Railway Station, designed by Eliel Saarinen in 1916. The sculptures are evocative of the monumental works of Pharaonaic Egypt. It has been copied endlessly ever since by avant-garde set designers of plays and films, including Batman.

After such a tour, you'll want to:

☕ **TAKE A BREAK**   From the railway station, head directly south until you reach Pohjoisesplanadi, site of a number of cafes. Our favorite is **Café Espan Ursula,** Pohjoisesplanadi 21 (☎ **09/2709-2940**), which is by the pulsating shopping street near the Market Place. In addition to ordering food and drink here, it's great for people-watching.

6 Organized Tours

CITY TOURS   A city tour lasting 1½ hours, offered by **Helsinki Expert** (☎ **09/2288-1222**), costs 105 FIM ($16.15) for adults, 50 FIM ($7.70) for children under 13. The tour covers all the main sights of Helsinki, including the Sibelius Monument. Tickets can be purchased from TourExpert at the Helsinki City Tourist Office or any of the departure points: the Olympia Terminal and Market Square. The Olympia Terminal tour departs at 10am daily year-round; the Market Square tour departs daily July through September at 2pm.

For an **orientation sightseeing trip** without a guide, catch tram no. 3T, which takes you past 35 major city buildings and monuments. The 45-minute trip is available only in summer. You can board tram no. 3T in front of the railway station or at Market Square Monday to Saturday 6am to 1am and Sunday 7:30am to 1am. The tram departs regularly at intervals ranging from 5 to 15 minutes. During rush hours, you might have difficulty finding a seat. A ticket costs 10 FIM ($1.55), 5 FIM (75¢) for children under 13.

HARBOR TOURS   For a waterside view of Helsinki and its nearby islands, contact the **Royal Line,** Meritullintori 6 (☎ **09/652-088**). It has two big-windowed ships (each accommodating up to 250 passengers): the MS *Katarina* and the MS *Natalia*. The most popular tours are "Traditional Helsinki by Sea" and "Helsinki Under the

Bridges," which explores the central and western views of the city, respectively, offering distant views of some of the more accessible islands of the archipelago. Each departs four times a day mid-May through August, lasts 90 minutes each, and costs 60 FIM ($9.25) per person. The tour with lunch sells for 125 FIM ($19.25).

There's also a 7-hour excursion departing between mid-May and mid-September on Monday, Wednesday, Friday, and Saturday at 10am, and returning at 6pm; it costs 175 FIM ($26.95) per person and includes a shore excursion in the historic town of Porvoo.

7 Spectator Sports & Outdoor Activities

Major sports events take place at the **Olympic Stadium,** Paavo Nurmi tie 1 (☎ 09/ 440-363), described under "Seeing the Sights," above. In summer, soccer games between Finland and other European countries are scheduled. Check *Helsinki This Week,* which lists the events taking place at the stadium at the time of your visit. Take tram no. 3B, 3T, 4, or 10.

JOGGING To keep fit, Finns are just as fond of jogging as Americans or Canadians. The best paths are close to **Olympic Stadium** (see above) and in **Kaivopuisto Park** (the southern part of Helsinki). There are also some good jogging trails around **Hesperia Park,** which is convenient if you're staying at a hotel in the city center.

SAUNAS & BEACHES Most hotels (at least, the better ones) have a sauna. If you want to sample a Finnish sauna and your hotel doesn't have one, the reception desk can direct you to the nearest sauna that's open to the general public.

Traditionally every Finnish city had a wood-heated public sauna. The only one wood-heated public sauna remaining in Helsinki is the **Kothiharjun Sauna,** Harjutorinkatu, near the Sörnäien metro station; ☎ 09/753-1537). Visitors are welcome to experience a real Finnish sauna in newly renovated premises, open Tuesday to Friday 1 to 8pm and Saturday noon to 6pm.

If you're in Helsinki in the summer, you'll find the best beaches at **Mustikkamaa, Uunisaari, Pihlajasaari, Hietaniemi,** and **Sevrasaari.** There's also a popular beach on Suomenlinna; you might combine a trip to the beach with a visit to Suomenlinna fortress. However, if you're from a warmer climate, you may find the waters of the Baltic, even in July, too chilly for your tastes.

TENNIS The best bet for playing tennis in Helsinki is to travel 3½ miles northwest of the railway station to the Pitäjämäki district. Here the **Tali Tennis Center,** Kutonokuja 3, Pitäjämäki (☎ 09/556-271), welcomes foreign visitors. Built in 1967, this is the largest, most modern, and most popular tennis complex in Helsinki. The center maintains 10 indoor tennis courts and 6 outdoor courts. In winter, 5 of the 6 outdoor courts are covered with a plastic "bubble." Depending on the time of day and season, indoor courts cost 68 to 112 FIM ($10.45 to $17.25) per hour; outdoor courts range from 68 to 92 FIM ($10.45 to $14.15) per hour. Use of outdoor courts is severely limited by the weather and the seasons. You can rent a tennis racquet for 10 FIM ($1.55) and buy tennis balls once you're here. Take bus no. 14 or 39 from the center of the city. It's open daily from 6am to 10:30pm, but call first to see if the courts are available.

8 Shopping

Finland has taken a bold, creative lead in the highly competitive world of interior design. Search out ceramics and glassware (Arabia is famous), hand-woven articles, hand-carved wood, jaunty fashions, and rugs.

Textiles and jewelry also bear the distinctive stamp of Finland, and toy stores brim with educational toys for each stage of a child's development. Souvenir possibilities include decorations made from reindeer skin, costumed dolls, baskets, and pungent berry liqueurs made from yellow cloudberries, cranberries, and Arctic brambleberries. Of course, you'll find all your sauna needs here as well.

THE SHOPPING SCENE

Most stores are open Monday to Friday 9am to 5pm and Saturday 9am to 2pm. Sometimes stores stay open until 4pm on Saturday, especially in the summer.

SHOPPING AREAS   The most important shopping neighborhoods are in the center of the city. They include **Esplanadi,** for those seeking the finest of Finnish design—but at high prices. Even if you don't buy anything, it's a delightful street for promenading in summer. Airline offices, banks, and travel agencies share the street with shops filled with the best of Finnish crafts, as well as a number of art galleries.

Esplanadi leads from the commercial heart of town all the way to the waterfront. Bordering the water is **Market Square (Kauppatori),** a fresh open-air market that's open Monday to Saturday. In summer, peddlers set up trolleys and tables to display their wares. Most of the goods for sale are produce (some of them ideal for picnic food), but there are souvenir and gift items as well.

The other main shopping section is called simply **Central,** beginning at Esplanadi and extending to the famous Helsinki Railway Station. Many of the big names in Finnish shopping are here, none more notable than the Stockmann Department Store. Many shopping complexes are also situated in this district, including the Forum. One of the main shopping streets here is **Aleksanterinkatu,** which runs parallel to Esplanadi, stretching from the harborfront to Mannerheimintie.

Other shopping streets, all in the center, include **Iso Roobertinkatu** and **Bulevardi,** lying off Esplanadi. Bulevardi, starting at the Klaus Kurki Hotel, winds its way to the water.

TAX REFUNDS   Tax-free shopping is available at stores that display Europe Tax-Free Shopping signs in their windows. It's available to all visitors who reside outside the European Union. The value-added tax (usually 22%) on articles bought in these shops is refunded to you when you leave Finland. The minimum tax-free purchase is 250 FIM ($38.50).

Most of the large department stores and shops can ship your purchases directly to your home address. That way you avoid having to file a claim at Customs. If you take the merchandise with you, ask for a check for the tax amount. This check can be cashed at the airport or harbor where you depart. The savings, which come to about 12% to 16%, apply to both cash and credit- and charge-card purchases. However, if you use your purchased goods before leaving Finland, you won't get a tax refund. Most international cards, such as American Express and Visa, are accepted at major shops, but always ask beforehand.

If you have any questions about tax-free shopping, contact **Europe Tax-Free Shopping (Finland) Ltd.,** Salomonkatu 17A (☎ **09/6132-9600**).

SHOPPING HOURS   Most stores are open Monday to Friday 9am to 6pm and on Saturday 9am to 1pm. A new government regulation allows shopping on Sunday in June, July, August, and December. As a result, Forum and Stockmann are open during those months on Sunday from noon to 4pm.

A PREVIEW OF FINNISH DESIGN   Before you begin to shop, you might want to survey modern Finnish design. Go to the **Museum of Art and Design,** Korkeavuorenkatu 23 (☎ **09/622-0540**), which is open Monday to Friday 10am to

7pm, Saturday and Sunday 10am to 6pm. The admission is 40 to 50 FIM ($6.15 to $7.70) for adults, 10 FIM ($1.55) for seniors, and free for children. In what used to be a schoolhouse, the museum has on permanent display the best of Finnish design in wood, textiles, ceramics, glass, and other materials. Other examples of Finnish design can be found at **Design Forum Finland,** Fabianinkatu 10 (☎ **09/629-290**), which is open Monday to Friday 10am to 6pm and Saturday and Sunday 11am to 4pm. Design Forum specializes in industrial design, applied arts, graphic arts, and interior architecture. A shop and a business gift service are available.

SHOPPING A TO Z
BOOKS
⊙ **Academic Bookstore.** Pohjoisesplanadi 39. ☎ **09/121-41.** Tram: 3B.

Sprawling over two floors crammed with books in many languages, this store (judging from the number of titles in stock) could be the largest bookstore in Europe. It offers many English-language books, along with a number of travel aids. It also has the finest stationery department in Finland and sells greeting cards as well as high-quality gift and hobby articles. If you're here on a Friday, you can attend a literary get-together in the store, which brings together writers and members of the reading public. All of Finland's major authors and leading politicians, and many foreign writers (including Kurt Vonnegut and Norwegian actress Liv Ullmann), have attended these meetings. The building, with large skylit windows and Carrara marble slabs, was designed by Aalto.

DEPARTMENT STORES
⊙ **Stockmann.** Aleksanterinkatu 52. ☎ **09/1211.** Tram: 3B.

Helsinki's largest department store is also Finland's finest and oldest. Its main entrance is on Aleksanterinkatu, with other entrances on Keskuskatu, Pohjoisesplanadi, and Mannerheimintie. Stockmann has a little bit of everything, the most diversified sampling of Finnish and imported merchandise of any store: glassware, stoneware, ceramics, lamps, furniture, furs, contemporary jewelry, clothes and textiles, handmade candles, reindeer hides—everything. Purchases made through the store's Export Service entitle you to a full and immediate 18% deduction, and you don't have to carry your purchases home with you.

FASHION
Annikki Karvinen. Pohjoisesplanadi 23. ☎ **09/6811-750.** Tram: 3B.

Ms. Karvinen became famous for elevating *poppana,* Finnish cotton, into the stellar peaks of fashion. All poppana fabrics are hand-woven, and Ms. Karvinen has adapted the same style to velvet, silk, and viscose for more formal and more expensive fashion. She designs jackets for both indoors and outdoors. In addition, her outlet offers tablecloths, bedspreads, and other household items for sale.

Lepisto Leather Boutique. Pohjoisesplandi 27. ☎ **09/625-558.** Tram: 3B, 3T, or 4. Bus: 18.

This boutique manufactures and sells high-quality leather garments for men and women. The organization is known for its Finnish leather fashion, especially reindeer skin (in both suede and leather). The creative force behind this ship, Kari Lepistö, is one of the most creative leather designers in the Nordic world.

Marimekko. Pohjoisesplanadi 2. ☎ **09/686-02-40.** Tram: 3B.

Ever since the early 1960s when Jacqueline Kennedy was photographed wearing Marimekko outfits, the name has been familiar to Americans. Meaning "Mary's frock," Marimekko offers a large variety of prints in vivid colors splashed against the gray Finnish landscape of winter. The company, founded in 1951 by Armi Ratia, now includes a collection of unusually textured fabrics sold by the yard for decorating homes and offices. Equally important are the dresses, suits, coats, bags, interior accessories, and many other goods that are sold here, including Marimekko's famous striped T-shirts and dresses. The inventory of shirts and colors changes with the season.

Pentik Boutique. Fabianinkatu 14. ☎ **09/174-320.** Tram: 3B or 3T.

Come here for clever inventions carved from Finnish wood, usually birch. Look for costume jewelry, kitchenware, dining plates, wall ornaments, and just about everything else that might be fashioned from whatever grows up through the rocky Finnish soil.

Ril's Concept Store. Pohjoisesplanadi 25. ☎ **09/174-500.** Tram: 3B, 3T, or 4. Bus: 18.

This women's boutique highlights the designs of Kuopio, Finland-born Ritva Lisa Pohjolainen, who is currently enjoying international attention from the fashion industry—and giving Marimekko some serious competition in the process. The designer creates innovative, daring styles, for business and social engagements, that are favored by various female members of the Finnish government and the media.

Tarja Niskanen. Korkovuorenkatu 4. ☎ **09/624-022.** Tram: 3B or 3T.

This is the most famous milliner in Finland, known for designing attractive head gear that protects women from the rigors of the Finnish winter. Don't expect delicate "picture hats" here—the emphasis is on warmth. Heavy-duty designs made from fur, leather, or velvet range in price from about 500 FIM ($77) for a velvet hat to about 3,000 FIM ($462) for something made from sable.

GIFTS

Anne's Shop. Fredrikinkatu 68. ☎ **09/445-823.** Tram: 3B or 3T.

Opposite the Temppeliaukio Church, this shop offers tax-free shopping. It also has some of the finest gifts in town, including Finnish knives, wood and ceramic products, dolls and hats from Lapland, wool sweaters, reindeer skin, and jewelry.

Kiseleff Bazaar Hall. Aleksanterinkatu 28. Tram: 3B, 3T, or 4.

This shopping quarter in the old center of Helsinki, between the cathedral and Market Square, contains a group of small, specialized shops that sell lots of unique gifts. Here you can find handcrafts, souvenirs, old-fashioned toys, antiques, sauna accessories, knives, and Christmas decorations.

GLASS, PORCELAIN & CERAMICS

✪ **Hackman Shop Arabia.** Pohjoisesplanadi 25. ☎ **0204/393-501.** Tram: 3B.

This shop assembles under one roof the products of some of the world's most prestigious manufacturers of household porcelain and art ceramics. Most of the goods are made by Arabia, although some Finnish-made glass and art glass by Nuutajarvi Ittala are also offered. Located in the center of Helsinki's most prestigious shopping district, it inventories first-rate household goods by Finland's leading designers. The multilingual staff can arrange for any of your purchases to be mailed home.

Arabia was established in a suburb of Helsinki (Arabia) in 1873. Today its ceramic factories are among the most modern in the world. Arabia's artists create their own works, sometimes in highly collectible limited editions.

Although most visitors buy their goods at the company's main store, Hackman Shop Arabia maintains a small museum and a spacious discount sales area at its factory 3 miles east of the center at Hämeentie 135 (☎ **0204/393-500**). Here, discontinued styles and slightly imperfect seconds are available at significant reductions off the regular prices. To reach the suburban factory, take tram no. 6 to the end of the line or, between June and mid-September, take Arabia's special bus (it's hard to miss, since it's covered with Arabia signs) from a point near the main store. The free bus runs hourly Monday to Saturday from 10am to 4pm.

HANDCRAFTS

Aarikka. Pohjoisesplanadi 25–27. ☎ **09/652-277.** Tram: 3B.

This shop carries one of Finland's best selections of gifts, wooden and silver jewelry, and wooden toys. Unusual household utensils, fashioned from wood, are also available.

Artisaani. Unioninkatu 28. ☎ **09/665-225.** Tram: 3B.

Near Market Square, Artisaani is a cooperative of about 20 artisans who sell their own arts and crafts direct from their country workshops. Ceramic sculptures; pottery; glassware; gold, silver, and bronze jewelry; leather goods; printed fabrics; and other textiles are displayed.

Kalevala Koru. Unioninkatu 25. ☎ **09/171-520.** Tram: 3B.

Although this store is best known for its collection of jewelry, it also offers a fine collection of handcrafts and gifts. Its extensive knitwear, in both traditional and modern designs, includes pullovers, caps, and mittens for both men and women.

Ryijypalvelu. Abrahamink 7, Esplanadi. ☎ **09/660-615.** Tram: 6.

A well-stocked second-floor shop specializing in *ryas* (Finnish woven goods) is operated by the Women's Organization of the Disabled War Veterans' Association to raise money for Finland's disabled veterans. You can also buy kits for producing the same rugs at home for about one-third the price.

Suomen Käsityön Ystävät (Friends of Finnish Handcraft). Runeberginkatu 40. ☎ **09/612-6050.** Tram: 3B or 3T.

Suomen Käsityön Ystävät was founded in 1879 to develop and preserve the traditions of Finnish handcrafts. Some of the designs are more than a century old, and others, introduced by well-known Finnish artists, are fresh and contemporary. If you want to save money and produce something with your own hands, you can purchase complete rug and embroidery kits. Here you can see a permanent exhibit of museum-quality *ryijy* tapestries. Textiles, table linens, towels, and gift items, such as shawls and embroidered work—including early 20th-century Jugendstil patterns—can be purchased here. Shipping service is available.

JEWELRY

Galerie Björn Weckström. Unioninkatu 30. ☎ **09/656-529.** Tram: 3T.

Specializing in Lapponia jewelry, as well as sculpture and glass, this store has won Grand Prix prizes in international jewelry competitions. Björn Weckström has earned a reputation for nature-inspired shapes, and the jewelry here has been called "miniature sculptures." The glass collection of bowls, vases, and sculptures sometimes comes in lovely, mysterious colors whose exact ingredients remain a secret of the manufacturer.

✪ **Kalevala Koru.** Unioninkatu 25. ☎ **09/68-60-400.** Tram: 3B.

Founded in 1937, this store is owned by the Association of Kalevala Women in Finland, whose aim is to preserve the best cultural traditions of a long-ago Finland. They accomplish this through educational programs and through sales of the most authentic reproductions of traditional designs and styles they can find. (See "Handcrafts," above, for some of their offerings.) The name of their organization is derived from the *Kalevala,* the Finnish national epic.

The store sells both traditional and modern jewelry in bronze, silver, and gold. Many of these pieces are based on originals uncovered in archaeological excavations that date from the 10th and 11th centuries. Each is produced by some of Finland's foremost artisans. Copies of Lapp jewelry are also sold. The store cooperates with the Finnish National Museum.

MUSIC

Digelius Music. Laivurinrinne 2. ☎ **09/666-375.** Tram: 3B or 3T.

This store has the best selection of Finnish folk music and jazz in the country, as well as one of the largest offerings of folk music in Europe (about 10,000 titles). The store provides mail-order service to customers worldwide.

Fuga. Kaisaniemenkatu 7. ☎ **09/7001-82-51.** Tram: 2, 3B, or 6.

This is one of the best music stores in Helsinki, with classical recordings from all over Europe, as well as folk and a smattering of jazz. One of the two Nuotio brothers can offer advice.

SAUNA

✪ **Sauna Soppi-Shop.** Eteläranta 14. ☎ **09/668-9970.** Tram: 3B.

Two Finnish women established this shop in 1974 because they believe in the therapeutic and emotional benefits of sauna rituals. Everything sold here is functionally important to the sauna. They offer buckets, ladles, thermometers, linen seat covers, washing mitts, loincloths, and even a sauna "visitors' book." This may be the most complete selection of sauna-related articles in the world.

SCULPTURE

Galleria Sculptor. Eteläranta 12. ☎ **09/621-6337.** Tram: 3B.

The organization that maintains this store, the Association of Finnish Sculptors, was originally established in 1910. Today it's the oldest artists' association in Finland, comprising 230 carefully screened members and 200 somewhat less active members. Works exhibited here must be by Finnish members who are living (or deceased within the past 2 years). Sculptures—crafted from wood, bronze, stone, plastic, aluminum, steel, or ceramics—range from small medallions to monumental pieces.

SHOPPING COMPLEXES

Forum Shopping Center. Mannerheimintie 20. Tram: 3B, 3T, 7A, or 7B.

Covering an entire block, the Forum includes 120 shops, restaurants, and service enterprises—making it the number-one shopping center in Finland. There's a seven-story atrium. You'll find a wide array of merchandise here, including art, gold, jewelry, food, decorating items, clothing, yarns, leather, records, glasses, rugs, watches, and sporting goods.

Itäkeskus Shopping Complex. Itäkeskus. ☎ **09/343-1005.** Metro: Itäkeskus.

This complex of shops and restaurants opened in 1992 in a residential suburb a 15-minute subway ride east of Helsinki's center. It has some resemblance to an American shopping mall, but the emphasis is on Scandinavian and Finnish merchandise. You'll find at least 180 shops, including about 20 kiosks and food stalls.

Kämp Galleria. Pohjoisesplanadi 33. Tram: 3B or 3T.

This is Helsinki's most desirable shopping arcade, with a cluster of about 50 mostly upscale shops, set close to the newly developed Hotel Kämp.

9 Helsinki After Dark

In recent years Helsinki has seen an explosion of nighttime possibilities. Friday and Saturday nights are impossibly overcrowded, so if you plan to go out, you need to show up early at a club, or you may not get in. The older crowd sticks mainly to bars in popular hotels, such as the Strand Inter-Continental.

Nearly all theatrical performances are presented in Finnish or Swedish. However, music is universal, and the Helsinki cultural landscape is always rich in music whatever the season. The major orchestral and concert performances take place in Finlandia Hall (see "Classical Music & Concerts," below). Operas at the Finnish National Opera are sung in their original languages.

The main agency for theater, concert, and opera tickets is **Ticket Service Finland (Lippupalvelu),** Mannerheimintie 5 (☎ **09/0600-100-20**), in the center.

Your best source of information—virtually your only source, other than Finnish newspapers—is a little magazine called *Helsinki Guide,* distributed free at most hotels and at the tourist office. It has complete listings, not only of cultural events, but of practically anything that's happening in the Finnish capital—from the Baltic herring market to body-building contests.

THE PERFORMING ARTS
THEATER

Suomen Kansallisteatteri (Finnish National Theater). Läntinen Teatterikuja 1B. ☎ **09/1733-1331.** Tickets 60–110 FIM ($9.25–$16.95). Tram: 3B.

The Finnish National Theater enjoys international fame because of its presentations of the classics of Finland and many other countries; each play, however, is performed in Finnish. The theater itself, one of the architectural gems of 19th-century Helsinki, was established in 1872 and stages about 10 premieres a year.

Svenska Teatern (Swedish Theater). Norra Esplanaden 2. ☎ **09/616-21411.** Tickets 90–150 FIM ($13.85–$23.10). Tram: 3B.

If you speak Swedish, you might want to attend a performance at the horseshoe-shaped Swedish Theater, which has been presenting plays since 1866. The theater is in the absolute center of Helsinki, opposite Stockmann Department Store. The theatrical season begins in early September and runs through May. The box office is open Monday 10am to 6pm, Tuesday to Friday 10am to 7pm, and Saturday noon to 7pm. The theater is closed on Sunday.

OPERA & BALLET

✪ **Finnish National Opera.** Helsinginkatu 58. ☎ **09/4030-2211.** Tickets 50–500 FIM ($7.70–$77). Tram: 3B.

The ballet and opera performances of the Finnish National Opera enjoy international fame. Operas are sung in their original languages. The original Finnish National Opera was built in the 1870s as a Russian garrison theater, but in 1993 the opera house moved to its new home. The ticket office is open Monday to Friday 9am to 6pm and Saturday 3 to 6pm. On performance nights, the ticket office stays open until the performance begins. The opera and ballet season runs from September to June.

CLASSICAL MUSIC & CONCERTS

Helsingin Kaupunginorkesteri (Helsinki Philharmonic Orchestra). Finlandia Hall, Karamzininkatu 4. ☎ **09/40-241.** Tickets 80–120 FIM ($12.30–$18.50). Tram: 3B.

The oldest symphony orchestra in Scandinavia performs from September to May in the gracefully modern Finlandia Hall, designed by Alvar Aalto of white Carrara marble.

Just a short distance from the town center, it's the musical nerve center of Finland. The box office opens at 6pm, and all concerts begin at 7pm. For information and reservations, call ☎ 09/6138-6246.

THE CLUB & MUSIC SCENE
NIGHTCLUBS/CABARET

Baker's Family. Mannerheimintie 12. ☎ **09/612-6330.** Cover Sept–May only, 30 FIM ($4.60). Tram: 3B.

Although it has been reconfigured, redecorated, and reincarnated many times since it was established in 1915, Baker's Family is the most deeply entrenched, long-lived drinking and dining complex in Helsinki. It sprawls across three floors, and on a busy night is often crammed with nightclubbers—many of them single. The effect sometimes resembles an upscale railway station, where food and drink are dispensed with gusto, dance music plays, and the roulette wheel of a small-stakes casino whirs. Most people come for the cafe, open daily 7am to 4am, or for one of the bars, open Monday to Saturday 11am to 4am. If you're hungry, a restaurant (which can be reached through the rest of the complex or from a separate entrance on Kalevankatu 2) serves fish dishes, such as salmon, and meat dishes, such as grilled steaks, Monday to Saturday 11am to 1am. Fixed-price menus cost 95 to 175 FIM ($14.65 to $26.95). If you want to dance, a club supplies hot music, sometimes Latino-derived, Wednesday to Saturday 9pm to 4am.

Club Cream. Erottajan 7. ☎ **09/680-2665.** Cover 20–40 FIM ($3.10–$6.15), depending on the night and act. Tram: 3B, 3T.

This, one of the newest dance clubs in Helsinki, offers two floors of space, two animated bars, lots of night owls under 35 from all Finnish subcultures, and powerful references to whatever's happening in nightlife circles of London and Los Angeles. Thursday night is Latino night; Friday and Saturday house and garage music reign supreme. Open nightly from 9pm to 4am.

Hesperia Hotel Nightclub. In the Radisson SAS Hesperia Hotel Helsinki, Mannerheimintie 50. ☎ **09/431-01.** Cover 30–40 FIM ($4.60–$6.15). Tram: 4, 7, and 10.

The largest nightclub in Helsinki fills most of the cellar of a well-known hotel along one of the city's showcase boulevards. Renovated and upgraded in 1998, and outfitted in pale grays with touches of red, it hosts live bands (jazz, rock, soul, blues, or whatever) every Tuesday, Wednesday, and Thursday, and a well-trained DJ every Friday and Saturday, when the focus is on high-energy dancing. No one under 24 is admitted inside, and the revelers range from 24 to around 38 years old. Open Wednesday to Sunday 9pm to 2am.

Storyville. Museokatu 8. ☎ **09/408-007.** Cover 30–45 FIM ($4.60–$6.95). Tram: 4, 7, or 10.

One of the busiest and most active live music venues in Helsinki was named after the fabled red-light district of New Orleans, and as such, focuses on a menu of Créole and Cajun specialties that match. It occupies the street level and cellar of a building in the heart of town, and has an open-minded policy that offers full restaurant service to anyone who wants it, but doesn't pressure anyone into dining who doesn't want to. Full meals average 100 to 200 FIM ($19 to $38) each. More important, live music—blues, jazz, Dixieland, soul, or funk—is heard nightly from 8pm to 3:30am.

Tenth Floor. Hotel Vaakuna, Asemaaukio 2. ☎ **09/131-181.** Cover 30 FIM ($4.60) Fri–Sat. Tram: 3, 4, 6, 7, or 10.

Set on the uppermost floor of a well-known Helsinki hotel, amid an unobtrusive decor with views that stretch out over the city, this is one of the capital's most popular and animated discos. Open Monday to Saturday 9pm to 4am, it plays the kind of dance music you might have expected in London or Los Angeles. No one under 24 is admitted. Although most of the clients are 24 to 35-ish, some clients in their 50s seem to enjoy the spectacle of the animated dancing from their bar-stool perches.

ROCK

Tavastia Club. Urho Kekkosenk 4–6. ☎ **09/694-3066.** Cover 50–150 FIM ($7.70–$23.10). Tram: 4 or 7.

The most visible emporium for rock and roll is Tavastia, a battered, all-purpose room whose venue changes with every rock group that performs. Don't expect any semblance of a regularly maintained schedule, as everything is very iffy, depending only on the ability of management to book acts from Finland and abroad, and then on that group's ability to show up on time. It includes everything from heavy metal to blues and soul, and is likely to attract many Finnish students, some of them into punk rock, in their early 20s. Local newspapers, plus flyers distributed in counterculture sites throughout the city, publicize this place's upcoming events.

DANCE CLUBS

Club König. Mikonkatu 4. ☎ **09/6844-0713.** No cover. Tram: 3B or 3T.

In the restaurant's cellar is a smoky, cramped, and convivial nightclub, the Club König, open Monday to Saturday from 9pm to 4am. Club-goers range in age from 25 to 55, and many of the regular barflies here seem to know one another since forever.

The Hype Club. In the Ramada Presidentti Hotel, Eteläranta Rautatiekatu 4. ☎ **09/6911.** Cover 30 FIM ($4.60); free for guests of the Ramada Presidentti Hotel. Tram: 3B or 3T.

In the cellar of one of the city's largest hotels, this is the place to go if you love to dance. The DJs play the latest hits in house music, and the crowd is young and energetic. It's open Friday to Saturday 10pm to 4am.

Kaarle XII. Kasarmikatu 40. ☎ **09/612-9990.** No cover. Tram: 3B.

This is a tried-and-true, much-visited, much-battered nightclub where a congenial crew of locals get together, get rowdy, sometimes drink too much, and generally try to flirt with newcomers. Some of them, according to management, even met their future partners here thanks to chance encounters on otherwise cold Helsinki nights. The most crowded nights, when lines form outside, are Thursday, Saturday, and to a lesser degree, Friday. Named in honor of a long-deceased Swedish king, the club contains a street-level pub, an upstairs disco, and a total of six bars. The decor is plush, albeit a bit battered, and nostalgic. It's open Tuesday and Wednesday from noon to 11pm, Thursday to Saturday from noon to 3am. Beer costs 25 FIM ($3.85) per mugful. The only food service here, other than sandwiches dispensed at the bars, is within a small-scale restaurant—a refuge from the milling crowd—that seats only 35 at a time. Open Tuesday to Saturday from 6pm to midnight, it charges from 92 to 125 FIM ($14.15 to $19.25) for a main course.

THE BAR SCENE
PUBS

Corona Bar for Billiards. Eerikinkatu 11. ☎ **09/642-002.** Tram: 1.

Although it has one of the largest collections of pool tables in Helsinki (nine of them, each positioned into a high-energy cluster at the back of the premises), most of the hip young people who gravitate here don't really bother with them. Gathered at the bar near the entrance are lots of actors and writers, most of them under 35, enjoying the raffish and sometimes raucous ambience that might remind you of an urban scene in Los Angeles or New York—except all the characters happen to be Finnish. Pints of beer cost from 22 to 30 FIM ($3.40 to $4.60) each; sandwiches are available if you're hungry. If you are interested in actually playing pool, a table rents for 35 to 44 FIM ($5.40 to $6.80) per hour, depending on the time of day. (*Caution:* Some Finns are avid gamblers, so be alert to the possibility that your friendly billiards game with a local might be riskier than you imagined.) The place is open daily 11am to 2am.

O'Malley's Pub. In the Sokos Torni Hotel, Yrjönkatu 26. ☎ **09/131-131.** Tram: 3B.

This is a cramped, convivial, and gregarious pub, one of the most popular, that evokes the spirit, legend, and lore of Ireland—despite the Finnish doorman and clientele. Bar snacks are available, although they appear to be an afterthought to an evening otherwise devoted to drinking and more drinking, which, along with animated conversation, rules the night. Beer costs 20 to 26 FIM ($3.10 to $4). O'Malley's is open Monday to Saturday from 10am to about 1 or 2am, depending on the night. Live music, usually from an Irish-derived rock band, is presented 2 nights a week, often Monday and Tuesday nights.

THE BARS

Atelier Bar. In the Sokos Torni Hotel, Yrjönkatu 26. ☎ **09/131-131.** Tram: 3, 4, or 10.

On the top floor of the famous old Sokos Torni Hotel (see "Accommodations," above), site of many well-documented episodes of espionage during the Second World War, this is one of Helsinki's most famous bars, yet many foreign visitors never find it. It welcomes many local artists and writers, who don't seem to mind the cramped space. The walls are decorated with original paintings, some of them by regular patrons. Take the elevator up as far as it will go, but then you must navigate a narrow iron staircase. Drinks cost 35 FIM ($5.40), and beer prices begin at 24 FIM ($3.70). It's open Monday to Saturday 3:30pm to 1am and Sunday 3pm to midnight.

König Restaurant Bar. Mikonkatu 4. ☎ **09/6844-0713.** Tram: 3B or 3T.

Visiting diplomats and the haute bourgeoisie like this landmark restaurant and bar (see "Dining," above). Established in 1892, the bar was designed by Eliel Saarinen, one of Finland's greatest architects. The bar is paneled with wood and sheathed in carefully restored leather wallpaper. Portraits of the most famous patrons of the 1930s hang on the walls (something of a historical gallery of Finland's famous), and the food is relatively inexpensive, considering the poshness of the place. You can come here just to drink, although a bar menu lists such items as club sandwiches and salads priced at 35 to 45 FIM ($5.40 to $6.95). It's open Monday to Wednesday 11:30am to midnight, Thursday and Friday 11:30am to 1am, and Saturday 1pm to 1am.

The Lobby Bar. In the Hotel Klaus Kurki, Bulevardi 2. ☎ **09/618-911.** Tram: 3B, 3T, or 6.

On the street level of the Hotel Klaus Kurki, this fashionable bar is vividly scarlet, with formal architectural details and a hanging collection of 19th-century engravings. Find yourself a cubbyhole in the labyrinth of seating arrangements and perhaps order the bartender's special, a "Finnish Marguerita" (Finnish vodka, Cointreau, and lemon juice). The bar is open Monday to Saturday 3 to 11pm.

Palace Bar. In the Palace Hotel, Eteläranta 10. ☎ **09/134-561.** Tram: 3B. Bus: 16.

It has been suggested that if Betty Grable and Marilyn Monroe were trying to figure out *How to Marry a Millionaire* today, they'd come to this lofty retreat. Now a fashionable bar in a fashionable hotel, this 11th-floor room actually dates from the 1960s when it was originally designed as a men's toilet! Those memories are all but forgotten today in this charming little bar with glowing paneling and nautical accessories. In summer, tables are placed on an outdoor terrace that overlooks the harbor. Special cocktails include Singapore Slings. Drinks cost 40 FIM ($6.15). The bar is open Monday to Thursday 11am to 1am, Friday 11am to 2am, and Saturday 1pm to 2am.

GAMBLING CASINOS

Several Helsinki nightclubs have small-stakes casinos—usually just a roulette wheel with an attractive croupier and a deliberately low maximum bet. For more serious action, head directly for Casino Ray (see below).

Casino Ray. In the Ramada Presidentti Hotel, Eteläinen Rautatiekatu 4. ☎ **09/680-800.** Tram: 3B or 3T.

This is Finland's only large-stakes casino (although a handful of betting parlors operate on cruise ships in offshore waters). Here, on the second floor of one of the city's largest hotels, maximum bets can range from 10 to 20,000 FIM ($1.55 to $3,080) in blackjack, *Punto Banco,* Red Dog, Money Wheel, and roulette; smaller sums can be used in nearly 120 slot machines on the premises. Non-Finns must show their passport at the door and pay a first-time registration fee of 10 FIM ($1.55) for a weekly casino card. Roulette and blackjack are played daily from noon to 4am; the slot machines are open daily from 2pm to 4am.

GAY & LESBIAN NIGHTLIFE

Con Hombres. Eerikinkatu 14. ☎ **09/608-826.** No cover. Tram: 3B or 4, 7, or 10.

Most of the clientele at this dark but accommodating bar are gay men, and although the energy level might be a bit lower than you might have expected, it's viewed as an important link in the small-scale world of Finnish gay life. You'll almost certainly be able to strike up a dialogue with someone here, at least after the second drink. The place has two bars on a single ground-floor setting: one blue, one green. Literally translated from Spanish, Con Hombres means "with guys" or "among guys." It's open daily from 4pm to 2am.

Don't Tell Mama. Annankatu 32. ☎ **09/694-1122.** Cover Fri–Sat nights only 25 FIM ($3.85). Tram: 1, 4.

This is the largest and most visible gay bar in Finland, with a central location and a two-story format that's painted a Nordic shade of blue. About 80% of the clientele is gay and male; the remaining 20% is for the most part lesbian. Look for two very active and busy bar areas, recorded music, Finns and other Europeans from every walk of life, and a particular emphasis on disco every Friday and Saturday, the only nights there's ever a cover charge imposed. It's open every night from 10pm to 4am. In some ways, this place is the envy of many straight folk who like to dance, as the energy on the dance floor, and the cutting-edge music, is said by insiders to be the best in Helsinki.

Lost & Found. Annankatu 6. ☎ **09/680-1010.** No cover. Tram: 1, 4.

This is Helsinki's "other" gay bar, although with a higher percentage of straight people than at Don't Tell Mama. You'll find a larger-than-expected disco that sprawls over two floors, each with a busy bar area and lots of Europeans from outside Finland. It's open nightly from 10pm till around 4am. There's no cover charge, but the coat check will cost you around 8 FIM ($1.25).

Nalle Pub. Kaarlenkatu 3–5. ☎ **09/701-5543.** No cover. Tram 3, 3B, or 3T.

This was the premier lesbian bar in Helsinki, with a devoted following and a reputation as a rendezvous site for the country's tightly knit network of gay women. Many gay men also like to patronize the place. Set about a half-mile north of the city's commercial core, it's open daily from 3pm to 2am, and has an active billiard table, a large bar area, recorded music, and a strong sense of community.

10 Side Trips from Helsinki

PORVOO (BORGÅ)

30 miles NE of Helsinki

This colorful hamlet gives visitors a look at what a small town in this area was like a century or so ago—it's the second-oldest town in Finland. Simply strolling the Old Quarter with its narrow, winding streets is a fun way to spend an afternoon.

Founded as a Swedish town in 1346 at the mouth of a river, Porvoo was already an important trading center in the Middle Ages. Even before the town was given its charter, the Swedes had a wooden fortress on a hill that helped control river and sea trade for several centuries. After Sweden finally relinquished Finland to Russia, Porvoo was the site of the first Finnish Diet in the early 19th century, when Tsar Alexander I made the little country a Grand Duchy.

Many of Porvoo's residents still consider themselves Swedes, and almost half the town's population speaks Swedish and clings to the old Swedish name for this town, Borgå.

The most important industry here today is the publishing firm of Werner Söderström, established in 1853, one of the largest in Scandinavia.

ESSENTIALS

GETTING THERE   The most interesting way to go to Porvoo is on the MS *J. L. Runeberg,* which sails May 19 to September 1 from Market Square in Helsinki on Wednesday to Tuesday only. A round-trip ticket costs 165 FIM ($25.40) for adults, 75 FIM ($11.55) for children. For bookings and inquiries, contact **J. L. Runeberg** (☎ **019/524-33-31**).

VISITOR INFORMATION   The **Porvoo Tourist Office** is at Rihkamakatu 20, SF-06100 Porvoo (☎ **019/520-2316**). In summer only, it's open Monday to Friday 10am to 6pm, and Saturday and Sunday 10am to 4pm. Otherwise, hours are Monday to Friday 10am to 4:30pm and Saturday 10am to 2pm.

SEEING THE SIGHTS

If you arrive in Porvoo by boat, you'll get a good view of the old merchants' houses and warehouses along the waterfront—most dating from the 18th century.

Cathedral of Porvoo. Kirkkotori. ☎ **019/661-1250.** Free admission. May–Sept, Mon–Fri 10am–6pm, Sat 10am–2pm, Sun 2–5pm; Oct–Apr, Tues–Sat 10am–2pm, Sun 2–4pm.

The oldest part of the present granite building dates from the late 13th century or early 14th century. The church has since been plundered or even burned down several times. It became a cathedral in 1723 when the Episcopal see was moved from Viipuri to Porvoo. The church was once attended by Alexander I of Russia.

Johan Ludvig Runeberg House. Aleksanterinkatu 3. ☎ **019/581-330.** Admission 20 FIM ($3.10) adults, 10 FIM ($1.55) children 5–15, free for children under 5. May–Aug, Mon–Sat 10am–4pm, Sun 11am–5pm; Sept–Apr, Wed–Sat 10am–4pm, Sun 11am–5pm.

Porvoo is particularly proud of its association with the Finnish national poet Johan Ludvig Runeberg, who spent the last 25 years of his life here. His home, in the center of town, is now a museum. Works of the poet's son, the sculptor Walter Runeberg, can be seen here, including an interesting statue of his father. Johan Ludvig Runeberg is buried in the old cemetery west of the river.

Porvoo Museum. Valikatu 11. ☎ **019/574-7589.** Admission 20 FIM ($3.10) adults, 5 FIM (75¢) children under 16. May–Aug, daily 11am–4pm; Sept–Apr, Wed–Sun noon–4pm.

This museum's collections are housed in two buildings, the **Historical Museum** in the Old Town Hall and the art collection in the **Edelfelt-Vallgren Museum,** originally a merchant's house. The stone buildings stand on Museum Square (also known as Old Town Hall Square) in the Old Town, and both buildings display artifacts from the 1700s that survived the big fires in 1760 and the 1800s. The art museum also has collections of Finnish art nouveau furniture and ceramics.

WHERE TO DINE

Wanha Laamanni. Vuorikatu 17. ☎ **019/523-04-55.** Reservations recommended. Main courses 90–129 FIM ($13.85–$19.85), 1-course fixed-price lunch (winter only) 95 FIM ($14.65). AE, DC, MC, V. Summer, daily 11am–midnight; off-season, Mon–Fri 11am–10pm, Sat–Sun noon–8pm. FINNISH.

Originally constructed as a private house near the medieval cathedral, this late Gustavian-style restaurant (whose name translates as "The Old Judge's Chambers") has an 18th-century decor. The chef turns out many excellent Finnish specialties. Begin with such appetizers as Russian blini with roe, or perhaps wild mushrooms in sour cream marinated in cloves of garlic, or even soup (possibly black salsify with sweet pepper). Main dishes include Baltic herring stewed in sour cream, a delectable grilled salmon with wild-mushroom sauce, and fillet of beef in a green-pepper and beetroot sauce.

HYVINKÄÄ
35 miles N of Helsinki

This young town, which received its charter as recently as 1960, has long been linked to Finland's railway network and is visited today chiefly because of its National Railway Museum (see below). Only 35 miles north of Helsinki, Hyvinkää can be reached by "H train," which leaves twice an hour from Helsinki's Central Station, and by car, which takes an hour on Route 3. Buses bearing the sign hyvinkää also arrive here from the Helsinki bus station.

This rapidly growing industrial and commercial center is in a very scenic part of Finland. Visitors can walk through **Hyvinkää Sveitsi,** the "Switzerland of Hyvinkää," a park within walking distance of the center of town, which has marked and lit walking paths and skiing tracks of various lengths. It also has a jogging track and ski slopes and jumps.

Hyvinkää's connection with the railway dates from 1862, when the link was added between Hämeenlinna and Helsinki. This railway culture is preserved in the **Finnish Railway Museum,** in the center of town at Hyvinkäänkatu 9 (☎ **019/456-4241**). The museum is housed in the original railway buildings dating from the 1870s. Exhibits include the oldest steam engine preserved in Finland, *Passi,* from 1868; Finland's oldest rail car, a Fiat from 1914; and a model railway, the largest of its kind in the country. But our favorite exhibit is a three-coach imperial train dating from the 1870s. Built for the Russian tsar, the imperial coach train originally consisted of five coaches: two for the tsar and tsarina, a saloon, a dining room, and a kitchen. The railway museum, established in Helsinki in 1898, was transferred to Hyvinkää in 1974. It's open June to August 15 daily 11am to 5pm; otherwise Tuesday to Saturday noon to 3pm and Sunday noon to 5pm. Admission is 30 FIM ($4.60) for 16 and over, 15 FIM ($2.30) for ages 7 to 15, and children 6 and under enter for free.

HÄMEENLINNA

61 miles N of Helsinki

Finland's oldest town (founded in 1639), Hämeenlinna (Tavastehus in Swedish) is one of the starting points for **cruises** on the Silja Line vessels (Suomen Hopealinja), which run to Tampere or along the scenic route to the ridge of Kangasala. Hämeenlinna is also the starting point for a series of 1-day cruises, the most popular of which goes to the Aulanko Tourist Center and to sculptor Emil Wikström's studio museum, Visavuori. If you go on one of these cruises, your car can be driven by the car-pilot service to await your arrival.

The **Hämeenlinna City Tourist Information Office,** Sibeliuksenkatu 5A (☎ 03/ 621-23-88), is open June to August, Monday to Friday 9am to 5pm and Saturday 9am to 2pm; September to May, Monday to Friday 9am to 5pm.

SEEING THE SIGHTS

The large park at **Aulanko,** about 2½ miles from the center of town, is one of the best-known tourist centers in Finland. Here you'll find a hotel (see "Where to Stay," below), a panoramic tower, tennis courts, a golf course, and a bathing beach.

Häme Castle. Kustaa III Katu 6. ☎ **03/675-6820.** Admission 20 FIM ($3.10) adults, 10 FIM ($1.55) children 7–17, free for children under 7. May to mid-Aug, daily 10am–6pm; mid-Aug to Apr, daily 10am–4pm. Bus: 5 or 12 from the marketplace.

Häme Castle dominates the town. Construction has been going on here for 700 years. The oldest sections date from the 1260s and are known as the fortified camp, including a square gray-stone wall with defensive towers at three corners. Once the residence of mighty nobles, the castle later became a strictly supervised outpost of the Swedish Crown. As the years went by, it served as both a granary and a prison. The main castle is now a historic monument. It houses exhibits and rents out its facilities for meetings and celebrations. There's also a summer cafe and a restaurant that can be booked for events in advance.

Sibelius Birthplace. Hallituskatu 11. ☎ **03/621-2755.** Admission 10 FIM ($1.55) adults, 5 FIM (75¢) students and children 7 and over, free for children under 7. May–Aug, daily 10am–4pm; Sept–Apr, daily noon–4pm.

The great composer Jean Sibelius was born at Hämeenlinna on December 8, 1865, in this wooden house. It stands in the center of town, about 50 yards from the marketplace. The museum is also the setting for small chamber concerts and sells tapes of Sibelius's music.

WHERE TO STAY

Hotel Cumulus. Raatihuoneenkatu 16–18, FIN-13100 Hämeenlinna (Aulanko). ☎ **03/ 648-81.** Fax 03/648-8299. 100 units. MINIBAR TV TEL. June 16–Aug 2 and Fri–Sun year-round, 430 FIM ($66.20) double; rest of year, 690 FIM ($106.25) double. Rates include breakfast and evening use of sauna. Children 13 and under stay free in parents' room with existing bedding. Additional bed 100 FIM ($15.40) extra. AE, DC, MC, V. Free parking. Bus: 2 or 13.

Next to the main commercial street of town, within walking distance of Kauppatori (Market Square), this early 1970s concrete-and-glass hotel has comfortable rooms with good beds and small bathrooms, plus an attractive Finnish restaurant, Hubiretky. There are two saunas on the premises plus a swimming pool. You can book a non-smoking room, but you must specifically request it when making your reservations. The breakfast is huge. There's a pub, Prince Albert, and a disco, Tiffany.

Rantasipi Aulanko. FIN-13210 Hämmenlinna (Aulanko). ☎ **03/658-801.** Fax 03/219-22. www.rantasipi.fi. 50 units. MINIBAR TV TEL. June 15–Aug 15 and selected weekends (Fri–Sun),

510 FIM ($78.55) double; rest of year, 710 FIM ($109.35) double. Year-round, 900 FIM ($138.60) suite. Rates include breakfast and morning use of sauna. AE, DC, MC, V. Free parking. Bus: 2 or 13.

This name is instantly recognizable throughout Finland because of the hotel's location in one of the country's best-known nature preserves. The hotel has been enlarged many times since it was originally built in the 1930s. It sits at the edge of Vanajavesi Lake near a sweep of open grassland surrounded by forested hillsides. Each room has an open-air balcony. Rooms for the most part are medium in size and functionally furnished. Bathrooms, though small, are beautifully maintained. On weekends year-round the dining room is likely to be overflowing. On the premises are tennis courts, a golf course, a labyrinth of walking paths, four saunas, a lakeside bathing beach, an indoor pool, riding stables, and a masseuse. In winter, cross-country skiing is popular. The hotel, a venue for important conferences, lies at the end of a series of prominent signs in Aulanko Park, 3 miles north of the train station at Hämeenlinna.

WHERE TO DINE

Restaurant Piparkakkutalo. In the Piparkakkutalo "Gingerbread" House, Kirkkorinne 2. ☎ **03/648040.** Reservations recommended. Main courses 60–120 FIM ($9.25–$18.50). AE, MC, V. Mon–Fri 11am–midnight, Sat noon–midnight, Sun noon–11pm. Basement-level pub, Sun–Thurs 3pm–midnight, Fri–Sat 3pm–2am. INTERNATIONAL.

The town's most charming restaurant, adjacent to the village church, within sight of the main square, occupies a historic manor house built during the 19th century as the home of a wealthy merchant. The building's name (Piparkakkutalo) translates from the Finnish as "the gingerbread cookie" because of its lavish ornamentation.

The same menu is offered on both floors of the restaurant but somehow the upstairs dining room has the distinction of being called "The Bistro." You can come here for flank steak with onions, chateaubriand, or pepper steak, but when in this part of the world, you can also try something more exotic like Lappish reindeer with juniperberry sauce. A recent pasta dish of tagliatelle with a cream and herb sauce was succulent. We followed the advice of some of the habitues and opted for a sautéed pike-perch for a main course and were glad we did. For a more raucous and sudsy time, consider dropping into O'Maggie's pub, an ode to Irish nationalism that's set in the building's cellar. Here, foaming mugs of beer are priced according to their alcohol content and a limited pub menu is available.

KOTKA

83 miles E of Helsinki

The ✪ **Langinkoski Imperial Fishing Lodge,** Langinkaski (☎ **05/228-1050**), 3 miles north of Kotka, was the imperial fishing lodge of the Russian tsar's family, the summer retreat for Alexander III from 1889 to 1894. This log house on the River Kymi offers an insight into how the last of the Romanovs lived their summers before they met violent deaths during the Russian Revolution. Near the Langinkoski Rapids (for which it was named), the lodge is open May to September only, daily 10am to 5pm; admission is 12 FIM ($1.85).

The mysterious Anastasia (youngest daughter of the assassinated Nicholas II) used to run wild along the turbulent rapids. Her girlish "A" can still be seen in the guest book.

The tsar chose a spot in Finland's premier salmon-fishing area to build the lodge (in 1889) on property consisting of half a dozen small islands connected by bridges. Its deliberately unpretentious architecture was in the Finnish style of hand-hewn pine logs, far removed from the grandeur of the family's 900-room palace outside St. Petersburg.

The tsarina often prepared the family meals herself, and the copper pots she used can still be seen. Alexander III died in 1894, and the lodge held little appeal for his son.

Information is available from the **Kotka Tourist Office,** Kyrkokatu 8 (☎ 05/ 234-4424), open June to August, Tuesday to Friday 9am to 6pm and Saturday 10am to 2pm; September to May, Monday to Friday 9am to 4pm. If you drive, Kotka is a 2-hour trip from Helsinki. There are five buses leaving Helsinki daily, traveling to Kotka in 2 hours. Once at the bus station at Kotka, you can take buses 12, 13, or 14 to the lodge at Langinkoski.

Appendix A:
Denmark in Depth

The Danes live in a small country, but they extend a big welcome to visitors. Americans and Canadians, as well as their longtime friends, the British, are enthusiastically greeted—in English. Denmark is an important stopover for any travelers who want to say they've seen the best of Europe.

Made up mostly of islands, Denmark is a heavily industrialized nation, known for its manufactured products as well as its arts and crafts. It also boasts a quarter of a million farmers.

The British novelist Evelyn Waugh (author of *Brideshead Revisited*) called the Danes "the most exhilarating people of Europe." Few Danes would dispute that—and neither would we.

1 Denmark Today

Denmark has been called a bridge because it links northern Europe with the Scandinavian peninsula. In 2000 that became truer than ever as the Øresund Bridge went across the sound connecting the island of Zealand, on which Copenhagen sits, with southern Sweden and the city of Malmö, for the first time in history.

The smallest of the Scandinavian countries, it has a total land mass of about 16,591 square miles, most of which is on the peninsula of Jutland (bordering Germany). The major islands are Zealand, Funen, and Bornholm. Denmark has adequate space for its 5.5 million or so residents, but its population density is much greater than that of the other Scandinavian countries. About 1.4 million Danes live in the capital city, Copenhagen, on the island of Zealand.

Only about 4.5% of Denmark's inhabitants are immigrants, primarily from other Nordic or European nations. About 98% of all Danes belong to the state church (Danish Lutheran), although church attendance is low. The second-largest group is Catholics (30,000), and there are about 6,500 Jews.

Technically, Denmark is a parliamentary democracy and constitutional monarchy. Its territories include the Faeroe Islands (an autonomous area) and Greenland (which was granted regional autonomy in 1985). The sovereign is Queen Margrethe II, who ascended to the throne in 1972; her husband is a Frenchman, Prince Henrik. Margrethe is the first female sovereign in Denmark in 6 centuries. Real power is vested in the unicameral parliament (the Folketing), which is

Did You Know?

- Denmark is a nation of nearly 500 islands.
- The reigning queen, Margrethe II, designs postage stamps and opera and ballet sets.
- The writings of Hans Christian Andersen are the second most widely translated literary works in the world (after the Bible).
- Some historians argue that the fairy-tale writer Andersen wasn't the son of a poor cobbler, but the child of Christian VIII.
- Denmark has the largest proportion of female clerics per population.
- The country has a celebration honoring America's Fourth of July.

elected every 4 years by all citizens over the age of 23. The royal family functions primarily in a ceremonial capacity.

Although it has been a NATO member since 1949, Denmark does not permit nuclear weapons to be deployed on its soil. Denmark became the first NATO country to grant women the right to serve in front-line units. Denmark enjoys harmonious relations with its Scandinavian neighbors and other European countries. It's also an active member of the European Union, but not part of the "Euro blanket," having voted in September 2000 to retain the Danish kroner.

Denmark enjoys one of the world's highest standards of living and has a comprehensive social welfare system, which is funded through extremely high taxes. Danes enjoy 7½-hour work days, cradle-to-grave security, state-funded hospitals and schools, and even a month-long annual vacation. During vacations, they tend to travel extensively. The Danes tend to be extremely well educated; they pioneered the establishment of adult education centers (for those ages 18 to 35), a movement that has spread to other European countries.

Although a progressive, modern, and liberal state (it was the first country to recognize same-sex marriage), Denmark has its share of problems, including high unemployment. The institution of marriage is increasingly rejected by the young, so common-law relationships are becoming the norm. The divorce rate is rising, too.

The "melancholy Dane" aspect of their character (if there is one) is reflected in a relatively high suicide rate. Otherwise, their general state of health is excellent—a Danish girl born today has a life expectancy of 78 years; a Danish boy, 72 years.

Culturally, Denmark is a world leader; its citizens are eager media consumers and avid readers. Even though it's a small country, Denmark publishes some 12,000 books a year. There are 42 newspapers; and the theater and film industries are thriving in spite of cutbacks in government funding.

Denmark in the late '90s built bridges to the world. On June 14, 1998, Queen Margrethe II cut a ribbon before driving across the Great Belt Bridge, a span that links the island of Zealand (on which Copenhagen sits) with the island of Funen. Because Funen is linked by bridge to Jutland (part of mainland Europe), Copenhageners can now drive to Germany without having to rely on ferries. Traveling time across the "Belt" has been cut by more than 1 hour compared to the ferries.

2 The Natural Environment

Denmark has more than 4,500 miles of irregular coastline and is linked geologically with northern Europe. It's a low-lying country—its highest elevation is only 565 feet above sea level. But that doesn't mean the country is flat. Most of its terrain consists of folds; undulations; small and often steep hills; and long, low rises. There are also forests, small rivers, lakes, and even beaches. Many are excellent for swimming, although the water may be too cold for some people.

The west coast of Jutland is on the North Sea, but it's not suitable for exploration by ship because it's obstructed by sand dunes and small sand banks. "Island hills" that rise from sandy plains represent the oldest glacial terrain in Denmark. Much of this landscape was formed during the last Ice Age, when icebergs carved the country into its present shape. The east coast of Jutland has fjords (such as Lim and Mariager), but they lack the drama of those on Norway's west coast. Denmark's longest river is the 80-mile Gudenå, which rises in north-central Jutland and feeds into Lake Lanso on the eastern side of the peninsula.

Winters in Denmark tend to be mild along the North Sea coast and harsh in the interior of Jutland. In general, eastern Denmark receives more precipitation than the west; in the winter, that situation is reversed.

In the east, Denmark opens toward the Baltic Sea, which surrounds its small offshore island of Bornholm. Bornholm's flora differs from that found elsewhere in the country.

Denmark's vegetation resembles that of the continent. The woods in southern Denmark are largely deciduous, with oak and birch forests. Major reforestation is under way, especially with coniferous forests, mostly pine and spruce. The most beautiful beech forests are on the island of Møn.

Humans and agriculture have reduced the living space for Denmark's native fauna, but roe, red deer, badgers, and foxes are still found. Fallow deer are widely scattered throughout the country. Birders can spot woodpeckers, robins, tits, chaffinches, and song thrushes in the Danish wetlands, which survive more or less in their natural state. The best place for bird-watching is near the Limfjord in North Jutland.

Denmark, a leader among environmentally conscious nations, has set aside 3.5% of its land mass as a protected nature reserve. That includes Rebild National Park in North Jutland, the chalk cliffs of Møn, and the tidal sands off the west coast of Jutland—one of the world's most valued wetlands.

3 History 101

Dateline

- 810 The reign of the first Danish king ends.
- 940–985 Harald Bluetooth brings Christianity to Denmark.
- 1013–42 The crowns of Denmark and England are united.
- 1397 The Union of Kalmar unites Denmark, Norway, and Sweden.

continues

The first recorded Danish king was Godfred, who died in 810. Little is known about him except that he played a significant role in halting the Frankish conquests of the Holy Roman Emperor Charlemagne. Godfred's successor, Hemming, made a treaty marking the Eider River as Denmark's southern border. It remained the border until 1864.

Two famous kings emerged in the 10th century: Gorm (883–940) and his son, Harald Bluetooth (940–985). They united Denmark, establishing its center at Jelling. Harald also introduced Christianity, which became the predominant religion.

Harald conquered Norway and attempted to conquer England. Harald's son, Sweyn I, took over England in 1013. Under Sweyn's son, Canute II (994–1035), England, Denmark, and part of Sweden came under the rule of one crown. After Canute's death, however, the kingdom was reduced to just Denmark. Canute's nephew, Sweyn II, ruled the Danish kingdom, and upon his death his five sons governed Denmark successively.

The Holy Roman Empire was the "overlord" of Denmark until the Danes established independent leadership under Archbishop Eskil (1100–1182) and King Waldemar I (1131–82). The monarchy was strong. During a celebration at Ringsted in 1190, church and state were united. Bishop Absalon (1128–1201), a soldier and statesman, is credited with restoring Danish political and ecclesiastical independence from German influences.

Waldemar II (1170–1241) helped strengthen the Danish government. His son, Eric IV (1216–50), succeeded him as king, but argued with his brothers and the church. Eric's brother, Duke Abel of Schleswig, proclaimed himself king and assassinated Eric in 1250. Civil wars ensued, and three of the four successive kings were killed in battle. Eric VI (1274–1319) also waged war with Norway and Sweden, which led to Denmark's debilitation. Between 1332 and 1340, Denmark had no king and was ruled by nobles. Waldemar IV Atterdag (1320–75) became king by signing the peace treaty of Stralsund in 1370.

UNITED SCANDINAVIA After Waldemar IV died in 1375, the dynasty was left without a male heir. Olaf, his grandson, succeeded him as king. Olaf helped unite the crowns of Denmark and Norway and inherited the Swedish throne. He was the son of Margaret (1353–1412), daughter of Waldemar, and wife of Haakon VI Magnusson (1339–80), king of Norway. Margaret actually ruled the country as regent. When both Haakon and Olaf died, she was acknowledged as queen of Norway and Denmark. An ambitious woman, she wanted to rule Norway, Sweden, and Denmark.

The Union of Kalmar came about in 1397. Margaret arranged for her nephew, Eric of

- **1471** Sweden bows out; Denmark and Norway are ruled by Christian I (1426–81).
- **1530** Lutheran preachers bring the Reformation to Denmark.
- **1577–1648** The long reign of Christian IV brings prosperity but ends in a losing war with Sweden.
- **1814** Denmark cedes Norway to Sweden.
- **1866** Denmark loses Schleswig-Holstein to Prussia.
- **1915** A new constitution gives Denmark universal suffrage.
- **1933** Denmark gains all of Greenland.
- **1940–45** Denmark is invaded and occupied by Nazi Germany.
- **1949** Over some protests, Denmark joins NATO.
- **1953** A new constitution provides for a single-chamber parliament.
- **1972** Denmark joins the European Economic Community; Margrethe, daughter of Frederik IX, becomes queen of Denmark.
- **1982** Paul Schluter becomes the first Conservative prime minister since 1894.
- **1989** Denmark becomes the first NATO country to allow women in front-line military units, and the first country to recognize same-sex marriages.
- **1992** Denmark votes against the Maastricht Treaty, which established the framework for the European Economic Union.
- **1993** Denmark resists the European Union for the first half of the year, then reverses its position and votes to support the Maastricht Treaty.

continues

- **1996** Copenhagen is designated the "Cultural Capital of Europe." The "Copenhagen 96" festival attracts artists and performers from all over the world, with more than 25,000 performances staged.
- **1998** By a narrow margin, Denmark votes to enlarge its ties with the European Union.
- **2000** Danes vote against the Euro; Øresund Bridge links the island of Zealand (Copenhagen) with Sweden.

Pomerania (1382–1459), to be crowned king of all three countries as Eric VII. Margaret, however, continued to rule until her death.

Eric VII had no heirs, so he tried to pass the kingdom on to one of his relatives in Pomerania. That didn't please the nobility, and he was dethroned in 1439. The Danish Privy Council chose Christopher of Bavaria (Eric's nephew) to become king in 1440.

Upon Christopher III's death, Sweden pressed for autonomy. It elected Charles VIII as king in 1471, and Denmark and Norway took a joint king, Christian I (1426–81).

THE 16TH CENTURY The unpopular Christian II (1481–1559) ascended the throne in 1513. Having no faith in democracy, he turned over control of the kingdom's finances to his mistress's mother. He recaptured Sweden in 1520 but was defeated a year later by Gustavus Vasa. Christian was deposed in 1522 and fled to the Netherlands.

His successor, Frederik I (1471–1533), signed a charter granting the nobility many privileges. Upon Frederik's death, the Reformation took hold in Denmark. Conflicts between Lutherans and Catholics erupted in a civil war, which ended in 1536 with the surrender of Copenhagen. The Danish Lutheran Church was founded in 1536 during the reign of Christian III (1534–59), who tried—but failed—to make the crown hereditary. Frederik II, Christian's son, was elected in 1559. Frederik launched a war against Eric XIV of Sweden, during a territorial dispute over Baltic provinces. This became the Seven Years' War of the North (1563–70), in which the Danes were overwhelmed.

WARS WITH SWEDEN Hostilities with Sweden continued, but the reign of Christian IV (1577–1648) was one of relative prosperity. Christiania (now Oslo) was named after him. However, in the closing years of his reign, Sweden invaded Jutland, defeating the Danes. Under the Treaty of Christianople, Denmark was forced to cede many of its possessions to Sweden.

Frederik III (1609–70) tried to regain the lost territories when Sweden went to war with Poland, but Charles X defeated him. Frederik ended up giving Sweden additional territory. Charles X attacked Denmark in an attempt to control the whole country, but this time Denmark won, regaining its lost territories. Sweden ended the war upon the death of Charles X in 1660.

Christian V (1646–99) started the Skaane War (1675–79), in which Denmark attempted to acquire additional territory, but it lost. Frederik IV (1671–1730), his successor, resumed the war with Sweden in 1699. Named the "Great Northern War," it raged from 1699 to 1730.

During the 18th century Denmark achieved many reforms; it also gained control of colonies in the West Indies (now the U.S. Virgin Islands) and Greenland. Agriculture and trade prospered.

THE 19TH CENTURY At the start of the Napoleonic wars, Denmark was neutral. In 1801 England destroyed the Danish fleet in Copenhagen, forcing Denmark to choose Napoleon's side. It was a disaster for Denmark. Napoleon lost the war in 1814, and peace was made at Kiel. Denmark was forced to yield

Norway to Sweden and Heligoland, an island in the North Sea, to England. Denmark sank into poverty.

Following the Napoleonic wars, the rulers Frederik VI and Christian VIII formed conservative governments. In 1848 the Danes demanded a more liberal constitution. Absolute rule was abolished, and Frederik VII established a government based on representation. The Danish constitution was signed on June 5, 1849.

In March 1848 the Schleswig-Holstein revolution began. It lasted 2 years. The Danes initially triumphed over Prussia, but in the 1866 Treaty of Prague, Denmark again lost Schleswig-Holstein to Prussia.

On July 28, 1866, a new constitution was adopted, but it was more conservative than the 1849 document. The Conservatives quickly gained power, instituting reforms and improving the economy.

THE 20TH CENTURY   When the First World War broke out, Denmark remained neutral. However, the Danes mined their waters for Germany. Denmark joined the other Scandinavian countries and adopted a uniform trade policy in November 1914. Unemployment and higher taxes marked the war years. A new constitution was signed on June 5, 1915, establishing a two-chamber parliament and granting equal voting rights to men and women. Because Germany lost the war, many people felt that all of Schleswig should be returned to Denmark, but ultimately it got only North Schleswig.

Iceland and Denmark agreed to a new treaty in 1918. Although separate sovereign states, the two countries were united under one king. The Danish armed forces represented Iceland.

Denmark participated in the creation of the League of Nations and officially joined it in 1920. A crisis arose in 1921 when Norway claimed jurisdiction over the territory of Greenland. On April 5, 1933, the Permanent Court of International Justice granted Denmark sovereignty over Greenland.

In May 1939, Hitler asked Denmark to sign a nonaggression pact. Denmark accepted; Norway and Sweden did not. The pact specified that Denmark and Germany would not go to war with each other for 10 years. When war broke out in 1939, Denmark declared its neutrality. Denmark's ties with Iceland were severed, and the United States and Great Britain occupied Greenland and the Faeroe Islands, respectively.

Despite the pact, Nazi forces invaded and occupied Denmark in 1940. In 1943 Hitler sent Gen. Hermann von Hanneken to impose martial law on Denmark. The heroic Danish resistance opposed the German occupying forces. When Germany surrendered in 1945, British troops occupied Denmark. Denmark joined the United Nations.

After the war, the Liberal Party, under Knud Kristensen, assumed control. In 1947 Kristensen resigned. The Social Democratic Party, under Hans Hedtoft, headed the new government under Frederik IX. The economy remained sluggish until 1948.

In 1949 Denmark joined NATO. In 1953 Denmark, Norway, Sweden, and Iceland formed the Scandinavian Council; it lasted until 1961. Also in 1953, Denmark adopted a new constitution, which provided for a single-chamber parliament.

In 1972 Denmark became the sole Nordic member of the European Economic Community. That year, Queen Margrethe, born in 1940 (the year of the Nazi invasion), became queen of Denmark upon the death of her father, Frederik IX.

In 1982 Denmark seemed to abandon its long-cherished liberalism when it elected Paul Schuler its first Conservative prime minister since 1894. However, by 1989 Denmark was leading the world in the development of a liberal social agenda. It became the first NATO country to allow women to join front-line military units. Later, it became the first country to recognize marriages between partners of the same sex.

The early 1990s were dominated by Denmark's continuing debate over its role (or lack of it) in the European Union. In 1992 Denmark rejected the Maastricht Treaty, which had established a framework for the European Economic Union. However, in a 1993 referendum Denmark reversed its position, voting to support the Maastricht Treaty and the country's limited involvement in it. Denmark presided over the European Union for the first part of that year.

Also in 1993, Denmark observed the 50th anniversary of the rescue of 8,000 of its Jewish citizens, who were smuggled out of the country into neutral Sweden virtually overnight. That year the Tivoli Gardens celebrated its 150th year, and *The Little Mermaid* turned 80.

In 1996 Copenhagen was named the "Cultural Capital of Europe." Following in the footsteps of Athens, Florence, Paris, and Madrid, Copenhagen celebrated with a year-long festival; exhibitions, performances, community events, and environmental programs attracted artists from around the world. The city staged more than 25,000 performances. A massive campaign of restoration and new construction revitalized the city.

In May 1998, Denmark conducted a referendum on extending its ties and connections with the European Union (EU). In a tight race, Denmark, including the North Atlantic territories of Greenland and the Faeroe Islands, voted for enlargement of its position within the EU. But the margin was so narrow that it indicated how divided Danes remain on this important issue.

THE 21ST CENTURY   Two major events occurred in the Danish republic in 2000, each expected to have far-reaching implications for the tiny nation.

It made headlines across Europe in the summer of 2000 when the Øresund Bridge officially opened, linking Sweden and Denmark. The 10-mile motor and railway link, on which construction began in the summer of 1995, gives the island of Zealand (the eastern part of Denmark) and Skåne (the southern part of Sweden) a shared bridge, serving some 3½ million inhabitants in the area.

The Øresund region, which encompasses parts of both Sweden and Denmark, is the largest domestic market in Northern Europe—larger than Stockholm and equal in size to Berlin, Hamburg, and Amsterdam combined. Built at a cost of $3 billion, it is the largest combined rail/road tunnel in the world. The price of a one-way fare in a passenger car is $30.

In theory, a vehicle can now travel in roughly a straight line from the Arctic coast of Norway to the Mediterranean shores of Spain. For centuries, it has been a dream to link the continent from its northern tip to its southern toe. The "Øresund Fixed Link" spans the city Øresund Sound between the cities of Copenhagen and Malmö.

Already the Danes, who like nicknames, have called the new span "The Beer Bridge." Denmark has cheaper prices and lower taxes than Sweden for alcoholic beverages, which sends many a Swedish motorist across the bridge to avail themselves of the lower tariffs.

The double-decker bridge, with a four-lane highway on top, plus a train link underneath, arches like a ribbon for about 5 miles over the water before descending to a 2-mile-long artificial island. From that point it drops beneath the sound into a tunnel at the Danish side.

In September of 2000, a majority of Danes voted "no" on joining the euro, the single currency of the European Union of which Denmark is a member. That "no" vote is expected to deter Britain and Sweden (two other EU countries) from participating. In Sweden, officials predicted that the Danish "no" could postpone their own entry into the euro zone indefinitely. Prime Minister Tony Blair predicted in London that the Danish vote would have no impact on Britain, but polls show public opinion hardening against the euro.

Supporters of the euro in Denmark claimed that their participation would help maintain Denmark's influence in Europe and perhaps gain the country a seat at the European Central Bank, which sets monetary police for the euro zone. Already Denmark pegs its kroner to the euro.

Opponents of the euro maintained successfully that Danish participation would end the country's independence, hasten the developing of an all-encompassing "superstate" of Europe, and eventually consume the identity of the little Danish nation.

Danes have been re-examining their political system as well, which some suggest is no longer workable or tenable. Currently, many small political parties join themselves into a series of politically expedient coalitions as the need arises. Some propose a merging of several small splinter groups into a smaller number of more powerful parties.

Denmark also bears the unusual problems of an economy that's one of the most affluent in the world. Despite an awesomely high standard of living, life in Denmark does not come without fiscal fears and neuroses. Families are burdened under a national debt that's equivalent to around 69,000 DKK ($8,625) per person; as a result, living standards are beginning to decline, subtly but inexorably.

Under pressure from growing foreign competition, Danish industry increasingly faces the need to streamline. Welfare payments, health services, and the quality of education have felt the strain of government cutbacks and austerity programs. As a result, racist condemnations of newly arrived immigrants from Asia and Africa have flared up, causing insiders to question the degree to which Denmark is really the ultra-liberal, ultra-secure nation everyone always assumed it was.

4 Dining with the Danes

Danish food is the best in Scandinavia—in fact, it's among the best in Europe.

Breakfast is usually big and hearty, just right before a day of sightseeing. It usually consists of homemade breads, Danish cheeses, and often a boiled egg or salami. In most establishments you can order bacon and eggs. However, you may prefer simply a continental breakfast of Danish *wienerbrød* (pastry) and coffee. The "danish" is moist, airy, and rich.

The favorite dish at midday, the ubiquitous *smørrebrød* (open-faced sandwiches), is a national institution. It means "bread and butter," but the Danes stack it as though it were the Leaning Tower of Pisa. Then they throw in a slice of curled cucumber and bits of parsley, or perhaps sliced peaches or a mushroom for color.

Two of these sandwiches can make a more-than-filling lunch. They're seen everywhere, from the grandest dining rooms to the lowliest pushcart. In restaurants, guests look over a checklist and mark the ones they want. Some are made with sliced pork (perhaps with a prune on top), roast beef with béarnaise sauce and crispy fried bits of onion, or liver paste adorned with an olive or cucumber slice and gelatin made from strong beef stock.

Smørrebrød is often served as an hors d'oeuvre. The most popular, most tempting, and usually most expensive of these delicacies is prepared with a mound of tiny Danish shrimp, on which a lemon slice and caviar often perch, perhaps with fresh dill. The "ugly duckling" of the smørrebrød family is anything with a cold sunny-side-up egg on top.

At dinner, the Danes tend to keep farmers' hours. Eating at 6:30pm is common, although restaurants remain open much later. Many main dishes are familiar to North Americans, but they're prepared with a distinct Danish flourish—for example, *lever med løg* (liver and fried onions), *bøf* (beef in a thousand different ways), *lammesteg* (roast lamb), or that old reliable, *flaeskesteg med rødkål* (roast pork with red cabbage).

Danish chefs are especially noted for fresh fish dishes. Tiny Danish shrimp, *rejer,* are splendid; herring and kippers are also greeted with enthusiasm. Favorites include *rodspaette* (plaice), *laks* (salmon), *makrel* (mackerel), and *kogt torsk* (boiled cod).

Danish cheese may be consumed at any meal, then eaten again on a late-night smørrebrød at the Tivoli. Danish blue is already familiar to most people. For something softer and milder, try Havarti.

Danish specialties that are worth sampling include *frikadeller* (meatballs or rissoles prepared in various ways); an omelet with a rasher of bacon covered with chopped chives and served in a skillet; and hamburger patties topped with fried onions and coated with rich brown gravy.

Two great desserts are apple Charlotte, best when decorated with whipped cream, dried breadcrumbs, and chopped almonds; and *rødgrød med fløde*—basically a jellied fruit-studded juice, served with thick cream.

Carlsberg or Tuborg beer is Denmark's national beverage. A bottle of Pilsner costs about half the price of the stronger export beer with the fancy label. Value-conscious Danes rely on the low-priced *fadøl* (draft beer); visitors on a modest budget might want to do the same.

You may gravitate more toward *aquavit* (schnapps, to the British), which comes from the city of Aalborg in northern Jutland. The Danes, who usually drink it at mealtime, follow it with a beer chaser. It should only be served icy cold.

For those with a daintier taste, the world-famous Danish liqueur, Cherry Heering, is a delightful drink; it can be consumed anytime except with meals.

Appendix B: Norway in Depth

The "Land of the Midnight Sun" is a special experience. Norwegians view their scrub-covered islands, snow-crested peaks, and glacier-born fjords as symbols of a wilderness culture. The majestic scenery inspired the symphonies of Grieg, the plays of Ibsen, and the paintings of Munch. The landscape has also shaped the Norwegians' view of themselves as pastoral dwellers in one of the world's most splendid countrysides.

The name Norway (in Norwegian, *Norge* or *Noreg*) is derived from *Norvegr*, meaning "the way to the north." The Vikings used the term more than 1,000 years ago to describe the shipping route along the west coast of Norway. Norwegians have been seafarers since the dawn of history, so it seems natural for the country to have a nautical name.

To the ancients, Norway was a mythical land. A journey held unspeakable perils. Writers called the mythical land "Ultima Thule," and feared that it was inhabited by strange, barbaric, even fabulous creatures. In the 4th century B.C., the Greek writer Pytheas thought the laws of nature did not apply there, and said that everything—water and earth included—floated in midair. In what may have been an attempt to describe a snowstorm, Herodotus claimed that in Norway feathers covered everything and constantly blew into one's face.

Norway is a land of tradition, exemplified by its rustic stave churches and its folk dances. But Norway is also modern. It's a technologically advanced nation, rich in petroleum and hydroelectric energy. Norwegians also enjoy a well-developed national social insurance system that provides pensions, health insurance, unemployment insurance, and rehabilitation assistance. The system is financed by contributions from the insured, which makes Norway one of the most heavily taxed nations on earth.

One of the last great natural frontiers of the world, Norway invites exploration, with its steep and jagged fjords, salmon-filled rivers, glaciers, mountains, and meadows. In the winter, the shimmering aurora borealis (northern lights) are the lure, before giving way to the midnight sun of summer.

1 Norway Today

The long, narrow country stretches some 1,100 miles north to south, but rarely more than 60 miles east to west. Norway is a land of raw nature. It occupies the western and extreme northern portion of the

Scandinavia peninsula, bordering Finland, Sweden, and Russia. In the west, its 13,000 miles of coastline confront the often-turbulent North Atlantic Ocean.

There's plenty of breathing room for everybody. When you factor in the Arctic desolation of the north, Norway averages about 20 people per square mile. Most of the 4 million inhabitants are concentrated in the south, where the weather is less severe. Even so, the population of Oslo, the capital, is less than half a million. Aside from Oslo, there are no really big cities; the populations of Bergen and Trondheim are 208,000 and 134,000, respectively.

Norway does not want to be a melting pot, and immigration is strictly controlled. The largest minority group is the Lapps (or Sami), who live in the far north; they have broad powers of self-government, including their own parliament. Although many people have emigrated from Norway—about 1 million to America alone—immigration to Norway from other countries has been limited. About 3.2% of the population originally came from Great Britain, Denmark, and Sweden.

Norway is a constitutional monarchy. Although without political power, Norway's royal family enjoys the subjects' unwavering support. The real power is in the Storting, or parliament. Women play a major role in government. Some 40% of all elected officials are women, and women head several government ministries. Many industries—especially energy—are fully or partially state controlled. Oil from the North Sea is a vital resource; the government has a Ministry of Oil and Energy. The government grants large subsidies to agriculture and fisheries.

As a result of their natural surroundings, Norwegians are among the most athletic people in Europe. Nearly every Norwegian child learns to ski as well as walk. They are also among the best-educated people in the world. Norway's educational standard has risen considerably since the Second World War, and some 90% of Norwegian young people take a 3-year course in academic or vocational school after completing their compulsory education.

About 90% of the population belongs to the national Lutheran church, of which the king is the titular head. Freedom of worship is guaranteed to all.

Because the economy depends significantly on foreign trade, most business is conducted in English. Norway has two official languages, Riksmal and Landsmal, both of Danish origin. The Lapps, the indigenous people of the north, have their own language.

Cultural activities are important in Norway. The government subsidizes book publishing, guaranteeing sales of 1,000 copies of each book published for distribution to public libraries. Encouraging Norwegian writers helps preserve the language. Movie production, limited by population and language, fares poorly, however. Opera is fairly new to the country, and Norway acquired its first professional ballet ensemble in 1948. Folk music, however, has roots going back to Norse times, and is still very much alive. Norway encourages the arts by providing a guaranteed income to active artists whose work has achieved and maintained a high standard over a period of years.

2 The Natural Environment

Norway is one of nature's last great frontiers in Europe—mountains, glaciers, and lakes cover 70% of its land. Less than 4% of its territory, mostly in the south-central area, is arable. Within Norway's Jotunheimen range are the highest mountain peaks in Europe north of the Alps. Norway has about 17,000

- Norwegians have one of the highest per capita incomes in the world.
- While medieval alchemists were trying to make gold, they discovered *akevitt* (aquavit, or schnapps), the national "firewater" of Norway.
- Norway has the world's largest foreign trade per capita.
- The average population density is only 13 inhabitants per square kilometer, compared with 96 for Europe as a whole.
- Norway and Russia share a short land border and have disputed control of a sea area the size of Belgium, Switzerland, and Austria combined.
- Hammerfest is the world's northernmost town.
- More people of Norwegian descent (5 million) live in the United States than in Norway (4.3 million in 1994).

glaciers. Along the western coast, some 50,000 islands protect the mainland from some of the worst storms in the North Atlantic.

Norway has a varied and changing climate. The coastal zones in the west and east normally experience cool summers and temperate winters. Inland, summers are warm, and winters cold and dry. In the extreme north, 100 days of annual snowfall each year isn't uncommon.

The fjords are not only a distinguishing feature of Norway's landscape, but a special attraction to visitors. The fjords were created thousands of years ago when the ocean flowed into glacial valleys. These "fingers" of water cut deep into the landscape. The most intriguing of the fjords, the Sognefjord, is more than 100 miles long and extremely deep.

Norway's rivers tend to be short and volatile. A smooth flow of water is often "agitated" by waterfalls and patches of white water. Because they're not suited for transportation, rivers are primarily sources of food, principally salmon. The longest river in Scandinavia, the Glomma, runs through southwestern Norway.

Norway's position on the globe has earned it the nickname "Land of the Midnight Sun." In summer, towns in northern Norway, such as Tromsø, experience 24 hours of sunshine, followed by 24 hours of darkness in winter. Even in southern Norway, the summer days are long, and the winter nights may last more than 17 hours.

Thick birch and pine forests cover the mountains; in the lowlands, oak forests abound. Spruce forests cover the southeast and middle regions. The steep mountains in the east are among the tallest in Europe and the site of some of the world's most challenging alpine ski runs. There is excellent hiking in the Vassafaret district around Flåm, where the mountains are rounded, gentle, and dotted with alpine lakes and rivers.

The mountains are also home to ravens, eagles, grouse, and gyrfalcons. They serve as a migratory home to the pure-white snowy owl. Norway's countryside and forests teem with Arctic animals such as reindeer, Arctic fox, wolves, bears, lynx, elk, beavers, and otters. Along the coast are nesting grounds for puffins and cormorants; whales, salmon, and cod frolic in the icy seas offshore. Through Norway's conservation efforts and strict regulations regarding the environment, these animals and fish flourish much as they have in the past.

Norway in Depth

Impressions

I would not enter Norway again for all the firs in Scandinavia. The blight of temperance has settled on the place.
—Archer Grant of Stroud, Gloucestershire, 1912

November always seemed to me the Norway of the year.
—Emily Dickinson, 1864

Norway is a hard country: hard to know, hard to shoot over, and hard—very hard—to fall down on: but hard to forsake and harder to forget.
—J. A. Lees, *Peaks and Pines, Another Norway Book,* 1899

3 History 101

Norway in Depth

Dateline

- **800–1050** The age of the Vikings, when Norsemen terrorized the coasts of Europe.
- **872** Harald Fairhair conquers many small provinces and reigns as first king.
- **1001** Leif Eriksson discovers America (or so the sagas claim).
- **1030** Christianity is firmly established; Olaf II is declared a saint.
- **1066** The Viking Age ends with the defeat of Harald III in England.
- **1350** The Black Death wipes out much of the population.
- **1397** Margaret becomes queen of Norway, Denmark, and Sweden at the Union of Kalmar.
- **1439** Danish rule is imposed on Norway.
- **1814** Norway breaks from Denmark and adopts a constitution, but comes under Swedish rule.
- **1905** The Norwegian parliament breaks from Sweden and declares independence.
- **1914** Norway declares its neutrality in the First World War.
- **1920** Norway joins the League of Nations, ending its isolation.

continues

Norway has been inhabited since the end of the Ice Age. The earliest Scandinavian settlers hunted reindeer and other game in these northern lands. Some 5,000 to 6,000 years ago, the inhabitants turned to agriculture, especially around the Oslofjord. Artifacts show that in the Roman era, Norway had associations with areas to the south.

THE AGE OF THE VIKINGS Prehistory ended during the Viking era, roughly A.D. 800 to 1050. Much of what is known about this era wasn't written down, but has been conveyed through sagas passed by word of mouth or revealed by archaeological finds. Some scholars consider the looting of the Lindisfarne monastery in northern England in 793 the beginning of the "age of the Vikings."

"The Vikings are coming!" became a dreadful cry along the coasts of Europe. The victims expected fire and sword. Scandinavian historians are usually kinder to the Vikings, citing the fact they often went abroad to trade and colonize. From Norway, the Vikings branched out to settle in the Orkney and Shetland Islands (now part of Scotland). They also settled in the Scottish Hebrides and on the Isle of Man. Viking settlements were established on Greenland and Iceland, which had previously been uninhabited. The Norse communities on Greenland eventually died out. The sagas claim that in 1001, Leif Eriksson discovered "wineland of the good," a reference to the American continent. Many scholars, however, claim that the Vikings' long ships reached America long before Leif Eriksson.

The road to unification of Norway was rough. In 872 Harald Fairhair, after winning a battle near Stavanger, conquered many of the provices, but other battles for unification took decades. Harald was followed by his son, Eric I—"Bloody Axe," to his enemies. Eric began his reign by assassinating two of his eight brothers, and later killed five other brothers. His one surviving brother, Haakon, succeeded him as king in 954. Haakon tried unsuccessfully to convert Norway to Christianity. After he died in the Battle of Fitjar (960), Harald II Graafell, one of Eric's sons, became king of Norway. Cruel and oppressive, he died in battle in 970.

Haakon, son of Sigurd of Lade, became the next king of Norway. He resisted Danish attacks and ruled for about 25 years, but died in a peasant riot in 995. After the Battle of Swold in 1000, Norway was divided between Denmark and the Jarl of Lade.

Olaf II Haraldsson was a Viking until 1015, when he became king of Norway. Although oppressive and often cruel, he continued to spread Christianity. Canute of Denmark invaded Norway in 1028, sending Olaf fleeing to England. Canute's son, Sweyn, ruled Norway from 1028 to 1035. Sweyn was forced out when Olaf II was proclaimed a saint and his son, Magnus I, was made king. Magnus was also king of Denmark, a position he lost when Canute's nephew led a revolt against him and he was killed. Olaf's sainthood firmly established Christianity in Norway.

Harald Sigurdsson (known as Harald III) ruled Norway from 1046 until his death in 1066. His death marks the end of the Viking Age.

- **1940** Nazi troops invade Norway; the king and government flee.
- **1945** Norway regains independence and executes its Nazi puppet ruler, Quisling.
- **1960s** Oil boom hits Norway.
- **1986** Labour Party installs first female prime minister, Gro Harlem Brundtland.
- **1989** Center-right coalition regains power.
- **1990** Brundtland becomes prime minister again.
- **1991** Harald V becomes king.
- **1994** Lillehammer plays host to XVII Olympic Winter Games.
- **1995** Norway wins Eurovision Song Contest, an annual cultural event observed by 600 million viewers.
- **1996** Eurovision Song Contest is held in Oslo; Norway takes second place.
- **1998** Oil prices fall, but Norway plunges ahead with costly engineering projects.
- **2000** Harald lets thousands of visitors see his home for the first time since 1920.

Norway in Depth

THE MIDDLE AGES Wars with Denmark continued, and civil wars raged from 1130 to 1227. Norwegian towns and the church continued to grow. Under Haakon V in the 13th century, Oslo became the capital of Norway. The Black Death reached Norway in 1350 and wiped out much of the population.

From 1362 to 1364 Norway and Sweden had a joint monarch, Haakon VI (1340–80), son of the Swedish king, Magnus Eriksson. Haakon married Margaret, daughter of the Danish king Valdemar Atterdag. Their son, Olaf, was chosen to be the Danish king upon Valdemar's death in 1375. He inherited the throne of Norway after his father died in 1380, bringing Norway into a union with Denmark. The union lasted until 1814.

UNION WITH DENMARK When Olaf died at the age of 17, Margaret became regent of Norway, Denmark, and Sweden. She ruled through her nephew, Eric of Pomerania, who had become king of Norway in 1389. He was recognized as a joint ruler at Kalmar. Margaret was actually the power behind the throne until her death, in 1412. Eric of Pomerania tried to rule the three countries, but Sweden and Norway rebelled. Eric fled in 1439 and Christopher III of Bavaria became the ruler, imposing Danish rule.

Denmark led Norway into the Seven Years' War of the North in 1563, and took unfair advantage of its position in trade, in the military, and even in surrendering Norwegian land to Sweden.

During the Napoleonic Wars (1807–14), Denmark and Norway were allied with France, although it created much economic hardship. Famine was widespread. In 1814 Frederik VI of Denmark surrendered to Napoléon's opponents and handed Norway over to Sweden. That officially ended 434 years of Danish rule over Norway.

SECESSION FROM SWEDEN   On May 17, 1814, an assembly adopted a constitution and chose Christian Frederik as the Norwegian king. May 17 is celebrated as Norwegian National Day. The Swedes objected and launched a military campaign, eventually subduing Norway. The Swedes accepted the Norwegian constitution, but only within a union of the two kingdoms. Christian Frederik fled.

Soon thereafter, Norway suffered through one of its greatest economic depressions. Norway's parliamentary assembly, the Storting (Stortinget), engaged in repeated conflicts with the Swedish monarchs. Bernadotte ruled over both Norway and Sweden as Charles XIV from 1818 to 1844.

By the 1830s the economy of Norway had improved. The first railway line was laid in 1854. Its merchant fleet grew significantly between 1850 and 1880.

From the 1880s on, the Liberals in the Storting brought much-needed reform to the country. But by the end of the century, the conflict with Sweden was growing as more and more Norwegians demanded independence.

In August 1905 the Storting decided to dissolve the union with Sweden. Sweden agreed to let Norway rule itself. In October 1905 Norway held an election, and the son of Denmark's king was proclaimed king of Norway. He chose the name Haakon VII.

AN INDEPENDENT NORWAY   Free at last, Norway enjoyed peace and prosperity until the beginning of the First World War. Even though the economy was satisfactory, thousands of Norwegians emigrated to the United States around the turn of the century. In 1914 Norway joined Sweden and Denmark in declaring a policy of neutrality. Despite the declaration, around 2,000 Norwegian seamen lost their lives in the war because of submarine attacks and underwater mines.

In 1920 Norway joined the League of Nations, ending its policy of isolation. At the outbreak of the Second World War, Norway again declared its neutrality. Nonetheless, Allied forces mined Norway's waters in 1940, and the Nazis attacked on April 9, 1940. Great Britain and France provided some military assistance, but Norway fell after a 2-month struggle. The government and the royal family fled into exile in England, taking 1,000 ships of the Norwegian merchant fleet. In spite of the resistance movement, Norway was occupied by the Nazis until the end of the war in 1945. Vidkun Quisling, the Norwegian minister of defense in the 1930s, served the Nazis as leader of the puppet government.

Quisling was executed following the Nazi retreat from Norway. On June 7, 1945, the government-in-exile returned from Britain. The retreating Nazis had followed a scorched-earth policy in Finnmark, destroying almost everything of value. In the late 1940s, Norway began to rebuild its shattered economy.

After an abortive attempt to form a Nordic defense alliance, Norway and Denmark joined NATO in 1949. The Communist Party tried to secure recognition in Norway, but failed.

A Sifter of Viking Secrets

The world press gave scant attention to the death, in 1997, of Norwegian archaeologist Anne-Stine Ingstad, but she was a pioneer, sifting through the sandy soil above a Newfoundland beach to uncover the remains of a Viking outpost.

She was the wife of Helge Ingstad, whose discovery of the site in 1961 produced the first conclusive evidence that Vikings had made a North American beachhead 500 years before Columbus. Vikings sailed from a colony in Greenland to reach the North American continent (today's Canada). Icelandic sagas had described the voyages in detail, and few scholars doubted that Leif Eriksson and other Vikings had made such voyages and explorations. But until the Ingstads made their startling discoveries, no hard evidence of a Viking presence existed—only a spate of spurious artifacts.

The initial discovery was met with skepticism. But once Anne-Stine Ingstad started to dig, most doubts evaporated. Her husband had used vivid geographic descriptions in Icelandic sagas to find the camp described by Eriksson and others. Once the site was discovered, she carried out excavations over several months. In time, she uncovered the foundations of eight buildings, including a large house almost identical to Eriksson's great hall in Greenland.

In 1964 she unearthed a tiny stone spinning wheel, suggesting that female Vikings had used the camp. In 1980 UNESCO designated the settlement, L'Anse aux Meadows, a World Heritage Site, along with the Pyramids of Egypt and the Grand Canyon.

By the 1960s oil prospecting in the North Sea had yielded rich finds, which led to a profound restructuring of Norwegian trade and industry. In 1972 Norway voted not to enter the Common Market, following a bitter political dispute.

Norway had a nonsocialist government from 1981 to 1986. In 1986, Labour Party leader Gro Harlem Brundtland headed a minority government as Norway's first female prime minister. She introduced 7 women into her 18-member cabinet. Soon, however, tumbling oil prices and subsequent unemployment led to a recession. The Labour government lost the 1989 elections. A center-right coalition assumed control of government. In November 1990, Brundtland returned to office as prime minister, this time with 9 women in her 19-member cabinet. In 1991 Olav V died and was succeeded by his son, Harald V.

Today the Norwegian government faces many of the same problems that confront other nations: violent crime, drugs, immigration control, unemployment, acid rain, and pollution. Concern about acid rain and pollution, much of which comes from Great Britain, was so great that riots erupted when Margaret Thatcher visited Norway in 1987.

Although some Conservatives objected, Norway applied for membership in the European Union (EU) in 1993. The country also began to assert itself more on the international scene. Thorvald Stoltenberg, the minister of foreign affairs, was named peace negotiator for ravaged Bosnia-Herzegovina, and in clandestine meetings held outside Oslo helped affect a rapprochement between the PLO and Israel. All these history-making events were eclipsed by the XVII Olympic Winter Games, held in Lillehammer in February 1994. In November 1994, Norwegians rejected a nonbinding referendum on EU membership. Following that, everyone waited for the Norwegian parliament to vote on whether the country would join. The parliament deliberately avoided the issue and did not vote on the matter. The referendum, though nonbinding, remains in force, and Norway is not a member of the EU. But that does not mean the country has no economic links with the rest of Europe. In 1994 Norway reinforced its commitments to membership in the EEAA (European Economic Area Agreement), an association initiated in 1992 to ensure its access to the EU's single market. It includes cooperation in a variety of cultural and economic areas.

In 1995 Norway won the Eurovision Song Contest for best songs evocative of a country, repeating its sweep of a decade earlier and ensuring that the event would be held there in 1996. As the host country, Norway captured second place.

By 1998 Norway was having its share of troubles, as oil prices plunged to their lowest levels in a decade. Turmoil in financial markets knocked the krone lower and prompted the central bank to double interest rates to 10%. The popular prime minister Kjell Magne Bondevik, who took over the office in 1997, stunned the country by taking a temporary leave from office. His doctors said he was having a "depressive reaction" to too much work and stress. In late 1998, Bondevik came back to his job—and is now running the country.

Today, Norway continues pushing forward with major engineering projects. The country is connecting its sparsely inhabited outcroppings and linking its interior fjordside villages in an effort to stem the flow of people to larger towns and villages. At Hitra, a largely barren island off the west coast, a new 3½-mile tunnel (the world's deepest and second longest) has been built at a cost of $41 million. It links mainland Norway to a hamlet with some 4,100 residents. On the North Cape at Norway's Arctic tip, a $140 million bridge and tunnel was constructed to Mager Island, home to only 3,600 people (and more than that many reindeer). An additional $135 million went into the earth in the mountains east of Bergen to link the towns of Aurland (population 1,900) and Laerdal (2,250). Its 15.2-mile length casts the previous world record-holder, the 10.1-mile St. Gotthard tunnel in Switzerland, into a distant second place.

Locally, the most interest generated in Oslo was the opening of Norway's royal palace for public tours for the first time since 1920. After an evaluation is made of the effect of all those visits on the structure, it will be determined if future tours will be permitted. But locals and visitors alike poured through the palace in the summer of 2000, finding it modest as royal palaces go, especially London's Buckingham Palace with its 600 rooms. Rubberneckers got to see 15 of the palace rooms, none of them private royal quarters. King Harald V and his Queen, Sonja, had fled to their summer residence with their children. Everything pocket-sized had been removed so as not to unduly tempt souvenir hunters.

4 Dining with the Norwegians

Norwegians are proud—and rightly so—of their many tempting specialties, ranging from *boiled cod* (considered a delicacy) to reindeer steak smothered in brown gravy and accompanied by tart little *lingonberries,* which resemble wild cranberries.

Fish, both fresh and saltwater, is at the center of Norwegian cuisine. Prepared in countless ways, dishes are always fresh and usually well prepared.

Besides the aforementioned cod, in early summer, *kokt laks* (boiled salmon) is a wonderful treat. *Kreps* (crayfish) and *ørret* (mountain trout) are also popular. For those willing to splurge, we recommend the delicately seasoned *fiskegratin* (fish soufflé). Norwegians love their *rølet al* (smoked fatty eel), although most visitors tend to bypass this one at the smörgåsbord table. The national appetizer is brine-cured herring with raw onions.

You may want to try *reindeer steak* or *faar-i-kaal,* the national dish, a heavily creamed cabbage-and-mutton stew with boiled potatoes. The *kjøttkaker,* Norwegian hamburger—often pork patties—served with sautéed onions, brown gravy, and boiled potatoes, is a great way to introduce the children to Norwegian cuisine.

The *boiled potato* is ubiquitous. The Norwegian prefers it without butter—just a bit of parsley. Nowadays, fresh vegetables and crisp salads are a regular feature of the Norwegian diet as well.

Rømmergrøt is a sour-cream porridge covered with melted butter, brown sugar, and cinnamon. If they're in season, try the tasty, amber-colored *muiter* (cloudberries). An additional treat is a pancake accompanied by lingonberries.

Frokost (breakfast) is often a whopping *koldtbord,* the famous cold board, consisting of herring and goat's milk cheese, and often salmon and soft-boiled eggs, plus *wienerbrød* (Danish pastry). Many visitors may not want to spend the extra kroner for this big spread, but those going on glacier expeditions need this early-morning fortification.

Incidentally, the multi-dish *smörgåsbord* and *smørrebrød* (*smørbrød* in Norway), an open-faced sandwich, are very popular in Norway, although they seem to be served here without the elaborate rituals associated with such events in Denmark and Sweden. Customarily, smörgåsbord in Norway is only a prelude to the main meal.

The chief criticism leveled against Norwegian cooking is that it's too bland. The food is always abundant (the Norwegians are known for their second helpings), substantial, and well prepared—but no threat to the French for a Cordon Bleu prize.

Appendix C:
Sweden in Depth

Sweden is one of the most paradoxical nations on earth. An essentially conservative country, it is nonetheless a leader in social welfare, prison reform, and equal opportunity for women.

Swedes have long enjoyed a very high standard of living in Europe and wages that are among the highest. During the worldwide recession in the 1990s, the country had trouble maintaining the value of its currency. It has also faced its highest unemployment rate since the Second World War. There's definitely trouble in paradise, but compared with the rest of the world, Sweden is better off than most nations.

The past and the future exist side by side in Sweden. Stockholm and some west coast cities have stunning modern shopping complexes and up-to-date hotels. But a journey to Dalarna and Värmland, or the historic walled city of Visby on the island of Gotland, transports you to a more distant time.

Many visitors come to explore "the Kingdom of Crystal" in Småland province, where dozens of so-called glass huts, such as Orrefors and Kosta Boda, are tucked away among lakes and forests.

The Swedes are responsible for many inventions that have changed modern life. They include the safety match, alternating current, the milk separator, the refrigerator, the vacuum cleaner, and the ball bearing—not to mention the zipper, which has led to all sorts of encounters between people all over the world.

1 Sweden Today

Sweden's 174,000 square miles of lush forests and more than 100,000 lakes make up a land where the urbane and the untamed are said to live harmoniously. There's ample space for the 8.3 million residents—it has a density of only 48 people per square mile. About 85% of the citizens live in the southern half of the country. The north is populated by the two chief minority groups: the Lapps (Sami), and the Finnish-speaking people of the northeast. Stockholm is the political capital, with a population of 1,435,000; Gothenburg, a major automobile manufacturing town, is home to 704,000; and Malmö, the port city, to 458,000.

Once an ethnically homogeneous society, Sweden has experienced a vast wave of immigration in the past several years. Today more than 10% of residents are immigrants or the children of immigrants. Most of the influx has come from other Scandinavian countries. Because of Sweden's strong stance on human rights, it has also become a major

❓ Did You Know?

- Sweden, today a symbol of neutrality, once pursued war. It has invaded Russia, conquered Britain, and grabbed Normandy.
- A survey showed that a large percentage of Americans confuse Sweden and Switzerland.
- Half the couples living together in Sweden are unmarried.
- Sweden has added two words to international gastronomy: smörgåsbord and Absolut.
- The world's longest smörgåsbord was prepared in Sweden. It stretched 798 yards.
- James Joyce, F. Scott Fitzgerald, George Orwell, Marcel Proust, and Aldous Huxley did *not* win Sweden's Nobel Prize for literature.
- Sweden is one of five nations that established colonies in North America.

destination for political and social refugees from Africa and the Middle East. Many immigrants seeking asylum come from the former Yugoslavia.

Sweden's government is a constitutional monarchy supported by a parliamentary government. The royal family functions primarily in a ceremonial capacity. The ruling body is a one-chamber parliament, whose members are popularly elected for 3-year terms. A Social Democrat, Goeran Persson, heads the present government. Because of Sweden's location, it has been active in promoting peace among its warring Baltic neighbors. The country is an active member of the United Nations and was admitted to the European Union as a full member in 1995.

Like other European countries, Sweden has seen its policy of cradle-to-grave welfare threatened in recent years. The main topic of debate in the Social Democrat–dominated parliament is how to sustain the generous welfare system while putting a curb on ever-increasing taxes. The state provides health insurance and many generous family benefits, including an allowance for care providers, 15 months of paid parental leave after the birth of a child (divided between both parents), tax-free child allowances, and education stipends for children. When they reach retirement (age 65), Swedes are entitled to a hefty pension that rises with inflation.

Education plays an important role in Sweden. Schools, run by municipalities, provide free tuition, books, and lunches. Although attendance is mandatory for only 9 years, 90% of Swedes pursue some form of higher education. Adult education and the university are funded by the state.

Sweden's high level of education complements its high-tech industrial economy. Although in years past the economy was based on agriculture, in the latter half of this century industry has become predominant, employing nearly 80% of all workers. More than 50% of exports are heavy machinery, including cars, trucks, and telecommunications equipment. Companies such as Saab and Volvo produce vehicles familiar throughout the world. Despite Sweden's industrial predominance, the country still produces some 80% of its own food.

Although such a highly industrialized nation depends on its factories, Sweden has enacted stringent environmental policies. Monitoring the environment is the responsibility of local governments. Each of Sweden's 286 municipalities has the right to limit pollutant emissions in its sector.

Sweden in Depth

The environment has always played an integral role in Swedish life. There are 20 national parks. Although not regulated by law, Sweden has a policy that entitles citizens to unlimited free access to the nation's wilderness areas.

Another important element is Sweden's strong focus on culture. Over the past 25 years Swedes have turned their attention to music. Today young people are purchasing more recorded music and attending more live concerts than they were even a decade ago. Reading is on the rise (more than 9,000 book titles are published in Sweden every year), museum attendance has increased, and there's greater interest in the media. The average Swede spends 6 hours a day immersed in some form of mass media (newspapers, magazines, television, radio, and so forth).

Many Swedes claim that their country—once the "world's conscience"—is drifting. "We are no longer exceptional," says Lars Sahlin, a bartender in a popular Stockholm nightclub and a self-styled philosopher. "Our unemployment remains. There have been social-spending scandals, a decline in competitiveness."

Sweden's per capita income standing has fallen from 4th to 15th in the world, behind its three Scandinavian neighbors. Once Sweden preached racial tolerance and was particularly critical of the United States. Now Stockholm suburbs have segregated communities for their 800,000 immigrants.

A certain nostalgia is sweeping the nation today, a desire to return to the way life was when Sweden was one of the three or four richest countries in the world.

The country is under increasing pressure to drop its neutrality and join an expanding NATO. It is firmly resisting that, but has taken part in Bosnia peacekeeping. Although Sweden has been a member of the European Union since 1995, polls indicate that the people would reject membership if a new election were held.

As Sweden moves into the 21st century, its problems continue. For example, businesses can't grow because it's too expensive to hire people. Observers have noted that young Swedes are starting to think internationally, and some of them are leaving Sweden to take positions elsewhere in the global economy. "The people leaving are the very people that Sweden needs the most," one Swedish businessman lamented to the press.

2 The Natural Environment

Sweden is the fourth-largest nation in Europe. It's roughly the size of California, but sparsely populated. It stretches about 990 miles from north to south, with a disproportionate amount of territory above the Arctic Circle. From north to south, Sweden lies at roughly the same latitude as Alaska. Forests cover more than half the land; it's a heavily industrialized nation, and less than 10% of its land is used for agriculture. Sweden can be divided into three main regions: the mountainous northern zone, Norrland; the lake-filled, hilly central region, Svealand; and the broad southern plateau, Götaland, home of most of the country's agricultural enterprises.

Sweden has more than 100,000 lakes, including Vänern, the largest in Western Europe. Lakes cover about 9% of the countryside, and play an important role in transporting goods from the Baltic ports to cities throughout Sweden and the rest of Scandinavia. Canals link many lakes to the sea. The most important is the 370-mile Göta Canal. Constructed in the 19th century, it links Gothenburg in the west to Stockholm in the east. Some 121 miles of canals were built to connect the lakes and rivers that make up the waterway.

Sweden appeared to me the country in the world most proper to form the botanist and natural historian; every object seemed to remind me of the creation of things, of the first efforts of sportive nature.

—Mary Wollstonecraft, letters written
during a short residence in Sweden, 1796

Sweden's rivers tend to be short, and usually empty into one of the numerous lakes. They're used for short-haul transportation and especially for providing hydroelectric power to fuel the many factories scattered throughout the countryside. The most important rivers are the Pite, the Lule, and the Indal.

Sweden's expansive seacoast is more than 1,550 miles long. The west is bounded by the Kattegat and the Skagerrak seas, and the east by the Gulf of Bothnia and the Baltic Sea. Numerous small islands and reefs dot the east and southwest coasts. If all the inlets and islands were included, the coastline of Sweden would measure 4,650 miles. Öland and Gotland, Sweden's largest, most populated islands, are in the Baltic Sea, off the eastern coast.

Sweden is a center for alpine activities (including skiing, hiking, and glacier walking), most of which take place in the mountainous regions of Norrland. The far northern area is home to many of the country's highest peaks, including its highest mountain, 6,946-foot Kebnekaise.

There are five climate zones, each supporting a distinct array of plant life: the tundra in the north, coniferous forests below the timberline, central Sweden's birch forests, deciduous forests in the south, and the beech and oak zones in the southernmost regions. The countryside teems with bears, elk, reindeer, foxes, wolves, and otters. Numerous game birds also make their home in Sweden's expansive forests.

3 History 101

The first mention of Swedish people is found in *Germania,* by the Roman historian Tacitus (A.D. 56–120). He called the tribe "Svear" and described them as a "militant Germanic race." Later historians would describe them as "skiing hunters." The word *Sverige* (or "the domain of the Svear") eventually became *Sweden.*

The early Swedes were Vikings who pursued a thriving slave trade. St. Anskar, a Frankish missionary, introduced Christianity in 829, hoping it would tame the Viking spirit. It took at least 2 centuries for paganism to die out, but by the second half of the 11th century, Christianity had gained a foothold. It finally became accepted under Eric IX, who ruled until 1160. He led a crusade to Finland and later became the patron saint of Sweden.

Sweden's greatest medieval statesman was Birger Jarl, who ruled from 1248 to 1266; during his reign, serfdom was abolished and Stockholm was founded. When his son, Magnus

Dateline

- **98** Sweden is first mentioned in a book, *Germania,* by Tacitus.
- **829** St. Anskar introduces Christianity.
- **1248** Birger Jarl abolishes serfdom and founds Stockholm.
- **1319** Magnus VII of Norway unites Sweden with Norway.
- **1350s** The Black Death decimates the population.
- **1397** Margaret rules Sweden, Norway, and Denmark after the Union of Kalmar.
- **1521** Gustavus Vasa founds the Vasa Dynasty.

Sweden in Depth

continues

- **1648** Treaty of Westphalia grants Sweden the possessions of Stettin, Bremen, and West Pomerania.
- **1809** Napoléon names Jean Bernadotte heir to the throne of Sweden.
- **1889** The Social Democratic Party is formed.
- **1905** Sweden grants independence to Norway.
- **1909** Suffrage for men is achieved.
- **1921** Suffrage for women and an 8-hour workday are established.
- **1940** Sweden declares its neutrality in the Second World War.
- **1946** Sweden joins the United Nations.
- **1953** Dag Hammarskjöld becomes secretary-general of the United Nations.
- **1973** Carl XVI Gustaf ascends the throne.
- **1986** Olof Palme, prime minister and leader of the Social Democrats, is assassinated.
- **1992** Sweden faces currency crisis.
- **1994** Refugees and the welfare system strain Sweden's budget.
- **1995** Sweden, Finland, and Austria gain full membership in the European Union.
- **1996** Social Democrat Goeran Persson, Sweden's finance minister, is elected prime minister.
- **1997** World headlines link Sweden to past sterilization programs and to Nazi gold.
- **1998** Social Democrats remain in power on a pledge to continue huge welfare programs.
- **2000** The $3 billion Øresund bridge links Denmark and Sweden for the first time.

Ladulås, became king in 1275, he granted extensive power to the Catholic church and founded a hereditary aristocracy.

A NORDIC UNION Magnus VII of Norway (1316–74) was only 3 when he was elected to the Swedish throne, but his election signaled a recognition of the benefits of increased cooperation within the Nordic world. During his reign, distinct social classes emerged. They included the aristocracy; the Catholic clergy (who owned more than 20% of the land); peasant farmers and laborers; and a commercial class of landowners, foresters, mine owners, and merchants. The merchants' fortunes and power were based on trade links with the Hanseatic League. The association consisted of a well-organized handful of trading cities scattered in Germany and along the Baltic coastline. As commerce increased, the league's trading partners (especially Visby, on the island of Gotland) and their residents flourished, and the league's power grew.

In 1389 the Swedish aristocracy, fearing the growing power of the Germans in the Hanseatic League, negotiated an intra-Nordic union with Denmark and the remaining medieval fiefdoms in Norway and Finland. The experimental process began in 1397 in Kalmar, Sweden, which gave its name to the brief but farsighted Union of Kalmar. A leading figure in its development was the Danish queen Margaret, who was also queen of Norway when the Swedish aristocracy offered her the throne in 1389. Despite its ideals, the union collapsed after about 40 years. Merchants, miners, and peasants staged a revolt in defense of Sweden's trade links with the Hanseatic League, and power struggles between Danish and Swedish nobles took a toll.

Although the union was a failure, one of its legacies was the establishment of a Riksdag (parliament). Created partly as a compromise among different political factions, it consisted of representatives from various towns and regions; the peasant classes also had limited representation.

Queen Margaret's heir, her nephew, Eric of Pomerania (1382–1459), became the crowned head of Norway, Denmark, and Sweden. He spent most of his reign fighting with the Hanseatic League. Deposed in 1439, he was replaced by Christopher of Bavaria, whose early death in 1448 led to a major conflict and the eventual dissolution of the Kalmar Union. King Christian II of Denmark invaded

Stockholm in 1520, massacred the leaders who opposed him, and established an unpopular reign; there was much civil disobedience until the emergence of the Vasa dynasty, which expelled the Danes.

THE VASA DYNASTY   In May 1520 a Swedish nobleman, Gustavus Vasa, returned from captivity in Denmark and immediately began planning the military expulsion of the Danes from Sweden. In 1523 he captured Stockholm, won official recognition of Swedish independence, and was elected king.

In a power struggle with the Catholic church, Gustavus confiscated most church-held lands (increasing the power of the state overnight) and established Lutheranism as the national religion. He commissioned a complete translation of the Bible and other religious works into Swedish, and forcefully put down uprisings in the provinces. He established the right of succession for his offspring and decreed that his son, Eric XIV, would follow him as king (which he did, in 1543).

Although at first Eric was a wise ruler, his eventual downfall came in part from his growing conflicts with noblemen and his marriage to his unpopular mistress, Karin Mansdotter. (He had previously tried to negotiate marriage with Queen Elizabeth I of England.) Eric eventually went insane.

The next 50 years were marked by Danish plots to regain control of Sweden and Swedish plots to conquer Poland, Estonia, and the Baltic trade routes leading to Russia. A dynastic link to the Polish royal families led to the ascension of Sigismund (son of the Swedish king Johan III) in Warsaw. When his father died, Sigismund became king of Sweden and Poland simultaneously. But Sweden opposed his Catholicism and expelled him; he was followed by Karl (Charles) IX, who led Sweden into a dangerous and expensive series of wars with Denmark, Russia, and Poland.

By 1611, as Sweden was fighting simply to survive, Gustavus II Adolphus (1594–1632) ascended the throne. Viewed today as a brilliant politician and military leader, he was one of the century's most stalwart Protestants at a time when political alliances often formed along religious lines. After organizing an army composed mainly of farmers and field hands (financed by money from the Falun copper mines), he secured Sweden's safety.

He died fighting the Hapsburg emperor's Catholic army near the city of Luützen in 1632. His heir and only child, Christina (1626–89), was 6 years old. Christina, who did not want to pursue war and had converted to Catholicism (against the advice of her counselors), abdicated the throne in 1654 in favor of her cousin, Charles X Gustav (1622–60).

Ten years after his rise to power, Charles X expelled the Danes from many of Sweden's southern provinces, establishing the country's borders approximately where they are today. The endless wars with Denmark (and other kingdoms in northern Germany) continued in the years that followed. An even greater problem was the growing power of the nobles, who had amassed (usually through outright purchase from the cash-poor monarchy) an estimated 72% of Sweden's land. In an acrimonious process, Charles XI (1655–97) redistributed the land into approximately equal shares held by the monarchy, the

Swedish Yankees

Waves of Swedes came to the United States in the 19th century and rushed to embrace Americanisms and the English language. Perhaps because they blend in so well, the descendants of those immigrants are among the least noticeable, least self-asserting national group in the country today. Despite their assimilation, Swedish immigrants have had an influence as profound as that of any other national group.

The Swedes first settled in North America in 1638, when the colony of New Sweden was established at the mouth of the Delaware River. The settlement was captured by the Dutch 17 years later, and the settlers evacuated to New Amsterdam, the town that became New York. Famous Swedes who left their mark included Capt. Jonas Bronck, whose homestead still bears a version of his name—the Bronx. Later, during the American Revolution, came such ideologues as Count Axel von Fersen (who reportedly trysted once or twice with Marie Antoinette) and John Mårtensson (John Morton), one of the signers of the Declaration of Independence. Sweden, lacking a base in the New World and eager to undermine Britain (one of its most powerful maritime rivals), was the first country to sign a trade agreement with the fledging United States.

Fascination with the New World overcame Sweden's population in earnest in 1846, and waves of Swedes set out to seek health, wealth, religious freedom, and a land of their own. During a 5-year period beginning

nobles, and the independent farmers. The position of small landowners has remained secure in Sweden ever since, although the absolute monarchy gained increased power. With Charles's newfound wealth, he greatly strengthened the country's military power.

Charles XII (1682–1718) came to the throne at the age of 4, with his mother, the queen, as regent. His war-torn reign may have signaled the collapse of the Swedish empire.

Under Frederick I (1676–1751), Sweden regained some of its former prestige and waged war against Russia. Gustavus III (1746–92) initiated many reforms, encouraged the arts, and transformed the architectural landscape of Stockholm, but he also revived the absolute power of the monarchy, perhaps as a reaction against the changes effected by the French Revolution. He was assassinated by a group of fanatical noblemen while attending a ball at the Opera.

THE 19TH CENTURY   The next king, Gustavus IV (1778–1837), hated Napoléon. He led Sweden into the Third Coalition against France (1805–07). For his efforts, he lost Stralsund and Swedish Pomerania; in the wars against Russia and Denmark, Sweden lost Finland in 1808. The next year, Gustavus IV was overthrown. He died in exile.

A new constitution was written in 1808, granting the Riksdag (parliament) equal power with the king. Charles XIII (1748–1818), the uncle of the deposed king, became the new monarch.

Napoléon arranged for his aide, Jean Bernadotte (1763–1844), to become heir to the Swedish throne. Bernadotte won a war with Denmark, forcing that country to cede Norway to Sweden (1814). Upon the death of Charles XIII, Bernadotte became king of Sweden and Norway, ruling as Charles XIV. During his reign Sweden adopted a policy of neutrality, and the royal line that he established is still on the throne. Charles XIV was succeeded by his son, in 1868, five annual crops failed in Sweden, leading to the migration of at least 100,000 people. Between 1846 and 1873, a total of 1.5 million Swedes emigrated to North America—a figure that's especially impressive considering that Sweden's entire population was only around 4 million. The drain on the country's human resources was disastrous. Of all European countries, only Ireland lost a larger proportion of its population to emigration.

It's noteworthy that Sweden's high literacy rate, which endured despite the famine that affected many immigrants, helped Swedes to assimilate in the New World. In some regions of the Midwest, Swedes tended to settle together, but there were never any urban ghettos inhabited mainly by Swedes.

The first, and among the best-publicized, group of Swedish immigrants was a 1,500-member religious sect known as Jansonists (Erikjansare), whose leader, Erik Jansson, founded a colony in Illinois known as Bishop's Hill. Conceived as a utopia where all goods and property would be shared in common, it attracted national journalistic attention until an enraged disciple, furious at the refusal of the group's leader to allow his wife to leave the community, shot Jansson. Jansson's disciples, who believed he was immortal and would soon be resurrected, scattered throughout the Midwest and eventually established their own farms.

Oscar I (1799–1859), who introduced many reforms, including freedom of worship and of the press.

The Industrial Revolution changed the face of Sweden. The Social Democratic Party was launched in 1889, leading to a universal suffrage movement. All males gained the right to vote in 1909.

THE 20TH CENTURY Norway declared its independence in 1905, and Sweden accepted the secession. Sweden adhered to a policy of neutrality during the First World War, although many Swedes were sympathetic to the German cause. Many Swedish volunteers enlisted in the White Army during the Russian Revolution of 1917.

In 1921 women gained the right to vote, and an 8-hour workday was established. The Social Democratic Party continued to grow in power, and after 1932, a welfare state was instituted.

Although Sweden offered weapons and volunteers to Finland during its Winter War against the Soviet Union in 1939, it declared its neutrality during the Second World War. Sweden provoked long-lived resentment from Norway, whose cities were leveled by Nazi troops that had been granted free passage across Swedish territory. Under heavy Allied threats against Sweden in 1943 and 1944, Nazi troop transports through the country were halted. Throughout the war Sweden accepted many refugees. Swedish diplomat Raoul Wallenberg's attempts to rescue Hungarian Jews have been recounted in books and films.

Sweden joined the United Nations in 1946 but refused to join NATO in 1949. More disturbing was Sweden's decision to return to the Soviet Union many German and Baltic refugees who had opposed Russia during the war. They were presumably killed on Stalin's orders.

Sweden in Depth

The Swede is, surely, the human blackbird, with his copious, rich and liquid voice, in a language that reaches the extreme of voluptuous volubility.
—Edmund Gosse, 1911

If ever there was a Yankeer than Yankee, he's a Swede.
—Henry Adams, 1901

Native son Dag Hammarskjöld became secretary-general of the United Nations in 1953, and he did much to help Sweden regain the international respect it had lost because of its wartime policies. In 1961, toward the end of his second 5-year term, he was killed in an airplane crash.

Sweden continued to institute social reforms in the 1950s and 1960s, including the establishment of a national health service.

Carl XVI Gustaf, who was just 27, became king in 1973, following the death of his grandfather, Gustaf VI Adolf. (The new king's father had been killed in an airplane crash.) In 1976 he married Silvia Sommerlath, who was born in Germany. King Carl XVI Gustaf and Queen Silvia have three children.

The leader of the Social Democrats, Olof Palme, was prime minister from 1969 to 1976 and again from 1982 until his assassination outside a movie theater in Stockholm in 1986. A pacifist, he was a staunch critic of the United States, especially during the Vietnam War. An arrest was made, but the murder remains unsolved.

In the early 1990s, Sweden's problems included an austerity program and slow economic growth. Inflation was severe. In 1992 the government experienced a currency crisis that made headlines around the world. In September 1994, the Social Democrats, led by Ingvar Carlsson (who had succeeded Olof Palme), were returned to office after 3 years of Conservative rule. The election brought the proportion of women in parliament to 41%, the highest in the world.

In 1995 Sweden was granted full membership in the European Union, providing the setting for much-needed economic growth. Prime Minister Ingvar Carlsson retired in 1996, and in an effort to control rapidly increasing taxes and cut government spending, Finance Minister Goeran Persson was elected prime minister of the ruling Social Democratic Party.

Just as Sweden's image of itself as one of the most progressive nations on earth was being questioned, a chilling chapter from the past was revealed in 1997. Sweden had as many as 60,000 of its citizens sterilized from 1935 to 1976. The ideas behind the program resembled Nazi ideas of racial superiority. Singled out were those judged to be inferior, flawed by bad eyesight, mental retardation, and otherwise "undesirable" racial characteristics. Some citizens were sterilized involuntarily. The respected newspaper *Dagens Nyheter* stirred national debate and worldwide headlines when it ran a series of articles about the program.

Sweden's reputation received more battering in 1997. There were revelations of wartime iron exports—which fed Hitler's military machine—and of postwar Swedish hoarding of the German gold received in payment, much of it looted from victims of the Nazis.

In the September 1998 elections, Social Democrats remained in power on a pledge to increase spending on the country's huge welfare program. The Social Democrats have been in power for 57 of the past 66 years. The government spends 46% of the gross national product on welfare, more than any other industrialized country. Income taxes take 59% of people's pay. Employers pay up to 41% of employee remuneration into social security and pension plans.

The former Communist Party is now called the Left Party, and it has been growing in approval with voters—enough so that district branches have removed photographs of Lenin from party office walls. The party secretary of the Moderates, Gunnar Hokmark, found little comfort in the 1998 election, saying, "It puts Swedes in a left lock that is stronger than in any other country of Europe."

In May of 2000, Sweden for the first time in its history became physically linked with the continent via the Øresund Bridge. Both Queen Margrethe of Denmark and King Carl Gustaf of Sweden inaugurated the span that links the Scandinavian peninsula with Europe. Construction on the 10-mile motor and railway link began in 1995.

The bridge gives the island of Zealand (the eastern part of Denmark) and Scania (the southern part of Sweden) a shared bridge, serving some 3½ million inhabitants in the area.

The Øresund region, which encompasses parts of both Sweden and Denmark, is the largest domestic market in Northern Europe—larger than Stockholm and equal in size to Berlin, Hamburg, and Amsterdam combined. Built at a cost of $3 billion, it is the largest combined rail/road tunnel in the world. The price of a one-way fare in a passenger car is $30.

In theory, a vehicle can now travel in roughly a straight line from the Arctic coast of Norway to the Mediterranean shores of Spain. For centuries, it has been a dream to link the continent from its northern tip to its southern toe. The "Øresund Fixed Link" spans the icy Øresund Sound between the cities of Copenhagen and Malmö.

4 Dining with the Swedes

The fame of the smörgåsbord is justly deserved. Incorporating a vast array of dishes—everything from Baltic herring to smoked reindeer—selections from the smörgåsbord may be eaten either as hors d'oeuvres or as a meal in itself.

One cardinal rule of the smörgåsbord: Don't mix fish and meat dishes. It is customary to begin with *sill* (herring), prepared in many ways. Herring is usually followed by other treats from the sea, such as jellied eel, smoked fish, or raw pickled salmon. Then diners proceed to the cold meat dishes, where baked ham, liver paste, and the like are accompanied by vegetable salads. Hot dishes, often Swedish meatballs, come next, backed up by cheese and crackers, and perhaps a fresh fruit salad.

The smörgåsbord is not served as often in Sweden as many visitors seem to expect, as it requires time-consuming preparation. Many Swedish families reserve it for special occasions. In lieu of the 40-dish smörgåsbord, some restaurants have taken to serving a plate of *assietter* (hors d'oeuvres). One of the tricks for enjoying smörgåsbord is timing. It's best to go early, when fish dishes are fresh. Late arrivals may be more fashionable, but the food is often stale.

Typical mealtimes in Sweden are 8 to 11am for the standard continental breakfast, noon to 2:30pm for lunch, and as early as 5:30pm to around 8 or 8:30pm for dinner. Many restaurants in Stockholm are open until midnight, but don't count on this in the small villages.

A Swedish breakfast at your hotel may consist of cheese, ham, sausage, egg, bread, and perhaps *filmjölk,* a kind of sour-milk yogurt. *Smörgas,* the famous Swedish open-faced sandwich, like the Danish *smørrebrød* and Norwegian *smørbrød*, is a slice of buttered bread with something on top. It is eaten at any time of day, and you'll find it varying in price, depending on what you order and where you order it.

Unless you decide to have smörgåsbord at lunch (it's never served in the evenings), you'll find that the Swedes do not go for lavish spreads in the middle of the day. The usual luncheon order consists of one course, as you'll observe on menus, especially in the larger towns. Dinner menus are for complete meals, with appetizer, main course and side dishes, and dessert.

Swedish chefs generally tend to be far more expert with fish dishes (freshwater pike and salmon are star choices) than meat courses. The Swedes go mad at the sight of *kraftor* (crayfish), in season from mid-August to mid-September. This succulent, dill-flavored delicacy is eaten with the fingers, and much of the fun is the elaborate ritual surrounding its consumption. A platter of thin pancakes, served with lingonberries (comparable to cranberries), is the traditional Thursday-night dinner in Sweden. It's good on any other night of the week—but somehow better on Thursday.

Swedish cuisine used to be deficient in fresh vegetables and fruits, relying heavily on the tin can, but this is no longer true. Potatoes are the staff of life, but fresh salad bars long ago peppered the landscape, especially in the big cities.

The calorie-laden Swedish pastry—the mainstay of the *konditori*—is tempting and fatal to weight watchers. *Kaffe* (coffee) is the universal drink in Sweden, although tea (taken straight) and milk are also popular. The water is perfectly safe to drink all over Sweden. Those who want a reprieve from alcohol might enjoy the fruit-flavored Pommac soft drink, and Coca-Cola is ubiquitous. The state monopoly, or Systembolaget, controls the sale of alcoholic beverages. Licensed restaurants may sell alcohol after noon only (1pm on Sunday). Schnapps or aquavit—served icy cold—is a superb Swedish drink, often used to accompany smörgåsbord. The run-of-the-mill Swedish beer (Pilsner) has only a small amount of alcohol. All restaurants serve *lättol* (light beer) and *folköl*, a somewhat stronger brew. Swedish vodka, or *brännvin*, is made from corn and potatoes and flavored with different spices. All brännvin is served ice cold in schnapps glasses. Keep in mind that aquavit is much stronger than it looks, and Sweden has strictly enforced rules about drinking and driving. Most Swedes seem to drink their liquor straight; mixed drinks are uncommon. Either way, the drink prices are sky-high.

Appendix D: Finland in Depth

One of the world's northernmost countries, Finland is the last frontier of Western Europe. Lapland, which makes up nearly one-third of Finland, is north of the Arctic Circle.

Technically, Finland is not part of Scandinavia, but it is in spirit, as reflected in its modern architecture; its high standard of living; its avant-garde designs in textiles, furniture, and ceramics; and its advances in education.

Geographically remote (although easily accessible), Finland does not attract the number of visitors that go to Denmark, Norway, and Sweden—and that's a shame, as Finland has much to offer the visitor in both summer and winter.

1 Finland Today

Covering an area of 130,000 square miles and home to 5 million people, Finland has a relatively low population density—about 38 people per square mile. More than one-third of its territory lies above the Arctic Circle, home to one of its large minority groups—the Lapps, or Sami. Helsinki, the capital, has a population of about half a million.

Finland is a republic; a president governs with a 200-member unicameral parliament. The president serves a 6-year term, and members of parliament are popularly elected for 4-year terms. Finland was the first nation to grant suffrage to women, so women have played an active role in government since the early 1900s. Women members compose about 40% of the parliament. In 1995, along with Sweden and Austria, Finland joined the European Union.

Finland's welfare system is among the best in the world. Universal health care is offered, supplemented by extensive preventive health education. Maternal health is stressed through free medical care and a "maternity package" consisting of either money for the infant's basic needs or the actual products, such as clothes, diapers, bottles, and bibs (only 15% of families choose the cash). Families with children under 17 also receive allowances from the state. Children get free medical and dental care through the age of 19.

Finland's literacy rate is nearly 100%. This has been achieved through an emphasis on bilingualism (Finnish and Swedish) as well as free schooling. All primary education and university courses are conducted in Finnish and Swedish—the two official languages. Because of the obscurity of the Finnish language, Finns have had to master other

Those Mysterious Genes

The Finns, partly from a justifiable sense of nationalism, have always felt themselves to be distinctly different from other Europeans. Poised uncomfortably between Russia and Sweden, the Finns have a mythology and literature that are quite different from those of their neighbors. Archaeologists, linguists, and anthropologists have struggled to trace the origins of the Finns, one of the most mysterious national groups in Europe.

The tongue-twisting Finnish language is radically different in its syntax, vocabulary, and grammar from the Teutonic and Slavic languages of its neighbors. Finnish belongs to the Finno-Ugric language group, which includes Hungarian, Estonian, Latvian, and the Sami dialect of the nomadic tribes in Finland's far north. Of all these, the Finnish language's link with Hungarian has especially fascinated anthropologists, some of whom have theorized that the Finns and Hungarians were prehistoric siblings that migrated simultaneously from the steppes of Central Asia and subsequently split into southern (Hungarian) and northern (Finnish and Estonian) branches. The Hungarians, however, are much less genetically "pure" than the Finns, in part because of their pivotal role as a partner during the 19th century in the Austrian Empire, and the cosmopolitan mingling of bloodlines that has occurred ever since.

The "separateness" of the Finns has fascinated more than the world's linguists. Geneticists have theorized that linguistic separateness implies a pool of "racially pure" genes that have been kept more or less isolated from those of other people.

In the 1970s and 1980s Professor Harri Nevanlinna performed exhaustive experiments on the range and distribution of the Finnish genotype by

languages, primarily English, French, and German. Students are required to attend 10 years of primary school, after which they can pursue vocational training or university studies. Finland is the best-educated nation in Europe.

Finland's economy relies primarily on exporting high-tech industrial goods. Metal and engineering products account for more than 40% of the country's exports. Many of these are computer-controlled mechanical goods and specialized vehicles, used mainly in the mining industry. Finland also exports a large amount of paper products from its birch forests. In fact, Finland is the primary supplier of paper products for all of Western Europe.

Finland's location in the Baltic, as well as its shared border with Russia, has opened the gates to a strong eastern trade. Many goods pass through Finland on their way to Russia and the rest of Asia. Since the demise of the Soviet Union and the rise of capitalism, Russian exports have also begun to move through Finland.

The Finnish government has taken steps to ensure Finland's role in northern European commerce. Through membership in the European Union and close ties to the recently liberated Baltic states (such as Estonia), Helsinki is rapidly expanding as the hub for commerce between the established nations in the West and the emerging Baltic states and Central and Eastern Europe.

The Finns are generally a homogenous group, having one of the most genetically pure gene pools in the world (see "Those Mysterious Genes" box, above). Most Finns live in the southern region, many in the Helsinki area. Finland's two principal minority groups—the Lapps in the north and the Roma (gypsies) in studying the distribution of various blood traits in the Finnish population. He found that although the Finns had the same general genetic characteristics as other Europeans, they also had some DNA strains that are almost completely lacking elsewhere in Europe. All in all, Finns appear to be very similar, genetically, to other Finns, but distinctly different from other genetic groups in Europe. Eventually it was concluded that 25% to 50% of Finnish genes are Baltic, 25% are Siberian, and 25% to 50% are Germanic.

An even higher incidence of genetic separateness was discovered among members of the Sami tribes (also known as Inuits or, less accurately, Eskimos) of Scandinavia's far north. These nomadic tribes have dialects that belong to the Finno-Ugric group. Their migration into what is now Finland occurred eons before the arrival of the Finns, and they possess a genetic makeup unique in Europe.

Are there any pathologies (or lack thereof) that affect the Finns more than they do the rest of humankind? Some 30 congenital (and often fairly serious) diseases carried by recessive genes occur within the Finnish population, an over-representation of unusual maladies that has sometimes been bitterly referred to as Finland's "pathological heritage." These diseases, susceptibility to which might have resulted simply from Finnish intermarriage and inbreeding during Finland's years of agrarian isolation, are extremely rare (and, in some cases, nonexistent) elsewhere in the world.

By contrast, there are some congenital diseases that the Finns seem to lack altogether, but which are relatively common in other peoples. So, although it can't be demonstrated that the Finnish immune system is better or worse than the rest of humankind's, it is nonetheless different.

the south—constitute less than 1% of the entire population. Immigration is discouraged; most of the country's present immigrant population—about 20,000—are refugees who have been assigned to Finland by the United Nations.

2 The Natural Environment

Suomi (its Finnish name) is one of the largest countries in Europe, about 700 miles long, with a maximum breadth of 335 miles. Finland's coastline is approximately 682 miles long.

Finland shares its border with Sweden, Norway, and Russia. Its geography can be divided into three distinct areas—the coastal plain, the lake district, and the highland in the north—each characterized by a slightly different climate and topography.

Most of the country is lowland, with the highest point at Halti, 4,344 feet above sea level. More than 65% of the land is forested; arable farmland makes up about 8% of the land mass.

Finland has more lakes than any other country—a total of 187,888 that cover some 10% of the country. Although abundant in number, most of the lakes are relatively shallow (around 25 feet), and none is more than 300 feet deep. The lakes are narrow, and many are dotted with islands; most of them are frozen in winter. The largest is Lake Saimaa, near the Russian border.

Finland's rivers tend to be short. The major rivers are the Kemi, Torne, Muonio, Oulu, and Vuoksi. The Kemi, Finland's longest river, is its primary

❓ Did You Know?

- Finland has some 188,000 lakes and 180,000 islands.
- Finland, in 1906, was the first country to grant women the right to vote.
- Finland has one of the highest per-capita Internet connection rates in the world.
- Two Finnish brothers hold the world's record for sitting on an anthill.
- The legendary bird of fairy tale and mythology—the whooper swan, *Cygnus musicus*—has been saved from extinction and once again nests in Finland.
- The world's northernmost film festival is held under the midnight sun of Lapland at Sodankyl.
- Finland has its own version of the tango, a far cry from Argentina's.
- Finland has launched news broadcasts in Latin.
- One of the most heavily forested regions on earth, Finland makes baseball bats out of fiberglass.
- Per capita, Finland is the leading book-publishing country in the world—17.1 titles are published per year for every 10,000 inhabitants.

source of hydroelectric power; it's also Finland's major salmon producer. The Vuoksi, which originates from Lake Saimaa, has Finland's most striking waterfall. All of Finland's waterways play a vital role in the logging industry.

Finland has a gentle coastline, with many bays and inlets. There is little tidal action, so the seashore resembles the shores of the country's many lakes. Off the coast are thousands of small islands, the most important of which are the Åland Islands, a chain of more than 6,500 islands located in the Gulf of Bothnia off Finland's southern coast.

As in Norway and Sweden, Finland's flora varies tremendously by region. The coastal zones are much milder than the interior and can sustain such species as oaks, elms, and maples. The central region is home to conifers, and the north, dominated by the tundra, can sustain little vegetation. Throughout Finland, there are some 1,000 varieties of flowering plants.

With more than two-thirds of Finland covered with forest, the countryside teems with wildlife. Forests are home to wolves, bears, lynx, and various species of birds. Wild reindeer still roam the extreme north, although their numbers have been significantly reduced for the usual reasons: unrestricted killing for most of the 20th century, the encroachment of human population, pollutants, and the loss of some natural breeding grounds. Finland's thousands of lakes are migratory stops and home to hundreds of species of birds; most come to dine on the trout and salmon found in the chilly streams and lakes.

Finns go to great lengths to protect their natural resources. The government has designated 30 areas as national parks. Wildlife areas have generally been left undisturbed, with simple trail markings and rustic campsites. National parks in the southern regions tend to be smaller and less rugged than their larger, wilder counterparts in the north.

The largest national park in Finland is Lemmenjoki, north of the Arctic Circle. This wilderness area is home to the magnificent Lemmenjoki River Valley, famed for its gold deposits. Cliffs rise dramatically on each side of the river.

As the Ice Age receded throughout Scandinavia, widely scattered Stone Age settlements emerged among the lakes and forests of what is now Finland. The tribes that established these communities were probably nomadic Lapps of Mongolian origin, although the mists of time have greatly obscured the exact nature of the communities.

With the arrival of new tribes of Finno-Ugric origin (starting in the 1st century A.D.) and other unrelated Germanic tribes from the southern edge of the Gulf of Finland, the original Lapps retreated farther and farther north. Recent genetic research into the distribution of blood groups points to evidence that about two-thirds of the Finnish population today is of Western (that is, European) origin (see "Those Mysterious Genes" box, above). Nonetheless, philologists stress the uniqueness of the Finnish language, Suomia, whose only close relative is Hungarian. Both languages belong to the Finno-Ugric subdivision of the Uralic subfamily of the Ural-Altaic family, unrelated to the Indo-European family to which almost all Western European languages belong.

The arrival of the Vikings, mentioned in written records beginning about A.D. 800, led to the establishment of cultural and trade routes as far east as Constantinople. Early in their recorded history, inhabitants of the region now known as Finland probably had many contacts with the Russian empire as well as the kingdoms of Estonia and Latvia. More important, they also established trade links with the shores of the southern Baltic—the area that's now Poland and part of Germany. Many different cultures and bloodlines met and mingled in Finland, leading to bloody wars among the Finnish tribes, until Sweden—fearing for the stability of its eastern neighbor—launched a series of attacks into the area.

SWEDISH INTRUSIONS In A.D. 1155, Eric IX, assisted by St. Henry, the English-born bishop of Uppsala, launched a crusade for the political and religious conversion of the Finnish tribes. Their major opposition was from the Novgorodians (a powerful Russian kingdom) in eastern Finland (Karelia), who were seizing land and spreading the Russian Orthodox faith from

Dateline

- **A.D. 100** Finland is inhabited by people from the southern Gulf of Finland and by Finno-Ugrians.
- **1155** Eric IX, king of Sweden, brings the Crusades to Finland.
- **1581** Johan III of Sweden makes Finland a Grand Duchy.
- **1713–21** Russia invades and occupies Finland.
- **1721** Sweden regains control of western Finland, but loses much Finnish territory in the east to Russia.
- **1809** Finland becomes a Grand Duchy of Russia under Tsar Alexander I.
- **1821** The capital is moved from Turku to Helsinki.
- **1878** Under Tsar Alexander II, Finland gains its own conscript army; Finnish replaces Swedish as the official language.
- **1905** Finns launch a national strike to oppose the oppressive policies of Tsar Nicholas II, who had revoked Finnish autonomy in 1899.
- **1906** Finland is allowed a single-chamber Diet with 200 elected deputies.
- **1917** Russia restores Finnish autonomy, as Finland declares its independence.
- **1918** Mannerheim succeeds in driving Russian forces out of Finland.
- **1919** Finland adopts a constitution.
- **1920** Finland joins the League of Nations.
- **1939–40** The first Russo-Finnish War begins.
- **1941–44** Russo-Finnish Continuation War rages, with Finland allied with Germany.

conti

- **1955** Helsinki hosts the Olympic Games, as Finland pursues a policy of neutrality.
- **1956** Urho Kekkonen becomes president of Finland and presides over the long and tense Cold War era.
- **1982** Kekkonen resigns; Mauno Koivisto is elected president.
- **1988** Koivisto is reelected to a second 6-year term, as Communists decline in power.
- **1992** Finland celebrates the 75th anniversary of its independence.
- **1994** Koivisto steps down; Martti Ahtisaari assumes the presidency.
- **1995** Finland, along with Sweden and Austria, joins the European Union.
- **1998** It's announced that Finland will chair the EU for last half of 1999; a "Northern Dimension" policy is planned.
- **2000** Tarja Halonen is elected Finland's first female president. Finland grants rights to same-sex couples to register their unions like heterosexual couples.

the East. A famous battle occurred in 1240 at the River Neva, when Alexander Nevski, a noted hero of Russian literature, defeated Sweden. Later, in 1323, a treaty between Sweden and the Novgorodians divided Finland's easternmost province of Karelia between Novgorod and Sweden. Eastern Finland, from that moment on, became part of the Russian-Byzantine world; although it shared a common language with the western sector, that region would not be reunited with the rest of Finland again except for a brief period early in the 20th century.

Meanwhile, with the largest portion of Finland under Swedish rule, most of the population enjoyed considerable autonomy and mercantile prosperity. The Swedish language became dominant. Under Sweden's king, Gustavus Vasa, Helsinki became one of the Swedish Empire's most important trading bases in the Baltic. Lutheranism was introduced into Finland by Michael Agricola (1506–57) who, because of his translation of the New Testament into Finnish and his compilation of a Finnish grammar, is called "the father of Finnish literature."

Sweden's King Johan III (1537–92) granted Finland the status of Grand Duchy in 1581. Unfortunately, Finland became a battleground in the continuing wars among Russia, Sweden, Denmark, and Poland. New boundaries were established in 1671, when Russia was forced to yield certain lands in Karelia.

Finland entered the Thirty Years' War on Sweden's side, to which it was subjugated, its own language and culture suppressed in favor of Sweden's. The great famine of 1676 killed one third of the population.

During the reign of Sweden's King Charles XII (1682–1718), Russia invaded and occupied Finland from 1713 to 1721. At the end of the war Sweden still ruled Finland, although some eastern territories, including southern Karelia, passed back to Russia. Russia gained new territories in another Swedish-Russian war, which raged from 1741 to 1743.

In 1808, at the peak of the Napoleonic wars, Russia finally seized all of Finland. Under Tsar Alexander I (1777–1825), Finland was granted the status of Grand Duchy, and throughout the 19th century it enjoyed broad autonomy, developing a democratic system without interference from St. Petersburg.

LIFE UNDER THE RUSSIANS Turku was the capital of Finland until 1821 when the tsar moved it to Helsinki. In 1878, under Tsar Alexander II (1818–81), Finland gained its own independent conscript army, and the Finnish language became the official language, replacing Swedish.

Although Tsar Alexander III (1845–94) tried to follow a liberal policy toward Finland, most of his advisers were opposed, preferring to keep Finland as a buffer zone between the Russian capital (then St. Petersburg) and the rest of Europe. Alexander's conservative and reactionary son, Nicholas II

(1868–1918), revoked Finnish autonomy in 1899 and began an intensive campaign of Russification. Russian became the official language in 1900, and the following year the separate Finnish army was abolished. Mass arrests followed. In 1905 Finland called a national strike to protest these conditions, forcing Nicholas II to ease some of his edicts. In 1906 Finland was permitted to have a unicameral parliament (the Diet) composed of 200 elected deputies, but it had little real power.

At the outbreak of World War I, Russia totally dominated Finland, and Finnish autonomy became just a memory. Finland lost its status as a Grand Duchy and became just a dominion of its more powerful neighbor to the east.

AN INDEPENDENT FINLAND   Finland was saved by the outbreak of the Russian Revolution and the collapse of tsarist rule. The Russian provisional government restored Finnish autonomy on March 20, 1917. Nevertheless, the Finns called a general strike, seeking total independence. A civil war followed, in which the leftist, pro-Russian Red Guard, supporting Russian troops in Finland, was opposed by the conservative-nationalist civil guard, the Whites.

On November 15, 1917, a proclamation placed control of the country's affairs in the hands of a Finnish government, and on December 6, President Svinhufvrud (1861–1944) declared the independence of Finland. Russia recognized Finnish independence on January 5, 1918, although 40,000 Russian troops were still stationed in Finland supporting the Red Guard.

Baron Carl Gustaf Emil von Mannerheim (1867–1951) assumed control of the Whites with the intention of driving Russia out of Finland. With the help of a German expeditionary force, he managed to win the civil war, which ended on May 16, 1918. At the end of the war, Finland was in dire economic circumstances and faced starvation.

On December 12, 1918, Mannerheim was named regent of Finland, and a constitution was adopted in June 1919, making Finland a republic. The new document called for the election of a president every 6 years. In his position, Mannerheim wielded supreme executive power, as did K. J. Stahlberg (1865–1952), the first president.

Russia and Finland signed a peace treaty at Tartu in October 1920. Russia got East Karelia. Finland joined the League of Nations on December 16, 1920, and the following year the League ruled that Finland—not Sweden—was entitled to the Åland Islands.

The 1920s saw continuing struggles between the government and Finnish communists. In 1923 the Communist Party was outlawed, but it returned under the title of the Democratic League. During the 1930s, many social and economic reforms were carried out.

WARS WITH RUSSIA   A Soviet-Finnish nonaggression pact was signed on January 12, 1932, but Russia continued to make demands on Finland, including the annexation of the Hanko peninsula for use as a Soviet naval base. When Finland refused, Russian troops invaded on November 30, 1939.

The Winter War of 1939–40 was one of the harshest ever in Finland, but the Finns, greatly outnumbered, resisted with bravery and courage. In March 1940 they accepted Russian terms, ceding territories in the north, the province of Viipuri, and the naval base at Hanko. The inhabitants of those districts left their homeland and moved within Finland's new borders.

Resentment against Russia led to a treaty with Germany. Hitler's request for transit rights across Finland was granted. Finland tried to remain neutral when the Nazis invaded Russia on June 22, 1941, but Russia bombed towns in southern Finland and Mannerheim launched the Russo-Finnish Continuation War. Territories that had been lost to Russia were retaken. But in 1944 Russi launched a large-scale attack, forcing Finland to ask for peace. Russia retook the territory it had ceded to Finland and imposed severe war reparations. The situation was complicated since German troops stationed in northern Finland refused to withdraw. Therefore, Finland had to launch a war against the Nazis in Lapland in 1945.

Mannerheim became president in 1944 but was obliged to step down in 1946 because of ill health. In Paris in 1947 Finland and Russia signed an armistice.

MODERN FINLAND   J. K. Paasikivi assumed the presidency of Finland in 1946, and concluded a mutual assistance treaty with the Soviet Union in 1948. In 1952 Helsinki became the site of the Olympic Games, focusing world attention on Finland, which in 1955 joined the United Nations.

In 1956 Urho Kekkonen became president of Finland; he continued in office during the long Cold War era, resigning in 1982 because of ill health. During his 25 years in office, Kekkonen successfully pursued a precarious policy of neutrality, earning a reputation for skillful diplomacy. At the end of his tenure, he saw the decline of the Communist Party in Finland. In 1975 he hosted the Conference on Security and Cooperation in Europe, where he received the heads of state and the heads of government of 35 countries who signed the Helsinki Agreement on international human rights.

Upon Kekkonen's resignation in 1982, Mauno Koivisto was elected president. Nearing the end of the long Cold War, Koivisto was re-elected to a second 6-year term in 1988. The country celebrated its 75th year of independence in 1992. After 12 years in office, the two-term Finnish president, Koivisto, stepped down in 1994. In his place, Martti Ahtisaari was elected president. In 1995 Finland, together with Austria and Sweden, joined the European Union.

The early 1990s witnessed epochal changes in Finland's neighbors to the east and south. Contacts, both commercial and social, with its formerly communist southern neighbor Estonia dramatically increased, and there was a modest increase in contacts with the other two Baltic countries, Latvia and Lithuania. As a result, there are now several daily flights, car ferries, and other ship connections between Helsinki and Tallinn (capital of Estonia), and direct air service to both Riga (Latvia) and Vilnius (Lithuania). Relations with Russia have also been improving since the fall of communism.

In 1998 Finland began plans to develop a "coherent strategy" toward Moscow on the part of the EU. This "coordinated" Russian policy was in place when Finland assumed the presidency of the EU in the last 6 months of 1999. This developing policy is known as the "Northern Dimension" to European policy, and it was the cornerstone at the EU summit meeting in Helsinki in December 1999, the last such major EU summit before the arrival of the millennium.

Finnish leaders continue to define the "common interests" of all the 15 EU members vis-a-vis Moscow. These are not just lofty words, but practical, too—for example, in less than 20 years EU countries will depend on deposits in Russia's Barents and Kara Sea areas for up to 70% of their natural gas.

While Sweden and Denmark have chosen to remain outside the Economic and Monetary Union, Finland continues to support a European single currency (Norway and Iceland aren't members of the EU). Although not a member of NATO, Finland has contributed troops to peacekeeping operations in Bosnia. Russia, according to one high-ranking Russian military official, would view Finland in NATO "as an extremely serious threat."

In step with the other advanced Scandinavian countries, Johannes Koskinen, the Finnish minister, backed a proposal in 2000 to allow same-sex couples to register their unions the same way as married straight couples. Finland has long been known as a gay-friendly nation—in fact, Tarja Halonen, the president of Finland, was a former chairman of the Finnish National Organization for Sexual Equality and has been speaking out on gay rights for years.

4 Dining with the Finns

Breakfast in Finland is usually served between 7 and 10am, lunch between 11am and 2pm, and dinner any time after 4pm. Some restaurants stay open as late as 1am; nightclubs and discos—some of which serve food—are often open until 3am.

In Finland, full-fledged restaurants are called *ravintola.* Inexpensive lunches are available at places called *kahvila* and *baari.* A baari serves light food and perhaps a mild beer, although coffee is more common. All well-known alcoholic beverages are available throughout Finland in fully licensed restaurants and bars.

Potatoes, meat, fish, milk, butter, and rye bread are the mainstays of the Finnish diet. Soups are popular, especially pea soup and rich meat soups, in which potatoes and vegetables are cooked with chunks of beef.

Every Finn looks forward to the crayfish season between July 20 and September, when some 225,000 pounds of this delicacy are caught in inland waters. Finns take special care in eating crayfish, sucking out every morsel of flavor. After devouring half a dozen, they down a glass of schnapps. Called *rapu,* the crayfish is usually boiled in salted water and seasoned with dill. Of course, with all this slurping and shelling, you'll need a bib.

The icy-cold waters of Finland produce very fine fish, some of which are unknown elsewhere in the world. A cousin to the salmon, the 2-inch-long *muikku fritti* is found in Finland's inland waters. This fish is highly praised by gastronomes, and its roe is a delicacy. The most common fish, however, is *silakka* (Baltic herring), which is consumed in vast quantities. Rarely larger than sardines, the herring is not only pickled, but fried or grilled. Sometimes it's baked between layers of potatoes in a sauce made with milk, cheese, and egg. The fish is usually spiced with dill; in fact, dill is the most popular herb in the country.

Finland's version of the Swedish smörgåsbord is called *voileipäpöytä* (which means "bread and butter table"). That definition is too literal. Expect not only bread and butter, but an array of dishes, including many varieties of fish (for example, pickled salt herring and fresh salted salmon) and several cold meat dishes, including smoked reindeer—all at a fixed price.

Along with elk, bear, and reindeer tongue, Finns like the sharp taste of *puolukka,* a lingonberry. The Arctic cloudberry is a rare delicacy.

The two most popular salads in Finland are beet and cucumber. Bread is invariably served, including whole wheat, white, black, and varieties of rye. The most typical is a dark, sour rye called *ruisleipa.* Those open-faced sandwiches, so familiar in all Scandinavian countries, are called *voileivat* here.

Fresh vegetables are plentiful in the summer, but they appear less often during the long winter months. Boiled new potatoes, the most common vegetable, are typically served with sprays of fresh dill. In elegant restaurants and homes, you may be served a convoluted morel known as "the black truffle of the north." It's the prize of all the mushrooms that grow in the forests of Finland.

Some Finnish hors d'oeuvres are especially good, particularly *vorschmack*. Herring is ground very fine, then blended with garlic, onions, and lamb; the mixture is then cooked in butter over a low flame for a long time, often several hours. Russian officers from St. Petersburg may have introduced this dish in the mid–19th century. In fact, the Russians have introduced a lot of dishes to Finland, and beef Stroganoff appears on many menus, especially in Helsinki. Borscht, a beet soup with sour cream, is available in many restaurants.

One of the best-known regional specialties comes from the province of Savo. *Kalakukko* is a mixture of a whitefish variety known only in Finland and pork baked in rye dough.

Another typical dish—this one from Karelia—is *karjalanpaisti*, a hot pot made with a combination of meats. Another Karelia specialty is *karjalan piirakka*—oval rye pasties made with either rice or potatoes.

The national beverage of Finland is milk (sometimes curdled), which is safe to drink (as is water) throughout the country. Two famous Finnish liqueurs should be tasted: *lakka,* made from the saffron-colored wild cloudberry, and *mesimarja,* made from the Arctic brambleberry.

Schnapps is a Finn's favorite, an all-around tipple. Hard liquor, often imported, is expensive—and anyone on a budget had better stick to a domestic beer (Koff and Lapinkulta are good local brands).

Index

Aalborg, 9, 153–156
Abisko, 462–463
Accommodations
  Denmark
    Ærø, 131
    best of, 7–8
    Copenhagen,
      46–56
    Dragør,
      102–104
    Nyborg, 120
    Odense,
      123–124
    Rønne,
      134–135
    Sandvig, 139
    Svendborg, 126
    Tåsinge,
      128–129
  Finland, 499–507
  Norway
    Balestrand,
      272–273
    Bergen,
      245–249
    Bodø, 284–285
    Flåm, 274
    Geilo, 275–276
    Hammerfest,
      262–263
    Honningsvåg,
      264
    Lofoten Islands,
      288–289
    Narvik, 290
    Oslo, 190–197
    Trondheim,
      279–280

  Ulvik, 268
  Voss, 270
  Sweden
    Abisko, 463
    Båstad,
      408–409
    best of, 295
    Falun, 442
    Gothenburg,
      387–390
    Gripsholm
      Castle, 379
    Helsingborg,
      413–416
    Jokkmokk, 458
    Kiruna, 462
    Kvikkjokk, 460
    Leksands,
      443–444
    Luleå, 454–457
    Lund, 430–431
    Malmö,
      421–424
    Mora, 447
    Rättvik, 445
    Sigtuna, 374
    Simrishamn,
      437
    Stockholm,
      323–332
    Uppsala,
      377–378
    Visby, 451–452
    Ystad, 434
Adventure trips, 17
Ærø, 129–131
**Ærøskøbing, 2, 10,
  130**

Ainola, 524
Airlines
  Denmark, 23–28
  Finland, 480–481
  Norway, 173
  Sweden, 305
Åjtte, 458
Åkirkeby, 136
Allinge, 136–139
Almindingen, 137
Alta, 164
Amber, 94
American Express
  Copenhagen, 44
  Denmark, 14
  Finland, 488
  Helsinki, 496
  Oslo, 188
  Stockholm, 320
**Andersen, Hans
  Christian**
    H. C. Andersen
      Barndomshjem,
      122
    H. C. Andersen
      Boulevard, 40
    H. C. Andersen
      Hus, 122
    Leksand, 442
    Odense, 121–122
**Ångelholm-Helsing-
  borg airport, 411**
**Anne Hvides Gård,
  126**
**Archaeological sites,
  138, 236, 277, 290,
  450, 565**

Architecture. *See also*
  Castles and palaces;
  Town halls
    Åkirkeby, 136
    Copenhagen, 40,
      80, 84
    Dragør, 2, 102
    Finland, 526–527,
      530
    Nyborg, 118
    Oslo, 218–219
    Ribe, 140–144
    Stockholm, 355
    Sweden, 398
    Trondheim, 276
    Visby, 448–449
    Voss, 269
Arctic Circle, 164,
  453
Area codes
    Bergen, 243
    Copenhagen, 44
    Denmark, 34
    Finland, 488
    Gothenburg, 385
    Helsinki, 496
    Norway, 180
    Oslo, 188
    Stockholm, 2320
    Sweden, 312
Århus, 9, 145–150
Aroksjokk, 460–461
Around Gotland
  Race, 302
Arrenjarka, 459
Art galleries, 94, 363
Assistens Kirkegård,
  83
ATM machines, 14
Auction houses, 94,
  363
Aula, 217
Aurungs, 450

Baby-sitters
    Copenhagen, 44
    Helsinki, 498

    Oslo, 188
    Stockholm, 320
Backakra, 436
Bakken Amusement
  Park, 84
Balder-Lisselby, 446
Balestrand, 272–273
Balke, 136
Baltic Herring
  Market, 478
Bander, 450
Banking, 243
Båstad, 405–410
Baths, 227
Beaches
    Copenhagen, 102
    Denmark, 16
    Finland, 534
    Norway, 164
    Oslo, 227
    Sweden, 450
Bergen
    accomodations,
      245–249
    itineraries, 251
    restaurants,
      249–251
    transportation,
      241–243
    traveling to,
      240–241
Bergen Airport, 240
Bergen Aquarium,
  251
Bergen Folklore, 258
Bergqvist, Yngve, 456
Berwaldhallen, 368
Biking
    Copenhagen, 92
    Denmark, 1, 4, 16
    Finland, 466, 478
    Norway, 170,
      265–266
    Sweden, 302
Bird-watching, 164,
  170, 288

Birkebeiner Race,
  168
Birkholm Island, 130
Bjåre Peninsula, 406
Bø, 169
Boating, 164
Boat travel, 30, 174,
  178, 261–266
Bodin Kirke, 283
Bodø, 158, 164,
  282–286
Bodø Domkirke, 283
Bohus Fortress, 439
Bookstores
    Bergen, 243
    Copenhagen, 44,
      94
    Gothenburg, 2385
    Helsinki, 496, 536
    Oslo, 188, 229
    Stockholm, 320,
      364
Boren lake, 439
Bornholm, 10,
  132–140
Børsen, 84
Borstova, 267
Botanical Gardens,
  78, 398, 428–429,
  449, 528
Bottarvegården, 450
British Airways, 173
Bryggen, 162
Bucket shops, 25
Bull, Ole, 255
Burgsvik, 450
Burmeisterska Huset,
  448
Business hours
    Bergen, 243
    Copenhagen, 44
    Denmark, 34
    Finland, 489
    Gothenburg, 385
    Helsinki, 496

Norway, 180
Sweden, 312
**Bus travel, 31, 176,
309, 484–485**

Café Opera, 369
Camping
Denmark, 4
Finland, 468
Canoeing
Finland, 466, 478
Sweden, 303
**Carl Larsson-gården,
441**
**Carl Nielsen Museet,
121**
**Carnival in Copen-
hagen, 15**
**Carolina Rediviva,
376**
Car rentals
Copenhagen, 44
Norway, 177
Stockholm, 320
Castles and palaces
Denmark
Amalienborg
Palace, 73
Christianborg
Palace, 5, 79
Clausholm, 146
Egeskov Castle,
4, 6, 122–123
Fredensborg
Slot, 108
Frederiksborg
Castle, 5,
106–107
Kronborg Slot,
5, 109–110
Ledreborg Park
Og Slot, 115
Marienlyst Slot,
110
Nyborg Slot,
120

Rosenborg
Castle, 5, 78
Rosenholm
Slot, 147
Valdemars Slot,
127–128
Finland
Häme Castle,
547
Norway
Alersjus Castle,
213
Gamiehaugen,
254
Slottsparken,
216
Stiftsgården, 278
Sweden
Castle of
Bosjökloster,
433
Drottningholm,
354
Gripsholm
Castle,
379–380
Kungliga Slottet,
346
Sofiero Slott,
412
Tullgarn Palace,
380
Vadstena Castle,
439
**Cathedral of Porvoo,
545**
**Cathedral of St.
Clemens, 146**
Ceramics
Finland, 469
Norway, 161
Sweden, 364,
412–413
Chalk stacks, 450
Charles IX, 439
Charter flights, 25

Children
Copenhagen,
84–85
Gothenburg, 399
Helsinki, 530
Lillehammer, 238
Oslo, 219
Stockholm, 355
Christiania, 41
**Christiania Bymo-
dell, 218–219**
Christianshavn, 41
Christiansø, 10, 138
Citicorp, 14
Climate
Denmark, 14
Finland, 476
Norway, 167–168
Oslo, 189
**Clothing & textiles,
Finland, 469**
**Coastal steamers,
178, 261–265**
Consulates
Finland, 489
Gothenburg, 386
Helsinki, 497
Norway, 180
Oslo, 188
Stockholm, 320
Sweden, 313
Copenhagen
accomodations,
47–56
itineraries, 70–71
neighborhoods,
39–42
nightlife, 97–101
organized tours,
91–92
restaurants
Indre By, 67–68
Nyhavn and
Kongens
Nytorv, 60–6
Rådhuspladse
64–67

Copenhagen *(cont.)*
Slotsholmen,
66–69
Tivoli Gardens,
56–60
shopping, 93–97
train travel, 174
transportation,
42–44
traveling to, 38–39
walking tours,
85–91
**Copenhagen Cathe-
dral, 80**
Copenhagen Zoo, 85
Costumes, 160
Counterculture, 6
Couriers, 26
**Covered wagons,
renting, 442**
Credit cards, 14
**Cruises and boat
tours**
North Cape, 262
Norway, 174
Crystal
Denmark, 7, 95
Norway, 161
Sweden, 365
Cunard, 174
Currency
Denmark, 10–13
Finland, 475–476
Norway, 166–167
Sweden, 298, 300
Currency exchange
Bergen, 243
Copenhagen, 44
Gothenburg, 386
Helsinki, 497
Oslo, 188
Stockholm, 320
Customs
Denmark, 35
Finland, 489

Norway, 180
Sweden, 312

Dala-Airport, 442
**Dalarna, 438,
440–447**
Dalarna horse, 447
Dalby Church, 432
Dalhem, 450
D'Artagnan, 161
Davids Samling, 77
**Den Fynske Landsby,
122**
**Den
Hirschsprungske
Samling, 78**
**Den Kongelige
Afstøbningssam-
ling, 81**
**Den Lille Havfrue,
76–77**
Denmark
accommodations
Ærø, 131
best of, 7–8
Copenhagen,
46–56
Dragør,
102–104
Nyborg, 120
Odense,
123–124
Rønne,
134–135
Sandvig, 139
Svendborg, 126
Tåsinge,
128–129
artisans, 6
climate, 14
crystal, 7
culture, 550–551
currency, 10–13
driver's license, 10
entry requirements,
10

environment, 551
farms, 1
food, 557–558
furniture, 7
history, 551–557
porcelain, 7
regions, 9–10
restaurants, 8
Ærø, 131
Copenhagen,
56–69
Dragør,
102–104
Helsingør, 111
Hillerød, 107
Humlebæk, 105
Nexø, 136
Nyborg,
120–121
Odense,
124–125
Rønne, 135
Roskilde,
115–116
Svendborg,
126–127
Tåsinge,
128–129
silver, 7
tours, 33–34
transportation,
31–32
traveling to, 23–30
**Denmark's
Aquarium, 85**
**Denmark's Tekniske
Museet, 110**
**Den National Scene,
258**
**Den Norske Opera,
231–232**
Dentists
Bergen, 243
Copenhagen, 45
Gothenburg, 386
Helsinki, 497

Norway, 180
Oslo, 188
Stockholm, 320
Sweden, 312
Department stores
Denmark, 94, 147
Finland, 536
Norway, 229, 256
Sweden, 364, 400
Design
Danish, 7
Finland, 465
Sweden, 295
**Det Gamle Rådhus,
141**
**Det Kongelige
Teater, 98**
**Det Norske
Folkloreshowet, 232**
Dining. *See*
Restaurants
Divan II, 8
**Djurgården, 318,
349–353**
Doctors
Bergen, 243
Copenhagen, 45
Denmark, 35
Gothenburg, 386
Helsinki, 497
Norway, 180
Oslo, 188
Stockholm, 320
Sweden, 312
Dogsledding, 265
Dolm Church, 278
**Dominican
Monastery of St.
Nicholas, 449**
**Domkyrkan, 429,
449**
**Dragør, 2, 42,
102–104**
Dr. Holms Hotel, 161
Driver's licenses
Denmark, 10
Finland, 474

Norway, 166
Sweden, 298
Driving tours, 450
**Drottningholm
Court Theater, 293,
301, 368**
**Drottning Kristinas
Jaktslott, 398**
Drug laws
Denmark, 35
Finland, 489
Sweden, 312
Drugstores
Bergen, 244
Copenhagen, 45
Denmark, 35
Finland, 489
Gothenburg, 386
Helsinki, 497
Norway, 180
Oslo, 188
Stockholm, 320
Sweden, 312
Dry cleaning
Copenhagen, 45
Gothenburg, 386
Norway, 180
Oslo, 188
Stockholm, 321
Dueodde, 136

Ebeltoft, 4, 152–153
Eduskuntatalo, 519
Electricity
Denmark, 35
Norway, 180
Sweden, 312
Electric train, 273
Elsinore, 109–111
Embassies
Bergen, 244
Denmark, 35
Finland, 489
Gothenburg, 386
Helsinki, 497
Norway, 180
Oslo, 188

Stockholm, 320
Sweden, 313
Emergencies
Bergen, 244
Copenhagen, 45
Denmark, 35
Finland, 489
Gothenburg, 386
Helsinki, 497
Norway, 180
Oslo, 188
Stockholm, 320
Sweden, 313
Enamelware, 229
Entry requirements
Denmark, 10
Sweden, 297–298
Erikson, Sören, 445
**Eurailpass, 29,
306–307, 482**
Experimentarium, 85
Eyeglass repair
Bergen, 244
Copenhagen, 45
Gothenburg, 386
Helsinki, 497
Oslo, 188
Stockholm, 320

**Faerder Sailing Race,
169**
Falsled Kro, 7, 8
**Falu Koppargruva,
441–442**
Falun, 440
**Falun Copper Mine,
441–442**
Families
Denmark, 23
Finland, 480
Fanø, 144–145
Farms, 1
Fårö, 449
Fårösund, 450
**Fashion, 94, 256,
401, 536**

Fax machines, 314, 322, 387, 491, 498

Ferries

Denmark, 132, 174

Finland, 486

Norway, 170, 177, 273

Sweden, 174, 308

Festivals

Denmark

Aalborg Carnival, 15

Århus Festival Week, 16

Ballet and Opera Festival, 15

Carnival in Copenhagen, 15

Copenhagen Jazz Festival, 5, 15

Fall Ballet Festival, 16

Fire Festival Regatta, 5, 16

Frederikssund, 106

Funen Festival, 15

July 4 Festival, 5, 15

Midsummer's Night, 15

Roskilde Festival, 15

Sønderborg Tilting Festival, 16

Viking Festival, 5, 15, 106

Finland

Helsinki Festival, 467

Kuopio Dance and Music Festival, 467, 477

May Day, 477

Midnight Sun Film Festival, 467, 477

Savonlinna Opera Festival, 467, 477–478

Tar Skiing Race, 467

Turku Music Festival, 478

Walpurgis Eve Celebration, 477

Norway

Bergen International Festival (Bergen Festspill), 159, 168

Chamber Music Festival, 169

Emigration Festival (Kvinesdal), 169

Emigration Festival (Stavanger), 169

Holmenkollen Ski Festival, 160, 168, 171

International Salmon Fishing Festival, 169

Kongsberg Jazz Festival, 169

Kristiansund Opera Festival, 168

Molde International Jazz Festival, 159, 169

Narvik Winter Festival, 168

Nobel Peace Prize Ceremony, 160

North Cape Festival, 264

Northern Lights Festival, 168

Oslo Jazz Festival, 169

Peer Gynt Festival, 169

Telemark Festival, 169

Voss Jazz Festival, 168

Sweden

Falun Folkmusik Festival, 293, 301, 440

Lucia, the Festival of Lights, 302

Medieval Week, 293, 302, 448

Midsummer, 301

Minnesota Day, 302

Music at Lake Siljan, 443

Nobel Day, 302

Rättviksdansen, 302

Stockholm
  Waterfestival,
  293, 302
  Walpurgis Eve,
  293, 301
Fidenäs, 450
**Filharmonikerna i
Konserthuset, 368**
Finland
  accommodations,
  499–507
  climate, 476
  culture, 579–581
  currency, 475–476
  entry requirements,
  474
  environment,
  581–582
  food, 587–588
  history, 582–587
  itineraries, 487–488
  regions, 472–474
  tourist informa-
  tion, 474
  transportation,
  484–486
  traveling to,
  480–484
**Finlandia Ski Race,
477**
**Finnegaardstuene,
162**
Finnesloftet, 269
**Finnish National
Opera, 540**
Finnmark, 164
**Finnmark Fylkes-
rederi, 263**
Fiolstræde, 39
Fishing
  Denmark, 4, 16
  Finland, 466, 478
  Norway, 159, 164,
  170–171, 255,
  272
  Sweden, 292, 302,
  458

Fitness, 92
**Fjords, 163, 178,
265–276**
Flåm, 273–274
**Flaskeskibssamlingen,
130**
Flea markets, 94
Fløibanen, 252
Fokstumyra, 170
**Folgefonn Glacier,
163**
Folk costumes, 229
Folkteatern, 401
Food
  Denmark,
  557–558
  Finland, 587–588
  Norway, 566–567
  Sweden, 577–578
Fornebu Airport, 173
Forsvarsmuseet, 134
**Fredensborg,
107–108**
Frederikskirke, 82
**Fredrikstad, 158,
164, 235**
Fregatten Jylland, 152
Frihedsmuseet, 77
Frilandsmuseet, 83
Frøya, 278
**Funen, 9–10,
117–131**
Funen Village, 122
Furniture, 7
Furs, 420–421

Gallow Hill, 448
Gambling, 101,544
**Gamie Aker Kirke,
219**
Gamie Bergen, 252
**Gamla Stan, 317,
346–347**
Gamlebyen, 235
Gammelgården, 445
Gammel Skagen, 156
Gammelstad, 454

**Gandolbanen cable
car, 289**
**Gay and lesbian
travelers**
  Denmark, 21–22
  Finland, 480
  Norway, 173
  Sweden, 304
**Gay and lesbian bars
and clubs**
  Bergen, 259
  Copenhagen, 101
  Gothenburg, 403
  Helsinki, 544-545
  Oslo, 234-235
  Stockholm,
  370–371
**Geilo, 163, 171,
274–276**
Geiranger, 163
Gems, 365
**Genealogy, tracing,
172**
Gervide, 450
Gifts, 230, 365, 537
**Gjenreisningsmuseet,
262**
Glaciers, 164
Glass
  Finland, 469, 537
  Norway, 95, 229,
  365
  Sweden, 229, 295,
  365
Glimmingehus, 436
Gløma river, 164
Glomfjord, 164
**Gold, panning for,
468**
Golf
  Copenhagen, 92
  Denmark, 4, 17
  Finland, 479
  Norway, 171, 255
  Sweden, 292, 294
  303, 362, 405,
  407–408, 461

Index

Göta Älv River, 439
Göta Canal, 438–440
Götaland, 297
Göteborg Maritime
  Center, 396
Göteborgsoperan,
  402
Gothenburg
  itineraries, 395
  neighborhoods,
    384–385
  nightlife, 401–403
  restaurants,
    387–390,
    391–394
  sightseeing,
    395–399
  transportation, 385
  traveling to,
    383–384
Gotland, 438,
  447–453
Gotlands Fornsal,
  449
Granberget, 443
Grand Hotel, 161,
  295
Great Belt, 117
Great Winter
  Market, 458
Greighallen, 257
Grener, 156
Grete Waitz Run,
  168
Gripsholms Värdshus
  Restaurant, 296
Gröna Lunds Tivoli,
  369
Grundtvigs Kirke
  (Grundtvig
  Church), 84
Gudbrandsdalen,
  164
Gudhjem, 137–138
Guldhedens Våtten-
  orn, 395
  ns, 227

Hafjell Alpine
  Center, 239
Hairdressers
  Bergen, 244
  Copenhagen, 45
  Gothenburg, 386
  Helsinki, 497
Håkonshallen, 254
Hallands Väderö,
  406
Hallingdall, 163
Hamburger Börs,
  469
Hämeenlinna,
  547–548
Hammeren, 139
Hammerfest, 164,
  261–263
Hammershus
  Fortress, 139
Hamresanden Beach,
  164
Handcrafts
  Finland, 538
  Norway, 228, 257
  Sweden, 295,
    365–366, 401,
    420
Hanseatic harbor,
  449
Hardangerfjord, 163,
  268
Hardangervidda
  National Park, 163,
  267
Havis Amanda, 470
Health insurance
  Denmark, 18–19
  Norway, 172
  Sweden, 304
Helsingborg,
  410–418
Helsingør, 9,
  109–111
Helsingør Bymuseet,
  110

Helsinin Kaupungi-
  norkesteri, 540
Helsinki
  accommodations,
    499–507
  itineraries,
    518–519
  neighborhoods,
    493–495
  nightlife, 540–545
  organized tours,
    533–534
  restaurants,
    508–518
  shopping, 534–539
  spectator sports,
    534
  transportation,
    495–496
  traveling to,
    492–493
  walking tours,
    531–533
Helsinki Marathon,
  478
Hembygdsgårdar,
  443
Hemse, 450
Heyerdahl, Thor, 214
Hiking
  Finland, 466, 479
  Norway, 159, 163,
    171
  Sweden, 292, 302
Hillerød, 105–107
Himmelbjerget, 150
Hirschsprung Collec-
  tion, 78
Hitra, 278
Hjalmar
  Lundbohmsgården,
  461
Hjorth's Fabrik,
  133–134
Hoburgen, 450
Hol, 274

Holidays
Denmark, 15, 35
Finland, 477
Norway, 168
Sweden, 300
Holmens Kirke, 82
Home furnishings,
96, 366
Honningsvåg,
263–266
Honnorrabatt, 176
Horseback riding
Denmark, 4
Norway, 171
Sweden, 303, 362
Hospitals
Bergen, 244
Copenhagen, 45
Helsinki, 497
Stockholm, 321
Høst, Olaf, 138
Hotel Dagmar, 7
Hotel d'Angleterre, 7
Hotel Hesselet, 8
Hotel Kämp, 470
Hotels. *See* Accommodations
Hoved Banegård, 39
Humlebæk, 104–105
Hunderfossen
Family Park, 238
Hyvinkää, 546

Ibsen, Henrik, 164
Ice hockey, 362
Ice Hotel, 456–457
Icelandair, 173
Indre By, 41
Insurance, 19–20
Internet access
Copenhagen, 45
Gothenburg, 386
Helsinki, 497
Oslo, 188
Stockholm, 320

InterRail Pass,
29–30, 307–308,
483
Ire, 450
Iron ore, 461
Islamic art, 77

Jelling, 9
Jewelry, 96–97, 229,
257
Finland, 469, 538
Jogging
Copenhagen, 92
Finland, 534
Sweden, 303
Johan Ludvig
Runeberg House,
545–546
Jokkmokk, 292,
457–460
Jons Kapel, 139
Jostedal Glacier, 272
Jukkasjärvi, 456
Jutland, 9, 140–156

Kaknästornet, 348
Kållandsö, 329
Kappelshamn, 450
Karl IX, 458
Karmeliterklostret,
110
Kärnan, 411–412
Kastrup Airport,
38–39
Kautokeino, 164
Kebnekaise, 461
Kebnekaise Mountain, 460
Kids. *See* Children
Kirkenes, 164
King Sigismund of
Poland, 439
King's Trail, 459
Kinsarvik Church,
267
Kiruna, 460–462
Kivik Tomb, 437

Klosterkyrkan, 439
Knitwear, 160
Kobenhavns
Bymuseet, 83
Købmagergade, 39
Køge, 9
Kommandanten, 8
Kongelige Bibliotek,
81
Kongens Nytorv, 40
Kongsten Fort, 164
Konserthuset, 402
Konsten Fort, 235
Kotka, 548–549
Kristiansand, 164,
168
Kristine Church, 440
Kultorvet, 39
Kungälv, 439
Kungliga Dramatiska
Teatern, 369
Kungsholmen, 318,
353
Kungsleden, 459,
463
Kunstindustrimuseet,
77
Kustaanmiekka,
525–526
Kvikkjokk, 459–460
Kvinesdal, 169

Läckö Slott, 439
Ladbyskibet, 123
Lady Hamilton
Hotel, 295
Lake Siljan, 442
Lake Vänern, 439
Lake Vättern, 439
Landvetter Airport,
383
Langholmen, 317
Language
Denmark, 35
Finland, 489
Sweden, 313
Lapp Church, 458

Index

Lappeenranta, 465
Lapps, 164, 266
Lärbro, 450
Larsson, Carl, 440, 446
Laundry
  Bergen, 244
  Copenhagen, 45
  Gothenburg, 386
  Helsinki, 497
  Norway, 180
  Oslo, 188
  Stockholm, 321
Learning vacations, 17–18
Lejre Research Center, 115
Leksand, 442–444
Libraries
  Bergen, 244
  Copenhagen, 45
  Oslo, 188
  Stockholm, 321
Lickershamn, 450
Lidköping, 439
Lilla Torg, 419
Lillehammer, 164, 168, 171, 238–239
Linens, 366–367
Linköping, 439
Liquor laws
  Denmark, 35
  Finland, 489–490
  Helsinki, 497
  Norway, 180
  Sweden, 313, 386
Liseberg Park, 396
Lisselby, 446
Little Mermaid, 76–77
Ljugarn, 450
LKAB Mining Company, 461
Lodging. See Accommodations

Lofoten Islands, 164, 170, 265–266, 286–289
Lofthus, 163
Log rafting, 294
Lost property
  Bergen, 244
  Copenhagen, 45
  Gothenburg, 386
  Helsinki, 498
  Oslo, 189
  Stockholm, 321
Lovund, 170
Luggage storage and lockers
  Bergen, 244
  Copenhagen, 45
  Gothenburg, 386
  Helsinki, 498
  Oslo, 189
  Stockholm, 321
Lummelunda Grottan, 449
Lund, 292, 428–433
Lutheran Cathedral, 522
Lyngs Alps, 164
Lysefjord, 164

Måbø Valley, 267
Madsebakke, 138
Mads Lerches Gård, 118
Maiden's Tower, 449
Mail
  Denmark, 36
  Finland, 490
  Helsinki, 498
  Norway, 181
  Sweden, 313
Malmö, 418–428
Maps
  Denmark, 36
  Finland, 490
  Norway, 181
  Sweden, 313, 364

Mariakirke, 254
Mariakyrkan, 406, 412
Marie Louise, 8
Marikollen, 169
Markets
  Copenhagen, 40–41
  Stockholm, 365, 367
Marstal, 130
Masexpresen, 440
Mattarahkka, 461
Medieval Week, 448
Midnight sun
  Finland, 476
  Norway, 164, 167–168
  Sweden, 291, 300, 463
Midnight Sun Marathon, 169
Midsummer's Night, 15, 169
Minerals, 365
Miniprice Ticket, 176
Mobil Bislett Games, 169
Molde, 163
Møn, 9
Monastery of St. Maria, 374
Moneygram, 14
Mora, 446–447
Mountain climbing, 159
Mount Mostadfjell, 288
Munch, Edvard, 217–218
Munkholmen Island, 278
Museet for Samtidskunst, 114
Museet Lysøen, 255

Museums

Denmark

Aebelholt
Kloster-
museum, 107

Ærø Museum,
131

Amager
Museum, 102

Arken Museum
of Modern
Art, 84

Bornholm
Ceramic
Museum,
133–134

Bornholms
Kunstmuseet,
138

Bornholms
Museum, 134

Carl Nielsen
Museet, 121

Christianborg
Palace, 79

Danmarks Jern-
banemuseum,
122

Davids Samling,
77

Den Fynske
Landsby, 122

Den Gamle By,
146

Den
Hirschsprungs-
ke Samling, 78

Den Kongelige
Afstøbnings-
samling, 81

Denmark's
Tekniske
Museet, 110

Det National-
historiske
Museum på

Frederiksborg,
106

Dragør
Museum, 102

Erotica
Museum, 6,
79–80

Experimentar-
ium, 85

Forsvarsmuseet,
134

Frihedsmuseet,
77

Frilandsmuseet,
83

Gudhjem
Museum, 138

Helsingør
Bymuseet, 110

Hirschsprung
Collection, 78

Hjorth's Fabrik,
133–134

Kobenhavns
Bymuseet, 83

Kunstindustri-
museet, 77

Landsbrugs
Museum, 138

Louisiana
Museum of
Modern Art,
103

Louis Tussaud
Wax Museum,
72–73

Mads Lerches
Gård, 118

Museet for
Samtidskunst,
114

Museum of
Danish Resis-
tance, 77

Museum of
Decorative

and Applied
Art, 77

Museums at
Gammel
Estrup, 147

Nationalmuseet
(National
Museum), 79

Nexø Museum,
137

Nordjyllands
Kunstmuseet,
154

Nordsjællandsk
Folkemuseet,
107

Nyborg Og
Omegns
Museet, 118

Ny Carlsberg
Glyptotek, 72

Orlogsmuseet,
81

Palæsamling-
erne, 114

Railway
Museum, 122

Roskilde
Museum, 114

Royal Arsenal
Museum, 80

Royal Museum
of Fine Arts,
78

Royal Naval
Museum, 81

Silkeborg
Museum, 151

Søfartssam-
lingerne I
Troense, 127

Statens Museum
for Kunst, 78

Thorvaldsen's
Museum, 8

Museums *(cont.)*
Tivoli Museum,
82
Tøjhusmuseet,
80
Tramway
Museum, 115
Viking Ship
Museum, 113
Finland
Ainola, 467
Coastal Artillery
Museum, 527
Ehrensvärd
Museum, 528
Finnish National
Gallery, 519
Gallen-Kallela
Museum, 468,
524–525
Helsinki City
Museum, 519
Klasma, 519
Mannerheim
Museum, 467,
522
Military
Museum of
Finland, 522
National
Museum of
Finland, 522
Sara Hildén Art
Museum, 467
Seurasaari
Open-Air
Museum, 525
Sinebrychoff
Art Museum,
523
Suerasaari
Open-Air
Museum, 467
Urho Kekkonen
Museum
Tamminiemi,
523–524

Norway
Astrup Fearnley
Museum of
Modern Art,
213
Bergen Art
Museum, 252
Bryggens
Museum, 252
Bu Museum,
267–268
Det Hanseatiske
Museum, 160,
252
Edvard Munch
Museum, 160,
217
Forsvarsmuseet,
213
Frammuseet,
214
Fredrikstad
Museum, 235
Gjenreisningsm
useet, 262
Henie-Onstad
Kunstsenter,
215–216
Historisk
Museum, 213
Ibsen Museum,
218
Kon-Tiki
Museum, 214
Kunstindustrim
useet, 212
Lillehammer
Art Museum,
238
Lofoten
Museum, 287
Malhaugen
Open-Air
Museum, 238
Museet for
Samtidskunst,
212–213

Museum of
Natural His-
tory and
Archaeology,
277
Museum of
Norwegian
Vehicle His-
tory, 239
Nasjonalgal-
leriet, 212
Nordkapp-
hallen, 264
Nordkapp-
museet, 264
Nordland-
museet, 283
Nordland Røde
Kors
Krigsmine-
museum,
289–290
Norges
Hjemmefront-
museum, 213
Norsk Arkitek-
turmuseum,
218
Norsk Sjøfarts-
museum, 215
Norwegian Folk
Museum, 160,
215
Norwegian
Olympic
Museum, 239
Ofoten
Museum, 290
Oslo Bymu-
seum, 218
Ringve
Museum, 277
Royal and
Ancient Polar
Bear Society,
262

Index

Skimuseet, 216
Trøndelag Folk
  Museum, 278
Vestlandske
  Kunstindustri
  museum, 255
Vigelandsparken,
  160, 213–214
Viking Ship
  Museum, 160
Vikingskip-
  huset, 214
Voss Folkse-
  museum, 269
Sweden
  Åjtte, 294
  Arkitektur
    Museet, 355
  Blase Limestone
    museum, 449
  Bunge open-air
    cultural
    museum, 449
  City Museum
    in the Grey
    Friars
    Monastery,
    434
  Drotten
    Museum, 429
  Fredriksdal
    Open-Air
    Museum and
    Botanical
    Garden, 411
  Göteborgs
    Konstmuseum,
    294, 395-396
  Hallwylska
    Museet, 348
  Historiska
    Museet, 349,
    429
  Hjalmar Lund-
    bohmsgården,
    461
Kommendant-
  huset, 419
Kulturen, 429
Linnaeus Gar-
  den and
  Museum,
  376–377
Malmö Museer,
  419
Millesgården,
  294, 354
Moderna
  Museet, 349
Museum Gusta-
  vianum, 377
Nationalmu-
  seum, 294,
  348–349
Nordiska
  Museet, 352
Norrbottens
  Museum,
  454–455
Östaslatiska-
  museet, 347
Prins Eugens
  Waldemar-
  sudde,
  352–353
Röhsska
  Museum of
  Arts and
  Crafts, 396
Royal Warship
  Vasa, 293
Sigtuna
  Museum, 374
Skansen, 349,
  352
Stadmuseet,
  353
Stockholm
  Medeltids-
  museum, 347
Teknik-Och
  Sjöfarts-
  museet, 419
Thielska Gal-
  leriet, 353
Vagnmusset,
  419
Vasamuseet,
  349, 352
Ystada Konst-
  museum,
  433–434
Zornmuseet,
  446
Music, 96, 230, 539
Musk oxen, 265

Narnsfjord, 163
Narvik, 164, 168,
  289–290
Nationalmuseet, 79
National parks
  Abisko National
    Park, 462–463
  Fokstumyra, 170
  Hardangervidda
    National Park,
    267
  Pihlajasaari Recre-
    ational Park, 528
  Rebild National
    Park, 153
  Sarek National
    Park, 459
  Vadvetjåkka
    National Park,
    462–463
Nationaltheatret, 231
Needlework, 96
Newspapers
  Copenhagen, 46
  Denmark, 36
  Finland, 490
  Oslo, 18946
  Sweden, 313
Nexø, 135–136

Nidaros Cathedral,
277
Nidaros Domen, 163
Nielsen, Carl, 121
Nielson, Kai, 446
Nightlife
Copenhagen,
97–101
Gothenburg,
401–403
Helsinki, 540–545
Norway, 271, 282
Oslo, 230–235
Stockholm,
367–373
Sweden, 432, 453
Nikkaluokta, 461
Nils Olsson Hems-
löjd, 447
Njavve, 459
Nobel Peace Prize,
160, 170, 302
Nordkapp, 266
Nordkapphallen, 264
Nordkappmuseet,
264
Nordlandmuseet,
283
Nordsjællandsk
Folkemuseet, 107
Nørrebro, 42
Nørreport Station,
42
Norrland, 297. See
Swedish Lapland
Norrmalm, 317,
348–349
Norrvikens Trädgår-
dar, 406
North Cape, 164,
169, 266
North Cape March,
169
Northern Light Pass,
175
North Vaerøy
Church, 288

Norway
accommodations
Balestrand,
272–273
Bodø, 284–285
Flåm, 274
Geilo, 275–276
Hammerfest,
262–263
Honningsvåg,
264
Lofoten Islands,
288–289
Narvik, 290
Oslo, 190–197
Sandhamn,
381–382
Sigtuna, 374
Trondheim,
279–280
Ulvik, 268
Uppsala,
377–378
Voss, 270
climate, 167–168
coastal steamers,
178, 261–266
culture, 559–560
currency, 166–167
environment,
560–561
events, 168–170
fjords, 178,
266–276
food, 566–567
history, 561–566
itineraries, 260
nightlife, 271
northern coast,
276–290
regions of,
163–164
restaurants
Bodø, 285–286
Geilo, 276
Hammerfest,
263

Honningsvåg,
264, 266
Lofoten Islands,
288–289
Narvik, 290
Trondheim,
280–282
Ulvik, 268
Voss, 271
tourist informa-
tion, 164–166
tours, 178–179
transportation,
175–178
traveling to,
173–174
Norway Cup Interna-
tional Youth Soccer
Tournament, 169
Norwegian Coastal
Voyage/Bergen
Line, 261
Norwegian Tourist
Board, 164
Numedal, 163
Nusnäs, 447
Nyborg, 118–121
Nyborg Voldspil, 118
Ny Carlsberg Glyp-
totek, 72
Nyhavn, 40
Nylarskirke, 135

Odense, 3–4, 9,
121–125
Oil, 164
Öja, 450
Olav the Holy, 138
Old man of Hobur-
gen, 450
Oldtidsveien, 236
Olivo, 470
Olskirke, 138
Olympiaparken, 239
Olympic Stadium,
522–523, 534
Operahauset, 368

Operakällaren, 296
Øre, 10
Organized tours
  Copenhagen,
    91–92
  Helsinki, 533–534
  Oslo, 226
  Stockholm, 361
Orlogsmuseet, 81
Oscars Teatern, 369
Oslo
  accomodations,
    190-197
  festivals, 168–169
  history, 183
  itineraries,
    208–209
  neighborhoods,
    185–186
  nightlife, 230–235
  parks and gardens,
    216
  regions, 164
  restaurants
    Aker Brygge,
      205–206
    At Bygdøy, 207
    Central,
      198–203
    Eastern, 206
    At Frogner, 208
    Holmenkollen,
      208
    Old Town,
      204–205
    Western,
      206-207
  transportation,
    186–187
  traveling to, 184
  walking tours,
    219–226
Oslo Domkirke, 209
Oslo Konserthus,
  231
Østerdal, 163
Østerlarskirke, 137

Östermalm, 318
Our Savior's Church,
  82–83

Palace Hotel, 470
Palæsamlingerne,
  114
Pantomime Theater,
  97
Passports
  Denmark, 10
  Finland, 474
  Norway, 166
  Sweden, 298
Paul & Norbert, 296
Pedersker, 136
Peer Gynt Road, 164
Pewter, 230
Pharmacies
  Copenhagen, 46
  Denmark, 36
Phoenix
  Copenhagen, 7
Photographic needs
  Bergen, 244
  Copenhagen, 46
  Denmark, 36
  Gothenburg, 386
  Helsinki, 498
  Oslo, 189
  Stockholm, 321
  Sweden, 312
Police
  Bergen, 244
  Denmark, 36
  Finland, 490
  Gothenburg, 386
  Helsinki, 498
  Norway, 181
  Oslo, 189
  Stockholm, 321
  Sweden, 313
Porcelain
  Denmark, 7
  Finland, 537
  Norway, 95

Porvoo, 466,
  545–546
Post office
  Bergen, 244
  Copenhagen, 46
  Gothenburg, 386
  Oslo, 189
  Stockholm, 321
Pottery, 125, 134,
  412–313
Powder Tower, 448
Prince Eugen, 446

Quedens Gaard, 141

Rådhus and World
  Clock, 72
Rådhuspladsen, 40
Radio and television
  Denmark, 36
  Finland, 490
  Helsinki, 498
  Norway, 181
  Stockholm, 321
  Sweden, 313, 386
Radisson SAS Hotel
  Norge, 161
Radisson SAS Park
  Avenue Hotel, 295
Radisson SAS Royal
  Garden Hotel, 161
Radisson SAS Scan-
  dinavia Hotel, 295
Rafting
  Norway, 265
  Sweden, 303
Rantasipi Pohjan-
  hovi, 470
Rapadel, 459
Rättvik, 292,
  444–446
Rättvika
  Hantverksby, 445
Rauma, 465
Rebaters, 25–26
Reindeer, 163
Religious services

Index

Rembrandt, 446
Restaurant Julia, 470
Restaurant Julius
Fritzner, 162
Restaurant
Oppipoika, 470
Restaurant Palace,
471
Restaurants
Denmark, 8
Ærø, 131
Copenhagen,
56–69
Dragør,
102–104
Helsingør, 111
Hillerød, 107
Humlebæk, 105
Nexø, 136
Nyborg,
120–121
Odense,
124–125
Rønne, 135
Roskilde,
115–116
Sandvig, 139
Svendborg,
126–127
Tåsinge,
128–129
Finland
Helsinki,
508–518
Norway
Bergen,
249–251
Bodø, 285–286
Geilo, 276
Hammerfest,
263
Honningsvåg,
264, 266
Lofoten Islands,
288–289
Narvik, 290

Trondheim,
280–282
Ulvik, 268
Voss, 271
Sweden
Båstad,
409–410
best of, 296
Gothenburg,
391–394
Gripsholm
Castle, 380
Helsingborg,
416–417
Leksands,
443–444
Lund, 431–432
Malmö,
424–427
Mora, 447
Oslo, 198–207
Rättvik,
445–446
Sandhamn, 382
Sigtuna, 374
Simrishamn,
437
Stockholm,
332–344
Tullgarn Palace,
380
Uppsala,
378–379
Visby, 452–453
Ystad, 435
Rest rooms
Copenhagen, 46
Denmark, 36
Finland, 490
Helsinki, 498
Norway, 181
Sweden, 313–314,
321
Ribe, 2, 9, 140–144
Riddarholm Church,
346–347
Riviera, 164

Rockne, Knute, 163
Roma, 450
Rønne, 10, 133–135
Røros, 163
Rörstrand porcelain,
439
Rosenkrantz Tower,
254
Roskilde, 9, 15,
111–116
Roxen lake, 439
Royal and Ancient
Polar Bear Society,
262
Royal Cast Collec-
tion, 81
Royal Library, 81
Royal Trail, 463
Rude, Olaf, 138
Runde, 170
Rundetårn, 80
Runeberg, Johan
Ludvig, 545–546

Safaris, 294, 469
Safety
Copenhagen, 46
Denmark, 36
Finland, 490
Oslo, 189
Sailing
Denmark, 17
Norway, 171
Sweden, 303
Salmon fishing, 458
Saltstaumen Eddy,
284
Samis, 164, 438,
458–459
Sandefjord, 164
Sandhamn, 381–382
Sandvig, 139–140
Santa complex, 446
Sarek National Park,
459
SAS, 173, 175

Index

Saunas
    Denmark, 47, 120,
        134–135,
        148–149, 155
    Finland, 464, 534,
        539
    Sweden, 323–324,
        328, 330, 362
Savonlinna, 465
Scandic hotel Kalas-
    tajatorppa, 470
Scandic Hotel
    Rosendahl, 470
Scanrail Pass, 28–29,
    306
Scantours, 440
Scuba diving,
    Norway, 171
Sculpture, 539
Seals, 464
Seniors
    Denmark, 22–23
    Finland, 22–23
    Sweden, 304
Seurasaari, 525
Shoe repair
    Bergen, 244
    Copenhagen, 46
    Gothenburg, 387
    Stockholm, 321
    Sweden, 314
Shopping
    Bergen, 256–257
    Copenhagen,
        93–97
    Denmark, 123
    Gothenburg,
        400–401
    Helsinki, 535–539
    Oslo, 228–230
    Stockholm,
        362–367
    Sweden, 450–451
Sibelius, Jean, 524,
    547
Siggur, 450

Sigtuna, 291,
    374–376
Silkeborg, 150–152
Silver
    Denmark, 7, 147
    Norway, 97, 229
Simrishamn,
    435–437
Sjömagasinet, 296
Skaftnes Section, 287
Skagen, 156
Skåne
    Båstad, 405–410
    Helsingborg,
        410–418
    Lund, 428–433
    Malmö, 418–428
    Simrishamn,
        435–437
    Ystad, 433–435
Skaneleden walking
    trail, 406
Skansen, 369
Skating, 227
Skien, 164
Skiing
    Finland, 466, 479
    Norway, 159, 163,
        171–172, 239,
        269
    Oslo, 227–228
    Sweden, 292, 443
Skiperstod, 267
Ski School, 274
Skt. Gertruds
    Kloster, 8
Skt. Ibs Kirke, 114
Skt. Jørgensbjerg
    Kirke, 114
Skt. Mariæ Church,
    110
Skt. Olai's Kirke,
    110
Slätbaken, 439
Slite, 450
Slotsholmen, 40, 41
Slottskogen, 398

Snogebæk, 136
Søby, 130
Soccer, 362
Södermalm, 318, 353
Søfartssamlingerne I
    Troense, 127
Sognefjord, 163,
    168, 259, 268, 271
Sojvide, 450
Souvenirs, 230, 365
Squash, 362
St. Birgitta of
    Sweden, 439
St. Canute's
    Cathedral, 122
St. Catherine's
    Church and
    Monastery,
    141–142
St. Jørgensbjerg
    quarter, 114
St. Jørgen's Church,
    126
St. Nicolaj Church,
    126
St. Olav church, 272
St. Peter's Church,
    419–420
Stadsbibliotek, 396
Stadshus, 461
Stadsteatern, 402
Statholdergaarden,
    161
Stavanger, 164, 168
Stock Exchange, 84
Stockholm
    accomodations,
        330-332
    archipelago,
        381–382
    itineraries,
        345—346
    neighborhoods,
        316–318
    nightlife, 367–373
    organized tours,
        361

Stockholm *(cont.)*
restaurants
Djurgården,
341–342
Gamla Stan,
338–341
Kungsholmen,
341
Langholmen,
343
Normmalm,
332–338
Södermalm,
342–343
Sollentuna,
343–344
Solna, 343
Vasaparken, 342
spectator sports,
362
tourist informa-
tion, 317
transportation,
318–320
traveling to,
315–316
walking tours,
355–361
S-tog, 39
Stone sculptures, 450
Storknabben, 458
Stortinget, 209
**Strindberg, August,
354**
Strøget, 40–41
**Submarine Vesikko,
528**
**Suemenlinna
Fortress, 525**
Suldal, 169
**Suomen
Kansallisteatteri,
540**
Svaneholm, 420
Svaneke, 137
Svartisen, 164, 284
Svealand, 297

**Svendborg, 10,
125–129**
Svenska Teatern, 540
Sweaters, 230
Swebus, 440
Sweden
accommodations
Abisko, 463
Falun, 442
Gothenburg,
387–390
Gripsholm
Castle, 379
Jokkmokk, 458
Kiruna, 462
Kvikkjokk, 460
Leksands,
443–444
Luleå, 455–457
Mora, 447
Rättvik, 445
Visby, 451–452
climate, 298
culture, 568–570
currency, 298
entry requirements,
297–298
environment,
570–571
history, 571–577
itineraries,
311–312
midnight sun, 300
nightlife, 410,
417–418,
427–428, 453
regions, 297
restaurants
Gothenburg,
391–394
Gripsholm
Castle, 380
Leksands,
443–444
Mora, 447
Oslo, 198–207

Rättvik,
445–446
Sandhamn, 382
Sigtuna, 374
Tullgarn Palace,
380
Uppsala,
378–379
Visby, 452–453
shopping, 450–451
tours, 310–311
transportation,
308–310
traveling to, 305
**Swedish Lapland,
438, 453–463**
Swedish Open, 405
**Swedish Touring
Club, 463**
Swimming
Copenhagen, 93
Norway, 255,
283–284
Stockholm, 362
Sweden, 303

Tar Skiing Race, 477
Tåsinge, 127–129
Taxes
Bergen, 244
Copenhagen, 46
Denmark, 36
Finland, 490
Gothenburg, 387
Helsinki, 498
Norway, 181
Oslo, 189
Sweden, 314
Taxis, 322, 485
Telegrams
Helsinki, 498
Norway, 181
Sweden, 387
Telephones
Bergen, 244
Denmark, 37
Finland, 491

Helsinki, 498
Norway, 181
Stockholm, 322
Sweden, 314
Television. *See* **Radio and television**
Telex, 314, 322, 387, 491, 498
Temppeliaukio Church, 523
Tennis
Bergen, 256
Copenhagen, 93
Finland, 534
Oslo, 228
Stockholm, 362
Textiles, 367, 451
Thomas Cook, 14
Tilleg i Tekst, 267
Time zones
Denmark, 37
Finland, 491
Norway, 181
Sweden, 314
Tipping
Denmark, 37
Finland, 491
Norway, 181
Sweden, 314
Tivoli Gardens, 40, 56–60, 71
Tjåmotis, 459
Tøjhusmuseet, 80
Tønsberg, 158, 164, 236–238
Torekov, 406
Tornio Gold Club, 461
Town halls
Århus, 146
Copenhagen, 4, 72
Ebeltoft, 4, 152
Helsingborg, 411
Rådhuset, 209
Ribe, 141
Stockholm, 353

Toys, 367
Trädgårdsföreningen, 398
Train travel
Denmark, 28–30
Finland, 481–483
Norway, 175–176
Sweden, 306
Transit information
Copenhagen, 46
Gothenburg, 387
Oslo, 189
Stockholm, 322
Travel clubs, 26
Traveler's checks, 13–14
Travelers with disabilities
Denmark, 20–21
Finland, 480
Norway, 172–173
Sweden, 304
Treks, 265
Troldhaugen, 254
Trolleskoe, 138
Trollhättan, 439
Tromsø, 164, 168–169
Trondheim, 158, 163, 276–282
Trondheimsfjord, 163
Tryvannstårnet, 215
Turku, 465, 472
Tycho Brahe Planetarium, 85
Tyholttårnet, 278

Ulvik, 266–268
Uppsala, 292, 376–379
Uppsala Domkyrka, 377

Vadstena, 439
Vadvetjåkka National Park, 462–463

Vaernes Airport, 276
Vaikijaur, 459
Valdres, 163
Value-added tax (VAT), 93, 228, 363
Vamlingbo, 450
Vangskyrkje, 269
Vardø, 164
Vasa, Gustavus, 439
Vasastaden, 317–318
Vaxholm, 381
Vesterbro, 41
Vesterbrogade, 40
Victory Hotel, 295
Vidablick, 445
Viebaeltegård, 125
Vigeland, Gustav, 214
Vik, 271
Viking Run, 168
Vikings
archaeology, 565
churches, 137
festivals, 5, 15
jewelry, 97, 123
museums, 113
Ribe, 2, 140–142
ships, 123
Vikingskiphuset, 214
Vindefjord, 164
Vinstra, 169
Visas
Denmark, 10
Finland, 474
Norway, 166
Sweden, 298
Visa Travelers Checks, 14
Visby, 292, 447–453
Vor Freslers Kirken, 82–83
Vor Frue Kirke, 80, 120
Voss, 163, 168, 171, 268–271

Index

Wagons, horse-
drawn, 294, 442
Walking
Denmark, 17
Norway, 256
Sweden, 303
Walking tours
Copenhagen,
85–91
Helsinki,
531–533
Oslo, 219–226
Stockholm,
355–361
Water
Denmark, 37
Norway, 181
Sweden, 314
Wedholms Fisk, 296
Weight lifting, 362
Whale watching,
171–172
White-water rafting,
293
Widerøe Airline,
175, 287
Wildlife, 265–266,
288
Witch burning,
164
World Cup Summer
Ski Jumping, 169

Yachting, 164
Ystad, 433–435

Zealand, 9
Zoologisk Have,
85
Zorn, Anders, 446
Zorngården, 447
Zornmuseet, 446

Index

FROMMER'S® COMPLETE TRAVEL GUIDES

Alaska
Amsterdam
Argentina & Chile
Arizona
Atlanta
Australia
Austria
Bahamas
Barcelona, Madrid & Seville
Beijing
Belgium, Holland &
  Luxembourg
Bermuda
Boston
British Columbia & the
  Canadian Rockies
Budapest & the Best of Hungary
California
Canada
Cancún, Cozumel & the
  Yucatán
Cape Cod, Nantucket &
  Martha's Vineyard
Caribbean
Caribbean Cruises & Ports
  of Call
Caribbean Ports of Call
Carolinas & Georgia
Chicago
China
Colorado
Costa Rica
Denmark
Denver, Boulder & Colorado
  Springs
England
Europe

European Cruises & Ports of Call
Florida
France
Germany
Greece
Greek Islands
Hawaii
Hong Kong
Honolulu, Waikiki & Oahu
Ireland
Israel
Italy
Jamaica
Japan
Las Vegas
London
Los Angeles
Maryland & Delaware
Maui
Mexico
Montana & Wyoming
Montréal & Québec City
Munich & the Bavarian Alps
Nashville & Memphis
Nepal
New England
New Mexico
New Orleans
New York City
New Zealand
Nova Scotia, New Brunswick &
  Prince Edward Island
Oregon
Paris
Philadelphia & the Amish
  Country
Portugal

Prague & the Best of the Czech
  Republic
Provence & the Riviera
Puerto Rico
Rome
San Antonio & Austin
San Diego
San Francisco
Santa Fe, Taos & Albuquerque
Scandinavia
Scotland
Seattle & Portland
Shanghai
Singapore & Malaysia
South Africa
Southeast Asia
South Florida
South Pacific
Spain
Sweden
Switzerland
Texas
Thailand
Tokyo
Toronto
Tuscany & Umbria
USA
Utah
Vancouver & Victoria
Vermont, New Hampshire
  & Maine
Vienna & the Danube Valley
Virgin Islands
Virginia
Walt Disney World & Orlando
Washington, D.C.
Washington State

FROMMER'S® DOLLAR-A-DAY GUIDES

Australia from $50 a Day
California from $70 a Day
Caribbean from $70 a Day
England from $70 a Day
Europe from $70 a Day

Florida from $70 a Day
Hawaii from $70 a Day
Ireland from $60 a Day
Italy from $70 a Day
London from $85 a Day

New York from $80 a Day
Paris from $80 a Day
San Francisco from $60 a Day
Washington, D.C.,
  from $70 a Day

FROMMER'S® PORTABLE GUIDES

Acapulco, Ixtapa &
  Zihuatanejo
Alaska Cruises & Ports
  of Call
Amsterdam
Australia's Great Barrier Reef
Bahamas
Baja & Los Cabos
Berlin
Boston
California Wine Country
Charleston & Savannah
Chicago

Dublin
Hawaii: The Big Island
Hong Kong
Houston
Las Vegas
London
Los Angeles
Maine Coast
Maui
Miami
New Orleans
New York City
Paris

Phoenix & Scottsdale
Portland
Puerto Rico
Puerto Vallarta, Manzanillo &
  Guadalajara
San Diego
San Francisco
Seattle
Sydney
Tampa & St. Petersburg
Vancouver
Venice
Washington, D.C.

FROMMER'S® NATIONAL PARK GUIDES

Family Vacations in the
  National Parks
Grand Canyon

National Parks of the American
  West
Rocky Mountain
Yellowstone & Grand Teton

Yosemite & Sequoia/
  Kings Canyon
Zion & Bryce Canyon

FROMMER'S® MEMORABLE WALKS

Chicago	New York	San Francisco
London	Paris	Washington, D.C.

FROMMER'S® GREAT OUTDOOR GUIDES

Arizona & New Mexico	Northern California	Southern New England
New England	Southern California & Baja	Vermont & New Hampshire

FROMMER'S® BORN TO SHOP GUIDES

Born to Shop: France	Born to Shop: Italy	Born to Shop: New York
Born to Shop: Hong Kong,	Born to Shop: London	Born to Shop: Paris
Shanghai & Beijing		

FROMMER'S® IRREVERENT GUIDES

Amsterdam	Los Angeles	Seattle & Portland
Boston	Manhattan	Vancouver
Chicago	New Orleans	Walt Disney World
Las Vegas	Paris	Washington, D.C.
London	San Francisco	

FROMMER'S® BEST-LOVED DRIVING TOURS

America	France	New England
Britain	Germany	Scotland
California	Ireland	Spain
Florida	Italy	Western Europe

THE UNOFFICIAL GUIDES®

Bed & Breakfasts in California	Golf Vacations in the	New Orleans
Bed & Breakfasts in	Eastern U.S.	New York City
New England	The Great Smoky &	Paris
Bed & Breakfasts in the	Blue Ridge Mountains	San Francisco
Northwest	Inside Disney	Skiing in the West
Bed & Breakfasts in Southeast	Hawaii	Southeast with Kids
Beyond Disney	Las Vegas	Walt Disney World
Branson, Missouri	London	Walt Disney World for
California with Kids	Mid-Atlantic with Kids	Grown-ups
Chicago	Mini Las Vegas	Walt Disney World for Kids
Cruises	Mini-Mickey	Washington, D.C.
Disneyland	New England with Kids	World's Best Diving Vacations
Florida with Kids		

SPECIAL-INTEREST TITLES

Frommer's Britain's Best Bed & Breakfasts and Country Inns	Hanging Out in Europe
Frommer's France's Best Bed & Breakfasts and Country Inns	Hanging Out in France
	Hanging Out in Ireland
Frommer's Italy's Best Bed & Breakfasts and Country Inns	Hanging Out in Italy
	Hanging Out in Spain
Frommer's Caribbean Hideaways	Israel Past & Present
Frommer's Adventure Guide to Australia & New Zealand	Frommer's The Moon
	Frommer's New York City with Kids
Frommer's Adventure Guide to Central America	The New York Times' Guide to Unforgettable Weekends
Frommer's Adventure Guide to India & Pakistan	Places Rated Almanac
Frommer's Adventure Guide to South America	Retirement Places Rated
Frommer's Adventure Guide to Southeast Asia	Frommer's Road Atlas Britain
Frommer's Adventure Guide to Southern Africa	Frommer's Road Atlas Europe
Frommer's Gay & Lesbian Europe	Frommer's Washington, D.C., with Kids
Frommer's Exploring America by RV	Frommer's What the Airlines Never Tell You
Hanging Out in England	

Let Us Hear From You!

Dear Frommer's Reader,

You are our greatest resource in keeping our guides relevant, timely, and lively. We'd love to hear from you about your travel experiences—good or bad. Want to recommend a great restaurant or a hotel off the beaten path—or register a complaint? Any thoughts on how to improve the guide itself?

Please use this page to share your thoughts with me and mail it to the address below. Or if you like, send a FAX or e-mail me at frommersfeedback@hungryminds.com. And so that we can thank you—and keep you up on the latest developments in travel—we invite you to sign up for a free daily Frommer's e-mail travel update. Just write your e-mail address on the back of this page. Also, if you'd like to take a moment to answer a few questions about yourself to help us improve our guides, please complete the following quick survey. (We'll keep that information confidential.)

Thanks for your insights.

Yours sincerely,

Michael Spring

Michael Spring, *Publisher*

Name (Optional) ————————————————————————————

Address————————————————————————————————

——

City————————————————————————————— **State**———— **ZIP**————

Name of Frommer's Travel Guide ————————————————————

Comments————————————————————————————————

——

——

——

——

——

——

——

——

Please tell us a little about yourself so that we can serve you and the Frommer's community better. We will keep this information confidential.

Age: ( )18-24; ( )25-39; ( )40-49; ( )50-55; ( )Over 55

Income: ( )Under $25,000; ( )$25,000-$50,000; ( )$50,000-$100,000; ( )Over $100,000

I am: ( )Single, never married; ( )Married, with children; ( )Married, without children; ( )Divorced; ( )Widowed

Number of people in my household: ( )1; ( )2; ( )3; ( )4; ( )5 or more

Number of people in my household under 18: ( )1; ( )2; ( )3; ( )4; ( )5 or more

I am ( )a student; ( )employed full-time; ( )employed part-time; ( )not employed at this time; ( )retired; ( )other

I took ( )0; ( )1; ( )2; ( )3; ( )4 or more leisure trips in the past 12 months

My last vacation was ( )a weekend; ( )1 week; ( )2 weeks; ( )3 or more weeks

My last vacation was to ( )the U.S.; ( )Canada; ( )Mexico; ( )Europe; ( )Asia; ( )South America; ( )Central America; ( )The Caribbean; ( )Africa; ( )Middle East; ( )Australia/New Zealand

( )I would; ( )would not buy a Frommer's Travel Guide for business travel

I access the Internet ( )at home; ( )at work; ( )both; ( )I do not use the Internet

I used the Internet to do research for my last trip. ( )Yes; ( )No

I used the Internet to book accommodations or air travel on my last trip. ( )Yes; ( )No

My favorite travel site is ( )frommers.com; ( )travelocity.com; ( )expedia.com; other _____

I use Frommer's Travel Guides ( )always; ( )sometimes; ( )seldom

I usually buy ( )1; ( )2; ( )more than 2 guides when I travel

Other guides I use include _____

What's the most important thing we could do to improve Frommer's Travel Guides?

_____

_____

_____

_____

Yes, please send me a daily e-mail travel update. My e-mail address is

_____

Mail to: Michael Spring, Publisher and Vice President, Frommer's Travel Guides
909 Third Ave., New York, NY 10022   FAX: 212.884.5432